Look for this iPod icon throughout the text.

Icons connect textbook content to your iPod or other MP3/MP4 device.

Images courtesy of Apple.

What if I Don't Have an iPod?

Content can be downloaded and viewed on any computer, with or without an iPod.

Visit this text's Web site for directions or use the DVD available for purchase with this text.

iPod content includes:

- Lecture presentations
  - *Audio-based*
  - *Video-based*
  - *Slideshow only*
- Demonstration problems+
- Interactive self quizzes
- Videos on various course topics

+Available with some textbooks

iPod® Content Installer DVD for use with

Managerial Accounting for Managers

NOREEN | BREWER | GARRISON

MEDIA-INTEGRATED EDITION

This DVD-rom will autostart on most machines. OR, from the start menu, select run, and type: D:\ Autorun.exe where D represents the letter of your DVD-rom drive.

MANAGERIAL ACCOUNTING for managers

NOREEN
BREWER
GARRISON

DVD ROM

MADE WITH macromedia

INCLUDES Adobe Acrobat

ISBN 978-0-07-723528-4
MHID 0-07-723528-2

McGraw-Hill Irwin

Want to see iPod in action?

Visit **www.mhhe.com/ipod** to view a demonstration of our iPod content.

McGraw-Hill's

HOMEWORK MANAGER PLUS™

THE COMPLETE SOLUTION

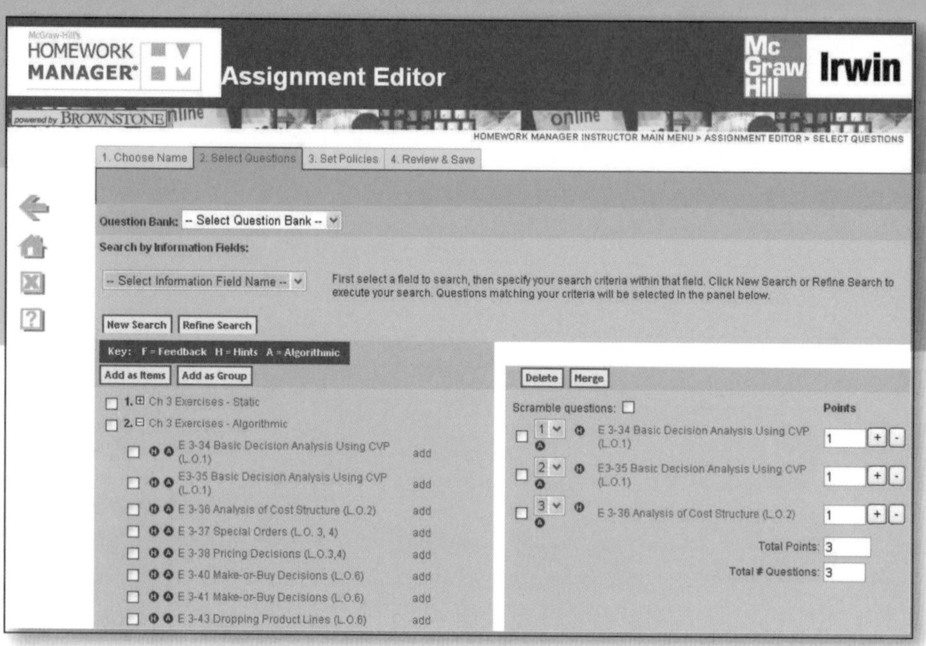

McGraw-Hill's **Homework** Manager®

This online homework management solution contains the textbook's end-of-chapter material. Now you have the option to build assignments from static and algorithmic versions of the text problems and exercises or to build self-graded quizzes from the additional questions provided in the online test bank.

Features:

- Assigns book-specific problems/exercises to students
- Provides integrated test bank questions for quizzes and tests
- Automatically grades assignments and quizzes, storing results in one grade book
- Dispenses immediate feedback to students regarding their work

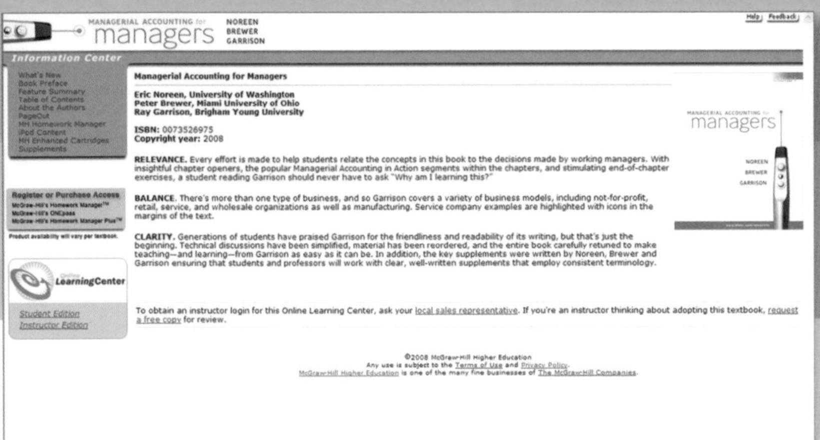

Interactive Online Version of the Textbook

In addition to the textbook, students can rely on this online version of the text for a convenient way to study. The interactive content is fully integrated with McGraw-Hill's Homework Manager® to give students quick access to relevant content as they work through problems, exercises, and practice quizzes.

Features:

- Online version of the text integrated with McGraw-Hill's Homework Manager
- Students referred to appropriate sections of the online book as they complete an assignment or take a practice quiz
- Direct link to related material that corresponds with the learning objective within the text

THE COMPLETE SOLUTION

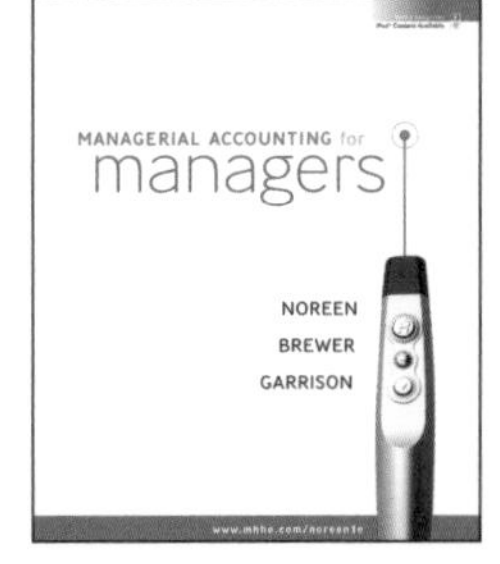

Noreen / Brewer / Garrison

Managerial Accounting for Managers

978-0-07-336851-1

1 TERM

McGraw-Hill's Homework Manager Plus™ combines the power of McGraw-Hill's Homework Manager® with the latest interactive learning technology to create a comprehensive, fully integrated online study package. Students working on assignments in McGraw-Hill's Homework Manager can click a simple hotlink and instantly review the appropriate material in the Interactive Online Textbook.

By including McGraw-Hill's Homework Manager Plus with your textbook adoption, you're giving your students a vital edge as they progress through the course and ensuring that the help they need is never more than a mouse click away. Contact your McGraw-Hill representative or visit the book's Web site to learn how to add McGraw-Hill's Homework Manager Plus to your adoption.

Imagine being able to create and access your test anywhere, at any time without installing the testing software. Now with **McGraw-Hill's EZ Test Online**, instructors can select questions from multiple McGraw-Hill test banks, author their own and then either print the test for paper distribution or give it online.

Use our EZ Test Online to help your students prepare to succeed with Apple® iPod® iQuiz.

Using our EZ Test Online you can make test and quiz content available for a student's Apple iPod.

Students must purchase the iQuiz game application from Apple for 99¢ in order to use the iQuiz content. It works on the iPod fifth generation iPods and better.

Instructors only need EZ Test Online to produce iQuiz ready content. Instructors take their existing tests and quizzes and export them to a file that can then be made available to the student to take as a self-quiz on their iPods. It's as simple as that.

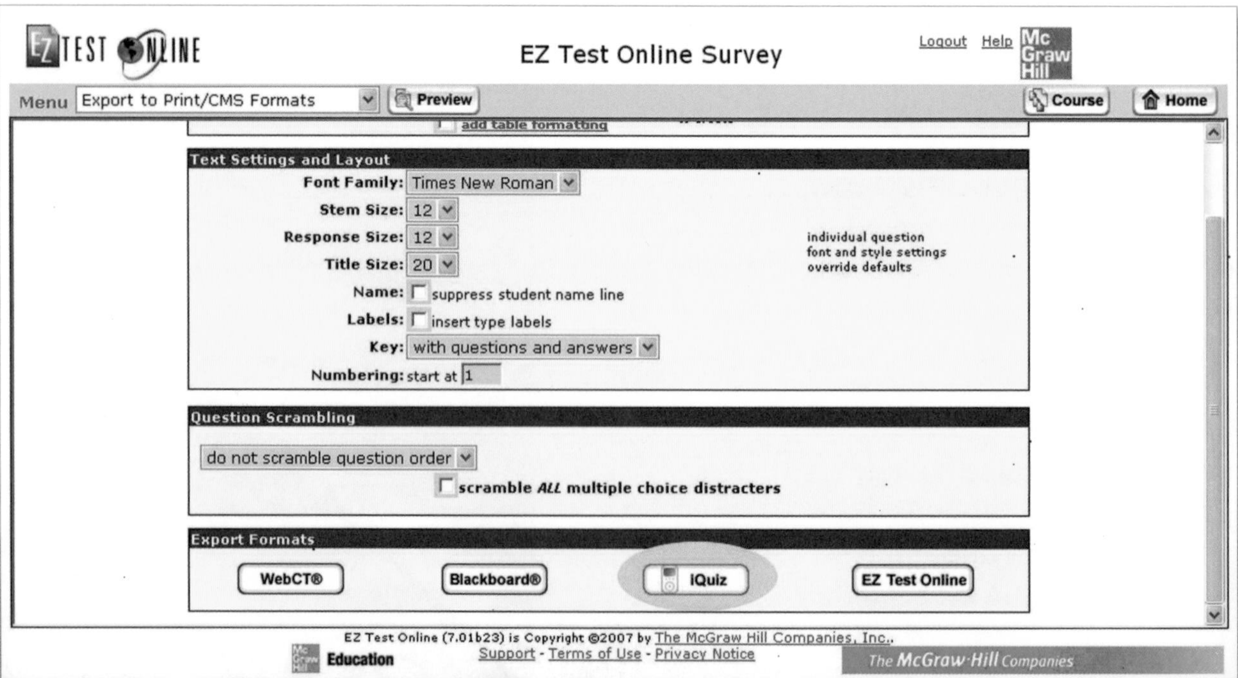

MANAGERIAL ACCOUNTING for managers

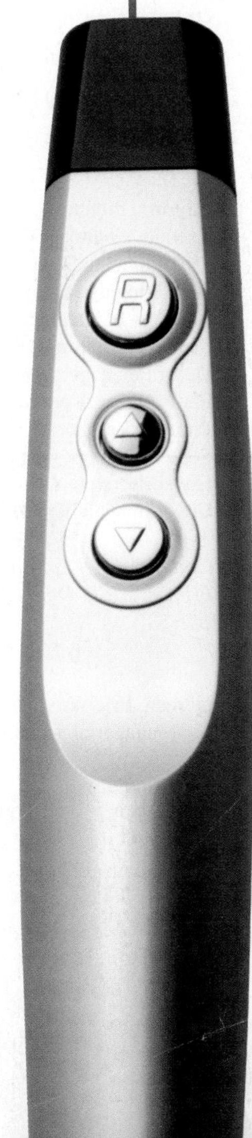

Eric W. Noreen, Ph.D., CMA
Professor Emeritus
University of Washington

Peter C. Brewer, Ph.D., CPA
Miami University—Oxford, Ohio

Ray H. Garrison, D.B.A., CPA
Professor Emeritus
Brigham Young University

Boston Burr Ridge, IL Dubuque, IA New York San Francisco St. Louis
Bangkok Bogotá Caracas Kuala Lumpur Lisbon London Madrid Mexico City
Milan Montreal New Delhi Santiago Seoul Singapore Sydney Taipei Toronto

Dedication

To our families and
to our many colleagues who use this book.

MANAGERIAL ACCOUNTING FOR MANAGERS

Published by McGraw-Hill/Irwin, a business unit of The McGraw-Hill Companies, Inc., 1221 Avenue of the Americas, New York, NY, 10020.

This book is printed on acid-free paper.

1 2 3 4 5 6 7 8 9 0 DOW/DOW 0 9 8 7

ISBN 978-0-07-352697-3
MHID 0-07-352697-5

Editorial director: *Stewart Mattson*
Executive editor: *Tim Vertovec*
Developmental editor: *Emily A. Hatteberg*
Marketing director: *Dan Silverburg*
Lead project manager: *Pat Frederickson*
Senior Production supervisor: *Debra R. Sylvester*
Design manager: *Kami Carter*
Photo research coordinator: *Lori Kramer*
Photo researcher: *Keri Johnson*
Senior media project manager: *Greg Bates*
Cover design: *Kami Carter*
Cover image: *© Jill Braaten*
Typeface: *10.5/12 Times Roman*
Compositor: *Aptara*
Printer: *R.R. Donnelley*

Library of Congress Cataloging-in-Publication Data

Noreen, Eric W.
Managerial accounting for managers / Eric W. Noreen, Peter C. Brewer, Ray H. Garrison.
p. cm.
Includes index.
ISBN-13: 978-0-07-352697-3 (alk. paper)
ISBN-10: 0-07-352697-5 (alk. paper)
1. Managerial accounting. I. Brewer, Peter C. II. Garrison, Ray H. III. Title.
HF5657.4.N668 2008
658.15'11--dc22 2007034085

www.mhhe.com

About the Authors

Eric W. Noreen has held appointments at institutions in the United States, Europe, and Asia. He is emeritus professor of accounting at the University of Washington.

He received his BA degree from the University of Washington and MBA and PhD degrees from Stanford University. A Certified Management Accountant, he was awarded a Certificate of Distinguished Performance by the Institute of Certified Management Accountants.

Professor Noreen has served as associate editor of *The Accounting Review* and the *Journal of Accounting and Economics*. He has numerous articles in academic journals including: the *Journal of Accounting Research*; the *Accounting Review*; the *Journal of Accounting and Economics*; *Accounting Horizons*; *Accounting, Organizations and Society*; *Contemporary Accounting Research*; the *Journal of Management Accounting Research*; and the *Review of Accounting Studies*.

Professor Noreen has won a number of awards from students for his teaching.

Peter C. Brewer is a professor in the Department of Accountancy at Miami University, Oxford, Ohio. He holds a BS degree in accounting from Penn State University, an MS degree in accounting from the University of Virginia, and a PhD from the University of Tennessee. He has published 30 articles in a variety of journals including: *Management Accounting Research, the Journal of Information Systems, Cost Management, Strategic Finance, the Journal of Accountancy, Issues in Accounting Education*, and *the Journal of Business Logistics*.

About the Authors

Professor Brewer is a member of the editorial boards of *Issues in Accounting Education* and the *Journal of Accounting Education*. His article "Putting Strategy into the Balanced Scorecard" won the 2003 International Federation of Accountants' Articles of Merit competition and his articles "Using Six Sigma to Improve the Finance Function" and "Lean Accounting: What's It All About?" were awarded the Institute of Management Accountants' Lybrand Gold and Silver Medals in 2005 and 2006. He has received Miami University's Richard T. Farmer School of Business Teaching Excellence Award and has been recognized on two occasions by the Miami University Associated Student Government for "making a remarkable commitment to students and their educational development." He is a leading thinker in undergraduate management accounting curriculum innovation and is a frequent presenter at various professional and academic conferences.

Prior to joining the faculty at Miami University, Professor Brewer was employed as an auditor for Touche Ross in the firm's Philadelphia office. He also worked as an internal audit manager for the Board of Pensions of the Presbyterian Church (U.S.A.). He frequently collaborates with companies such as Harris Corporation, Ghent Manufacturing, Cintas, Ethicon Endo-Surgery, Schneider Electric, Lenscrafters, and Fidelity Investments in a consulting or case writing capacity.

Ray H. Garrison

Ray H. Garrison is emeritus professor of accounting at Brigham Young University, Provo, Utah. He received his BS and MS degrees from Brigham Young University and his DBA degree from Indiana University.

As a certified public accountant, Professor Garrison has been involved in management consulting work with both national and regional accounting firms. He has published articles in *The Accounting Review*, *Management Accounting*, and other professional journals. Innovation in the classroom has earned Professor Garrison the Karl G. Maeser Distinguished Teaching Award from Brigham Young University.

NOREEN BREWER GARRISON

Focusing on the Future Manager

For decades, Garrison's **Managerial Accounting** has successfully guided students through the rough waters of accounting. Now, the same authors who brought you the quality and reliability of Garrison are taking managerial accounting to the next level in **Managerial Accounting for Managers.**

Noreen/Brewer/Garrison includes Garrison's great coverage of managerial accounting topics such as relevant costs for decision making, capital budgeting decisions, and segment reporting and decentralization; however, all journal entries that appear in the Garrison book have been removed from the Noreen book. For example, the job-order costing chapter has been extensively rewritten to remove all journal entries. Furthermore, the chapters dealing with process costing, the statement of cash flows, and financial statement analysis have been dropped to enable you to focus your attention on the bedrocks of managerial accounting—planning, control, and decision making.

By removing journal entries, the authors have crafted a streamlined managerial accounting book that is perfect for non-accounting majors who intend to move into managerial positions. Noreen/Brewer/Garrison focuses on the fundamentals, allowing students to develop the conceptual framework managers need to succeed.

Most important, in **Managerial Accounting for Managers,** both students and professors will find the same core standards that have made Garrison the best text on the market:

"I LOVE the removal of the journal entries . . ."
—*Tom Hrubec, Franklin University*

"This book focuses on management decisions, and discusses concepts and applications clearly and concisely."
—*Alfonso R. Oddo, Niagara University*

"...this text really has good illustrations of Managerial Accounting usage in the 'real world.'"
—*Tamara Phelan, Northern Illinois University*

FOCUS. Noreen/Brewer/Garrison pinpoints the key managerial concepts students will need in their future careers. With no journal entries or financial accounting topics to worry about, students can focus on the fundamental principles of managerial accounting.

RELEVANCE. With its insightful Business Focus features to begin each chapter, current In Business examples throughout the text, and tried-and-true end-of-chapter material, a student will always see the real-world applicability of Noreen/Brewer/Garrison.

BALANCE. There is more than one type of business, and so Noreen/Brewer/Garrison covers a variety of business models, including nonprofit, retail, service, wholesale, and manufacturing organizations. Service company examples are highlighted with icons in the margins of the text.

Noreen's Powerful Pedagogy

Managerial Accounting for Managers is full of pedagogy designed to make studying productive and hassle free.

Opening Vignette

Each chapter opens with a Business Focus feature that provides a real-world example for students, allowing them to see how the chapter's information and insights apply to the world outside the classroom. **Learning Objectives** alert students to what they should expect as they progress through the chapter.

Chapter 2

Learning Objectives

After studying Chapter 2, you should be able to:

LO1 Identify and give examples of each of the three basic manufacturing cost categories.

LO2 Distinguish between product costs and period costs and give examples of each.

LO3 Prepare an income statement including calculation of the cost of goods sold.

LO4 Prepare a schedule of cost of goods manufactured.

LO5 Understand the differences between variable costs and fixed costs.

LO6 Understand the differences between direct and indirect costs.

LO7 Define and give examples of cost classifications used in making decisions: differential costs, opportunity costs, and sunk costs.

LP 2

Cost Terms, Concepts, and Classifications

Costs Add Up

BUSINESS FOCUS

Understanding costs and how they behave is critical in business. Labor Ready is a company based in Tacoma, Washington, that fills temporary manual labor jobs throughout the United States, Canada, and the UK—issuing over 6 million paychecks each year to more than half a million laborers. For example, food vendors at the Seattle Mariners' Safeco Field hire Labor Ready workers to serve soft drinks and food at baseball games. Employers are charged about $11 per hour for this service. Since Labor Ready pays its workers only about $6.50 per hour and offers no fringe benefits and has no national competitors, this business would appear to be a gold mine generating about $4.50 per hour in profit. However, the company must maintain 687 hiring offices, each employing a permanent staff of four to five persons. Those costs, together with payroll taxes, workmen's compensation insurance, and other administrative costs, result in a margin of only about 5%, or a little over 50¢ per hour. ■

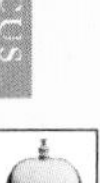

Source: Catie Golding, "Short-Term Work, Long-Term Profits," *Washington CEO*, January 2000, pp. 10–12.

"Excellent... Easy to read with interesting and relevant 'real-world' examples."

—John Reisch, East Carolina University

IN BUSINESS

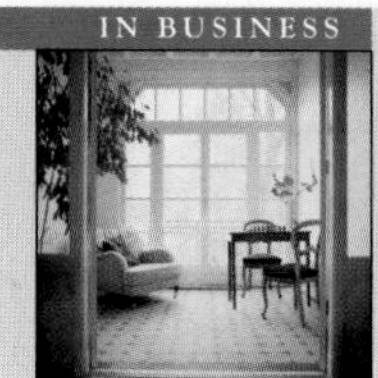

MANAGING DIVERSITY WITH TECHNOLOGY

Andersen Windows, Inc. of Bayport, Minnesota, has a software program that enables it to produce just about any window configuration that a customer might order. The program—which works on most standard Microsoft® Windows platforms—allows customers to select from any of the company's large selection of standard window and door sizes and styles. Customers can add the features and options they want with an easy "point-and-click" until they've configured the desired units. Placing the order after final selections are made is just as easy—the window order can be sent electronically into Andersen's back office system where it is automatically fulfilled. The entire process is highly automated and very efficient, yet it enables the customer a high degree of flexibility.

Source: Andersen® Intelligent Quote, used by permission of Andersen Windows, Inc.

In Business Boxes

These helpful boxed features offer a glimpse into how real companies use the managerial accounting concepts discussed within the chapter. Each chapter contains from three to fourteen of these current examples.

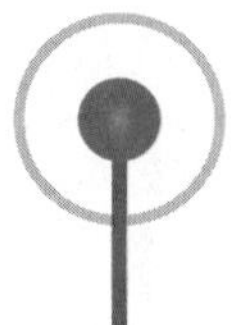

Segment Reporting and Decentralization 443

MANAGERIAL ACCOUNTING IN ACTION
The Issue

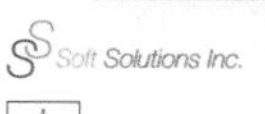

SoftSolutions, Inc., is a rapidly growing computer software company founded by Lori Saffer, who had previously worked in a large software company, and Marjorie Matsuo, who had previously worked in the hotel industry as a general manager. They formed the company to develop and market user-friendly accounting and operations software designed specifically for hotels. They quit their jobs, pooled their savings, hired several programmers, and got down to work.

The first sale was by far the most difficult. No hotel wanted to be the first to use an untested product from an unknown company. After overcoming this obstacle with persistence, good luck, dedication to customer service, and a very low introductory price, the company's sales grew.

The company quickly developed similar business software for other specialized markets and then branched out into clip art and computer games. Within four years of its founding, the organization had grown to the point where Saffer and Matsuo were no longer able to personally direct all of the company's activities. Decentralization had become a necessity.

Accordingly, the company was split into two divisions—Business Products and Consumer Products. By mutual consent, Matsuo took the title president and Saffer took the title vice president of the Business Products Division. Chris Worden, a programmer who had spearheaded the drive into the clip art and computer games markets, was designated vice president of the Consumer Products Division.

Almost immediately, the issue arose of how best to evaluate the performance of the divisions. Matsuo called a meeting to consider this issue and asked Saffer, Worden, and the controller, Bill Carson, to attend. The following discussion took place at that meeting:

Marjorie: We need to find a better way to measure the performance of our divisions.

Chris: I agree. Consumer Products has been setting the pace in this company for the last two years, and we should be getting more recognition.

Lori: Chris, we are delighted with the success of the Consumer Products Division.

Chris: I know. But it is hard to figure out just how successful we are with the present accounting reports. All we have are sales and cost of goods sold figures for the division.

Bill: What's the matter with those figures? They are prepared using generally accepted accounting principles.

Chris: The sales figures are fine. However, cost of goods sold includes some costs that really aren't the costs of our division, and it excludes some costs that are. Let's take a simple example. Everything we sell in the Consumer Products Division has to pass through the automatic bar-coding machine, which applies a unique bar code to the product.

Lori: That's true for items from the Business Products Division as well as for items from the Consumer Products Division.

Chris: That's precisely the point. Whether an item comes from the Business Products Division or the Consumer Products Division, it must pass through the automatic bar-coding machine after the software has been packaged. How much of the cost of the automatic bar coder would be saved if we didn't have any consumer products?

Marjorie: Since we have only one automatic bar coder and we would need it anyway to code the business products, I guess none of the cost would be saved.

Chris: That's right. And since none of the cost could be saved even if the entire Consumer Products Division were eliminated, how can we logically say that some of the cost of the automatic bar coder is a cost of the Consumer Products Division?

Lori: Just a minute, Chris, are you saying that my Business Products Division should be charged with the entire cost of the automatic bar coder?

Chris: No, that's not what I am saying.

Marjorie: But Chris, I don't see how we can have sensible performance reports without making someone responsible for costs like the cost of the automatic bar coder. Bill, as our accounting expert, what do you think?

Bill: I have some ideas for handling issues like the automatic bar coder. The best approach would probably be for me to put together a draft performance report. We can discuss it at the next meeting when everyone has something concrete to look at.

Marjorie: Okay, let's see what you come up with.

Managerial Accounting in Action Vignettes

These vignettes depict cross-functional teams working together in real-life settings, working with the products and services that students recognize from their own lives. Students are shown step-by-step how accounting concepts are implemented in organizations and how these concepts are applied to solve everyday business problems. First, "The Issue" is introduced through a dialogue; the student then walks through the implementation process; finally, "The Wrap-up" summarizes the big picture.

Service Examples

To reflect our service-based economy, the text is replete with examples from service-based businesses. A helpful icon distinguishes service-related examples in the text.

End-of-Chapter Material

Building on Garrison/Noreen/Brewer's reputation for the best end-of-chapter review and discussion material of any text on the market, Noreen's problem and case material continues to conform to AICPA and AACSB recommendations and makes a great starting point for class discussions and group projects. Other helpful features include:

- **Research and Application Cases** using 10-K data from companies such as Whole Foods Market, Dell, and FedEx, offer end-of-chapter learning opportunities for students to identify strategy and business risks and evaluate managerial accounting concepts within a real world context.
- **Excel® Spreadsheet Templates** are available for use with selected problems and cases.
- **Ethics assignments** serve as a reminder that good conduct is vital in business.
- The **Writing Icon** denotes problems that require students to use critical thinking as well as writing skills to explain their decisions.

Author-Written Supplements

Unlike other managerial accounting texts, Noreen, Brewer, and Garrison write all of the text's major supplements, ensuring a perfect fit between text and supplement. For more information on **Managerial Accounting for Managers** supplements package, see page xiv.

"Good overview for managers that can be used for teaching the subject at both undergraduate and graduate levels to managers in non-accounting disciplines."

—Kamala Rafhavan, Robert Morris University

". . . a very good text that needs to be considered seriously."

—Kashi R. Balachandran, New York University

Market-Leading Technology

iPod Content

Harness the power of one of the most popular technology tools students use today–the Apple iPod®. Our innovative approach allows students to download audio and video presentations right into their iPod and take learning materials with them wherever they go.

Students just need to visit the Online Learning Center at **www.mhhe.com/noreen1e** to download our iPod content. For each chapter of the book, they will be able to download audio narrated lecture presentations, managerial accounting videos, and even self-quizzes designed for use on various versions of iPods. The iPod content can be downloaded quickly and easily from the enclosed DVD without the need to spend the additional download time.

It makes review and study time as easy as putting on headphones.

McGraw-Hill's Homework Manager® is a Web-based supplement that duplicates problems directly from the textbook end-of-chapter material, using algorithms to provide a limitless supply of online self-graded practice for students, or assignments and tests with unique versions of every problem. Say goodbye to cheating in your classroom; say hello to the power and flexibility you've been waiting for in creating assignments.

The enhanced version of McGraw-Hill's Homework Manager integrates all of Noreen/Brewer/Garrison's online and multimedia assets to allow your students to brush up on a topic before doing their homework. You now have the option to give your students pre-populated hints and feedback. The test bank has been added to McGraw-Hill's Homework Manager so you can create online quizzes and exams and have them autograded and recorded in the same gradebook as your homework assignments. Lastly, the enhanced version provides you with the option of incorporating the complete online version of the textbook, so your students can easily reference the chapter material as they do their homework assignment, even when their textbook is far away.

McGraw-Hill's Homework Manager is also a useful grading tool. All assignments can be delivered over the Web and are graded automatically, with the results stored in your private gradebook. Detailed results let you see at a glance how each student does on an assignment or an individual problem—you can even see how many tries it took them to solve it.

Students receive full access to McGraw-Hill's Homework Manager when they purchase Homework Manager Plus®, or you can have McGraw-Hill's Homework Manager pass codes shrinkwrapped with the textbook: Students can also purchase access to McGraw-Hill's Homework Manager directly from your class home page.

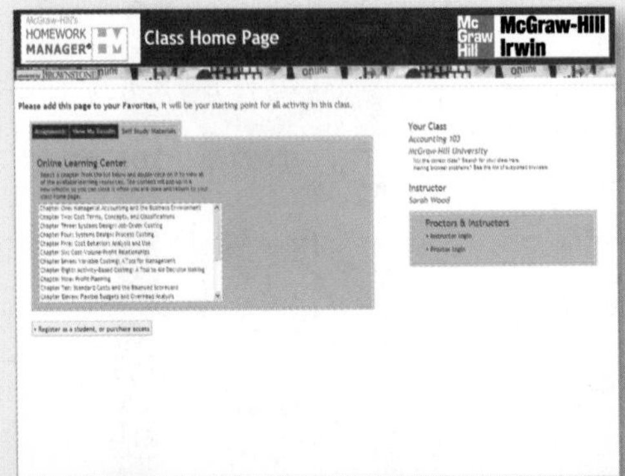

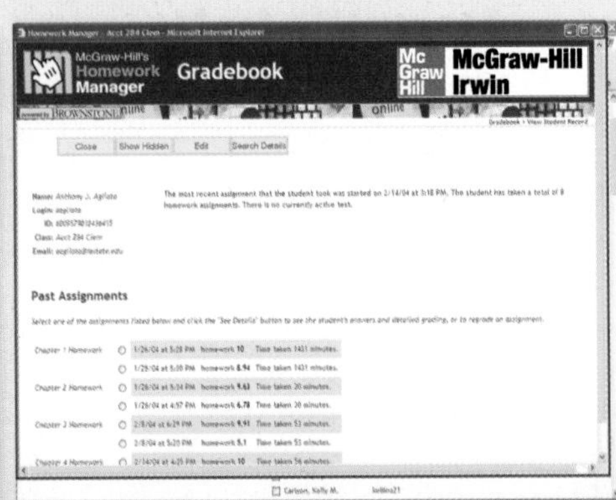

McGraw-Hill's Homework Manager Plus™

combines the power of McGraw-Hill's Homework Manager with the latest interactive learning technology to create a comprehensive, fully integrated online study package.

Students using McGraw-Hill's Homework Manager Plus can access not only McGraw-Hill's Homework Manager® itself, but the interactive online textbook as well. Far more than a textbook on a screen, this resource is completely integrated into McGraw-Hill's Homework Manager, allowing students working on assignments to click a hotlink and instantly review the appropriate material in the textbook.

By including McGraw-Hill's Homework Manager Plus with your textbook adoption, you're giving your students a vital edge as they progress through the course and ensuring that the help they need is never more than a mouse click away.

Students receive full access to McGraw-Hill's Homework Manager when they purchase Homework Manager Plus.

Online Learning Center (OLC) www.mhhe.com/Noreen1e

More and more students are studying online. That's why we offer an Online Learning Center (OLC) that follows **Managerial Accounting for Managers** chapter by chapter. It doesn't require any building or maintenance on your part. It's ready to go the moment you and your students type in the URL.

As your students study, they can refer to the OLC Web site for such benefits as:

- Internet-based activities
- Self-grading quizzes
- Links to professional resources on the Web and job opportunity information
- Learning objectives
- Chapter overviews
- Internet factory tours
- Excel spreadsheets
- PowerPoint® slides
- Excel walkthroughs

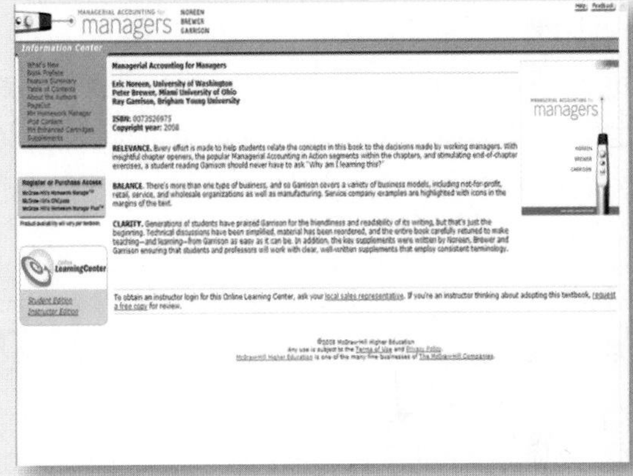

A secured Instructor Resource Center stores your essential course materials to save you prep time before class. The Instructor's Manual, solutions, and PowerPoint slides are now just a couple of clicks away. You will also find useful packaging information and transition notes.

The OLC also serves as a doorway to other technology solutions like PageOut, which is free to **Managerial Accounting for Managers** adopters.

Topic Tackler Plus

This program is a complete tutorial focusing on those areas in the managerial accounting course that give students the most trouble. Providing extensive help on two key topics for every single chapter, this program delves into the material via the following:

- Video Clips
- PowerPoint slide shows
- Interactive exercises
- Self-grading quizzes
- Web site hotlinks

This highly engaging presentation will give your students command of the aspects of managerial accounting. Students can access Topic Tackler Plus via the Online Learning Center.

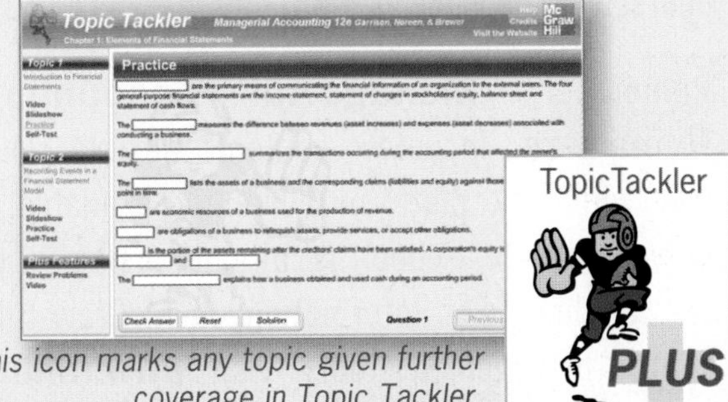

This icon marks any topic given further coverage in Topic Tackler.

Creating an Online Course is Easy—with the Right Guide

For the instructor needing to educate students online, we offer **Managerial Accounting for Managers** content for complete online courses. To make this possible, we have joined forces with the most popular delivery platforms currently available. These platforms are designed for instructors who want complete control over course content and how it is presented to students. You can customize the **Managerial Accounting for Managers** Online Learning Center content and author your own course materials. It's entirely up to you.

eCollege.com

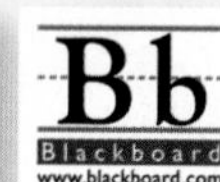

Products like WebCT, Blackboard, and eCollege expand the reach of your course. Online discussion and message boards will now complement your office hours. Thanks to a sophisticated tracking system, you will know which students need more attention—even if they don't ask for help. That's because online testing scores are recorded and automatically placed in your gradebook, and if a student is struggling with coursework, a special alert message lets you know.

Remember, **Managerial Accounting for Managers** includes content flexible enough to use with any platform currently available. If your department or school is already using a platform, we can help. For information on McGraw-Hill/Irwin's course management tools, visit **www.mhhe.com/solutions**.

PageOut—McGraw-Hill's Course Management System

PageOut is the easiest way to create a Web site for your accounting course.

There's no need for HTML coding, graphic design, or a thick how-to book. Just fill in a series of boxes with simple English and click on one of our professional designs. In no time, your course is online with a Web site that contains your syllabus!

Should you need assistance in preparing your Web site, we can help. Our team of product specialists is ready to take your course materials and build a custom Web site to your specifications; you simply need to call a McGraw-Hill/Irwin PageOut specialist (1-800-634-3963) to start the process. Best of all, PageOut is free when you adopt **Managerial Accounting for Managers**! To learn more, please visit **www.pageout.net**.

Enhanced Cartridge

The Enhanced Cartridge is developed to help you get your course up and running with much less time and effort. The content, enhanced with more assignments and more study materials than a standard cartridge, is pre-populated into appropriate chapters and content categories. Now there's no need to cut and paste our content into your course — it's already there!

In addition to the standard instructor supplement content, this cartridge also includes:

- Pre-populated course syllabus
- iPod/MP3 content
- Chapter pre- and post-tests
- Midterm and final tests
- Discussion boards
- Additional assignments
- Personalized graphics/banners/icons for your school
- Gradebook functionality

The Enhanced Cartridge allows students to access their course anytime, anywhere. For students the Enhanced Cartridge includes:

- Key term flashcards
- Excel templates
- Narrated review problems
- Topic Tackler Plus
- PowerPoint slides

CPS Classroom Performance System by eInstruction

This is a revolutionary system that brings ultimate interactivity to the classroom. CPS is a wireless response system that gives you immediate feedback from every student in the class. CPS units include easy-to-use software for creating and delivering questions and assessments to your class. With CPS you can ask subjective and objective questions. Then every student simply responds with their individual, wireless response pad, providing instant results. CPS is the perfect tool for engaging students while gathering important assessment data.

Instructor Supplements

Assurance of Learning Ready

Many educational institutions today are focused on the notion of assurance of learning, an important element of some accreditation standards. *Managerial Accounting for Managers* is designed specifically to support your assurance of learning initiatives with a simple, yet powerful, solution.

Each test bank question for *Managerial Accounting for Managers* maps to a specific chapter learning outcome/objective listed in the text. You can use our test bank software, *EZ Test,* to easily query for learning outcomes/objectives that directly relate to the learning objectives for your course. You can then use the reporting features of *EZ Test* to aggregate student results in similar fashion, making the collection and presentation of assurance of learning data simple and easy. You can also use our Algorithmic-Diploma Test Bank to do this.

AACSB Statement

McGraw-Hill Companies is a proud corporate member of AACSB International. Recognizing the importance and value of AACSB accreditation, we have sought to recognize the curricula guidelines detailed in AACSB standards for business accreditation by connecting selected test bank questions in *Managerial Accounting for Managers* to the general knowledge and skill guidelines found in the AACSB standards.

The statements contained in *Managerial Accounting for Managers* are provided only as a guide for the users of this text. The AACSB leaves content coverage and assessment clearly within the realm and control of individual schools, the mission of the school, and the faculty. The AACSB also charges schools with the obligation of doing assessment against their own content and learning goals. While *Managerial Accounting for Managers* and its teaching package make no claim of any specific AACSB qualification or evaluation, we have labeled selected questions according to the six general knowledge and skills areas.

Instructor CD-ROM

MHID: 0073368490
ISBN-13: 9780073368498

Allowing instructors to create a customized multimedia presentation, this all-in-one resource incorporates the Test Bank, PowerPoint® Slides, Instructor's Resource Guide, Solutions Manual, Teaching Transparency Masters, links to PageOut, and the Excel Templates.

Algorithmic-Diploma Test Bank

MHID: 0073262536
ISBN-13: 9780073262536

This computerized test bank is an algorithmic problem generator that enables instructors to create similarly structured problems with different values, allowing every student to be assigned a unique quiz or test. The user-friendly interface gives faculty the ability to easily create different versions of the same test, change the answer order, edit or add questions, and even conduct online testing.

Instructor's Resource Guide

(Available on the password-protected Instructor OLC and Instructor's Resource CD)

Extensive chapter-by-chapter lecture notes help with classroom presentations and contain useful suggestions for presenting key concepts and ideas. The lecture notes coordinate closely with the PowerPoint Slides, making lesson planning even easier.

Solutions Manual

(Available on the password-protected Instructor OLC and Instructor's Resource CD)

This supplement contains completely worked-out solutions to all assignment material and a general discussion of the use of group exercises. In addition, the manual contains suggested course outlines and a listing of exercises, problems, and cases scaled according to difficulty.

Computerized Test Bank

(Available on the Instructor's Resource CD)

This test bank utilizes McGraw-Hill's *EZ Test* software to quickly create customized exams. This user-friendly program allows instructors to sort questions by format, edit existing questions, or add new ones. It also can scramble questions for multiple versions of the same test.

Microsoft Excel® Template Solutions

(Available on the password-protected Instructor OLC and Instructor's Resource CD)

Prepared by Jack Terry of ComSource Associates, Inc., these Excel templates offer solutions to the student version.

Test Bank

(Available on the Instructor's Resource CD)

Over 2,000 questions are organized by chapter and include true/false, multiple-choice, and essay questions and computational problems.

PowerPoint® Slides

(Available on OLC and Instructor's Resource CD)

Prepared by Jon Booker and Charles Caldwell of Tennessee Technological University, and Susan Galbreath of Lipscomb University, these slides offer a great visual complement for your lectures. A complete set of slides covers each chapter.

Student Supplements

McGraw-Hill's Homework Manager® and McGraw-Hill's Homework Manager Plus™

This Web-based software duplicates problem structures directly from the end-of-chapter material in the textbook. It uses algorithms to provide a Limitless supply of self-graded practice.

Homework Manager Plus combines the power of McGraw-Hill's Homework Manager with the latest interactive learning technology to create a comprehensive, fully integrated online study package.

Online Learning Center (OLC)

www.mhhe.com/noreen1e

See page xi for details.

iPod® Content

See page x for details.

Topic Tackler Plus

(Available on the OLC)

Available on the text Web site, Topic Tackler Plus helps you master difficult concepts in managerial accounting through a creative, interactive learning process. Designed for study outside the classroom, this material delves into chapter concepts with graphical slides and diagrams, Web links, video clips, and animations, all centered around engaging exercises designed to put you in control of your learning of managerial accounting topics.

Workbook/Study Guide

MHID: 0073368547
ISBN-13: 9780073368542

This study aid provides suggestions for studying chapter material, summarizes essential points in each chapter, and tests your knowledge using self-test questions and exercises.

Managerial Accounting Practice Set

MHID: 0073396192
ISBN-13: 9780073396194

Authored by Janice L. Cobb of Texas Christian University, *Doing the Job of the Managerial Accountant* is a real-world application for the Introductory Managerial Accounting student. The case is based on an actual growing, entrepreneurial manufacturing company that is complex enough to demonstrate the decisions management must make, yet simple enough that a sophomore student can easily understand the entire operations of the company. The case requires the student to do tasks they would perform working as the managerial accountant for the company. The required tasks are directly related to the concepts learned in all managerial accounting classes. The practice set can be used by the professor as a teaching tool for class lectures, as additional homework assignments, or as a semester project.

Media Integration

iPod icons throughout the text link content back to chapter-specific quizzes, audio and visual lecture presentations, review problems, and course-related videos. This gives students access to a portable, electronic learning option to support their classroom instruction.

Working Papers

MHID: 0073368555
ISBN-13: 9780073368559

This study aid contains forms that help you organize your solutions to homework problems.

Excel® Templates

(Available on the OLC)

Prepared by Jack Terry of ComSource Associates, Inc., this spreadsheet-based software uses Excel to solve selected problems and cases in the text. These selected problems and cases are identified in the margin of the text with an appropriate icon.

Check Figures

These provide key answers for selected problems and cases. They are available on the text Web site.

Acknowledgments

Suggestions have been received from many of our colleagues throughout the world. Each of those who have offered comments and suggestions has our thanks.

The efforts of many people are needed to develop and improve a text. Among these people are the reviewers and consultants who point out areas of concern, cite areas of strength, and make recommendations for change. In this regard, the following professors provided feedback that was enormously helpful in preparing the first edition of ***Managerial Accounting for Managers***:

Frank Aquilino, Montclair State University
Kashi R. Balachandran, New York University
Surasakdi Bhamornsiri, University of North Carolina-Charlotte
Janet Butler, Texas State University-san Marcos
Rusty Calk, New Mexico State University
Cathy Claiborne, Texas Southern Univiversity
Nancy Coulmas, Bloomsburg University of Pennsylvania
Jean Crawford, Alabama State University
Andrea Drake, University of Cincinnati-cincinnati
Jan Duffy, Iowa State University
Cindy Easterwood, Virginia Tech
Janice Fergusson, University of South Carolina
Ananda Ganguly, Clairmont College
Olen Greer, Missouri State University
Ken Harmon, Kennesaw State University
Kathy Ho, Niagara University
Maggie Houston, Wright State University
Tom Hrubec, Franklin University
Robyn Jarnagin, Montana State University
Randy Johnston, Michigan State University
Nancy Jones, California State University
Carl Keller, Indiana University–Purdue University Fort Wayne
James Kinard, Ohio State University-Columbus
Kathy Long, University of Tennessee at Chattanooga
Patti Lopez, Valencia Comm College East
Jim Lukawitz, University of Memphis
Anna Lusher, Slippery Rock University
Laurie Mcwhorter, Mississippi State University
James Meddaugh, Ohio University
Alfonso R. Oddo, Niagara University
Tamara Phelan, Northern Illinois University
Les Price, Pierce College
Kamala Raghavan, Robert Morris University
Raul Ramos, Lorain County Community College
John Reisch, East Carolina University
Michelle Reisch, East Carolina University
Pamela Rouse, Butler University
Amy Santos, Manatee Community College
Ellen Sweatt, Georgia Perimeter College
Rick Tabor, Auburn University
Diane Tanner, University of North Florida
Chuck Thompson, University of Massachusetts
Marjorie E. Yuschak, Rutgers Business School

We are grateful for the outstanding support from McGraw-Hill. In particular, we would like to thank Stewart Mattson, Editorial Director; Tim Vertovec, Executive Editor; Emily Hatteberg, Developmental Editor; Dan Silverburg, Marketing Director; Pat Frederickson, Lead Project Manager; Debra Sylvester, Production Supervisor; Kami Carter, Design Manager; Gregory Bates, Senior Media Project Manager; and Lori Kramer, Photo Research Coordinator.

Finally, we would like to thank Beth Woods and Barbara Schnathorst for working so hard to ensure an error-free first edition. The authors also wish to thank Linda and Michael Bamber for inspiring the creation of the 10-K Research and Application exercises that are included in the end-of-chapter materials throughout the book.

We are grateful to the Institute of Certified Management Accountants for permission to use questions and/or unofficial answers from past Certificate in Management Accounting (CMA) examinations. Likewise, we thank the American Institute of Certified Public Accountants, the Society of Management Accountants of Canada, and the Chartered Institute of Management Accountants (United Kingdom) for permission to use (or to adapt) selected problems from their examinations. These problems bear the notations CPA, SMA, and CIMA respectively.

Eric W. C. Noreen • Peter Brewer • Ray H. Garrison

Brief Contents

Contents

Chapter 3 Systems Design: Job-Order Costing 78

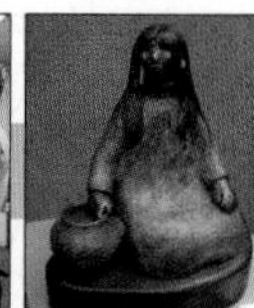

Chapter 4 Cost Behavior: Analysis and Use 120

Chapter 5

Cost-Volume-Profit Relationships 165

Chapter 6

Variable Costing: A Tool for Management 208

Activity-Based Costing: A Tool to Aid Decision Making 242

Chapter 8
Profit Planning 297

Standard Costs and the Balanced Scorecard 343

Chapter 10

Flexible Budgets and Overhead Analysis 396

Chapter 11 Segment Reporting and Decentralization 437

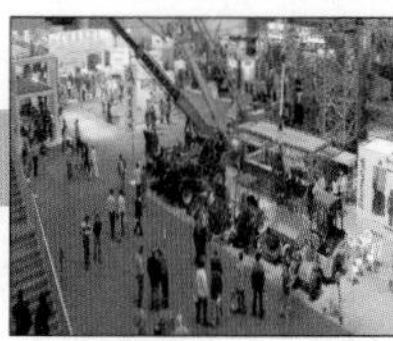

Chapter 12 Relevant Costs for Decision Making 499

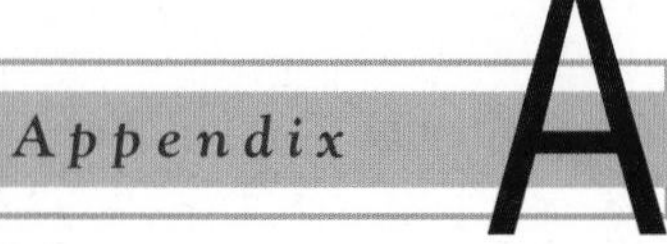

Appendix A

Pricing Products and Services 605

Appendix B

Profitability Analysis 621

Chapter

1

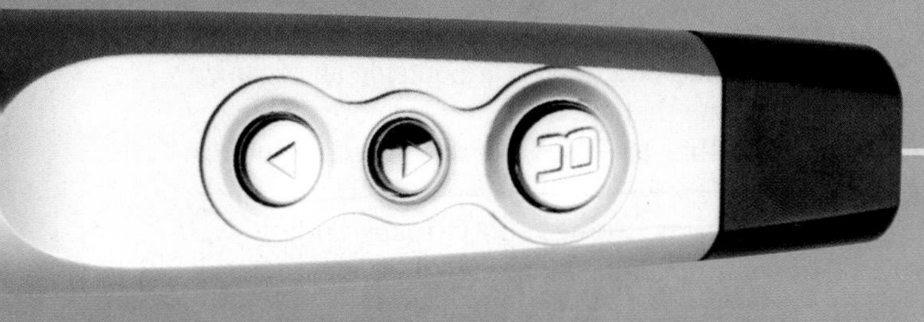

Managerial Accounting and the Business Environment

The Role of Management Accounting

BUSINESS FOCUS

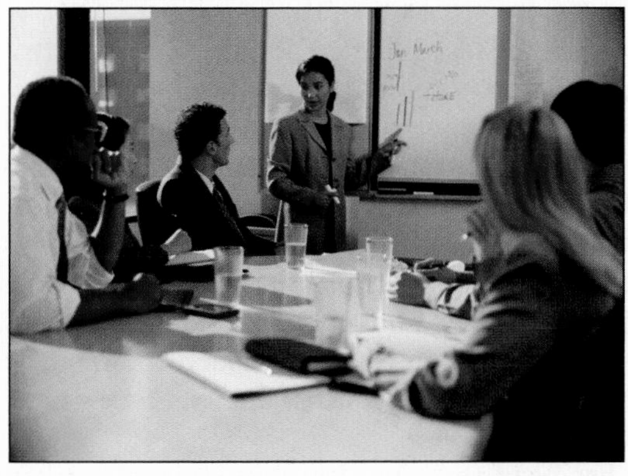

It is estimated that 95% of all finance professionals work inside corporations, governments, and other organizations, integrating accounting with operations and reporting to the outside world. While some of the effort expended by these people relates to financial accounting, the profession needs to further stress the role management accountants play within organizations supporting decision making, planning, and control. In short, the emphasis in business and the role of accounting should be more about *doing* business rather than tabulating and reporting historical financial results.

Management accounting is undergoing a renaissance in response to technological changes, globalization, and growing risk management concerns. In these challenging times, management accountants help "steady the ship" by acting as their organizations' interpreters, sage advisors, and ethical "keepers of the numbers." Managers understand that good business results come from dynamic processes, procedures, and practices that are well designed and properly implemented and managed. Certified Management Accountants are qualified to help their fellow managers achieve good business results because they have earned an advanced certification that addresses all important aspects of accounting inside organizations. ■

Source: Conversation with Paul Sharman, CEO of the Institute of Management Accountants.

Learning Objectives

After studying Chapter 1, you should be able to:

LO1 Identify the major differences and similarities between financial and managerial accounting.

LO2 Understand the role of management accountants in an organization.

LO3 Understand the basic concepts underlying Lean Production, the Theory of Constraints (TOC), and Six Sigma.

LO4 Understand the importance of upholding ethical standards.

LP 1

Managerial accounting is concerned with providing information to managers—that is, people inside an organization who direct and control its operations. In contrast, **financial accounting** is concerned with providing information to stockholders, creditors, and others who are outside an organization. Managerial accounting provides the essential data that are needed to run organizations. Financial accounting provides the essential data that are used by outsiders to judge a company's past financial performance.

Managerial accountants prepare a variety of reports. Some reports focus on how well managers or business units have performed—comparing actual results to plans and to benchmarks. Some reports provide timely, frequent updates on key indicators such as orders received, order backlog, capacity utilization, and sales. Other analytical reports are prepared as needed to investigate specific problems such as a decline in the profitability of a product line. And yet other reports analyze a developing business situation or opportunity. In contrast, financial accounting is oriented toward producing a limited set of specific prescribed annual and quarterly financial statements in accordance with generally accepted accounting principles (GAAP).

The chapter begins with discussions of globalization and the meaning of strategy. Next, it describes the information needs of management and how the role of managerial accounting differs from financial accounting. Finally, the chapter provides an overview of the organizational context within which management accounting operates—including discussions of organizational structure, process management, technology in business, the importance of ethics, corporate governance, and enterprise risk management.

Globalization

Video 1–1

The world has become much more intertwined over the last 20 years. Reductions in tariffs, quotas, and other barriers to free trade; improvements in global transportation systems; explosive expansion in Internet usage; and increasing sophistication in international markets have created a truly global marketplace. Exhibit 1–1 illustrates this tremendous growth in international trade from the standpoint of the United States and some of its key trading partners. Panel A of the exhibit shows the dollar value of imports (stated in billions of dollars) into the United States from six countries; Panel B shows the dollar value of exports from the United States to those same six countries. As you can see, the increase in import and export activity from 1990 to 2004 was huge. In particular, trade with China expanded enormously as did trade with Mexico and Canada, which participate in the North American Free Trade Agreement (NAFTA).

In a global marketplace, a company that has been very successful in its local market may suddenly find itself facing competition from halfway around the globe. For example, in the 1980s American automobile manufacturers began losing market share to Japanese competitors who offered American consumers higher quality cars at lower prices. For consumers, this type of heightened international competition promises a greater variety of goods and services, at higher quality and lower prices. However, heightened international competition threatens companies that may have been quite profitable in their own local markets.

Although globalization leads to greater competition, it also means greater access to new markets, customers, and workers. For example, the emerging markets of China, India, Russia, and Brazil contain more than 2.5 billion potential customers and workers.[1] Many companies such as FedEx, McDonald's, and Nike are actively seeking to grow

[1] *The Economist: Pocket World in Figures 2004*, Profile Books Ltd., London, U.K.

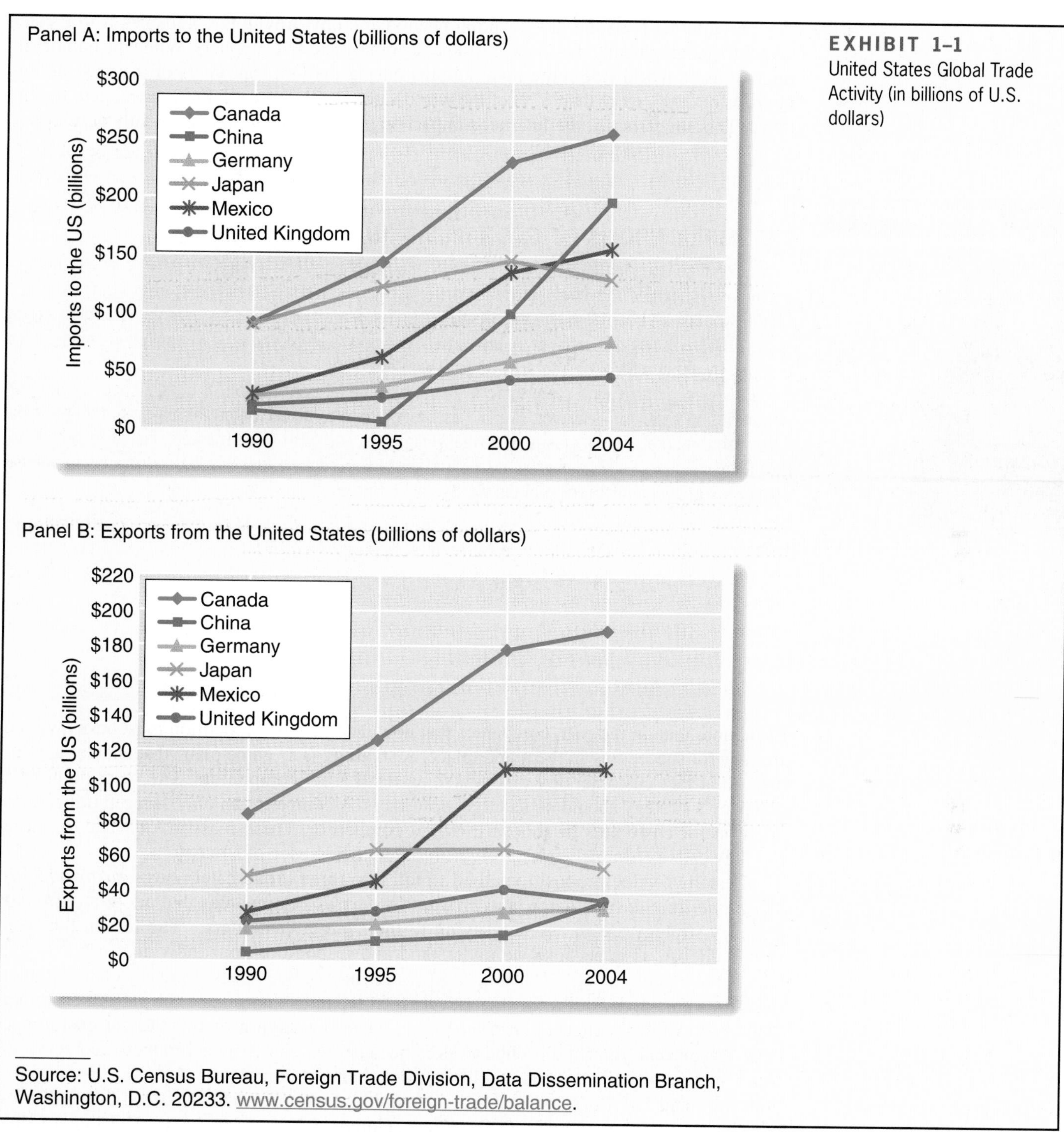

EXHIBIT 1–1
United States Global Trade Activity (in billions of U.S. dollars)

their sales by investing in emerging markets. In addition, the movement of jobs from the United States and Western Europe to other parts of the world has been notable in recent years. For example, one study estimates that by the end of the decade more than 825,000 financial services and high-tech jobs will transfer from Western Europe to less expensive labor markets such as India, China, Africa, Eastern Europe, and Latin America.[2]

[2] "Job Exports: Europe's Turn," *BusinessWeek,* April 19, 2004, p. 50.

The Internet fuels the globalization phenomenon by providing companies with greater access to geographically dispersed customers, employees, and suppliers. While the number of Internet users worldwide more than doubled during the first four years of the new millennium, as of 2004, more than 87% of the world's population was still not connected to the Internet. This suggests that the Internet's impact on global business has yet to fully develop.

IN BUSINESS

THE IMPLICATIONS OF GLOBALIZATION

International competition goes hand-in-hand with globalization. China's entrance into the global marketplace has highlighted this stark reality for many U.S. companies. For example, from 2000 to 2003, China's wooden bedroom furniture exports to the United States increased by more than 233% to a total of $1.2 billion. During this same time, the number of workers employed by U.S. furniture manufacturers dropped by about a third, or a total of 35,000 workers.

However, globalization means more than international competition. It brings opportunities for companies to enter new markets. FedEx has pushed hard to be an important player in the emerging Asian cargo market. FedEx makes 622 weekly flights to and from Asian markets, including service to 224 Chinese cities. FedEx currently has 39% of the U.S.–China express market and it plans to pursue continuous growth in that region of the world.

Sources: Ted Fishman, "How China Will Change Your Business," *Inc.* magazine, March 2005, pp. 70–84; Matthew Boyle, "Why FedEx Is Flying High," *Fortune*, November 1, 2004, pp. 145–150.

Strategy

Even more than in the past, companies that now face global competition must have a viable *strategy* for succeeding in the marketplace. A **strategy** is a "game plan" that enables a company to attract customers by distinguishing itself from competitors. The focal point of a company's strategy should be its target customers. A company can only succeed if it creates a reason for customers to choose it over a competitor. These reasons, or what are more formally called *customer value propositions,* are the essence of strategy.

Customer value propositions tend to fall into three broad categories—*customer intimacy, operational excellence,* and *product leadership*. Companies that adopt a *customer intimacy* strategy are in essence saying to their target customers, "The reason that you should choose us is because we understand and respond to your individual needs better than our competitors." Ritz-Carlton, Nordstrom, and Starbucks rely primarily on a customer intimacy value proposition for their success. Companies that pursue the second customer value proposition, called *operational excellence,* are saying to their target customers, "The reason that you should choose us is because we can deliver products and services faster, more conveniently, and at a lower price than our competitors." Southwest Airlines, Wal-Mart, and The Vanguard Group are examples of companies that succeed first and foremost because of their operational excellence. Companies pursuing the third customer value proposition, called *product leadership,* are saying to their target customers, "The reason that you should choose us is because we offer higher quality products than our competitors." BMW, Cisco Systems, and W.L. Gore (the creator of GORE-TEX® fabrics) are examples of companies that succeed because of their product leadership. Although one company may offer its customers a combination of these three customer value propositions, one usually outweighs the others in terms of importance.[3]

---

[3] These three customer value propositions were defined by Michael Treacy and Fred Wiersema in "Customer Intimacy and Other Value Disciplines," *Harvard Business Review,* January/February 1993, pp. 84–93.

IN BUSINESS

OPERATIONAL EXCELLENCE COMES TO THE DIAMOND BUSINESS

An average engagement ring purchased from Blue Nile, an Internet diamond retailer, costs $5,200 compared to $9,500 if purchased from Tiffany & Co., a bricks-and-mortar retailer. Why is there such a difference? There are three reasons. First, Blue Nile allows wholesalers to sell directly to customers using its website. In the brick-and-mortar scenario, diamonds change hands as many as seven times before being sold to a customer—passing through various cutters, wholesalers, brokers, and retailers, each of whom demands a profit. Second, Blue Nile carries very little inventory and incurs negligible overhead. Diamonds are shipped directly from wholesalers after they have been purchased by a customer—no retail outlets are necessary. Bricks-and-mortar retailers tie up large amounts of money paying for the inventory and employees on their showroom floors. Third, Blue Nile generates a high volume of transactions by selling to customers anywhere in the world; therefore, it can accept a lower profit margin per transaction than local retailers, who complete fewer transactions with customers within a limited geographic radius.

Perhaps you are wondering why customers are willing to trust an Internet retailer when buying an expensive item such as a diamond. The answer is that all of the diamonds sold through Blue Nile's website are independently certified by the Gemological Institute of America in four categories—carat count, type of cut, color, and clarity. In essence, Blue Nile has turned diamonds into a commodity and is using an operational excellence customer value proposition to generate annual sales of $154 million.

Source: Victoria Murphy, "Romance Killer," *Forbes*, November 29, 2004, pp. 97–101.

The Work of Management and the Need for Managerial Accounting Information

Video 1–1

Every organization—large and small—has managers. Someone must be responsible for formulating strategy, making plans, organizing resources, directing personnel, and controlling operations. This is true of the Bank of America, the Peace Corps, the University of Illinois, the Red Cross, and the Coca-Cola Corporation, as well as the local 7-Eleven convenience store. In this chapter, we will use a particular organization—Good Vibrations, Inc.—to illustrate the work of management. What we have to say about the management of Good Vibrations, however, is very general and can be applied to virtually any organization.

Good Vibrations runs a chain of retail outlets that sells a full range of music CDs. The chain's stores are concentrated in Pacific Rim cities such as Sydney, Singapore, Hong Kong, Beijing, Tokyo, and Vancouver. The company has found that the best way to generate sales, and profits, is to create an exciting shopping environment following a customer intimacy strategy. Consequently, the company puts a great deal of effort into planning the layout and decor of its stores—which are often quite large and extend over several floors in key downtown locations. Management knows that different types of clientele are attracted to different kinds of music. The international rock section is generally decorated with bold, brightly colored graphics, and the aisles are purposely narrow to create a crowded feeling much like one would experience at a popular nightclub on Friday night. In contrast, the classical music section is wood-paneled and fully sound insulated, with the rich, spacious feeling of a country club meeting room.

Managers at Good Vibrations, like managers everywhere, carry out three major activities—*planning, directing and motivating,* and *controlling*. **Planning** involves establishing a basic strategy, selecting a course of action, and specifying how the action will be implemented. **Directing and motivating** involves mobilizing people to carry out plans and run routine operations. **Controlling** involves ensuring that the plan is actually carried out and is appropriately modified as circumstances change. Management accounting information plays a vital role in these basic management activities—but most particularly in the planning and control functions.

Planning

An important part of planning is to identify alternatives and then to select from among the alternatives the one that best fits the organization's strategy and objectives. The basic objective of Good Vibrations is to earn profits for the owners of the company by providing superior service at competitive prices in as many markets as possible. To further this strategy, every year top management carefully considers a range of options, or alternatives, for expanding into new geographic markets. This year management is considering opening new stores in Shanghai, Los Angeles, and Auckland.

When making this choice, management must balance the potential benefits of opening a new store against the costs and demands on the company's resources. Management knows from bitter experience that opening a store in a major new market is a big step that cannot be taken lightly. It requires enormous amounts of time and energy from the company's most experienced, talented, and busy professionals. When the company attempted to open stores in both Beijing and Vancouver in the same year, resources were stretched too thin. The result was that neither store opened on schedule, and operations in the rest of the company suffered. Therefore, Good Vibrations plans very carefully before entering a new market.

Among other data, top management looks at the sales volumes, profit margins, and costs of the company's established stores in similar markets. These data, supplied by the management accountant, are combined with projected sales volume data at the proposed new locations to estimate the profits that would be generated by the new stores. In general, virtually all important alternatives considered by management in the planning process impact revenues or costs, and management accounting data are essential in estimating those impacts.

After considering all of the alternatives, Good Vibrations' top management decided to open a store in the booming Shanghai market in the third quarter of the year, but to defer opening any other new stores to another year. As soon as this decision was made, detailed plans were drawn up for all parts of the company that would be involved in the Shanghai opening. For example, the Personnel Department's travel budget was increased, since it would be providing extensive on-site training to the new personnel hired in Shanghai.

As in the case of the Personnel Department, the plans of management are often expressed formally in **budgets,** and the term *budgeting* is generally used to describe this part of the planning process. Budgets are usually prepared under the direction of the **controller,** who is the manager in charge of the Accounting Department. Typically, budgets are prepared annually and represent management's plans in specific, quantitative terms. In addition to a travel budget, the Personnel Department will be given goals in terms of new hires, courses taught, and detailed breakdowns of expected expenses. Similarly, the store managers will be given targets for sales volume, profit, expenses, pilferage losses, and employee training. Good Vibrations' management accountants will collect, analyze, and summarize these data in the form of budgets.

Directing and Motivating

In addition to planning for the future, managers oversee day-to-day activities and try to keep the organization functioning smoothly. This requires motivating and directing people. Managers assign tasks to employees, arbitrate disputes, answer questions, solve on-the-spot problems, and make many small decisions that affect customers and employees. In effect, directing is that part of a manager's job that deals with the routine and the here and now. Managerial accounting data, such as daily sales reports, are often used in this type of day-to-day activity.

Controlling

In carrying out the **control** function, managers seek to ensure that the plan is being followed. **Feedback,** which signals whether operations are on track, is the key to effective control. In sophisticated organizations, this feedback is provided by various detailed reports. One of these reports, which compares budgeted to actual results, is called a **performance report.** Performance reports suggest where operations are not proceeding as planned and where some parts of the organization may require additional attention. For example, the manager of the new Shanghai store will be given sales volume, profit, and expense targets. As the year progresses, performance reports will be constructed that compare actual sales volume, profit, and expenses to the targets. If the actual results fall below the targets, top management will be alerted that the Shanghai store requires more attention. Experienced personnel can be flown in to help the new manager, or top management may conclude that its plans need to be revised. As we shall see in later chapters, one of the central purposes of managerial accounting is to provide this kind of feedback to managers.

The End Results of Managers' Activities

When a customer enters a Good Vibrations store, the results of management's planning, directing and motivating, and controlling activities will be evident in the many details that make the difference between a pleasant and an irritating shopping experience. The store will be clean, fashionably decorated, and logically laid out. Featured artists' videos will be displayed on TV monitors throughout the store, and the background rock music will be loud enough to send older patrons scurrying for the classical music section. Popular CDs will be in stock, and the latest hits will be available for private listening on earphones. Specific titles will be easy to find. Regional music, such as CantoPop in Hong Kong, will be prominently featured. Checkout clerks will be alert, friendly, and efficient. In short, what the customer experiences doesn't simply happen; it is the result of the efforts of managers who must visualize and then fit together the processes that are needed to get the job done.

The Planning and Control Cycle

Exhibit 1–2 (page 8) depicts the work of management in the form of the *planning and control cycle*. The **planning and control cycle** involves the smooth flow of management activities from planning through directing and motivating, controlling, and then back to planning again. All of these activities involve decision making, which is the hub around which the other activities revolve.

Comparison of Financial and Managerial Accounting

LEARNING OBJECTIVE 1
Identify the major differences and similarities between financial and managerial accounting.

Financial accounting reports are prepared for external parties such as shareholders and creditors, whereas managerial accounting reports are prepared for managers inside the organization. This contrast in orientation results in a number of major differences between financial and managerial accounting, even though they often rely on the same underlying financial data. Exhibit 1–3 (page 8) summarizes these differences.

As shown in Exhibit 1–3, financial and managerial accounting differ not only in their user orientation but also in their emphasis on the past and the future, in the type of data provided to users, and in several other ways. These differences are discussed in the following paragraphs.

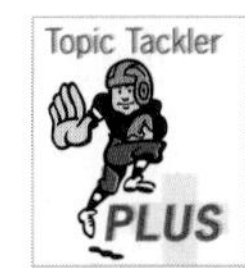

1–1

Emphasis on the Future

Since *planning* is such an important part of the manager's job, managerial accounting has a strong future orientation. In contrast, financial accounting primarily summarizes past financial transactions. These summaries may be useful in planning, but only to a point. The future is not simply a reflection of what has happened in the past. Changes are constantly taking place in economic conditions, customer needs and desires, competitive conditions, and so on. All of these changes demand that the manager's planning be based in large part on estimates of what will happen rather than on summaries of what has already happened.

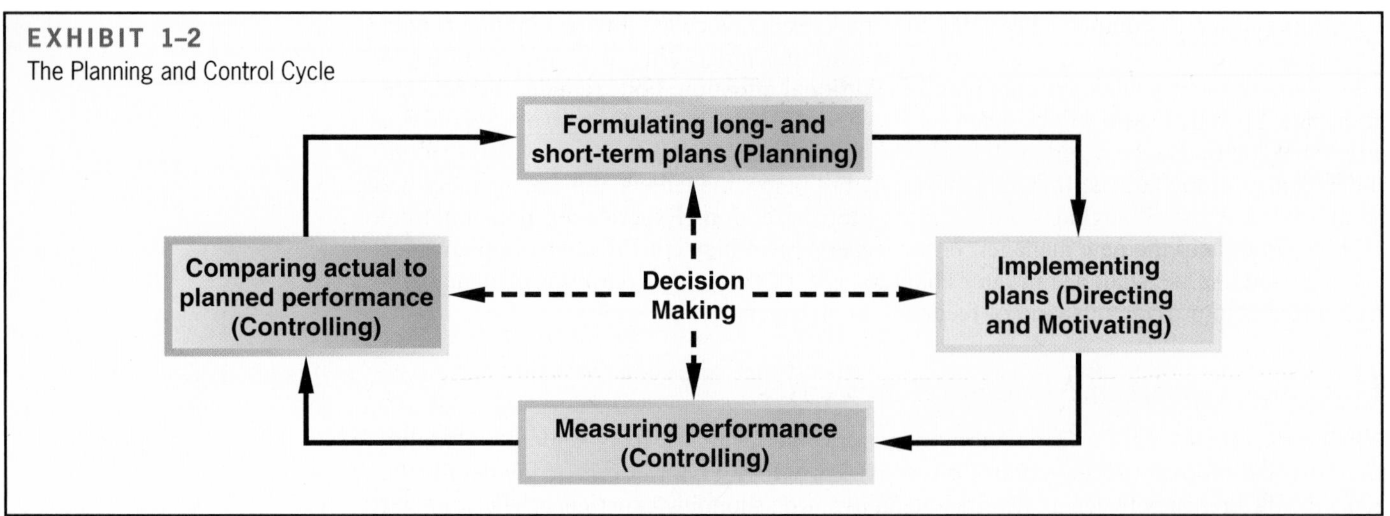

EXHIBIT 1–2
The Planning and Control Cycle

Formulating long- and short-term plans (Planning)
Implementing plans (Directing and Motivating)
Measuring performance (Controlling)
Comparing actual to planned performance (Controlling)
Decision Making

EXHIBIT 1–3
Comparison of Financial and Managerial Accounting

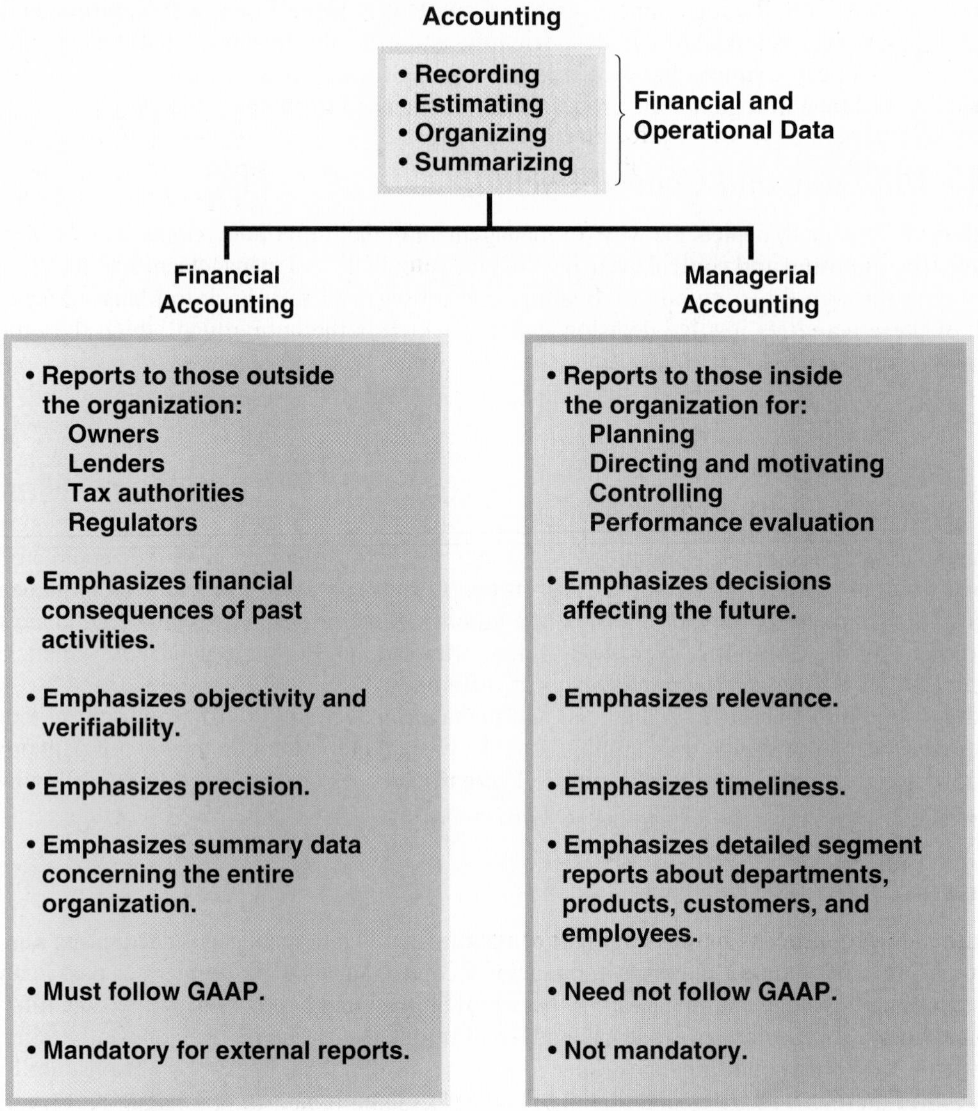
Accounting
• Recording
• Estimating
• Organizing
• Summarizing
Financial and Operational Data
Financial Accounting
• Reports to those outside the organization:
Owners
Lenders
Tax authorities
Regulators
• Emphasizes financial consequences of past activities.
• Emphasizes objectivity and verifiability.
• Emphasizes precision.
• Emphasizes summary data concerning the entire organization.
• Must follow GAAP.
• Mandatory for external reports.
Managerial Accounting
• Reports to those inside the organization for:
Planning
Directing and motivating
Controlling
Performance evaluation
• Emphasizes decisions affecting the future.
• Emphasizes relevance.
• Emphasizes timeliness.
• Emphasizes detailed segment reports about departments, products, customers, and employees.
• Need not follow GAAP.
• Not mandatory.

Relevance of Data

Financial accounting data should be objective and verifiable. However, for internal uses managers want information that is relevant even if it is not completely objective or verifiable. By relevant, we mean *appropriate for the problem at hand.* For example, it is difficult to verify estimated sales volumes for a proposed new store at Good Vibrations, but this is exactly the type of information that is most useful to managers. Managerial accounting should be flexible enough to provide whatever data are relevant for a particular decision.

Less Emphasis on Precision

Making sure that dollar amounts are accurate down to the last dollar or penny takes time and effort. While that kind of accuracy is required for external reports, most managers would rather have a good estimate immediately than wait for a more precise answer later. For this reason, managerial accountants often place less emphasis on precision than financial accountants do. For example, in a decision involving hundreds of millions of dollars, estimates that are rounded off to the nearest million dollars are probably good enough. In addition to placing less emphasis on precision than financial accounting, managerial accounting places much more weight on nonmonetary data. For example, data about customer satisfaction may be routinely used in managerial accounting reports.

Segments of an Organization

Financial accounting is primarily concerned with reporting for the company as a whole. By contrast, managerial accounting focuses much more on the parts, or **segments,** of a company. These segments may be product lines, sales territories, divisions, departments, or any other categorization that management finds useful. Financial accounting does require some breakdowns of revenues and costs by major segments in external reports, but this is a secondary emphasis. In managerial accounting, segment reporting is the primary emphasis.

Generally Accepted Accounting Principles (GAAP)

Financial accounting statements prepared for external users must comply with generally accepted accounting principles (GAAP). External users must have some assurance that the reports have been prepared in accordance with a common set of ground rules. These common ground rules enhance comparability and help reduce fraud and misrepresentation, but they do not necessarily lead to the type of reports that would be most useful in internal decision making. For example, if management at Good Vibrations is considering selling land to finance a new store, they need to know the current market value of the land. However, GAAP requires that the land be stated at its original, historical cost on financial reports. The more relevant data for the decision—the current market value—is ignored under GAAP.

Managerial accounting is not bound by GAAP. Managers set their own rules concerning the content and form of internal reports. The only constraint is that the expected benefits from using the information should outweigh the costs of collecting, analyzing, and summarizing the data. Nevertheless, as we shall see in subsequent chapters, it is undeniably true that financial reporting requirements have heavily influenced management accounting practice.

Managerial Accounting—Not Mandatory

Financial accounting is mandatory; that is, it must be done. Various outside parties such as the Securities and Exchange Commission (SEC) and the tax authorities require periodic financial statements. Managerial accounting, on the other hand, is not mandatory. A company is completely free to do as much or as little as it wishes. No regulatory bodies or other outside agencies specify what is to be done, or, for that matter, whether anything is to be done at all. Since managerial accounting is completely optional, the important question is always, "Is the information useful?" rather than, "Is the information required?"

Organizational Structure

LEARNING OBJECTIVE 2
Understand the role of management accountants in an organization.

Management must accomplish its objectives by working through people. Presidents of companies like Good Vibrations could not possibly execute all of their company's strategies alone; they must rely on other people. This is done by creating an organizational structure that permits effective *decentralization.*

Decentralization

Decentralization is the delegation of decision-making authority throughout an organization by giving managers the authority to make decisions relating to their area of responsibility. Some organizations are more decentralized than others. Because of Good Vibrations' geographic dispersion and the peculiarities of local markets, the company is highly decentralized.

Good Vibrations' president (often synonymous with the term chief executive officer, or CEO) sets the broad strategy for the company and makes major strategic decisions such as opening stores in new markets; however, much of the remaining decision-making authority is delegated to managers at various levels throughout the organization. Each of the company's numerous retail stores has a store manager as well as a separate manager for each music category such as international rock and classical/jazz. In addition, the company has support departments such as a central Purchasing Department and a Personnel Department.

The Functional View of Organizations

Exhibit 1–4 shows Good Vibrations' organizational structure in the form of an **organization chart.** The purpose of an organization chart is to show how responsibility is divided among

EXHIBIT 1–4
Organization Chart, Good Vibrations, Inc.

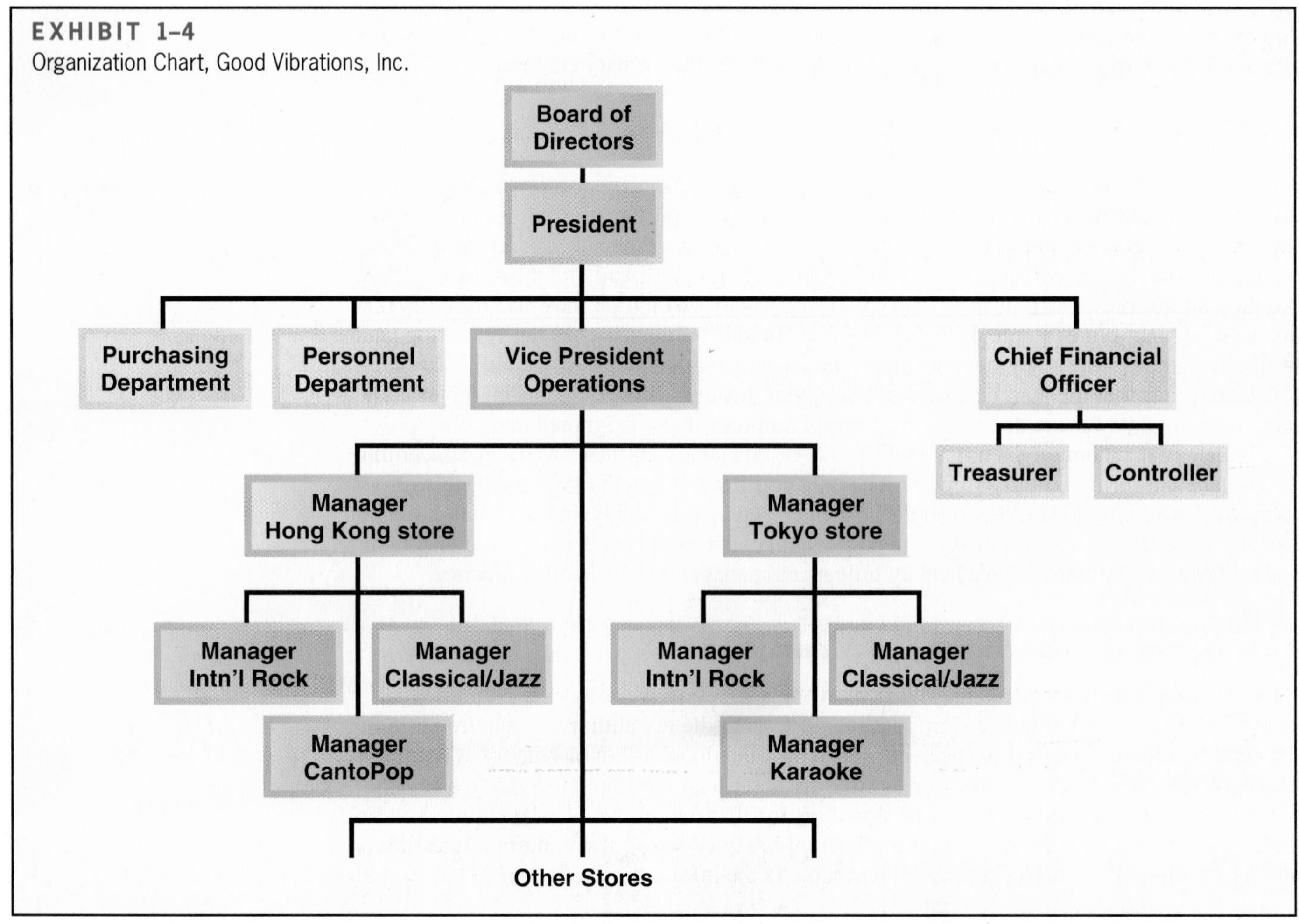

managers and to show formal lines of reporting and communication, or *chain of command*. Each box depicts an area of management responsibility, and the lines between the boxes show the lines of formal authority between managers. The chart tells us, for example, that the store managers are responsible to the operations vice president. In turn, the operations vice president is responsible to the company president, who in turn is responsible to the board of directors. Following the lines of authority and communication on the organization chart, we can see that the manager of the Hong Kong store would ordinarily report to the operations vice president rather than directly to the president of the company.

Informal relationships and channels of communication often develop outside the formal reporting relationships on the organization chart as a result of personal contacts between managers. The informal structure does not appear on the organization chart, but it is often vital to effective operations.

Line and Staff Relationships

An organization chart also depicts *line* and *staff* positions in an organization. A person in a **line** position is *directly* involved in achieving the basic objectives of the organization. A person in a **staff** position, by contrast, is only *indirectly* involved in achieving those basic objectives. Staff positions provide assistance to line positions or other parts of the organization, but they do not have direct authority over line positions. Refer again to the organization chart in Exhibit 1–4. Because the basic objective of Good Vibrations is to sell recorded music at a profit, those managers whose areas of responsibility are directly related to selling music occupy line positions. These positions, which are shown in a darker color in the exhibit, include the managers of the various music departments in each store, the store managers, the operations vice president, the president, and the board of directors.

By contrast, the manager of the central Purchasing Department occupies a staff position, since the only purpose of the Purchasing Department is to serve the line departments by doing their purchasing for them. However, both line and staff managers have authority over the employees in their own departments.

The Chief Financial Officer

As previously mentioned, in the United States the manager of the accounting department is often known as the *controller*. The controller in turn reports to the *Chief Financial Officer (CFO)*. The **Chief Financial Officer** is the member of the top management team who is responsible for providing timely and relevant data to support planning and control activities and for preparing financial statements for external users. An effective CFO is considered a key member of the top management team whose advice is sought in all major decisions. The CFO is a highly paid professional who has command over the technical details of accounting and finance, who can provide leadership to other professionals in his or her department, who can analyze new and evolving situations, who can communicate technical data to others in a simple and clear manner, and who is able to work well with top managers from other disciplines. More than ever, the accountants who work under the CFO focus their efforts on supporting the needs of their co-workers in line positions:

> Growing numbers of management accountants spend the bulk of their time as internal consultants or business analysts within their companies. Technological advances have liberated them from the mechanical aspects of accounting. They spend less time preparing standardized reports and more time analyzing and interpreting information. Many have moved from the isolation of accounting departments to be physically positioned in the operating departments with which they work. Management accountants work on cross-functional teams, have extensive face-to-face communications with people throughout their organizations, and are actively involved in decision making. . . . They are trusted advisors.[4]

[4] Gary Siegel Organization, *Counting More, Counting Less: Transformations in the Management Accounting Profession, The 1999 Practice Analysis of Management Accounting,* Institute of Management Accountants, Montvale, NJ, August 1999, p. 3.

IN BUSINESS

WHAT DOES IT TAKE?

A controller at McDonald's describes the characteristics needed by its most successful management accountants as follows:

> [I]t's a given that you know your accounting cold. You're expected to know the tax implications of proposed courses of action. You need to understand cost flows and information flows. You have to be very comfortable with technology and be an expert in the company's business and accounting software. You have to be a generalist. You need a working knowledge of what people do in marketing, engineering, human resources, and other departments. You need to understand how the processes, departments, and functions work together to run the business. You'll be expected to contribute ideas at planning meetings, so you have to see the big picture, keep a focus on the bottom line, and think strategically.

Source: Gary Siegel, James E. Sorensen, and Sandra B. Richtermeyer, "Becoming a Business Partner: Part 2," *Strategic Finance*, October 2003, pp. 37–41. Used with permission from the Institute of Management Accountants (IMA), Montvale, N.J., USA, www.imanet.org.

Process Management

LEARNING OBJECTIVE 3
Understand the basic concepts underlying Lean Production, the Theory of Constraints (TOC), and Six Sigma.

Video 1–1

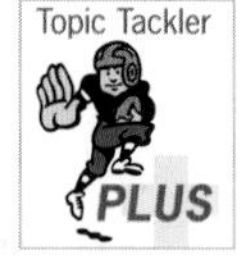

1–2

As discussed at the beginning of this chapter, the last two decades have been a period of tremendous turmoil and change in the business environment. Competition in many industries has become worldwide in scope, and the pace of innovation in products and services has accelerated. This has been good news for consumers, since intensified competition has generally led to lower prices, higher quality, and more choices. However, for businesses intensified global competition has presented serious challenges. More than ever companies are realizing that they must complement the functional view of their operations with a cross-functional orientation that seeks to improve the *business processes* that deliver customer value.

A **business process** is a series of steps that are followed in order to carry out some task in a business. It is quite common for the linked set of steps comprising a business process to span departmental boundaries. The term *value chain* is often used when we look at how the functional departments of an organization interact with one another to form business processes. A **value chain,** as shown in Exhibit 1–5, consists of the major business functions that add value to a company's products and services. The customer's needs are most effectively met by coordinating the business processes that span these functions.

This section discusses three different approaches to managing and improving business processes—Lean Production, the Theory of Constraints (TOC), and Six Sigma. Although each is unique in certain respects, they all share the common theme of focusing on managing and improving business processes.

EXHIBIT 1–5
Business Functions Making Up the Value Chain

Research and Development	Product Design	Manufacturing	Marketing	Distribution	Customer Service

Lean Production

Traditionally, managers in manufacturing companies have sought to maximize production so as to spread the costs of investments in equipment and other assets over as many units as possible. In addition, managers have traditionally felt that an important part of their jobs was to keep everyone busy on the theory that idleness wastes money. These traditional views, often aided and abetted by traditional management accounting practices, resulted in a number of practices that have come under criticism in recent years.

In a traditional manufacturing company, work is *pushed* through the system in order to produce as much as possible and to keep everyone busy—even if products cannot be immediately sold. This almost inevitably results in large inventories of *raw materials, work in process,* and *finished* goods. **Raw materials** are the materials that are used to make a product. **Work in process** inventories consist of units of product that are only partially complete and will require further work before they are ready for sale to a customer. **Finished goods** inventories consist of units of product that have been completed but have not yet been sold to customers.

The *push* process in traditional manufacturing starts by accumulating large amounts of raw material inventories from suppliers so that operations can proceed smoothly even if unanticipated disruptions occur. Next, enough materials are released to workstations to keep everyone busy. When a workstation completes its tasks, the partially completed goods (i.e., work in process) are "pushed" forward to the next workstation regardless of whether that workstation is ready to receive them. The result is that partially completed goods stack up, waiting for the next workstation to become available. They may not be completed for days, weeks, or even months. Additionally, when the units are finally completed, customers may or may not want them. If finished goods are produced faster than the market will absorb, the result is bloated finished goods inventories.

Although some may argue that maintaining large amounts of inventory has its benefits, it clearly has its costs. According to experts, in addition to tying up money, maintaining inventories encourages inefficient and sloppy work, results in too many defects, and dramatically increases the amount of time required to complete a product. For example, when partially completed goods are stored for long periods of time before being processed by the next workstation, defects introduced by the preceding workstation go unnoticed. If a machine is out of calibration or incorrect procedures are being followed, many defective units will be produced before the problem is discovered. And when the defects are finally discovered, it may be very difficult to track down the source of the problem. In addition, units may be obsolete or out of fashion by the time they are finally completed.

Large inventories of partially completed goods create many other problems that are best discussed in more advanced courses. These problems are not obvious—if they were, companies would have long ago reduced their inventories. Managers at Toyota are credited with the insight that large inventories often create many more problems than they solve. Toyota pioneered what is known today as *Lean Production.*

The Lean Thinking Model

The **lean thinking model** is a five-step management approach that organizes resources such as people and machines around the flow of business processes and that pulls units through these processes in response to customer orders. The result is lower inventories, fewer defects, less wasted effort, and quicker customer response times. Exhibit 1–6 (page 14) depicts the five stages of the lean thinking model.

The first step is to identify the value to customers in specific products and services. The second step is to identify the *business process* that delivers this value to customers.[5] As discussed earlier, the linked set of steps comprising a business process typically span the departmental boundaries that are specified in an organization chart. The third step is to organize work arrangements around the flow of the business process. This is often accomplished by creating what is known as a *manufacturing cell.* The cellular approach takes employees

[5] The Lean Production literature uses the term *value stream* rather than *business process.*

EXHIBIT 1–6
The Lean Thinking Model

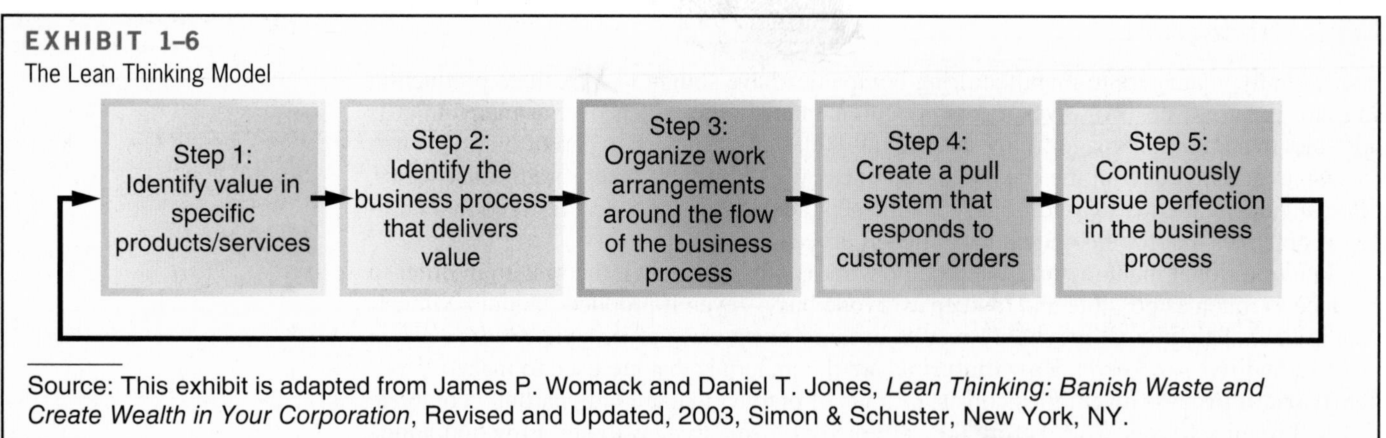

Source: This exhibit is adapted from James P. Womack and Daniel T. Jones, *Lean Thinking: Banish Waste and Create Wealth in Your Corporation*, Revised and Updated, 2003, Simon & Schuster, New York, NY.

and equipment from departments that were previously separated from one another and places them side-by-side in a work space called a *cell*. The equipment within the cell is aligned in a sequential manner that follows the steps of the business process. Each employee is trained to perform all the steps within his or her own manufacturing cell.

The fourth step in the lean thinking model is to create a pull system where production is not initiated until a customer has ordered a product. Inventories are reduced to a minimum by purchasing raw materials and producing units only as needed to meet customer demand. Under ideal conditions, a company operating a pull system would purchase only enough materials each day to meet that day's needs. Moreover, the company would have no goods still in process at the end of the day, and all goods completed during the day would be shipped immediately to customers. As this sequence suggests, work takes place "just-in-time" in the sense that raw materials are received by each manufacturing cell just in time to go into production, manufactured parts are completed just in time to be assembled into products, and products are completed just in time to be shipped to customers. Not surprisingly, this facet of the lean thinking model is often called **just-in-time** production, or **JIT** for short.

The change from *push* to *pull* production is more profound than it may appear. Among other things, producing only in response to a customer order means that workers will be idle whenever demand falls below the company's production capacity. This can be an extremely difficult cultural change for an organization. It challenges the core beliefs of many managers and raises anxieties in workers who have become accustomed to being kept busy all of the time.

The fifth step of the lean thinking model is to continuously pursue perfection in the business process. In a traditional company, parts and materials are inspected for defects when they are received from suppliers, and assembled units are inspected as they progress along the production line. In a Lean Production system, the company's suppliers are responsible for the quality of incoming parts and materials. And instead of using quality inspectors, the company's production workers are directly responsible for spotting defective units. A worker who discovers a defect immediately stops the flow of production. Supervisors and other workers go to the cell to determine the cause of the problem and correct it before any further defective units are produced. This procedure ensures that problems are quickly identified and corrected.

The lean thinking model can also be used to improve the business processes that link companies together. The term **supply chain management** is commonly used to refer to the coordination of business processes across companies to better serve end consumers. For example Procter & Gamble and Costco coordinate their business processes to ensure that Procter & Gamble's products, such as Bounty, Tide, and Crest, are on Costco's shelves when customers want them. Both Procter & Gamble and Costco realize that their mutual success depends on working together to ensure Procter & Gamble's products are available to Costco's customers.

IN BUSINESS

THE POWER OF LEAN

Lean thinking can benefit all types of businesses. For example, Dell Inc.'s lean production system can produce a customized personal computer within 36 hours. Even more impressive, Dell doesn't start ordering components and assembling computers until orders are booked. By ordering right before assembly, Dell's parts are on average 60 days newer than those of its competitors, which translates into a 6% profit advantage in components alone.

In the service arena, Jefferson Pilot Financial (JPF) realized that "[l]ike an automobile on the assembly line, an insurance policy goes through a series of processes, from initial application to underwriting, or risk assessment, to policy issuance. With each step, value is added to the work in progress—just as a car gets doors or a coat of paint." Given this realization, JPF organized its work arrangements into a cellular layout and synchronized the rate of output to the pace of customer demand. JPF's lean thinking enabled it to reduce attending physician statement turnaround times by 70%, decrease labor costs 26%, and reduce reissue errors by 40%.

Sources: Gary McWilliams, "Whirlwind on the Web," *BusinessWeek*, April 7, 1997, p. 134; Stephen Pritchard, "Inside Dell's Lean Machine," *Works Management*, December 2002, pp. 14–16; and Cynthia Karen Swank, "The Lean Service Machine," *Harvard Business Review*, October 2003, pp. 123–129.

The Theory of Constraints (TOC)

A **constraint** is anything that prevents you from getting more of what you want. Every individual and every organization faces at least one constraint, so it is not difficult to find examples of constraints. You may not have enough time to study thoroughly for every subject *and* to go out with your friends on the weekend, so time is your constraint. United Airlines has only a limited number of loading gates available at its busy Chicago O'Hare hub, so its constraint is loading gates. Vail Resorts has only a limited amount of land to develop as homesites and commercial lots at its ski areas, so its constraint is land.

The **Theory of Constraints (TOC)** is based on the insight that effectively managing the constraint is a key to success. As an example, long waiting periods for surgery are a chronic problem in the National Health Service (NHS), the government-funded provider of health care in the United Kingdom. The diagram in Exhibit 1–7 illustrates a simplified version of the steps followed by a surgery patient. The number of patients who can be processed through each step in a day is indicated in the exhibit. For example, appointments for outpatient visits can be made for as many as 100 referrals from general practitioners in a day.

The constraint, or *bottleneck,* in the system is determined by the step that has the smallest capacity—in this case surgery. The total number of patients processed through the entire system cannot exceed 15 per day—the maximum number of patients who can be treated in surgery. No matter how hard managers, doctors, and nurses try to improve the processing rate elsewhere in the system, they will never succeed in driving down wait lists until the capacity

EXHIBIT 1–7
Processing Surgery Patients at an NHS Facility (simplified)*

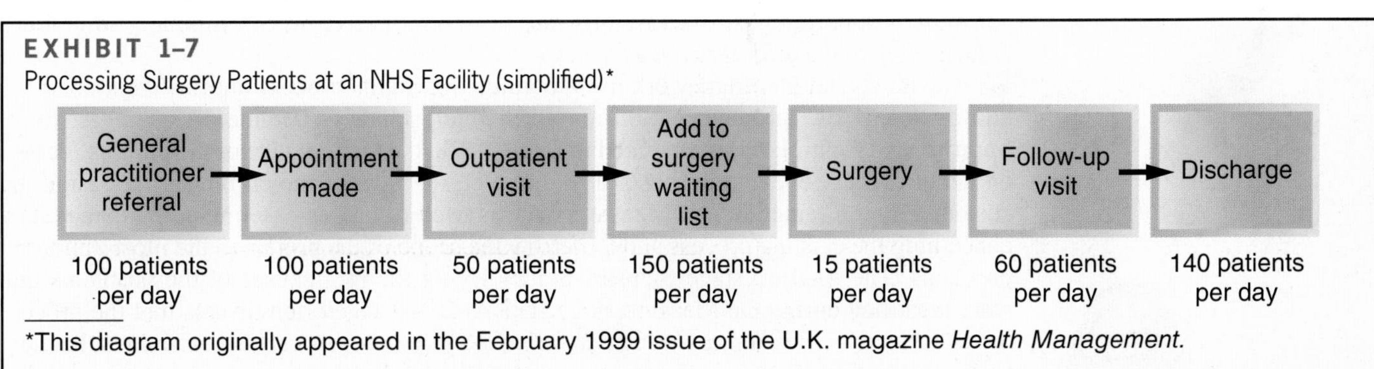

*This diagram originally appeared in the February 1999 issue of the U.K. magazine *Health Management.*

of surgery is increased. In fact, improvements elsewhere in the system—particularly before the constraint—are likely to result in even longer waiting times and more frustrated patients and health care providers. Thus, to be effective, improvement efforts must be focused on the constraint. A business process, such as the process for serving surgery patients, is like a chain. If you want to increase the strength of a chain, what is the most effective way to do this? Should you concentrate your efforts on strengthening the strongest link, all the links, or the weakest link? Clearly, focusing your effort on the weakest link will bring the biggest benefit.

The procedure to follow to strengthen the chain is clear. First, identify the weakest link, which is the constraint. In the case of the NHS, the constraint is surgery. Second, do not place a greater strain on the system than the weakest link can handle—if you do, the chain will break. In the case of the NHS, more referrals than surgery can accommodate lead to unacceptably long waiting lists. Third, concentrate improvement efforts on strengthening the weakest link. In the case of the NHS, this means finding ways to increase the number of surgeries that can be performed in a day. Fourth, if the improvement efforts are successful, eventually the weakest link will improve to the point where it is no longer the weakest link. At that point, the new weakest link (i.e., the new constraint) must be identified, and improvement efforts must be shifted over to that link. This simple sequential process provides a powerful strategy for optimizing business processes.

IN BUSINESS

WATCH WHERE YOU CUT COSTS

At one hospital, the emergency room became so backlogged that its doors were closed to the public and patients were turned away for over 36 hours in the course of a single month. It turned out, after investigation, that the constraint was not the emergency room itself; it was the housekeeping staff. To cut costs, managers at the hospital had laid off housekeeping workers. This created a bottleneck in the emergency room because rooms were not being cleaned as quickly as the emergency room staff could process new patients. Thus, laying off some of the lowest paid workers at the hospital had the effect of forcing the hospital to idle some of its most highly paid staff and most expensive equipment!

Source: Tracey Burton-Houle, "AGI Continues to Steadily Make Advances with the Adaptation of TOC into Healthcare," www.goldratt.com/toctquarterly/august2002.htm.

Six Sigma

Six Sigma is a process improvement method that relies on customer feedback and fact-based data gathering and analysis techniques to drive process improvement. Motorola and General Electric are closely identified with the emergence of the Six Sigma movement. Technically, the term Six Sigma refers to a process that generates no more than 3.4 defects per million opportunities. Because this rate of defects is so low, Six Sigma is sometimes associated with the term *zero defects*.

The most common framework used to guide Six Sigma process improvement efforts is known as DMAIC (pronounced: du-may-ik), which stands for Define, Measure, Analyze, Improve, and Control. As summarized in Exhibit 1–8, the Define stage of the process focuses on defining the scope and purpose of the project, the flow of the current process, and the customer's requirements. The Measure stage is used to gather baseline performance data concerning the existing process and to narrow the scope of the project to the most important problems. The Analyze stage focuses on identifying the root causes of the problems that were identified during the Measure stage. The Analyze stage often reveals that the process includes many *activities that do not add value to the product or service*. Activities that customers are not willing to pay for because they add no value are known as **non-value-added**

EXHIBIT 1–8
The Six Sigma DMAIC Framework

Stage	Goals
Define	Establish the scope and purpose of the project. Diagram the flow of the current process. Establish the customer's requirements for the process.
Measure	Gather baseline performance data related to the existing process. Narrow the scope of the project to the most important problems.
Analyze	Identify the root cause(s) of the problems identified in the Measure stage.
Improve	Develop, evaluate, and implement solutions to the problems.
Control	Ensure that problems remain fixed. Seek to improve the new methods over time.

Source: Peter C. Brewer and Nancy A. Bagranoff, "Near Zero-Defect Accounting with Six Sigma," *Journal of Corporate Accounting and Finance,* January-February 2004, pp. 67–72.

activities and such activities should be eliminated wherever possible. During the Improve stage potential solutions are developed, evaluated, and implemented to eliminate non-value-added activities and any other problems uncovered in the Analyze stage. Finally, the objective in the Control stage is to ensure that the problems remain fixed and that the new methods are improved over time.[6]

Managers must be very careful when attempting to translate Six Sigma improvements into financial benefits. There are only two ways to increase profits—decrease costs or increase sales. Cutting costs may seem easy—lay off workers who are no longer needed because of improvements such as eliminating non-value-added activities. However, if this approach is taken, employees quickly get the message that process improvements lead to job losses and they will understandably resist further improvement efforts. If improvement is to continue, employees must be convinced that the end result of improvement will be more secure rather than less secure jobs. This can only happen if management uses tools such as Six Sigma to generate more business rather than to cut the workforce.

Technology in Business

Technology is being harnessed in many ways by businesses. In this section we will discuss two of these ways—e-commerce and enterprise systems.

Video 1–1

E-Commerce

E-commerce refers to business that is conducted using the Internet. At the start of the new millennium, e-commerce was riding high. The stock prices of dot.com companies (companies that focus on generating revenue exclusively through the Internet) were climbing by leaps and bounds. On January 30, 2000, more than 20 dot.com companies, such as Pets.com and Epidemic.com, paid as much as $3 million for 30-second commercials during the Super Bowl. However, by November of that same year, prospects for dot.com companies began to worsen as companies such as Pets.com, Garden.com and Furniture.com all failed. By the spring of 2001, EToys had folded and monthly statistics for dot.com layoffs and closures had peaked at 17,554 and 64, respectively. In short, the dot.com collapse was under way.[7]

[6] Peter C. Brewer, "Six Sigma Helps a Company Create a Culture of Accountability," *Journal of Organizational Excellence,* Summer 2004, pp. 45–59.

[7] Time line published by BBC News at http://news.bbc.co.uk.

Since the collapse of the dot.com bubble in 2001, e-commerce has slowly been rebuilding momentum. Internet advertising is projected to exceed $12 billion per year before the end of the decade.[8] And while e-commerce has already had a major impact on the sale of books, music, and airline tickets, it appears that companies such as Blue Nile, eBay, Amazon.com, Lending Tree, and Expedia will continue to disrupt and redefine other markets such as the jewelry, real estate, and hotel industries.[9] In addition to dot.com companies, established brick-and-mortar companies such as General Electric, Wells Fargo, and Target will undoubtedly continue to expand into cyberspace—both for business-to-business transactions and for retailing.

The growth in e-commerce is occurring because the Internet has important advantages over more conventional marketplaces for many kinds of transactions. For example, the Internet is an ideal technology for streamlining the mortgage lending process. Customers can complete loan applications over the Internet rather than tying up the time of a staffperson in an office. And data and funds can be sent back and forth electronically.

Nevertheless, while building a successful dot.com business remains a tenuous and high-risk proposition, e-commerce is here to stay. The stock prices of dot.com companies will rise and fall, but the benefits that the Internet provides to businesses and their customers will ensure that e-commerce grows.

IN BUSINESS

INTERNET INNOVATIONS

Companies continue to develop new ways of using the Internet to improve their performance. Below is a summary of intriguing Internet applications categorized into four descriptive groups.

1. Collaboration
   - Eli Lilly has a website where scientific problems are posed to its global workforce. The best solutions earn cash rewards.
   - Lockheed Martin used the Internet to help 80 of its suppliers from around the world to collaborate in designing and building a new stealth fighter plane.
2. Customer Service
   - General Motors uses the Internet to auction off vehicles with expired leases.
   - IndyMac Bancorp uses the Internet to link its nationwide network of loan brokers to its central computers. Using these links, the brokers can electronically submit and then monitor their clients' loan applications.
3. Management
   - CareGroup's approximately 2,500 doctors are rated on 20 criteria related to the care they provide for insured patients. The results are summarized on digital report cards that have helped spot inefficiencies, saving the company $4 million annually.
   - Bristol-Myers Squibb uses the Internet to speed up drug research and development. The Web-based system has reduced by one-third the time needed to develop new medications.
4. Cutting Edge
   - Fresh Direct is an on-line grocer in New York City. Using the Internet to streamline order processing, the company is able to charge prices as much as 35% below its competitors.
   - eArmyU is a virtual Internet-based university that provides educational opportunities to 40,000 geographically dispersed U.S. soldiers.

Source: Heather Green, "The Web Smart 50," *BusinessWeek*, November 24, 2003, pp. 82–106.

[8] Stephen Baker, "Where the Real Internet Money Is Made," *BusinessWeek,* December 27, 2004, p. 99.

[9] Timothy J. Mullaney, "E-Biz Strikes Again!" *BusinessWeek,* May 10, 2004, pp. 80–90.

Enterprise Systems[10]

Historically, most companies implemented specific software programs to support specific business functions. The accounting department would select its own software applications to meet its needs, while manufacturing would select different software programs to support its needs. The separate systems were not integrated and could not easily pass data back and forth. The end result was data duplication and data inconsistencies coupled with lengthy customer response times and high costs.

An **enterprise system** is designed to overcome these problems by integrating data across an organization into a single software system that enables all employees to have simultaneous access to a common set of data. There are two keys to the data integration inherent in an enterprise system. First, all data are recorded only once in the company's centralized digital data repository known as a database. When data are added to the database or are changed, the new information is simultaneously and immediately available to everyone across the organization. Second, the unique data elements contained within the database can be linked together. For example, one data element, such as a customer identification number, can be related to other data elements, such as that customer's address, billing history, shipping history, merchandise returns history, and so on. The ability to forge such relationships among data elements explains why this type of database is called a *relational database*.

Data integration helps employees communicate with one another and it also helps them communicate with their suppliers and customers. For example, consider how the *customer relationship management* process is improved when enterprise-wide information resides in one location. Whether meeting the customer's needs requires accessing information related to billing (an accounting function), delivery status (a distribution function), price quotes (a marketing function), or merchandise returns (a customer service function) the required information is readily available to the employee interacting with the customer. Though expensive and risky to install, the benefits of data integration have led many companies to invest in enterprise systems.

IN BUSINESS

THE BENEFITS OF DATA INTEGRATION

Nike's old supply-chain system was tenuously connected by 27 different computer systems, most of which could not talk to one another. The results for Nike were predictable—retailers ran out of hot-selling sneakers and were saddled with duds that didn't sell. Nike spent $500 million to fix the problem and the results have been impressive—the lead time for getting new sneaker styles to retail shelves has been cut from nine to six months. The percentage of shoes that Nike makes without a firm order from a retailer has dropped from 30% to 3%.

Agri Beef Company's enterprise system enables its accounts payable process to accomplish in two check runs what used to require 22 check runs. As Treasurer Kim Stuart commented: "Now we can post transactions straight through to another division's general ledger account . . . That change alone saves us 200 [labor] hours a month."

Sources: Stanley Holmes, "The New Nike," *BusinessWeek*, September 20, 2004, pp. 78–86; Doug Bartholomew, "The ABC's of ERP," *CFO-IT*, Fall 2004, pp. 19–21.

The Importance of Ethics in Business

LEARNING OBJECTIVE 4
Understand the importance of upholding ethical standards.

A series of major financial scandals involving Enron, Tyco International, HealthSouth, Adelphia Communications, WorldCom, Global Crossing, Rite Aid, and other companies have raised deep concerns about ethics in business. The managers and companies involved in these scandals have suffered mightily—from huge fines to jail terms and financial

[10] *Enterprise systems* is a broad term that encompasses many enterprise-wide computer applications such as customer relationship management and supply chain management systems. Perhaps the most frequently mentioned type of enterprise system is an Enterprise Resource Planning (ERP) system.

collapse. And the recognition that ethical behavior is absolutely essential for the functioning of our economy has led to numerous regulatory changes—some of which we will discuss in a later section on corporate governance. But why is ethical behavior so important? This is not a matter of just being "nice." Ethical behavior is the lubricant that keeps the economy running. Without that lubricant, the economy would operate much less efficiently—less would be available to consumers, quality would be lower, and prices would be higher.

Take a very simple example. Suppose that dishonest farmers, distributors, and grocers knowingly tried to sell wormy apples as good apples and that grocers refused to take back wormy apples. What would you do as a consumer of apples? Go to another grocer? But what if all grocers acted this way? What would you do then? You would probably either stop buying apples or you would spend a lot of time inspecting apples before buying them. So would everyone else. Now notice what has happened. Because farmers, distributors, and grocers could not be trusted, sales of apples would plummet and those who did buy apples would waste a lot of time inspecting them minutely. Everyone loses. Farmers, distributors; and grocers make less money; consumers enjoy fewer apples; and consumers waste time looking for worms. In other words, without fundamental trust in the integrity of businesses, the economy would operate much less efficiently. James Surowiecki summed up this point as follows:

> [F]lourishing economies require a healthy level of trust in the reliability and fairness of everyday transactions. If you assumed every potential deal was a rip-off or that the

IN BUSINESS

NO TRUST—NO ENRON

Jonathan Karpoff reports on a particularly important, but often overlooked, aspect of the Enron debacle:

> As we know, some of Enron's reported profits in the late 1990s were pure accounting fiction. But the firm also had legitimate businesses and actual assets. Enron's most important businesses involved buying and selling electricity and other forms of energy. [Using Enron as an intermediary, utilities that needed power bought energy from producers with surplus generating capacity.] Now when an electric utility contracts to buy electricity, the managers of the utility want to make darned sure that the seller will deliver the electrons exactly as agreed, at the contracted price. There is no room for fudging on this because the consequences of not having the electricity when consumers switch on their lights are dire. . . .
>
> This means that the firms with whom Enron was trading electricity . . . had to trust Enron. And trust Enron they did, to the tune of billions of dollars of trades every year. But in October 2001, when Enron announced that its previous financial statements overstated the firm's profits, it undermined such trust. As everyone recognizes, the announcement caused investors to lower their valuations of the firm. Less understood, however, was the more important impact of the announcement; by revealing some of its reported earnings to be a house of cards, Enron sabotaged its reputation. The effect was to undermine even its legitimate and (previously) profitable operations that relied on its trustworthiness.
>
> This is why Enron melted down so fast. Its core businesses relied on the firm's reputation. When that reputation was wounded, energy traders took their business elsewhere. . . .

Energy traders lost their faith in Enron, but what if no other company could be trusted to deliver on its commitments to provide electricity as contracted? In that case, energy traders would have nowhere to turn. As a direct result, energy producers with surplus generating capacity would be unable to sell their surplus power. As a consequence, their existing customers would have to pay higher prices. And utilities that did not have sufficient capacity to meet demand on their own would have to build more capacity, which would also mean higher prices for their consumers. So a general lack of trust in companies such as Enron would ultimately result in overinvestment in energy-generating capacity and higher energy prices for consumers.

Source: Jonathan M. Karpoff, "Regulation vs. Reputation in Preventing Corporate Fraud," *UW Business*, Spring 2002, pp. 28–30

> products you were buying were probably going to be lemons, then very little business would get done. More important, the costs of the transactions that did take place would be exorbitant, since you'd have to do enormous work to investigate each deal and you'd have to rely on the threat of legal action to enforce every contract. For an economy to prosper, what's needed is not a Pollyannaish faith that everyone else has your best interests at heart—"caveat emptor" [buyer beware] remains an important truth—but a basic confidence in the promises and commitments that people make about their products and services.[11]

Thus, for the good of everyone—including profit-making companies—it is vitally important that business be conducted within an ethical framework that builds and sustains trust.

The Institute of Management Accountants (IMA) of the United States has adopted an ethical code called the *Statement of Ethical Professional Practice* that describes in some detail the ethical responsibilities of management accountants. Even though the code was specifically developed for management accountants, it has much broader application.

Code of Conduct for Management Accountants

The IMA's Statement of Ethical Professional Practice consists of two parts that are presented in full in Exhibit 1–9 (page 22). The first part provides general guidelines for ethical behavior. In a nutshell, a management accountant has ethical responsibilities in four broad areas: first, to maintain a high level of professional competence; second, to treat sensitive matters with confidentiality; third, to maintain personal integrity; and fourth, to disclose information in a credible fashion. The second part of the code specifies what should be done if an individual finds evidence of ethical misconduct. We recommend that you stop at this point and read all of Exhibit 1–9.

The IMA's code of conduct provides sound, practical advice for management accountants and managers. Most of the rules in the code are motivated by a very practical consideration—if these rules were not generally followed in business, then the economy and all of us would suffer. Consider the following specific examples of the consequences of not abiding by the code:

- Suppose employees could not be trusted with confidential information. Then top managers would be reluctant to distribute such information within the company and, as a result, decisions would be based on incomplete information and operations would deteriorate.
- Suppose employees accepted bribes from suppliers. Then contracts would tend to go to suppliers who pay the highest bribes rather than to the most competent suppliers. Would you like to fly in aircraft whose wings were made by the subcontractor who paid the highest bribe? Would you fly as often? What would happen to the airline industry if its safety record deteriorated due to shoddy workmanship on contracted parts and assemblies?
- Suppose the presidents of companies routinely lied in their annual reports and financial statements. If investors could not rely on the basic integrity of a company's financial statements, they would have little basis for making informed decisions. Suspecting the worst, rational investors would pay less for securities issued by companies and may not be willing to invest at all. As a consequence, companies would have less money for productive investments—leading to slower economic growth, fewer goods and services, and higher prices.

---

[11] James Surowiecki, "A Virtuous Cycle," *Forbes*, December 23, 2002, pp. 248–256. Reprinted by Permission of Forbes Magazine©2006 Forbes Inc.

EXHIBIT 1–9
IMA Statement of Ethical Professional Practice

Members of IMA shall behave ethically. A commitment to ethical professional practice includes: overarching principles that express our values, and standards that guide our conduct.

PRINCIPLES

IMA's overarching ethical principles include: Honesty, Fairness, Objectivity, and Responsibility. Members shall act in accordance with these principles and shall encourage others within their organizations to adhere to them.

STANDARDS

A member's failure to comply with the following standards may result in disciplinary action.

I. COMPETENCE

Each member has a responsibility to:

1. Maintain an appropriate level of professional expertise by continually developing knowledge and skills.
2. Perform professional duties in accordance with relevant laws, regulations, and technical standards.
3. Provide decision support information and recommendations that are accurate, clear, concise, and timely.
4. Recognize and communicate professional limitations or other constraints that would preclude responsible judgment or successful performance of an activity.

II. CONFIDENTIALITY

Each member has a responsibility to:

1. Keep information confidential except when disclosure is authorized or legally required.
2. Inform all relevant parties regarding appropriate use of confidential information. Monitor subordinates' activities to ensure compliance.
3. Refrain from using confidential information for unethical or illegal advantage.

III. INTEGRITY

Each member has a responsibility to:

1. Mitigate actual conflicts of interest. Regularly communicate with business associates to avoid apparent conflicts of interest. Advise all parties of any potential conflicts.
2. Refrain from engaging in any conduct that would prejudice carrying out duties ethically.
3. Abstain from engaging in or supporting any activity that might discredit the profession.

IV. CREDIBILITY

Each member has a responsibility to:

1. Communicate information fairly and objectively.
2. Disclose all relevant information that could reasonably be expected to influence an intended user's understanding of the reports, analyses, or recommendations.
3. Disclose delays or deficiencies in information, timeliness, processing, or internal controls in conformance with organization policy and/or applicable law.

RESOLUTION OF ETHICAL CONFLICT

In applying the Standards of Ethical Professional Practice, you may encounter problems identifying unethical behavior or resolving an ethical conflict. When faced with ethical issues, you should follow your organization's established policies on the resolution of such conflict. If these policies do not resolve the ethical conflict, you should consider the following courses of action:

1. Discuss the issue with your immediate supervisor except when it appears that the supervisor is involved. In that case, present the issue to the next level. If you cannot achieve a satisfactory resolution, submit the issue to the next management level. If your immediate superior is the chief executive officer or equivalent, the acceptable reviewing authority may be a group such as the audit committee, executive committee, board of directors, board of trustees, or owners. Contact with levels above the immediate superior should be initiated only with your superior's knowledge, assuming he or she is not involved. Communication of such problems to authorities or individuals not employed or engaged by the organization is not considered appropriate, unless you believe there is a clear violation of the law.
2. Clarify relevant ethical issues by initiating a confidential discussion with an IMA Ethics Counselor or other impartial advisor to obtain a better understanding of possible courses of action.
3. Consult your own attorney as to legal obligations and rights concerning the ethical conflict.

As these examples suggest, if ethical standards were not generally adhered to, everyone would suffer—businesses as well as consumers. Essentially, abandoning ethical standards would lead to a lower standard of living with lower-quality goods and services, less to choose from, and higher prices. In short, following ethical rules such as those in the Statement of Ethical Professional Practice is absolutely essential for the smooth functioning of an advanced market economy.

IN BUSINESS

WHO IS TO BLAME?

Don Keough, a retired Coca-Cola executive, recalls that, "In my time, CFOs [Chief Financial Officers] were basically tough, smart, and mean. Bringing good news wasn't their function. They were the truth-tellers." But that had changed by the late 1990s in some companies. Instead of being truth-tellers, CFOs became corporate spokesmen, guiding stock analysts in their quarterly earnings estimates—and then making sure those earnings estimates were beaten using whatever means necessary, including accounting tricks and in some cases outright fraud. But does the buck stop there?

A survey of 179 CFOs published in May 2004 showed that only 38% of those surveyed believed that pressure to use aggressive accounting techniques to improve results had lessened relative to three years earlier. And 20% of those surveyed said the pressure had increased over the past three years. Where did the respondents say the pressure was coming from? Personal greed, weak boards of directors, and overbearing Chief Executive Officers (CEOs) topped the list. Who is to blame? Perhaps that question is less important than focusing on what is needed—greater personal integrity and less emphasis on meeting quarterly earnings estimates.

Sources: Jeremy Kahn, "The Chief Freaked Out Officer," *Fortune*, December 9, 2002, pp. 197–202, and Don Durfee, "After the Scandals: It's Better (and Worse) Than You Think," *CFO*, May 2004, p. 29.

Company Codes of Conduct

Many companies have adopted formal ethical codes of conduct. These codes are generally broad-based statements of a company's responsibilities to its employees, its customers, its suppliers, and the communities in which the company operates. Codes rarely spell out specific do's and don'ts or suggest proper behavior in a specific situation. Instead, they give broad guidelines. For example, Exhibit 1–10 (page 24) shows Johnson & Johnson's code of ethical conduct, which it refers to as a Credo. Johnson & Johnson created its Credo in 1943 and today it is translated into 36 languages. Johnson & Johnson surveys its employees every two to three years to obtain their impressions of how well the company adheres to its ethical principles. If the survey reveals shortcomings, corrective actions are taken.[12]

It bears emphasizing that establishing a code of ethical conduct, such as Johnson & Johnson's Credo, is meaningless if employees, and in particular top managers, do not adhere to it when making decisions. If top managers continue to say, in effect, that they will only be satisfied with bottom-line results and will accept no excuses, they are building a culture that implicitly coerces employees to engage in unethical behavior to get ahead. This type of unethical culture is contagious. In fact, one survey showed that "[t]hose who engage in unethical behavior often justify their actions with one or more of the following reasons: (1) the organization expects unethical behavior, (2) everyone else is unethical, and/or (3) behaving unethically is the only way to get ahead."[13]

---

[12] www.jnj.com/our_company/our_credo

[13] Michael K. McCuddy, Karl E. Reichardt, and David Schroeder, "Ethical Pressures: Fact or Fiction?" *Management Accounting* 74, no. 10, pp. 57–61.

EXHIBIT 1–10
The Johnson & Johnson Credo

Johnson & Johnson Credo

We believe our first responsibility is to the doctors, nurses and patients, to mothers and fathers and all others who use our products and services. In meeting their needs everything we do must be of high quality. We must constantly strive to reduce our costs in order to maintain reasonable prices. Customers' orders must be serviced promptly and accurately. Our suppliers and distributors must have an opportunity to make a fair profit.

We are responsible to our employees, the men and women who work with us throughout the world. Everyone must be considered as an individual. We must respect their dignity and recognize their merit. They must have a sense of security in their jobs. Compensation must be fair and adequate, and working conditions clean, orderly and safe. We must be mindful of ways to help our employees fulfill their family responsibilities. Employees must feel free to make suggestions and complaints. There must be equal opportunity for employment, development and advancement for those qualified. We must provide competent management, and their actions must be just and ethical.

We are responsible to the communities in which we live and work and to the world community as well. We must be good citizens—support good works and charities and bear our fair share of taxes. We must encourage civic improvements and better health and education. We must maintain in good order the property we are privileged to use, protecting the environment and natural resources.

Our final responsibility is to our stockholders. Business must make a sound profit. We must experiment with new ideas. Research must be carried on, innovative programs developed and mistakes paid for. New equipment must be purchased, new facilities provided and new products launched. Reserves must be created to provide for adverse times. When we operate according to these principles, the stockholders should realize a fair return.

IN BUSINESS

WHERE WOULD YOU LIKE TO WORK?

Nearly all executives claim that their companies maintain high ethical standards; however, not all executives walk the talk. Employees usually know when top executives are saying one thing and doing another and they also know that these attitudes spill over into other areas. Working in companies where top managers pay little attention to their own ethical rules can be extremely unpleasant. Several thousand employees in many different organizations were asked if they would recommend their company to prospective employees. Overall, 66% said that they would. Among those employees who believed that their top management strives to live by the company's stated ethical standards, the number of recommenders jumped to 81%. But among those who believed top management did not follow the company's stated ethical standards, the number was just 21%.

Source: Jeffrey L. Seglin, "Good for Goodness' Sake," *CFO,* October 2002, pp. 75–78.

Codes of Conduct on the International Level

The Code of Ethics for Professional Accountants, issued by the International Federation of Accountants (IFAC), governs the activities of all professional accountants throughout the world, regardless of whether they are practicing as independent CPAs, employed in government service, or employed as internal accountants.[14]

In addition to outlining ethical requirements in matters dealing with integrity and objectivity, resolution of ethical conflicts, competence, and confidentiality, the IFAC's code also outlines the accountant's ethical responsibilities in other matters such as those relating to

[14] A copy of this code can be obtained on the International Federation of Accountants' website www.ifac.org.

taxes, independence, fees and commissions, advertising and solicitation, the handling of monies, and cross-border activities. Where cross-border activities are involved, the IFAC ethical requirements must be followed if they are stricter than the ethical requirements of the country in which the work is being performed.

Corporate Governance

Effective *corporate governance* enhances stockholders' confidence that a company is being run in their best interests rather than in the interests of top managers. **Corporate governance** is the system by which a company is directed and controlled. If properly implemented, the corporate governance system should provide incentives for the board of directors and top management to pursue objectives that are in the interests of the company's owners and it should provide for effective monitoring of performance.[15] Many would argue that, in addition to protecting the interests of stockholders, an effective corporate governance system also should protect the interests of the company's many other *stakeholders*—its customers, creditors, employees, suppliers, and the communities within which it operates. These parties are referred to as stakeholders because their welfare is tied to the company's performance.

Unfortunately, history has repeatedly shown that unscrupulous top managers, if unchecked, can exploit their power to defraud stakeholders. This unpleasant reality became all too clear in 2001 when the fall of Enron kicked off a wave of corporate scandals. These scandals were characterized by financial reporting fraud and misuse of corporate funds at the very highest levels—including CEOs and CFOs. While this was disturbing in itself, it also indicated that the institutions intended to prevent such abuses weren't working, thus raising fundamental questions about the adequacy of the existing corporate governance system. In an attempt to respond to these concerns, the U.S. Congress passed the most important reform of corporate governance in many decades—*The Sarbanes-Oxley Act of 2002*.

IN BUSINESS

SPILLED MILK AT PARMALAT

Corporate scandals have not been limited to the United States. In 2003, Parmalat, a publicly traded dairy company in Italy, went bankrupt. The CEO, Calisto Tanzi, admitted to manipulating the books for more than a decade so that he could skim off $640 million to cover losses at various of his family businesses. But the story doesn't stop there. Parmalat's balance sheet contained $13 billion in nonexistent assets, including a $5 billion Bank of America account that didn't exist. All in all, Parmalat was the biggest financial fraud in European history.

Source: Gail Edmondson, David Fairlamb, and Nanette Byrnes, "The Milk Just Keeps on Spilling," *BusinessWeek*, January 26, 2004, pp. 54–58.

The Sarbanes-Oxley Act of 2002

The **Sarbanes-Oxley Act of 2002** was intended to protect the interests of those who invest in publicly traded companies by improving the reliability and accuracy of corporate financial reports and disclosures. We would like to highlight six key aspects of the legislation.[16]

15 This definition of corporate governance was adapted from the 2004 report titled OECD Principles of Corporate Governance published by the Organization for Economic Co-Operation and Development.

16 A summary of the Sarbanes-Oxley Act of 2002 can be obtained from the American Institute of Certified Public Accountants (AICPA) website www.aicpa.org/info/sarbanes_oxley_summary.

First, the Act requires that both the CEO and CFO certify in writing that their company's financial statements and accompanying disclosures fairly represent the results of operations—with possible jail time if a CEO or CFO certifies results that they know are false. This creates very powerful incentives for the CEO and CFO to ensure that the financial statements contain no misrepresentations.

Second, the Act established the Public Company Accounting Oversight Board to provide additional oversight over the audit profession. The Act authorizes the Board to conduct investigations, to take disciplinary actions against audit firms, and to enact various standards and rules concerning the preparation of audit reports.

Third, the Act places the power to hire, compensate, and terminate the public accounting firm that audits a company's financial reports in the hands of the audit committee of the board of directors. Previously, management often had the power to hire and fire its auditors. Furthermore, the Act specifies that all members of the audit committee must be independent, meaning that they do not have an affiliation with the company they are overseeing, nor do they receive any consulting or advisory compensation from the company.

Fourth, the Act places important restrictions on audit firms. Historically, public accounting firms earned a large part of their profits by providing consulting services to the companies that they audited. This provided the appearance of a lack of independence since a client that was dissatisfied with an auditor's stance on an accounting issue might threaten to stop using the auditor as a consultant. To avoid this possible conflict of interests, the Act prohibits a public accounting firm from providing a wide variety of nonauditing services to an audit client.

Fifth, the Act requires that a company's annual report contain an *internal control report.* Internal controls are put in place by management to provide assurance to investors that financial disclosures are reliable. The report must state that it is management's responsibility to establish and maintain adequate internal controls and it must contain an assessment by management of the effectiveness of its internal control structure. The internal control report is accompanied by an opinion from the company's audit firm as to whether management's assessment of its internal control over financial reporting is fairly stated.[17]

Finally, the Act establishes severe penalties of as many as 20 years in prison for altering or destroying any documents that may eventually be used in an official proceeding and as many as 10 years in prison for managers who retaliate against a so-called whistle-blower who goes outside the chain of command to report misconduct. Collectively, these six aspects of the Sarbanes-Oxley Act of 2002 should help reduce the incidence of fraudulent financial reporting.

IN BUSINESS

SARBANES-OXLEY: AN EXPENSIVE PIECE OF LEGISLATION

You wouldn't think 169 words could be so expensive! But that is the case with what is known as Section 404 of The Sarbanes-Oxley Act of 2002 that requires a publicly traded company's annual report to contain an internal control report certified by its auditors. Estimates indicate that compliance with this provision will cost the Fortune 1000 companies alone about $6 billion annually—much of which will go to public accounting firms in fees. With the increased demand for audit services, public accounting firms such as KPMG, PricewaterhouseCoopers, Ernst & Young, and Deloitte are returning to campuses to hire new auditors in large numbers and students are flocking to accounting classes.

Source: Holman W. Jenkins Jr., "Thinking Outside the Sarbox," *The Wall Street Journal,* November 24, 2004, p. A13.

[17] The Public Company Accounting Oversight Board's Auditing Standard No. 2 requires the audit firm to issue a second opinion on whether its client maintained effective internal control over the financial reporting process. This opinion is in addition to the opinion regarding the fairness of management's assessment of the effectiveness of its own internal controls.

Enterprise Risk Management

Businesses face risks every day. Some risks are foreseeable. For example, a company could reasonably be expected to foresee the possibility of a natural disaster or a fire destroying its centralized data storage facility. Companies respond to this type of risk by maintaining off-site backup data storage facilities. Other risks are unforeseeable. For example, in 1982 Johnson & Johnson never could have imagined that a deranged killer would insert poison into bottles of Tylenol and then place these tainted bottles on retail shelves, ultimately killing seven people.[18] Johnson & Johnson—guided by the first line of its Credo (see page 24)—responded to this crisis by acting to reduce the risks faced by its customers and itself. First, it immediately recalled and destroyed 31 million bottles of Tylenol with a retail value of $100 million to reduce the risk of additional fatalities. Second, it developed the tamper-resistant packaging that we take for granted today to reduce the risk that the same type of crime could be repeated in the future.

Every business strategy or decision involves risks. **Enterprise risk management** is a process used by a company to proactively identify and manage those risks.

Identifying and Controlling Business Risks

Companies should identify foreseeable risks before they occur rather than react to unfortunate events that have already happened. The left-hand column of Exhibit 1–11 (page 28) provides 12 examples of business risks. This list is not exhaustive, rather its purpose is to illustrate the diverse nature of business risks that companies face. Whether the risks relate to the weather, computer hackers, complying with the law, employee theft, financial reporting, or strategic decision making, they all have one thing in common. If the risks are not managed effectively, they can infringe on a company's ability to meet its goals.

Once a company identifies its risks, it can respond to them in various ways such as accepting, avoiding, sharing, or reducing the risk. Perhaps the most common risk management tactic is to reduce risks by implementing specific controls. The right-hand column of Exhibit 1–11 provides an example of a control that could be implemented to help reduce each of the risks mentioned in the left-hand column of the exhibit.

In conclusion, a sophisticated enterprise risk management system cannot guarantee that all risks are eliminated. Nonetheless, many companies understand that managing risks is a superior alternative to reacting, perhaps too late, to unfortunate events.

IN BUSINESS

MANAGING WEATHER RISK

The National Oceanic and Atmospheric Administration claims that the weather influences one-third of the U.S. gross domestic product. In 2004, the word *unseasonable* was used by more than 120 publicly traded companies to explain unfavorable financial performance. Indeed, it would be easy to conclude that the weather poses an uncontrollable risk to businesses, right? Wrong! Weather risk management is a growing industry with roughly 80 companies offering weather risk management services to clients.

For example, Planalytics is a weather consulting firm that helps Wise Metal Group, a manufacturer of aluminum can sheeting, to manage its natural gas purchases. Wise's $3 million monthly gas bill fluctuates sharply depending on the weather. Planalytics' software helps Wise plan its gas purchases in advance of changing temperatures. Beyond influencing natural gas purchases, the weather can also delay the boats that deliver Wise's raw materials and it can affect Wise's sales to the extent that cooler weather conditions lead to a decline in canned beverage sales.

Source: Abraham Lustgarten, "Getting Ahead of the Weather," *Fortune*, February 7, 2005, pp. 87–94.

---

[18] Tamara Kaplan, "The Tylenol Crisis: How Effective Public Relations Saved Johnson & Johnson," in Glen Broom, Allen Center, and Scott Cutlip, *Effective Public Relations,* Prentice Hall, Upper Saddle River, NJ.

EXHIBIT 1–11
Identifying and Controlling Business Risks

Examples of Business Risks	Examples of Controls to Reduce Business Risks
• Intellectual assets being stolen from computer files	• Create firewalls that prohibit computer hackers from corrupting or stealing intellectual property
• Products harming customers	• Develop a formal and rigorous new product testing program
• Losing market share due to the unforeseen actions of competitors	• Develop an approach for legally gathering information about competitors' plans and practices
• Poor weather conditions shutting down operations	• Develop contingency plans for overcoming weather-related disruptions
• A website malfunctioning	• Thoroughly test the website before going "live" on the Internet
• A supplier strike halting the flow of raw materials	• Establish a relationship with two companies capable of providing needed raw materials
• A poorly designed incentive compensation system causing employees to make bad decisions	• Create a balanced set of performance measures that motivates the desired behavior
• Financial statements unfairly reporting the value of inventory	• Count the physical inventory on hand to make sure that it agrees with the accounting records
• An employee stealing assets	• Segregate duties so that the same employee does not have physical custody of an asset and the responsibility of accounting for it
• An employee accessing unauthorized information	• Create password-protected barriers that prohibit employees from obtaining information not needed to do their jobs
• Inaccurate budget estimates causing excessive or insufficient production	• Implement a rigorous budget review process
• Failing to comply with equal employment opportunity laws	• Create a report that tracks key metrics related to compliance with the laws

The Certified Management Accountant (CMA)

An individual who possesses the necessary qualifications and who passes a rigorous professional exam earns the right to be known as a *Certified Management Accountant (CMA).* In addition to the prestige that accompanies a professional designation, CMAs are often given greater responsibilities and higher compensation than those who do not have such a designation. Information about becoming a CMA and the CMA program can be accessed on the Institute of Management Accountants' (IMA) website www.imanet.org or by calling 1-800-638-4427.

To become a Certified Management Accountant, the following four steps must be completed:

1. File an Application for Admission and register for the CMA examination.
2. Pass all four parts of the CMA examination within a three-year period.
3. Satisfy the experience requirement of two continuous years of professional experience in management and/or financial accounting prior to or within seven years of passing the CMA examination.
4. Comply with the Statement of Ethical Professional Practice.

IN BUSINESS

HOW'S THE PAY?

The Institute of Management Accountants has created the following table that allows an individual to estimate what his salary would be as a management accountant. (The table below applies specifically to men. A similar table exists for women.)

			Your Calculation
Start with this base amount		$74,779	$74,779
If you are top-level management.	ADD	$15,893	
OR, if you are senior-level management	ADD	$6,369	
OR, if you are entry-level management	SUBTRACT	$21,861	
Number of years in the field _______	TIMES	$355	
If you have an advanced degree.	ADD	$13,861	
OR, if you have no degree.	SUBTRACT	$19,289	
If you hold the CMA	ADD	$13,619	
If you hold the CPA	ADD	$6,832	
If you have had one or more career interruptions	SUBTRACT	$13,367	_______
Your estimated salary level			=======

For example, if you make it to top-level management in 10 years, have an advanced degree and a CMA, and no career interruptions, your estimated salary would be $121,702 [$74,779 + $15,893 + (10 × $355) + $13,861 + $13,619].

Source: David L. Schroeder and Karl E. Reichardt, "2004 Salary Survey," *Strategic Finance*, June 2005, pp. 28–43.

Summary

Successful companies follow strategies that differentiate themselves from competitors. Strategies often focus on three customer value propositions—customer intimacy, operational excellence, and product leadership.

Most organizations rely on decentralization to some degree. Decentralization is formally depicted in an organization chart that shows who works for whom and which units perform line and staff functions.

Lean Production, the Theory of Constraints, and Six Sigma are three management approaches that focus on business processes. Lean Production organizes resources around business processes and pulls units through those processes in response to customer orders. The result is lower inventories, fewer defects, less wasted effort, and quicker customer response times. The Theory of Constraints emphasizes the importance of managing an organization's constraints. Since the constraint is whatever is holding back the organization, improvement efforts usually must be focused on the constraint to be effective. Six Sigma uses the DMAIC (Define, Measure, Analyze, Improve, and Control) framework to eliminate non-value-added activities and to improve processes.

E-commerce and enterprise systems are being used to reshape business practices. An enterprise system integrates data across the organization in a single software system that makes the same data available to all managers.

Ethical behavior is the foundation of a successful market economy. If we cannot trust others to act ethically in their business dealings with us, we will be inclined to invest less, scrutinize purchases more, and generally waste time and money trying to protect ourselves from the unscrupulous—resulting in fewer goods available to consumers at higher prices and lower quality.

Unfortunately, trust in our corporate governance system has been undermined in recent years by numerous high-profile financial reporting scandals. The Sarbanes-Oxley Act of 2002 was passed with the objective of improving the reliability of the financial disclosures provided by publicly traded companies.

Glossary

At the end of each chapter, a list of key terms for review is given, along with the definition of each term. (These terms are printed in boldface where they are defined in the chapter.) Carefully study each term to be sure you understand its meaning. The list for Chapter 1 follows.

Budget A detailed plan for the future, usually expressed in formal quantitative terms. (p. 6)

Business process A series of steps that are followed to carry out some task in a business. (p. 11)

Chief Financial Officer (CFO) The member of the top management team who is responsible for providing timely and relevant data to support planning and control activities and for preparing financial statements for external users. (p. 11)

Constraint Anything that prevents an organization or individual from getting more of what it wants. (p. 15)

Control The process of instituting procedures and then obtaining feedback to ensure that all parts of the organization are functioning effectively and moving toward overall company goals. (p. 6)

Controller The member of the top management team who is responsible for providing relevant and timely data to managers and for preparing financial statements for external users. The controller reports to the CFO. (p. 6)

Controlling Ensuring that the plan is actually carried out and is appropriately modified as circumstances change. (p. 5)

Corporate governance The system by which a company is directed and controlled. If properly implemented it should provide incentives for top management to pursue objectives that are in the interests of the company and it should effectively monitor performance. (p. 25)

Decentralization The delegation of decision-making authority throughout an organization by providing managers with the authority to make decisions relating to their area of responsibility. (p.10)

Directing and motivating Mobilizing people to carry out plans and run routine operations. (p. 5)

Enterprise system A software system that integrates data from across an organization into a single centralized database that enables all employees to access a common set of data. (p. 19)

Enterprise risk management A process used by a company to help identify the risks that it faces and to develop responses to those risks that enable the company to be reasonably assured of meeting its goals. (p. 27)

Feedback Accounting and other reports that help managers monitor performance and focus on problems and/or opportunities that might otherwise go unnoticed. (p. 6)

Financial accounting The phase of accounting concerned with providing information to stockholders, creditors, and others outside the organization. (p. 2)

Finished goods Units of product that have been completed but have not yet been sold to customers. (p. 13)

Just-in-time (JIT) A production and inventory control system in which materials are purchased and units are produced only as needed to meet actual customer demand. (p. 14)

Lean thinking model A five-step management approach that organizes resources around the flow of business processes and that pulls units through these processes in response to customer orders. (p. 13)

Line A position in an organization that is directly related to the achievement of the organization's basic objectives. (p. 11)

Managerial accounting The phase of accounting concerned with providing information to managers for use inside the organization. (p. 2)

Non-value-added activities Activities that consume resources but do not add value for which customers are willing to pay. (p. 16)

Organization chart A diagram of a company's organizational structure that depicts formal lines of reporting, communication, and responsibility between managers. (p. 10)

Performance report A detailed report comparing budgeted data to actual data. (p. 7)

Planning Selecting a course of action and specifying how the action will be implemented. (p. 5)

Planning and control cycle The flow of management activities through planning, directing and motivating, and controlling, and then back to planning again. (p. 7)

Raw materials Materials that are used to make a product. (p. 13)

Sarbanes-Oxley Act of 2002 Legislation enacted to protect the interests of stockholders who invest in publicly traded companies by improving the reliability and accuracy of the disclosures provided to them. (p. 25)

Segment Any part of an organization that can be evaluated independently of other parts and about which the manager seeks financial data. Examples include a product line, a sales territory, a division, or a department. (p. 9)

Six Sigma A method that relies on customer feedback and objective data gathering and analysis techniques to drive process improvement. (p. 16)

Staff A position in an organization that is only indirectly related to the achievement of the organization's basic objectives. Such positions provide service or assistance to line positions or to other staff positions. (p.11)

Strategy A "game plan" that enables a company to attract customers by distinguishing itself from competitors. (p. 4)

Supply chain management A management approach that coordinates business processes across companies to better serve end consumers. (p. 14)

Theory of Constraints (TOC) A management approach that emphasizes the importance of managing constraints. (p. 15)

Value chain The major business functions that add value to a company's products and services such as research and development, product design, manufacturing, marketing, distribution, and customer service. (p. 11)

Work in process Units of product that are only partially complete and will require further work before they are ready for sale to a customer. (p. 13)

Quiz 1

Multiple-choice questions are provided on the text Web site at www.mhhe.com/noreen1e.

Questions

1-1 What is the basic difference in orientation between financial and managerial accounting?
1-2 What is meant by a business strategy?
1-3 Describe the three broad categories of customer value propositions.
1-4 Describe the three major activities of a manager.
1-5 What are the four steps in the planning and control cycle?
1-6 What are the major differences between financial and managerial accounting?
1-7 Distinguish between line and staff positions in an organization.
1-8 Describe the basic responsibilities of the Chief Financial Officer.
1-9 What are the three main categories of inventories in a manufacturing company?
1-10 What are the five steps in the lean thinking model?
1-11 What are the major benefits from successful implementation of the lean thinking model?
1-12 Describe what is meant by a "pull" production system.
1-13 Where does the Theory of Constraints recommend that improvement efforts be focused?
1-14 Briefly describe Six Sigma.
1-15 Describe the five stages in the Six Sigma DMAIC Framework.
1-16 What is an enterprise system supposed to accomplish?
1-17 Why is adherence to ethical standards important for the smooth functioning of an advanced market economy?
1-18 Describe what is meant by corporate governance.
1-19 Briefly describe what is meant by enterprise risk management.

Exercises

EXERCISE 1-1 The Roles of Managers and Management Accountants [LO1, LO2]

A number of terms that relate to organizations, the work of management, and the role of managerial accounting are listed below:

budgets	controller
decentralization	directing and motivating
feedback	financial accounting
line	managerial accounting
nonmonetary data	planning
performance report	staff
precision	Chief Financial Officer

Choose the term or terms above that most appropriately complete the following statements.

1. ____________________ is concerned with providing information for the use of those who are inside the organization, whereas ____________________ is concerned with providing information for the use of those who are outside the organization.
2. ____________________ consists of identifying alternatives, selecting from among the alternatives the one that is best for the organization, and specifying what actions will be taken to implement the chosen alternative.
3. When ____________________, managers oversee day-to-day activities and keep the organization functioning smoothly.
4. The accounting and other reports coming to management that are used in controlling the organization are called ____________________.
5. The delegation of decision-making authority throughout an organization by allowing managers at various operating levels to make key decisions relating to their area of responsibility is called ____________________.
6. A position on the organization chart that is directly related to achieving the basic objectives of an organization is called a ____________________ position.
7. A ____________________ position provides service or assistance to other parts of the organization and does not directly achieve the basic objectives of the organization.
8. The manager in charge of the accounting department is generally known as the ____________________.
9. The plans of management are expressed formally in ____________________.
10. A detailed report to management comparing budgeted data to actual data for a specific time period is called a ____________________.
11. The ____________________ is the member of the top management team who is responsible for providing timely and relevant data to support planning and control activities and for preparing financial statements for external users.
12. Managerial accounting places less emphasis on ____________________ and more emphasis on ____________________ than financial accounting.

EXERCISE 1-2 The Business Environment [LO3]

A number of terms are listed below:

value chain	Six Sigma	enterprise risk management
supply chain management	budget	Internet
lean thinking model	nonconstraint	pulls
customer value proposition	business process	constraint
corporate governance	Theory of Constraints	enterprise system
strategy	non-value-added activity	Just-In-Time

Required:

Choose the term or terms from the above list that most appropriately completes each of the following statements:

1. A(n) ____________________ is a game plan that enables a company to attract customers by distinguishing itself from competitors.
2. ____________________ is a method that relies on customer feedback and objective data gathering and analysis techniques to drive process improvement.
3. A(n) ____________________ is a series of steps that are followed to carry out some task in a business.
4. The system by which a company is directed and controlled is called ____________________.
5. The process used by a company to help identify the risks that it faces and to develop responses to those risks so that the company is reasonably assured of meeting its goals is known as ____________________.
6. A production and inventory control system in which materials are purchased and units are produced only as needed to meet actual customer demand is known as ____________________.
7. The ____________________ fuels the globalization phenomenon by providing companies with greater access to geographically dispersed customers, employees, and suppliers.
8. A(n) ____________________ is anything that prevents an organization or individual from getting more of what it wants.
9. Increasing the rate of output of a(n) ____________________ as the result of an improvement effort is unlikely to have much effect on profits.
10. A(n) ____________________ consists of business functions that add value to a company's products and services such as research and development, product design, manufacturing, marketing, distribution, and customer service.

11. A(n) ____________ integrates data from across an organization into a single centralized database that enables all employees to access a common set of data.
12. A management approach that coordinates business processes across companies to better serve end consumers is known as ____________.
13. The ____________ is a five-step management approach that organizes resources around the flow of business processes and that ____________ units through those processes in response to customer orders.
14. A company can only succeed if it creates a reason for customers to choose it over a competitor; in short, a ____________.
15. A(n) ____________ is a detailed plan for the future, usually expressed in formal quantitative terms.
16. A(n) ____________ consumes resources but does not add value for which customers are willing to pay.
17. The management approach that emphasizes the importance of managing constraints is known as the ____________.

EXERCISE 1-3 Ethics in Business [LO4]

Andy Morio was hired by a popular fast-food restaurant as an order-taker and cashier. Shortly after taking the job, he was shocked to overhear an employee bragging to a friend about shortchanging customers. He confronted the employee who then snapped back: "Mind your own business. Besides, everyone does it and the customers never miss the money." Andy didn't know how to respond to this aggressive stance.

Required:

What would be the practical consequences on the fast-food industry and on consumers if cashiers generally shortchanged customers at every opportunity?

Problems

PROBLEM 1-4 Ethics in Business [LO4]

Paul Sarver is the controller of a corporation whose stock is not listed on a national stock exchange. The company has just received a patent on a product that is expected to yield substantial profits in a year or two. At the moment, however, the company is experiencing financial difficulties; and because of inadequate working capital, it is on the verge of defaulting on a note held by its bank.

At the end of the most recent fiscal year, the company's president instructed Sarver not to record several invoices as accounts payable. Sarver objected since the invoices represented bona fide liabilities. However, the president insisted that the invoices not be recorded until after year-end, at which time it was expected that additional financing could be obtained. After several very strenuous objections—expressed to both the president and other members of senior management—Sarver finally complied with the president's instructions.

Required:

1. Did Sarver act in an ethical manner? Explain.
2. If the new product fails to yield substantial profits and the company becomes insolvent, can Sarver's actions be justified by the fact that he was following orders from a superior? Explain.

PROBLEM 1-5 Preparing an Organization Chart [LO2]

Ridell University is a large private school located in the Midwest. The university is headed by a president who has five vice presidents reporting to him. These vice presidents are responsible for auxiliary services, admissions and records, academics, financial services (controller), and the physical plant.

In addition, the university has managers who report to these vice presidents. These include managers for central purchasing, the university press, and the university bookstore, all of whom report to the vice president for auxiliary services; managers for computer services and for accounting and finance, who report to the vice president for financial services; and managers for grounds and custodial services and for plant and maintenance, who report to the vice president for the physical plant.

The university has four colleges—business, humanities, fine arts, and engineering and quantitative methods—and a law school. Each of these units has a dean who is responsible to the academic vice president. Each college has several departments.

Required:

1. Prepare an organization chart for Ridell University.
2. Which of the positions on your chart would be line positions? Why would they be line positions? Which would be staff positions? Why?
3. Which of the positions on your chart would have a need for accounting information? Explain.

PROBLEM 1-6 Ethics in Business [LO4]

Adam Williams was recently hired as assistant controller of GroChem, Inc., which processes chemicals for use in fertilizers. Williams was selected for this position because of his past experience in chemical processing. During his first month on the job, Williams made a point of getting to know the people responsible for the plant operations and learning how things are done at GroChem.

During a conversation with the plant supervisor, Williams asked about the company procedures for handling toxic waste materials. The plant supervisor replied that he was not involved with the disposal of wastes and suggested that Williams might be wise to ignore this issue. This response strengthened Williams' determination to probe this area further to be sure that the company was not vulnerable to litigation.

Upon further investigation, Williams discovered evidence that GroChem was using a nearby residential landfill to dump toxic wastes—an illegal activity. It appeared that some members of GroChem's management team were aware of this situation and may have been involved in arranging for this dumping; however, Williams was unable to determine whether his superior, the controller, was involved.

Uncertain how he should proceed, Williams began to consider his options by outlining the following three alternative courses of action:

- Seek the advice of his superior, the controller.
- Anonymously release the information to the local newspaper.
- Discuss the situation with an outside member of the board of directors with whom he is acquainted.

Required:

1. Discuss why Adam Williams has an ethical responsibility to take some action in the matter of GroChem, Inc., and the dumping of toxic wastes. Refer to the specific standards (competence, confidentiality, integrity, and/or credibility) in the Statement of Ethical Professional Practice established by the Institute of Management Accountants to support your answer.
2. For each of the three alternative courses of action that Adam Williams has outlined, explain whether or not the action is appropriate according to the Statement of Ethical Professional Practice established by the Institute of Management Accountants.
3. Assume that Adam Williams sought the advice of his superior, the controller, and discovered that the controller was involved in the dumping of toxic wastes. Describe the steps that Williams should take to resolve this situation.

(CMA, adapted)

PROBLEM 1-7 Ethics in Business [LO4]

Consumers and attorney generals in more than 40 states accused a prominent nationwide chain of auto repair shops of misleading customers and selling them unnecessary parts and services, from brake jobs to front-end alignments. Lynn Sharpe Paine reported the situation as follows in "Managing for Organizational Integrity," *Harvard Business Review,* March-April, 1994:

> In the face of declining revenues, shrinking market share, and an increasingly competitive market . . . management attempted to spur performance of its auto centers. . . . The automotive service advisers were given product-specific sales quotas—sell so many springs, shock absorbers, alignments, or brake jobs per shift—and paid a commission based on sales. . . . [F]ailure to meet quotas could lead to a transfer or a reduction in work hours. Some employees spoke of the "pressure, pressure, pressure" to bring in sales.
>
> This pressure-cooker atmosphere created conditions under which employees felt that the only way to satisfy top management was by selling products and services to customers that they didn't really need.

Suppose all automotive repair businesses routinely followed the practice of attempting to sell customers unnecessary parts and services.

Required:

1. How would this behavior affect customers? How might customers attempt to protect themselves against this behavior?
2. How would this behavior probably affect profits and employment in the automotive service industry?

PROBLEM 1-8 Line and Staff Positions; Organization Chart [LO2]

The Association of Medical Personnel (AMP) is a membership/educational organization that serves a wide range of individuals who work for medical institutions including hospitals, clinics, and medical practices. The membership is composed of doctors, nurses, medical assistants, and professional administrators. The purpose of the organization is to provide individuals in the medical field with a professional organization that offers educational and training opportunities through local chapters, a monthly magazine (*AMP Review*), continuing education programs, seminars, self-study courses, and research publications.

AMP is governed by a board of directors who are members elected to these positions by the membership. The chairperson of the board is the highest ranking volunteer member and presides over the board; the board establishes policy for the organization. The policies are administered and carried out by AMP's paid professional staff. The president's chief responsibility is to manage the operations of the professional staff. Like any organization, the professional staff of AMP is composed of line and staff positions. A partial organization chart of the AMP professional staff is shown in Exhibit A.

EXHIBIT A

Partial Organization Chart for the Association of Medical Personnel

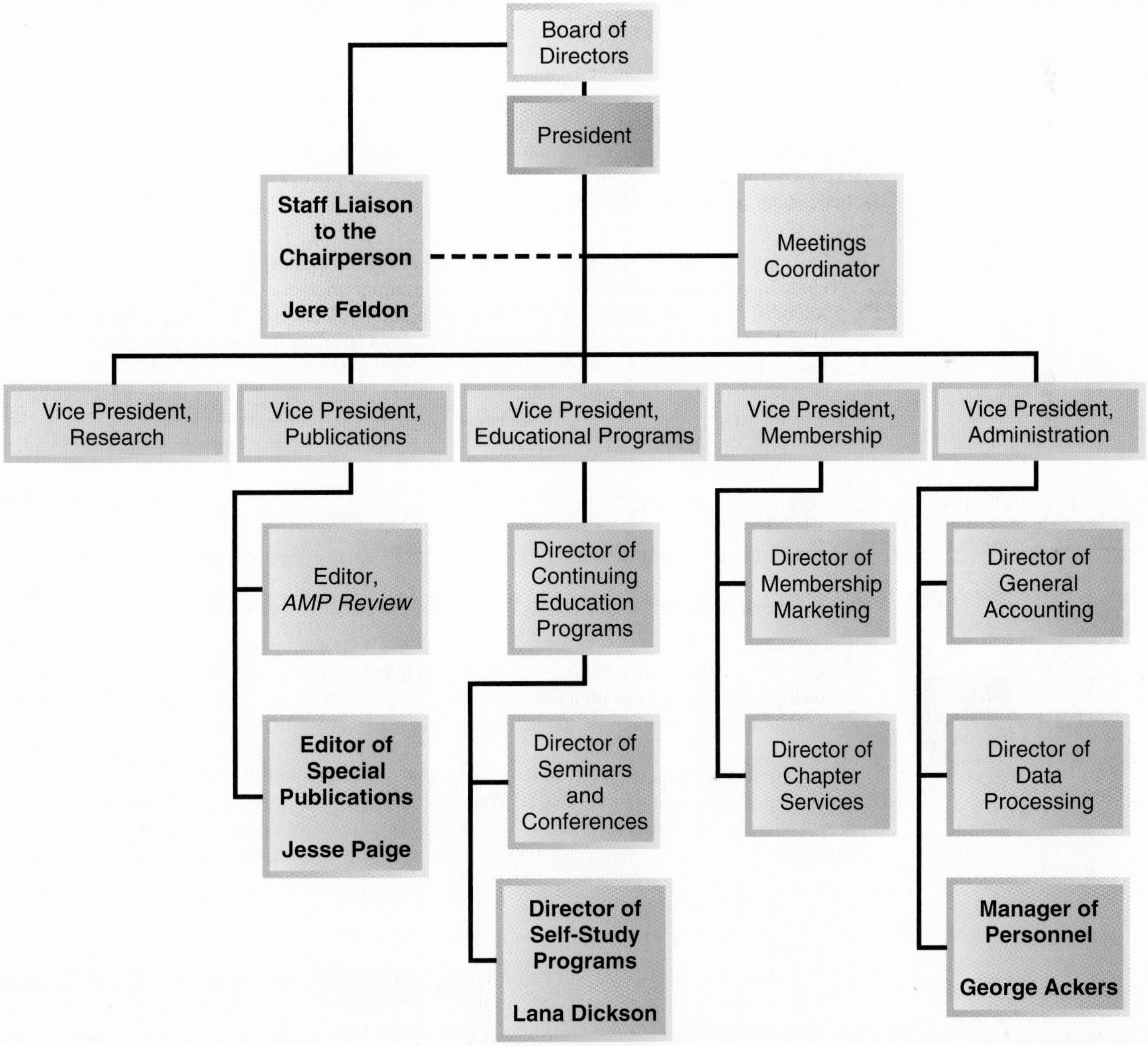

Four of the positions appearing in the organization chart are described below.

Jere Feldon, Staff Liaison to the Chairperson

Feldon is assigned to work with the chairperson of AMP by serving as an intermediary between the chairperson and the professional staff. All correspondence to the chairperson is funneled through Feldon. Feldon also works very closely with the president of AMP, especially on any matters that have to be brought to the attention of the chairperson and the board.

Lana Dickson, Director of Self-Study Programs

Dickson is responsible for developing and marketing the self-study programs offered by AMP. Self-study courses consist of cassette tapes and a workbook. Most of the courses are developed by outside contractors who work under her direction. Dickson relies on the director of membership marketing to assist her in marketing these courses.

Jesse Paige, Editor of Special Publications

Paige is primarily responsible for the publication and sale of any research monographs that are generated by the research department. In addition, he coordinates the publication of any special projects that may be prepared by any other AMP committees or departments. Paige also works with AMP's Publication Committee which sets policy on the types of publications that AMP should publish.

George Ackers, Manager of Personnel

Ackers works with all of the departments of AMP in hiring professional and clerical staff. The individual departments screen and interview prospective employees for professional positions, but Ackers is responsible for advertising open positions. Ackers plays a more active role in the hiring of clerical personnel by screening individuals before they are sent to the departments for interviews. In addition, Ackers coordinates the employee performance evaluation program and administers AMP's salary schedule and fringe benefit program.

Required:

1. Distinguish between line positions and staff positions in an organization by defining each. Include in your discussion the role, purpose, and importance of each.
2. Many times, conflicts will arise between line and staff managers in organizations. Discuss the characteristics of line and staff managers that may cause conflicts between the two.
3. For each of the four individuals identified by name in the text,
   a. Identify whether the individual's position is a line or staff position and explain why.
   b. Identify potential problems that could arise in each individual's position, either due to the type of position (i.e., line or staff) or to the location of the individual's position within the organization.

(CMA, adapted)

RESEARCH AND APPLICATION 1–9 [LO1, LO2, and LO4]

The questions in this exercise are based on one of the fastest growing food retailers in the United States—Whole Foods Market, Inc. To answer the questions, you will need to download Whole Foods Market's 2004 annual report at www.wholefoodsmarket.com/investor/annualreports.html and its 10-K/A for the fiscal year ended September 26, 2004 by going to www.sec.gov/edgar/searchedgar/companysearch.html. Input CIK code 865436 and hit enter. In the gray box on the right-hand side of your computer screen define the scope of your search by inputting 10-K and then pressing enter. Select the 10-K/A with a filing date of May 18, 2005. In addition, you'll need to download the company's mission statement (which it refers to as a Declaration of Interdependence) at www.wholefoodsmarket.com/company/declaration.html and its code of conduct and ethics at www.wholefoodsmarket.com/investor/codeofconduct.pdf. You do not need to print these documents to answer the questions.

Required:

1. What is Whole Foods Market's strategy for success in the marketplace? Does the company rely primarily on a customer intimacy, operational excellence, or product leadership customer value proposition? What evidence supports your conclusion?

2. What business risks does Whole Foods Market face that may threaten its ability to satisfy stockholder expectations? What are some examples of control activities that the company could use to reduce these risks? (Hint: Focus on pages 11–15 of the 10-K/A.)
3. Create an excerpt of an organization chart for Whole Foods Market. Do not try to create an organization chart for the entire company—it would be overwhelming! Pick a portion of the company and depict how the company organizes itself. (Hint: Study the 2004 Global All-Stars mentioned in the annual report and refer to page 16 of the 10-K/A.) Mention by name three employees that occupy line positions and three employees that occupy staff positions.
4. Compare and contrast Whole Foods Market's mission statement with the Johnson & Johnson Credo shown on page 24.
5. Compare and contrast Whole Foods Market's mission statement and its code of conduct and ethics.
6. Is Whole Foods Market's Annual Report and 10-K/A primarily a financial accounting document or a managerial accounting document? What evidence supports your conclusion? (Hint: Refer to Exhibit 1–2 in the text.)

Chapter

2

Cost Terms, Concepts, and Classifications

Learning Objectives

After studying Chapter 2, you should be able to:

LO1 Identify and give examples of each of the three basic manufacturing cost categories.

LO2 Distinguish between product costs and period costs and give examples of each.

LO3 Prepare an income statement including calculation of the cost of goods sold.

LO4 Prepare a schedule of cost of goods manufactured.

LO5 Understand the differences between variable costs and fixed costs.

LO6 Understand the differences between direct and indirect costs.

LO7 Define and give examples of cost classifications used in making decisions: differential costs, opportunity costs, and sunk costs.

LP 2

Costs Add Up

BUSINESS FOCUS

Understanding costs and how they behave is critical in business. Labor Ready is a company based in Tacoma, Washington, that fills temporary manual labor jobs throughout the United States, Canada, and the UK—issuing over 6 million paychecks each year to more than half a million laborers. For example, food vendors at the Seattle Mariners' Safeco Field hire Labor Ready workers to serve soft drinks and food at baseball games. Employers are charged about $11 per hour for this service. Since Labor Ready pays its workers only about $6.50 per hour and offers no fringe benefits and has no national competitors, this business would appear to be a gold mine generating about $4.50 per hour in profit. However, the company must maintain 687 hiring offices, each employing a permanent staff of four to five persons. Those costs, together with payroll taxes, workmen's compensation insurance, and other administrative costs, result in a margin of only about 5%, or a little over 50¢ per hour. ■

Source: Catie Golding, "Short-Term Work, Long-Term Profits," *Washington CEO*, January 2000, pp. 10–12.

As explained in Chapter 1, the work of management focuses on (1) planning, which includes setting objectives and outlining how to attain these objectives; and (2) control, which includes the steps taken to ensure that objectives are realized. To carry out these planning and control responsibilities, managers need *information* about the organization. This information often relates to the *costs* of the organization.

In managerial accounting, the term *cost* is used in many different ways. The reason is that there are many types of costs, and these costs are classified differently according to the immediate needs of management. For example, managers may want cost data to prepare external financial reports, to prepare planning budgets, or to make decisions. Each different use of cost data demands a different classification and definition of costs. For example, the preparation of external financial reports requires the use of historical cost data, whereas decision making may require predictions about future costs.

In this chapter, we discuss many of the possible uses of cost data and how costs are defined and classified for each use. Our first task is to explain how costs are classified for the purpose of preparing external financial reports—particularly in manufacturing companies. To set the stage for this discussion, we begin the chapter by defining some terms commonly used in manufacturing.

General Cost Classifications

All types of organizations incur costs—governmental, not-for-profit, manufacturing, retail, and service. Generally, the kinds of costs that are incurred and the way in which these costs are classified depend on the type of organization. For this reason, we will consider in our discussion the cost characteristics of a variety of organizations—manufacturing, merchandising, and service.

2–1

Our initial focus in this chapter is on manufacturing companies, since their basic activities include most of the activities found in other types of organizations. Manufacturing companies such as Texas Instruments, Ford, and DuPont are involved in acquiring raw materials, producing finished goods, marketing, distributing, billing, and almost every other business activity. Therefore, an understanding of costs in a manufacturing company can be very helpful in understanding costs in other types of organizations.

In this chapter, we introduce cost concepts that apply to diverse organizations including fast-food outlets such as Kentucky Fried Chicken, Pizza Hut, and Taco Bell; movie studios such as Disney, Paramount, and United Artists; consulting firms such as Accenture and McKinsey; and your local hospital. The exact terms used in these industries may not be the same as those used in manufacturing, but the same basic concepts apply. With some slight modifications, these basic concepts also apply to merchandising companies such as Wal-Mart, The Gap, 7-Eleven, Nordstrom, and Tower Records. With that in mind, let's begin our discussion of manufacturing costs.

Manufacturing Costs

Most manufacturing companies separate manufacturing costs into three broad categories: direct materials, direct labor, and manufacturing overhead. A discussion of each of these categories follows.

LEARNING OBJECTIVE 1
Identify and give examples of each of the three basic manufacturing cost categories.

Direct Materials The materials that go into the final product are called **raw materials.** This term is somewhat misleading, since it seems to imply unprocessed natural resources like wood pulp or iron ore. Actually, raw materials refer to any materials that are used in the final product; and the finished product of one company can become the raw materials of another company. For example, the plastics produced by Du Pont are a raw material used by Compaq Computer in its personal computers. One study of 37 manufacturing industries found that materials costs averaged about 55% of sales revenues.[1]

Raw materials may include both *direct* and *indirect materials*. **Direct materials** are those materials that become an integral part of the finished product and whose costs can be conveniently traced to the finished product. This would include, for example, the seats that Airbus purchases from subcontractors to install in its commercial aircraft and the tiny electric motor Panasonic uses in its DVD players.

Sometimes it isn't worth the effort to trace the costs of relatively insignificant materials to end products. Such minor items would include the solder used to make electrical connections in a Sony TV or the glue used to assemble an Ethan Allen chair. Materials such as solder and glue are called **indirect materials** and are included as part of manufacturing overhead, which is discussed later in this section.

Direct Labor **Direct labor** consists of labor costs that can be easily (i.e., physically and conveniently) traced to individual units of product. Direct labor is sometimes called *touch labor,* since direct labor workers typically touch the product while it is being made. Examples of direct labor include assembly-line workers at Toyota, carpenters at the home builder Kaufman and Broad, and electricians who install equipment on aircraft at Bombardier Learjet.

Labor costs that cannot be physically traced to the creation of products, or that can be traced only at great cost and inconvenience, are termed **indirect labor.** Just like indirect materials, indirect labor is treated as part of manufacturing overhead. Indirect labor includes the labor costs of janitors, supervisors, materials handlers, and night security guards. Although the efforts of these workers are essential to production, it would be either impractical or impossible to accurately trace their costs to specific units of product. Hence, such labor costs are treated as indirect labor.

IN BUSINESS

IS SENDING JOBS OVERSEAS ALWAYS A GOOD IDEA?

In recent years, many companies have sent jobs from high labor-cost countries such as the United States to lower labor-cost countries such as India and China. But is chasing labor cost savings always the right thing to do? In manufacturing, the answer is no. Typically, total direct labor costs are around 7% to 15% of cost of goods sold. Since direct labor is such a small part of overall costs, the labor savings realized by "offshoring" jobs can easily be overshadowed by a decline in supply chain efficiency that occurs simply because production facilities are located farther from the ultimate customers. The increase in inventory carrying costs and obsolescence costs coupled with slower response to customer orders, not to mention foreign currency exchange risks, can more than offset the benefits of employing geographically dispersed low-cost labor.

One manufacturer of casual wear in Los Angeles, California, understands the value of keeping jobs close to home in order to maintain a tightly knit supply chain. The company can fill orders for as many as 160,000 units in 24 hours. In fact, the company carries less than 30 days' inventory and is considering fabricating clothing only after orders are received from customers rather than attempting to forecast what items will sell and making them in advance. How would they do this? The company's entire supply chain—including weaving, dyeing, and sewing—is located in downtown Los Angeles, eliminating shipping delays.

Source: Robert Sternfels and Ronald Ritter, "When Offshoring Doesn't Make Sense," *The Wall Street Journal*, October 19, 2004, p. B8.

[1] Germain Boer and Debra Jeter, "What's New About Modern Manufacturing? Empirical Evidence on Manufacturing Cost Changes," *Journal of Management Accounting Research* 5, pp. 61–83.

Major shifts have taken place and continue to take place in the structure of labor costs in some industries. Sophisticated automated equipment, run and maintained by skilled indirect workers, is increasingly replacing direct labor. Indeed, direct labor averages only about 10% of sales revenues in manufacturing. In some companies, direct labor has become such a minor element of cost that it has disappeared altogether as a separate cost category. Nevertheless, the vast majority of manufacturing and service companies throughout the world continue to recognize direct labor as a separate cost category.

Manufacturing Overhead **Manufacturing overhead,** the third element of manufacturing cost, includes all costs of manufacturing except direct materials and direct labor. Manufacturing overhead includes items such as indirect materials; indirect labor; maintenance and repairs on production equipment; and heat and light, property taxes, depreciation, and insurance on manufacturing facilities. A company also incurs costs for heat and light, property taxes, insurance, depreciation, and so forth, associated with its selling and administrative functions, but these costs are not included as part of manufacturing overhead. Only those costs associated with *operating the factory* are included in manufacturing overhead. Across large numbers of manufacturing companies, manufacturing overhead averages about 16% of sales revenues.[2]

Various names are used for manufacturing overhead, such as *indirect manufacturing cost, factory overhead,* and *factory burden.* All of these terms are synonyms for *manufacturing overhead.*

Nonmanufacturing Costs

Nonmanufacturing costs are often divided into two categories: (1) *selling costs* and (2) *administrative costs.* **Selling costs** include all costs that are incurred to secure customer orders and get the finished product to the customer. These costs are sometimes called *order-getting* and *order-filling* costs. Examples of selling costs include advertising, shipping, sales travel, sales commissions, sales salaries, and costs of finished goods warehouses.

Administrative costs include all executive, organizational, and clerical costs associated with the *general management* of an organization rather than with manufacturing or selling. Examples of administrative costs include executive compensation, general accounting, secretarial, public relations, and similar costs involved in the overall, general administration of the organization *as a whole.*

Nonmanufacturing costs are also often called selling, general, and administrative (SG&A) costs.

Product Costs versus Period Costs

LEARNING OBJECTIVE 2
Distinguish between product costs and period costs and give examples of each.

In addition to classifying costs as manufacturing or nonmanufacturing costs, there are other ways to look at costs. For instance, they can also be classified as either *product costs* or *period costs.* To understand the difference between product costs and period costs, we must first discuss the matching principle from financial accounting.

Generally, costs are recognized as expenses on the income statement in the period that benefits from the cost. For example, if a company pays for liability insurance in advance for

[2] J. Miller, A. DeMeyer, and J. Nakane, *Benchmarking Global Manufacturing* (Homewood, IL: Richard D. Irwin), Chapter 2. The Boer and Jeter article cited on the previous page contains a similar finding concerning the magnitude of manufacturing overhead.

two years, the entire amount is not considered an expense of the year in which the payment is made. Instead, one-half of the cost would be recognized as an expense each year. The reason is that both years—not just the first year—benefit from the insurance payment. The unexpensed portion of the insurance payment is carried on the balance sheet as an asset called prepaid insurance.

The *matching principle* is based on the *accrual* concept that *costs incurred to generate a particular revenue should be recognized as expenses in the same period that the revenue is recognized.* This means that if a cost is incurred to acquire or make something that will eventually be sold, then the cost should be recognized as an expense only when the sale takes place—that is, when the benefit occurs. Such costs are called *product costs.*

Product Costs

For financial accounting purposes, **product costs** include all costs involved in acquiring or making a product. In the case of manufactured goods, these costs consist of direct materials, direct labor, and manufacturing overhead. Product costs "attach" to units of product as the goods are purchased or manufactured, and they remain attached as the goods go into inventory awaiting sale. Product costs are initially assigned to an inventory account on the balance sheet. When the goods are sold, the costs are released from inventory as expenses (typically called cost of goods sold) and matched against sales revenue. Since product costs are initially assigned to inventories, they are also known as **inventoriable costs.**

We want to emphasize that product costs are not necessarily treated as expenses in the period in which they are incurred. Rather, as explained above, they are treated as expenses in the period in which the related products *are sold.* This means that a product cost such as direct materials or direct labor might be incurred during one period but not recorded as an expense until a following period when the completed product is sold.

Period Costs

Period costs are all the costs that are not product costs. For example, sales commissions and the rental costs of administrative offices are period costs. Period costs are not included as part of the cost of either purchased or manufactured goods; instead, period costs are expensed on the income statement in the period in which they are incurred using the usual rules of accrual accounting. Keep in mind that the period in which a cost is incurred is not necessarily the period in which cash changes hands. For example, as discussed earlier, the costs of liability insurance are spread across the periods that benefit from the insurance—regardless of the period in which the insurance premium is paid.

As suggested above, *all selling and administrative expenses are considered to be period costs.* Advertising, executive salaries, sales commissions, public relations, and other nonmanufacturing costs discussed earlier are all examples of period costs. They will appear on the income statement as expenses in the period in which they are incurred.

Prime Cost and Conversion Cost

Two more cost categories are often used in discussions of manufacturing costs—*prime cost* and *conversion cost*. These terms are quite easy to define. **Prime cost** is the sum of direct materials cost and direct labor cost. **Conversion cost** is the sum of direct labor cost and manufacturing overhead cost. The term *conversion cost* is used to describe direct labor and manufacturing overhead because these costs are incurred to convert materials into the finished product.

Exhibit 2–1 (page 44) contains a summary of the cost terms that we have introduced so far.

IN BUSINESS

DISSECTING THE VALUE CHAIN

United Colors of Benetton, an Italian apparel company headquartered in Ponzano, is unusual in that it is involved in all activities in the "value chain" from clothing design through manufacturing, distribution, and ultimate sale to customers in Benetton retail outlets. Most companies are involved in only one or two of these activities. Looking at this company allows us to see how costs are distributed across the entire value chain. A recent income statement from the company contained the following data:

	Millions of Euros	Percent of Revenues
Revenue	1,686	100.0%
Cost of sales	929	55.1
Selling and administrative expenses:		
Payroll and related cost	125	7.4
Distribution and transport	30	1.8
Sales commissions	74	4.4
Advertising and promotion	54	3.2
Depreciation and amortization	78	4.6
Other expenses	179	10.6
Total selling and administrative expenses	540	32.0%

Even though this company spends large sums on advertising and runs its own shops, the cost of sales is still quite high in relation to the revenue—55.1% of revenue. And despite the company's lavish advertising campaigns, advertising and promotion costs amounted to only 3.2% of revenue. (Note: One U.S. dollar was worth about 0.7331 euros at the time of this financial report.)

IN BUSINESS

PRODUCT COSTS AND PERIOD COSTS: A LOOK ACROSS INDUSTRIES

Cost of goods sold and selling and administrative expenses expressed as a percentage of sales differ across companies and industries. For example, the data below summarize the median cost of goods sold as a percentage of sales and the median selling and administrative expense as a percentage of sales for eight different industries. Why do you think the percentages in each column differ so dramatically?

Industry	Cost of Goods Sold ÷ Sales	Selling and Administrative Expense ÷ Sales
Aerospace and Defense	79%	9%
Beverages	52%	34%
Computer Software and Services	34%	38%
Electrical Equipment and Components	64%	21%
Healthcare Services	82%	6%
Oil and Gas	90%	3%
Pharmaceuticals	31%	41%
Restaurants	78%	8%

Source: Lori Calabro, "Controlling the Flow," CFO, February 2005, p. 46–50.

EXHIBIT 2–1
Summary of Cost Terms

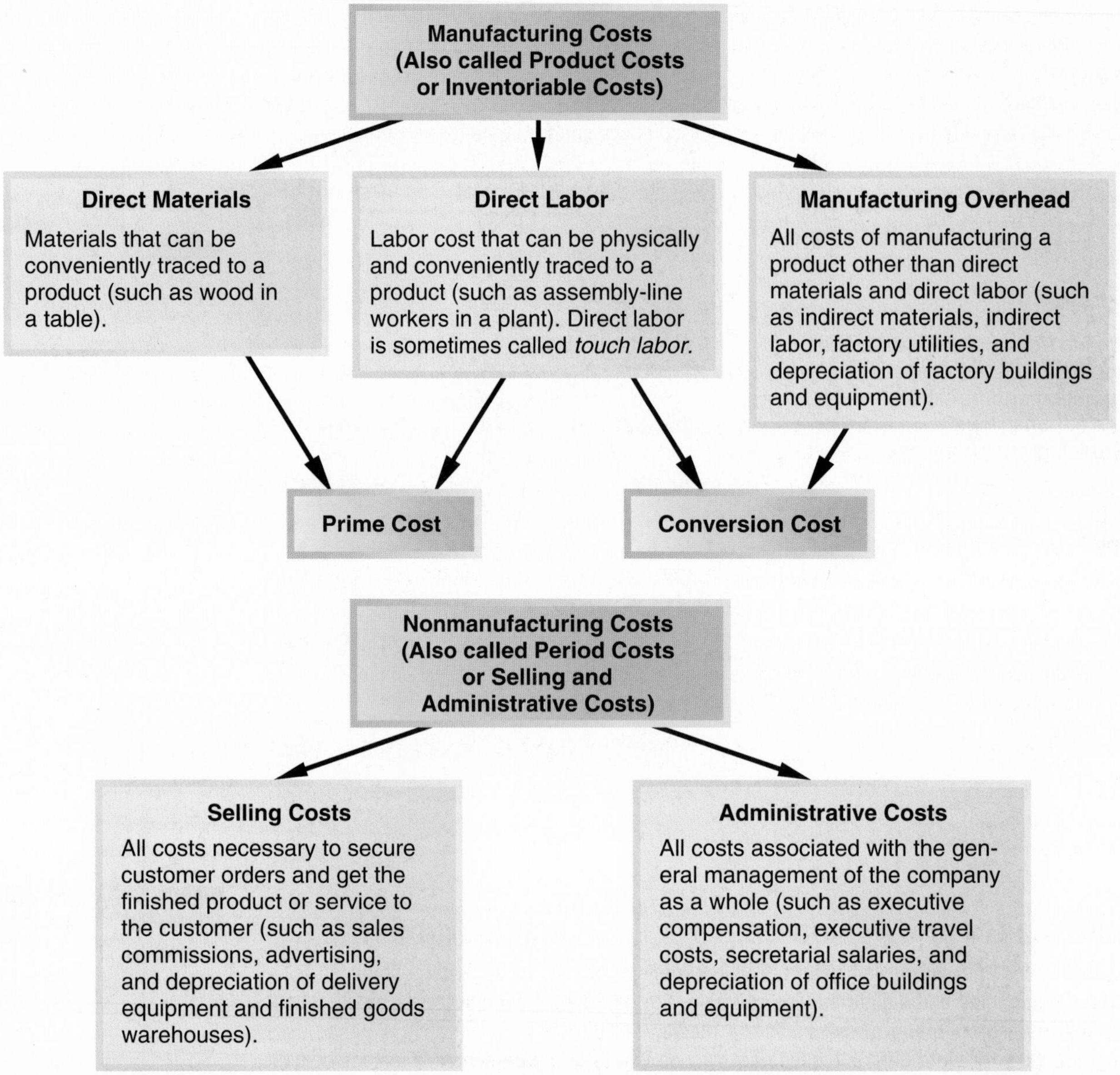

Manufacturing Costs (Also called Product Costs or Inventoriable Costs)

Direct Materials
Materials that can be conveniently traced to a product (such as wood in a table).

Direct Labor
Labor cost that can be physically and conveniently traced to a product (such as assembly-line workers in a plant). Direct labor is sometimes called *touch labor.*

Manufacturing Overhead
All costs of manufacturing a product other than direct materials and direct labor (such as indirect materials, indirect labor, factory utilities, and depreciation of factory buildings and equipment).

Prime Cost (Direct Materials + Direct Labor)

Conversion Cost (Direct Labor + Manufacturing Overhead)

Nonmanufacturing Costs (Also called Period Costs or Selling and Administrative Costs)

Selling Costs
All costs necessary to secure customer orders and get the finished product or service to the customer (such as sales commissions, advertising, and depreciation of delivery equipment and finished goods warehouses).

Administrative Costs
All costs associated with the general management of the company as a whole (such as executive compensation, executive travel costs, secretarial salaries, and depreciation of office buildings and equipment).

IN BUSINESS

BLOATED SELLING AND ADMINISTRATIVE EXPENSES

Selling and administrative expenses tend to creep up during economic booms—creating problems when the economy falls into recession. Ron Nicol, a partner at the Boston Consulting Group, found that selling and administrative expenses at America's 1,000 largest companies grew at an average rate of 1.7% per year between 1985 and 1996 and then exploded to an average of 10% growth per year between 1997 and 2000. If companies had maintained their historical balance between sales revenues on the one hand and selling and administrative expenses on the other hand, Nicol calculates that selling and administrative expenses would have been about $500 million lower in the year 2000 for the average company on his list.

Source: Jon E. Hilsenrath, "The Outlook: Corporate Dieting Is Far from Over," *The Wall Street Journal,* July 9, 2001, p. A1.

Cost Classifications on Financial Statements

In this section of the chapter, we compare the cost classifications used on the financial statements of manufacturing and merchandising companies. The financial statements prepared by a *manufacturing* company are more complex than the statements prepared by a merchandising company because a manufacturing company must produce its goods as well as market them. The production process involves many costs that do not exist in a merchandising company, and these costs must be properly accounted for on the manufacturing company's financial statements. We begin by explaining how these costs are shown on the balance sheet followed by the income statement.

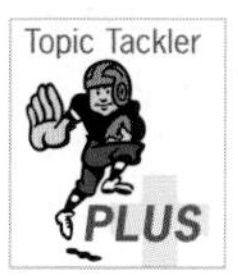

2–2

The Balance Sheet

The balance sheet, or statement of financial position, of a manufacturing company is similar to that of a merchandising company. However, their inventory accounts differ. A merchandising company has only one class of inventory—goods purchased from suppliers for resale to customers. In contrast, manufacturing companies have three classes of inventories—*raw materials, work in process*, and *finished goods*. **Raw materials** are the materials that are used to make a product. **Work in process** consists of units of product that are only partially complete and will require further work before they are ready for sale to a customer. **Finished goods** consist of completed units of product that have not yet been sold to customers. Ordinarily, the sum total of these three categories of inventories is the only amount shown on the balance sheet in external reports. However, the footnotes to the financial statements often provide more detail.

We will use two companies—Graham Manufacturing and Reston Bookstore—to illustrate the concepts discussed in this section. Graham Manufacturing is located in Portsmouth, New Hampshire, and makes precision brass fittings for yachts. Reston Bookstore is a small bookstore in Reston, Virginia, specializing in books about the Civil War.

The footnotes to Graham Manufacturing's Annual Report reveal the following information concerning its inventories:

Graham Manufacturing Corporation
Inventory Accounts

	Beginning Balance	Ending Balance
Raw materials	$ 60,000	$ 50,000
Work in process	90,000	60,000
Finished goods	125,000	175,000
Total inventory accounts	$275,000	$285,000

Graham Manufacturing's raw materials inventory consists largely of brass rods and brass blocks. The work in process inventory consists of partially completed brass fittings. The finished goods inventory consists of brass fittings that are ready to be sold to customers.

In contrast, the inventory account at Reston Bookstore consists entirely of the costs of books the company has purchased from publishers for resale to the public. In merchandising companies like Reston, these inventories may be called *merchandise inventory*. The beginning and ending balances in this account appear as follows:

Reston Bookstore
Inventory Account

	Beginning Balance	Ending Balance
Merchandise Inventory	$100,000	$150,000

LEARNING OBJECTIVE 3
Prepare an income statement including calculation of the cost of goods sold.

The Income Statement

Exhibit 2–2 compares the income statements of Reston Bookstore and Graham Manufacturing. For purposes of illustration, these statements contain more detail about cost of goods sold than you will generally find in published financial statements.

At first glance, the income statements of merchandising and manufacturing companies like Reston Bookstore and Graham Manufacturing are very similar. The only apparent difference is in the labels of some of the entries in the computation of the cost of goods sold. In the exhibit, the computation of cost of goods sold relies on the following basic equation for inventory accounts:

Basic Equation for Inventory Accounts

$$\text{Beginning balance} + \text{Additions to inventory} = \text{Ending balance} + \text{Withdrawals from inventory}$$

The logic underlying this equation, which applies to any inventory account, is illustrated in Exhibit 2–3. The beginning inventory consists of any units that are in the inventory at the beginning of the period. Additions are made to the inventory during the period. The sum of the beginning balance and the additions to the account is the total amount of inventory available. During the period, withdrawals are made from inventory. The ending balance is whatever is left at the end of the period after the withdrawals.

EXHIBIT 2–2
Comparative Income Statements: Merchandising and Manufacturing Companies

The cost of merchandise inventory purchased from outside suppliers during the period. →

Merchandising Company Reston Bookstore		
Sales		$1,000,000
Cost of goods sold:		
Beginning merchandise inventory	$100,000	
Add: Purchases	650,000	
Goods available for sale	750,000	
Deduct: Ending merchandise inventory	150,000	600,000
Gross margin		400,000
Selling and administrative expenses:		
Selling expense	100,000	
Administrative expense	200,000	300,000
Net operating income		$ 100,000

The manufacturing costs associated with the goods that were finished during the period. (See Exhibit 2–4 for details.) →

Manufacturing Company Graham Manufacturing		
Sales		$1,500,000
Costs of goods sold:		
Beginning finished goods inventory	$125,000	
Add: Cost of goods manufactured	850,000	
Goods available for sale	975,000	
Deduct: Ending finished goods inventory	175,000	800,000
Gross margin		700,000
Selling and administrative expenses:		
Selling expense	250,000	
Administrative expense	300,000	550,000
Net operating income		$ 150,000

EXHIBIT 2–3
Inventory Flows

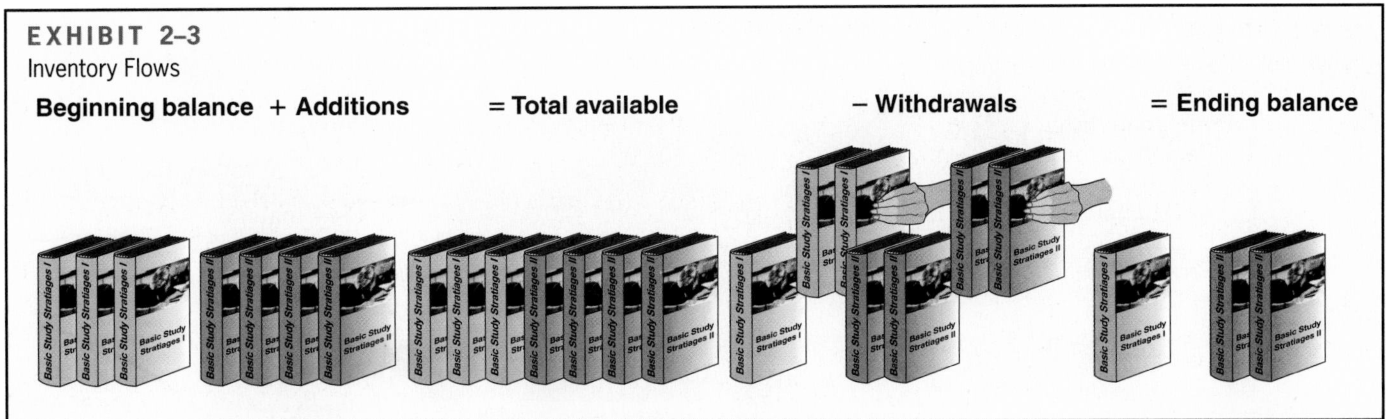

These concepts are used to determine the cost of goods sold for a merchandising company like Reston Bookstore as follows:

Cost of Goods Sold in a Merchandising Company

$$\text{Beginning merchandise inventory} + \text{Purchases} = \text{Ending merchandise inventory} + \text{Cost of goods sold}$$

or

$$\text{Cost of goods sold} = \text{Beginning merchandise inventory} + \text{Purchases} - \text{Ending merchandise inventory}$$

To determine the cost of goods sold in a merchandising company, we only need to know the beginning and ending balances in the Merchandise Inventory account and the purchases. Total purchases can be easily determined in a merchandising company by simply adding together all purchases from suppliers.

The cost of goods sold for a manufacturing company like Graham Manufacturing is determined as follows:

Cost of Goods Sold in a Manufacturing Company

$$\text{Beginning finished goods inventory} + \text{Cost of goods manufactured} = \text{Ending finished goods inventory} + \text{Cost of goods sold}$$

or

$$\text{Cost of goods sold} = \text{Beginning finished goods inventory} + \text{Cost of goods manufactured} - \text{Ending finished goods inventory}$$

To determine the cost of goods sold in a manufacturing company, we need to know the *cost of goods manufactured* and the beginning and ending balances in the Finished Goods inventory account. The **cost of goods manufactured** consists of the manufacturing costs associated with goods that were *finished* during the period. The cost of goods manufactured for Graham Manufacturing is derived in the *schedule of cost of goods manufactured* shown in Exhibit 2–4 (page 48).

Schedule of Cost of Goods Manufactured

LEARNING OBJECTIVE 4
Prepare a schedule of cost of goods manufactured.

At first glance, the **schedule of cost of goods manufactured** in Exhibit 2–4 appears complex and perhaps even intimidating. However, it is all quite logical. The schedule of cost of goods manufactured contains the three elements of product costs that we discussed earlier—direct materials, direct labor, and manufacturing overhead.

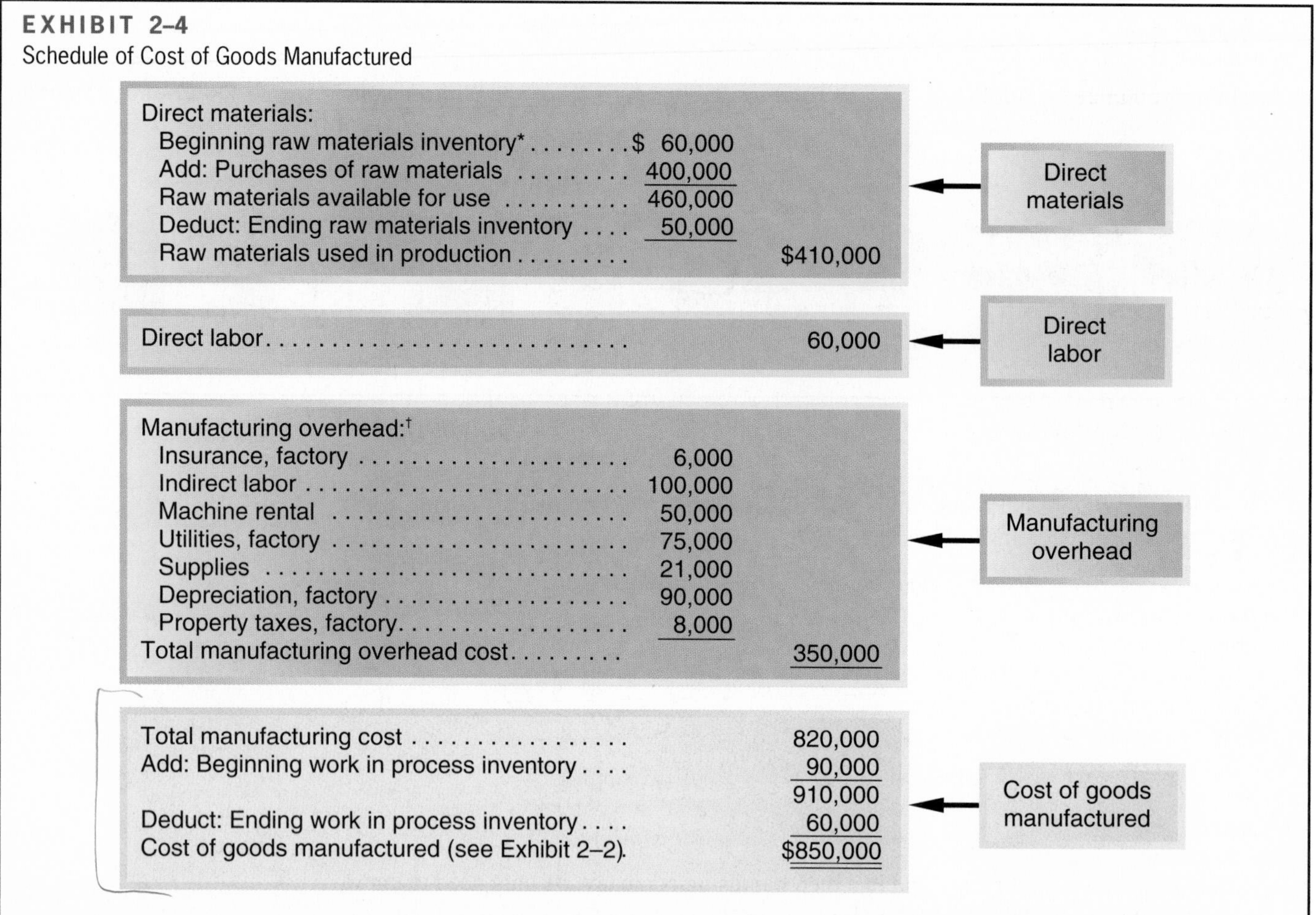

EXHIBIT 2–4
Schedule of Cost of Goods Manufactured

Direct materials:		
Beginning raw materials inventory*	$ 60,000	
Add: Purchases of raw materials	400,000	
Raw materials available for use	460,000	
Deduct: Ending raw materials inventory	50,000	
Raw materials used in production		$410,000
Direct labor		60,000
Manufacturing overhead:†		
Insurance, factory	6,000	
Indirect labor	100,000	
Machine rental	50,000	
Utilities, factory	75,000	
Supplies	21,000	
Depreciation, factory	90,000	
Property taxes, factory	8,000	
Total manufacturing overhead cost		350,000
Total manufacturing cost		820,000
Add: Beginning work in process inventory		90,000
		910,000
Deduct: Ending work in process inventory		60,000
Cost of goods manufactured (see Exhibit 2–2)		$850,000

*We assume in this example that the Raw Materials inventory account contains only direct materials and that indirect materials are carried in a separate Supplies account. Using a Supplies account for indirect materials is a common practice. In Chapter 3, we discuss the procedure to be followed if *both* direct and indirect materials are carried in a single account.

†In Chapter 3 we will see that the manufacturing overhead section of the Schedule of Cost of Goods Manufactured can be considerably simplified by using a *predetermined manufacturing overhead rate.*

The direct materials cost of $410,000 is not the cost of raw materials purchased during the period—it is the cost of raw materials *used* during the period. The purchases of raw materials are added to the beginning balance to determine the cost of the materials available for use. The ending raw materials inventory is deducted from this amount to arrive at the cost of raw materials used in production. The sum of the three manufacturing cost elements—materials, direct labor, and manufacturing overhead—is the total manufacturing cost of $820,000. However, you'll notice that this is *not* the same thing as the cost of goods manufactured for the period of $850,000. The subtle distinction between the total manufacturing cost and the cost of goods manufactured is very easy to miss. Some of the materials, direct labor, and manufacturing overhead costs incurred during the period relate to goods that are not yet completed. As stated above, the cost of goods manufactured consists of the manufacturing costs associated with the goods that were finished during the period. Consequently, adjustments need to be made to the total manufacturing cost of the period for the partially completed goods that were in process at the beginning and at the end of the period. The costs that relate to goods that are not yet completed are shown in the work in process inventory figures at the bottom of the schedule. Note that the beginning work in process inventory must be added to the manufacturing costs of the period, and the ending work in process inventory must be deducted, to arrive at the cost of goods manufactured. Since the Work in Process account declined by $30,000 during the year ($90,000 − $60,000), this explains the $30,000 difference between the total manufacturing cost and the cost of goods manufactured.

Product Cost Flows

Earlier in the chapter, we defined product costs as costs incurred to either purchase or manufacture goods. For manufactured goods, these costs consist of direct materials, direct labor, and manufacturing overhead. It will be helpful at this point to look briefly at the flow of costs in a manufacturing company. This will help us understand how product costs move through the various accounts and how they affect the balance sheet and the income statement.

Exhibit 2–5 illustrates the flow of costs in a manufacturing company. Raw materials purchases are recorded in the Raw Materials inventory account. When raw materials are used in production, their costs are transferred to the Work in Process inventory account as direct materials. Notice that direct labor cost and manufacturing overhead cost are added directly to Work in Process. Work in Process can be viewed most simply as products on an assembly line. The direct materials, direct labor, and manufacturing overhead costs added to Work in Process in Exhibit 2–5 are the costs needed to complete these products as they move along this assembly line.

Notice from the exhibit that as goods are completed, their costs are transferred from Work in Process to Finished Goods. Here the goods await sale to customers. As goods are sold, their costs are transferred from Finished Goods to Cost of Goods Sold. At this point the various costs required to make the product are finally recorded as an expense. Until that point, these costs are in inventory accounts on the balance sheet.

EXHIBIT 2–5
Cost Flows and Classifications in a Manufacturing Company

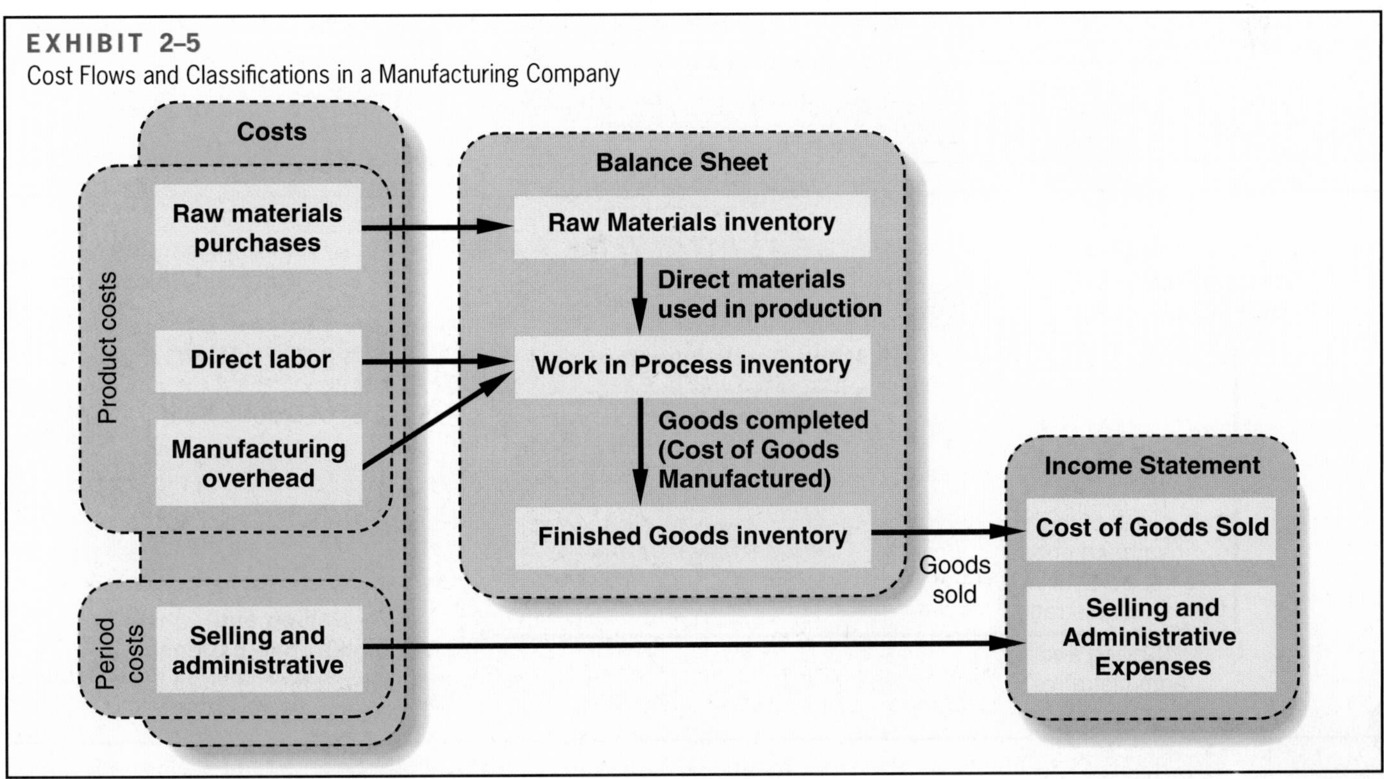

Inventoriable Costs

As stated earlier, product costs are often called inventoriable costs. The reason is that these costs go directly into inventory accounts as they are incurred (first into Work in Process and then into Finished Goods), rather than going into expense accounts. Thus, they are termed *inventoriable costs. This is a key concept because such costs can end up on the balance sheet as assets if goods are only partially completed or are unsold at the end of a period.* To illustrate this point, refer again to Exhibit 2–5. At the end of the period, the materials, labor, and overhead costs that are associated with the units in the Work in Process and Finished Goods inventory accounts will appear on the balance sheet as assets. As explained earlier, these costs will not become expenses until the goods are completed and sold.

Selling and administrative expenses are not involved in making a product. For this reason, they are not treated as product costs but rather as period costs that are expensed as they are incurred, as shown in Exhibit 2–5.

An Example of Cost Flows

To provide an example of cost flows in a manufacturing company, assume that a company's annual insurance cost is $2,000. Three-fourths of this amount ($1,500) applies to factory operations, and one-fourth ($500) applies to selling and administrative activities. Therefore, $1,500 of the $2,000 insurance cost would be a product (inventoriable) cost and would be added to the cost of the goods produced during the year. This concept is illustrated in Exhibit 2–6, where $1,500 of insurance cost is added to Work in Process.

EXHIBIT 2–6
An Example of Cost Flows in a Manufacturing Company

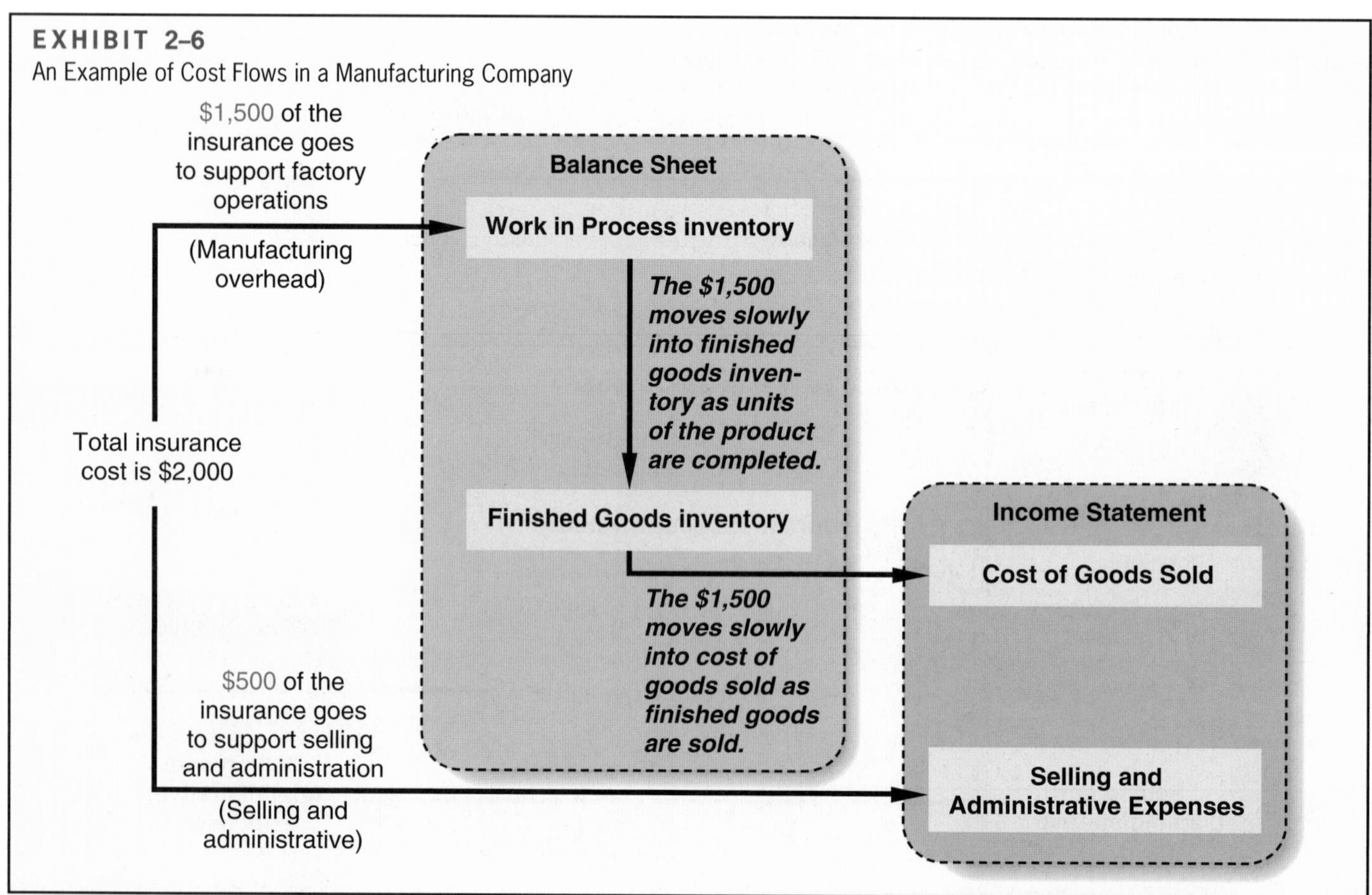

EXHIBIT 2–7
Summary of Cost Classifications

Purpose of Cost Classification	Cost Classifications

Preparing external financial statements	• Product costs (inventoriable)
	  • Direct materials
	  • Direct labor
	  • Manufacturing overhead
	• Period costs (expensed)
	  • Nonmanufacturing costs
	    • Selling costs
	    • Administrative costs

Predicting cost behavior in response to changes in activity	• Variable cost (proportional to activity) • Fixed cost (constant in total)
Assigning costs to cost objects such as departments or products	• Direct cost (can be easily traced) • Indirect cost (cannot be easily traced)
Making decisions	• Differential cost (differs between alternatives) • Sunk cost (past cost not affected by a decision) • Opportunity cost (forgone benefit)

As shown in the exhibit, this portion of the year's insurance cost will not become an expense until the goods that are produced during the year are sold—which may not happen until the following year or even later. Until the goods are sold, the $1,500 will be part of inventories—either Work in Process or Finished Goods—along with the other costs of producing the goods.

By contrast, the $500 of insurance cost that applies to the company's selling and administrative activities will be expensed immediately.

Thus far, we have been mainly concerned with classifications of manufacturing costs for the purpose of determining inventory valuations on the balance sheet and cost of goods sold on the income statement in external financial reports. However, costs are used for many other purposes, and each purpose requires a different classification of costs. We will consider several different purposes for cost classifications in the remaining sections of this chapter. These purposes and the corresponding cost classifications are summarized in Exhibit 2–7. To help keep the big picture in mind, we suggest that you refer back to this exhibit frequently as you progress through the rest of this chapter.

Cost Classifications for Predicting Cost Behavior

LEARNING OBJECTIVE 5
Understand the differences between variable costs and fixed costs.

Video 2–1

Quite frequently, it is necessary to predict how a certain cost will behave in response to a change in activity. For example, a manager at Qwest may want to estimate the impact a 5% increase in long-distance calls would have on the company's total electric bill. **Cost behavior** refers to how a cost reacts to changes in the level of activity. As the activity level rises and falls, a particular cost may rise and fall as well—or it may remain constant. For planning purposes, a manager must be able to anticipate which of these will happen; and if a cost can be expected to change, the manager must be able to estimate how much it will change. To help make such distinctions, costs are often categorized as variable or fixed.

Variable Cost

A **variable cost** is a cost that varies, in total, in direct proportion to changes in the level of activity. The activity can be expressed in many ways, such as units produced, units sold, miles driven, beds occupied, lines of print, hours worked, and so forth. A good example of a variable cost is direct materials. The cost of direct materials used during a period will vary, in total, in direct proportion to the number of units that are produced. To illustrate this idea, consider the Saturn Division of GM. Each auto requires one battery. As the output of autos increases and decreases, the number of batteries used will increase and decrease proportionately. If auto production goes up 10%, then the number of batteries used will also go up 10%. The concept of a variable cost is shown graphically in Exhibit 2–8.

The graph on the left-hand side of Exhibit 2–8 illustrates that the *total* variable cost rises and falls as the activity level rises and falls. This idea is presented below, assuming that a Saturn's battery costs $24:

Number of Autos Produced	Cost per Battery	Total Variable Cost—Batteries
1	$24	$24
500	$24	$12,000
1,000	$24	$24,000

While total variable costs change as the activity level changes, it is important to note that a variable cost is constant if expressed on a *per unit* basis. For example, the per unit cost of batteries remains constant at $24 even though the total cost of the batteries increases and decreases with activity.

There are many examples of costs that are variable with respect to the products and services provided by a company. In a manufacturing company, variable costs include items such as direct materials, shipping costs, and sales commissions and some elements of manufacturing overhead such as lubricants. We will also usually assume that direct labor is a variable cost, although direct labor may act more like a fixed cost in some situations as we shall see in a later chapter. In a merchandising company, the variable costs of carrying and selling products include items such as cost of goods sold,

EXHIBIT 2–8
Variable and Fixed Cost Behavior

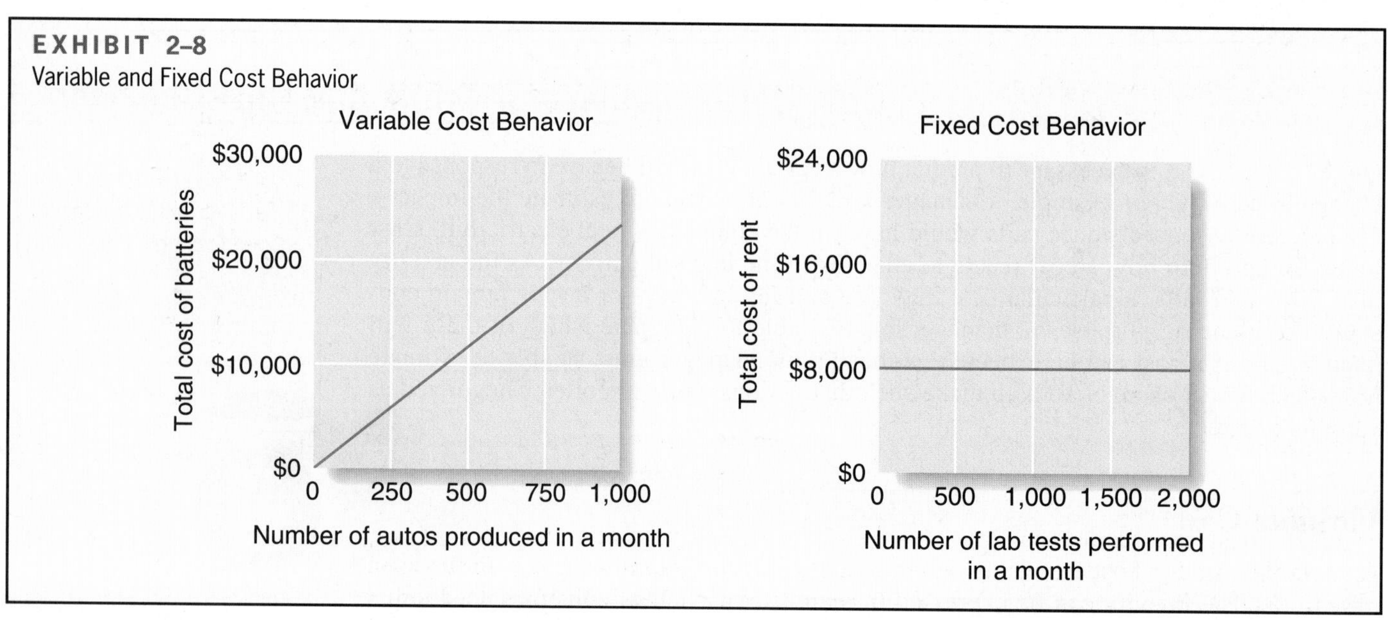

sales commissions, and billing costs. In a hospital, the variable costs of providing health care services to patients would include the costs of the supplies, drugs, meals, and perhaps nursing services.

When we say that a cost is variable, we ordinarily mean that it is variable with respect to the amount of goods or services the organization produces. However, costs can be variable with respect to other things. For example, the wages paid to employees at a Blockbuster Video outlet will depend on the number of hours the store is open and not strictly on the number of videos rented. In this case, we would say that wage costs are variable with respect to the hours of operation. Nevertheless, when we say that a cost is variable, we ordinarily mean it is variable with respect to the amount of goods and services produced. This could be how many Jeep Cherokees are produced, how many videos are rented, how many patients are treated, and so on.

IN BUSINESS

BROWN IS THINKING GREEN

United Parcel Service (UPS) truck drivers travel more than 1.3 billion miles annually to deliver more than 4.5 billion packages. Therefore, it should come as no surprise that fuel is a huge variable cost for the company. Even if UPS can shave just a penny of cost from each mile driven, the savings can be enormous. This explains why UPS is so excited about swapping its old diesel powered trucks for diesel-electric hybrid vehicles, which have the potential to cut fuel costs by 50%. Beyond the savings for UPS, the environment would also benefit from the switch since hybrid vehicles cut emissions by 90%. As UPS television commercials ask, "What can Brown do for you?" Thanks to diesel-electric technology, the answer is that Brown can help make the air you breathe a little bit cleaner.

Source: Charles Haddad and Christine Tierney, "FedEx and Brown Are Going Green," *BusinessWeek*, August 4, 2003, pp. 60–62.

Fixed Cost

A **fixed cost** is a cost that remains constant, in total, regardless of changes in the level of activity. Unlike variable costs, fixed costs are not affected by changes in activity. Consequently, as the activity level rises and falls, total fixed costs remain constant unless influenced by some outside force, such as a price change. Rent is a good example of a fixed cost. Suppose the Mayo Clinic rents a machine for $8,000 per month that tests blood samples for the presence of leukemia cells. The $8,000 monthly rental cost will be incurred regardless of the number of tests that may be performed during the month. The concept of a fixed cost is shown graphically on the right-hand side of Exhibit 2–8.

Very few costs are completely fixed. Most will change if activity changes enough. For example, suppose that the capacity of the leukemia diagnostic machine at the Mayo Clinic is 2,000 tests per month. If the clinic wishes to perform more than 2,000 tests in a month, it would be necessary to rent an additional machine, which would cause a jump in the fixed costs. When we say a cost is fixed, we mean it is fixed within some *relevant range*. The **relevant range** is the range of activity within which the assumptions about variable and fixed costs are valid. For example, the assumption that the rent for diagnostic machines is $8,000 per month is valid within the relevant range of 0 to 2,000 tests per month.

Fixed costs can create confusion if they are expressed on a per unit basis. This is because the average fixed cost per unit increases and decreases *inversely* with changes in activity. In the Mayo Clinic, for example, the average cost per test will fall as the number

IN BUSINESS

FOOD COSTS AT A LUXURY HOTEL

The Sporthotel Theresa (http://www.theresa.at/), owned and operated by the Egger family, is a four star hotel located in Zell im Zillertal, Austria. The hotel features access to hiking, skiing, biking, and other activities in the Ziller alps as well as its own fitness facility and spa.

Three full meals a day are included in the hotel room charge. Breakfast and lunch are served buffet-style while dinner is a more formal affair with as many as six courses. A sample dinner menu appears below:

Tyrolean cottage cheese with homemade bread
***
Salad bar
***
Broccoli-terrine with saddle of venison and smoked goose-breast
Or
Chicken-liver parfait with gorgonzola-cheese ravioli and port-wine sauce
***
Clear vegetable soup with fine vegetable strips
Or
Whey-yoghurt juice
***
Roulade of pork with zucchini, ham and cheese on pesto ribbon noodles and saffron sauce
Or
Roasted filet of Irish salmon and prawn with spring vegetables and sesame mash
Or
Fresh white asparagus with scrambled egg, fresh herbs, and parmesan
Or
Steak of Tyrolean organic beef
***
Strawberry terrine with homemade chocolate ice cream
Or
Iced Viennese coffee

The chef, Stefan Egger, believes that food costs are roughly proportional to the number of guests staying at the hotel; that is, they are a variable cost. He must order food from suppliers two or three days in advance, but he adjusts his purchases to the number of guests who are currently staying at the hotel and their consumption patterns. In addition, guests make their selections from the dinner menu early in the day, which helps Stefan plan which foodstuffs will be required for dinner. Consequently, he is able to prepare just enough food so that all guests are satisfied and yet waste is held to a minimum.

Source: Conversation with Stefan Egger, chef at the Sporthotel Theresa.

of tests performed increases because the $8,000 rental cost will be spread over more tests. Conversely, as the number of tests performed in the clinic declines, the average cost per test will rise as the $8,000 rental cost is spread over fewer tests. This concept is illustrated in the table below:

Monthly Rental Cost	Number of Tests Performed	Average Cost per Test
$8,000	10	$800
$8,000	500	$16
$8,000	2,000	$4

Cost	Behavior of the Cost (within the relevant range) In Total	Per Unit
Variable cost	Total variable cost increases and decreases in proportion to changes in the activity level.	Variable cost per unit remains constant.
Fixed cost	Total fixed cost is not affected by changes in the activity level within the relevant range.	Fixed cost per unit decreases as the activity level rises and increases as the activity level falls.

EXHIBIT 2–9
Summary of Variable and Fixed Cost Behavior

Note that if the Mayo Clinic performs only 10 tests each month, the rental cost of the equipment will average $800 per test. But if 2,000 tests are performed each month, the average cost will drop to only $4 per test. More will be said later about the misunderstandings created by this variation in average unit costs.

Examples of fixed costs include straight-line depreciation, insurance, property taxes, rent, supervisory salaries, administrative salaries, and advertising.

A summary of both variable and fixed cost behavior is presented in Exhibit 2–9.

IN BUSINESS

THE POWER OF SHRINKING AVERAGE FIXED COST PER UNIT

Intel has recently built five new computer chip manufacturing facilities that have put its competitors on the defensive. Each plant can produce chips using a 12-inch wafer that is imprinted with 90-nanometer circuit lines that are 0.1% of the width of a human hair. These plants can produce 1.25 million chips a day, or about 375 million chips a year. Better yet, these new plants slash Intel's production costs in half since each plant's volume of output is 2.5 times greater than any of Intel's seven older plants. Building a computer chip manufacturing facility is a very expensive undertaking due to the required investment in fixed equipment costs. So why are Intel's competitors on the defensive? Because they are struggling to match Intel's exceptionally low average fixed cost per unit of output. Or, in an economist's terms, they are struggling to match Intel's economies of scale.

Source: Cliff Edwards, "Intel," *BusinessWeek*, March 8, 2004, pp. 56–64.

Cost Classifications for Assigning Costs to Cost Objects

LEARNING OBJECTIVE 6
Understand the differences between direct and indirect costs.

Costs are assigned to cost objects for a variety of purposes including pricing, preparing profitability studies, and controlling spending. A **cost object** is anything for which cost data are desired—including products, customers, jobs, and organizational subunits. For purposes of assigning costs to cost objects, costs are classified as either *direct* or *indirect.*

Direct Cost

A **direct cost** is a cost that can be easily and conveniently traced to a specified cost object. The concept of direct cost extends beyond just direct materials and direct labor. For example, if Reebok is assigning costs to its various regional and national sales offices, then the salary of the sales manager in its Tokyo office would be a direct cost of that office.

Indirect Cost

An **indirect cost** is a cost that cannot be easily and conveniently traced to a specified cost object. For example, a Campbell Soup factory may produce dozens of varieties of canned soups. The factory manager's salary would be an indirect cost of a particular variety such as chicken noodle soup. The reason is that the factory manager's salary is incurred as a consequence of running the entire factory—it is not incurred to produce any one soup variety. *To be traced to a cost object such as a particular product, the cost must be caused by the cost object.* The factory manager's salary is called a *common cost* of producing the various products of the factory. A **common cost** is a cost that is incurred to support a number of cost objects but cannot be traced to them individually. A common cost is a type of indirect cost.

A particular cost may be direct or indirect, depending on the cost object. While the Campbell Soup factory manager's salary is an *indirect* cost of manufacturing chicken noodle soup, it is a *direct* cost of the manufacturing division. In the first case, the cost object is chicken noodle soup. In the second case, the cost object is the entire manufacturing division.

Cost Classifications for Decision Making

LEARNING OBJECTIVE 7
Define and give examples of cost classifications used in making decisions: differential costs, opportunity costs, and sunk costs.

Costs are an important feature of many business decisions. In making decisions, it is essential to have a firm grasp of the concepts *differential cost, opportunity cost,* and *sunk cost.*

Differential Cost and Revenue

Decisions involve choosing between alternatives. In business decisions, each alternative will have costs and benefits that must be compared to the costs and benefits of the other available alternatives. A difference in costs between any two alternatives is known as a **differential cost.** A difference in revenues between any two alternatives is known as **differential revenue.**

Video 2–1

A differential cost is also known as an **incremental cost,** although technically an incremental cost should refer only to an increase in cost from one alternative to another; decreases in cost should be referred to as *decremental costs.* Differential cost is a broader term, encompassing both cost increases (incremental costs) and cost decreases (decremental costs) between alternatives.

The accountant's differential cost concept can be compared to the economist's marginal cost concept. In speaking of changes in cost and revenue, the economist uses the terms *marginal cost* and *marginal revenue.* The revenue that can be obtained from selling one more unit of product is called marginal revenue, and the cost involved in producing one more unit of product is called marginal cost. The economist's marginal concept is basically the same as the accountant's differential concept applied to a single unit of output.

IN BUSINESS

THE COST OF A HEALTHIER ALTERNATIVE

McDonald's is under pressure from critics to address the health implications of its menu. In response, McDonald's switched from partially hydrogenated vegetable oil to fry foods to a new soybean oil that cuts trans-fat levels by 48% even though the soybean oil is much more expensive than the partially hydrogenated vegetable oil and it lasts only half as long. What were the cost implications of this change? A typical McDonald's restaurant uses 500 pounds of the relatively unhealthy oil per week at a cost of about $186. In contrast, the same restaurant would need to use 1,000 pounds of the new soybean oil per week at a cost of about $571. This is a differential cost of $385 per restaurant per week. This may seem like a small amount of money until the calculation is expanded to include 13,000 McDonald's restaurants operating 52 weeks a year. Now, the total tab for a more healthy frying oil rises to about $260 million per year.

Source: Matthew Boyle, "Can You Really Make Fast Food Healthy?" *Fortune,* August 9, 2004, pp. 134–139.

Differential costs can be either fixed or variable. To illustrate, assume that Nature Way Cosmetics, Inc., is thinking about changing its marketing method from distribution through retailers to distribution by a network of neighborhood sales representatives. Present costs and revenues are compared to projected costs and revenues in the following table:

	Retailer Distribution (present)	Sales Representatives (proposed)	Differential Costs and Revenues
Revenues (Variable)	$700,000	$800,000	$100,000
Cost of goods sold (Variable)	350,000	400,000	50,000
Advertising (Fixed)	80,000	45,000	(35,000)
Commissions (Variable)	0	40,000	40,000
Warehouse depreciation (Fixed)	50,000	80,000	30,000
Other expenses (Fixed)	60,000	60,000	0
Total expenses	540,000	625,000	85,000
Net operating income	$160,000	$175,000	$ 15,000

According to the above analysis, the differential revenue is $100,000 and the differential costs total $85,000, leaving a positive differential net operating income of $15,000 under the proposed marketing plan.

The decision of whether Nature Way Cosmetics should stay with the present retail distribution or switch to sales representatives could be made on the basis of the net operating incomes of the two alternatives. As we see in the above analysis, the net operating income under the present distribution method is $160,000, whereas the net operating income with sales representatives is estimated to be $175,000. Therefore, using sales representatives is preferred, since it would result in $15,000 higher net operating income. Note that we would have arrived at exactly the same conclusion by simply focusing on the differential revenues, differential costs, and differential net operating income, which also show a $15,000 advantage for sales representatives.

In general, only the differences between alternatives are relevant in decisions. Those items that are the same under all alternatives and that are not affected by the decision can be ignored. For example, in the Nature Way Cosmetics example above, the "Other expenses" category, which is $60,000 under both alternatives, can be ignored, since it has no effect on the decision. If it were removed from the calculations, the sales representatives would still be preferred by $15,000. This is an extremely important principle in management accounting that we will revisit in later chapters.

IN BUSINESS

USING THOSE EMPTY SEATS

Cancer patients who seek specialized or experimental treatments must often travel far from home. Flying on a commercial airline can be an expensive and grueling experience for these patients. Priscilla Blum noted that many corporate jets fly with empty seats and she wondered why these seats couldn't be used for cancer patients. Taking the initiative, she founded Corporate Angel Network (www.corpangelnetwork.org), an organization that arranges free flights on some 1,500 jets from over 500 companies. There are no tax breaks for putting cancer patients in empty corporate jet seats, but filling an empty seat with a cancer patient doesn't involve any significant incremental cost. Since its founding, Corporate Angel Network has provided over 16,000 free flights.

Sources: Scott McCormack, "Waste Not, Want Not," *Forbes*, July 26, 1999, p. 118. Roger McCaffrey, "A True Tale of Angels in the Sky," *The Wall Street Journal*, February, 2002, p. A14. Helen Gibbs, Communication Director, Corporate Angel Network, private communication.

Opportunity Cost

Opportunity cost is the potential benefit that is given up when one alternative is selected over another. To illustrate this important concept, consider the following examples:

Example 1 Vicki has a part-time job that pays $200 per week while attending college. She would like to spend a week at the beach during spring break, and her employer has agreed to give her the time off, but without pay. The $200 in lost wages would be an opportunity cost of taking the week off to be at the beach.

Example 2 Suppose that Neiman Marcus is considering investing a large sum of money in land that may be a site for a future store. Rather than invest the funds in land, the company could invest the funds in high-grade securities. If the land is acquired, the opportunity cost is the investment income that could have been realized by purchasing the securities instead.

Example 3 Steve is employed by a company that pays him a salary of $38,000 per year. He is thinking about leaving the company and returning to school. Since returning to school would require that he give up his $38,000 salary, the forgone salary would be an opportunity cost of seeking further education.

Opportunity costs are not usually found in the accounting records of an organization, but they are costs that must be explicitly considered in every decision a manager makes. Virtually every alternative involves an opportunity cost. In Example 3 above, for instance, the higher income that could be realized in future years as a result of returning to school is an opportunity cost of staying in his present job.

Sunk Cost

A **sunk cost** is a cost *that has already been incurred* and that cannot be changed by any decision made now or in the future. Because sunk costs cannot be changed by any decision, they are not differential costs. And because only differential costs are relevant in a decision, sunk costs can and should be ignored.

To illustrate a sunk cost, assume that a company paid $50,000 several years ago for a special-purpose machine. The machine was used to make a product that is now obsolete and is no longer being sold. Even though in hindsight purchasing the machine may have been unwise, the $50,000 cost has already been incurred and cannot be undone. And it would be folly to continue making the obsolete product in a misguided attempt to "recover" the original cost of the machine. In short, the $50,000 originally paid for the machine is a sunk cost that should be ignored in current decisions.

IN BUSINESS

THE SUNK COST TRAP

Hal Arkes, a psychologist at Ohio University, asked 61 college students to assume they had mistakenly purchased tickets for both a $50 and a $100 ski trip for the same weekend. They could go on only one of the ski trips and would have to throw away the unused ticket. He further asked them to assume that they would actually have more fun on the $50 trip. Most of the students reported that they would go on the less enjoyable $100 trip. The larger cost mattered more to the students than having more fun. However, the sunk costs of the tickets should have been totally irrelevant in this decision. No matter which trip was selected, the actual total cost was $150—the cost of both tickets. And since this cost does not differ between the alternatives, it should be ignored. Like these students, most people have a great deal of difficulty ignoring sunk costs when making decisions.

Source: John Gourville and Dilip Soman, "Pricing and the Psychology of Consumption," *Harvard Business Review*, September 2002, pp. 92–93.

Summary

In this chapter, we have looked at some of the ways in which managers classify costs. How the costs will be used—for preparing external reports, predicting cost behavior, assigning costs to cost objects, or decision making—will dictate how the costs are classified.

For purposes of valuing inventories and determining expenses for the balance sheet and income statement, costs are classified as either product costs or period costs. Product costs are assigned to inventories and are considered assets until the products are sold. At the point of sale, product costs become cost of goods sold on the income statement. In contrast, period costs are taken directly to the income statement as expenses in the period in which they are incurred.

In a merchandising company, product cost is whatever the company paid for its merchandise. For external financial reports in a manufacturing company, product costs consist of all manufacturing costs. In both kinds of companies, selling and administrative costs are considered to be period costs and are expensed as incurred.

For purposes of predicting how costs will react to changes in activity, costs are classified into two categories—variable and fixed. Variable costs, in total, are strictly proportional to activity. The variable cost per unit is constant. Fixed costs, in total, remain at the same level for changes in activity that occur within the relevant range. The average fixed cost per unit decreases as the number of units increases.

For purposes of assigning costs to cost objects such as products or departments, costs are classified as direct or indirect. Direct costs can be conveniently traced to cost objects. Indirect costs cannot be conveniently traced to cost objects.

For purposes of making decisions, the concepts of differential cost and revenue, opportunity cost, and sunk cost are vitally important. Differential costs and revenues are the costs and revenues that differ between alternatives. Opportunity cost is the benefit that is forgone when one alternative is selected over another. Sunk cost is a cost that occurred in the past and cannot be altered. Differential costs and opportunity costs should be carefully considered in decisions. Sunk costs are always irrelevant in decisions and should be ignored.

These various cost classifications are *different* ways of looking at costs. A particular cost, such as the cost of cheese in a taco served at Taco Bell, could be a manufacturing cost, a product cost, a variable cost, a direct cost, and a differential cost—all at the same time. Taco Bell is a manufacturer of fast food. The cost of the cheese in a taco is a manufacturing cost and, as such, it would be a product cost as well. In addition, the cost of cheese is variable with respect to the number of tacos served and it is a direct cost of serving tacos. Finally, the cost of the cheese in a taco is a differential cost of making and serving the taco.

Review Problem 1: Cost Terms

Many new cost terms have been introduced in this chapter. It will take you some time to learn what each term means and how to properly classify costs in an organization. Consider the following example: Chippen Corporation manufactures furniture, including tables. Selected costs are given below:

1. The tables are made of wood that costs $100 per table.
2. The tables are assembled by workers, at a wage cost of $40 per table.
3. Workers making the tables are supervised by a factory supervisor who is paid $38,000 per year.
4. Electrical costs are $2 per machine-hour. Four machine-hours are required to produce a table.
5. The depreciation on the machines used to make the tables totals $10,000 per year. The machines have no resale value and do not wear out through use.
6. The salary of the president of the company is $100,000 per year.
7. The company spends $250,000 per year to advertise its products.
8. Salespersons are paid a commission of $30 for each table sold.
9. Instead of producing the tables, the company could rent its factory space for $50,000 per year.

Required:

Classify these costs according to the various cost terms used in the chapter. *Carefully study the classification of each cost.* If you don't understand why a particular cost is classified the way it is, reread the section of the chapter discussing the particular cost term. The terms *variable cost* and *fixed cost* refer to how costs behave with respect to the number of tables produced in a year.

Solution to Review Problem 1

	Variable Cost	Fixed Cost	Period (Selling and Administrative) Cost	Product Cost: Direct Materials	Product Cost: Direct Labor	Product Cost: Manufacturing Overhead	Sunk Cost	Opportunity Cost
1. Wood used in a table ($100 per table)	X			X				
2. Labor cost to assemble a table ($40 per table)	X				X			
3. Salary of the factory supervisor ($38,000 per year)		X				X		
4. Cost of electricity to produce tables ($2 per machine-hour)	X					X		
5. Depreciation of machines used to produce tables ($10,000 per year)		X				X	X*	
6. Salary of the company president ($100,000 per year)		X	X					
7. Advertising expense ($250,000 per year)		X	X					
8. Commissions paid to salespersons ($30 per table sold)	X		X					
9. Rental income forgone on factory space								X†

*This is a sunk cost because the outlay for the equipment was made in a previous period.

†This is an opportunity cost because it represents the potential benefit that is lost or sacrificed as a result of using the factory space to produce tables. Opportunity cost is a special category of cost that is not ordinarily recorded in an organization's accounting books. To avoid possible confusion with other costs, we will not attempt to classify this cost in any other way except as an opportunity cost.

Review Problem 2: Schedule of Cost of Goods Manufactured and Income Statement

The following information has been taken from the accounting records of Klear-Seal Corporation for last year:

Selling expenses	$140,000
Raw materials inventory, January 1	$90,000
Raw materials inventory, December 31	$60,000
Utilities, factory	$36,000
Direct labor cost	$150,000
Depreciation, factory	$162,000
Purchases of raw materials	$750,000
Sales	$2,500,000
Insurance, factory	$40,000
Supplies, factory	$15,000
Administrative expenses	$270,000
Indirect labor	$300,000
Maintenance, factory	$87,000
Work in process inventory, January 1	$180,000
Work in process inventory, December 31	$100,000
Finished goods inventory, January 1	$260,000
Finished goods inventory, December 31	$210,000

Management wants these data organized in a better format so that financial statements can be prepared for the year.

Required:

1. Prepare a schedule of cost of goods manufactured as in Exhibit 2–4.
2. Compute the cost of goods sold as in Exhibit 2–2.
3. Prepare an income statement.

Solution to Review Problem 2

1.

Klear-Seal Corporation Schedule of Cost of Goods Manufactured For the Year Ended December 31		
Direct materials:		
Raw materials inventory, January 1	$ 90,000	
Add: Purchases of raw materials	750,000	
Raw materials available for use	840,000	
Deduct: Raw materials inventory, December 31	60,000	
Raw materials used in production		$ 780,000
Direct labor		150,000
Manufacturing overhead:		
Utilities, factory	36,000	
Depreciation, factory	162,000	
Insurance, factory	40,000	
Supplies, factory	15,000	
Indirect labor	300,000	
Maintenance, factory	87,000	
Total manufacturing overhead cost		640,000
Total manufacturing cost		1,570,000
Add: Work in process inventory, January 1		180,000
		1,750,000
Deduct: Work in process inventory, December 31		100,000
Cost of goods manufactured		$1,650,000

2. The cost of goods sold would be computed as follows:

Finished goods inventory, January 1	$ 260,000
Add: Cost of goods manufactured	1,650,000
Goods available for sale	1,910,000
Deduct: Finished goods inventory, December 31	210,000
Cost of goods sold	$1,700,000

3.

Klear-Seal Corporation Income Statement For the Year Ended December 31		
Sales		$2,500,000
Cost of goods sold (above)		1,700,000
Gross margin		800,000
Selling and administrative expenses:		
Selling expenses	$140,000	
Administrative expenses	270,000	410,000
Net operating income		$ 390,000

Glossary

Administrative costs All executive, organizational, and clerical costs associated with the general management of an organization rather than with manufacturing or selling. (p. 41)

Common cost A cost that is incurred to support a number of cost objects but that cannot be traced to them individually. For example, the wage cost of the pilot of a 747 airliner is a common cost of all of the passengers on the aircraft. Without the pilot, there would be no flight and no passengers. But no part of the pilot's wage is caused by any one passenger taking the flight. (p. 56)

Conversion cost Direct labor cost plus manufacturing overhead cost. (p. 42)

Cost behavior The way in which a cost reacts to changes in the level of activity. (p. 51)

Cost object Anything for which cost data are desired. Examples of cost objects are products, customers, jobs, and parts of the organization such as departments or divisions. (p. 55)

Cost of goods manufactured The manufacturing costs associated with the goods that were finished during the period. (p. 47)

Differential cost A difference in cost between two alternatives. Also see *Incremental cost.* (p. 56)

Differential revenue The difference in revenue between two alternatives. (p. 56)

Direct cost A cost that can be easily and conveniently traced to a specified cost object. (p. 55)

Direct labor Factory labor costs that can be easily traced to individual units of product. Also called *touch labor.* (p. 40)

Direct materials Materials that become an integral part of a finished product and whose costs can be conveniently traced to it. (p. 40)

Finished goods Units of product that have been completed but not yet sold to customers. (p. 45)

Fixed cost A cost that remains constant, in total, regardless of changes in the level of activity within the relevant range. If a fixed cost is expressed on a per unit basis, it varies inversely with the level of activity. (p. 53)

Incremental cost An increase in cost between two alternatives. Also see *Differential cost.* (p. 56)

Indirect cost A cost that cannot be easily and conveniently traced to a specified cost object. (p. 56)

Indirect labor The labor costs of janitors, supervisors, materials handlers, and other factory workers that cannot be conveniently traced to particular products. (p. 40)

Indirect materials Small items of material such as glue and nails that may be an integral part of a finished product, but whose costs cannot be easily or conveniently traced to it. (p. 40)

Inventoriable costs Synonym for *product costs.* (p. 42)

Manufacturing overhead All manufacturing costs except direct materials and direct labor. (p. 41)

Opportunity cost The potential benefit that is given up when one alternative is selected over another. (p. 58)

Period costs Costs that are taken directly to the income statement as expenses in the period in which they are incurred or accrued. (p. 42)

Prime cost Direct materials cost plus direct labor cost. (p. 42)

Product costs All costs that are involved in acquiring or making a product. In the case of manufactured goods, these costs consist of direct materials, direct labor, and manufacturing overhead. Also see *Inventoriable costs.* (p. 42)

Raw materials Any materials that go into the final product. (pp. 39, 45)

Relevant range The range of activity within which assumptions about variable and fixed cost behavior are valid. (p. 53)

Schedule of cost of goods manufactured A schedule showing the direct materials, direct labor, and manufacturing overhead costs incurred during a period and the portion of those costs that are assigned to Work in Process and Finished Goods. (p. 47)

Selling costs All costs that are incurred to secure customer orders and get the finished product or service into the hands of the customer. (p. 41)

Sunk cost A cost that has already been incurred and that cannot be changed by any decision made now or in the future. (p. 58)

Variable cost A cost that varies, in total, in direct proportion to changes in the level of activity. A variable cost is constant per unit. (p. 51)

Work in process Units of product that are only partially complete. (p. 45)

Quiz 2

Multiple-choice questions are provided on the text Web site at www.mhhe.com/noreen1e.

Questions

2-1 What are the three major elements of product costs in a manufacturing company?

2-2 Distinguish between the following: (a) direct materials, (b) indirect materials, (c) direct labor, (d) indirect labor, and (e) manufacturing overhead.

2-3 Explain the difference between a product cost and a period cost.

2-4 Describe how the income statement of a manufacturing company differs from the income statement of a merchandising company.

2-5 Describe the schedule of cost of goods manufactured. How does it tie into the income statement?

2-6 Describe how the inventory accounts of a manufacturing company differ from the inventory account of a merchandising company.

2-7 Why are product costs sometimes called inventoriable costs? Describe the flow of such costs in a manufacturing company from the point of incurrence until they finally become expenses on the income statement.

2-8 Is it possible for costs such as salaries or depreciation to end up as assets on the balance sheet? Explain.

2-9 What is meant by the term *cost behavior?*

2-10 "A variable cost is a cost that varies per unit of product, whereas a fixed cost is constant per unit of product." Do you agree? Explain.

2-11 How do fixed costs create difficulties in costing units of product?

2-12 Why is manufacturing overhead considered an indirect cost of a unit of product?

2-13 Define the following terms: differential cost, opportunity cost, and sunk cost.

2-14 Only variable costs can be differential costs. Do you agree? Explain.

Exercises

EXERCISE 2-1 Classifying Manufacturing Costs [LO1]

Your Boat, Inc., assembles custom sailboats from components supplied by various manufacturers. The company is very small and its assembly shop and retail sales store are housed in a Gig Harbor, Washington, boathouse. Below are listed some of the costs that are incurred at the company.

Required:

For each cost, indicate whether it would most likely be classified as direct labor, direct materials, manufacturing overhead, selling, or an administrative cost.

1. The wages of employees who build the sailboats.
2. The cost of advertising in the local newspapers.
3. The cost of an aluminum mast installed in a sailboat.
4. The wages of the assembly shop's supervisor.
5. Rent on the boathouse.
6. The wages of the company's bookkeeper.
7. Sales commissions paid to the company's salespeople.
8. Depreciation on power tools.

EXERCISE 2-2 Classification of Costs as Period or Product Costs [LO2]

Suppose that you have been given a summer job at Fairwings Avionics, a company that manufactures sophisticated radar sets for commercial aircraft. The company, which is privately owned, has approached a bank for a loan to help finance its tremendous growth. The bank requires financial statements before approving such a loan. You have been asked to help prepare the financial statements and were given the following list of costs:

1. The cost of the memory chips used in a radar set.
2. Factory heating costs.
3. Factory equipment maintenance costs.
4. Training costs for new administrative employees.
5. The cost of the solder that is used in assembling the radar sets.
6. The travel costs of the company's salespersons.
7. Wages and salaries of factory security personnel.
8. The cost of air-conditioning executive offices.
9. Wages and salaries in the department that handles billing customers.

10. Depreciation on the equipment in the fitness room used by factory workers.
11. Telephone expenses incurred by factory management.
12. The costs of shipping completed radar sets to customers.
13. The wages of the workers who assemble the radar sets.
14. The president's salary.
15. Health insurance premiums for factory personnel.

Required:

Classify the above costs as either product (inventoriable) costs or period (noninventoriable) costs for purposes of preparing the financial statements for the bank.

EXERCISE 2-3 Constructing an Income Statement [LO3]

Last month Mountain High, a mountain sporting goods retailer, had total sales of $3,200,000, selling expenses of $110,000, and administrative expenses of $470,000. The company had beginning merchandise inventory of $140,000, purchased additional merchandise inventory for $2,550,000, and had ending merchandise inventory of $180,000.

Required:

Prepare an income statement for the company for the month.

EXERCISE 2-4 Prepare a Schedule of Cost of Goods Manufactured [LO4]

Mannerman Fabrication manufactures a variety of products in its factory. Data for the most recent month's operations appear below:

Beginning raw materials inventory	$55,000
Purchases of raw materials	$440,000
Ending raw materials inventory	$65,000
Direct labor	$215,000
Manufacturing overhead	$380,000
Beginning work in process inventory	$190,000
Ending work in process inventory	$220,000

Required:

Prepare a schedule of cost of goods manufactured for the company for the month.

EXERCISE 2-5 Classification of Costs as Fixed or Variable [LO5]

Below are costs and measures of activity in a variety of organizations.

Required:

Classify each cost as variable or fixed with respect to the indicated measure of activity by placing an X in the appropriate column.

		Cost Behavior	
Cost	Measure of Activity	Variable	Fixed
1. The cost of small glass plates used for lab tests in a medical lab	Number of lab tests performed		
2. A boutique jewelry store's cost of leasing retail space in a mall	Dollar sales		
3. Top management salaries at FedEx	Total sales		
4. Electrical costs of running production equipment at a Toyota factory	Number of vehicles produced		
5. The cost of insuring a dentist's office against fire	Patient-visits		
6. The cost of commissions paid to salespersons at a Honda dealer	Total sales		
7. The cost of heating the intensive care unit at Swedish Hospital	Patient-days		
8. The cost of batteries installed in trucks produced at a GM factory	Number of trucks produced		
9. The salary of a university professor	Number of students taught by the professor		
10. The costs of cleaning supplies used at a fast-food restaurant to clean the kitchen and dining areas at the end of the day	Number of customers served		

EXERCISE 2-6 Identifying Direct and Indirect Costs [LO6]

The Empire Hotel is a four-star hotel located in downtown Seattle.

Required:

For each of the following costs incurred at the Empire Hotel, indicate whether it would most likely be a direct cost or an indirect cost of the specified cost object by placing an X in the appropriate column.

	Cost	Cost Object	Direct Cost	Indirect Cost
Ex.	Room service beverages	A particular hotel guest	X	
1.	The salary of the head chef	The hotel's restaurant		
2.	The salary of the head chef	A particular restaurant customer		
3.	Room cleaning supplies	A particular hotel guest		
4.	Flowers for the reception desk	A particular hotel guest		
5.	The wages of the doorman	A particular hotel guest		
6.	Room cleaning supplies	The housecleaning department		
7.	Fire insurance on the hotel building	The hotel's gym		
8.	Towels used in the gym	The hotel's gym		

EXERCISE 2-7 Differential, Opportunity, and Sunk Costs [LO7]

The Sorrento Hotel is a four-star hotel located in downtown Seattle. The hotel's operations vice president would like to replace the hotel's antiquated computer terminals at the registration desk with attractive state-of-the-art flat-panel displays. The new displays would take less space, would consume less power than the old computer terminals, and would provide additional security since they can only be viewed from a restrictive angle. The new computer displays would not require any new wiring. The hotel's chef believes the funds would be better spent on a new bulk freezer for the kitchen.

Required:

For each of the items below, indicate by placing an X in the appropriate column whether it should be considered a differential cost, an opportunity cost, or a sunk cost in the decision to replace the old computer terminals with new flat-panel displays. If none of the categories apply for a particular item, leave all columns blank.

	Item	Differential Cost	Opportunity Cost	Sunk Cost
Ex.	Cost of electricity to run the terminals	X		
1.	Cost of the new flat-panel displays			
2.	Cost of the old computer terminals			
3.	Rent on the space occupied by the registration desk . . .			
4.	Wages of registration desk personnel			
5.	Benefits from a new freezer			
6.	Costs of maintaining the old computer terminals			
7.	Cost of removing the old computer terminals			
8.	Cost of existing registration desk wiring			

EXERCISE 2-8 Product Cost Flows; Product versus Period Costs [LO2, LO3]

Ryser Company was organized on May 1. On that date the company purchased 35,000 plastic emblems, each with a peel-off adhesive backing. The front of the emblems contained the company's name, accompanied by an attractive logo. Each emblem cost Ryser Company $2.

During May, 31,000 emblems were drawn from the Raw Materials inventory account. Of these, 1,000 were taken by the sales manager to an important sales meeting with prospective customers and handed out as an advertising gimmick. The remaining emblems drawn from inventory were affixed to units of the company's product that were being manufactured during May. Of the units of product having emblems affixed during May, 90% were completed and transferred from

Work in Process to Finished Goods. Of the units completed during the month, 75% were sold and shipped to customers.

Required:

1. Determine the cost of emblems that would be in each of the following accounts at May 31:
   a. Raw Materials.
   b. Work in Process.
   c. Finished Goods.
   d. Cost of Goods Sold.
   e. Advertising Expense.
2. Specify whether each of the above accounts would appear on the balance sheet or on the income statement at May 31.

EXERCISE 2-9 Preparation of a Schedule of Cost of Goods Manufactured and Cost of Goods Sold [LO1, LO3, LO4]

The following cost and inventory data for the just completed year are taken from the accounting records of Eccles Company:

Costs incurred:	
Advertising expense	$100,000
Direct labor cost	$90,000
Purchases of raw materials	$132,000
Rent, factory building	$80,000
Indirect labor	$56,300
Sales commissions	$35,000
Utilities, factory	$9,000
Maintenance, factory equipment	$24,000
Supplies, factory	$700
Depreciation, office equipment	$8,000
Depreciation, factory equipment	$40,000

	Beginning of Year	End of Year
Inventories:		
Raw materials	$8,000	$10,000
Work in process	$5,000	$20,000
Finished goods	$70,000	$25,000

Required:

1. Prepare a schedule of cost of goods manufactured.
2. Prepare the cost of goods sold section of Eccles Company's income statement for the year.

EXERCISE 2-10 Classification of Costs as Variable or Fixed and as Selling and Administrative or Product [LO2, LO5]

Below are listed various costs that are found in organizations.

1. The costs of turn signal switches used at a General Motors plant. These are one of the parts installed in the steering columns assembled at the plant.
2. Interest expense on CBS's long-term debt.
3. Salespersons' commissions at Avon Products, a company that sells cosmetics door to door.
4. Insurance on one of Cincinnati Milacron's factory buildings.
5. The costs of shipping brass fittings from Graham Manufacturing's plant in New Hampshire to customers in California.
6. Depreciation on the bookshelves at Reston Bookstore.
7. The costs of X-ray film at the Mayo Clinic's radiology lab.
8. The cost of leasing an 800 telephone number at L. L. Bean. The monthly charge for the 800 number is independent of the number of calls taken.
9. The depreciation on the playground equipment at a McDonald's outlet.
10. The cost of mozzarella cheese used at a Pizza Hut outlet.

Required:

Classify each cost as either variable or fixed with respect to the volume of goods or services produced and sold by the organization. Also classify each cost as a selling and administrative cost or a product cost. Prepare your answer sheet as shown below. Place an X in the appropriate columns to show the proper classifications of each cost.

Cost Item	Cost Behavior		Selling and Administrative Cost	Product Cost
	Variable	Fixed		

 **Problems**

PROBLEM 2-11 Cost Classification [LO2, LO5, LO6]

Listed below are costs found in various organizations.

1. Depreciation, executive jet.
2. Costs of shipping finished goods to customers.
3. Wood used in manufacturing furniture.
4. Sales manager's salary.
5. Electricity used in manufacturing furniture.
6. Secretary to the company president.
7. Aerosol attachment placed on a spray can produced by the company.
8. Billing costs.
9. Packing supplies for shipping products overseas.
10. Sand used in manufacturing concrete.
11. Supervisor's salary, factory.
12. Executive life insurance.
13. Sales commissions.
14. Fringe benefits, assembly-line workers.
15. Advertising costs.
16. Property taxes on finished goods warehouses.
17. Lubricants for production equipment.

Required:

Prepare an answer sheet with column headings as shown below. For each cost item, indicate whether it would be variable or fixed with respect to the number of units produced and sold; and then whether it would be a selling cost, an administrative cost, or a manufacturing cost. If it is a manufacturing cost, indicate whether it would typically be treated as a direct or indirect cost with respect to units of product. Three sample answers are provided for illustration.

Cost Item	Variable or Fixed	Selling Cost	Administrative Cost	Manufacturing (Product) Cost	
				Direct	Indirect
Direct labor	V			X	
Executive salaries	F		X		
Factory rent	F				X

PROBLEM 2-12 Cost Classification [LO1, LO2, LO5, LO7]

Several years ago Medex Company purchased a small building adjacent to its manufacturing plant in order to have room for expansion when needed. Since the company had no immediate need for the extra space, the building was rented out to another company for a rental revenue of $40,000 per year. The renter's lease will expire next month, and rather than renewing the lease, Medex Company has decided to use the building itself to manufacture a new product.

Direct materials cost for the new product will total $40 per unit. It will be necessary to hire a supervisor to oversee production. Her salary will be $2,500 per month. Workers will be hired to manufacture the new product, with direct labor cost amounting to $18 per unit. Manufacturing operations will occupy all of the building space, so it will be necessary to rent space in a warehouse nearby in order to store finished units of product. The rental cost will be $1,000 per month. In addition, the company will need to rent equipment for use in producing the new product; the rental cost will be $3,000 per month. The company will continue to depreciate the building on a straight-line basis, as in past years. Depreciation on the building is $10,000 per year.

Advertising costs for the new product will total $50,000 per year. Costs of shipping the new product to customers will be $10 per unit. Electrical costs of operating machines will be $2 per unit.

To have funds to purchase materials, meet payrolls, and so forth, the company will have to liquidate some temporary investments. These investments are presently yielding a return of $6,000 per year.

Required:

Prepare an answer sheet with the following column headings:

Name of the Cost	Variable Cost	Fixed Cost	Product Cost			Period (Selling and Administrative) Cost	Opportunity Cost	Sunk Cost
			Direct Materials	Direct Labor	Manufacturing Overhead			

List the different costs associated with the new product decision down the extreme left column (under Name of the Cost). Then place an X under each heading that helps to describe the type of cost involved. There may be X's under several column headings for a single cost. (For example, a cost may be a fixed cost, a period cost, and a sunk cost; you would place an X under each of these column headings opposite the cost.)

PROBLEM 2-13 Classification of Costs as Variable or Fixed and Direct or Indirect [LO5, LO6]

Various costs associated with manufacturing operations are given below:

1. Plastic washers used to assemble autos.
2. Production superintendent's salary.
3. Wages of workers who assemble a product.
4. Electricity to run production equipment.
5. Janitorial salaries.
6. Clay used to make bricks.
7. Rent on a factory building.
8. Wood used to make skis.
9. Screws used to make furniture.
10. A supervisor's salary.
11. Cloth used to make shirts.
12. Depreciation of cafeteria equipment.
13. Glue used to make textbooks.
14. Lubricants for production equipment.
15. Paper used to make textbooks.

Required:

Classify each cost as being either variable or fixed with respect to the number of units produced and sold. Also indicate whether each cost would typically be treated as a direct cost or an indirect cost with respect to units of product. Prepare your answer sheet as shown below:

Cost Item	Cost Behavior		To Units of Product	
	Variable	Fixed	Direct	Indirect
Example: Factory insurance		X		X

PROBLEM 2-14 Schedule of Cost of Goods Manufactured; Income Statement; Cost Behavior [LO1, LO2, LO3, LO4, LO5]

Various cost and sales data for Medco, Inc., are given below for the just completed year:

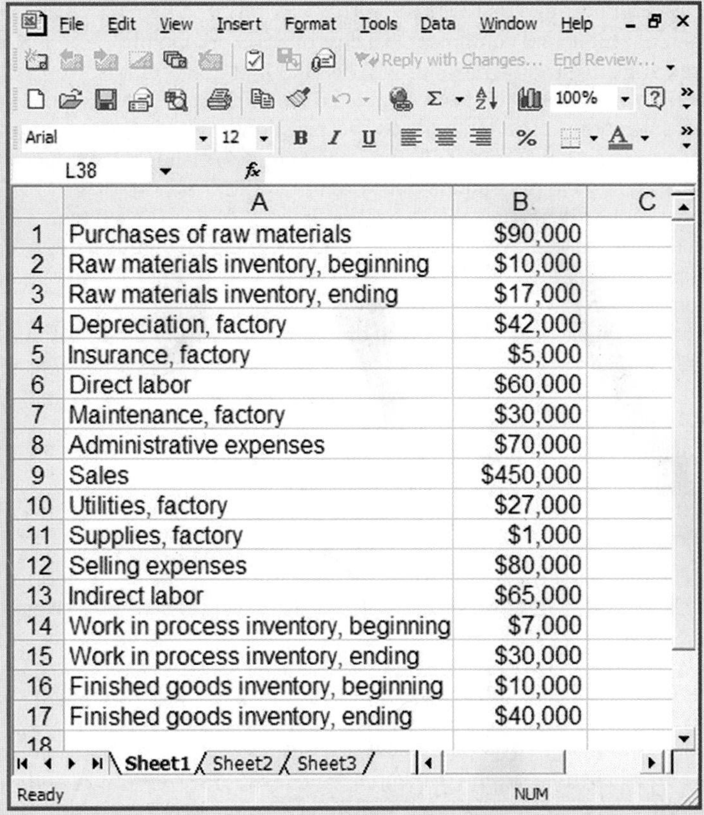

	A	B	C
1	Purchases of raw materials	$90,000	
2	Raw materials inventory, beginning	$10,000	
3	Raw materials inventory, ending	$17,000	
4	Depreciation, factory	$42,000	
5	Insurance, factory	$5,000	
6	Direct labor	$60,000	
7	Maintenance, factory	$30,000	
8	Administrative expenses	$70,000	
9	Sales	$450,000	
10	Utilities, factory	$27,000	
11	Supplies, factory	$1,000	
12	Selling expenses	$80,000	
13	Indirect labor	$65,000	
14	Work in process inventory, beginning	$7,000	
15	Work in process inventory, ending	$30,000	
16	Finished goods inventory, beginning	$10,000	
17	Finished goods inventory, ending	$40,000	
18			

Required:

1. Prepare a schedule of cost of goods manufactured.
2. Prepare an income statement.
3. Assume that the company produced the equivalent of 10,000 units of product during the year. What was the average cost per unit for direct materials? What was the average cost per unit for factory depreciation?
4. Assume that the company expects to produce 15,000 units of product during the coming year. What average cost per unit and what total cost would you expect the company to incur for direct materials at this level of activity? For factory depreciation? (In preparing your answer, assume that direct materials is a variable cost and that depreciation is a fixed cost; also assume that depreciation is computed on a straight-line basis.)
5. As the manager responsible for production costs, explain to the president any difference in the average costs per unit between (3) and (4) above.

PROBLEM 2-15 Classification of Salary Cost as a Period or Product Cost [LO2]

You have just been hired by EduRom Company, which was organized on January 2 of the current year. The company manufactures and sells a variety of educational DVDs for personal computers. It is your responsibility to supervise the employees who take orders from customers over the phone and to arrange for shipping orders via Federal Express, UPS, and other freight carriers.

The company is unsure how to classify your annual salary in its cost records. The company's cost analyst says that your salary should be classified as a manufacturing (product) cost; the controller says that it should be classified as a selling expense; and the president says that it doesn't matter which way your salary cost is classified.

Required:

1. Which viewpoint is correct? Why?
2. From the point of view of the reported net operating income for the year, is the president correct in saying that it doesn't matter which way your salary cost is classified? Explain.

PROBLEM 2-16 Classification of Various Costs [LO1, LO2, LO5, LO7]

Frieda Bronkowski has invented a new type of flyswatter. After giving the matter much thought, Frieda has decided to quit her $4,000 per month job with a consulting firm and produce and sell the flyswatters full time. Frieda will rent a garage that will be used as a production plant. The rent will be $150 per month. Frieda will rent production equipment at a cost of $500 per month.

The cost of materials for each flyswatter will be $0.30. Frieda will hire workers to produce the flyswatters. They will be paid $0.50 for each completed unit. Frieda will rent a room in the house next door for use as her sales office. The rent will be $75 per month. She has arranged for the telephone company to attach a recording device to her home phone to get off-hours messages from customers. The device will increase her monthly phone bill by $20.

Frieda has some money in savings that is earning interest of $1,000 per year. These savings will be withdrawn and used for about a year to get the business going. To sell her flyswatters, Frieda will advertise heavily in the local area. Advertising costs will be $400 per month. In addition, Frieda will pay a sales commission of $0.10 for each flyswatter sold.

For the time being, Frieda does not intend to draw any salary from the new company.

Frieda has already paid the legal and filing fees to incorporate her business. These fees amounted to $600.

Required:

1. Prepare an answer sheet with the following column headings:

Name of the Cost	Variable Cost	Fixed Cost	Product Cost			Period (Selling and Administrative) Cost	Opportunity Cost	Sunk Cost
			Direct Materials	Direct Labor	Manufacturing Overhead			

   List the different costs associated with the new company down the extreme left column (under Name of Cost). Then place an X under each heading that helps to describe the type of cost involved. There may be X's under several column headings for a single cost. (That is, a cost may be a fixed cost, a period cost, and a sunk cost; you would place an X under each of these column headings opposite the cost.) Under the variable cost column, list only those costs that would be variable with respect to the number of flyswatters that are produced and sold.

2. All of the costs you have listed above, except one, would be differential costs between the alternatives of Frieda producing flyswatters or staying with the consulting firm. Which cost is *not* differential? Explain.

PROBLEM 2-17 Cost Classification and Cost Behavior [LO2, LO5, LO6]

Heritage Company manufactures a beautiful bookcase that enjoys widespread popularity. The company has a backlog of orders that is large enough to keep production going indefinitely at the plant's full capacity of 4,000 bookcases per year. Annual cost data at full capacity follow:

Direct materials used (wood and glass)	$430,000
General office salaries	$110,000
Factory supervision	$70,000
Sales commissions	$60,000
Depreciation, factory building	$105,000
Depreciation, office equipment	$2,000
Indirect materials, factory	$18,000
Factory labor (cutting and assembly)	$90,000
Advertising	$100,000
Insurance, factory	$6,000
General office supplies (billing)	$4,000
Property taxes, factory	$20,000
Utilities, factory	$45,000

Required:

1. Prepare an answer sheet with the column headings shown below. Enter each cost item on your answer sheet, placing the dollar amount under the appropriate headings. As examples, this has been done already for the first two items in the list above. Note that each cost item is classified in two ways: first, as either variable or fixed with respect to the number of units produced and sold; and second, as either a selling and administrative cost or a product cost. (If the item is a product cost, it should also be classified as either direct or indirect as shown.)

Cost Item	Cost Behavior		Selling or Administrative Cost	Product Cost	
	Variable	Fixed		Direct	Indirect*
Materials used	$430,000			$430,000	
General office salaries.		$110,000	$110,000		

*To units of product.

2. Total the dollar amounts in each of the columns in (1) above. Compute the average product cost per bookcase.
3. Due to a recession, assume that production drops to only 2,000 bookcases per year. Would you expect the average product cost per bookcase to increase, decrease, or remain unchanged? Explain. No computations are necessary.
4. Refer to the original data. The president's next-door neighbor has considered making himself a bookcase and has priced the necessary materials at a building supply store. He has asked the president whether he could purchase a bookcase from the Heritage Company "at cost," and the president has agreed to let him do so.
   a. Would you expect any disagreement between the two men over the price the neighbor should pay? Explain. What price does the president probably have in mind? The neighbor?
   b. Since the company is operating at full capacity, what cost term used in the chapter might be justification for the president to charge the full, regular price to the neighbor and still be selling "at cost"? Explain.

PROBLEM 2-18 Variable and Fixed Costs; Subtleties of Direct and Indirect Costs [LO5, LO6]

The Central Area Well-Baby Clinic provides a variety of health services to newborn babies and their parents. The clinic is organized into a number of departments, one of which is the Immunization Center. A number of costs of the clinic and the Immunization Center are listed below.

Example: The cost of polio immunization tablets

a. The salary of the head nurse in the Immunization Center.
b. Costs of incidental supplies consumed in the Immunization Center, such as paper towels.
c. The cost of lighting and heating the Immunization Center.
d. The cost of disposable syringes used in the Immunization Center.
e. The salary of the Central Area Well-Baby Clinic's information systems manager.
f. The costs of mailing letters soliciting donations to the Central Area Well-Baby Clinic.
g. The wages of nurses who work in the Immunization Center.
h. The cost of medical malpractice insurance for the Central Area Well-Baby Clinic.
i. Depreciation on the fixtures and equipment in the Immunization Center.

Required:

For each cost listed above, indicate whether it is a direct or indirect cost of the Immunization Center, whether it is a direct or indirect cost of immunizing particular patients, and whether it is variable or fixed with respect to the number of immunizations administered. Use the form shown below for your answer.

Item Description	Direct or Indirect Cost of the Immunization Center		Direct or Indirect Cost of Particular Patients		Variable or Fixed with Respect to the Number of Immunizations Administered	
	Direct	Indirect	Direct	Indirect	Variable	Fixed
Example: The cost of polio immunization tablets	X		X		X	

PROBLEM 2-19 Schedule of Cost of Goods Manufactured; Income Statement [LO1, LO2, LO3, LO4]
Skyler Company was organized on November 1 of the previous year. After seven months of start-up losses, management had expected to earn a profit during June, the most recent month. Management was disappointed, however, when the income statement for June also showed a loss. June's income statement follows:

Skyler Company Income Statement For the Month Ended June 30		
Sales		$600,000
Less operating expenses:		
Selling and administrative salaries	$ 35,000	
Rent on facilities	40,000	
Purchases of raw materials	190,000	
Insurance	8,000	
Depreciation, sales equipment	10,000	
Utilities costs	50,000	
Indirect labor	108,000	
Direct labor	90,000	
Depreciation, factory equipment	12,000	
Maintenance, factory	7,000	
Advertising	80,000	630,000
Net operating loss		$(30,000)

After seeing the $30,000 loss for June, Skyler's president stated, "I was sure we'd be profitable within six months, but after eight months we're still spilling red ink. Maybe it's time for us to throw in the towel and accept one of those offers we've had for the company. To make matters worse, I just heard that Linda won't be back from her surgery for at least six more weeks."

Linda is the company's controller; in her absence, the statement above was prepared by a new assistant who has had little experience in manufacturing operations. Additional information about the company follows:

a. Only 80% of the rent on facilities applies to factory operations; the remainder applies to selling and administrative activities.
b. Inventory balances at the beginning and end of the month were as follows:

	June 1	June 30
Raw materials	$17,000	$42,000
Work in process	$70,000	$85,000
Finished goods	$20,000	$60,000

c. Some 75% of the insurance and 90% of the utilities cost apply to factory operations; the remaining amounts apply to selling and administrative activities.

The president has asked you to check over the above income statement and make a recommendation as to whether the company should continue operations.

Required:
1. As one step in gathering data for a recommendation to the president, prepare a schedule of cost of goods manufactured for June.
2. As a second step, prepare a new income statement for the month.
3. Based on your statements prepared in (1) and (2) above, would you recommend that the company continue operations?

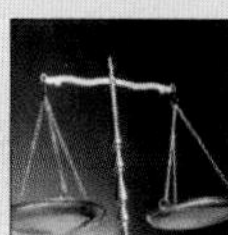

PROBLEM 2-20 Ethics and the Manager [LO2]
The top management of General Electronics, Inc., is well known for "managing by the numbers." With an eye on the company's desired growth in overall net profit, the company's CEO (chief executive officer) sets target profits at the beginning of the year for each of the company's divisions. The CEO has stated her policy as follows: "I won't interfere with operations in the divisions. I am available for advice, but the division vice presidents are free to do anything they want so long as they hit the target profits for the year."

In November, Stan Richart, the vice president in charge of the Cellular Telephone Technologies Division, saw that making the current year's target profit for his division was going to be very difficult. Among other actions, he directed that discretionary expenditures be delayed until the beginning of the new year. On December 30, he was angered to discover that a warehouse clerk had ordered $350,000 of cellular telephone parts earlier in December even though the parts weren't really needed by the assembly department until January or February. Contrary to common accounting practice, the General Electronics, Inc., Accounting Policy Manual states that such parts are to be recorded as an expense when delivered. To avoid recording the expense, Mr. Richart asked that the order be canceled, but the purchasing department reported that the parts had already been delivered and the supplier would not accept returns. Since the bill had not yet been paid, Mr. Richart asked the accounting department to correct the clerk's mistake by delaying recognition of the delivery until the bill is paid in January.

Required:

1. Are Mr. Richart's actions ethical? Explain why they are or are not ethical.
2. Do the general management philosophy and accounting policies at General Electronics encourage or discourage ethical behavior? Explain.

PROBLEM 2-21 Schedule of Cost of Goods Manufactured; Income Statement; Cost Behavior [LO1, LO2, LO3, LO4, LO5]

The following selected account balances for the year ended December 31 are provided for Valenko Company:

Advertising expense	$215,000
Insurance, factory equipment	$8,000
Depreciation, sales equipment	$40,000
Rent, factory building	$90,000
Utilities, factory	$52,000
Sales commissions	$35,000
Cleaning supplies, factory	$6,000
Depreciation, factory equipment	$110,000
Selling and administrative salaries	$85,000
Maintenance, factory	$74,000
Direct labor	?
Purchases of raw materials	$260,000

Inventory balances at the beginning and end of the year were as follows:

	Beginning of Year	End of Year
Raw materials	$50,000	$40,000
Work in process	?	$33,000
Finished goods	$30,000	?

The total manufacturing costs for the year were $675,000; the goods available for sale totaled $720,000; and the cost of goods sold totaled $635,000.

Required:

1. Prepare a schedule of cost of goods manufactured and the cost of goods sold section of the company's income statement for the year.
2. Assume that the dollar amounts given above are for the equivalent of 30,000 units produced during the year. Compute the average cost per unit for direct materials used, and compute the average cost per unit for rent on the factory building.
3. Assume that in the following year the company expects to produce 50,000 units. What average cost per unit and total cost would you expect to be incurred for direct materials? For rent on the factory building? (Assume that direct materials is a variable cost and that rent is a fixed cost.)
4. As the manager in charge of production costs, explain to the president the reason for any difference in the average costs per unit between (2) and (3) above.

PROBLEM 2-22 Working with Incomplete Data from the Income Statement and Schedule of Cost of Goods Manufactured [LO3, LO4]

Supply the missing data in the four cases below. Each case is independent of the others.

	Case			
	1	2	3	4
Schedule of Cost of Goods Manufactured				
Direct materials	$7,000	$9,000	$6,000	$8,000
Direct labor	$2,000	$4,000	?	$3,000
Manufacturing overhead	$10,000	?	$7,000	$21,000
Total manufacturing costs	?	$25,000	$18,000	?
Beginning work in process inventory	?	$1,000	$2,000	?
Ending work in process inventory	$4,000	$3,500	?	$2,000
Cost of goods manufactured	$18,000	$?	$16,000	$31,500
Income Statement				
Sales	$25,000	$40,000	$30,000	$50,000
Beginning finished goods inventory	$6,000	?	$7,000	$9,000
Cost of goods manufactured	$18,000	?	$16,000	$31,500
Goods available for sale	?	?	?	?
Ending finished goods inventory	$9,000	$4,000	?	$7,000
Cost of goods sold	?	$26,500	$18,000	?
Gross margin	?	?	?	?
Selling and administrating expenses	$6,000	?	?	$10,000
Net operating income	$?	$5,500	$3,000	$?

PROBLEM 2-23 Income Statement; Schedule of Cost of Goods Manufactured [LO1, LO2, LO3, LO4]
Hickey Corporation is a manufacturer that produces a single product. The following information has been taken from the company's production, sales, and cost records for the just completed year:

Production in units	30,000
Sales in units	?
Ending finished goods inventory in units	?
Sales in dollars	$650,000
Costs:	
Advertising	$50,000
Direct labor	$80,000
Indirect labor	$60,000
Raw materials purchased	$160,000
Building rent (production uses 80% of the space; administrative and sales offices use the rest)	$50,000
Utilities, factory	$35,000
Royalty paid for use of production patent, $1 per unit produced	?
Maintenance, factory	$25,000
Rent for special production equipment, $6,000 per year plus $0.10 per unit produced	?
Selling and administrative salaries	$140,000
Other factory overhead costs	$11,000
Other selling and administrative expenses	$20,000

	Beginning of Year	End of Year
Inventories:		
Raw materials	$20,000	$10,000
Work in process	$30,000	$40,000
Finished goods	$0	?

The finished goods inventory is being carried at the average unit production cost for the year. The selling price of the product is $25 per unit.

Required:

1. Prepare a schedule of cost of goods manufactured for the year.
2. Compute the following:
   a. The number of units in the finished goods inventory at the end of the year.
   b. The cost of the units in the finished goods inventory at the end of the year.
3. Prepare an income statement for the year.

Cases

CASE 2-24 Missing Data; Income Statement; Schedule of Cost of Goods Manufactured
[LO1, LO2, LO3, LO4]

"I know I'm a pretty good scientist, but I guess I still have some things to learn about running a business," said Staci Morales, founder and president of Medical Technology, Inc. "Demand has been so strong for our heart monitor that I was sure we'd be profitable immediately, but just look at the gusher of red ink for the first quarter. At this rate we'll be out of business in a year." The data to which Staci was referring are shown below:

Medical Technology, Inc. Income Statement For the Quarter Ended June 30		
Sales (16,000 monitors)		$ 975,000
Less operating expenses:		
Selling and administrative salaries	$ 90,000	
Advertising	200,000	
Cleaning supplies, factory	6,000	
Indirect labor cost	135,000	
Depreciation, office equipment	18,000	
Direct labor cost	80,000	
Raw materials purchased	310,000	
Maintenance, factory	47,000	
Rental cost, facilities	65,000	
Insurance, factory	9,000	
Utilities	40,000	
Depreciation, production equipment	75,000	
Travel, salespersons	60,000	1,135,000
Net operating loss		$ (160,000)

Medical Technology was organized on April 1 of the current year to produce and market a revolutionary new heart monitor. The company's accounting system was set up by Staci's brother-in-law who had taken an accounting course about 10 years ago.

"We may not last a year if the insurance company doesn't pay the $227,000 it owes us for the 4,000 monitors lost in the truck accident last week," said Staci. "The agent says our claim is inflated, but that's a lot of baloney."

Just after the end of the quarter, a truck carrying 4,000 monitors wrecked and burned, destroying the entire load. The monitors were part of the 20,000 units completed during the quarter ended June 30. They were in a warehouse awaiting sale at quarter-end and were sold and shipped on July 3 (this sale is *not* included on the income statement above). The trucking company's insurer is liable for the cost of the goods lost. Staci's brother-in-law has determined this cost as follows:

$$\frac{\text{Total costs for the quarter}}{\text{Monitors produced during the quarter}} = \$1{,}135{,}000/20{,}000 \text{ units} = \$56.75 \text{ per unit}$$

$$4{,}000 \text{ units} \times \$56.75 \text{ per unit} = \$227{,}000$$

The following additional information is available on the company's activities during the quarter ended June 30:

a. Inventories at the beginning and end of the quarter were as follows:

	Beginning of the Quarter	End of the Quarter
Raw materials	$0	$40,000
Work in process.	$0	$30,000
Finished goods	$0	?

b. Eighty percent of the rental cost for facilities and 90% of the utilities cost relate to manufacturing operations. The remaining amounts relate to selling and administrative activities.

Required:

1. What conceptual errors, if any, were made in preparing the income statement above?
2. Prepare a schedule of cost of goods manufactured for the quarter.
3. Prepare a corrected income statement for the quarter. Your statement should show in detail how the cost of goods sold is computed.
4. Do you agree that the insurance company owes Medical Technology, Inc., $227,000? Explain your answer.

CASE 2-25 Inventory Computations from Incomplete Data [LO3, LO4]

While snoozing at the controls of his Pepper Six airplane, Dunse P. Sluggard leaned heavily against the door; suddenly, the door flew open and a startled Dunse tumbled out. As he parachuted to the ground, Dunse watched helplessly as the empty plane smashed into Operex Products' plant and administrative offices.

"The insurance company will never believe this," cried Mercedes Juliet, the company's controller, as she watched the ensuing fire burn the building to the ground. "The entire company is wiped out!"

"There's no reason to even contact the insurance agent," replied Ford Romero, the company's operations manager. "We can't file a claim without records, and all we have left is this copy of last year's annual report. It shows that raw materials at the beginning of this year (January 1) totaled $30,000, work in process totaled $50,000, and finished goods totaled $90,000. But what we need is a record of these inventories as of today, and our records are up in smoke."

"All except this summary page I was working on when the plane hit the building," said Mercedes. "It shows that our sales to date this year have totaled $1,350,000 and that manufacturing overhead cost has totaled $520,000."

"Hey! This annual report is more helpful than I thought," exclaimed Ford. "I can see that our gross margin was 40% of sales. I can also see that direct labor cost is one-quarter of the manufacturing overhead cost."

"We may have a chance after all," cried Mercedes. "My summary sheet lists the sum of direct labor and direct materials at $510,000 for the year, and it says that our goods available for sale to customers this year has totaled $960,000 at cost. Now if we just knew the amount of raw materials purchased so far this year."

"I know that figure," yelled Ford. "It's $420,000! The purchasing agent gave it to me in our planning meeting yesterday."

"Fantastic," shouted Mercedes. "We'll have our claim ready before the day is over!"

To file a claim with the insurance company, Operex Products must determine the amount of cost in its inventories as of the date of the accident. You may assume that all of the materials used in production during the year were direct materials.

Required:

Determine the amount of cost in the raw materials, work in process, and finished goods inventories as of the date of the accident. (Hint: One way to proceed would be to reconstruct the various schedules and statements that would have been affected by the company's inventory accounts during the year.)

RESEARCH AND APPLICATION 2-26 [LO1, LO2, LO5, LO6]

The questions in this exercise are based on Dell, Inc. To answer the questions, you will need to download Dell's Form 10-K for the fiscal year ended January 28, 2005 by going to www.sec.gov/edgar/searchedgar/companysearch.html. Input CIK code 826083 and hit enter. In the gray box on the right-hand side of your computer screen define the scope of your search by inputting 10-K and then pressing enter. Select the 10-K with a filing date of March 8, 2005. You do not need to print this document in order to answer the questions.

Required:

1. What is Dell's strategy for success in the marketplace? Does the company rely primarily on a customer intimacy, operational excellence, or product leadership customer value proposition? What evidence supports your conclusion?
2. What business risks does Dell face that may threaten its ability to satisfy stockholder expectations? What are some examples of control activities that the company could use to reduce these risks? (Hint: Focus on pages 7–10 of the 10-K.)
3. How has the Sarbanes-Oxley Act of 2002 explicitly affected the disclosures contained in Dell's 10-K report? (Hint: Focus on pages 34–35, 59, and 76–78.)
4. Is Dell a merchandiser or a manufacturer? What information contained in the 10-K supports your answer?
5. What are some examples of direct and indirect inventoriable costs for Dell? Why has Dell's gross margin (in dollars) steadily increased from 2003 to 2005, yet the gross margin as a percent of net revenue has only increased slightly?
6. What is the inventory balance on Dell's January 28, 2005 balance sheet? Why is the inventory balance so small compared to the other current asset balances? What competitive advantage does Dell derive from its low inventory levels? Page 27 of Dell's 10-K reports a figure called the cash conversion cycle. The cash conversion cycle for Dell has consistently been negative. Is this a good sign for Dell or a bad sign? Why?
7. Describe some of the various types of operating expenses incurred by Dell. Why are these expenses treated as period costs?
8. List four different cost objects for Dell. For each cost object, mention one example of a direct cost and an indirect cost.

Chapter

3

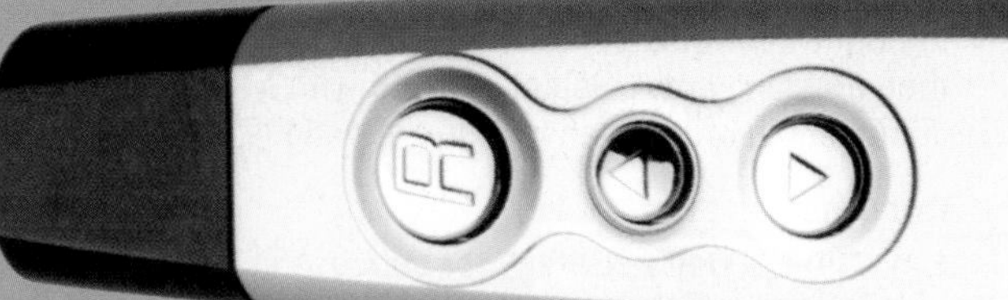

Learning Objectives

After studying Chapter 3, you should be able to:

LO1 Distinguish between process costing and job-order costing and identify companies that would use each costing method.

LO2 Identify the documents used in a job-order costing system.

LO3 Compute predetermined overhead rates and explain why estimated overhead costs (rather than actual overhead costs) are used in the costing process.

LO4 Apply overhead cost to jobs using a predetermined overhead rate.

LO5 Determine underapplied or overapplied overhead.

LO6 Use the direct method to determine cost of goods sold.

LO7 Use the indirect method to determine cost of goods sold.

LO8 (Appendix 3A) Understand the implications of basing the predetermined overhead rate on activity at capacity rather than on estimated activity for the period.

LP 3

Systems Design: Job-Order Costing

Two College Students Succeeding as Entrepreneurs

BUSINESS FOCUS

When the University of Dayton athletic department needed 2,000 customized T-shirts to give away at its first home basketball game of the year, it chose University Tees to provide the shirts. A larger competitor could have been chosen, but University Tees won the order because of its fast customer response time, low price, and high quality.

University Tees is a small business that was started in February 2003 by two Miami University seniors—Joe Haddad and Nick Dadas (see the company's website at www.universitytees.com). The company creates the artwork for customized T-shirts and then relies on carefully chosen suppliers to manufacture the product.

Accurately calculating the cost of each potential customer order is critically important to University Tees because the company needs to be sure that the price exceeds the cost associated with satisfying the order. The costs include the cost of the T-shirts themselves, printing costs (which vary depending on the quantity of shirts produced and the number of colors printed per shirt), silk screen costs (which also vary depending on the number of colors included in a design), shipping costs, and the artwork needed to create a design. The company also takes into account its competitors' pricing strategies when developing its own price quotes. ■

Source: Conversation with Joe Haddad, cofounder of University Tees.

As discussed in Chapter 2, product costing is the process of assigning costs to the products and services provided by a company. An understanding of this costing process is vital to managers, because the way in which a product or service is costed can have a substantial impact on reported profits, as well as on key management decisions.

The essential purpose of any managerial costing system should be to provide cost data to help managers plan, control, direct, and make decisions. Nevertheless, external financial reporting and tax reporting requirements often heavily influence how costs are accumulated and summarized on managerial reports. This is true of product costing.

In this chapter, we use *absorption costing* to determine product costs. This method was also used in Chapter 2. In **absorption costing,** all manufacturing costs, both fixed and variable, are assigned to units of product—units are said to *fully absorb manufacturing costs*. Later, in Chapter 6, we look at an alternative to absorption costing known as *variable costing*. Chapter 6 also discusses the strengths and weaknesses of the two approaches.

Most countries—including the United States—require some form of absorption costing for both external financial reporting and tax reporting. In addition, the vast majority of companies throughout the world also use absorption costing for managerial accounting purposes. Since absorption costing is the most common approach to product costing, we discuss it first and then deal with alternatives in subsequent chapters.

Process and Job-Order Costing

LEARNING OBJECTIVE 1
Distinguish between process costing and job-order costing and identify companies that would use each costing method.

In computing the cost of a product or a service, managers are faced with a difficult problem. Many costs (such as rent) do not change much from month to month, whereas production may change frequently, with production going up in one month and then down in another. In addition to variations in the level of production, several different products or services may be produced in a given period in the same facility. Under these conditions, how is it possible to accurately determine the cost of a product or service? In practice, assigning costs to products and services involves averaging across time and across products. The way in which this averaging is carried out depends heavily on the type of production process. Two costing systems are commonly used in manufacturing and in many service companies; these two systems are known as *process costing* and *job-order costing.*

Process Costing

A **process costing system** is used in situations where the company produces many units of a single product for long periods. Examples include producing paper at Weyerhaeuser, refining aluminum ingots at Reynolds Aluminum, mixing and bottling beverages at Coca-Cola, and making wieners at Oscar Meyer. All of these industries are characterized by an essentially homogeneous product that flows through the production process on a continuous basis.

Process costing systems accumulate costs in a particular operation or department for an entire period (month, quarter, year) and then divide this total cost by the number of units produced during the period. The basic formula for process costing is:

$$\text{Unit product cost} = \frac{\text{Total manufacturing cost}}{\text{Total units produced}}$$

Since one unit of product is indistinguishable from any other unit of product, each unit produced during the period is assigned the same average cost. This costing technique results in a broad, average unit cost figure that applies to homogeneous units flowing in a continuous stream out of the production process.

Job-Order Costing

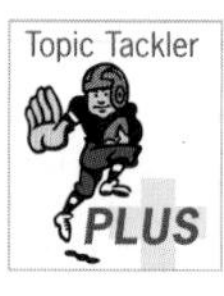

3–1

A **job-order costing system** is used in situations where many *different* products are produced each period. For example, a Levi Strauss clothing factory would typically make many different types of jeans for both men and women during a month. A particular order might consist of 1,000 stonewashed men's blue denim jeans, style number A312. This order of 1,000 jeans is called a *batch* or a *job.* In a job-order costing system, costs are traced and allocated to jobs and then the costs of the job are divided by the number of units in the job to arrive at an average cost per unit.

Other examples of situations where job-order costing would be used include large-scale construction projects managed by Bechtel International, commercial aircraft produced by Boeing, greeting cards designed and printed by Hallmark, and airline meals prepared by LSG SkyChefs. All of these examples are characterized by diverse outputs. Each Bechtel project is unique and different from every other—the company may be simultaneously constructing a dam in Zaire and a bridge in Indonesia. Likewise, each airline orders a different type of meal from LSG SkyChefs' catering service.

Job-order costing is also used extensively in service industries. Hospitals, law firms, movie studios, accounting firms, advertising agencies, and repair shops, for example, all use a variation of job-order costing to accumulate costs for accounting and billing purposes. Although the detailed example of job-order costing provided in the following section deals with a manufacturing company, the same basic concepts and procedures are used by many service organizations.

The record-keeping and cost assignment problems are more complex when a company sells many different products and services than when it has only a single product. Since the products are different, the costs are typically different. Consequently, cost records must be maintained for each distinct product or job. For example, an attorney in a large criminal law practice would ordinarily keep separate records of the costs of advising and defending each client. And the Levi Strauss factory mentioned above would keep separate track of the costs of filling orders for particular styles of jeans. Thus, a job-order costing system requires more effort than a process costing system. Nevertheless, job-order costing is used by more than half the manufacturers in the United States.

Job-Order Costing—An Overview

LEARNING OBJECTIVE 2
Identify the documents used in a job-order costing system.

To introduce job-order costing, we will follow a specific job as it progresses through the manufacturing process. This job consists of two experimental couplings that Yost Precision Machining has agreed to produce for Loops Unlimited, a manufacturer of roller coasters. Couplings connect the cars on the roller coaster and are a critical component in the performance and safety of the ride. Before we begin our discussion, recall from the previous chapter that companies generally classify manufacturing costs into three broad categories: (1) direct materials, (2) direct labor, and (3) manufacturing overhead. As we study the operation of a job-order costing system, we will see how each of these three types of costs is assigned to jobs.

Video 3–1

MANAGERIAL ACCOUNTING IN ACTION
The Issue

Yost Precision Machining is a small company in Michigan that specializes in fabricating precision metal parts that are used in a variety of applications ranging from deep-sea exploration vehicles to the inertial triggers in automobile air bags. The company's top managers gather every morning at 8:00 A.M. in the company's conference room for the daily planning meeting. Attending the meeting this morning are: Jean Yost, the company's president; David Cheung, the marketing manager; Debbie Turner, the production manager; and Marcus White, the company controller. The president opened the meeting:

Jean: The production schedule indicates we'll be starting Job 2B47 today. Isn't that the special order for experimental couplings, David?

David: That's right. That's the order from Loops Unlimited for two couplings for their new roller coaster ride for Magic Mountain.

Debbie: Why only two couplings? Don't they need a coupling for every car?

David: Yes. But this is a completely new roller coaster. The cars will go faster and will be subjected to more twists, turns, drops, and loops than on any other existing roller coaster. To hold up under these stresses, Loops Unlimited's engineers had to completely redesign the cars and couplings. They want to thoroughly test the design before proceeding to large-scale production. So they want us to make just two of these new couplings for testing purposes. If the design works, then we'll have the inside track on the order to supply couplings for the whole ride.

Jean: We agreed to take on this initial order at our cost just to get our foot in the door. Marcus, will there be any problem documenting our cost so we can get paid?

Marcus: No problem. The contract with Loops stipulates that they will pay us an amount equal to our cost of goods sold. With our job-order costing system, I can tell you that number on the day the job is completed.

Jean: Good. Is there anything else we should discuss about this job at this time? No? Well then let's move on to the next item of business.

Measuring Direct Materials Cost

Yost Precision Machining will require four G7 Connectors and two M46 Housings to make the two experimental couplings for Loops Unlimited. If this were a standard product, it already would have a *bill of materials*. A **bill of materials** is a document that lists the type and quantity of each type of direct material needed to complete a unit of product. In this case, there is no established bill of materials, so Yost's production staff determined the materials requirements from the blueprints submitted by the customer. Each coupling requires two connectors and one housing, so to make two couplings, four connectors and two housings are required.

A *production order* is issued when an agreement has been reached with the customer concerning the quantities, prices, and shipment date for the order. The Production Department then prepares a *materials requisition form* similar to the form in Exhibit 3–1. The **materials requisition form** is a detailed source document that specifies the type and quantity of materials to be drawn from the storeroom and identifies the job that will be charged for the cost of the materials. The form is used to control the flow of materials into production and also for making entries in the accounting records.

The Yost Precision Machining materials requisition form in Exhibit 3–1 shows that the company's Milling Department has requisitioned two M46 Housings and four G7 Connectors for the Loops Unlimited job, which has been designated as Job 2B47. A production worker presents the completed form to the storeroom clerk who then issues the specified

EXHIBIT 3–1
Materials Requisition Form

Materials Requistion Number 14873 Date March 2
Job Number to Be Charged 2B47
Department Milling

Description	Quantity	Unit Cost	Total Cost
M46 Housing	2	$124	$248
G7 Connector	4	$103	412
			$660

Authorized Signature *Bill White*

EXHIBIT 3–2
Job Cost Sheet

JOB COST SHEET

Job Number 2B47 | Date Initiated March 2
Date Completed
Department Milling | Units Completed
Item Special order coupling
For Stock

Direct Materials		Direct Labor			Manufacturing Overhead		
Req. No.	Amount	Ticket	Hours	Amount	Hours	Rate	Amount
14873	$660	843	5	$45			

Cost Summary	
Direct Materials	$
Direct Labor	$
Manufacturing Overhead	$
Total Cost	$
Unit Product Cost	$

Units Shipped		
Date	Number	Balance

materials to the worker. The storeroom clerk is not allowed to release materials without a completed and properly authorized materials requisition form.

Job Cost Sheet

After being notified that the production order has been issued, the Accounting Department prepares a *job cost sheet* like the one presented in Exhibit 3–2. A **job cost sheet** is a form prepared for a job that records the materials, labor, and manufacturing overhead costs charged to that job.

After direct materials are issued, the Accounting Department records their costs directly on the job cost sheet. Note from Exhibit 3–2, for example, that the $660 cost for direct materials shown earlier on the materials requisition form has been charged to Job 2B47 on its job cost sheet. The requisition number 14873 from the materials requisition form is also recorded on the job cost sheet to make it easier to identify the source document for the direct materials charge.

Measuring Direct Labor Cost

Direct labor cost is handled similarly to direct materials cost. Direct labor consists of labor charges that are easily traced to a particular job. Labor charges that cannot be easily traced directly to any job are treated as part of manufacturing overhead. As discussed in the previous chapter, this latter category of labor costs is called *indirect labor* and includes tasks such as maintenance, supervision, and cleanup.

Workers use *time tickets* to record the time they spend on each job and task. A completed **time ticket** is an hour-by-hour summary of the employee's activities throughout the day. An example of an employee time ticket is shown in Exhibit 3–3. When working on a specific job, the employee enters the job number on the time ticket and notes the amount of time spent on

EXHIBIT 3–3
Employee Time Ticket

Time Ticket No. 843 | Date March 3
Employee Mary Holden | Station 4

Started	Ended	Time Completed	Rate	Amount	Job Number
7:00	12:00	5.0	$9	$45	2B47
12:30	2:30	2.0	9	18	2B50
2:30	3:30	1.0	9	9	Maintenance
Totals		8.0		$72	

Supervisor R. W. Pace

that job. When not assigned to a particular job, the employee records the nature of the indirect labor task (such as cleanup and maintenance) and the amount of time spent on the task.

At the end of the day, the time tickets are gathered and the Accounting Department enters the direct labor-hours and costs on individual job cost sheets. (See Exhibit 3–2 for an example of how direct labor costs are entered on the job cost sheet.)

The system we have just described is a manual method for recording and posting labor costs. Today many companies rely on computerized systems and no longer record labor time by hand on sheets of paper. One computerized approach uses bar codes to capture data. Each employee and each job has a unique bar code. When beginning work on a job, the employee scans three bar codes using a handheld device much like the bar code readers at grocery store checkout stands. The first bar code indicates that a job is being started; the second is the unique bar code on the employee's identity badge; and the third is the unique bar code of the job itself. This information is fed automatically via an electronic network to a computer that notes the time and records all of the data. When the task is completed, the employee scans a bar code indicating the task is complete, the bar code on his or her identity badge, and the bar code attached to the job. This information is relayed to the computer that again notes the time, and a time ticket is automatically prepared. Since all of the source data is already in computer files, the labor costs can be automatically posted to job cost sheets (or their electronic equivalents). Computers, coupled with technology such as bar codes, can eliminate much of the drudgery involved in routine bookkeeping activities while at the same time increasing timeliness and accuracy.

IN BUSINESS

BUCKING THE TREND: USING PEOPLE INSTEAD OF MACHINES

For decades overhead costs have been going up and labor costs have been going down as companies have replaced people with machines. However, at the French automaker Renault, the exact opposite has been happening with its new, no-frills vehicle called the Logan. The Logan was intentionally stripped of costly design elements and unnecessary technology so that the car could be sold for $6,000 in emerging Eastern European markets. The car's simplified design enables Renault's manufacturing plant in Romania to assemble the car almost entirely with people instead of robots. The monthly pay for a line worker at Renault's Romanian plant is $324 versus an average of more than $4,700 per worker in Western European countries. Thanks in part to low-cost labor, Logan's production costs are estimated to be just $1,089 per unit.

The Logan is finding buyers not only in emerging markets but also in more advanced Western European nations where customers have been clamoring for the car. Renault expects sales for the Logan to climb to one million vehicles by 2010—adding $341 million to its profits.

Source: Gail Edmondson and Constance Faivre d'Arcier, "Got 5,000 Euros? Need a New Car?" *BusinessWeek*, July 4, 2005, p. 49.

Application of Manufacturing Overhead

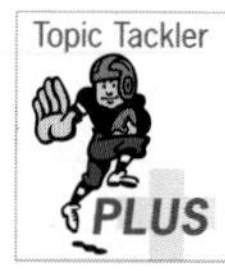

3–2

LEARNING OBJECTIVE 3
Compute predetermined overhead rates and explain why estimated overhead costs (rather than actual overhead costs) are used in the costing process.

Recall that product costs include manufacturing overhead as well as direct materials and direct labor. Therefore, manufacturing overhead also needs to be recorded on the job cost sheet. However, assigning manufacturing overhead to a specific job involves some difficulties. There are three reasons for this:

1. Manufacturing overhead is an *indirect cost.* This means that it is either impossible or difficult to trace these costs to a particular product or job.
2. Manufacturing overhead consists of many different items ranging from the grease used in machines to the annual salary of the production manager.
3. Even though output may fluctuate due to seasonal or other factors, total manufacturing overhead costs tend to remain relatively constant due to the presence of fixed costs.

Given these problems, overhead costs are usually assigned to products using an allocation process. This allocation of overhead costs is accomplished by selecting an *allocation base* that is common to all of the company's products and services. An **allocation base** is a measure such as direct labor-hours (DLH) or machine-hours (MH) that is used to assign overhead costs to products and services.

The most widely used allocation bases are direct labor-hours and direct labor cost, with machine-hours and even units of product (where a company has only a single product) also used to some extent.

Manufacturing overhead is commonly applied to products using *a predetermined overhead rate*. The **predetermined overhead rate** is computed by dividing the total estimated manufacturing overhead cost for the period by the estimated total amount of the allocation base as follows:

$$\text{Predetermined overhead rate} = \frac{\text{Estimated total manufacturing overhead cost}}{\text{Estimated total amount of the allocation base}}$$

We will have more to say in later chapters concerning how the predetermined overhead rate is computed. At this point, it is sufficient to note that the first step in computing the predetermined overhead rate is to estimate the level of production for the period. The second step is to estimate the total amount of the allocation base in the denominator that would be required for that level of production. The third step is to estimate the total manufacturing overhead cost in the numerator that would be incurred for the estimated amount of the allocation base. Roughly speaking, the greater the expected production, the greater the estimated amount of the allocation base and the greater the expected total manufacturing overhead cost, although the relation between these three estimates is not usually strictly proportional.

Note that the predetermined overhead rate is based on estimates rather than actual results. This is because the *predetermined* overhead rate is computed *before* the period begins and is used to *apply* overhead cost to jobs throughout the period. The process of assigning overhead cost to jobs is called **overhead application.** The formula for determining the amount of overhead cost to apply to a particular job is:

$$\begin{matrix}\text{Overhead applied to} \\ \text{a particular job}\end{matrix} = \begin{matrix}\text{Predetermined} \\ \text{overhead rate}\end{matrix} \times \begin{matrix}\text{Amount of the allocation} \\ \text{base incurred by the job}\end{matrix}$$

For example, if the predetermined overhead rate is \$8 per direct labor-hour, then \$8 of overhead cost is *applied* to a job for each direct labor-hour incurred by the job. When the allocation base is direct labor-hours, the formula becomes:

$$\begin{matrix}\text{Overhead applied to} \\ \text{a particular job}\end{matrix} = \begin{matrix}\text{Predetermined} \\ \text{overhead rate}\end{matrix} \times \begin{matrix}\text{Actual direct labor-hours} \\ \text{charged to the job}\end{matrix}$$

LEARNING OBJECTIVE 4
Apply overhead cost to jobs using a predetermined overhead rate.

Using the Predetermined Overhead Rate

To illustrate the steps involved in computing and using a predetermined overhead rate, let's return to Yost Precision Machining. The company has estimated its total manufacturing overhead costs will be \$320,000 for the year and its total direct labor-hours will be 40,000. Its predetermined overhead rate for the year would be $8 per direct labor-hour, as shown below:

$$\text{Predetermined overhead rate} = \frac{\text{Estimated total manufacturing overhead cost}}{\text{Estimated total amount of the allocation base}}$$

$$= \frac{\$320{,}000}{40{,}000 \text{ direct labor-hours}}$$

$$= \$8 \text{ per direct labor-hour}$$

The job cost sheet in Exhibit 3–4 indicates that 27 direct labor-hours (i.e., DLHs) were charged to Job 2B47. Therefore, a total of $216 of manufacturing overhead cost would be applied to the job:

$$\begin{array}{c}\text{Overhead applied to}\\ \text{Job 2B47}\end{array} = \begin{array}{c}\text{Predetermined}\\ \text{overhead rate}\end{array} \times \begin{array}{c}\text{Actual direct labor-hours}\\ \text{charged to Job 2B47}\end{array}$$

$$= \$8 \text{ per DLH} \times 27 \text{ DLHs}$$

$$= \$216 \text{ of overhead applied to Job 2B47}$$

This amount of overhead has been entered on the job cost sheet in Exhibit 3–4. Note that this is *not* the actual amount of overhead caused by the job. Actual overhead costs are *not* assigned to jobs—if that could be done, the costs would be direct costs, not overhead. The overhead assigned to the job is simply a share of the total overhead that was estimated at the beginning of the year. A **normal cost system,** which we have been describing, applies overhead to jobs by multiplying a predetermined overhead rate by the actual amount of the allocation base incurred by the jobs.

Overhead may be applied as direct labor-hours are charged to jobs, or all of the overhead can be applied at once when the job is completed. The choice is up to the company. However, if a job is not completed at the end of the accounting period, overhead should be applied to that job so as to value work in process inventory.

The Need for a Predetermined Rate

Instead of using a predetermined rate, a company could wait until the end of the accounting period to compute an actual overhead rate based on the *actual* total manufacturing costs and the *actual* total units in the allocation base for the period. However, managers cite several reasons for using predetermined overhead rates instead of actual overhead rates:

1. They would like to know the accounting system's valuation of completed jobs *before* the end of the accounting period. Suppose, for example, that Yost Precision Machining waits until the end of the year to compute its overhead rate. Then the cost of goods sold for Job 2B47 would not be known until the close of the year, even though the job was completed and shipped to the customer in March. This problem can be reduced by computing the actual overhead rate more frequently, but that immediately leads to another problem as discussed below.

2. If actual overhead rates are computed frequently, seasonal factors in overhead costs or in the allocation base can produce fluctuations in the overhead rates. For example, the costs of heating and cooling a production facility in Illinois will be highest in the winter and summer months and lowest in the spring and fall. If an overhead rate were computed each month or each quarter, the predetermined overhead rate would go up in the winter and summer and down in the spring and fall. Two identical jobs, one completed in the winter and one completed in the spring, would be assigned different costs if the overhead rate were computed on a monthly or quarterly basis. Managers generally feel that such fluctuations in overhead rates and costs serve no useful purpose and are misleading.

3. The use of a predetermined overhead rate simplifies record keeping. To determine the overhead cost to apply to a job, the accounting staff at Yost Precision Machining simply

EXHIBIT 3–4
A Completed Job Cost Sheet

JOB COST SHEET

Job Number 2B47 — Date Initiated March 2
Date Completed March 8
Department Milling
Item Special order coupling — Units Completed 2
For Stock

Direct Materials		Direct Labor			Manufacturing Overhead		
Req. No.	Amount	Ticket	Hours	Amount	Hours	Rate	Amount
14873	$ 660	843	5	$ 45	27	$8/DLH	$216
14875	506	846	8	60			
14912	238	850	4	21			
	$1,404	851	10	54			
			27	$180			

Cost Summary		Units Shipped		
		Date	Number	Balance
Direct Materials	$1,404			
Direct Labor	$ 180	March 8	—	2
Manufacturing Overhead	$ 216			
Total Product Cost	$1,800			
Unit Product Cost	$ 900*			

*$1,800 ÷ 2 units = $900 per unit.

multiplies the direct labor-hours recorded for the job by the predetermined overhead rate of $8 per direct labor-hour.

For these reasons, most companies use predetermined overhead rates rather than actual overhead rates in their cost accounting systems.

Choice of an Allocation Base for Overhead Cost

Ideally, the allocation base used in the predetermined overhead rate should *drive* the overhead cost. A **cost driver** is a factor, such as machine-hours, beds occupied, computer time, or flight-hours, that causes overhead costs. If a base is used to compute overhead rates that does not "drive" overhead costs, then the result will be inaccurate overhead rates and distorted product costs. For example, if direct labor-hours is used to allocate overhead, but in reality overhead has little to do with direct labor-hours, then products with high direct labor-hour requirements will be overcosted.

Most companies use direct labor-hours or direct labor cost as the allocation base for manufacturing overhead. However, as discussed in earlier chapters, major shifts are taking place in the structure of costs. In the past, direct labor accounted for up to 60% of the cost of many products, with overhead cost making up only a portion of the remainder. This situation has been changing for two reasons. First, sophisticated automated equipment has taken over functions that used to be performed by direct labor workers. Since the costs of acquiring and maintaining such equipment are classified as overhead, this increases overhead while decreasing direct labor. Second, products are becoming more sophisticated and complex and are changed more frequently. This increases the need for highly skilled indirect workers such as engineers. As a result of these two trends, direct labor is decreasing relative to overhead as a component of product costs.

In companies where direct labor and overhead costs have been moving in opposite directions, it would be difficult to argue that direct labor "drives" overhead costs. Accordingly, managers in some companies use *activity-based costing* principles to redesign their cost accounting systems. Activity-based costing is designed to more accurately reflect the demands that products, customers, and other cost objects make on overhead resources. The activity-based approach is discussed in more detail in Chapter 7.

We hasten to add that although direct labor may not be an appropriate allocation base in some industries, in others it continues to be a significant driver of manufacturing overhead. Indeed, most manufacturing companies in the United States continue to use direct labor as the primary or secondary allocation base for manufacturing overhead. The key point is that the allocation base used by the company should really drive, or cause, overhead costs, and direct labor is not always an appropriate allocation base.

IN BUSINESS

WAIST MANAGEMENT

Research from the University of Michigan suggests that a company's health-care costs are driven to a significant extent by the weight of its employees. Workers who are overweight can cost as much as $1,500 more per year to insure than other workers. So what is a company to do? Park Place Entertainment, a casino operator with more than 7,000 employees, decided to attack the problem by holding a weight-loss contest. Over two years, the company's workforce dropped 20 tons of weight. After the contest, 12 diabetics were able to stop using medications that cost $13,300 per year per employee. Additionally, the company believes that its contest caused a decline in absenteeism and an increase in productivity.

Source: Jill Hecht Maxwell, "Worker Waist Management," *Inc.*, August 2004, p. 32; Jessi Hempel, "Dieting for Dollars," *BusinessWeek*, November 3, 2003, p. 10.

IN BUSINESS

UNDERSTANDING COST DRIVERS CAN BE TRICKY BUSINESS

Conventional wisdom in the health-care industry was that costs could be reduced by reducing a patient's length of stay in a hospital. It seemed logical that reducing the number of days that a patient spends in the hospital should reduce the cost of treating that patient. However, researchers John Evans, Yuhchang Hwang, and Nandu Nagarajan provide evidence within one hospital that when doctors were motivated to reduce length of stay, it did not reduce costs. Doctors compensated for a reduction in length of stay by increasing the number of procedures performed per patient per day. Thus, any potential savings from reducing one cost driver—length of stay—were offset by cost increases caused by increasing another cost driver—number of procedures performed per patient per day.

Source: John H. Evans, Yuhchang Hwang, and Nandu J. Nagarajan, "Management Control and Hospital Cost Reduction: Additional Evidence," *Journal of Accounting and Public Policy*, Spring 2001, pp. 73–88.

Computation of Unit Costs

With the application of Yost Precision Machining's $216 of manufacturing overhead to the job cost sheet in Exhibit 3–4, the job cost sheet is complete except for two final steps. First, the totals for direct materials, direct labor, and manufacturing overhead are transferred to the Cost Summary section of the job cost sheet and added together to obtain the total cost for the job. Then the total product cost ($1,800) is divided by the number of units (2) to obtain the unit product cost ($900). As indicated earlier, *this unit product cost is an average cost and should not be interpreted as the cost that would actually be incurred if another unit were produced.* Much of the actual overhead costs would not change if another unit were produced, so the incremental cost of an additional unit is something less than the average unit cost of $900.

The completed job cost sheet will serve as the basis for valuing unsold units in ending inventory and for determining cost of goods sold.

Summary of Document Flows

The sequence of events discussed above is summarized in Exhibit 3–5. A careful study of the flow of documents in this exhibit provides a good overview of the overall operation of a job-order costing system.

MANAGERIAL ACCOUNTING IN ACTION
The Wrap-up

In the 8:00 A.M. daily planning meeting on March 9, Jean Yost, the president of Yost Precision Machining, once again drew attention to Job 2B47, the experimental couplings:

Jean: I see Job 2B47 is completed. Let's get those couplings shipped immediately to Loops Unlimited so they can get their testing program under way. Marcus, how much are we going to bill Loops for those two units?

Marcus: Because we agreed to sell the experimental couplings at cost, we will be charging Loops Unlimited just $900 a unit.

Jean: Fine. Let's hope the couplings work out and we make some money on the big order later.

An Extended Example of Job-Order Costing

We are now ready to take a more detailed look at the flow of costs in job-order costing. To illustrate, let's consider activity for the month of April for Rand Company, a producer of gold and silver commemorative medallions. At the beginning of the month, Rand Company had no finished goods inventory and one job in process—Job A, a special minting of 1,000 gold medallions commemorating the invention of motion pictures. Some work had been completed on this job prior to April; therefore, a total of $30,000 in manufacturing costs had already been recorded on Job A's cost sheet. This job will be completed in April. In addition, Job B, an order for 10,000 silver medallions commemorating the fall of the Berlin Wall, will be started in April and completed in a subsequent month.

In this example, we will track the flow of Rand Company's raw materials, labor, and overhead costs for April and prepare an income statement for the month.

Direct and Indirect Materials

During April, $52,000 in raw materials were requisitioned from the storeroom for use in production. These raw materials included $28,000 of direct materials for Job A, $22,000 of direct materials for Job B, and $2,000 of indirect materials. As shown in Exhibit 3–6, these costs are recorded on the appropriate job cost sheets and in an account we will call Manufacturing Overhead Incurred. Specifically, $28,000 of direct materials is charged to Job A's cost sheet and $22,000 is charged to Job B's cost sheet. Note that the $2,000 of indirect materials has *not* been assigned to either of the two jobs—instead, it is charged to the account we call Manufacturing Overhead Incurred. We will be charging all of the actual manufacturing overhead costs that are incurred to this account.

Notice from Exhibit 3–6 that the job cost sheet for Job A contains a beginning balance of $30,000. We stated earlier that this balance represents the cost of work done on this job prior to April. This cost would be classified on the company's balance sheet as Work in Process inventory at the beginning of April.

EXHIBIT 3–5
The Flow of Documents in a Job-Order Costing System

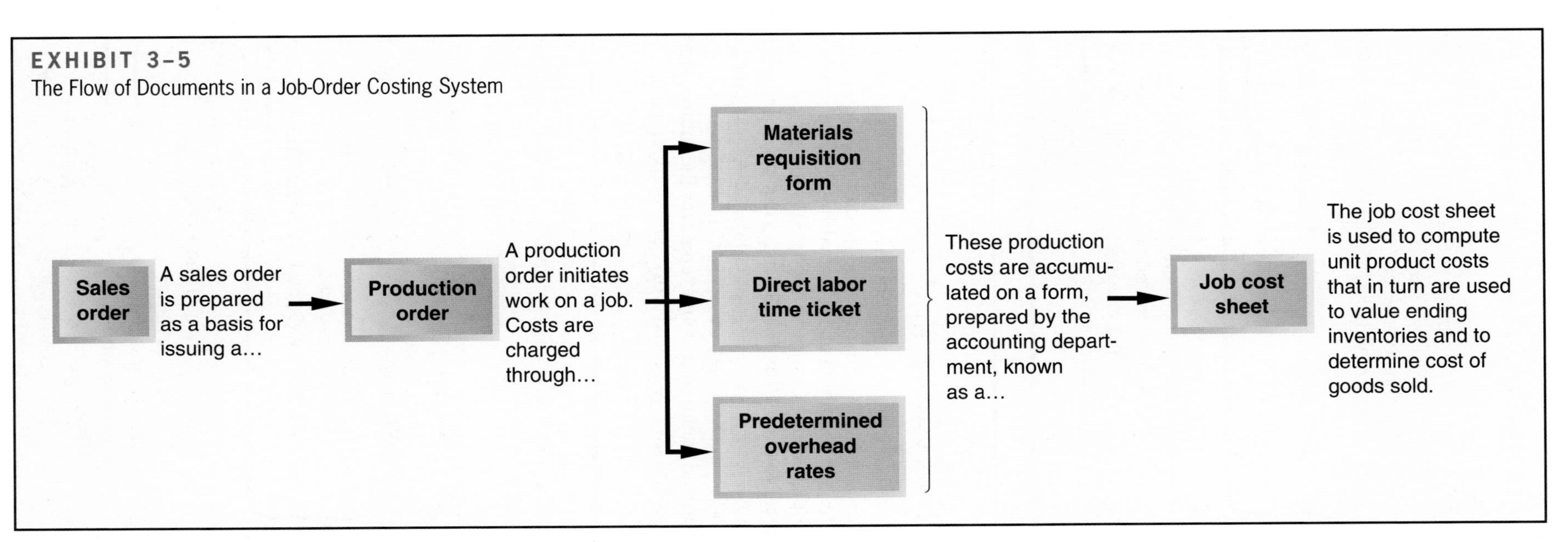

EXHIBIT 3–6
Raw Materials Cost Flows

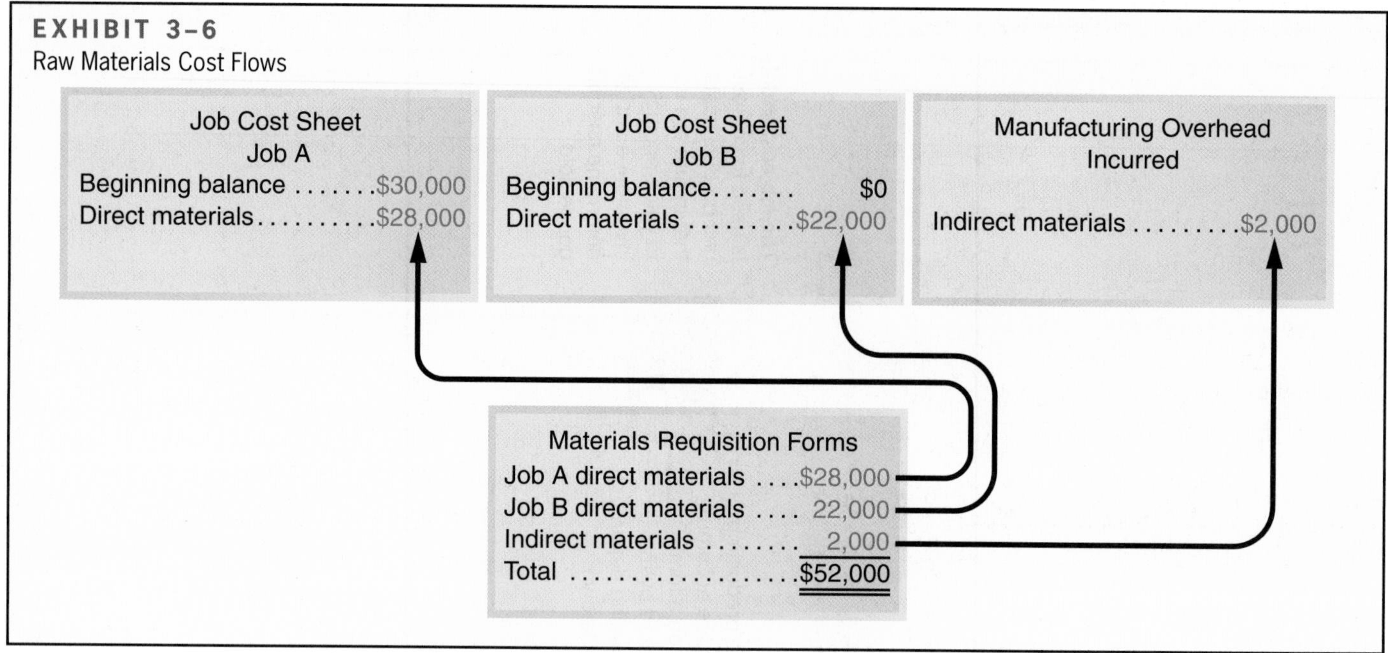

Labor Cost

As work is performed each day, employee time tickets are filled out by workers, collected, and forwarded to the Accounting Department. In the Accounting Department, wages are computed and the resulting costs are classified as either direct or indirect labor. In April, Rand Company incurred $40,000 of direct labor cost for Job A, $20,000 of direct labor cost for Job B, and $15,000 of indirect labor cost. Exhibit 3–7 shows that during April, $40,000 of direct labor cost was charged to Job A and $20,000 to Job B on their job cost sheets. The $15,000 of indirect labor costs charged to the Manufacturing Overhead Incurred account represent the indirect labor costs incurred during April, such as supervision, janitorial work, and maintenance.

EXHIBIT 3–7
Labor Cost Flows

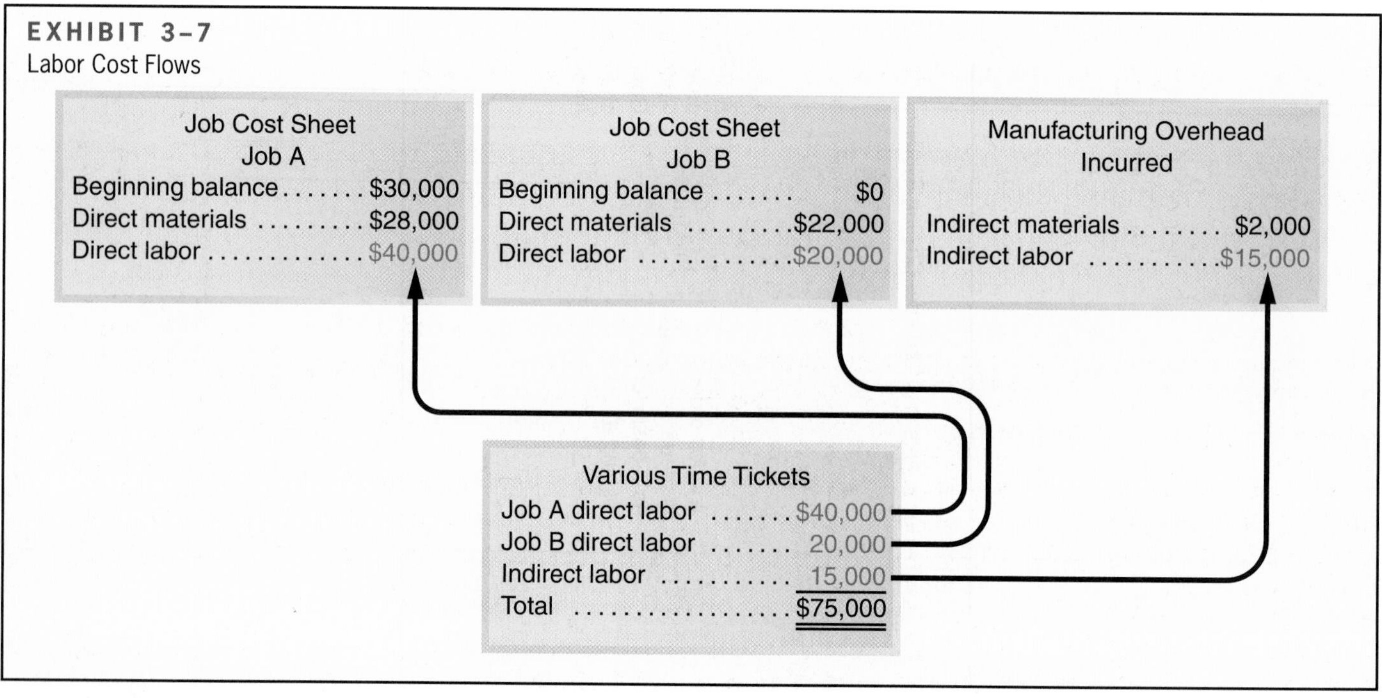

EXHIBIT 3–8
Manufacturing Overhead Cost Flows

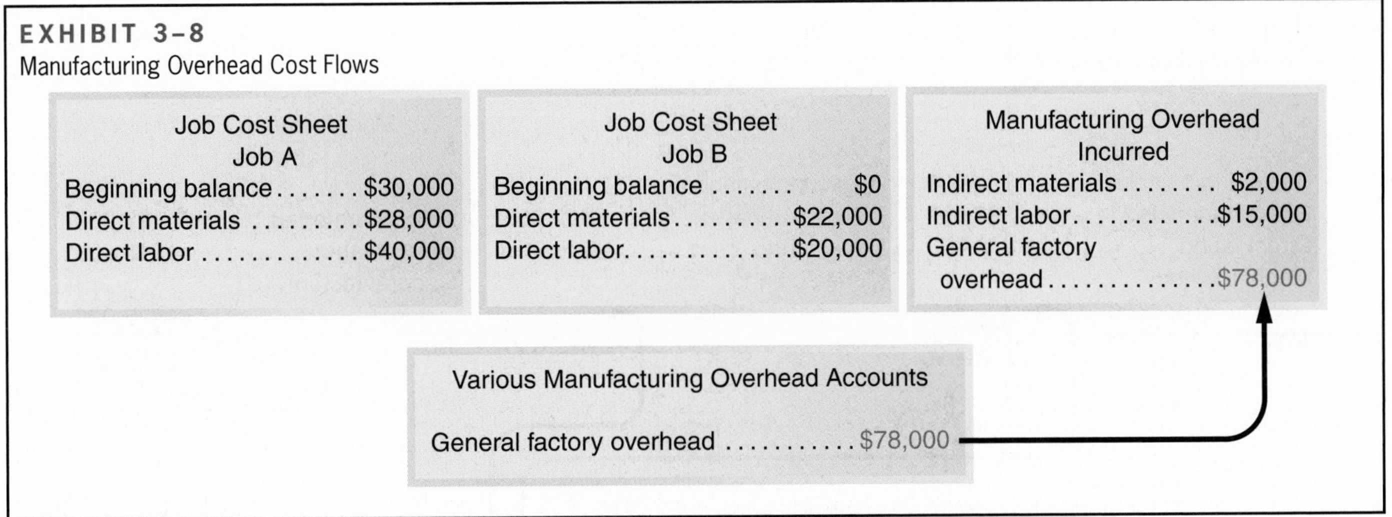

Manufacturing Overhead Cost

Recall that all manufacturing costs other than direct materials and direct labor are classified as manufacturing overhead costs. These costs are charged directly to the Manufacturing Overhead Incurred account as they are incurred. To illustrate, assume that Rand Company incurred the following general factory overhead costs during April:

Factory utilities (heat, water, and power)	$21,000
Rent on factory equipment..................	16,000
Factory property taxes	13,000
Factory insurance.........................	7,000
Manufacturing depreciation	18,000
Miscellaneous factory overhead costs.........	3,000
Total general factory overhead	$78,000

Exhibit 3–8 shows how these costs are recorded.

Applying Manufacturing Overhead

Since actual manufacturing costs are charged to the Manufacturing Overhead Incurred account rather than to the job cost sheets, how are manufacturing overhead costs assigned to jobs? The answer is, by means of the predetermined overhead rate. Recall from our discussion earlier in the chapter that a predetermined overhead rate is established at the beginning of each year. The rate is calculated by dividing the estimated total manufacturing overhead cost for the year by the estimated amount of the allocation base (measured in machine-hours, direct labor-hours, or some other base). The predetermined overhead rate is then used to apply overhead costs to jobs. For example, if direct labor-hours is the allocation base, overhead cost is applied to each job by multiplying the predetermined overhead rate by the number of direct labor-hours charged to the job. To illustrate, assume that Rand Company's predetermined overhead rate is $6 per machine-hour. Also assume that during April, 10,000 machine-hours were worked on Job A and 5,000 machine-hours were worked on Job B. Thus, $60,000 in manufacturing overhead cost ($6 per machine-hour × 10,000 machine-hours) would be applied to Job A and $30,000 in manufacturing overhead cost ($6 per machine-hour × 5,000 machine-hours) would be applied to Job B. Exhibit 3–9 shows how these costs are applied to jobs.

EXHIBIT 3–9
Applying Manufacturing Overhead to Jobs

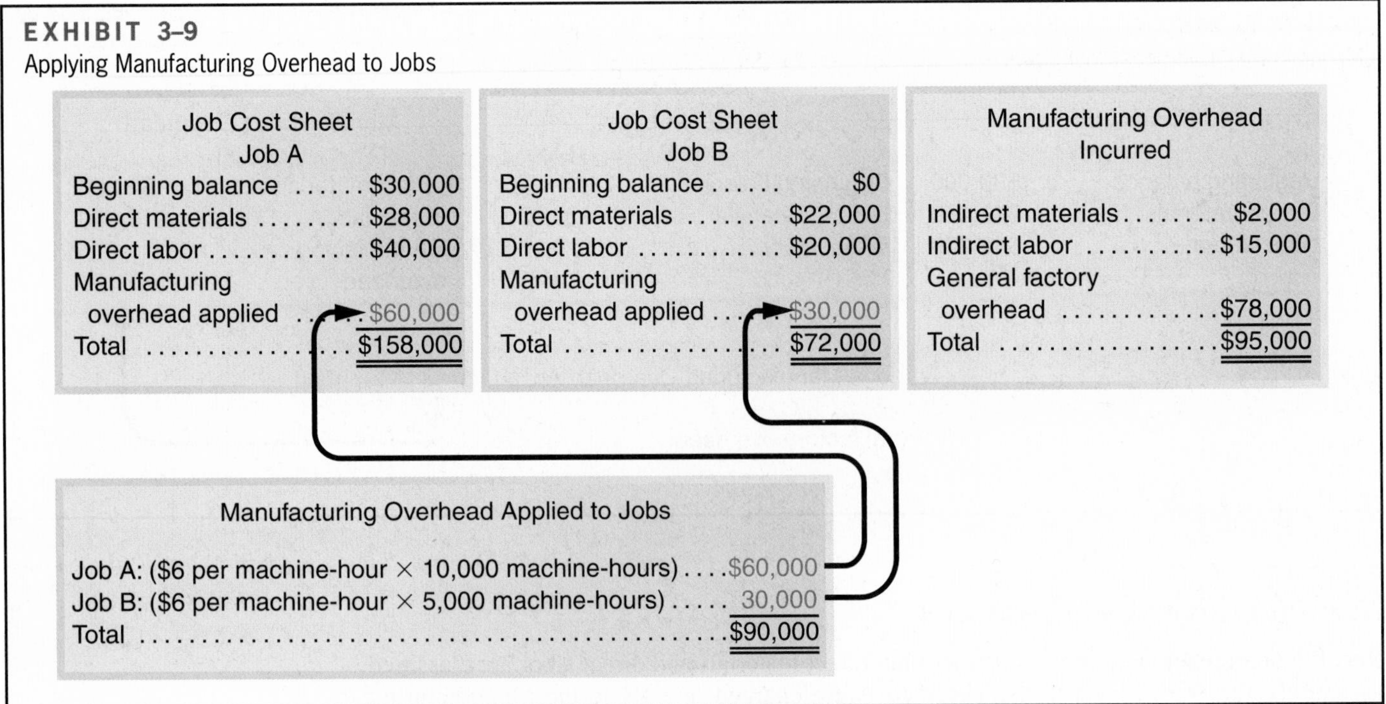

Job Cost Sheet Job A	
Beginning balance	$30,000
Direct materials	$28,000
Direct labor	$40,000
Manufacturing overhead applied	$60,000
Total	$158,000

Job Cost Sheet Job B	
Beginning balance	$0
Direct materials	$22,000
Direct labor	$20,000
Manufacturing overhead applied	$30,000
Total	$72,000

Manufacturing Overhead Incurred	
Indirect materials	$2,000
Indirect labor	$15,000
General factory overhead	$78,000
Total	$95,000

Manufacturing Overhead Applied to Jobs	
Job A: ($6 per machine-hour × 10,000 machine-hours)	$60,000
Job B: ($6 per machine-hour × 5,000 machine-hours)	30,000
Total	$90,000

Notice that Job A has been assigned total manufacturing costs of $158,000. Since Job A was completed in April, we can now compute the unit product cost for each of the 1,000 gold medallions included in the job. The unit product cost for Job A is $158 ($158,000 ÷ 1,000 units). This figure will be referred to later when we turn our attention to computing Rand Company's cost of goods sold. Also notice in Exhibit 3–9 that Job B has been assigned $72,000 of manufacturing costs; however, its unit product cost cannot be determined yet because the job is still in progress at the end of April. The $72,000 assigned to Job B will be reported as Work in Process inventory on the balance sheet at the end of April.

Underapplied or Overapplied Overhead

LEARNING OBJECTIVE 5
Determine underapplied or overapplied overhead.

You may have noted a discrepancy in Exhibit 3–9. The actual manufacturing overhead incurred during April was $95,000, but only $90,000 in manufacturing overhead cost was applied to the two jobs in process during the month. This discrepancy occurs because the manufacturing overhead applied to jobs is based on the predetermined overhead rate, which is itself based on estimates that were made before the month began of the total manufacturing overhead cost and the total machine-hours. Except under very special circumstances, if either of these estimates is off, the actual manufacturing overhead costs that are incurred will not equal the manufacturing overhead cost that is applied to jobs using the predetermined overhead rate.

The difference between the manufacturing overhead cost applied to jobs and the actual manufacturing overhead costs of a period is called either **underapplied** or **overapplied overhead.** For Rand Company, overhead was underapplied because the applied cost ($90,000) was $5,000 less than the actual cost ($95,000). If the situation had been reversed and the company had applied $95,000 in manufacturing overhead cost to jobs while incurring actual manufacturing overhead costs of only $90,000, then the overhead would have been overapplied.

What is the cause of the underapplied or overapplied overhead? The causes can be complex. To illustrate what can happen, suppose that two companies—Turbo Crafters and Black & Huang—have prepared the following estimates for the coming year:

	Turbo Crafters	Black & Huang
Allocation base	Machine-hours	Direct materials cost
Estimated manufacturing overhead cost (a)	$300,000	$120,000
Estimated total amount of the allocation base (b)	75,000 machine-hours	$80,000 direct materials cost
Predetermined overhead rate (a) ÷ (b)	$4 per machine-hour	150% of direct materials cost

Note that when the allocation base is dollars (such as direct materials cost in the case of Black & Huang) the predetermined overhead rate is expressed as a percentage of the allocation base. When dollars are divided by dollars, the result is a percentage.

Now assume that because of unexpected changes in overhead spending and changes in demand for the companies' products, the *actual* overhead cost and the actual activity recorded during the year in each company are as follows:

	Turbo Crafters	Black & Huang
Actual manufacturing overhead cost	$290,000	$130,000
Actual total amount of the allocation base	68,000 machine-hours	$90,000 direct materials cost

For each company, note that the actual data for both cost and the allocation base differ from the estimates used in computing the predetermined overhead rate. This results in underapplied and overapplied overhead as follows:

	Turbo Crafters	Black & Huang
Actual manufacturing overhead cost	$290,000	$130,000
Manufacturing overhead cost applied to jobs during the year:		
Predetermined overhead rate (a)	$4 per machine-hour	150% of direct materials cost
Actual total amount of the allocation base (b)	68,000 machine-hours	$ 90,000 direct materials cost
Manufacturing overhead applied (a) × (b)	$272,000	$135,000
Underapplied (overapplied) manufacturing overhead	$ 18,000	$ (5,000)

For Turbo Crafters, the $272,000 of manufacturing overhead cost applied to jobs is less than the $290,000 actual manufacturing overhead cost for the year. Therefore, overhead is underapplied. Notice that the original $300,000 estimate of manufacturing overhead for Turbo Crafters is not directly involved in this computation. Its impact is felt only through the $4 predetermined overhead rate.

For Black & Huang, the $135,000 of manufacturing overhead cost applied to jobs is greater than the $130,000 actual manufacturing overhead cost for the year, so overhead is overapplied. A summary of the concepts discussed above is presented in Exhibit 3–10.

Disposition of Underapplied or Overapplied Overhead

Note that the manufacturing overhead cost that is applied to jobs is an estimate—it does not represent actual costs incurred. The company's accounts must be adjusted at the end of the period so that they reflect actual costs rather than this estimate. This is accomplished in one of two ways: either (1) the underapplied or overapplied overhead at the end of a period is closed out to Cost of Goods Sold; or (2) it is allocated between Work in Process, Finished Goods, and Cost of Goods Sold in proportion to the overhead applied during the current period that is in the ending balances of these accounts. The latter method takes us further into the details of bookkeeping than we would like to go in this book, so we will always assume that the underapplied or overapplied overhead is closed out to Cost of Goods Sold.

EXHIBIT 3–10
Summary of Overhead Concepts

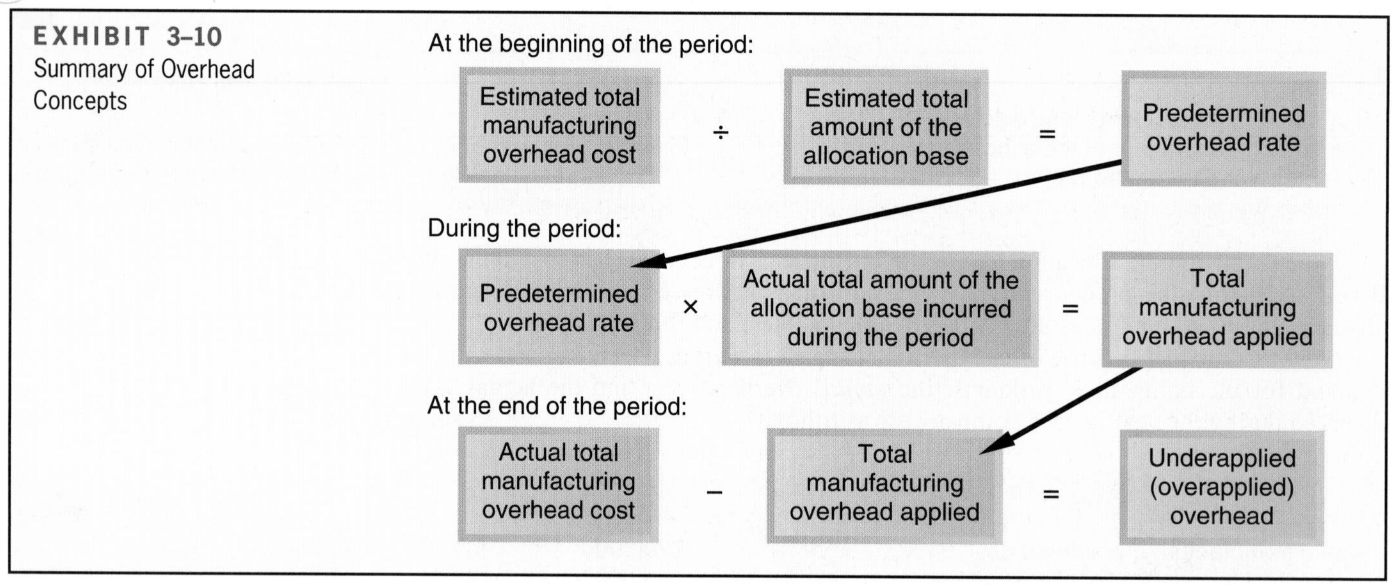

In other words, Cost of Goods Sold is adjusted for the amount of underapplied or overapplied overhead.

The procedure for closing out underapplied or overapplied overhead to Cost of Goods Sold is quite simple. Underapplied overhead is added to Cost of Goods Sold. Overapplied overhead is deducted from Cost of Goods Sold. The reasoning is that if overhead is underapplied, not enough manufacturing overhead was applied to jobs and hence their costs are understated. Therefore, Cost of Goods Sold must be increased to compensate for this understatement. Likewise, if overhead is overapplied, too much manufacturing overhead was applied to jobs and hence their costs are overstated. Therefore, Cost of Goods Sold must be decreased to compensate for this overstatement. In short, adding to or deducting from Cost of Goods Sold corrects the misstatement of cost that occurs as a result of using a predetermined overhead rate.

Prepare an Income Statement

Cost of Goods Sold

LEARNING OBJECTIVE 6
Use the direct method to determine cost of goods sold.

Recall from Chapter 2 that Cost of Goods Sold consists of the costs of the products sold to customers. It can be determined directly or indirectly. The indirect method was used in Chapter 2. The direct method is simpler and quicker when the necessary data are available, but that is not always the case. We will illustrate both approaches for Rand Company.

The Direct Method of Determining Cost of Goods Sold Recall that Job A, which consisted of 1,000 gold medallions, was completed during April, but Job B was not completed. Also recall that we already computed the unit product cost for each of the 1,000 gold medallions included in Job A—$158 ($158,000 ÷ 1,000 units). If we assume that 750 of the 1,000 gold medallions included in Job A were shipped to customers by the end of April, then the cost of the medallions sold to customers would be $118,500 (=750 units × $158 per unit). This amount must be adjusted for the $5,000 underapplied overhead to arrive at the cost of goods sold for the period ($123,500). Exhibit 3–11 illustrates the direct method of determining the cost of goods sold.

EXHIBIT 3–11
The Direct Method of Determining Cost of Goods Sold

Unadjusted cost of goods sold (750 units × $158 per unit)	$118,500
Add: Underapplied overhead	5,000
Cost of goods sold	$123,500

LEARNING OBJECTIVE 7
Use the indirect method to determine cost of goods sold.

The Indirect Method of Determining Cost of Goods Sold The indirect method introduced in Chapter 2 relies on the following formulas:

Cost of goods manufactured = Total manufacturing cost charged to jobs
+ Beginning work in process inventory
− Ending work in process inventory

Cost of goods sold = Beginning finished goods inventory
+ Cost of goods manufactured
− Ending finished goods inventory

To determine the cost of goods sold with these formulas, we will need to know five items: (1) the beginning work in process inventory; (2) the total manufacturing cost charged to jobs for the period; (3) the ending work in process inventory; (4) the beginning finished goods inventory; and (5) the ending finished goods inventory. These costs are detailed below:

1. The beginning work in process inventory was $30,000—the beginning balance on Job A's job cost sheet.
2. The total manufacturing cost charged to jobs consists of direct materials, direct labor, and manufacturing overhead charged to jobs during the period. From Exhibit 3–9, the total manufacturing cost can be determined as follows:

	Job A	Job B	Total
Direct materials	$28,000	$22,000	$ 50,000
Direct labor	$40,000	$20,000	60,000
Manufacturing overhead applied	$60,000	$30,000	90,000
Total manufacturing cost charged to jobs			$200,000

3. The ending work in process inventory consists of $72,000—the accumulated cost of Job B.
4. At the start of the Rand Company example, we stated that the company had no beginning finished goods inventories.
5. The ending finished goods inventory consists of the costs of any completed units that have not been sold at the end of the month. Job A consisted of 1,000 units, 750 of which were sold. Therefore, the ending finished goods inventory consists of 250 units (= 1,000 units − 750 units). Recall that the unit product cost of Job A is $158 per unit. Consequently, the total cost of these 250 unsold, but completed, units is $39,500 (= 250 units × $158 per unit).

Using this data, Exhibit 3–12 illustrates the indirect method of determining the cost of goods sold.

Note two things from Exhibit 3–11 and Exhibit 3–12. First, the cost of goods sold is identical under the two methods—and always will be. Second, under both methods, the underapplied overhead is added to the unadjusted cost of goods sold to determine the cost of goods sold. Remember the reason for this. Underapplied overhead means that not enough overhead was applied to jobs—the actual manufacturing overhead exceeded the amount of manufacturing overhead applied to jobs using the predetermined overhead rate. We must add the underapplied overhead to the unadjusted cost of goods sold to remove this discrepancy.

EXHIBIT 3–12
The Indirect Method of Determining Cost of Goods Sold

Manufacturing costs charged to jobs:	
Direct materials*	$ 50,000
Direct labor	60,000
Manufacturing overhead applied	90,000
Total manufacturing cost charged to jobs	200,000
Add: Beginning work in process inventory	30,000
	230,000
Deduct: Ending work in process inventory	72,000
Cost of goods manufactured	$158,000
Beginning finished goods inventory	$ 0
Add: Cost of goods manufactured (see above)	158,000
Goods available for sale	158,000
Deduct: Ending finished goods inventory,	39,500
Unadjusted cost of goods sold	118,500
Add: Underapplied overhead	5,000
Cost of goods sold	$123,500

*Further details concerning materials could be included in the statement as shown in the Schedule of Cost of Goods Manufactured from Chapter 2.

Income Statement

Now that we know the cost of goods sold ($123,500), all we need to construct the company's income statement for April is the total sales revenue and the selling and administrative expenses. We will assume that Rand Company's total sales revenue is $225,000 and that it has supplied the following data concerning its selling and administrative expenses in April:

Rand Company
Selling and Administrative Expenses
For the Month Ending April 30

Salaries expense	$30,000
Depreciation expense	7,000
Advertising expense	42,000
Other expense	8,000
Total selling and administrative expense	$87,000

Exhibit 3–13 combines these selling and administrative expenses with the sales and cost of goods sold data to create the company's income statement for the month.

EXHIBIT 3–13
Income Statement*

Rand Company
Income Statement
For the Month Ending April 30

Sales	$225,000
Cost of goods sold	123,500
Gross margin	101,500
Selling and administrative expense	87,000
Net operating income	$ 14,500

*Note: This is an abbreviated version of the Income Statement from Chapter 2. Details concerning the cost of goods sold and the selling and administrative expenses could be included in the income statement.

Multiple Predetermined Overhead Rates

Our discussion in this chapter has assumed that there is a single predetermined overhead rate for an entire factory called a **plantwide overhead rate.** This is a fairly common practice—particularly in smaller companies. But in larger companies, *multiple predetermined overhead rates* are often used. In a **multiple predetermined overhead rate** system each production department may have its own predetermined overhead rate. Such a system, while more complex, is more accurate, since it can reflect differences across departments in how overhead costs are incurred. For example, overhead might be allocated based on direct labor-hours in departments that are relatively labor intensive and based on machine-hours in departments that are relatively machine intensive. When multiple predetermined overhead rates are used, overhead is applied in each department according to its own overhead rate as a job proceeds through the department.

Job-Order Costing in Service Companies

Job-order costing is also used in service organizations such as law firms, movie studios, hospitals, and repair shops, as well as in manufacturing companies. In a law firm, for example, each client is considered to be a "job," and the costs of that job are accumulated day by day on a job cost sheet as the client's case is handled by the firm. Legal forms and similar inputs represent the direct materials for the job; the time expended by attorneys represents the direct labor; and the costs of secretaries, clerks, rent, depreciation, and so forth, represent the overhead.

In a movie studio such as Columbia Pictures, each film produced by the studio is a "job," and costs for direct materials (costumes, props, film, etc.) and direct labor (actors, directors, and extras) are charged to each film's job cost sheet. A share of the studio's overhead costs, such as utilities, depreciation of equipment, wages of maintenance workers, and so forth, is also charged to each film.

In sum, job-order costing is a versatile and widely used costing method that may be encountered in virtually any organization that provides diverse products or services.

Use of Information Technology

Earlier in the chapter we discussed how bar code technology can be used to record labor time—reducing the drudgery in that task and increasing accuracy. Bar codes have many other uses.

In a company with a well-developed bar code system, the manufacturing cycle begins with the receipt of a customer's order in electronic form. Until very recently, the order would have been received via electronic data interchange (EDI), which involves a network of computers linking organizations. An EDI network allows companies to electronically exchange business documents and other information that extend into all areas of business activity from ordering raw materials to shipping completed goods. Recently, EDI has been challenged by a far cheaper web-based alternative—XML (Extensible Markup Language), an extension of HTML (Hypertext Markup Language). HTML uses codes to tell your web browser how to display information on your screen, but the computer doesn't know what the information is—it just displays it. XML provides additional tags that identify the kind of information that is being exchanged. For example, price data might be coded as <price> 14.95 <price>. When your computer reads this data and sees the tags <price> surrounding 14.95, your computer will immediately know that this is a price. XML tags can designate many different kinds of information—customer orders, medical records, bank statements, and so on—and the tags will indicate to your computer how to display, store, and retrieve the information. Office Depot is an early adopter of XML, which it is using to facilitate e-commerce with its big customers.

Once an order has been received via EDI or in the form of an XML file, the computer draws up a list of required raw materials and sends out electronic purchase orders to suppliers. When materials arrive at the company's plant from the suppliers, bar codes that have been applied by the suppliers are scanned to update inventory records and to trigger payment for the materials. A unique bar code is also assigned to each job. When the materials are requisitioned for use in production, the bar codes for the materials are scanned again along with the bar code for the job. At that point, the computer adds the cost of the materials to a computer record that is the digital equivalent of a job cost sheet. Similarly, bar codes are used to update the job's digital records for labor and other costs incurred in the manufacturing process. When goods are completed, another scan is performed to update the Finished Goods inventory account. When goods are sold, another scan is performed to update the Cost of Goods Sold account.

Goods ready to be shipped are packed into containers that are bar coded with information that includes the customer number, the type and quantity of goods being shipped, and the order number. This bar code is then used for preparing billing information and for tracking the packed goods until placed on a carrier for shipment to the customer. Some customers require that the packed goods be bar coded with point-of-sale labels that can be scanned at retail checkout counters. These scans allow the retailer to update inventory records, verify price, and generate a customer receipt.

IN BUSINESS

RFID: THE NEXT GENERATION BEYOND BAR CODES

Bar code technology has revolutionized how organizations gather data. However, bar code readers cannot read a bar code more than a few feet away nor can they read a bar code that is not visible. This creates inefficiencies when companies attempt to track large amounts of raw materials, finished goods or merchandise inventory. Radio Frequency Identification Systems (RFID) overcome these inherent limitations of bar codes. For example, a tractor trailer full of merchandise with RFID tags can be "read" without even opening the trailer doors.

According to Kurt Salmon Associates, RFID technology can lower warehousing and distribution costs by 3% to 5% largely because employees no longer need to scan the bar code on each item. Companies such as Home Depot, Marks & Spencer, Metro AG, Procter & Gamble, and Wal-Mart are moving quickly to adopt RFID technology. In fact, Wal-Mart is requiring its top 100 suppliers to "put RFID tags on all of their pallets, cases, cartons and high margin items."

A survey conducted by *PC* Magazine indicates that more than half of the companies in the automotive, consumer goods, and transportation and logistics industries plan to adopt RFID. Some experts believe that, once technological advances drop the cost of an RFID tag from 25–30 cents down to 5 cents, this technology will be very widely adopted.

Sources: Meredith Levinson, "The RFID Imperative," *CIO* Magazine, December 2003 (www.cio.com/archive/120103/retail.html) and "Here Comes RFID Chips," *PC* Magazine, October 18, 2005, pp. 31–33.

In short, bar code technology is being integrated into many areas of business activity. When combined with EDI or XML, it eliminates a lot of clerical drudgery and allows companies to capture and exchange more data and to analyze and report information much more quickly and completely and with less error than with manual systems.

IN BUSINESS

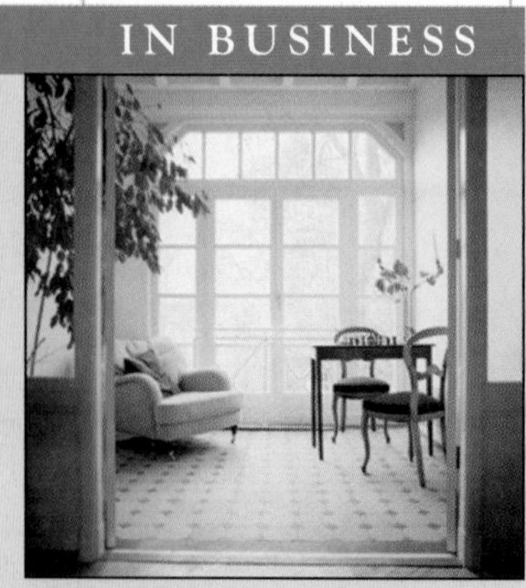

MANAGING DIVERSITY WITH TECHNOLOGY

Andersen Windows, Inc. of Bayport, Minnesota, has a software program that enables it to produce just about any window configuration that a customer might order. The program—which works on most standard Microsoft® Windows platforms—allows customers to select from any of the company's large selection of standard window and door sizes and styles. Customers can add the features and options they want with an easy "point-and-click" until they've configured the desired units. Placing the order after final selections are made is just as easy—the window order can be sent electronically into Andersen's back office system where it is automatically fulfilled. The entire process is highly automated and very efficient, yet it enables the customer a high degree of flexibility.

Source: Andersen® Intelligent Quote, used by permission of Andersen Windows, Inc.

Summary

Job-order costing and process costing are widely used to track costs. Job-order costing is used in situations where the organization offers many different products or services, such as in furniture manufacturing, hospitals, and legal firms. Process costing is used where units of product are homogeneous, such as in flour milling or cement production.

Materials requisition forms and labor time tickets are used to assign direct materials and direct labor costs to jobs in a job-order costing system. Manufacturing overhead costs are assigned to jobs using a predetermined overhead rate. The predetermined overhead rate is determined before the period begins by dividing the estimated total manufacturing cost for the period by the estimated total amount of the allocation base for the period. The most frequently used allocation bases are direct labor-hours and machine-hours. Overhead is applied to jobs by multiplying the predetermined overhead rate by the actual amount of the allocation base used by the job.

Because the predetermined overhead rate is based on estimates, the actual overhead cost incurred during a period may be more or less than the amount of overhead cost applied to production. Such a difference is referred to as underapplied or overapplied overhead. The underapplied or overapplied overhead for a period can be either closed out to Cost of Goods Sold or allocated between Work in Process, Finished Goods, and Cost of Goods Sold. When overhead is underapplied, manufacturing overhead costs have been understated and therefore inventories and/or expenses must be adjusted upwards. When overhead is overapplied, manufacturing overhead costs have been overstated and therefore inventories and/or expenses must be adjusted downwards.

Review Problem: Job-Order Costing

Hogle Corporation uses job-order costing and applies overhead cost to jobs on the basis of machine-hours worked. For the just completed year, the company estimated that it would work 75,000 machine-hours and incur $450,000 in manufacturing overhead cost. The company actually worked 80,000 machine-hours.

The company has provided the following financial data concerning its operations for the year:

Direct materials	$360,000
Indirect materials	$20,000
Direct labor	$75,000
Indirect labor	$110,000
Sales commissions	$90,000
Administrative salaries	$200,000
General selling expenses	$17,000
Factory utility costs	$43,000
Advertising costs	$180,000
Factory depreciation	$280,000
Selling and administrative depreciation	$70,000
Factory insurance	$7,000
Selling and administrative insurance	$3,000
Cost of goods sold (not adjusted for underapplied or overapplied overhead)	$870,000
Sales	$1,500,000

Required:

1. Is overhead underapplied or overapplied for the year? By how much?
2. Prepare an income statement for the year.

Solution to Review Problem

1. To determine the underapplied or overapplied overhead for the year, we must know the actual manufacturing overhead cost incurred and the manufacturing overhead applied to jobs. The actual manufacturing overhead cost incurred can be determined by adding together all of the manufacturing overhead items in the financial data provided by the company as follows:

Manufacturing overhead costs incurred:	
Indirect materials	$ 20,000
Indirect labor	110,000
Factory utility costs	43,000
Factory depreciation	280,000
Factory insurance	7,000
Total manufacturing overhead cost incurred	$460,000

The predetermined overhead rate for the year would be computed as follows:

$$\text{Predetermined overhead rate} = \frac{\text{Estimated total manufacturing overhead cost}}{\text{Estimated total amount of the allocation base}}$$

$$= \frac{\$450{,}000}{75{,}000 \text{ machine-hours}}$$

$$= \$6 \text{ per machine-hour}$$

Based on the 80,000 machine-hours actually worked during the year, the company would have applied $480,000 in overhead cost to production: $6 per machine-hour × 80,000 machine hours. The actual manufacturing overhead cost incurred was $460,000, whereas the manufacturing overhead applied to jobs using the company's predetermined overhead rate was $480,000. Therefore, overhead was overapplied by $20,000 (= $480,000 − $460,000).

2. To construct the income statement, we will need the sales (which is given), the adjusted cost of goods sold, and the total selling and administrative expenses. The latter can be determined as follows:

Selling and administrative expenses incurred:	
Sales commissions	$ 90,000
Administrative salaries	200,000
General selling expenses	17,000
Advertising costs	180,000
Selling and administrative depreciation	70,000
Selling and administrative insurance	3,000
Total selling and administrative expense	$560,000

The adjusted cost of goods sold is determined as follows:

Unadjusted cost of goods sold	$870,000
Deduct: Overapplied overhead	20,000
Cost of goods sold	$850,000

Finally, the income statement is constructed as follows:

HOGLE CORPORATION Income Statement	
Sales	$1,500,000
Cost of goods sold	850,000
Gross margin	650,000
Selling and administrative expense	560,000
Net operating income	$ 90,000

Glossary

Absorption costing A costing method that includes all manufacturing costs—direct materials, direct labor, and both variable and fixed manufacturing overhead—in the cost of a product. (p. 79)

Allocation base A measure of activity such as direct labor-hours or machine-hours that is used to assign costs to cost objects. (p. 84)

Bill of materials A document that shows the quantity of each type of direct material required to make a product. (p. 81)

Cost driver A factor, such as machine-hours, beds occupied, computer time, or flight-hours, that causes overhead costs. (p. 86)

Job cost sheet A form prepared for a job that records the materials, labor, and manufacturing overhead costs charged to that job. (p. 82)

Job-order costing system A costing system used in situations where many different products, jobs, or services are produced each period. (p. 80)

Materials requisition form A detailed source document that specifies the type and quantity of materials to be drawn from the storeroom and that identifies the job that will be charged for the cost of those materials. (p. 81)

Multiple predetermined overhead rate A costing system with multiple overhead cost pools with a different predetermined overhead rate for each cost pool, rather than a single predetermined overhead rate for the entire company. Each production department is often treated as a separate overhead cost pool. (p. 97)

Normal cost system A costing system in which overhead costs are applied to a job by multiplying a predetermined overhead rate by the actual amount of the allocation base incurred by the job. (p. 85)

Overapplied overhead The amount by which overhead cost applied to jobs exceeds the amount of overhead cost actually incurred during a period. (p. 92)

Overhead application The process of charging manufacturing overhead cost to job cost sheets. (p. 84)

Plantwide overhead rate A single predetermined overhead rate that is used throughout a plant. (p. 97)

Predetermined overhead rate A rate used to charge manufacturing overhead cost to jobs that is established in advance for each period. It is computed by dividing the estimated total manufacturing overhead cost for the period by the estimated total amount of the allocation base for the period. (p. 84)

Process costing system A costing system used in situations where a single, homogeneous product (such as cement or flour) is produced for long periods of time. (p. 79)

Time ticket A detailed source document that is used to record the amount of time an employee spends on various activities. (p. 82)

Underapplied overhead The amount by which overhead cost actually incurred exceeds the amount of overhead cost applied to jobs during a period. (p. 92)

Appendix 3A: The Predetermined Overhead Rate and Capacity

LEARNING OBJECTIVE 8
Understand the implications of basing the predetermined overhead rate on activity at capacity rather than on estimated activity for the period.

Companies typically base their predetermined overhead rates on the estimated, or budgeted, amount of the allocation base for the upcoming period. This is the method that is used in the chapter, but it is a practice that has come under severe criticism.[1] An example will be very helpful in understanding why. Prahad Corporation manufactures music CDs for local recording studios. The company's CD duplicating machine is capable of producing a new CD every 10 seconds from a master CD. The company leases the CD duplicating machine for $180,000 per year, and this is the company's only manufacturing overhead cost.

[1] Institute of Management Accountants, *Measuring the Cost of Capacity: Statements on Management Accounting, Number 4Y*, Montvale, NJ; Thomas Klammer, ed., *Capacity Measurement and Improvement: A Manager's Guide to Evaluating and Optimizing Capacity Productivity* (Chicago: CAM-I, Irwin Professional Publishing); and C. J. McNair, "The Hidden Costs of Capacity," *The Journal of Cost Management* (Spring 1994), pp. 12–24.

With allowances for setups and maintenance, the machine is theoretically capable of producing up to 900,000 CDs per year. However, due to weak retail sales of CDs, the company's commercial customers are unlikely to order more than 600,000 CDs next year. The company uses machine time as the allocation base for applying manufacturing overhead to CDs. These data are summarized below:

Prahad Corporation Data	
Total manufacturing overhead cost.	\$180,000 per year
Allocation base—machine time per CD	10 seconds per CD
Capacity	900,000 CDs per year
Budgeted output for next year.	600,000 CDs

If Prahad follows common practice and computes its predetermined overhead rate using estimated or budgeted figures, then its predetermined overhead rate for next year would be \$0.03 per second of machine time computed as follows:

$$\text{Predetermined overhead rate} = \frac{\text{Estimated total manufacturing overhead cost}}{\text{Estimated total amount of the allocation base}}$$

$$= \frac{\$180{,}000}{600{,}000 \text{ CDs} \times 10 \text{ seconds per CD}}$$

$$= \$0.03 \text{ per second}$$

Since each CD requires 10 seconds of machine time, each CD will be charged for \$0.30 of overhead cost.

Critics charge that there are two problems with this procedure. First, if predetermined overhead rates are based on budgeted activity, then the unit product costs will fluctuate depending on the budgeted level of activity for the period. For example, if the budgeted output for the year was only 300,000 CDs, the predetermined overhead rate would be \$0.06 per second of machine time or \$0.60 per CD rather than \$0.30 per CD. In general, if budgeted output falls, the overhead cost per unit will increase; it will appear that the CDs cost more to make. Managers may then be tempted to increase prices at the worst possible time—just as demand is falling.

Second, critics charge that under the traditional approach, products are charged for resources that they don't use. When the fixed costs of capacity are spread over estimated activity, the units that are produced must shoulder the costs of unused capacity. That is why the applied overhead cost per unit increases as the level of activity falls. The critics argue that products should be charged only for the capacity that they use; they should not be charged for the capacity they don't use. This can be accomplished by basing the predetermined overhead rate on capacity as follows:

$$\text{Predetermined overhead rate based on capacity} = \frac{\text{Estimated total manufacturing overhead cost at capacity}}{\text{Estimated total amount of the allocation base at capacity}}$$

$$= \frac{\$180{,}000}{900{,}000 \text{ CDs} \times 10 \text{ seconds per CD}}$$

$$= \$0.02 \text{ per second}$$

Since the predetermined overhead rate is \$0.02 per second, the overhead cost applied to each CD would be \$0.20. This charge is constant and would not be affected by the level of activity during a period. If output falls, the charge would still be \$0.20 per CD.

This method will almost certainly result in underapplied overhead. If actual output at Prahad Corporation is 600,000 CDs, then only \$120,000 of overhead cost would be applied to products (\$0.20 per CD × 600,000 CDs). Since the actual overhead cost is \$180,000, there would be underapplied overhead of \$60,000. In another departure from tradition, the critics suggest that the underapplied overhead that results from idle capacity should be separately disclosed as a period expense on the income statement to reflect the cost of unused capacity. Disclosing this cost as a lump sum on the income statement, rather than burying it in Cost of Goods Sold or ending inventories, makes it much more visible to managers.

To illustrate, suppose that Prahad Corporation's sales are $207,000, its cost of goods sold is $134,000, and its selling and administrative expenses are $24,000 in a period in which its overhead is underapplied by $60,000. Then its income statement would appear as follows:

Prahad Corporation Income Statement		
Sales		$207,000
Cost of goods sold		134,000
Gross margin		73,000
Underapplied manufacturing overhead	$60,000	
Selling and administrative expenses	24,000	84,000
Net operating income		($ 11,000)

Note that the underapplied overhead is prominently displayed in this income statement, bringing attention to the cost of the company's unused capacity.

Official pronouncements do not prohibit basing predetermined overhead rates on capacity for external reports.[2] Nevertheless, basing the predetermined overhead rate on estimated or budgeted activity is a long-established practice in industry, and some managers and accountants may object to the large amounts of underapplied overhead that would often result from using capacity to determine predetermined overhead rates. And some may insist that the underapplied overhead be allocated among Cost of Goods Sold and ending inventories—which would defeat the purpose of basing the predetermined overhead rate on capacity.

IN BUSINESS

RESOURCE CONSUMPTION ACCOUNTING

Clopay Plastic Products Company, headquartered in Cincinnati, Ohio, recently implemented a pilot application of a German cost accounting system known in the United States as Resource Consumption Accounting (RCA). One of the benefits of RCA is that it uses the estimated total amount of the allocation base at capacity to calculate overhead rates and to assign costs to cost objects. This makes idle capacity visible to managers who can react to this information by either growing sales or taking steps to reduce the amount and cost of available capacity. It also ensures that products are only charged for the resources used to produce them.

Clopay's old cost system spread all of the company's manufacturing overhead costs over the units produced. So, if Clopay's senior managers decided to discontinue what appeared to be an unprofitable product, the unit costs of the remaining products would increase as the fixed overhead costs of the newly idled capacity were spread over the remaining products.

Source: B. Douglas Clinton and Sally A. Webber, "Here's Innovation in Management Accounting with Resource Consumption Accounting," *Strategic Finance*, October 2004, pp. 21–26.

[2] Institute of Management Accountants, *Measuring the Cost of Capacity*, pp. 46–47.

Questions

3-1 Why aren't actual manufacturing overhead costs traced to jobs just as direct materials and direct labor costs are traced to jobs?

3-2 When would job-order costing be used instead of process costing?

3-3 What is the purpose of the job cost sheet in a job-order costing system?

3-4 What is a predetermined overhead rate, and how is it computed?

3-5 Explain how a sales order, a production order, a materials requisition form, and a labor time ticket are involved in producing and costing products.

3-6 Explain why some production costs must be assigned to products through an allocation process.

3-7 Why do companies use predetermined overhead rates rather than actual manufacturing overhead costs to apply overhead to jobs?

3-8 What factors should be considered in selecting a base to be used in computing the predetermined overhead rate?

3-9 If a company fully allocates all of its overhead costs to jobs, does this guarantee that a profit will be earned for the period?

3-10 Would you expect the amount of overhead applied for a period to equal the actual overhead costs of the period? Why or why not?

3-11 What is underapplied overhead? Overapplied overhead? What disposition is made of these amounts at the end of the period?

3-12 Provide two reasons why overhead might be underapplied in a given year.

3-13 What adjustment to cost of goods sold is made for underapplied overhead? What adjustment is made for overapplied overhead?

3-14 Sigma Company applies overhead cost to jobs on the basis of direct labor cost. Job A, which was started and completed during the current period, shows charges of $5,000 for direct materials, $8,000 for direct labor, and $6,000 for overhead on its job cost sheet. Job B, which is still in process at year-end, shows charges of $2,500 for direct materials and $4,000 for direct labor. Should any overhead cost be added to Job B at year-end? Explain.

3-15 A company assigns overhead cost to completed jobs on the basis of 125% of direct labor cost. The job cost sheet for Job 313 shows that $10,000 in direct materials has been used on the job and that $12,000 in direct labor cost has been incurred. If 1,000 units were produced in Job 313, what is the unit product cost?

3-16 What is a plantwide overhead rate? Why are multiple overhead rates, rather than a plantwide overhead rate, used in some companies?

3-17 What happens to overhead rates based on direct labor when automated equipment replaces direct labor?

3-18 (Appendix 3A) If the plant is operated at less than capacity and the predetermined overhead rate is based on the estimated total amount of the allocation base at capacity, will overhead ordinarily be overapplied or underapplied?

3-19 (Appendix 3A) Rather than netting underapplied overhead against Cost of Goods Sold or Cost of Goods Sold and ending inventories, some critics suggest an alternative way to disclose underapplied overhead. What is this alternative method?

Quiz 3

Multiple-choice questions are provided on the text Web site at www.mhhe.com/noreen1e.

Exercises 

EXERCISE 3-1 Process Costing and Job-Order Costing [LO1]

Which would be more appropriate in each of the following situations—job-order costing or process costing?

a. A custom yacht builder.
b. A golf course designer.
c. A potato chip manufacturer.
d. A business consultant.
e. A plywood manufacturer.
f. A soft-drink bottler.
g. A film studio.
h. A firm that supervises bridge construction projects.
i. A manufacturer of fine custom jewelry.
j. A made-to-order clothing factory.
k. A factory making one personal computer model.
l. A fertilizer factory.

EXERCISE 3-2 Job-Order Costing Documents [LO2]

Mountain Gearing Company has incurred the following costs on Job ES34, an order for 40 gearing wheels to be delivered at the end of next month.

Direct materials:

On March 5, requisition number 870 was issued for 40 titanium blanks to be used in the special order. The blanks cost $8.00 each.

On March 8, requisition number 873 was issued for 960 hardened nibs also to be used in the special order. The nibs cost $0.60 each.

Direct labor:

On March 9, Harry Kerst worked from 9:00 A.M. until 12:15 P.M. on Job ES34. He is paid $12.00 per hour.

On March 21, Mary Rosas worked from 2:15 P.M. until 4:30 P.M. on Job ES34. She is paid $14.00 per hour.

Required:

1. On what documents would these costs be recorded?
2. How much cost should have been recorded on each of the documents for Job ES34?

EXERCISE 3-3 Compute the Predetermined Overhead Rate [LO3]

Logan Products computes its predetermined overhead rate annually on the basis of direct labor-hours. At the beginning of the year it estimated that its total manufacturing overhead would be $586,000 and the total direct labor would be 40,000 hours. Its actual total manufacturing overhead for the year was $713,400 and its actual total direct labor was 41,000 hours.

Required:

Compute the company's predetermined overhead rate for the year.

EXERCISE 3-4 Apply Overhead [LO4]

Westan Corporation uses a predetermined overhead rate of $23.10 per direct labor-hour. This predetermined rate was based on 12,000 estimated direct labor-hours and $277,200 of estimated total manufacturing overhead.

The company incurred actual total manufacturing overhead costs of $266,000 and 12,600 total direct labor-hours during the period.

Required:

Determine the amount of manufacturing overhead that would have been applied to units of product during the period.

EXERCISE 3-5 Determine Underapplied or Overapplied Overhead [LO5]

Kirkaid Company recorded the following transactions for the just completed month.

a. $84,000 in raw materials were requisitioned for use in production. Of this amount, $72,000 was for direct materials and the remainder was for indirect materials.
b. Total labor wages of $108,000 were incurred. Of this amount, $105,000 was for direct labor and the remainder was for indirect labor.
c. Additional actual manufacturing overhead costs of $197,000 were incurred.
d. A total of $218,000 in manufacturing overhead was applied to jobs.

Required:

Determine the underapplied or overapplied overhead for the month.

EXERCISE 3-6 Direct Method of Determining Cost of Goods Sold [LO6]

Uxmaiz Corporation had only one job in process during May—Job X32Z—and had no finished goods inventory on May 1. Job X32Z was started in April and finished during May. Data concerning that job appear below:

	Job X32Z
Beginning balance	$5,000
Charged to the job during May:	
Direct materials	$8,000
Direct labor	$2,000
Manufacturing overhead applied	$4,000
Units completed	100
Units in process at the end of May	0
Units sold during May	40

In May, overhead was overapplied by $300. The company adjusts its cost of goods sold every month for the amount of the overhead that was underapplied or overapplied.

Required:

1. Using the direct method, what is the cost of goods sold for May?
2. What is the total value of the finished goods inventory at the end of May?
3. What is the total value of the work in process inventory at the end of May?

EXERCISE 3-7 Indirect Method of Determining Cost of Goods Sold [LO7]

Refer to the data for Uxmaiz Corporation in Exercise 3–6.

Required:

Using the indirect method, determine the cost of goods sold for May.

EXERCISE 3-8 (Appendix 3A) Overhead Rate Based on Capacity [LO8]

Samanca Cabinets makes custom wooden cabinets for high-end stereo systems from specialty woods. The company uses a job-order costing system. The capacity of the plant is determined by the capacity of its constraint, which is time on the automated bandsaw that makes finely beveled cuts in wood according to the preprogrammed specifications of each cabinet. The bandsaw can operate up to 150 hours per month. The estimated total manufacturing overhead at capacity is $11,100 per month. The company bases its predetermined overhead rate on capacity, so its predetermined overhead rate is $74 per hour of bandsaw use.

The results of a recent month's operations appear below:

Sales	$39,860
Beginning inventories	$0
Ending inventories	$0
Direct materials	$4,820
Direct labor (all variable)	$9,640
Manufacturing overhead incurred	$10,870
Selling and administrative expense	$9,350
Actual hours of bandsaw use	124

Required:

1. Prepare an income statement following the example in Appendix 3A in which any underapplied overhead is directly recorded on the income statement as an expense.
2. Why is overhead ordinarily underapplied when the predetermined overhead rate is based on capacity?

EXERCISE 3-9 Applying Overhead; Cost of Goods Manufactured [LO4, LO5, LO6]

The following cost data relate to the manufacturing activities of Black Company during the just completed year:

Actual manufacturing overhead costs:	
Property taxes, factory	$ 3,000
Utilities, factory	5,000
Indirect labor	10,000
Depreciation, factory	24,000
Insurance, factory	6,000
Total actual manufacturing overhead costs	$48,000
Other costs charged to jobs:	
Direct materials	$33,000
Direct labor	$40,000
Inventories:	
Work in process, beginning	$6,000
Work in process, ending	$7,500

The company uses a predetermined overhead rate to apply overhead cost to production. The rate for the year was $5 per machine-hour; a total of 10,000 machine-hours was recorded for the year. All raw materials ultimately become direct materials—none are classified as indirect materials.

Required:
1. Compute the amount of underapplied or overapplied overhead cost for the year.
2. Determine the cost of goods manufactured for the year using the indirect method.

EXERCISE 3-10 Varying Predetermined Overhead Rates [LO3, LO4]

Javadi Company makes a composting bin that is subject to wide seasonal variations in demand. Unit product costs are computed on a quarterly basis by dividing each quarter's manufacturing costs (materials, labor, and overhead) by the quarter's production in units. The company's estimated costs, by quarter, for the coming year are given below:

	Quarter			
	First	Second	Third	Fourth
Direct materials	$240,000	$120,000	$ 60,000	$180,000
Direct labor	96,000	48,000	24,000	72,000
Manufacturing overhead	228,000	204,000	192,000	216,000
Total manufacturing costs	$564,000	$372,000	$276,000	$468,000
Number of units to be produced	80,000	40,000	20,000	60,000
Estimated unit product cost	$7.05	$9.30	$13.80	$7.80

Management finds the variation in unit product costs to be confusing and difficult to work with. It has been suggested that the problem lies with manufacturing overhead, since it is the largest element of cost. Accordingly, you have been asked to find a more appropriate way of assigning manufacturing overhead cost to units of product. After some analysis, you have determined that the company's overhead costs are mostly fixed and therefore show little sensitivity to changes in the level of production.

Required:
1. The company uses a job-order costing system. How would you recommend that manufacturing overhead cost be assigned to production? Be specific, and show computations.
2. Recompute the company's unit product costs in accordance with your recommendations in (1) above.

EXERCISE 3-11 Underapplied and Overapplied Overhead [LO5]

Cretin Enterprises uses a predetermined overhead rate of $21.40 per direct labor-hour. This predetermined rate was based on 8,000 estimated direct labor-hours and $171,200 of estimated total manufacturing overhead.

The company incurred actual total manufacturing overhead costs of $172,500 and 8,250 total direct labor-hours during the period.

Required:
1. Determine the amount of underapplied or overapplied manufacturing overhead for the period.
2. Assuming that the entire amount of the underapplied or overapplied overhead is closed out to Cost of Goods Sold, what would be the effect of the underapplied or overapplied overhead on the company's gross margin for the period?

EXERCISE 3-12 (Appendix 3A) Overhead Rates and Capacity Issues [LO3, LO4, LO5, LO8]

Estate Pension Services helps clients set up and administer pension plans that are in compliance with tax laws and regulatory requirements. The firm uses a job-order costing system in which overhead is applied to clients' accounts on the basis of professional staff hours charged to the accounts. Data concerning two recent years appear below:

	2005	2006
Estimated professional staff hours to be charged to clients' accounts	2,400	2,250
Estimated overhead cost	$144,000	$144,000
Professional staff hours available	3,000	3,000

"Professional staff hours available" is a measure of the capacity of the firm. Any hours available that are not charged to clients' accounts represent unused capacity.

Required:

1. Jennifer Miyami is an established client whose pension plan was set up many years ago. In both 2005 and 2006, only five hours of professional staff time were charged to Ms. Miyami's account. If the company bases its predetermined overhead rate on the estimated overhead cost and the estimated professional staff hours to be charged to clients, how much overhead cost would have been applied to Ms. Miyami's account in 2005? In 2006?
2. Suppose that the company bases its predetermined overhead rate on the estimated overhead cost and the estimated professional staff hours to be charged to clients as in (1) above. Also suppose that the actual professional staff hours charged to clients' accounts and the actual overhead costs turn out to be exactly as estimated in both years. By how much would the overhead be underapplied or overapplied in 2005? In 2006?
3. Refer back to the data concerning Ms. Miyami in (1) above. If the company bases its predetermined overhead rate on the estimated overhead cost and the professional staff hours available, how much overhead cost would have been applied to Ms. Miyami's account in 2005? In 2006?
4. Suppose that the company bases its predetermined overhead rate on the estimated overhead cost and the professional staff hours available as in (3) above. Also suppose that the actual professional staff hours charged to clients' accounts and the actual overhead costs turn out to be exactly as estimated in both years. By how much would the overhead be underapplied or overapplied in 2005? In 2006?

EXERCISE 3-13 Departmental Overhead Rates [LO2, LO3, LO4]

Diewold Company has two departments, Milling and Assembly. The company uses a job-order costing system and computes a predetermined overhead rate in each department. The Milling Department bases its rate on machine-hours, and the Assembly Department bases its rate on direct labor cost. At the beginning of the year, the company made the following estimates:

	Department	
	Milling	Assembly
Direct labor-hours	8,000	75,000
Machine-hours	60,000	3,000
Manufacturing overhead cost.	$510,000	$800,000
Direct labor cost	$72,000	$640,000

Required:

1. Compute the predetermined overhead rate to be used in each department.
2. Assume that the overhead rates you computed in (1) above are in effect. The job cost sheet for Job 407, which was started and completed during the year, showed the following:

	Department	
	Milling	Assembly
Direct labor-hours	5	20
Machine-hours	90	4
Materials requisitioned	$800	$370
Direct labor cost	$45	$160

   Compute the total overhead cost applied to Job 407.
3. Would you expect substantially different amounts of overhead cost to be charged to some jobs if the company used a plantwide overhead rate based on direct labor cost instead of using departmental rates? Explain. No computations are necessary.

EXERCISE 3-14 Predetermined Overhead Rate; Applying Overhead; Underapplied or Overapplied Overhead [LO3, LO4, LO5]

Medusa Products uses a job-order costing system. Overhead costs are applied to jobs on the basis of machine-hours. At the beginning of the year, management estimated that the company would work 85,000 machine-hours and incur $170,000 in manufacturing overhead costs for the year.

Required:

1. Compute the company's predetermined overhead rate.
2. Assume that during the year the company actually worked only 80,000 machine-hours and incurred $168,000 of manufacturing overhead costs. Compute the amount of underapplied or overapplied overhead for the year.
3. Explain why the manufacturing overhead was underapplied or overapplied for the year.

Problems

PROBLEM 3-15 Multiple Departments; Overhead Rates; Underapplied or Overapplied Overhead [LO3, LO4, LO5]

Winkle, Kotter, and Zale is a small law firm that contains 10 partners and 10 support persons. The firm employs a job-order costing system to accumulate costs chargeable to each client, and it is organized into two departments—the Research and Documents Department and the Litigation Department. The firm uses predetermined overhead rates to charge the costs of these departments to its clients. At the beginning of the current year, the firm's management made the following estimates for the year:

	Department	
	Research and Documents	Litigation
Research-hours	20,000	—
Direct attorney-hours	9,000	16,000
Materials and supplies	$18,000	$5,000
Direct attorney cost	$430,000	$800,000
Departmental overhead cost	$700,000	$320,000

The predetermined overhead rate in the Research and Documents Department is based on research-hours, and the rate in the Litigation Department is based on direct attorney cost.

The costs charged to each client are made up of three elements: materials and supplies used, direct attorney costs incurred, and an applied amount of overhead from each department in which work is performed on the case.

Case 618-3 was initiated on February 10 and completed on June 30. During this period, the following costs and time were recorded on the case:

	Department	
	Research and Documents	Litigation
Research-hours	18	—
Direct attorney-hours	9	42
Materials and supplies	$50	$30
Direct attorney cost	$410	$2,100

Required:

1. Compute the predetermined overhead rates used during the year in the Research and Documents Department and the Litigation Department.
2. Using the rates you computed in (1) above, compute the total overhead cost applied to Case 618-3.
3. What would be the total cost charged to Case 618-3? Show computations by department and in total for the case.
4. At the end of the year, the firm's records revealed the following *actual* cost and operating data for all cases handled during the year:

	Department	
	Research and Documents	Litigation
Research-hours	23,000	—
Direct attorney-hours	8,000	15,000
Materials and supplies	$19,000	$6,000
Direct attorney cost	$400,000	$725,000
Departmental overhead cost	$770,000	$300,000

Determine the amount of underapplied or overapplied overhead cost in each department for the year.

PROBLEM 3-16 Predetermined Overhead Rate; Applying Overhead; Underapplied or Overapplied Overhead [LO4, LO5, LO6]

Ravsten Company uses a job-order costing system.

The company applies overhead cost to jobs on the basis of machine-hours. For the current year, the company estimated that it would work 36,000 machine-hours and incur $153,000 in manufacturing overhead cost. The following transactions occurred during the year:

a. Raw materials requisitioned for use in production, $190,000 (80% direct and 20% indirect).
b. The following costs were incurred for employee services:

Direct labor	$160,000
Indirect labor	$27,000
Sales commissions	$36,000
Administrative salaries	$80,000

c. Heat, power, and water costs incurred in the factory, $42,000.
d. Insurance costs, $10,000 (90% relates to factory operations, and 10% relates to selling and administrative activities).
e. Advertising costs incurred, $50,000.
f. Depreciation recorded for the year, $60,000 (85% relates to factory operations, and 15% relates to selling and administrative activities).
g. The company used 40,000 machine-hours during the year.
h. Goods that cost $480,000 to manufacture according to their job cost sheets were transferred to the finished goods warehouse.
i. Sales for the year totaled $700,000. The total cost to manufacture these goods according to their job cost sheets was $475,000.

Required:

1. Determine the underapplied or overapplied overhead for the year.
2. Prepare an income statement for the year. (Hint: No calculations are required to determine the cost of goods sold before any adjustment for underapplied or overapplied overhead.)

PROBLEM 3-17 Direct Method of Determining Cost of Goods Sold [LO6]

Techuxia Corporation worked on four jobs during October: Job A256, Job A257, Job A258, and Job A260. At the end of October, the job cost sheets for these jobs contained the following data:

	Job A256	Job A257	Job A258	Job A260
Beginning balance	$1,200	$500	$0	$0
Charged to the jobs during October:				
Direct materials	$2,600	$3,500	$1,400	$3,500
Direct labor	$800	$1,000	$600	$400
Manufacturing overhead applied	$1,200	$1,500	$900	$600
Units completed	100	0	200	0
Units in process at the end of October	0	400	0	500
Units sold during October	80	0	40	0

Jobs A256 and A258 were completed during October. The other two jobs had not yet been completed at the end of October. There was no finished goods inventory on October 1.

In October, overhead was overapplied by $800. The company adjusts its cost of goods sold every month for the amount of the underapplied or overapplied overhead.

Required:

1. Using the direct method, what is the cost of goods sold for October?
2. What is the total value of the finished goods inventory at the end of October?
3. What is the total value of the work in process inventory at the end of October?

PROBLEM 3-18 Indirect Method of Determining Cost of Goods Sold [LO7]

Refer to the data for Techuxia Corporation in Problem 3-17.

Required:

Using the indirect method, what is the cost of goods sold for October?

PROBLEM 3-19 Multiple Departments; Applying Overhead [LO3, LO4, LO5]

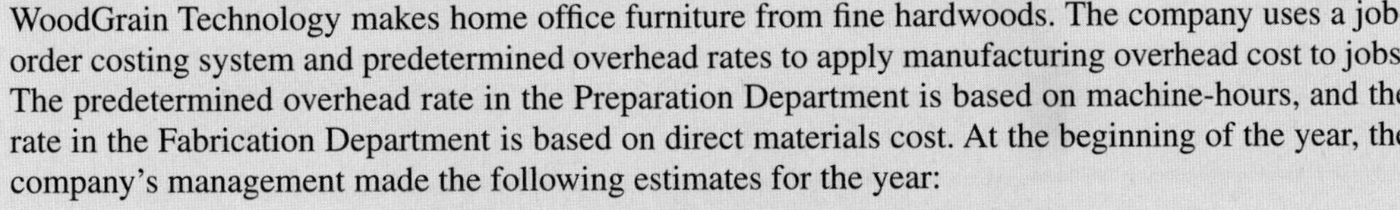

WoodGrain Technology makes home office furniture from fine hardwoods. The company uses a job-order costing system and predetermined overhead rates to apply manufacturing overhead cost to jobs. The predetermined overhead rate in the Preparation Department is based on machine-hours, and the rate in the Fabrication Department is based on direct materials cost. At the beginning of the year, the company's management made the following estimates for the year:

	Department	
	Preparation	Fabrication
Machine-hours	80,000	21,000
Direct labor-hours	35,000	65,000
Direct materials cost	$190,000	$400,000
Direct labor cost	$280,000	$530,000
Manufacturing overhead cost	$416,000	$720,000

The following information pertains to Job 127, which was started on April 1 and completed on May 12.

	Department	
	Preparation	Fabrication
Machine-hours	350	70
Direct labor-hours	80	130
Direct materials cost	$940	$1,200
Direct labor cost	$710	$980

Required:

1. Compute the predetermined overhead rates used during the year in the Preparation Department and the Fabrication Department.
2. Compute the total overhead cost applied to Job 127.
3. What would be the total cost recorded for Job 127? If the job contained 25 units, what would be the unit product cost?
4. At the end of the year, the records of WoodGrain Technology revealed the following *actual* cost and operating data for all jobs worked on during the year:

	Department	
	Preparation	Fabrication
Machine-hours	73,000	24,000
Direct labor-hours	30,000	68,000
Direct materials cost	$165,000	$420,000
Manufacturing overhead cost	$390,000	$740,000

What was the amount of underapplied or overapplied overhead in each department at the end of the year?

PROBLEM 3-20 (Appendix 3A) Predetermined Overhead Rate and Capacity [LO3, LO4, LO5, LO8]
Skid Road Recording, Inc., is a small audio recording studio located in Seattle. The company handles work for advertising agencies—primarily for radio ads—and has a few singers and bands as clients. Skid Road Recording handles all aspects of recording from editing to making a digital master from which CDs can be copied. The competition in the audio recording industry in Seattle has always been tough, but it has been getting even tougher over the last several years. The studio has been losing customers to newer studios that are equipped with more up-to-date equipment and that are able to offer very attractive prices and excellent service. Summary data concerning the last two years of operations follow:

	2005	2006
Estimated hours of studio service	1,000	750
Estimated studio overhead cost	$90,000	$90,000
Actual hours of studio service provided	900	600
Actual studio overhead cost incurred	$90,000	$90,000
Hours of studio service at capacity	1,800	1,800

The company applies studio overhead to recording jobs based on the hours of studio service provided. For example, 30 hours of studio time were required to record, edit, and master the *Slug Fest* music CD for a local band. All of the studio overhead is fixed, and the actual overhead cost incurred was exactly as estimated at the beginning of the year in both 2005 and 2006.

Required:

1. Skid Road Recording computes its predetermined overhead rate at the beginning of each year based on the estimated studio overhead and the estimated hours of studio service for the year. How much overhead would have been applied to the *Slug Fest* job if it had been done in 2005? In 2006? By how much would overhead have been underapplied or overapplied in 2005? In 2006?
2. The president of Skid Road Recording has heard that some companies in the industry have changed to a system of computing the predetermined overhead rate at the beginning of each year based on the estimated studio overhead for the year and the hours of studio service that could be provided at capacity. He would like to know what effect this method would have on job costs. How much overhead would have been applied using this method to the *Slug Fest* job if it had been done in 2005? In 2006? By how much would overhead have been underapplied or overapplied in 2005 using this method? In 2006?
3. How would you interpret the underapplied or overapplied overhead that results from using studio hours at capacity to compute the predetermined overhead rate?
4. What fundamental business problem is Skid Road Recording resolving? Which method of computing the predetermined overhead rate is likely to be more helpful in resolving this problem? Explain.

PROBLEM 3-21 Applying Overhead in a Service Company [LO4, LO5]
Heritage Gardens provides complete garden design and landscaping services. The company uses a job-order costing system to track the costs of its landscaping projects. The table below provides data concerning the three landscaping projects that were in progress during May. There was no work in process at the beginning of May.

	Project		
	Williams	Chandler	Nguyen
Designer-hours	200	80	120
Direct materials	$4,800	$1,800	$3,600
Direct labor	$2,400	$1,000	$1,500

Actual overhead costs were $16,000 for May. Overhead costs are applied to projects on the basis of designer-hours because most of the overhead is related to the costs of the garden design studio. The predetermined overhead rate is $45 per designer-hour. The Williams and Chandler projects were completed in May; the Nguyen project was not completed by the end of the month. No other jobs were in process during May.

Required:

1. Compute the amount of overhead cost that would have been applied to each project during May.
2. Determine the cost of goods manufactured for May.
3. What is the accumulated cost of the work in process at the end of the month?
4. Determine the underapplied or overapplied overhead for May.

PROBLEM 3-22 Applying Overhead; Underapplied or Overapplied Overhead; Income Statement [LO4, LO5, LO6]

Durham Company uses a job-order costing system. The following transactions took place last year:

a. Raw materials requisitioned for use in production, $40,000 (80% direct and 20% indirect).
b. Factory utility costs incurred, $14,600.
c. Depreciation recorded on plant and equipment, $28,000. Three-fourths of the depreciation relates to factory equipment, and the remainder relates to selling and administrative equipment.
d. Costs for salaries and wages were incurred as follows:

Direct labor	$40,000
Indirect labor	$18,000
Sales commissions	$10,400
Administrative salaries	$25,000

e. Insurance costs incurred, $3,000 (80% relates to factory operations, and 20% relates to selling and administrative activities).
f. Miscellaneous selling and administrative expenses incurred, $18,000.
g. Manufacturing overhead was applied to production. The company applies overhead on the basis of 150% of direct labor cost.
h. Goods that cost $130,000 to manufacture according to their job cost sheets were transferred to the finished goods warehouse.
i. Goods that had cost $120,000 to manufacture according to their job cost sheets were sold for $200,000.

Required:

1. Determine the underapplied or overapplied overhead for the year.
2. Prepare an income statement for the year. (Hint: No calculations are required to determine the cost of goods sold before any adjustment for underapplied or overapplied overhead.)

PROBLEM 3-23 Predetermined Overhead Rate; Underapplied or Overapplied Overhead [LO3, LO5]

Savallas Company is highly automated and uses computers to control manufacturing operations. The company uses a job-order costing system and applies manufacturing overhead cost to products on the basis of computer-hours. The following estimates were used in preparing the predetermined overhead rate at the beginning of the year:

Computer-hours	85,000
Manufacturing overhead cost	$1,530,000

During the year, a severe economic recession resulted in cutting back production and a buildup of inventory in the company's warehouse. The company recorded the following actual cost and operating data for the year:

Computer-hours	60,000
Manufacturing overhead cost	$1,350,000
Cost of goods sold (not adjusted for underapplied or overapplied overhead)	$2,800,000

Required:

1. Compute the company's predetermined overhead rate for the year.
2. Compute the underapplied or overapplied overhead for the year.
3. Determine the cost of goods sold for the year after any adjustment for underapplied or overapplied overhead.

PROBLEM 3-24 Applying Overhead in a Service Company [LO2, LO3, LO4]

Pearson Architectural Design uses a job-order costing system and applies studio overhead to jobs on the basis of direct staff costs. Because Pearson Architectural Design is a service firm, the names of the accounts it uses are different from the names used in manufacturing companies. The following costs were recorded in January:

Cost of subcontracted work (comparable to direct materials)	$90,000
Direct staff costs (comparable to direct labor)	$200,000
Studio overhead (comparable to manufacturing overhead cost applied)	$320,000
Cost of work completed (comparable to cost of goods manufactured)	$570,000

There were no beginning inventories in January.

At the end of January, only one job was still in process. This job (the Krimmer Corporation Headquarters project) had been charged with $13,500 in direct staff costs.

Required:

1. Compute the predetermined overhead rate that was used during January.
2. Complete the following job cost sheet for the partially completed Krimmer Corporation Headquarters project. (Hint: Cost of goods manufactured equals beginning work in process inventory plus manufacturing costs incurred less ending work in process inventory.)

Job Cost Sheet Krimmer Corporation Headquarters Project	
Costs of subcontracted work	$?
Direct staff costs	?
Studio overhead	?
Total cost to January 31	$?

PROBLEM 3-25 Plantwide versus Departmental Overhead Rates; Underapplied or Overapplied Overhead [LO3, LO4, LO5]

"Don't tell me we've lost another bid!" exclaimed Sandy Kovallas, president of Lenko Products, Inc. "I'm afraid so," replied Doug Martin, the operations vice president. "One of our competitors underbid us by about $10,000 on the Hastings job." "I just can't figure it out," said Kovallas. "It seems we're either too high to get the job or too low to make any money on half the jobs we bid any more. What's happened?"

Lenko Products manufactures specialized goods to customers' specifications and operates a job-order costing system. Manufacturing overhead cost is applied to jobs on the basis of direct labor cost. The following estimates were made at the beginning of the year:

	Department			
	Cutting	Machining	Assembly	Total Plant
Direct labor	$300,000	$200,000	$400,000	$900,000
Manufacturing overhead	$540,000	$800,000	$100,000	$1,440,000

Jobs require varying amounts of work in the three departments. The Hastings job, for example, would have required manufacturing costs in the three departments as follows:

	Department			
	Cutting	Machining	Assembly	Total Plant
Direct materials	$12,000	$900	$5,600	$18,500
Direct labor	$6,500	$1,700	$13,000	$21,200
Manufacturing overhead	?	?	?	?

The company uses a plantwide overhead rate to apply manufacturing overhead cost to jobs.

Required:

1. Assuming the use of a plantwide overhead rate:
   a. Compute the rate for the current year.
   b. Determine the amount of manufacturing overhead cost that would have been applied to the Hastings job.
2. Suppose that instead of using a plantwide overhead rate, the company had used a separate predetermined overhead rate in each department. Under these conditions:
   a. Compute the rate for each department for the current year.
   b. Determine the amount of manufacturing overhead cost that would have been applied to the Hastings job.
3. Explain the difference between the manufacturing overhead that would have been applied to the Hastings job using the plantwide rate in question 1(b) above and using the departmental rates in question 2(b).
4. Assume that it is customary in the industry to bid jobs at 150% of total manufacturing cost (direct materials, direct labor, and applied overhead). What was the company's bid price on the Hastings job? What would the bid price have been if departmental overhead rates had been used to apply overhead cost?
5. At the end of the year, the company assembled the following *actual* cost data relating to all jobs worked on during the year:

	Department			
	Cutting	Machining	Assembly	Total Plant
Direct materials	$760,000	$90,000	$410,000	$1,260,000
Direct labor	$320,000	$210,000	$340,000	$870,000
Manufacturing overhead	$560,000	$830,000	$92,000	$1,482,000

Compute the underapplied or overapplied overhead for the year (*a*) assuming that a plantwide overhead rate is used, and (*b*) assuming that departmental overhead rates are used.

Cases

CASE 3-26 (Appendix 3A) Ethics; Predetermined Overhead Rate and Capacity [LO4, LO5, LO8]
Melissa Ostwerk, the new controller of TurboDrives, Inc., has just returned from a seminar on the choice of the activity level in the predetermined overhead rate. Even though the subject did not sound exciting at first, she found that there were some important ideas presented that should get a hearing at her company. After returning from the seminar, she arranged a meeting with the production manager, Jan Kingman, and the assistant production manager, Lonny Chan.

Melissa: I ran across an idea that I wanted to check out with both of you. It's about the way we compute predetermined overhead rates.

Jan: We're all ears.

Melissa: We compute the predetermined overhead rate by dividing the estimated total factory overhead for the coming year by the estimated total units produced for the coming year.

Lonny: We've been doing that as long as I've been with the company.

Jan: And it has been done that way at every other company I've worked at, except at most places they divide by direct labor-hours.

Melissa: We use units because it is simpler and we basically make one product with minor variations. But, there's another way to do it. Instead of dividing the estimated total factory overhead by the estimated total units produced for the coming year, we could divide by the total units produced at capacity.

Lonny: Oh, the Marketing Department will love that. It will drop the costs on all of our products. They'll go wild over there cutting prices.

Melissa: That is a worry, but I wanted to talk to both of you first before going over to Marketing.

Jan: Aren't you always going to have a lot of underapplied overhead?

Melissa: That's correct, but let me show you how we would handle it. Here's an example based on our budget for next year.

Budgeted (estimated) production	80,000 units
Budgeted sales	80,000 units
Capacity	100,000 units
Selling price	$70 per unit
Variable manufacturing cost	$18 per unit
Total manufacturing overhead cost (all fixed)	$2,000,000
Selling and administrative expenses (all fixed)	$1,950,000
Beginning inventories	$0

Traditional approach to computation of the predetermined overhead rate:

$$\text{Predetermined overhead rate} = \frac{\text{Estimated total manufacturing overhead cost}}{\text{Estimated total amount of the allocation base}}$$

$$= \frac{\$2{,}000{,}000}{80{,}000 \text{ units}} = \$25 \text{ per unit}$$

Budgeted Income Statement		
Revenue (80,000 units × $70 per unit)		$5,600,000
Cost of goods sold:		
Variable manufacturing		
(80,000 units × $18 per unit)	$1,440,000	
Manufacturing overhead applied		
(80,000 units × $25 per unit)	2,000,000	3,440,000
Gross margin		2,160,000
Selling and administrative expenses		1,950,000
Net operating income		$ 210,000

New approach to computation of the predetermined overhead rate using capacity in the denominator:

$$\text{Predetermined overhead rate} = \frac{\text{Estimated total manufacturing overhead cost at capacity}}{\text{Estimated total amount of the allocation base at capacity}}$$

$$= \frac{\$2{,}000{,}000}{100{,}000 \text{ units}} = \$20 \text{ per unit}$$

Budgeted Income Statement		
Revenue (80,000 units × $70 per unit)		$5,600,000
Cost of goods sold:		
Variable manufacturing		
(80,000 units × $18 per unit)	$1,440,000	
Manufacturing overhead applied		
(80,000 units × $20 per unit)	1,600,000	3,040,000
Gross margin		2,560,000
Cost of unused capacity		
[(100,000 units − 80,000 units) × $20 per unit]		400,000
Selling and administrative expenses		1,950,000
Net operating income		$ 210,000

Jan: Whoa!! I don't think I like the looks of that "Cost of unused capacity." If that thing shows up on the income statement, someone from headquarters is likely to come down here looking for some people to lay off.

Lonny: I'm worried about something else, too. What happens when sales are not up to expectations? Can we pull the "hat trick"?

Melissa: I'm sorry, I don't understand.

Jan: Lonny's talking about something that happens fairly regularly. When sales are down and profits look like they are going to be lower than the president told the owners they were going to be, the president comes down here and asks us to deliver some more profits.

Lonny: And we pull them out of our hat.

Jan: Yeah, we just increase production until we get the profits we want.

Melissa: I still don't understand. You mean you increase sales?

Jan: Nope, we increase production. We're the production managers, not the sales managers.

Melissa: I get it. Since you have produced more, the sales force has more units it can sell.

Jan: Nope, the marketing people don't do a thing. We just build inventories and that does the trick.

Required:

In all of the questions below, assume that the predetermined overhead rate under the traditional method is $25 per unit, and under the new method it is $20 per unit. Also assume that under the traditional method any underapplied or overapplied overhead is taken directly to the income statement as an adjustment to Cost of Goods Sold.

1. Suppose actual production is 80,000 units. Compute the net operating incomes that would be realized under the traditional and new methods if actual sales are 75,000 units and everything else turns out as expected.
2. How many units would have to be produced under each of the methods in order to realize the budgeted net operating income of $210,000 if actual sales are 75,000 units and everything else turns out as expected?
3. What effect does the new method based on capacity have on the volatility of net operating income?
4. Will the "hat trick" be easier or harder to perform if the new method based on capacity is used?
5. Do you think the "hat trick" is ethical?

CASE 3-27 Critical Thinking; Interpretation of Manufacturing Overhead Rates [LO3, LO4]

Sharpton Fabricators Corporation manufactures a variety of parts for the automotive industry. The company uses a job-order costing system with a plantwide predetermined overhead rate based on direct labor-hours. On December 10, 2006, the company's controller made a preliminary estimate of the predetermined overhead rate for 2007. The new rate was based on the estimated total manufacturing overhead cost of $2,475,000 and the estimated 52,000 total direct labor-hours for 2007:

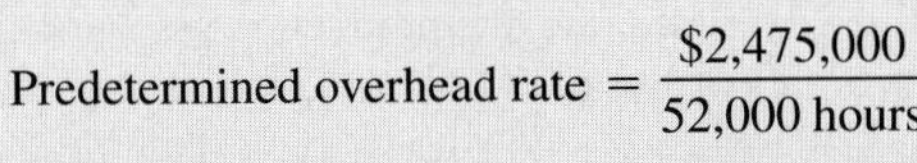

$$\text{Predetermined overhead rate} = \frac{\$2{,}475{,}000}{52{,}000 \text{ hours}}$$

$$= \$47.60 \text{ per direct labor-hour}$$

This new predetermined overhead rate was communicated to top managers in a meeting on December 11. The rate did not cause any comment because it was within a few pennies of the overhead rate that had been used during 2006. One of the subjects discussed at the meeting was a proposal by the production manager to purchase an automated milling machine built by Central Robotics. The president of Sharpton Fabricators, Kevin Reynolds, agreed to meet with the regional sales representative from Central Robotics to discuss the proposal.

On the day following the meeting, Mr. Reynolds met with Jay Warner, Central Robotics' sales representative. The following discussion took place:

Reynolds: Larry Winter, our production manager, asked me to meet with you because he is interested in installing an automated milling machine. Frankly, I am skeptical. You're going to have to show me this isn't just another expensive toy for Larry's people to play with.

Warner: That shouldn't be too difficult, Mr. Reynolds. The automated milling machine has three major advantages. First, it is much faster than the manual methods you are using. It can process about twice as many parts per hour as your present milling machines. Second, it is much more flexible. There are some up-front programming costs, but once those have been incurred, almost no setup is required on the machines for standard operations. You just punch in the code of the standard operation, load the machine's hopper with raw material, and the machine does the rest.

Reynolds: Yeah, but what about cost? Having twice the capacity in the milling machine area won't do us much good. That center is idle much of the time anyway.

Warner: I was getting there. The third advantage of the automated milling machine is lower cost. Larry Winters and I looked over your present operations, and we estimated that the automated equipment would eliminate the need for about 6,000 direct labor-hours a year. What is your direct labor cost per hour?

Reynolds: The wage rate in the milling area averages about $21 per hour. Fringe benefits raise that figure to about $30 per hour.

Warner: Don't forget your overhead.

Reynolds: Next year the overhead rate will be about $48 per hour.

Warner: So including fringe benefits and overhead, the cost per direct labor-hour is about $78.

Reynolds: That's right.

Warner: Since you can save 6,000 direct labor-hours per year, the cost savings would amount to about $468,000 a year.

Reynolds: That's pretty impressive, but you aren't giving away this equipment are you?

Warner: Several options are available, including leasing and outright purchase. Just for comparison purposes, our 60-month lease plan would require payments of only $300,000 per year.

Reynolds: Sold! When can you install the equipment?

Shortly after this meeting, Mr. Reynolds informed the company's controller of the decision to lease the new equipment, which would be installed over the Christmas vacation period. The controller realized that this decision would require a recomputation of the predetermined overhead rate for the year 2007 since the decision would affect both the manufacturing overhead and the direct labor-hours for the year. After talking with both the production manager and the sales representative from Central Robotics, the controller discovered that in addition to the annual lease cost of $300,000, the new machine would also require a skilled technician/programmer who would have to be hired at a cost of $45,000 per year to maintain and program the equipment. Both of these costs would be included in factory overhead. There would be no other changes in total manufacturing overhead cost, which is almost entirely fixed. The controller assumed that the new machine would result in a reduction of 6,000 direct labor-hours for the year from the levels that had initially been planned.

When the revised predetermined overhead rate for the year 2007 was circulated among the company's top managers, there was considerable dismay.

Required:

1. Recompute the predetermined rate assuming that the new machine will be installed. Explain why the new predetermined overhead rate is higher (or lower) than the rate that was originally estimated for the year 2007.
2. What effect (if any) would this new rate have on the cost of jobs that do not use the new automated milling machine?
3. Why would managers be concerned about the new overhead rate?
4. After seeing the new predetermined overhead rate, the production manager admitted that he probably wouldn't be able to eliminate all of the 6,000 direct labor-hours. He had been hoping to accomplish the reduction by not replacing workers who retire or quit, but that would not be possible. As a result, the real labor savings would be only about 2,000 hours—one worker. Given this additional information, evaluate the original decision to acquire the automated milling machine from Central Robotics.

CASE 3-28 Ethics and the Manager [LO3, LO4, LO5]

Cristin Madsen has recently been transferred to the Appliances Division of Solequin Corporation. Shortly after taking over her new position as divisional controller, she was asked to develop the division's predetermined overhead rate for the upcoming year. The accuracy of the rate is important because it is used throughout the year and any overapplied or underapplied overhead is closed out to Cost of Goods Sold at the end of the year. Solequin Corporation uses direct labor-hours in all of its divisions as the allocation base for manufacturing overhead.

To compute the predetermined overhead rate, Cristin divided her estimate of the total manufacturing overhead for the coming year by the production manager's estimate of the total direct labor-hours for the coming year. She took her computations to the division's general manager for approval but was quite surprised when he suggested a modification in the base. Her conversation with the general manager of the Appliances Division, Lance Jusic, went like this:

Madsen: Here are my calculations for next year's predetermined overhead rate. If you approve, we can enter the rate into the computer on January 1 and be up and running in the job-order costing system right away this year.

Jusic: Thanks for coming up with the calculations so quickly, and they look just fine. There is, however, one slight modification I would like to see. Your estimate of the total direct labor-hours for the year is 110,000 hours. How about cutting that to about 105,000 hours?

Madsen: I don't know if I can do that. The production manager says she will need about 110,000 direct labor-hours to meet the sales projections for next year. Besides, there are going to be over 108,000 direct labor-hours during the current year and sales are projected to be higher next year.

Jusic: Cristin, I know all of that. I would still like to reduce the direct labor-hours in the base to something like 105,000 hours. You probably don't know that I had an agreement with your predecessor as divisional controller to shave 5% or so off the estimated direct labor-hours every year. That way, we kept a reserve that usually resulted in a big boost to net operating income at the end of the fiscal year in December. We called it our Christmas bonus. Corporate headquarters always seemed pleased that we could pull off such a miracle at the end of the year. This system has worked well for many years, and I don't want to change it now.

Required:

1. Explain how shaving 5% off the estimated direct labor-hours in the base for the predetermined overhead rate usually results in a big boost in net operating income at the end of the fiscal year.
2. Should Cristin Madsen go along with the general manager's request to reduce the direct labor-hours in the predetermined overhead rate computation to 105,000 direct labor-hours?

RESEARCH AND APPLICATION 3-29 [LO1, LO2, LO3]

The questions in this exercise are based on Toll Brothers, Inc., one of the largest home builders in the United States. To answer the questions, you will need to download Toll Brothers' 2004 annual report (www.tollbrothers.com/homesearch/servlet/HomeSearch?app=IRannual) and Form 10-K. To access the 10-K report, go to www.sec.gov/edgar/searchedgar/companysearch.html. Input CIK code 794170 and hit enter. In the gray box on the right-hand side of your computer screen define the scope of your search by inputting 10-K and then pressing enter. Select the 10-K with a filing date of January 13, 2005. You do not need to print these documents to answer the questions.

Required:

1. What is Toll Brothers' strategy for success in the marketplace? Does the company rely primarily on a customer intimacy, operational excellence, or product leadership customer value proposition? What evidence supports your conclusion?
2. What business risks does Toll Brothers face that may threaten the company's ability to satisfy stockholder expectations? What are some examples of control activities that the company could use to reduce these risks? (Hint: Focus on pages 10–11 of the 10-K.)
3. Would Toll Brothers be more likely to use process costing or job-order costing? Why?
4. What are some examples of Toll Brothers' direct material costs? Would you expect the bill of materials for each of Toll Brothers' homes to be the same or different? Why?
5. Describe the types of direct labor costs incurred by Toll Brothers. Would Toll Brothers use employee time tickets at their home sites under construction? Why or why not?
6. What are some examples of overhead costs that are incurred by Toll Brothers?
7. Some companies establish prices for their products by marking up their full manufacturing cost (i.e., the sum of direct materials, direct labor, and manufacturing overhead costs). For example, a company may set prices at 150% of each product's full manufacturing cost. Does Toll Brothers price its houses using this approach?
8. How does Toll Brothers assign manufacturing overhead costs to cost objects? From a financial reporting standpoint, why does the company need to assign manufacturing overhead costs to cost objects?

Chapter

4

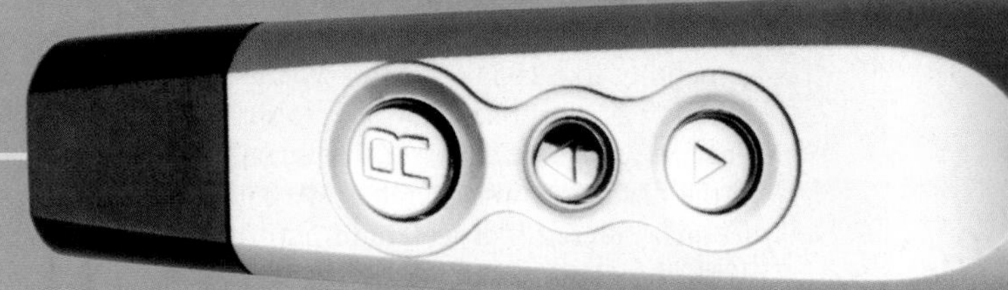

Learning Objectives

After studying Chapter 4, you should be able to:

LO1 Understand how fixed and variable costs behave and how to use them to predict costs.

LO2 Use a scattergraph plot to diagnose cost behavior.

LO3 Analyze a mixed cost using the high-low method.

LO4 Prepare an income statement using the contribution format.

LO5 (Appendix 4A) Analyze a mixed cost using the least-squares regression method.

LP 4

Source: Conversations with Shidoni personnel, including Bill Rogers and Harry Gold, and Shidoni literature. See www.shidoni.com for more information concerning the company.

Cost Behavior: Analysis and Use

The Business of Art Sculpture

BUSINESS FOCUS

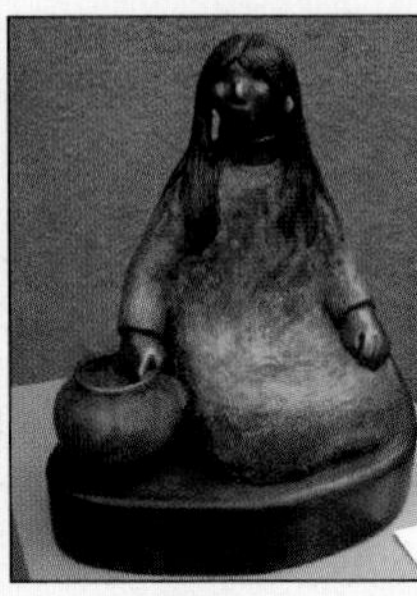

Shidoni Foundry, located in Tesuque, New Mexico, is a fine art casting and fabrication facility. The process of creating a bronze or other metal sculpture is complex. The artist creates the sculpture using modeling clay and then hires a foundry such as Shidoni to produce the actual metal sculpture. Shidoni craftspeople make a rubber mold from the clay model then use that mold to make a wax version of the original. The wax is in turn used to make a ceramic casting mold, and finally the bronze version is cast. Both the wax and the ceramic casting mold are destroyed in the process of making the metal casting, but the rubber mold is not and can be reused to make additional castings.

The surface of the metal sculpture can be treated with various patinas. One of the accompanying photos shows Harry Gold, the shop's patina artist, applying a patina to a metal sculpture with brush and blowtorch. The other photo shows a finished sculpture with patinas applied.

The artist is faced with a difficult business decision. The rubber mold for a small figure such as the seated Indian in the accompanying photo costs roughly $500; the mold for a life-size figure such as the cowboy costs $3,800 to $5,000. This is just for the mold! Fortunately, as discussed above, a number of metal castings can be made from each mold. However, each life-size casting costs $8,500 to $11,000. In contrast, a casting of the much smaller Indian sculpture would cost about $750. Given the fixed costs of the mold and variable costs of the casting, finish treatments, and bases, the artist must decide how many castings to produce and how to price them. The fewer the castings, the greater the rarity factor, and hence the higher the price that can be charged to art lovers. However, in that case, the fixed costs of making the mold must be spread across fewer items. The artist must make sure not to price the sculptures so high that the investment in molds and in the castings cannot be recovered. ■

In Chapter 2, we stated that costs can be classified by behavior. Cost behavior refers to how a cost will change as the level of activity changes. Managers who understand how costs behave can predict how costs will change under various alternatives. Conversely, attempting to make decisions without a thorough understanding of cost behavior patterns can lead to disaster. For example, cutting back production of a product line might result in far less cost savings than managers assume if they confuse fixed costs with variable costs—leading to a drop in profits. To avoid such problems, managers must be able to accurately predict what costs will be at various activity levels.

This chapter briefly reviews the definitions of variable and fixed costs and then discusses the behavior of these costs in greater depth than in Chapter 2. The chapter also introduces the concept of a mixed cost, which is a cost that has both variable and fixed cost elements. The chapter concludes by introducing a new income statement format—called the *contribution format*—in which costs are organized by behavior rather than by the traditional functions of production, sales, and administration.

Types of Cost Behavior Patterns

In Chapter 2 we mentioned only variable and fixed costs. In this chapter we will examine a third cost behavior pattern, known as a *mixed* or *semivariable* cost. All three cost behavior patterns—variable, fixed, and mixed—are found in most organizations. The relative proportion of each type of cost in an organization is known as its **cost structure.** For example, an organization might have many fixed costs but few variable or mixed costs. Alternatively, it might have many variable costs but few fixed or mixed costs. In this chapter, we will concentrate on gaining a fuller understanding of the behavior of each type of cost. In the next chapter, we explore how cost structure impacts decisions.

4–1

IN BUSINESS

COST STRUCTURE: A MANAGEMENT CHOICE

Some managers are thriftier than others. Kenneth Iverson built Nucor Steel into the most successful U.S. steel company of recent years by developing a whole new approach to steel-making using cost-efficient minimills. Iverson ran his company with few layers of management and a commitment to employees that everyone would be treated alike. Workers were "dissuaded from joining a union by high wages and a series of No's—no management dining rooms, no company yachts, no company planes, no first-class travel for executives, and no support staff to pamper the upper echelons." Iverson ran the largest steel company in the U.S. with only 20 people in his headquarters. "By responding to market signals, focusing on a single major product line, and treating his employees with respect and compassion, Mr. Iverson contributed immensely to the industrial rebirth in this country."

Source: Donald F. Barnett and Robert W. Crandall, "Remembering a Man of Steel," *The Wall Street Journal*, April 23, 2002, p. B4.

Variable Costs

LEARNING OBJECTIVE 1
Understand how fixed and variable costs behave and how to use them to predict costs.

We explained in Chapter 2 that a variable cost is a cost whose total dollar amount varies in direct proportion to changes in the activity level. If the activity level doubles, the total variable cost also doubles. If the activity level increases by only 10%, then the total variable cost increases by 10% as well.

IN BUSINESS

ADVERTISING ON THE WEB

Many companies spend a growing portion of their advertising budgets on web-based contextual advertising. Here is an example of how it works. A tour company specializing in trips to Belize would like to steer consumers interested in Belize vacations to its website. The tour company partners with National Geographic and Quigo Technologies, a software company, to ensure that every time a visitor reads a National Geographic article mentioning the word Belize, a pop-up advertisement contains a link to the tour company's website. The tour company pays 50 cents each time a visitor clicks on that link. The 50 cents is split between iExplore.com, National Geographic's on-line business, and Quigo Technologies. For the tour company, this form of advertising is a clear example of a variable cost. The cost per click is constant at 50 cents per unit, but the total advertising cost rises as the number of clicks increases.

The challenge for software developers at companies such as Quigo Technologies, Google, and Yahoo is to write programs that intelligently select ads that are relevant to the context of a given web page. Providing superior contextual relevance increases the likelihood that web surfers will click on an advertisement, which in turn increases the revenue generated. Quigo Technologies' Michael Yavonditte claims that his company's ads are clicked on 0.7% of the time versus 0.2% for competitors.

Source: Chana R. Schoenberger, "Out of Context" *Forbes*, November 29, 2004, pp. 64–68.

We also found in Chapter 2 that a variable cost remains constant if expressed on a *per unit* basis. To provide an example, consider Nooksack Expeditions, a small company that provides daylong whitewater rafting excursions on rivers in the North Cascade Mountains. The company provides all of the necessary equipment and experienced guides, and it serves gourmet meals to its guests. The meals are purchased from an exclusive caterer for $30 a person for a daylong excursion. If we look at the cost of the meals on a *per person* basis, it remains constant at $30. This $30 cost per person will not change, regardless of how many people participate in a daylong excursion. The behavior of this variable cost, on both a per unit and a total basis, is tabulated as follows:

Number of Guests	Cost of Meals per Guest	Total Cost of Meals
250	$30	$7,500
500	$30	$15,000
750	$30	$22,500
1,000	$30	$30,000

The idea that a variable cost is constant per unit but varies in total with the activity level is crucial to understanding cost behavior patterns. We shall rely on this concept repeatedly in this chapter and in chapters ahead.

Exhibit 4–1 illustrates variable cost behavior. Note that the graph of the total cost of the meals slants upward to the right. This is because the total cost of the meals is directly proportional to the number of guests. In contrast, the graph of the per unit cost of meals is flat because the cost of the meals per guest is constant at $30.

The Activity Base For a cost to be variable, it must be variable *with respect to something.* That "something" is its *activity base.* An **activity base** is a measure of whatever causes the incurrence of variable cost. An activity base is sometimes referred to as a *cost driver.* Some of the most common activity bases are direct labor-hours, machine-hours, units produced, and units sold. Other examples of activity bases (cost drivers) include the number of miles driven by salespersons, the number of pounds of laundry cleaned by a hotel, the

EXHIBIT 4–1
Variable Cost Behavior

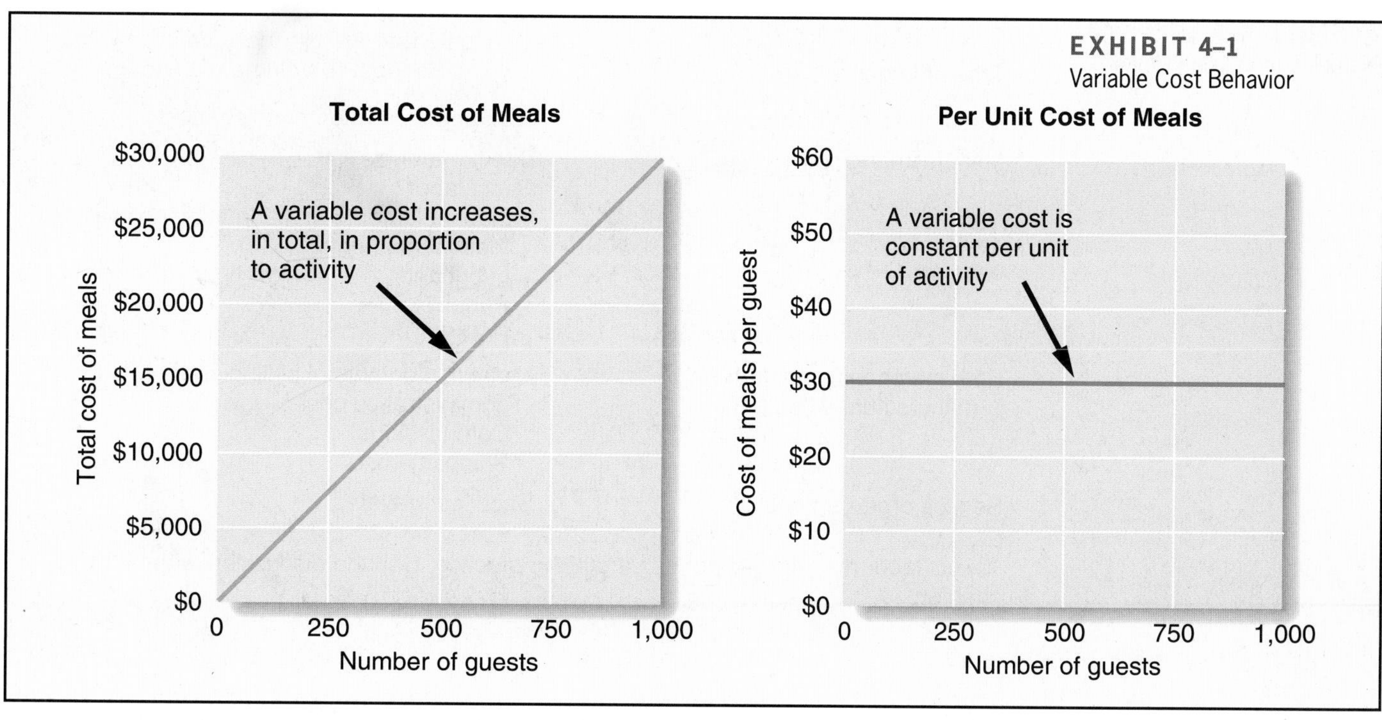

number of calls handled by technical support staff at a software company, and the number of beds occupied in a hospital.

People sometimes get the notion that if a cost doesn't vary with production or with sales, then it is not a variable cost. This is not correct. As suggested by the range of bases listed above, costs are caused by many different activities within an organization. Whether a cost is variable or fixed depends on whether it is caused by the activity under consideration. For example, when analyzing the cost of service calls under a product warranty, the relevant activity measure is the number of service calls made. Those costs that vary in total with the number of service calls made are the variable costs of making service calls.

Nevertheless, unless stated otherwise, you can assume that the activity base under consideration is the total volume of goods and services provided by the organization. So, for example, if we ask whether direct materials at Ford is a variable cost, the answer is yes, since the cost of direct materials is variable with respect to Ford's total volume of output. We will specify the activity base only when it is something other than total output.

IN BUSINESS

COPING WITH THE FALLOUT FROM SEPTEMBER 11

Costs can change for reasons that have nothing to do with changes in volume. Filterfresh is a company that services coffee machines located in commercial offices—providing milk, sugar, cups, and coffee. The company's operations were profoundly affected by the security measures many companies initiated after the terrorist attacks on the World Trade Center and the Pentagon on September 11, 2001. Heightened security at customer locations means that Filterfresh's 250 deliverymen can no longer casually walk through a customer's lobby with a load of supplies. Now a guard typically checks the deliveryman's identification and paperwork at the loading dock and may search the van before permitting the deliveryman access to the customer's building. These delays have added an average of about an hour per day to each route, which means that Filterfresh needs 24 more delivery people to do the same work it did prior to September 11. That's a 10% increase in cost without any increase in the amount of coffee sold.

Source: Anna Bernasek, "The Friction Economy," *Fortune*, February 18, 2002, pp. 104–112.

EXHIBIT 4–2
Examples of Variable Costs

Type of Organization	Costs that Are Normally Variable with Respect to Volume of Output
Merchandising company	Cost of goods (merchandise) sold
Manufacturing company	Direct materials Direct labor* Variable elements of manufacturing overhead: Indirect materials Lubricants Supplies Power
Both merchandising and manufacturing companies	Variable elements of selling and administrative costs: Commissions Shipping costs
Service organizations	Supplies, travel

*Direct labor may or may not be variable in practice. See the discussion later in this chapter.

Extent of Variable Costs The number and type of variable costs in an organization will depend in large part on the organization's structure and purpose. A public utility like Florida Power and Light, with large investments in equipment, will tend to have few variable costs. Most of the costs are associated with its plant, and these costs tend to be insensitive to changes in levels of service provided. A manufacturing company like Black and Decker, by contrast, will often have many variable costs; these costs will be associated with both manufacturing and distributing its products to customers.

A merchandising company like Wal-Mart or J. K. Gill will usually have a high proportion of variable costs in its cost structure. In most merchandising companies, the cost of merchandise purchased for resale, a variable cost, constitutes a very large component of total cost. Service companies, by contrast, have diverse cost structures. Some service companies, such as the Skippers restaurant chain, have fairly large variable costs because of the costs of their raw materials. On the other hand, service companies involved in consulting, auditing, engineering, dental, medical, and architectural activities have very large fixed costs in the form of expensive facilities and highly trained salaried employees.

Some of the more frequently encountered variable costs are listed in Exhibit 4–2 above. This exhibit is not a complete listing of all costs that can be considered variable. Moreover, some of the costs listed in the exhibit may behave more like fixed than variable costs in some organizations and in some circumstances. We will see examples of this later in the chapter. Nevertheless, Exhibit 4–2 provides a useful listing of many of the costs that normally would be considered variable with respect to the volume of output.

True Variable versus Step-Variable Costs

Not all variable costs have exactly the same behavior pattern. Some variable costs behave in a *true variable* or *proportionately variable* pattern. Other variable costs behave in a *step-variable* pattern.

True Variable Costs Direct materials is a true or proportionately variable cost because the amount used during a period will vary in direct proportion to the level of production activity. Moreover, any amounts purchased but not used can be stored and carried forward to the next period as inventory.

Step-Variable Costs The cost of a resource that is obtainable only in large chunks and that increases or decreases only in response to fairly wide changes in activity is known as a **step-variable cost.** For example, the wages of skilled repair technicians are often considered

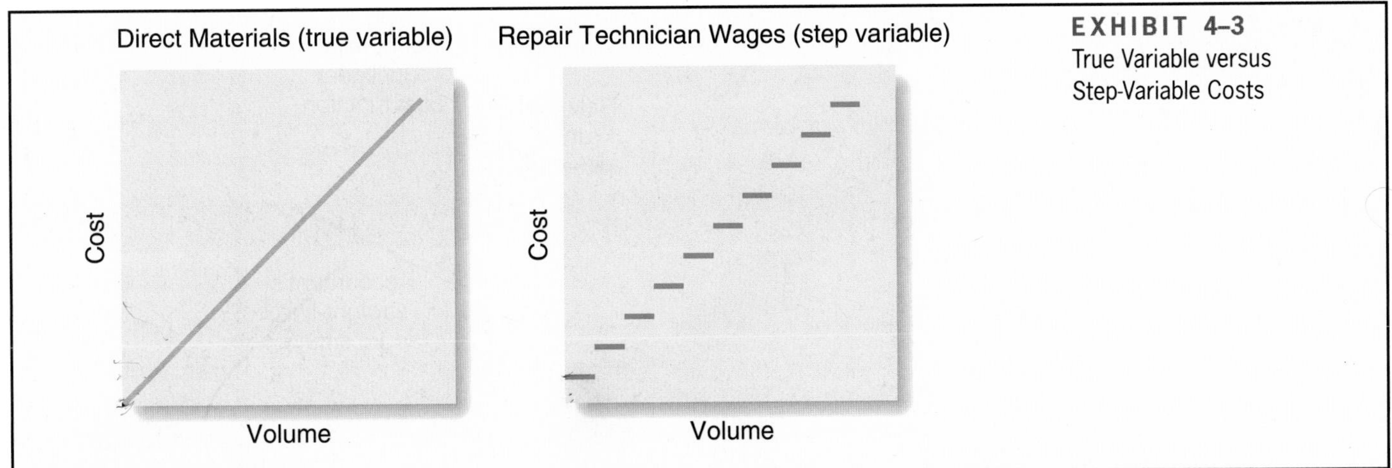

EXHIBIT 4–3
True Variable versus Step-Variable Costs

to be a step-variable cost. Such a technician's time can only be obtained in large chunks—it is difficult to hire a skilled technician on anything other than a full-time basis. Moreover, any technician's time not currently used cannot be stored as inventory and carried forward to the next period. If the time is not used effectively, it is gone forever. Furthermore, a repair technician can work at a leisurely pace if pressures are light but intensify his or her efforts if pressures build up. For this reason, small changes in the level of production may have no effect on the number of technicians employed by the company.

Exhibit 4–3 contrasts the behavior of a step-variable cost with the behavior of a true variable cost. Notice that the cost of repair technicians changes only with fairly wide changes in volume and that additional technicians come in large, indivisible chunks. Great care must be taken in working with these kinds of costs to prevent "fat" from building up in an organization. There may be a tendency to employ additional help more quickly than needed, and there is a natural reluctance to lay people off when volume declines.

IN BUSINESS

WHAT GOES UP DOESN'T NECESSARILY COME DOWN

The traditional view of variable costs is that they behave similarly in response to either increases or decreases in activity. However, the results of a research study using data from 7,629 companies spanning a 20-year period suggests otherwise. In this study, a 1% increase in sales corresponded with a 0.55% increase in selling and administrative costs, while a 1% decrease in sales corresponded with a 0.35% decrease in selling and administrative costs. These results suggest that many costs do not mechanistically increase or decrease in response to changes in the activity base; rather they change in response to managers' decisions about how to react to changes in the level of the activity base.

"When volume falls, managers must decide whether to maintain committed resources and bear the costs of operating with unutilized capacity or reduce committed resources and incur the adjustment costs of retrenching and, if volume is restored, replacing committed resources at a later date." Managers faced with these choices are less likely to reduce expenses when they perceive that a decrease in activity level is temporary or when the cost of adjusting committed resources is high.

Source: Mark C. Anderson, Rajiv D. Banker, and Surya N. Janakiraman, "Are Selling, General, and Administrative Costs 'Sticky'?" *Journal of Accounting Research*, March 2003, pp. 47–63.

The Linearity Assumption and the Relevant Range Except in the case of step-variable costs, we ordinarily assume a strictly linear relationship between cost and volume. Economists correctly point out that many costs that the accountant classifies as variable actually behave in a *curvilinear* fashion; that is, the relation between cost and activity is a curve. A curvilinear cost is illustrated in Exhibit 4–4.

Although many costs are not strictly linear, a curvilinear cost can be satisfactorily approximated with a straight line within a narrow band of activity known as the *relevant range.* The **relevant range** is that range of activity within which the assumptions made about cost behavior

EXHIBIT 4–4
Curvilinear Costs and the Relevant Range

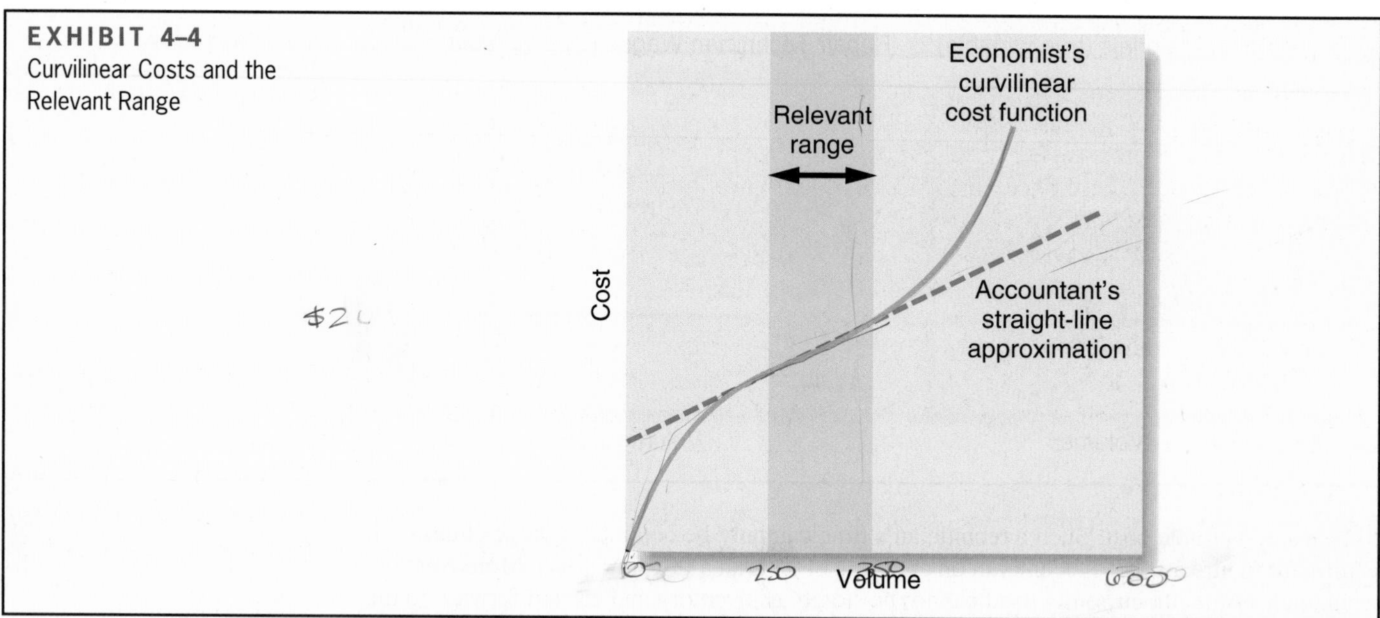

are reasonably valid. For example, note that the dashed line in Exhibit 4–4 approximates the curvilinear cost with very little loss of accuracy within the shaded relevant range. However, outside of the relevant range this particular straight line is a poor approximation to the curvilinear cost relationship. Managers should always keep in mind that assumptions made about cost behavior may be invalid if activity falls outside of the relevant range.

Fixed Costs

In our discussion of cost behavior patterns in Chapter 2, we stated that total fixed costs remain constant within the relevant range of activity. To continue the Nooksack Expeditions example, assume the company rents a building for $500 per month to store its equipment. Within the relevant range, the total amount of rent paid is the same regardless of the number of guests the company takes on its expeditions during any given month. Exhibit 4–5 depicts this cost behavior pattern.

EXHIBIT 4–5
Fixed Cost Behavior

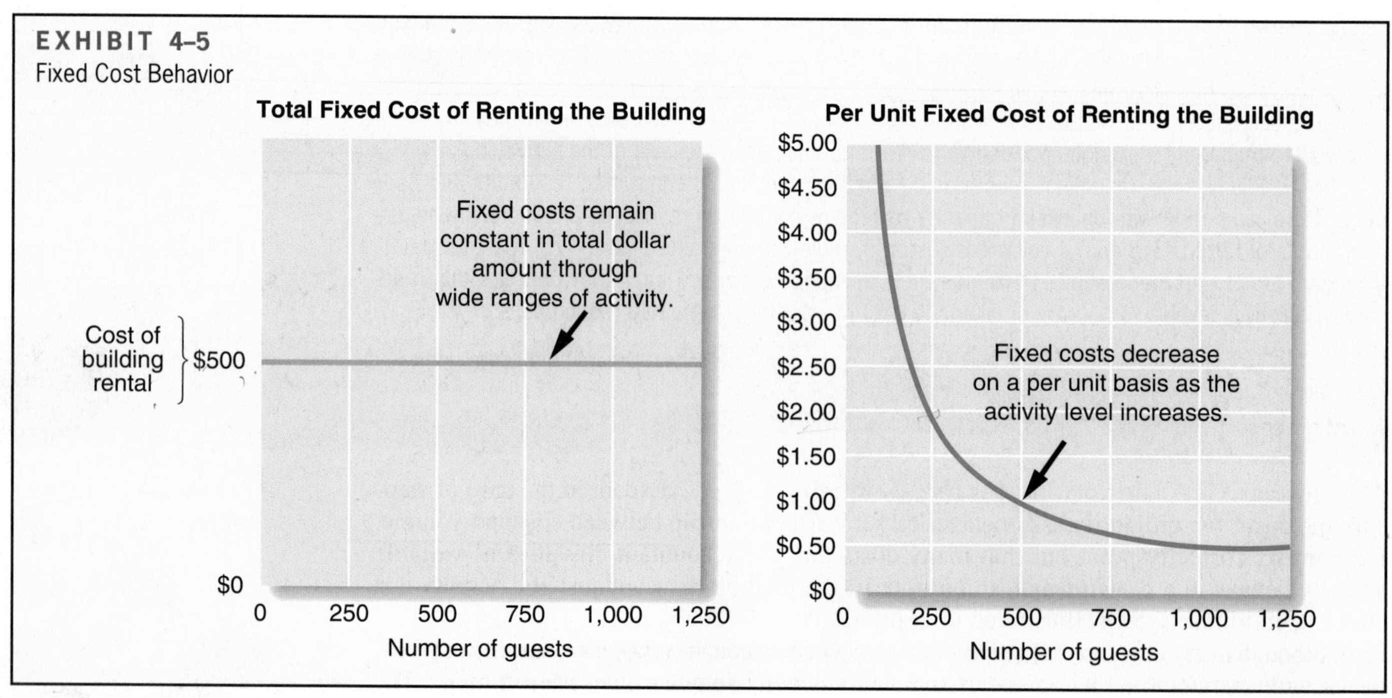

Since fixed costs remain constant in total, the average fixed cost *per unit* becomes progressively smaller as the level of activity increases. If Nooksack Expeditions has only 250 guests in a month, the $500 fixed rental cost would amount to an average of $2 per guest. If there are 1,000 guests, the fixed rental cost would average only 50 cents per guest. Exhibit 4–5 illustrates this aspect of the behavior of fixed costs. Note that as the number of guests increases, the average fixed cost per unit drops, but it drops at a decreasing rate. The first guests have the biggest impact on the average fixed cost per unit.

It is necessary in some contexts to express fixed costs on an average per unit basis. For example, in Chapter 2 we showed how unit product costs computed for use in external financial statements contain both variable and fixed costs. As a general rule, however, we caution against expressing fixed costs on an average per unit basis in internal reports because it creates the false impression that fixed costs are like variable costs and that total fixed costs actually change as the level of activity changes. To avoid confusion in internal reporting and decision-making situations, fixed costs should be expressed in total rather than on a per unit basis.

IN BUSINESS

COSTING THE TREK

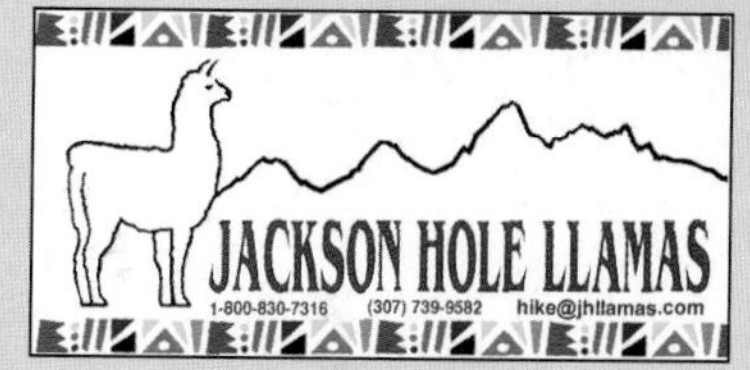

Jackson Hole Llamas is owned and operated by Jill Aanonsen/Hodges and David Hodges. The company provides guided tours to remote areas of Yellowstone National Park and the Jedediah Smith Wilderness, with the llamas carrying the baggage for the multiday treks.

Jill and David operate out of their ranch in Jackson Hole, Wyoming, leading about 10 trips each summer season. All food is provided as well as tents and sleeping pads. Based on the number of guests on a trip, Jill and David will decide how many llamas will go on the trip and how many will remain on the ranch. Llamas are transported to the trailhead in a special trailer.

The company has a number of costs, some of which are listed below:

Cost	Cost Behavior
Food and beverage costs	Variable with respect to the number of guests and the length of the trip in days.
Truck and trailer operating costs	Variable with respect to the number of miles to the trailhead.
Guide wages	Step variable; Jill and David serve as the guides on most trips and hire guides only for larger groups.
Costs of providing tents	Variable with respect to the number of guests and length of the trip in days. Jackson Hole Llamas owns its tents, but they wear out through use and must be repaired or eventually replaced.
Cost of feeding llamas	Variable with respect to the number of guests, and hence the number of llamas, on a trip. [Actually, the cost of feeding llamas may *decrease* with the number of guests on a trip. When a llama is on a trek, it lives off the land—eating grasses and other vegetation found in meadows and along the trail. When a llama is left on the ranch, it may have to be fed purchased feed.]
Property taxes	Fixed.

Source: Jill Aanonsen/Hodges and David Hodges, owners and operators of Jackson Hole Llamas, www.jhllamas.com.

Types of Fixed Costs

Fixed costs are sometimes referred to as capacity costs, since they result from outlays made for buildings, equipment, skilled professional employees, and other items needed to provide the basic capacity for sustained operations. For planning purposes, fixed costs can be viewed as either *committed* or *discretionary.*

Committed Fixed Costs Investments in facilities, equipment, and the basic organization that can't be significantly reduced even for short periods of time without making fundamental changes are referred to as **committed fixed costs.** Examples of such costs include depreciation of buildings and equipment, real estate taxes, insurance expenses, and salaries of top management and operating personnel. Even if operations are interrupted or cut back, committed fixed costs remain largely unchanged in the short term. During a recession, for example, a company won't usually eliminate key executive positions or sell off key facilities—the basic organizational structure and facilities ordinarily are kept intact. The costs of restoring them later are likely to be far greater than any short-run savings that might be realized.

Once a decision is made to acquire committed fixed resources, the company may be locked into that decision for many years to come. Consequently, such commitments should be made only after careful analysis of the available alternatives. Investment decisions involving committed fixed costs will be examined in Chapter 13.

Discretionary Fixed Costs **Discretionary fixed costs** (often referred to as *managed fixed costs*) usually arise from *annual* decisions by management to spend on certain fixed cost items. Examples of discretionary fixed costs include advertising, research, public relations, management development programs, and internships for students.

Two key differences exist between discretionary fixed costs and committed fixed costs. First, the planning horizon for a discretionary fixed cost is short term—usually a single year. By contrast, committed fixed costs have a planning horizon that encompasses many years. Second, discretionary fixed costs can be cut for short periods of time with minimal damage to the long-run goals of the organization. For example, spending on management development programs can be reduced because of poor economic conditions. Although some unfavorable consequences may result from the cutback, it is doubtful that these consequences would be as great as those that would result if the company decided to economize by laying off key personnel.

Whether a particular cost is regarded as committed or discretionary may depend on management's strategy. For example, during recessions when the level of home building is down, many construction companies lay off most of their workers and virtually disband operations. Other construction companies retain large numbers of employees on the payroll, even though the workers have little or no work to do. While these latter companies may be faced with short-term cash flow problems, it will be easier for them to respond quickly when economic conditions improve. And the higher morale and loyalty of their employees may give these companies a significant competitive advantage.

The most important characteristic of discretionary fixed costs is that management is not locked into its decisions regarding such costs. Discretionary costs can be adjusted from year to year or even perhaps during the course of a year if necessary.

IN BUSINESS

A TWIST ON FIXED AND VARIABLE COSTS

Mission Controls designs and installs automation systems for food and beverage manufacturers. At most companies, when sales drop and cost cutting is necessary, top managers lay off workers. The founders of Mission Controls decided to do something different when sales drop—they slash their own salaries before they even consider letting any of their employees go. This makes their own salaries somewhat variable, while the wages and salaries of workers act more like fixed costs. The payoff is a loyal and committed workforce.

Source: Christopher Caggiano, "Employment, Guaranteed for Life," *Inc.* magazine, October 15, 2002, p. 74.

The Trend toward Fixed Costs The trend in many industries is toward greater fixed costs relative to variable costs. Chores that used to be performed by hand have been taken over by machines. For example, grocery clerks at stores like Safeway and Kroger used to key in prices by hand on cash registers. Now, most stores are equipped with barcode readers that enter price and other product information automatically. In general, competition has created pressure to give customers more value for their money—a demand that often can only be satisfied by automating business processes. For example, an H & R Block employee used to fill out tax returns for customers by hand and the advice given to a customer largely depended on the knowledge of that particular employee. Now, sophisticated computer software based on the accumulated knowledge of many experts is used to complete tax returns, and the software provides tax planning and other advice tailored to the customer's needs.

As automation intensifies, the demand for "knowledge" workers—those who work primarily with their minds rather than their muscles—has grown tremendously. Since knowledge workers tend to be salaried, highly trained, and difficult to replace, the costs of compensating these workers are often relatively fixed and are committed rather than discretionary.

IN BUSINESS

A NEW TWIST ON SENDING JOBS OFFSHORE

SeaCode (www.sea-code.com) is a San Diego based company that offers a new twist on the popular practice of outsourcing jobs from the United States to foreign countries with lower labor costs. The company houses 600 computer programmers from around the world on a cruise ship three miles off the coast of Los Angeles. This "floating tech factory" is subject to the labor laws of whatever flag the boat chooses to fly rather than to U.S. labor laws. SeaCode pays its "knowledge workers" $1,500 to $1,800 per month, which is below prevailing salaries on the U.S. mainland but exceeds the salaries in many countries. The company claims that it has been inundated with resumes of college graduates from across the globe.

SeaCode's clients get access to highly skilled labor at a lower cost than would have to be paid for similar jobs housed on U.S. soil. In addition, rather than having to fly half way around the world to places such as India or China to oversee projects, U.S. managers can fly to Los Angeles and in a brief time be three miles off the California coast checking on the status of "offshore" operations.

Source: Reed Tucker, "Will a Floating Tech Factory Fly?" *Fortune*, September 5, 2005, p. 28.

Is Labor a Variable or a Fixed Cost? As the preceding discussion suggests, wages and salaries may be fixed or variable. The behavior of wage and salary costs will differ from one country to another, depending on labor regulations, labor contracts, and custom. In some countries, such as France, Germany, and Japan, management has little flexibility in adjusting the labor force to changes in business activity. In countries such as the United States and the United Kingdom, management typically has much greater latitude. However, even in these less restrictive environments, managers may choose to treat employee compensation as a fixed cost for several reasons.

First, many managers are reluctant to decrease their workforce in response to short-term declines in sales. These managers realize that the success of their businesses hinges on retaining highly skilled and trained employees. If these valuable workers are laid off, it is unlikely that they would ever return or be easily replaced. Furthermore, laying off workers undermines the morale of those employees who remain.

Second, managers do not want to be caught with a bloated payroll in an economic downturn. Therefore, managers are reluctant to add employees in response to short-term increases in sales. Instead, more and more companies rely on temporary and part-time workers to take up the slack when their permanent, full-time employees are unable to handle all of the demand for their products and services. In such companies, labor costs are a complex mixture of fixed and variable costs.

IN BUSINESS

LABOR AT SOUTHWEST AIRLINES

Starting with a $10,000 investment in 1966, Herb Kelleher built Southwest Airlines into the most profitable airline in the United States. Prior to stepping down as president and CEO of the airline in 2001, Kelleher wrote: "The thing that would disturb me most to see after I'm no longer CEO is layoffs at Southwest. Nothing kills your company's culture like layoffs. Nobody has ever been furloughed here, and that is unprecedented in the airline industry. It's been a huge strength of ours . . . We could have furloughed at various times and been more profitable, but I always thought that was shortsighted. You want to show your people that you value them and you're not going to hurt them just to get a little money in the short run."

Because of this commitment by management to the company's employees, all wages and salaries are basically committed fixed costs at Southwest Airlines.

Source: Herb Kelleher, "The Chairman of the Board Looks Back," *Fortune*, May 28, 2001, pp. 63–76.

Many major companies have undergone waves of downsizing in recent years in which large numbers of employees—particularly managers—have lost their jobs. This downsizing may seem to suggest that even management salaries should be regarded as variable costs, but this would not be a valid conclusion. Downsizing has largely been the result of attempts to reengineer business processes and cut costs rather than a response to a decline in sales activity. This underscores an important, but subtle, point. Fixed costs can change—they just don't change in response to small changes in activity.

In sum, there is no clear-cut answer to the question "Is labor a variable or fixed cost?" It depends on how much flexibility management has to adjust the workforce and management's strategy. Nevertheless, unless otherwise stated, we will assume in this text that direct labor is a variable cost. This assumption is more likely to be valid for companies in the United States than in countries where employment laws permit much less flexibility.

IN BUSINESS

THE REGULATORY BURDEN

The late Peter F. Drucker, a renowned observer of business and society, claimed that "the driving force behind the steady growth of temps [and outsourcing of work] . . . is the growing burden of rules and regulations for employers." U.S. laws and regulations concerning employees require companies to file multiple reports—and any breach, even if unintentional, can result in punishment. According to the Small Business Administration, the owner of a small or midsize business spends up to a quarter of his or her time on employment-related paperwork and the cost of complying with government regulations (including tax report preparation) is over $5,000 per employee per year. "No wonder that employers . . . complain bitterly that they have no time to work on products and services. . . . They no longer chant the old mantra 'People are our greatest asset.' Instead, they claim 'People are our greatest liability.'" To the extent that the regulatory burden leads to a decline in permanent full-time employees and an increase in the use of temporary employees and outsourcing, labor costs are converted from fixed to variable costs. While this is not the intent of the regulations, it is a consequence.

Source: Peter F. Drucker, "They're Not Employees, They're People," *Harvard Business Review*, February 2002.

Fixed Costs and the Relevant Range

The concept of the relevant range, which was introduced in the discussion of variable costs, is also important in understanding fixed costs—particularly discretionary fixed costs. The levels of discretionary fixed costs are typically decided at the beginning of the year and depend on the needs of planned programs such as advertising and training. The scope of these programs will depend, in turn, on the overall anticipated level of activity for the year. At very high levels of activity, programs are often broadened or expanded. For example, if the company hopes to increase sales by 25%, it would probably plan for much larger advertising costs than if no sales increase were planned. So the *planned* level of activity might affect total discretionary fixed costs. However, once the total discretionary fixed costs have been budgeted, they are unaffected by the *actual* level of activity. For example, once the advertising budget has been established and spent, it will not be affected by how many units are actually sold. Therefore, the cost is fixed with respect to the *actual* number of units sold.

Discretionary fixed costs are easier to adjust than committed fixed costs. They also tend to be less "lumpy." Committed fixed costs consist of costs such as buildings, equipment, and the salaries of key personnel. It is difficult to buy half a piece of equipment or to hire a quarter of a product-line manager, so the step pattern depicted in Exhibit 4–6 is typical for such costs. The relevant range of activity for a fixed cost is the range of activity over which the graph of the cost is flat as in Exhibit 4–6. As a company expands its level of activity, it may outgrow its present facilities, or the key management team may need to be expanded. The result, of course, will be increased committed fixed costs as larger facilities are built and as new management positions are created.

One reaction to the step pattern depicted in Exhibit 4–6 is to conclude that discretionary and committed fixed costs are really just step-variable costs. To some extent this is true, since *almost* all costs can be adjusted in the long run. There are two major differences, however, between the step-variable costs depicted earlier in Exhibit 4–3 and the fixed costs depicted in Exhibit 4–6.

The first difference is that the step-variable costs can often be adjusted quickly as conditions change, whereas once fixed costs have been set, they usually can't be changed easily. A step-variable cost such as the wages of repair technicians, for example, can be adjusted upward or downward by hiring and laying off technicians. By contrast, once a company has signed a lease for a building, it is locked into that level of lease cost for the life of the contract.

The second difference is that the *width of the steps* depicted for step-variable costs is much narrower than the width of the steps depicted for the fixed costs in Exhibit 4–6. The width of the steps relates to volume or level of activity. For step-variable costs, the width of a step might be 40 hours of activity per week in the case of repair technicians. For fixed costs, however, the width of a step might be *thousands* or even *tens of thousands* of hours of activity. In essence, the width of the steps for step-variable costs is generally so narrow that these costs can be treated essentially as variable costs for most purposes. The width of the steps for fixed costs, on the other hand, is so wide that these costs should be treated as entirely fixed within the relevant range.

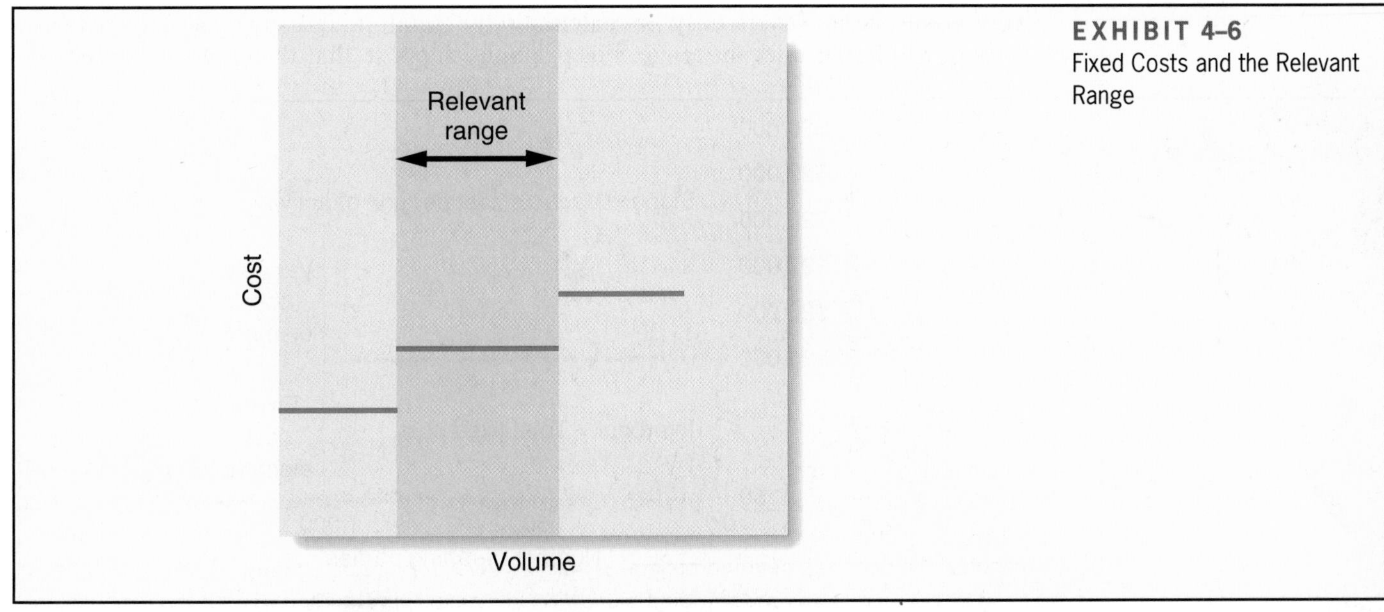

EXHIBIT 4–6
Fixed Costs and the Relevant Range

Mixed Costs

A **mixed cost** contains both variable and fixed cost elements. Mixed costs are also known as semivariable costs. To continue the Nooksack Expeditions example, the company must pay a license fee of $25,000 per year plus $3 per rafting party to the state's Department of Natural Resources. If the company runs 1,000 rafting parties this year, then the total fees paid to the state would be $28,000, made up of $25,000 in fixed cost plus $3,000 in variable cost. Exhibit 4–7 depicts the behavior of this mixed cost.

Even if Nooksack fails to attract any customers, the company will still have to pay the license fee of $25,000. This is why the cost line in Exhibit 4–7 intersects the vertical cost axis at the $25,000 point. For each rafting party the company organizes, the total cost of the state fees will increase by $3. Therefore, the total cost line slopes upward as the variable cost of $3 per party is added to the fixed cost of $25,000 per year.

Since the mixed cost in Exhibit 4–7 is represented by a straight line, the following equation for a straight line can be used to express the relationship between a mixed cost and the level of activity:

$$Y = a + bX$$

In this equation,

Y = The total mixed cost

a = The total fixed cost (the vertical intercept of the line)

b = The variable cost per unit of activity (the slope of the line)

X = The level of activity

Since the variable cost per unit equals the slope of the straight line, the steeper the slope, the higher the variable cost per unit.

In the case of the state fees paid by Nooksack Expeditions, the equation is written as follows:

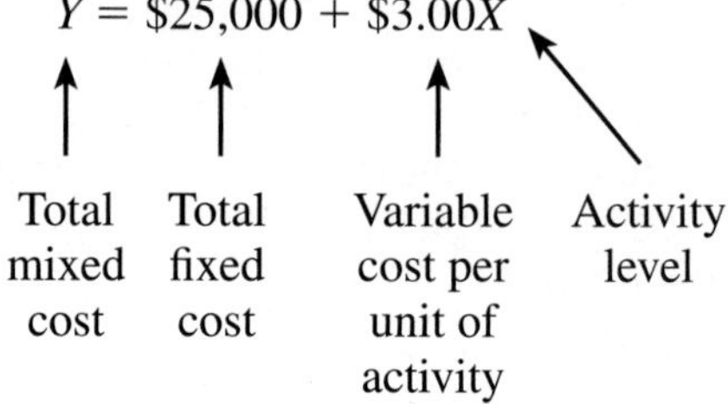

This equation makes it easy to calculate the total mixed cost for any level of activity within the relevant range. For example, suppose that the company expects to

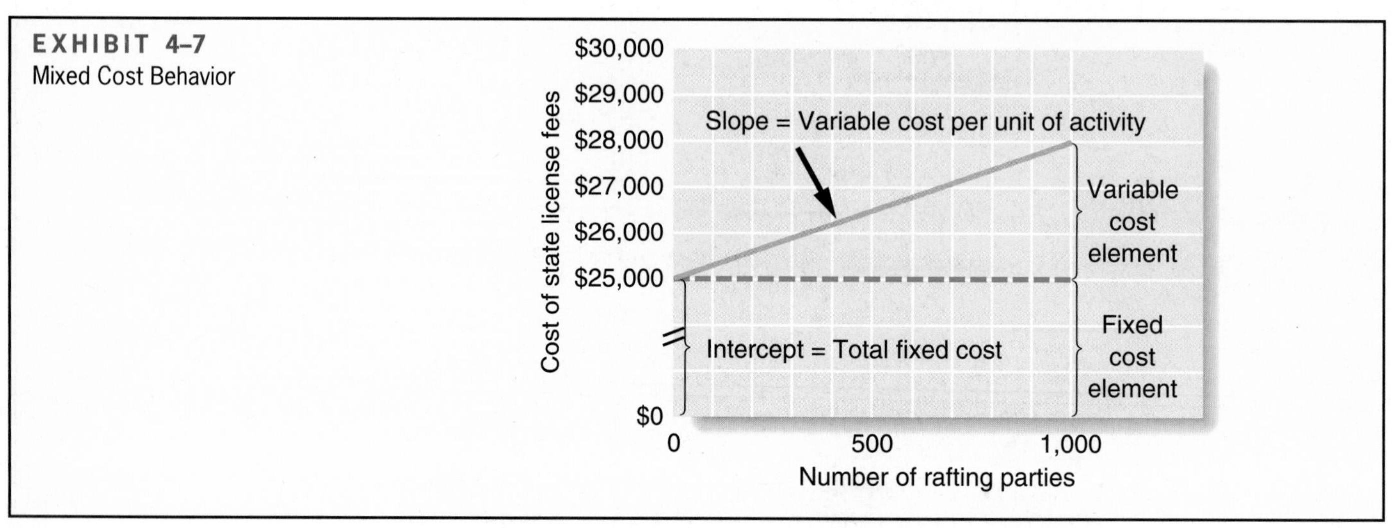

EXHIBIT 4–7
Mixed Cost Behavior

organize 800 rafting parties in the next year. The total state fees would be calculated as follows:

$$Y = \$25{,}000 + (\$3.00 \text{ per rafting party} \times 800 \text{ rafting parties})$$
$$= \$27{,}400$$

IN BUSINESS

COST BEHAVIOR IN THE U.S. AND JAPAN

A total of 257 American and 40 Japanese manufacturing companies responded to a questionnaire concerning their management accounting practices. Among other things, the companies were asked whether they classified certain costs as variable, semivariable, or fixed. Some of the results are summarized in Exhibit 4–8. Note that companies do not all classify costs in the same way. For example, roughly 45% of the U.S. companies classify material-handling labor costs as variable, 35% as semivariable, and 20% as fixed. Also note that the Japanese companies are much more likely than U.S. companies to classify labor costs as fixed.

Source: NAA Tokyo Affiliate, "Management Accounting in the Advanced Management Surrounding—Comparative Study on Survey in Japan and U.S.A."

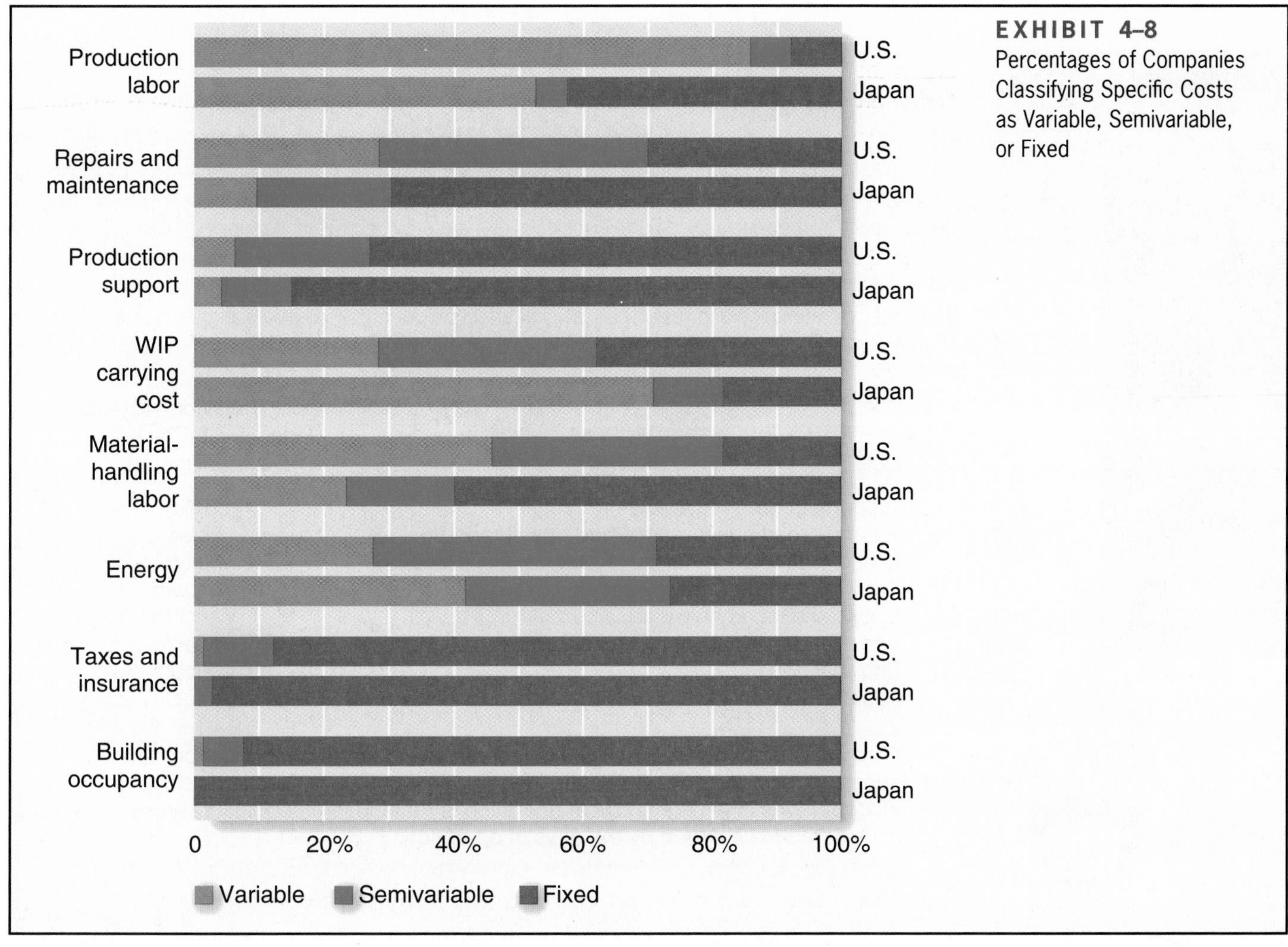

EXHIBIT 4–8
Percentages of Companies Classifying Specific Costs as Variable, Semivariable, or Fixed

The Analysis of Mixed Costs

Mixed costs are very common. For example, the cost of providing X-ray services to patients at the Harvard Medical School Hospital is a mixed cost. The costs of equipment depreciation and radiologists' and technicians' salaries are fixed, but the costs of X-ray film, power, and supplies are variable. At Southwest Airlines, maintenance costs are a mixed cost. The company incurs fixed costs for renting maintenance facilities and for keeping skilled mechanics on the payroll, but the costs of replacement parts, lubricating oils, tires, and so forth, are variable with respect to how often and how far the company's aircraft are flown.

The fixed portion of a mixed cost represents the minimum cost of having a service *ready and available* for use. The variable portion represents the cost incurred for *actual consumption* of the service, thus it varies in proportion to the amount of service actually consumed.

How does management go about actually estimating the fixed and variable components of a mixed cost? The most common methods used in practice are *account analysis* and the *engineering approach.*

In **account analysis,** an account is classified as either variable or fixed based on the analyst's prior knowledge of how the cost in the account behaves. For example, direct materials would be classified as variable and a building lease cost would be classified as fixed because of the nature of those costs. The total fixed cost of an organization is the sum of the costs for the accounts that have been classified as fixed. The variable cost per unit is estimated by dividing the sum of the costs for the accounts that have been classified as variable by the total activity.

The **engineering approach** to cost analysis involves a detailed analysis of what cost behavior should be, based on an industrial engineer's evaluation of the production methods

IN BUSINESS

OPERATIONS DRIVE COSTS

White Grizzly Adventures is a snowcat skiing and snowboarding company in Meadow Creek, British Columbia, that is owned and operated by Brad and Carole Karafil. The company shuttles 12 guests to the top of the company's steep and tree-covered terrain in a single snowcat. Guests stay as a group at the company's lodge for a fixed number of days and are provided healthy gourmet meals.

Brad and Carole must decide each year when snowcat operations will begin in December and when they will end in early spring, and how many nonoperating days to schedule between groups of guests for maintenance and rest. This decision affects a variety of costs. Examples of costs that are fixed and variable with respect to the number of days of operation at White Grizzly include:

Cost	Cost Behavior—Fixed or Variable with Respect to Days of Operation
Property taxes	Fixed
Summer road maintenance and tree clearing	Fixed
Lodge depreciation	Fixed
Snowcat operator and guides	Variable
Cooks and lodge help	Variable
Snowcat depreciation	Variable
Snowcat fuel	Variable
Food*	Variable

*The costs of food served to guests theoretically depend on the number of guests in residence. However, the lodge is almost always filled to its capacity of 12 persons when the snowcat operation is running, so food costs can be considered to be driven by the days of operation.

Source: Brad & Carole Karafil, owners and operators of White Grizzly Adventures, www.whitegrizzly.com.

to be used, the materials specifications, labor requirements, equipment usage, production efficiency, power consumption, and so on. For example, Pizza Hut might use the engineering approach to estimate the cost of preparing and serving a particular take-out pizza. The cost of the pizza would be estimated by carefully costing the specific ingredients used to make the pizza, the power consumed to cook the pizza, and the cost of the container the pizza is delivered in. The engineering approach must be used in those situations where no past experience is available concerning activity and costs. In addition, it is sometimes used together with other methods to improve the accuracy of cost analysis.

Account analysis works best when analyzing costs at a fairly aggregated level, such as the cost of serving patients in the emergency room (ER) of Cook County General Hospital. The costs of drugs, supplies, forms, wages, equipment, and so on, can be roughly classified as variable or fixed and a mixed cost formula for the overall cost of the emergency room can be estimated fairly quickly. However, this method does not recognize that some of the accounts may have both fixed and variable cost elements. For example, the cost of electricity for the ER is a mixed cost. Most of the electricity is a fixed cost because it is used for heating and lighting. However, the consumption of electricity increases with activity in the ER since diagnostic equipment, operating theater lights, defibrillators, and so on, all consume electricity. The most effective way to estimate the fixed and variable elements of such a mixed cost may be to analyze past records of cost and activity data. These records should reveal whether electrical costs vary significantly with the number of patients and if so, by how much. The remainder of this section explains how to conduct such an analysis of past cost and activity data.

Dr. Derek Chalmers, the chief executive officer of Brentline Hospital, motioned Kinh Nguyen, the chief financial officer of the hospital, into his office.

MANAGERIAL ACCOUNTING IN ACTION
The Issue

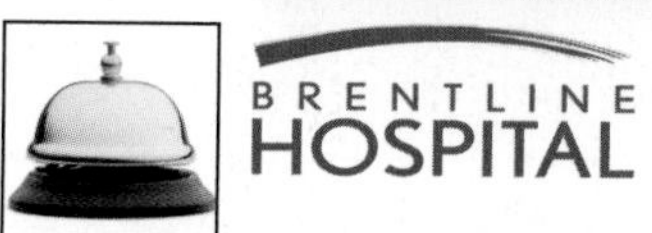

Derek: I wanted to talk to you about our maintenance expenses. They seem to be bouncing around a lot. Over the last half year or so they have been as low as $7,400 and as high as $9,800 per month.

Kinh: That type of variation is normal for maintenance expenses.

Derek: But we budgeted a constant $8,400 a month. Can't we do a better job of predicting what these costs are going to be? And how do we know when we've spent too much in a month? Shouldn't there be some explanation for these variations?

Kinh: Now that you mention it, we are in the process of tightening up our budgeting process. Our first step is to break all of our costs down into fixed and variable components.

Derek: How will that help?

Kinh: Well, it will permit us to predict what the level of costs will be. Some costs are fixed and shouldn't change much. Other costs go up and down as our activity goes up and down. The trick is to figure out what is driving the variable component of the costs.

Derek: What about the maintenance costs?

Kinh: My guess is that the variations in maintenance costs are being driven by our overall level of activity. When we treat more patients, our equipment is used more intensively, which leads to more maintenance expense.

Derek: How would you measure the level of overall activity? Would you use patient-days?

Kinh: I think so. Each day a patient is in the hospital counts as one patient-day. The greater the number of patient-days in a month, the busier we are. Besides, our budgeting is all based on projected patient-days.

Derek: Okay, so suppose you are able to break the maintenance costs down into fixed and variable components. What will that do for us?

Kinh: Basically, I will be able to predict what maintenance costs should be as a function of the number of patient-days.

Derek: I can see where that would be useful. We could use it to predict costs for budgeting purposes.

Kinh: We could also use it as a benchmark. Based on the actual number of patient-days for a period, I can predict what the maintenance costs should have been. We can compare this to the actual spending on maintenance.

Derek: Sounds good to me. Let me know when you get the results.

LEARNING OBJECTIVE 2
Use a scattergraph plot to diagnose cost behavior.

Diagnosing Cost Behavior with a Scattergraph Plot

Kinh Nguyen began his analysis of maintenance costs by collecting cost and activity data for a number of recent months. Those data are displayed below:

Month	Activity Level: Patient-Days	Maintenance Cost Incurred
January	5,600	$7,900
February	7,100	$8,500
March	5,000	$7,400
April	6,500	$8,200
May	7,300	$9,100
June	8,000	$9,800
July	6,200	$7,800

The first step in analyzing the cost and activity data is to plot the data on a scattergraph. This plot immediately reveals any nonlinearities or other problems with the data. The scattergraph of maintenance costs versus patient-days at Brentline Hospital is shown in the top half of Exhibit 4–9. Two things should be noted about this scattergraph:

1. The total maintenance cost, *Y*, is plotted on the vertical axis. Cost is known as the **dependent variable,** since the amount of cost incurred during a period depends on the level of activity for the period. (That is, as the level of activity increases, total cost will also ordinarily increase.)
2. The activity, *X* (patient-days in this case), is plotted on the horizontal axis. Activity is known as the **independent variable,** since it causes variations in the cost.

From the scattergraph, it is evident that maintenance costs do increase with the number of patient-days. In addition, the scattergraph reveals that the relation between maintenance costs and patient-days is approximately *linear*. In other words, the points lie more or less along a straight line. Such a straight line has been drawn using a ruler in the bottom half of Exhibit 4–9. Cost behavior is considered **linear** whenever a straight line is a reasonable approximation for the relation between cost and activity. Note that the data points do not fall exactly on the straight line. This will almost always happen in practice; the relation is seldom perfectly linear.

Note that the straight line in Exhibit 4–9 has been drawn through the point representing 7,300 patient-days and a total maintenance cost of $9,100. Drawing the straight line through one of the data points helps make a quick-and-dirty estimate of variable and fixed costs. The vertical intercept where the straight line crosses the *Y* axis—in this case, about $3,300—is the rough estimate of the fixed cost. The variable cost can be quickly estimated by subtracting the estimated fixed cost from the total cost at the point lying on the straight line.

Total maintenance cost for 7,300 patient-days (a point falling on the straight line)	$9,100
Less estimated fixed cost (the vertical intercept)	3,300
Estimated total variable cost for 7,300 patient-days	$5,800

The average variable cost per unit at 7,300 patient-days is computed as follows:

Variable cost per unit = $5,800 ÷ 7,300 patient-days
= $0.79 per patient-day (rounded)

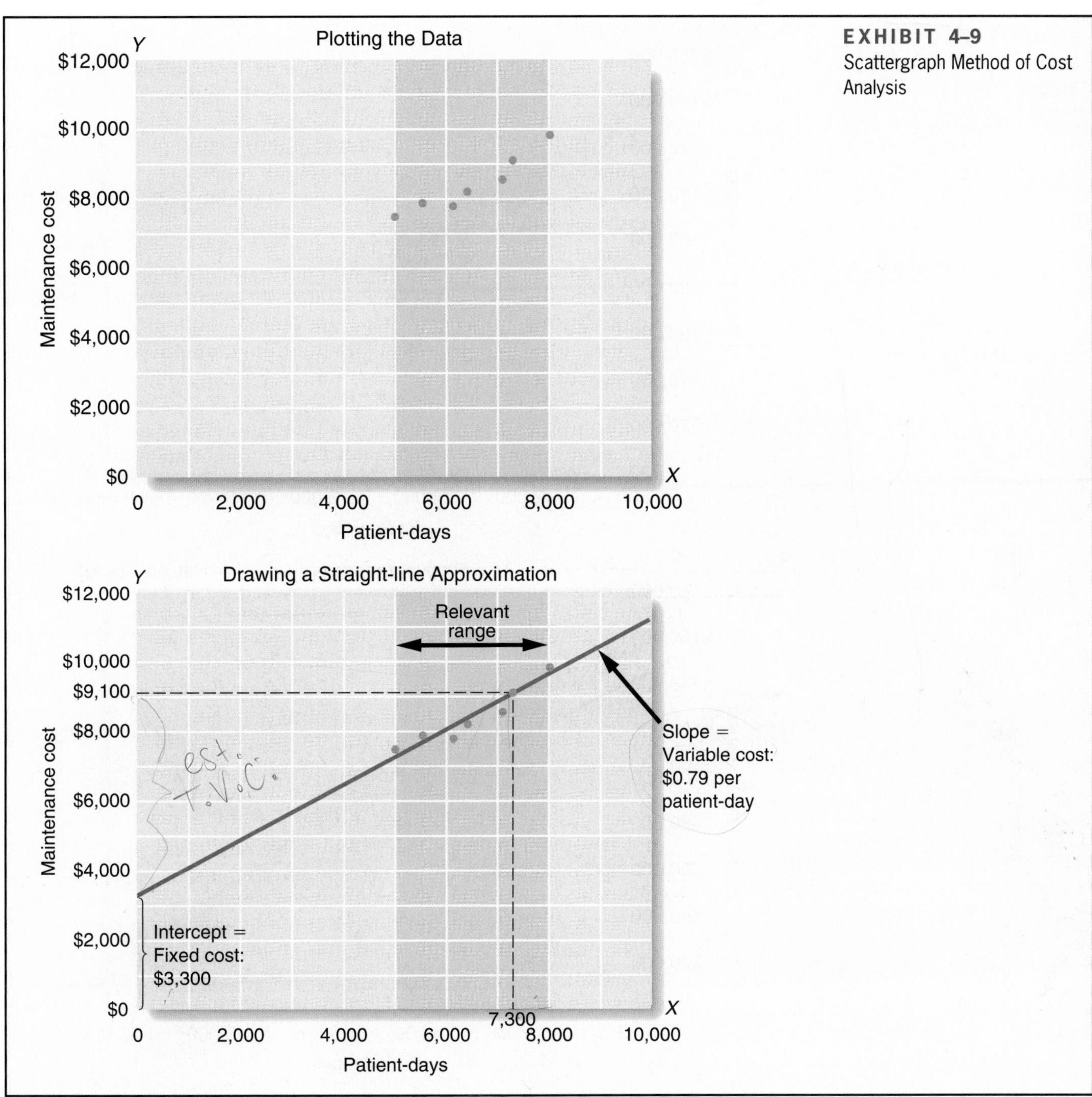

EXHIBIT 4–9
Scattergraph Method of Cost Analysis

Combining the estimate of the fixed cost and the estimate of the variable cost per patient-day, we can express the relation between cost and activity as follows:

$$Y = \$3{,}300 + \$0.79X$$

where X is the number of patient-days.

We hasten to add that this *is* a quick-and-dirty method of estimating the fixed and variable cost elements of a mixed cost; it is seldom used in practice when the financial implications of a decision based on the data are significant. However, setting aside the estimates of the fixed and variable cost elements, plotting the data on a scattergraph is an essential diagnostic step that is too often overlooked. Suppose, for example, we had

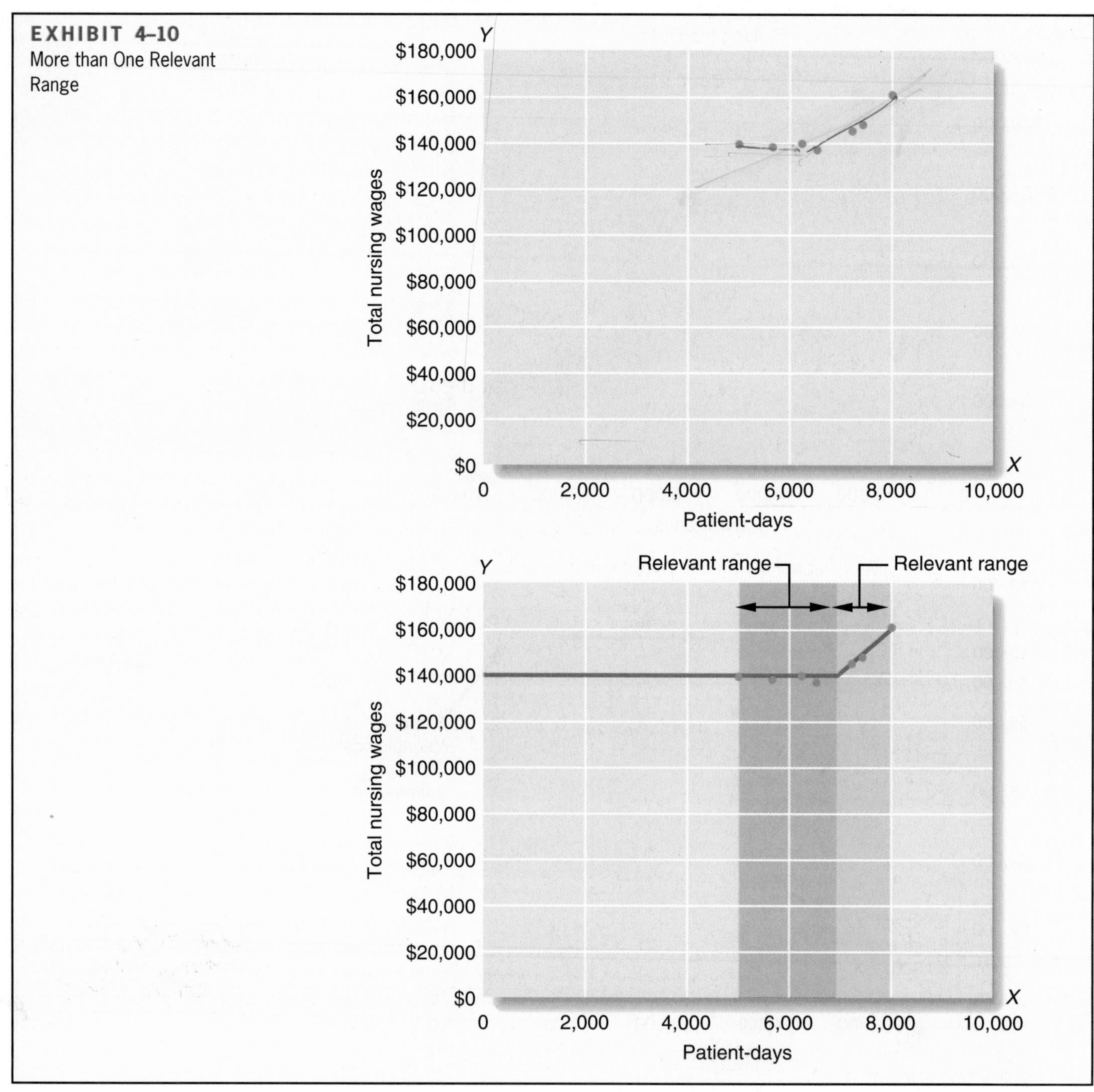

EXHIBIT 4–10
More than One Relevant Range

been interested in the relation between total nursing wages and the number of patient-days at the hospital. The permanent, full-time nursing staff can handle up to 7,000 patient-days in a month. Beyond that level of activity, part-time nurses must be called in to help out. The cost and activity data for nurses are plotted on the scattergraph in Exhibit 4–10. Looking at that scattergraph, it is evident that two straight lines would do a much better job of fitting the data than a single straight line. Up to 7,000 patient-days, total nursing wages are essentially a fixed cost. Above 7,000 patient-days, total nursing wages are a mixed cost. This happens because, as stated above, the permanent, full-time nursing staff can handle up to 7,000 patient-days in a month. Above that level, part-time nurses are called in to help, which adds to the cost. Consequently, two straight lines (and two equations) would be used to represent total nursing wages—one for the relevant

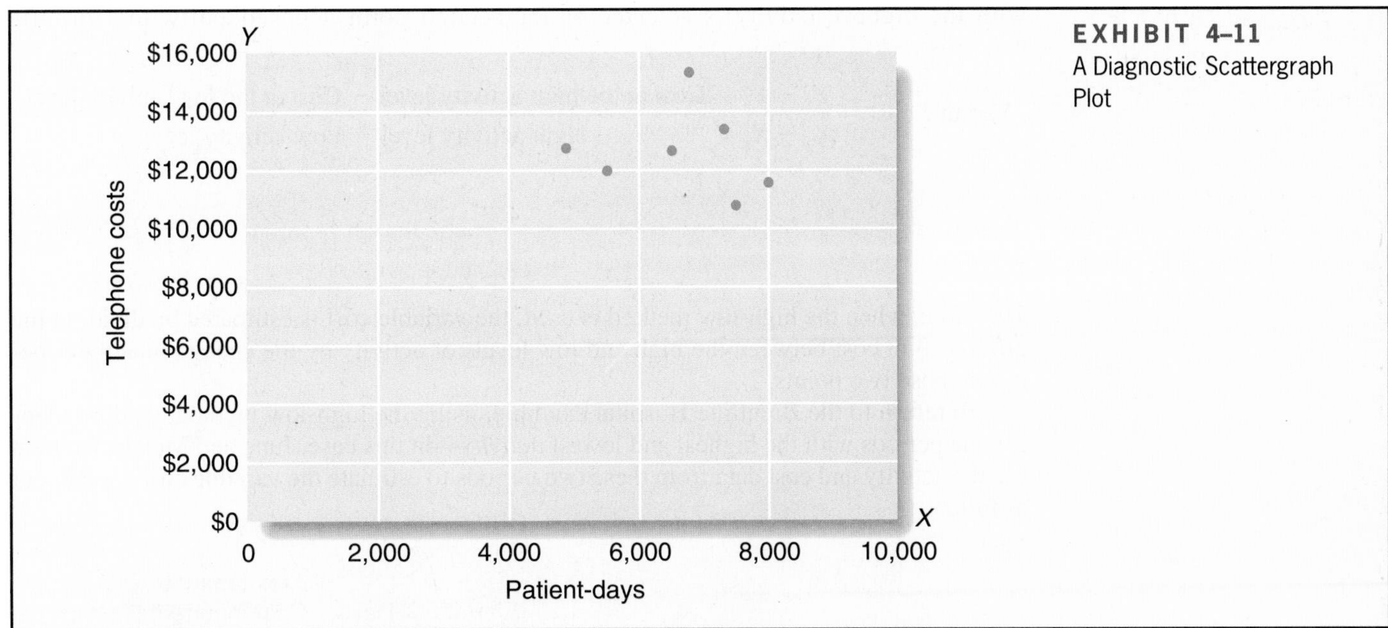

EXHIBIT 4–11
A Diagnostic Scattergraph Plot

range of 5,600 to 7,000 patient-days and one for the relevant range of 7,000 to 8,000 patient-days.

As another example, suppose that Brentline Hospital's management is interested in the relation between the hospital's telephone costs and patient-days. Patients are billed directly for their use of telephones, so those costs do not appear on the hospital's cost records. Rather, management is concerned about the charges for the staff's use of telephones. The data for this cost are plotted in Exhibit 4–11. It is evident from that plot that while the telephone costs do vary from month to month, they are not related to patient-days. Something other than patient-days is driving the telephone bills. Therefore, it would not make sense to analyze this cost any further by attempting to estimate a variable cost per patient-day for telephone costs. Plotting the data helps diagnose such situations.

The High-Low Method

LEARNING OBJECTIVE 3
Analyze a mixed cost using the high-low method.

In addition to the quick-and-dirty method described in the preceding section, more precise methods are available for estimating fixed and variable costs. However, it must be emphasized that fixed and variable costs should be computed only if a scattergraph plot confirms that the relation is approximately linear. In the case of maintenance costs at Brentline Hospital, the relation does appear to be linear. In the case of telephone costs, there isn't any clear relation between telephone costs and patient-days, so there is no point in estimating how much of the cost varies with patient-days.

Assuming that the scattergraph plot indicates a linear relation between cost and activity, the fixed and variable cost elements of a mixed cost can be estimated using the *high-low method* or the *least-squares regression method.* The high-low method is based on the rise-over-run formula for the slope of a straight line. As discussed above, if the relation between cost and activity can be represented by a straight line, then the slope of the straight line is equal to the variable cost per unit of activity. Consequently, the following formula can be used to estimate the variable cost.

$$\text{Variable cost} = \text{Slope of the line} = \frac{\text{Rise}}{\text{Run}} = \frac{Y_2 - Y_1}{X_2 - X_1}$$

To analyze mixed costs with the **high-low method,** begin by identifying the period with the lowest level of activity and the period with the highest level of activity. The period with the lowest activity is selected as the first point in the above formula and the period with the highest activity is selected as the second point. Consequently, the formula becomes:

$$\text{Variable cost} = \frac{Y_2 - Y_1}{X_2 - X_1} = \frac{\text{Cost at the high activity level} - \text{Cost at the low activity level}}{\text{High activity level} - \text{Low activity level}}$$

or

$$\text{Variable cost} = \frac{\text{Change in cost}}{\text{Change in activity}}$$

Therefore, when the high-low method is used, the variable cost is estimated by dividing the difference in cost between the high and low levels of activity by the change in activity between those two points.

To return to the Brentline Hospital example, using the high-low method, we first identify the periods with the highest and lowest *activity*—in this case, June and March. We then use the activity and cost data from these two periods to estimate the variable cost component as follows:

	Patient-Days	Maintenance Cost Incurred
High activity level (June)	8,000	$9,800
Low activity level (March).	5,000	7,400
Change.	3,000	$2,400

$$\text{Variable cost} = \frac{\text{Change in cost}}{\text{Change in activity}} = \frac{\$2{,}400}{3{,}000 \text{ patient-days}} = \$0.80 \text{ per patient-day}$$

Having determined that the variable maintenance cost is 80 cents per patient-day, we can now determine the amount of fixed cost. This is done by taking the total cost at *either* the high or the low activity level and deducting the variable cost element. In the computation below, total cost at the high activity level is used in computing the fixed cost element:

$$\begin{aligned}\text{Fixed cost element} &= \text{Total cost} - \text{Variable cost element}\\ &= \$9{,}800 - (\$0.80 \text{ per patient-day} \times 8{,}000 \text{ patient-days})\\ &= \$3{,}400\end{aligned}$$

Both the variable and fixed cost elements have now been isolated. The cost of maintenance can be expressed as $3,400 per month plus 80 cents per patient-day or as:

$$Y = \$3{,}400 + \$0.80X$$

↑ Y: Total maintenance cost

↑ X: Total patient-days

The data used in this illustration are shown graphically in Exhibit 4–12. Notice that a straight line has been drawn through the points corresponding to the low and high levels of activity. In essence, that is what the high-low method does—it draws a straight line through those two points.

Sometimes the high and low levels of activity don't coincide with the high and low amounts of cost. For example, the period that has the highest level of activity may not have the highest amount of cost. Nevertheless, the costs at the highest and lowest levels of *activity* are always used to analyze a mixed cost under the high-low method. The reason is that the analyst would like to use data that reflect the greatest possible variation in activity.

EXHIBIT 4–12
High-Low Method of Cost Analysis

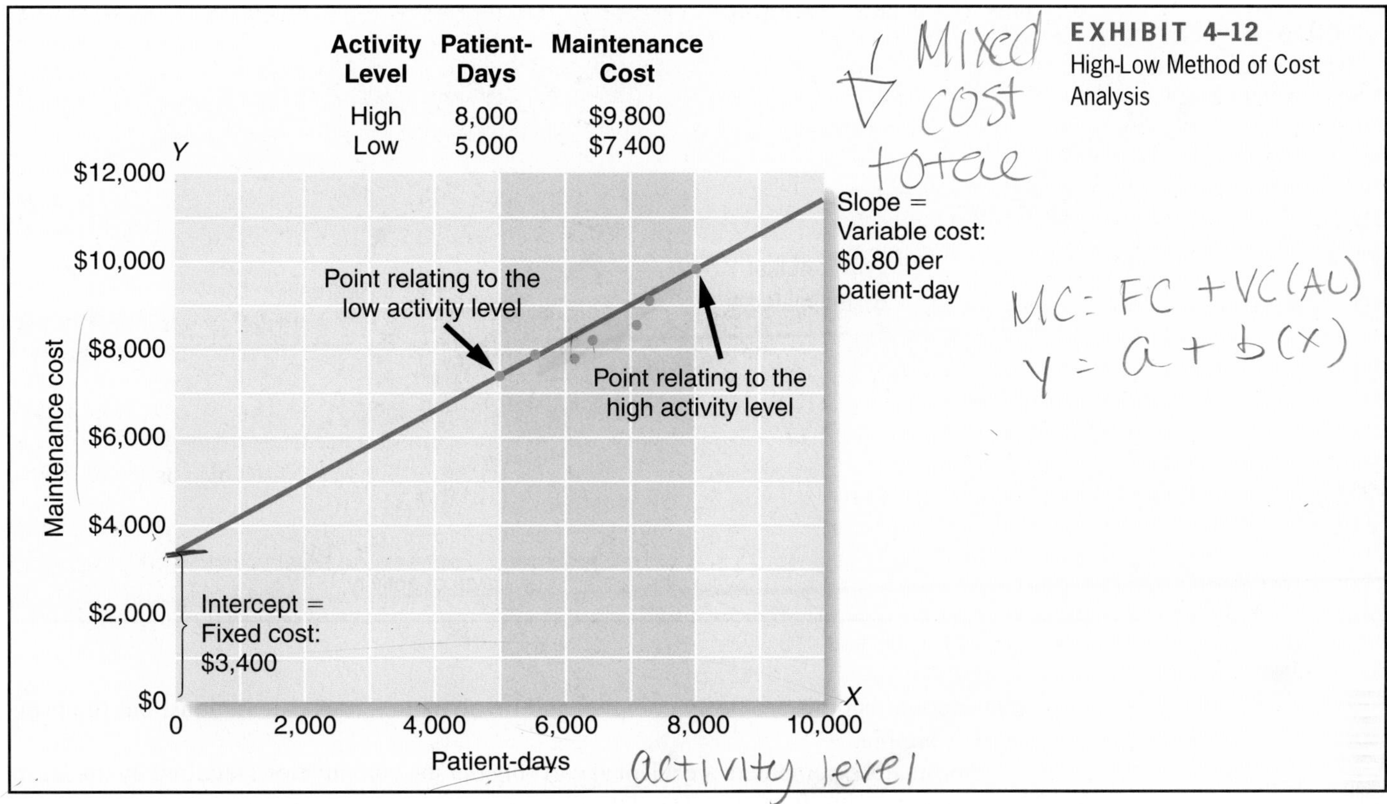

The high-low method is very simple to apply, but it suffers from a major (and sometimes critical) defect—it utilizes only two data points. Generally, two data points are not enough to produce accurate results. Additionally, the periods with the highest and lowest activity tend to be unusual. A cost formula that is estimated solely using data from these unusual periods may misrepresent the true cost behavior during normal periods. Such a distortion is evident in Exhibit 4–12. The straight line should probably be shifted down somewhat so that it is closer to more of the data points. For these reasons, other methods of cost analysis that use all of the data will generally be more accurate than the high-low method. A manager who chooses to use the high-low method should do so with a full awareness of its limitations.

Fortunately, computer software makes it very easy to use sophisticated statistical methods, such as *least-squares regression,* that use all of the data and that are capable of providing much more information than just the estimates of variable and fixed costs. The details of these statistical methods are beyond the scope of this text, but the basic approach is discussed below. Nevertheless, even if the least-squares regression approach is used, it is always a good idea to plot the data in a scattergraph. By simply looking at the scattergraph, you can quickly verify whether it makes sense to fit a straight line to the data using least-squares regression or some other method.

The Least-Squares Regression Method

The **least-squares regression method,** unlike the high-low method, uses all of the data to separate a mixed cost into its fixed and variable components. A *regression line* of the form $Y = a + bX$ is fitted to the data, where a represents the total fixed cost and b represents the variable cost per unit of activity. The basic idea underlying the least-squares regression method is illustrated in Exhibit 4–13 using hypothetical data points. Notice from the exhibit that the deviations from the plotted points to the regression line are measured vertically on the graph. These vertical deviations are called the regression errors. There is nothing mysterious about the least-squares regression method. It simply computes the regression line that minimizes the sum of these squared errors. The formulas

EXHIBIT 4–13
The Concept of Least-Squares Regression

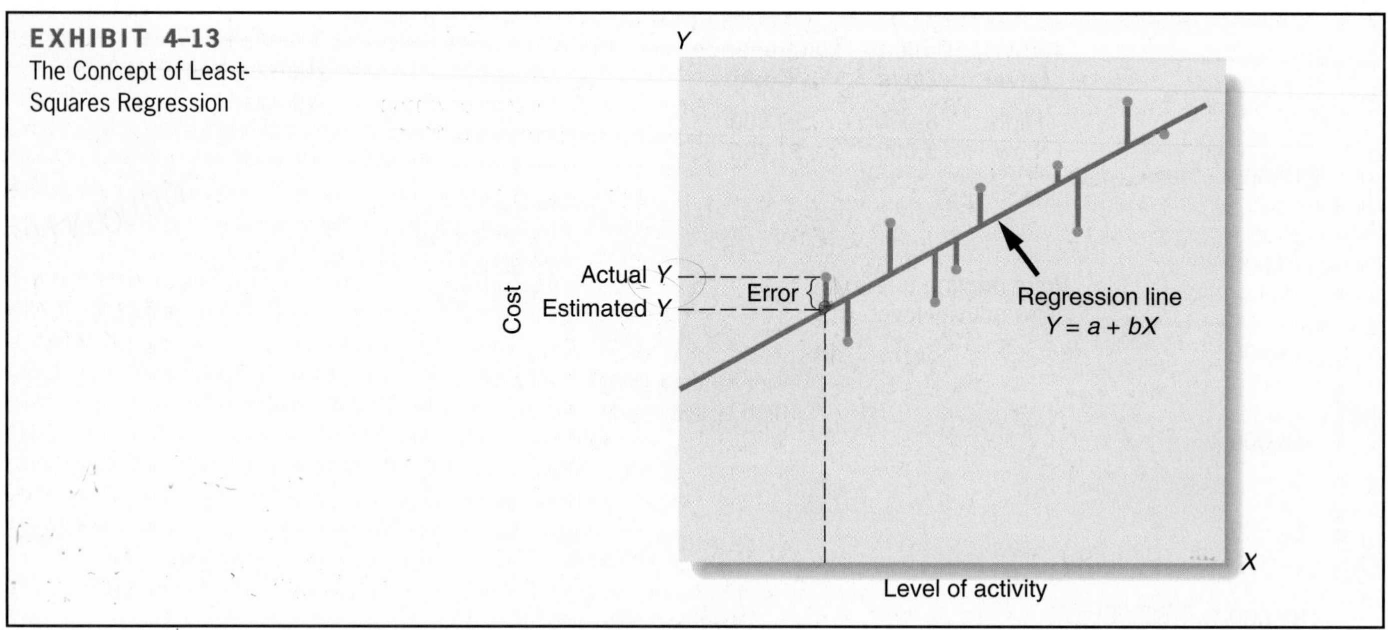

that accomplish this are fairly complex and involve numerous calculations, but the principle is simple.

Fortunately, computers are adept at carrying out the computations required by the least-squares regression formulas. The data—the observed values of X and Y—are entered into the computer, and software does the rest. In the case of the Brentline Hospital maintenance cost data, a statistical software package on a personal computer can calculate the following least-squares regression estimates of the total fixed cost (a) and the variable cost per unit of activity (b):

$$a = \$3{,}431$$
$$b = \$0.759$$

Therefore, using the least-squares regression method, the fixed element of the maintenance cost is \$3,431 per month and the variable portion is 75.9 cents per patient-day.

In terms of the linear equation $Y = a + bX$, the cost formula can be written as

$$Y = \$3{,}431 + \$0.759X$$

where activity (X) is expressed in patient-days.

While a statistical software application was used in this example to calculate the values of a and b, the estimates can also be computed using a spreadsheet application such as Microsoft® Excel. In Appendix 4A to this chapter, we show how this can be done.

In addition to estimates of the intercept (fixed cost) and slope (variable cost per unit), least-squares regression software ordinarily provides a number of other very useful statistics. One of these statistics is the R^2, which is a measure of "goodness of fit." The $\boldsymbol{R^2}$ tells us the percentage of the variation in the dependent variable (cost) that is explained by variation in the independent variable (activity). The R^2 varies from 0% to 100%, and the higher the percentage, the better. In the case of the Brentline Hospital maintenance cost data, the R^2 is 0.90, which indicates that 90% of the variation in maintenance costs is explained by the variation in patient-days. This is reasonably high and is an indication of a good fit. On the other hand, a low R^2 would be an indication of a poor fit. You should always plot the data in a scattergraph, but it is particularly important to check the data visually when the R^2 is low. A quick look at the scattergraph can reveal that there is little relation between the cost and the activity or that the relation is something other than a simple straight line. In such cases, additional analysis would be required.

After completing the analysis of maintenance costs, Kinh Nguyen met with Dr. Derek Chalmers to discuss the results.

Kinh: We used least-squares regression analysis to estimate the fixed and variable components of maintenance costs. According to the results, the fixed cost per month is $3,431 and the variable cost per patient-day is 75.9 cents.

Derek: Okay, so if we plan for 7,800 patient-days next month, what is your estimate of the maintenance costs?

Kinh: That will take just a few seconds to figure out. [Kinh wrote the following calculations on a pad of paper.]

Fixed costs	$3,431
Variable costs:	
7,800 patient-days × $0.759 per patient-day.	5,920
Total expected maintenance costs	$9,351

Derek: Nine thousand three hundred and fifty *one* dollars; isn't that a bit *too* precise?

Kinh: Sure. I don't really believe the maintenance costs will be exactly this figure. However, based on the information we have, this is the best estimate we can come up with.

Derek: This type of estimate will be a lot better than just guessing like we have done in the past. Thanks. I hope to see more of this kind of analysis.

Multiple Regression Analysis

In the discussion thus far, we have assumed that a single factor such as patient-days drives the variable cost component of a mixed cost. This assumption is acceptable for many mixed costs, but in some situations the variable cost element may be driven by a number of factors. For example, shipping costs may depend on both the number of units shipped *and* the weight of the units. In a situation such as this, *multiple regression* is necessary. **Multiple regression** is an analytical method that is used when the dependent variable (i.e., cost) is caused by more than one factor. Although adding more factors, or variables, makes the computations more complex, the principles involved are the same as in the simple least-squares regressions discussed above.

The Contribution Format Income Statement

LEARNING OBJECTIVE 4
Prepare an income statement using the contribution format.

Separating costs into fixed and variable elements helps to predict costs and provide benchmarks. As we will see in later chapters, separating costs into fixed and variable elements is also often crucial in making decisions. This crucial distinction between fixed and variable costs is at the heart of the **contribution approach** to constructing income statements. The unique thing about the contribution approach is that it provides managers with an income statement that clearly distinguishes between fixed and variable costs and therefore facilitates planning, control, and decision making.

Why a New Income Statement Format?

An income statement prepared using the *traditional approach,* as illustrated in Chapter 2, is organized in a "functional" format—emphasizing the functions of production, administration, and sales. No attempt is made to distinguish between fixed and variable costs. Under the heading "Administrative expense," for example, both variable and fixed costs are lumped together.

Although an income statement prepared in the functional format may be useful for external reporting purposes, it has serious limitations when used for internal purposes. Internally, managers need cost data organized in a format that will facilitate planning, control, and decision making. As we shall see in chapters ahead, these tasks are much easier when cost data are available in a fixed and variable format. The contribution format income statement has been developed in response to these needs.

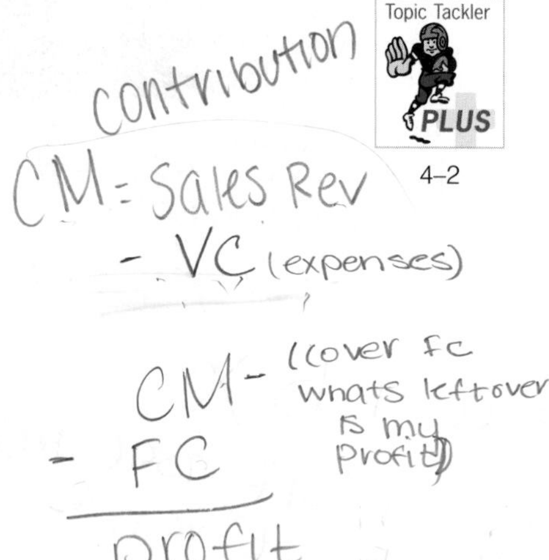

The Contribution Approach

Exhibit 4–14 uses a simple example to compare a contribution approach income statement to the traditional approach discussed in Chapter 2.

Notice that the contribution approach separates costs into fixed and variable categories, first deducting variable expenses from sales to obtain the *contribution margin.* The **contribution margin** is the amount remaining from sales revenues after variable expenses have been deducted. This amount *contributes* toward covering fixed expenses and then toward profits for the period.

The contribution format income statement is used as an internal planning and decision-making tool. Its emphasis on cost behavior facilitates cost-volume-profit analysis (such as we shall be doing in the next chapter), management performance appraisals, and budgeting. Moreover, the contribution approach helps managers organize data pertinent to numerous decisions such as product-line analysis, pricing, use of scarce resources, and make or buy analysis. All of these topics are covered in later chapters.

EXHIBIT 4–14

Comparison of the Contribution Income Statement with the Traditional Income Statement (the data are given)

Traditional Approach (costs organized by function)		
Sales		$12,000
Cost of goods sold		6,000*
Gross margin		6,000
Selling and administrative expenses:		
Selling	$3,100*	
Administrative	1,900*	5,000
Net operating income		$ 1,000

Contribution Approach (costs organized by behavior)		
Sales		$12,000
Variable expenses:		
Variable production	$2,000	
Variable selling	600	
Variable administrative	400	3,000
Contribution margin		9,000
Fixed expenses:		
Fixed production	4,000	
Fixed selling	2,500	
Fixed administrative	1,500	8,000
Net operating income		$ 1,000

*Contains both variable and fixed expenses. This is the income statement for a manufacturing company; thus, when the income statement is placed in the contribution format, the "cost of goods sold" is divided between variable production costs and fixed production costs. If this were the income statement for a *merchandising* company (which simply purchases completed goods from a supplier), then the cost of goods sold would be *all* variable.

Summary

As we shall see in later chapters, the ability to predict how costs respond to changes in activity is critical for making decisions, controlling operations, and evaluating performance. Three major classifications of costs were discussed in this chapter—variable, fixed, and mixed. Mixed costs consist of variable and fixed elements and can be expressed in equation form as $Y = a + bX$, where X is the activity, Y is the cost, a is the fixed cost element, and b is the variable cost per unit of activity.

Several methods can be used to estimate the fixed and variable cost components of a mixed cost using past records of cost and activity. If the relation between cost and activity appears to be linear based on a scattergraph plot, then the variable and fixed components of the mixed cost can be estimated using the quick-and-dirty method, the high-low method, or the least-squares regression method. The quick-and-dirty method is based on drawing a straight line and then using the slope and the intercept of the straight line to estimate the variable and fixed cost components of the mixed cost. The high-low method implicitly draws a straight line through the points of lowest activity and highest activity. In most situations, the least-squares regression method is preferred to both the quick-and-dirty and high-low methods. Computer software is widely available for using the least-squares regression method. These software applications provide a variety of useful statistics along with estimates of the intercept (fixed cost) and slope (variable cost per unit). Nevertheless, even when least-squares regression is used, the data should be plotted to confirm that the relationship is really a straight line.

Managers use costs organized by behavior to help make many decisions. The contribution format income statement can aid decision making because it classifies costs by cost behavior (i.e., variable versus fixed) rather than by the functions of production, administration, and sales.

Review Problem 1: Cost Behavior

Neptune Rentals operates a boat rental service. Consider the following costs of the company over the relevant range of 5,000 to 8,000 hours of operating time for its boats:

	Hours of Operating Time			
	5,000	6,000	7,000	8,000
Total costs:				
Variable costs	$ 20,000	$?	$?	$?
Fixed costs	168,000	?	?	?
Total costs	$188,000	$?	$?	$?
Cost per hour:				
Variable cost	$?	$?	$?	$?
Fixed cost	?	?	?	?
Total cost per hour	$?	$?	$?	$?

Required:

Compute the missing amounts, assuming that cost behavior patterns remain unchanged within the relevant range of 5,000 to 8,000 hours.

Solution to Review Problem 1

The variable cost per hour can be computed as follows:

$$\$20{,}000 \div 5{,}000 \text{ hours} = \$4 \text{ per hour}$$

Therefore, the missing amounts are as follows:

	Hours of Operating Time			
	5,000	6,000	7,000	8,000
Total costs:				
Variable costs				
(@ $4 per hour)	$ 20,000	$ 24,000	$ 28,000	$ 32,000
Fixed costs	168,000	168,000	168,000	168,000
Total costs	$188,000	$192,000	$196,000	$200,000
Cost per hour:				
Variable cost	$ 4.00	$ 4.00	$ 4.00	$ 4.00
Fixed cost	33.60	28.00	24.00	21.00
Total cost per hour	$ 37.60	$ 32.00	$ 28.00	$ 25.00

Observe that the total variable costs increase in proportion to the number of hours of operating time, but that these costs remain constant at $4 if expressed on a per hour basis.

In contrast, the total fixed costs do not change with changes in the level of activity. They remain constant at $168,000 within the relevant range. With increases in activity, however, the fixed cost per hour decreases, dropping from $33.60 per hour when the boats are operated 5,000 hours a period to only $21.00 per hour when the boats are operated 8,000 hours a period. *Because of this troublesome aspect of fixed costs, they are most easily (and most safely) dealt with on a total basis, rather than on a unit basis, in cost analysis work.*

Review Problem 2: High-Low Method

The administrator of Azalea Hills Hospital would like a cost formula linking the administrative costs involved in admitting patients to the number of patients admitted during a month. The admitting department's costs and the number of patients admitted during the immediately preceding eight months are given in the following table:

Month	Number of Patients Admitted	Admitting Department Costs
May	1,800	$14,700
June	1,900	$15,200
July	1,700	$13,700
August	1,600	$14,000
September	1,500	$14,300
October	1,300	$13,100
November	1,100	$12,800
December	1,500	$14,600

Required:

1. Use the high-low method to establish the fixed and variable components of admitting costs.
2. Express the fixed and variable components of admitting costs as a cost formula in the form $Y = a + bX$.

Solution to Review Problem 2

1. The first step in the high-low method is to identify the periods of the lowest and highest activity. Those periods are November (1,100 patients admitted) and June (1,900 patients admitted).

   The second step is to compute the variable cost per unit using those two data points:

Month	Number of Patients Admitted	Admitting Department Costs
High activity level (June)	1,900	$15,200
Low activity level (November)	1,100	12,800
Change	800	$ 2,400

$$\text{Variable cost} = \frac{\text{Change in cost}}{\text{Change in activity}} = \frac{\$2{,}400}{800 \text{ patients admitted}} = \$3 \text{ per patient admitted}$$

   The third step is to compute the fixed cost element by deducting the variable cost element from the total cost at either the high or low activity. In the computation below, the high point of activity is used:

$$\begin{aligned}\text{Fixed cost element} &= \text{Total cost} - \text{Variable cost element}\\ &= \$15{,}200 - (\$3 \text{ per patient admitted} \times 1{,}900 \text{ patients admitted})\\ &= \$9{,}500\end{aligned}$$

2. The cost formula is $Y = \$9{,}500 + \$3X$.

Glossary

Account analysis A method for analyzing cost behavior in which an account is classified as either variable or fixed based on the analyst's prior knowledge of how the cost in the account behaves. (p. 134)

Activity base A measure of whatever causes the incurrence of a variable cost. For example, the total cost of X-ray film in a hospital will increase as the number of X-rays taken increases. Therefore, the number of X-rays is the activity base that explains the total cost of X-ray film. (p. 122)

Committed fixed costs Investments in facilities, equipment, and basic organizational structure that can't be significantly reduced even for short periods of time without making fundamental changes. (p. 128)

Contribution approach An income statement format that organizes costs by their behavior. Costs are separated into variable and fixed categories rather than being separated according to organizational functions. (p. 143)

Contribution margin The amount remaining from sales revenues after all variable expenses have been deducted. (p. 144)

Cost structure The relative proportion of fixed, variable, and mixed costs in an organization. (p. 121)

Dependent variable A variable that responds to some causal factor; total cost is the dependent variable, as represented by the letter Y, in the equation $Y = a + bX$. (p. 136)

Discretionary fixed costs Those fixed costs that arise from annual decisions by management to spend on certain fixed cost items, such as advertising and research. (p. 128)

Engineering approach A detailed analysis of cost behavior based on an industrial engineer's evaluation of the inputs that are required to carry out a particular activity and of the prices of those inputs. (p. 134)

High-low method A method of separating a mixed cost into its fixed and variable elements by analyzing the change in cost between the high and low activity levels. (p. 139)

Independent variable A variable that acts as a causal factor; activity is the independent variable, as represented by the letter X, in the equation $Y = a + bX$. (p. 136)

Least-squares regression method A method of separating a mixed cost into its fixed and variable elements by fitting a regression line that minimizes the sum of the squared errors. (p. 141)

Linear cost behavior Cost behavior is said to be linear whenever a straight line is a reasonable approximation for the relation between cost and activity. (p. 136)

Mixed cost A cost that contains both variable and fixed cost elements. (p. 132)

Multiple regression An analytical method required when variations in a dependent variable are caused by more than one factor. (p. 143)

R^2 A measure of goodness of fit in least-squares regression analysis. It is the percentage of the variation in the dependent variable that is explained by variation in the independent variable. (p. 142)

Relevant range The range of activity within which assumptions about variable and fixed cost behavior are reasonably valid. (p. 125)

Step-variable cost The cost of a resource that is obtainable only in large chunks and that increases and decreases only in response to fairly wide changes in activity. (p. 124)

Appendix 4A: Least-Squares Regression Using Microsoft® Excel

LEARNING OBJECTIVE 5
Analyze a mixed cost using the least-squares regression method.

The least-squares regression method for estimating a linear relationship is based on the equation for a straight line:

$$Y = a + bX$$

As explained in the chapter, least-squares regression selects the values for the intercept a and the slope b that minimize the sum of the squared errors. The following formulas, which are derived in statistics and calculus texts, accomplish that objective:

$$b = \frac{n(\Sigma XY) - (\Sigma X)(\Sigma Y)}{n(\Sigma X^2) - (\Sigma X)^2}$$

$$a = \frac{(\Sigma Y) - b(\Sigma X)}{n}$$

where:

X = The level of activity (independent variable)

Y = The total mixed cost (dependent variable)

a = The total fixed cost (the vertical intercept of the line)

b = The variable cost per unit of activity (the slope of the line)

n = Number of observations

Σ = Sum across all n observations

Manually performing the calculations required by the formulas is tedious at best. Fortunately, statistical software packages are widely available that perform the calculations automatically. Spreadsheet software, such as Microsoft® Excel, can also be used to do least-squares regression—although it requires a little more work than using a specialized statistical application.

To illustrate how Excel can be used to calculate the intercept *a,* the slope *b,* and the R^2, we will use the Brentline Hospital data for maintenance costs on page 136. The worksheet in Exhibit 4A–1 contains the data and the calculations.

As you can see, the *X* values (the independent variable) have been entered in cells B4 through B10. The *Y* values (the dependent variable) have been entered in cells C4 through C10. The slope, intercept, and R^2 are computed using the Excel functions INTERCEPT, SLOPE, and RSQ. You must specify the range of cells for the *Y* values and for the *X* values. In Exhibit 4A–1, cell B12 contains the formula =INTERCEPT(C4:C10,B4:B10); cell B13

EXHIBIT 4A–1
The Least-Squares Regression Worksheet for Brentline Hospital

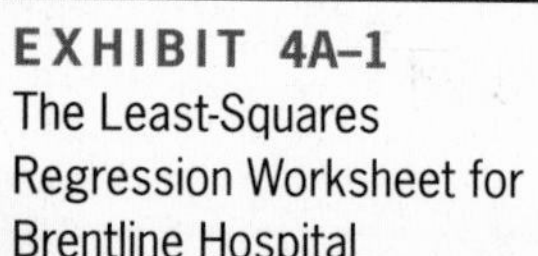

Microsoft Excel - Appendix 5A.xls

	A	B	C	D
1		*Patient*	*Maintenance*	
2		*Days*	*Costs*	
3	*Month*	*X*	*Y*	
4	January	5,600	$7,900	
5	February	7,100	$8,500	
6	March	5,000	$7,400	
7	April	6,500	$8,200	
8	May	7,300	$9,100	
9	June	8,000	$9,800	
10	July	6,200	$7,800	
11				
12	Intercept	$3,431		
13	Slope	$0.759		
14	RSQ	0.90		
15				

Least-squares regression

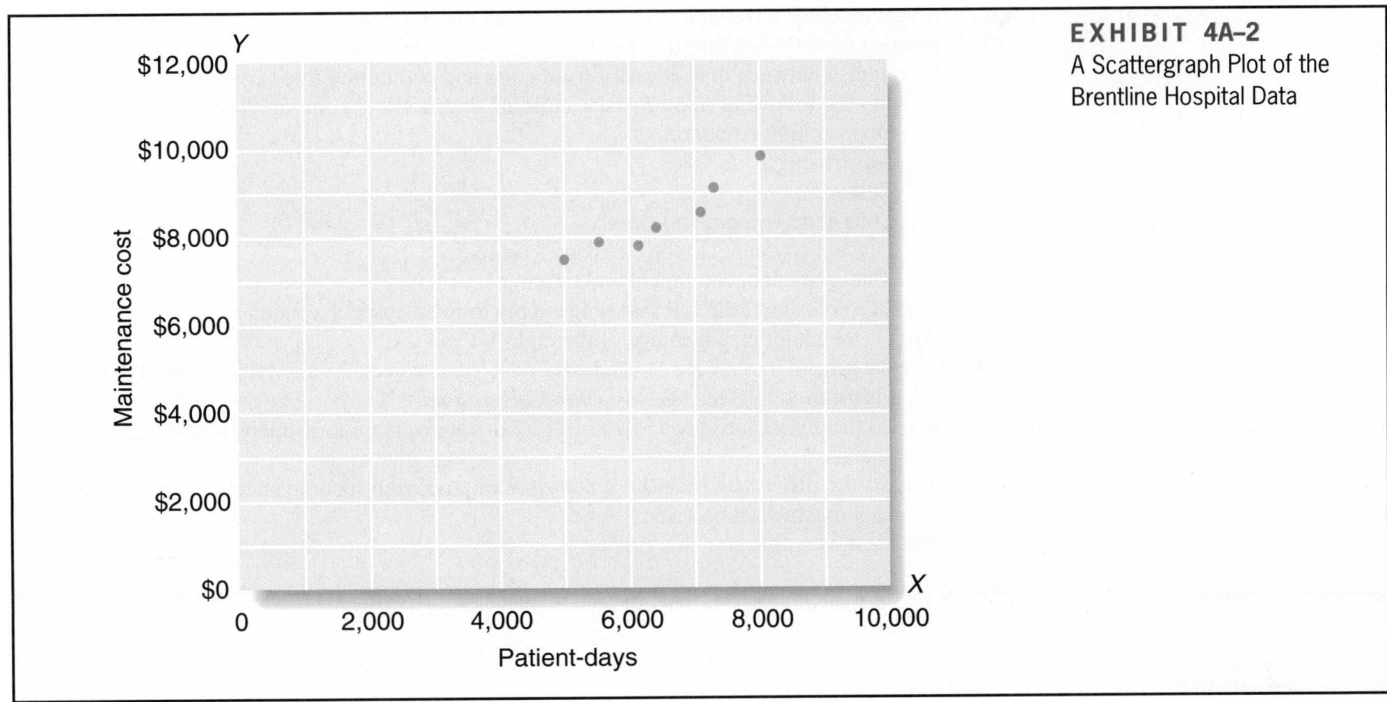

EXHIBIT 4A–2
A Scattergraph Plot of the Brentline Hospital Data

contains the formula =SLOPE(C4:C10,B4:B10); and cell B14 contains the formula =RSQ(C4:C10,B4:B10).

According to the calculations carried out by Excel, the fixed maintenance cost (the intercept) is $3,431 per month and the variable cost (the slope) is $0.759 per patient-day. Therefore, the cost formula for maintenance cost is:

$$Y = a + bX$$

$$Y = \$3{,}431 + \$0.759X$$

Note that the R^2 (i.e., RSQ) is 0.90, which—as previously discussed—is quite good and indicates that 90% of the variation in maintenance costs is explained by the variation in patient-days.

Plotting the data is easy in Excel. Select the range of values that you would like to plot—in this case, cells B4:C10. Then select the Chart Wizard tool on the toolbar and make the appropriate choices in the various dialogue boxes that appear. When you are finished, you should have a scattergraph that looks like the plot in Exhibit 4A–2. Note that the relation between cost and activity is approximately linear, so it is reasonable to fit a straight line to the data as we have implicitly done with the least-squares regression.

Questions

4-1 Distinguish between (*a*) a variable cost, (*b*) a fixed cost, and (*c*) a mixed cost.

4-2 What effect does an increase in volume have on—
- *a.* Unit fixed costs?
- *b.* Unit variable costs?
- *c.* Total fixed costs?
- *d.* Total variable costs?

4-3 Define the following terms: (*a*) cost behavior and (*b*) relevant range.

4-4 What is meant by an *activity base* when dealing with variable costs? Give several examples of activity bases.

4-5 Distinguish between (*a*) a variable cost, (*b*) a mixed cost, and (*c*) a step-variable cost. Plot the three costs on a graph, with activity plotted horizontally and cost plotted vertically.

4-6 Managers often assume a strictly linear relationship between cost and volume. How can this practice be defended in light of the fact that many costs are curvilinear?

4-7 Distinguish between discretionary fixed costs and committed fixed costs.

4-8 Classify the following fixed costs as normally being either committed or discretionary:

a. Depreciation on buildings.
b. Advertising.
c. Research.
d. Long-term equipment leases.
e. Pension payments to the company's retirees.
f. Management development and training.

4-9 Does the concept of the relevant range apply to fixed costs? Explain.

4-10 What is the major disadvantage of the high-low method?

4-11 Give the general formula for a mixed cost. Which term represents the variable cost? The fixed cost?

4-12 What is meant by the term *least-squares regression?*

4-13 What is the difference between ordinary least-squares regression analysis and multiple regression analysis?

4-14 What is the difference between a contribution approach income statement and a traditional approach income statement?

4-15 What is the contribution margin?

Quiz 4

Multiple-choice questions are provided on the text Web site at www.mhhe.com/noreen1e.

Exercises

EXERCISE 4-1 Fixed and Variable Cost Behavior [LO1]

Koffee Express operates a number of espresso coffee stands in busy suburban malls. The fixed weekly expense of a coffee stand is $1,100 and the variable cost per cup of coffee served is $0.26.

Required:

1. Fill in the following table with your estimates of total costs and cost per cup of coffee at the indicated levels of activity for a coffee stand. Round off the cost of a cup of coffee to the nearest tenth of a cent.

	Cups of Coffee Served in a Week		
	1,800	1,900	2,000
Fixed cost	?	?	?
Variable cost	?	?	?
Total cost.	?	?	?
Cost per cup of coffee served.	?	?	?

2. Does the cost per cup of coffee served increase, decrease, or remain the same as the number of cups of coffee served in a week increases? Explain.

EXERCISE 4-2 Scattergraph Analysis [LO2]

The data below have been taken from the cost records of the Atlanta Processing Company. The data relate to the cost of operating one of the company's processing facilities at various levels of activity:

Month	Units Processed	Total Cost
January	8,000	$14,000
February.	4,500	$10,000
March.	7,000	$12,500
April	9,000	$15,500
May	3,750	$10,000
June	6,000	$12,500
July.	3,000	$8,500
August	5,000	$11,500

Required:

1. Prepare a scattergraph using the above data. Plot cost on the vertical axis and activity on the horizontal axis. Fit a line to your plotted points using a ruler.
2. Using the quick-and-dirty method, what is the approximate monthly fixed cost? The approximate variable cost per unit processed? Show your computations.

EXERCISE 4-3 High-Low Method [LO3]

The Edelweiss Hotel in Vail, Colorado, has accumulated records of the total electrical costs of the hotel and the number of occupancy-days over the last year. An occupancy-day represents a room rented out for one day. The hotel's business is highly seasonal, with peaks occurring during the ski season and in the summer.

Month	Occupancy-Days	Electrical Costs
January	2,604	$6,257
February.	2,856	$6,550
March.	3,534	$7,986
April	1,440	$4,022
May	540	$2,289
June.	1,116	$3,591
July.	3,162	$7,264
August	3,608	$8,111
September.	1,260	$3,707
October	186	$1,712
November	1,080	$3,321
December	2,046	$5,196

Required:

1. Using the high-low method, estimate the fixed cost of electricity per month and the variable cost of electricity per occupancy-day. Round off the fixed cost to the nearest whole dollar and the variable cost to the nearest whole cent.
2. What other factors other than occupancy-days are likely to affect the variation in electrical costs from month to month?

EXERCISE 4-4 Contribution Format Income Statement [LO4]

Haaki Shop, Inc., is a large retailer of water sports equipment. An income statement for the company's surfboard department for a recent quarter is presented below:

The Haaki Shop, Inc. Income Statement—Surfboard Department For The Quarter Ended May 31		
Sales		$800,000
Cost of goods sold		300,000
Gross margin		500,000
Selling and administrative expenses:		
Selling expenses	$250,000	
Administrative expenses	160,000	410,000
Net operating income.		$ 90,000

The surfboards sell, on the average, for $400 each. The department's variable selling expenses are $50 per surfboard sold. The remaining selling expenses are fixed. The administrative expenses are 25% variable and 75% fixed. The company purchases its surfboards from a supplier at a cost of $150 per surfboard.

Required:

1. Prepare an income statement for the quarter using the contribution approach.
2. What was the contribution toward fixed expenses and profits from each surfboard sold during the quarter? (State this figure in a single dollar amount per surfboard.)

EXERCISE 4-5 (Appendix 4A) Least-Squares Regression [LO5]

EZ Rental Car offers rental cars in an off-airport location near a major tourist destination in Florida. Management would like to better understand the behavior of the company's costs. One of those costs is the cost of washing cars. The company operates its own car wash facility in which each rental car that is returned is thoroughly cleaned before being released for rental to another customer. Management believes that the costs of operating the car wash should be related to the number of rental returns. Accordingly, the following data have been compiled:

Month	Rental Returns	Car Wash Costs
January	2,310	$10,113
February.	2,453	$12,691
March.	2,641	$10,905
April	2,874	$12,949
May	3,540	$15,334
June	4,861	$21,455
July.	5,432	$21,270
August	5,268	$19,930
September	4,628	$21,860
October	3,720	$18,383
November	2,106	$9,830
December	2,495	$11,081

Required:

Using least-squares regression, estimate the fixed cost and variable cost elements of monthly car wash costs. The fixed cost element should be estimated to the nearest dollar and the variable cost element to the nearest cent.

EXERCISE 4-6 Cost Behavior; Contribution Format Income Statement [LO1, LO4]

Parker Company manufactures and sells a single product. A partially completed schedule of the company's total and per unit costs over a relevant range of 60,000 to 100,000 units produced and sold each year is given below:

	Units Produced and Sold		
	60,000	80,000	100,000
Total costs:			
Variable costs.	$150,000	?	?
Fixed costs	360,000	?	?
Total costs	$510,000	?	?
Cost per unit:			
Variable cost.	?	?	?
Fixed cost.	?	?	?
Total cost per unit	?	?	?

Required:

1. Complete the schedule of the company's total and unit costs above.
2. Assume that the company produces and sells 90,000 units during the year at the selling price of $7.50 per unit. Prepare a contribution format income statement for the year.

EXERCISE 4-7 High-Low Method; Scattergraph Analysis [LO2, LO3]

Zerbel Company, a wholesaler of large, custom-built air conditioning units for commercial buildings, has noticed considerable fluctuation in its shipping expense from month to month, as shown below:

Month	Units Shipped	Total Shipping Expense
January	4	$2,200
February.	7	$3,100
March.	5	$2,600
April	2	$1,500
May	3	$2,200
June	6	$3,000
July.	8	$3,600

Required:

1. Using the high-low method, estimate the cost formula for shipping expense.
2. The president has no confidence in the high-low method and would like you to "check out" your results using the scattergraph method. Do the following:
   a. Prepare a scattergraph using the data given above. Plot cost on the vertical axis and activity on the horizontal axis. Use a ruler to fit a straight line to your plotted points.
   b. Using your scattergraph, estimate the approximate variable cost per unit shipped and the approximate fixed cost per month with the quick-and-dirty method.
3. What factors, other than the number of units shipped, are likely to affect the company's shipping expense? Explain.

EXERCISE 4-8 (Appendix 4A) Least-Squares Regression [LO5]

Refer to the data for Zerbel Company in Exercise 4-7.

Required:

1. Using the least-squares regression method, estimate the cost formula for shipping expense.
2. If you also completed Exercise 4-7, prepare a simple table comparing the variable and fixed cost elements of shipping expense as computed under the quick-and-dirty scattergraph method, the high-low method, and the least-squares regression method.

EXERCISE 4-9 Cost Behavior; High-Low Method [LO1, LO3]

Speedy Parcel Service operates a fleet of delivery trucks in a large metropolitan area. A careful study by the company's cost analyst has determined that if a truck is driven 120,000 miles during a year, the average operating cost is 11.6 cents per mile. If a truck is driven only 80,000 miles during a year, the average operating cost increases to 13.6 cents per mile.

Required:

1. Using the high-low method, estimate the variable and fixed cost elements of the annual cost of truck operation.
2. Express the variable and fixed costs in the form $Y = a + bX$.
3. If a truck were driven 100,000 miles during a year, what total cost would you expect to be incurred?

EXERCISE 4-10 High-Low Method; Predicting Cost [LO1, LO3]

The number of X-rays taken and X-ray costs over the last nine months in Beverly Hospital are given below:

Month	X-Rays Taken	X-Ray Costs
January	6,250	$28,000
February.	7,000	$29,000
March.	5,000	$23,000
April	4,250	$20,000
May	4,500	$22,000
June	3,000	$17,000
July.	3,750	$18,000
August	5,500	$24,000
September	5,750	$26,000

Required:

1. Using the high-low method, estimate the cost formula for X-ray costs.
2. Using the cost formula you derived above, what X-ray costs would you expect to be incurred during a month in which 4,600 X-rays are taken?

EXERCISE 4-11 Scattergraph Analysis; High-Low Method [LO2, LO3]

Refer to the data in Exercise 4-10 for Beverly Hospital.

Required:

1. Prepare a scattergraph using the data from Exercise 4-10. Plot cost on the vertical axis and activity on the horizontal axis. Using a ruler, fit a line to your plotted points.
2. Using the quick-and-dirty method, what is the approximate monthly fixed cost for X-rays? The approximate variable cost per X-ray taken?
3. Scrutinize the points on your graph, and explain why the high-low method would or would not yield an accurate cost formula in this situation.

EXERCISE 4-12 High-Low Method; Predicting Cost [LO1, LO3]

Resort Inns, Inc., has a total of 2,000 rooms in its nationwide chain of motels. On average, 70% of the rooms are occupied each day. The company's operating costs are $21 per occupied room per day at this occupancy level, assuming a 30-day month. This $21 figure contains both variable and fixed cost elements. During October, the occupancy rate dropped to only 45%. A total of $792,000 in operating cost was incurred during October.

Required:

1. Estimate the variable cost per occupied room per day.
2. Estimate the total fixed operating costs per month.
3. Assume that the occupancy rate increases to 60% during November. What total operating costs would you expect the company to incur during November?

EXERCISE 4-13 (Appendix 4A) Least-Squares Regression [LO1, LO5]

One of Varic Company's products goes through a glazing process. The company has observed glazing costs as follows over the last six weeks:

Week	Units Produced	Total Glazing Cost
1	8	$270
2	5	$200
3	10	$310
4	4	$190
5	6	$240
6	9	$290

For planning purposes, the company's management must know the amount of variable glazing cost per unit and the total fixed glazing cost per week.

Required:

1. Using the least-squares regression method, estimate the variable and fixed elements of the glazing cost.
2. Express the cost data in (1) above in the form $Y = a + bX$.
3. If the company processes seven units next week, what would be the expected total glazing cost?

Problems 

PROBLEM 4-14 (Appendix 4A) Scattergraph; Cost Behavior; Least-Squares Regression Method [LO1, LO2, LO5]

Amanda King has just been appointed director of recreation programs for Highland Park, a rapidly growing community in Connecticut. In the past, the city has sponsored a number of softball leagues in the summer months. From the city's cost records, Amanda has found the following total costs associated with the softball leagues over the last five years:

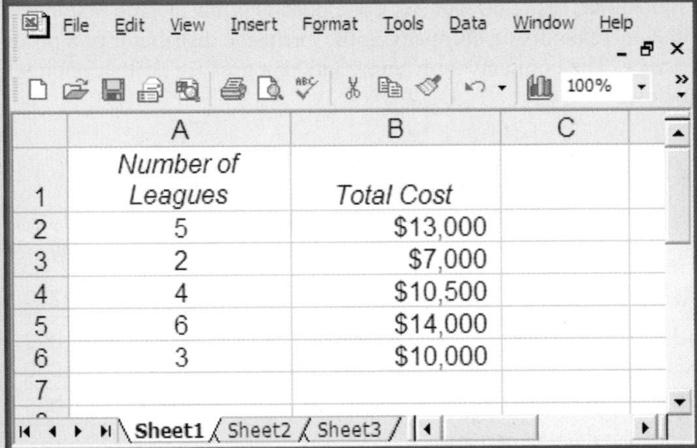

	A	B	C
1	Number of Leagues	Total Cost	
2	5	$13,000	
3	2	$7,000	
4	4	$10,500	
5	6	$14,000	
6	3	$10,000	
7			

Each league requires its own paid supervisor and paid umpires as well as printed schedules and other copy work. Therefore, Amanda knows that some variable costs are associated with the leagues. She would like to know the amount of variable cost per league and the total fixed cost per year associated with the softball program. This information would help her for planning purposes.

Required:

1. Using the least-squares regression method, estimate the variable cost per league and the total fixed cost per year for the softball program.
2. Express the cost data derived in (1) above in the form $Y = a + bX$.
3. Assume that Amanda would like to expand the softball program during the coming year to involve a total of seven leagues. Compute the expected total cost for the softball program. Can you see any problem with using the cost formula from (2) above to derive this total cost figure? Explain.
4. Prepare a scattergraph, and fit a line to the plotted points using the cost formula expressed in (2) above.

PROBLEM 4-15 Contribution Format versus Traditional Income Statement [LO4]

House of Organs, Inc., purchases organs from a well-known manufacturer and sells them at the retail level. The organs sell, on the average, for $2,500 each. The average cost of an organ from the manufacturer is $1,500.

House of Organs, Inc., has always kept careful records of its costs. The costs that the company incurs in a typical month are presented below in the form of a spreadsheet:

Costs	Cost Formula
Selling:	
Advertising	$950 per month
Delivery of organs	$60 per organ sold
Sales salaries and commissions	$4,800 per month, plus 4% of sales
Utilities	$650 per month
Depreciation of sales facilities	$5,000 per month
Administrative:	
Executive salaries	$13,500 per month
Depreciation of office equipment	$900 per month
Clerical	$2,500 per month, plus $40 per organ sold
Insurance	$700 per month

During November, the company sold and delivered 60 organs.

Required:

1. Prepare an income statement for November using the traditional format with costs organized by function.
2. Redo (1) above, this time using the contribution format with costs organized by behavior. Show costs and revenues on both a total and a per unit basis down through contribution margin.
3. Refer to the income statement you prepared in (2) above. Why might it be misleading to show the fixed costs on a per unit basis?

PROBLEM 4-16 Cost Behavior; High-Low Method; Contribution Format Income Statement [LO1, LO3, LO4]
Frankel Ltd., a British merchandising company, is the exclusive distributor of a product that is gaining rapid market acceptance. The company's revenues and expenses (in British pounds) for the last three months are given below:

Frankel Ltd. Comparative Income Statements For the Three Months Ended June 30	April	May	June
Sales in units	3,000	3,750	4,500
Sales revenue	£420,000	£525,000	£630,000
Cost of goods sold	168,000	210,000	252,000
Gross margin	252,000	315,000	378,000
Selling and administrative expenses:			
Shipping expense	44,000	50,000	56,000
Advertising expense	70,000	70,000	70,000
Salaries and commissions	107,000	125,000	143,000
Insurance expense	9,000	9,000	9,000
Depreciation expense	42,000	42,000	42,000
Total selling and administrative expenses	272,000	296,000	320,000
Net operating income (loss)	£ (20,000)	£ 19,000	£ 58,000

(Note: Frankel Ltd.'s income statement has been recast in the functional format common in the United States. The British currency is the pound, denoted by £.)

Required:

1. Identify each of the company's expenses (including cost of goods sold) as either variable, fixed, or mixed.
2. Using the high-low method, separate each mixed expense into variable and fixed elements. State the cost formula for each mixed expense.
3. Redo the company's income statement at the 4,500-unit level of activity using the contribution format.

PROBLEM 4-17 Identifying Cost Behavior Patterns [LO1]
A number of graphs displaying cost behavior patterns are shown below. The vertical axis on each graph represents total cost and the horizontal axis represents the level of activity (volume).

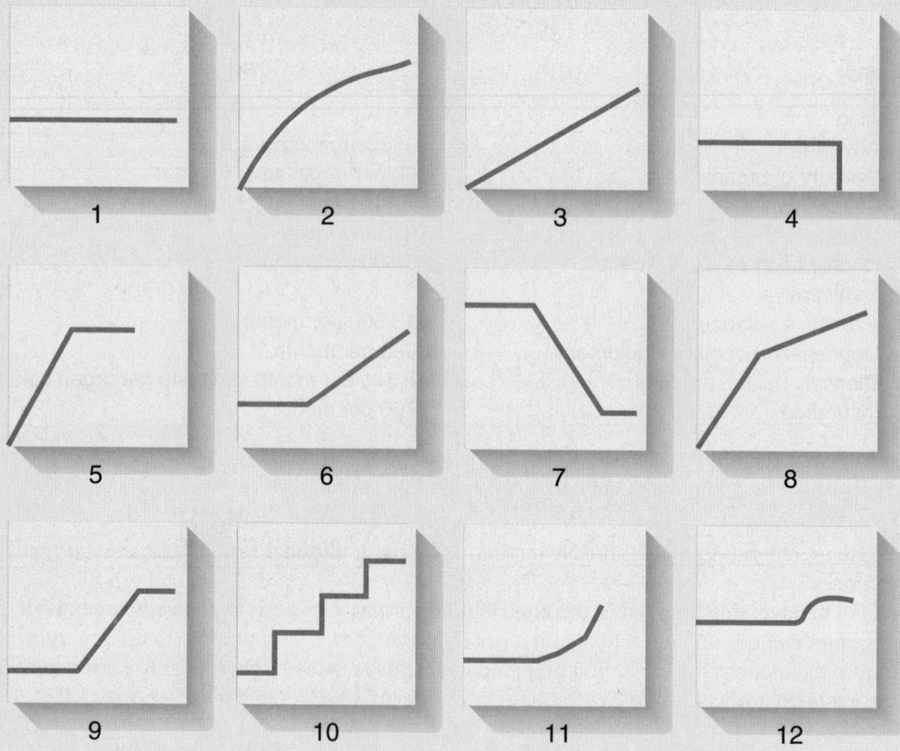

Required:

1. For each of the following situations, identify the graph that illustrates the cost behavior pattern involved. Any graph may be used more than once.
   a. Electricity bill—a flat fixed charge, plus a variable cost after a certain number of kilowatt-hours are used.
   b. City water bill, which is computed as follows:

First 1,000,000 gallons or less	$1,000 flat fee
Next 10,000 gallons	$0.003 per gallon used
Next 10,000 gallons	$0.006 per gallon used
Next 10,000 gallons	$0.009 per gallon used
Etc.	Etc.

   c. Depreciation of equipment, where the amount is computed by the straight-line method. When the depreciation rate was established, it was anticipated that the obsolescence factor would be greater than the wear and tear factor.
   d. Rent on a factory building donated by the city, where the agreement calls for a fixed fee payment unless 200,000 labor-hours or more are worked, in which case no rent need be paid.
   e. Cost of raw materials, where the cost starts at $7.50 per unit and then decreases by 5 cents per unit for each of the first 100 units purchased, after which it remains constant at $2.50 per unit.
   f. Salaries of maintenance workers, where one maintenance worker is needed for every 1,000 hours of machine-hours or less (that is, 0 to 1,000 hours requires one maintenance worker, 1,001 to 2,000 hours requires two maintenance workers, etc.).
   g. Cost of raw material used.
   h. Rent on a factory building donated by the county, where the agreement calls for rent of $100,000 less $1 for each direct labor-hour worked in excess of 200,000 hours, but a minimum rental payment of $20,000 must be paid.
   i. Use of a machine under a lease, where a minimum charge of $1,000 is paid for up to 400 hours of machine time. After 400 hours of machine time, an additional charge of $2 per hour is paid up to a maximum charge of $2,000 per period.
2. How would a knowledge of cost behavior patterns such as those above be of help to a manager in analyzing the cost structure of his or her company?

(CPA, adapted)

PROBLEM 4-18 High-Low and Scattergraph Analysis [LO2, LO3]

Sebolt Wire Company heats copper ingots to very high temperatures by placing the ingots in a large heat coil. The heated ingots are then run through a shaping machine that shapes the soft ingot into wire. Due to the long heat-up time, the coil is never turned off. When an ingot is placed in the coil, the temperature is raised to an even higher level, and then the coil is allowed to drop to the "waiting" temperature between ingots. Management needs to know the variable cost of power involved in heating an ingot and the fixed cost of power during "waiting" periods. The following data on ingots processed and power costs are available:

Month	Ingots	Power Cost
January	110	$5,500
February.	90	$4,500
March.	80	$4,400
April	100	$5,000
May	130	$6,000
June.	120	$5,600
July.	70	$4,000
August	60	$3,200
September	50	$3,400
October	40	$2,400

Required:

1. Using the high-low method, estimate a cost formula for power cost. Express the formula in the form $Y = a + bX$.
2. Prepare a scattergraph by plotting ingots processed and power cost on a graph. Fit a straight line to the plotted points using a ruler, and estimate a cost formula for power cost using the quick-and-dirty method.

PROBLEM 4-19 (Appendix 4A) Least-Squares Regression Method [LO5]
Refer to the data for Sebolt Wire Company in Problem 4-18.

Required:

1. Using the least-squares regression method, estimate a cost formula for power cost. (Round the variable cost to the nearest cent and the fixed cost to the nearest dollar.)
2. Prepare a table showing the total fixed cost per month and the variable cost per ingot under each of the three methods used in Problems 4-18 and 4-19. Then comment on the accuracy and usefulness of the data derived by each method.

PROBLEM 4-20 (Appendix 4A) Least-Squares Regression Analysis; Contribution Format Income Statement [LO4, LO5]
Alden Company has decided to use a contribution approach income statement for internal planning purposes. The company has analyzed its expenses and has developed the following cost formulas:

Cost	Cost Formula
Cost of goods sold	$20 per unit sold
Advertising expense.	$170,000 per quarter
Sales commissions	5% of sales
Administrative salaries.	$80,000 per quarter
Shipping expense	?
Depreciation expense	$50,000 per quarter

Management has concluded that shipping expense is a mixed cost, containing both variable and fixed cost elements. Units sold and the related shipping expense over the last eight quarters are given below:

Quarter	Units Sold (000)	Shipping Expense
Year 1:		
First	16	$160,000
Second	18	$175,000
Third	23	$210,000
Fourth	19	$180,000
Year 2:		
First	17	$170,000
Second	20	$190,000
Third	25	$230,000
Fourth	22	$205,000

Management would like a cost formula derived for shipping expense so that a budgeted income statement using the contribution approach can be prepared for the next quarter.

Required:

1. Using the least-squares regression method, estimate a cost formula for shipping expense. (Since the Units Sold above are in thousands of units, the variable cost you compute will also be in thousands of units. It can be left in this form, or you can convert your variable cost to a per unit basis by dividing it by 1,000.)
2. In the first quarter of Year 3, the company plans to sell 21,000 units at a selling price of $50 per unit. Prepare a contribution format income statement for the quarter.

PROBLEM 4-21 High-Low Method; Predicting Cost [LO1, LO3]
Golden Company's total overhead cost at various levels of activity are presented below:

Month	Machine-Hours	Total Overhead Cost
March	50,000	$194,000
April	40,000	$170,200
May	60,000	$217,800
June	70,000	$241,600

Assume that the overhead cost above consists of utilities, supervisory salaries, and maintenance. The breakdown of these costs at the 40,000 machine-hour level of activity is as follows:

Utilities (variable)	$ 52,000
Supervisory salaries (fixed)	60,000
Maintenance (mixed)	58,200
Total overhead cost	$170,200

The company wants to break down the maintenance cost into its variable and fixed cost elements.

Required:

1. Estimate how much of the $241,600 of overhead cost in June was maintenance cost. (Hint: To do this, it may be helpful to first determine how much of the $241,600 consisted of utilities and supervisory salaries. Think about the behavior of variable and fixed costs within the relevant range.)
2. Using the high-low method, estimate a cost formula for maintenance.
3. Express the company's total overhead cost in the form $Y = a + bX$.
4. What total overhead cost would you expect to be incurred at an activity level of 45,000 machine-hours?

PROBLEM 4-22 High-Low Method; Cost of Goods Manufactured [LO1, LO3]

NuWay, Inc., manufactures a single product. Selected data from the company's cost records for two recent months are given below:

	Level of Activity	
	July—Low	October—High
Number of units produced	9,000	12,000
Cost of goods manufactured	$285,000	$390,000
Work in process inventory, beginning	$14,000	$22,000
Work in process inventory, ending	$25,000	$15,000
Direct materials cost per unit	$15	$15
Direct labor cost per unit	$6	$6
Manufacturing overhead cost, total	?	?

The company's manufacturing overhead cost consists of both variable and fixed cost elements. To have data available for planning, management wants to determine how much of the overhead cost is variable with units produced and how much of it is fixed per year.

Required:

1. For both July and October, estimate the amount of manufacturing overhead cost added to production. The company had no underapplied or overapplied overhead in either month. (Hint: A useful way to proceed might be to construct a schedule of cost of goods manufactured.)
2. Using the high-low method, estimate a cost formula for manufacturing overhead. Express the variable portion of the formula in terms of a variable rate per unit of product.
3. If 9,500 units are produced during a month, what would be the cost of goods manufactured? (Assume that the company's beginning work in process inventory for the month is $16,000 and that its ending work in process inventory is $19,000. Also assume that there is no underapplied or overapplied overhead cost for the month.)

PROBLEM 4-23 High-Low Method; Predicting Cost [LO1, LO3]

Echeverria SA is an Argentinian manufacturing company whose total factory overhead costs fluctuate somewhat from year to year according to the number of machine-hours worked in its production facility. These costs (in Argentinian pesos) at high and low levels of activity over recent years are given below:

	Level of Activity	
	Low	High
Machine-hours	60,000	80,000
Total factory overhead costs	274,000 pesos	312,000 pesos

The factory overhead costs above consist of indirect materials, rent, and maintenance. The company has analyzed these costs at the 60,000 machine-hours level of activity as follows:

Indirect materials (variable)	90,000 pesos
Rent (fixed)	130,000
Maintenance (mixed)	54,000
Total factory overhead costs	274,000 pesos

For planning purposes, the company wants to break down the maintenance cost into its variable and fixed cost elements.

Required:

1. Estimate how much of the factory overhead cost of 312,000 pesos at the high level of activity consists of maintenance cost. (Hint: To do this, it may be helpful to first determine how much of the 312,000 pesos cost consists of indirect materials and rent. Think about the behavior of variable and fixed costs.)
2. Using the high-low method, estimate a cost formula for maintenance.
3. What *total* overhead costs would you expect the company to incur at an operating level of 65,000 machine-hours?

Cases

CASE 4-24 Scattergraph Analysis; Selection of an Activity Base [LO2]

Mapleleaf Sweepers of Toronto manufactures replacement rotary sweeper brooms for the large sweeper trucks that clear leaves and snow from city streets. The business is seasonal, with the largest demand during and just preceding the fall and winter months. Since there are so many different kinds of sweeper brooms used by its customers, Mapleleaf Sweepers makes all of its brooms to order.

The company has been analyzing its overhead accounts to determine fixed and variable components for planning purposes. Below are data for the company's janitorial labor costs over the last nine months. (Cost data are in Canadian dollars.)

	Number of Units Produced	Number of Janitorial Workdays	Janitorial Labor Cost
January	115	21	$3,840
February.	109	19	$3,648
March.	102	23	$4,128
April	76	20	$3,456
May	69	23	$4,320
June.	108	22	$4,032
July.	77	16	$2,784
August	71	14	$2,688
September	127	21	$3,840

The number of workdays varies from month to month due to the number of weekdays, holidays, days of vacation, and sick leave taken in the month. The number of units produced in a month varies depending on demand and the number of workdays in the month.

There are two janitors who each work an eight-hour shift each workday. They each can take up to 10 days of paid sick leave each year. Their wages on days they call in sick and their wages during paid vacations are charged to miscellaneous overhead rather than to the janitorial labor cost account.

Required:

1. Plot the janitorial labor cost and units produced on a scattergraph. (Place cost on the vertical axis and units produced on the horizontal axis.)
2. Plot the janitorial labor cost and number of workdays on a scattergraph. (Place cost on the vertical axis and the number of workdays on the horizontal axis.)

3. Which measure of activity—number of units produced or janitorial workdays—should be used as the activity base for explaining janitorial labor cost?

CASE 4-25 (Appendix 4A) Least-Squares Regression; Scattergraph; Comparison of Activity Bases [LO2, LO5]

The Hard Rock Mining Company is developing cost formulas for management planning and decision-making purposes. The company's cost analyst has concluded that utilities cost is a mixed cost, and he is attempting to find a base with which the cost might be closely correlated. The controller has suggested that tons mined might be a good base to use in developing a cost formula. The production superintendent disagrees; she thinks that direct labor-hours would be a better base. The cost analyst has decided to try both bases and has assembled the following information:

Quarter	Tons Mined (000)	Direct Labor-Hours (000)	Utilities Cost
Year 1:			
First	15	5	$50,000
Second	11	3	$45,000
Third	21	4	$60,000
Fourth	12	6	$75,000
Year 2:			
First	18	10	$100,000
Second	25	9	$105,000
Third	30	8	$85,000
Fourth	28	11	$120,000

Required:

1. Using tons mined as the independent (X) variable:
   a. Determine a cost formula for utilities cost using the least-squares regression method. (The variable cost you compute will be in thousands of tons. It can be left in this form, or you can convert your variable cost to a per ton basis by dividing it by 1,000.)
   b. Prepare a scattergraph and plot the tons mined and utilities cost. (Place cost on the vertical axis and tons mined on the horizontal axis.) Fit a straight line to the plotted points using the cost formula determined in (*a*) above.
2. Using direct labor-hours as the independent (X) variable, repeat the computations in (*a*) and (*b*) above.
3. Would you recommend that the company use tons mined or direct labor-hours as a base for planning utilities cost?

CASE 4-26 (Appendix 4A) Analysis of Mixed Costs, Job-Order Costing, and Activity-Based Costing [LO1, LO2, LO5]

Ruedi Bärlach PLC, a company located in Gümligen, Switzerland, manufactures custom-designed high-precision industrial tools. The company has a traditional job-order costing system in which direct labor and direct materials costs are assigned directly to jobs, but factory overhead is applied to jobs using a predetermined overhead rate based on direct labor-hours. Management uses this job cost data for valuing cost of goods sold and inventories for external reports. For internal decision-making, management has largely ignored this cost data since direct labor costs are basically fixed and management believes overhead costs actually have little to do with direct labor-hours. Recently, management has become interested in activity-based costing (ABC) as a way of estimating job costs and other costs for decision-making purposes.

Management assembled a cross-functional team to design a prototype ABC system. Electrical costs were among the first factory overhead costs investigated by the team. Electricity is used to provide light, to power equipment, and to heat the building in the winter. The ABC team proposed allocating electrical costs to jobs based on machine-hours since running the machines consumes significant amounts of electricity. Data assembled by the team concerning actual direct labor-hours, machine-hours, and electrical costs over a recent eight-week period have been entered into the spreadsheet that appears below. (The Swiss currency is the Swiss franc, which is denoted by SFr.)

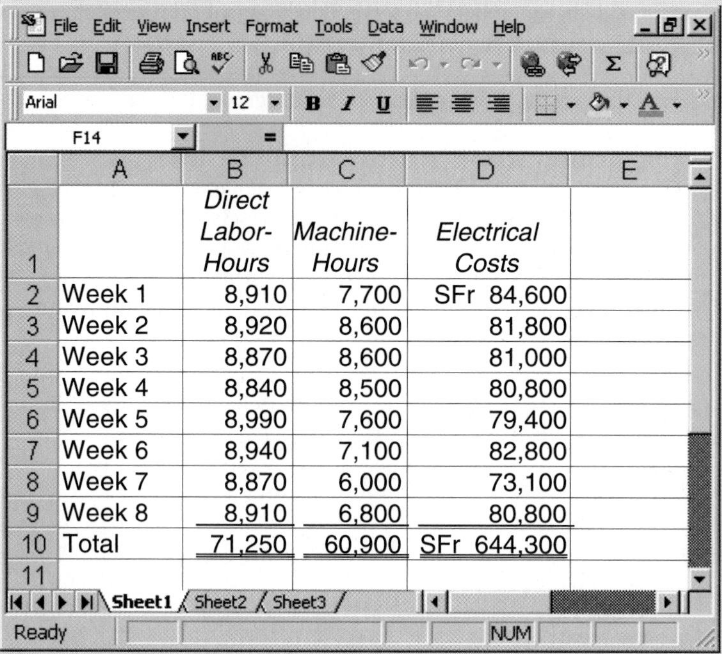

	A	B	C	D	E
1		Direct Labor-Hours	Machine-Hours	Electrical Costs	
2	Week 1	8,910	7,700	SFr 84,600	
3	Week 2	8,920	8,600	81,800	
4	Week 3	8,870	8,600	81,000	
5	Week 4	8,840	8,500	80,800	
6	Week 5	8,990	7,600	79,400	
7	Week 6	8,940	7,100	82,800	
8	Week 7	8,870	6,000	73,100	
9	Week 8	8,910	6,800	80,800	
10	Total	71,250	60,900	SFr 644,300	
11					

To help assess the effect of the proposed change to machine-hours as the allocation base, the above eight-week totals were converted to annual figures by multiplying them by six.

	Direct Labor-Hours	Machine-Hours	Electrical Costs
Estimated annual total (eight-week total above × 6)	427,500	365,400	SFr 3,865,800

Required:

1. Assume that the estimated annual totals shown above are used to compute the company's predetermined overhead rate. What would be the predetermined overhead rate for electrical costs if the allocation base is direct labor-hours? machine-hours?
2. Management intends to bid on a job for a set of custom tools for a watchmaker that would require 30 direct labor-hours and 25 machine-hours. How much electrical cost would be charged to this job using the predetermined overhead rate computed in part (1) above if the allocation base is direct labor-hours? machine-hours?
3. Prepare a scattergraph in which you plot direct labor-hours on the horizontal axis and electrical costs on the vertical axis. Prepare another scattergraph in which you plot machine-hours on the horizontal axis and electrical costs on the vertical axis. Do you agree with the ABC team that machine-hours is a better allocation base for electrical costs than direct labor-hours? Why?
4. Using machine-hours as the measure of activity and the least-squares regression method, estimate the fixed and variable components of electrical costs.
5. How much electrical cost do you think would actually be caused by the custom tool job for the toolmaker in part (2) above? Explain.
6. What factors, apart from direct labor-hours and machine-hours, are likely to affect consumption of electrical power in the company?

CASE 4-27 Analysis of Mixed Costs in a Pricing Decision [LO1, LO2 **or** LO3 **or** LO5]

Jasmine Lee owns a catering company that serves food and beverages at exclusive parties and business functions. Lee's business is seasonal, with a heavy schedule during the summer months and holidays and a lighter schedule at other times.

One of the major events that Lee's customers request is a cocktail party. She offers a standard cocktail party and has estimated the cost per guest for this party as follows:

Food and beverages	$17.00
Labor (0.5 hour @ $10.00 per hour)	5.00
Overhead (0.5 hour @ $18.63 per hour)	9.32
Total cost per guest	$31.32

This standard cocktail party lasts three hours and Lee hires one worker for every six guests, which is one-half hour of labor per guest. These workers are hired only as needed and are paid only for the hours they actually work.

Lee ordinarily charges $45 per guest. She is confident about her estimates of the costs of food and beverages and labor, but is not as comfortable with the estimate of overhead cost. The $18.63 overhead cost per labor-hour was determined by dividing total overhead expenses for the last 12 months by total labor-hours for the same period. Monthly data concerning overhead costs and labor-hours appear below:

Month	Labor Hours	Overhead Expenses
January	1,500	$ 44,000
February.	1,680	47,200
March.	1,800	48,000
April	2,520	51,200
May	2,700	53,600
June.	3,300	56,800
July.	3,900	59,200
August	4,500	61,600
September	4,200	60,000
October	2,700	54,400
November	1,860	49,600
December	3,900	58,400
Total.	34,560	$644,000

Lee has received a request to bid on a 120-guest fund-raising cocktail party to be given next month by an important local charity. (The party would last the usual three hours.) She would like to win this contract because the guest list for this charity event includes many prominent individuals that she would like to land as future clients. Lee is confident that these potential customers would be favorably impressed by her company's services at the charity event.

Required:

1. Estimate the contribution to profit of a standard 120-guest cocktail party if Lee charges her usual price of $45 per guest. (In other words, by how much would her overall profit increase?)
2. How low could Lee bid for the charity event, in terms of a price per guest, and still not lose money on the event itself?
3. The individual who is organizing the charity's fund-raising event has indicated that he has already received a bid under $42 from another catering company. Do you think Lee should bid below her normal $45 per guest price for the charity event? Why or why not?

(CMA, adapted)

RESEARCH AND APPLICATION 4-28 (APPENDIX 4A) [LO1, LO2, LO3, LO4, LO5]

The questions in this exercise are based on Blue Nile, Inc. To answer the questions, you will need to download Blue Nile's Form 10-K for the fiscal year ended January 2, 2005 at www.sec.gov/edgar/searchedgar/companysearch.html. Once at this website, input CIK code 1091171 and hit enter. In the gray box on the right-hand side of your computer screen define the scope of your search by inputting 10-K and then pressing enter. Select the 10-K with a filing date of March 25, 2005. You do not need to print this document to answer the questions. You will need the information below to answer the questions.

	2004				2005	
	Quarter 1	Quarter 2	Quarter 3	Quarter 4	Quarter 1	Quarter 2
Net sales	?	?	?	?	$44,116	$43,826
Cost of sales	?	?	?	?	$34,429	$33,836
Gross profit	?	?	?	?	$9,687	$9,990
Selling, general, and administrative expense	$5,308	$5,111	$5,033	$7,343	$6,123	$6,184
Operating income. . .	?	?	?	?	$3,564	$3,806

Required:

1. What is Blue Nile's strategy for success in the marketplace? Does the company rely primarily on a customer intimacy, operational excellence, or product leadership customer value proposition? What evidence from the 10-K supports your conclusion?
2. What business risks does Blue Nile face that may threaten its ability to satisfy stockholder expectations? What are some examples of control activities that the company could use to reduce these risks? (Hint: Focus on pages 8–19 of the 10-K.) Are some of the risks faced by Blue Nile difficult to reduce through control activities? Explain.
3. Is Blue Nile a merchandiser or a manufacturer? What information contained in the 10-K supports your answer?
4. Using account analysis, would you label cost of sales and selling, general, and administrative expense as variable, fixed, or mixed costs? Why? (Hint: focus on pages 24–26 and 38 of the 10-K.) Cite one example of a variable cost, step-variable cost, discretionary fixed cost, and committed fixed cost for Blue Nile.
5. Fill in the blanks in the table above based on information contained in the 10-K. Using the high-low method, estimate the variable and fixed cost elements of the quarterly selling, general, and administrative expense. Express Blue Nile's variable and fixed selling, general, and administrative expenses in the form $Y = a + bX$.
6. Using the least-squares regression method, estimate a cost formula for selling, general, and administrative expense. Are these estimates the same or different from those obtained using the high-low method? Why?
7. Prepare a contribution format income statement for the third quarter of 2005 assuming that Blue Nile's net sales were $45,500 and its cost of sales as a percentage of net sales remained unchanged from the prior quarter.
8. How would you describe Blue Nile's cost structure? Is Blue Nile's cost of sales as a percentage of sales higher or lower than competitors with bricks and mortar jewelry stores?

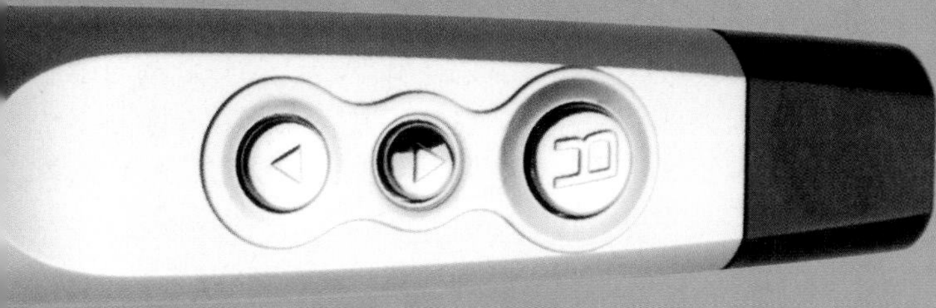

Chapter 5

Cost-Volume-Profit Relationships

What Happened to the Profit?

BUSINESS FOCUS

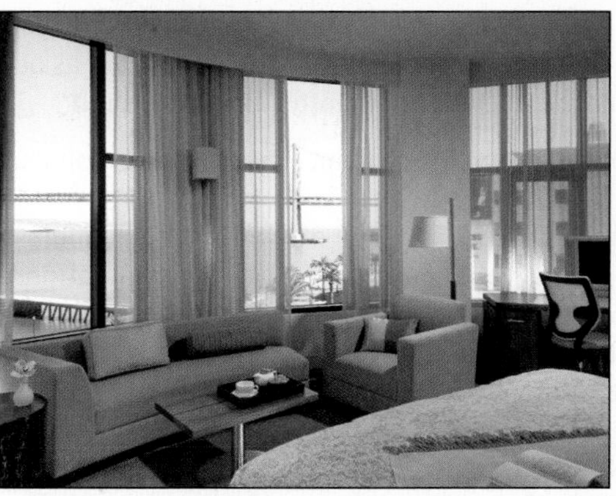

Chip Conley is CEO of Joie de Vivre Hospitality, a company that owns and operates 28 hospitality businesses in northern California. Conley summed up the company's experience after the dot.com crash and 9/11 as follows: "In the history of American hotel markets, no hotel market has ever seen a drop in revenues as precipitous as the one in San Francisco and Silicon Valley in the last two years. On average, hotel revenues . . . dropped 40% to 45%. . . . We've been fortunate that our breakeven point is lower than our competition's. . . . But the problem is that the hotel business is a fixed-cost business. So in an environment where you have those precipitous drops and our costs are moderately fixed, our net incomes—well, they're not incomes anymore, they're losses." ■

Source: Karen Dillon, "Shop Talk," *Inc* magazine, December 2002, pp. 111–114.

Learning Objectives

After studying Chapter 5, you should be able to:

LO1 Explain how changes in activity affect contribution margin and net operating income.

LO2 Prepare and interpret a cost-volume-profit (CVP) graph.

LO3 Use the contribution margin ratio (CM ratio) to compute changes in contribution margin and net operating income resulting from changes in sales volume.

LO4 Show the effects on contribution margin of changes in variable costs, fixed costs, selling price, and volume.

LO5 Compute the break-even point in unit sales and sales dollars.

LO6 Determine the level of sales needed to achieve a desired target profit.

LO7 Compute the margin of safety and explain its significance.

LO8 Compute the degree of operating leverage at a particular level of sales and explain how it can be used to predict changes in net operating income.

LO9 Compute the break-even point for a multiproduct company and explain the effects of shifts in the sales mix on contribution margin and the break-even point.

Cost-volume-profit (CVP) analysis is a powerful tool that helps managers understand the relationships among cost, volume, and profit. CVP analysis focuses on how profits are affected by the following five factors:

1. Selling prices.
2. Sales volume.
3. Unit variable costs.
4. Total fixed costs.
5. Mix of products sold.

Because CVP analysis helps managers understand how profits are affected by these key factors, it is a vital tool in many business decisions. These decisions include what products and services to offer, what prices to charge, what marketing strategy to use, and what cost structure to implement. To help understand the role of CVP analysis in business decisions, consider the case of Acoustic Concepts, Inc., a company founded by Prem Narayan.

MANAGERIAL ACCOUNTING IN ACTION
The Issue

Prem, who was a graduate student in engineering at the time, started Acoustic Concepts to market a radical new speaker he had designed for automobile sound systems. The speaker, called the Sonic Blaster, uses an advanced microprocessor and proprietary software to boost amplification to awesome levels. Prem contracted with a Taiwanese electronics manufacturer to produce the speaker. With seed money provided by his family, Prem placed an order with the manufacturer and ran advertisements in auto magazines.

The Sonic Blaster was an almost immediate success, and sales grew to the point that Prem moved the company's headquarters out of his apartment and into rented quarters in a nearby industrial park. He also hired a receptionist, an accountant, a sales manager, and a small sales staff to sell the speakers to retail stores. The accountant, Bob Luchinni, had worked for several small companies where he had acted as a business advisor as well as accountant and bookkeeper. The following discussion occurred soon after Bob was hired:

Prem: Bob, I've got a lot of questions about the company's finances that I hope you can help answer.

Bob: We're in great shape. The loan from your family will be paid off within a few months.

Prem: I know, but I am worried about the risks I've taken on by expanding operations. What would happen if a competitor entered the market and our sales slipped? How far could sales drop without putting us into the red? Another question I've been trying to resolve is how much our sales would have to increase to justify the big marketing campaign the sales staff is pushing for.

Bob: Marketing always wants more money for advertising.

Prem: And they are always pushing me to drop the selling price on the speaker. I agree with them that a lower price will boost our volume, but I'm not sure the increased volume will offset the loss in revenue from the lower price.

Bob: It sounds like these questions are all related in some way to the relationships among our selling prices, our costs, and our volume. I shouldn't have a problem coming up with some answers.

Prem: Can we meet again in a couple of days to see what you have come up with?

Bob: Sounds good. By then I'll have some preliminary answers for you as well as a model you can use for answering similar questions in the future.

The Basics of Cost-Volume-Profit (CVP) Analysis

Bob Luchinni's preparation for his forthcoming meeting with Prem begins where our study of cost behavior in the preceding chapter left off—with the contribution income statement. The contribution income statement emphasizes the behavior of costs and therefore is extremely helpful to managers in judging the impact on profits of changes in selling price, cost, or volume. Bob will base his analysis on the following contribution income statement he prepared last month:

Acoustic Concepts, Inc. Contribution Income Statement For the Month of June		
	Total	Per Unit
Sales (400 speakers)	$100,000	$250
Variable expenses	60,000	150
Contribution margin	40,000	$100
Fixed expenses	35,000	
Net operating income	$ 5,000	

Notice that sales, variable expenses, and contribution margin are expressed on a per unit basis as well as in total on this contribution income statement. The per unit figures will be very helpful to Bob in some of his calculations. Note that this contribution income statement has been prepared for management's use inside the company and would not ordinarily be made available to those outside the company.

Contribution Margin

LEARNING OBJECTIVE 1
Explain how changes in activity affect contribution margin and net operating income.

As explained in the previous chapter, contribution margin is the amount remaining from sales revenue after variable expenses have been deducted. Thus, it is the amount available to cover fixed expenses and then to provide profits for the period. Notice the sequence here—contribution margin is used *first* to cover the fixed expenses, and then whatever remains goes toward profits. If the contribution margin is not sufficient to cover the fixed expenses, then a loss occurs for the period. To illustrate with an extreme example, assume that Acoustic Concepts sells only one speaker during a particular month. The company's income statement would appear as follows:

Contribution Income Statement Sales of 1 Speaker		
	Total	Per Unit
Sales (1 speaker)	$ 250	$250
Variable expenses	150	150
Contribution margin	100	$100
Fixed expenses	35,000	
Net operating loss	$(34,900)	

For each additional speaker the company sells during the month, $100 more in contribution margin becomes available to help cover the fixed expenses. If a second speaker is sold, for example, then the total contribution margin will increase by $100 (to a total of $200) and the company's loss will decrease by $100, to $34,800:

Contribution Income Statement Sales of 2 Speakers		
	Total	Per Unit
Sales (2 speakers)	$ 500	$250
Variable expenses	300	150
Contribution margin	200	$100
Fixed expenses	35,000	
Net operating loss	$(34,800)	

If enough speakers can be sold to generate $35,000 in contribution margin, then all of the fixed expenses will be covered and the company will *break even* for the month—that is, it will show neither profit nor loss but just cover all of its costs. To reach the break-even point, the company will have to sell 350 speakers in a month, since each speaker sold yields $100 in contribution margin:

Contribution Income Statement Sales of 350 Speakers		
	Total	Per Unit
Sales (350 speakers)	$87,500	$250
Variable expenses	52,500	150
Contribution margin	35,000	$100
Fixed expenses	35,000	
Net operating income	$ 0	

Computation of the break-even point is discussed in detail later in the chapter; for the moment, note that the **break-even point** is the level of sales at which profit is zero.

Once the break-even point has been reached, net operating income will increase by the amount of the unit contribution margin for each additional unit sold. For example, if 351 speakers are sold in a month, then the net operating income for the month will be $100, since the company will have sold 1 speaker more than the number needed to break even:

Contribution Income Statement Sales of 351 Speakers		
	Total	Per Unit
Sales (351 speakers)	$87,750	$250
Variable expenses	52,650	150
Contribution margin	35,100	$100
Fixed expenses	35,000	
Net operating income	$ 100	

If 352 speakers are sold (2 speakers above the break-even point), the net operating income for the month will be $200. If 353 speakers are sold (3 speakers above the break-even point), the net operating income for the month will be $300, and so forth. To estimate the profit at any sales volume above the break-even point, simply multiply the number of units sold in excess of the break-even point by the unit contribution margin. The result represents the anticipated profits for the period. Or, to estimate the effect of a planned increase in sales on profits, simply multiply the increase in units sold by the unit contribution margin. The result will be the expected increase in profits. To illustrate, if Acoustic Concepts is currently selling 400 speakers per month and plans to increase sales to 425 speakers per month, the anticipated impact on profits can be computed as follows:

Increased number of speakers to be sold	25
Contribution margin per speaker	× $100
Increase in net operating income	$2,500

These calculations can be verified as follows:

	Sales Volume			
	400 Speakers	425 Speakers	Difference (25 Speakers)	Per Unit
Sales (@ $250 per speaker)	$100,000	$106,250	$6,250	$250
Variable expenses (@ $150 per speaker)	60,000	63,750	3,750	150
Contribution margin	40,000	42,500	2,500	$100
Fixed expenses	35,000	35,000	0	
Net operating income	$ 5,000	$ 7,500	$2,500	

To summarize, if sales are zero, the company's loss would equal its fixed expenses. Each unit that is sold reduces the loss by the amount of the unit contribution margin. Once the break-even point has been reached, each additional unit sold increases the company's profit by the amount of the unit contribution margin.

CVP Relationships in Graphic Form

LEARNING OBJECTIVE 2
Prepare and interpret a cost-volume-profit (CVP) graph.

The relationships among revenue, cost, profit, and volume are illustrated on a **cost-volume-profit (CVP) graph.** A CVP graph highlights CVP relationships over wide ranges of activity. To help explain his analysis to Prem Narayan, Bob Luchinni decided to prepare a CVP graph for Acoustic Concepts.

Video 5–1

Preparing the CVP Graph

In a CVP graph (sometimes called a *break-even chart*), unit volume is represented on the horizontal (X) axis and dollars on the vertical (Y) axis. Preparing a CVP graph involves three steps as depicted in Exhibit 5–1:

1. Draw a line parallel to the volume axis to represent total fixed expense. For Acoustic Concepts, total fixed expenses are $35,000.

EXHIBIT 5–1
Preparing the CVP Graph

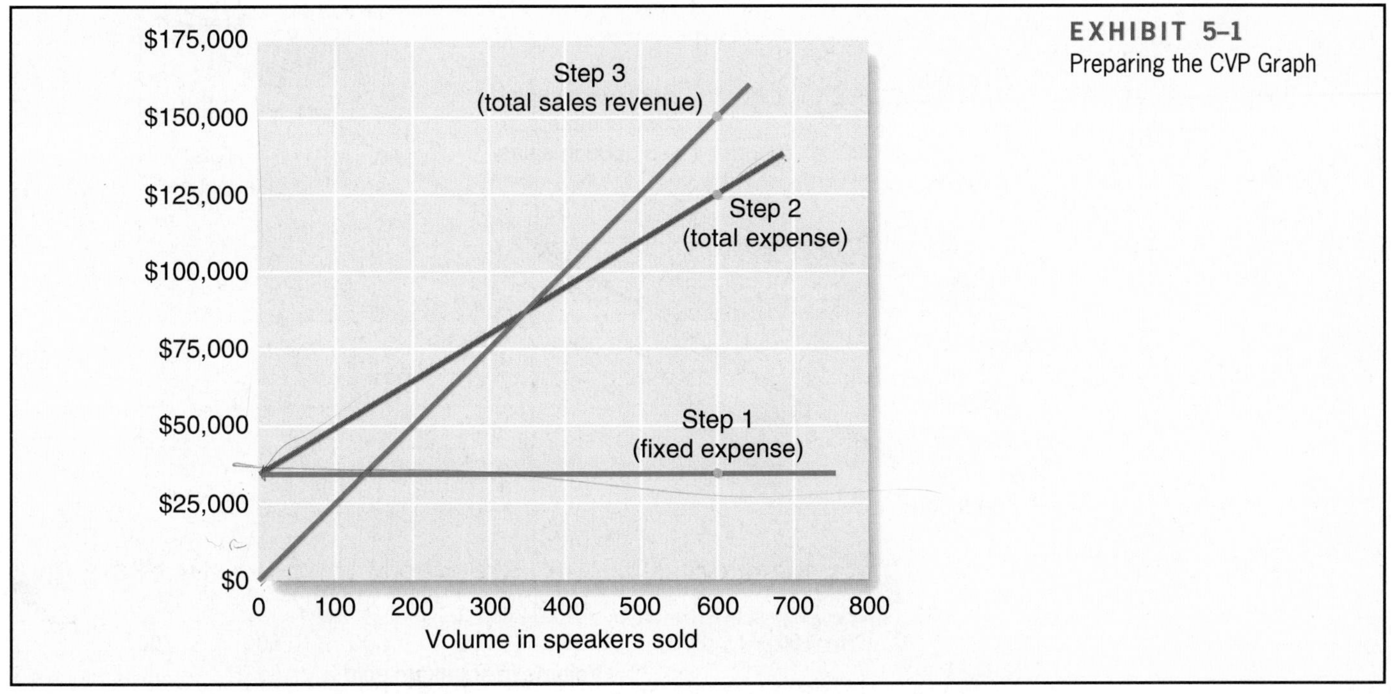

2. Choose some volume of unit sales and plot the point representing total expense (fixed and variable) at the activity level you have selected. In Exhibit 5–1, Bob Luchinni chose a volume of 600 speakers. Total expense at that activity level is:

Fixed expense	$35,000
Variable expense (600 speakers × $150 per speaker)	90,000
Total expense	$125,000

After the point has been plotted, draw a line through it back to the point where the fixed expense line intersects the dollars axis.

3. Again choose some volume of unit sales and plot the point representing total sales dollars at the activity level you have selected. In Exhibit 5–1, Bob Luchinni again chose a volume of 600 speakers. Sales at that activity level total $150,000 (600 speakers × $250 per speaker). Draw a line through this point back to the origin.

The interpretation of the completed CVP graph is given in Exhibit 5–2. The anticipated profit or loss at any given level of sales is measured by the vertical distance between the total revenue line (sales) and the total expense line (variable expense plus fixed expense).

The break-even point is where the total revenue and total expense lines cross. The break-even point of 350 speakers in Exhibit 5–2 agrees with the break-even point computed earlier.

As discussed earlier, when sales are below the break-even point—in this case, 350 units—the company suffers a loss. Note that the loss (represented by the vertical distance between the total expense and total revenue lines) gets bigger as sales decline. When sales are above the break-even point, the company earns a profit and the size of the profit (represented by the vertical distance between the total revenue and total expense lines) increases as sales increase.

EXHIBIT 5–2
The Completed CVP Graph

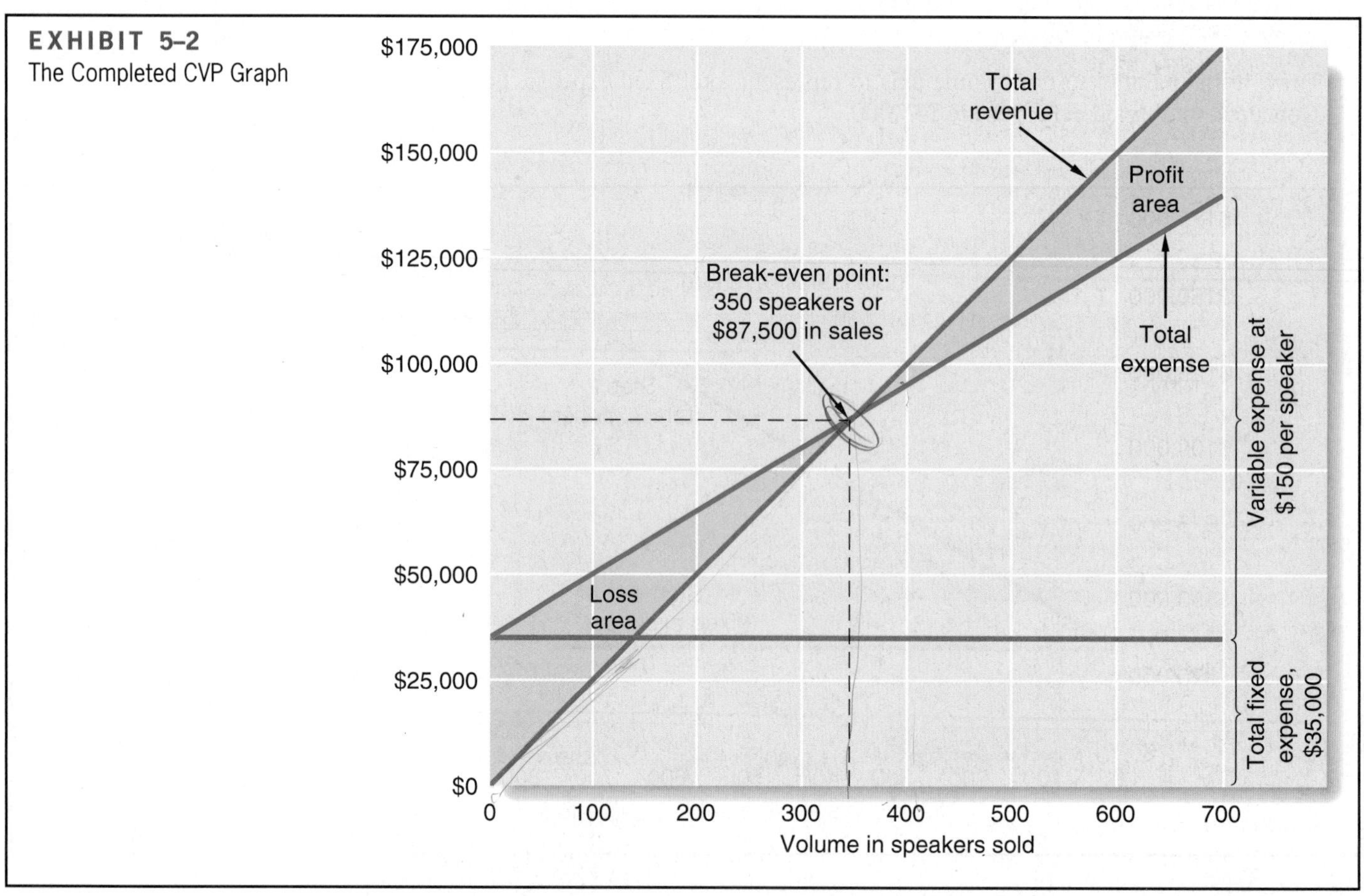

Contribution Margin Ratio (CM Ratio)

LEARNING OBJECTIVE 3
Use the contribution margin ratio (CM ratio) to compute changes in contribution margin and net operating income resulting from changes in sales volume.

In the previous section, we explored how cost-volume-profit relationships can be visualized. In this section, we show how the *contribution margin ratio* can be used in cost-volume-profit calculations. As the first step, we have added a column to Acoustic Concepts' contribution format income statement in which sales revenues, variable expenses, and contribution margin are expressed as a percentage of sales:

	Total	Per Unit	Percent of Sales
Sales (400 speakers)	$100,000	$250	100%
Variable expenses	60,000	150	60%
Contribution margin	40,000	$100	40%
Fixed expenses	35,000		
Net operating income	$ 5,000		

The contribution margin as a percentage of sales is referred to as the **contribution margin ratio (CM ratio).** This ratio is computed as follows:

$$\text{CM ratio} = \frac{\text{Contribution margin}}{\text{Sales}}$$

For Acoustic Concepts, the computations are:

$$\text{CM ratio} = \frac{\text{Total contribution margin}}{\text{Total sales}} = \frac{\$40{,}000}{\$100{,}000} = 40\%$$

In a company such as Acoustic Concepts that has only one product, the CM ratio can also be computed on a per unit basis as follows:

$$\text{CM ratio} = \frac{\text{Unit contribution margin}}{\text{Unit selling price}} = \frac{\$100}{\$250} = 40\%$$

The CM ratio shows how the contribution margin will be affected by a change in total sales. Acoustic Concepts' CM ratio of 40% means that for each dollar increase in sales, total contribution margin will increase by 40 cents ($1 sales × CM ratio of 40%). Net operating income will also increase by 40 cents, assuming that fixed costs are not affected by the increase in sales.

As this illustration suggests, *the impact on net operating income of any given dollar change in total sales can be computed by simply applying the CM ratio to the dollar change.* For example, if Acoustic Concepts plans a $30,000 increase in sales during the coming month, the contribution margin should increase by $12,000 ($30,000 increase in sales × CM ratio of 40%). As we noted above, net operating income will also increase by $12,000 if fixed costs do not change. This is verified by the following table:

	Sales Volume			Percent of Sales
	Present	Expected	Increase	
Sales	$100,000	$130,000	$30,000	100%
Variable expenses	60,000	78,000*	18,000	60%
Contribution margin	40,000	52,000	12,000	40%
Fixed expenses	35,000	35,000	0	
Net operating income	$ 5,000	$ 17,000	$12,000	

*$130,000 expected sales ÷ $250 per unit = 520 units. 520 units × $150 per unit = $78,000.

The CM ratio is particularly valuable in situations where the dollar sales of one product must be traded off against the dollar sales of another product. In this situation, products that yield the greatest amount of contribution margin per dollar of sales should be emphasized.

Some Applications of CVP Concepts

LEARNING OBJECTIVE 4
Show the effects on contribution margin of changes in variable costs, fixed costs, selling price, and volume.

Bob Luchinni, the accountant at Acoustic Concepts, wanted to demonstrate to the company's president Prem Narayan how the concepts developed on the preceding pages can be used in planning and decision making. Bob gathered the following basic data:

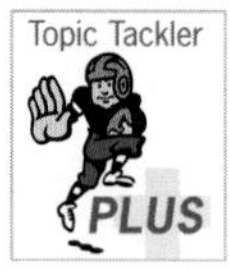

5–1

	Per Unit	Percent of Sales
Selling price	$250	100%
Variable expenses	150	60%
Contribution margin	$100	40%

Recall that fixed expenses are $35,000 per month. Bob Luchinni will use these data to show the effects of changes in variable costs, fixed costs, sales price, and sales volume on the company's profitability in a variety of situations.

Change in Fixed Cost and Sales Volume Acoustic Concepts is currently selling 400 speakers per month at $250 per speaker for total monthly sales of $100,000. The sales manager feels that a $10,000 increase in the monthly advertising budget would increase monthly sales by $30,000 to a total of 520 units. Should the advertising budget be increased? The following table shows the financial impact of the proposed change in the monthly advertising budget:

	Current Sales	Sales with Additional Advertising Budget	Difference	Percent of Sales
Sales	$100,000	$130,000	$30,000	100%
Variable expenses	60,000	78,000*	18,000	60%
Contribution margin	40,000	52,000	12,000	40%
Fixed expenses	35,000	45,000†	10,000	
Net operating income	$ 5,000	$ 7,000	$ 2,000	

*520 units × $150 per unit = $78,000.
†$35,000 + additional $10,000 monthly advertising budget = $45,000.

Assuming no other factors need to be considered, the increase in the advertising budget should be approved because it would increase net operating income by $2,000. There are two shorter ways to arrive at this solution. The first alternative solution follows:

Alternative Solution 1

Expected total contribution margin:	
$130,000 × 40% CM ratio	$52,000
Present total contribution margin:	
$100,000 × 40% CM ratio	40,000
Incremental contribution margin	12,000
Change in fixed expenses:	
Less incremental advertising expense	10,000
Increased net operating income	$ 2,000

Because in this case only the fixed costs and the sales volume change, the solution can be presented in an even shorter format, as follows:

Alternative Solution 2

Incremental contribution margin:	
$30,000 × 40% CM ratio	$12,000
Less incremental advertising expense	10,000
Increased net operating income	$ 2,000

Notice that this approach does not depend on knowledge of previous sales. Also note that it is unnecessary under either shorter approach to prepare an income statement. Both of the alternative solutions involve an **incremental analysis**—they consider only those items of revenue, cost, and volume that will change if the new program is implemented. Although in each case a new income statement could have been prepared, the incremental approach is simpler and more direct and focuses attention on the specific changes that would occur as a result of the decision.

Change in Variable Costs and Sales Volume Refer to the original data. Recall that Acoustic Concepts is currently selling 400 speakers per month. Prem is considering the use of higher-quality components, which would increase variable costs (and thereby reduce the contribution margin) by $10 per speaker. However, the sales manager predicts that using higher-quality components would increase sales to 480 speakers per month. Should the higher-quality components be used?

The $10 increase in variable costs would decrease the unit contribution margin by $10—from $100 down to $90.

Solution

Expected total contribution margin with higher-quality components:	
480 speakers × $90 per speaker	$43,200
Present total contribution margin:	
400 speakers × $100 per speaker	40,000
Increase in total contribution margin	$ 3,200

According to this analysis, the higher-quality components should be used. Since fixed costs would not change, the $3,200 increase in contribution margin shown above should result in a $3,200 increase in net operating income.

IN BUSINESS

GROWING SALES AT AMAZON.COM

Amazon.com was deciding between two tactics for growing sales and profits. The first approach was to invest in television advertising. The second approach was to offer free shipping on larger orders. To evaluate the first option, Amazon.com invested in television ads in two markets—Minneapolis, Minnesota, and Portland, Oregon. The company quantified the profit impact of this choice by subtracting the increase in fixed advertising costs from the increase in contribution margin. The profit impact of television advertising paled in comparison to the free "super saver shipping" program, which the company introduced on orders over $99. In fact, the free shipping option proved to be so popular and profitable that within two years Amazon.com dropped its qualifying threshold to $49 and then again to a mere $25. At each stage of this progression, Amazon.com used cost-volume-profit analysis to determine whether the extra volume from liberalizing the free shipping offer more than offset the associated increase in shipping costs.

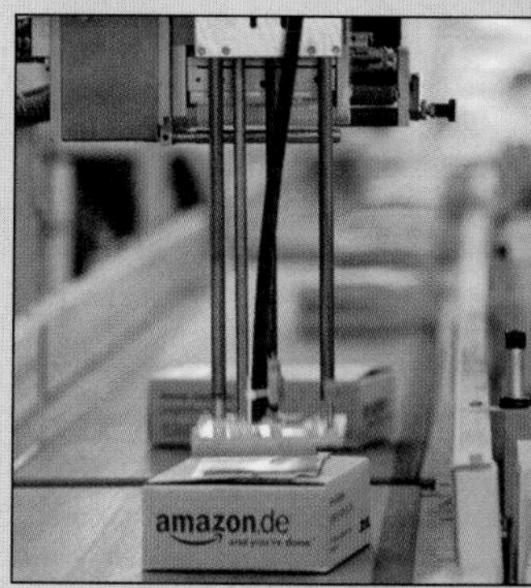

Source: Rob Walker, "Because 'Optimism is Essential,'" *Inc.* magazine, April 2004 pp. 149–150.

Change in Fixed Cost, Sales Price, and Sales Volume Refer to the original data and recall again that Acoustic Concepts is currently selling 400 speakers per month. To increase sales, the sales manager would like to cut the selling price by $20 per speaker and increase the advertising budget by $15,000 per month. The sales manager believes that if these two steps are taken, unit sales will increase by 50% to 600 speakers per month. Should the changes be made?

A decrease in the selling price of $20 per speaker would decrease the unit contribution margin by $20 down to $80.

Solution

Expected total contribution margin with lower selling price:	
600 speakers × $80 per speaker	$48,000
Present total contribution margin:	
400 speakers × $100 per speaker	40,000
Incremental contribution margin	8,000
Change in fixed expenses:	
Less incremental advertising expense	15,000
Reduction in net operating income	$ (7,000)

According to this analysis, the changes should not be made. The $7,000 reduction in net operating income that is shown above can be verified by preparing comparative income statements as follows:

	Present 400 Speakers per Month		Expected 600 Speakers per Month		
	Total	Per Unit	Total	Per Unit	Difference
Sales	$100,000	$250	$138,000	$230	$38,000
Variable expenses	60,000	150	90,000	150	30,000
Contribution margin	40,000	$100	48,000	$ 80	8,000
Fixed expenses	35,000		50,000*		15,000
Net operating income (loss)	$ 5,000		$ (2,000)		$ (7,000)

*35,000 + Additional monthly advertising budget of $15,000 = $50,000.

IN BUSINESS

DELTA ATTEMPTS TO BOOST TICKET SALES

The United States Transportation Department ranked the Cincinnati/Northern Kentucky International Airport (CNK) as the second most expensive airport in the country. Because of its high ticket prices, CNK airport officials estimated that they were losing 28% of Cincinnati-area travelers—about 2,500 people per day—to five surrounding airports that offered lower fares. Delta Airlines, which has 90% of the traffic at CNK, attempted to improve the situation by introducing SimpliFares. The program, which Delta touted with a $2 million media campaign, not only lowered fares but also reduced the ticket change fee from $100 to $50. From a cost-volume-profit standpoint, Delta was hoping that the increase in discretionary fixed advertising costs and the decrease in sales revenue realized from lower ticket prices would be more than offset by an increase in sales volume.

Source: James Pilcher, "New Delta Fares Boost Ticket Sales," *The Cincinnati Enquirer*, September 3, 2004, pp. A1 and A12.

Change in Variable Cost, Fixed Cost, and Sales Volume Refer to Acoustic Concepts' original data. As before, the company is currently selling 400 speakers per month. The sales manager would like to pay salespersons a sales commission of $15 per speaker sold, rather than the flat salaries that now total $6,000 per month. The sales manager is confident that the change would increase monthly sales by 15% to 460 speakers per month. Should the change be made?

Solution Changing the sales staff's compensation from salaries to commissions would affect both fixed and variable expenses. Fixed expenses would decrease by $6,000, from $35,000 to $29,000. Variable expenses per unit would increase by $15, from $150 to $165, and the unit contribution margin would decrease from $100 to $85.

Expected total contribution margin with sales staff on commissions:	
460 speakers × $85 per speaker	$39,100
Present total contribution margin:	
400 speakers × $100 per speaker	40,000
Decrease in total contribution margin	(900)
Change in fixed expenses:	
Add salaries avoided if a commission is paid	6,000
Increase in net operating income	$ 5,100

According to this analysis, the changes should be made. Again, the same answer can be obtained by preparing comparative income statements:

	Present 400 Speakers per Month		Expected 460 Speakers per Month		
	Total	Per Unit	Total	Per Unit	Difference
Sales	$100,000	$250	$115,000	$250	$15,000
Variable expenses	60,000	150	75,900	165	15,900
Contribution margin	40,000	$100	39,100	$ 85	900
Fixed expenses	35,000		29,000		(6,000)*
Net operating income	$ 5,000		$ 10,100		$ 5,100

*Note: A *reduction* in fixed expenses has the effect of *increasing* net operating income.

Change in Selling Price Refer to the original data where Acoustic Concepts is currently selling 400 speakers per month. The company has an opportunity to make a bulk sale of 150 speakers to a wholesaler if an acceptable price can be negotiated. This sale would not disturb the company's regular sales and would not affect the company's total fixed expenses. What price per speaker should be quoted to the wholesaler if Acoustic Concepts wants to increase its total monthly profits by $3,000?

Solution

Variable cost per speaker	$150
Desired profit per speaker:	
$3,000 ÷ 150 speakers	20
Quoted price per speaker	$170

Notice that fixed expenses are not included in the computation. This is because fixed expenses are not affected by the bulk sale, so all of the additional contribution margin increases the company's profits.

Break-Even Analysis

LEARNING OBJECTIVE 5
Compute the break-even point in unit sales and sales dollars.

Video 5–1

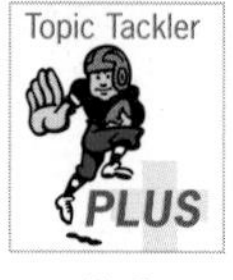

5–2

Break-even analysis is an aspect of CVP analysis that is designed to answer questions such as how far could sales drop before the company begins to lose money?

Break-Even Computations

Earlier in the chapter we defined the break-even point as the level of sales at which the company's profit is zero. The break-even point can be computed using either the *equation method* or the *contribution margin method*—the two methods are equivalent.

The Equation Method The **equation method** translates the contribution format income statement illustrated earlier in the chapter into equation form as follows:

$$\text{Profits} = (\text{Sales} - \text{Variable expenses}) - \text{Fixed expenses}$$

Rearranging this equation slightly yields the following equation, which is widely used in CVP analysis:

$$\text{Sales} = \text{Variable expenses} + \text{Fixed expenses} + \text{Profits}$$

At the break-even point, profits are zero. Therefore, the break-even point can be computed by finding the point where sales equal the total of the variable expenses plus the fixed expenses. For Acoustic Concepts, the break-even point in unit sales, Q, can be computed as follows:

$$\text{Sales} = \text{Variable expenses} + \text{Fixed expenses} + \text{Profits}$$

$$\$250Q = \$150Q + \$35{,}000 + \$0$$
$$\$100Q = \$35{,}000$$
$$Q = \$35{,}000 \div \$100 \text{ per speaker}$$
$$Q = 350 \text{ speakers}$$

where:

$$Q = \text{Quantity of speakers sold}$$
$$\$250 = \text{Unit selling price}$$
$$\$150 = \text{Unit variable expenses}$$
$$\$35{,}000 = \text{Total fixed expenses}$$

The break-even point in total sales dollars can be computed by multiplying the break-even level of unit sales by the selling price per unit:

$$350 \text{ speakers} \times \$250 \text{ per speaker} = \$87{,}500$$

The break-even point in total sales dollars, X, can also be computed as follows:

$$\text{Sales} = \text{Variable expenses} + \text{Fixed expenses} + \text{Profits}$$

$$X = 0.60X + \$35{,}000 + \$0$$
$$0.40X = \$35{,}000$$
$$X = \$35{,}000 \div 0.40$$
$$X = \$87{,}500$$

where:

$$X = \text{Total sales dollars}$$
$$0.60 = \text{Variable expense ratio (Variable expenses} \div \text{Sales)}$$
$$\$35{,}000 = \text{Total fixed expenses}$$

Note that in the above analysis the *variable expense ratio* is used. The **variable expense ratio** is the ratio of variable expense to sales. It can be computed by dividing the total variable expense by the total sales, or in a single product analysis, it can be computed by dividing the variable cost per unit by the unit selling price.

Also note that the use of the ratios in the above analysis yields a break-even point expressed in sales dollars rather than in units sold. If desired, the break-even point in units sold can be computed as follows:

$$\$87{,}500 \div \$250 \text{ per speaker} = 350 \text{ speakers}$$

The Contribution Margin Method The **contribution margin method** is a shortcut version of the equation method already described. The approach centers on the idea discussed earlier that each unit sold provides a certain amount of contribution margin that goes toward covering fixed costs. To find how many units must be sold to break even, divide the total fixed expenses by the unit contribution margin:

$$\text{Break-even point in units sold} = \frac{\text{Fixed expenses}}{\text{Unit contribution margin}}$$

Each speaker generates a contribution margin of $100 ($250 selling price, less $150 variable expenses). Since the total fixed expenses are $35,000, the break-even point in unit sales is computed as follows:

$$\frac{\text{Fixed expenses}}{\text{Unit contribution margin}} = \frac{\$35{,}000}{\$100 \text{ per speaker}} = 350 \text{ speakers}$$

A variation of this method uses the CM ratio instead of the unit contribution margin. The result is the break-even point in total sales dollars rather than in total units sold.

$$\text{Break-even point in total sales dollars} = \frac{\text{Fixed expenses}}{\text{CM ratio}}$$

In the Acoustic Concepts example, the calculation is as follows:

$$\frac{\text{Fixed expenses}}{\text{CM ratio}} = \frac{\$35{,}000}{0.40} = \$87{,}500$$

This approach, based on the CM ratio, is particularly useful when a company has multiple products and wishes to compute a single break-even point for the company as a whole. More is said on this point later in the chapter.

LEARNING OBJECTIVE 6
Determine the level of sales needed to achieve a desired target profit.

Target Profit Analysis

CVP formulas can be used to determine the sales volume needed to achieve a target profit. Suppose that Prem Narayan of Acoustic Concepts wishes to earn a target profit of $40,000 per month. How many speakers would have to be sold?

The CVP Equation One approach is to use the equation method. Instead of solving for the unit sales where profits are zero, solve for the unit sales where profits are $40,000.

$$\text{Sales} = \text{Variable expenses} + \text{Fixed expenses} + \text{Profits}$$
$$\$250Q = \$150Q = \$35{,}000 = \$40{,}000$$
$$\$100Q = \$75{,}000$$
$$Q = \$75{,}000 \div \$100 \text{ per speaker}$$
$$Q = 750 \text{ speakers}$$

where:

$$Q = \text{Quantity of speakers sold}$$
$$\$250 = \text{Unit selling price}$$
$$\$150 = \text{Unit variable expenses}$$
$$\$35{,}000 = \text{Total fixed expenses}$$
$$\$40{,}000 = \text{Target profit}$$

Thus, the target profit can be achieved by selling 750 speakers per month, which represents \$187,500 in total sales (\$250 per speaker × 750 speakers).

IN BUSINESS

COSTS ON THE INTERNET

The company eToys, which sells toys over the Internet, lost \$190 million in 1999 on sales of \$151 million. One big cost was advertising. eToys spent about \$37 on advertising for each \$100 of sales. (Other e-tailers were spending even more—in some cases, up to \$460 on advertising for each \$100 in sales!)

eToys did have some advantages relative to bricks-and-mortar stores such as Toys "R" Us. eToys had much lower inventory costs since it only needed to keep on hand one or two of a slow-moving item, whereas a traditional store has to fully stock its shelves. And bricks-and-mortar retail spaces in malls and elsewhere do cost money—on average, about 7% of sales. However, e-tailers such as eToys have their own set of disadvantages. Customers "pick and pack" their own items at a bricks-and-mortar outlet, but e-tailers have to pay employees to carry out this task. This costs eToys about \$33 for every \$100 in sales. And the technology to sell over the Internet is not free. eToys spent about \$29 on its website and related technology for every \$100 in sales. However, many of these costs of selling over the Internet are fixed. Toby Lenk, the CEO of eToys, estimated that the company would pass its break-even point somewhere between \$750 and \$900 million in sales—representing less than 1% of the market for toys. eToys did not make this goal and laid off 70% of its employees in January 2001. Subsequently, eToys was acquired by KBToys.com.

Sources: Erin Kelly, "The Last e-Store on the Block," *Fortune*, September 18, 2000, pp. 214–220; Jennifer Couzin, *The Industry Standard*, January 4, 2001.

The Contribution Margin Approach A second approach involves expanding the contribution margin formula to include the target profit:

$$\text{Unit sales to attain the target profit} = \frac{\text{Fixed expenses} + \text{Target profit}}{\text{Unit contribution margin}}$$
$$= \frac{\$35{,}000 + \$40{,}000}{\$100 \text{ per speaker}}$$
$$= 750 \text{ speakers}$$

This approach gives the same answer as the equation method because it is simply a shortcut version of the equation method. Similarly, the dollar sales needed to attain the target profit can be computed as follows:

$$\text{Dollar sales to attain target profit} = \frac{\text{Fixed expenses} + \text{Target profit}}{\text{CM ratio}}$$
$$= \frac{\$35{,}000 + \$40{,}000}{0.40}$$
$$= \$187{,}500$$

The Margin of Safety

LEARNING OBJECTIVE 7
Compute the margin of safety and explain its significance.

The **margin of safety** is the excess of budgeted (or actual) sales dollars over the break-even volume of sales dollars. It is the amount by which sales can drop before losses are incurred. The higher the margin of safety, the lower the risk of not breaking even and incurring a loss. The formula for its calculation is:

$$\text{Margin of safety} = \text{Total budgeted (or actual) sales} - \text{Break-even sales}$$

The margin of safety can also be expressed in percentage form by dividing the margin of safety in dollars by total dollar sales:

$$\text{Margin of safety percentage} = \frac{\text{Margin of safety in dollars}}{\text{Total budgeted (or actual) sales in dollars}}$$

The calculation of the margin of safety for Acoustic Concepts is:

Sales (at the current volume of 400 speakers) (a)	$100,000
Break-even sales (at 350 speakers)	87,500
Margin of safety (in dollars) (b)	$ 12,500
Margin of safety as a percentage of sales, (b) ÷ (a)	12.5%

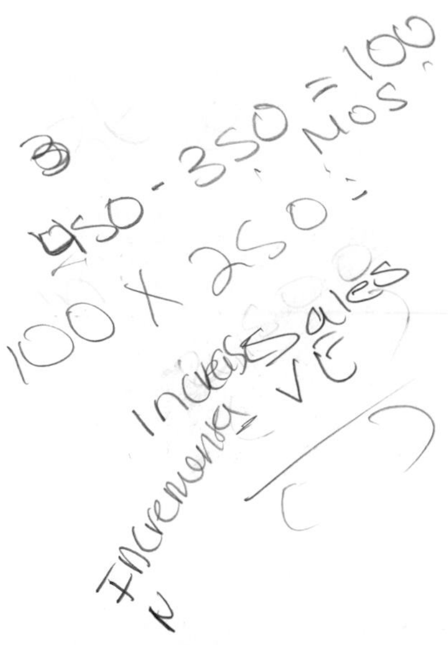

This margin of safety means that at the current level of sales and with the company's current prices and cost structure, a reduction in sales of $12,500, or 12.5%, would result in just breaking even.

In a single-product company like Acoustic Concepts, the margin of safety can also be expressed in terms of the number of units sold by dividing the margin of safety in dollars by the selling price per unit. In this case, the margin of safety is 50 speakers ($12,500 ÷ $250 per speaker = 50 speakers).

IN BUSINESS

COMPUTING MARGIN OF SAFETY FOR A SMALL BUSINESS

Sam Calagione owns Dogfish Head Craft Brewery, a microbrewery in Rehobeth Beach, Delaware. He charges distributors as much as $100 per case for his premium beers such as World Wide Stout. The high-priced microbrews bring in $800,000 in operating income on revenue of $7 million. Calagione reports that his raw ingredients and labor costs for one case of World Wide Stout are $30 and $16, respectively. Bottling and packaging costs are $6 per case. Gas and electric costs are about $10 per case.

If we assume that World Wide Stout is representative of all Dogfish microbrews, then we can compute the company's margin of safety in five steps. First, variable cost as a percentage of sales is 62% [($30 + $16 + $6 + $10)/$100]. Second, the contribution margin ratio is 38% (1 − 0.62). Third, Dogfish's total fixed cost is $1,860,000 [($7,000,000 × 0.38) − $800,000]. Fourth, the break-even point in sales dollars is $4,894,737 ($1,860,000/0.38). Fifth, the margin of safety is $2,105,263 ($7,000,000 − $4,894,737).

Source: Patricia Huang, "Château Dogfish," *Forbes*, February 28, 2005, pp. 57–59.

MANAGERIAL ACCOUNTING IN ACTION
The Wrap-up

Prem Narayan and Bob Luchinni met to discuss the results of Bob's analysis.

Prem: Bob, everything you have shown me is pretty clear. I can see what impact some of the sales manager's suggestions would have on our profits. Some of those suggestions are quite good and others are not so good. I am concerned that our margin of safety is only 50 speakers. What can we do to increase this number?

Bob: Well, we have to increase total sales or decrease the break-even point or both.

Prem: And to decrease the break-even point, we have to either decrease our fixed expenses or increase our unit contribution margin?

Bob: Exactly.

Prem: And to increase our unit contribution margin, we must either increase our selling price or decrease the variable cost per unit?

Bob: Correct.

Prem: So what do you suggest?

Bob: Well, the analysis doesn't tell us which of these to do, but it does indicate we have a potential problem here.

Prem: If you don't have any immediate suggestions, I would like to call a general meeting next week to discuss ways we can work on increasing the margin of safety. I think everyone will be concerned about how vulnerable we are to even small downturns in sales.

CVP Considerations in Choosing a Cost Structure

Video 5–1

Cost structure refers to the relative proportion of fixed and variable costs in an organization. Managers often have some latitude in trading off between these two types of costs. For example, fixed investments in automated equipment can reduce variable labor costs. In this section, we discuss the choice of a cost structure. We introduce the concept of *operating leverage,* which plays a key role in determining the impact of cost structure on profit stability.

Cost Structure and Profit Stability

Which cost structure is better—high variable costs and low fixed costs, or the opposite? No single answer to this question is possible; each approach has its advantages. To show what we mean, refer to the income statements given below for two blueberry farms. Bogside Farm depends on migrant workers to pick its berries by hand, whereas Sterling Farm has invested in expensive berry-picking machines. Consequently, Bogside Farm has higher variable costs, but Sterling Farm has higher fixed costs:

	Bogside Farm		Sterling Farm	
	Amount	Percent	Amount	Percent
Sales	$100,000	100%	$100,000	100%
Variable expenses	60,000	60%	30,000	30%
Contribution margin	40,000	40%	70,000	70%
Fixed expenses	30,000		60,000	
Net operating income	$ 10,000		$ 10,000	

Which farm has the better cost structure? The answer depends on many factors, including the long-run trend in sales, year-to-year fluctuations in the level of sales, and the attitude of the owners toward risk. If sales are expected to exceed $100,000 in the future, then Sterling Farm probably has the better cost structure. The reason is that its CM ratio is higher, and its profits will therefore increase more rapidly as sales increase. To illustrate, assume that each farm experiences a 10% increase in sales without any increase in fixed costs. The new income statements would be as follows:

	Bogside Farm		Sterling Farm	
	Amount	Percent	Amount	Percent
Sales	$110,000	100%	$110,000	100%
Variable expenses	66,000	60%	33,000	30%
Contribution margin	44,000	40%	77,000	70%
Fixed expenses	30,000		60,000	
Net operating income	$ 14,000		$ 17,000	

Sterling Farm has experienced a greater increase in net operating income due to its higher CM ratio even though the increase in sales was the same for both farms.

What if sales drop below $100,000? What are the farms' break-even points? What are their margins of safety? The computations needed to answer these questions are shown below using the contribution margin method:

	Bogside Farm	Sterling Farm
Fixed expenses	$ 30,000	$ 60,000
Contribution margin ratio	÷ 0.40	÷ 0.70
Break-even in total sales dollars	$ 75,000	$ 85,714
Total current sales (a)	$100,000	$100,000
Break-even sales	75,000	85,714
Margin of safety in sales dollars (b)	$ 25,000	$ 14,286
Margin of safety as a percentage of sales, (b) ÷ (a)	25.0%	14.3%

Bogside Farm's margin of safety is greater and its contribution margin ratio is lower than Sterling Farm. Therefore Bogside Farm is less vulnerable to downturns than Sterling Farm. Due to its lower contribution margin ratio, Bogside Farm will not lose contribution margin as rapidly as Sterling Farm when sales decline. Thus, Bogside Farm's profit will be less volatile. We saw earlier that this is a drawback when sales increase, but it provides more protection when sales drop. And because its break-even point is lower, Bogside Farm can suffer a larger sales decline before losses emerge.

To summarize, without knowing the future, it is not obvious which cost structure is better. Both have advantages and disadvantages. Sterling Farm, with its higher fixed costs and lower variable costs, will experience wider swings in net operating income as sales fluctuate, with greater profits in good years and greater losses in bad years. Bogside Farm, with its lower fixed costs and higher variable costs, will enjoy greater profit stability and will be more protected from losses during bad years, but at the cost of lower net operating income in good years.

IN BUSINESS

A LOSING COST STRUCTURE

Both JetBlue and United Airlines use an Airbus 235 to fly from Dulles International Airport near Washington, DC, to Oakland, California. Both planes have a pilot, copilot, and four flight attendants. That is where the similarity ends. Based on 2002 data, the pilot on the United flight earned $16,350 to $18,000 a month compared to $6,800 per month for the JetBlue pilot. United's senior flight attendants on the plane earned more than $41,000 per year; whereas the JetBlue attendants were paid $16,800 to $27,000 per year. Largely because of the higher labor costs at United, its costs of operating the flight were more than 60% higher than JetBlue's costs. Due to intense fare competition from JetBlue and other low-cost carriers, United was unable to cover its higher operating costs on this and many other flights. Consequently, United went into bankruptcy at the end of 2002.

Source: Susan Carey, "Costly Race in the Sky," *The Wall Street Journal,* September 9, 2002, pp. B1 and B3.

Operating Leverage

LEARNING OBJECTIVE 8
Compute the degree of operating leverage at a particular level of sales and explain how it can be used to predict changes in net operating income.

A lever is a tool for multiplying force. Using a lever, a massive object can be moved with only a modest amount of force. In business, *operating leverage* serves a similar purpose. **Operating leverage** is a measure of how sensitive net operating income is to a given percentage change in dollar sales. Operating leverage acts as a multiplier. If operating leverage is high, a small percentage increase in sales can produce a much larger percentage increase in net operating income.

Operating leverage can be illustrated by returning to the data for the two blueberry farms. We previously showed that a 10% increase in sales (from $100,000 to $110,000 in each farm) results in a 70% increase in the net operating income of Sterling Farm (from $10,000 to $17,000) and only a 40% increase in the net operating income of Bogside Farm (from $10,000 to $14,000). Thus, for a 10% increase in sales, Sterling Farm experiences a much greater percentage increase in profits than does Bogside Farm. Therefore, Sterling Farm has greater operating leverage than Bogside Farm.

The **degree of operating leverage** at a given level of sales is computed by the following formula:

$$\text{Degree of operating leverage} = \frac{\text{Contribution margin}}{\text{Net operating income}}$$

The degree of operating leverage is a measure, at a given level of sales, of how a percentage change in sales volume will affect profits. To illustrate, the degree of operating leverage for the two farms at $100,000 sales would be computed as follows:

$$\text{Bogside Farm: } \frac{\$40,000}{\$10,000} = 4$$

$$\text{Sterling Farm: } \frac{\$70,000}{\$10,000} = 7$$

Since the degree of operating leverage for Bogside Farm is 4, the farm's net operating income grows four times as fast as its sales. Similarly, Sterling Farm's net operating income grows seven times as fast as its sales. Thus, if sales increase by 10%, then we can expect the net operating income of Bogside Farm to increase by four times this amount, or by 40%, and the net operating income of Sterling Farm to increase by seven times this amount, or by 70%.

	(1) Percent Increase in Sales	(2) Degree of Operating Leverage	Percent Increase in Net Operating Income (1) × (2)
Bogside Farm.	10%	4	40%
Sterling Farm	10%	7	70%

What is responsible for the higher operating leverage at Sterling Farm? The only difference between the two farms is their cost structure. If two companies have the same total revenue and same total expense but different cost structures, then the company with the higher proportion of fixed costs in its cost structure will have higher operating leverage. Referring back to the original example on page 180, when both farms have sales of $100,000 and total expenses of $90,000, one-third of Bogside Farm's costs are fixed but two-thirds of Sterling Farm's costs are fixed. As a consequence, Sterling's degree of operating leverage is higher than Bogside's.

The degree of operating leverage is not a constant; it is greatest at sales levels near the break-even point and decreases as sales and profits rise. The following table shows the degree of operating leverage for Bogside Farm at various sales levels. (Data used earlier for Bogside Farm are shown in color.)

Sales	$75,000	$80,000	$100,000	$150,000	$225,000
Variable expenses	45,000	48,000	60,000	90,000	135,000
Contribution margin (a)	30,000	32,000	40,000	60,000	90,000
Fixed expenses	30,000	30,000	30,000	30,000	30,000
Net operating income (b)	$ 0	$ 2,000	$ 10,000	$ 30,000	$ 60,000
Degree of operating leverage, (a) ÷ (b)	∞	16	4	2	1.5

Thus, a 10% increase in sales would increase profits by only 15% (10% × 1.5) if sales were previously $225,000, as compared to the 40% increase we computed earlier at the $100,000 sales level. The degree of operating leverage will continue to decrease the farther the company moves from its break-even point. At the break-even point, the degree of operating leverage is infinitely large ($30,000 contribution margin ÷ $0 net operating income = ∞).

IN BUSINESS

OPERATING LEVERAGE: A KEY TO PROFITABLE E-COMMERCE

Did you ever wonder why Expedia and eBay were among the first Internet companies to become profitable? One big reason is because they sell information products rather than physical products. For example, when somebody buys a physical product, such as a book from Amazon.com, the company needs to purchase a copy of the book from the publisher, process it, and ship it; hence, Amazon.com's gross margins are around 26%. However, once Expedia covers its fixed overhead costs, the extra expense incurred to provide service to one more customer is practically zero; therefore, the incremental revenue provided by that customer "falls to the bottom line."

In the first quarter of 2002, Expedia doubled its sales to $116 million and reported net income of $5.7 million compared to a loss of $17.6 million in the first quarter of 2001. This is the beauty of having a high degree of operating leverage. Sales growth can quickly translate to profit growth when variable costs are negligible. Of course, operating leverage has a dark side—if Expedia's sales plummet, its profits will nosedive as well.

Source: Timothy J. Mullaney and Robert D. Hof, "Finally, the Pot of Gold," *BusinessWeek*, June 24, 2002, pp. 104–106.

The degree of operating leverage can be used to quickly estimate what impact various percentage changes in sales will have on profits, without the necessity of preparing detailed income statements. As shown by our examples, the effects of operating leverage can be dramatic. If a company is near its break-even point, then even small percentage increases in sales can yield large percentage increases in profits. *This explains why management will often work very hard for only a small increase in sales volume.* If the degree of operating leverage is 5, then a 6% increase in sales would translate into a 30% increase in profits.

Structuring Sales Commissions

Companies usually compensate salespeople by paying them a commission based on sales, a salary, or a combination of the two. Commissions based on sales dollars can lead to lower profits. To illustrate, consider Pipeline Unlimited, a producer of surfing equipment. Salespeople for the company sell the company's products to retail sporting goods stores throughout

North America and the Pacific Basin. Data for two of the company's surfboards, the XR7 and Turbo models, appear below:

	Model	
	XR7	Turbo
Selling price	$695	$749
Variable expenses	344	410
Contribution margin	$351	$339

Which model will salespeople push hardest if they are paid a commission of 10% of sales revenue? The answer is the Turbo, since it has the higher selling price and hence the larger commission. On the other hand, from the standpoint of the company, profits will be greater if salespeople steer customers toward the XR7 model since it has the higher contribution margin.

To eliminate such conflicts, commissions can be based on contribution margin rather than on selling price. If this is done, the salespersons will want to sell the mix of products that maximizes contribution margin. Providing that fixed costs are not affected by the sales mix, maximizing the contribution margin will also maximize the company's profit.[1] In effect, by maximizing their own compensation, salespersons will also maximize the company's profit.

IN BUSINESS

AN ALTERNATIVE APPROACH TO SALES COMMISSIONS

Thrive Networks, located in Concord, Massachusetts, used to pay its three salesmen based on individually earned commissions. This system seemed to be working fine as indicated by the company's sales growth from $2.7 million in 2002 to $3.6 million in 2003. However, the company felt there was a better way to motivate and compensate its salesmen. It pooled commissions across the three salesmen and compensated them collectively. The new approach was designed to build teamwork and leverage each salesman's individual strengths. Jim Lippie, the director of business development, was highly skilled at networking and generating sales leads. John Barrows, the sales director, excelled at meeting with prospective clients and producing compelling proposals. Nate Wolfson, the CEO and final member of the sales team, was the master at closing the deal. The new approach has worked so well that Wolfson plans to use three-person sales teams in his offices nationwide.

Source: Cara Cannella, "Kill the Commissions," *Inc.* magazine, August 2004, p. 38.

Sales Mix

LEARNING OBJECTIVE 9
Compute the break-even point for a multiproduct company and explain the effects of shifts in the sales mix on contribution margin and the break-even point.

Before concluding our discussion of CVP concepts, we need to consider the impact of changes in *sales mix* on a company's profit.

The Definition of Sales Mix

The term **sales mix** refers to the relative proportions in which a company's products are sold. The idea is to achieve the combination, or mix, that will yield the greatest amount of profits. Most companies have many products, and often these products are not equally profitable.

[1] This also assumes the company has no production constraint. If it does, the sales commissions should be modified. See the Profitability Appendix at the end of the book.

Hence, profits will depend to some extent on the company's sales mix. Profits will be greater if high-margin rather than low-margin items make up a relatively large proportion of total sales.

Changes in the sales mix can cause perplexing variations in a company's profits. A shift in the sales mix from high-margin items to low-margin items can cause total profits to decrease even though total sales may increase. Conversely, a shift in the sales mix from low-margin items to high-margin items can cause the reverse effect—total profits may increase even though total sales decrease. It is one thing to achieve a particular sales volume; it is quite another to sell the most profitable mix of products.

IN BUSINESS

KODAK: GOING DIGITAL

Kodak dominates the film industry in the U.S., selling two out of every three rolls of film. It also processes 40% of all film dropped off for developing. Unfortunately for Kodak, this revenue stream is rapidly declining due to competition from digital cameras, which do not use film at all. To counter this threat, Kodak has moved into the digital market with its own line of digital cameras and various services, but sales of digital products undeniably cut into the company's film business. "Chief Financial Officer Robert Brust has 'stress-tested' profit models based on how quickly digital cameras may spread. If half of homes go digital, . . . Kodak's sales would rise 10% a year—but profits would go up only 8% a year. Cost cuts couldn't come fast enough to offset a slide in film sales and the margin pressure from selling cheap digital cameras." The sales mix is moving in the wrong direction, given the company's current cost structure and competitive prices.

Source: Bruce Upbin, "Kodak's Digital Moment," *Forbes*, August 21, 2000, pp. 106–112.

Sales Mix and Break-Even Analysis

If a company sells more than one product, break-even analysis is more complex than discussed to this point. The reason is that different products will have different selling prices, different costs, and different contribution margins. Consequently, the break-even point depends on the mix in which the various products are sold. To illustrate, consider Sound Unlimited, a small company that imports DVDs from France. At present, the company sells two DVDs: the Le Louvre DVD, a multimedia free-form tour of the famous art museum in Paris; and the Le Vin DVD, which features the wines and wine-growing regions of France. The company's September sales, expenses, and break-even point are shown in Exhibit 5–3.

As shown in the exhibit, the break-even point is $60,000 in sales, which was computed by dividing the company's fixed expenses of $27,000 by its overall CM ratio of 45%. However, this is the break-even only if the company's sales mix does not change. Currently, the Le Louvre DVD is responsible for 20% and the Le Vin DVD for 80% of the company's dollar sales. Assuming this sales mix does not change, if total sales are $60,000, the sales of the Le Louvre DVD would be $12,000 (20% of $60,000) and the sales of the Le Vin DVD would be $48,000 (80% of $60,000). As shown in Exhibit 5–3, at these levels of sales, the company would indeed break even. But $60,000 in sales represents the break-even point for the company only if the sales mix does not change. *If the sales mix changes, then the break-even point will also usually change.* This is illustrated by the results for October in which the sales mix shifted away from the more profitable Le Vin DVD (which has a 50% CM ratio) toward the less profitable Le Louvre CD (which has a 25% CM ratio). These results appear in Exhibit 5–4.

Although sales have remained unchanged at $100,000, the sales mix is exactly the reverse of what it was in Exhibit 5–3, with the bulk of the sales now coming from the less profitable Le Louvre DVD. Notice that this shift in the sales mix has caused both the overall CM ratio and total profits to drop sharply from the prior month even though total sales are the same. The overall CM ratio has dropped from 45% in September to only 30% in October, and net operating income has dropped from $18,000 to only $3,000. In addition, with the

EXHIBIT 5–3
Multiproduct Break-Even Analysis

Sound Unlimited
Contribution Income Statement
For the Month of September

	Le Louvre DVD		Le Vin DVD		Total	
	Amount	Percent	Amount	Percent	Amount	Percent
Sales	$20,000	100%	$80,000	100%	$100,000	100%
Variable expenses	15,000	75%	40,000	50%	55,000	55%
Contribution margin	$ 5,000	25%	$40,000	50%	45,000	45%
Fixed expenses					27,000	
Net operating income					$ 18,000	

Computation of the break-even point:

$$\frac{\text{Fixed expenses}}{\text{Overall CM ratio}} = \frac{\$27{,}000}{0.45} = \$60{,}000$$

Verification of the break-even point:

	Le Louvre DVD	Le Vin DVD	Total
Current dollar sales	$20,000	$80,000	$100,000
Percentage of total dollar sales	20%	80%	100%
Sales at the break-even point	$12,000	$48,000	$60,000

	Le Louvre DVD		Le Vin DVD		Total	
	Amount	Percent	Amount	Percent	Amount	Percent
Sales	$12,000	100%	$48,000	100%	$ 60,000	100%
Variable expenses	9,000	75%	24,000	50%	33,000	55%
Contribution margin	$ 3,000	25%	$24,000	50%	27,000	45%
Fixed expenses					27,000	
Net operating income					$ 0	

EXHIBIT 5–4
Multiproduct Break-Even Analysis: A Shift in Sales Mix (see Exhibit 5–3)

Sound Unlimited
Contribution Income Statement
For the Month of October

	Le Louvre DVD		Le Vin DVD		Total	
	Amount	Percent	Amount	Percent	Amount	Percent
Sales	$80,000	100%	$20,000	100%	$100,000	100%
Variable expenses	60,000	75%	10,000	50%	70,000	70%
Contribution margin	$20,000	25%	$10,000	50%	30,000	30%
Fixed expenses					27,000	
Net operating income					$ 3,000	

Computation of the break-even point:

$$\frac{\text{Fixed expenses}}{\text{Overall CM ratio}} = \frac{\$27{,}000}{0.30} = \$90{,}000$$

drop in the overall CM ratio, the company's break-even point is no longer $60,000 in sales. Since the company is now realizing less average contribution margin per dollar of sales, it takes more sales to cover the same amount of fixed costs. Thus, the break-even point has increased from $60,000 to $90,000 in sales per year.

In preparing a break-even analysis, some assumption must be made concerning the sales mix. Usually the assumption is that it will not change. However, if the sales mix is expected to change, then this must be explicitly considered in any CVP computations.

IN BUSINESS

PLAYING THE CVP GAME

In 2002, General Motors (GM) gave away almost $2,600 per vehicle in customer incentives such as price cuts and 0% financing. "The pricing sacrifices have been more than offset by volume gains, most of which have come from trucks and SUVs, like the Chevy Suburban and the GMC Envoy, which generate far more profit for the company than cars. Lehman Brothers analysts estimate that GM will sell an additional 395,000 trucks and SUVs and an extra 75,000 cars in 2002. The trucks, however, are the company's golden goose, hauling in an average [contribution margin] . . . of about $7,000, compared with just $4,000 for the cars. All told, the volume gains could bring in an additional $3 billion [in profits]."

Source: Janice Revell, "GM's Slow Leak," *Fortune*, October 28, 2002, pp. 105–110.

Assumptions of CVP Analysis

A number of assumptions commonly underlie CVP analysis:

1. Selling price is constant. The price of a product or service will not change as volume changes.
2. Costs are linear and can be accurately divided into variable and fixed elements. The variable element is constant per unit, and the fixed element is constant in total over the entire relevant range.
3. In multiproduct companies, the sales mix is constant.
4. In manufacturing companies, inventories do not change. The number of units produced equals the number of units sold.

While these assumptions may be violated in practice, the results of CVP analysis are often "good enough" to be quite useful. Perhaps the greatest danger lies in relying on simple CVP analysis when a manager is contemplating a large change in volume that lies outside of the relevant range. For example, a manager might contemplate increasing the level of sales far beyond what the company has ever experienced before. However, even in these situations the model can be adjusted as we have done in this chapter to take into account anticipated changes in selling prices, fixed costs, and the sales mix that would otherwise violate the assumptions mentioned above. For example, in a decision that would affect fixed costs, the change in fixed costs can be explicitly taken into account as illustrated earlier in the chapter in the Acoustic Concepts example on pages 172–175.

Summary

CVP analysis is based on a simple model of how profits respond to prices, costs, and volume. This model can be used to answer a variety of critical questions such as what is the company's break-even volume, what is its margin of safety, and what is likely to happen if specific changes are made in prices, costs, and volume.

A CVP graph depicts the relationships between sales volume in units on the one hand and fixed expenses, variable expenses, total expenses, total sales, and profits on the other hand. The CVP graph is useful for developing intuition about how costs and profits respond to changes in sales volume.

The contribution margin ratio is the ratio of the total contribution margin to total sales. This ratio can be used to quickly estimate what impact a change in total sales would have on net operating income. The ratio is also useful in break-even analysis.

The break-even point is the level of sales (in units or in dollars) at which the company just breaks even. The break-even point can be computed using several different techniques that are all based on the simple CVP model. With slight modifications, the same techniques can be used to compute the level of sales required to attain a target profit.

The margin of safety is the amount by which the company's current sales exceeds break-even sales.

The degree of operating leverage allows quick estimation of what impact a given percentage change in sales would have on the company's net operating income. The higher the degree of operating leverage, the greater is the impact on the company's profits. The degree of operating leverage is not constant—it depends on the company's current level of sales.

The profits of a multiproduct company are affected by its sales mix. Changes in the sales mix can affect the break-even point, margin of safety, and other critical factors.

Review Problem: CVP Relationships

Voltar Company manufactures and sells a specialized cordless telephone for high electromagnetic radiation environments. The company's contribution format income statement for the most recent year is given below:

	Total	Per Unit	Percent of Sales
Sales (20,000 units)	$1,200,000	$60	100%
Variable expenses	900,000	45	? %
Contribution margin	300,000	$15	? %
Fixed expenses	240,000		
Net operating income	$ 60,000		

Management is anxious to increase the company's profit and has asked for an analysis of a number of items.

Required:

1. Compute the company's CM ratio and variable expense ratio.
2. Compute the company's break-even point in both units and sales dollars. Use the equation method.
3. Assume that sales increase by $400,000 next year. If cost behavior patterns remain unchanged, by how much will the company's net operating income increase? Use the CM ratio to compute your answer.
4. Refer to the original data. Assume that next year management wants the company to earn a profit of at least $90,000. How many units will have to be sold to meet this target profit?
5. Refer to the original data. Compute the company's margin of safety in both dollar and percentage form.
6. *a.* Compute the company's degree of operating leverage at the present level of sales.
   b. Assume that through a more intense effort by the sales staff, the company's sales increase by 8% next year. By what percentage would you expect net operating income to increase? Use the degree of operating leverage to obtain your answer.
   c. Verify your answer to (*b*) by preparing a new contribution format income statement showing an 8% increase in sales.
7. In an effort to increase sales and profits, management is considering the use of a higher-quality speaker. The higher-quality speaker would increase variable costs by $3 per unit, but management could eliminate one quality inspector who is paid a salary of $30,000 per year. The sales manager estimates that the higher-quality speaker would increase annual sales by at least 20%.
   a. Assuming that changes are made as described above, prepare a projected contribution format income statement for next year. Show data on a total, per unit, and percentage basis.
   b. Compute the company's new break-even point in both units and dollars of sales. Use the contribution margin method.
   c. Would you recommend that the changes be made?

Solution to Review Problem

1.

$$\text{CM ratio} = \frac{\text{Unit contribution margin}}{\text{Selling price}} = \frac{\$15}{\$60} = 25\%$$

$$\text{Variable expense ratio} = \frac{\text{Variable expense}}{\text{Selling price}} = \frac{\$45}{\$60} = 75\%$$

2.

$$\text{Sales} = \text{Variable expenses} + \text{Fixed expenses} + \text{Profits}$$

$$\$60Q = \$45Q + \$240{,}000 + \$0$$

$$\$15Q = \$240{,}000$$

$$Q = \$240{,}000 \div \$15 \text{ per unit}$$

$$Q = 16{,}000 \text{ units; or at \$60 per unit, \$960,000}$$

Alternative solution:

$$X = 0.75X + \$240{,}000 + \$0$$

$$0.25X = \$240{,}000$$

$$X = \$240{,}000 \div 0.25$$

$$X = \$960{,}000\text{; or at \$60 per unit, 16,000 units}$$

3.

Increase in sales	$400,000
Multiply by the CM ratio	× 25%
Expected increase in contribution margin	$100,000

Since the fixed expenses are not expected to change, net operating income will increase by the entire $100,000 increase in contribution margin computed above.

4. Equation method:

$$\text{Sales} = \text{Variable expenses} + \text{Fixed expenses} + \text{Profits}$$

$$\$60Q = \$45Q + \$240{,}000 + \$90{,}000$$

$$\$15Q = \$330{,}000$$

$$Q = \$330{,}000 \div \$15 \text{ per unit}$$

$$Q = 22{,}000 \text{ units}$$

Contribution margin method:

$$\frac{\text{Fixed expenses} + \text{Target profit}}{\text{Contribution margin per unit}} = \frac{\$240{,}000 + \$90{,}000}{\$15 \text{ per unit}} = 22{,}000 \text{ units}$$

5.

$$\text{Margin of safety in dollars} = \text{Total sales} - \text{Break-even sales}$$

$$= \$1{,}200{,}000 - \$960{,}000 = \$240{,}000$$

$$\text{Margin of safety percentage} = \frac{\text{Margin of safety in dollars}}{\text{Total sales}} = \frac{\$240{,}000}{\$1{,}200{,}000} = 20\%$$

6. *a.*

$$\text{Degree of operating leverage} = \frac{\text{Contribution margin}}{\text{Net operating income}} = \frac{\$300{,}000}{\$60{,}000} = 5$$

b.

Expected increase in sales	8%
Degree of operating leverage	× 5
Expected increase in net operating income	40%

c. If sales increase by 8%, then 21,600 units (20,000 × 1.08 = 21,600) will be sold next year. The new contribution format income statement would be as follows:

	Total	Per Unit	Percent of Sales
Sales (21,600 units)	$1,296,000	$60	100%
Variable expenses	972,000	45	75%
Contribution margin	324,000	$15	25%
Fixed expenses	240,000		
Net operating income	$ 84,000		

Thus, the $84,000 expected net operating income for next year represents a 40% increase over the $60,000 net operating income earned during the current year:

$$\frac{\$84{,}000 - \$60{,}000}{\$60{,}000} = \frac{\$24{,}000}{\$60{,}000} = 40\% \text{ increase}$$

Note from the income statement above that the increase in sales from 20,000 to 21,600 units has increased *both* total sales and total variable expenses. It is a common error to overlook the increase in variable expenses when preparing a projected contribution format income statement.

7. *a.* A 20% increase in sales would result in 24,000 units being sold next year: 20,000 units × 1.20 = 24,000 units.

	Total	Per Unit	Percent of Sales
Sales (24,000 units)	$1,440,000	$60	100%
Variable expenses	1,152,000	48*	80%
Contribution margin	288,000	$12	20%
Fixed expenses	210,000†		
Net operating income	$ 78,000		

*$45 + $3 = $48; $48 ÷ $60 = 80%.
†$240,000 − $30,000 = $210,000.

Note that the change in per unit variable expenses results in a change in both the per unit contribution margin and the CM ratio.

b.

$$\text{Break-even point in unit sales} = \frac{\text{Fixed expenses}}{\text{Unit contribution margin}}$$

$$= \frac{\$210{,}000}{\$12 \text{ per unit}} = 17{,}500 \text{ units}$$

$$\text{Break-even point in dollar sales} = \frac{\text{Fixed expenses}}{\text{CM ratio}}$$

$$= \frac{\$210{,}000}{0.20} = \$1{,}050{,}000$$

c. Yes, based on these data the changes should be made. The changes increase the company's net operating income from the present $60,000 to $78,000 per year. Although the changes also result in a higher break-even point (17,500 units as compared to the present 16,000 units), the company's margin of safety actually becomes greater than before:

$$\text{Margin of safety in dollars} = \text{Total sales} - \text{Break-even sales}$$

$$= \$1{,}440{,}000 - \$1{,}050{,}000 = \$390{,}000$$

As shown in (5) above, the company's present margin of safety is only $240,000. Thus, several benefits will result from the proposed changes.

Glossary

Break-even point The level of sales at which profit is zero. The break-even point can also be defined as the point where total sales equals total expenses or as the point where total contribution margin equals total fixed expenses. (p. 168)

Contribution margin method A method of computing the break-even point in which the fixed expenses are divided by the contribution margin per unit. (p. 177)

Contribution margin ratio (CM ratio) A ratio computed by dividing contribution margin by dollar sales. (p. 171)

Cost-volume-profit (CVP) graph A graphical representation of the relationships between an organization's revenues, costs, and profits on the one hand and its sales volume on the other hand. (p. 169)

Degree of operating leverage A measure, at a given level of sales, of how a percentage change in sales will affect profits. The degree of operating leverage is computed by dividing contribution margin by net operating income. (p. 182)

Equation method A method of computing the break-even point that relies on the equation Sales = Variable expenses + Fixed expenses + Profits. (p. 176)

Incremental analysis An analytical approach that focuses only on those costs and revenues that change as a result of a decision. (p. 173)

Margin of safety The excess of budgeted (or actual) dollar sales over the break-even dollar sales. (p. 179)

Operating leverage A measure of how sensitive net operating income is to a given percentage change in dollar sales. (p. 182)

Sales mix The relative proportions in which a company's products are sold. Sales mix is computed by expressing the sales of each product as a percentage of total sales. (p. 184)

Variable expense ratio A ratio computed by dividing variable expenses by dollar sales (p. 177)

Quiz 5

Multiple-choice questions are provided on the text Web site at www.mhhe.com/noreen1e.

Questions

5-1 What is meant by a product's contribution margin ratio? How is this ratio useful in planning business operations?

5-2 Often the most direct route to a business decision is an incremental analysis. What is meant by an *incremental analysis?*

5-3 Company A's costs are mostly variable, whereas Company B's costs are mostly fixed. When sales increase, which company will tend to realize the greatest increase in profits? Explain.

5-4 What is meant by the term *operating leverage?*

5-5 What is meant by the term *break-even point?*

5-6 Name three approaches to break-even analysis. Briefly explain how each approach works.

5-7 In response to a request from your immediate supervisor, you have prepared a CVP graph portraying the cost and revenue characteristics of your company's product and operations. Explain how the lines on the graph and the break-even point would change if (*a*) the selling price per unit decreased, (*b*) fixed cost increased throughout the entire range of activity portrayed on the graph, and (*c*) variable cost per unit increased.

5-8 What is meant by the margin of safety?

5-9 What is meant by the term *sales mix?* What assumption is usually made concerning sales mix in CVP analysis?

5-10 Explain how a shift in the sales mix could result in both a higher break-even point and a lower net income.

Exercises

EXERCISE 5-1 Preparing a Contribution Format Income Statement [LO1]

Wheeler Corporation's most recent income statement follows:

	Total	Per Unit
Sales (8,000 units)	$208,000	$26.00
Variable expenses	144,000	18.00
Contribution margin	64,000	$ 8.00
Fixed expenses	56,000	
Net operating income	$ 8,000	

Required:

Prepare a new contribution format income statement under each of the following conditions (consider each case independently):

1. The sales volume increases by 50 units.
2. The sales volume declines by 50 units.
3. The sales volume is 7,000 units.

EXERCISE 5-2 Prepare a Cost-Volume-Profit (CVP) Graph [LO2]

Katara Enterprises distributes a single product whose selling price is $36 and whose variable cost is $24 per unit. The company's monthly fixed expense is $12,000.

Required:

1. Prepare a cost-volume-profit graph for the company up to a sales level of 2,000 units.
2. Estimate the company's break-even point in unit sales using your cost-volume-profit graph.

EXERCISE 5-3 Computing and Using the CM Ratio [LO3]

Last month when Harrison Creations, Inc., sold 40,000 units, total sales were $300,000, total variable expenses were $240,000, and total fixed expenses were $45,000.

Required:

1. What is the company's contribution margin (CM) ratio?
2. Estimate the change in the company's net operating income if it were to increase its total sales by $1,500.

EXERCISE 5-4 Changes in Variable Costs, Fixed Costs, Selling Price, and Volume [LO4]

Data for Herron Corporation are shown below:

	Per Unit	Percent of Sales
Selling price	$75	100%
Variable expenses	45	60%
Contribution margin	$30	40%

Fixed expenses are $75,000 per month and the company is selling 3,000 units per month.

Required:

1. The marketing manager argues that an $8,000 increase in the monthly advertising budget would increase monthly sales by $15,000. Should the advertising budget be increased?
2. Refer to the original data. Management is considering using higher-quality components that would increase the variable cost by $3 per unit. The marketing manager believes the higher-quality product would increase sales by 15% per month. Should the higher-quality components be used?

EXERCISE 5-5 Compute the Break-Even Point [LO5]

Maxson Products distributes a single product, a woven basket whose selling price is $8 and whose variable cost is $6 per unit. The company's monthly fixed expense is $5,500.

Required:

1. Solve for the company's break-even point in unit sales using the equation method.
2. Solve for the company's break-even point in sales dollars using the equation method and the CM ratio.
3. Solve for the company's break-even point in unit sales using the contribution margin method.
4. Solve for the company's break-even point in sales dollars using the contribution margin method and the CM ratio.

EXERCISE 5-6 Compute the Level of Sales Required to Attain a Target Profit [LO6]
Liman Corporation has a single product whose selling price is $140 and whose variable cost is $60 per unit. The company's monthly fixed expense is $40,000.

Required:
1. Using the equation method, solve for the unit sales that are required to earn a target profit of $6,000.
2. Using the contribution margin approach, solve for the dollar sales that are required to earn a target profit of $8,000.

EXERCISE 5-7 Compute the Margin of Safety [LO7]
Mohan Corporation is a distributor of a sun umbrella used at resort hotels. Data concerning the next month's budget appear below:

Selling price	$25 per unit
Variable expense	$15 per unit
Fixed expense	$8,500 per month
Unit sales	1,000 units per month

Required:
1. Compute the company's margin of safety.
2. Compute the company's margin of safety as a percentage of its sales.

EXERCISE 5-8 Compute and Use the Degree of Operating Leverage [LO8]
Eneliko Company installs home theater systems. The company's most recent monthly contribution format income statement appears below:

	Amount	Percent of Sales
Sales	$120,000	100%
Variable expenses	84,000	70%
Contribution margin	36,000	30%
Fixed expenses	24,000	
Net operating income.	$ 12,000	

Required:
1. Compute the company's degree of operating leverage.
2. Using the degree of operating leverage, estimate the impact on net operating income of a 10% increase in sales.
3. Verify your estimate from part (2) above by constructing a new contribution format income statement for the company assuming a 10% increase in sales.

EXERCISE 5-9 Compute the Break-Even Point for a Multiproduct Company [LO9]
Lucky Products markets two computer games: Predator and Runway. A contribution format income statement for a recent month for the two games appears below:

	Predator	Runway	Total
Sales	$100,000	$50,000	$150,000
Variable expenses	25,000	5,000	30,000
Contribution margin	$ 75,000	$45,000	120,000
Fixed expenses			90,000
Net operating income			$ 30,000

Required:
1. Compute the overall contribution margin (CM) ratio for the company.
2. Compute the overall break-even point for the company in sales dollars.
3. Verify the overall break-even point for the company by constructing a contribution format income statement showing the appropriate levels of sales for the two products.

EXERCISE 5-10 Break-Even Analysis; Target Profit; Margin of Safety; CM Ratio [LO1, LO3, LO5, LO6, LO7]
Pringle Company distributes a single product. The company's sales and expenses for a recent month follow:

	Total	Per Unit
Sales	$600,000	$40
Variable expenses	420,000	28
Contribution margin	180,000	$12
Fixed expenses	150,000	
Net operating income	$ 30,000	

Required:
1. What is the monthly break-even point in units sold and in sales dollars?
2. Without resorting to computations, what is the total contribution margin at the break-even point?
3. How many units would have to be sold each month to earn a target profit of $18,000? Use the contribution margin method. Verify your answer by preparing a contribution format income statement at the target level of sales.
4. Refer to the original data. Compute the company's margin of safety in both dollar and percentage terms.
5. What is the company's CM ratio? If monthly sales increase by $80,000 and there is no change in fixed expenses, by how much would you expect monthly net operating income to increase?

EXERCISE 5-11 Break-Even Analysis and CVP Graphing [LO2, LO4, LO5]
Chi Omega Sorority is planning its annual Riverboat Extravaganza. The Extravaganza committee has assembled the following expected costs for the event:

Dinner (per person)	$7
Favors and program (per person)	$3
Band	$1,500
Tickets and advertising	$700
Riverboat rental	$4,800
Floorshow and strolling entertainers	$1,000

The committee members would like to charge $30 per person for the evening's activities.

Required:
1. Compute the break-even point for the Extravaganza (in terms of the number of persons that must attend).
2. Assume that only 250 persons attended the Extravaganza last year. If the same number attend this year, what price per ticket must be charged to break even?
3. Refer to the original data ($30 ticket price per person). Prepare a CVP graph for the Extravaganza from zero tickets up to 600 tickets sold.

EXERCISE 5-12 Using a Contribution Format Income Statement [LO1, LO4]
Porter Company's most recent contribution format income statement is shown below:

	Total	Per Unit
Sales (30,000 units)	$150,000	$5
Variable expenses	90,000	3
Contribution margin	60,000	$2
Fixed expenses	50,000	
Net operating income	$ 10,000	

Required:
Prepare a new contribution format income statement under each of the following conditions (consider each case independently):
1. The number of units sold increases by 15%.
2. The selling price decreases by 50 cents per unit, and the number of units sold increases by 20%.

3. The selling price increases by 50 cents per unit, fixed expenses increase by $10,000, and the number of units sold decreases by 5%.
4. Variable expenses increase by 20 cents per unit, the selling price increases by 12%, and the number of units sold decreases by 10%.

EXERCISE 5-13 Missing Data; Basic CVP Concepts [LO1, LO9]

Fill in the missing amounts in each of the eight case situations below. Each case is independent of the others. (Hint: One way to find the missing amounts would be to prepare a contribution format income statement for each case, enter the known data, and then compute the missing items.)

a. Assume that only one product is being sold in each of the four following case situations:

Case	Units Sold	Sales	Variable Expenses	Contribution Margin per Unit	Fixed Expenses	Net Operating Income (Loss)
1	9,000	$270,000	$162,000	$?	$90,000	$?
2	?	$350,000	?	$15	$170,000	$40,000
3	20,000	?	$280,000	$6	?	$35,000
4	5,000	$160,000	?	?	$82,000	($12,000)

b. Assume that more than one product is being sold in each of the four following case situations:

Case	Sales	Variable Expenses	Average Contribution Margin (Percent)	Fixed Expenses	Net Operating Income (Loss)
1	$450,000	$?	40%	$?	$65,000
2	$200,000	$130,000	?	$60,000	?
3	?	?	80%	$470,000	$90,000
4	$300,000	$90,000	?	?	($15,000)

EXERCISE 5-14 Break-Even and Target Profit Analysis [LO3, LO4, LO5, LO6]

Super Sales Company is the exclusive distributor for a revolutionary bookbag. The product sells for $60 per unit and has a CM ratio of 40%. The company's fixed expenses are $360,000 per year.

Required:

1. What are the variable expenses per unit?
2. Using the equation method:
   a. What is the break-even point in units and in sales dollars?
   b. What sales level in units and in sales dollars is required to earn an annual profit of $90,000?
   c. Assume that through negotiation with the manufacturer the Super Sales Company is able to reduce its variable expenses by $3 per unit. What is the company's new break-even point in units and in sales dollars?
3. Repeat (2) above using the contribution margin method.

EXERCISE 5-15 Operating Leverage [LO4, LO8]

Superior Door Company sells prehung doors to home builders. The doors are sold for $60 each. Variable costs are $42 per door, and fixed costs total $450,000 per year. The company is currently selling 30,000 doors per year.

Required:

1. Prepare a contribution format income statement for the company at the present level of sales and compute the degree of operating leverage.
2. Management is confident that the company can sell 37,500 doors next year (an increase of 7,500 doors, or 25%, over current sales). Compute the following:
   a. The expected percentage increase in net operating income for next year.
   b. The expected net operating income for next year. (Do not prepare an income statement; use the degree of operating leverage to compute your answer.)

EXERCISE 5-16 Break-Even and Target Profit Analysis [LO4, LO5, LO6]

Reveen Products sells camping equipment. One of the company's products, a camp lantern, sells for $90 per unit. Variable expenses are $63 per lantern, and fixed expenses associated with the lantern total $135,000 per month.

Required:

1. Compute the company's break-even point in number of lanterns and in total sales dollars.
2. If the variable expenses per lantern increase as a percentage of the selling price, will it result in a higher or a lower break-even point? Why? (Assume that the fixed expenses remain unchanged.)
3. At present, the company is selling 8,000 lanterns per month. The sales manager is convinced that a 10% reduction in the selling price will result in a 25% increase in the number of lanterns sold each month. Prepare two contribution income statements, one under present operating conditions, and one as operations would appear after the proposed changes. Show both total and per unit data on your statements.
4. Refer to the data in (3) above. How many lanterns would have to be sold at the new selling price to yield a minimum net operating income of $72,000 per month?

EXERCISE 5-17 Multiproduct Break-Even Analysis [LO9]

Okabee Enterprises is the distributor for two products, Model A100 and Model B900. Monthly sales and the contribution margin ratios for the two products follow:

	Product		
	Model A100	Model B900	Total
Sales	$700,000	$300,000	$1,000,000
Contribution margin ratio	60%	70%	?

The company's fixed expenses total $598,500 per month.

Required:

1. Prepare a contribution format income statement for the company as a whole.
2. Compute the break-even point for the company based on the current sales mix.
3. If sales increase by $50,000 per month, by how much would you expect net operating income to increase? What are your assumptions?

Problems

PROBLEM 5-18 Basic CVP Analysis [LO1, LO3, LO4, LO5, LO8]

Stratford Company distributes a lightweight lawn chair that sells for $15 per unit. Variable costs are $6 per unit, and fixed costs total $180,000 annually.

Required:

Answer the following independent questions:

1. What is the product's CM ratio?
2. Use the CM ratio to determine the break-even point in sales dollars.
3. The company estimates that sales will increase by $45,000 during the coming year due to increased demand. By how much should net operating income increase?
4. Assume that the operating results for last year were as follows:

Sales	$360,000
Variable expenses	144,000
Contribution margin	216,000
Fixed expenses	180,000
Net operating income	$ 36,000

   a. Compute the degree of operating leverage at the current level of sales.
   b. The president expects sales to increase by 15% next year. By how much should net operating income increase?

5. Refer to the original data. Assume that the company sold 28,000 units last year. The sales manager is convinced that a 10% reduction in the selling price, combined with a $70,000 increase in

advertising expenditures, would cause annual sales in units to increase by 50%. Prepare two contribution format income statements, one showing the results of last year's operations and one showing what the results of operations would be if these changes were made. Would you recommend that the company do as the sales manager suggests?

6. Refer to the original data. Assume again that the company sold 28,000 units last year. The president feels that it would be unwise to change the selling price. Instead, he wants to increase the sales commission by $2 per unit. He thinks that this move, combined with some increase in advertising, would cause annual sales to double. By how much could advertising be increased with profits remaining unchanged? Do not prepare an income statement; use the incremental analysis approach.

PROBLEM 5-19 Basics of CVP Analysis; Cost Structure [LO1, LO3, LO4, LO5, LO6]

Memofax, Inc., produces memory enhancement kits for fax machines. Sales have been very erratic, with some months showing a profit and some months showing a loss. The company's contribution format income statement for the most recent month is given below:

Sales (13,500 units at $20 per unit)	$270,000
Variable expenses	189,000
Contribution margin	81,000
Fixed expenses	90,000
Net operating loss	$ (9,000)

Required:

1. Compute the company's CM ratio and its break-even point in both units and dollars.
2. The sales manager feels that an $8,000 increase in the monthly advertising budget, combined with an intensified effort by the sales staff, will result in a $70,000 increase in monthly sales. If the sales manager is right, what will be the effect on the company's monthly net operating income or loss? (Use the incremental approach in preparing your answer.)
3. Refer to the original data. The president is convinced that a 10% reduction in the selling price, combined with an increase of $35,000 in the monthly advertising budget, will cause unit sales to double. What will the new contribution format income statement look like if these changes are adopted?
4. Refer to the original data. The company's advertising agency thinks that a new package would help sales. The new package being proposed would increase packaging costs by $0.60 per unit. Assuming no other changes, how many units would have to be sold each month to earn a profit of $4,500?
5. Refer to the original data. By automating certain operations, the company could slash its variable expenses in half. However, fixed costs would increase by $118,000 per month.
   a. Compute the new CM ratio and the new break-even point in both units and dollars.
   b. Assume that the company expects to sell 20,000 units next month. Prepare two contribution format income statements, one assuming that operations are not automated and one assuming that they are.
   c. Would you recommend that the company automate its operations? Explain.

PROBLEM 5-20 Sales Mix; Multiproduct Break-Even Analysis [LO9]

Marlin Company, a wholesale distributor, has been operating for only a few months. The company sells three products—sinks, mirrors, and vanities. Budgeted sales by product and in total for the coming month are shown below:

	Product							
	Sinks		Mirrors		Vanities		Total	
Percentage of total sales	48%		20%		32%		100%	
Sales	$240,000	100%	$100,000	100%	$160,000	100%	$500,000	100%
Variable expenses	72,000	30%	80,000	80%	88,000	55%	240,000	48%
Contribution margin	$168,000	70%	$ 20,000	20%	$ 72,000	45%	260,000	52%
Fixed expenses							223,600	
Net operating income							$ 36,400	

$$\text{Break-even point in sales dollars} = \frac{\text{Fixed expenses}}{\text{CM ratio}} = \frac{\$223{,}600}{0.52} = \$430{,}000$$

As shown by these data, net operating income is budgeted at $36,400 for the month, and break-even sales at $430,000.

Assume that actual sales for the month total $500,000 as planned. Actual sales by product are: sinks, $160,000; mirrors, $200,000; and vanities, $140,000.

Required:

1. Prepare a contribution format income statement for the month based on actual sales data. Present the income statement in the format shown above.
2. Compute the break-even point in sales dollars for the month, based on your actual data.
3. Considering the fact that the company met its $500,000 sales budget for the month, the president is shocked at the results shown on your income statement in (1) above. Prepare a brief memo for the president explaining why both the operating results and the break-even point in sales dollars are different from what was budgeted.

PROBLEM 5-21 Basic CVP Analysis; Graphing [LO1, LO2, LO4, LO5]

Shirts Unlimited operates a chain of shirt stores around the country. The stores carry many styles of shirts that are all sold at the same price. To encourage sales personnel to be aggressive in their sales efforts, the company pays a substantial sales commission on each shirt sold. Sales personnel also receive a small basic salary.

The following worksheet contains cost and revenue data for Store 36. These data are typical of the company's many outlets:

Microsoft Excel - Problem 5-21 screen captur...

	A	B
1		*Per Shirt*
2	Selling price	$ 40.00
3		
4	Variable expenses:	
5	Invoice cost	$ 18.00
6	Sales commission	7.00
7	Total variable expenses	$ 25.00
8		
9		*Annual*
10	Fixed expenses:	
11	Rent	$ 80,000
12	Advertising	150,000
13	Salaries	70,000
14	Total fixed expenses	$300,000
15		
16		

Shirts Unlimited is a fairly new organization. The company has asked you, as a member of its planning group, to assist in some basic analysis of its stores and company policies.

Required:

1. Calculate the annual break-even point in dollar sales and in unit sales for Store 36.
2. Prepare a CVP graph showing cost and revenue data for Store 36 from zero shirts up to 30,000 shirts sold each year. Clearly indicate the break-even point on the graph.
3. If 19,000 shirts are sold in a year, what would be Store 36's net operating income or loss?

4. The company is considering paying the store manager of Store 36 an incentive commission of $3 per shirt (in addition to the salespersons' commissions). If this change is made, what will be the new break-even point in dollar sales and in unit sales?
5. Refer to the original data. As an alternative to (4) above, the company is considering paying the store manager a $3 commission on each shirt sold in excess of the break-even point. If this change is made, what will be the store's net operating income or loss if 23,500 shirts are sold in a year?
6. Refer to the original data. The company is considering eliminating sales commissions entirely in its stores and increasing fixed salaries by $107,000 annually.
   a. If this change is made, what will be the new break-even point in dollar sales and in unit sales in Store 36?
   b. Would you recommend that the change be made? Explain.

PROBLEM 5-22 Break-Even Analysis; Pricing [LO1, LO4, LO5]

Detmer Holdings AG of Zurich, Switzerland, has just introduced a new fashion watch for which the company is trying to find an optimal selling price. Marketing studies suggest that the company can increase sales by 5,000 units for each SFr2 per unit reduction in the selling price. (SFr2 denotes 2 Swiss francs.) The company's present selling price is SFr90 per unit, and variable expenses are SFr60 per unit. Fixed expenses are SFr840,000 per year. The present annual sales volume (at the SFr90 selling price) is 25,000 units.

Required:
1. What is the present yearly net operating income or loss?
2. What is the present break-even point in units and in Swiss franc sales?
3. Assuming that the marketing studies are correct, what is the *maximum* profit that the company can earn yearly? At how many units and at what selling price per unit would the company generate this profit?
4. What would be the break-even point in units and in Swiss franc sales using the selling price you determined in (3) above (i.e., the selling price at the level of maximum profits)? Why is this break-even point different from the break-even point you computed in (2) above?

PROBLEM 5-23 Graphing; Incremental Analysis; Operating Leverage [LO2, LO4, LO5, LO6, LO8]

Teri Hall has recently opened Sheer Elegance, Inc., a store specializing in fashionable stockings. Ms. Hall has just completed a course in managerial accounting, and she believes that she can apply certain aspects of the course to her business. She is particularly interested in adopting the cost-volume-profit (CVP) approach to decision making. Thus, she has prepared the following analysis:

Sales price per pair of stockings	$2.00
Variable expense per pair of stockings	0.80
Contribution margin per pair of stockings	$1.20
Fixed expense per year:	
Building rental	$12,000
Equipment depreciation	3,000
Selling	30,000
Administrative	15,000
Total fixed expense	$60,000

Required:
1. How many pairs of stockings must be sold to break even? What does this represent in total dollar sales?
2. Prepare a CVP graph for the store from zero pairs up to 70,000 pairs of stockings sold each year. Indicate the break-even point on the graph.
3. How many pairs of stockings must be sold to earn a $9,000 target profit for the first year?
4. Ms. Hall now has one full-time and one part-time salesperson working in the store. It will cost her an additional $8,000 per year to convert the part-time position to a full-time position. Ms. Hall believes that the change would bring in an additional $20,000 in sales each year. Should she convert the position? Use the incremental approach. (Do not prepare an income statement.)

5. Refer to the original data. Actual operating results for the first year are as follows:

Sales	$125,000
Variable expenses	50,000
Contribution margin	75,000
Fixed expenses	60,000
Net operating income	$ 15,000

a. What is the store's degree of operating leverage?

b. Ms. Hall is confident that with some effort she can increase sales by 20% next year. What would be the expected percentage increase in net operating income? Use the degree of operating leverage concept to compute your answer.

PROBLEM 5-24 Break-Even and Target Profit Analysis [LO5, LO6]

The Marbury Stein Shop sells steins from all parts of the world. The owner of the shop, Clint Marbury, is thinking of expanding his operations by hiring local college students, on a commission basis, to sell steins at the local college. The steins will bear the school emblem.

These steins must be ordered from the manufacturer three months in advance, and because of the unique emblem of each college, they cannot be returned. The steins would cost Mr. Marbury $15 each with a minimum order of 200 steins. Any additional steins would have to be ordered in increments of 50.

Since Mr. Marbury's plan would not require any additional facilities, the only costs associated with the project would be the cost of the steins and the cost of sales commissions. The selling price of the steins would be $30 each. Mr. Marbury would pay the students a commission of $6 for each stein sold.

Required:

1. To make the project worthwhile in terms of his own time, Mr. Marbury would require a $7,200 profit for the first six months of the venture. What level of sales in units and dollars would be required to attain this target net operating income? Show all computations.
2. Assume that the venture is undertaken and an order is placed for 200 steins. What would be Mr. Marbury's break-even point in units and in sales dollars? Show computations, and explain the reasoning behind your answer.

PROBLEM 5-25 Sales Mix; Break-Even Analysis; Margin of Safety [LO7, LO9]

Puleva Milenario SA, a company located in Toledo, Spain, manufactures and sells two models of luxuriously finished cutlery—Alvaro and Bazan. Present revenue, cost, and unit sales data for the two products appear below. All currency amounts are stated in terms of euros, which are indicated by the symbol €.

	Alvaro	Bazan
Selling price per unit	€4.00	€6.00
Variable expenses per unit	€2.40	€1.20
Number of units sold monthly	200 units	80 units

Fixed expenses are €660 per month.

Required:

1. Assuming the sales mix above, do the following:
   a. Prepare a contribution format income statement showing both euro and percent columns for each product and for the company as a whole.
   b. Compute the break-even point in euros for the company as a whole and the margin of safety in both euros and percent of sales.
2. The company has developed another product, Cano, that the company plans to sell for €8 each. At this price, the company expects to sell 40 units per month of the product. The variable expense would be €6 per unit. The company's fixed expenses would not change.
   a. Prepare another contribution format income statement, including sales of Cano (sales of the other two products would not change).
   b. Compute the company's new break-even point in euros for the company as a whole and the new margin of safety in both euros and percent of sales.

3. The president of the company was puzzled by your analysis. He did not understand why the break-even point has gone up even though there has been no increase in fixed expenses and the addition of the new product has increased the total contribution margin. Explain to the president what has happened.

PROBLEM 5-26 Sales Mix; Multiproduct Break-Even Analysis [LO9]

Topper Sports, Inc., produces high-quality sports equipment. The company's Racket Division manufactures three tennis rackets—the Standard, the Deluxe, and the Pro—that are widely used in amateur play. Selected information on the rackets is given below:

	Standard	Deluxe	Pro
Selling price per racket	$40.00	$60.00	$90.00
Variable expenses per racket:			
Production	$22.00	$27.00	$31.50
Selling (5% of selling price)	$2.00	$3.00	$4.50

All sales are made through the company's own retail outlets. The Racket Division has the following fixed costs:

	Per Month
Fixed production costs.	$120,000
Advertising expense	100,000
Administrative salaries.	50,000
Total.	$270,000

Sales, in units, over the past two months have been as follows:

	Standard	Deluxe	Pro	Total
April	2,000	1,000	5,000	8,000
May	8,000	1,000	3,000	12,000

Required:

1. Using the contribution approach, prepare an income statement for April and an income statement for May, with the following headings:

	Standard		Deluxe		Pro		Total	
	Amount	Percent	Amount	Percent	Amount	Percent	Amount	Percent
Sales . . .								
Etc.								

   Place the fixed expenses only in the Total column. Do not show percentages for the fixed expenses.

2. Upon seeing the income statements in (1) above, the president stated, "I can't believe this! We sold 50% more rackets in May than in April, yet profits went down. It's obvious that costs are out of control in that division." What other explanation can you give for the drop in net operating income?
3. Compute the Racket Division's break-even point in dollar sales for April.
4. Has May's break-even point in dollar sales gone up or down from April's break-even point? Explain without computing a break-even point for May.

5. Assume that sales of the Standard racket increase by $20,000. What would be the effect on net operating income? What would be the effect if Pro racket sales increased by $20,000? Do not prepare income statements; use the incremental analysis approach in determining your answer.

PROBLEM 5-27 Various CVP Questions: Break-Even Point; Cost Structure; Target Sales [LO1, LO3, LO4, LO5, LO6, LO8]

Tyrene Products manufactures recreational equipment. One of the company's products, a skateboard, sells for $37.50. The skateboards are manufactured in an antiquated plant that relies heavily on direct labor workers. Thus, variable costs are high, totaling $22.50 per skateboard.

Over the past year the company sold 40,000 skateboards, with the following operating results:

Sales (40,000 skateboards)	$1,500,000
Variable expenses	900,000
Contribution margin	600,000
Fixed expenses	480,000
Net operating income	$ 120,000

Management is anxious to maintain and perhaps even improve its present level of income from the skateboards.

Required:

1. Compute (*a*) the CM ratio and the break-even point in skateboards, and (*b*) the degree of operating leverage at last year's level of sales.
2. Due to an increase in labor rates, the company estimates that variable costs will increase by $3 per skateboard next year. If this change takes place and the selling price per skateboard remains constant at $37.50, what will be the new CM ratio and the new break-even point in skateboards?
3. Refer to the data in (2) above. If the expected change in variable costs takes place, how many skateboards will have to be sold next year to earn the same net operating income ($120,000) as last year?
4. Refer again to the data in (2) above. The president has decided that the company may have to raise the selling price of its skateboards. If Tyrene Products wants to maintain *the same CM ratio as last year,* what selling price per skateboard must it charge next year to cover the increased labor costs?
5. Refer to the original data. The company is considering the construction of a new, automated plant. The new plant would slash variable costs by 40%, but it would cause fixed costs to increase by 90%. If the new plant is built, what would be the company's new CM ratio and new break-even point in skateboards?
6. Refer to the data in (5) above.
   a. If the new plant is built, how many skateboards will have to be sold next year to earn the same net operating income, $120,000, as last year?
   b. Assume that the new plant is constructed and that next year the company manufactures and sells 40,000 skateboards (the same number as sold last year). Prepare a contribution format income statement, and compute the degree of operating leverage.
   c. If you were a member of top management, would you have been in favor of constructing the new plant? Explain.

PROBLEM 5-28 Interpretive Questions on the CVP Graph [LO2, LO5]

A CVP graph, as illustrated on the next page, is a useful technique for showing relationships between an organization's costs, volume, and profits.

Required:

1. Identify the numbered components in the CVP graph.
2. State the effect of each of the following actions on line 3, line 9, and the break-even point. For line 3 and line 9, state whether the action will cause the line to:
   Remain unchanged.
   Shift upward.
   Shift downward.

Have a steeper slope (i.e., rotate upward).
Have a flatter slope (i.e., rotate downward).
Shift upward *and* have a steeper slope.

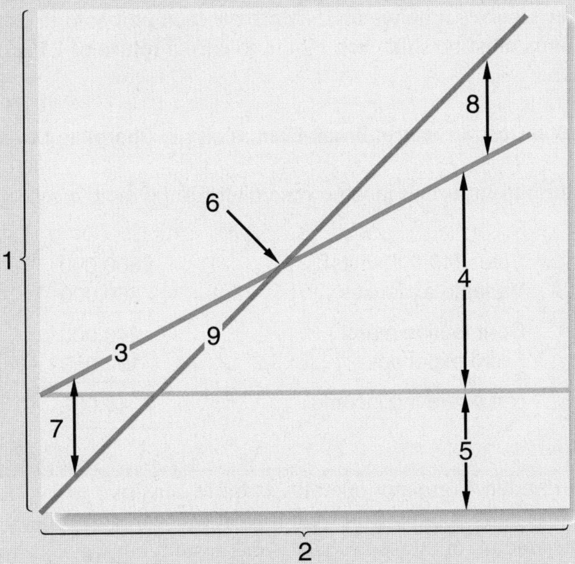

Shift upward *and* have a flatter slope.
Shift downward *and* have a steeper slope.
Shift downward *and* have a flatter slope.

In the case of the break-even point, state whether the action will cause the break-even point to:
Remain unchanged.
Increase.
Decrease.
Probably change, but the direction is uncertain.

Treat each case independently.

x. *Example*. Fixed costs are increased by $20,000 each period.
Answer (see choices above): Line 3: Shift upward.
Line 9: Remain unchanged.
Break-even point: Increase.

a. The unit selling price is decreased from $30 to $27.
b. The per unit variable costs are increased from $12 to $15.
c. The total fixed costs are reduced by $40,000.
d. Five thousand fewer units are sold during the period than were budgeted.
e. Due to purchasing a robot to perform a task that was previously done by workers, fixed costs are increased by $25,000 per period, and variable costs are reduced by $8 per unit.
f. As a result of a decrease in the cost of materials, both unit variable costs and the selling price are decreased by $3.
g. Advertising costs are increased by $50,000 per period, resulting in a 10% increase in the number of units sold.
h. Due to paying salespersons a commission rather than a flat salary, fixed costs are reduced by $21,000 per period, and unit variable costs are increased by $6.

PROBLEM 5-29 Changes in Fixed and Variable Costs; Break-Even and Target Profit Analysis [LO4, LO5, LO6]

Novelties, Inc., produces and sells highly faddish products directed toward the preteen market. A new product has come onto the market that the company is anxious to produce and sell. Enough capacity exists in the company's plant to produce 30,000 units each month. Variable costs to manufacture and sell one unit would be $1.60, and fixed costs would total $40,000 per month.

The Marketing Department predicts that demand for the product will exceed the 30,000 units that the company is able to produce. Additional production capacity can be rented from another company at a fixed cost of $2,000 per month. Variable costs in the rented facility would total $1.75 per unit, due to somewhat less efficient operations than in the main plant. The product would sell for $2.50 per unit.

Required:

1. Compute the monthly break-even point for the new product in units and in total dollar sales. Show all computations in good form.
2. How many units must be sold each month to make a monthly profit of $9,000?
3. If the sales manager receives a bonus of 15 cents for each unit sold in excess of the break-even point, how many units must be sold each month to earn a return of 25% on the monthly investment in fixed costs?

PROBLEM 5-30 Changes in Cost Structure; Break-Even Analysis; Operating Leverage; Margin of Safety [LO4, LO5, LO7, LO8]

Frieden Company's contribution format income statement for the most recent month is given below:

Sales (40,000 units)	$800,000
Variable expenses	560,000
Contribution margin	240,000
Fixed expenses	192,000
Net operating income	$ 48,000

The industry in which Frieden Company operates is quite sensitive to cyclical movements in the economy. Thus, profits vary considerably from year to year according to general economic conditions. The company has a large amount of unused capacity and is studying ways of improving profits.

Required:

1. New equipment has come on the market that would allow Frieden Company to automate a portion of its operations. Variable costs would be reduced by $6 per unit. However, fixed costs would increase to a total of $432,000 each month. Prepare two contribution format income statements, one showing present operations and one showing how operations would appear if the new equipment is purchased. Show an Amount column, a Per Unit column, and a Percent column on each statement. Do not show percentages for the fixed costs.
2. Refer to the income statements in (1) above. For both present operations and the proposed new operations, compute (*a*) the degree of operating leverage, (*b*) the break-even point in dollars, and (*c*) the margin of safety in both dollar and percentage terms.
3. Refer again to the data in (1) above. As a manager, what factor would be paramount in your mind in deciding whether to purchase the new equipment? (You may assume that ample funds are available to make the purchase.)
4. Refer to the original data. Rather than purchase new equipment, the marketing manager argues that the company's marketing strategy should be changed. Instead of paying sales commissions, which are included in variable expenses, the marketing manager suggests that salespersons be paid fixed salaries and that the company invest heavily in advertising. The marketing manager claims that this new approach would increase unit sales by 50% without any change in selling price; the company's new monthly fixed expenses would be $240,000; and its net operating income would increase by 25%. Compute the break-even point in dollar sales for the company under the new marketing strategy. Do you agree with the marketing manager's proposal?

Cases

CASE 5-31 Break-Evens for Individual Products in a Multiproduct Company [LO5, LO9]

Jasmine Park encountered her boss, Rick Gompers, at the pop machine in the lobby. Rick is the vice president of marketing at Down South Lures Corporation. Jasmine was puzzled by some calculations she had been doing, so she asked him:

Jasmine: "Rick, I'm not sure how to go about answering the questions that came up at the meeting with the president yesterday."

Rick: "What's the problem?"

Jasmine: "The president wanted to know the break even for each of the company's products, but I am having trouble figuring them out."

Rick: "I'm sure you can handle it, Jasmine. And, by the way, I need your analysis on my desk tomorrow morning at 8:00 sharp so I can look at it before the follow-up meeting at 9:00."

Down South Lures makes three fishing lures in its manufacturing facility in Alabama. Data concerning these products appear below.

	Frog	Minnow	Worm
Normal annual sales volume	100,000	200,000	300,000
Unit selling price	$2.00	$1.40	$0.80
Variable cost per unit	$1.20	$0.80	$0.50

Total fixed expenses for the entire company are $282,000 per year.

All three products are sold in highly competitive markets, so the company is unable to raise its prices without losing unacceptable numbers of customers.

The company has no work in process or finished goods inventories due to an extremely effective just-in-time manufacturing system.

Required:

1. What is the company's overall break-even point in total sales dollars?
2. Of the total fixed costs of $282,000, $18,000 could be avoided if the Frog lure product were dropped, $96,000 if the Minnow lure product were dropped, and $60,000 if the Worm lure product were dropped. The remaining fixed costs of $108,000 consist of common fixed costs such as administrative salaries and rent on the factory building that could be avoided only by going out of business entirely.
   a. What is the break-even point in units for each product?
   b. If the company sells exactly the break-even quantity of each product, what will be the overall profit of the company? Explain this result.

CASE 5-32 Cost Structure; Break-Even Point; Target Profits [LO4, LO5, LO6]

Marston Corporation manufactures disposable thermometers that are sold to hospitals through a network of independent sales agents located in the United States and Canada. These sales agents sell a variety of products to hospitals in addition to Marston's disposable thermometer. The sales agents are currently paid an 18% commission on sales, and this commission rate was used when Marston's management prepared the following budgeted income statement for the upcoming year.

Marston Corporation Budgeted Income Statement		
Sales		$30,000,000
Cost of goods sold:		
Variable	$17,400,000	
Fixed	2,800,000	20,200,000
Gross margin		9,800,000
Selling and administrative expenses:		
Commissions	5,400,000	
Fixed advertising expense	800,000	
Fixed administrative expense	3,200,000	9,400,000
Net operating income		$ 400,000

Since the completion of the above statement, Marston's management has learned that the independent sales agents are demanding an increase in the commission rate to 20% of sales for the upcoming year. This would be the third increase in commissions demanded by the independent sales agents in five years. As a result, Marston's management has decided to investigate the possibility of hiring its own sales staff to replace the independent sales agents.

Marston's controller estimates that the company will have to hire eight salespeople to cover the current market area, and the total annual payroll cost of these employees will be about $700,000, including fringe benefits. The salespeople will also be paid commissions of 10% of sales. Travel and entertainment expenses are expected to total about $400,000 for the year. The company will also have to hire a sales manager and support staff whose salaries and fringe benefits will come to $200,000 per year. To make up for the promotions that the independent sales agents had been running on behalf of Marston, management believes that the company's budget for fixed advertising expenses should be increased by $500,000.

Required:

1. Assuming sales of $30,000,000, construct a budgeted contribution format income statement for the upcoming year for each of the following alternatives:
   a. The independent sales agents' commission rate remains unchanged at 18%.
   b. The independent sales agents' commission rate increases to 20%.
   c. The company employs its own sales force.
2. Calculate Marston Corporation's break-even point in sales dollars for the upcoming year assuming the following:
   a. The independent sales agents' commission rate remains unchanged at 18%.
   b. The independent sales agents' commission rate increases to 20%.
   c. The company employs its own sales force.
3. Refer to your answer to (1)(b) above. If the company employs its own sales force, what volume of sales would be necessary to generate the net operating income the company would realize if sales are $30,000,000 and the company continues to sell through agents (at a 20% commission rate)?
4. Determine the volume of sales at which net operating income would be equal regardless of whether Marston Corporation sells through agents (at a 20% commission rate) or employs its own sales force.
5. Prepare a graph on which you plot the profits for both of the following alternatives.
   a. The independent sales agents' commission rate increases to 20%.
   b. The company employs its own sales force.
   On the graph, use total sales revenue as the measure of activity.
6. Write a memo to the president of Marston Corporation in which you make a recommendation as to whether the company should continue to use independent sales agents (at a 20% commission rate) or employ its own sales force. Fully explain the reasons for your recommendation in the memo.

(CMA, adapted)

CASE 5-33 Break-Even Analysis with Step Fixed Costs [LO5, LO6]

The Cardiac Care Department at St. Andrew's General Hospital has a capacity of 70 beds and operates 24 hours a day year-around. The measure of activity in the department is patient-days, where one patient-day represents one patient occupying a bed for one day. The average revenue per patient-day is $480 and the average variable cost per patient-day is $180. The fixed cost of the department (not including personnel costs) is $2,740,000.

The only personnel directly employed by the Cardiac Care Department are aides, nurses, and supervising nurses. The hospital has minimum staffing requirements for the department based on total annual patient-days in Cardiac Care. Hospital requirements, beginning at the minimum expected level of activity, follow:

Annual Patient-Days	Aides	Nurses	Supervising Nurses
10,000–12,000	7	15	3
12,001–13,750	8	15	3
13,751–16,500	9	16	4
16,501–18,250	10	16	4
18,251–20,750	10	17	5
20,751–23,000	11	18	5

These staffing levels represent full-time equivalents, and it should be assumed that the Cardiac Care Department always employs only the minimum number of required full-time equivalent personnel.

Average annual salaries for each class of employee are: aides, $36,000; nurses, $58,000; and supervising nurses, $76,000.

Required:

1. Compute the total fixed costs (including the salaries of aides, nurses, and supervising nurses) in the Cardiac Care Department for each level of activity shown above (i.e., total fixed costs at the 10,000–12,000 patient-day level of activity, total fixed costs at the 12,001–13,750 patient-day level of activity, etc.).

2. Compute the minimum number of patient-days required for the Cardiac Care Department to break even.
3. Determine the minimum number of patient-days required for the Cardiac Care Department to earn an annual "profit" of $720,000.

(CPA, adapted)

RESEARCH AND APPLICATION 5-34 [LO3, LO4, LO5, LO6, LO7, LO8, LO9]

The questions in this exercise are based on the Benetton Group, a company headquartered in Italy and known in the United States primarily for one of its brands of fashion apparel—United Colors of Benetton. To answer the questions, you will need to download the Benetton Group's 2004 Annual Report at www.benetton.com/investors. You do not need to print this document to answer the questions.

Required:

1. How do the formats of the income statements shown on pages 33 and 50 of Benetton's annual report differ from one another (disregard everything beneath the line titled "income from operations")? Which expenses shown on page 50 appear to have been reclassified as variable selling costs on page 33?
2. Why do you think cost of sales is included in the computation of contribution margin on page 33?
3. Perform two separate computations of Benetton's break-even point in euros. For the first computation, use data from 2003. For the second computation, use data from 2004. Why do the numbers that you computed differ from one another?
4. What sales volume would have been necessary in 2004 for Benetton to attain a target income from operations of €300 million?
5. Compute Benetton's margin of safety using data from 2003 and 2004. Why do your answers for the two years differ from one another?
6. What is Benetton's degree of operating leverage in 2004? If Benetton's sales in 2004 had been 6% higher than what is shown in the annual report, what income from operations would the company have earned? What percentage increase in income from operations does this represent?
7. What income from operations would Benetton have earned in 2004 if it had invested an additional €10 million in advertising and promotions and realized a 3% increase in sales? As an alternative, what income from operations would Benetton have earned if it not only invested an additional €10 million in advertising and promotions but also raised its sales commission rate to 6% of sales, thereby generating a 5% increase in sales? Which of these two scenarios would have been preferable for Benetton?
8. Assume that total sales in 2004 remained unchanged at €1,686 million (as shown on pages 33 and 50); however, the Casual sector sales were €1,554 million, the Sportswear and Equipment sector sales were €45million, and the Manufacturing and Other sector sales were €87 million. What income from operations would Benetton have earned with this sales mix? (Hint: look at pages 36 and 37 of the annual report.) Why is the income from operations under this scenario different from what is shown in the annual report?

Chapter 6

Learning Objectives

After studying Chapter 6, you should be able to:

LO1 Explain how variable costing differs from absorption costing and compute unit product costs under each method.

LO2 Prepare income statements using both variable and absorption costing.

LO3 Reconcile variable costing and absorption costing net operating incomes and explain why the two amounts differ.

LO4 Understand the advantages and disadvantages of both variable and absorption costing.

LP 6

Variable Costing: A Tool for Management

IBM's $2.5 Billion Investment in Technology

BUSINESS FOCUS

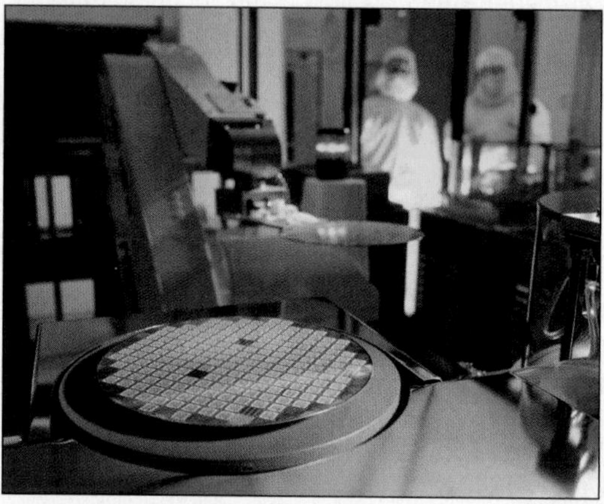

When it comes to state-of-the-art in automation, IBM's $2.5 billion semiconductor manufacturing facility in East Fishkill, New York, is tough to beat. The plant uses wireless networks, 600 miles of cable, and more than 420 servers to equip itself with what IBM claims is more computing power than NASA uses to launch a space shuttle.

Each batch of 25 wafers (one wafer can be processed into 1,000 computer chips) travels through the East Fishkill plant's manufacturing process without ever being touched by human hands. A computer system "looks at orders and schedules production runs . . . adjusts schedules to allow for planned maintenance and . . . feeds vast reams of production data into enterprise-wide management and financial-reporting systems." The plant can literally run itself as was the case a few years ago when a snowstorm hit and everyone went home while the automated system continued to manufacture computer chips until it ran out of work.

In a manufacturing environment such as this, labor costs are insignificant and fixed overhead costs are huge. There is a strong temptation to build inventories and increase profits without increasing sales. How can this be done you ask? It would seem logical that producing more units would have no impact on profits unless the units were sold, right? Wrong! As we will discover in this chapter, absorption costing—the most widely used method of determining product costs—can artificially increase profits by increasing the quantity of units produced. ■

Source: Ghostwriter, "Big Blue's $2.5 Billion Sales Tool," *Fortune,* September 19, 2005, pp. 316F–316J.

Two general approaches are used in manufacturing companies for costing products for the purposes of valuing inventories and cost of goods sold. One approach, called *absorption costing,* was discussed in Chapter 3. Absorption costing is generally used for external financial reports. The other approach, called *variable costing,* is preferred by some managers for internal decision making and must be used when an income statement is prepared in the contribution format. Ordinarily, absorption costing and variable costing produce different figures for net operating income, and the difference can be quite large. In addition to showing how these two methods differ, we will consider the arguments for and against each costing method and we will show how management decisions can be affected by the costing method chosen.

Overview of Absorption and Variable Costing

LEARNING OBJECTIVE 1
Explain how variable costing differs from absorption costing and compute unit product costs under each method.

As discussed in the last two chapters, the contribution format income statement and cost-volume-profit (CVP) analysis are valuable management tools. Both of these tools emphasize cost behavior and require that managers carefully distinguish between variable and fixed costs. Absorption costing, which was discussed in Chapters 2 and 3, assigns both variable and fixed manufacturing costs to products—mingling them in a way that makes it difficult for managers to distinguish between them. In contrast, variable costing focuses on *cost behavior*—clearly separating fixed from variable costs. One of the strengths of variable costing is that it harmonizes with both the contribution approach and the CVP concepts discussed in the preceding chapter.

Absorption Costing

Video 6–1

As discussed in Chapter 3, **absorption costing** treats *all* manufacturing costs as product costs, regardless of whether they are variable or fixed. The cost of a unit of product under the absorption costing method consists of direct materials, direct labor, and *both* variable and fixed manufacturing overhead. Thus, absorption costing allocates a portion of fixed manufacturing overhead cost to each unit of product, along with the variable manufacturing costs. Because absorption costing includes all manufacturing costs in product costs, it is frequently referred to as the *full cost* method.

Variable Costing

Under **variable costing,** only those manufacturing costs that vary with output are treated as product costs. This would usually include direct materials, direct labor, and the variable portion of manufacturing overhead. Fixed manufacturing overhead is not treated as a product cost under this method. Rather, fixed manufacturing overhead is treated as a period cost and, like selling and administrative expenses, it is expensed in its entirety each period. Consequently, the cost of a unit of product in inventory or in cost of goods sold under the variable costing method does not contain any fixed manufacturing overhead cost. Variable costing is sometimes referred to as *direct costing* or *marginal costing.*

Selling and Administrative Expense

To complete this summary comparison of absorption and variable costing, we need to briefly consider the handling of selling and administrative expenses. These expenses are never treated as product costs, regardless of the costing method. Thus, under absorption and variable costing, variable and fixed selling and administrative expenses are always treated as period costs and are expensed as incurred.

Exhibit 6–1 summarizes the classification of costs under both absorption and variable costing.

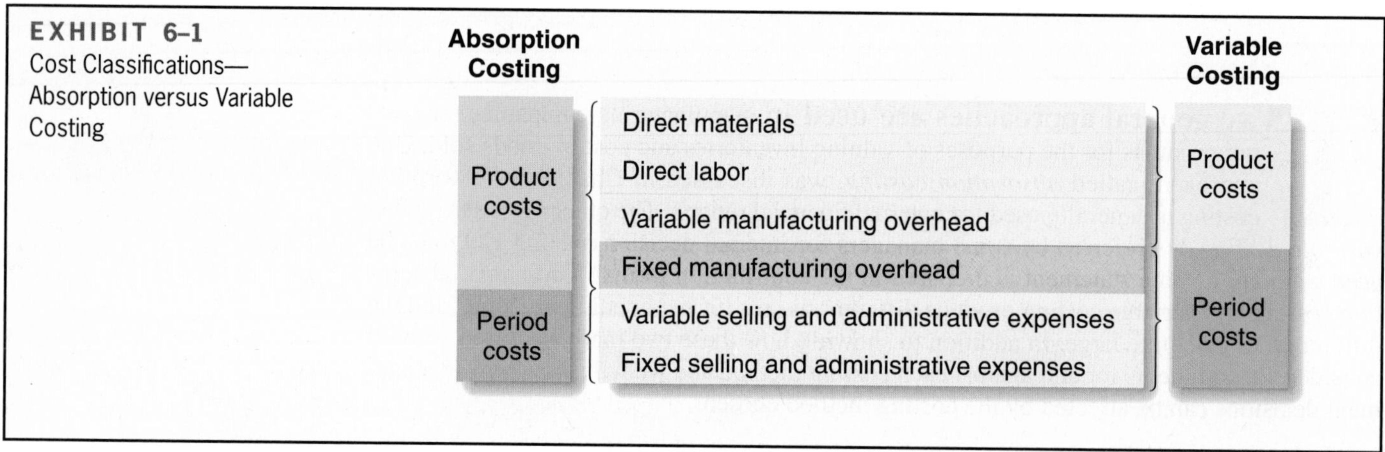

EXHIBIT 6–1
Cost Classifications—Absorption versus Variable Costing

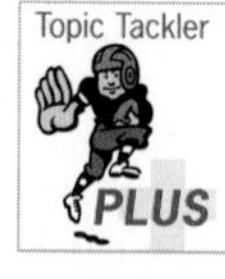

6–1

Unit Cost Computations

To illustrate the computation of unit product costs under both absorption and variable costing, consider Boley Company, a small company that produces a single product and that has the following cost structure:

Number of units produced each year	6,000
Variable costs per unit:	
Direct materials	$2
Direct labor	$4
Variable manufacturing overhead	$1
Variable selling and administrative expenses	$3
Fixed costs per year:	
Fixed manufacturing overhead	$30,000
Fixed selling and administrative expenses	$10,000

Required:

1. Compute the unit product cost under absorption costing.
2. Compute the unit product cost under variable costing.

Solution

Absorption Costing	
Direct materials	$ 2
Direct labor	4
Variable manufacturing overhead	1
Total variable manufacturing cost	7
Fixed manufacturing overhead ($30,000 ÷ 6,000 units of product)	5
Unit product cost	$12
Variable Costing	
Direct materials	$ 2
Direct labor	4
Variable manufacturing overhead	1
Unit product cost	$ 7

(Under variable costing, the $30,000 fixed manufacturing overhead is a period expense along with selling and administrative expenses.)

Under the absorption costing method, *all* manfacturing costs, variable and fixed, are included when determining the unit product cost. Thus, if the company sells a unit of product and absorption costing is being used, then $12 (consisting of $7 variable cost and $5 fixed cost) will be deducted on the income statement as cost of goods sold. Similarly, any unsold units will be carried as inventory on the balance sheet at $12 each.

Under the variable costing method, only the variable manfacturing costs are included in product costs. Thus, if the company sells a unit of product, only $7 will be deducted as cost of goods sold, and unsold units will be carried as inventory on the balance sheet at only $7 each.

IN BUSINESS

THE BEHAVIORAL SIDE OF CALCULATING UNIT PRODUCT COSTS

In 2004, Andreas STIHL, a manufacturer of chain saws and other landscaping products, asked its U.S. subsidiary, STIHL Inc., to replace its absorption costing income statements with the variable costing approach. From a computer systems standpoint, the change was not disruptive because STIHL used an enterprise system called SAP that accommodates both absorption and variable costing. However, from a behavioral standpoint, STIHL felt the change could be very disruptive. For example, STIHL's senior managers were keenly aware that the variable costing approach reported lower unit product costs than the absorption costing approach. Given this reality, the sales force might be inclined to erroneously conclude that each product had magically become more profitable, thereby justifying ill-advised price reductions. Because of behavioral concerns such as this, STIHL worked hard to educate its employees how to interpret a variable costing income statement.

Source: Carl S. Smith, "Going for GPK: STIHL Moves Toward This Costing System in the United States," *Strategic Finance*, April 2005, pp. 36–39.

IN BUSINESS

SCRUTINIZING VARIABLE MANUFACTURING COSTS AT FORD

Jim Padilla, the chief operating officer at the Ford Motor Company, believes in ranking vehicles by the amount of contribution margin earned. In other words, for internal decision-making purposes he views direct materials, direct labor, and variable manufacturing overhead as product costs and fixed manufacturing overhead as a period cost. Historically, Ford has been willing to sell small cars that get good gas mileage at a loss to boost the company's average fuel economy and air-pollution emission ratings. Padilla is committed to scaling back this practice. He believes the company should give serious consideration to discontinuing any car that cannot generate enough sales to cover its variable production costs.

Source: Alex Taylor III, "Bill's Brand-New Ford," *Fortune*, June 28, 2004, pp. 68–76.

Income Comparison of Absorption and Variable Costing

LEARNING OBJECTIVE 2
Prepare income statements using both variable and absorption costing.

Exhibit 6–2 displays income statements prepared under the absorption and variable costing approaches. In preparing these statements, we use the data for Boley Company presented earlier, along with other information about the company as given below:

Units in beginning inventory	0
Units produced	6,000
Units sold	5,000
Units in ending inventory	1,000
Selling price per unit	$20
Selling and administrative expenses:	
Variable per unit	$3
Fixed per year	$10,000

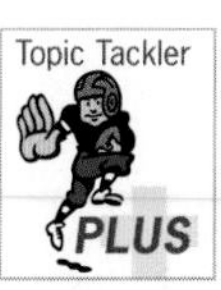

6–2

EXHIBIT 6–2
Comparison of Absorption and Variable Costing—Boley Company

Absorption Costing		
Sales (5,000 units × $20 per unit)		$100,000
Cost of goods sold:		
Beginning inventory	$ 0	
Add cost of goods manufactured (6,000 units × $12 per unit)	72,000	
Goods available for sale	72,000	
Less ending inventory (1,000 units × $12 per unit)	12,000	
Cost of goods sold		60,000
Gross margin		40,000
Selling and administrative expenses: (5,000 units × $3 per unit variable + $10,000 fixed)		25,000
Net operating income		$ 15,000
Variable Costing		
Sales (5,000 units × $20 per unit)		$100,000
Variable expenses:		
Variable cost of goods sold:		
Beginning inventory	$ 0	
Add variable manufacturing costs (6,000 units × $7 per unit)	42,000	
Goods available for sale	42,000	
Less ending inventory (1,000 units × $7 per unit)	7,000	
Variable cost of goods sold	35,000	
Variable selling and administrative expenses (5,000 units × $3 per unit)	15,000	50,000
Contribution margin		50,000
Fixed expenses:		
Fixed manufacturing overhead	30,000	
Fixed selling and administrative expenses	10,000	40,000
Net operating income		$ 10,000

Note the difference in ending inventories. Fixed manufacturing overhead cost at $5 per unit is included under the absorption approach. This explains the difference in ending inventory and in net operating income (1,000 units × $5 per unit = $5,000).

Several observations should be made concerning the income statements in Exhibit 6–2. First, the net operating incomes under the two costing methods are not the same. The net operating income under absorption costing is higher than under variable costing by $5,000. Why is this? Under absorption costing, each of the units produced during the period is assigned $5 of fixed manufacturing overhead cost (see the unit cost computations on page 210). This is true of the 1,000 units in ending inventory as well as the 5,000 units that were sold. Consequently, the ending inventory under absorption costing contains $5,000 of fixed manufacturing overhead and the cost of goods sold contains $25,000 of fixed manufacturing overhead. In contrast, the entire $30,000 of fixed manufacturing overhead is expensed under variable costing. As a direct result, the net operating income under variable costing is $5,000 lower than under absorption costing. In effect, the $5,000 of fixed manufacturing overhead in ending inventory under absorption costing is deferred to the future period in which these units are sold. This $5,000 of fixed manufacturing overhead cost in the ending inventory is referred to as **fixed manufacturing overhead cost deferred in inventory.** In general, under absorption costing, when inventories increase, some of the fixed manufacturing costs of the current period are reported on the balance sheet as part of the ending inventories rather than on the income statement as part of cost of goods sold.

Second, the absorption costing income statement makes no distinction between fixed and variable costs—a distinction that is crucial for CVP analysis and for much of the planning and control concepts discussed in later chapters. It is difficult or even impossible to determine from an absorption costing income statement which costs are variable and which are fixed. In contrast, on a variable costing income statement the fixed and variable costs are explicitly identified—making CVP analysis far easier.

The difference between the absorption and variable costing approaches to accounting for fixed manufacturing costs centers on timing. Advocates of variable costing say that fixed manufacturing costs should be expensed immediately in total, whereas advocates of absorption costing say that fixed manufacturing costs should be charged against revenues gradually as units of product are sold. Any units of product not sold under absorption costing result in fixed manfacturing costs being inventoried and carried forward on the balance sheet *as assets* to the next period.

The following discussion of Emerald Isle Knitters expands on the discussion of the absorption and variable costing approaches to accounting for fixed manufacturing costs.

Extended Comparison of Income Data

MANAGERIAL ACCOUNTING IN ACTION
The Issue

Mary O'Meara is the owner and manager of Emerald Isle Knitters, Ltd., located in the Republic of Ireland. Mary started the company three years ago with cash loaned to her by a local bank. The company, which has only 10 employees, manufactures a traditional wool fisherman's sweater from a pattern Mary learned from her grandmother. Like most apparel manufacturers, Emerald Isle Knitters sells its product to department stores and clothing store chains rather than to retail customers.

The sweater was an immediate success, and the company sold all of its first year's production. However, in the second year of operations, one of the company's major customers canceled its order due to bankruptcy, and the company ended the year with a large inventory of unsold sweaters. The third year of operations was a great year in contrast to the disastrous second year. Sales rebounded dramatically, and all of the unsold production carried over from the second year was sold by the end of the third year.

Shortly after the close of the third year, Mary met with her accountant Sean MacLafferty to discuss the results for the year. (Note: All of the company's business is transacted using the euro, denoted by €, as the currency. The euro is the common currency of many member countries of the European Union.)

Mary: Sean, I am confused! Last year, we reported a net operating income of €30,000, which was higher than I expected given the big order that was cancelled by a major customer. This year we reported a net operating income of €90,000, which is lower than I expected given our dramatic rebound in sales. My intuition in terms of predicting our financial performance has been dead wrong for two years in a row. What's going on?

Sean: I think the source of confusion is the rules of financial accounting that we must follow when preparing financial statements for the bank. I have always felt that complying with these rules may be necessary for external reporting purposes, but that relying on them for internal decision-making purposes is misleading.

Mary: What other options do we have? Frankly, I have always assumed that there is only one way to prepare an income statement.

Sean: Most people make the same assumption. However, when it comes to internal reporting, we can use another income statement approach that I think you'll find more intuitive. How about if I prepare income statements for the last three years using what is called the variable costing approach and we'll compare them to the income statements that we have been using for the bank—which, by the way, are called absorption costing income statements. You can compare the two sets of numbers and decide which approach you prefer.

Mary: Sounds good. Let me know when you are ready to meet again.

EXHIBIT 6–3
Basic Data for Absorption and Variable Costing Income Statements—Emerald Isle Knitters, Ltd.

Basic Data	
Selling price per unit sold	€20
Variable manufacturing cost per unit produced	€7
Fixed manufacturing overhead costs per year	€150,000
Variable selling and administrative expenses per unit sold	€1
Fixed selling and administrative expenses per year	€90,000

	Year 1	Year 2	Year 3	Three Years Together
Units in beginning inventory	0	0	5,000	0
Units produced	25,000	25,000	25,000	75,000
Units sold	25,000	20,000	30,000	75,000
Units in ending inventory	0	5,000	0	0

Unit Product Costs	Year 1	Year 2	Year 3
Under variable costing (variable manufacturing costs only)	€7	€7	€7
Under absorption costing:			
Variable manufacturing costs	€7	€7	€7
Fixed manufacturing overhead costs (€150,000 spread over the number of units produced in each year)	6	6	6
Total absorption cost per unit	€13	€13	€13

LEARNING OBJECTIVE 3
Reconcile variable costing and absorption costing net operating incomes and explain why the two amounts differ.

Immediately after the meeting with Mary, Sean put together the data and financial reports that appear in Exhibit 6–3. (All financial statements have been reformatted to be closer to U.S. standards.)

The basic data needed to prepare both income statements appear in Exhibit 6–3. The absorption costing income statements as reported to the bank for the last three years appear in the top half of Exhibit 6–4. The variable costing income statements that Sean prepared for the last three years appear in the bottom half of Exhibit 6–4.

Note that Emerald Isle Knitters maintained a steady rate of production of 25,000 sweaters per year. However, sales varied from year to year. In Year 1, production and sales were equal. In Year 2, production exceeded sales due to the canceled order. In Year 3, sales recovered and exceeded production. As a consequence, inventories did not change during Year 1, inventories increased during Year 2, and inventories decreased during Year 3. The change in inventories during the year is the key to understanding how absorption costing differs from variable costing. Note that when inventories increase in Year 2, absorption costing net operating income exceeds variable costing net operating income. When inventories decrease in Year 3, the opposite occurs—variable costing net operating income exceeds absorption costing net operating income. And when inventories do not change as in Year 1, there is no difference in net operating income between the two methods. Why is this? The reasons are discussed below and are briefly summarized in Exhibit 6–5.[1]

1. When production and sales are equal, as in Year 1 for Emerald Isle Knitters, net operating income will generally be the same regardless of whether absorption or variable costing is used. The reason is as follows: The *only* difference that can exist between absorption and variable costing net operating income is the amount of fixed manufacturing

[1] The discussions in this chapter concerning differences between absorption and variable costing net operating incomes assume that the LIFO inventory flow assumption is used.

EXHIBIT 6–4
Absorption and Variable Costing Income Statements—Emerald Isle Knitters, Ltd.

	Year 1		Year 2		Year 3		Three Years Together	
Absorption Costing								
Sales		€500,000		€400,000		€600,000		€1,500,000
Cost of goods sold:								
Beginning inventory	€ 0		€ 0		€ 65,000		€ 0	
Add cost of goods manufactured (25,000 units × €13 per unit)	325,000		325,000		325,000		975,000	
Goods available for sale	325,000		325,000		390,000		975,000	
Less ending inventory (5,000 units × €13 per unit)	0		65,000		0		0	
Cost of goods sold		325,000		260,000		390,000		975,000
Gross margin		175,000		140,000		210,000		525,000
Selling and administrative expenses		115,000*		110,000*		120,000*		345,000
Net operating income		€ 60,000		€ 30,000		€ 90,000		€ 180,000

*The selling and administrative expenses are computed as follows:
Year 1: 25,000 units × €1 per unit variable + €90,000 fixed = €115,000.
Year 2: 20,000 units × €1 per unit variable + €90,000 fixed = €110,000.
Year 3: 30,000 units × €1 per unit variable + €90,000 fixed = €120,000.

	Year 1		Year 2		Year 3		Three Years Together	
Variable Costing								
Sales		€500,000		€400,000		€600,000		€1,500,000
Variable expenses:								
Variable cost of goods sold:								
Beginning inventory	€ 0		€ 0		€ 35,000		€ 0	
Add variable manufacturing costs (25,000 units × €7 per unit)	175,000		175,000		175,000		525,000	
Goods available for sale	175,000		175,000		210,000		525,000	
Less ending inventory (5,000 units × €7 per unit)	0		35,000		0		0	
Variable cost of goods sold	175,000*		140,000*		210,000*		525,000	
Variable selling and administrative expenses (€1 per unit *sold*)	25,000	200,000	20,000	160,000	30,000	240,000	75,000	600,000
Contribution margin		300,000		240,000		360,000		900,000
Fixed expenses:								
Fixed manufacturing overhead	150,000		150,000		150,000		450,000	
Fixed selling and administrative expenses	90,000	240,000	90,000	240,000	90,000	240,000	270,000	720,000
Net operating income		€ 60,000		€ 0		€120,000		€ 180,000

*The variable cost of goods sold could have been computed more simply as follows:
Year 1: 25,000 units sold × €7 per unit = €175,000.
Year 2: 20,000 units sold × €7 per unit = €140,000.
Year 3: 30,000 units sold × €7 per unit = €210,000.

EXHIBIT 6–5
Comparative Income Effects—Absorption and Variable Costing

Relation between Production and Sales for the Period	Effect on Inventories	Relation between Absorption and Variable Costing Net Operating Incomes
Production = Sales	No change in inventories	Absorption costing net operating income = Variable costing net operating income
Production > Sales	Inventories increase	Absorption costing net operating income > Variable costing net operating income*
Production < Sales	Inventories decrease	Absorption costing net operating income < Variable costing net operating income†

*Net operating income is higher under absorption costing, since fixed manufacturing overhead cost is *deferred* in inventory under absorption costing as inventories increase.
†Net operating income is lower under absorption costing, since fixed manufacturing overhead cost is *released* from inventory under absorption costing as inventories decrease.

overhead recognized as expense on the income statement. When everything that is produced in the year is sold, all of the fixed manufacturing overhead assigned to units of product under absorption costing becomes part of the current year's cost of goods sold. Under variable costing, the total fixed manufacturing overhead flows directly to the income statement as an expense. So under either method, when production equals sales (and hence inventories do not change), all the fixed manufacturing overhead incurred during the year flows through to the income statement as an expense. And therefore, the net operating income under the two methods is the same.

2. When production exceeds sales, the net operating income reported under absorption costing will generally be higher than the net operating income reported under variable costing (see Year 2 in Exhibit 6–4). This occurs because under absorption costing, part of the fixed manufacturing overhead cost of the current period is deferred in inventory. In Year 2, for example, €30,000 of fixed manufacturing overhead cost (5,000 units × €6 per unit) has been applied to units in ending inventory. These costs are excluded from cost of goods sold.

   Under variable costing, however, *all* of the fixed manufacturing overhead cost of Year 2 has been immediately expensed. As a result, the net operating income for Year 2 under variable costing is €30,000 *lower* than it is under absorption costing. Exhibit 6–6

EXHIBIT 6–6
Reconciliation of Variable Costing and Absorption Costing—Net Operating Income Data from Exhibit 6–4

	Year 1	Year 2	Year 3
Variable costing net operating income	€60,000	€ 0	€120,000
Add fixed manufacturing overhead costs deferred in inventory under absorption costing (5,000 units × €6 per unit)		30,000	
Deduct fixed manufacturing overhead costs released from inventory under absorption costing (5,000 units × €6 per unit)			(30,000)
Absorption costing net operating income	€60,000	€30,000	€ 90,000

contains a reconciliation of the variable costing and absorption costing net operating incomes.

3. When production is less than sales, the net operating income reported under the absorption costing approach will generally be less than the net operating income reported under the variable costing approach (see Year 3 in Exhibit 6–4). This happens with absorption costing because fixed manufacturing overhead costs that were previously deferred in the prior period's inventory are released as part of the current period's cost of goods sold. This is known as **fixed manufacturing overhead cost released from inventory.** In Year 3, for example, the €30,000 in fixed manufacturing overhead cost deferred in inventory under the absorption approach from Year 2 to Year 3 is released from inventory because these units were sold. As a result, the cost of goods sold for Year 3 contains not only all of the fixed manufacturing overhead cost for Year 3 (since all that was produced in Year 3 was sold in Year 3) but €30,000 of fixed manufacturing overhead cost from Year 2 as well.

   By contrast, under variable costing only the fixed manufacturing overhead cost of Year 3 have been charged against Year 3. The result is that net operating income under variable costing is €30,000 *higher* than it is under absorption costing. Exhibit 6–6 contains a reconciliation of the variable costing and absorption costing net operating incomes for Year 3.

4. Over an *extended* period of time, the cumulative net operating incomes reported under absorption costing and variable costing will tend to be the same. The reason is that over the long run sales can't exceed production, nor can production much exceed sales. The shorter the time period, the more the net operating incomes will tend to differ.

IN BUSINESS

THE HOUSE OF CARDS AT GILLETTE

Alfred M. Zeien was the successful CEO of Gillette Co. for eight years, leading the company to earnings growth rates of 15% to 20% per year. However, as his successor discovered, some of this profit growth was an illusion based on building inventories. William H. Steele, an analyst with Bank of America Securities, alleges: "There is no question Gillette was making its numbers (in part) by aggressively selling to the trade, and building inventories." Within a three-year period, Gillette's inventories of finished goods had increased by over 40% (to $1.3 billion) even though Gillette's sales had barely increased.

How can building inventories increase profits without any increase in sales? It's fairly simple. When a company produces more units than it sells fixed manufacturing overhead is deferred in ending inventory, thereby increasing profits.

Source: William C. Symonds, "The Big Trim at Gillette," *BusinessWeek*, November 8, 1999, p. 42.

Effect of Changes in Production on Net Operating Income

Video 6–1

In the Emerald Isle Knitters example in the preceding section, production was constant and sales fluctuated over the three-year period. Since sales fluctuated, the income statements Sean MacLafferty presented in Exhibit 6–4 allowed us to see the effect of changes in sales on net operating income under both variable and absorption costing.

To further investigate the differences between variable and absorption costing, Sean next put together the hypothetical example in Exhibit 6–7. In this hypothetical example, sales are constant and production fluctuates (the opposite of Exhibits 6–3 and 6–4). The purpose of Exhibit 6–7 and the income statements shown in Exhibit 6–8 is to illustrate for Mary O'Meara the effect of changes in *production* on net operating income under both variable and absorption costing.

EXHIBIT 6–7
Basic Data to Demonstrate the Sensitivity of Costing Methods to Changes in Production

Basic Data			
Selling price per unit sold			€20
Variable manufacturing cost per unit produced			€7
Fixed manufacturing overhead costs per year			€150,000
Variable selling and administrative expenses per unit sold			€1
Fixed selling and administrative expenses per year			€90,000
	Year 1	Year 2	Year 3
Units in beginning inventory	0	0	5,000
Units produced	25,000	30,000	20,000
Units sold	25,000	25,000	25,000
Units in ending inventory	0	5,000	0
Unit Product Costs	Year 1	Year 2	Year 3
Under variable costing (variable manufacturing costs only)	€ 7.00	€ 7.00	€ 7.00
Under absorption costing			
Variable manufacturing costs	€ 7.00	€ 7.00	€ 7.00
Fixed manufacturing overhead costs (€150,000 spread over the number of units produced in each year)	6.00	5.00	7.50
Total absorption cost per unit	€13.00	€12.00	€14.50

Variable Costing

Net operating income is *not* affected by changes in production under variable costing. Notice from Exhibit 6–8 that net operating income is the same for all three years under variable costing, although production exceeds sales in one year and is less than sales in another year. In short, a change in production has no impact on net operating income when variable costing is used.

Absorption Costing

Net operating income *is* affected by changes in production under absorption costing. As shown in Exhibit 6–8, net operating income under absorption costing goes up in Year 2 and then goes down in Year 3. Note particularly that net operating income goes up and down between these two years *even though the same number of units is sold in each year.* The reason for this effect can be traced to fixed manufacturing overhead costs that shift between periods under absorption costing as a result of changes in inventory.

As shown in Exhibit 6–7, production exceeds sales in Year 2, resulting in an increase of 5,000 units in inventory. Each unit produced during Year 2 is assigned €5 in fixed manufacturing overhead costs (see the unit cost computations in Exhibit 6–7). Therefore, €25,000 (5,000 units × €5 per unit) of the fixed manufacturing overhead costs of Year 2 are not expensed in that year but rather are added to the inventory account (along with the variable manufacturing costs). The net operating income of Year 2 rises sharply, because these costs are deferred in inventories, even though the same number of units is sold in Year 2 as in the other years.

The reverse effect occurs in Year 3. Since sales exceed production in Year 3, that year is forced to cover all of its own fixed manufacturing overhead costs as well as the fixed manufacturing overhead costs carried forward in inventory from Year 2. A substantial drop in net operating income during Year 3 results from the release of fixed manufacturing overhead costs from inventories despite the fact that the same number of units is sold in that year as in the other years.

EXHIBIT 6–8

Absorption and Variable Costing Income Statements—Changes in Production Scenario.

	Year 1		Year 2		Year 3	
Absorption Costing						
Sales (25,000 units)		€500,000		€500,000		€500,000
Cost of goods sold:						
Beginning inventory	€ 0		€ 0		€ 60,000	
Add cost of goods manufactured	325,000*		360,000*		290,000*	
Goods available for sale	325,000		360,000		350,000	
Less ending inventory	0		60,000†		0	
Cost of goods sold		325,000		300,000		350,000
Gross margin		175,000		200,000		150,000
Selling and administrative expenses (25,000 units × €1 per unit variable + €90,000 fixed)		115,000		115,000		115,000
Net operating income		€ 60,000		€ 85,000		€ 35,000

*Cost of goods manufactured:
Year 1: 25,000 units × €13.00 per unit = €325,000.
Year 2: 30,000 units × €12.00 per unit = €360,000.
Year 3: 20,000 units × €14.50 per unit = €290,000.
†Ending inventory, Year 2: 5,000 units × €12 per unit = €60,000.

	Year 1		Year 2		Year 3	
Variable Costing						
Sales (25,000 units)		€500,000		€500,000		€500,000
Variable expenses:						
Variable cost of goods sold:						
Beginning inventory	€ 0		€ 0		€ 35,000	
Add variable manufacturing costs at €7 per unit produced	175,000		210,000		140,000	
Goods available for sale	175,000		210,000		175,000	
Less ending inventory	0		35,000*		0	
Variable cost of goods sold	175,000		175,000		175,000	
Variable selling and administrative expenses	25,000	200,000	25,000	200,000	25,000	200,000
Contribution margin		300,000		300,000		300,000
Fixed expenses:						
Fixed manufacturing overhead	150,000		150,000		150,000	
Fixed selling and administrative expenses	90,000	240,000	90,000	240,000	90,000	240,000
Net operating income		€ 60,000		€ 60,000		€ 60,000

*Ending inventory, Year 2: 5,000 units × €7 per unit = €35,000.

EXHIBIT 6–9
Reconciliation of Variable Costing and Absorption Costing—Net Operating Income Data from Exhibit 6–8

	Year 1	Year 2	Year 3
Variable costing net operating income	€60,000	€60,000	€60,000
Add fixed manufacturing overhead costs deferred in inventory under absorption costing (5,000 units × €5 per unit)		25,000	
Deduct fixed manufacturing overhead costs released from inventory under absorption costing (5,000 units × €5 per unit).			(25,000)
Absorption costing net operating income	€60,000	€85,000	€35,000

The variable costing and absorption costing net operating incomes are reconciled in Exhibit 6–9. This exhibit shows that the differences in net operating income can be traced to the effects of changes in inventories on absorption costing net operating income. Under absorption costing, fixed manufacturing overhead costs are deferred in inventory when inventories increase and are released from inventory when inventories decrease.

IN BUSINESS

eBAY EASES THE PAIN OF EXCESS INVENTORY

Companies can accumulate excess inventory for numerous reasons. For example, overly optimistic sales forecasts can result in too much inventory. Or, as we have learned in this chapter, managers can inflate absorption costing net income by producing excess inventory. Regardless of the cause, eBay is coming to the rescue of companies whose warehouses are bursting at the seams. More than 71 companies, including Motorola, Dell, and IBM, are selling outdated inventory using eBay's auction services. Using eBay enables these companies to recoup 45% of the product's usual selling price compared to 15–20% using other disposal methods. eBay estimates that big company sales on its website now total $500 million a year. In fact, eBay reports that Motorola alone unloads $1 million of outdated cell phones per month.

Source: Brian Grow and Sheridan Prasso, "Excess Inventory? eBay to the Rescue," *BusinessWeek*, September 9, 2002, p. 8.

MANAGERIAL ACCOUNTING IN ACTION
The Wrap-up

After checking all of his work, Sean discussed his results with Mary.

Sean: I have some calculations I would like to show you. These exhibits should help explain why our net operating income didn't increase this year as much as you thought it should have.

Mary: This first exhibit (i.e., Exhibit 6–4) looks like it just summarizes our income statements for the last three years.

Sean: Not exactly. There are actually two sets of income statements on this exhibit. The absorption costing income statements are the ones I originally prepared and we submitted to the bank. Below the absorption costing income statements is another set of income statements.

Mary: Those are the ones labeled variable costing.

Sean: That's right. You can see that the net operating incomes are the same for the two sets of income statements in our first year of operations, but they differ for the other two years.

Mary: I'll say! The variable costing statements indicate that we just broke even in the second year instead of earning a €30,000 profit. And the increase in net operating income between the second and third years is €120,000 instead of just €60,000. I don't know how you came up with two different net operating income figures, but the variable costing net operating income seems to be much closer to the truth. The second year was almost a disaster. We barely sold enough sweaters to cover all of our fixed costs.

Sean: You and I both know that, but the accounting rules view the situation a little differently. If we produce more than we sell, the accounting rules require that we take some of the fixed manufacturing cost and assign it to the units that end up on the balance sheet in ending inventories.

Mary: That surprises me given that I thought accountants were always supposed to err on the side of being conservative. Since when is it conservative to call an expense an asset?

Sean: While I tend to agree with you, some accountants would argue otherwise because . . .

Mary: Honestly, I am not interested in the various arguments. All I know is that we don't make any money just producing sweaters. If absorption costing lets a company boost its net operating income by making more sweaters—and not selling any of them—that makes no sense to me.

Sean: Me neither.

Mary: Well, if our bank wants us to use absorption costing, then that is what we'll continue to do for it. However, is there any reason why we can't use the variable costing method inside the company? The statements are easier for me to understand, and the net operating income figures make more sense to me.

Sean: I don't see why we can't do both. Making the adjustment from one method to the other is very simple.

Mary: Good. Let's make the switch.

Choosing a Costing Method

The Impact on the Manager

LEARNING OBJECTIVE 4
Understand the advantages and disadvantages of both variable and absorption costing.

Like Mary O'Meara, opponents of absorption costing argue that shifting fixed manufacturing overhead cost between periods can be confusing and can lead to misinterpretations and even to faulty decisions. Look again at the data in Exhibit 6–8; a manager might wonder why net operating income went up substantially in Year 2 under absorption costing when sales remained the same as in the prior year. Was it a result of lower selling costs, more efficient operations, or was some other factor involved? One cannot say by simply looking at the absorption costing income statement. Then in Year 3, net operating income drops sharply, even though the same number of units is sold as in the other two years. Why would income rise in one year and then drop in the next? The figures seem erratic and contradictory and can lead to confusion and a loss of confidence in the integrity of the financial data.

By contrast, the variable costing income statements in Exhibit 6–8 are clear and easy to understand. Sales remain constant over the three-year period covered in the exhibit, so both contribution margin and net operating income also remain constant. The statements are consistent with what managers would expect to see under the circumstances, so they tend to generate confidence rather than confusion.

To avoid mistakes when absorption costing is used, readers of financial statements should be alert to changes in inventory levels. Under absorption costing, if inventories increase, fixed manufacturing overhead costs are deferred in inventories, which in turn increases net operating income. If inventories decrease, fixed manufacturing overhead costs are released from inventories, which in turn decreases net operating income. Thus, when absorption costing is used, fluctuations in net operating income can be due to changes in inventories rather than to changes in sales.

IN BUSINESS

THE PERVERSE EFFECTS OF ABSORPTION COSTING AT NISSAN

Jed Connelly, the top American executive at Nissan North America, admits: "We had a lot of excess production that we had to force on the market." Nissan liked to run its factories at capacity, regardless of how well the cars were selling, because under its bookkeeping rules (presumably absorption costing), the factories would then generate a profit. As a consequence, Nissan dealers had to slash prices and offer big rebates to sell their cars. According to *Fortune* magazine, "Years of discounting and distress sales seriously undercut the value of the Nissan brand. While Toyota stood for quality, customers came to Nissan to get a better deal."

Source: Alex Taylor III, "The Man Who Wants to Change Japan Inc.," *Fortune*, December 20, 1999, pp. 189–198.

CVP Analysis and Absorption Costing

Absorption costing is widely used for both internal and external reports. Many companies use the absorption approach exclusively because of its focus on *full* costing of units of product. A weakness of the method, however, is its inability to work well with CVP analysis.

To illustrate, refer again to Exhibit 6–3. Let us compute the break-even point for Emerald Isle Knitters. To obtain the break-even point, we divide total fixed costs by the contribution margin per unit:

Selling price per unit	€ 20
Variable costs per unit (manufacturing and selling)	8
Contribution margin per unit	€ 12
Fixed manufacturing overhead costs	€150,000
Fixed selling and administrative costs	90,000
Total fixed costs	€240,000

$$\frac{\text{Break-even point}}{\text{in unit sales}} = \frac{\text{Total fixed expenses}}{\text{Contribution margin per unit}} = \frac{€240{,}000}{€12 \text{ per unit}} = 20{,}000 \text{ units}$$

The break-even point is 20,000 units. Notice from Exhibit 6–3 that in Year 2 the company sold exactly 20,000 units, the break-even volume. Under the contribution approach, using variable costing, the company does break even in Year 2, showing zero net operating income. *Under absorption costing, however, the company shows a positive net operating income of €30,000 for Year 2* (see Exhibit 6–4). How can this be? How can absorption costing produce a positive net operating income when the company sold exactly the break-even volume of units?

The answer lies in the fact that €30,000 in fixed manufacturing overhead costs were deferred in inventory during Year 2 under absorption costing and therefore did not appear as expenses. By deferring these fixed manufacturing overhead costs in inventory, the income statement shows a profit even though the company sold exactly the break-even volume of units. Absorption costing runs into similar kinds of difficulty in other areas of CVP analysis, which assumes that variable costing is being used.

Decision Making

Under absorption costing, fixed manufacturing overhead costs appear to be variable with respect to the number of units sold, but they are not. For example, in Exhibit 6–3, the absorption unit product cost is €13, but the variable portion of this cost is only €7. Since the product costs are stated on a per unit basis, managers may mistakenly believe that if another unit is produced, it will cost the company €13.

The misperception that absorption unit product costs are variable can lead to many problems, including inappropriate pricing decisions and decisions to drop products that are in fact profitable. These problems with absorption costing product costs will be discussed more fully in later chapters.

External Reporting and Income Taxes

Practically speaking, absorption costing is required for external reports in the United States. A company that attempts to use variable costing on its external financial reports runs the risk that its auditors may not accept the financial statements as conforming to generally accepted accounting principles (GAAP).[2] Tax law on this issue is clear-cut. Under the Tax Reform Act of 1986, a form of absorption costing must be used when filling out income tax forms.

Even if a company must use absorption costing for its external reports, a manager can, as Mary O'Meara suggests, use variable costing income statements for internal reports. No particular accounting problems are created by using *both* costing methods—the variable costing method for internal reports and the absorption costing method for external reports. As we demonstrated earlier in Exhibits 6–6 and 6–9, the adjustment from variable costing net operating income to absorption costing net operating income is a simple one that can be easily made at the end of the accounting period.

Top executives are typically evaluated based on the earnings reported to shareholders on the company's external financial reports. This creates a problem for top executives who might otherwise favor using variable costing for internal reports. They may feel that since they are evaluated based on absorption costing reports, decisions should also be based on absorption costing data.

IN BUSINESS

ABSORPTION COSTING AROUND THE WORLD

Absorption costing is the norm for external financial reports around the world. After the fall of communism, accounting methods were changed in Russia to bring them into closer agreement with accounting methods used in the West. One result was the adoption of absorption costing.

Source: Adolf J. H. Enthoven, "Russia's Accounting Moves West," *Strategic Finance*, July 1999, pp. 32–37.

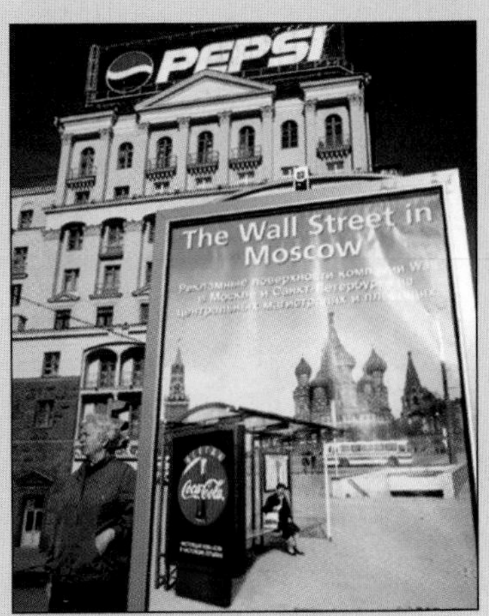

---

[2] The situation is actually slightly ambiguous concerning whether absorption costing is strictly required. Official pronouncements do not actually prohibit variable costing. And some companies expense significant elements of their fixed manufacturing costs on their external reports. Nevertheless, the reality is that most accountants believe that absorption costing is required for external reporting and a manager who argues otherwise is likely to be unsuccessful.

Advantages of Variable Costing and the Contribution Approach

As stated earlier, even if the absorption approach is used for external reporting purposes, variable costing, together with the contribution format income statement, is an appealing alternative for internal reports. The advantages of variable costing can be summarized as follows:

1. Data required for CVP analysis can be taken directly from a contribution format income statement. These data are not available on a conventional absorption costing income statement.
2. Under variable costing, the profit for a period is not affected by changes in inventories. Other things remaining the same (i.e., selling prices, costs, sales mix, etc.), profits move in the same direction as sales when variable costing is used.
3. Managers often assume that unit product costs are variable costs. This is a problem under absorption costing, since unit product costs are a combination of both fixed and variable costs. Under variable costing, unit product costs do not contain fixed costs.
4. The impact of fixed costs on profits is emphasized under the variable costing and contribution approach. The total amount of fixed costs appears explicitly on the income statement, highlighting that the whole amount of fixed costs must be covered for the company to be truly profitable. In contrast, under absorption costing, the fixed costs are mingled together with the variable costs and are buried in cost of goods sold and ending inventories.
5. Variable costing data make it easier to estimate the profitability of products, customers, and other business segments. With absorption costing, profitability is obscured by arbitrary fixed cost allocations. These issues will be discussed in later chapters.
6. Variable costing ties in with cost control methods such as standard costs and flexible budgets, which will be covered in later chapters.
7. Variable costing net operating income is closer to net cash flow than absorption costing net operating income. This is particularly important for companies with potential cash flow problems.

With all of these advantages, one might wonder why absorption costing continues to be used almost exclusively for external reporting and why it is the predominant choice for internal reports as well. This is partly due to tradition, but absorption costing is also attractive to many accountants and managers because they believe it better matches costs with revenues. Advocates of absorption costing argue that *all* manufacturing costs must be assigned to products in order to properly match the costs of producing units of product with their revenues when they are sold. The fixed costs of depreciation, taxes, insurance, supervisory salaries, and so on, are just as essential to manufacturing products as are the variable costs.

Advocates of variable costing argue that fixed manufacturing costs are not really the costs of any particular unit of product. These costs are incurred to have the *capacity* to make products during a particular period and will be incurred even if nothing is made during the period. Moreover, whether a unit is made or not, the fixed manufacturing costs will be exactly the same. Therefore, variable costing advocates argue that fixed manufacturing costs are not part of the costs of producing a particular unit of product and thus the matching principle dictates that fixed manufacturing costs should be charged to the current period.

At any rate, absorption costing is the generally accepted method for preparing mandatory external financial reports and income tax returns. Probably because of the cost and possible confusion of maintaining two separate costing systems—one for external reporting and one for internal reporting—most companies use absorption costing for both external and internal reports.

Variable Costing and the Theory of Constraints

The Theory of Constraints (TOC), which was introduced in Chapter 1, suggests that the key to improving a company's profits is managing its constraints. For reasons that will be discussed in Chapter 12, this requires careful identification of each product's variable costs.

Consequently, companies involved in TOC use a form of variable costing. One difference is that the TOC approach generally considers direct labor to be a fixed cost. As discussed in earlier chapters, in many companies direct labor is not really a variable cost. Even though direct labor workers may be paid on an hourly basis, many companies have a commitment—sometimes enforced in labor contracts or by law—to guarantee workers a minimum number of paid hours. In TOC companies, there are two additional reasons to consider direct labor a fixed cost.

First, direct labor is not usually the constraint. In the simplest cases, the constraint is a machine. In more complex cases, the constraint is a policy (such as a poorly designed compensation scheme for salespersons) that prevents the company from using its resources more effectively. If direct labor is not the constraint, there is no reason to increase it. Hiring more direct labor would increase costs without increasing the output of salable products and services.

Second, TOC emphasizes continuous improvement to maintain competitiveness. Without committed and enthusiastic employees, sustained continuous improvement is virtually impossible. Since layoffs often have devastating effects on employee morale, managers involved in TOC are extremely reluctant to lay off employees.

For these reasons, most managers in TOC companies regard direct labor as a committed fixed cost rather than a variable cost. Hence, in the modified form of variable costing used in TOC companies, direct labor is not usually classified as a product cost.

Impact of Lean Production

As discussed in this chapter, variable and absorption costing will produce different net operating incomes whenever the number of units produced is different from the number of units sold—in other words, whenever there is a change in the number of units in inventory. We have also learned that absorption costing net operating income can be erratic, sometimes moving in a direction that is opposite from the movement in sales.

When companies use Lean Production methods, these problems are reduced. The erratic movement of net operating income under absorption costing and the difference in net operating income between absorption and variable costing occur because of changes in the number of units in inventory. Under Lean Production, goods are produced to customers' orders and the goal is to eliminate finished goods inventories entirely and reduce work in process inventory to almost nothing. If there is very little inventory, then changes in inventories will be very small and both variable and absorption costing will show basically the same net operating income. With very little inventory, absorption costing net operating income usually moves in the same direction as movements in sales.

Of course, the cost of a unit of product will still be different between variable and absorption costing, as explained earlier in the chapter. But when Lean Production is used, the differences in net operating income will largely disappear.

Summary

Variable and absorption costing are alternative methods of determining unit product costs. Under variable costing, only those manufacturing costs that vary with output are treated as product costs. This includes direct materials, variable overhead, and ordinarily direct labor. Fixed manufacturing overhead is treated as a period cost and it is expensed on the income statement as incurred. By contrast, absorption costing treats fixed manufacturing overhead as a product cost, along with direct materials, direct labor, and variable overhead. Under both costing methods, selling and administrative expenses are treated as period costs and they are expensed on the income statement as incurred.

Since absorption costing treats fixed manufacturing overhead as a product cost, a portion of fixed manufacturing overhead is assigned to each unit as it is produced. If units of product are unsold at the end of a period, then the fixed manufacturing overhead cost attached to those units is carried with them into the inventory account and deferred to a future period. When these units are later sold, the fixed manufacturing overhead cost attached to them is released from the inventory account and charged against income as part of cost of goods sold. Thus, under absorption costing, it is possible to defer a portion of the fixed manufacturing overhead cost from one period to a future period through the inventory account.

Unfortunately, this shifting of fixed manufacturing overhead cost between periods can cause erratic fluctuations in net operating income and can result in confusion and unwise decisions. To guard against mistakes when they interpret income statement data, managers should be alert to changes in inventory levels or unit product costs during the period.

Practically speaking, variable costing can't be used externally for either financial or tax reporting. However, it may be used internally by managers for planning and control purposes. The variable costing approach works well with CVP analysis.

Review Problem: Contrasting Variable and Absorption Costing

Dexter Corporation produces and sells a single product, a wooden hand loom for weaving small items such as scarves. Selected cost and operating data relating to the product for two years are given below:

Selling price per unit	$50
Manufacturing costs:	
Variable per unit produced:	
Direct materials	$11
Direct labor	$6
Variable overhead	$3
Fixed per year	$120,000
Selling and administrative costs:	
Variable per unit sold	$4
Fixed per year	$70,000

	Year 1	Year 2
Units in beginning inventory	0	2,000
Units produced during the year	10,000	6,000
Units sold during the year	8,000	8,000
Units in ending inventory	2,000	0

Required:

1. Assume the company uses absorption costing.
   a. Compute the unit product cost in each year.
   b. Prepare an income statement for each year.
2. Assume the company uses variable costing.
   a. Compute the unit product cost in each year.
   b. Prepare an income statement for each year.
3. Reconcile the variable costing and absorption costing net operating incomes.

Solution to Review Problem

1. *a.* Under absorption costing, all manufacturing costs, variable and fixed, are included in unit product costs:

	Year 1	Year 2
Direct materials	$11	$11
Direct labor	6	6
Variable manufacturing overhead	3	3
Fixed manufacturing overhead		
($120,000 ÷ 10,000 units)	12	
($120,000 ÷ 6,000 units)		20
Unit product cost	$32	$40

b. The absorption costing income statements follow:

	Year 1		Year 2	
Sales (8,000 units × $50 per unit)		$400,000		$400,000
Cost of goods sold:				
Beginning inventory	$0		$ 64,000	
Add cost of goods manufactured (10,000 units × $32 per unit; 6,000 units × $40 per unit)	320,000		240,000	
Goods available for sale	320,000		304,000	
Less ending inventory (2,000 units × $32 per unit; 0 units × $40 per unit)	64,000	256,000	0	304,000
Gross margin		144,000		96,000
Selling and administrative expenses (8,000 units × $4 per unit + $70,000)		102,000		102,000
Net operating income		$ 42,000		$ (6,000)

2. *a.* Under variable costing, only the variable manufacturing costs are included in unit product costs:

	Year 1	Year 2
Direct materials	$11	$11
Direct labor	6	6
Variable manufacturing overhead	3	3
Unit product cost	$20	$20

b. The variable costing income statements follow. Notice that the variable cost of goods sold is computed in a simpler, more direct manner than in the examples provided earlier. On a variable costing income statement, this simple approach or the more complex approach illustrated earlier is acceptable for computing the cost of goods sold.

	Year 1		Year 2	
Sales (8,000 units × $50 per unit)		$400,000		$400,000
Variable expenses:				
Variable cost of goods sold (8,000 units × $20 per unit)	$160,000		$160,000	
Variable selling and administrative expenses (8,000 units × $4 per unit)	32,000	192,000	32,000	192,000
Contribution margin		208,000		208,000
Fixed expenses:				
Fixed manufacturing overhead	120,000		120,000	
Fixed selling and administrative expenses	70,000	190,000	70,000	190,000
Net operating income		$ 18,000		$ 18,000

3. The reconciliation of the variable and absorption costing net operating incomes follows:

	Year 1	Year 2
Variable costing net operating income	$18,000	$18,000
Add fixed manufacturing overhead costs deferred in inventory under absorption costing (2,000 units × $12 per unit)	24,000	
Deduct fixed manufacturing overhead costs released from inventory under absorption costing (2,000 units × $12 per unit)		(24,000)
Absorption costing net operating income	$42,000	$(6,000)

Quiz 6

Multiple-choice questions are provided on the text Web site at www.mhhe.com/noreen1e.

Glossary

Absorption costing A costing method that includes all manufacturing costs—direct materials, direct labor, and both variable and fixed manufacturing overhead—in unit product costs. (p. 209)

Fixed manufacturing overhead cost deferred in inventory The portion of the fixed manufacturing overhead cost of a period that goes into ending inventory under the absorption costing method. (p. 212)

Fixed manufacturing overhead cost released from inventory The fixed manufacturing overhead cost of a *prior* period that becomes an expense of the current period under the absorption costing method. (p. 217)

Variable costing A costing method that includes only variable manufacturing costs—direct materials, direct labor, and variable manufacturing overhead—in unit product costs. (p. 209)

Questions

6-1 What is the basic difference between absorption costing and variable costing?

6-2 Are selling and administrative expenses treated as product costs or as period costs under variable costing?

6-3 Explain how fixed manufacturing overhead costs are shifted from one period to another under absorption costing.

6-4 What arguments can be advanced in favor of treating fixed manufacturing overhead costs as product costs?

6-5 What arguments can be advanced in favor of treating fixed manufacturing overhead costs as period costs?

6-6 If production and sales are equal, which method would you expect to show the higher net operating income, variable costing or absorption costing? Why?

6-7 If production exceeds sales, which method would you expect to show the higher net operating income, variable costing or absorption costing? Why?

6-8 If fixed manufacturing overhead costs are released from inventory under absorption costing, what does this tell you about the level of production in relation to the level of sales?

6-9 Parker Company had $5,000,000 in sales and reported a $300,000 loss in its annual report to stockholders. According to a CVP analysis prepared for management's use, $5,000,000 in sales is the break-even point for the company. Did the company's inventory level increase, decrease, or remain unchanged? Explain.

6-10 Under absorption costing, how is it possible to increase net operating income without increasing sales?

6-11 How is the use of variable costing limited?

6-12 How does Lean Production reduce or eliminate the difference in reported net operating income between absorption and variable costing?

Exercises

EXERCISE 6-1 Variable and Absorption Costing Unit Product Costs [LO1]
Shastri Bicycle of Bombay, India, produces an inexpensive, yet rugged, bicycle for use on the city's crowded streets that it sells for 500 rupees. (Indian currency is denominated in rupees, denoted by R.) Selected data for the company's operations last year follow:

Units in beginning inventory	0
Units produced	10,000
Units sold	8,000
Units in ending inventory	2,000
Variable costs per unit:	
Direct materials	R120
Direct labor	R140
Variable manufacturing overhead	R50
Variable selling and administrative	R20
Fixed costs:	
Fixed manufacturing overhead	R600,000
Fixed selling and administrative	R400,000

Required:
1. Assume that the company uses absorption costing. Compute the unit product cost for one bicycle.
2. Assume that the company uses variable costing. Compute the unit product cost for one bicycle.

EXERCISE 6-2 Variable Costing Income Statement; Explanation of Difference in Net Operating Income [LO2]
Refer to the data in Exercise 6-1 for Shastri Bicycle. An absorption costing income statement prepared by the company's accountant appears below:

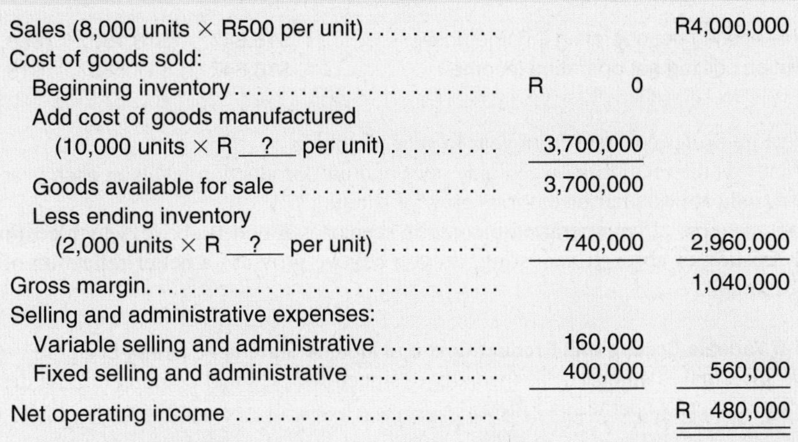

Sales (8,000 units × R500 per unit)		R4,000,000
Cost of goods sold:		
Beginning inventory	R 0	
Add cost of goods manufactured (10,000 units × R __?__ per unit)	3,700,000	
Goods available for sale	3,700,000	
Less ending inventory (2,000 units × R __?__ per unit)	740,000	2,960,000
Gross margin		1,040,000
Selling and administrative expenses:		
Variable selling and administrative	160,000	
Fixed selling and administrative	400,000	560,000
Net operating income		R 480,000

Required:
1. Determine how much of the ending inventory of R740,000 above consists of fixed manufacturing overhead cost deferred in inventory to the next period.
2. Prepare an income statement for the year using the variable costing method. Explain the difference in net operating income between the two costing methods.

EXERCISE 6-3 Reconciliation of Absorption and Variable Costing Net Operating Incomes [LO3]
High Tension Transformers, Inc., manufactures heavy-duty transformers for electrical switching stations. The company uses variable costing for internal management reports and absorption costing for external reports to shareholders, creditors, and the government. The company has provided the following data:

	Year 1	Year 2	Year 3
Inventories:			
Beginning (units)	180	150	160
Ending (units)	150	160	200
Variable costing net operating income	$292,400	$269,200	$251,800

The company's fixed manufacturing overhead per unit was constant at $450 for all three years.

Required:

1. Determine each year's absorption costing net operating income. Present your answer in the form of a reconciliation report such as the one shown in Exhibit 6–6.
2. In Year 4, the company's variable costing net operating income was $240,200 and its absorption costing net operating income was $267,200. Did inventories increase or decrease during Year 4? How much fixed manufacturing overhead cost was deferred or released from inventory during Year 4?

EXERCISE 6-4 Evaluating Absorption and Variable Costing as Alternative Costing Methods [LO4]

The questions below pertain to two different scenarios involving a manufacturing company. In each scenario, the cost structure of the company is constant from year to year. Selling prices, unit variable costs, and total fixed costs are the same in every year. However, unit sales and/or unit production levels may vary from year to year.

Required:

1. Consider the following data for scenario A:

	Year 1	Year 2	Year 3
Variable costing net operating income	$16,847	$16,847	$16,847
Absorption costing net operating income	$16,847	$29,378	$6,018

   a. Were unit sales constant from year to year? Explain.
   b. What was the relation between unit sales and unit production levels in each year? For each year, indicate whether inventories grew or shrank.

2. Consider the following data for scenario B:

	Year 1	Year 2	Year 3
Variable costing net operating income (loss)	$16,847	($18,153)	($53,153)
Absorption costing net operating income	$16,847	$17,583	$18,318

   a. Were unit sales constant from year to year? Explain.
   b. What was the relation between unit sales and unit production levels in each year? For each year, indicate whether inventories grew or shrank.

3. Given the patterns of net operating income in scenarios A and B above, which costing method, variable costing or absorption costing, do you believe provides a better reflection of economic reality? Explain.

EXERCISE 6-5 Variable Costing Unit Product Cost and Income Statement; Break-Even [LO1, LO2]

CompuDesk, Inc., makes an oak desk specially designed for personal computers. The desk sells for $200. Data for last year's operations follow:

Units in beginning inventory	0
Units produced	10,000
Units sold	9,000
Units in ending inventory	1,000
Variable costs per unit:	
Direct materials	$ 60
Direct labor	30
Variable manufacturing overhead	10
Variable selling and administrative	20
Total variable cost per unit	$ 120
Fixed costs:	
Fixed manufacturing overhead	$300,000
Fixed selling and administrative	450,000
Total fixed costs	$750,000

Required:

1. Assume that the company uses variable costing. Compute the unit product cost for one computer desk.
2. Assume that the company uses variable costing. Prepare a contribution format income statement for the year.
3. What is the company's break-even point in terms of units sold?

EXERCISE 6-6 Absorption Costing Unit Product Cost and Income Statement [LO1, LO2]

Refer to the data in Exercise 6-5 for CompuDesk. Assume in this exercise that the company uses absorption costing.

Required:

1. Compute the unit product cost for one computer desk.
2. Prepare an income statement for the year.

EXERCISE 6-7 Variable and Absorption Costing Unit Product Costs and Income Statements [LO1, LO2]

Maxwell Company manufactures and sells a single product. The following costs were incurred during the company's first year of operations:

Variable costs per unit:	
Manufacturing:	
Direct materials.	$18
Direct labor	$7
Variable manufacturing overhead.	$2
Variable selling and administrative.	$5
Fixed costs per year:	
Fixed manufacturing overhead.	$160,000
Fixed selling and administrative expenses.	$110,000

During the year, the company produced 20,000 units and sold 16,000 units. The selling price of the company's product is $50 per unit.

Required:

1. Assume that the company uses absorption costing:
   a. Compute the unit product cost.
   b. Prepare an income statement for the year.
2. Assume that the company uses variable costing:
   a. Compute the unit product cost.
   b. Prepare an income statement for the year.

EXERCISE 6-8 Inferring Costing Method; Unit Product Cost [LO1, LO4]

Amcor, Inc., incurs the following costs to produce and sell a single product.

Variable costs per unit:	
Direct materials	$10
Direct labor.	$5
Variable manufacturing overhead	$2
Variable selling and administrative expenses	$4
Fixed costs per year:	
Fixed manufacturing overhead.	$90,000
Fixed selling and administrative expenses.	$300,000

During the last year, 30,000 units were produced and 25,000 units were sold. The Finished Goods inventory account at the end of the year shows a balance of $85,000 for the 5,000 unsold units.

Required:

1. Is the company using absorption costing or variable costing to cost units in the Finished Goods inventory account? Show computations to support your answer.
2. Assume that the company wishes to prepare financial statements for the year to issue to its stockholders.
   a. Is the $85,000 figure for Finished Goods inventory the correct amount to use on these statements for external reporting purposes? Explain.
   b. At what dollar amount *should* the 5,000 units be carried in inventory for external reporting purposes?

EXERCISE 6-9 Variable Costing Income Statement; Reconciliation [LO2, LO3]
Morey Company has just completed its first year of operations. The company's absorption costing income statement for the year appears below:

Morey Company Income Statement		
Sales (40,000 units at $33.75 per unit)		$1,350,000
Cost of goods sold:		
Beginning inventory	$ 0	
Add cost of goods manufactured (50,000 units at $21 per unit)	1,050,000	
Goods available for sale	1,050,000	
Less ending inventory (10,000 units at $21 per unit)	210,000	840,000
Gross margin		510,000
Selling and administrative expenses		420,000
Net operating income		$ 90,000

The company's selling and administrative expenses consist of $300,000 per year in fixed expenses and $3 per unit sold in variable expenses. The company's $21 per unit product cost given above is computed as follows:

Direct materials	$10
Direct labor	4
Variable manufacturing overhead	2
Fixed manufacturing overhead ($250,000 ÷ 50,000 units)	5
Unit product cost	$21

Required:
1. Redo the company's income statement in the contribution format using variable costing.
2. Reconcile any difference between the net operating income on your variable costing income statement and the net operating income on the absorption costing income statement above.

Problems 

PROBLEM 6-10 Variable Costing Income Statement; Reconciliation [LO2, LO3]
During Denton Company's first two years of operations, the company reported absorption costing net operating income as follows:

	Year 1	Year 2
Sales (at $50 per unit)	$1,000,000	$1,500,000
Cost of goods sold:		
Beginning inventory	0	170,000
Add cost of goods manufactured (at $34 per unit)	850,000	850,000
Goods available for sale	850,000	1,020,000
Less ending inventory (at $34 per unit)	170,000	0
Cost of goods sold	680,000	1,020,000
Gross margin	320,000	480,000
Selling and administrative expenses*	310,000	340,000
Net operating income	$ 10,000	$ 140,000

*$3 per unit variable; $250,000 fixed each year.

The company's $34 unit product cost is computed as follows:

Direct materials	$ 8
Direct labor	10
Variable manufacturing overhead	2
Fixed manufacturing overhead ($350,000 ÷ 25,000 units)	14
Unit product cost	$34

Production and cost data for the two years are given below:

	Year 1	Year 2
Units produced	25,000	25,000
Units sold	20,000	30,000

Required:

1. Prepare a variable costing income statement for each year in the contribution format.
2. Reconcile the absorption costing and variable costing net operating income figures for each year.

PROBLEM 6-11 Variable and Absorption Costing Unit Product Costs and Income Statements; Explanation of Difference in Net Operating Income [LO1, LO2, LO3]

Wiengot Antennas, Inc., produces and sells a unique type of TV antenna. The company has just opened a new plant to manufacture the antenna, and the following cost and revenue data have been provided for the first month of the plant's operation in the form of a worksheet.

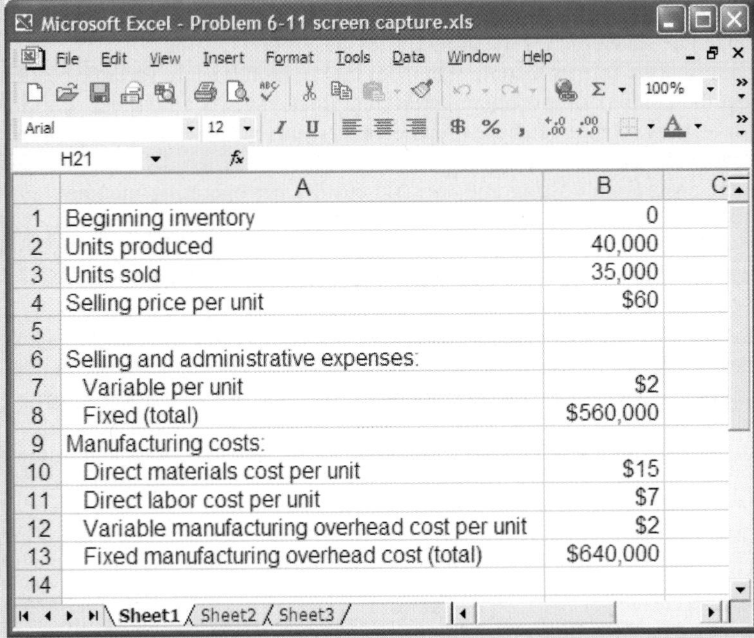

Microsoft Excel - Problem 6-11 screen capture.xls

	A	B
1	Beginning inventory	0
2	Units produced	40,000
3	Units sold	35,000
4	Selling price per unit	$60
5		
6	Selling and administrative expenses:	
7	Variable per unit	$2
8	Fixed (total)	$560,000
9	Manufacturing costs:	
10	Direct materials cost per unit	$15
11	Direct labor cost per unit	$7
12	Variable manufacturing overhead cost per unit	$2
13	Fixed manufacturing overhead cost (total)	$640,000
14		

Since the new antenna is unique in design, management is anxious to see how profitable it will be and has asked that an income statement be prepared for the month.

Required:

1. Assume that the company uses absorption costing.
   a. Determine the unit product cost.
   b. Prepare an income statement for the month.
2. Assume that the company uses variable costing.
   a. Determine the unit product cost.
   b. Prepare a contribution format income statement for the month.
3. Explain the reason for any difference in the ending inventory balances under the two costing methods and the impact of this difference on reported net operating income.

PROBLEM 6-12 Comprehensive Problem with Labor Fixed [LO1, LO2, LO3, LO4]

Advance Products, Inc., has just organized a new division to manufacture and sell specially designed tables using select hardwoods for personal computers. The division's monthly costs are shown in the schedule below:

Manufacturing costs:	
Variable costs per unit:	
Direct materials	$86
Variable manufacturing overhead	$4
Fixed manufacturing overhead costs (total)	$240,000
Selling and administrative costs:	
Variable	15% of sales
Fixed (total)	$160,000

Advance Products regards all of its workers as full-time employees and the company has a long-standing no-layoff policy. Furthermore, production is highly automated. Accordingly, the company includes its labor costs in its fixed manufacturing overhead. The tables sell for $250 each.

During the first month of operations, the following activity was recorded:

Units produced	4,000
Units sold	3,200

Required:

1. Compute the unit product cost under:
   a. Absorption costing.
   b. Variable costing.
2. Prepare an income statement for the month using absorption costing.
3. Prepare a contribution format income statement for the month using variable costing.
4. Assume that the company must obtain additional financing. As a member of top management, which of the statements that you have prepared in (2) and (3) above would you prefer to take with you as you negotiate with the bank? Why?
5. Reconcile the absorption costing and variable costing net operating income figures in (2) and (3) above.

PROBLEM 6-13 Absorption and Variable Costing; Production Constant, Sales Fluctuate [LO1, LO2, LO3, LO4]

Sandi Scott obtained a patent on a small electronic device and organized Scott Products, Inc., to produce and sell the device. During the first month of operations, the device was very well received on the market, so Ms. Scott looked forward to a healthy profit. For this reason, she was surprised to see a loss for the month on her income statement. This statement was prepared by her accounting service, which takes great pride in providing its clients with timely financial data. The statement follows:

Scott Products, Inc. Income Statement		
Sales (40,000 units)		$200,000
Variable expenses:		
Variable cost of goods sold*	$80,000	
Variable selling and administrative expenses	30,000	110,000
Contribution margin		90,000
Fixed expenses:		
Fixed manufacturing overhead	75,000	
Fixed selling and administrative expenses	20,000	95,000
Net operating loss		$ (5,000)

*Consists of direct materials, direct labor, and variable manufacturing overhead.

Ms. Scott is discouraged over the loss shown for the month, particularly since she had planned to use the statement to encourage investors to purchase stock in the new company. A friend, who is a CPA, insists that the company should be using absorption costing rather than variable costing. He argues that if absorption costing had been used, the company would probably have reported a profit for the month.

Selected cost data relating to the product and to the first month of operations follow:

Units produced	50,000
Units sold	40,000
Variable costs per unit:	
Direct materials	$1.00
Direct labor	$0.80
Variable manufacturing overhead	$0.20
Variable selling and administrative expenses	$0.75

Required:

1. Complete the following:
   a. Compute the unit product cost under absorption costing.
   b. Redo the company's income statement for the month using absorption costing.
   c. Reconcile the variable and absorption costing net operating income (loss) figures.
2. Was the CPA correct in suggesting that the company really earned a "profit" for the month? Explain.
3. During the second month of operations, the company again produced 50,000 units but sold 60,000 units. (Assume no change in total fixed costs.)
   a. Prepare a contribution format income statement for the month using variable costing.
   b. Prepare an income statement for the month using absorption costing.
   c. Reconcile the variable costing and absorption costing net operating income figures.

PROBLEM 6-14 Prepare and Reconcile Variable Costing Statements [LO1, LO2, LO3, LO4]

Linden Company manufactures and sells a single product. Cost data for the product follow:

Variable costs per unit:	
Direct materials	$ 6
Direct labor	12
Variable factory overhead	4
Variable selling and administrative	3
Total variable costs per unit	$25
Fixed costs per month:	
Fixed manufacturing overhead	$240,000
Fixed selling and administrative	180,000
Total fixed cost per month	$420,000

The product sells for $40 per unit. Production and sales data for May and June, the first two months of operations, are as follows:

	Units Produced	Units Sold
May	30,000	26,000
June	30,000	34,000

Income statements prepared by the Accounting Department, using absorption costing, are presented below:

	May	June
Sales	$1,040,000	$1,360,000
Cost of goods sold:		
Beginning inventory	0	120,000
Add cost of goods manufactured	900,000	900,000
Goods available for sale	900,000	1,020,000
Less ending inventory	120,000	0
Cost of goods sold	780,000	1,020,000
Gross margin	260,000	340,000
Selling and administrative expenses	258,000	282,000
Net operating income	$ 2,000	$ 58,000

Required:

1. Determine the unit product cost under:
   a. Absorption costing.
   b. Variable costing.
2. Prepare variable costing income statements for May and June using the contribution approach.
3. Reconcile the variable costing and absorption costing net operating income figures.
4. The company's Accounting Department has determined the break-even point to be 28,000 units per month, computed as follows:

$$\frac{\text{Fixed cost per month}}{\text{Unit contribution margin}} = \frac{\$420{,}000}{\$15 \text{ per unit}} = 28{,}000 \text{ units}$$

Upon receiving this figure, the president commented, "There's something peculiar here. The controller says that the break-even point is 28,000 units per month. Yet we sold only 26,000 units in May, and the income statement we received showed a $2,000 profit. Which figure do we believe?" Prepare a brief explanation of what happened on the May income statement.

PROBLEM 6-15 Incentives Created by Absorption Costing; Ethics and the Manager [LO2, LO4]
Aristotle Constantinos, the manager of DuraProducts' Australian Division, is trying to set the production schedule for the last quarter of the year. The Australian Division had planned to sell 100,000 units during the year, but current projections indicate sales will be only 78,000 units in total. By September 30 the following activity had been reported:

	Units
Inventory, January 1	0
Production	72,000
Sales	60,000
Inventory, September 30	12,000

Demand has been soft, and the sales forecast for the last quarter is only 18,000 units.

The division can rent warehouse space to store up to 30,000 units. The division should maintain a minimum inventory level of at least 1,500 units. Mr. Constantinos is aware that production must be at least 6,000 units per quarter in order to retain a nucleus of key employees. Maximum production capacity is 45,000 units per quarter.

Due to the nature of the division's operations, fixed manufacturing overhead is a major element of product cost.

Required:

1. Assume that the division is using variable costing. How many units should be scheduled for production during the last quarter of the year? (The basic formula for computing the required production for a period in a company is: Expected sales + Desired ending inventory − Beginning inventory = Required production.) Show computations and explain your answer. Will the number of units scheduled for production affect the division's reported profit for the year? Explain.
2. Assume that the division is using absorption costing and that the divisional manager is given an annual bonus based on the division's net operating income. If Mr. Constantinos wants to maximize his division's net operating income for the year, how many units should be scheduled for production during the last quarter? [See the formula in (1) above.] Explain.
3. Identify the ethical issues involved in the decision Mr. Constantinos must make about the level of production for the last quarter of the year.

PROBLEM 6-16 Variable Costing Income Statements; Sales Constant; Production Varies; Lean Production [LO1, LO2, LO3, LO4]

"Can someone explain to me what's wrong with these statements?" asked Cheri Reynolds, president of Milex Corporation. "They just don't make sense. We sold the same number of units this year as we did last year, yet our profits have tripled! Who messed up the calculations?"

The absorption costing income statements to which Ms. Reynolds was referring are shown below:

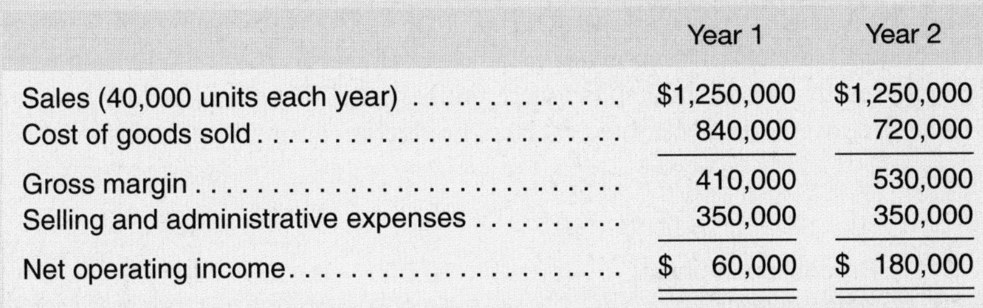

	Year 1	Year 2
Sales (40,000 units each year)	$1,250,000	$1,250,000
Cost of goods sold	840,000	720,000
Gross margin	410,000	530,000
Selling and administrative expenses	350,000	350,000
Net operating income	$ 60,000	$ 180,000

In the first year, the company produced and sold 40,000 units; in the second year, the company again sold 40,000 units, but it increased production to 50,000 units, as shown below:

	Year 1	Year 2
Production in units	40,000	50,000
Sales in units	40,000	40,000
Variable manufacturing cost per unit produced	$6	$6
Variable selling and administrative expense per unit sold	$2	$2
Fixed manufacturing overhead costs (total)	$600,000	$600,000

Milex Corporation applies fixed manufacturing overhead costs to its only product on the basis of each year's production. (Thus, a new fixed manufacturing overhead rate is computed each year, as in Exhibit 6–7.)

Required:

1. Compute the unit product cost for each year under:
   a. Absorption costing.
   b. Variable costing.
2. Prepare a contribution format income statement for each year using variable costing.
3. Reconcile the variable costing and absorption costing net operating income figures for each year.
4. Explain to the president why the net operating income for Year 2 was higher than for Year 1 under absorption costing, although the same number of units was sold in each year.
5. *a.* Explain how operations would have differed in Year 2 if the company had been using Lean Production and inventories had been eliminated.
   b. If Lean Production had been in use during Year 2 and ending inventories were zero, what would the company's net operating income have been under absorption costing? Explain the reason for any difference between this income figure and the figure reported by the company in the statements above.

PROBLEM 6-17 Prepare and Interpret Statements; Changes in Both Sales and Production; Lean Production [LO1, LO2, LO3, LO4]

Memotec, Inc., manufactures and sells a unique electronic part. Operating results for the first three years of activity were as follows (absorption costing basis):

	Year 1	Year 2	Year 3
Sales	$1,000,000	$800,000	$1,000,000
Cost of goods sold:			
Beginning inventory	0	0	280,000
Add cost of goods manufactured	800,000	840,000	760,000
Goods available for sale	800,000	840,000	1,040,000
Less ending inventory	0	280,000	190,000
Cost of goods sold	800,000	560,000	850,000
Gross margin	200,000	240,000	150,000
Selling and administrative expenses	170,000	150,000	170,000
Net operating income (loss)	$ 30,000	$ 90,000	$ (20,000)

Sales dropped by 20% during Year 2 due to the entry of several foreign competitors into the market. Memotec had expected sales to remain constant at 50,000 units for the year; production was set at 60,000 units in order to build a buffer of protection against unexpected spurts in demand. By the start of Year 3, management could see that spurts in demand were unlikely and that the inventory was excessive. To work off the excessive inventories, Memotec cut back production during Year 3, as shown below:

	Year 1	Year 2	Year 3
Production in units	50,000	60,000	40,000
Sales in units	50,000	40,000	50,000

Additional information about the company follows:

a. The company's plant is highly automated. Variable manufacturing costs (direct materials, direct labor, and variable manufacturing overhead) total only $4 per unit, and fixed manufacturing overhead costs total $600,000 per year.

b. Fixed manufacturing overhead costs are applied to units of product on the basis of each year's production. (That is, a new fixed overhead rate is computed each year, as in Exhibit 6–7).

c. Variable selling and administrative expenses are $2 per unit sold. Fixed selling and administrative expenses total $70,000 per year.

d. The company uses a FIFO inventory flow assumption.

Memotec's management can't understand why profits tripled during Year 2 when sales dropped by 20%, and why a loss was incurred during Year 3 when sales recovered to previous levels.

Required:

1. Prepare a contribution format income statement for each year using variable costing.
2. Refer to the absorption costing income statements above.
   a. Compute the unit product cost in each year under absorption costing. (Show how much of this cost is variable and how much is fixed.)
   b. Reconcile the variable costing and absorption costing net operating income figures for each year.
3. Refer again to the absorption costing income statements. Explain why net operating income was higher in Year 2 than it was in Year 1 under the absorption approach, in light of the fact that fewer units were sold in Year 2 than in Year 1.
4. Refer again to the absorption costing income statements. Explain why the company suffered a loss in Year 3 but reported a profit in Year 1, although the same number of units was sold in each year.
5. *a.* Explain how operations would have differed in Year 2 and Year 3 if the company had been using Lean Production with the result that ending inventory was zero.
   b. If Lean Production had been in use during Year 2 and Year 3, what would the company's net operating income (or loss) have been in each year under absorption costing? Explain the reason for any differences between these income figures and the figures reported by the company in the statements above.

Cases

CASE 6-18 Ethics and the Manager; Absorption Costing Income Statements [LO2, LO4]

Michael Lee was hired as chief executive officer (CEO) in late November by the board of directors of Hunter Electronics, a company that produces a state-of-the-art DVD drive for personal computers. The previous CEO had been fired by the board due to a series of questionable business practices including prematurely recording revenues on products that had not yet been shipped to customers.

Michael felt that his first priority on the job was to restore employee morale—which had suffered during the previous CEO's reign. He was particularly anxious to build a sense of trust between himself and the company's employees. His second priority was to prepare the budget for the coming year, which the board of directors wanted to review in their December 15 meeting.

After hammering out the details in meetings with key managers, Michael was able to put together a budget that he felt the company could realistically meet during the coming year. That budget appears below:

Basic Budget Data	
Units in beginning inventory	0
Units produced	200,000
Units sold	200,000
Units in ending inventory	0
Variable costs per unit:	
Direct materials	$ 50
Direct labor	40
Variable manufacturing overhead	20
Variable selling and administrative	10
Total variable cost per unit	$120
Fixed costs:	
Fixed manufacturing overhead	$ 8,400,000
Fixed selling and administrative	3,600,000
Total fixed costs	$12,000,000

Hunter Electronics Budgeted Income Statement (Absorption Method)		
Sales (200,000 units)		$40,000,000
Cost of goods sold:		
Beginning inventory	$ 0	
Add cost of goods manufactured (200,000 × $152 per unit)	30,400,000	
Goods available for sale	30,400,000	
Less ending inventory	0	30,400,000
Gross margin		9,600,000
Selling and administrative expenses:		
Variable selling and administrative	2,000,000	
Fixed selling and administrative	3,600,000	5,600,000
Net operating income		$ 4,000,000

While the board of directors did not oppose the budget, they made it clear that the budget was not as ambitious as they had hoped. The most influential member of the board stated that "managers should have to really stretch to meet profit goals." After some discussion, the board decided to set a profit goal of $4,800,000 for the coming year. To provide strong incentives and a win-win situation, the board agreed to pay out bonuses to top managers of $200,000 if this profit goal was eventually met. Michael's share of the bonus pool would be $50,000. The bonus would be all-or-nothing. If actual net operating income turned out to be $4,800,000 or more, the bonus would be paid. Otherwise, no bonus would be allowed.

Required:

1. Assuming that the company does not build up its inventory (i.e., production equals sales) and its selling price and cost structure remain the same, how many units of the DVD drive would have to be sold to meet the target net operating income of $4,800,000?
2. Verify your answer to (1) above by constructing a revised budget and budgeted absorption costing income statement that yields a net operating income of $4,800,000.
3. Unfortunately, by October of the next year it had become clear that the company would not be able to make the $4,800,000 target profit. In fact, it looked like the company would wind up the year as originally planned, with sales of 200,000 units, no ending inventories, and a profit of $4,000,000.

   Several managers who were reluctant to lose their year-end bonuses approached Michael and suggested that the company could still show a profit of $4,800,000. The managers argued that at the present rate of sales, there was enough capacity to produce tens of thousands of additional DVD drives for the warehouse. Overtime costs might have to be incurred, but all of this additional cost would be assigned to the DVD drives in ending inventory.

   If sales are 200,000 units for the year and the selling price and cost structure remain the same, how many units would have to be produced to show a profit of at least $4,800,000 under absorption costing? (Round your answer up to the nearest whole unit.)
4. Verify your answer to (3) above by constructing an absorption costing income statement.
5. Do you think Michael Lee should approve the plan to build ending inventories in order to attain the target profit?
6. What advice would you give to the board of directors concerning how they determine bonuses in the future?

CASE 6-19 The Case of the Perplexed President; Lean Production [LO2, LO3, LO4]

John Ovard, president of Mylar, Inc., was looking forward to receiving the company's second quarter income statement. He knew that the sales budget of 20,000 units sold had been met during the second quarter and that this represented a 25% increase in sales over the first quarter. He was especially happy about the increase in sales, since Mylar was about to approach its bank for additional loan money for expansion purposes. He anticipated that the strong second-quarter results would be a real plus in persuading the bank to extend the additional credit.

For this reason, Mr. Ovard was shocked when he received the second-quarter income statement below, which showed a substantial drop in absorption costing net operating income from the first quarter.

Mylar, Inc.
Income Statements
For the First Two Quarters

	First Quarter		Second Quarter	
Sales		$1,600,000		$2,000,000
Cost of goods sold:				
Beginning inventory	$ 210,000		$ 490,000	
Add cost of goods manufactured	1,400,000		980,000	
Goods available for sale	1,610,000		1,470,000	
Less ending inventory	490,000		70,000	
Cost of goods sold	1,120,000		1,400,000	
Add underapplied overhead	0	1,120,000	240,000	1,640,000
Gross margin		480,000		360,000
Selling and administrative expenses		310,000		330,000
Net operating income		$ 170,000		$ 30,000

Mr. Ovard was certain there had to be an error somewhere and immediately called the controller into his office to find the problem. The controller stated, "That net operating income is correct, John. Sales went up during the second quarter, but the problem is in production. You see, we budgeted to produce 20,000 units each quarter, but a strike in one of our supplier's plants forced us to cut production back to only 14,000 units in the second quarter. That's what caused the drop in net operating income."

Mr. Ovard was angered by the controller's explanation. "I call you in here to find out why income dropped when sales went up, and you talk about production! So what if production was off? What does that have to do with the sales that we made? If sales go up, then income ought to go up. If your statements can't show a simple thing like that, then we're due for some changes in your area!"

Budgeted production and sales for the year, along with actual production and sales for the first two quarters, are given below:

	Quarter			
	First	Second	Third	Fourth
Budgeted sales (units)	16,000	20,000	20,000	24,000
Actual sales (units)	16,000	20,000	—	—
Budgeted production (units)	20,000	20,000	20,000	20,000
Actual production (units)	20,000	14,000	—	—

The company's plant is heavily automated, so fixed manufacturing overhead costs total $800,000 per quarter. Variable manufacturing costs are $30 per unit. The fixed manufacturing overhead cost is applied to units of product at the rate of $40 per unit (based on the budgeted production shown above). Any underapplied or overapplied overhead is closed directly to cost of goods sold for the quarter.

The company had 3,000 units in inventory to start the first quarter and uses the FIFO inventory flow assumption. Variable selling and administrative expenses are $5 per unit sold.

Required:

1. What characteristic of absorption costing caused the drop in net operating income for the second quarter and what could the controller have said to explain the problem?
2. Prepare a contribution format income statement for each quarter using variable costing.
3. Reconcile the absorption costing and the variable costing net operating income figures for each quarter.
4. Identify and discuss the advantages and disadvantages of using the variable costing method for internal reporting purposes.
5. Assume that the company had introduced Lean Production methods at the beginning of the second quarter, resulting in zero ending inventory. (Sales and production during the first quarter were as shown above.)
   a. How many units would have been produced during the second quarter under Lean Production?
   b. Starting with the third quarter, would you expect any difference between the net operating income reported under absorption costing and under variable costing? Explain why there would or would not be any difference.

Chapter 7

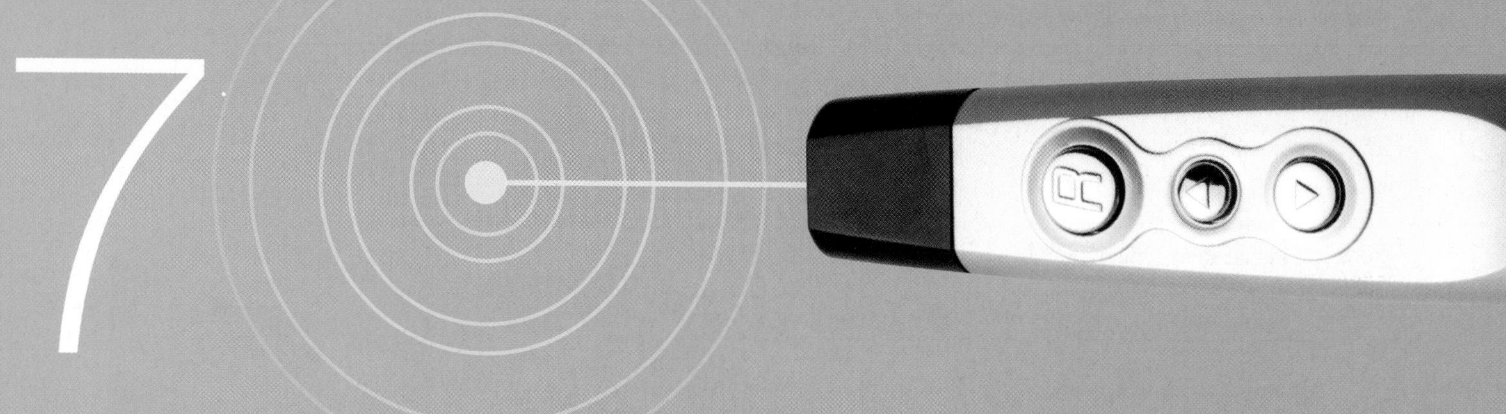

Learning Objectives

After studying Chapter 7, you should be able to:

LO1 Understand activity-based costing and how it differs from a traditional costing system.

LO2 Assign costs to cost pools using a first-stage allocation.

LO3 Compute activity rates for cost pools.

LO4 Assign costs to a cost object using a second-stage allocation.

LO5 Use activity-based costing to compute product and customer margins.

LO6 (Appendix 7A) Prepare an action analysis report using activity-based costing data and interpret the report.

LP 7

Activity-Based Costing: A Tool to Aid Decision Making

The Payoff from Activity-Based Costing

BUSINESS FOCUS

Implementing an activity-based costing system can be expensive. To be worth the cost, the system must actually be used to make decisions and increase profits. Insteel Industries manufactures a range of products, such as concrete reinforcing steel, industrial wire, and bulk nails, for the construction, home furnishings, appliance, and tire manufacturing industries. The company implemented an activity-based costing system at its manufacturing plant in Andrews, South Carolina, and immediately began using activity-based data to make strategic and operating decisions.

In terms of strategic decisions, Insteel dropped some unprofitable products, raised prices on others, and in some cases even discontinued relationships with unprofitable customers. Insteel realized that simply discontinuing products and customers does not improve profits. The company needed to either redeploy its freed-up capacity to increase sales or eliminate its freed-up capacity to reduce costs. Insteel chose to redeploy its freed-up capacity and used its activity-based costing system to identify which new business opportunities to pursue.

In terms of operational improvements, Insteel's activity-based costing system revealed that its 20 most expensive activities consumed 87% of the plant's $21.4 million in costs. Almost $4.9 million was being consumed by non-value-added activities. Teams were formed to reduce scrap costs, material handling and freight costs, and maintenance costs. Within one year, scrap and maintenance costs had been cut by $1,800,000 and freight costs by $550,000. Overall, non-value-added activity costs dropped from 23% to 17% of total costs. ■

Source: V.G. Narayanan and R. Sarkar, "The Impact of Activity-Based Costing on Managerial Decisions at Insteel Industries—A Field Study," *Journal of Economics & Management Strategy,* Summer 2002, pp. 257–288.

This chapter introduces the concept of *activity-based costing* which has been embraced by a wide variety of manufacturing, service, and nonprofit organizations including American Express, The Association of Neurological Surgeons, Cambridge Hospital Community Health Network, Carrier Corporation, Dana Corporation, Dialysis Clinic, GE Medical Systems, Hallmark, ITT Automotive North America, Maxwell Appliance Controls, Pillsbury, Tampa Electric Company, and the U.S. Postal Service. **Activity-based costing (ABC)** is a costing method that is designed to provide managers with cost information for strategic and other decisions that potentially affect capacity and therefore "fixed" as well as variable costs. Activity-based costing is ordinarily used as a supplement to, rather than as a replacement for, a company's usual costing system. Most organizations that use activity-based costing have two costing systems—the official costing system that is used for preparing external financial reports and the activity-based costing system that is used for internal decision making and for managing activities.

This chapter focuses primarily on ABC applications in manufacturing to provide a contrast with the material presented in earlier chapters. More specifically, Chapters 2 and 3 focused on traditional absorption costing systems used by manufacturing companies to calculate unit product costs for the purpose of valuing inventories and determining cost of goods sold for external financial reports. In contrast, this chapter explains how manufacturing companies can use activity-based costing rather than traditional methods to calculate unit product costs for the purposes of managing overhead and making decisions. Chapter 6 had a similar purpose. That chapter focused on how to use variable costing to aid decisions that do not affect fixed costs. This chapter extends that idea to show how activity-based costing can be used to aid decisions that potentially affect fixed costs as well as variable costs.

Activity-Based Costing: An Overview

LEARNING OBJECTIVE 1
Understand activity-based costing and how it differs from a traditional costing system.

As stated above, traditional absorption costing is designed to provide data for external financial reports. In contrast, activity-based costing is designed to be used for internal decision making. As a consequence, activity-based costing differs from traditional cost accounting in three ways. In activity-based costing:

1. Nonmanufacturing as well as manufacturing costs may be assigned to products, but only on a cause-and-effect basis.
2. Some manufacturing costs may be excluded from product costs.
3. Numerous overhead cost pools are used, each of which is allocated to products and other cost objects using its own unique measure of activity.

Each of these departures from traditional cost accounting practice will be discussed in turn.

IN BUSINESS

SHEDDING LIGHT ON PRODUCT PROFITABILITY

Reichhold, Inc., one of the world's leading suppliers of synthetic materials, adopted activity-based costing to help shed light on the profitability of its various products. Reichhold's prior cost system used one allocation base, reactor hours, to assign overhead costs to products. The ABC system uses four additional activity measures—preprocess preparation hours, thin-tank hours, filtration hours, and waste disposal costs per batch—to assign costs to products. Reichhold has rolled out ABC to all 19 of its North American plants because the management team believes that ABC helps improve the company's "capacity management, cycle times, value-added pricing decisions, and analysis of product profitability."

Source: Edward Blocher, Betty Wong, and Christopher McKittrick, "Making Bottom-Up ABC Work at Reichhold, Inc.," *Strategic Finance,* April 2002, pp. 51–55.

How Costs Are Treated under Activity-Based Costing

Video 7–1

Nonmanufacturing Costs and Activity-Based Costing

In traditional cost accounting, only manufacturing costs are assigned to products. Selling and administrative expenses are treated as period expenses and are not assigned to products. However, many of these nonmanufacturing costs are also part of the costs of producing, selling, distributing, and servicing specific products. For example, commissions paid to salespersons, shipping costs, and warranty repair costs can be easily traced to individual products. In this chapter, we will use the term *overhead* to refer to nonmanufacturing costs as well as to indirect manufacturing costs. In activity-based costing, products are assigned all of the overhead costs—nonmanufacturing as well as manufacturing—that they can reasonably be supposed to have caused. In essence, we will be determining the entire cost of a product rather than just its manufacturing cost. The focus in Chapters 2 and 3 was on determining just the manufacturing cost of a product.

Manufacturing Costs and Activity-Based Costing

In traditional cost accounting systems, *all* manufacturing costs are assigned to products—even manufacturing costs that are not caused by the products. For example, in Chapter 3 we learned that a predetermined plantwide overhead rate is computed by dividing *all* budgeted manufacturing overhead costs by a measure of budgeted activity such as direct labor-hours. This approach spreads *all* manufacturing overhead costs across products based on each product's direct labor-hour usage. In contrast, activity-based costing systems purposely do not assign two types of manufacturing overhead costs to products.

Manufacturing overhead includes costs such as the factory security guard's wages, the plant controller's salary, and the cost of supplies used by the plant manager's secretary. These types of costs are assigned to products in a traditional absorption costing system even though they are totally unaffected by which products are made during a period. In contrast, activity-based costing systems do not arbitrarily assign these types of costs, which are called *organization-sustaining* costs, to products. Activity-based costing treats these types of costs as period expenses rather than product costs.

Additionally, in a traditional absorption costing system, the costs of unused, or idle, capacity are assigned to products. If the budgeted level of activity declines, the overhead rate and unit product costs increase as the increasing costs of idle capacity are spread over a smaller base. In contrast, in activity-based costing, products are only charged for the costs of the capacity they use—not for the costs of capacity they don't use. This provides more stable unit product costs and is consistent with the goal of assigning to products only the costs of the resources that they use.[1]

Cost Pools, Allocation Bases, and Activity-Based Costing

Throughout the 19th century and most of the 20th century, cost system designs were simple and satisfactory. Typically, either one plantwide overhead cost pool or a number of departmental overhead cost pools was used to assign overhead costs to products. The plantwide and departmental approaches always had one thing in common—they relied on allocation bases such as direct labor-hours and machine-hours for allocating overhead costs to products. In the labor-intensive production processes of many years ago, direct labor was the most common choice for an overhead allocation base because it represented a large component of product costs, direct labor-hours were closely tracked, and many managers believed that direct labor-hours, the total volume of units produced, and overhead costs were highly

[1] Appendix 3A discusses how the costs of idle capacity can be accounted for as a period cost in an income statement. This treatment highlights the cost of idle capacity rather than burying it in inventory and cost of goods sold. The procedures laid out in this chapter for activity-based costing have the same end effect.

correlated. (Three variables, such as direct labor-hours, the total volume of units produced, and overhead costs, are highly correlated if they tend to move together.) Given that most companies at the time were producing a very limited variety of products that required similar resources to produce, allocation bases such as direct labor-hours, or even machine-hours, worked fine because in fact there was probably little difference in the overhead costs attributable to different products.

Then conditions began to change. As a percentage of total cost, direct labor began declining and overhead began increasing. Many tasks previously done by direct laborers were being performed by automated equipment—a component of overhead. Companies began creating new products and services at an ever-accelerating rate that differed in volume, batch size, and complexity. Managing and sustaining this product diversity required investing in many more overhead resources, such as production schedulers and product design engineers, that had no obvious connection to direct labor-hours or machine-hours. In this new environment, continuing to rely exclusively on a limited number of overhead cost pools and traditional allocation bases posed the risk that reported unit product costs would be distorted and, therefore, misleading when used for decision-making purposes.

Activity-based costing, thanks to advances in technology that make more complex cost systems feasible, provides an alternative to the traditional plantwide and departmental approaches to defining cost pools and selecting allocation bases. The activity-based approach has appeal in today's business environment because it uses more cost pools and unique measures of activity to better understand the costs of managing and sustaining product diversity.

In activity-based costing, an **activity** is any event that causes the consumption of overhead resources. An **activity cost pool** is a "bucket" in which costs are accumulated that relate to a single activity measure in the ABC system. An **activity measure** is an allocation base in an activity-based costing system. The term *cost driver* is also used to refer to an activity measure because the activity measure should "drive" the cost being allocated. The two most common types of activity measures are *transaction drivers* and *duration drivers.* **Transaction drivers** are simple counts of the number of times an activity occurs such as the number of bills sent out to customers. **Duration drivers** measure the amount of time required to perform an activity such as the time spent preparing individual bills for customers. In general, duration drivers are more accurate measures of resource consumption than transaction drivers, but they take more effort to record. For that reason, transaction drivers are often used in practice.

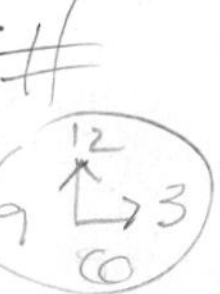

Traditional cost systems rely exclusively on allocation bases that are driven by the volume of production. On the other hand, activity-based costing defines five levels of activity—unit-level, batch-level, product-level, customer-level, and organization-sustaining—that largely do *not* relate to the volume of units produced. The costs and corresponding activity measures for unit-level activities do relate to the volume of units produced; however, the remaining categories do not. These levels are described as follows:[2]

1. **Unit-level activities** are performed each time a unit is produced. The costs of unit-level activities should be proportional to the number of units produced. For example, providing power to run processing equipment would be a unit-level activity since power tends to be consumed in proportion to the number of units produced.
2. **Batch-level activities** are performed each time a batch is handled or processed, regardless of how many units are in the batch. For example, tasks such as placing purchase orders, setting up equipment, and arranging for shipments to customers are batch-level activities. They are incurred once for each batch (or customer order). Costs at the batch level depend on the number of batches processed rather than on the number of units produced, the number of units sold, or other measures of volume. For example, the cost of setting up a machine for batch processing is the same regardless of whether the batch contains one or thousands of items.
3. **Product-level activities** relate to specific products and typically must be carried out regardless of how many batches are run or units of product are produced or sold. For

[2] Robin Cooper, "Cost Classification in Unit-Based and Activity-Based Manufacturing Cost Systems," *Journal of Cost Management,* Fall 1990, pp. 4–14.

example, activities such as designing a product, advertising a product, and maintaining a product manager and staff are all product-level activities.

4. **Customer-level activities** relate to specific customers and include activities such as sales calls, catalog mailings, and general technical support that are not tied to any specific product.
5. **Organization-sustaining activities** are carried out regardless of which customers are served, which products are produced, how many batches are run, or how many units are made. This category includes activities such as heating the factory, cleaning executive offices, providing a computer network, arranging for loans, preparing annual reports to shareholders, and so on.

Many companies throughout the world continue to base overhead allocations on direct labor-hours or machine-hours. In situations where overhead costs and direct labor-hours are highly correlated or in situations where the goal of the overhead allocation process is to prepare external financial reports, this practice makes sense. However, if plantwide overhead costs do not move in tandem with plantwide direct labor-hours or machine-hours, product costs will be distorted—with the potential of distorting decisions made within the company.

IN BUSINESS

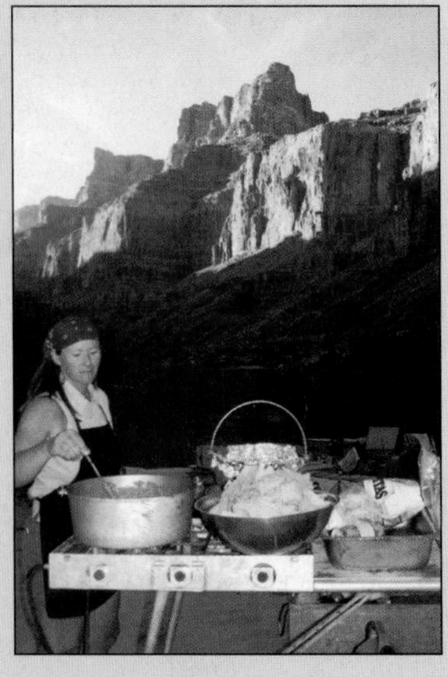

DINING IN THE CANYON

Western River Expeditions (www.westernriver.com) runs river rafting trips on the Colorado, Green, and Salmon rivers. One of its most popular trips is a six-day trip down the Grand Canyon, which features famous rapids such as Crystal and Lava Falls as well as the awesome scenery accessible only from the bottom of the Grand Canyon. The company runs trips of one or two rafts, each of which carries two guides and up to 18 guests. The company provides all meals on the trip, which are prepared by the guides.

In terms of the hierarchy of activities, a guest can be considered as a unit and a raft as a batch. In that context, the wages paid to the guides are a batch-level cost since each raft requires two guides regardless of the number of guests in the raft. Each guest is given a mug to use during the trip and to take home at the end of the trip as a souvenir. The cost of the mug is a unit-level cost since the number of mugs given away is strictly proportional to the number of guests on a trip.

What about the costs of food served to guests and guides—is this a unit-level cost, a batch-level cost, a product-level cost, or an organization-sustaining cost? At first glance, it might be thought that food costs are a unit-level cost—the greater the number of guests, the higher the food costs. However, that is not quite correct. Standard menus have been created for each day of the trip. For example, the first night's menu might consist of shrimp cocktail, steak, cornbread, salad, and cheesecake. The day before a trip begins, all of the food needed for the trip is taken from the central warehouse and packed in modular containers. It isn't practical to finely adjust the amount of food for the actual number of guests planned to be on a trip—most of the food comes prepackaged in large lots. For example, the shrimp cocktail menu may call for two large bags of frozen shrimp per raft and that many bags will be packed regardless of how many guests are expected on the raft. Consequently, the costs of food are not a unit-level cost that varies with the number of guests actually on a trip. Instead, the costs of food are a batch-level cost.

Source: Conversations with Western River Expeditions personnel.

Designing an Activity-Based Costing (ABC) System

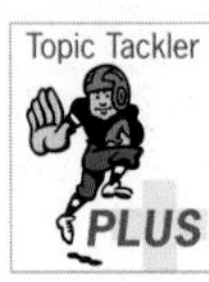

7–1

Experts agree on several essential characteristics of any successful implementation of activity-based costing. First, the initiative to implement activity-based costing must be strongly supported by top management. Second, the design and implementation of an ABC system should be the responsibility of a cross-functional team rather than of the accounting department. The team should include representatives from each area that will use the data provided by the ABC system. Ordinarily, this would include representatives from marketing, production, engineering, and top management as well as technically trained accounting staff. An outside consultant who specializes in activity-based costing may serve as an advisor to the team. And third, the ABC data should be linked to how people are evaluated and rewarded. This ensures that the system will not be ignored.

The reason for insisting on strong top-management support and a multifunction team approach is rooted in the fact that it is difficult to implement changes in organizations unless those changes have the full support of those who are affected. This is particularly true if, as recommended above, the ABC system is used in evaluating and rewarding managers. Unless the managers who are directly affected by these changes have a say, resistance will be inevitable. In addition, designing a good ABC system requires intimate knowledge of many parts of the organization's overall operations. This knowledge can only come from the people who are familiar with those operations.

Top managers must support the initiative for two reasons. First, without leadership from top management, some managers may not see any reason to change. Second, if top managers do not support the ABC system and continue to evaluate and reward employees based on traditional (non-ABC) cost data, their subordinates will quickly get the message that ABC is not important and they will abandon the ABC initiative. Time after time, when accountants have attempted to implement an ABC system on their own without top-management support and active cooperation from other managers, the results have been ignored.

MANAGERIAL ACCOUNTING IN ACTION
The Issue

Classic Brass, Inc. makes two main product lines for luxury yachts—standard stanchions and custom compass housings. The president of the company, John Towers, recently attended a management conference at which activity-based costing was discussed. Following the conference, he called a meeting of the company's top managers to discuss what he had learned. Attending the meeting were production manager Susan Richter, the marketing manager Tom Olafson, and the accounting manager Mary Goodman. He began the conference by distributing the company's income statement that Mary Goodman had prepared a few hours earlier (see Exhibit 7–1):

John: Well, it's official. Our company has sunk into the red for the first time in its history—a loss of $1,250.

Tom: I don't know what else we can do! Given our successful efforts to grow sales of the custom compass housings, I was expecting to see a boost to our bottom line, not a net loss. Granted, we have been losing even more bids than usual for standard stanchions because of our recent price increase, but . . .

EXHIBIT 7–1
Classic Brass Income Statement

Classic Brass
Income Statement
Year Ended December 31, 2005

Sales		$3,200,000
Cost of goods sold:		
Direct materials	$ 975,000	
Direct labor	351,250	
Manufacturing overhead*	1,000,000	2,326,250
Gross margin		873,750
Selling and administrative expenses:		
Shipping expenses	65,000	
Marketing expenses	300,000	
General administrative expenses	510,000	875,000
Net operating income		($ 1,250)

*The company's traditional cost system allocates manufacturing overhead to products using a plantwide overhead rate and machine-hours as the allocation base. Inventory levels did not change during the year.

John: Do you think our prices for standard stanchions are too high?

Tom: No, I don't think our prices are too high. I think our competitors' prices are too low. In fact, I'll bet they are pricing below their cost.

Susan: Why would our competitors price below their cost?

Tom: They are out to grab market share.

Susan: What good is more market share if they are losing money on every unit sold?

John: I think Susan has a point. Mary, what is your take on this?

Mary: If our competitors are pricing standard stanchions below cost, shouldn't they be losing money rather than us? If our company is the one using accurate information to make informed decisions while our competitors are supposedly clueless, then why is our "bottom line" taking a beating? Unfortunately, I think we may be the ones shooting in the dark, not our competitors.

John: Based on what I heard at the conference that I just attended, I am inclined to agree. One of the presentations at the conference dealt with activity-based costing. As the speaker began describing the usual insights revealed by activity-based costing systems, I was sitting in the audience getting an ill feeling in my stomach.

Mary: Honestly John, I have been claiming for years that our existing cost system is okay for external reporting, but it is dangerous to use it for internal decision making. It sounds like you are on board now, right?

John: Yes.

Mary: Well then, how about if all of you commit the time and energy to help me build a fairly simple activity-based costing system that may shed some light on the problems we are facing?

John: Let's do it. I want each of you to appoint one of your top people to a special "ABC team" to investigate how we cost products.

Like most other ABC implementations, the ABC team decided that its new ABC system would supplement, rather than replace, the existing cost accounting system, which would continue to be used for external financial reports. The new ABC system would be used to prepare special reports for management decisions such as bidding on new business.

The accounting manager drew the chart appearing in Exhibit 7–2 to explain the general structure of the ABC model to her team members. Cost objects such as products generate activities. For example, a customer order for a custom compass housing requires the activity of preparing a production order. Such an activity consumes resources. A production order uses a sheet of paper and takes time to fill out. And consumption of resources causes costs. The greater the number of sheets used to fill out production orders and the greater the amount of time devoted to filling out such orders, the greater the cost. Activity-based costing attempts to trace through these relationships to identify how products and customers affect costs.

EXHIBIT 7–2
The Activity-Based Costing Model

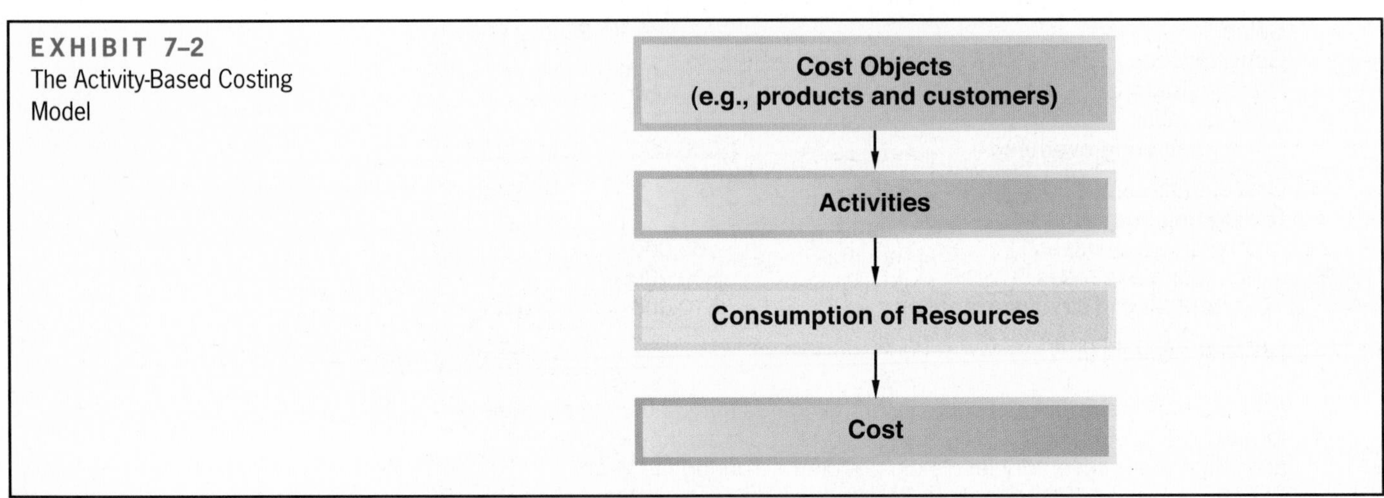

As in most other companies, the ABC team at Classic Brass felt that the company's traditional cost accounting system adequately measured the direct materials and direct labor costs of products since these costs are directly traced to products. Therefore, the ABC study would be concerned solely with the other costs of the company—manufacturing overhead and selling and administrative costs.

The team felt it was important to carefully plan how it would go about implementing the new ABC system at Classic Brass. Accordingly, it broke down the implementation process into five steps:

Steps for Implementing Activity-Based Costing:

1. Define activities, activity cost pools, and activity measures.
2. Assign overhead costs to activity cost pools.
3. Calculate activity rates.
4. Assign overhead costs to cost objects using the activity rates and activity measures.
5. Prepare management reports.

Step 1: Define Activities, Activity Cost Pools, and Activity Measures

The first major step in implementing an ABC system is to identify the activities that will form the foundation for the system. This can be difficult, time-consuming, and involves a great deal of judgment. A common procedure is for the individuals on the ABC implementation team to interview people who work in overhead departments and ask them to describe their major activities. Ordinarily, this results in a very long list of activities.

IN BUSINESS

IS E-TAILING REALLY EASIER?

The company art.com™ sells prints and framed prints over the web. An activity-based costing study identified the following 12 activities carried out in the company:

1. Service customers
2. Website optimization
3. Merchandise inventory selection and management
4. Purchasing and receiving
5. Customer acquisition and retention—paid-for marketing
6. Customer acquisition and retention—revenue share marketing (affiliate group)
7. Sustain information system
8. Sustain business—administration
9. Sustain business—production
10. Maintain facility—administrative
11. Maintain facility—production
12. Sustain business—executive

For example, the activity "merchandise inventory selection and management" involves scanning, describing, classifying, and linking each inventory item to search options on the company's website. "Staff must carefully manage each change to the database, which is similar to adding and removing inventory items from the shelf of a store. They annotate added inventory items and upload them into the system, as well as remove obsolete and discontinued items. . . . The number of inventory items for an e-tailer is typically much greater than for a brick-and-mortar [store], which is a competitive advantage, but experience shows managing a large inventory consumes substantial resources."

Source: Thomas L. Zeller, David R. Kublank, and Philip G. Makris, " How art.com™ Uses ABC to Succeed," *Strategic Finance*, March 2001, pp. 25–31. Reprinted with permission from the IMA, Montvale, NJ, USA, www.imanet.org.

The length of such lists of activities poses a problem. On the one hand, the greater the number of activities tracked in the ABC system, the more accurate the costs are likely to be. On the other hand, a complex system involving large numbers of activities is costly to design, implement, maintain, and use. Consequently, the original lengthy list of activities is usually reduced to a handful by combining similar activities. For example, several actions may be involved in handling and moving raw materials—from receiving raw materials on the loading dock to sorting them into the appropriate bins in the storeroom. All of these activities might be combined into a single activity called material handling.

When combining activities in an ABC system, activities should be grouped together at the appropriate level. Batch-level activities should not be combined with unit-level activities or product-level activities with batch-level activities and so on. In general, it is best to combine only those activities that are highly correlated with each other within a level. For example, the number of customer orders received is likely to be highly correlated with the number of completed customer orders shipped, so these two batch-level activities (receiving and shipping orders) can usually be combined with little loss of accuracy.

At Classic Brass, the ABC team, in consultation with top managers, selected the following *activity cost pools* and *activity measures:*

Activity Cost Pools at Classic Brass

Activity Cost Pool	Activity Measure
Customer orders	Number of customer orders
Product design	Number of product designs
Order size	Machine-hours
Customer relations	Number of active customers
Other	Not applicable

The *Customer Orders* cost pool will be assigned all costs of resources that are consumed by taking and processing customer orders, including costs of processing paperwork and any costs involved in setting up machines for specific orders. The activity measure for this cost pool is simply the number of customer orders received. This is a batch-level activity, since each order generates work that occurs regardless of whether the order is for one unit or 1,000 units.

The *Product Design* cost pool will be assigned all costs of resources consumed by designing products. The activity measure for this cost pool is the number of products designed. This is a product-level activity because the amount of design work on a new product does not depend on the number of units ultimately ordered or batches ultimately run.

The *Order Size* cost pool will be assigned all costs of resources consumed as a consequence of the number of units produced, including the costs of miscellaneous factory supplies, power to run machines, and some equipment depreciation. This is a unit-level activity since each unit requires some of these resources. The activity measure for this cost pool is machine-hours.

The *Customer Relations* cost pool will be assigned all costs associated with maintaining relations with customers, including the costs of sales calls and the costs of entertaining customers. The activity measure for this cost pool is the number of customers the company has on its active customer list. The Customer Relations cost pool represents a customer-level activity.

The *Other* cost pool will be assigned all overhead costs that are not associated with customer orders, product design, the size of the orders, or customer relations. These costs mainly consist of organization-sustaining costs and the costs of unused, idle capacity. These costs *will not* be assigned to products because they represent resources that are *not* consumed by products.

It is unlikely that any other company would use exactly the same activity cost pools and activity measures that were selected by Classic Brass. Because of the amount of judgment involved, the number and definitions of the activity cost pools and activity measures used by companies vary considerably.

The Mechanics of Activity-Based Costing

Step 2: Assign Overhead Costs to Activity Cost Pools

LEARNING OBJECTIVE 2
Assign costs to cost pools using a first-stage allocation.

Exhibit 7–3 shows the annual overhead costs (both manufacturing and nonmanufacturing) that Classic Brass intends to assign to its activity cost pools. Notice the data in the exhibit are organized by department (e.g., Production, Marketing, and General Administrative). This is because the data have been extracted from the company's general ledger. General ledgers usually classify costs within the departments where the costs are incurred. For example, salaries, supplies, rent, and so forth incurred in the marketing department are charged to that department. The functional orientation of the general ledger mirrors the presentation of costs in the absorption income statement in Exhibit 7–1. In fact, you'll notice the total costs for the Production Department in Exhibit 7–3 ($1,000,000) equal the total manufacturing overhead costs from the income statement in Exhibit 7–1. Similarly, the total costs for the General Administrative and Marketing Departments in Exhibit 7–3 ($510,000 and $300,000) equal the marketing and general and administrative expenses shown in Exhibit 7–1.

Three costs included in the income statement in Exhibit 7–1—direct materials, direct labor, and shipping—are excluded from the costs shown in Exhibit 7–3. The ABC team purposely excluded these costs from Exhibit 7–3 because the existing cost system can accurately trace direct materials, direct labor, and shipping costs to products. There is no need to incorporate these direct costs in the activity-based allocations of indirect costs.

Classic Brass's activity-based costing system will divide the nine types of overhead costs in Exhibit 7–3 among its activity cost pools via an allocation process called *first-stage allocation.* The **first-stage allocation** in an ABC system is the process of assigning functionally organized overhead costs derived from a company's general ledger to the activity cost pools.

First-stage allocations are usually based on the results of interviews with employees who have first-hand knowledge of the activities. For example, Classic Brass needs to allocate $500,000 of indirect factory wages to its five activity cost pools. These allocations will be more accurate if the employees who are classified as indirect factory workers (e.g., supervisors, engineers, and quality inspectors) are asked to estimate what percentage of their time is spent dealing with customer orders, with product design, with processing units of product (i.e., order size), and with customer relations. These interviews are conducted with considerable care. Those who are interviewed must thoroughly understand what the activities encompass and what is expected of them in the interview. In addition, departmental managers are typically interviewed to determine how the nonpersonnel costs should be distributed across the activity cost pools. For example, the Classic Brass production manager would be interviewed to determine how the $300,000 of factory equipment depreciation (shown in

Production Department:		
Indirect factory wages.	$500,000	
Factory equipment depreciation	300,000	
Factory utilities	120,000	
Factory building lease.	80,000	$1,000,000
General Administrative Department:		
Administrative wages and salaries	400,000	
Office equipment depreciation	50,000	
Administrative building lease	60,000	510,000
Marketing Department:.		
Marketing wages and salaries	250,000	
Selling expenses	50,000	300,000
Total overhead cost		$1,810,000

EXHIBIT 7–3
Annual Overhead Costs (both Manufacturing and Nonmanufacturing) at Classic Brass

IN BUSINESS

ABC HELPS A DAIRY UNDERSTAND ITS COSTS

Kemps LLC, headquartered in Minneapolis, Minnesota, produces dairy products such as milk, yogurt, and ice cream. The company implemented an ABC system that helped managers understand the impact of product and customer diversity on profit margins. The ABC model "captured differences in how the company entered orders from customers (customer phone call, salesperson call, fax, truck-driver entry, EDI, or Internet), how it packaged orders (full stacks of six cases, individual cases, or partial break-pack cases for small orders), how it delivered orders (commercial carriers or its own fleet, including route miles), and time spent by the driver at each customer location."

Kemps' ABC system helped the company acquire a large national customer because it identified "the specific manufacturing, distribution, and order handling costs associated with serving this customer." The ability to provide the customer with accurate cost information built a trusting relationship that distinguished Kemps from other competitors. Kemps also used its ABC data to transform unprofitable customers into profitable ones. For example, one customer agreed to accept a 13% price increase, to eliminate two low-volume products, and to begin placing full truckload orders rather than requiring partial truckload shipments, thereby lowering Kemps' costs by $150,000 per year.

Source: Robert S. Kaplan and Steven R. Anderson, "Time-Driven Activity-Based Costing," *Harvard Business Review*, November 2004, pp. 131–139.

Exhibit 7–3) should be allocated to the activity cost pools. The key question that the production manager would need to answer is "What percentage of the available machine capacity is consumed by each activity such as the number of customer orders or the number of units processed (i.e., size of orders)?"

The results of the interviews at Classic Brass are displayed in Exhibit 7–4. For example, factory equipment depreciation is distributed 20% to Customer Orders, 60% to Order Size, and 20% to the Other cost pool. The resource in this instance is machine time. According to the estimates made by the production manager, 60% of the total available machine time was used to actually process units to fill orders. This percentage is entered in the Order Size column. Each customer order requires setting up, which also requires machine time. This activity consumes 20% of the total available machine time and is entered under the Customer Orders column. The remaining 20% of available machine time represents idle time and is entered under the Other column.

Exhibit 7–4 and many of the other exhibits in this chapter are presented in the form of Excel spreadsheets. All of the calculations required in activity-based costing can be done by hand. Nevertheless, setting up an activity-based costing system on a spreadsheet or using special ABC software can save a lot of work—particularly in situations involving many activity cost pools and in organizations that periodically update their ABC systems.

We will not go into the details of how all of the percentages in Exhibit 7–4 were determined. However, note that 100% of the factory building lease has been assigned to the Other cost pool. Classic Brass has a single production facility. It has no plans to expand or to sublease any excess space. The cost of this production facility is treated as an organization-sustaining cost because there is no way to avoid even a portion of this cost if a particular product or customer were to be dropped. (Remember that organization-sustaining costs are assigned to the Other cost pool and are not allocated to products.) In contrast, some companies have separate facilities for manufacturing specific products. The costs of these separate facilities could be directly traced to the specific products.

Once the percentage distributions in Exhibit 7–4 have been established, it is easy to allocate costs to the activity cost pools. The results of this first-stage allocation are displayed in Exhibit 7–5. Each cost is allocated across the activity cost pools by multiplying it by the percentages in Exhibit 7–4. For example, the indirect factory wages of $500,000 are

EXHIBIT 7–4

Results of Interviews: Distribution of Resource Consumption across Activity Cost Pools

	Customer Orders	Product Design	Order Size	Customer Relations	Other	Totals
	Activity Cost Pools					
Production Department:						
Indirect factory wages	25%	40%	20%	10%	5%	100%
Factory equipment depreciation	20%	0%	60%	0%	20%	100%
Factory utilities	0%	10%	50%	0%	40%	100%
Factory building lease	0%	0%	0%	0%	100%	100%
General Administrative Department:						
Administrative wages and salaries	15%	5%	10%	30%	40%	100%
Office equipment depreciation	30%	0%	0%	25%	45%	100%
Administrative building lease	0%	0%	0%	0%	100%	100%
Marketing Department:						
Marketing wages and salaries	22%	8%	0%	60%	10%	100%
Selling expenses	10%	0%	0%	70%	20%	100%

EXHIBIT 7–5

First-Stage Allocations to Activity Cost Pools

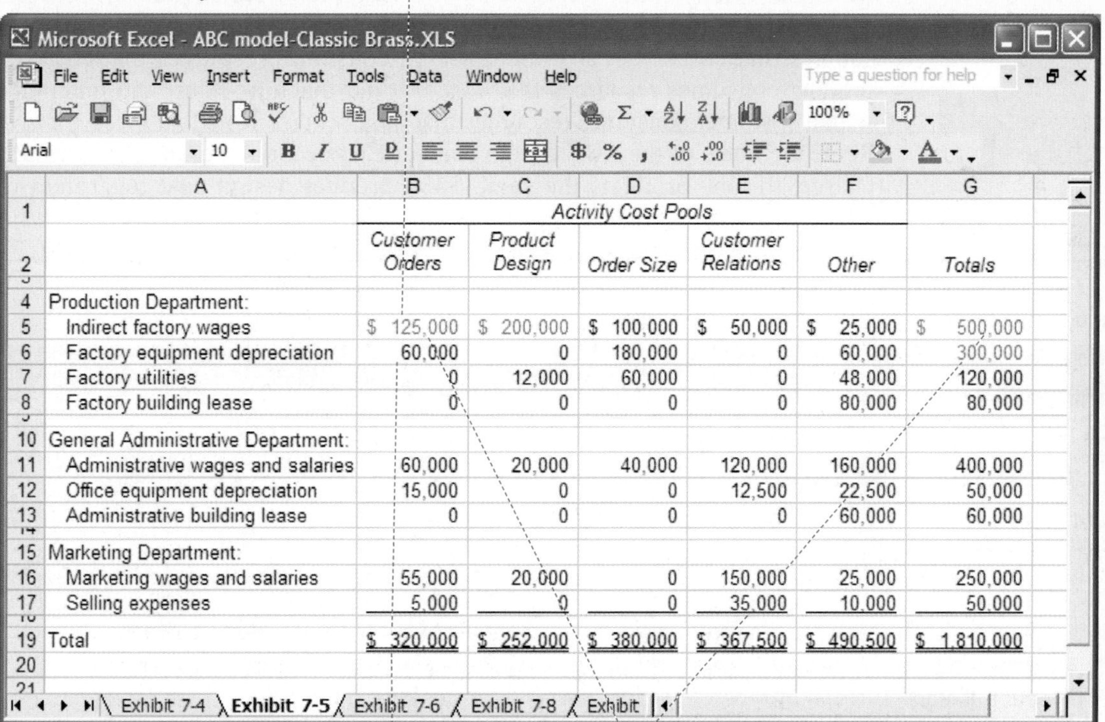

	Customer Orders	Product Design	Order Size	Customer Relations	Other	Totals
	Activity Cost Pools					
Production Department:						
Indirect factory wages	$ 125,000	$ 200,000	$ 100,000	$ 50,000	$ 25,000	$ 500,000
Factory equipment depreciation	60,000	0	180,000	0	60,000	300,000
Factory utilities	0	12,000	60,000	0	48,000	120,000
Factory building lease	0	0	0	0	80,000	80,000
General Administrative Department:						
Administrative wages and salaries	60,000	20,000	40,000	120,000	160,000	400,000
Office equipment depreciation	15,000	0	0	12,500	22,500	50,000
Administrative building lease	0	0	0	0	60,000	60,000
Marketing Department:						
Marketing wages and salaries	55,000	20,000	0	150,000	25,000	250,000
Selling expenses	5,000	0	0	35,000	10,000	50,000
Total	$ 320,000	$ 252,000	$ 380,000	$ 367,500	$ 490,500	$ 1,810,000

Exhibit 7–4 shows that Customer Orders consume 25% of the resources represented by the $500,000 of indirect factory wages.

25% × $500,000 = $125,000

Other entries in the table are computed in a similar fashion.

multiplied by the 25% entry under Customer Orders in Exhibit 7–4 to arrive at the $125,000 entry under Customer Orders in Exhibit 7–5. Similarly, the indirect factory wages of $500,000 are multiplied by the 40% entry under Product Design in Exhibit 7–4 to arrive at the $200,000 entry under Product Design in Exhibit 7–5. All of the entries in Exhibit 7–5 are computed in this way.

Now that the first-stage allocations to the activity cost pools have been completed, the next step is to compute the activity rates.

Step 3: Calculate Activity Rates

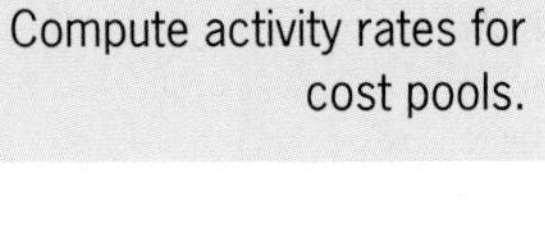

The activity rates that will be used for assigning overhead costs to products and customers are computed in Exhibit 7–6. The ABC team determined the total activity for each cost pool that would be required to produce the company's present product mix and to serve its present customers. These numbers are listed in Exhibit 7–6. For example, the ABC team found that 400 new product designs are required each year to serve the company's present customers. The activity rates are computed by dividing the *total* cost for each activity by its *total* activity. For example, the $320,000 total annual cost for the Customer Orders cost pool (which was computed in Exhibit 7–5) is divided by the total of 1,000 customer orders per year to arrive at the activity rate of $320 per customer order. Similarly, the $252,000 *total* cost for the Product Design cost pool is divided by the *total* number of designs (i.e., 400 product designs) to determine the activity rate of $630 per design. Note that an activity rate is not computed for the *Other* category of costs. This is because the Other cost pool consists of organization-sustaining costs and costs of idle capacity that are not allocated to products and customers. Overall profits must be large enough to cover these unallocated costs. Also note that the activity rates represent *average* costs. For example, the average cost of a customer order is $320.

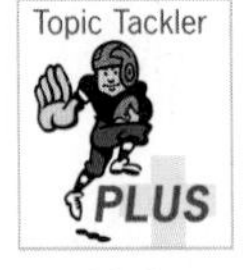

7–2

The rates in Exhibit 7–6 indicate that *on average* a customer order consumes resources that cost $320; a product design consumes resources that cost $630; a unit of product consumes resources that cost $19 per machine-hour; and maintaining relations with a customer consumes resources that cost $1,470. Note that these are *average* figures. Some members of the ABC design team at Classic Brass argued that it would be unfair to charge all new products the same $630 product design cost regardless of how much

EXHIBIT 7–6
Computation of Activity Rates

Microsoft Excel - ABC model-Classic Brass.XLS

	A	B	C	D	E	F
1	*Activity Cost Pools*	*(a)* *Total Cost**	*(b)* *Total Activity*		*(a) ÷ (b)* *Activity Rate*	
2	Customer orders	$320,000	1,000	orders	$320	per order
3	Product design	$252,000	400	designs	$630	per design
4	Order size	$380,000	20,000	MHs	$19	per MH
5	Customer relations	$367,500	250	customers	$1,470	per customer
6	Other	$490,500	Not applicable		Not applicable	
7						
8	*From Exhibit 7-5.					
9						

Exhibit 7-4 / Exhibit 7-5 / Exhibit 7-6 / Exhibit 7

design time they actually require. After discussing the pros and cons, the team concluded that it would not be worth the effort at the present time to keep track of actual design time spent on each new product. They felt that the benefits of increased accuracy would not be great enough to justify the higher cost of implementing and maintaining the more detailed costing system. Similarly, some team members were uncomfortable assigning the same $1,470 cost to each customer. Some customers are undemanding—ordering standard products well in advance of their needs. Others are very demanding and consume large amounts of marketing and administrative staff time. These are generally customers who order customized products, who tend to order at the last minute, and who change their minds. While everyone agreed with this observation, the data that would be required to measure individual customers' demands on resources was not currently available. Rather than delay implementation of the ABC system, the team decided to defer such refinements to a later date.

Before proceeding further, it would be helpful to get a better idea of the overall process of assigning costs to products and other cost objects in an ABC system. Exhibit 7–7 provides a visual perspective of the ABC system at Classic Brass. We recommend that you carefully go over this exhibit. In particular, note that the Other category, which contains organization-sustaining costs and costs of idle capacity, is not allocated to products or customers.

Step 4: Assign Overhead Costs to Cost Objects

LEARNING OBJECTIVE 4
Assign costs to a cost object using a second-stage allocation.

The fourth step in the implementation of activity-based costing is called *second-stage allocation.* In the **second-stage allocation,** activity rates are used to apply overhead costs to products and customers. First, we will illustrate how to assign costs to products followed by an example of how to assign costs to customers.

The data needed by the ABC team to assign overhead costs to Classic Brass's two products—standard stanchions and custom compass housings—are as follows:

Standard Stanchions

1. This product line does not require any new design resources.
2. 30,000 units were ordered during the year, comprising 600 separate orders.
3. Each stanchion requires 35 minutes of machine time for a total of 17,500 machine-hours.

EXHIBIT 7–7
The Activity-Based Costing Model at Classic Brass

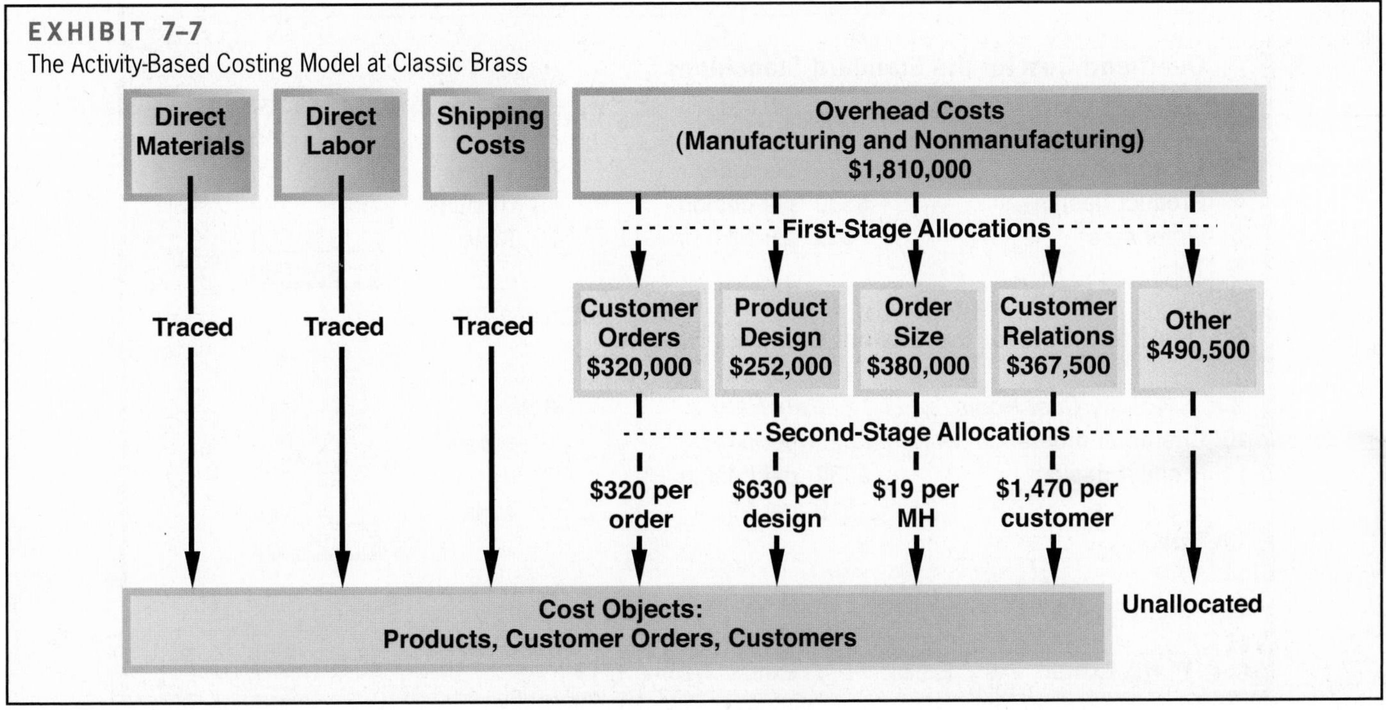

Custom Compass Housings

1. This is a custom product that requires new design resources.
2. There were 400 orders for custom compass housings. Orders for this product are placed separately from orders for standard stanchions.
3. There were 400 custom designs prepared. One custom design was prepared for each order.
4. Since some orders were for more than one unit, a total of 1,250 custom compass housings were produced during the year. A custom compass housing requires an average of 2 machine-hours for a total of 2,500 machine-hours.

Notice, 600 customer orders were placed for standard stanchions and 400 customer orders were placed for custom compass housings, for a total of 1,000 customer orders. All 400 product designs related to custom compass housings; none related to standard stanchions. Producing 30,000 standard stanchions required 17,500 machine-hours and producing 1,250 custom compass housings required 2,500 machine-hours, for a total of 20,000 machine-hours.

Exhibit 7–8 illustrates how overhead costs are assigned to the standard stanchions and custom compass housings. For example, the exhibit shows that $192,000 of overhead costs are assigned from the Customer Orders activity cost pool to the standard stanchions ($320 per order × 600 orders). Similarly, $128,000 of overhead costs are assigned from the Customer Orders activity cost pool to the custom compass housings ($320 per order × 400 orders). The Customer Orders cost pool contained a total of $320,000 (see Exhibit 7–5 or 7–6) and this total amount has been assigned to the two products ($192,000 + $128,000 = $320,000).

EXHIBIT 7–8
Assigning Overhead Costs to Products

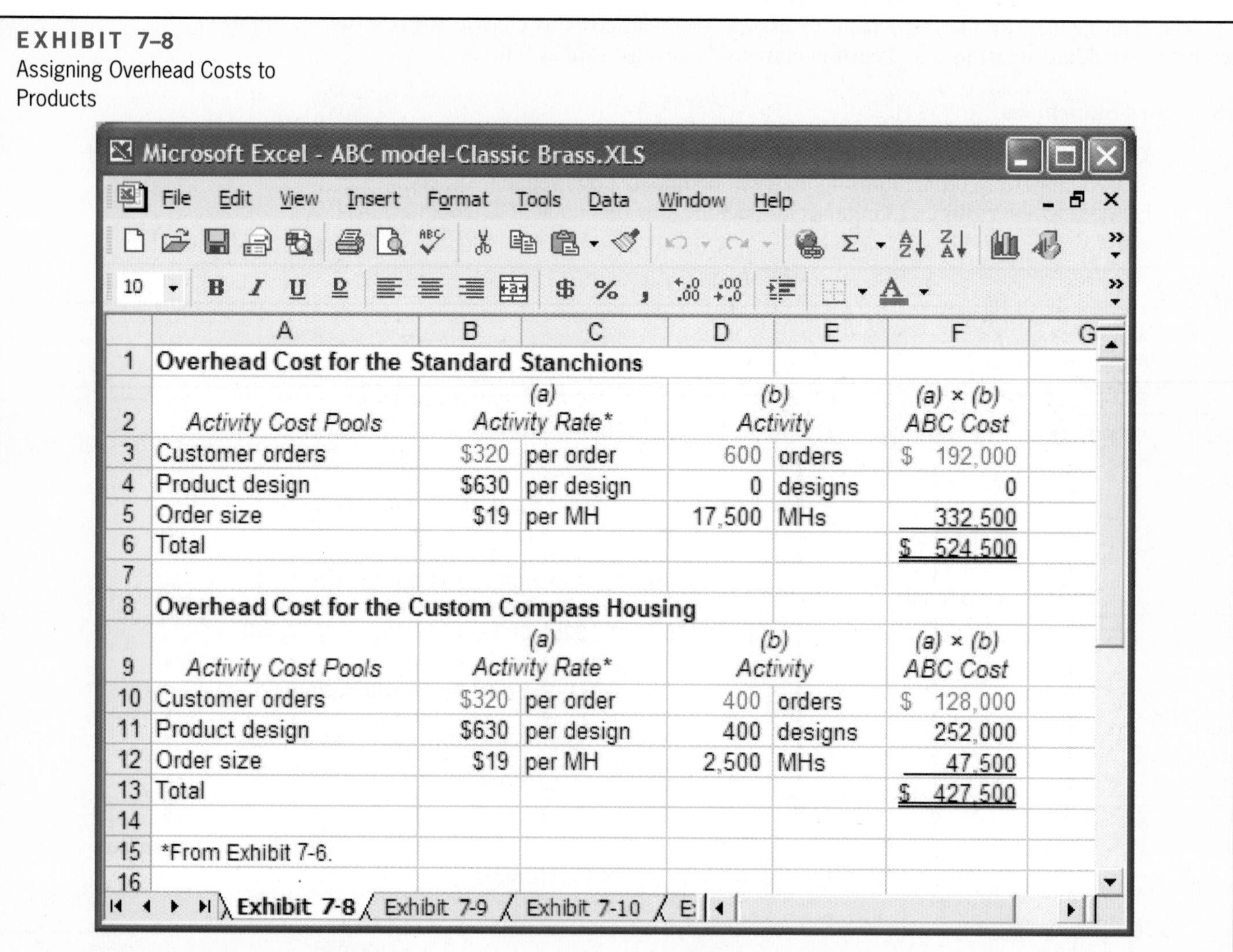

Microsoft Excel - ABC model-Classic Brass.XLS

	A	B	C	D	E	F
1	**Overhead Cost for the Standard Stanchions**					
2	*Activity Cost Pools*	*(a) Activity Rate**		*(b) Activity*		*(a) × (b) ABC Cost*
3	Customer orders	$320	per order	600	orders	$ 192,000
4	Product design	$630	per design	0	designs	0
5	Order size	$19	per MH	17,500	MHs	332,500
6	Total					$ 524,500
7						
8	**Overhead Cost for the Custom Compass Housing**					
9	*Activity Cost Pools*	*(a) Activity Rate**		*(b) Activity*		*(a) × (b) ABC Cost*
10	Customer orders	$320	per order	400	orders	$ 128,000
11	Product design	$630	per design	400	designs	252,000
12	Order size	$19	per MH	2,500	MHs	47,500
13	Total					$ 427,500
14						
15	*From Exhibit 7-6.					
16						

Exhibit 7–8 shows that a total of $952,000 of overhead costs is assigned to Classic Brass's two product lines—$524,500 to standard stanchions and $427,500 to custom compass housings. This amount is less than the $1,810,000 of overhead costs included in the ABC system. Why? The total amount of overhead assigned to products does not match the total amount of overhead cost in the ABC system because the ABC team purposely did not assign the $367,500 of Customer Relations and $490,500 of Other costs to products. The Customer Relations activity is a customer-level activity and the Other activity is an organization-sustaining activity—neither activity is caused by products. As shown below, when the Customer Relations and Other activity costs are added to the $952,000 of overhead costs assigned to products, the total is $1,810,000.

	Standard Stanchions	Custom Compass Housings	Total
Overhead Costs Assigned to Products			
Customer orders	$192,000	$128,000	$ 320,000
Product design	0	252,000	252,000
Order size	332,500	47,500	380,000
Subtotal	$524,500	$427,500	952,000
Overhead Costs not Assigned to Products			
Customer relations			367,500
Other			490,500
Subtotal			858,000
Total overhead cost			$1,810,000

Next, we describe another example of second-stage allocation—assigning activity costs to customers.

The data needed by the design team to assign overhead costs to one of its company's customers—Windward Yachts—are as follows:

Windward Yachts

1. The company placed a total of three orders.
   a. Two orders were for 150 standard stanchions per order.
   b. One order was for a single custom compass housing unit.
2. A total of 177 machine-hours were used to fulfill the three customer orders.
   a. The 300 standard stanchions required 175 machine-hours.
   b. The custom compass housing required 2 machine-hours.
3. Windward Yachts is one of 250 customers served by Classic Brass.

(#/order)(# of orders) = OH costs

Exhibit 7–9 illustrates how the ABC system assigns overhead costs to this customer. As shown in Exhibit 7–9, the ABC team calculated that $6,423 of overhead costs should be assigned to Windward Yachts. The exhibit shows that Windward Yachts is assigned $960 ($320 per order × 3 orders) of overhead costs from the Customer Orders activity cost pool; $630 ($630 per design × 1 design) from the Product Design cost pool; $3,363 ($19 per machine-hour × 177 machine-hours) from the Order Size cost pool; and $1,470 ($1,470 per customer × 1 customer) from the Customer Relations cost pool.

With second-stage allocations complete, the ABC design team was ready to turn its attention to creating reports that would help explain the company's first ever net operating loss.

Step 5: Prepare Management Reports

The most common management reports prepared with ABC data are product and customer profitability reports. These reports help companies channel their resources to their most profitable

EXHIBIT 7–9
Assigning Overhead Costs to Customers

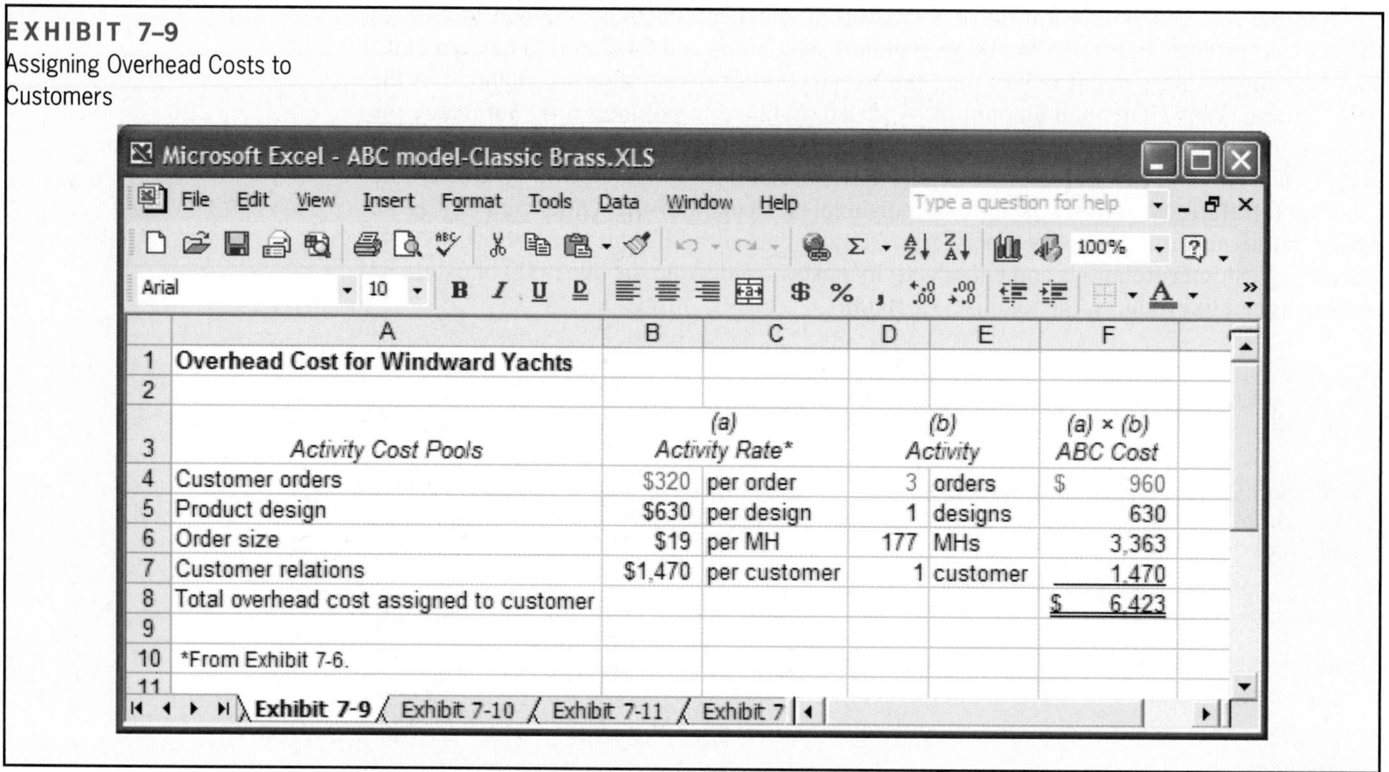

Microsoft Excel - ABC model-Classic Brass.XLS

	A	B	C	D	E	F
1	**Overhead Cost for Windward Yachts**					
2						
3	*Activity Cost Pools*	*(a) Activity Rate**		*(b) Activity*		*(a) × (b) ABC Cost*
4	Customer orders	$320	per order	3	orders	$ 960
5	Product design	$630	per design	1	designs	630
6	Order size	$19	per MH	177	MHs	3,363
7	Customer relations	$1,470	per customer	1	customer	1,470
8	Total overhead cost assigned to customer					$ 6,423
9						
10	*From Exhibit 7-6.					

Exhibit 7-9 / Exhibit 7-10 / Exhibit 7-11 / Exhibit 7

LEARNING OBJECTIVE 5
Use activity-based costing to compute product and customer margins.

growth opportunities while at the same time highlighting products and customers that drain profits. We begin by illustrating a product profitability report followed by a customer profitability report.

The Classic Brass ABC team realized that the profit from a product, also called the *product margin,* is a function of the product's sales and the direct and indirect costs that the product causes. The ABC cost allocations shown in Exhibit 7–8 only summarize each product's indirect (i.e., overhead) costs. Therefore, to compute a product's profit (i.e., product margin), the design team needed to gather each product's sales and direct costs in addition to the overhead costs previously computed. The pertinent sales and direct cost data for each product are shown below. Notice the numbers in the total column agree with the income statement in Exhibit 7–1.

	Standard Stanchions	Custom Compass Housings	Total
Sales	$2,660,000	$540,000	$3,200,000
Direct costs:			
Direct materials.	$905,500	$69,500	$975,000
Direct labor	$263,750	$87,500	$351,250
Shipping	$60,000	$5,000	$65,000

Having gathered the above data, the design team created the product profitability report shown in Exhibit 7–10. The report revealed that standard stanchions are profitable, with a positive product margin of $906,250, whereas the custom compass housings are unprofitable, with a negative product margin of $49,500. Keep in mind that the product profitability report purposely does not include the costs in the Customer Relations and Other activity cost pools. These costs, which total $858,000, were excluded from the report because they are not caused by the products. Customer Relations costs are caused by customers, not products. The Other costs are organization-sustaining costs that are not caused by any particular product.

EXHIBIT 7–10
Product Margins—Activity-Based Costing

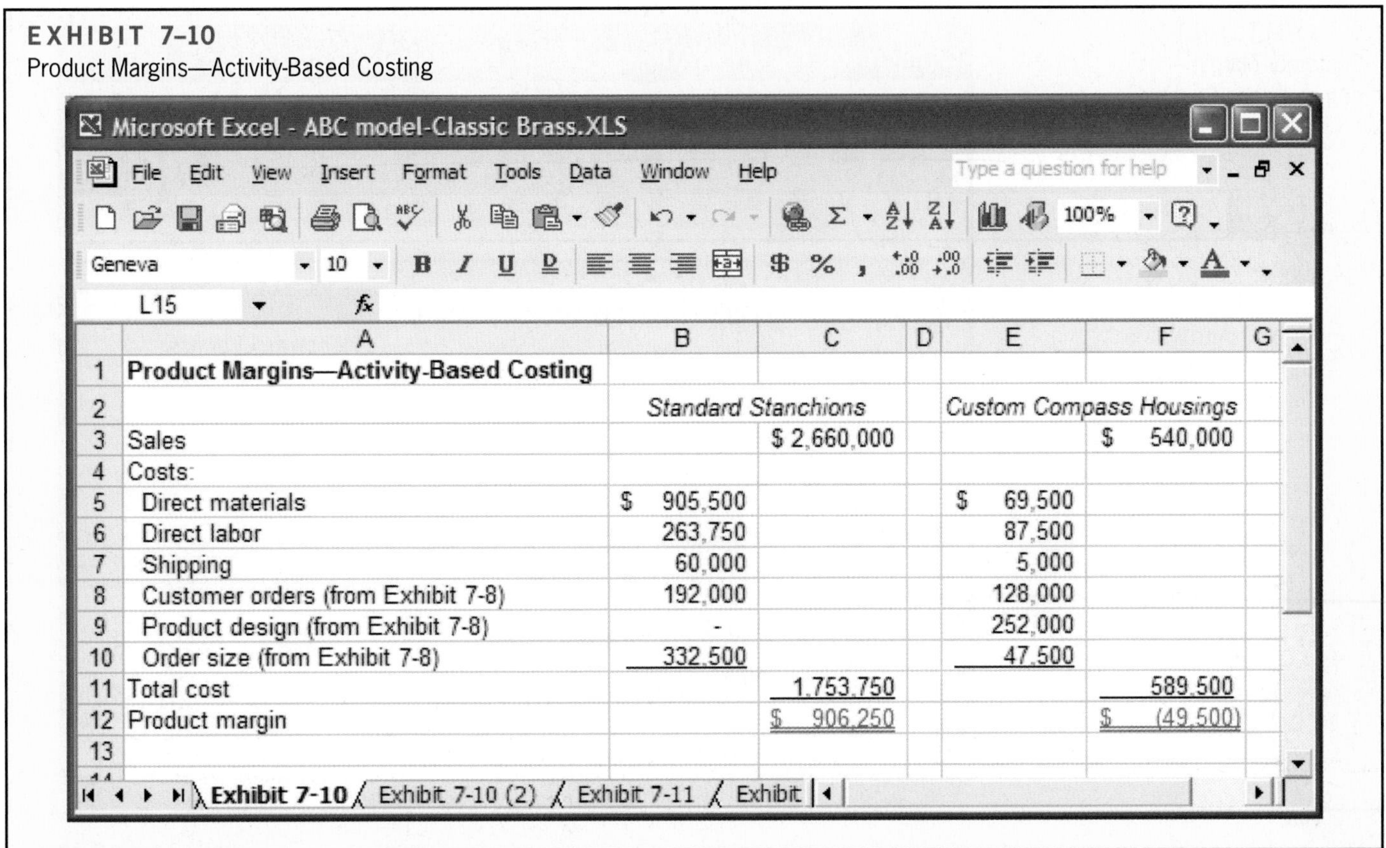

	A	B	C	D	E	F
1	**Product Margins—Activity-Based Costing**					
2		*Standard Stanchions*			*Custom Compass Housings*	
3	Sales		$ 2,660,000			$ 540,000
4	Costs:					
5	Direct materials	$ 905,500			$ 69,500	
6	Direct labor	263,750			87,500	
7	Shipping	60,000			5,000	
8	Customer orders (from Exhibit 7-8)	192,000			128,000	
9	Product design (from Exhibit 7-8)	-			252,000	
10	Order size (from Exhibit 7-8)	332,500			47,500	
11	Total cost		1,753,750			589,500
12	Product margin		$ 906,250			$ (49,500)

The product margins can be reconciled with the company's net operating income as follows:

	Standard Stanchions	Custom Compass Housings	Total
Sales (See Exhibit 7–10)	$2,660,000	$540,000	$3,200,000
Total costs (See Exhibit 7–10)	1,753,750	589,500	2,343,250
Product margins (See Exhibit 7–10).	$ 906,250	$ (49,500)	856,750
Overhead costs not assigned to products:			
Customer relations			367,500
Other.			490,500
Total			858,000
Net operating income			$ (1,250)

Next, the design team created a customer profitability report for Windward Yachts. Similar to the product profitability report, the design team needed to gather data concerning sales to Windward Yachts and the direct material, direct labor, and shipping costs associated with those sales. Those data are presented below:

	Windward Yachts
Sales	$11,350
Direct costs:	
Direct material costs	$2,123
Direct labor costs	$1,900
Shipping costs	$205

EXHIBIT 7–11
Customer Margin—Activity-Based Costing

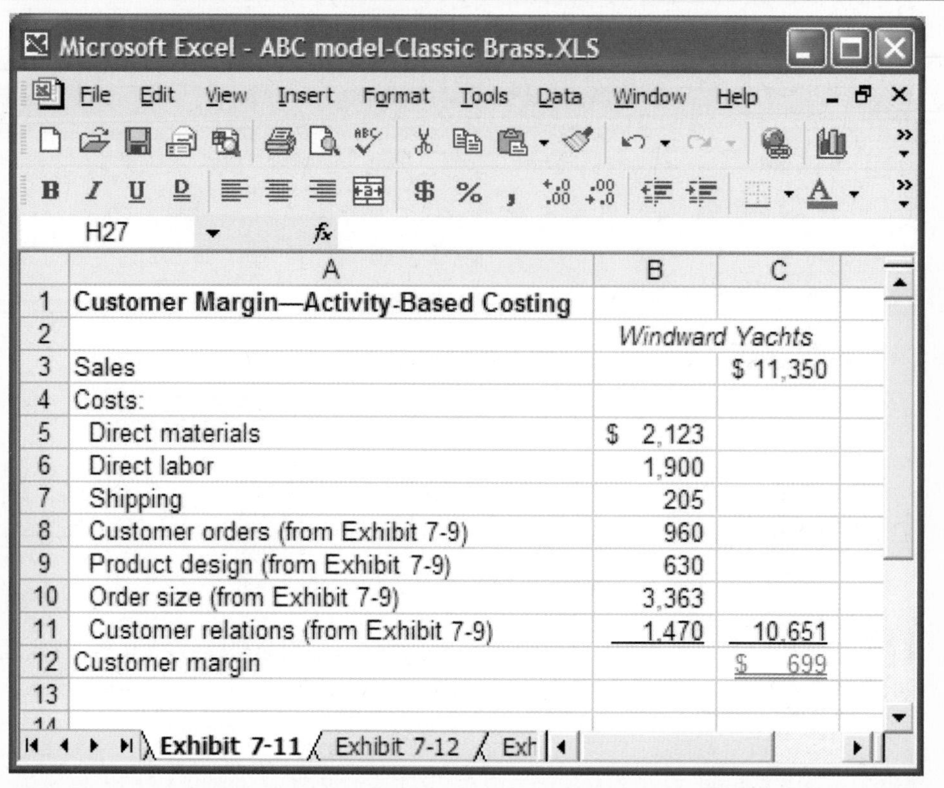

	A	B	C
1	**Customer Margin—Activity-Based Costing**		
2		*Windward Yachts*	
3	Sales		$ 11,350
4	Costs:		
5	Direct materials	$ 2,123	
6	Direct labor	1,900	
7	Shipping	205	
8	Customer orders (from Exhibit 7-9)	960	
9	Product design (from Exhibit 7-9)	630	
10	Order size (from Exhibit 7-9)	3,363	
11	Customer relations (from Exhibit 7-9)	1,470	10,651
12	Customer margin		$ 699
13			

Using these data and the data from Exhibit 7–9, the design team created the customer profitability report shown in Exhibit 7–11. The report revealed that the customer margin for Windward Yachts is $699. A similar report could be prepared for each of Classic Brass's 250 customers, thereby enabling the company to cultivate relationships with its most profitable customers, while taking steps to reduce the negative impact of unprofitable customers.

IN BUSINESS

FINDING THAT GOLDEN TOP 20%

According to Meridien Research of Newton, Massachusetts, 20% of a bank's customers generate about 150% of its profits. At the other end of the spectrum, 30% of a bank's customers drain 50% of its profits. The question becomes how do banks identify which customers are in that golden top 20%? For many banks, the answer is revealed through customer relationship management software that provides activity-based costing capability.

"We had some customers that we thought, on the surface, would be very profitable, with an average of $300,000 in business accounts," said Jerry Williams, chairman and chief executive officer of First Bancorp. "What we didn't pull out was the fact that some write more than 275 checks a month. Once you apply the labor costs, it's not a profitable customer."

Meridien Research estimates that large commercial banks are increasing their spending on customer profitability systems by 14% a year with total annual expenditures exceeding $6 billion dollars.

Source: Joseph McKendrick, "Your Best Customers May Be Different Tomorrow," *Bank Technology News*, July 2001, pp. 1–4.

Comparison of Traditional and ABC Product Costs

Video 7–1

The ABC team used a two-step process to compare its traditional and ABC product costs. First, the team reviewed the product margins reported by the traditional cost system. Then, they contrasted the differences between the traditional and ABC product margins.

EXHIBIT 7–12
Product Margins—Traditional Costing System

	A	B	C	D	E	F	G	H	I
1	**Product Margins—Traditional Cost System**								
2		*Standard Stanchions*			*Custom Compass Housings*			*Total*	
3	Sales		$2,660,000			$ 540,000			$3,200,000
4	Cost of goods sold:								
5	Direct materials	$ 905,500			$ 69,500			$ 975,000	
6	Direct labor	263,750			87,500			351,250	
7	Manufacturing overhead	875,000	2,044,250		125,000	282,000		1,000,000	2,326,250
8	Product margin		$ 615,750			$ 258,000			873,750
9	Selling and administrative								875,000
10	Net operating income								$ (1,250)
11									

Product Margins Computed Using the Traditional Cost System

Classic Brass's traditional cost system assigns only manufacturing costs to products—this includes direct materials, direct labor, and manufacturing overhead. Selling and administrative costs are not assigned to products. Exhibit 7–12 shows the product margins reported by Classic Brass's traditional cost system. We will explain how these margins were calculated in three steps. First, the sales and direct materials and direct labor cost data are the same numbers used by the ABC team to prepare Exhibit 7–10. In other words, the traditional cost system and the ABC system treat these three pieces of revenue and cost data identically.

Second, the traditional cost system uses a plantwide overhead rate to assign manufacturing overhead costs to products. The numerator for the plantwide overhead rate is $1,000,000, which is the total amount of manufacturing overhead shown on the income statement in Exhibit 7–1. The footnote in Exhibit 7–1 mentions that the traditional cost system uses machine-hours to assign manufacturing overhead costs to products. The Order Size activity in Exhibit 7–6 used 20,000 machine-hours as its level of activity. These same 20,000 machine-hours would be used in the denominator of the plantwide overhead rate, which is computed as follows:

$$\text{Plantwide overhead rate} = \frac{\text{Total estimated manufacturing overhead}}{\text{Total estimated machine-hours}}$$

$$= \frac{\$1{,}000{,}000}{20{,}000 \text{ machine-hours}}$$

$$= \$50 \text{ per machine-hour}$$

Since 17,500 machine-hours were worked on standard stanchions, this product line is assigned $875,000 (17,500 machine-hours × $50 per machine-hour) of manufacturing overhead cost. Similarly, the custom compass housings required 2,500 machine-hours, so this product line is assigned $125,000 (2,500 machine-hours × $50 per machine-hour) of manufacturing overhead cost. The sales of each product minus its cost of goods sold equals the product margin of $615,750 for standard stanchions and $258,000 for custom compass housings.

Notice, the net operating loss of $1,250 shown in Exhibit 7–12 agrees with the loss reported in the income statement in Exhibit 7–1 and with the loss shown in the table immediately benneath Exhibit 7–10. The company's *total* sales, *total* costs, and its resulting net operating loss are the same regardless of whether you are looking at the absorption income statement in Exhibit 7–1, the ABC product profitability analysis, or the traditional product profitability analysis in Exhibit 7–12. Although the "total pie" remains constant across the traditional and ABC systems, what differs is how the pie is divided between the two product lines. The traditional product margin calculations suggest that standard stanchions are generating a product margin of $615,750 and the custom compass housings a product margin of $258,000. However, these product margins differ from the ABC product margins reported in Exhibit 7–10. Indeed, the traditional cost system is sending misleading signals to Classic Brass's managers about each product's profitability. Let's explain why.

The Differences between ABC and Traditional Product Costs

The changes in product margins caused by switching from the traditional cost system to the activity-based costing system are shown below:

	Standard Stanchions	Custom Compass Housings
Product margins—traditional	$615,750	$258,000
Product margins—ABC	906,250	(49,500)
Change in reported product margins	$290,500	($307,500)

The traditional cost system overcosts the standard stanchions and consequently reports an artificially low product margin for this product. The switch to an activity-based view of product profitability increases the product margin on standard stanchions by $290,500. In contrast, the traditional cost system undercosts the custom compass housings and reports an artificially high product margin for this product. The switch to activity-based costing decreases the product margin on custom compass housings by $307,500.

The reasons for the change in reported product margins between the two costing methods are revealed in Exhibit 7–13 (page 263). The top portion of the exhibit shows each product's direct and indirect cost assignments as reported by the traditional cost system in Exhibit 7–12. For example, Exhibit 7–13 includes the following costs for standard stanchions: direct materials, $905,500; direct labor, $263,750; and manufacturing overhead, $875,000. Each of these costs corresponds with those reported in Exhibit 7–12. Notice, the selling and administrative costs of $875,000 are purposely not allocated to products because these costs are considered to be period costs. Similarly, the bottom portion of Exhibit 7–13 summarizes the direct and indirect cost assignments as reported by the activity-based costing system in Exhibit 7–10. The only new information in Exhibit 7–13 is shown in the two columns of percentages. The first column of percentages shows the percentage of each cost assigned to standard stanchions. For example, the $905,500 of direct materials cost traced to standard stanchions is 92.9% of the company's total direct materials cost of $975,000. The second column of percentages does the same thing for custom compass housings.

There are three reasons why the traditional and activity-based costing systems report different product margins. First, Classic Brass's traditional cost system allocates *all* manufacturing overhead costs to products. This forces both products to absorb all manufacturing overhead costs regardless of whether they actually consumed the costs that were allocated to them. The ABC system does not assign the manufacturing overhead costs consumed by the Customer Relations activity to products because these costs are caused by customers, not specific products. It also does not assign the manufacturing overhead costs included in the Other activity to products because these organization-sustaining and unused capacity costs

EXHIBIT 7–13
A Comparison of Traditional and Activity-Based Cost Assignments

	Standard Stanchions		Custom Compass Housings		Total
Traditional Cost System	(a) Amount	(a) ÷ (c) %	(b) Amount	(b) ÷ (c) %	(c) Amount
Direct materials	$ 905,500	92.9%	$ 69,500	7.1%	$ 975,000
Direct labor	263,750	75.1%	87,500	24.9%	351,250
Manufacturing overhead	875,000	87.5%	125,000	12.5%	1,000,000
Total cost assigned to products	$2,044,250		$282,000		2,326,250
Selling and administrative					875,000
Total cost					$3,201,250
Activity-Based Costing System					
Direct costs:					
Direct materials	$ 905,500	92.9%	$ 69,500	7.1%	$ 975,000
Direct labor	263,750	75.1%	87,500	24.9%	351,250
Shipping	60,000	92.3%	5,000	7.7%	65,000
Indirect costs:					
Customer orders	192,000	60.0%	128,000	40.0%	320,000
Product design	0	0.0%	252,000	100.0%	252,000
Order size	332,500	87.5%	47,500	12.5%	380,000
Total cost assigned to products	$1,753,750		$589,500		2,343,250
Costs not assigned to products:					
Customer relations					367,500
Other					490,500
Total cost					$3,201,250

are not caused by any particular product. From an ABC point of view, assigning these costs to products is inherently arbitrary and counterproductive.

Second, Classic Brass's traditional cost system allocates all of the manufacturing overhead costs using a volume-related allocation base—machine-hours—that may or may not reflect what actually causes the costs. In other words, in the traditional system, 87.5% of each manufacturing overhead cost is implicitly assigned to standard stanchions and 12.5% is assigned to custom compass housings. For example, the traditional cost system inappropriately assigns 87.5% of costs of the Customer Orders activity (a batch-level activity) to standard stanchions even though the ABC system revealed that standard stanchions caused only 60% of these costs. Conversely, the traditional cost system assigns only 12.5% of these costs to custom compass housings even though this product caused 40% of these costs. Similarly, the traditional cost system assigns 87.5% of the costs of the Product Design activity (a product-level activity) to standard stanchions even though the standard stanchions caused none of these costs. All of the costs of the Product Design activity, rather than just 12.5%, should be assigned to custom compass housings. The result is that traditional cost systems overcost high-volume products (such as the standard stanchions) and undercost low-volume products (such as the custom compass housings) because they assign batch-level and product-level costs using volume-related allocation bases.

The third reason the product margins differ between the two cost systems is that the ABC system assigns the nonmanufacturing overhead costs caused by products to those products on a cause-and-effect basis. The traditional cost system disregards these costs because they are classified as period costs. The ABC system directly traces shipping costs to products and includes the nonmanufacturing overhead costs caused by products in the activity cost pools that are assigned to products.

IN BUSINESS

COMPARING ACTIVITY-BASED AND TRADITIONAL PRODUCT COSTS

Airco Heating and Air Conditioning (Airco), located in Van Buren, Arkansas, implemented an ABC system to better understand the profitability of its products. The ABC system assigned $4,458,605 of overhead costs to eight activities as follows:

Activity Cost Pool	Total Cost	Total Activity	Activity Rate
Machines	$ 435,425	73,872 machine-hours	$5.89
Data record maintenance	132,597	14 products administered	$9,471.21
Material handling	1,560,027	16,872 products	$92.46
Product changeover	723,338	72 setup hours	$10,046.36
Scheduling	24,877	2,788 production runs	$8.92
Raw material receiving	877,107	2,859 receipts	$306.79
Product shipment	561,014	13,784,015 miles	$0.04
Customer service	144,220	2,533 customer contacts	$56.94
Total	$4,458,605		

Airco's managers were surprised by the fact that 55% [($1,560,027 + $877,107) ÷ $4,458,605] of its overhead resources were consumed by material handling and receiving activities. They responded by reducing the raw material and part transport distances within the facility. In addition, they compared the traditional and ABC product margin percentages (computed by dividing each product's margin by the sales of the product) for the company's seven product lines of air conditioners as summarized below:

	Product						
	5-Ton	6-Ton	7.5 Ton	10-Ton	12.5 Ton	15-Ton	20-Ton
Traditional product margin %	−20%	4%	40%	−4%	20%	42%	70%
ABC product margin %	−15%	−8%	50%	1%	−6%	40%	69%

In response to the ABC data, Airco decided to explore the possibility of raising prices on 5-ton, 6-ton, and 12.5-ton air conditioners while at the same time seeking to reduce overhead consumption by these products.

Source: Copyright 2004 From "An Application of Activity-Based Costing in the Air Conditioner Manufacturing Industry," *The Engineering Economist* 49, Issue 3, pp. 221–236 by Heather Nachtmann and Mohammad Hani Al-Rifai. Reproduced by permission of Taylor & Francis group, LLC., http://www.taylorandfrancis.com.

MANAGERIAL ACCOUNTING IN ACTION
The Wrap-up

The ABC design team presented the results of its work in a meeting attended by all of the top managers of Classic Brass, including the president John Towers, the production manager Susan Richter, the marketing manager Tom Olafson, and the accounting manager Mary Goodman. The ABC team brought with them copies of the chart showing the ABC design (Exhibit 7–7), and the table comparing the traditional and ABC cost assignments (Exhibit 7–13). After the formal presentation by the ABC team, the following discussion took place:

John: I would like to personally thank the ABC team for all of the work they have done and for an extremely interesting presentation. I am now beginning to wonder about a lot of the decisions we have made in the past using our old cost accounting system. According to the ABC analysis, we had it all backwards. We are losing money on the custom products and making a fistful on the standard products.

Mary: I have to admit that I had no idea that the Product Design work for custom compass housings was so expensive! I knew burying these costs in our plantwide overhead rate was penalizing standard stanchions, but I didn't understand the magnitude of the problem.

Susan: I never did believe we were making a lot of money on the custom jobs. You ought to see all of the problems they create for us in production.

Tom: I hate to admit it, but the custom jobs always seem to give us headaches in marketing, too.

John: If we are losing money on custom compass housings, why not suggest to our customers that they go elsewhere for that kind of work?

Tom: Wait a minute, we would lose a lot of sales.

Susan: So what, we would save a lot more costs.

Mary: Maybe yes, maybe no. Some of the costs would not disappear if we were to drop the custom business.

Tom: Like what?

Mary: Well Tom, I believe you said that about 10% of your time is spent dealing with new products. As a consequence, 10% of your salary was allocated to the Product Design cost pool. If we were to drop all of the products requiring design work, would you be willing to take a 10% pay cut?

Tom: I trust you're joking.

Mary: Do you see the problem? Just because 10% of your time is spent on custom products doesn't mean that the company would save 10% of your salary if the custom products were dropped. Before we take a drastic action like dropping the custom products, we should identify which costs are really relevant.

John: I think I see what you are driving at. We wouldn't want to drop a lot of products only to find that our costs really haven't changed much. It is true that dropping the products would free up resources like Tom's time, but we had better be sure we have some good use for those resources *before* we take such an action.

As this discussion among the managers of Classic Brass illustrates, caution should be exercised before taking an action based on an ABC analysis such as the one shown in Exhibits 7–10 and 7–11. The product and customer margins computed in these exhibits are a useful starting point for further analysis, but managers need to know what costs are really affected before taking any action such as dropping a product or customer or changing the prices of products or services. Appendix 7A shows how an *action analysis report* can be constructed to help managers make such decisions. An **action analysis report** provides more detail about costs and how they might adjust to changes in activity than the ABC analysis presented in Exhibits 7–10 and 7–11.

Targeting Process Improvements

Activity-based costing can also be used to identify activities that would benefit from process improvements. Indeed, this is the most widely cited benefit of activity-based costing by managers.[3] When used in this way, activity-based costing is often called *activity-based management.* Basically, **activity-based management** involves focusing on activities to eliminate waste, decrease processing time, and reduce defects. Activity-based management is used in organizations as diverse as manufacturing companies, hospitals, and the U.S. Marine Corps. When "40 percent of the cost of running a hospital involves storing, collecting and moving information," there is obviously a great deal of room for eliminating waste.[4]

The first step in any improvement program is to decide what to improve. The Theory of Constraints approach discussed in Chapter 1 is a powerful tool for targeting the area in an organization whose improvement will yield the greatest benefit. Activity-based management provides another approach. The activity rates computed in activity-based costing can provide valuable clues concerning where there is waste and opportunity for improvement. For example, looking at the activity rates in Exhibit 7–6, managers at Classic Brass may conclude that $320 to process a customer order is far too expensive for an activity that adds

[3] Dan Swenson, "The Benefits of Activity-Based Cost Management to the Manufacturing Industry," *Journal of Management Accounting Research* 7, pp. 167–180.

[4] Kambiz Foroohar, "Rx: Software," *Forbes,* April 7, 1997, p. 114.

no value to the product. As a consequence, they may target customer order processing for process improvement using Six Sigma as discussed in Chapter 1.

Benchmarking is another way to leverage the information in activity rates. **Benchmarking** is a systematic approach to identifying the activities with the greatest room for improvement. It is based on comparing the performance in an organization with the performance of other, similar organizations known for their outstanding performance. If a particular part of the organization performs far below the world-class standard, managers will be likely to target that area for improvement.

IN BUSINESS

COSTS IN HEALTH CARE

Owens & Minor, a $3 billion medical supplies distributor, offers an activity-based billing option to its customers. Instead of charging a fixed amount for items that are ordered by customers, the charges are based on activities required to fill the order as well as on the cost of the item ordered. For example, Owens & Minor charges extra for weekend deliveries. These charges encourage customers to reduce their weekend delivery requests. This results in decreased costs for Owens & Minor, which can then be passed on to customers in the form of lower charges for the specific items that are ordered. As many as 25% of Owens & Minor's 4,000 health care customers have used this billing option to identify and realize cost reduction opportunities. For example, Bill Wright of Sutter Health in Sacramento, California, said that Owens & Minor's activity-based billing has motivated his company to eliminate weekend deliveries, place more items per order, align purchase quantities with prepackaged specifications, and transmit orders electronically. The end result is that one Sutter affiliate decreased its purchasing costs from 4.25% of product costs to 3.75%. In all, Owens & Minor has identified about 250 activity-driven procurement costs that hospitals can manage more efficiently to reduce costs.

Source: Todd Shields, "Hospitals Turning to Activity-Based Costing to Save and Measure Distribution Costs," *Healthcare Purchasing News,* November 2001, pp. 14–15.

IN BUSINESS

PROCESS IMPROVEMENTS HELP NURSES

Providence Portland Medical Center (PPMC) used ABC to improve one of the most expensive and error-prone processes within its nursing units—ordering, distributing, and administering medications to patients. To the surprise of everyone involved, the ABC data showed that "medication-related activities made up 43% of the nursing unit's total operating costs." The ABC team members knew that one of the root causes of this time-consuming process was the illegibility of physician orders that are faxed to the pharmacy. Replacing the standard fax machine with a much better $5,000 machine virtually eliminated unreadable orders and decreased follow-up telephone calls by more than 90%—saving the hospital $500,000 per year. In total, the ABC team generated improvement ideas that offered $1 million of net savings in redeployable resources. "This amount translates to additional time that nurses and pharmacists can spend on direct patient care."

Source: "How ABC Analysis Will Save PPMC Over $1 Million a Year," *Financial Analysis, Planning & Reporting,* November 2003, pp. 6–10.

Activity-Based Costing and External Reports

Since activity-based costing generally provides more accurate product costs than traditional costing methods, why isn't it used for external reports? Some companies *do* use activity-based costing in their external reports, but most do not. There are a number of reasons for this. First, external reports are less detailed than internal reports prepared for decision making. On the external reports, individual product costs are not reported. Cost of goods sold and inventory valuations are disclosed, but these accounts are not broken down by product. If some products are undercosted and some are overcosted, the errors tend to cancel each other when the product costs are added together.

Second, it is often very difficult to make changes in a company's accounting system. The official cost accounting systems in most large companies are usually embedded in complex computer programs that have been modified in-house over the course of many years. It is extremely difficult to make changes in such computer programs without causing numerous bugs.

Third, an ABC system such as the one described in this chapter does not conform to generally accepted accounting principles (GAAP). As discussed in Chapter 2, product costs computed for external reports must include all of the manufacturing costs and only manufacturing costs; but in an ABC system as described in this chapter, product costs exclude some manufacturing costs and include some nonmanufacturing costs. It is possible to adjust the ABC data at the end of the period to conform to GAAP, but that requires more work.

Fourth, auditors are likely to be uncomfortable with allocations that are based on interviews with the company's personnel. Such subjective data can be easily manipulated by management to make earnings and other key variables look more favorable.

For all of these reasons, most companies confine their ABC efforts to special studies for management, and they do not attempt to integrate activity-based costing into their formal cost accounting systems.

The Limitations of Activity-Based Costing

Implementing an activity-based costing system is a major project that requires substantial resources. And once implemented, an activity-based costing system is more costly to maintain than a traditional costing system—data concerning numerous activity measures must be periodically collected, checked, and entered into the system. The benefits of increased accuracy may not outweigh these costs.

Activity-based costing produces numbers, such as product margins, that are at odds with the numbers produced by traditional costing systems. But managers are accustomed to using traditional costing systems to run their operations and traditional costing systems are often used in performance evaluations. Essentially, activity-based costing changes the rules of the game. It is a fact of human nature that changes in organizations, particularly those that alter the rules of the game, inevitably face resistance. This underscores the importance of top management support and the full participation of line managers, as well as the accounting staff, in any activity-based costing initiative. If activity-based costing is viewed as an accounting initiative that does not have the full support of top management, it is doomed to failure.

In practice, most managers insist on fully allocating all costs to products, customers, and other costing objects in an activity-based costing system—including the costs of idle capacity and organization-sustaining costs. This results in overstated costs and understated margins and mistakes in pricing and other critical decisions.

Activity-based costing data can easily be misinterpreted and must be used with care when used in making decisions. Costs assigned to products, customers, and other cost objects are only *potentially* relevant. Before making any significant decisions using activity-based costing data, managers must identify which costs are really relevant for the decision at hand. See Appendix 7A for more details.

As discussed in the previous section, reports generated by the best activity-based costing systems do not conform to generally accepted accounting principles. Consequently, an organization involved in activity-based costing should have two cost systems—one for internal use and one for preparing external reports. This is costlier than maintaining just one system and may cause confusion about which system is to be believed and relied on.

IN BUSINESS

A CRITICAL PERSPECTIVE OF ABC

Marconi is a Portuguese telecommunications company that encountered problems with its ABC system. The company's production managers felt that 23% of the costs included in the system were common costs that should not be allocated to products and that allocating these costs to products was not only inaccurate, but also irrelevant to their operational cost reduction efforts. Furthermore, Marconi's front-line workers resisted the ABC system because they felt it might be used to weaken their autonomy and to justify downsizing, outsourcing, and work intensification. They believed that ABC created a "turkeys queuing for Christmas syndrome" because they were expected to volunteer information to help create a cost system that could eventually lead to their demise. These two complications created a third problem—the data necessary to build the ABC cost model was provided by disgruntled and distrustful employees. Consequently, the accuracy of the data was questionable at best. In short, Marconi's experiences illustrate some of the challenges that complicate real-world ABC implementations.

Source: Maria Major and Trevor Hopper, "Managers Divided: Implementing ABC in a Portuguese Telecommunications Company," *Management Accounting Research,* June 2005, pp. 205–229.

IN BUSINESS

THE SURVEY SAYS . . .

Professors John Innes, Falconer Mitchell, and Donald Sinclair have conducted two surveys designed to study ABC adoption trends within the United Kingdom across a five-year time span. The professors' initial survey results are based on responses from 352 of the U.K.'s largest companies, while the follow-up survey results obtained five years later are based on responses from 177 of the U.K.'s largest companies.

The initial survey results indicated that 21% of respondents were currently using ABC, 29.6% were considering ABC adoption, 13.3% had rejected ABC after considering its implementation, and 36.1% were not considering ABC. Five years later the follow-up survey showed that 17.5% of respondents were currently using ABC, 20.3% were considering ABC adoption, 15.3% had rejected ABC after considering implementation, and 46.9% were not considering ABC. The professors summarized their findings by saying "These results are indicative of no growth in the popularity of ABC, and are consistent with both a leveling off in interest in it and the adoption of it over this five-year period."

Source: John Innes, Falconer Mitchell, and Donald Sinclair, "Activity-Based Costing in the U.K.'s Largest Companies: A Comparison of 1994 and 1999 Survey Results," *Management Accounting Research,* September 2000, pp. 349–362.

Summary

Traditional cost accounting methods suffer from several defects that can result in distorted costs for decision-making purposes. All manufacturing costs—even those that are not caused by any specific product—are allocated to products. And nonmanufacturing costs that are caused by products are not assigned to products. Traditional methods also allocate the costs of idle capacity to products. In effect, products are charged for resources that they don't use. And finally, traditional methods tend to place too much reliance on unit-level allocation bases such as direct labor and machine-hours. This results in overcosting high-volume products and undercosting low-volume products and can lead to mistakes when making decisions.

Activity-based costing estimates the costs of the resources consumed by cost objects such as products and customers. The activity-based costing approach assumes that cost objects generate activities that in turn consume costly resources. Activities form the link between costs and cost objects.

Activity-based costing is concerned with overhead—both manufacturing overhead and selling and administrative overhead. The accounting for direct labor and direct materials is usually the same under traditional and ABC costing methods.

To build an ABC system, companies typically choose a small set of activities that summarize much of the work performed in overhead departments. Associated with each activity is an activity cost pool. To the extent possible, overhead costs are directly traced to these activity cost pools. The remaining overhead costs are allocated to the activity cost pools in the first-stage allocation. Interviews with managers often form the basis for these allocations.

An activity rate is computed for each cost pool by dividing the costs assigned to the cost pool by the measure of activity for the cost pool. Activity rates provide useful information to managers concerning the costs of performing overhead activities. A particularly high cost for an activity may trigger efforts to improve the way the activity is carried out in the organization.

In the second-stage allocation, the activity rates are used to apply costs to cost objects such as products and customers. The costs computed under activity-based costing are often quite different from the costs generated by a company's traditional cost accounting system. While the ABC system is almost certainly more accurate, managers should nevertheless exercise caution before making decisions based on the ABC data. Some of the costs may not be avoidable and hence would not be relevant.

Review Problem: Activity-Based Costing

Ferris Corporation makes a single product—a fire-resistant commercial filing cabinet—that it sells to office furniture distributors. The company has a simple ABC system that it uses for internal decision making. The company has two overhead departments whose costs are listed below:

Manufacturing overhead	$500,000
Selling and administrative overhead	300,000
Total overhead costs	$800,000

The company's ABC system has the following activity cost pools and activity measures:

Activity Cost Pool	Activity Measure
Assembling units	Number of units
Processing orders	Number of orders
Supporting customers	Number of customers
Other	Not applicable

Costs assigned to the "Other" activity cost pool have no activity measure; they consist of the costs of unused capacity and organization-sustaining costs—neither of which are assigned to orders, customers, or the product.

Ferris Corporation distributes the costs of manufacturing overhead and of selling and administrative overhead to the activity cost pools based on employee interviews, the results of which are reported below:

Distribution of Resource Consumption Across Activity Cost Pools					
	Assembling Units	Processing Orders	Supporting Customers	Other	Total
Manufacturing overhead	50%	35%	5%	10%	100%
Selling and administrative overhead	10%	45%	25%	20%	100%
Total activity.	1,000 units	250 orders	100 customers		

Required:

1. Perform the first-stage allocation of overhead costs to the activity cost pools as in Exhibit 7–5.
2. Compute activity rates for the activity cost pools as in Exhibit 7–6.
3. OfficeMart is one of Ferris Corporation's customers. Last year, OfficeMart ordered filing cabinets four different times. OfficeMart ordered a total of 80 filing cabinets during the year. Construct a table as in Exhibit 7–9 showing the overhead costs attributable to OfficeMart.
4. The selling price of a filing cabinet is $595. The cost of direct materials is $180 per filing cabinet, and direct labor is $50 per filing cabinet. What is the customer margin of OfficeMart? See Exhibit 7–11 for an example of how to complete this report.

Solution to Review Problem

1. The first-stage allocation of costs to the activity cost pools appears below:

	Activity Cost Pools				
	Assembling Units	Processing Orders	Supporting Customers	Other	Total
Manufacturing overhead	$250,000	$175,000	$25,000	$50,000	$500,000
Selling and administrative overhead	30,000	135,000	75,000	60,000	300,000
Total cost..................	$280,000	$310,000	$100,000	$110,000	$800,000

2. The activity rates for the activity cost pools are:

Activity Cost Pools	(a) Total Cost	(b) Total Activity	(a) ÷ (b) Activity Rate
Assembling units...........	$280,000	1,000 units	$280 per unit
Processing orders..........	$310,000	250 orders	$1,240 per order
Supporting customers........	$100,000	100 customers	$1,000 per customer

3. The overhead cost attributable to OfficeMart would be computed as follows:

Activity Cost Pools	(a) Activity Rate	(b) Activity	(a) × (b) ABC Cost
Assembling units	$280 per unit	80 units	$22,400
Processing orders	$1,240 per order	4 orders	$4,960
Supporting customers	$1,000 per customer	1 customer	$1,000

4. The customer margin can be computed as follows:

Sales ($595 per unit × 80 units)		$47,600
Costs:		
Direct materials ($180 per unit × 80 units)	$14,400	
Direct labor ($50 per unit × 80 units)...........	4,000	
Unit-related overhead (above)	22,400	
Order-related overhead (above)...............	4,960	
Customer-related overhead (above)	1,000	46,760
Customer margin		$ 840

Glossary

Action analysis report A report showing what costs have been assigned to a cost object, such as a product or customer, and how difficult it would be to adjust the cost if there is a change in activity. (p. 265)

Activity An event that causes the consumption of overhead resources in an organization. (p. 245)

Activity-based costing (ABC) A costing method based on activities that is designed to provide managers with cost information for strategic and other decisions that potentially affect capacity and therefore fixed as well as variable costs. (p. 243)

Activity-based management (ABM) A management approach that focuses on managing activities as a way of eliminating waste and reducing delays and defects. (p. 265)

Activity cost pool A "bucket" in which costs are accumulated that relate to a single activity measure in an activity-based costing system. (p. 245)

Activity measure An allocation base in an activity-based costing system; ideally, a measure of the amount of activity that drives the costs in an activity cost pool. (p. 245)

Batch-level activities Activities that are performed each time a batch of goods is handled or processed, regardless of how many units are in the batch. The amount of resource consumed depends on the number of batches run rather than on the number of units in the batch. (p. 245)

Benchmarking A systematic approach to identifying the activities with the greatest potential for improvement. (p. 266)

Customer-level activities Activities that are carried out to support customers but that are not related to any specific product. (p. 246)

Duration driver A measure of the amount of time required to perform an activity. (p. 245)

First-stage allocation The process by which overhead costs are assigned to activity cost pools in an activity-based costing system. (p. 251)

Organization-sustaining activities Activities that are carried out regardless of which customers are served, which products are produced, how many batches are run, or how many units are made. (p. 246)

Product-level activities Activities that relate to specific products that must be carried out regardless of how many units are produced and sold or batches run. (p. 245)

Second-stage allocation The process by which activity rates are used to apply costs to products and customers in activity-based costing. (p. 255)

Transaction driver A simple count of the number of times an activity occurs. (p. 245)

Unit-level activities Activities that are performed each time a unit is produced. (p. 245)

Appendix 7A: ABC Action Analysis

LEARNING OBJECTIVE 6
Prepare an action analysis report using activity-based costing data and interpret the report.

A conventional ABC analysis, such as the one presented in Exhibits 7–10 and 7–11 in the chapter, has several important limitations. Referring back to Exhibit 7–10, recall that the custom compass housings show a negative product margin of $49,500. Because of this apparent loss, managers were considering dropping this product. However, as the discussion among the managers revealed, it is unlikely that all of the $589,500 cost of the product would be avoided if it were dropped. Some of these costs would continue even if the product were totally eliminated. *Before* taking action, it is vital to identify which costs would be avoided and which costs would continue. Only those costs that can be avoided are relevant in the decision. Moreover, many of the costs are managed costs that would require explicit management action to eliminate. If the custom compass housings product line were eliminated, the direct materials cost would be avoided without any explicit management action—the materials simply wouldn't be ordered. On the other hand, if the custom compass housings were dropped, explicit management action would be required to eliminate the salaries of overhead workers that are assigned to this product.

Simply shifting these managed costs to other products would not solve anything. These costs would have to be eliminated or the resources *shifted to the constraint* to have any benefit to the company. While eliminating the cost is obviously beneficial, redeploying the resources is only beneficial if the resources are shifted to the constraint in the process. If the resources are redeployed to a work center that is not a constraint, it would increase the excess capacity in that work center—which has no direct benefit to the company.

In addition, if some overhead costs need to be eliminated as a result of dropping a product, specific managers must be held responsible for eliminating those costs or the reductions are unlikely to occur. If no one is specifically held responsible for eliminating the costs, they will almost certainly continue to be incurred. Without external pressure, managers usually avoid cutting costs in their areas of responsibility. The action analysis report developed in this appendix is intended to help top managers identify what costs are relevant in a decision and to place responsibility for the elimination of those costs on the appropriate managers.

Activity Rates—Action Analysis Report

Constructing an action analysis report begins with the results of the first-stage allocation, which is reproduced as Exhibit 7A–1. In contrast to the conventional ABC analysis covered in the chapter, the calculation of the activity rates for an action analysis report is a bit more involved. In addition to computing an overall activity rate for each activity cost pool, an activity rate is computed for each cell in Exhibit 7A–1. The computations of activity rates for the action analysis are carried out in Exhibit 7A–2. For example, the $125,000 cost of indirect factory wages for the Customer Orders cost pool is divided by the total activity for that cost pool—1,000 orders—to arrive at the activity rate of $125 per customer order for indirect factory wages. Similarly, the $200,000 cost of indirect factory wages for the Product Design cost pool is divided by the total activity for that cost pool—400 designs—to arrive at the activity rate of $500 per design for indirect factory wages. Note that the totals at the bottom of Exhibit 7A–2 agree with the overall activity rates in Exhibit 7–6 in the chapter. Exhibit 7A–2, which shows the activity rates for the action analysis report, contains more detail than Exhibit 7–6, which contains the activity rates for the conventional ABC analysis.

Assignment of Overhead Costs to Products—Action Analysis Report

Similarly, computing the overhead costs to be assigned to products for an action analysis report involves more detail than for a conventional ABC analysis. The computations for Classic Brass are carried out in Exhibit 7A–3. For example, the activity rate of $125 per customer order for indirect factory wages is multiplied by 600 orders for the standard stanchions to arrive at the cost of $75,000 for indirect factory wages in Exhibit 7A–3. Instead of just a single cost number for each cost pool as in the conventional ABC analysis, we now have an entire cost matrix showing much more detail. Note that the column totals for the cost matrix in Exhibit 7A–3 agree with the ABC costs for stanchions in Exhibit 7–8. Indeed, the conventional ABC analysis of Exhibit 7–10 can be easily constructed using the column totals at the bottom of the cost matrices in Exhibit 7A–3. In contrast, the action analysis report will be based on the row totals at the right of the cost matrices in Exhibit 7A–3. In addition, the action analysis report will include a simple color-coding scheme that will help managers identify how easily the various costs can be adjusted.

EXHIBIT 7A–1
First-Stage Allocations to Activity Cost Pools

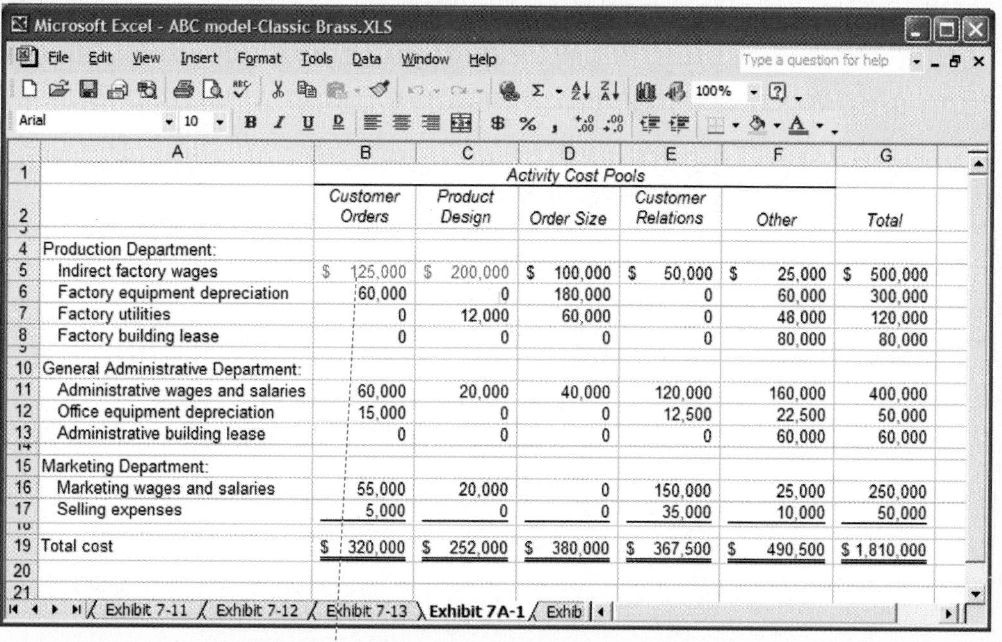

	Customer Orders	Product Design	Order Size	Customer Relations	Other	Total
	Activity Cost Pools					
Production Department:						
Indirect factory wages	$ 125,000	$ 200,000	$ 100,000	$ 50,000	$ 25,000	$ 500,000
Factory equipment depreciation	60,000	0	180,000	0	60,000	300,000
Factory utilities	0	12,000	60,000	0	48,000	120,000
Factory building lease	0	0	0	0	80,000	80,000
General Administrative Department:						
Administrative wages and salaries	60,000	20,000	40,000	120,000	160,000	400,000
Office equipment depreciation	15,000	0	0	12,500	22,500	50,000
Administrative building lease	0	0	0	0	60,000	60,000
Marketing Department:						
Marketing wages and salaries	55,000	20,000	0	150,000	25,000	250,000
Selling expenses	5,000	0	0	35,000	10,000	50,000
Total cost	$ 320,000	$ 252,000	$ 380,000	$ 367,500	$ 490,500	$ 1,810,000

EXHIBIT 7A–2
Computation of the Activity Rates for the Action Analysis Report

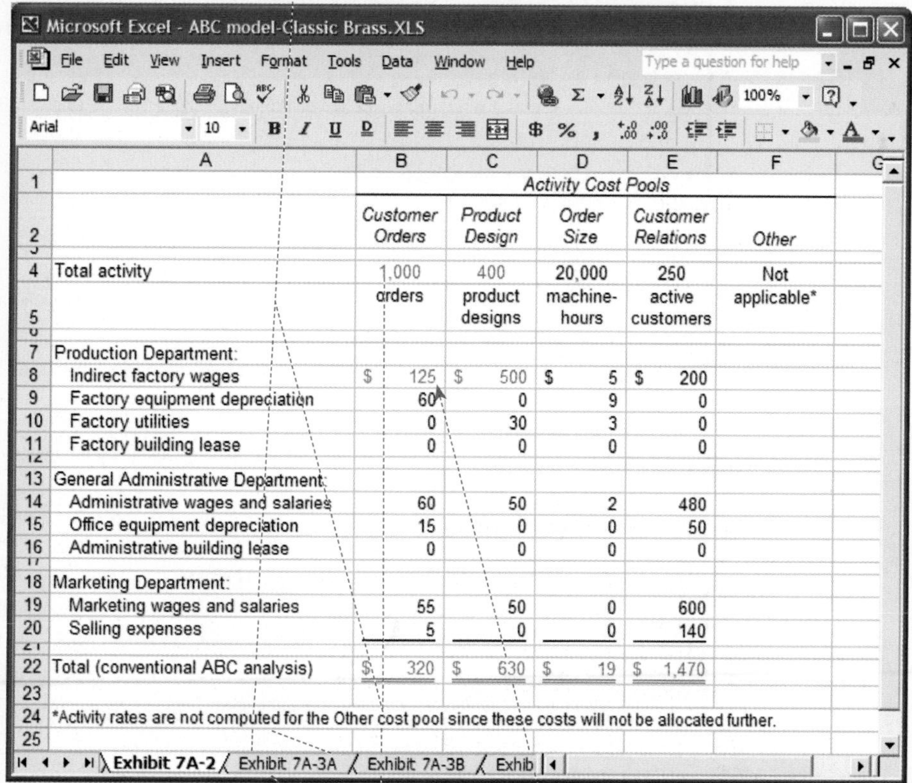

	Customer Orders	Product Design	Order Size	Customer Relations	Other
	Activity Cost Pools				
Total activity	1,000 orders	400 product designs	20,000 machine-hours	250 active customers	Not applicable*
Production Department:					
Indirect factory wages	$ 125	$ 500	$ 5	$ 200	
Factory equipment depreciation	60	0	9	0	
Factory utilities	0	30	3	0	
Factory building lease	0	0	0	0	
General Administrative Department:					
Administrative wages and salaries	60	50	2	480	
Office equipment depreciation	15	0	0	50	
Administrative building lease	0	0	0	0	
Marketing Department:					
Marketing wages and salaries	55	50	0	600	
Selling expenses	5	0	0	140	
Total (conventional ABC analysis)	$ 320	$ 630	$ 19	$ 1,470	

*Activity rates are not computed for the Other cost pool since these costs will not be allocated further.

$125,000 ÷ 1,000 orders = $125 per order.
Other entries in the table are computed similarly.

EXHIBIT 7A–3
Action Analysis Cost Matrices

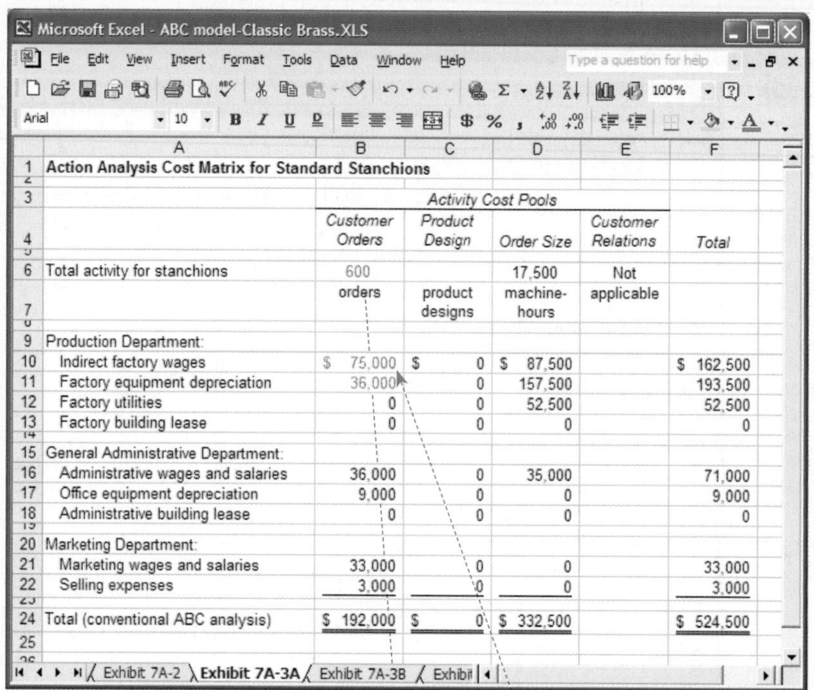

Microsoft Excel - ABC model-Classic Brass.XLS

Action Analysis Cost Matrix for Standard Stanchions

	Activity Cost Pools				
	Customer Orders	*Product Design*	*Order Size*	*Customer Relations*	*Total*
Total activity for stanchions	600 orders	product designs	17,500 machine-hours	Not applicable	
Production Department:					
Indirect factory wages	$ 75,000	$ 0	$ 87,500		$ 162,500
Factory equipment depreciation	36,000	0	157,500		193,500
Factory utilities	0	0	52,500		52,500
Factory building lease	0	0	0		0
General Administrative Department:					
Administrative wages and salaries	36,000	0	35,000		71,000
Office equipment depreciation	9,000	0	0		9,000
Administrative building lease	0	0	0		0
Marketing Department:					
Marketing wages and salaries	33,000	0	0		33,000
Selling expenses	3,000	0	0		3,000
Total (conventional ABC analysis)	$ 192,000	$ 0	$ 332,500		$ 524,500

Exhibit 7A-2 | Exhibit 7A-3A | Exhibit 7A-3B | Exhibit

From Exhibit 7A–2, the activity rate for indirect factory wages for the Customer Orders cost pool is $125 per order.

$125 per order × 600 orders = $75,000

Other entries in the table are computed in a similar way.

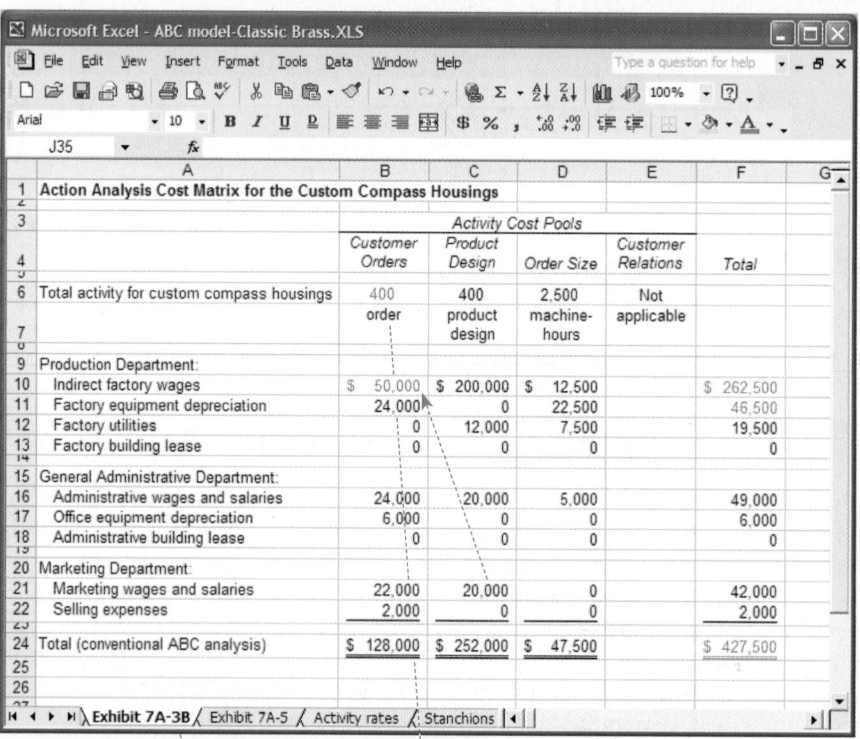

Microsoft Excel - ABC model-Classic Brass.XLS

Action Analysis Cost Matrix for the Custom Compass Housings

	Activity Cost Pools				
	Customer Orders	*Product Design*	*Order Size*	*Customer Relations*	*Total*
Total activity for custom compass housings	400 order	400 product design	2,500 machine-hours	Not applicable	
Production Department:					
Indirect factory wages	$ 50,000	$ 200,000	$ 12,500		$ 262,500
Factory equipment depreciation	24,000	0	22,500		46,500
Factory utilities	0	12,000	7,500		19,500
Factory building lease	0	0	0		0
General Administrative Department:					
Administrative wages and salaries	24,000	20,000	5,000		49,000
Office equipment depreciation	6,000	0	0		6,000
Administrative building lease	0	0	0		0
Marketing Department:					
Marketing wages and salaries	22,000	20,000	0		42,000
Selling expenses	2,000	0	0		2,000
Total (conventional ABC analysis)	$ 128,000	$ 252,000	$ 47,500		$ 427,500

Exhibit 7A-3B | Exhibit 7A-5 | Activity rates | Stanchions

From Exhibit 7A–2, the activity rate for indirect factory wages for the Customer Orders cost pool is $125 per order.

$125 per order × 400 order = $50,000

Other entries in the table are computed in a similar way.

EXHIBIT 7A–4
Ease of Adjustment Codes

Green: *Costs that adjust automatically to changes in activity without management action.*

Direct materials
Shipping costs

Yellow: *Costs that could, in principle, be adjusted to changes in activity, but management action would be required.*

Direct labor
Indirect factory wages
Factory utilities
Administrative wages and salaries
Office equipment depreciation
Marketing wages and salaries
Selling expenses

Red: *Costs that would be very difficult to adjust to changes in activity and management action would be required.*

Factory equipment depreciation
Factory building lease
Administrative building lease

Ease of Adjustment Codes

The ABC team constructed Exhibit 7A–4 to aid managers in the use of the ABC data. In this exhibit, each cost has been assigned an *ease of adjustment code*—Green, Yellow, or Red. The **ease of adjustment code** reflects how easily the cost could be adjusted to changes in activity.[5] "Green" costs are those costs that would adjust more or less automatically to changes in activity without any action by managers. For example, direct materials costs would adjust to changes in orders without any action being taken by managers. If a customer does not order stanchions, the direct materials for the stanchions would not be required and would not be ordered. "Yellow" costs are those costs that could be adjusted in response to changes in activity, but such adjustments require management action; the adjustment is not automatic. The ABC team believes, for example, that direct labor costs should be included in the Yellow category. Managers must make difficult decisions and take explicit action to increase or decrease, in aggregate, direct labor costs—particularly since the company has a no lay-off policy. "Red" costs are costs that could be adjusted to changes in activity only with a great deal of difficulty, and the adjustment would require management action. The building leases fall into this category, since it would be very difficult and expensive to break the leases.

The Action Analysis View of the ABC Data

Looking at Exhibit 7A–3, the totals on the right-hand side of the table indicate that the $427,500 of overhead cost for the custom compass housings consists of $262,500 of indirect factory wages, $46,500 of factory equipment depreciation, and so on. These data are displayed in Exhibit 7A–5, which shows an action analysis of the custom compass housings product. An action analysis report shows what costs have been assigned to the cost object, such as a product or customer, and how difficult it would be to adjust the cost if there is a change in activity. Note that the Red margin at the bottom of Exhibit 7A–5, ($49,500), is exactly the same as the product margin for the custom compass housings in Exhibit 7–10 in the chapter.

The cost data in the action analysis in Exhibit 7A–5 are arranged by the color coded ease of adjustment. All of the Green costs—those that adjust more or less automatically

[5] The idea of using colors to code how easily costs can be adjusted was suggested to us at a seminar put on by Boeing and by an article by Alfred King, "Green Dollars and Blue Dollars: The Paradox of Cost Reduction," *Journal of Cost Management,* Fall 1993, pp. 44–52.

EXHIBIT 7A–5
Action Analysis of Custom Compass Housings: Activity-Based Costing System

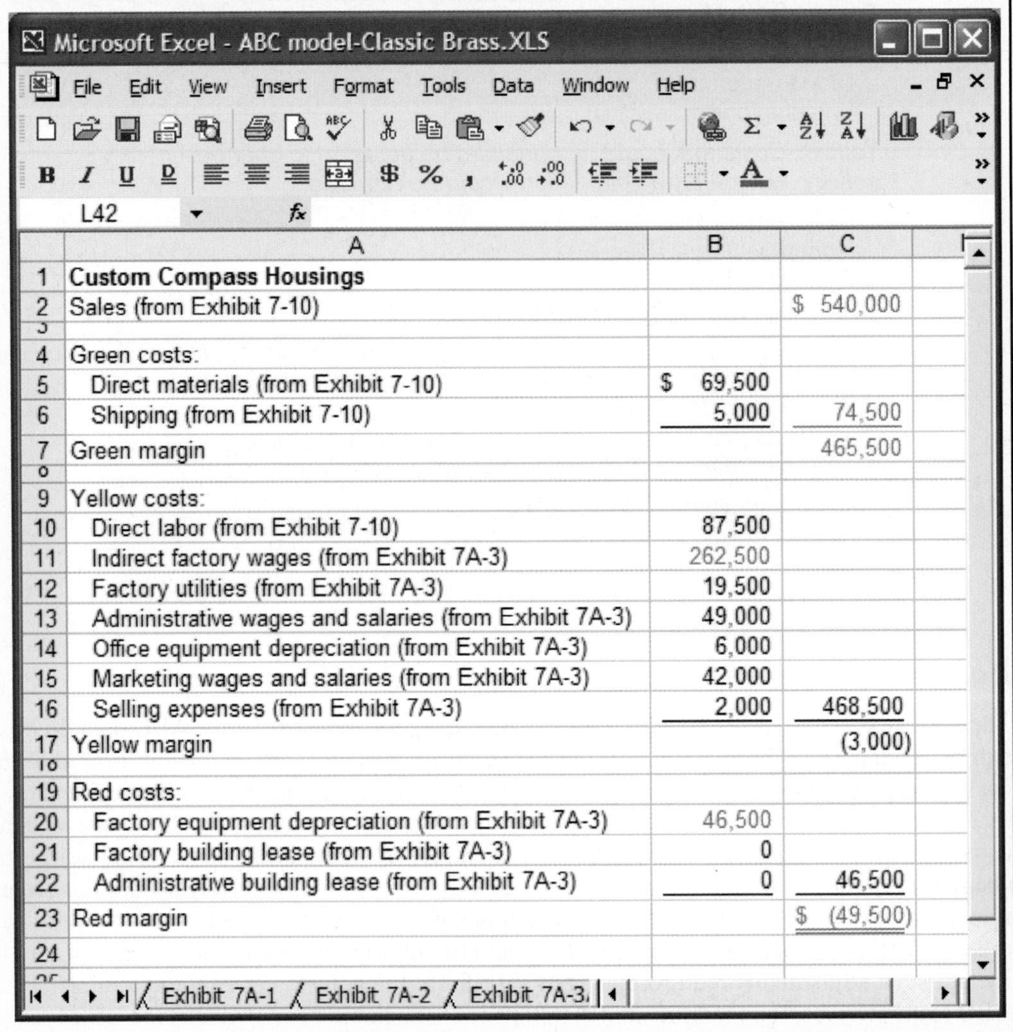

	A	B	C
1	**Custom Compass Housings**		
2	Sales (from Exhibit 7-10)		$ 540,000
3			
4	Green costs:		
5	Direct materials (from Exhibit 7-10)	$ 69,500	
6	Shipping (from Exhibit 7-10)	5,000	74,500
7	Green margin		465,500
8			
9	Yellow costs:		
10	Direct labor (from Exhibit 7-10)	87,500	
11	Indirect factory wages (from Exhibit 7A-3)	262,500	
12	Factory utilities (from Exhibit 7A-3)	19,500	
13	Administrative wages and salaries (from Exhibit 7A-3)	49,000	
14	Office equipment depreciation (from Exhibit 7A-3)	6,000	
15	Marketing wages and salaries (from Exhibit 7A-3)	42,000	
16	Selling expenses (from Exhibit 7A-3)	2,000	468,500
17	Yellow margin		(3,000)
18			
19	Red costs:		
20	Factory equipment depreciation (from Exhibit 7A-3)	46,500	
21	Factory building lease (from Exhibit 7A-3)	0	
22	Administrative building lease (from Exhibit 7A-3)	0	46,500
23	Red margin		$ (49,500)

to changes in activity—appear together at the top of the list of costs. These costs total $74,500 and are subtracted from the sales of $540,000 to yield a Green margin of $465,500. The same procedure is followed for the Yellow and Red costs. This action analysis indicates what costs would have to be cut and how difficult it would be to cut them if the custom compass housings product were dropped. Prior to making any decision about dropping products, the managers responsible for the costs must agree to either eliminate the resources represented by those costs or to transfer the resources to an area in the organization that really needs the resources—namely, a constraint. If managers do not make such a commitment, it is likely that the costs would continue to be incurred. As a result, the company would lose the sales from the products without really saving the costs.

MANAGERIAL ACCOUNTING IN ACTION
The Wrap-up

After the action analysis was prepared by the ABC team, top management at Classic Brass met once again to review the results of the ABC analysis.

John: When we last met, we had discussed the advisability of discontinuing the custom compass housings product line. I understand that the ABC team has done some additional analysis to help us in making this decision.

Mary: That's right. The action analysis report we put together indicates how easy it would be to adjust each cost and where specific cost savings would have to come from if we were to drop the custom compass housings.

John: What's this red margin at the bottom of the action analysis? Isn't that a product margin?

Mary: Yes, it is. However, we call it a red margin because we should stop and think very, very carefully before taking any actions based on that margin.

John: Why is that?

Mary: As an example, we subtracted the costs of factory equipment depreciation to arrive at that red margin. We doubt that we could avoid any of that cost if we were to drop custom orders. We use the same machines on custom orders that we use on standard products. The factory equipment has no resale value, and it does not wear out through use.

John: What about this yellow margin?

Mary: Yellow means proceed with a great deal of caution. To get to the yellow margin we deducted from sales numerous costs that could be adjusted only if the managers involved are willing to eliminate resources or shift them to the constraint.

John: If I understand the yellow margin correctly, the apparent loss of $3,000 on the custom compass housings is the result of the indirect factory wages of $262,500.

Susan: Right, that's basically the wages of our design engineers.

John: I am uncomfortable with the idea of laying off any of our designers for numerous reasons. So where does that leave us?

Mary: What about raising prices on our custom products?

Tom: We should be able to do that. We have been undercutting the competition to make sure that we won bids on custom work because we thought it was a very profitable thing to do.

John: Why don't we just charge directly for design work?

Tom: Some of our competitors already do that. However, I don't think we would be able to charge enough to cover our design costs.

John: Can we do anything to make our design work more efficient so it costs us less? I'm not going to lay anyone off, but if we make the design process more efficient, we could lower the charge for design work and spread those costs across more customers.

Susan: That may be possible. I'll form a Six Sigma team to look at it.

John: Let's get some benchmark data on design costs. If we set our minds to it, I'm sure we can be world class in no time.

Susan: Okay. Mary, will you help with the benchmark data?

Mary: Sure.

John: Let's meet again in about a week to discuss our progress. Is there anything else on the agenda for today?

The points raised in the preceding discussion are extremely important. By measuring the resources consumed by products (and other cost objects), an ABC system provides a much better basis for decision making than a traditional cost accounting system that spreads overhead costs around without much regard for what might be causing the overhead. A well-designed ABC system provides managers with estimates of potentially relevant costs that can be a very useful starting point for management analysis.

Summary (Appendix 7A)

The action analysis report illustrated in this appendix is a valuable addition to the ABC toolkit. An action analysis report provides more information for decision making than a conventional ABC analysis. The action analysis report makes it clear where costs would have to be adjusted in the organization as a result of an action. In a conventional ABC analysis, a cost such as $320 for processing an order represents costs from many parts of the organization. If an order is dropped, there will be little pressure to actually eliminate the $320 cost unless it is clear where the costs are incurred and which managers would be responsible for reducing the cost. In contrast, an action analysis report traces the costs

EXHIBIT 7A–6
Summary of the Steps to Produce an Action Analysis Report

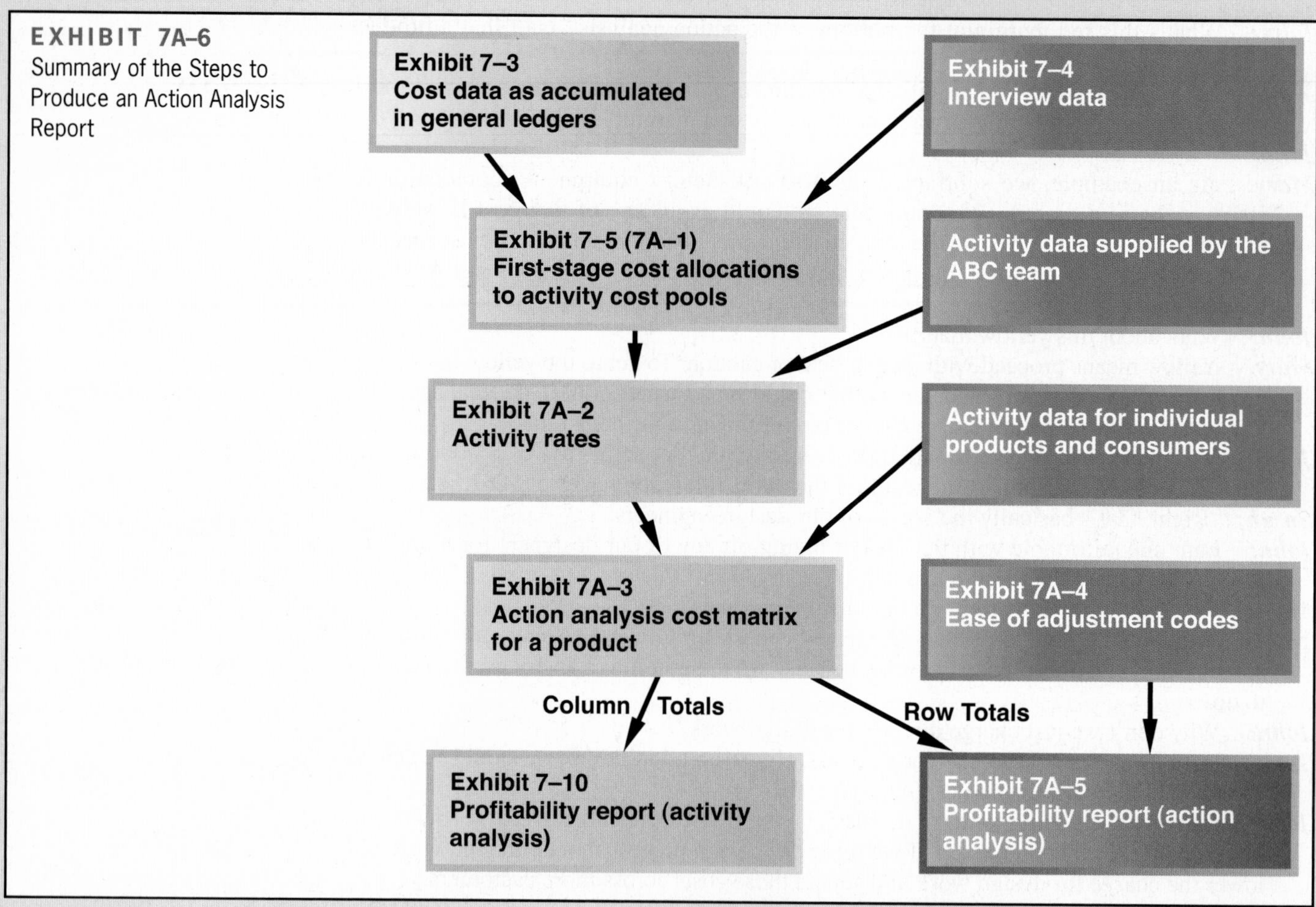

to where they are incurred in the organization and makes it much easier to assign responsibility to managers for reducing costs. In addition, an action analysis report provides information concerning how easily a cost can be adjusted. Costs that cannot be adjusted are not relevant in a decision.

Exhibit 7A–6 summarizes all of the steps required to create both an action analysis report as illustrated in this appendix and an activity analysis as shown in the chapter.

Review Problem: Activity Analysis Report

Refer to the data for Ferris Corporation in the Review Problem at the end of the chapter on pages 269–270.

Required:

1. Compute activity rates for Ferris Corporation as in Exhibit 7A–2.
2. Using Exhibit 7A–3 as a guide, construct a table showing the overhead costs for the OfficeMart orders described in requirement (3) of the Review Problem at the end of the chapter.
3. The management of Ferris Corporation has assigned ease of adjustment codes to costs as follows:

Cost	Ease of Adjustment Code
Direct materials	Green
Direct labor.	Yellow
Manufacturing overhead	Yellow
Selling and administrative overhead	Red

Using Exhibit 7A–5 as a guide, prepare an action analysis of the OfficeMart orders.

Solution to Review Problem

1. The activity rates for the activity cost pools are:

	Assembling Units	Processing Orders	Supporting Customers
Total activity	1,000 units	250 orders	100 customers
Manufacturing overhead	$250	$ 700	$ 250
Selling and administrative overhead	30	540	750
Total	$280	$1,240	$1,000

2. The overhead cost for the four orders of a total of 80 filing cabinets would be computed as follows:

	Assembling Units	Processing Orders	Supporting Customers	Total
Activity	80 units	4 orders	1 customer	
Manufacturing overhead	$20,000	$2,800	$ 250	$23,050
Selling and administrative overhead	2,400	2,160	750	5,310
Total	$22,400	$4,960	$1,000	$28,360

3. The action analysis report is:

Sales		$47,600
Green costs:		
Direct materials	$14,400	14,400
Green margin		33,200
Yellow costs:		
Direct labor	4,000	
Manufacturing overhead	23,050	27,050
Yellow margin		6,150
Red costs:		
Selling and administrative overhead	5,310	5,310
Red margin		$ 840

Glossary (Appendix 7A)

Ease of adjustment codes Costs are coded as Green, Yellow, or Red—depending on how easily the cost could be adjusted to changes in activity. "Green" costs adjust automatically to changes in activity. "Yellow" costs could be adjusted in response to changes in activity, but such adjustments require management action; the adjustment is not automatic. "Red" costs could be adjusted to changes in activity only with a great deal of difficulty and would require management action. (p. 275)

Questions

7-1 In what fundamental ways does activity-based costing differ from traditional costing methods such as those described in Chapters 2 and 3?

7-2 Why is direct labor a poor base for allocating overhead in many companies?

7-3 Why is top management support crucial when attempting to implement an activity-based costing system?

7-4 What are unit-level, batch-level, product-level, customer-level, and organization-sustaining activities?

7-5 What types of costs should not be assigned to products in an activity-based costing system?

7-6 Why are there two stages of allocation in activity-based costing?

7-7 Why is the first stage of the allocation process in activity-based costing often based on interviews?

7-8 When activity-based costing is used, why do manufacturing overhead costs often shift from high-volume products to low-volume products?

7-9 How can the activity rates (i.e., cost per activity) for the various activities be used to target process improvements?

7-10 Why is the activity-based costing described in this chapter unacceptable for external financial reports?

7-11 (Appendix 7A) Why should reports such as those in Exhibits 7–10 and 7–11 be supplemented with an action analysis report such as in Exhibit 7A–5 when making decisions about products or customers?

Quiz 7

Multiple-choice questions are provided on the text Web site at www.mhhe.com/noreen1e.

Exercises 

EXERCISE 7-1 ABC Cost Hierarchy [LO1]

The following activities occur at Greenwich Corporation, a company that manufactures a variety of products.

a. Various individuals manage the parts inventories.
b. A clerk in the factory issues purchase orders for a job.
c. The personnel department trains new production workers.
d. The factory's general manager meets with other department heads such as marketing to coordinate plans.
e. Direct labor workers assemble products.
f. Engineers design new products.
g. The materials storekeeper issues raw materials to be used in jobs.
h. The maintenance department performs periodic preventive maintenance on general-use equipment.

Required:

Classify each of the activities above as either a unit-level, batch-level, product-level, or organization-sustaining activity.

EXERCISE 7-2 First-Stage Allocation [LO2]

VaultOnWheels Corporation operates a fleet of armored cars that make scheduled pickups and deliveries for its customers in the Phoenix area. The company is implementing an activity-based costing system that has four activity cost pools: Travel, Pickup and Delivery, Customer Service, and Other. The activity measures are miles for the Travel cost pool, number of pickups and deliveries for the Pickup and Delivery cost pool, and number of customers for the Customer Service cost pool. The Other cost pool has no activity measure. The following costs will be assigned using the activity-based costing system:

Driver and guard wages	$ 840,000
Vehicle operating expense	270,000
Vehicle depreciation	150,000
Customer representative salaries and expenses	180,000
Office expenses	40,000
Administrative expenses	340,000
Total cost	$1,820,000

The distribution of resource consumption across the activity cost pools is as follows:

	Travel	Pickup and Delivery	Customer Service	Other	Totals
Driver and guard wages	40%	45%	10%	5%	100%
Vehicle operating expense	75%	5%	0%	20%	100%
Vehicle depreciation	70%	10%	0%	20%	100%
Customer representative salaries and expenses	0%	0%	85%	15%	100%
Office expenses	0%	25%	35%	40%	100%
Administrative expenses	0%	5%	55%	40%	100%

Required:
Carry out the first-stage allocations of costs to activity cost pools as illustrated in Exhibit 7–5.

EXERCISE 7-3 Compute Activity Rates [LO3]

As You Like It Gardening is a small gardening service that uses activity-based costing to estimate costs for pricing and other purposes. The proprietor of the company believes that costs are driven primarily by the size of customer lawns, the size of customer garden beds, the distance to travel to customers, and the number of customers. In addition, the costs of maintaining garden beds depends on whether the beds are low-maintenance beds (mainly ordinary trees and shrubs) or high-maintenance beds (mainly flowers and exotic plants). Accordingly, the company uses the five activity cost pools listed below:

Activity Cost Pool	Activity Measure
Caring for lawn	Square feet of lawn
Caring for garden beds—low maintenance	Square feet of low-maintenance beds
Caring for garden beds—high maintenance	Square feet of high-maintenance beds
Travel to jobs	Miles
Customer billing and service	Number of customers

The company has already carried out its first-stage allocations of costs. The company's annual costs and activities are summarized as follows:

Activity Cost Pool	Estimated Overhead Cost	Expected Activity
Caring for lawn	$77,400	180,000 square feet of lawn
Caring for garden beds—low maintenance	$30,000	24,000 square feet of low-maintenance beds
Caring for garden beds—high maintenance	$57,600	18,000 square feet of high-maintenance beds
Travel to jobs	$4,200	15,000 miles
Customer billing and service	$8,700	30 customers

Required:
Compute the activity rate for each of the activity cost pools.

EXERCISE 7-4 Second-Stage Allocation [LO4]

Larner Corporation is a diversified manufacturer of industrial goods. The company's activity-based costing system contains the following six activity cost pools and activity rates:

Activity Cost Pool	Activity Rates
Supporting direct labor.	$7.00 per direct labor-hour
Machine processing	$3.00 per machine-hour
Machine setups	$40.00 per setup
Production orders	$160.00 per order
Shipments	$120.00 per shipment
Product sustaining	$800 per product

Activity data have been supplied for the following products:

	Total Expected Activity	
	J78	W52
Direct labor-hours	1,000	40
Machine-hours	3,200	30
Machine setups	5	1
Production orders	5	1
Shipments	10	1
Product sustaining	1	1

Required:

Determine the total overhead cost that would be assigned to each of the products listed above in the activity-based costing system.

EXERCISE 7-5 Product and Customer Profitability Analysis [LO4, LO5]

Updraft Systems, Inc., makes paragliders for sale through specialty sporting goods stores. The company has a standard paraglider model, but also makes custom-designed paragliders. Management has designed an activity-based costing system with the following activity cost pools and activity rates:

Activity Cost Pool	Activity Rate
Supporting manufacturing	$18 per direct labor-hour
Order processing	$192 per order
Custom designing	$261 per custom design
Customer service	$426 per customer

Management would like an analysis of the profitability of a particular customer, Eagle Wings, which has ordered the following products over the last 12 months:

	Standard Model	Custom Design
Number of gliders	10	2
Number of orders	1	2
Number of custom designs	0	2
Direct labor-hours per glider	28.5	32.0
Selling price per glider	$1,650	$2,300
Direct materials cost per glider	$462	$576

The company's direct labor rate is $19 per hour.

Required:

Using the company's activity-based costing system, compute the customer margin of Eagle Wings.

EXERCISE 7-6 (Appendix 7A) Preparing an Action Analysis Report [LO6]

Pro Golf Corporation produces private label golf clubs for pro shops throughout North America. The company uses activity-based costing to evaluate the profitability of serving its customers. This analysis is based on categorizing the company's costs as follows, using the ease of adjustment color coding scheme described in Appendix 7A:

	Ease of Adjustment Code
Direct materials	Green
Direct labor	Yellow
Indirect labor	Yellow
Factory equipment depreciation	Red
Factory administration	Red
Selling and administrative wages and salaries	Red
Selling and administrative depreciation	Red
Marketing expenses	Yellow

Management would like to evaluate the profitability of a particular customer—the Peregrine Golf Club of Eagle, Colorado. Over the last 12 months this customer submitted one order for 80 golf clubs that had to be produced in two batches due to differences in product labeling requested by the customer. Summary data concerning the order appear below:

Number of clubs	80
Number of orders	1
Number of batches	2
Direct labor-hours per club	0.3
Selling price per club	$48.00
Direct materials cost per club	$25.40
Direct labor rate per hour	$21.50

A cost analyst working in the controller's office at the company has already produced the action analysis cost matrix for the Peregrine Golf Club that follows:

Action Analysis Cost Matrix for Peregrine Golf Club

	Activity Cost Pools				
	Volume	Batch Processing	Order Processing	Customer Service	Total
Activity	24 direct labor-hours	2 batches	1 order	1 customer	
Manufacturing overhead:					
Indirect labor	$ 33.60	$51.60	$ 4.80	$ 0.00	$ 90.00
Factory equipment depreciation	105.60	0.80	0.00	0.00	106.40
Factory administration	16.80	0.60	14.00	231.00	262.40
Selling and administrative overhead:					
Wages and salaries	12.00	0.00	38.00	386.00	436.00
Depreciation	0.00	0.00	5.00	25.00	30.00
Marketing expenses	115.20	0.00	57.00	368.00	540.20
Total	$283.20	$53.00	$118.80	$1,010.00	$1,465.00

Required:

Prepare an action analysis report showing the profitability of the Peregrine Golf Club. Include direct materials and direct labor costs in the report. Use Exhibit 7A–5 as a guide for organizing the report.

EXERCISE 7-7 Activity Measures [LO1]

Various activities at Morales Corporation, a manufacturing company, are listed below. Each activity has been classified as unit-level, batch-level, product-level, customer-level, or organization-sustaining.

	Activity	Activity Classification	Examples of Activity Measures
a.	Materials are moved from the receiving dock to the assembly area by a material-handling crew	Batch-level	
b.	Direct labor workers assemble various products	Unit-level	
c.	Diversity training is provided to all employees in the company	Organization-sustaining	
d.	A product is designed by a cross-functional team	Product-level	
e.	Equipment is set up to process a batch	Batch-level	
f.	A customer is billed for all products delivered during the month	Customer-level	

Required:

Complete the above table by listing an example of an activity measure for each activity.

EXERCISE 7-8 Computing ABC Product Costs [LO3, LO4]

Performance Products Corporation makes two products, titanium Rims and Posts. Data regarding the two products follow:

	Direct Labor-Hours per Unit	Annual Production
Rims	0.40	20,000 units
Posts	0.20	80,000 units

Additional information about the company follows:

a. Rims require $17 in direct materials per unit, and Posts require $10.
b. The direct labor wage rate is $16 per hour.
c. Rims are more complex to manufacture than Posts, and they require special equipment.
d. The ABC system has the following activity cost pools:

Activity Cost Pool	Activity Measure	Estimated Overhead Cost	Activity		
			Rims	Posts	Total
Machine setups	Number of setups	$21,600	100	80	180
Special processing	Machine-hours	$180,000	4,000	0	4,000
General factory	Direct labor-hours	$288,000	8,000	16,000	24,000

Required:

1. Compute the activity rate for each activity cost pool.
2. Determine the unit cost of each product according to the ABC system, including direct materials and direct labor.

EXERCISE 7-9 First-Stage Allocations [LO2]

The operations vice president of First Bank of Eagle, Kristin Wu, has been interested in investigating the efficiency of the bank's operations. She has been particularly concerned about the costs of handling routine transactions at the bank and would like to compare these costs at the bank's various branches. If the branches with the most efficient operations can be identified, their methods can be studied and then replicated elsewhere. While the bank maintains meticulous records of wages and other costs, there has been no attempt thus far to show how those costs are related to the various services provided by the bank. Ms. Wu has asked your help in conducting an activity-based costing study of bank operations. In particular, she would like to know the cost of opening an account, the cost of processing deposits and withdrawals, and the cost of processing other customer transactions.

The Avon branch of First Bank of Eagle has submitted the following cost data for last year:

Teller wages	$150,000
Assistant branch manager salary	70,000
Branch manager salary	85,000
Total	$305,000

Virtually all of the other costs of the branch—rent, depreciation, utilities, and so on—are organization-sustaining costs that cannot be meaningfully assigned to individual customer transactions such as depositing checks.

In addition to the cost data above, the employees of the Avon branch have been interviewed concerning how their time was distributed last year across the activities included in the activity-based costing study. The results of those interviews appear below:

	Distribution of Resource Consumption Across Activities				
	Opening Accounts	Processing Deposits and Withdrawals	Processing Other Customer Transactions	Other Activities	Totals
Teller wages	0%	75%	15%	10%	100%
Assistant branch manager salary	10%	15%	25%	50%	100%
Branch manager salary	0%	0%	20%	80%	100%

Required:

Prepare the first-stage allocation for Ms. Wu as illustrated in Exhibit 7–5.

EXERCISE 7-10 Computing and Interpreting Activity Rates [LO3]

(This exercise is a continuation of Exercise 7-9; it should be assigned *only* if Exercise 7-9 is also assigned.) The manager of the Avon branch of First Bank of Eagle has provided the following data concerning the transactions of the branch during the past year:

Activity	Total Activity at the Avon Branch
Opening accounts	200 accounts opened
Processing deposits and withdrawals	50,000 deposits and withdrawals
Processing other customer transactions	1,000 other customer transactions

The lowest costs reported by other branches for these activities are displayed below:

Activity	Lowest Cost Among All First Bank of Eagle Branches
Opening accounts	$24.35 per account opened
Processing deposits and withdrawals	$2.72 per deposit or withdrawal
Processing other customer transactions	$48.90 per other customer transaction

Required:

1. Using the first-stage allocation from Exercise 7-9 and the above data, compute the activity rates for the activity-based costing system. (Use Exhibit 7–6 as a guide.) Round all computations to the nearest whole cent.
2. What do these results suggest to you concerning operations at the Avon branch?

EXERCISE 7-11 Second-Stage Allocation to an Order [LO4]

Transvaal Mining Tools Ltd. of South Africa makes specialty tools used in the mining industry. The company uses an activity-based costing system for internal decision-making purposes. The company has four activity cost pools as listed below:

Activity Cost Pool	Activity Measure	Activity Rate
Order size	Number of direct labor-hours	R17.60 per direct labor-hour*
Customer orders	Number of customer orders	R360 per customer order
Product testing	Number of testing hours	R79 per testing hour
Selling	Number of sales calls	R1,494 per sales call

*(The currency in South Africa is the rand, denoted here by R.)

The managing director of the company would like information concerning the cost of a recently completed order for hard-rock drills. The order required 150 direct labor-hours, 18 hours of product testing, and three sales calls.

Required:

Prepare a report showing the overhead cost of the order for hard-rock drills according to the activity-based costing system. What is the total overhead cost assigned to the order?

EXERCISE 7-12 (Appendix 7A) Second-Stage Allocation to an Order Using the Action Analysis Approach [LO4, LO6]

This exercise should be assigned in conjunction with Exercise 7-11.

The results of the first-stage allocation of the activity-based costing system at Transvaal Mining Tools Ltd., in which the activity rates were computed, appear below:

	Order Size	Customer Orders	Product Testing	Selling
Manufacturing overhead:				
Indirect labor	R 9.60	R 231.00	R 36.00	R 0.00
Factory depreciation	7.00	0.00	18.00	0.00
Factory utilities	0.20	0.00	1.00	0.00
Factory administration	0.00	46.00	24.00	12.00
Selling and administrative:				
Wages and salaries	0.80	72.00	0.00	965.00
Depreciation	0.00	11.00	0.00	36.00
Taxes and insurance	0.00	0.00	0.00	49.00
Selling expenses	0.00	0.00	0.00	432.00
Total overhead cost	R 17.60	R 360.00	R 79.00	R 1,494.00

Required:

1. Using Exhibit 7A–3 as a guide, prepare a report showing the overhead cost of the order for hard-rock drills discussed in Exercise 7-11. What is the total overhead cost of the order?
2. Explain the two different perspectives this report gives to managers concerning the nature of the overhead costs involved in the order. (Hint: Look at the row and column totals of the report you have prepared.)

EXERCISE 7-13 Cost Hierarchy [LO1]

Green Glider Corporation makes golf carts that it sells directly to golf courses throughout the world. Several basic models are available, which are modified to suit the needs of each particular golf course. A golf course located in the Pacific Northwest, for example, would typically specify that its golf carts come equipped with retractable rain-proof covers. In addition, each customer (i.e., golf course) customizes its golf carts with its own color scheme and logo. The company typically makes all of the golf carts for a customer before starting work on the next customer's golf carts. Below are listed a number of activities and costs at Green Glider Corporation:

a. The purchasing department orders the specific color of paint specified by the customer from the company's supplier.
b. A steering wheel is installed in a golf cart.

c. An outside attorney draws up a new generic sales contract for the company limiting Green Glider's liability in case of accidents that involve its golf carts.
d. The company's paint shop makes a stencil for a customer's logo.
e. A sales representative visits an old customer to check on how the company's golf carts are working out and to try to make a new sale.
f. The accounts receivable department prepares the bill for a completed order.
g. Electricity is used to heat and light the factory and the administrative offices.
h. A golf cart is painted.
i. The company's engineer modifies the design of a model to eliminate a potential safety problem.
j. The marketing department has a catalogue printed and then mails copies to golf course managers.
k. Completed golf carts are individually tested on the company's test track.
l. A new model golf cart is shipped to the leading golfing trade magazine to be evaluated for the magazine's annual rating of golf carts.

Required:

Classify each of the costs or activities above as unit-level, batch-level, product-level, customer-level, or organization-sustaining. In this case, customers are golf courses, products are models of the golf cart, a batch is a specific order from a customer, and units are individual golf carts.

EXERCISE 7-14 Second-Stage Allocation and Margin Calculations [LO4, LO5]

Theatre Seating, Inc., makes high-quality adjustable seats for theaters. The company's activity-based costing system has four activity cost pools, which are listed below along with their activity measures and activity rates:

Activity Cost Pool	Activity Measure	Activity Rate
Supporting direct labor.	Number of direct labor-hours	$12 per direct labor-hour
Batch processing	Number of batches	$96 per batch
Order processing	Number of orders	$284 per order
Customer service	Number of customers	$2,620 per customer

The company just completed a single order from CineMax Entertainment Corporation for 2,400 custom seats. The order was produced in four batches. Each seat required 0.8 direct labor-hours. The selling price was $137.95 per seat, the direct materials cost was $112.00 per seat, and the direct labor cost was $14.40 per seat. This was the only order from CineMax Entertainment for the year.

Required:

Using Exhibit 7–11 as a guide, prepare a report showing the customer margin on sales to CineMax Entertainment for the year.

EXERCISE 7-15 (Appendix 7A) Second-Stage Allocations and Margin Calculations Using the Action Analysis Approach [LO4, LO6]

Refer to the data for Theatre Seating, Inc., in Exercise 7-14 and the following additional details concerning the activity rates:

	Activity Rates			
	Supporting Direct Labor	Batch Processing	Order Processing	Customer Service
Manufacturing overhead:				
Indirect labor	$ 1.80	$72.00	$ 18.00	$ 0.00
Factory equipment depreciation	7.35	3.25	0.00	0.00
Factory administration	2.10	7.00	28.00	268.00
Selling and administrative:				
Wages and salaries	0.50	13.00	153.00	1,864.00
Depreciation	0.00	0.75	6.00	26.00
Marketing expenses	0.25	0.00	79.00	462.00
Total activity rate	$12.00	$96.00	$284.00	$2,620.00

Management has provided their ease of adjustment codes for purposes of preparing action analyses.

	Ease of Adjustment Codes
Direct materials	Green
Direct labor	Yellow
Manufacturing overhead:	
Indirect labor	Yellow
Factory equipment depreciation	Red
Factory administration	Red
Selling and administrative:	
Wages and salaries	Red
Depreciation	Red
Marketing expenses	Yellow

Required:

Using Exhibit 7A–5 as a guide, prepare an action analysis report for CineMax Entertainment similar to those prepared for products.

EXERCISE 7-16 Cost Hierarchy and Activity Measures [LO1]

Various activities at Companhia de Textils, S.A., a manufacturing company located in Brazil, are listed below. The company makes a variety of products in its plant outside Sao Paulo.

a. Preventive maintenance is performed on general-purpose production equipment.
b. Products are assembled by hand.
c. Reminder notices are sent to customers who are late in making payments.
d. Purchase orders are issued for materials to be used in production.
e. Modifications are made to product designs.
f. New employees are hired by the personnel office.
g. Machine settings are changed between batches of different products.
h. Parts inventories are maintained in the storeroom. (Each product requires its own unique parts.)
i. Insurance costs are incurred on the company's facilities.

Required:

1. Classify each of the activities as either unit-level, batch-level, product-level, customer-level, or organization-sustaining.
2. Where possible, name one or more activity measures that could be used to assign costs generated by the activity to products or customers.

EXERCISE 7-17 Comprehensive Activity-Based Costing Exercise [LO2, LO3, LO4, LO5]

Silicon Optics has supplied the following data for use in its activity-based costing system:

Overhead Costs	
Wages and salaries	$350,000
Other overhead costs	200,000
Total overhead costs	$550,000

Activity Cost Pool	Activity Measure	Total Activity
Direct labor support	Number of direct labor-hours	10,000 DLHs
Order processing	Number of orders	500 orders
Customer support	Number of customers	100 customers
Other	These costs are not allocated to products or customers	Not applicable

	Distribution of Resource Consumption Across Activity Cost Pools				
	Direct Labor Support	Order Processing	Customer Support	Other	Total
Wages and salaries	30%	35%	25%	10%	100%
Other overhead costs	25%	15%	20%	40%	100%

During the year, Silicon Optics completed an order for a special optical switch for a new customer, Indus Telecom. This customer did not order any other products during the year. Data concerning that order follow:

Data Concerning the Indus Telecom Order	
Selling price	$295 per unit
Units ordered	100 units
Direct materials	$264 per unit
Direct labor-hours	0.5 DLH per unit
Direct labor rate	$25 per DLH

Required:

1. Using Exhibit 7–5 as a guide, prepare a report showing the first-stage allocations of overhead costs to the activity cost pools.
2. Using Exhibit 7–6 as a guide, compute the activity rates for the activity cost pools.
3. Prepare a report showing the overhead costs for the order from Indus Telecom, including customer support costs.
4. Using Exhibit 7–11 as a guide, prepare a report showing the customer margin for Indus Telecom.

EXERCISE 7-18 (Appendix 7A) Comprehensive Activity-Based Costing Exercise [LO2, LO3, LO4, LO6]

Refer to the data for Silicon Optics in Exercise 7-17.

Required:

1. Using Exhibit 7A–1 as a guide, prepare a report showing the first-stage allocations of overhead costs to the activity cost pools.
2. Using Exhibit 7A–2 as a guide, compute the activity rates for the activity cost pools.
3. Using Exhibit 7A–3 as a guide, prepare a report showing the overhead costs for the order from Indus Telecom including customer support costs.
4. Using Exhibit 7–11 as a guide, prepare a report showing the customer margin for Indus Telecom.
5. Using Exhibit 7A–5 as a guide, prepare an action analysis report showing the customer margin for Indus Telecom. Direct materials should be coded as a Green cost, direct labor and wages and salaries as Yellow costs, and other overhead costs as a Red cost.
6. What action, if any, do you recommend as a result of the above analyses?

EXERCISE 7-19 Calculating and Interpreting Activity-Based Costing Data [LO3, LO4]

Sven's Cookhouse is a popular restaurant located on Lake Union in Seattle. The owner of the restaurant has been trying to better understand costs at the restaurant and has hired a student intern to conduct an activity-based costing study. The intern, in consultation with the owner, identified three major activities. She then completed the first-stage allocations of costs to the activity cost pools, using data from last month's operations. The results appear below:

Activity Cost Pool	Activity Measure	Total Cost	Total Activity
Serving a party of diners	Number of parties served	$12,000	5,000 parties
Serving a diner	Number of diners served	$90,000	12,000 diners
Serving a drink	Number of drinks ordered	$26,000	10,000 drinks

The above costs include all of the costs of the restaurant except for organization-sustaining costs such as rent, property taxes, and top-management salaries. A group of diners who ask to sit at the same table are counted as a party. Some costs, such as the costs of cleaning linen, are the same whether one person is at a table or the table is full. Other costs, such as washing dishes, depend on the number of diners served.

Prior to the activity-based costing study, the owner knew very little about the costs of the restaurant. He knew that the total cost for the month (including organization-sustaining costs) was $180,000 and that 12,000 diners had been served. Therefore, the average cost per diner was $15.

Required:

1. According to the activity-based costing system, what is the total cost of serving each of the following parties of diners?
   a. A party of four diners who order three drinks in total.
   b. A party of two diners who do not order any drinks.
   c. A lone diner who orders two drinks.
2. Convert the total costs you computed in (1) above to costs per diner. In other words, what is the average cost per diner for serving each of the following parties?
   a. A party of four diners who order three drinks in total.
   b. A party of two diners who do not order any drinks.
   c. A lone diner who orders two drinks.
3. Why do the costs per diner for the three different parties differ from each other and from the overall average cost of $15.00 per diner?

Problems 

PROBLEM 7-20 Evaluating the Profitability of Services [LO2, LO3, LO4, LO5]
Gore Range Carpet Cleaning is a small, family-owned business operating out of Eagle-Vail, Colorado. For its services, the company has always charged a flat fee per hundred square feet of carpet cleaned. The current fee is $22.95 per hundred square feet. However, there is some question about whether the company is actually making any money on jobs for some customers—particularly those located on more remote ranches that require considerable travel time. The owner's daughter, home for the summer from college, has suggested investigating this question using activity-based costing. After some discussion, a simple system consisting of four activity cost pools seemed to be adequate. The activity cost pools and their activity measures appear below:

Activity Cost Pool	Activity Measure	Activity for the Year
Cleaning carpets.	Square feet cleaned (00s)	10,000 hundred square feet
Travel to jobs	Miles driven	50,000 miles
Job support.	Number of jobs	1,800 jobs
Other (costs of idle capacity and organization-sustaining costs)	None	Not applicable

The total cost of operating the company for the year is $340,000, which includes the following costs:

Wages	$140,000
Cleaning supplies	25,000
Cleaning equipment depreciation	10,000
Vehicle expenses.	30,000
Office expenses.	60,000
President's compensation	75,000
Total cost	$340,000

Resource consumption is distributed across the activities as follows:

	Distribution of Resource Consumption Across Activity Cost Pools				
	Cleaning Carpets	Travel to Jobs	Job Support	Other	Total
Wages	75%	15%	0%	10%	100%
Cleaning supplies	100%	0%	0%	0%	100%
Cleaning equipment depreciation	70%	0%	0%	30%	100%
Vehicle expenses	0%	80%	0%	20%	100%
Office expenses	0%	0%	60%	40%	100%
President's compensation	0%	0%	30%	70%	100%

Job support consists of receiving calls from potential customers at the home office, scheduling jobs, billing, resolving issues, and so on.

Required:

1. Using Exhibit 7–5 as a guide, prepare the first-stage allocation of costs to the activity cost pools.
2. Using Exhibit 7–6 as a guide, compute the activity rates for the activity cost pools.
3. The company recently completed a 6 hundred square-foot carpet-cleaning job at the Lazy Bee Ranch—a 52-mile round-trip journey from the company's offices in Eagle-Vail. Compute the cost of this job using the activity-based costing system.
4. The revenue from the Lazy Bee Ranch was $137.70 (6 hundred square-feet at $22.95 per hundred square feet). Using Exhibit 7–11 as a guide, prepare a report showing the margin from this job.
5. What do you conclude concerning the profitability of the Lazy Bee Ranch job? Explain.
6. What advice would you give the president concerning pricing jobs in the future?

PROBLEM 7-21 (Appendix 7A) Evaluating the Profitability of Services Using an Action Analysis [LO2, LO3, LO4, LO6]

Refer to the data for Gore Range Carpet Cleaning in Problem 7-20.

Required:

1. Using Exhibit 7A–1 as a guide, prepare the first-stage allocation of costs to the activity cost pools.
2. Using Exhibit 7A–2 as a guide, compute the activity rates for the activity cost pools.
3. The company recently completed a 6 hundred square-foot carpet-cleaning job at the Lazy Bee Ranch—a 52-mile round-trip journey from the company's offices in Eagle-Vail. Compute the cost of this job using the activity-based costing system.
4. The revenue from the Lazy Bee Ranch was $137.70 (6 hundred square-feet at $22.95 per hundred square feet). Using Exhibit 7A–5 as a guide, prepare an action analysis report of the Lazy Bee Ranch job. The president of Gore Range Carpet Cleaning considers all of the company's costs to be Green costs except for office expenses, which are coded Yellow, and his own compensation, which is coded Red. The people who do the actual carpet cleaning are all trained part-time workers who are paid only for work actually done.
5. What do you conclude concerning the profitability of the Lazy Bee Ranch job? Explain.
6. What advice would you give the president concerning pricing jobs in the future?

PROBLEM 7-22 Activity-Based Costing and Bidding on Jobs [LO2, LO3, LO4]

Denny Asbestos Removal Company removes potentially toxic asbestos insulation and related products from buildings. The company's estimator has been involved in a long-simmering dispute with the on-site work supervisors. The on-site supervisors claim that the estimator does not adequately distinguish between routine work such as removal of asbestos insulation around heating pipes in older homes and nonroutine work such as removing asbestos-contaminated ceiling plaster in industrial buildings. The on-site supervisors believe that nonroutine work is far more expensive than routine work and should bear higher customer charges. The estimator sums up his position in this way: "My job is to measure the area to be cleared of asbestos. As directed by top management, I simply multiply the square footage by $4,000 per thousand square feet to determine the bid price. Since our average cost is only $3,000 per thousand square feet, that leaves enough cushion to take care of the additional costs of nonroutine work that shows up. Besides, it is difficult to know what is routine or not routine until you actually start tearing things apart."

To shed light on this controversy, the company initiated an activity-based costing study of all of its costs. Data from the activity-based costing system follow:

Activity Cost Pool	Activity Measure	Total Activity
Removing asbestos	Thousands of square feet	500 thousand square feet
Estimating and job setup	Number of jobs	200 jobs*
Working on nonroutine jobs	Number of nonroutine jobs	25 nonroutine jobs
Other (costs of idle capacity and organization-sustaining costs)	Not applicable; these costs are not allocated to jobs	

*The total number of jobs includes nonroutine jobs as well as routine jobs. Nonroutine jobs as well as routine jobs require estimating and setup work.

Wages and salaries	$ 200,000
Disposal fees	600,000
Equipment depreciation	80,000
On-site supplies	60,000
Office expenses	190,000
Licensing and insurance	370,000
Total cost	$1,500,000

	Distribution of Resource Consumption Across Activity Cost Pools				
	Removing Asbestos	Estimating and Job Setup	Working on Nonroutine Jobs	Other	Total
Wages and salaries	40%	10%	35%	15%	100%
Disposal fees	70%	0%	30%	0%	100%
Equipment depreciation	50%	0%	40%	10%	100%
On-site supplies	55%	15%	20%	10%	100%
Office expenses	10%	40%	30%	20%	100%
Licensing and insurance	50%	0%	40%	10%	100%

Required:

1. Using Exhibit 7–5 as a guide, perform the first-stage allocation of costs to the activity cost pools.
2. Using Exhibit 7–6 as a guide, compute the activity rates for the activity cost pools.
3. Using the activity rates you have computed, determine the total cost and the average cost per thousand square feet of each of the following jobs according to the activity-based costing system.
   a. A routine 2,000-square-foot asbestos removal job.
   b. A routine 4,000-square-foot asbestos removal job.
   c. A nonroutine 2,000-square-foot asbestos removal job.
4. Given the results you obtained in (3) above, do you agree with the estimator that the company's present policy for bidding on jobs is adequate?

PROBLEM 7-23 Second-Stage Allocations and Product Margins [LO4, LO5]

AnimPix, Inc., is a small company that creates computer-generated animations for films and television. Much of the company's work consists of short commercials for television, but the company also does realistic computer animations for special effects in movies.

The young founders of the company have become increasingly concerned with the economics of the business—particularly since many competitors have sprung up recently in the local area. To help understand the company's cost structure, an activity-based costing system has been designed. Three major activities are carried out in the company: animation concept, animation production, and contract administration. The animation concept activity is carried out at the contract proposal stage when the company bids on projects. This is an intensive activity that involves individuals from all parts of the company in creating storyboards and prototype stills to be shown to the prospective client. After the client has accepted a project, the animation goes into production and contract administration begins. Technical staff do almost all of the work involved in animation production, whereas the administrative staff is largely responsible for contract administration. The activity cost pools and their activity measures and rates are listed below:

Activity Cost Pool	Activity Measure	Activity Rate
Animation concept	Number of proposals	$6,000 per proposal
Animation production	Minutes of animation	$7,700 per minute of animation
Contract administration	Number of contracts	$6,600 per contract

These activity rates include all of the costs of the company, except for the costs of idle capacity and organization-sustaining costs. There are no direct labor or direct materials costs.

Preliminary analysis using these activity rates has indicated that the local commercials segment of the market may be unprofitable. This segment is highly competitive. Producers of local commercials may ask several companies like AnimPix to bid, which results in an unusually low ratio of accepted contracts to bids. Furthermore, the animation sequences tend to be much shorter for local commercials than for other work. Since animation work is billed at standard rates according to the running time of the completed animation, the revenues from these short projects tend to be below average. Data concerning activity in the local commercials market appear below:

The total sales for local commercials amounted to $240,000.

Required:

1. Determine the cost of the local commercials market. (Think of the local commercials market as a product.)
2. Prepare a report showing the product margin of the local commercials market. (Remember, this company has no direct materials or direct labor costs.)
3. What would you recommend to management concerning the local commercials market?

Activity Measure	Local Commercials
Number of proposals	20
Minutes of animation	12
Number of contracts	8

PROBLEM 7-24 (Appendix 7A) Second-Stage Allocations and Product Margins [LO4, LO6]

Refer to the data for AnimPix, Inc., in Problem 7-23. In addition, the company has provided the following details concerning its activity rates:

	Activity Rates		
	Animation Concept	Animation Production	Contract Administration
Technical staff salaries	$3,500	$5,000	$1,800
Animation equipment depreciation	600	1,500	0
Administrative wages and salaries	1,400	200	4,600
Supplies costs	300	600	100
Facility costs	200	400	100
Total	$6,000	$7,700	$6,600

Management has provided the following ease of adjustment codes for the various costs:

	Ease of Adjustment Code
Technical staff salaries.	Red
Animation equipment depreciation	Red
Administrative wages and salaries	Yellow
Supplies costs	Green
Facility costs	Red

These codes created some controversy. In particular, some administrators objected to coding their own salaries Yellow, while the technical staff salaries were coded Red. However, the founders of the firm overruled these objections by pointing out that "our technical staff is our most valuable asset. Good animators are extremely difficult to find, and they would be the last to go if we had to cut back."

Required:

1. Using Exhibit 7A–3 as a guide, determine the cost of the local commercials market. (Think of the local commercials market as a product.)
2. Using Exhibit 7A–5 as a guide, prepare an action analysis report concerning the local commercials market. (This company has no direct materials or direct labor costs.)
3. What would you recommend to management concerning the local commercials market?

Cases 

CASE 7-25 (Appendix 7A) Comprehensive Activity-Based Costing Case [LO2, LO3, LO4, LO6]
Victorian Windows is a small company that builds specialty wooden windows for local builders. For years the company assigned overhead costs to products based on direct labor-hours (DLHs). However, the company's president became interested in activity-based costing after reading an article about it in a trade journal. An activity-based costing design team was put together, and within a few months a simple system consisting of four activity cost pools had been designed. The activity cost pools and their activity measures appear below:

Activity Cost Pool	Activity Measure	Total Activity for the Year
Making windows	Direct labor-hours	80,000 DLHs
Processing orders	Number of orders	1,000 orders
Customer relations	Number of customers	200 customers
Other (costs of idle capacity and organization-sustaining costs)	None	Not applicable

The Processing Orders activity includes order taking, job setup, job scheduling, and so on. Direct materials and direct labor are directly assigned to jobs in both the traditional and activity-based costing systems. The total overhead cost (both nonmanufacturing and manufacturing) for the year is $1,180,000 and includes the following costs:

Manufacturing overhead costs:		
Indirect factory wages	$240,000	
Production equipment depreciation	250,000	
Other factory costs	110,000	$ 600,000
Selling and administrative expenses:		
Administrative wages and salaries	240,000	
Office expenses	60,000	
Marketing expenses	280,000	580,000
Total overhead cost		$1,180,000

Based largely on interviews with employees, the distribution of resource consumption across the activities has been estimated as follows:

	Distribution of Resource Consumption Across Activities				
	Making Windows	Processing Orders	Customer Relations	Other	Total
Indirect factory wages	25%	50%	10%	15%	100%
Production equipment depreciation	80%	0%	0%	20%	100%
Other factory costs	40%	0%	0%	60%	100%
Administrative wages and salaries	0%	25%	35%	40%	100%
Office expenses	0%	20%	30%	50%	100%
Marketing expenses	0%	0%	75%	25%	100%

Management of the company is particularly interested in measuring the profitability of two customers. One of the customers, Avon Construction, is a low-volume purchaser. The other, Lynx Builders, is a relatively high-volume purchaser. Details of these two customers' orders for the year follow:

	Avon Construction	Lynx Builders
Number of orders during the year	2 orders	3 orders
Total direct labor-hours	250 DLHs	1,500 DLHs
Total sales	$9,995	$54,995
Total direct materials	$3,400	$17,200
Total direct labor cost	$4,500	$27,000

Required:

1. The company's traditional costing system applies manufacturing overhead to jobs strictly on the basis of direct labor-hours. Using this traditional approach, carry out the following steps:
   a. Compute the predetermined manufacturing overhead rate.
   b. Compute the total margin for all of the windows ordered by Avon Construction according to the traditional costing system. Do the same for Lynx Builders.
2. Using activity-based costing, do the following:
   a. Using Exhibit 7–5 as a guide, perform the first-stage allocation of costs to the activity cost pools.
   b. Using Exhibit 7A–2 as a guide, compute the activity rates for the activity cost pools.
   c. Compute the overhead costs of serving each of the two customers. (You will need to construct a table like Exhibit 7A–3 for each customer. However, unlike Exhibit 7A–3, you should fill in the column for Customer Relations as well as the other columns. Exhibit 7A–3 was constructed for a product; in this case we are interested in a customer.)
   d. Management has provided the following ease of adjustment codes to use in action analysis reports:

	Ease of Adjustment Code
Direct materials	Green
Direct labor	Yellow
Indirect factory wages	Yellow
Production equipment depreciation	Yellow
Other factory costs	Yellow
Administrative wages and salaries	Red
Office expenses	Yellow
Marketing expenses	Yellow

   Using Exhibit 7A–5 as a guide, prepare an action analysis report showing the margin on business with Avon Construction. Repeat for Lynx Builders.
3. Does Victorian Windows appear to be losing money on either customer? Do the traditional and activity-based costing systems agree concerning the profitability of the customers? If they do not agree, which costing system do you believe? Why?

RESEARCH AND APPLICATION 7-26 [LO1, LO2, LO3]

The questions in this exercise are based on JetBlue Airways Corporation. To answer the questions, you will need to download JetBlue's Form 10-K/A for the year ended December 31, 2004 at www.sec.gov/edgar/searchedgar/companysearch.html. Once at this website, input CIK code 1158463 and hit enter. In the gray box on the right-hand side of your computer screen define the scope of your search by inputting 10-K and then pressing enter. Select the 10-K/A with a filing date of March 8, 2005. You do not need to print the 10-K/A to answer the questions.

Required:

1. What is JetBlue's strategy for success in the marketplace? Does the company rely primarily on a customer intimacy, operational excellence, or product leadership customer value proposition? What evidence supports your conclusion?

2. What business risks does JetBlue face that may threaten the company's ability to satisfy stockholder expectations? What are some examples of control activities that the company could use to reduce these risks? (Hint: Focus on pages 17–23 of the 10-K/A).
3. How can the concept of unit-level activities be applied to an airline? More specifically, what are two examples of unit-level activities for JetBlue? What steps has JetBlue taken to manage these unit-level activities more efficiently?
4. How can the concept of batch-level activities be applied to an airline? What are two examples of batch-level activities for JetBlue? What steps has JetBlue taken to manage these batch-level activities more efficiently?
5. What is one example of a customer-level activity and an organization-sustaining activity for JetBlue?
6. Give an example of a transaction driver and a duration driver that could be used to assign fuel costs to a particular flight departure. Which of the two activity measures would be more accurate and why?

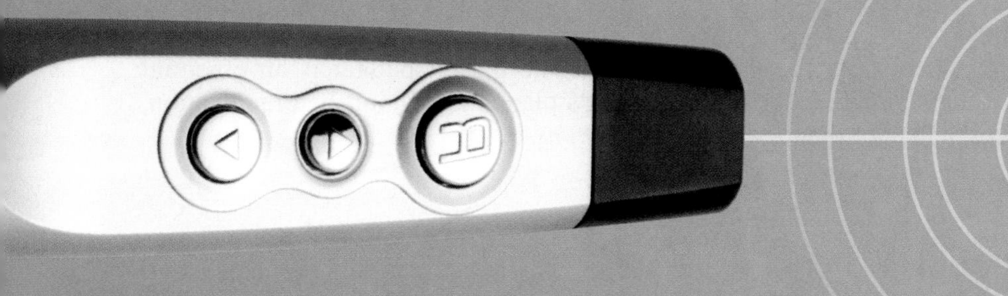

Chapter 8

Profit Planning

Lilo & Stitch on Budget

BUSINESS FOCUS

The full-length feature cartoon *Tarzan* grossed about $450 million worldwide for the Walt Disney Company. However, production costs got out of control. The company traditionally manages film production by focusing on meeting the planned release date—paying little attention to costs. In the case of *Tarzan*, production fell behind schedule due to the tendency of animation teams to add more eye-dazzling complexity to each production. At one point, it was estimated that 190,000 individual drawings would be needed to complete the film in contrast to the 130,000 drawings needed to complete *The Lion King*. To meet *Tarzan*'s release date, workers were pulled off other productions and were often paid at overtime rates. The size of the film crew eventually reached 573, which was nearly twice the size of the crew that had made *The Lion King*. With animators earning salaries in the hundreds of thousands of dollars, the cost implications were staggering.

Thomas S. Schumacher, Disney's feature-animation chief, was charged with dramatically reducing the cost of future films while making sure that the audience wouldn't notice any decline in quality. *Lilo & Stitch* was the first film to be produced with this goal in mind. The process began by prioritizing where the money was to be spent. The budget for music was kept generous; animation costs were cut by controlling the small details that add big costs with little effect on the quality of the film. For example, animators wanted to draw cute designs on the shirts worn by Nani, Lilo's big sister. However, adding this level of detail on every frame in which Nani appears in the film would have added about $250,000 in cost. By controlling such details, *Lilo & Stitch* was finished on time and at a cost of about $80 million. This contrasted with a cost of more than $150 million for *Tarzan*. ■

Source: Bruce Orwall, "Comics Stripped: At Disney, String of Weak Cartoons Leads to Cost Cuts," *The Wall Street Journal*, June 18, 2002, pp. A1 and A8.

Learning Objectives

After studying Chapter 8, you should be able to:

LO1 Understand why organizations budget and the processes they use to create budgets.

LO2 Prepare a sales budget, including a schedule of expected cash collections.

LO3 Prepare a production budget.

LO4 Prepare a direct materials budget, including a schedule of expected cash disbursements for purchases of materials.

LO5 Prepare a direct labor budget.

LO6 Prepare a manufacturing overhead budget.

LO7 Prepare a selling and administrative expense budget.

LO8 Prepare a cash budget.

LO9 Prepare a budgeted income statement.

LO10 Prepare a budgeted balance sheet.

LP 8

In this chapter, we focus on the steps taken by businesses to achieve their planned levels of profits—a process called *profit planning.* Profit planning is accomplished by preparing a number of budgets that together form an integrated business plan known as the *master budget.* The master budget is an essential management tool that communicates management's plans throughout the organization, allocates resources, and coordinates activities.

The Basic Framework of Budgeting

LEARNING OBJECTIVE 1
Understand why organizations budget and the processes they use to create budgets.

A **budget** is a quantitative plan for acquiring and using resources over a specified time period. Individuals often create household budgets that balance their income and expenditures for food, clothing, housing, and so on while providing for some savings. Once the budget is established, actual spending is compared to the budget to make sure the plan is being followed. Companies use budgets in a similar way, although the amount of work and underlying details involved far exceed a personal budget.

In an organization, the term **master budget** refers to a summary of a company's plans including specific targets for sales, production, and financing activities. The master budget—which culminates in a cash budget, a budgeted income statement, and a budgeted balance sheet—formally lays out the financial aspects of management's plans for the future and assists in monitoring actual expenditures relative to those plans.

Budgets are used for two distinct purposes—*planning* and *control.* **Planning** involves developing goals and preparing various budgets to achieve those goals. **Control** involves the steps taken by management to increase the likelihood that all parts of the organization are working together to achieve the goals set down at the planning stage. To be effective, a good budgeting system must provide for both planning and control. Good planning without effective control is a waste of time and effort.

Advantages of Budgeting

Organizations realize many benefits from budgeting including:

1. Budgets *communicate* management's plans throughout the organization.
2. Budgets force managers to *think about* and plan for the future. In the absence of the necessity to prepare a budget, many managers would spend all of their time dealing with daily emergencies.
3. The budgeting process provides a means of *allocating resources* to those parts of the organization where they can be used most effectively.
4. The budgeting process can uncover potential *bottlenecks* before they occur.
5. Budgets *coordinate* the activities of the entire organization by *integrating* the plans of its various parts. Budgeting helps to ensure that everyone in the organization is pulling in the same direction.
6. Budgets define goals and objectives that can serve as *benchmarks* for evaluating subsequent performance.

Responsibility Accounting

Most of what we say in this chapter and in the next three chapters is concerned with *responsibility accounting.* The basic idea underlying **responsibility accounting** is that a manager should be held responsible for those items—and *only* those items—that the manager can actually control to a significant extent. Each line item (i.e., revenue or cost) in the budget is made the responsibility of a manager who is held responsible for subsequent deviations between

BRINGING ORDER OUT OF CHAOS

Consider the following situation encountered by one of the authors at a mortgage banking company: For years, the company operated with virtually no system of budgets whatsoever. Management contended that budgeting wasn't well suited to the company's type of operation. Moreover, management pointed out that the company was already profitable. Indeed, outwardly the company gave every appearance of being a well-managed, smoothly operating organization. A careful look within, however, disclosed that day-to-day operations were far from smooth, and often approached chaos. The average day involved putting out one brush fire after another. The Cash account was always at crisis levels. At the end of a day, no one ever knew whether enough cash would be available the next day to cover required loan closings. Departments were uncoordinated, and it was not uncommon to find that one department was pursuing a course of action that conflicted with the goals of another department. Employee morale was low, and turnover was high. Employees complained bitterly that when a job was well done, nobody ever knew about it.

The company was bought out by a new group of stockholders who required that an integrated budgeting system be established to control operations. Within one year's time, significant changes were evident. Brush fires were rare. Careful planning virtually eliminated the problems that had been experienced with cash, and departmental efforts were coordinated and directed toward predetermined overall company goals. Although the employees were initially wary of the new budgeting program, they became "converted" when they experienced its positive effects. The more efficient operations caused profits to jump dramatically. Communication increased throughout the organization. When a job was well done, everybody knew about it. As one employee stated, "For the first time, we know what the company expects of us."

budgeted goals and actual results. In effect, responsibility accounting *personalizes* accounting information by holding individuals responsible for revenues and costs. This concept is central to any effective profit planning and control system. Someone must be held responsible for each cost or else no one will be responsible and the cost will inevitably grow out of control.

Being held responsible for financial performance does not mean that the manager is penalized if actual results do not measure up to the budgeted goals. However, the manager should take the initiative to correct any unfavorable discrepancies, should understand the source of significant favorable or unfavorable discrepancies, and should be prepared to explain the reasons for discrepancies to higher management. The point of an effective responsibility accounting system is to make sure that nothing "falls through the cracks," that the organization reacts quickly and appropriately to deviations from its plans, and that the organization learns from the feedback it gets by comparing budgeted goals to actual results. The point is *not* to penalize individuals for missing targets.

Choosing a Budget Period

Operating budgets ordinarily cover a one-year period corresponding to the company's fiscal year. Many companies divide their budget year into four quarters. The first quarter is then subdivided into months, and monthly budgets are developed. The last three quarters may be carried in the budget as quarterly totals only. As the year progresses, the figures for the second quarter are broken down into monthly amounts, then the third-quarter figures are broken down, and so forth. This approach has the advantage of requiring periodic review and reappraisal of budget data throughout the year.

Continuous or *perpetual budgets* are used by a significant number of organizations. A **continuous** or **perpetual budget** is a 12-month budget that rolls forward one month (or quarter) as the current month (or quarter) is completed. In other words, one month (or quarter) is added to the end of the budget as each month (or quarter) comes to a close. This approach keeps managers focused at least one year ahead so that they do not become too narrowly focused on short-term results.

In this chapter, we will look at one-year operating budgets. However, using basically the same techniques, operating budgets can be prepared for periods that extend over many years. It may be difficult to accurately forecast sales and required data much beyond a year, but even rough estimates can be invaluable in uncovering potential problems and opportunities that would otherwise be overlooked.

IN BUSINESS

KEEPING CURRENT

Jim Bell, Hunstman Corp.'s director of corporate finance, says that his company must frequently update its budgets and its forecasts to meet the demands of investors, creditors, and others. The company updates its annual budget each month, using the most recent data, to provide greater accuracy as the year unfolds. The budget is also used together with sophisticated modeling software to evaluate what effects decisions and various changes in input prices and other parameters might have on future results.

Source: Tim Reason, "Partial Clearing," *CFO*, December 2002, pp. 73–76.

The Self-Imposed Budget

The success of a budget program is largely determined by the way a budget is developed. In the most successful budget programs, managers actively participate in preparing their own budgets rather than having them imposed from above. The participative approach is particularly effective when budgets are used to evaluate a manager's performance because imposing expectations from above and then penalizing employees who do not meet those expectations will generate resentment rather than cooperation and commitment. In fact, many managers believe that being empowered to create their own *self-imposed budgets* is the most effective method of budget preparation. A **self-imposed budget** or **participative budget,** as illustrated in Exhibit 8–1, is a budget that is prepared with the full cooperation and participation of managers at all levels.

EXHIBIT 8–1
The Initial Flow of Budget Data in a Participative Budgeting System

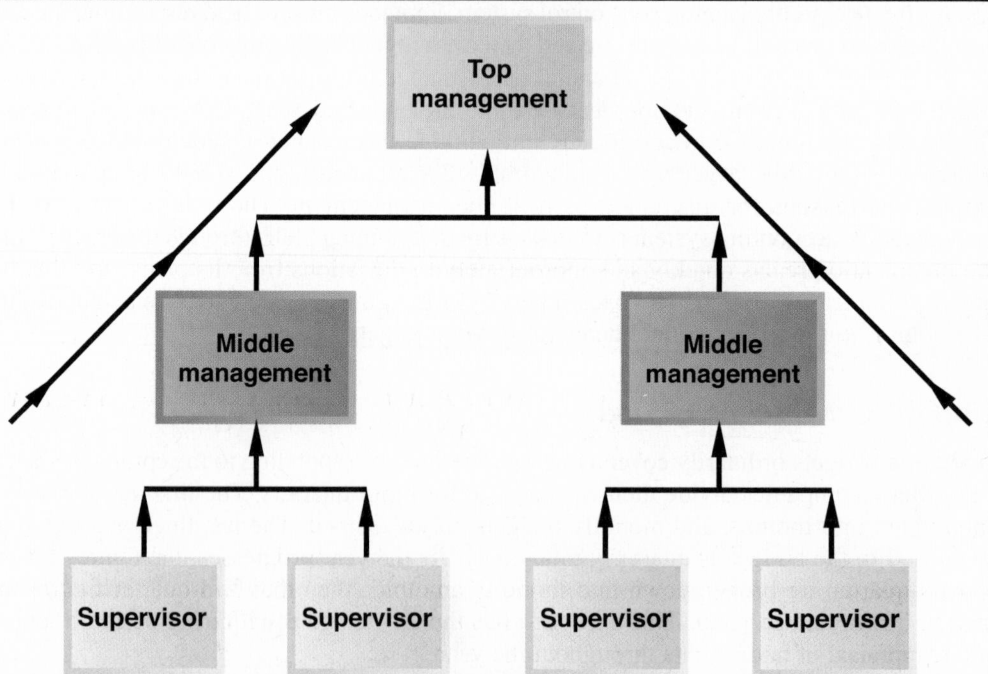

The initial flow of budget data in a participative system is from lower levels of responsibility to higher levels of responsibility. Each person with responsibility for cost control will prepare his or her own budget estimates and submit them to the next higher level of management. These estimates are reviewed and consolidated as they move upward in the organization.

Self-imposed budgets have a number of advantages:

1. Individuals at all levels of the organization are recognized as members of the team whose views and judgments are valued by top management.
2. Budget estimates prepared by front-line managers are often more accurate and reliable than estimates prepared by top managers who have less intimate knowledge of markets and day-to-day operations.
3. Motivation is generally higher when individuals participate in setting their own goals than when the goals are imposed from above. Self-imposed budgets create commitment.
4. A manager who is not able to meet a budget that has been imposed from above can always say that the budget was unrealistic and impossible to meet. With a self-imposed budget, this excuse is not available.

One important limitation of self-imposed budgeting is that lower-level managers may allow too much *budgetary slack.* Since the manager who creates the budget will be held accountable for actual results that deviate from the budget, the manager will have a natural tendency to submit a budget that is easy to attain (i.e., the manager will build slack into the budget). For this reason, budgets prepared by lower-level managers should be scrutinized by higher levels of management. Questionable items should be discussed and modified as appropriate. Without such a review, self-imposed budgets may be too slack, resulting in suboptimal performance.

As these comments suggest, all levels in the organization should work together to produce the budget. Lower-level managers are more familiar with day-to-day operations than top managers. Top managers should have a more strategic perspective than lower-level managers. Each level of responsibility in an organization should contribute its unique knowledge and perspective in a cooperative effort to develop an integrated budget. Nevertheless, a self-imposed approach to setting budgets works best when all managers understand the organization's strategy. Otherwise, the budgets proposed by the lower-level managers will lack coherent direction. Chapter 9 discusses in greater detail how a company can go about formulating its strategy and communicating it throughout the organization.

Unfortunately, most companies do not follow the budgeting process we have described. Typically, top managers initiate the budgeting process by issuing profit targets. Lower-level managers are directed to prepare budgets that meet those targets. The difficulty is that the targets set by top managers may be unrealistically high or may allow too much slack. If the targets are too high and employees know they are unrealistic, motivation will suffer. If the targets allow too much slack, waste will occur. Unfortunately, top managers are often not in a position to know whether the targets are appropriate. Admittedly, a self-imposed budgeting system may lack sufficient strategic direction and lower-level managers may be tempted to build slack into their budgets. Nevertheless, because of the motivational advantages of self-imposed budgets, top managers should be cautious about imposing inflexible targets from above.

Human Factors in Budgeting

The success of a budget program also depends on the degree to which top management accepts the budget program as a vital part of the company's activities and the way in which top management uses budgeted data.

If a budget program is to be successful, it must have the complete acceptance and support of the persons who occupy key management positions. If lower or middle management personnel sense that top management is lukewarm about budgeting, or if they sense that top management simply tolerates budgeting as a necessary evil, then their own attitudes will reflect a similar lack of enthusiasm. Budgeting is hard work, and if top management is not enthusiastic about and committed to the budget program, then it is unlikely that anyone else in the organization will be either.

In administering the budget program, it is particularly important that top management not use the budget to pressure or blame employees. Using budgets in such negative ways will breed hostility, tension, and mistrust rather than cooperation and productivity. Unfortunately, the budget is too often used as a pressure device and excessive emphasis is placed on "meeting the budget" under all circumstances. Rather than being used as a weapon, the budget should be used as a positive instrument to assist in establishing goals, measuring operating results, and isolating areas that need attention.

The human aspects of budgeting are extremely important. The remainder of the chapter deals with technical aspects of budgeting, but do not lose sight of the human aspects. The purpose of the budget is to motivate people and to coordinate their efforts. This purpose is undermined if managers become preoccupied with the technical aspects or if the budget is used in a rigid and inflexible manner to control people.

IN BUSINESS

WHO CARES ABOUT BUDGETS?

Towers Perrin, a consulting firm, reports that the bonuses of more than two out of three corporate managers are based on meeting targets set in annual budgets. "Under this arrangement, managers at the beginning of a year all too often argue that their targets should be lowered because of tough business conditions, when in fact conditions are better than projected. If their arguments are successful, they can easily surpass the targets."

Source: Ronald Fink and Towers Perrin, "Riding the Bull: The 2000 Compensation Survey," *CFO,* June 2000, pp. 45–60.

How challenging should budget targets be? Some experts argue that budget targets should be very challenging and should require managers to stretch to meet goals. Even the most capable managers may have to scramble to meet such a "stretch budget" and they may not always succeed. In practice, most companies set their budget targets at a "highly achievable" level. A highly achievable budget may be challenging, but it can almost always be met by competent managers exerting reasonable effort.

Bonuses based on meeting and exceeding budgets are often a key element of management compensation. Typically, no bonus is paid unless the budget is met. The bonus often increases when the budget target is exceeded, but the bonus is usually capped out at some level. For obvious reasons, managers who have such a bonus plan or whose performance is evaluated based on meeting budget targets usually prefer to be evaluated based on highly achievable budgets rather than on stretch budgets. Moreover, highly achievable budgets may help build a manager's confidence and generate greater commitment to the budget. And finally, highly achievable budgets may result in less undesirable behavior at the end of budgetary periods by managers who are intent on earning their bonuses. Examples of such undesirable behaviors are presented in several of the In Business boxes in this chapter.

IN BUSINESS

BIASING FORECASTS

A manager's compensation is often tied to the budget. Typically, no bonus is paid unless a minimum performance hurdle such as 80% of the budget target is attained. Once that hurdle is passed, the manager's bonus increases until a cap is reached. That cap is often set at 120% of the budget target.

This common method of tying a manager's compensation to the budget has some serious negative side effects. For example, a marketing manager for a big beverage company intentionally grossly understated demand for the company's products for an upcoming major holiday so that the budget target for revenues would be low and easy to beat. Unfortunately, the company tied its production to this biased forecast and ran out of products to sell during the height of the holiday selling season.

As another example, near the end of the year another group of managers announced a price increase of 10% effective January 2 of the following year. Why would they do this? By announcing this price increase, managers hoped that customers would order before the end of the year, helping managers meet their sales targets for the current year. Sales in the following year would, of course, drop. What trick would managers pull to meet their sales targets next year in the face of this drop in demand?

Sources: Michael C. Jensen, "Corporate Budgeting Is Broken—Let's Fix It," *Harvard Business Review,* November 2001; and Michael C. Jensen, "Why Pay People to Lie?" *The Wall Street Journal,* January 8, 2001, p. A32.

The Budget Committee

A standing **budget committee** is usually responsible for overall policy relating to the budget program and for coordinating the preparation of the budget itself. This committee may consist of the president; vice presidents in charge of various functions such as sales, production, and purchasing; and the controller. Difficulties and disputes relating to the budget are resolved by the budget committee. In addition, the budget committee approves the final budget.

Disputes can (and do) erupt over budget matters. Because budgets allocate resources, the budgeting process determines to a large extent which departments get more resources and which get less. Also, the budget sets the benchmarks used to evaluate managers and their departments. Therefore, it should not be surprising that managers take the budgeting process very seriously and invest considerable energy and emotion in ensuring that their interests, and those of their departments, are protected. Because of this, the budgeting process can easily degenerate into an interoffice brawl in which the ultimate goal of working together toward common goals is forgotten.

Running a successful budgeting program that avoids interoffice battles requires considerable interpersonal skills in addition to purely technical skills. But even the best interpersonal skills will fail if, as discussed earlier, top management uses the budget process to inappropriately pressure employees or to assign blame.

IN BUSINESS

BETTER THAN BUDGETS?

Borealis is a company headquartered in Copenhagen, Denmark, that produces polymers for the plastics industry. Thomas Boesen, the company's financial controller, felt that the traditional budgeting process had outlived its usefulness—markets were changing so fast that the budget was out of date within weeks of its publication. Moreover, since budgets were used to control and evaluate the performance of managers, they were subject to considerable gaming behavior that reduced their accuracy and usefulness. So over a five-year period the company phased out its traditional budgets and replaced them with rolling forecasts and several other management tools. Instead of holding managers to a budget, targets based on competitors' performance were set for variable costs, fixed costs, and operating margins. Managers were given the freedom to spend money as needed to meet these competitive benchmarks. Since the rolling forecasts of financial results were not used to control spending or to evaluate managers' performance, managers had little incentive to "game the system," and hence the forecasts were more accurate than those obtained through the traditional budgeting process.

Source: Professor Bjorn Jorgensen, *Borealis,* Harvard Business School Case 9-102-048, Rev: May 9, 2002.

The Master Budget: An Overview

Topic Tackler

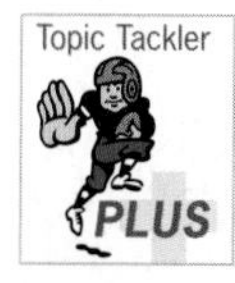

8–1

The master budget consists of a number of separate but interdependent budgets. Exhibit 8–2 (page 304) provides an overview of the various parts of the master budget and how they are related.

The first step in the budgeting process is the preparation of the **sales budget,** which is a detailed schedule showing the expected sales for the budget period. An accurate sales budget is the key to the entire budgeting process. As illustrated in Exhibit 8–2, all other parts of the master budget depend on the sales budget. If the sales budget is inaccurate, the rest of the budget will be inaccurate. The sales budget is based on the company's sales forecast, which may require the use of sophisticated mathematical models and statistical tools. We will not go into the details of how sales forecasts are made. This is a subject that is most appropriately covered in marketing courses.

The sales budget helps determine how many units need to be produced. Thus, the production budget is prepared after the sales budget. The production budget in turn is used to determine the budgets for manufacturing costs including the direct materials budget, the

EXHIBIT 8–2
The Master Budget Interrelationships

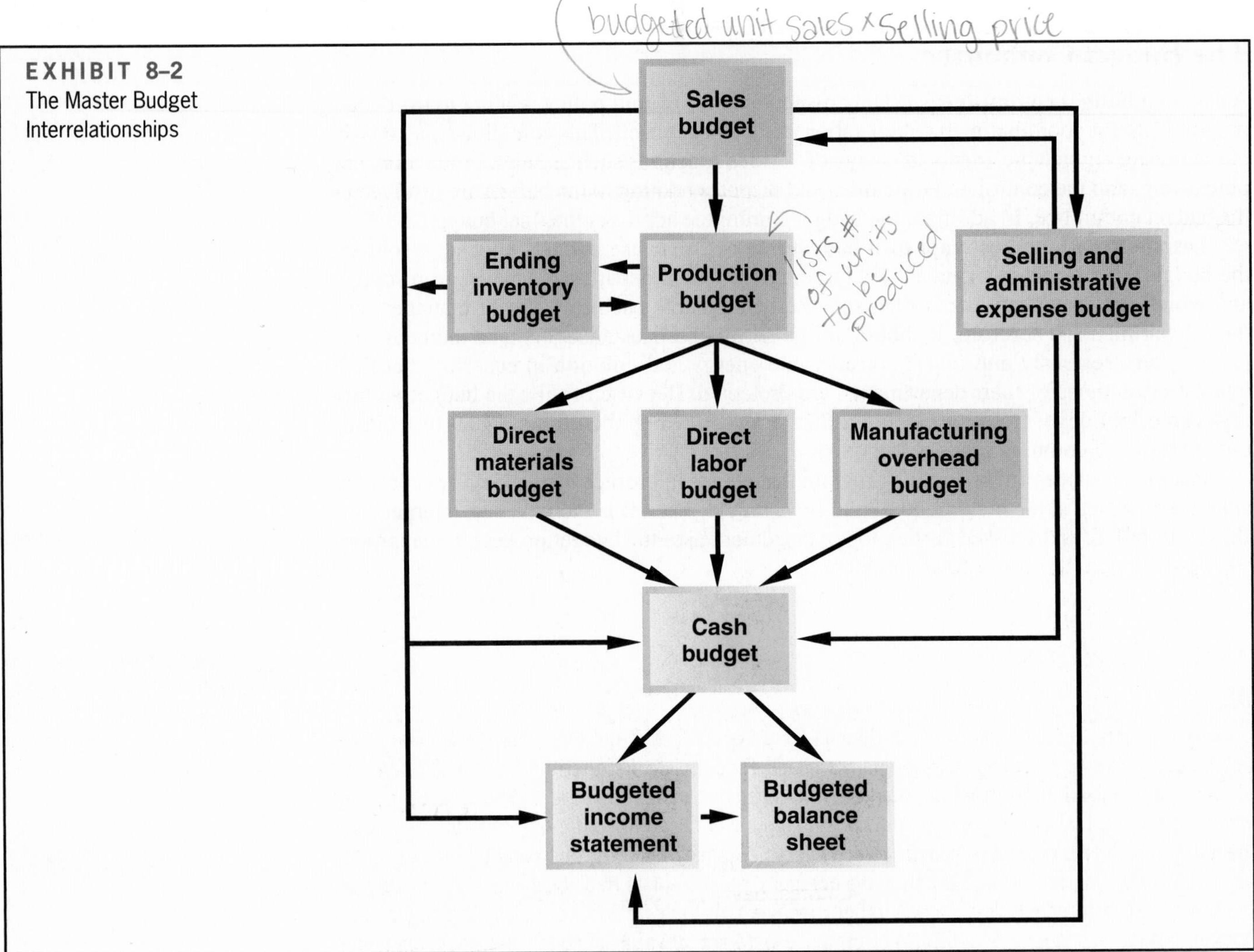

direct labor budget, and the manufacturing overhead budget. These budgets are then combined with data from the sales budget and the selling and administrative expense budget to determine the *cash budget.* A **cash budget** is a detailed plan showing how cash resources will be acquired and used. Observe from Exhibit 8–2 that all of the operating budgets have an impact on the cash budget. After the cash budget is prepared, the budgeted income statement and then the budgeted balance sheet can be prepared.

IN BUSINESS

BE REALISTIC

Gillette, the company that makes razors and other consumer products, got into trouble trying to meet increasingly unrealistic sales targets. The buyer at one of the company's big retail customers told Gillette's new CEO, Jim Kilts, that "he always waited until the last week of the quarter to order anything from Gillette 'because I know that you will always cut a deal.' To hit their numbers each quarter, [the Gillette salepersons] were willing to do anything—offer cut-rate deals, rearrange product packaging—whatever it took to make the sale." This resulted in artificially large sales at the end of the quarter—disrupting production schedules and loading the retail stores with excess inventory at discounted prices that would have to be sold off before more inventory would be ordered from Gillette.

Source: Katrina Brooker, "Jim Kilts Is an Old-School Curmudgeon," *Fortune,* December 30, 2002, pp. 95–102.

Preparing the Master Budget

MANAGERIAL ACCOUNTING IN ACTION
The Issue

Tom Wills is the majority stockholder and chief executive officer of Hampton Freeze, Inc., a company he started in 2006. The company makes premium popsicles using only natural ingredients and featuring exotic flavors such as tangy tangerine and minty mango. The company's business is highly seasonal, with most of the sales occurring in spring and summer.

In 2007, the company's second year of operations, a major cash crunch in the first and second quarters almost forced the company into bankruptcy. In spite of this cash crunch, 2007 turned out to be a very successful year in terms of both cash flow and net income. Partly as a result of that harrowing experience, Tom decided toward the end of 2007 to hire a professional financial manager. Tom interviewed several promising candidates for the job and settled on Larry Giano, who had considerable experience in the packaged foods industry. In the job interview, Tom questioned Larry about the steps he would take to prevent a recurrence of the 2007 cash crunch:

Video 8–1

Tom: As I mentioned earlier, we are going to end 2007 with a very nice profit. What you may not know is that we had some very big financial problems this year.

Larry: Let me guess. You ran out of cash sometime in the first or second quarter.

Tom: How did you know?

Larry: Most of your sales are in the second and third quarter, right?

Tom: Sure, everyone wants to buy popsicles in the spring and summer, but nobody wants them when the weather turns cold.

Larry: So you don't have many sales in the first quarter?

Tom: Right.

Larry: And in the second quarter, which is the spring, you are producing like crazy to fill orders?

Tom: Sure.

Larry: Do your customers, the grocery stores, pay you the day you make your deliveries?

Tom: Are you kidding? Of course not.

Larry: So in the first quarter, you don't have many sales. In the second quarter, you are producing like crazy, which eats up cash, but you aren't paid by your customers until long after you have paid your employees and suppliers. No wonder you had a cash problem. I see this pattern all the time in food processing because of the seasonality of the business.

Tom: So what can we do about it?

Larry: The first step is to predict the magnitude of the problem before it occurs. If we can predict early in the year what the cash shortfall is going to be, we can go to the bank and arrange for credit before we really need it. Bankers tend to be leery of panicky people who show up begging for emergency loans. They are much more likely to make the loan if you look like you are in control of the situation.

Tom: How can we predict the cash shortfall?

Larry: You can put together a cash budget. While you're at it, you might as well do a master budget. You'll find it is well worth the effort.

Tom: I don't like budgets. They are too confining. My wife budgets everything at home, and I can't spend what I want.

Larry: Can I ask a personal question?

Tom: What?

Larry: Where did you get the money to start this business?

Tom: Mainly from our family's savings. I get your point. We wouldn't have had the money to start the business if my wife hadn't been forcing us to save every month.

Larry: Exactly. I suggest you use the same discipline in your business. It is even more important here because you can't expect your employees to spend your money as carefully as you would.

With the full backing of Tom Wills, Larry Giano set out to create a master budget for the company for the year 2008. In his planning for the budgeting process, Larry drew up the following list of documents that would be a part of the master budget:

1. A sales budget, including a schedule of expected cash collections.
2. A production budget (a merchandise purchases budget would be used in a merchandising company).
3. A direct materials budget, including a schedule of expected cash disbursements for purchases of materials.
4. A direct labor budget.
5. A manufacturing overhead budget.
6. An ending finished goods inventory budget.
7. A selling and administrative expense budget.
8. A cash budget.
9. A budgeted income statement.
10. A budgeted balance sheet.

Larry felt it was important to have everyone's cooperation in the budgeting process, so he asked Tom to call a companywide meeting to explain the budgeting process. At the meeting there was initially some grumbling, but Tom was able to convince nearly everyone of the necessity for planning and getting better control over spending. It helped that the cash crisis earlier in the year was still fresh in everyone's minds. As much as some people disliked the idea of budgets, they liked their jobs more.

In the months that followed, Larry worked closely with all of the managers involved in the master budget, gathering data from them and making sure that they understood and fully supported the parts of the master budget that would affect them. In subsequent years, Larry hoped to turn the whole budgeting process over to the managers and to take a more advisory role.

The interdependent documents that Larry Giano prepared for Hampton Freeze are Schedules 1 through 10 of his company's master budget. In this section, we will study these schedules.

LEARNING OBJECTIVE 2
Prepare a sales budget, including a schedule of expected cash collections.

The Sales Budget

The sales budget is the starting point in preparing the master budget. As shown earlier in Exhibit 8–2, all other items in the master budget, including production, purchases, inventories, and expenses, depend on it.

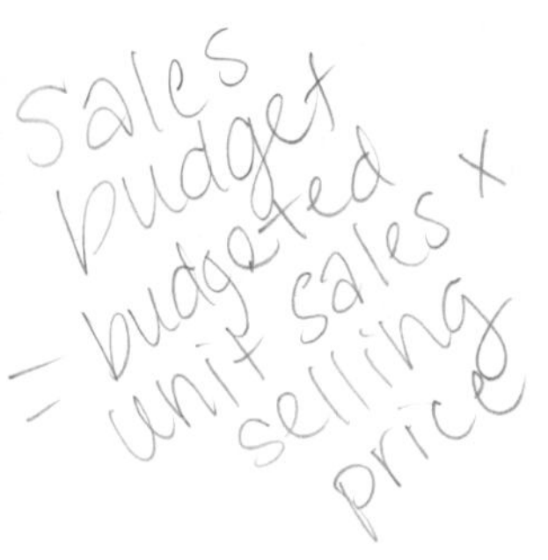

The sales budget is constructed by multiplying budgeted unit sales by the selling price. Schedule 1 contains the quarterly sales budget for Hampton Freeze for the year 2008. Notice from the schedule that the company plans to sell 100,000 cases of popsicles during the year, with sales peaking in the third quarter.

A schedule of expected cash collections, such as the one that appears in Schedule 1 for Hampton Freeze, is prepared after the sales budget. This schedule will be needed later to prepare the cash budget. Cash collections consist of collections on credit sales made to customers in prior periods plus collections on sales made in the current budget period. At Hampton Freeze all sales are on credit; furthermore, experience has shown that 70% of sales are collected in the quarter in which the sale is made and the remaining 30% are collected in the following quarter. For example, 70% of the first quarter sales of $200,000 (or $140,000) is collected during the first quarter and 30% (or $60,000) is collected during the second quarter.

IN BUSINESS

PREDICTING DEMAND

O'Reilly Auto Parts uses sophisticated demand software from Nonstop Solutions to forecast seasonal variations in sales. For example, monthly sales of windshield wiper blades vary from 25,000 in the summer to 50,000 in the winter. Demand software uses weather data, economic trends, and other information to make forecasts and can even learn from its past mistakes.

Source: Chana R. Schoenberger, "The Weakest Link," *Forbes*, October 1, 2001, pp. 114–115.

SCHEDULE 1

Microsoft Excel - Hampton Freeze.xls

	A	B	C	D	E	F
1		**Hampton Freeze, Inc.**				
2		**Sales Budget**				
3		**For the Year Ended December 31, 2008**				
4						
5				*Quarter*		
6		*1*	*2*	*3*	*4*	*Year*
7	Budgeted sales in cases	10,000	30,000	40,000	20,000	100,000
8	Selling price per case	$ 20.00	$ 20.00	$ 20.00	$ 20.00	$ 20.00
9	Total sales	$200,000	$600,000	$800,000	$400,000	$ 2,000,000
10						
11	Percentage of sales collected in the period of the sale			70%		
12	Percentage of sales collected in the period after the sale			30%		
13		70%	30%			
14		**Schedule of Expected Cash Collections**				
15	Accounts receivable, beginning balance[1]	$ 90,000				$ 90,000
16	First-quarter sales[2]	140,000	$ 60,000			200,000
17	Second-quarter sales[3]		420,000	$ 180,000		600,000
18	Third-quarter sales[4]			560,000	$ 240,000	800,000
19	Fourth-quarter sales[5]	-	-	-	280,000	280,000
20	Total cash collections[6]	$230,000	$480,000	$740,000	$520,000	$ 1,970,000

Schedule 1 / Schedule 2 / Schedule 3 / Schedule 4 / Schedule 5

[1]Cash collections from last year's fourth-quarter sales. See the beginning-of-year balance sheet on page 320.
[2]$200,000 × 70%; $200,000 × 30%.
[3]$600,000 × 70%; $600,000 × 30%.
[4]$800,000 × 70%; $800,000 × 30%.
[5]$400,000 × 70%.
[6]Uncollected fourth-quarter sales appear as accounts receivable on the company's end-of-year balance sheet (see Schedule 10 on page 321).

The Production Budget

LEARNING OBJECTIVE 3
Prepare a production budget.

The production budget is prepared after the sales budget. The **production budget** lists the number of units that must be produced to satisfy sales needs and to provide for the desired ending inventory. Production needs can be determined as follows:

Budgeted unit sales	XXXX
Add desired ending inventory	XXXX
Total needs	XXXX
Less beginning inventory	XXXX
Required production	XXXX

Note that production requirements are influenced by the desired level of the ending inventory. Inventories should be carefully planned. Excessive inventories tie up funds and create storage problems. Insufficient inventories can lead to lost sales or last-minute, high-cost production efforts. At Hampton Freeze, management believes that an ending inventory equal to 20% of the next quarter's sales strikes the appropriate balance.

Schedule 2 contains the production budget for Hampton Freeze. The first row in the production budget contains the budgeted sales, which have been taken directly from the sales budget (Schedule 1). The total needs for the first quarter are determined by adding together the budgeted sales of 10,000 cases for the quarter and the desired ending inventory of 6,000 cases. As discussed above, the ending inventory is intended to provide some cushion in case problems develop in production or sales increase unexpectedly. Since the budgeted sales for the second quarter are 30,000 cases and management would like the ending inventory in each quarter to equal 20% of the following quarter's sales, the desired ending inventory for the first quarter is 6,000 cases (20% of 30,000 cases). Consequently, the total needs for the first quarter are 16,000 cases. However, since the company already has 2,000 cases in beginning inventory, only 14,000 cases need to be produced in the first quarter.

Pay particular attention to the Year column to the right of the production budget in Schedule 2. In some cases (e.g., budgeted sales, total needs, and required production), the amount listed for the year is the sum of the quarterly amounts for the item. In other

SCHEDULE 2

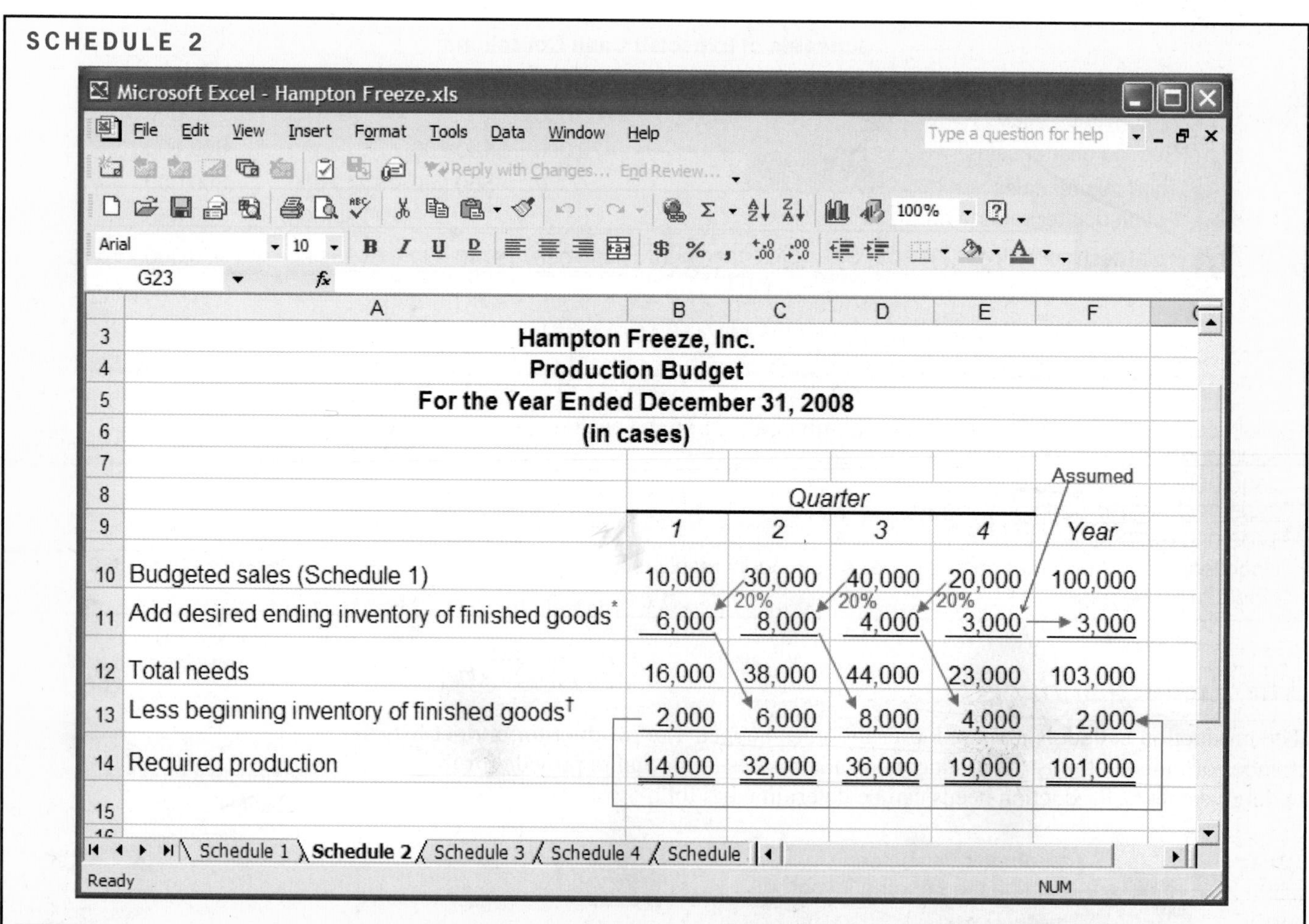

Microsoft Excel - Hampton Freeze.xls

Hampton Freeze, Inc.
Production Budget
For the Year Ended December 31, 2008
(in cases)

	Quarter 1	Quarter 2	Quarter 3	Quarter 4	Year
Budgeted sales (Schedule 1)	10,000	30,000	40,000	20,000	100,000
Add desired ending inventory of finished goods*	6,000	8,000	4,000	3,000	3,000
Total needs	16,000	38,000	44,000	23,000	103,000
Less beginning inventory of finished goods†	2,000	6,000	8,000	4,000	2,000
Required production	14,000	32,000	36,000	19,000	101,000

*Twenty percent of the next quarter's sales. The ending inventory of 3,000 cases is assumed.
†The beginning inventory in each quarter is the same as the prior quarter's ending inventory.

cases (e.g., desired ending inventory of finished goods and beginning inventory of finished goods), the amount listed for the year is not simply the sum of the quarterly amounts. From the standpoint of the entire year, the beginning finished goods inventory is the same as the beginning finished goods inventory for the first quarter—it is *not* the sum of the beginning finished goods inventories for all quarters. Similarly, from the standpoint of the entire year, the ending finished goods inventory is the same as the ending finished goods inventory for the fourth quarter—it is *not* the sum of the ending finished goods inventories for all four quarters. It is important to pay attention to such distinctions in all of the schedules that follow.

Inventory Purchases—Merchandising Company

Hampton Freeze prepares a production budget because it is a *manufacturing* company. If it were a *merchandising* company, it would prepare instead a **merchandise purchases budget** showing the amount of goods to be purchased from suppliers during the period. The merchandise purchases budget has the same basic format as the production budget, as shown below:

Budgeted sales	XXXXX
Add desired ending merchandise inventory	XXXXX
Total needs	XXXXX
Less beginning merchandise inventory	XXXXX
Required purchases	XXXXX

A merchandising company would prepare a merchandise purchases budget such as the one above for each item carried in stock. The merchandise purchases budget can be expressed in terms of either units or the purchase cost of those units.

The Direct Materials Budget

LEARNING OBJECTIVE 4
Prepare a direct materials budget, including a schedule of expected cash disbursements for purchases of materials.

A *direct materials budget* is prepared after the production requirements have been computed. The **direct materials budget** details the raw materials that must be purchased to fulfill the production budget and to provide for adequate inventories. The required purchases of raw materials are computed as follows:

Raw materials needed to meet the production schedule	XXXXX
Add desired ending inventory of raw materials	XXXXX
Total raw materials needs	XXXXX
Less beginning inventory of raw materials	XXXXX
Raw materials to be purchased	XXXXX

Schedule 3 contains the direct materials budget for Hampton Freeze. The only raw material included in that budget is high fructose sugar, which is the major ingredient in popsicles other than water. The remaining raw materials are relatively insignificant and are included in variable manufacturing overhead. As with finished goods, management would like to maintain some inventories of raw materials to act as a cushion. In this case, management

SCHEDULE 3

Microsoft Excel - Hampton Freeze.xls

	A	B	C	D	E	F
3	Hampton Freeze, Inc.					
4	Direct Materials Budget					
5	For the Year Ended December 31, 2008					
6						Assumed
7		Quarter				
8		1	2	3	4	Year
9	Required production in cases (Schedule 2)	14,000	32,000	36,000	19,000	101,000
10	Raw materials needed per case (pounds)	15	15	15	15	15
11	Production needs (pounds)	210,000	480,000	540,000	285,000	1,515,000
12	Add desired ending inventory of raw materials[1]	48,000	54,000	28,500	22,500	22,500
13	Total needs	258,000	534,000	568,500	307,500	1,537,500
14	Less beginning inventory of raw materials	21,000	48,000	54,000	28,500	21,000
15	Raw materials to be purchased	237,000	486,000	514,500	279,000	1,516,500
16	Cost of raw materials per pound	$ 0.20	$ 0.20	$ 0.20	$ 0.20	$ 0.20
17	Cost of raw materials to be purchased	$ 47,400	$ 97,200	$ 102,900	$ 55,800	$ 303,300
18						
19	Percentage of purchases paid for in the period of the purchase			50%		
20	Percentage of purchases paid for in the period after purchase			50%		
21		50%	50%			
22	Schedule of Expected Cash Disbursements for Materials					
23						
24	Accounts payable, beginning balance[2]	$ 25,800				$ 25,800
25	First-quarter purchases[3]	23,700	$ 23,700			47,400
26	Second-quarter purchases[4]		48,600	$ 48,600		97,200
27	Third-quarter purchases[5]			51,450	$ 51,450	102,900
28	Fourth-quarter purchases[6]	-	-	-	27,900	27,900
29	Total cash disbursements for materials	$ 49,500	$ 72,300	$ 100,050	$ 79,350	$ 301,200
30						

Schedule 1 / Schedule 2 / Schedule 3 / Schedule 4 / Schedule 5 / Sche

[1]Ten percent of the next quarter's production needs. For example, the second-quarter production needs are 480,000 pounds. Therefore, the desired ending inventory for the first quarter would be 10% × 480,000 pounds = 48,000 pounds. The ending inventory of 22,500 pounds for the fourth quarter is assumed.
[2]Cash payments for last year's fourth-quarter material purchases. See the beginning-of-year balance sheet on page 320.
[3]$47,400 × 50%; $47,400 × 50%.
[4]$97,200 × 50%; $97,200 × 50%.
[5]$102,900 × 50%; $102,900 × 50%.
[6]$55,800 × 50%. Unpaid fourth-quarter purchases appear as accounts payable on the company's end-of-year balance sheet.

would like to maintain ending inventories of sugar equal to 10% of the following quarter's production needs.

The first line in the direct materials budget contains the required production for each quarter, which is taken directly from the production budget (Schedule 2). Looking at the first quarter, since the production schedule calls for production of 14,000 cases of popsicles and each case requires 15 pounds of sugar, the total production needs are 210,000 pounds of sugar (14,000 cases × 15 pounds per case). In addition, management wants to have ending inventories of 48,000 pounds of sugar, which is 10% of the following quarter's needs of 480,000 pounds. Consequently, the total needs are 258,000 pounds (210,000 pounds for the current quarter's production plus 48,000 pounds for the desired ending inventory). However, since the company already has 21,000 pounds in beginning inventory, only 237,000 pounds of sugar (258,000 pounds − 21,000 pounds) will need to be purchased. Finally, the cost of the raw materials purchases is determined by multiplying the amount of raw material to be purchased by its unit cost. In this case, since 237,000 pounds of sugar will need to be purchased during the first quarter and sugar costs $0.20 per pound, the total cost will be $47,400 (237,000 pounds × $0.20 per pound).

As with the production budget, the amounts listed under the Year column are not always the sum of the quarterly amounts. The desired ending raw materials inventory for the year is the same as the desired ending raw materials inventory for the fourth quarter. Likewise, the beginning raw materials inventory for the year is the same as the beginning raw materials inventory for the first quarter.

The direct materials budget (or the merchandise purchases budget for a merchandising company) is usually accompanied by a schedule of expected cash disbursements for raw materials (or merchandise purchases). This schedule is needed to prepare the overall cash budget. Disbursements for raw materials (or merchandise purchases) consist of payments for purchases on account in prior periods plus any payments for purchases in the current budget period. Schedule 3 contains such a schedule of cash disbursements for Hampton Freeze.

Ordinarily, companies do not immediately pay their suppliers. At Hampton Freeze, the policy is to pay for 50% of purchases in the quarter in which the purchase is made and 50% in the following quarter, so while the company intends to purchase $47,400 worth of sugar in the first quarter, the company will only pay for half, $23,700, in the first quarter and the other half will be paid in the second quarter. The company will also pay $25,800 in the first quarter for sugar that was purchased on account in the previous quarter, but not yet paid for. This is the beginning balance in the accounts payable. Therefore, the total cash disbursements for sugar in the first quarter are $49,500—the $25,800 payment for sugar acquired in the previous quarter plus the $23,700 payment for sugar acquired during the first quarter.

The Direct Labor Budget

LEARNING OBJECTIVE 5
Prepare a direct labor budget.

The **direct labor budget** shows the direct labor-hours required to satisfy the production budget. By knowing in advance how much labor time will be needed throughout the budget year, the company can develop plans to adjust the labor force as the situation requires. Companies that neglect to budget run the risk of facing labor shortages or having to hire and lay off workers at awkward times. Erratic labor policies lead to insecurity, low morale, and inefficiency.

The direct labor budget for Hampton Freeze is shown in Schedule 4. The first line in the direct labor budget consists of the required production for each quarter, which is taken directly from the production budget (Schedule 2). The direct labor requirement for each quarter is computed by multiplying the number of units to be produced in that quarter by the number of direct labor-hours required to make a unit. For example, 14,000 cases are to be produced in the first quarter and each case requires 0.40 direct labor-hour, so a total of 5,600 direct labor-hours (14,000 cases × 0.40 direct labor-hour per case) will be required in the first quarter. The direct labor requirements can then be translated into budgeted direct labor costs. How this is done will depend on the company's labor policy. In Schedule 4, Hampton Freeze has assumed that the direct labor force will be adjusted as the work requirements change from quarter to quarter. In that case, the direct labor cost is computed by simply multiplying the direct labor-hour requirements by the direct labor rate per hour. For example, the direct labor cost in the first quarter is $84,000 (5,600 direct labor-hours × $15 per direct labor-hour).

SCHEDULE 4

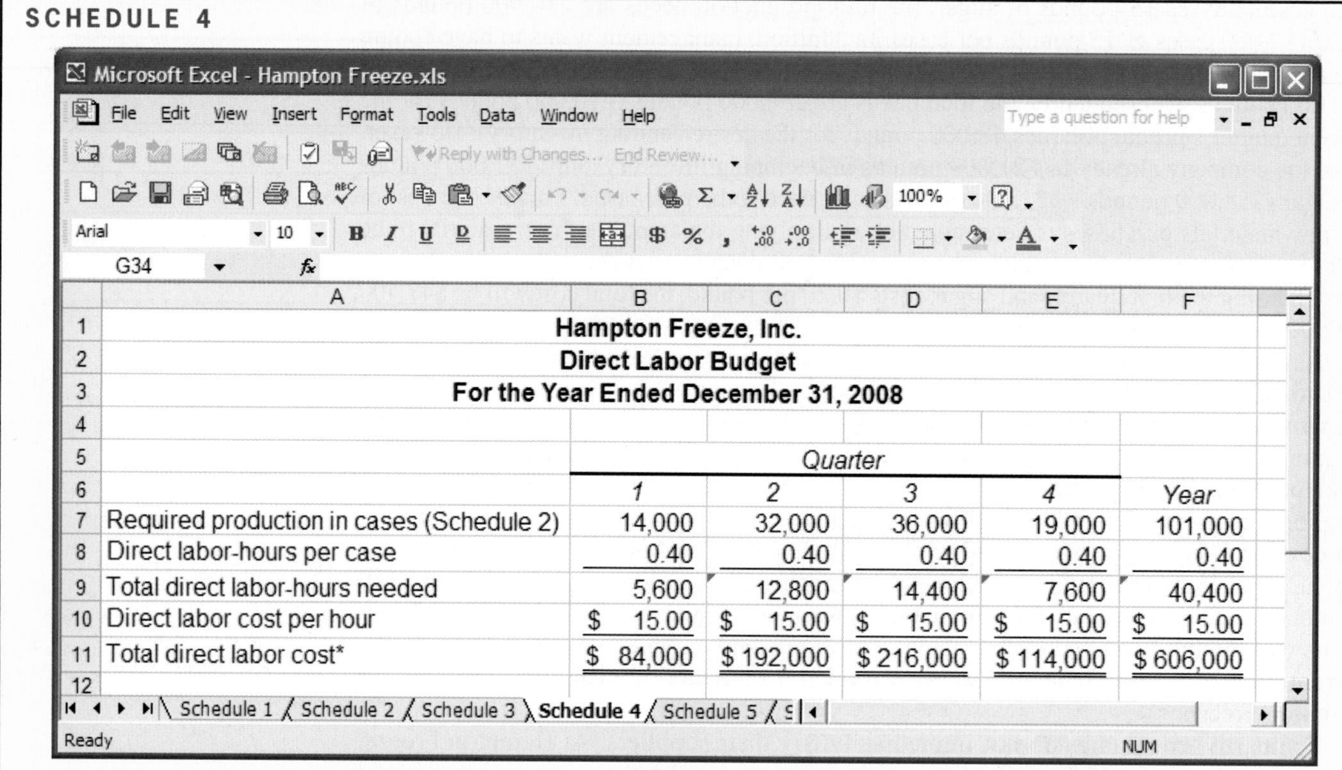

	Hampton Freeze, Inc.				
	Direct Labor Budget				
	For the Year Ended December 31, 2008				
	Quarter				
	1	*2*	*3*	*4*	*Year*
Required production in cases (Schedule 2)	14,000	32,000	36,000	19,000	101,000
Direct labor-hours per case	0.40	0.40	0.40	0.40	0.40
Total direct labor-hours needed	5,600	12,800	14,400	7,600	40,400
Direct labor cost per hour	$ 15.00	$ 15.00	$ 15.00	$ 15.00	$ 15.00
Total direct labor cost*	$ 84,000	$ 192,000	$ 216,000	$ 114,000	$ 606,000

*This schedule assumes that the direct labor workforce will be fully adjusted to the total direct labor-hours needed each quarter.

However, many companies have employment policies or contracts that prevent them from laying off and rehiring workers as needed. Suppose, for example, that Hampton Freeze has 25 workers who are classified as direct labor, but each of them is guaranteed at least 480 hours of pay each quarter at a rate of $15 per hour. In that case, the minimum direct labor cost for a quarter would be as follows:

$$25 \text{ workers} \times 480 \text{ hours per worker} \times \$15 \text{ per hour} = \$180{,}000$$

Note that in this case the direct labor costs for the first and fourth quarters would have to be increased to $180,000.

The Manufacturing Overhead Budget

LEARNING OBJECTIVE 6
Prepare a manufacturing overhead budget.

The **manufacturing overhead budget** lists all costs of production other than direct materials and direct labor. Schedule 5 shows the manufacturing overhead budget for Hampton Freeze. At Hampton Freeze, manufacturing overhead is separated into variable and fixed components. The variable component is $4 per direct labor-hour and the fixed component is $60,600 per quarter. Because the variable component of manufacturing overhead depends on direct labor, the first line in the manufacturing overhead budget consists of the budgeted direct labor-hours from the direct labor budget (Schedule 4). The budgeted direct labor-hours in each quarter are multiplied by the variable rate to determine the variable component of manufacturing overhead. For example, the variable manufacturing overhead for the first quarter is $22,400 (5,600 direct labor-hours × $4.00 per direct labor-hour). This is added to the fixed manufacturing overhead for the quarter to determine the total manufacturing overhead for the quarter of $83,000 ($22,400 + $60,600).

SCHEDULE 5

Microsoft Excel - Hampton Freeze.xls

	A	B	C	D	E	F
1	Hampton Freeze, Inc.					
2	Manufacturing Overhead Budget					
3	For the Year Ended December 31, 2008					
4						
5		Quarter				
6		1	2	3	4	Year
7	Budgeted direct labor-hours (Schedule 4)	5,600	12,800	14,400	7,600	40,400
8	Variable manufacturing overhead rate	$ 4.00	$ 4.00	$ 4.00	$ 4.00	$ 4.00
9	Variable manufacturing overhead	$ 22,400	$ 51,200	$ 57,600	$ 30,400	$ 161,600
10	Fixed manufacturing overhead	60,600	60,600	60,600	60,600	242,400
11	Total manufacturing overhead	83,000	111,800	118,200	91,000	404,000
12	Less depreciation	15,000	15,000	15,000	15,000	60,000
13	Cash disbursements for manufacturing overhead	$ 68,000	$ 96,800	$ 103,200	$ 76,000	$ 344,000
14						
15	Total manufacturing overhead (a)					$ 404,000
16	Budgeted direct labor-hours (b)					40,400
17	Predetermined overhead rate for the year (a)÷(b)					$ 10.00
18						

Schedule 5 / Schedule 6 / Schedule 7 / Schedule 8 / Schedule 9 / Sched

A few words about fixed costs and the budgeting process are in order. In most cases, fixed costs are the costs of supplying capacity to make products, process purchase orders, handle customer calls, and so on. The amount of capacity that will be required depends on the expected level of activity for the period. If the expected level of activity is greater than the company's current capacity, then fixed costs may have to be increased. Or, if the expected level is appreciably below the company's current capacity, then it may be desirable to decrease fixed costs if possible. However, once the level of the fixed costs has been determined in the budget, the costs really are fixed. The time to adjust fixed costs is during the budgeting process. An activity-based costing system can help to determine the appropriate level of fixed costs at budget time by answering questions like, "How many clerks will we need to hire to process the anticipated number of purchase orders next year?" For simplicity, in all of the budgeting examples in this book assume that the appropriate levels of fixed costs have already been determined.

The last line of Schedule 5 for Hampton Freeze shows the budgeted cash disbursements for manufacturing overhead. Since some of the overhead costs are not cash outflows, the total budgeted manufacturing overhead costs must be adjusted to determine the cash disbursements for manufacturing overhead. At Hampton Freeze, the only significant noncash manufacturing overhead cost is depreciation, which is $15,000 per quarter. These noncash depreciation charges are deducted from the total budgeted manufacturing overhead to determine the expected cash disbursements. Hampton Freeze pays all overhead costs involving cash disbursements in the quarter incurred. Note that the company's predetermined overhead rate for the year is $10 per direct labor-hour, which is determined by dividing the total budgeted manufacturing overhead for the year by the total budgeted direct labor-hours for the year.

The Ending Finished Goods Inventory Budget

After completing Schedules 1–5, Larry Giano had all of the data he needed to compute unit product costs. This computation was needed for two reasons: first, to determine cost of goods sold on the budgeted income statement; and second, to know what amount to put on the balance sheet inventory account for unsold units. The carrying cost of the unsold units is computed on the **ending finished goods inventory budget.**

Larry Giano considered using variable costing to prepare Hampton Freeze's budget statements, but he decided to use absorption costing instead because the bank would very likely require absorption costing. He also knew that it would be easy to convert the absorption costing financial statements to a variable costing basis later. At this point, the primary concern was to determine what financing, if any, would be required in 2008 and then to arrange for that financing from the bank.

The unit product cost computations are shown in Schedule 6. For Hampton Freeze, the absorption costing unit product cost is $13 per case of popsicles—consisting of $3 of direct materials, $6 of direct labor, and $4 of manufacturing overhead. The manufacturing overhead is applied to units of product at the rate of $10 per direct labor-hour. The budgeted carrying cost of the ending inventory is $39,000.

LEARNING OBJECTIVE 7
Prepare a selling and administrative expense budget.

The Selling and Administrative Expense Budget

The **selling and administrative expense budget** lists the budgeted expenses for areas other than manufacturing. In large organizations, this budget would be a compilation of many smaller, individual budgets submitted by department heads and other persons responsible for

SCHEDULE 6

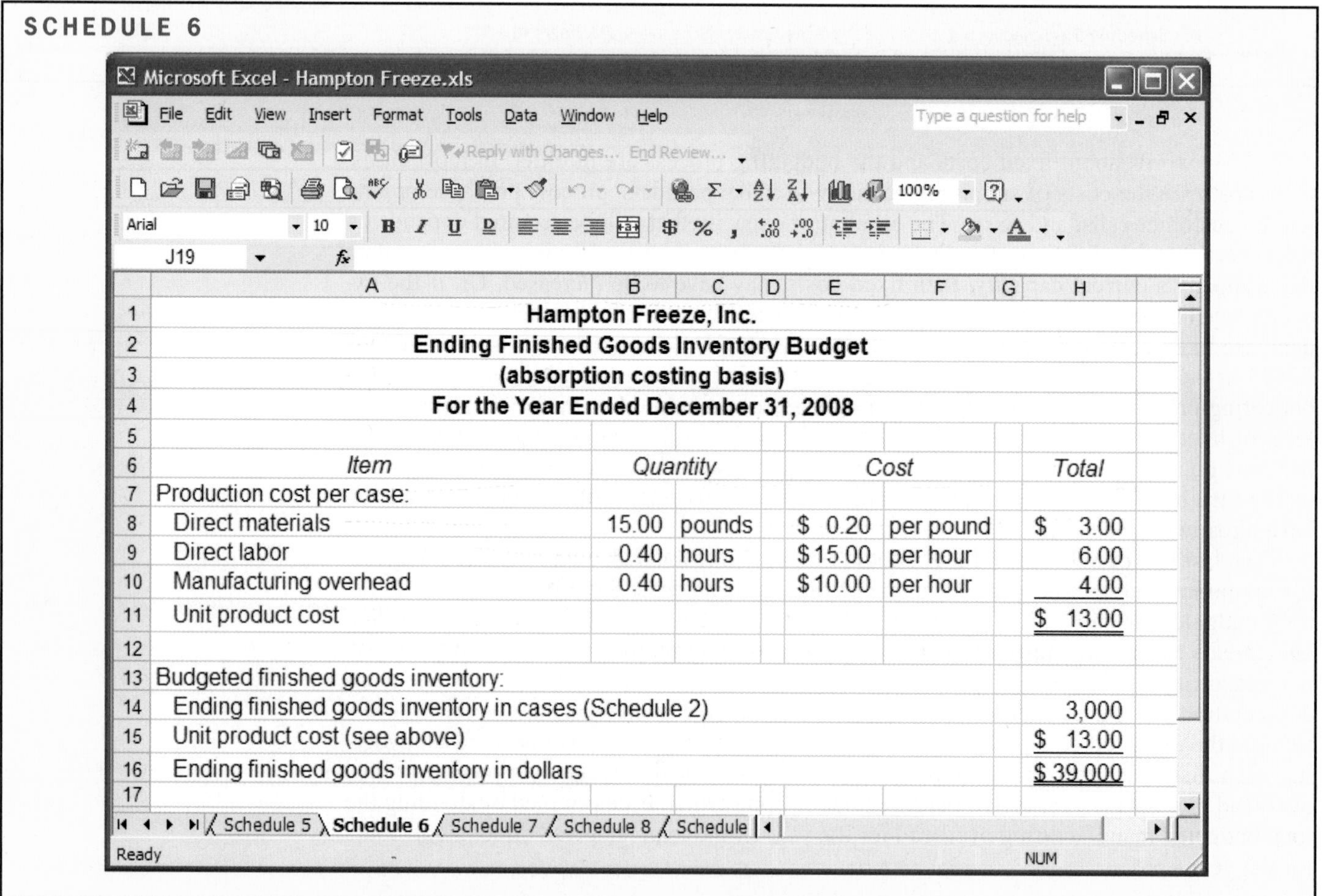

Hampton Freeze, Inc.
Ending Finished Goods Inventory Budget
(absorption costing basis)
For the Year Ended December 31, 2008

Item	Quantity		Cost		Total
Production cost per case:					
Direct materials	15.00	pounds	$ 0.20	per pound	$ 3.00
Direct labor	0.40	hours	$15.00	per hour	6.00
Manufacturing overhead	0.40	hours	$10.00	per hour	4.00
Unit product cost					$ 13.00
Budgeted finished goods inventory:					
Ending finished goods inventory in cases (Schedule 2)					3,000
Unit product cost (see above)					$ 13.00
Ending finished goods inventory in dollars					$ 39,000

SCHEDULE 7

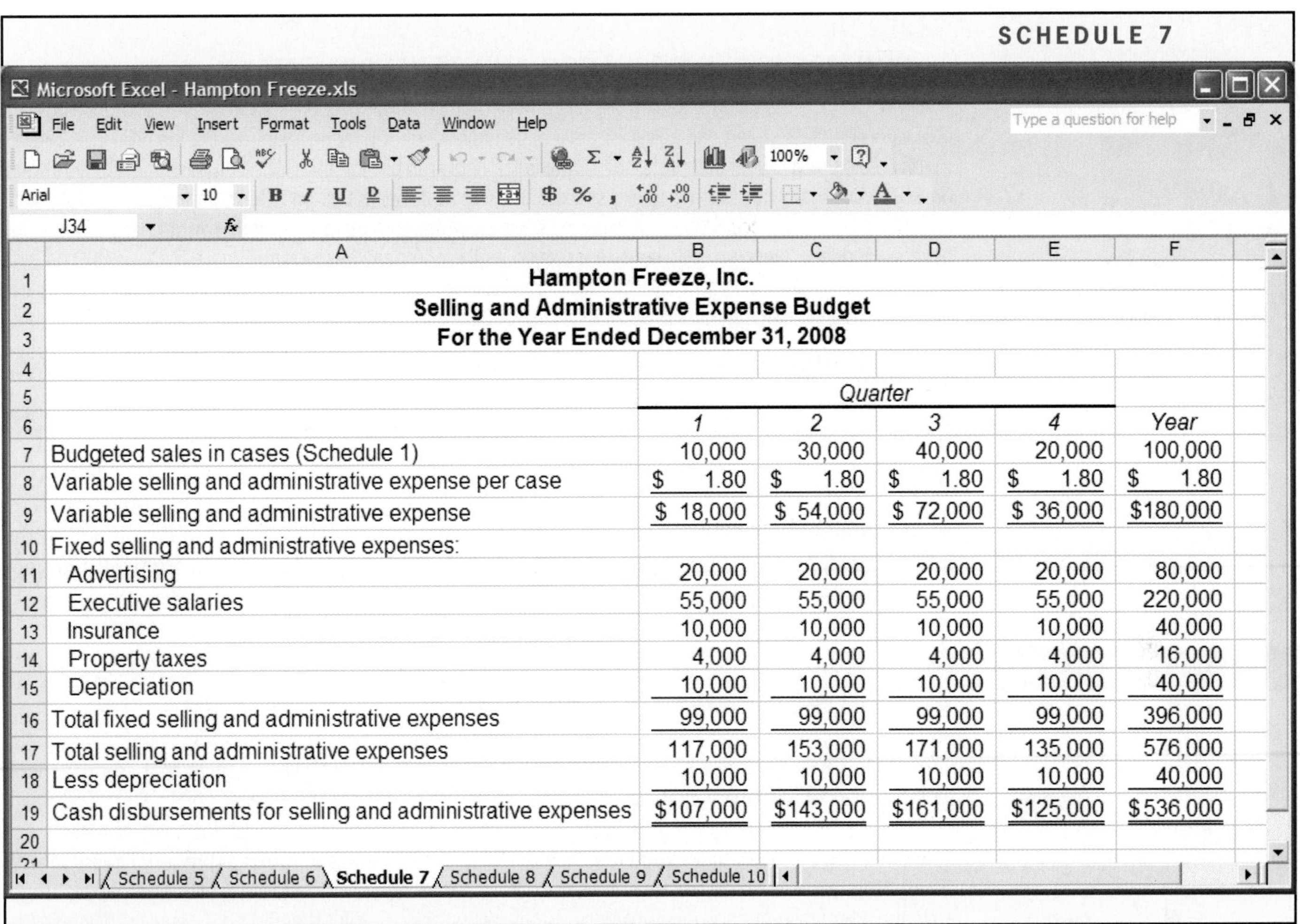

		Quarter			
Hampton Freeze, Inc. Selling and Administrative Expense Budget For the Year Ended December 31, 2008	1	2	3	4	Year
Budgeted sales in cases (Schedule 1)	10,000	30,000	40,000	20,000	100,000
Variable selling and administrative expense per case	$ 1.80	$ 1.80	$ 1.80	$ 1.80	$ 1.80
Variable selling and administrative expense	$ 18,000	$ 54,000	$ 72,000	$ 36,000	$180,000
Fixed selling and administrative expenses:					
Advertising	20,000	20,000	20,000	20,000	80,000
Executive salaries	55,000	55,000	55,000	55,000	220,000
Insurance	10,000	10,000	10,000	10,000	40,000
Property taxes	4,000	4,000	4,000	4,000	16,000
Depreciation	10,000	10,000	10,000	10,000	40,000
Total fixed selling and administrative expenses	99,000	99,000	99,000	99,000	396,000
Total selling and administrative expenses	117,000	153,000	171,000	135,000	576,000
Less depreciation	10,000	10,000	10,000	10,000	40,000
Cash disbursements for selling and administrative expenses	$107,000	$143,000	$161,000	$125,000	$536,000

selling and administrative expenses. For example, the marketing manager would submit a budget detailing the advertising expenses for each budget period.

Schedule 7 contains the selling and administrative expense budget for Hampton Freeze. Like the manufacturing overhead budget, the selling and administrative expense budget is divided into variable and fixed cost components. In the case of Hampton Freeze, the variable selling and administrative expense is $1.80 per case. Consequently, budgeted sales in cases for each quarter are entered at the top of the schedule. These data are taken from the sales budget (Schedule 1). The budgeted variable selling and administrative expenses are determined by multiplying the budgeted cases sold by the variable selling and administrative expense per case. For example, the budgeted variable selling and administrative expense for the first quarter is $18,000 (10,000 cases × $1.80 per case). The fixed selling and administrative expenses (all given data) are then added to the variable selling and administrative expenses to arrive at the total budgeted selling and administrative expenses. Finally, to determine the cash disbursements for selling and administrative items, the total budgeted selling and administrative expense is adjusted by subtracting any noncash selling and administrative expenses (in this case, just depreciation).[1]

[1] Other adjustments might need to be made for differences between cash flows on the one hand and revenues and expenses on the other hand. For example, if property taxes are paid twice a year in installments of $8,000 each, the expense for property tax would have to be "backed out" of the total budgeted selling and administrative expenses and the cash installment payments added to the appropriate quarters to determine the cash disbursements. Similar adjustments might also need to be made in the manufacturing overhead budget. We generally ignore these complications in this chapter.

IN BUSINESS

CANON INVESTS IN RESEARCH AND DEVELOPMENT

When Canon Inc., the world's leading digital camera manufacturer, prepares the research and development (R&D) portion of its selling and administrative expense budget, the focus is on making long-run investments to grow sales rather than cutting costs to maximize short-run profits. In 2005, Canon spent 8% of its sales on R&D while many of its competitors spent 6% to 7.5% of their sales on R&D. Canon's CEO Fujio Mitarai described his company's R&D philosophy by saying "we have to plant the seeds for the next decade and beyond." Indeed, Canon's seeds have blossomed as the company has secured more than 17,000 patents since 1995—second only to IBM. Canon's commitment to R&D helps explain why its digital cameras are delivering healthy earnings at a time when many of its competitors are losing money.

Source: Ian Rowley, Hiroko Tashiro, and Louise Lee, "Canon: Combat-Ready," *BusinessWeek*, September 5, 2005, pp. 48–49.

The Cash Budget

LEARNING OBJECTIVE 8
Prepare a cash budget.

As illustrated in Exhibit 8–2, the cash budget combines much of the data developed in the preceding steps. It is a good idea to review Exhibit 8–2 to get the big picture firmly in your mind before moving on.

IN BUSINESS

CONCENTRATING ON THE CASH FLOW

Burlington Northern Santa Fe (BNSF) operates the second largest railroad in the United States. The company's senior vice president, CFO, and treasurer is Tom Hunt, who reports that "As a general theme, we've become very cash-flow-oriented." After the merger of the Burlington Northern and Santa Fe railroads, the company went through a number of years of heavy investments and negative cash flows. To keep on top of the company's cash position, Hunt has a cash forecast prepared every month. "Everything falls like dominoes from free cash flow," Hunt says. "It provides us with alternatives. Right now, the alternative of choice is buying back our own stock . . . [b]ut it could be increasing dividends or making acquisitions. All those things are not even on the radar screen if you don't have free cash flow."

Source: Randy Myers, "Cash Crop: The 2000 Working Capital Survey," *CFO*, August 2000, pp. 59–82.

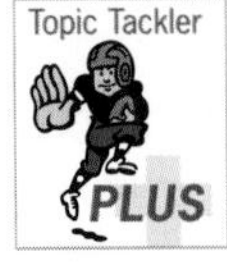

8–2

The cash budget is composed of four major sections:

1. The receipts section.
2. The disbursements section
3. The cash excess or deficiency section.
4. The financing section.

The receipts section lists all of the cash inflows, except from financing, expected during the budget period. Generally, the major source of receipts are from sales.

The disbursements section summarizes all cash payments that are planned for the budget period. These payments include raw materials purchases, direct labor payments, manufacturing overhead costs, and so on, as contained in their respective budgets. In addition, other cash disbursements such as equipment purchases and dividends are listed.

The cash excess or deficiency section is computed as follows:

Cash balance, beginning	XXXX
Add receipts	XXXX
Total cash available	XXXX
Less disbursements	XXXX
Excess (deficiency) of cash available over disbursements	XXXX

SCHEDULE 8

Microsoft Excel - Hampton Freeze.xls

	Hampton Freeze, Inc.						
	Cash Budget						
	For the Year Ended December 31, 2008						
			Quarter				
		Schedule	1	2	3	4	Year
7	Cash balance, beginning		$42,500	$36,000	$ 33,900	$165,650	$ 42,500
8	Add receipts:						
9	Collections from customers	1	230,000	480,000	740,000	520,000	1,970,000
10	Total cash available		272,500	516,000	773,900	685,650	2,012,500
11	Less disbursements:						
12	Direct materials	3	49,500	72,300	100,050	79,350	301,200
13	Direct labor	4	84,000	192,000	216,000	114,000	606,000
14	Manufacturing overhead	5	68,000	96,800	103,200	76,000	344,000
15	Selling and administrative	7	107,000	143,000	161,000	125,000	536,000
16	Equipment purchases		50,000	40,000	20,000	20,000	130,000
17	Dividends		8,000	8,000	8,000	8,000	32,000
18	Total disbursements		366,500	552,100	608,250	422,350	1,949,200
19	Excess (deficiency) of cash available over disbursements		(94,000)	(36,100)	165,650	263,300	63,300
20	Financing:						
21	Borrowings (at the beginnings of quarters)		130,000	70,000	-	-	200,000
22	Repayments (at end of the year)		-	-	-	(200,000)	(200,000)
23	Interest		-	-	-	(21,900)	(21,900)
24	Total financing		130,000	70,000	-	(221,900)	(21,900)
25	Cash balance, ending		$36,000	$33,900	$165,650	$ 41,400	$ 41,400

If a cash deficiency exists during any budget period, the company will need to borrow funds. If there is a cash excess during any budget period, funds borrowed in previous periods can be repaid or the excess funds can be invested.

The financing section details the borrowings and repayments projected to take place during the budget period. It also lists interest payments that will be due on money borrowed.

The cash balances at both the beginning and end of the year may be adequate even though a serious cash deficit occurs at some point during the year. Consequently, the cash budget should be broken down into time periods that are short enough to capture major fluctuations in cash balances. While a monthly cash budget is most common, some organizations budget cash on a weekly or even daily basis. Larry Giano has prepared a quarterly cash budget for Hampton Freeze that can be further refined as necessary. This budget appears in Schedule 8. The cash budget builds on the earlier schedules and on additional data that are provided below:

- The beginning cash balance is $42,500.
- Management plans to spend $130,000 during the year on equipment purchases: $50,000 in the first quarter; $40,000 in the second quarter; $20,000 in the third quarter; and $20,000 in the fourth quarter.
- The board of directors has approved cash dividends of $8,000 per quarter.
- Management would like to have a cash balance of at least $30,000 at the beginning of each quarter for contingencies.

- Hampton Freeze has an agreement with a local bank that allows the company to borrow in increments of $10,000 at the beginning of each quarter, up to a total loan balance of $250,000. The interest rate on these loans is 1% per month and for simplicity we will assume that interest is not compounded. The company would, as far as it is able, repay the loan plus accumulated interest at the end of the year.

The cash budget is prepared one quarter at a time, starting with the first quarter. Larry began the cash budget by entering the beginning balance of cash for the first quarter of $42,500—a number that is given on the prior page. Receipts—in this case, just the $230,000 in cash collections from customers—are added to the beginning balance to arrive at the total cash available of $272,500. Since the total disbursements are $366,500 and the total cash available is only $272,500, there is a shortfall of $94,000. Since management would like to have a beginning cash balance of at least $30,000 for the second quarter, the company will need to borrow at least $124,000.

Required Borrowings at the Beginning of the First Quarter	
Desired ending cash balance	$ 30,000
Plus deficiency of cash available over disbursements	94,000
Minimum required borrowings	$124,000

Recall that the bank requires that loans be made in increments of $10,000. Because Hampton Freeze needs to borrow at least $124,000, it will have to borrow $130,000.

The second quarter of the cash budget is handled similarly. Note that the ending cash balance for the first quarter is brought forward as the beginning cash balance for the second quarter. Also note that additional borrowing is required in the second quarter because of the continued cash shortfall.

Required Borrowings at the Beginning of the Second Quarter	
Desired ending cash balance	$30,000
Plus deficiency of cash available over disbursements	36,100
Minimum required borrowings	$66,100

Again, recall that the bank requires that loans be made in increments of $10,000. Because Hampton Freeze needs to borrow at least $66,100 at the beginning of the second quarter, the company will have to borrow $70,000 from the bank.

In the third quarter, the cash flow situation improves dramatically and the excess of cash available over disbursements is $165,650. Therefore, the company will end the quarter with ample cash and no further borrowing is necessary.

At the end of the fourth quarter, the loan and accumulated interest must be repaid. The accumulated interest can be computed as follows:

Interest on $130,000 borrowed at the beginning of the first quarter:	
$130,000 × 0.01 per month × 12 months*	$15,600
Interest on $70,000 borrowed at the beginning of the second quarter:	
$70,000 × 0.01 per month × 9 months*	6,300
Total interest accrued to the end of the fourth quarter	$21,900

*Simple, rather than compounded, interest is assumed for simplicity.

Note that the loan repayment of $200,000 ($130,000 + $70,000) appears in the financing section for the fourth quarter along with the interest payment of $21,900 computed above.

As with the production and raw materials budgets, the amounts under the Year column in the cash budget are not always the sum of the amounts for the four quarters. In particular, the beginning cash balance for the year is the same as the beginning cash balance for the first quarter and the ending cash balance for the year is the same as the ending cash balance for the fourth quarter. Also note the beginning cash balance in any quarter is the same as the ending cash balance for the previous quarter.

IN BUSINESS

CASH CRISIS AT A START-UP COMPANY

Good Home Co., headquartered in New York City, sells home cleaning and laundry products through merchandisers such as Restoration Hardware and Nordstrom. In 2001, the company's sales were $2.1 million. Then in September 2002, the company's founder Christine Dimmick appeared on the cable shopping network QVC and in a few hours she sold more than $300,000 worth of merchandise. However, euphoria turned to panic when Christine realized that she needed $200,000 in short-term financing to fill those orders. When attempts to renegotiate payment terms with suppliers failed, Christine realized that she needed to hire a finance professional. Jerry Charlup, who was hired as Good Home's part-time CFO, spent $6,000 to create a cash flow forecasting system using Excel. As Good Home's annual sales have grown to $4 million, Charlup says the new forecasting system is giving the company "a far clearer fix on how much operating capital it needs at any given time."

Source: Susan Hansen, "The Rent-To-Own CFO Program," *Inc.* magazine, February 2004, pp. 28–29.

The Budgeted Income Statement

LEARNING OBJECTIVE 9
Prepare a budgeted income statement.

A budgeted income statement can be prepared from the data developed in Schedules 1–8. *The budgeted income statement is one of the key schedules in the budget process.* It shows the company's planned profit and serves as a benchmark against which subsequent company performance can be measured.

Schedule 9 contains the budgeted income statement for Hampton Freeze.

SCHEDULE 9

Microsoft Excel - Hampton Freeze.xls

	A	B	C
1	**Hampton Freeze, Inc.**		
2	**Budgeted Income Statement**		
3	**For the Year Ended December 31, 2008**		
4			
5		*Schedules*	
6	Sales	1	$ 2,000,000
7	Cost of goods sold*	1,6	1,300,000
8	Gross margin		700,000
9	Selling and administrative expenses	7	576,000
10	Net operating Income		124,000
11	Interest expense	8	21,900
12	Net Income		$ 102,100
13			
14			

Schedule 8 | Schedule 9 | Schedule 10

*100,000 cases sold × $13 per case = $1,300,000.

The Budgeted Balance Sheet

LEARNING OBJECTIVE 10
Prepare a budgeted balance sheet.

The budgeted balance sheet is developed using data from the balance sheet from the beginning of the budget period and data contained in the various schedules. Hampton Freeze's budgeted balance sheet is presented in Schedule 10. Some of the data on the budgeted balance sheet have been taken from the company's previous end-of-year balance sheet for 2007 which appears below:

Hampton Freeze, Inc.
Balance Sheet
December 31, 2007

Assets		
Current assets:		
Cash	$ 42,500	
Accounts receivable	90,000	
Raw materials inventory (21,000 pounds)	4,200	
Finished goods inventory (2,000 cases)	26,000	
Total current assets		$162,700
Plant and equipment:		
Land	80,000	
Buildings and equipment	700,000	
Accumulated depreciation	(292,000)	
Plant and equipment, net		488,000
Total assets		$650,700
Liabilities and Stockholders' Equity		
Current liabilities:		
Accounts payable (raw materials)		$ 25,800
Stockholders' equity:		
Common stock, no par	$175,000	
Retained earnings	449,900	
Total stockholders' equity		624,900
Total liabilities and stockholders' equity		$650,700

MANAGERIAL ACCOUNTING IN ACTION
The Wrap-up

After completing the master budget, Larry Giano took the documents to Tom Wills, chief executive officer of Hampton Freeze, for his review.

Larry: Here's the budget. Overall, the net income is excellent, and the net cash flow for the entire year is positive.

Tom: Yes, but I see on this cash budget that we have the same problem with negative cash flows in the first and second quarters that we had last year.

Larry: That's true. I don't see any way around that problem. However, there is no doubt in my mind that if you take this budget to the bank today, they'll approve an open line of credit that will allow you to borrow enough to make it through the first two quarters without any problem.

Tom: Are you sure? They didn't seem very happy to see me last year when I came in for an emergency loan.

Larry: Did you repay the loan on time?

Tom: Sure.

Larry: I don't see any problem. You won't be asking for an emergency loan this time. The bank will have plenty of warning. And with this budget, you have a solid plan that shows when and how you are going to pay off the loan. Trust me, they'll go for it.

SCHEDULE 10

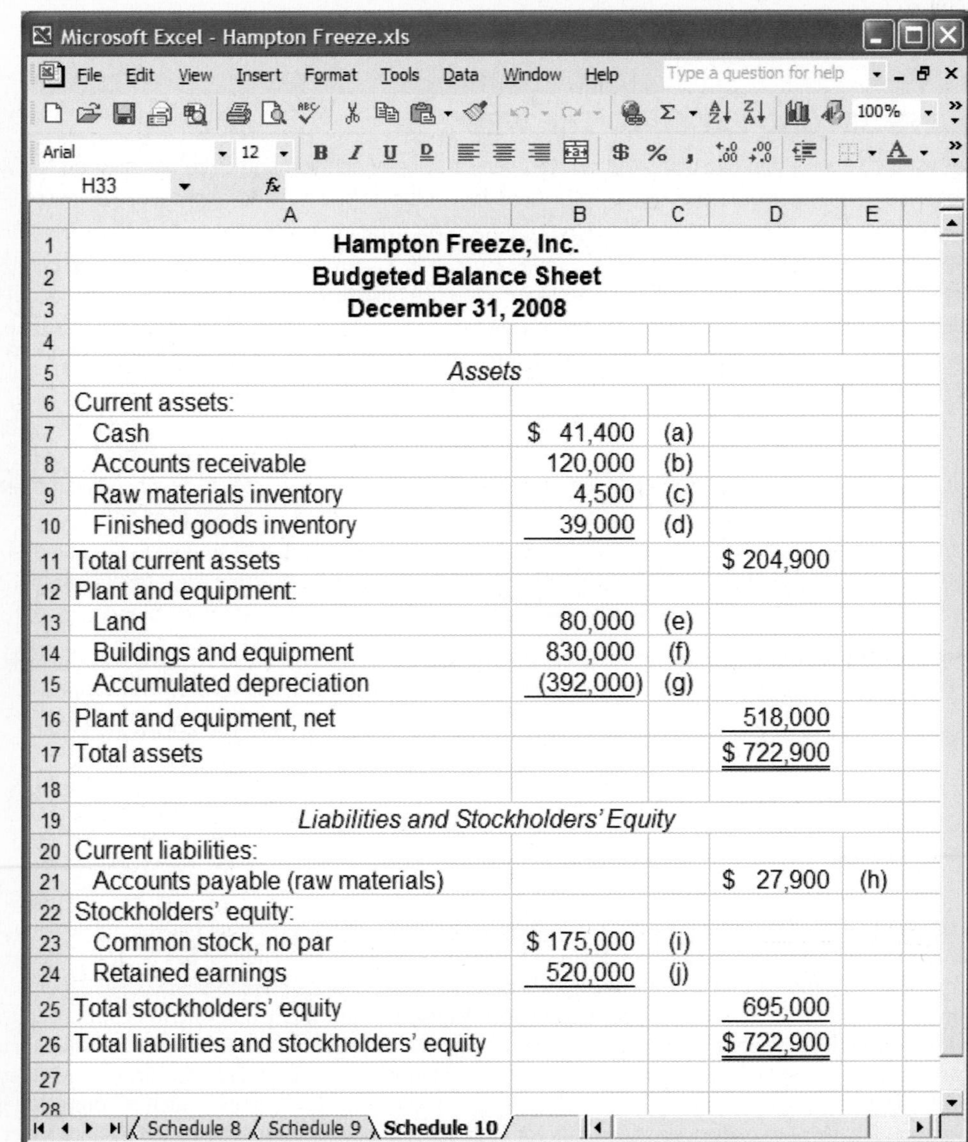

	A	B	C	D	E
1	**Hampton Freeze, Inc.**				
2	**Budgeted Balance Sheet**				
3	**December 31, 2008**				
4					
5	*Assets*				
6	Current assets:				
7	Cash	$ 41,400	(a)		
8	Accounts receivable	120,000	(b)		
9	Raw materials inventory	4,500	(c)		
10	Finished goods inventory	39,000	(d)		
11	Total current assets			$ 204,900	
12	Plant and equipment:				
13	Land	80,000	(e)		
14	Buildings and equipment	830,000	(f)		
15	Accumulated depreciation	(392,000)	(g)		
16	Plant and equipment, net			518,000	
17	Total assets			$ 722,900	
18					
19	*Liabilities and Stockholders' Equity*				
20	Current liabilities:				
21	Accounts payable (raw materials)			$ 27,900	(h)
22	Stockholders' equity:				
23	Common stock, no par	$ 175,000	(i)		
24	Retained earnings	520,000	(j)		
25	Total stockholders' equity			695,000	
26	Total liabilities and stockholders' equity			$ 722,900	

Explanation of December 31, 2008, balance sheet figures:

(a) The ending cash balance, as projected by the cash budget in Schedule 8.

(b) Thirty percent of fourth-quarter sales, from Schedule 1 ($400,000 × 30% = $120,000).

(c) From Schedule 3, the ending raw materials inventory will be 22,500 pounds. This material costs $0.20 per pound. Therefore, the ending inventory in dollars will be 22,500 pounds × $0.20 per pound = $4,500.

(d) From Schedule 6.

(e) From the December 31, 2007, balance sheet (no change).

(f) The December 31, 2007, balance sheet indicated a balance of $700,000. During 2008, $130,000 of additional equipment will be purchased (see Schedule 8), bringing the December 31, 2008, balance to $830,000.

(g) The December 31, 2007, balance sheet indicated a balance of $292,000. During 2008, $100,000 of depreciation will be taken ($60,000 on Schedule 5 and $40,000 on Schedule 7), bringing the December 31, 2008, balance to $392,000.

(h) One-half of the fourth-quarter raw materials purchases, from Schedule 3.

(i) From the December 31, 2007, balance sheet (no change).

(j)

December 31, 2007, balance	$449,900
Add net income, from Schedule 9	102,100
	552,000
Deduct dividends paid, from Schedule 8	32,000
December 31, 2008, balance	$520,000

IN BUSINESS

MOVING BEYOND EXCEL TO THE WEB

While research shows that two-thirds of U.S. companies still rely on Microsoft Excel for their budgeting process, some companies are evolving to a more technologically advanced approach. For example, Hendrick Motorsports has vaulted to the top of the NASCAR racing circuit thanks in part to its new budgeting process. Scott Lampe, Hendrick's CFO, discarded Excel in favor of Forecaster, a web-based budgeting program. He commented "with a spreadsheet, you can build the model the way you want it . . . The problem is, only you understand that model. Then you have to explain it to everyone, one at a time." The web-based approach enables Lampe to involve his crew chiefs, chassis guys, and engine guys in the budgeting process.

The Facilities & Operations (F&O) Business Office of the Battelle, Pacific Northwest National Laboratory has over 130 budget activities—each of which requires the preparation of an annual budget. In 2001, F&O replaced its spreadsheet-driven budget with a web-based approach. The new system enables F&O "management and their support staff to directly input their business plan and budget requests, eliminating the need for central business planning and budgeting staff to upload the numerous budget requests and subsequent changes." The web-based budgeting system saves F&O personnel more than 500 hours that were previously spent preparing Excel spreadsheets and uploading data.

Source: John Goff, "In The Fast Lane," *CFO*, December 2004, pp. 53–58; Peter T. Smith, Craig A. Goranson, and Mary F. Astley, "Intranet Budgeting Does the Trick," *Strategic Finance*, May 2003, pp. 30–33.

Summary

This chapter describes the budgeting process and shows how the various operating budgets relate to each other. The sales budget is the foundation for profit planning. Once the sales budget has been set, the production budget and the selling and administrative expense budget can be prepared since they depend on how many units are to be sold. The production budget determines how many units are to be produced, so after it is prepared, the various manufacturing cost budgets can be prepared. All of these budgets feed into the cash budget and the budgeted income statement and balance sheet. The parts of the master budget are connected in many ways. For example, the schedule of expected cash collections, which is completed in connection with the sales budget, provides data for both the cash budget and the budgeted balance sheet.

The material in this chapter is just an introduction to budgeting and profit planning. In later chapters, we will see how budgets are used to control day-to-day operations and how they are used in performance evaluation.

Review Problem: Budget Schedules

Mynor Corporation manufactures and sells a seasonal product that has peak sales in the third quarter. The following information concerns operations for Year 2—the coming year—and for the first two quarters of Year 3:

a. The company's single product sells for $8 per unit. Budgeted sales in units for the next six quarters are as follows (all sales are on credit):

	Year 2 Quarter				Year 3 Quarter	
	1	2	3	4	1	2
Budgeted unit sales	40,000	60,000	100,000	50,000	70,000	80,000

b. Sales are collected in the following pattern: 75% in the quarter the sales are made, and the remaining 25% in the following quarter. On January 1, Year 2, the company's balance sheet showed $65,000 in accounts receivable, all of which will be collected in the first quarter of the year. Bad debts are negligible and can be ignored.

c. The company desires an ending finished goods inventory at the end of each quarter equal to 30% of the budgeted unit sales for the next quarter. On December 31, Year 1, the company had 12,000 units on hand.

d. Five pounds of raw materials are required to complete one unit of product. The company requires ending raw materials inventory at the end of each quarter equal to 10% of the following quarter's production needs. On December 31, Year 1, the company had 23,000 pounds of raw materials on hand.

e. The raw material costs $0.80 per pound. Raw material purchases are paid for in the following pattern: 60% paid in the quarter the purchases are made, and the remaining 40% paid in the following quarter. On January 1, Year 2, the company's balance sheet showed $81,500 in accounts payable for raw material purchases, all of which will be paid for in the first quarter of the year.

Required:

Prepare the following budgets and schedules for the year, showing both quarterly and total figures:

1. A sales budget and a schedule of expected cash collections.
2. A production budget.
3. A direct materials budget and a schedule of expected cash payments for purchases of materials.

Solution to Review Problem

1. The sales budget is prepared as follows:

	Year 2 Quarter				
	1	2	3	4	Year
Budgeted unit sales	40,000	60,000	100,000	50,000	250,000
Selling price per unit	× $8	× $8	× $8	× $8	× $8
Total sales	$320,000	$480,000	$800,000	$400,000	$2,000,000

Based on the budgeted sales above, the schedule of expected cash collections is prepared as follows:

	Year 2 Quarter				
	1	2	3	4	Year
Accounts receivable, beginning balance	$ 65,000				$ 65,000
First-quarter sales ($320,000 × 75%, 25%)	240,000	$ 80,000			320,000
Second-quarter sales ($480,000 × 75%, 25%)		360,000	$120,000		480,000
Third-quarter sales ($800,000 × 75%, 25%)			600,000	$200,000	800,000
Fourth-quarter sales ($400,000 × 75%)				300,000	300,000
Total cash collections	$305,000	$440,000	$720,000	$500,000	$1,965,000

2. Based on the sales budget in units, the production budget is prepared as follows:

	Year 2 Quarter					Year 3 Quarter	
	1	2	3	4	Year	1	2
Budgeted unit sales	40,000	60,000	100,000	50,000	250,000	70,000	80,000
Add desired ending finished goods inventory*	18,000	30,000	15,000	21,000†	21,000	24,000	
Total needs	58,000	90,000	115,000	71,000	271,000	94,000	
Less beginning finished goods inventory	12,000	18,000	30,000	15,000	12,000	21,000	
Required production	46,000	72,000	85,000	56,000	259,000	73,000	

*30% of the following quarter's budgeted sales in units.
†30% of the budgeted Year 3 first-quarter sales.

3. Based on the production budget, raw materials will need to be purchased during the year as follows:

	Year 2 Quarter					Year 3 Quarter
	1	2	3	4	Year 2	1
Required production (units)	46,000	72,000	85,000	56,000	259,000	73,000
Raw materials needed per unit (pounds)	× 5	× 5	× 5	× 5	× 5	× 5
Production needs (pounds)	230,000	360,000	425,000	280,000	1,295,000	365,000
Add desired ending inventory of raw materials (pounds)*	36,000	42,500	28,000	36,500†	36,500	
Total needs (pounds)	266,000	402,500	453,000	316,500	1,331,500	
Less beginning inventory of raw materials (pounds)	23,000	36,000	42,500	28,000	23,000	
Raw materials to be purchased (pounds)	243,000	366,500	410,500	288,500	1,308,500	

*10% of the following quarter's production needs in pounds.
†10% of the Year 3 first-quarter production needs in pounds.

Based on the raw material purchases above, expected cash payments are computed as follows:

	Year 2 Quarter				
	1	2	3	4	Year 2
Cost of raw materials to be purchased at $0.80 per pound	$194,400	$293,200	$328,400	$230,800	$1,046,800
Accounts payable, beginning balance	$ 81,500				$ 81,500
First-quarter purchases ($194,400 × 60%, 40%)	116,640	$ 77,760			194,400
Second-quarter purchases ($293,200 × 60%, 40%)		175,920	$117,280		293,200
Third-quarter purchases ($328,400 × 60%, 40%)			197,040	$131,360	328,400
Fourth-quarter purchases ($230,800 × 60%)				138,480	138,480
Total cash disbursements	$198,140	$253,680	$314,320	$269,840	$1,035,980

Glossary

Budget A quantitative plan for acquiring and using resources over a specified time period. (p. 298)

Budget committee A group of key managers who are responsible for overall budgeting policy and for coordinating the preparation of the budget. (p. 303)

Cash budget A detailed plan showing how cash resources will be acquired and used over a specific time period. (p. 304)

Continuous budget A 12-month budget that rolls forward one month as the current month is completed. (p. 299)

Control Those steps taken by management to increase the likelihood that all parts of the organization are working together to achieve the goals set down at the planning stage. (p. 298)

Direct labor budget A detailed plan that shows the direct labor-hours required to fulfill the production budget. (p. 311)

Direct materials budget A detailed plan showing the amount of raw materials that must be purchased to fulfill the production budget and to provide for adequate inventories. (p. 309)

Ending finished goods inventory budget A budget showing the dollar amount of unsold finished goods inventory that will appear on the ending balance sheet. (p. 314)

Manufacturing overhead budget A detailed plan showing the production costs, other than direct materials and direct labor, that will be incurred over a specified time period. (p. 312)

Master budget A summary of a company's plans that sets specific targets for sales, production, and financing activities and that generally culminates in a cash budget, budgeted income statement, and budgeted balance sheet. (p. 298)

Merchandise purchases budget A detailed plan used by a merchandising company that shows the amount of goods that must be purchased from suppliers during the period. (p. 309)

Participative budget See *Self-imposed budget.* (p. 300)

Perpetual budget See *Continuous budget.* (p. 299)

Planning Developing goals and preparing budgets to achieve those goals. (p. 298)

Production budget A detailed plan showing the number of units that must be produced during a period in order to satisfy both sales and inventory needs. (p. 307)

Responsibility accounting A system of accountability in which managers are held responsible for those items of revenue and cost—and only those items—over which they can exert significant control. The managers are held responsible for differences between budgeted and actual results. (p. 298)

Sales budget A detailed schedule showing expected sales expressed in both dollars and units. (p. 303)

Self-imposed budget A method of preparing budgets in which managers prepare their own budgets. These budgets are then reviewed by higher-level managers, and any issues are resolved by mutual agreement. (p. 300)

Selling and administrative expense budget A detailed schedule of planned expenses that will be incurred in areas other than manufacturing during a budget period. (p. 314)

Questions

8-1 What is a budget? What is budgetary control?

8-2 Discuss some of the major benefits to be gained from budgeting.

8-3 What is meant by the term *responsibility accounting?*

8-4 What is a master budget? Briefly describe its contents.

8-5 Why is the sales forecast the starting point in budgeting?

8-6 "As a practical matter, planning and control mean exactly the same thing." Do you agree? Explain.

8-7 Describe the flow of budget data in an organization. Who are the participants in the budgeting process, and how do they participate?

8-8 What is a self-imposed budget? What are the major advantages of self-imposed budgets? What caution must be exercised in their use?

8-9 How can budgeting assist a company in planning its workforce staffing levels?

8-10 "The principal purpose of the cash budget is to see how much cash the company will have in the bank at the end of the year." Do you agree? Explain.

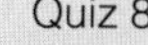

Quiz 8

Multiple-choice questions are provided on the text Web site at www.mhhe.com/noreen1e.

Exercises

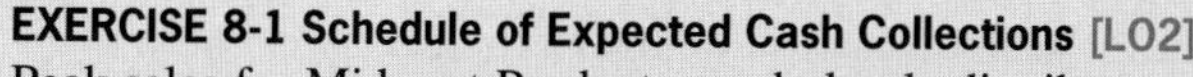

EXERCISE 8-1 Schedule of Expected Cash Collections [LO2]

Peak sales for Midwest Products, a wholesale distributor of leaf rakes, occur in August. The company's sales budget for the third quarter showing these peak sales is given below:

	July	August	September	Total
Budgeted sales (all on account)	$600,000	$900,000	$500,000	$2,000,000

From past experience, the company has learned that 20% of a month's sales are collected in the month of sale, another 70% are collected in the month following sale, and the remaining 10% are collected in the second month following sale. Bad debts are negligible and can be ignored. May sales totaled $430,000, and June sales totaled $540,000.

Required:

1. Prepare a schedule of expected cash collections from sales, by month and in total, for the third quarter.
2. Assume that the company will prepare a budgeted balance sheet as of September 30. Compute the accounts receivable as of that date.

EXERCISE 8-2 Production Budget [LO3]

Crystal Telecom has budgeted the sales of its innovative mobile phone over the next four months as follows:

	Sales in Units
July.	30,000
August	45,000
September	60,000
October	50,000

The company is now in the process of preparing a production budget for the third quarter. Past experience has shown that end-of-month inventories of finished goods must equal 10% of the next month's sales. The inventory at the end of June was 3,000 units.

Required:

Prepare a production budget for the third quarter showing the number of units to be produced each month and for the quarter in total.

EXERCISE 8-3 Direct Materials Budget [LO4]

Micro Products, Inc., has developed a very powerful electronic calculator. Each calculator requires three small "chips" that cost $2 each and are purchased from an overseas supplier. Micro Products has prepared a production budget for the calculator by quarters for Year 2 and for the first quarter of Year 3, as shown below:

	Year 2				Year 3
	First	Second	Third	Fourth	First
Budgeted production, in calculators	60,000	90,000	150,000	100,000	80,000

The chip used in production of the calculator is sometimes hard to get, so it is necessary to carry large inventories as a precaution against stockouts. For this reason, the inventory of chips at the end of a quarter must be equal to 20% of the following quarter's production needs. Some 36,000 chips will be on hand to start the first quarter of Year 2.

Required:

Prepare a direct materials budget for chips, by quarter and in total, for Year 2. At the bottom of your budget, show the dollar amount of purchases for each quarter and for the year in total.

EXERCISE 8-4 Direct Labor Budget [LO5]

The Production Department of the Riverside Plant of Junnen Corporation has submitted the following forecast of units to be produced at the plant for each quarter of the upcoming fiscal year. The plant produces high-end outdoor barbecue grills.

	1st Quarter	2nd Quarter	3rd Quarter	4th Quarter
Units to be produced	5,000	4,400	4,500	4,900

Each unit requires 0.40 direct labor-hours and direct labor-hour workers are paid $11 per hour.

Required:

1. Construct the company's direct labor budget for the upcoming fiscal year, assuming that the direct labor workforce is adjusted each quarter to match the number of hours required to produce the forecasted number of units produced.
2. Construct the company's direct labor budget for the upcoming fiscal year, assuming that the direct labor workforce is *not* adjusted each quarter. Instead, assume that the company's direct labor workforce consists of permanent employees who are guaranteed to be paid for at least 1,800 hours of work each quarter. If the number of required direct labor-hours is less than this number, the workers are paid for 1,800 hours anyway. Any hours worked in excess of 1,800 hours in a quarter are paid at the rate of 1.5 times the normal hourly rate for direct labor.

EXERCISE 8-5 Manufacturing Overhead Budget [LO6]

The direct labor budget of Krispin Corporation for the upcoming fiscal year contains the following details concerning budgeted direct labor-hours.

	1st Quarter	2nd Quarter	3rd Quarter	4th Quarter
Budgeted direct labor-hours	5,000	4,800	5,200	5,400

The company's variable manufacturing overhead rate is $1.75 per direct labor-hour and the company's fixed manufacturing overhead is $35,000 per quarter. The only noncash item included in the fixed manufacturing overhead is depreciation, which is $15,000 per quarter.

Required:

1. Construct the company's manufacturing overhead budget for the upcoming fiscal year.
2. Compute the company's manufacturing overhead rate (including both variable and fixed manufacturing overhead) for the upcoming fiscal year. Round off to the nearest whole cent.

EXERCISE 8-6 Selling and Administrative Expense Budget [LO7]

The budgeted unit sales of Haerve Company for the upcoming fiscal year are provided below:

	1st Quarter	2nd Quarter	3rd Quarter	4th Quarter
Budgeted unit sales........	12,000	14,000	11,000	10,000

The company's variable selling and administrative expenses per unit are $2.75. Fixed selling and administrative expenses include advertising expenses of $12,000 per quarter, executive salaries of $40,000 per quarter, and depreciation of $16,000 per quarter. In addition, the company will make insurance payments of $6,000 in the 2nd Quarter and $6,000 in the 4th Quarter. Finally, property taxes of $6,000 will be paid in the 3rd Quarter.

Required:

Prepare the company's selling and administrative expense budget for the upcoming fiscal year.

EXERCISE 8-7 Cash Budget Analysis [LO8]

A cash budget, by quarters, is given below for a retail company (000 omitted). The company requires a minimum cash balance of $5,000 to start each quarter.

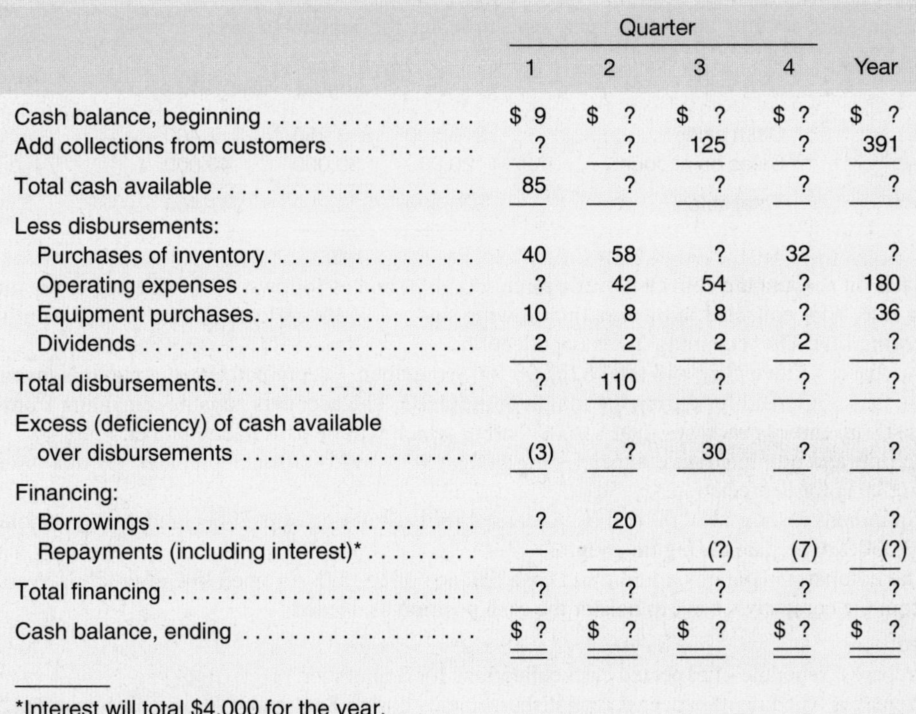

	Quarter 1	Quarter 2	Quarter 3	Quarter 4	Year
Cash balance, beginning	$ 9	$?	$?	$?	$?
Add collections from customers............	?	?	125	?	391
Total cash available......................	85	?	?	?	?
Less disbursements:					
Purchases of inventory..................	40	58	?	32	?
Operating expenses......................	?	42	54	?	180
Equipment purchases.....................	10	8	8	?	36
Dividends...............................	2	2	2	2	?
Total disbursements.......................	?	110	?	?	?
Excess (deficiency) of cash available over disbursements	(3)	?	30	?	?
Financing:					
Borrowings..............................	?	20	—	—	?
Repayments (including interest)*........	—	—	(?)	(7)	(?)
Total financing...........................	?	?	?	?	?
Cash balance, ending	$?	$?	$?	$?	$?

*Interest will total $4,000 for the year.

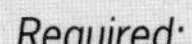

Required:

Fill in the missing amounts in the table above.

Problems 

PROBLEM 8-8 Behavioral Aspects of Budgeting [LO1]

Five years ago, Jack Cadence left his position at a large company to start Advanced Technologies Co. (ATC), a software design company. ATC's first product was a unique software package that seamlessly integrates networked PCs. Robust sales of this initial product permitted the company to begin development of other software products and to hire additional personnel. The staff at ATC quickly grew from three people working out of Cadence's basement to over 70 individuals working in leased spaces at an industrial park. Continued growth led Cadence to hire seasoned marketing, distribution, and production managers and an experienced accountant, Bill Cross.

Recently, Cadence decided that the company had become too large to run on an informal basis and that a formalized planning and control program centered around a budget was necessary. Cadence asked the accountant, Bill Cross, to work with him in developing the initial budget for ATC.

Cadence forecasted sales revenues based on his projections for both the market growth for the initial software and successful completion of new products. Cross used this data to construct the master budget for the company, which he then broke down into departmental budgets. Cadence and Cross met a number of times over a three-week period to hammer out the details of the budgets.

When Cadence and Cross were satisfied with their work, the various departmental budgets were distributed to the department managers with a cover letter explaining ATC's new budgeting system. The letter requested everyone's assistance in working together to achieve the budget objectives.

Several of the department managers were displeased with how the budgeting process was undertaken. In discussing the situation among themselves, they felt that some of the budget projections were overly optimistic and not realistically attainable.

Required:

1. How does the budgeting process Cadence and Cross used at ATC differ from recommended practice?
2. What are the behavioral implications of the way Cadence and Cross went about preparing the master budget?

(CMA, adapted)

PROBLEM 8-9 Schedules of Expected Cash Collections and Disbursements [LO2, LO4, LO8]

Calgon Products, a distributor of organic beverages, needs a cash budget for September. The following information is available:

a. The cash balance at the beginning of September is $9,000.

b. Actual sales for July and August and expected sales for September are as follows:

	July	August	September
Cash sales	$ 6,500	$ 5,250	$ 7,400
Sales on account	20,000	30,000	40,000
Total sales	$26,500	$35,250	$47,400

Sales on account are collected over a three-month period as follows: 10% collected in the month of sale, 70% collected in the month following sale, and 18% collected in the second month following sale. The remaining 2% is uncollectible.

c. Purchases of inventory will total $25,000 for September. Twenty percent of a month's inventory purchases are paid for during the month of purchase. The accounts payable remaining from August's inventory purchases total $16,000, all of which will be paid in September.

d. Selling and administrative expenses are budgeted at $13,000 for September. Of this amount, $4,000 is for depreciation.

e. Equipment costing $18,000 will be purchased for cash during September, and dividends totaling $3,000 will be paid during the month.

f. The company maintains a minimum cash balance of $5,000. An open line of credit is available from the company's bank to bolster the cash position as needed.

Required:

1. Prepare a schedule of expected cash collections for September.
2. Prepare a schedule of expected cash disbursements during September for inventory purchases.
3. Prepare a cash budget for September. Indicate in the financing section any borrowing that will be needed during September.

PROBLEM 8-10 Behavioral Aspects of Budgeting; Ethics and the Manager [LO1]

Granger Stokes, managing partner of the venture capital firm of Halston and Stokes, was dissatisfied with the top management of PrimeDrive, a manufacturer of computer disk drives. Halston and Stokes had invested $20 million in PrimeDrive, and the return on their investment had been unsatisfactory for several years. In a tense meeting of the board of directors of PrimeDrive, Stokes exercised his firm's rights as the major equity investor in PrimeDrive and fired PrimeDrive's chief executive officer (CEO). He then quickly moved to have the board of directors of PrimeDrive appoint himself as the new CEO.

Stokes prided himself on his hard-driving management style. At the first management meeting, he asked two of the managers to stand and fired them on the spot, just to show everyone who was in control of the company. At the budget review meeting that followed, he ripped up the departmental budgets that had been submitted for his review and yelled at the managers for their "wimpy, do nothing targets." He then ordered everyone to submit new budgets calling for at least a 40% increase in sales volume and announced that he would not accept excuses for results that fell below budget.

Keri Kalani, an accountant working for the production manager at PrimeDrive, discovered toward the end of the year that her boss had not been scrapping defective disk drives that had been returned by customers. Instead, he had been shipping them in new cartons to other customers to avoid booking losses. Quality control had deteriorated during the year as a result of the push for increased volume, and returns of defective TRX drives were running as high as 15% of the new drives shipped. When she confronted her boss with her discovery, he told her to mind her own business. And then, to justify his actions, he said, "All of us managers are finding ways to hit Stokes's targets."

Required:

1. Is Granger Stokes using budgets as a planning and control tool?
2. What are the behavioral consequences of the way budgets are being used at PrimeDrive?
3. What, if anything, do you think Keri Kalani should do?

PROBLEM 8-11 Production and Direct Materials Budgets [LO3, LO4]

Tonga Toys manufactures and distributes a number of products to retailers. One of these products, Playclay, requires three pounds of material A135 in the manufacture of each unit. The company is now planning raw materials needs for the third quarter—July, August, and September. Peak sales of Playclay occur in the third quarter of each year. To keep production and shipments moving smoothly, the company has the following inventory requirements:

a. The finished goods inventory on hand at the end of each month must be equal to 5,000 units plus 30% of the next month's sales. The finished goods inventory on June 30 is budgeted to be 17,000 units.
b. The raw materials inventory on hand at the end of each month must be equal to one-half of the following month's production needs for raw materials. The raw materials inventory on June 30 for material A135 is budgeted to be 64,500 pounds.
c. The company maintains no work in process inventories.

A sales budget for Playclay for the last six months of the year follows.

	Budgeted Sales in Units
July.	40,000
August	50,000
September	70,000
October	35,000
November	20,000
December	10,000

Required:

1. Prepare a production budget for Playclay for the months July, August, September, and October.
2. Examine the production budget that you prepared. Why will the company produce more units than it sells in July and August and less units than it sells in September and October?
3. Prepare a direct materials budget showing the quantity of material A135 to be purchased for July, August, and September and for the quarter in total.

PROBLEM 8-12 Direct Materials and Direct Labor Budgets [LO4, LO5]

The production department of Priston Company has submitted the following forecast of units to be produced by quarter for the upcoming fiscal year.

	1st Quarter	2nd Quarter	3rd Quarter	4th Quarter
Units to be produced	6,000	7,000	8,000	5,000

In addition, the beginning raw materials inventory for the 1st Quarter is budgeted to be 3,600 pounds and the beginning accounts payable for the 1st Quarter is budgeted to be $11,775.

Each unit requires three pounds of raw material that costs $2.50 per pound. Management desires to end each quarter with a raw materials inventory equal to 20% of the following quarter's production needs. The desired ending inventory for the 4th Quarter is 3,700 pounds. Management plans to pay for 70% of raw material purchases in the quarter acquired and 30% in the following quarter. Each unit requires 0.50 direct labor-hours and direct labor-hour workers are paid $12 per hour.

Required:

1. Prepare the company's direct materials budget and schedule of expected cash disbursements for materials for the upcoming fiscal year.
2. Prepare the company's direct labor budget for the upcoming fiscal year, assuming that the direct labor workforce is adjusted each quarter to match the number of hours required to produce the forecasted number of units produced.

PROBLEM 8-13 Direct Labor and Manufacturing Overhead Budgets [LO5, LO6]

The Production Department of Harveton Corporation has submitted the following forecast of units to be produced by quarter for the upcoming fiscal year.

	1st Quarter	2nd Quarter	3rd Quarter	4th Quarter
Units to be produced	16,000	15,000	14,000	15,000

Each unit requires 0.80 direct labor-hours and direct labor-hour workers are paid $11.50 per hour.

In addition, the variable manufacturing overhead rate is $2.50 per direct labor-hour. The fixed manufacturing overhead is $90,000 per quarter. The only noncash element of manufacturing overhead is depreciation, which is $34,000 per quarter.

Required:

1. Prepare the company's direct labor budget for the upcoming fiscal year, assuming that the direct labor workforce is adjusted each quarter to match the number of hours required to produce the forecasted number of units produced.
2. Prepare the company's manufacturing overhead budget.

PROBLEM 8-14 Schedule of Expected Cash Collections; Cash Budget [LO2, LO8]

Jodi Horton, president of the retailer Crestline Products, has just approached the company's bank with a request for a $30,000, 90-day loan. The purpose of the loan is to assist the company in acquiring inventories in support of peak April sales. Since the company has had some difficulty in paying off its loans in the past, the loan officer has asked for a cash budget to help determine whether the loan should be made. The following data are available for the months April–June, during which the loan will be used:

a. On April 1, the start of the loan period, the cash balance will be $26,000. Accounts receivable on April 1 will total $151,500, of which $141,000 will be collected during April and $7,200 will be collected during May. The remainder will be uncollectible.
b. Past experience shows that 20% of a month's sales are collected in the month of sale, 75% in the month following sale, and 4% in the second month following sale. The other 1% represents bad debts that are never collected. Budgeted sales and expenses for the three-month period follow:

	April	May	June
Sales (all on account)	$200,000	$300,000	$250,000
Merchandise purchases.	$120,000	$180,000	$150,000
Payroll	$9,000	$9,000	$8,000
Lease payments.	$15,000	$15,000	$15,000
Advertising	$70,000	$80,000	$60,000
Equipment purchases	$8,000	—	—
Depreciation.	$10,000	$10,000	$10,000

c. Merchandise purchases are paid in full during the month following purchase. Accounts payable for merchandise purchases on March 31, which will be paid during April, total $108,000.
d. In preparing the cash budget, assume that the $30,000 loan will be made in April and repaid in June. Interest on the loan will total $1,200.

Required:
1. Prepare a schedule of expected cash collections for April, May, and June and for the three months in total.
2. Prepare a cash budget, by month and in total, for the three-month period.
3. If the company needs a minimum cash balance of $20,000 to start each month, can the loan be repaid as planned? Explain.

PROBLEM 8-15 Cash Budget; Income Statement; Balance Sheet [LO2, LO4, LO8, LO9, LO10]

The balance sheet of Phototec, Inc., a distributor of photographic supplies, as of May 31 is given below:

Phototec, Inc. Balance Sheet May 31	
Assets	
Cash	$ 8,000
Accounts receivable	72,000
Inventory	30,000
Buildings and equipment, net of depreciation	500,000
Total assets	$610,000
Liabilities and Stockholders' Equity	
Accounts payable	$ 90,000
Note payable	15,000
Capital stock	420,000
Retained earnings	85,000
Total liabilities and stockholders' equity	$610,000

Phototec, Inc., has not budgeted previously, and for this reason it is limiting its master budget planning horizon to just one month ahead—namely, June. The company has assembled the following budgeted data relating to June:

a. Sales are budgeted at $250,000. Of these sales, $60,000 will be for cash; the remainder will be credit sales. One-half of a month's credit sales are collected in the month the sales are made, and the remainder is collected the following month. All of the May 31 accounts receivable will be collected in June.
b. Purchases of inventory are expected to total $200,000 during June. These purchases will all be on account. Forty percent of all inventory purchases are paid for in the month of purchase; the remainder are paid in the following month. All of the May 31 accounts payable to suppliers will be paid during June.
c. The June 30 inventory balance is budgeted at $40,000.
d. Selling and administrative expenses for June are budgeted at $51,000, exclusive of depreciation. These expenses will be paid in cash. Depreciation is budgeted at $2,000 for the month.
e. The note payable on the May 31 balance sheet will be paid during June. The company's interest expense for June (on all borrowing) will be $500, which will be paid in cash.
f. New warehouse equipment costing $9,000 will be purchased for cash during June.
g. During June, the company will borrow $18,000 from its bank by giving a new note payable to the bank for that amount. The new note will be due in one year.

Required:
1. Prepare a cash budget for June. Support your budget with a schedule of expected cash collections from sales and a schedule of expected cash disbursements for inventory purchases.
2. Prepare a budgeted income statement for June. Use the absorption costing income statement format as shown in Schedule 9.
3. Prepare a budgeted balance sheet as of June 30.

PROBLEM 8-16 Integration of Sales, Production, and Direct Materials Budgets [LO2, LO3, LO4]

Crydon, Inc., manufactures an advanced swim fin for scuba divers. Management is now preparing detailed budgets for the third quarter, July through September, and has assembled the following information to assist in preparing the budget:

a. The Marketing Department has estimated sales as follows for the remainder of the year (in pairs of swim fins):

July.	6,000	October.	4,000
August	7,000	November.	3,000
September	5,000	December.	3,000

The selling price of the swim fins is $50 per pair.

b. All sales are on account. Based on past experience, sales are expected to be collected in the following pattern:

40% in the month of sale
50% in the month following sale
10% uncollectible

The beginning accounts receivable balance (excluding uncollectible amounts) on July 1 will be $130,000.

c. The company maintains finished goods inventories equal to 10% of the following month's sales. The inventory of finished goods on July 1 will be 600 pairs.

d. Each pair of swim fins requires 2 pounds of geico compound. To prevent shortages, the company would like the inventory of geico compound on hand at the end of each month to be equal to 20% of the following month's production needs. The inventory of geico compound on hand on July 1 will be 2,440 pounds.

e. Geico compound costs $2.50 per pound. Crydon pays for 60% of its purchases in the month of purchase; the remainder is paid for in the following month. The accounts payable balance for geico compound purchases will be $11,400 on July 1.

Required:

1. Prepare a sales budget, by month and in total, for the third quarter. (Show your budget in both pairs of swim fins and dollars.) Also prepare a schedule of expected cash collections, by month and in total, for the third quarter.
2. Prepare a production budget for each of the months July through October.
3. Prepare a direct materials budget for geico compound, by month and in total, for the third quarter. Also prepare a schedule of expected cash disbursements for geico compound, by month and in total, for the third quarter.

PROBLEM 8-17 Completing a Master Budget [LO2, LO4, LO7, LO8, LO9, LO10]

Nordic Company, a merchandising company, prepares its master budget on a quarterly basis. The following data have been assembled to assist in preparation of the master budget for the second quarter.

a. As of March 31 (the end of the prior quarter), the company's balance sheet showed the following account balances:

Cash.	$ 9,000	
Accounts receivable.	48,000	
Inventory	12,600	
Buildings and equipment (net)	214,100	
Accounts payable.		$ 18,300
Capital stock		190,000
Retained earnings		75,400
	$283,700	$283,700

b. Actual sales for March and budgeted sales for April–July are as follows:

March (actual)	$60,000
April	$70,000
May	$85,000
June	$90,000
July...............	$50,000

c. Sales are 20% for cash and 80% on credit. All payments on credit sales are collected in the month following the sale. The accounts receivable at March 31 are a result of March credit sales.
d. The company's gross margin percentage is 40% of sales. (In other words, cost of goods sold is 60% of sales.)
e. Monthly expenses are budgeted as follows: salaries and wages, $7,500 per month; shipping, 6% of sales; advertising, $6,000 per month; other expenses, 4% of sales. Depreciation, including depreciation on new assets acquired during the quarter, will be $6,000 for the quarter.
f. Each month's ending inventory should equal 30% of the following month's cost of goods sold.
g. Half of a month's inventory purchases are paid for in the month of purchase and half in the following month.
h. Equipment purchases during the quarter will be as follows: April, $11,500; and May, $3,000.
i. Dividends totaling $3,500 will be declared and paid in June.
j. Management wants to maintain a minimum cash balance of $8,000. The company has an agreement with a local bank that allows the company to borrow in increments of $1,000 at the beginning of each month, up to a total loan balance of $20,000. The interest rate on these loans is 1% per month, and for simplicity, we will assume that interest is not compounded. The company would, as far as it is able, repay the loan plus accumulated interest at the end of the quarter.

Required:
Using the data above, complete the following statements and schedules for the second quarter:
1. Schedule of expected cash collections:

	April	May	June	Total
Cash sales............	$14,000			
Credit sales	48,000			
Total collections........	$62,000			

2. *a.* Merchandise purchases budget:

	April	May	June	Total
Budgeted cost of goods sold	$42,000*	$51,000		
Add desired ending inventory........	15,300†			
Total needs	57,300			
Less beginning inventory	12,600			
Required purchases...............	$44,700			

*$70,000 sales × 60% = $42,000.
†$51,000 × 30% = $15,300.

b. Schedule of expected cash disbursements for merchandise purchases:

	April	May	June	Total
For March purchases..............	$18,300			$18,300
For April purchases	22,350	$22,350		44,700
For May purchases				
For June purchases...............				
Total cash disbursements for purchases....................	$40,650			

3. Schedule of expected cash disbursements for selling and administrative expenses:

	April	May	June	Total
Salaries and wages	$ 7,500			
Shipping.	4,200			
Advertising	6,000			
Other expenses	2,800			
Total cash disbursements for operating expenses	$20,500			

4. Cash budget:

	April	May	June	Total
Cash balance, beginning	$ 9,000			
Add cash collections	62,000			
Total cash available	71,000			
Less cash disbursements:				
For inventory purchases.	40,650			
For selling and administrative expenses	20,500			
For equipment purchases.	11,500			
For dividends	—			
Total cash disbursements	72,650			
Excess (deficiency) of cash	(1,650)			
Financing				
Etc.				

5. Prepare an absorption costing income statement for the quarter ending June 30 as shown in Schedule 9 in the chapter.
6. Prepare a balance sheet as of June 30.

PROBLEM 8-18 Cash Budget with Supporting Schedules [LO2, LO4, LO7, LO8]

The president of Univax, Inc., has just approached the company's bank seeking short-term financing for the coming year, Year 2. Univax is a distributor of commercial vacuum cleaners. The bank has stated that the loan request must be accompanied by a detailed cash budget that shows the quarters in which financing will be needed, as well as the amounts that will be needed and the quarters in which repayments can be made.

To provide this information for the bank, the president has directed that the following data be gathered from which a cash budget can be prepared:

a. Budgeted sales and merchandise purchases for Year 2, as well as actual sales and purchases for the last quarter of Year 1, are as follows:

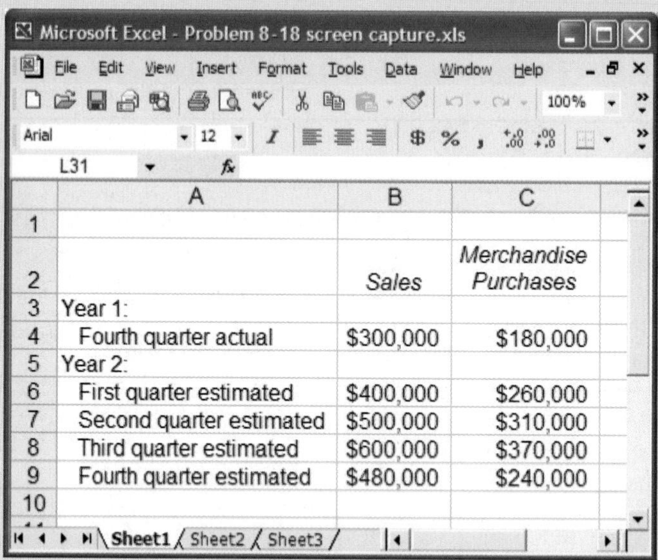

	A	B	C
1			
2		*Sales*	*Merchandise Purchases*
3	Year 1:		
4	Fourth quarter actual	$300,000	$180,000
5	Year 2:		
6	First quarter estimated	$400,000	$260,000
7	Second quarter estimated	$500,000	$310,000
8	Third quarter estimated	$600,000	$370,000
9	Fourth quarter estimated	$480,000	$240,000
10			

b. The company typically collects 33% of a quarter's sales before the quarter ends and another 65% in the following quarter. The remainder is uncollectible. This pattern of collections is now being experienced in the actual data for the Year 1 fourth quarter.
c. Some 20% of a quarter's merchandise purchases are paid for within the quarter. The remainder is paid in the following quarter.
d. Operating expenses for Year 2 are budgeted at $90,000 per quarter plus 12% of sales. Of the fixed amount, $20,000 each quarter is depreciation.
e. The company will pay $10,000 in cash dividends each quarter.
f. Land purchases will be made as follows during the year: $80,000 in the second quarter and $48,500 in the third quarter.
g. The Cash account contained $20,000 at the end of Year 1. The company must maintain a minimum cash balance of at least $18,000.
h. The company has an agreement with a local bank that allows the company to borrow in increments of $10,000 at the beginning of each quarter, up to a total loan balance of $100,000. The interest rate on these loans is 1% per month, and for simplicity, we will assume that interest is not compounded. The company would, as far as it is able, repay the loan plus accumulated interest at the end of the year.
i. At present, the company has no loans outstanding.

Required:

1. Prepare the following, by quarter and in total, for Year 2:
   a. A schedule of expected cash collections on sales.
   b. A schedule of expected cash disbursements for merchandise purchases.
2. Compute the expected cash disbursements for operating expenses, by quarter and in total, for Year 2.
3. Prepare a cash budget by quarter and in total for Year 2.

PROBLEM 8-19 Cash Budget with Supporting Schedules [LO2, LO4, LO8]

Janus Products, Inc., is a merchandising company that sells binders, paper, and other school supplies. The company is planning its cash needs for the third quarter. In the past, Janus Products has had to borrow money during the third quarter to support peak sales of back-to-school materials, which occur during August. The following information has been assembled to assist in preparing a cash budget for the quarter:

a. Budgeted monthly absorption costing income statements for July–October are as follows:

	July	August	September	October
Sales	$40,000	$70,000	$50,000	$45,000
Cost of goods sold	24,000	42,000	30,000	27,000
Gross margin	16,000	28,000	20,000	18,000
Selling and administrative expenses:				
Selling expense	7,200	11,700	8,500	7,300
Administrative expense*	5,600	7,200	6,100	5,900
Total expenses	12,800	18,900	14,600	13,200
Net operating income	$ 3,200	$ 9,100	$ 5,400	$ 4,800

*Includes $2,000 depreciation each month.

b. Sales are 20% for cash and 80% on credit.
c. Credit sales are collected over a three-month period with 10% collected in the month of sale, 70% in the month following sale, and 20% in the second month following sale. May sales totaled $30,000, and June sales totaled $36,000.
d. Inventory purchases are paid for within 15 days. Therefore, 50% of a month's inventory purchases are paid for in the month of purchase. The remaining 50% is paid in the following month. Accounts payable for inventory purchases at June 30 total $11,700.
e. The company maintains its ending inventory levels at 75% of the cost of the merchandise to be sold in the following month. The merchandise inventory at June 30 is $18,000.
f. Land costing $4,500 will be purchased in July.
g. Dividends of $1,000 will be declared and paid in September.
h. The cash balance on June 30 is $8,000; the company must maintain a cash balance of at least this amount at the end of each month.

i. The company has an agreement with a local bank that allows the company to borrow in increments of $1,000 at the beginning of each month, up to a total loan balance of $40,000. The interest rate on these loans is 1% per month, and for simplicity, we will assume that interest is not compounded. The company would, as far as it is able, repay the loan plus accumulated interest at the end of the quarter.

Required:

1. Prepare a schedule of expected cash collections for July, August, and September and for the quarter in total.
2. Prepare the following for merchandise inventory:
   a. A merchandise purchases budget for July, August, and September.
   b. A schedule of expected cash disbursements for merchandise purchases for July, August, and September and for the quarter in total.
3. Prepare a cash budget for July, August, and September and for the quarter in total.

PROBLEM 8-20 Integrated Operating Budgets [LO3, LO4, LO5, LO6]

The East Division of Kensic Company manufactures a vital component that is used in one of Kensic's major product lines. The East Division has been experiencing some difficulty in coordinating activities between its various departments, which has resulted in some shortages of the component at critical times. To overcome the shortages, the manager of East Division has decided to initiate a monthly budgeting system that is integrated between departments.

The first budget is to be for the second quarter of the current year. To assist in creating the budget, the divisional controller has accumulated the following information:

Sales. Sales through the first three months of the current year were 30,000 units. Actual sales in units for January, February, and March, and planned sales in units over the next five months, are given below:

January (actual)	6,000
February (actual)	10,000
March (actual)	14,000
April (planned)	20,000
May (planned)	35,000
June (planned)	50,000
July (planned)	45,000
August (planned)	30,000

In total, the East Division expects to produce and sell 250,000 units during the current year.

Direct Material. Two different materials are used in the production of the component. Data regarding these materials are given below:

Direct Material	Units of Direct Materials per Finished Component	Cost per Unit	Inventory at March 31
No. 208	4 pounds	$5.00	46,000 pounds
No. 311	9 feet	$2.00	69,000 feet

Material No. 208 is sometimes in short supply. Therefore, the East Division requires that enough of the material be on hand at the end of each month to provide for 50% of the following month's production needs. Material No. 311 is easier to get, so only one-third of the following month's production needs must be on hand at the end of each month.

Direct Labor. The East Division has three departments through which the components must pass before they are completed. Information relating to direct labor in these departments is given below:

Department	Direct Labor-Hours per Finished Component	Cost per Direct Labor-Hour
Shaping	0.25	$18.00
Assembly	0.70	$16.00
Finishing	0.10	$20.00

Direct labor is adjusted to the workload each month.

Manufacturing Overhead. East Division manufactured 32,000 components during the first three months of the current year. The actual variable overhead costs incurred during this three-month period are shown below. East Division's controller believes that the variable overhead costs incurred during the last nine months of the year will be at the same rate per component as experienced during the first three months.

Utilities	$ 57,000
Indirect labor	31,000
Supplies	16,000
Other	8,000
Total variable overhead	$112,000

The actual fixed manufacturing overhead costs incurred during the first three months was $1,170,000. The East Division has budgeted fixed manufacturing overhead costs for the entire year as follows:

Supervision	$ 872,000
Property taxes	143,000
Depreciation	2,910,000
Insurance	631,000
Other	72,000
Total fixed manufacturing overhead	$4,628,000

Finished Goods Inventory. The desired monthly ending finished goods inventory is 20% of the next month's estimated sales. The East Division has 4,000 units in finished goods inventory on March 31.

Required:

1. Prepare a production budget for the East Division for the second quarter ending June 30. Show computations by month and in total for the quarter.
2. Prepare a direct materials budget for each type of material for the second quarter ending June 30. Again show computations by month and in total for the quarter.
3. Prepare a direct labor budget for the second quarter ending June 30. This time it is *not* necessary to show monthly figures; show quarterly totals only. Assume that the workforce is adjusted as work requirements change.
4. Assume that the company plans to produce a total of 250,000 units for the year. Prepare a manufacturing overhead budget for the nine-month period ending December 31. (Do not compute a predetermined overhead rate.) Again, it is *not* necessary to show monthly figures.

(CMA, adapted)

PROBLEM 8-21 Completing a Master Budget [LO2, LO4, LO7, LO8, LO9, LO10]

The following data relate to the operations of Picanuy Corporation, a wholesale distributor of consumer goods:

Current assets as of December 31:	
Cash	$6,000
Accounts receivable	$36,000
Inventory	$9,800
Buildings and equipment, net	$110,885
Accounts payable	$32,550
Capital stock	$100,000
Retained earnings	$30,135

a. The gross margin is 30% of sales. (In other words, cost of goods sold is 70% of sales.)
b. Actual and budgeted sales data are as follows:

December (actual)	$60,000
January	$70,000
February.	$80,000
March.	$85,000
April	$55,000

c. Sales are 40% for cash and 60% on credit. Credit sales are collected in the month following sale. The accounts receivable at December 31 are the result of December credit sales.
d. Each month's ending inventory should equal 20% of the following month's budgeted cost of goods sold.
e. One-quarter of a month's inventory purchases is paid for in the month of purchase; the other three-quarters is paid for in the following month. The accounts payable at December 31 are the result of December purchases of inventory.
f. Monthly expenses are as follows: commissions, $12,000; rent, $1,800; other expenses (excluding depreciation), 8% of sales. Assume that these expenses are paid monthly. Depreciation is $2,400 for the quarter and includes depreciation on new assets acquired during the quarter.
g. Equipment will be acquired for cash: $3,000 in January and $8,000 in February.
h. Management would like to maintain a minimum cash balance of $5,000 at the end of each month. The company has an agreement with a local bank that allows the company to borrow in increments of $1,000 at the beginning of each month, up to a total loan balance of $50,000. The interest rate on these loans is 1% per month, and for simplicity, we will assume that interest is not compounded. The company would, as far as it is able, repay the loan plus accumulated interest at the end of the quarter.

Required:
Using the data above:
1. Complete the following schedule:

Schedule of Expected Cash Collections	January	February	March	Quarter
Cash sales.	$28,000			
Credit sales	36,000			
Total collections.	$64,000			

2. Complete the following:

Merchandise Purchases Budget	January	February	March	Quarter
Budgeted cost of goods sold	$49,000*			
Add desired ending inventory	11,200†			
Total needs	60,200			
Less beginning inventory.	9,800			
Required purchases.	$50,400			

*$70,000 sales × 70% = $49,000.
†$80,000 × 70% × 20% = $11,200.

Schedule of Expected Cash Disbursements—Merchandise Purchases	January	February	March	Quarter
December purchases	$32,550*			$32,550
January purchases	12,600	$37,800		50,400
February purchases				
March purchases				
Total disbursements	$45,150			

*Beginning balance of the accounts payable.

3. Complete the following schedule:

Schedule of Expected Cash Disbursements—Selling and Administrative Expenses	January	February	March	Quarter
Commissions	$12,000			
Rent	1,800			
Other expenses	5,600			
Total disbursements	$19,400			

4. Complete the following cash budget:

Cash Budget	January	February	March	Quarter
Cash balance, beginning	$ 6,000			
Add cash collections	64,000			
Total cash available	70,000			
Less cash disbursements:				
For inventory	45,150			
For operating expenses	19,400			
For equipment	3,000			
Total cash disbursements	67,550			
Excess (deficiency) of cash	2,450			
Financing				
Etc.				

5. Prepare an absorption costing income statement, similar to the one shown in Schedule 9 on page 319, for the quarter ended March 31.
6. Prepare a balance sheet as of March 31.

Cases

CASE 8-22 Evaluating a Company's Budget Procedures [LO1]

Tom Emory and Jim Morris strolled back to their plant from the administrative offices of Ferguson & Son Manufacturing Company. Tom is manager of the machine shop in the company's factory; Jim is manager of the equipment maintenance department.

The men had just attended the monthly performance evaluation meeting for plant department heads. These meetings had been held on the third Tuesday of each month since Robert Ferguson, Jr., the president's son, had become plant manager a year earlier.

As they were walking, Tom Emory spoke: "Boy, I hate those meetings! I never know whether my department's accounting reports will show good or bad performance. I'm beginning to expect the worst. If the accountants say I saved the company a dollar, I'm called 'Sir,' but if I spend even a little too much—boy, do I get in trouble. I don't know if I can hold on until I retire."

Tom had just been given the worst evaluation he had ever received in his long career with Ferguson & Son. He was the most respected of the experienced machinists in the company. He had been with Ferguson & Son for many years and was promoted to supervisor of the machine shop when the company expanded and moved to its present location. The president (Robert Ferguson, Sr.) had often stated that the company's success was due to the high-quality work of machinists like Tom. As supervisor, Tom stressed the importance of craftsmanship and told his workers that he wanted no sloppy work coming from his department.

When Robert Ferguson, Jr., became the plant manager, he directed that monthly performance comparisons be made between actual and budgeted costs for each department. The departmental budgets were intended to encourage the supervisors to reduce inefficiencies and to seek cost reduction opportunities. The company controller was instructed to have his staff "tighten" the budget slightly whenever a department attained its budget in a given month; this was done to reinforce the plant manager's desire to reduce costs. The young plant manager often stressed the importance of continued progress toward attaining the budget; he also made it known that he kept a file of these performance reports for future reference when he succeeded his father.

Tom Emory's conversation with Jim Morris continued as follows:

Emory: I really don't understand. We've worked so hard to meet the budget, and the minute we do so they tighten it on us. We can't work any faster and still maintain quality. I think my men are ready to quit trying. Besides, those reports don't tell the whole story. We always seem to be interrupting the big jobs for all those small rush orders. All that setup and machine adjustment time is killing us. And quite frankly, Jim, you were no help. When our hydraulic press broke down last month, your people were nowhere to be found. We had to take it apart ourselves and got stuck with all that idle time.

Morris: I'm sorry about that, Tom, but you know my department has had trouble making budget, too. We were running well behind at the time of that problem, and if we'd spent a day on that old machine, we would never have made it up. Instead we made the scheduled inspections of the forklift trucks because we knew we could do those in less than the budgeted time.

Emory: Well, Jim, at least you have some options. I'm locked into what the scheduling department assigns to me and you know they're being harassed by sales for those special orders. Incidentally, why didn't your report show all the supplies you guys wasted last month when you were working in Bill's department?

Morris: We're not out of the woods on that deal yet. We charged the maximum we could to other work and haven't even reported some of it yet.

Emory: Well, I'm glad you have a way of getting out of the pressure. The accountants seem to know everything that's happening in my department, sometimes even before I do. I thought all that budget and accounting stuff was supposed to help, but it just gets me into trouble. It's all a big pain. I'm trying to put out quality work; they're trying to save pennies.

Required:

1. Identify the problems that appear to exist in Ferguson & Son Manufacturing Company's budgetary control system and explain how the problems are likely to reduce the effectiveness of the system.
2. Explain how Ferguson & Son Manufacturing Company's budgetary control system could be revised to improve its effectiveness.

(CMA, adapted)

CASE 8-23 Master Budget with Supporting Schedules [LO2, LO4, LO8, LO9, LO10]

You have just been hired as a management trainee by Cravat Sales Company, a nationwide distributor of a designer's silk ties. The company has an exclusive franchise on the distribution of the ties, and sales have grown so rapidly over the last few years that it has become necessary to add new members to the management team. You have been given responsibility for all planning and budgeting. Your first assignment is to prepare a master budget for the next three months, starting April 1. You are anxious to make a favorable impression on the president and have assembled the information below.

The company desires a minimum ending cash balance each month of $10,000. The ties are sold to retailers for $8 each. Recent and forecasted sales in units are as follows:

January (actual)	20,000	June	60,000
February (actual)	24,000	July	40,000
March (actual)	28,000	August	36,000
April	35,000	September	32,000
May	45,000		

The large buildup in sales before and during June is due to Father's Day. Ending inventories are supposed to equal 90% of the next month's sales in units. The ties cost the company $5 each.

Purchases are paid for as follows: 50% in the month of purchase and the remaining 50% in the following month. All sales are on credit, with no discount, and payable within 15 days. The company has found, however, that only 25% of a month's sales are collected by month-end. An additional 50% is collected in the following month, and the remaining 25% is collected in the second month following sale. Bad debts have been negligible.

The company's monthly operating expenses are given below:

Variable:	
Sales commissions	$1 per tie
Fixed:	
Wages and salaries	$22,000
Utilities	$14,000
Insurance	$1,200
Depreciation	$1,500
Miscellaneous	$3,000

All operating expenses are paid during the month, in cash, with the exception of depreciation and insurance expired. Land will be purchased during May for $25,000 cash. The company declares dividends of $12,000 each quarter, payable in the first month of the following quarter. The company's balance sheet at March 31 is given below:

Assets	
Cash	$ 14,000
Accounts receivable ($48,000 February sales; $168,000 March sales)	216,000
Inventory (31,500 units)	157,500
Prepaid insurance	14,400
Fixed assets, net of depreciation	172,700
Total assets	$574,600
Liabilities and Stockholders' Equity	
Accounts payable	$ 85,750
Dividends payable	12,000
Capital stock	300,000
Retained earnings	176,850
Total liabilities and stockholders' equity	$574,600

The company has an agreement with a bank that allows the company to borrow in increments of $1,000 at the beginning of each month, up to a total loan balance of $40,000. The interest rate on these loans is 1% per month, and for simplicity, we will assume that interest is not compounded. At the end of the quarter, the company would pay the bank all of the accumulated interest on the loan and as much of the loan as possible (in increments of $1,000), while still retaining at least $10,000 in cash.

Required:

Prepare a master budget for the three-month period ending June 30. Include the following detailed budgets:

1. *a.* A sales budget by month and in total.
   b. A schedule of expected cash collections from sales, by month and in total.
   c. A merchandise purchases budget in units and in dollars. Show the budget by month and in total.
   d. A schedule of expected cash disbursements for merchandise purchases, by month and in total.
2. A cash budget. Show the budget by month and in total.
3. A budgeted income statement for the three-month period ending June 30. Use the contribution approach.
4. A budgeted balance sheet as of June 30.

RESEARCH AND APPLICATION 8-24 [LO1]

The questions in this exercise give you an appreciation for the complexity of budgeting in a large multinational corporation. To answer the questions, you will need to download the Procter & Gamble (P&G) 2005 Annual Report at www.pg.com/investors/annualreports.jhtml and briefly refer to "Item 2: Properties" in P&G's Form 10-K for the fiscal year ended June 30, 2005. To access the 10-K report, go to www.sec.gov/edgar/searchedgar/companysearch.html. Input CIK code 80424 and hit enter. In the gray box on the right-hand side of your computer screen define the scope of your search by inputting 10-K and then pressing enter. Select the 10-K with a filing date of August 29, 2005. You will also need to briefly refer to the Macy's Inc. Form 10-K for the fiscal year ended January 29, 2005. Macy's CIK code is 794367 and its filing date is March 28. 2005. You do not need to print any documents to answer the questions.

Required:

1. What is P&G's strategy for success in the marketplace? Does the company rely primarily on a customer intimacy, operational excellence, or product leadership customer value proposition? What evidence supports your conclusion?
2. What business risks does P&G face that may threaten its ability to satisfy stockholder expectations? What are some examples of control activities that the company could use to reduce these risks? (Hint: Focus on page 28 of the annual report).
3. What were P&G's quarterly net sales for the fiscal year ended June 30, 2005? What were Federated Department Stores' quarterly net sales for 2004? (Hint: see page 79 of its 10-K.) How does P&G's quarterly sales trend compare to Federated Department Stores' quarterly sales trend? Which of the two quarterly sales trends is likely to cause greater cash budgeting concerns? Why?
4. Describe the scope of P&G's business in three respects—physical facilities, products, and customers. More specifically, how many manufacturing facilities does P&G operate globally? What are P&G's three Global Business Units (GBUs)? Which of P&G's 17 "billion dollar brands" are included in each of these GBU's? How many brands does P&G offer in total and in how many countries do they sell these brands? How many countries does P&G's Market Development Organization operate in?
5. Describe five uncertainties that complicate P&G's efforts to accurately forecast its sales and expenses.
6. Although not specifically discussed in P&G's annual report, how could an Enterprise System as described in Chapter 1 help a globally dispersed, highly complex company such as P&G improve its budgeting process?
7. P&G's annual report briefly discusses the acquisition of Gillette (see pages 10–11). It acknowledges that Gillette has some different cultural norms in terms of how it defines accountability and communicates internally. Although not discussed in the annual report, how could differences in two organization's budgeting practices be responsible for these types of divergent cultural norms?

Chapter 9

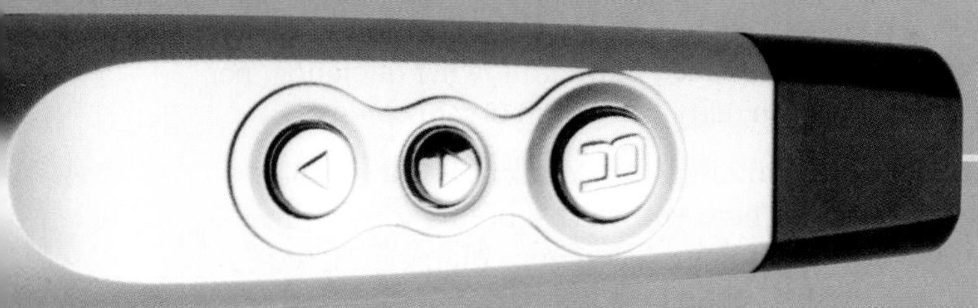

Standard Costs and the Balanced Scorecard

Managing Materials and Labor

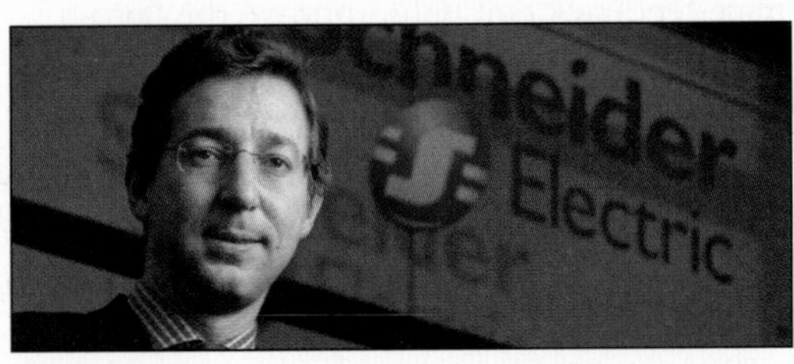

BUSINESS FOCUS

Schneider Electric's Oxford, Ohio, plant manufactures *busways* that transport electricity from its point of entry into a building to remote locations throughout the building. The plant's managers pay close attention to direct material costs because they are more than half of the plant's total manufacturing costs. To help control scrap rates for direct material inputs such as copper, steel, and aluminum, the accounting department prepares direct materials quantity variances. These variances compare the standard quantity of direct materials that should have been used to make a product (according to computations by the plant's engineers) to the amount of direct materials that were actually used. Keeping a close eye on these differences helps to identify and deal with the causes of excessive scrap, such as an inadequately trained machine operator, poor quality raw material inputs, or a malfunctioning machine.

Because direct labor is also a significant component of the plant's total manufacturing costs, the management team daily monitors the direct labor efficiency variance. This variance compares the standard amount of labor time allowed to make a product to the actual amount of labor time used. When idle workers cause an unfavorable labor efficiency variance, managers temporarily move workers from departments with slack to departments with a backlog of work to be done. ■

Source: Author's conversation with Doug Taylor, plant controller, Schneider Electric's Oxford, Ohio, plant.

Learning Objectives

After studying Chapter 9, you should be able to:

LO1 Explain how direct materials standards and direct labor standards are set.

LO2 Compute the direct materials price and quantity variances and explain their significance.

LO3 Compute the direct labor rate and efficiency variances and explain their significance.

LO4 Compute the variable manufacturing overhead spending and efficiency variances.

LO5 Understand how a balanced scorecard fits together and how it supports a company's strategy.

LO6 Compute delivery cycle time, throughput time, and manufacturing cycle efficiency (MCE).

LP 9

In this chapter we begin our study of management control and performance measures. Quite often, these terms carry with them negative connotations. Indeed, performance measurements can be used counterproductively to create fear, to cast blame, and to punish. However, if used properly, as explained in the following quotation, performance measurement serves a vital function in both daily life and in organizations:

> Imagine you want to improve your basketball shooting skill. You know that practice will help, so you [go] to the basketball court. There you start shooting toward the hoop, but as soon as the ball gets close to the rim your vision goes blurry for a second, so that you cannot observe where the ball ended up in relation to the target (left, right, in front, too far back, inside the hoop?). It would be pretty difficult to improve under those conditions. . . . (And by the way, how long would [shooting baskets] sustain your interest if you couldn't observe the outcome of your efforts?)
>
> Or imagine someone engaging in a weight loss program. A normal step in such programs is to purchase a scale to be able to track one's progress: Is this program working? Am I losing weight? A positive answer would be encouraging and would motivate me to keep up the effort, while a negative answer might lead me to reflect on the process: Am I working on the right diet and exercise program? Am I doing everything I am supposed to?, etc. Suppose you don't want to set up a sophisticated measurement system and decide to forgo the scale. You would still have some idea of how well you are doing from simple methods such as clothes feeling looser, a belt that fastens at a different hole, or simply via observation in a mirror! Now, imagine trying to sustain a weight loss program without any feedback on how well you are doing.
>
> In these . . . examples, availability of quantitative measures of performance can yield two types of benefits: First, performance feedback can help improve the "production process" through a better understanding of what works and what doesn't; e.g., shooting this way works better than shooting that way. Secondly, feedback on performance can sustain motivation and effort, because it is encouraging and/or because it suggests that more effort is required for the goal to be met.[1]

In the same way, performance measurement can be helpful in an organization. It can provide feedback concerning what works and what does not work, and it can help motivate people to sustain their efforts.

IN BUSINESS

FOCUSING ON THE NUMBERS

Joe Knight is the CEO of Setpoint, a company that designs and builds factory-automation equipment. Knight uses a large whiteboard, with about 20 rows and 10 columns, to focus worker attention on key factors involved in managing projects. A visitor to the plant, Steve Petersen, asked Knight to explain the board, but Knight instead motioned one of his workers to come over. The young man, with a baseball cap turned backward on his head, proceeded to walk the visitor through the board, explaining the calculation of gross margin and other key indicators on the board.

"'I was just amazed,' Petersen recalls. 'He knew that board inside and out. He knew every number on it. He knew exactly where the company was and where they had to focus their attention. There was no hesitation . . . . I was so impressed . . . that the people on the shop floor had it down like that. It was their scoreboard. It was the way they could tell if they were winning or losing. I talked to several of them, and I just couldn't get over the positive attitude they had and their understanding of the numbers.'"

Source: Bo Burlinghan, "What's Your Culture Worth?," *Inc.* magazine, September 2001, pp. 124–133.

[1] Soumitra Dutta and Jean-François Manzoni, *Process Reengineering, Organizational Change and Performance Improvement* (New York: McGraw-Hill), Chapter IV.

Our study of performance measurement begins with the lowest levels in the organization. We work our way up the organizational ladder in subsequent chapters. In this chapter we see how various measures are used to control operations and to evaluate performance. Even though we are starting with the lowest levels in the organization, keep in mind that performance measures should be derived from the organization's overall strategy. For example, a company like Sony that bases its strategy on rapid introduction of innovative consumer products should use different performance measures than a company like Federal Express where on-time delivery, customer convenience, and low cost are key competitive advantages. Sony may want to keep close track of the percentage of revenues from products introduced within the last year; whereas Federal Express may want to closely monitor the percentage of packages delivered on time. Later in this chapter when we discuss the *balanced scorecard,* we will have more to say concerning the role of strategy in the selection of performance measures. But first we will see how *standard costs* are used by managers to help control costs.

Companies in highly competitive industries like Federal Express, Southwest Airlines, Dell, and Toyota must be able to provide high-quality goods and services at low cost. If they do not, their customers will buy from more efficient competitors. Stated in the starkest terms, managers must obtain inputs such as raw materials and electricity at the lowest possible prices and must use them as effectively as possible—while maintaining or increasing the quality of what they sell. If inputs are purchased at prices that are too high or more input is used than is really necessary, higher costs will result.

How do managers control the prices that are paid for inputs and the quantities that are used? They could examine every transaction in detail, but this obviously would be an inefficient use of management time. For many companies, the answer to this control problem lies at least partially in *standard costs.*

Standard Costs—Management by Exception

Video 9–1

A *standard* is a benchmark or "norm" for measuring performance. Standards are found everywhere. Your doctor evaluates your weight using standards for individuals of your age, height, and gender. The food we eat in restaurants is prepared under specified standards of cleanliness. The buildings we live in conform to standards set in building codes. Standards are also widely used in managerial accounting where they relate to the *quantity* and *cost* (or acquisition price) of inputs used in manufacturing goods or providing services.

Quantity and cost standards are set for each major input such as raw materials and labor time. *Quantity standards* specify how much of an input should be used to make a product or provide a service. *Cost (price) standards* specify how much should be paid for each unit of the input. Actual quantities and actual costs of inputs are compared to these standards. If either the quantity or the cost of inputs departs significantly from the standards, managers investigate the discrepancy to find the cause of the problem and eliminate it. This process is called **management by exception.**

In our daily lives, we operate in a management by exception mode most of the time. Consider what happens when you sit down in the driver's seat of your car. You put the key in the ignition, you turn the key, and your car starts. Your expectation (standard) that the car will start is met; you do not have to open the car hood and check the battery, the connecting cables, the fuel lines, and so on. If you turn the key and the car does not start, then you have a discrepancy (variance). Your expectations are not met, and you need to investigate why. Note that even if the car starts after a second try, it still would be wise to investigate. The fact that the expectation was not met should be viewed as an opportunity to uncover the cause of the problem rather than as simply an annoyance. If the underlying cause is not discovered and corrected, the problem may recur and become much worse.

EXHIBIT 9–1
The Variance Analysis Cycle

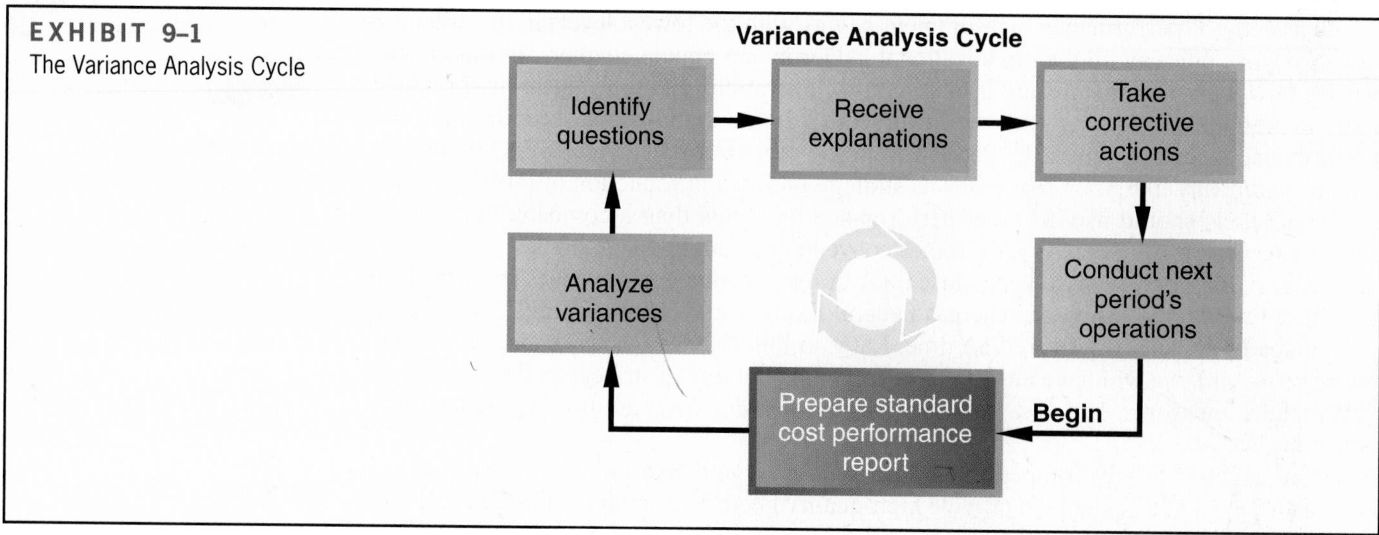

This basic approach to identifying and solving problems is the essence of the *variance analysis cycle,* which is illustrated in Exhibit 9–1. The cycle begins with the preparation of standard cost performance reports in the accounting department. These reports highlight the *variances,* which are the differences between actual results and what should have occurred according to the standards. The variances raise questions. Why did this variance occur? Why is this variance larger than it was last period? The significant variances are investigated to discover their root causes. Corrective actions are taken. And then next period's operations are carried out. The cycle begins again with the preparation of a new standard cost performance report for the latest period. The emphasis should be on highlighting problems, finding their root causes, and then taking corrective action. The goal is to improve operations—not to assign blame.

Who Uses Standard Costs?

Manufacturing, service, food, and not-for-profit organizations all make use of standards to some extent. Auto service centers like Firestone and Sears, for example, often set specific labor time standards for the completion of certain tasks, such as installing a carburetor or doing a valve job, and then measure actual performance against these standards. Fast-food outlets such as McDonald's have exacting standards for the quantity of meat going into a sandwich, as well as standards for the cost of the meat. Hospitals have standard costs for food, laundry, and other items, as well as standard time allowances for certain routine activities, such as laboratory tests. In short, you are likely to run into standard costs in virtually any line of business.

IN BUSINESS

STANDARD COSTING AT PARKER BRASS

The Brass Products Division at Parker Hannifin Corporation, known as Parker Brass, is a world-class manufacturer of tube and brass fittings, valves, hose and hose fittings. Management at the company uses variances from its standard costing system to target problem areas for improvement. If a production variance exceeds 5% of sales, the responsible manager is required to explain the variance and to propose a plan of action to correct the detected problems. In the past, variances were reported at the end of the month—often several weeks after a particular job had been completed. Now, a variance report is generated the day after a job is completed and summary variance reports are prepared weekly. These more frequent reports help managers take more timely corrective action.

Source: David Johnsen and Parvez Sopariwala, "Standard Costing Is Alive and Well at Parker Brass," *Management Accounting Quarterly,* Winter 2000, pp. 12–20.

Manufacturing companies often have highly developed standard costing systems in which standards for direct materials, direct labor, and overhead are created for each product. A **standard cost card** shows the standard quantities and costs of the inputs required to produce a unit of a specific product. In the following section, we provide a detailed example of setting standard costs and preparing a standard cost card.

Setting Standard Costs

Setting price and quantity standards ideally combines the expertise of everyone who has responsibility for purchasing and using inputs. In a manufacturing setting, this might include accountants, purchasing managers, engineers, production supervisors, line managers, and production workers. Past records of purchase prices and input usage can be helpful in setting standards. However, the standards should be designed to encourage efficient *future* operations, not just a repetition of *past* operations that may or may not have been efficient.

Ideal versus Practical Standards

Should standards be attainable all of the time, part of the time, or almost none of the time? Opinions vary, but standards tend to fall into one of two categories—either ideal or practical.

Ideal standards can be attained only under the best circumstances. They allow for no machine breakdowns or other work interruptions, and they call for a level of effort that can be attained only by the most skilled and efficient employees working at peak effort 100% of the time. Some managers feel that such standards spur continual improvement. These managers argue that even though employees know they will rarely meet the standard, it is a constant reminder of the need for ever-increasing efficiency and effort. Few organizations use ideal standards. Most managers feel that ideal standards tend to discourage even the most diligent workers. Moreover, variances from ideal standards are difficult to interpret. Large variances from the ideal are normal and it is therefore difficult to "manage by exception."

Practical standards are standards that are "tight but attainable." They allow for normal machine downtime and employee rest periods, and they can be attained through reasonable, though highly efficient, efforts by the average worker. Variances from practical standards typically signal a need for management attention because they represent deviations that fall outside of normal operating conditions. Furthermore, practical standards can serve multiple purposes. In addition to signaling abnormal conditions, they can also be used in forecasting cash flows and in planning inventory. By contrast, ideal standards cannot be used for these purposes because they do not allow for normal inefficiencies and result in unrealistic forecasts.

Throughout the remainder of this chapter, we will assume that practical rather than ideal standards are in use.

MANAGERIAL ACCOUNTING IN ACTION
The Issue

The Colonial Pewter Company was organized a year ago. The company's only product is a reproduction of an 18th century pewter bookend. The bookend is made largely by hand, using traditional metalworking tools. Consequently, the manufacturing process is labor intensive and requires a high level of skill.

Colonial Pewter has recently expanded its workforce to take advantage of unexpected demand for the bookends as gifts. The company started with a small cadre of experienced pewter workers but has had to hire less experienced workers as a result of the expansion. The president of the company, J. D. Wriston, has called a meeting to discuss production problems. Attending the meeting are Tom Kuchel, the production manager; Janet Warner, the purchasing manager; and Terry Sherman, the corporate controller.

J. D.: I've got a feeling that we aren't getting the production we should out of our new people.

Tom: Give us a chance. Some of the new people have been with the company for less than a month.

Janet: Let me add that production seems to be wasting an awful lot of material—particularly pewter. That stuff is very expensive.

Tom: What about the shipment of defective pewter that you bought a couple of months ago—the one with the iron contamination? That caused us major problems.

Janet: That's ancient history. How was I to know it was off-grade? Besides, it was a great deal.

J. D.: Calm down everybody. Let's get the facts before we start sinking our fangs into each other.

Tom: I agree. The more facts the better.

J. D.: Okay, Terry, it's your turn. Facts are the controller's department.

Terry: I'm afraid I can't provide the answers off the top of my head, but it won't take me too long to set up a system that can routinely answer questions relating to worker productivity, material waste, and input prices.

J. D.: How long is "not too long"?

Terry: I will need all of your cooperation, but how about a week from today?

J. D.: That's okay with me. What about everyone else?

Tom: Sure.

Janet: Fine with me.

J. D.: Let's mark it on our calendars.

Setting Direct Materials Standards

LEARNING OBJECTIVE 1
Explain how direct materials standards and direct labor standards are set.

Video 9–1

Terry Sherman's first task was to prepare price and quantity standards for the company's only significant raw material, pewter ingots. The **standard price per unit** for direct materials should reflect the final, delivered cost of the materials, net of any discounts taken. After consulting with purchasing manager Janet Warner, Terry prepared the following documentation for the standard price of a pound of pewter in ingot form:

Purchase price, top-grade pewter ingots, in 40-pound ingots	$3.85
Freight, by truck, from the supplier's warehouse	0.24
Less purchase discount	(0.09)
Standard price per pound	$4.00

Notice that the standard price reflects a particular grade of material (top grade), purchased in particular lot sizes (40-pound ingots), and delivered by a particular type of carrier (truck). Allowances have also been made for discounts. If everything proceeds according to these expectations, the net cost of a pound of pewter should be $4.00.

The **standard quantity per unit** for direct materials should reflect the amount of material required for each unit of finished product, as well as an allowance for unavoidable waste, spoilage, and other normal inefficiencies. After consulting with the production manager, Tom Kuchel, Terry Sherman prepared the following documentation for the standard quantity of pewter in a pair of bookends:

Material requirements as specified in the bill of materials for a pair of bookends, in pounds	2.7
Allowance for waste and spoilage, in pounds	0.2
Allowance for rejects, in pounds	0.1
Standard quantity per pair of bookends, in pounds	3.0

As discussed in Chapter 3, the bill of materials details the quantity of each type of material that should be used in a product. As shown above, the material requirements listed on the bill of materials should be adjusted for waste and other factors when determining the standard quantity per unit of product. "Waste and spoilage" refers to materials that are wasted as a normal part of the production process or that spoil before they are used. "Rejects" refers to the direct material contained in defective units that must be scrapped.

Although allowances for waste, spoilage, and rejects are often built into standards, this practice is often criticized because it contradicts the zero defects goal that underlies improvement programs such as Six Sigma. If allowances for waste, spoilage, and rejects are built into the standard cost, those allowances should be periodically reviewed and reduced over time to reflect improved processes, better training, and better equipment.

Once the price and quantity standards have been set, the standard cost of material per unit of the finished product can be computed as follows:

$$3.0 \text{ pounds per unit} \times \$4.00 \text{ per pound} = \$12.00 \text{ per unit}$$

This $12.00 cost will appear on the product's standard cost card.

Setting Direct Labor Standards

Direct labor price and quantity standards are usually expressed in terms of a labor rate and labor-hours. The **standard rate per hour** for direct labor includes wages, employment taxes, and fringe benefits. Using wage records and in consultation with the production manager, Terry Sherman determined the standard rate per direct labor-hour at the Colonial Pewter Company as follows:

Video 9–1

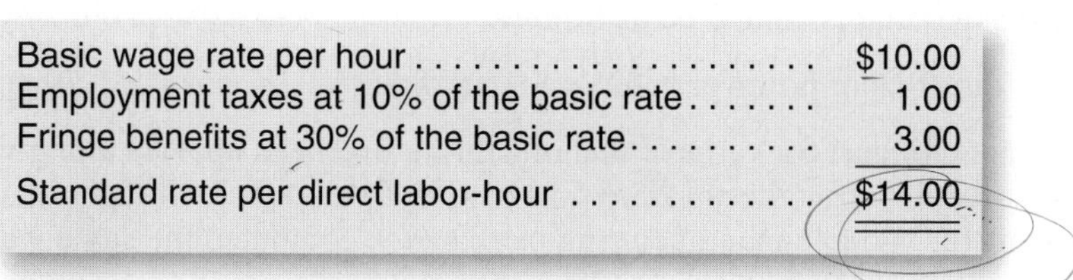

Basic wage rate per hour	$10.00
Employment taxes at 10% of the basic rate	1.00
Fringe benefits at 30% of the basic rate	3.00
Standard rate per direct labor-hour	$14.00

Many companies prepare a single standard rate per hour for all employees in a department. This standard rate reflects the expected "mix" of workers, even though the actual wage rates may vary somewhat from individual to individual due to differing skills or seniority. According to the standard computed above, the direct labor rate for Colonial Pewter should average $14 per hour.

The standard direct labor time required to complete a unit of product (called the **standard hours per unit**) is perhaps the single most difficult standard to determine. One approach is to break down each task into elemental body movements (such as reaching, pushing, and turning over). Published tables of standard times for such movements can be used to estimate the total time required to complete the task. Another approach is for an industrial engineer to do a time and motion study, actually clocking the time required for each task. As stated earlier, the standard time should include allowances for breaks, personal needs of employees, cleanup, and machine downtime.

After consulting with the production manager, Terry Sherman prepared the following documentation for the standard direct labor hours per unit:

Basic labor time per unit, in hours	1.9
Allowance for breaks and personal needs	0.1
Allowance for cleanup and machine downtime	0.3
Allowance for rejects	0.2
Standard direct labor-hours per unit of product	2.5

EXHIBIT 9–2
Standard Cost Card—Variable Manufacturing Costs

Inputs	(1) Standard Quantity or Hours	(2) Standard Price or Rate	Standard Cost (1) × (2)
Direct materials.	3.0 pounds	$4.00 per pound	$12.00
Direct labor	2.5 hours	$14.00 per hour	35.00
Variable manufacturing overhead.	2.5 hours	$3.00 per hour	7.50
Total standard cost per unit.			$54.50

Once the rate and time standards have been set, the standard direct labor cost per unit of product can be computed as follows:

2.5 direct labor-hours per unit × $14 per direct labor-hour = $35 per unit

This $35 per unit standard direct labor cost appears along with direct materials on the standard cost card for a pair of pewter bookends.

Setting Variable Manufacturing Overhead Standards

As with direct labor, the price and quantity standards for variable manufacturing overhead are usually expressed in terms of rate and hours. The rate represents *the variable portion of the predetermined overhead rate* discussed in Chapter 3; the hours relate to the activity base that is used to apply overhead to units of product (usually machine-hours or direct labor-hours, as we learned in Chapter 3). At Colonial Pewter, the variable portion of the predetermined overhead rate is $3 per direct labor-hour. Therefore, the standard variable manufacturing overhead cost per unit is computed as follows:

2.5 direct labor-hours per unit × $3 per direct labor-hour = $7.50 per unit

This $7.50 per unit cost for variable manufacturing overhead appears along with direct materials and direct labor on the standard cost card in Exhibit 9–2. Observe that the **standard cost per unit** for variable manufacturing overhead is computed the same way as for direct materials or direct labor—the standard quantity allowed per unit of the output is multiplied by the standard price. In this case, the standard quantity is expressed as 2.5 direct labor-hours per unit and the standard price (or rate) is expressed as $3 per direct labor-hour.

Are Standards the Same as Budgets?

Standards and budgets are very similar. The major distinction between the two terms is that a standard is a *unit* amount, whereas a budget is a *total* amount. The standard cost for direct materials at Colonial Pewter is $12 per pair of bookends. If 1,000 pairs of bookends are to be made, then the budgeted cost of direct materials would be $12,000. In effect, *a standard can be viewed as the budgeted cost for one unit of product.*

A General Model for Variance Analysis

Video 9–1

Why are standards separated into two categories—price and quantity? Different managers are usually responsible for buying and for using inputs. For example, in the case of a raw material, a purchasing manager is responsible for its price. However, the production manager is responsible for the amount of the raw material actually used to make products. As we shall see, setting up separate standards for price and quantity allows us to better separate the responsibilities of these two managers. It also allows us to prepare more timely reports. The purchasing manager's tasks are completed when the material is delivered for use in the factory. A performance report for the purchasing manager can be prepared at that point. However, the production manager's responsibilities have just begun at that point. A performance

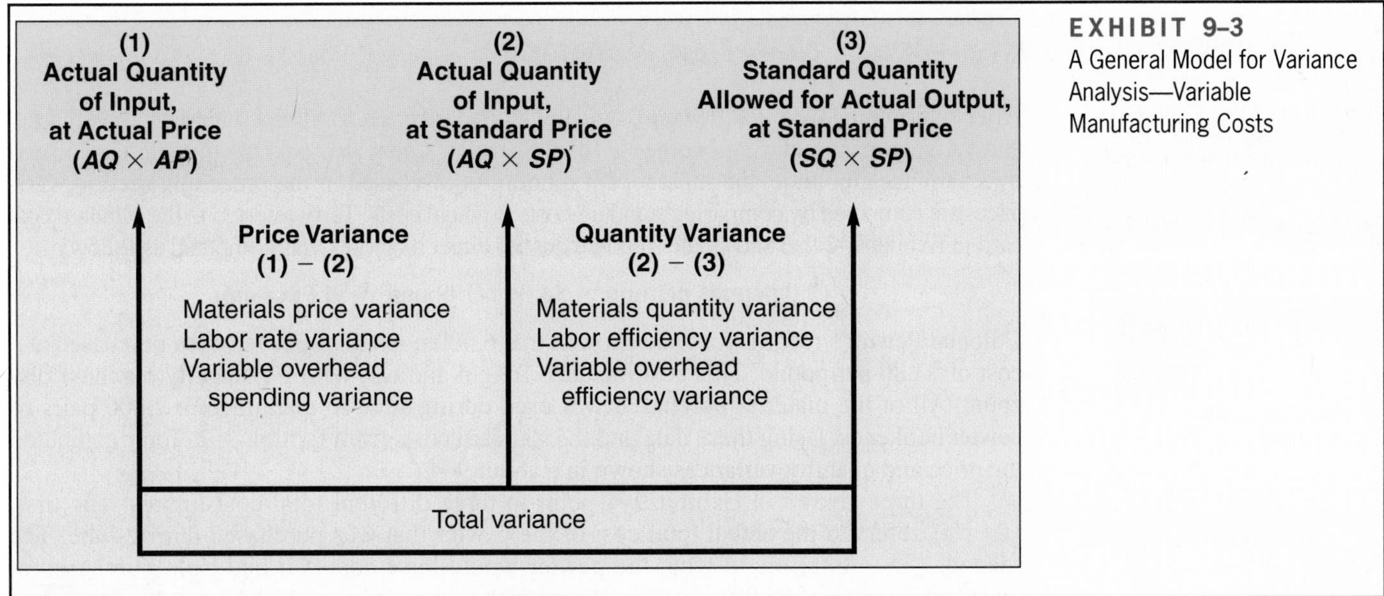

EXHIBIT 9–3
A General Model for Variance Analysis—Variable Manufacturing Costs

report for the production manager must be delayed until production is completed and it is known how much raw material was used in the final product. Therefore, it is important to clearly distinguish between deviations from price standards (the responsibility of the purchasing manager) and deviations from quantity standards (the responsibility of the production manager). Differences between *standard* prices and *actual* prices and between *standard* quantities and *actual* quantities are called **variances.** The act of computing and interpreting variances is called *variance analysis.*

Price and Quantity Variances

Exhibit 9–3 presents a general model for computing standard cost variances for variable costs. This model isolates price variances from quantity variances and shows how each of these variances is computed.[2] We will be using this model throughout the chapter to compute variances for direct materials, direct labor, and variable manufacturing overhead.

Three things should be noted from Exhibit 9–3. First, a price variance and a quantity variance can be computed for each of the three variable cost elements—direct materials, direct labor, and variable manufacturing overhead—even though the variances have different names. For example, a price variance is called a *materials price variance* in the case of direct materials but a *labor rate variance* in the case of direct labor and an *overhead spending variance* in the case of variable manufacturing overhead.

Second, the price variance—regardless of what it is called—is computed in exactly the same way regardless of whether one is dealing with direct materials, direct labor, or variable manufacturing overhead. The same is true of the quantity variance.

Third, the input is the actual quantity of direct materials, direct labor, and variable manufacturing overhead purchased or used; the output is the good production of the period, expressed in terms of the *standard quantity* (or the *standard hours) allowed for the actual output* (see column 3 in Exhibit 9–3). The **standard quantity allowed** or **standard hours allowed** means the amount of an input *that should have been used* to produce the actual output of the period. This could be more or less than the actual amount of the input, depending on the efficiency or inefficiency of operations. The standard quantity allowed is computed by multiplying the actual output in units by the standard input allowed per unit of output.

With this general model as the foundation, we will now calculate Colonial Pewter's price and quantity variances.

[2] Variance analysis of fixed costs will be discussed in the next chapter.

Using Standard Costs—Direct Materials Variances

LEARNING OBJECTIVE 2
Compute the direct materials price and quantity variances and explain their significance.

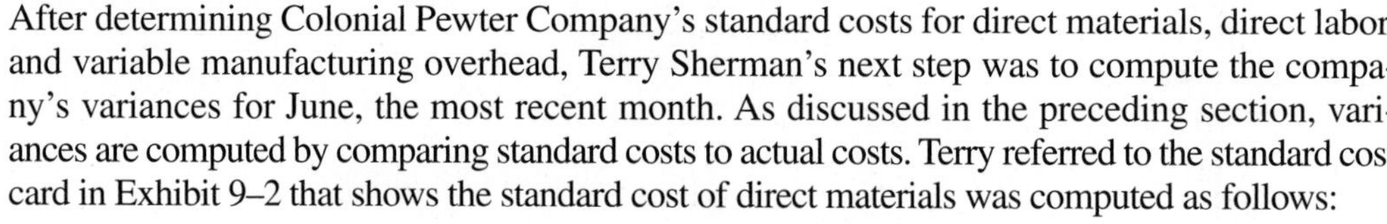

After determining Colonial Pewter Company's standard costs for direct materials, direct labor, and variable manufacturing overhead, Terry Sherman's next step was to compute the company's variances for June, the most recent month. As discussed in the preceding section, variances are computed by comparing standard costs to actual costs. Terry referred to the standard cost card in Exhibit 9–2 that shows the standard cost of direct materials was computed as follows:

$$3.0 \text{ pounds per unit} \times \$4.00 \text{ per pound} = \$12 \text{ per unit}$$

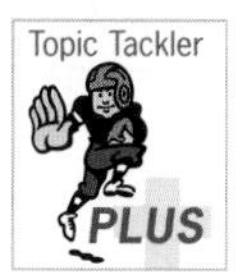

9–1

Colonial Pewter's records for June showed that 6,500 pounds of pewter were purchased at a cost of $3.80 per pound. This cost included freight and was net of a quantity purchase discount. All of the material purchased was used during June to manufacture 2,000 pairs of pewter bookends. Using these data and the standard costs from Exhibit 9–2, Terry computed the price and quantity variances shown in Exhibit 9–4.

The three arrows in Exhibit 9–4 point to three different total cost figures. The first, $24,700, refers to the actual total cost of the pewter that was purchased during June. The second, $26,000, refers to what the pewter would have cost if it had been purchased at the standard price of $4.00 a pound rather than the actual price of $3.80 a pound. The difference between these two figures, $1,300 ($26,000 − $24,700), is the price variance. It exists because the actual purchase price was $0.20 per pound less than the standard purchase price. Since 6,500 pounds were purchased, the total amount of the variance is $1,300 ($0.20 per pound × 6,500 pounds). This variance is labeled favorable (denoted by F), since the actual purchase price was less than the standard purchase price. A price variance is labeled unfavorable (denoted by U) if the actual purchase price exceeds the standard purchase price.

The third arrow in Exhibit 9–4 points to $24,000—the cost if the pewter had been purchased at the standard price *and* only the standard quantity allowed per unit had been used. The standards call for 3 pounds of pewter per unit. Since 2,000 units were produced, 6,000 pounds of pewter should have been used. This is referred to as the standard quantity allowed for the actual output. If this 6,000 pounds of pewter had been purchased at the standard price of $4.00 per pound, the company would have spent $24,000. The difference between this figure, $24,000, and the figure at the end of the middle arrow in Exhibit 9–4, $26,000, is the quantity variance of $2,000.

To understand this quantity variance, note that the actual amount of pewter used in production was 6,500 pounds. However, the standard amount of pewter allowed for the actual

EXHIBIT 9–4
Variance Analysis—Direct Materials

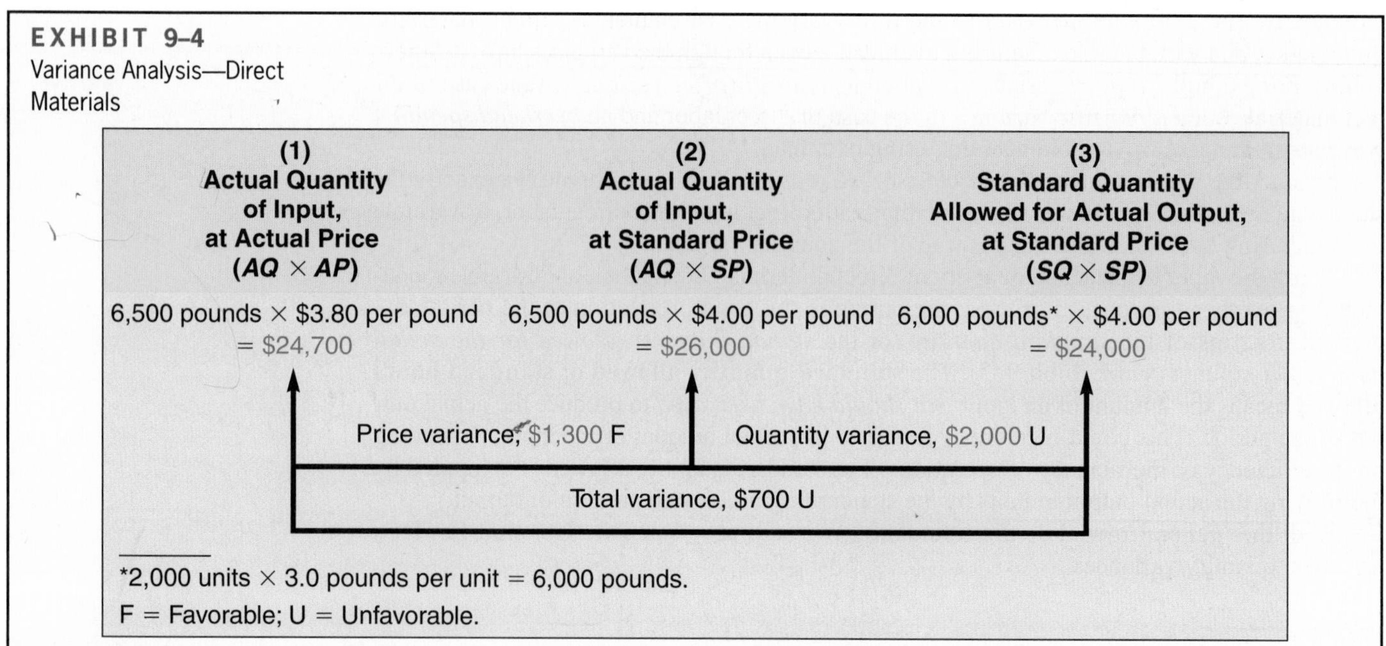

output is 6,000 pounds. Therefore, too much pewter was used to produce the actual output—by a total of 500 pounds. To express this in dollar terms, the 500 pounds is multiplied by the standard price of $4.00 per pound to yield the quantity variance of $2,000. Why is the standard price, rather than the actual price, of the pewter used in this calculation? The production manager is ordinarily responsible for the quantity variance. If the actual price were used in the calculation of the quantity variance, the production manager would be held responsible for the efficiency or inefficiency of the purchasing manager. Apart from being unfair, fruitless arguments between the production manager and purchasing manager would occur every time the actual price of an input was above its standard price. To avoid these arguments, the standard price is used when computing the quantity variance.

The quantity variance in Exhibit 9–4 is labeled unfavorable (denoted by U). This is because more pewter was used to produce the actual output than the standard allows. A quantity variance is labeled favorable (F) if the actual quantity is less than the standard quantity.

The computations in Exhibit 9–4 reflect the fact that all of the material purchased during June was also used during June. How are the variances computed if the amount of material purchased differs from the amount that is used? To illustrate, assume that during June the company purchased 6,500 pounds of materials, as before, but that it used only 5,000 pounds of material during the month and produced only 1,600 units. In this case, the price variance and quantity variance would be computed as shown in Exhibit 9–5.

Most companies compute the materials price variance when materials are *purchased* rather than when they are used in production. There are two reasons for this practice. First, delaying the computation of the price variance until the materials are used would result in less timely variance reports. Second, computing the price variance when the materials are purchased allows materials to be carried in the inventory accounts at their standard cost. This greatly simplifies bookkeeping.

Note from the exhibit that the price variance is computed on the entire amount of material purchased (6,500 pounds), as before, whereas the quantity variance is computed only on

EXHIBIT 9–5
Variance Analysis—Direct Materials, When the Amount Purchased Differs from the Amount Used

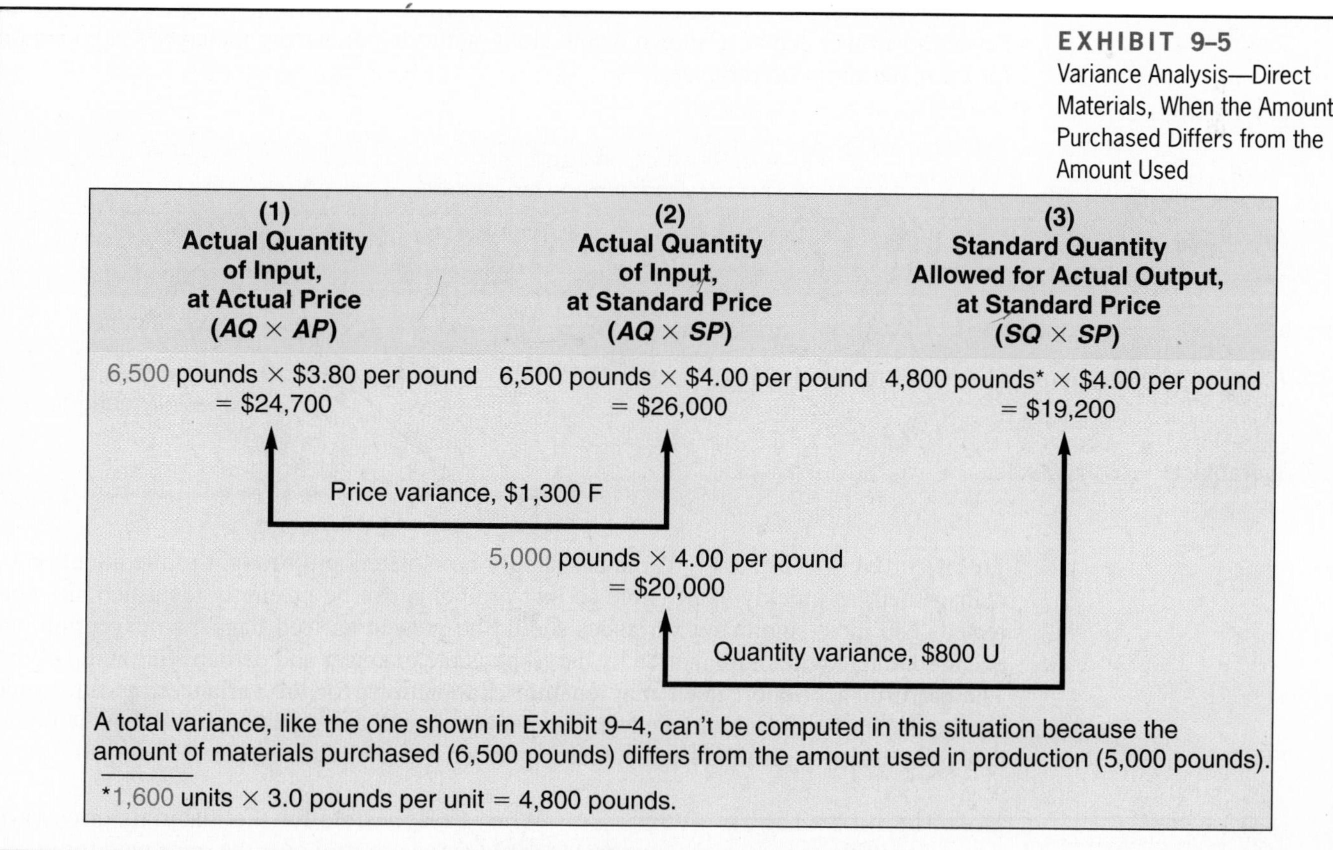

the portion of this material used in production during the month (5,000 pounds). What about the other 1,500 pounds of material that were purchased during the period, but that have not yet been used? When those materials are used in future periods, a quantity variance will be computed. However, a price variance will not be computed when the materials are finally used because the price variance was computed when the materials were purchased. The situation illustrated in Exhibit 9–5 is common for companies that purchase materials well in advance of when they are used in production.

Materials Price Variance—A Closer Look

A **materials price variance** measures the difference between what is paid for a given quantity of materials and what should have been paid according to the standard. From Exhibit 9–4, this difference can be expressed by the following formula:

$$\text{Materials price variance} = (AQ \times AP) - (AQ \times SP)$$

Actual quantity; Actual price; Standard price

The formula can be factored as follows:

$$\text{Materials price variance} = AQ(AP - SP)$$

Using the data from Exhibit 9–4 in this formula, we have the following:

6,500 pounds (\$3.80 per pound − \$4.00 per pound) = \$1,300 F

Notice that the answer is the same as that shown in Exhibit 9–4. Also note that when using this formula approach, a negative variance is always labeled as favorable (F) and a positive variance is always labeled as unfavorable (U). This will be true of all variance formulas in this and later chapters.

Variance reports are often presented in the form of a table. An excerpt from Colonial Pewter's variance report is shown below along with the purchasing manager's explanation for the materials price variance.

Colonial Pewter Company
Performance Report—Purchasing Department

Item Purchased	(1) Quantity Purchased	(2) Actual Price	(3) Standard Price	(4) Difference in Price (2) − (3)	Total Price Variance (1) × (4)	Explanation
Pewter	6,500 pounds	\$3.80	\$4.00	\$0.20	\$1,300 F	Bargained for an especially good price.

F = Favorable; U = Unfavorable.

Isolation of Variances Variances should be isolated and brought to the attention of management as quickly as possible so that problems can be promptly identified and corrected. The most significant variances should be viewed as "red flags"; an exception has occurred that requires explanation by the responsible manager and perhaps follow-up effort. The performance report itself may contain explanations for the variances, as illustrated above. In the case of Colonial Pewter Company, the purchasing manager said that the favorable price variance resulted from bargaining for an especially good price.

Responsibility for the Variance Who is responsible for the materials price variance? Generally speaking, the purchasing manager has control over the price paid for goods and is therefore responsible for the materials price variance. Many factors influence the prices paid for goods including how many units are ordered, how the order is delivered, whether the order is a rush order, and the quality of materials purchased. If any of these factors deviates from what was assumed when the standards were set, a price variance can result. For example, purchasing second-grade materials rather than top-grade materials may result in a favorable price variance, since the lower-grade materials may be less costly. However, we should keep in mind that the lower-grade materials may be less suitable for production.

However, someone other than the purchasing manager could be responsible for a materials price variance. Production may be scheduled in such a way, for example, that the purchasing manager must request express delivery. In these cases, the production manager should be held responsible for the resulting price variances.

A word of caution is in order. Variance analysis should not be used to assign blame. The emphasis should be on *supporting* the line managers and *assisting* them in meeting the goals that they have participated in setting for the company. In short, the emphasis should be positive rather than negative. Excessive dwelling on what has already happened, particularly in terms of trying to find someone to blame, can destroy morale and kill any cooperative spirit.

Materials Quantity Variance—A Closer Look

The **materials quantity variance** measures the difference between the quantity of materials used in production and the quantity that should have been used according to the standard. Although the variance is concerned with the physical usage of materials, as shown in Exhibit 9–4, it is generally stated in dollar terms to help gauge its importance. The formula for the materials quantity variance is as follows:

$$\text{Materials quantity variance} = (AQ \times SP) - (SQ \times SP)$$

Actual quantity; Standard price; Standard quantity allowed for actual output

same thing

Again, the formula can be factored as follows:

$$\text{Materials quantity variance} = SP(AQ - SQ)$$

Using the data from Exhibit 9–4 in the formula, we have the following:

$4.00 per pound (6,500 pounds − 6,000 pounds*) = $2,000 U

*2,000 units × 3.0 pounds per unit = 6,000 pounds.

The answer, of course, is the same as that shown in Exhibit 9–4.

The data might appear as follows if a formal performance report were prepared:

Colonial Pewter Company
Performance Report—Production Department

Type of Materials	(1) Standard Price	(2) Actual Quantity	(3) Standard Quantity Allowed	(4) Difference in Quantity (2) − (3)	Total Quantity Variance (1) × (4)	Explanation
Pewter	$4.00	6,500 pounds	6,000 pounds	500 pounds	$2,000 U	Low-quality materials unsuitable for production.

F = Favorable; U = Unfavorable.

The materials quantity variance is best isolated when materials are used in production. Materials are drawn for the number of units to be produced, according to the standard bill of materials for each unit. Any additional materials are usually drawn with an excess materials requisition slip, which is different in color from the normal requisition slips. This procedure calls attention to the excessive usage of materials *while production is still in process* and provides an opportunity to correct any developing problem.

Excessive materials usage can result from many factors, including faulty machines, inferior materials quality, untrained workers, and poor supervision. Generally speaking, it is the responsibility of the production department to see that material usage is kept in line with standards. There may be times, however, when the *purchasing* department is responsible for an unfavorable materials quantity variance. For example, if the purchasing department buys inferior materials at a lower price, the materials may be unsuitable for use and may result in excessive waste. Thus, purchasing rather than production would be responsible for the quantity variance. At Colonial Pewter, the production manager, Tom Kuchel, claimed on the Production Department's Performance Report that low-quality materials were the cause of the unfavorable materials quantity variance for June.

IN BUSINESS

WHAT HAPPENED TO THE RAISINS?

Management at an unnamed breakfast cereal company became concerned about the apparent waste of raisins in one of its products. A box of the product was supposed to contain 10 ounces of cereal and 2 ounces of raisins. However, the production process had been using an average of 2.5 ounces of raisins per box. To correct the problem, a bonus was offered to employees if the consumption of raisins dropped to 2.1 ounces per box or less—which would allow for about 5% waste. Within a month, the target was hit and bonuses were distributed. However, another problem began to appear. Market studies indicated that customers had become dissatisfied with the amount of raisins in the product. Workers had hit the 2.1-ounce per box target by drastically reducing the amount of raisins in rush orders. Boxes of the completed product are ordinarily weighed and if the weight is less than 12 ounces, the box is rejected. However, rush orders aren't weighed since that would slow down the production process. Consequently, workers were reducing the raisins in rush orders so as to hit the overall target of 2.1 ounces of raisins per box. This resulted in substandard boxes of cereal in rush orders and customer complaints. Clearly, managers need to be very careful when they set targets and standards. They may not get what they bargained for. Subsequent investigation by an internal auditor revealed that, due to statistical fluctuations, an average of about 2.5 ounces of raisins must be used to ensure that every box contains at least 2 ounces of raisins.

Source: Harper A. Roehm and Joseph R. Castellano, "The Danger of Relying on Accounting Numbers Alone," *Management Accounting Quarterly*, Fall 1999, pp. 4–9.

Using Standard Costs—Direct Labor Variances

LEARNING OBJECTIVE 3
Compute the direct labor rate and efficiency variances and explain their significance.

Terry Sherman's next step in determining Colonial Pewter's variances for June was to compute the direct labor variances for the month. Recall from Exhibit 9–2 that the standard direct labor cost per unit of product is $35, computed as follows:

2.5 hours per unit × $14.00 per hour = $35 per unit

During June, the company paid its direct labor workers $74,250, including employment taxes and fringe benefits, for 5,400 hours of work. This was an average of $13.75 per hour.

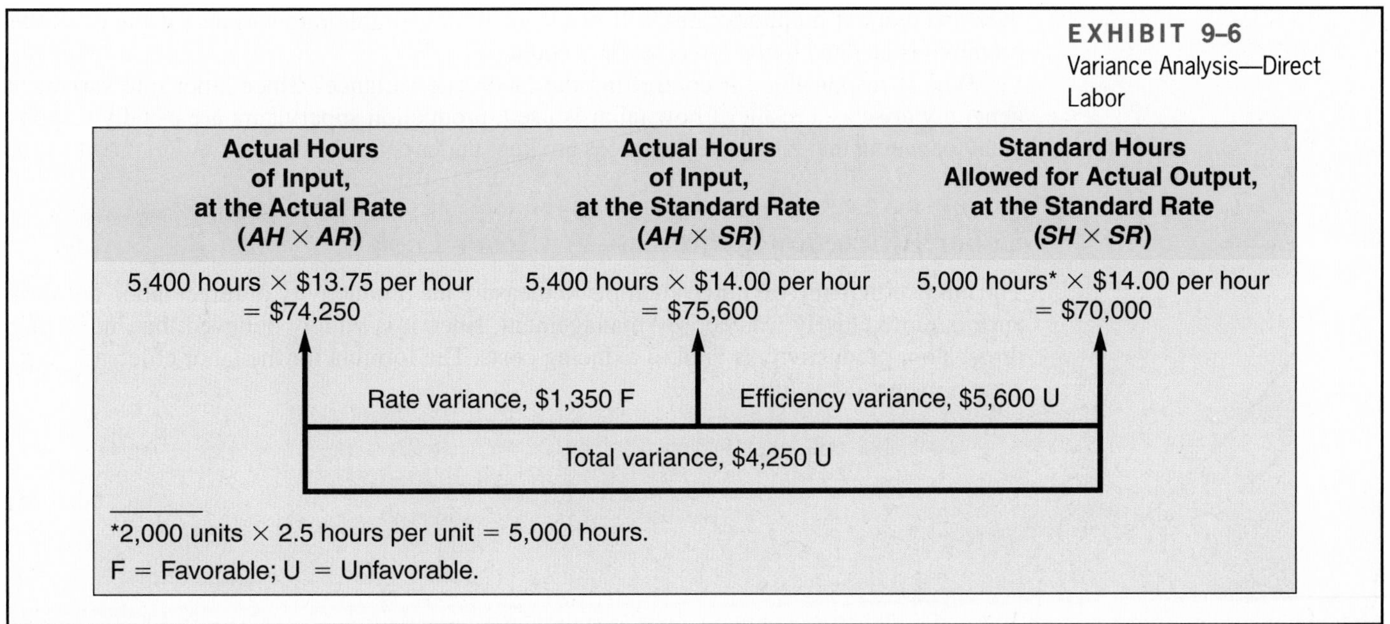

EXHIBIT 9–6
Variance Analysis—Direct Labor

Using these data and the standard costs from Exhibit 9–2, Terry computed the direct labor rate and efficiency variances that appear in Exhibit 9–6.

Notice that the column headings in Exhibit 9–6 are the same as those used in the prior two exhibits, except that in Exhibit 9–6 the terms *hours* and *rate* are used in place of the terms *quantity* and *price.*

Labor Rate Variance—A Closer Look

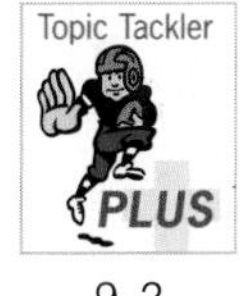

9–2

As explained earlier, the price variance for direct labor is commonly termed a **labor rate variance.** This variance measures any deviation from standard in the average hourly rate paid to direct labor workers. The formula for the labor rate variance is expressed as follows:

$$\text{Labor rate variance} = (AH \times AR) - (AH \times SR)$$

Actual hours — Actual rate — Standard rate

The formula can be factored as follows:

$$\text{Labor rate variance} = AH(AR - SR)$$

Using the data from Exhibit 9–6 in the formula, the labor rate variance can be computed as follows:

$$5{,}400 \text{ hours } (\$13.75 \text{ per hour} - \$14.00 \text{ per hour}) = \$1{,}350 \text{ F}$$

In most companies, the wage rates paid to workers are quite predictable. Nevertheless, rate variances can arise because of the way labor is used. Skilled workers with high hourly rates of pay may be given duties that require little skill and call for lower hourly rates of pay. This will result in an unfavorable labor rate variance, since the actual hourly rate of pay will exceed the standard rate specified for the particular task. In contrast, a favorable rate variance would result when workers who are paid at a rate lower than specified in the standard are assigned to the task. However, the lower-paid workers may not be as efficient. Finally, overtime work at premium rates will result in an unfavorable rate variance if the overtime premium is charged to the direct labor account.

Who is responsible for controlling the labor rate variance? Since labor rate variances generally arise as a result of how labor is used, production supervisors are usually responsible for seeing that labor rate variances are kept under control.

Labor Efficiency Variance—A Closer Look

The **labor efficiency variance** attempts to measure the productivity of direct labor. No variance is more closely watched by management, since it is widely believed that increasing direct labor productivity is vital to reducing costs. The formula for the labor efficiency variance is expressed as follows:

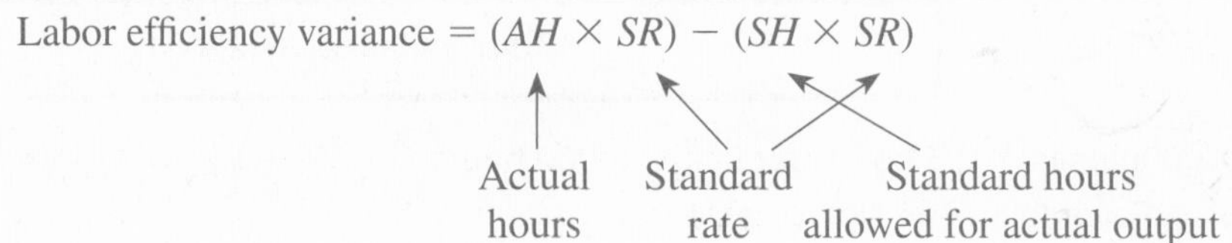

The formula can be factored as follows:

$$\text{Labor efficiency variance} = SR(AH - SH)$$

Using the data from Exhibit 9–6 in the formula, we have the following:

$$\$14.00 \text{ per hour } (5{,}400 \text{ hours} - 5{,}000 \text{ hours*}) = \$5{,}600 \text{ U}$$

*2,000 units × 2.5 hours per unit = 5,000 hours.

Possible causes of an unfavorable labor efficiency variance include poorly trained or motivated workers; poor quality materials, requiring more labor time; faulty equipment, causing breakdowns and work interruptions; poor supervision of workers; and inaccurate standards. The managers in charge of production would usually be responsible for control of the labor efficiency variance. However, the purchasing manager could be held responsible if the purchase of poor-quality materials resulted in excessive labor processing time.

Another important cause of an unfavorable labor efficiency variance may be insufficient demand for the company's products. Managers in some companies argue that it is difficult, and perhaps unwise, to constantly adjust the workforce in response to changes in the amount of work that needs to be done. In such companies, the direct labor workforce is essentially fixed in the short run. If demand is insufficient to keep everyone busy, workers are not laid off. In this case, if demand falls below the level needed to keep everyone busy, an unfavorable labor efficiency variance will often be recorded.

If customer orders are insufficient to keep the workers busy, the work center manager has two options—either accept an unfavorable labor efficiency variance or build inventory.[3] A central lesson of Lean Production is that building inventory with no immediate prospect of sale is a bad idea. Excessive inventory—particularly work in process inventory—leads to high defect rates, obsolete goods, and inefficient operations. As a consequence, when the workforce is basically fixed in the short term, managers must be cautious about how labor efficiency variances are used. Some experts advocate eliminating labor efficiency variances in such situations—at least for the purposes of motivating and controlling workers on the shop floor.

[3] For further discussion, see Eliyahu M. Goldratt and Jeff Cox, *The Goal,* 2nd rev. ed. (Croton-on-Hudson, NY: North River Press).

IN BUSINESS

DOES DIRECT LABOR VARIANCE REPORTING INCREASE PRODUCTIVITY?

Professors Rajiv Banker, Sarv Devaraj, Roger Schroeder, and Kingshuk Sinha studied the direct labor variance reporting practices at 18 plants of a Fortune 500 manufacturing company. Seven of the plants eliminated direct labor variance reporting and the other 11 plants did not. The group of seven plants that eliminated direct labor variance reporting experienced an 11% decline in labor productivity, which was significantly greater than the decline experienced by the other 11 plants. The authors estimated that the annual loss due to the decline in labor productivity across the seven plants of $1,996,000 was only partially offset by the $200,000 saved by eliminating the need to track direct labor variances.

While these findings suggest that direct labor variance reporting is a useful tool for monitoring direct labor workers, advocates of Lean Production would argue otherwise. They would claim that direct labor variance reporting is a non-value-added activity that encourages excessive production and demoralizes direct labor workers. The two points of view provide an interesting opportunity to debate the appropriate role of management accounting within organizations.

Source: Rajiv Banker, Sarv Devaraj, Roger Schroeder, and Kingshuk Sinha, "Performance Impact of the Elimination of Direct Labor Variance Reporting: A Field Study," *Journal of Accounting Research*, September 2002, pp. 1013–1036.

Using Standard Costs—Variable Manufacturing Overhead Variances

LEARNING OBJECTIVE 4
Compute the variable manufacturing overhead spending and efficiency variances.

The final step in Terry Sherman's analysis of Colonial Pewter's variances for June was to compute the variable manufacturing overhead variances. The variable portion of manufacturing overhead can be analyzed using the same basic formulas that are used to analyze direct materials and direct labor. Recall from Exhibit 9–2 that the standard variable manufacturing overhead is $7.50 per unit of product, computed as follows:

$$2.5 \text{ hours per unit} \times \$3.00 \text{ per hour} = \$7.50 \text{ per unit}$$

Colonial Pewter's cost records showed that the total actual variable manufacturing overhead cost for June was $15,390. Recall from the earlier discussion of the direct labor variances that 5,400 hours of direct labor time were recorded during the month and that the company produced 2,000 pairs of bookends. Terry's analysis of this overhead data appears in Exhibit 9–7.

EXHIBIT 9–7
Variance Analysis—Variable Manufacturing Overhead

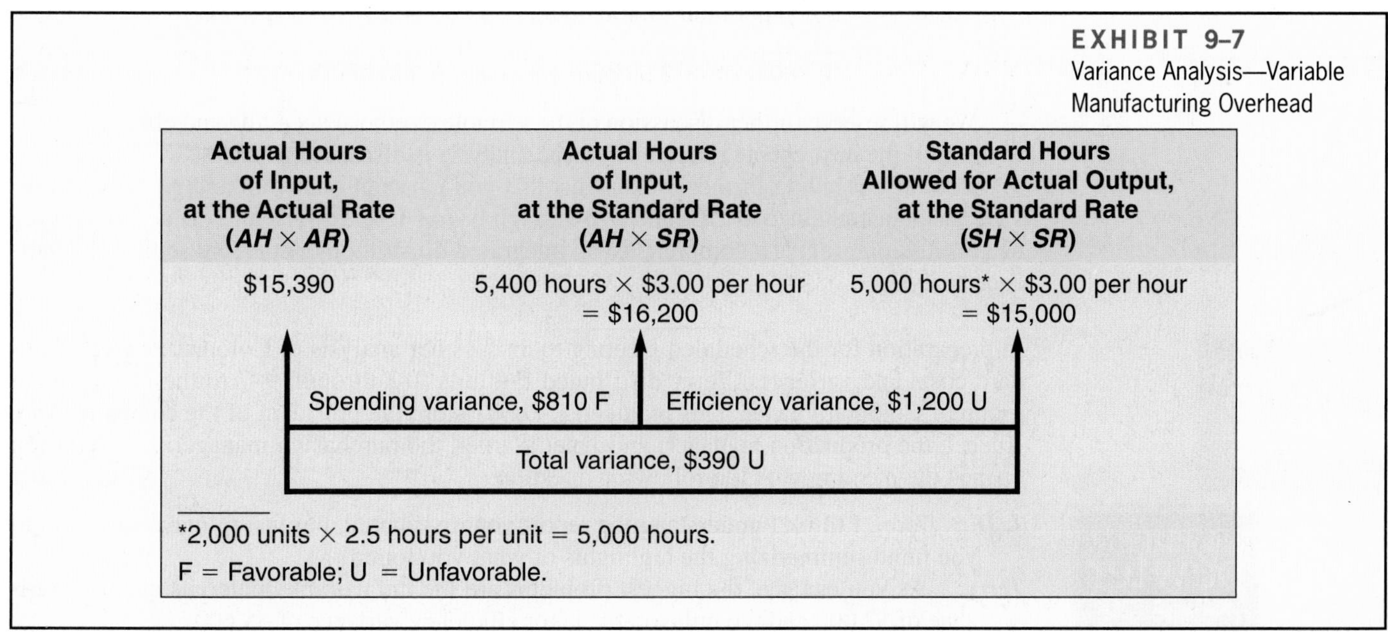

Notice the similarities between Exhibits 9–6 and 9–7. These similarities arise from the fact that direct labor-hours are being used as the base for allocating overhead cost to units of product; thus, the same hourly figures appear in Exhibit 9–7 for variable manufacturing overhead as in Exhibit 9–6 for direct labor. The main difference between the two exhibits is in the standard hourly rate being used, which in this company is much lower for variable manufacturing overhead than for direct labor.

Manufacturing Overhead Variances—A Closer Look

The formula for the **variable overhead spending variance** is expressed as follows:

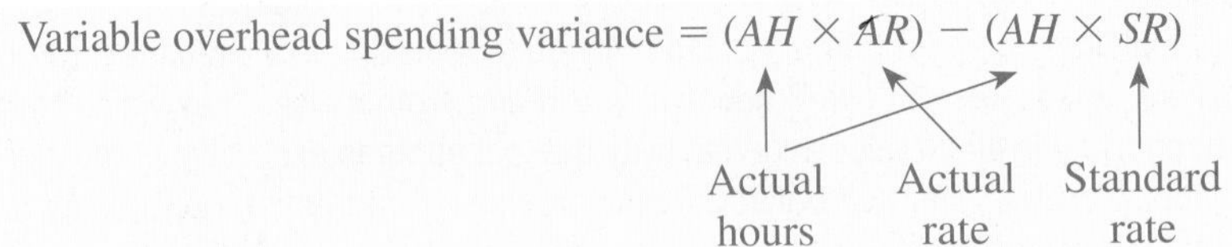

This formula can be factored as follows:

$$\text{Variable overhead spending variance} = AH(AR - SR)$$

Using the data from Exhibit 9–7 in the formula, the variable overhead spending variance can be computed as follows:

5,400 hours ($2.85 per hour* − $3.00 per hour) = $810 F

*$15,390 ÷ 5,400 hours = $2.85 per hour.

The formula for the **variable overhead efficiency variance** is expressed as follows:

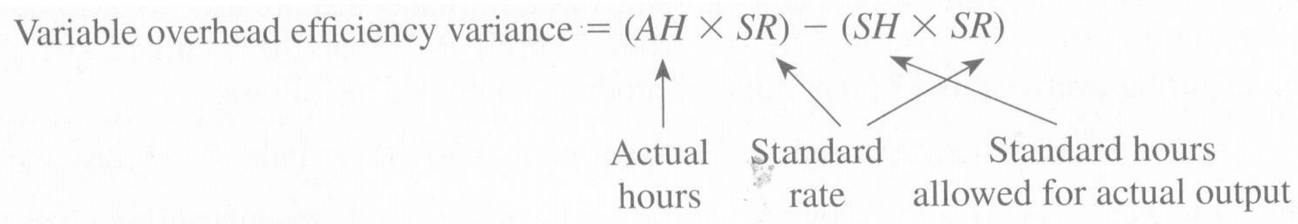

This formula can be factored as follows:

$$\text{Variable overhead efficiency variance} = SR(AH - SH)$$

Again using the data from Exhibit 9–7, the variance can be computed as follows:

$3.00 per hour (5,400 hours − 5,000 hours*) = $1,200 U

*2,000 units × 2.5 hours per unit = 5,000 hours.

We will reserve further discussion of the variable overhead spending and efficiency variances until the next chapter, where overhead analysis is discussed in depth.

Before proceeding further, we suggest that you pause at this point and go back and review the data contained in Exhibits 9–2 through 9–7. These exhibits and the accompanying text discussion provide a comprehensive, integrated illustration of standard setting and variance analysis.

MANAGERIAL ACCOUNTING IN ACTION
The Wrap-up

In preparation for the scheduled meeting to discuss her analysis of Colonial Pewter's standard costs and variances, Terry distributed Exhibits 9–2 through 9–7 to the management group of Colonial Pewter. This included J. D. Wriston, the president of the company; Tom Kuchel, the production manager; and Janet Warner, the purchasing manager. J. D. Wriston opened the meeting with the following question:

J. D.: Terry, I think I understand the report you distributed, but just to make sure, would you mind summarizing the highlights of what you found?

Terry: As you can see, the biggest problems are the unfavorable materials quantity variance of $2,000 and the unfavorable labor efficiency variance of $5,600.

J. D.: Tom, you're the production boss. What do you think is causing the unfavorable labor efficiency variance?

Tom: It has to be the new production workers. Our experienced workers shouldn't have much problem meeting the standard of 2.5 hours per unit. We all knew that there would be some inefficiency for a while as we brought new people on board. My plan for overcoming the problem is to pair up each of the new guys with one of our old-timers and have them work together for a while. It would slow down our older guys a bit, but I'll bet the unfavorable variance disappears and our new workers would learn a lot.

J. D.: Sounds good. Now, what about that $2,000 unfavorable materials quantity variance?

Terry: Tom, are the new workers generating a lot of scrap?

Tom: Yeah, I guess so.

J. D.: I think that could be part of the problem. Can you do anything about it?

Tom: I can watch the scrap closely for a few days to see where it's being generated. If it is the new workers, I can have the old-timers work with them on the problem when I team them up.

J. D.: Janet, the favorable materials price variance of $1,300 isn't helping us if it is contributing to the unfavorable materials quantity and labor efficiency variances. Let's make sure that our raw material purchases conform to our quality standards.

Janet: Fair enough.

J. D.: Good. Let's reconvene in a few weeks to see what has happened. Hopefully, we can get those unfavorable variances under control.

Variance Analysis and Management by Exception

Variance analysis and performance reports are important elements of *management by exception,* which is an approach that emphasizes focusing on those areas of responsibility where goals and expectations are not being met.

The budgets and standards discussed in this chapter and in the preceding chapter reflect management's plans. If all goes according to plan, there will be little difference between actual results and the results that would be expected according to the budgets and standards. If this happens, managers can concentrate on other issues. However, if actual results do not conform to the budget and to standards, the performance reporting system sends a signal to managers that an "exception" has occurred. This signal is in the form of a variance from the budget or standards.

However, are all variances worth investigating? The answer is no. Differences between actual results and what was expected will almost always occur. If every variance were investigated, management would waste a great deal of time tracking down nickel-and-dime differences. Variances may occur for a variety of reasons—only some of which are significant and worthy of management's attention. For example, hotter-than-normal weather in the summer may result in higher-than-expected electrical bills for air conditioning. Or, workers may work slightly faster or slower on a particular day. Because of unpredictable random factors, one can expect that virtually every cost category will produce a variance of some kind.

How should managers decide which variances are worth investigating? One clue is the size of the variance. A variance of $5 is probably not big enough to warrant attention, whereas a variance of $5,000 might well be worth tracking down. Another clue is the size of the variance relative to the amount of spending. A variance that is only 0.1% of spending on an item is likely to be well within the bounds one would normally expect due to random factors. On the other hand, a variance of 10% of spending is much more likely to be a signal that something is wrong.

A more dependable approach is to plot variance data on a statistical control chart, such as illustrated in Exhibit 9–8 (page 362). The basic idea underlying a statistical control

EXHIBIT 9–8
A Statistical Control Chart

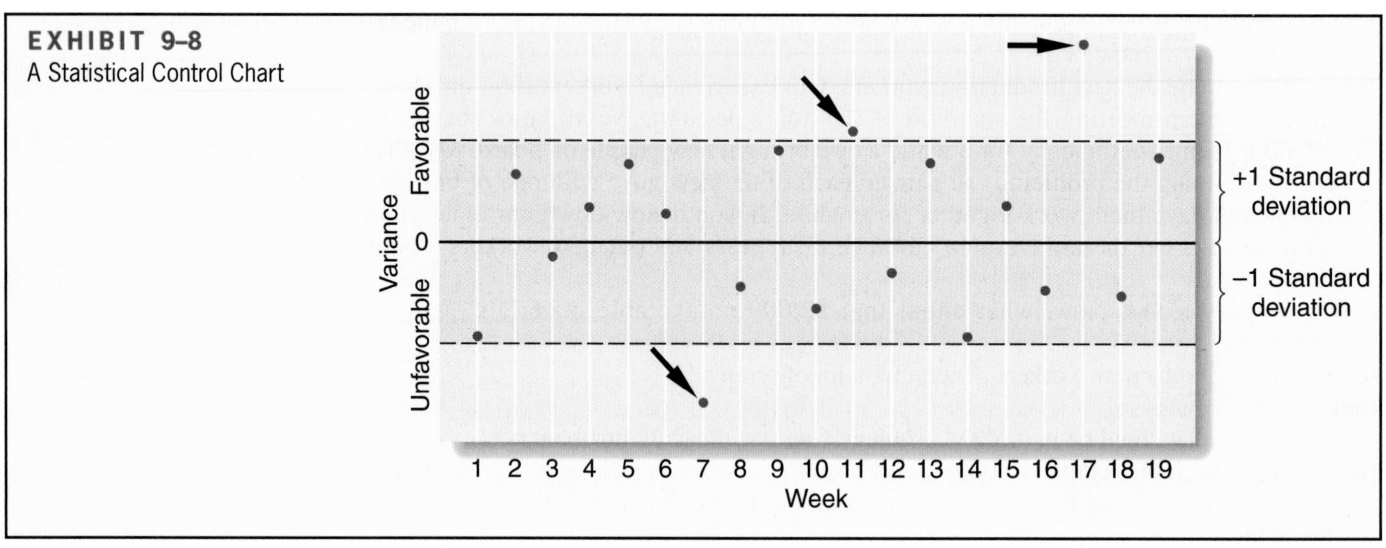

chart is that some random fluctuations in variances from period to period are normal. A variance should only be investigated when it is unusual relative to that normal level of random fluctuation. Typically, the standard deviation of the variances is used as the measure of the normal level of fluctuations. A rule of thumb is adopted such as "investigate all variances that are more than *X* standard deviations from zero." In the control chart in Exhibit 9–8, *X* is 1.0. That is, the rule of thumb in this company is to investigate all variances that are more than one standard deviation in either direction (favorable or unfavorable) from zero. This means that the variances in weeks 7, 11, and 17 would have been investigated, but none of the others.

What value of *X* should be chosen? The bigger the value of *X,* the wider the band of acceptable variances that would not be investigated. Thus, the bigger the value of *X,* the less time will be spent tracking down variances, but the more likely it is that a real out-of-control situation will be overlooked. Ordinarily, if *X* is selected to be 1.0, roughly 30% of all variances will trigger an investigation even though there is no real problem. If *X* is set at 1.5, the figure drops to about 13%. If *X* is set at 2.0, the figure drops all the way to about 5%. Don't forget, however, that selecting a big value of *X* will result not only in fewer false alarms but also a higher probability that a real problem will be overlooked.

In addition to watching for unusually large variances, the pattern of the variances should be monitored. For example, a run of steadily mounting variances should trigger an investigation even though none of the variances is large enough by itself to warrant investigation.

International Uses of Standard Costs

Standard costs are used by companies throughout the world. One study found that three-fourths of the companies surveyed in the United Kingdom, two-thirds of the companies surveyed in Canada, and 40% of the companies surveyed in Japan used standard cost systems.[4]

Standard costs were first introduced in Japan after World War II, with Nippon Electronics Company (NEC) being one of the first Japanese companies to adopt standard costs for all of its products. Many other Japanese companies followed NEC's lead and developed standard

[4] Shin'ichi Inoue, "Comparative Studies of Recent Development of Cost Management Problems in U.S.A., U.K., Canada, and Japan," Research Paper No. 29, Kagawa University, p. 17. The study included 95 United States companies, 52 United Kingdom companies, 82 Canadian companies, and 646 Japanese companies.

EXHIBIT 9–9
Uses of Standard Costs in Four Countries

	United States	United Kingdom	Canada	Japan
Cost management	1*	2	2	1
Budgetary planning and control†	2	3	1	3
Pricing decisions	3	1	3	2
Financial statement preparation	4	4	4	4

*The numbers 1 through 4 denote importance of use, from greatest to least.
†Includes management planning.
Source: Compiled from data in a study by Shin'ichi Inoue, "Comparative Studies of Recent Development of Cost Management Problems in U.S.A., U.K., Canada, and Japan," Research Paper No. 29, Kagawa University, p. 20.

cost systems. The ways in which these standard costs are used in Japan—and also in the other countries cited above—are shown in Exhibit 9–9.

Over time, the pattern of use shown in Exhibit 9–9 may change, but at present managers can expect to encounter standard costs in most industrialized nations. Moreover, the most important uses are for cost management and budgetary planning purposes.

Evaluation of Controls Based on Standard Costs

Advantages of Standard Costs

Standard cost systems have a number of advantages.

1. Standard costs are a key element in a management by exception approach. If costs conform to the standards, managers can focus on other issues. When costs are significantly outside the standards, managers are alerted that problems may exist that require attention. This approach helps managers focus on important issues.
2. Standards that are viewed as reasonable by employees can promote economy and efficiency. They provide benchmarks that individuals can use to judge their own performance.
3. Standard costs can greatly simplify bookkeeping. Instead of recording actual costs for each job, the standard costs for direct materials, direct labor, and overhead can be charged to jobs.
4. Standard costs fit naturally in an integrated system of "responsibility accounting." The standards establish what costs should be, who should be responsible for them, and whether actual costs are under control.

Potential Problems with the Use of Standard Costs

The improper use of standard costs can present a number of potential problems.

1. Standard cost variance reports are usually prepared on a monthly basis and often are released days or even weeks after the end of the month. As a consequence, the information in the reports may be so outdated that it is almost useless. Timely, frequent reports that are approximately correct are better than infrequent reports that are very precise but out of date by the time they are released. Some companies are now reporting variances and other key operating data daily or even more frequently.
2. If managers are insensitive and use variance reports as a club, morale will suffer. Employees should receive positive reinforcement for work well done. Management by exception, by its nature, tends to focus on the negative. If variances are used as a club, subordinates may be tempted to cover up unfavorable variances or take actions that are not in the best interests of the company to make sure the variances are favorable. For

example, workers may put on a crash effort to increase output at the end of the month to avoid an unfavorable labor efficiency variance. In the rush to produce more output, quality may suffer.

3. Labor quantity standards and efficiency variances make two important assumptions. First, they assume that the production process is labor-paced; if labor works faster, output will go up. However, output in many companies is not determined by how fast labor works; rather, it is determined by the processing speed of machines. Second, the computations assume that labor is a variable cost. However, direct labor may be essentially fixed. If labor is fixed, then an undue emphasis on labor efficiency variances creates pressure to build excess inventories.
4. In some cases, a "favorable" variance can be as bad or worse than an "unfavorable" variance. For example, McDonald's has a standard for the amount of hamburger meat that should be in a Big Mac. A "favorable" variance would mean that less meat was used than the standard specifies. The result is a substandard Big Mac and possibly a dissatisfied customer.
5. Too much emphasis on meeting the standards may overshadow other important objectives such as maintaining and improving quality, on-time delivery, and customer satisfaction. This tendency can be reduced by using supplemental performance measures that focus on these other objectives.
6. Just meeting standards may not be sufficient; continual improvement may be necessary to survive in a competitive environment. For this reason, some companies focus on the trends in the standard cost variances—aiming for continual improvement rather than just meeting the standards. In other companies, engineered standards are replaced either by a rolling average of actual costs, which is expected to decline, or by very challenging target costs.

In sum, managers should exercise considerable care when using a standard cost system. It is particularly important that managers go out of their way to focus on the positive, rather than just on the negative, and to be aware of possible unintended consequences.

Nevertheless, standard costs are found in the vast majority of manufacturing companies and in many service companies, although their use is changing. For evaluating performance, standard cost variances are often complemented by a performance measurement system called the *balanced scorecard,* which is discussed in the next section. The balanced scorecard concept has been eagerly embraced by a wide variety of organizations including Analog Devices, KPMG, Tenneco, Allstate, AT&T, Elf Atochem, Conair-Franklin, CIGNA Corporation, London Life Insurance Co., Southern Gardens Citrus Processing, Duke Children's Hospital, JP Morgan Chase, 3COM, Rockwater, Apple Computer, Advanced Micro Devices (AMD), FMC, Bank of Montreal, Massachusetts Special Olympics, United Way of Southeastern New England, Boston Lyric Opera, Bridgeport Hospital and Healthcare Services, Housing Authority of Fiji, and Verizon Communications. It has been estimated that about half of all Fortune 1000 companies have implemented a balanced scorecard.

Balanced Scorecard

LEARNING OBJECTIVE 5
Understand how a balanced scorecard fits together and how it supports a company's strategy.

A **balanced scorecard** consists of an integrated set of performance measures that are derived from and support the company's strategy throughout the organization. A strategy is essentially a theory about how to achieve the organization's goals. For example, Southwest Airlines' strategy is to offer an *operational excellence* customer value proposition that has three key components—low ticket prices, convenience, and reliability. The company operates only one type of aircraft, the Boeing 737, to reduce maintenance and training costs and simplify scheduling. It further reduces costs by not offering meals, seat assignments, or baggage transfers and by booking a large portion of its passenger revenue over the Internet. Southwest also uses point-to-point flights rather than the hub-and-spoke approach of its larger competitors, thereby providing customers convenient, nonstop service to their final destination. Since Southwest serves many less-congested airports such as Chicago Midway, Burbank, Manchester, Oakland, and Providence, it offers quicker passenger check-ins and reliable departures, while maintaining high asset utilization (i.e., the company's average gate turnaround time of 25 minutes enables it to function with fewer planes and gates). Overall, the company's strategy has worked. At a time when Southwest Airlines' larger competitors are struggling, it continues to earn substantial profits.

Under the balanced scorecard approach, top management translates its strategy into performance measures that employees can understand and influence. For example, the amount of time passengers have to wait in line to have their baggage checked might be a performance measure for the supervisor in charge of the Southwest Airlines check-in counter at the Burbank airport. This performance measure is easily understood by the supervisor, and can be improved by the supervisor's actions.

IN BUSINESS

WHY DO COMPANIES FAIL TO EXECUTE THEIR STRATEGIES?

Robert Paladino served as the vice president and global leader of the Telecommunications and Utility Practice for the Balanced Scorecard Collaborative—a consulting organization that works with companies to implement balanced scorecards. He offers four reasons why nine out of ten organizations fail to execute their business strategies.

First, only 5% of a company's workforce understands their organization's strategy. Paladino commented "if employees don't understand the strategic objectives, then they could be focused on closing the wrong performance gaps." Second, 85% of management teams spend less than one hour per month discussing strategy. Managers cannot effectively implement strategies if they do not spend enough time talking about them. Third, 60% of organizations do not link their budgets to strategy. The inevitable result is that companies pursue "financial strategies that differ from or, worse, may be in conflict with their business and customer quality strategies." Finally, only 25% of managers have their incentives linked to strategy. Thus, most managers are working to maximize their compensation by improving strategically misguided metrics.

Paladino says the balanced scorecard overcomes these four barriers because it helps employees focus their actions on executing organizational strategies.

Source: Robert E. Paladino, "Balanced Forecasts Drive Value," *Strategic Finance,* January 2005, pp. 37–42.

Common Characteristics of Balanced Scorecards

Performance measures used in the balanced scorecard approach tend to fall into the four groups illustrated in Exhibit 9–10 (page 366): financial, customer, internal business processes, and learning and growth. Internal business processes are what the company does in an attempt to satisfy customers. For example, in a manufacturing company, assembling a product is an internal business process. In an airline, handling baggage is an internal business process. The idea underlying these groupings (as indicated by the vertical arrows in Exhibit 9–10) is that learning is necessary to improve internal business processes; improving business processes is necessary to improve customer satisfaction; and improving customer satisfaction is necessary to improve financial results.

Note that the emphasis in Exhibit 9–10 is on *improvement*—not on just attaining some specific objective such as profits of $10 million. In the balanced scorecard approach, continual improvement is encouraged. If an organization does not continually improve, it will eventually lose out to competitors that do.

Financial performance measures appear at the top of Exhibit 9–10. Ultimately, most companies exist to provide financial rewards to owners. There are exceptions. Some companies—for example, The Body Shop—may have loftier goals such as providing environmentally friendly

EXHIBIT 9–10
From Strategy to Performance Measures: The Balanced Scorecard

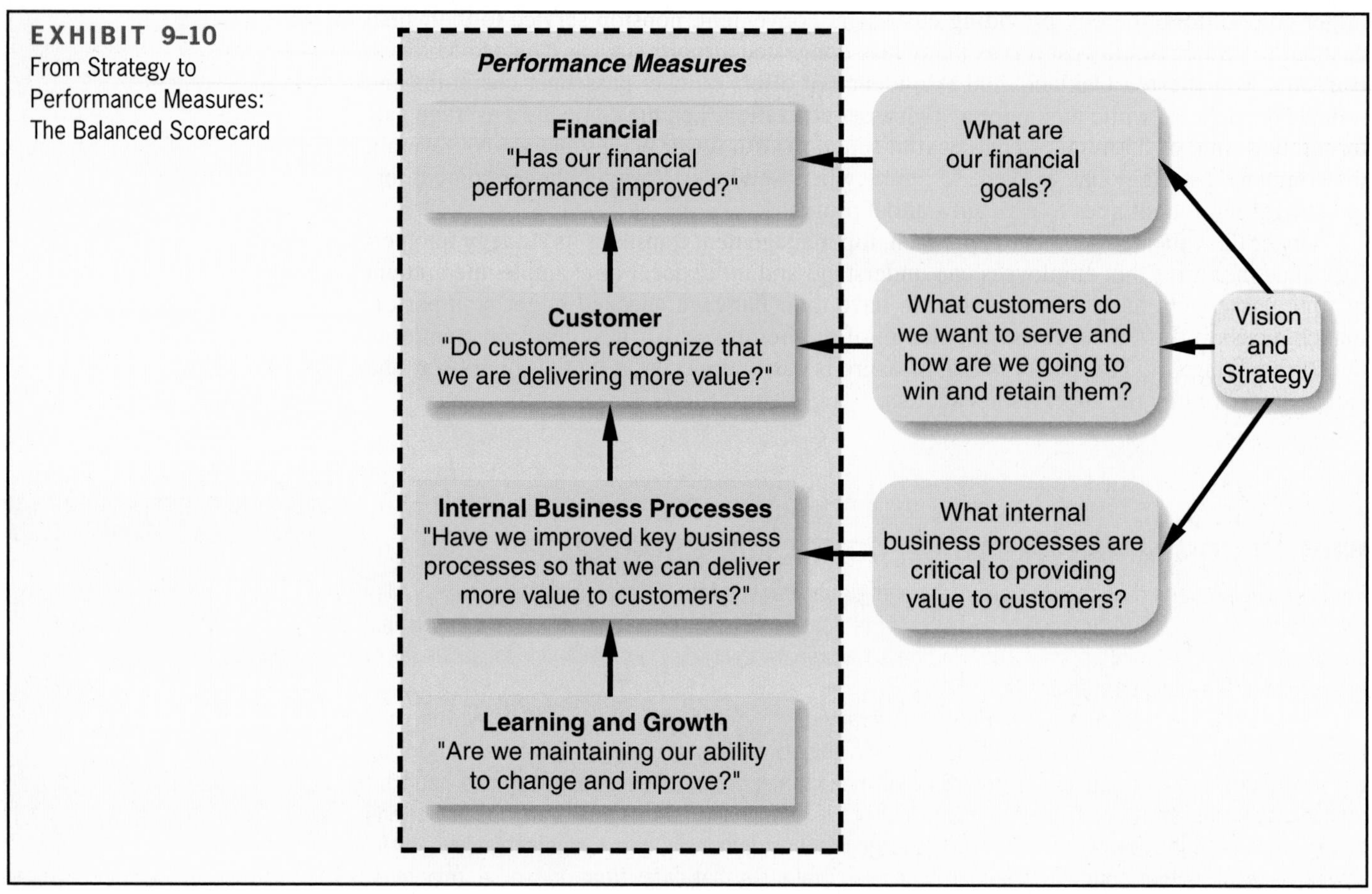

products to consumers. However, even nonprofit organizations must generate enough financial resources to stay in operation.

However, for several reasons, financial performance measures are not sufficient in themselves—they should be integrated with nonfinancial measures in a well-designed balanced scorecard. First, financial measures are lag indicators that report on the results of past actions. In contrast, nonfinancial measures of key success drivers such as customer satisfaction are leading indicators of future financial performance. Second, top managers are ordinarily responsible for the financial performance measures—not lower-level managers. The supervisor in charge of checking in passengers can be held responsible for how long passengers have to wait in line. However, this supervisor cannot reasonably be held responsible for the entire company's profit. That is the responsibility of the airline's top managers. We will have more to say about financial performance measures in later chapters.

Exhibit 9–11 lists some examples of performance measures that can be found on the balanced scorecards of companies. However, few companies, if any, would use all of these performance measures, and almost all companies would add other performance measures. Managers should carefully select performance measures for their own company's balanced scorecard, keeping the following points in mind. First and foremost, the performance measures should be consistent with, and follow from, the company's strategy. If the performance measures are not consistent with the company's strategy, people will find themselves working at cross-purposes. Second, the performance measures should be understandable and controllable to a significant extent by those being evaluated. Third, the scorecard should not have too many performance measures. This can lead to a lack of focus and confusion.

While the entire organization will have an overall balanced scorecard, each responsible individual will have his or her own personal scorecard as well. This scorecard should

EXHIBIT 9–11
Examples of Performance Measures for Balanced Scorecards

Customer Perspective	
Performance Measure	**Desired Change**
Customer satisfaction as measured by survey results	+
Number of customer complaints	–
Market share	+
Product returns as a percentage of sales	–
Percentage of customers retained from last period	+
Number of new customers	+

Internal Business Processes Perspective	
Performance Measure	**Desired Change**
Percentage of sales from new products	+
Time to introduce new products to market	–
Percentage of customer calls answered within 20 seconds	+
On-time deliveries as a percentage of all deliveries	+
Work in process inventory as a percentage of sales	–
Unfavorable standard cost variances	–
Defect-free units as a percentage of completed units	+
Delivery cycle time*	–
Throughput time*	–
Manufacturing cycle efficiency*	+
Quality costs	–
Setup time	–
Time from call by customer to repair of product	–
Percent of customer complaints settled on first contact	+
Time to settle a customer claim	–

Learning and Growth Perspective	
Performance Measure	**Desired Change**
Suggestions per employee	+
Value-added per employee†	+
Employee turnover	–
Hours of in-house training per employee	+

*Explained later in this chapter.
†Value-added is revenue less externally purchased materials, supplies, and services.

consist of items the individual can personally influence that relate directly to the performance measures on the overall balanced scorecard. The performance measures on this personal scorecard should not be overly influenced by actions taken by others in the company or by events that are outside of the individual's control. And, focusing on the performance measure should not lead an individual to take actions that are counter to the organization's objectives.

With those broad principles in mind, we will now take a look at how a company's strategy affects its balanced scorecard.

IN BUSINESS

LOSING SIGHT OF THE CUSTOMER

Understanding customer needs sounds simple enough, but it is surprising how often companies lose sight of what their customers want. For example, Waste Management, one of the largest trash haulers in the United States, assumed that its customers were most interested in receiving low prices. However, when the company actually surveyed its customers, it found out that they were more concerned about billing errors and missed garbage pickups. Waste Management responded to this feedback by upgrading its billing program—as a result customers are paying their bills in an average of 47 days instead of 71. Not only are customers happier with fewer billing errors, but shaving 24 days off the accounts receivable collection cycle is worth $30 million per day to the company!

Waste Management also addressed the issue of missed garbage pickups by initiating a program called Haul or Call. When a garbage truck driver sees an impediment blocking a garbage bin, his home office calls the customer to see when they can reschedule a pickup. Customers have been so impressed with this level of service that their defection rate has dropped from 12% to 8.6% in less than one year.

Waste Management has found that the key to improving bottom-line results is gathering information from its customers about the underlying drivers of financial performance.

Source: Julie Creswell, "Scandal Hits—Now What?" *Fortune*, July 7, 2003, pp. 127–130.

IN BUSINESS

IN DENIAL

Larry Bossidy, the long-time CEO of Allied Signal, reports that "When I took over at Allied Signal . . . I got two different pictures from our people and our customers. While our people were saying that we were delivering an order-fill rate of 98%, our customers thought we were at 60%. The irony was, instead of trying to address the customers' complaints, we seemed to think we had to show that we were right and they were wrong." Note the two messages contained in this short quotation. First, make sure you measure the right thing. Apparently, the internal measure of order-fill rates that had been used at Allied Signal was deficient—it did not capture customer perceptions, which are of paramount importance. Second, if customers are unhappy, don't tell them they are wrong. Try to figure out why they are unhappy.

Source: Larry Bossidy and Ram Charan, "How Did Honeywell Chairman Larry Bossidy Turn the Company Around? By His Maniacal Focus on Just One Thing: Execution," *Fortune*, June 10, 2002, pp. 149–152.

A Company's Strategy and the Balanced Scorecard

Returning to the performance measures in Exhibit 9–10, each company must decide which customers to target and what internal business processes are crucial to attracting and retaining those customers. Different companies, having different strategies, will target different customers with different kinds of products and services. Take the automobile industry as an example. BMW stresses engineering and handling; Volvo, safety; Jaguar, luxury detailing; Corvette, racy styling; and Toyota, reliability. Because of these differences in emphases, a one-size-fits-all approach to performance measurement won't work even within this one industry. Performance measures must be tailored to the specific strategy of each company.

Suppose, for example, that Jaguar's strategy is to offer distinctive, richly finished luxury automobiles to wealthy individuals who prize handcrafted, individualized products. To deliver this customer intimacy value proposition to its wealthy target customers, Jaguar might create such a large number of options for details, such as leather seats, interior and exterior color combinations, and wooden dashboards, that each car becomes virtually one of a kind. For example, instead of just offering tan or blue leather seats in standard cowhide, the company may offer customers the choice of an almost infinite palette of colors in any of a number of different exotic leathers. For such a system to work effectively, Jaguar would have to be able to deliver a completely customized car within a reasonable amount of time—and without incurring more cost for this customization than the customer is willing to pay. Exhibit 9–12 suggests how Jaguar might reflect this strategy in its balanced scorecard.

If the balanced scorecard is correctly constructed, the performance measures should be linked together on a cause-and-effect basis. Each link can then be read as a hypothesis in the form "If we improve this performance measure, then this other performance measure should also improve." Starting from the bottom of Exhibit 9–12, we can read the links between performance measures as follows. If employees acquire the skills to install new options more effectively, then the company can offer more options and the options can be installed in less time. If more options are available and they are installed in less time, then customer surveys should show greater satisfaction with the range of options available. If customer satisfaction improves, then the number of cars sold should increase. In addition, if customer satisfaction improves, the company should be able to maintain or increase its selling prices, and if the time to install options decreases, the costs of installing the options should decrease. Together, this should result in an increase in the contribution margin

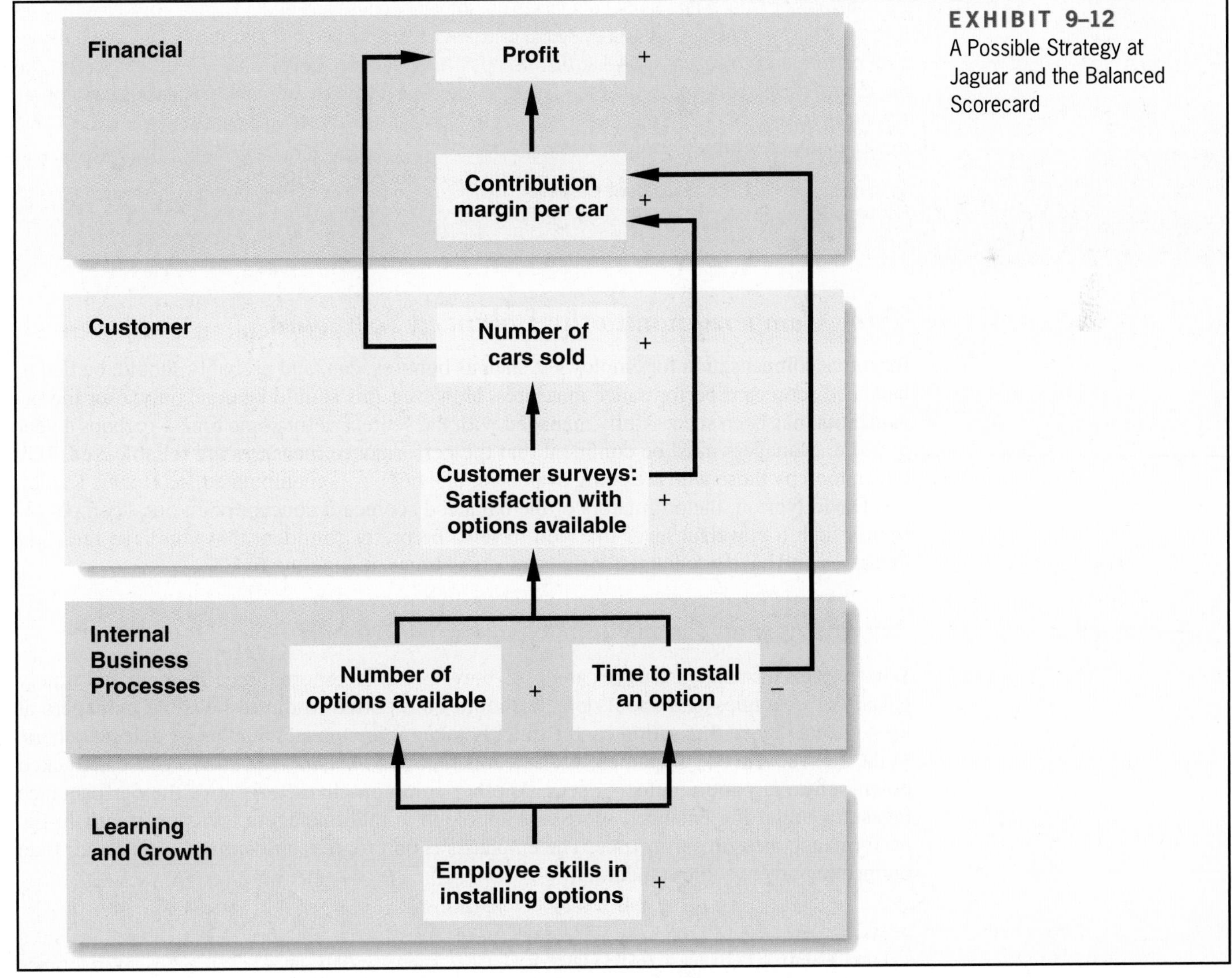

EXHIBIT 9–12
A Possible Strategy at Jaguar and the Balanced Scorecard

per car. If the contribution margin per car increases and more cars are sold, the result should be an increase in profits.

In essence, the balanced scorecard lays out a theory of how the company can take concrete actions to attain its desired outcomes (financial, in this case). While the strategy laid out in Exhibit 9–12 seems plausible, it should be regarded as only a theory. For example, if the company succeeds in increasing the number of options available and in decreasing the time required to install options and yet there is no increase in customer satisfaction, the number of cars sold, the contribution margin per car, or profits, the strategy would have to be reconsidered. One of the advantages of the balanced scorecard is that it continually tests the theories underlying management's strategy. If a strategy is not working, it should become evident when some of the predicted effects (i.e., more car sales) don't occur. Without this feedback, the organization may drift on indefinitely with an ineffective strategy based on faulty assumptions.

IN BUSINESS

CAUSE-AND-EFFECT IS THE KEY

Professors Christopher D. Ittner and David F. Larcker surveyed 157 companies and found that only 23% consistently verified the hypothesized cause-and-effect linkages embedded in their balanced scorecards. These companies earned a 5.14% higher return on common stockholders' equity than the 77% of companies that did not verify their cause-and-effect linkages.

The authors found that most companies do not verify cause-and-effect linkages because they erroneously believe that they are self-evident. For example, one fast-food chain chose employee turnover as a performance measure believing that its positive effects on profits were obvious. However, the professors' research revealed that the fast-food chain's profitability was only influenced by turnover among its supervisors, not lower-level employees. A broad measure of employee turnover did not help explain differences in profitability across restaurants.

Source: Christopher D. Ittner and David F. Larcker, "Coming Up Short on Nonfinancial Performance Measurement," *Harvard Business Review,* November 2003, pp. 88–95.

Tying Compensation to the Balanced Scorecard

Incentive compensation for employees, such as bonuses, can, and probably should, be tied to balanced scorecard performance measures. However, this should be done only after the organization has been successfully managed with the scorecard for some time—perhaps a year or more. Managers must be confident that the performance measures are reliable, sensible, understood by those who are being evaluated, and not easily manipulated. As Robert Kaplan and David Norton, the originators of the balanced scorecard concept point out, "compensation is such a powerful lever that you have to be pretty confident that you have the right measures and have good data for the measures before making the link."[5]

Advantages of Timely and Graphic Feedback

Whatever performance measures are used, they should be reported on a frequent and timely basis. For example, data about defects should be reported to the responsible managers at least once a day so that action can be quickly taken if an unusual number of defects occurs. In the most advanced companies, any defect is reported *immediately,* and its cause is tracked down before any more defects occur. Another common characteristic of the performance measures under the balanced scorecard approach is that managers focus on *trends* in the performance measures over time. The emphasis is on progress and *improvement* rather than on meeting any specific standard.

---

[5] Lori Calabro, "On Balance: A CFO Interview," *CFO,* February 2001, pp. 73–78.

For tracking trends and improvement over time, graphic displays are often far more informative than rows or columns of numbers. Consider, for example, the problem of passengers who reserve seats but do not show up to buy their tickets. Because of these "no-show" passengers, airlines routinely overbook popular flights. The airlines gamble that the number of overbooked passengers will be offset by the number of no-shows. Sometimes airlines lose this gamble. This results in the airline incurring substantial additional costs to either pay passengers to relinquish their reservations or to house and feed excess passengers until suitable replacement flights can be found. Because of these costs (and the ill will created among passengers), airlines carefully monitor the percentage of overbooked seats that actually turn out to be a problem and result in a passenger being bumped from a flight. Suppose, for example, that an airline has recorded the following data over the last 20 weeks:

Bumped passengers per hundred overbooked seats		Bumped passengers per hundred overbooked seats	
Week 1	7.1	Week 11	6.4
Week 2	6.5	Week 12	6.3
Week 3	6.7	Week 13	6.7
Week 4	7.2	Week 14	5.8
Week 5	7.0	Week 15	6.6
Week 6	7.3	Week 16	6.6
Week 7	6.7	Week 17	6.9
Week 8	6.5	Week 18	7.1
Week 9	6.2	Week 19	7.4
Week 10	5.8	Week 20	7.8

These data are plotted in Exhibit 9–13. Note how much easier it is to spot trends and unusual points when the data are plotted than when they are displayed in the form of a table. In particular, the worrisome increase in bumped passengers over the final seven weeks is very evident in the plotted data.

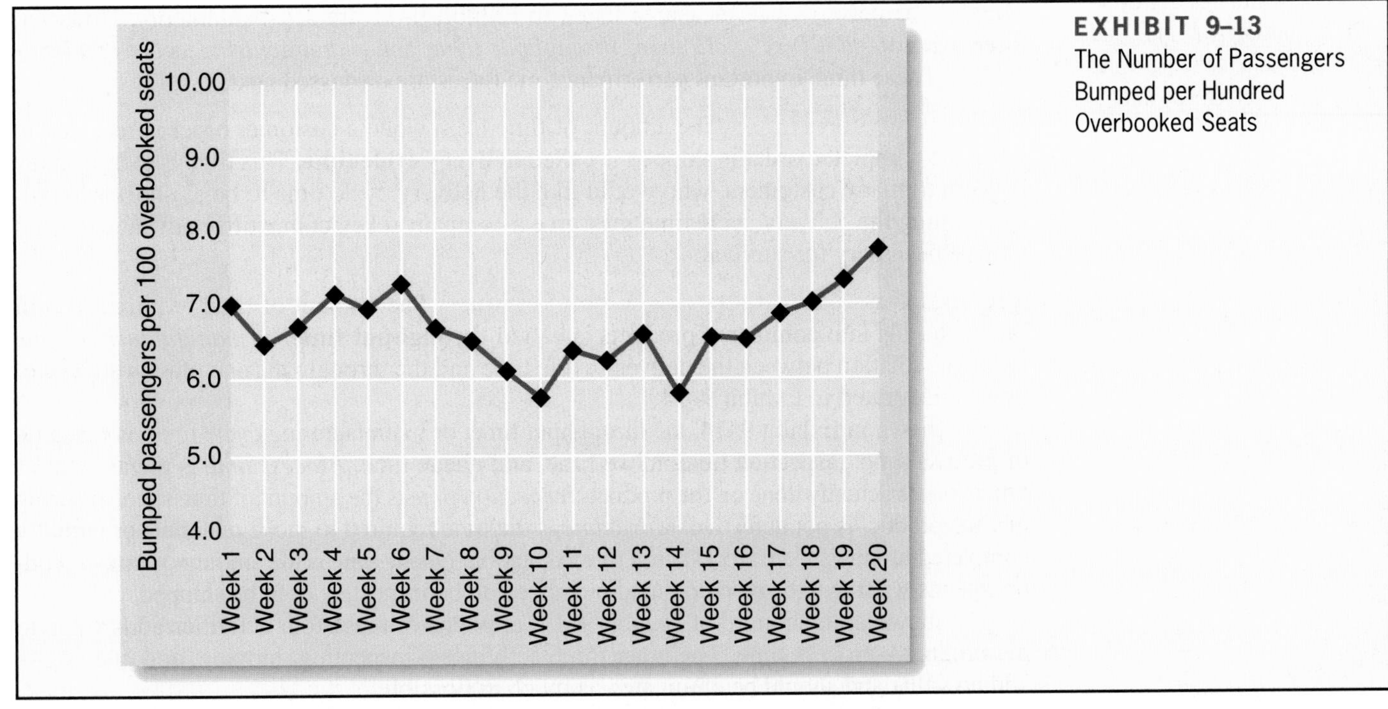

EXHIBIT 9–13
The Number of Passengers Bumped per Hundred Overbooked Seats

IN BUSINESS

A PICTURE IS WORTH A THOUSAND NUMBERS

Graphics are routinely integrated in Balanced Scorecard reports, with data often displayed on a "dashboard" with representations of gauges and digital readouts. At Beverage Can Americas Co. in Chicago, a division of London-based Rexam Plc., executive dashboards and scorecards are being rolled out to thousands of employees. "Each worker sees a handful of metrics that pertain to his or her job, which are represented as green, yellow, or red icons depending on whether they are satisfactory, borderline, or subpar."

Source: Scott Leibs, "Now You See It," *CFO*, July 2002, pp. 61–66.

IN BUSINESS

CORPORATE GOVERNANCE AND THE BALANCED SCORECARD

Historically, the board of directors of First Commonwealth Financial Corporation of Pennsylvania had only been given access to financial measures that were required for regulatory purposes. In the aftermath of corporate scandals such as Enron, Tyco, and WorldCom, the board decided to improve its oversight of the corporation by creating a balanced scorecard that not only helped ensure regulatory compliance but that also included forward-looking information about the company's strategy execution.

The board's scorecard had four main perspectives—learning and growth, internal, stakeholder, and financial. The internal perspective included three main processes—performance oversight, executive enhancement, and compliance and communication. For performance oversight, the board created measures related to approving strategies and overseeing execution and approving and monitoring funding for strategic initiatives. The executive enhancement measures focused on evaluating and rewarding executive performance and overseeing succession planning for key positions. The compliance and communication measures related to ensuring clear and reliable corporate disclosures and actively monitoring risk and regulatory compliance.

Source: Robert S. Kaplan and Michael Nagel, "First Commonwealth Financial Corporation," *Harvard Business School Publishing*, 2003, pp. 1–30.

LEARNING OBJECTIVE 6
Compute delivery cycle time, throughput time, and manufacturing cycle efficiency (MCE).

Some Measures of Internal Business Process Performance

Most of the performance measures listed in Exhibit 9–11 are self-explanatory. However, three are not—*delivery cycle time, throughput time,* and *manufacturing cycle efficiency (MCE).* These three important performance measures are discussed next.

Delivery Cycle Time The amount of time from when a customer order is received to when the completed order is shipped is called **delivery cycle time.** This time is clearly a key concern to many customers, who would like the delivery cycle time to be as short as possible. Cutting the delivery cycle time may give a company a key competitive advantage—and may be necessary for survival.

Throughput (Manufacturing Cycle) Time The amount of time required to turn raw materials into completed products is called **throughput time,** or *manufacturing cycle time.* The relation between the delivery cycle time and the throughput (manufacturing cycle) time is illustrated in Exhibit 9–14.

As shown in Exhibit 9–14, the throughput time, or manufacturing cycle time, is made up of process time, inspection time, move time, and queue time. *Process time* is the amount of time work is actually done on the product. *Inspection time* is the amount of time spent ensuring that the product is not defective. *Move time* is the time required to move materials or partially completed products from workstation to workstation. *Queue time* is the amount of time a product spends waiting to be worked on, to be moved, to be inspected, or to be shipped.

As shown at the bottom of Exhibit 9–14, only one of these four activities adds value to the product—process time. The other three activities—inspecting, moving, and queuing—add no value and should be eliminated as much as possible.

EXHIBIT 9–14
Delivery Cycle Time and Throughput (Manufacturing Cycle) Time

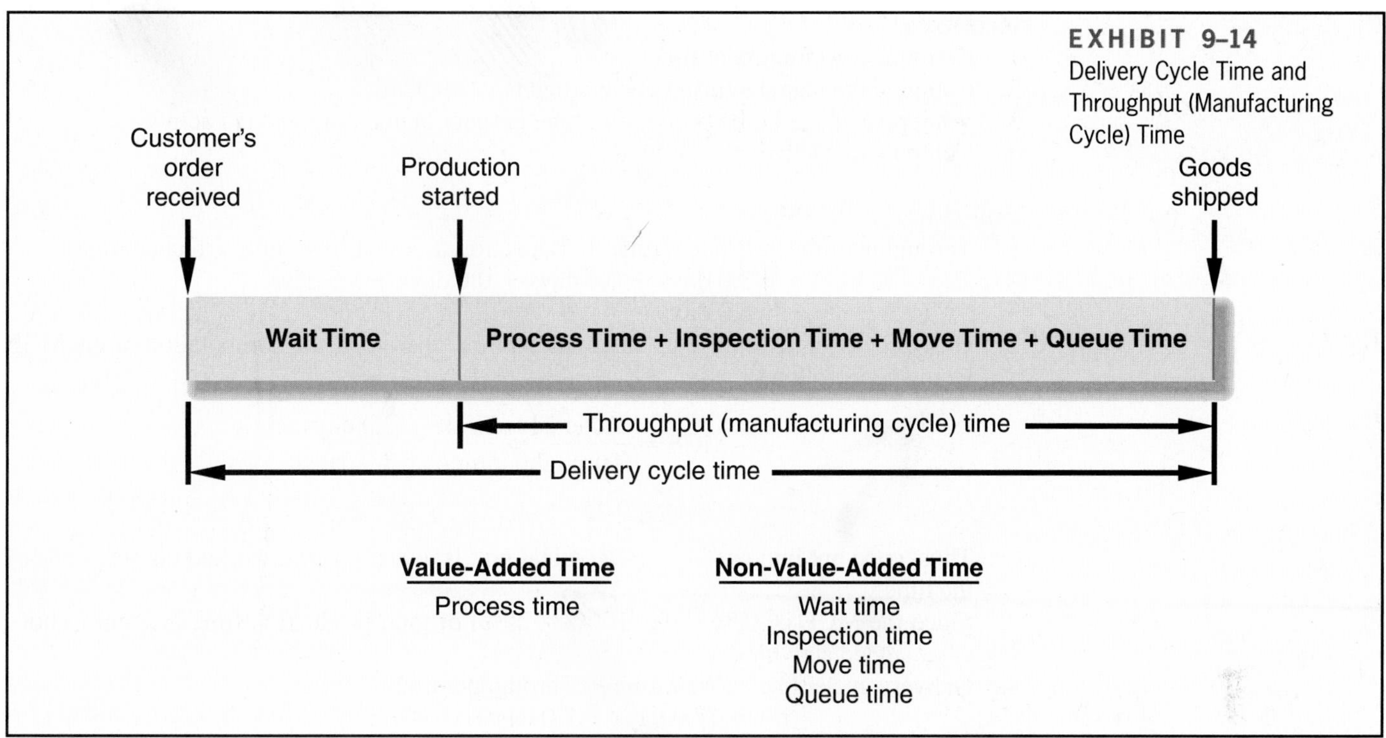

Manufacturing Cycle Efficiency (MCE) Through concerted efforts to eliminate the *non-value-added* activities of inspecting, moving, and queuing, some companies have reduced their throughput time to only a fraction of previous levels. In turn, this has helped to reduce the delivery cycle time from months to only weeks or hours. Throughput time, which is considered to be a key measure in delivery performance, can be put into better perspective by computing the **manufacturing cycle efficiency (MCE).** The MCE is computed by relating the value-added time to the throughput time. The formula is:

$$\text{MCE} = \frac{\text{Value-added time (Process time)}}{\text{Throughput (manufacturing cycle) time}}$$

Any non-value-added time results in an MCE of less than 1. An MCE of 0.5, for example, would mean that half of the total production time consists of inspection, moving, and similar non-value-added activities. In many manufacturing companies, the MCE is less than 0.1 (10%), which means that 90% of the time a unit is in process is spent on activities that do not add value to the product. Monitoring the MCE helps companies to reduce non-value-added activities and thus get products into the hands of customers more quickly and at a lower cost.

Example To provide an example of these measures, consider the following data for Novex Company:

Novex Company keeps careful track of the time to complete customer orders. During the most recent quarter, the following average times were recorded for each unit or order:

	Days
Wait time	17.0
Inspection time	0.4
Process time	2.0
Move time	0.6
Queue time	5.0

Goods are shipped as soon as production is completed.

Required:

1. Compute the throughput time.
2. Compute the manufacturing cycle efficiency (MCE).
3. What percentage of the production time is spent in non-value-added activities?
4. Compute the delivery cycle time.

Solution

1. Throughput time = Process time + Inspection time + Move time + Queue time
   = 2.0 days + 0.4 days + 0.6 days + 5.0 days
   = 8.0 days
2. Only process time represents value-added time; therefore, the computation of the MCE would be as follows:

$$\text{MCE} = \frac{\text{Value-added time}}{\text{Throughput time}} = \frac{2.0 \text{ days}}{8.0 \text{ days}}$$
$$= 0.25$$

   Thus, once put into production, a typical unit is actually being worked on only 25% of the time.
3. Since the MCE is 25%, 75% (100% – 25%) of total production time is spent in non-value-added activities.
4. Delivery cycle time = Wait time + Throughput time
   = 17.0 days + 8.0 days
   = 25.0 days

Some Final Observations Concerning the Balanced Scorecard We would like to emphasize a few points concerning the balanced scorecard. First, the balanced scorecard should be tailored to the company's strategy; each company's balanced scorecard should be unique. The examples given in this chapter are just that—examples. They should not be interpreted as general templates to be fitted to each company. Second, the balanced scorecard reflects a particular strategy, or theory, about how a company can further its objectives by taking specific actions. The theory should be viewed as tentative and subject to change if the actions do not in fact result in improvements in the company's financial and other goals. If the theory (i.e., strategy) changes, then the performance measures on the balanced scorecard should also change. The balanced scorecard should be viewed as a dynamic system that evolves as the company's strategy evolves.

IN BUSINESS

DELIVERY CYCLE TIMES IN THE DARK AGES

Have you ever ordered a new magazine and counted how many days it took for the first issue to arrive? Chances are that your delivery cycle time was somewhere between four to six weeks—a glacial pace in today's Internet environment. One of the root causes of the problem is fragmented organizational structures where circulation, fulfillment, production, manufacturing, and distribution focus on their departmental agendas instead of the customer. Most circulation directors agree that removing non-value-added time from the process of responding to customer orders would certainly have its benefits. For example, customers who receive their first issue of the magazine sooner are likely to pay their bill sooner. Furthermore, they are less likely to cancel their subscription or issue complaints that are costly to resolve.

One way to reduce the problem is for publishers to mail the first issue to customers using first class mail rather than periodical mail. This would shave six to seven days off of their delivery cycle time, but it would also cost an extra 80 to 90 cents for each first issue mailed. Do you think the time saved is worth the money spent?

Source: William B. Dugan, "Thanks for Ordering our Magazine . . . Now Don't Expect to See It for Five Weeks," *Circulation Management*, May 1, 2004, pp. 24–29.

Summary

A standard is a benchmark or "norm" for measuring performance. Standards are set for both the cost and the quantity of inputs needed to manufacture goods or to provide services. Quantity standards indicate how much of an input, such as labor time or raw materials, should be used to make a product or provide a service. Cost standards indicate what the cost of the input should be.

Standards are normally set so that they can be attained by reasonable, though highly efficient, efforts. Such "practical" standards are believed to positively motivate employees.

When standards are compared to actual performance, the difference is referred to as a *variance.* Variances are computed and reported to management on a regular basis for both the price and the quantity elements of direct materials, direct labor, and overhead. Price variances are computed by taking the difference between actual and standard prices and multiplying the result by the amount of input purchased. Quantity variances are computed by taking the difference between the actual amount of the input used and the amount of input that is allowed for the actual output, and then multiplying the result by the standard price of the input.

Not all variances require management time or attention. Only unusual or particularly significant variances should be investigated—otherwise a great deal of time would be spent investigating unimportant matters. Additionally, it should be emphasized that the point of the investigation should not be to find someone to blame. The point of the investigation is to pinpoint the problem so that it can be fixed and operations improved.

Traditional standard cost variance reports are often supplemented with other performance measures. Overemphasis on standard cost variances may lead to problems in other critical areas such as product quality, inventory levels, and on-time delivery.

A balanced scorecard consists of an integrated system of performance measures that are derived from and support the company's strategy. Different companies will have different balanced scorecards because they have different strategies. A well-constructed balanced scorecard provides a means for guiding the company and also provides feedback concerning the effectiveness of the company's strategy.

Review Problem: Standard Costs

Xavier Company produces a single product. Variable manufacturing overhead is applied to products on the basis of direct labor-hours. The standard costs for one unit of product are as follows:

Direct material: 6 ounces at $0.50 per ounce	$3
Direct labor: 1.8 hours at $10 per hour	18
Variable manufacturing overhead: 1.8 hours at $5 per hour	9
Total standard variable cost per unit	$30

During June, 2,000 units were produced. The costs associated with June's operations were as follows:

Material purchased: 18,000 ounces at $0.60 per ounce	$10,800
Material used in production: 14,000 ounces	—
Direct labor: 4,000 hours at $9.75 per hour	$39,000
Variable manufacturing overhead costs incurred	$20,800

Required:

Compute the direct materials, direct labor, and variable manufacturing overhead variances.

Solution to the Review Problem

Direct Materials Variances

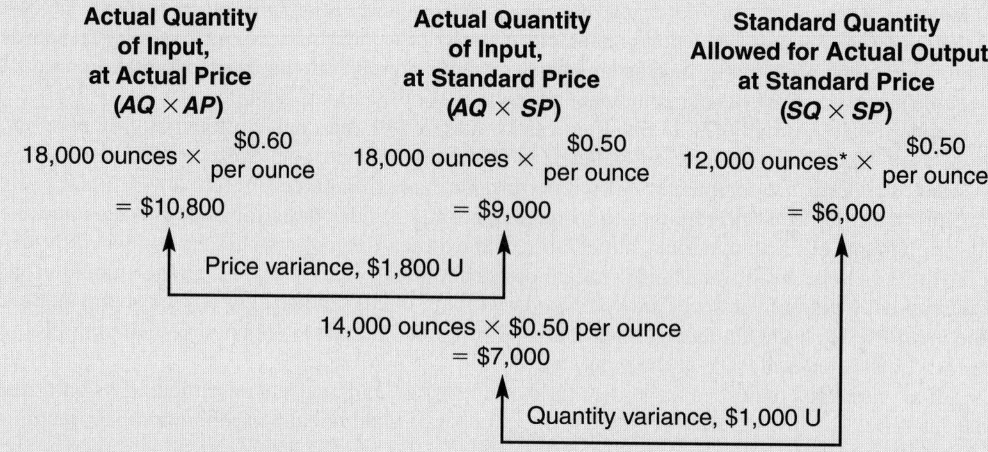

*2,000 units × 6 ounces per unit = 12,000 ounces.

Using the formulas in the chapter, the same variances would be computed as follows:

Materials price variance = $AQ(AP - SP)$

18,000 ounces ($0.60 per ounce − $0.50 per ounce) = $1,800 U

Materials quantity variance = $SP(AQ - SQ)$

$0.50 per ounce (14,000 ounces − 12,000 ounces) = $1,000 U

Direct Labor Variances

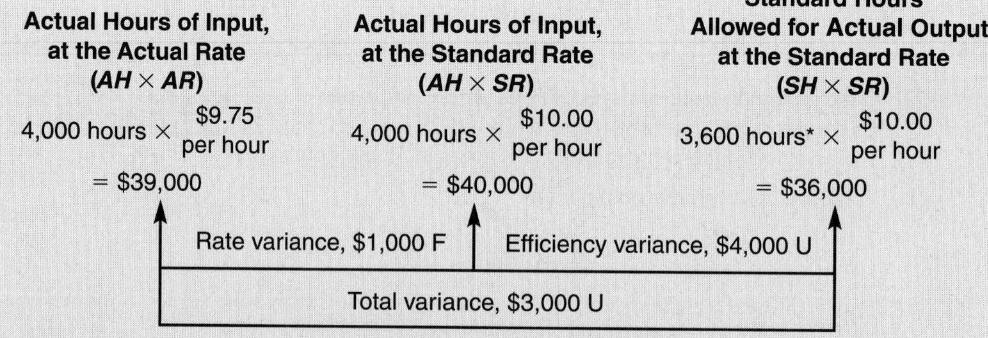

*2,000 units × 1.8 hours per unit = 3,600 hours.

Using the formulas in the chapter, the same variances would be computed as:

Labor rate variance = $AH(AR - SR)$

4,000 hours ($9.75 per hour − $10.00 per hour) = $1,000 F

Labor efficiency variance = $SR(AH - SH)$

$10.00 per hour (4,000 hours − 3,600 hours) = $4,000 U

Variable Manufacturing Overhead Variances

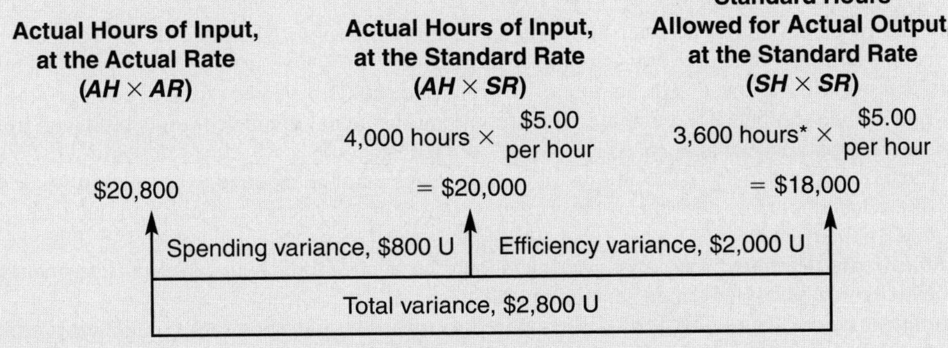

*2,000 units × 1.8 hours per unit = 3,600 hours.

Using the formulas in the chapter, the same variances would be computed as follows:

$$\text{Variable overhead spending variance} = AH(AR - SR)$$

$$\text{4,000 hours (\$5.20 per hour* } - \text{ \$5.00 per hour)} = \text{\$800 U}$$

*$20,800 ÷ 4,000 hours = $5.20 per hour.

$$\text{Variable overhead efficiency variance} = SR(AH - SH)$$

$$\text{\$5.00 per hour (4,000 hours} - \text{3,600 hours)} = \text{\$2,000 U}$$

Glossary

Balanced scorecard An integrated set of performance measures that are derived from and support the organization's strategy. (p. 364)

Delivery cycle time The elapsed time from receipt of a customer order to when the completed goods are shipped to the customer. (p. 372)

Ideal standards Standards that assume peak efficiency at all times. (p. 347)

Labor efficiency variance The difference between the actual hours taken to complete a task and the standard hours allowed for the actual output, multiplied by the standard hourly labor rate. (p. 358)

Labor rate variance The difference between the actual hourly labor rate and the standard rate, multiplied by the number of hours worked during the period. (p. 357)

Management by exception A management system in which standards are set for various activities, with actual results compared to these standards. Significant deviations from standards are flagged as exceptions. (p. 345)

Manufacturing cycle efficiency (MCE) Process (value-added) time as a percentage of throughput time. (p. 372)

Materials price variance The difference between the actual unit price paid for an item and the standard price, multiplied by the quantity purchased. (p. 354)

Materials quantity variance The difference between the actual quantity of materials used in production and the standard quantity allowed for the actual output, multiplied by the standard price per unit of materials. (p. 355)

Practical standards Standards that allow for normal machine downtime and other work interruptions and that can be attained through reasonable, though highly efficient, efforts by the average worker. (p. 347)

Standard cost card A detailed listing of the standard amounts of inputs and their costs that are required to produce a unit of a specific product. (p. 347)

Standard cost per unit The standard quantity allowed of an input per unit of a specific product, multiplied by the standard price of the input. (p. 350)

Standard hours allowed The time that should have been taken to complete the period's output. It is computed by multiplying the actual number of units produced by the standard hours per unit. (p. 351)

Standard hours per unit The amount of direct labor time that should be required to complete a single unit of product, including allowances for breaks, machine downtime, cleanup, rejects, and other normal inefficiencies. (p. 349)

Standard price per unit The price that should be paid for an input. The price should be net of discounts and should include any shipping costs. (p. 348)

Standard quantity allowed The amount of an input that should have been used to complete the period's actual output. It is computed by multiplying the actual number of units produced by the standard quantity per unit. (p. 351)

Standard quantity per unit The amount of an input that should be required to complete a single unit of product, including allowances for normal waste, spoilage, rejects, and other normal inefficiencies. (p. 348)

Standard rate per hour The labor rate that should be incurred per hour of labor time, including employment taxes and fringe benefits. (p. 349)

Throughput time The amount of time required to turn raw materials into completed products. (p. 372)

Variable overhead efficiency variance The difference between the actual level of activity (direct labor-hours, machine-hours, or some other base) and the standard activity allowed, multiplied by the variable part of the predetermined overhead rate. (p. 360)

Variable overhead spending variance The difference between the actual variable overhead cost incurred during a period and the standard cost that should have been incurred based on the actual activity of the period. (p. 360)

Variances The differences between standard prices and actual prices and between standard quantities and actual quantities. (p. 351)

Quiz 9

Multiple-choice questions are provided on the text Web site at www.mhhe.com/noreen1e.

Questions

9-1 What is a quantity standard? What is a price standard?

9-2 Distinguish between ideal and practical standards.

9-3 If employees are chronically unable to meet a standard, what effect would you expect this to have on their productivity?

9-4 What is the difference between a standard and a budget?

9-5 What is meant by the term *variance?*

9-6 What is meant by the term *management by exception?*

9-7 Why are separate price and quantity variances computed?

9-8 Who is generally responsible for the materials price variance? The materials quantity variance? The labor efficiency variance?

9-9 The materials price variance can be computed at what two different points in time? Which point is better? Why?

9-10 If the materials price variance is favorable but the materials quantity variance is unfavorable, what might this indicate?

9-11 Should standards be used to identify who to blame for problems?

9-12 "Our workers are all under labor contracts; therefore, our labor rate variance is bound to be zero." Discuss.

9-13 What effect, if any, would you expect poor-quality materials to have on direct labor variances?

9-14 If variable manufacturing overhead is applied to production on the basis of direct labor-hours and the direct labor efficiency variance is unfavorable, will the variable overhead efficiency variance be favorable or unfavorable, or could it be either? Explain.

9-15 What is a statistical control chart, and how is it used?

9-16 Why can undue emphasis on labor efficiency variances lead to excess work in process inventories?

9-17 Why do the measures used in a balanced scorecard differ from company to company?

9-18 Why does the balanced scorecard include financial performance measures as well as measures of how well internal business processes are doing?

9-19 What is the difference between delivery cycle time and throughput time? What four elements make up throughput time? Into what two classes can these four elements be placed?

9-20 If a company has a manufacturing cycle efficiency (MCE) of less than 1, what does it mean? How would you interpret an MCE of 0.40?

Exercises

EXERCISE 9-1 Setting Standards; Preparing a Standard Cost Card [LO1]

Svenska Pharmicia, a Swedish pharmaceutical company, makes an anticoagulant drug. The main ingredient in the drug is a raw material called Alpha SR40. Information concerning the purchase and use of Alpha SR40 follows:

Purchase of Alpha SR40: The raw material Alpha SR40 is purchased in 2-kilogram containers at a cost of 3,000 Kr per kilogram. (The Swedish currency is the krona, which is abbreviated as Kr.) A discount of 2% is offered by the supplier for payment within 10 days and Svenska Pharmicia takes all discounts. Shipping costs, which Svenska Pharmicia must pay, amount to 1,000 Kr for an average shipment of ten 2-kilogram containers.

Use of Alpha SR40: The bill of materials calls for 6 grams of Alpha SR40 per capsule of the anticoagulant drug. (A kilogram equals 1,000 grams.) About 4% of all Alpha SR40 purchased is rejected as unsuitable before being used to make the anticoagulant drug. In addition, after the addition of Alpha SR40, about 1 out of every 26 capsules is rejected at final inspection, due to defects of one sort or another in the capsule.

Required:

1. Compute the standard purchase price for one gram of Alpha SR40.
2. Compute the standard quantity of Alpha SR40 (in grams) per capsule that passes final inspection. (Carry computations to two decimal places.)
3. Using the data from (1) and (2) above, prepare a standard cost card showing the standard cost of Alpha SR40 per capsule of the anticoagulant drug.

EXERCISE 9-2 Material Variances [LO2]

Harmon Household Products, Inc., manufactures a number of consumer items for general household use. One of these products, a chopping board, requires an expensive hardwood. During a recent month, the company manufactured 4,000 chopping boards using 11,000 board feet of hardwood. The hardwood cost the company $18,700.

The company's standards for one chopping board are 2.5 board feet of hardwood, at a cost of $1.80 per board foot.

Required:

1. What cost for wood should have been incurred to make 4,000 chopping blocks? How much greater or less is this than the cost that was incurred?
2. Break down the difference computed in (1) above into a materials price variance and a materials quantity variance.

EXERCISE 9-3 Direct Labor Variances [LO3]

AirMeals, Inc., prepares in-flight meals for a number of major airlines. One of the company's products is stuffed cannelloni with roasted pepper sauce, fresh baby corn, and spring salad. During the most recent week, the company prepared 6,000 of these meals using 1,150 direct labor-hours. The company paid these direct labor workers a total of $11,500 for this work, or $10 per hour.

According to the standard cost card for this meal, it should require 0.20 direct labor-hours at a cost of $9.50 per hour.

Required:

1. What direct labor cost should have been incurred to prepare 6,000 meals? How much does this differ from the actual direct labor cost?
2. Break down the difference computed in (1) above into a labor rate variance and a labor efficiency variance.

EXERCISE 9-4 Variable Overhead Variances [LO4]

Order Up, Inc., provides order fulfillment services for dot.com merchants. The company maintains warehouses that stock items carried by its dot.com clients. When a client receives an order from a customer, the order is forwarded to Order Up, which pulls the item from storage, packs it, and ships it to the customer. The company uses a predetermined variable overhead rate based on direct labor-hours.

In the most recent month, 140,000 items were shipped to customers using 5,800 direct labor-hours. The company incurred a total of $15,950 in variable overhead costs.

According to the company's standards, 0.04 direct labor-hours are required to fulfill an order for one item and the variable overhead rate is $2.80 per direct labor-hour.

Required:

1. What variable overhead cost should have been incurred to fill the orders for the 140,000 items? How much does this differ from the actual variable overhead cost?
2. Break down the difference computed in (1) above into a variable overhead spending variance and a variable overhead efficiency variance.

EXERCISE 9-5 Creating a Balanced Scorecard [LO5]

Mason Paper Company (MPC) manufactures commodity grade papers for use in computer printers and photocopiers. MPC has reported net operating losses for the last two years due to intense price pressure from much larger competitors. The MPC management team—including Kristen Townsend (CEO), Mike Martinez (vice president of Manufacturing), Tom Andrews (vice president of Marketing), and Wendy Chen (CFO)—is contemplating a change in strategy to save the company from impending bankruptcy. Excerpts from a recent management team meeting are shown below:

Townsend: As we all know, the commodity paper manufacturing business is all about economies of scale. The largest competitors with the lowest cost per unit win. The limited capacity of our older machines prohibits us from competing in the high-volume commodity paper grades. Furthermore, expanding our capacity by acquiring a new paper-making machine is out of the question given the extraordinarily high price tag. Therefore, I propose that we abandon cost reduction as a strategic goal and instead pursue manufacturing flexibility as the key to our future success.

Chen: Manufacturing flexibility? What does that mean?

Martinez: It means we have to abandon our "crank out as many tons of paper as possible" mentality. Instead, we need to pursue the low-volume business opportunities that exist in the nonstandard, specialized paper grades. To succeed in this regard, we'll need to improve our flexibility in three ways. First, we must improve our ability to switch between paper grades. Right now, we require an average of four hours to change over to another paper grade. Timely customer deliveries are a function of changeover performance. Second, we need to expand the range of paper grades that we can manufacture. Currently, we can only manufacture three paper grades. Our customers must perceive that we are a "one-stop shop" that can meet all of their paper grade needs. Third, we will need to improve our yields (e.g., tons of acceptable output relative to total tons processed) in the nonstandard paper grades. Our percentage of waste within these grades will be unacceptably high unless we do something to improve our processes. Our variable costs will go through the roof if we cannot increase our yields!

Chen: Wait just a minute! These changes are going to destroy our equipment utilization numbers!

Andrews: You're right Wendy; however, equipment utilization is not the name of the game when it comes to competing in terms of flexibility. Our customers don't care about our equipment utilization. Instead, as Mike just alluded to, they want just-in-time delivery of smaller quantities of a full range of paper grades. If we can shrink the elapsed time from order placement to order delivery and expand our product offerings, it will increase sales from current customers and bring in new customers. Furthermore, we will be able to charge a premium price because of the limited competition within this niche from our cost-focused larger competitors. Our contribution margin per ton should drastically improve!

Martinez: Of course, executing the change in strategy will not be easy. We'll need to make a substantial investment in training because ultimately it is our people who create our flexible manufacturing capabilities.

Chen: If we adopt this new strategy, it is definitely going to impact how we measure performance. We'll need to create measures that motivate our employees to make decisions that support our flexibility goals.

Townsend: Wendy, you hit the nail right on the head. For our next meeting, could you pull together some potential measures that support our new strategy?

Required:

1. Contrast MPC's previous manufacturing strategy with its new manufacturing strategy.
2. Generally speaking, why would a company that changes its strategic goals need to change its performance measurement system as well? What are some examples of measures that would have been appropriate for MPC prior to its change in strategy? Why would those measures fail to support MPC's new strategy?
3. Using Exhibit 9–12 as a guide, construct a balanced scorecard that would support MPC's new manufacturing strategy. Use arrows to show the causal links between the performance measures and show whether the performance measure should increase or decrease over time. Feel free to create measures that may not be specifically mentioned in the chapter, but nonetheless make sense given the strategic goals of the company.
4. What hypotheses are built into MPC's balanced scorecard? Which of these hypotheses do you believe are most questionable and why?

EXERCISE 9-6 Measures of Internal Business Process Performance [LO6]
Lipex, Ltd., of Birmingham, England, is interested in cutting the amount of time between when a customer places an order and when the order is completed. For the first quarter of the year, the following data were reported:

Inspection time	0.5 days
Process time	2.8 days
Wait time	16.0 days
Queue time	4.0 days
Move time	0.7 days

Required:
1. Compute the throughput time.
2. Compute the manufacturing cycle efficiency (MCE) for the quarter.
3. What percentage of the throughput time was spent in non-value-added activities?
4. Compute the delivery cycle time.
5. If by using Lean Production all queue time can be eliminated in production, what will be the new MCE?

EXERCISE 9-7 Setting Standards (LO1)
Czar Nicholas Chocolatier, Ltd., makes premium handcrafted chocolate confections in London. The owner of the company is setting up a standard cost system and has collected the following data for one of the company's products, the Imperial Truffle. This product is made with the finest white chocolate and various fillings. The data below pertain only to the white chocolate used in the product. (The currency in the United Kingdom is the pound, which is denoted by £.):

Material requirements, kilograms of white chocolate per dozen truffles	0.80 kilograms
Allowance for waste, kilograms of white chocolate per dozen truffles.	0.02 kilograms
Allowance for rejects, kilograms of white chocolate per dozen truffles	0.03 kilograms
Purchase price, finest grade white chocolate	£9.00 per kilogram
Purchase discount	5% of purchase price
Shipping cost from the supplier in Belgium	£0.20 per kilogram
Receiving and handling cost	£0.05 per kilogram

Required:
1. Determine the standard price of a kilogram of white chocolate.
2. Determine the standard quantity of white chocolate for a dozen truffles.
3. Determine the standard cost of the white chocolate in a dozen truffles.

EXERCISE 9-8 Material and Labor Variances [LO2, LO3]
Topper Toys has developed a new toy called the Brainbuster. The company has a standard cost system to help control costs and has established the following standards for the Brainbuster toy:

Direct materials: 8 diodes per toy at $0.30 per diode
Direct labor: 1.2 hours per toy at $7 per hour

During August, the company produced 5,000 Brainbuster toys. Production data on the toy for August follow:

Direct materials: 70,000 diodes were purchased at a cost of $0.28 per diode. 20,000 of these diodes were still in inventory at the end of the month.
Direct labor: 6,400 direct labor-hours were worked at a cost of $48,000.

Required:

1. Compute the following variances for August:
   a. Direct materials price and quantity variances.
   b. Direct labor rate and efficiency variances.
2. Prepare a brief explanation of the possible causes of each variance.

EXERCISE 9-9 Material and Labor Variances [LO2, LO3]

Sonne Company produces a perfume called Whim. The direct materials and direct labor standards for one bottle of Whim are given below:

	Standard Quantity or Hours	Standard Price or Rate	Standard Cost
Direct materials.	7.2 ounces	$2.50 per ounce	$18.00
Direct labor	0.4 hours	$10.00 per hour	$4.00

During the most recent month, the following activity was recorded:

a. Twenty thousand ounces of material were purchased at a cost of $2.40 per ounce.
b. All of the material was used to produce 2,500 bottles of Whim.
c. Nine hundred hours of direct labor time were recorded at a total labor cost of $10,800.

Required:

1. Compute the direct materials price and quantity variances for the month.
2. Compute the direct labor rate and efficiency variances for the month.

EXERCISE 9-10 Material Variances [LO2]

Refer to the data in Exercise 9-9. Assume that instead of producing 2,500 bottles of Whim during the month, the company produced only 2,000 bottles using 16,000 ounces of material. (The rest of the material purchased remained in raw materials inventory.)

Required:

Compute the direct materials price and quantity variances for the month.

EXERCISE 9-11 Labor and Variable Manufacturing Overhead Variances [LO3, LO4]

Hollowell Audio, Inc., manufactures military-specification compact discs. The company uses standards to control its costs. The labor standards that have been set for one disc are as follows:

Standard Hours	Standard Rate per Hour	Standard Cost
24 minutes	$6.00	$2.40

During July, 8,500 hours of direct labor time were recorded to make 20,000 discs. The direct labor cost totaled $49,300 for the month.

Required:

1. What direct labor cost should have been incurred to make the 20,000 discs? By how much does this differ from the cost that was incurred?
2. Break down the difference in cost from (1) above into a labor rate variance and a labor efficiency variance.
3. The budgeted variable manufacturing overhead rate is $4 per direct labor-hour. During July, the company incurred $39,100 in variable manufacturing overhead cost. Compute the variable overhead spending and efficiency variances for the month.

EXERCISE 9-12 Creating a Balanced Scorecard [LO5]

Ariel Tax Services prepares tax returns for individual and corporate clients. As the company has gradually expanded to 10 offices, the founder Max Jacobs has begun to feel as though he is losing control of operations. In response to this concern, he has decided to implement a performance measurement system that will help control current operations and facilitate his plans of expanding to 20 offices.

Jacobs describes the keys to the success of his business as follows:

"Our only real asset is our people. We must keep our employees highly motivated and we must hire the 'cream of the crop.' Interestingly, employee morale and recruiting success are both driven by the same two factors—compensation and career advancement. In other words, providing superior compensation relative to the industry average coupled with fast-track career advancement opportunities keeps morale high and makes us a very attractive place to work. It drives a high rate of job offer acceptances relative to job offers tendered."

"Hiring highly qualified people and keeping them energized ensures operational success, which in our business is a function of productivity, efficiency, and effectiveness. Productivity boils down to employees being billable rather idle. Efficiency relates to the time required to complete a tax return. Finally, effectiveness is critical to our business in the sense that we cannot tolerate errors. Completing a tax return quickly is meaningless if the return contains errors."

"Our growth depends on acquiring new customers through word-of-mouth from satisfied repeat customers. We believe that our customers come back year after year because they value error-free, timely, and courteous tax return preparation. Common courtesy is an important aspect of our business! We call it service quality, and it all ties back to employee morale in the sense that happy employees treat their clients with care and concern."

"While sales growth is obviously important to our future plans, growth without a corresponding increase in profitability is useless. Therefore, we understand that increasing our profit margin is a function of cost-efficiency as well as sales growth. Given that payroll is our biggest expense, we must maintain an optimal balance between staffing levels and the revenue being generated. As I alluded to earlier, the key to maintaining this balance is employee productivity. If we can achieve cost-efficient sales growth, we should eventually have 20 profitable offices!"

Required:

1. Create a balanced scorecard for Ariel Tax Services. Link your scorecard measures using the framework from Exhibit 9–12. Indicate whether each measure is expected to increase or decrease. Feel free to create measures that may not be specifically mentioned in the chapter, but make sense given the strategic goals of the company.
2. What hypotheses are built into the balanced scorecard for Ariel Tax Services? Which of these hypotheses do you believe are most questionable and why?
3. Discuss the potential advantages and disadvantages of implementing an internal business process measure called *total dollar amount of tax refunds generated.* Would you recommend using this measure in Ariel's balanced scorecard?
4. Would it be beneficial to attempt to measure each office's individual performance with respect to the scorecard measures that you created? Why or why not?

EXERCISE 9-13 Working Backwards from Labor Variances [LO3]

The Worldwide Credit Card, Inc., uses standards to control the labor time involved in opening mail from card holders and recording the enclosed remittances. Incoming mail is gathered into batches, and a standard time is set for opening and recording each batch. The labor standards relating to one batch are as follows:

	Standard Hours	Standard Rate	Standard Cost
Per batch	2.5	$6.00	$15.00

The record showing the time spent last week in opening batches of mail has been misplaced. However, the batch supervisor recalls that 168 batches were received and opened during the week, and the controller recalls the following variance data relating to these batches:

Total labor variance	$330 U
Labor rate variance	$150 F

Required:

1. Determine the number of actual labor-hours spent opening batches during the week.
2. Determine the actual hourly rate paid to employees for opening batches last week.

(Hint: A useful way to proceed would be to work from known to unknown data either by using the variance formulas or by using the columnar format shown in Exhibit 9–6.)

Problems 

PROBLEM 9-14 Comprehensive Variance Analysis [LO2, LO3, LO4]
Portland Company's Ironton Plant produces precast ingots for industrial use. Carlos Santiago, who was recently appointed general manager of the Ironton Plant, has just been handed the plant's income statement for October. The statement is shown below:

	Budgeted	Actual
Sales (5,000 ingots)	$250,000	$250,000
Variable expenses:		
Variable cost of goods sold*	80,000	96,390
Variable selling expenses	20,000	20,000
Total variable expenses	100,000	116,390
Contribution margin	150,000	133,610
Fixed expenses:		
Manufacturing overhead	60,000	60,000
Selling and administrative	75,000	75,000
Total fixed expenses	135,000	135,000
Net operating income (loss)	$ 15,000	$ (1,390)

*Contains direct materials, direct labor, and variable manufacturing overhead.

Mr. Santiago was shocked to see the loss for the month, particularly since sales were exactly as budgeted. He stated, "I sure hope the plant has a standard cost system in operation. If it doesn't, I won't have the slightest idea of where to start looking for the problem."

The plant does use a standard cost system, with the following standard variable cost per ingot:

	Standard Quantity or Hours	Standard Price or Rate	Standard Cost
Direct materials	4.0 pounds	$2.50 per pound	$10.00
Direct labor	0.6 hours	$9.00 per hour	5.40
Variable manufacturing overhead	0.3 hours*	$2.00 per hour	0.60
Total standard variable cost			$16.00

*Based on machine-hours.

Mr. Santiago has determined that during October the plant produced 5,000 ingots and incurred the following costs:

a. Purchased 25,000 pounds of materials at a cost of $2.95 per pound. There were no raw materials in inventory at the beginning of the month.
b. Used 19,800 pounds of materials in production. (Finished goods and work in process inventories are insignificant and can be ignored.)
c. Worked 3,600 direct labor-hours at a cost of $8.70 per hour.
d. Incurred a total variable manufacturing overhead cost of $4,320 for the month. A total of 1,800 machine-hours was recorded.

It is the company's policy to close all variances to cost of goods sold on a monthly basis.

Required:

1. Compute the following variances for October:
   a. Direct materials price and quantity variances.
   b. Direct labor rate and efficiency variances.
   c. Variable manufacturing overhead spending and efficiency variances.

2. Summarize the variances that you computed in (1) above by showing the net overall favorable or unfavorable variance for October. What impact did this figure have on the company's income statement?
3. Pick out the two most significant variances that you computed in (1) above. Explain to Mr. Santiago possible causes of these variances.

PROBLEM 9-15 Variance Analysis in a Hospital [LO2, LO3, LO4]

"What's going on in that lab?" asked Derek Warren, chief administrator for Cottonwood Hospital, as he studied the prior month's reports. "Every month the lab teeters between a profit and a loss. Are we going to have to increase our lab fees again?"

"We can't," replied Lois Ankers, the controller. "We're getting *lots* of complaints about the last increase, particularly from the insurance companies and governmental health units. They're now paying only about 80% of what we bill. I'm beginning to think the problem is on the cost side."

To determine if lab costs are in line with other hospitals, Mr. Warren has asked you to evaluate the costs for the past month. Ms. Ankers has provided you with the following information:

a. Two basic types of tests are performed in the lab—smears and blood tests. During the past month, 2,700 smears and 900 blood tests were performed in the lab.
b. Small glass plates are used in both types of tests. During the past month, the hospital purchased 16,000 plates at a cost of $38,400. This cost is net of a 4% purchase discount. A total of 2,000 of these plates were unused at the end of the month; no plates were on hand at the beginning of the month.
c. During the past month, 1,800 hours of labor time were used in performing smears and blood tests. The cost of this labor time was $18,450.
d. The lab's variable overhead cost last month totaled $11,700.

Cottonwood Hospital has never used standard costs. By searching industry literature, however, you have determined the following nationwide averages for hospital labs:

Plates: Three plates are required per lab test. These plates cost $2.50 each and are disposed of after the test is completed.

Labor: Each smear should require 0.3 hours to complete, and each blood test should require 0.6 hours to complete. The average cost of this lab time is $12 per hour.

Overhead: Overhead cost is based on direct labor-hours. The average rate of variable overhead is $6 per hour.

Required:

1. Compute the materials price variance for the plates purchased last month, and compute a materials quantity variance for the plates used last month.
2. For labor cost in the lab:
   a. Compute a labor rate variance and a labor efficiency variance.
   b. In most hospitals, three-fourths of the workers in the lab are certified technicians and one-fourth are assistants. In an effort to reduce costs, Cottonwood Hospital employs only one-half certified technicians and one-half assistants. Would you recommend that this policy be continued? Explain.
3. Compute the variable overhead spending and efficiency variances. Is there any relation between the variable overhead efficiency variance and the labor efficiency variance? Explain.

PROBLEM 9-16 Basic Variance Analysis [LO2, LO3, LO4]

Barberry, Inc., manufactures a product called Fruta. The company uses a standard cost system and has established the following standards for one unit of Fruta:

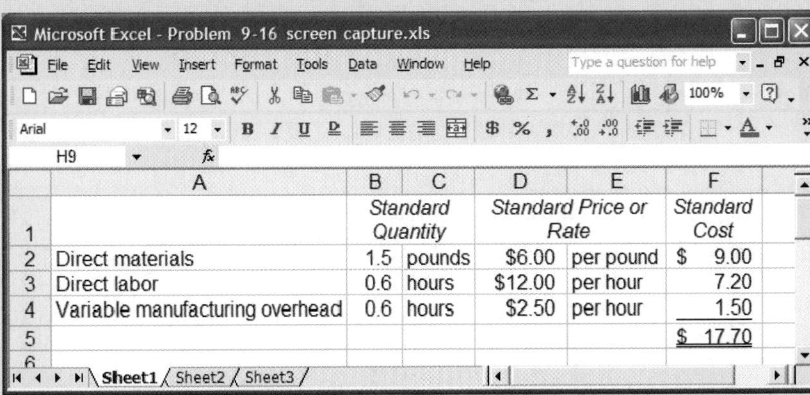

Microsoft Excel - Problem 9-16 screen capture.xls

	A	B	C	D	E	F
1		Standard Quantity		Standard Price or Rate		Standard Cost
2	Direct materials	1.5	pounds	$6.00	per pound	$ 9.00
3	Direct labor	0.6	hours	$12.00	per hour	7.20
4	Variable manufacturing overhead	0.6	hours	$2.50	per hour	1.50
5						$ 17.70

Sheet1 / Sheet2 / Sheet3

During June, the company recorded this activity relative to production of Fruta:

a. The company produced 3,000 units during June.
b. A total of 8,000 pounds of material were purchased at a cost of $46,000.
c. There was no beginning inventory of materials; however, at the end of the month, 2,000 pounds of material remained in ending inventory.
d. The company employs 10 persons to work on the production of Fruta. During June, each worked an average of 160 hours at an average rate of $12.50 per hour.
e. Variable manufacturing overhead is assigned to Fruta on the basis of direct labor-hours. Variable manufacturing overhead costs during June totaled $3,600.

The company's management is anxious to determine the efficiency of the Fruta production activities.

Required:

1. For direct materials used in the production of Fruta:
   a. Compute the price and quantity variances.
   b. The materials were purchased from a new supplier who is anxious to enter into a long-term purchase contract. Would you recommend that the company sign the contract? Explain.
2. For labor employed in the production of Fruta:
   a. Compute the rate and efficiency variances.
   b. In the past, the 10 persons employed in the production of Fruta consisted of 4 senior workers and 6 assistants. During June, the company experimented with 5 senior workers and 5 assistants. Would you recommend that the new labor mix be continued? Explain.
3. Compute the variable overhead spending and efficiency variances. What relation can you see between this efficiency variance and the labor efficiency variance?

PROBLEM 9-17 Measures of Internal Business Process Performance [LO6]

MacIntyre Fabrications, Ltd., of Aberdeen, Scotland, has recently begun a continuous improvement campaign in conjunction with a move toward Lean Production. Management has developed new performance measures as part of this campaign. The following operating data have been gathered over the last four months:

	Month			
	1	2	3	4
Throughput time	?	?	?	?
Manufacturing cycle efficiency	?	?	?	?
Delivery cycle time	?	?	?	?
Percentage of on-time deliveries	72%	73%	78%	85%
Total sales (units)	10,540	10,570	10,550	10,490

Management would like to know the company's throughput time, manufacturing cycle efficiency, and delivery cycle time. The data to compute these measures have been gathered and appear below:

	Month			
	1	2	3	4
Move time per unit, in days	0.5	0.5	0.4	0.5
Process time per unit, in days	0.6	0.5	0.5	0.4
Wait time per order before start of production, in days	9.6	8.7	5.3	4.7
Queue time per unit, in days	3.6	3.6	2.6	1.7
Inspection time per unit, in days	0.7	0.7	0.4	0.3

Required:

1. For each month, compute the following:
   a. The throughput time.
   b. The manufacturing cycle efficiency (MCE).
   c. The delivery cycle time.
2. Using the performance measures given in the problem and those you computed in (1) above, identify whether the trend over the four months is generally favorable, generally unfavorable, or mixed. What areas apparently require improvement and how might they be improved?
3. Refer to the move time, process time, and so forth, given above for month 4.
   a. Assume that in month 5 the move time, process time, and so forth, are the same as for month 4, except that through the implementation of Lean Production, the company is able to completely eliminate the queue time during production. Compute the new throughput time and MCE.
   b. Assume that in month 6 the move time, process time, and so forth, are the same as for month 4, except that the company is able to completely eliminate both the queue time during production and the inspection time. Compute the new throughput time and MCE.

PROBLEM 9-18 Perverse Effects of Some Performance Measures [LO5]

There is often more than one way to improve a performance measure. Unfortunately, some of the actions taken by managers to make their performance look better may actually harm the organization. For example, suppose the marketing department is held responsible only for increasing the performance measure "total revenues." Increases in total revenues may be achieved by working harder and smarter, but they can also usually be achieved by simply cutting prices. The increase in volume from cutting prices almost always results in greater total revenues; however, it does not always lead to greater total profits. Those who design performance measurement systems need to keep in mind that managers who are under pressure to perform may take actions to improve performance measures that have negative consequences elsewhere.

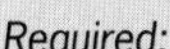

Required:

For each of the following situations, describe actions that managers might take to show improvement in the performance measure but which do not actually lead to improvement in the organization's overall performance.

1. Concerned with the slow rate at which new products are brought to market, top management of a consumer electronics company introduces a new performance measure—speed-to-market. The research and development department is given responsibility for this performance measure, which measures the average amount of time a product is in development before it is released to the market for sale.
2. The CEO of a telephone company has been under public pressure from city officials to fix the large number of public pay phones that do not work. The company's repair people complain that the problem is vandalism and damage caused by theft of coins from coin boxes—particularly in high-crime areas in the city. The CEO says she wants the problem solved and has pledged to city officials that there will be substantial improvement by the end of the year. To ensure that this is done, she makes the managers in charge of installing and maintaining pay phones responsible for increasing the percentage of public pay phones that are fully functional.
3. A manufacturing company has been plagued by the chronic failure to ship orders to customers by the promised date. To solve this problem, the production manager has been given the responsibility of increasing the percentage of orders shipped on time. When a customer calls in an order, the production manager and the customer agree to a delivery date. If the order is not completed by that date, it is counted as a late shipment.
4. Concerned with the productivity of employees, the board of directors of a large multinational corporation has dictated that the manager of each subsidiary will be held responsible for increasing the revenue per employee of his or her subsidiary.

PROBLEM 9-19 Setting Standards [LO1]

L'Essence is a small cosmetics company located in the perfume center of Grasse in southern France. The company plans to introduce a new body oil, called Energique, for which it needs to develop a standard product cost. The following information is available on the production of Energique:

a. The Energique base is made by mixing select lanolin and alcohol. Some loss in volume occurs for both the lanolin and the alcohol during the mixing process. As a result, each 100-liter batch of Energique base requires 100 liters of lanolin and 8 liters of alcohol.
b. After the base has been prepared, a highly concentrated lilac powder is added to impart a pleasing scent. Only 200 grams of the powder are added to each 100-liter batch. The addition of the lilac powder does not affect the total liquid volume.

c. Both the lanolin and the lilac powder are subject to some contamination from naturally occurring materials. For example, the lilac powder often contains some traces of insects that are not detected and removed when the lilac petals are processed. Occasionally such contaminants interact in ways that result in an unacceptable product with an unpleasant odor. About one 100-liter batch in twenty-one is rejected as unsuitable for sale for this reason and is thrown away.
d. It takes a worker two hours to process one 100-liter batch of Energique. Employees work an eight-hour day, including two hours per day for lunch, rest breaks, and cleanup.

Required:

1. Determine the standard quantity for each of the raw materials needed to produce an acceptable 100-liter batch of Energique.
2. Determine the standard labor time allowed to produce an acceptable 100-liter batch of Energique.
3. The standard prices for direct materials and direct labor in euros (€) appear below:

Lanolin	€16 per liter
Alcohol	€2 per liter
Lilac powder	€1 per gram
Direct labor cost	€12 per hour

Prepare a standard cost card for materials and labor for one acceptable 100-liter batch of Energique.

(CMA, adapted)

PROBLEM 9-20 Creating Balanced Scorecards that Support Different Strategies [LO5]

The Midwest Consulting Group (MCG) helps companies build balanced scorecards. As part of its marketing efforts, MCG conducts an annual balanced scorecard workshop for prospective clients. As MCG's newest employee, your boss has asked you to participate in this year's workshop by explaining to attendees how a company's strategy determines the measures that are appropriate for its balanced scorecard. Your boss has provided you with the excerpts below from the annual reports of two current MCG clients. She has asked you to use these excerpts in your portion of the workshop.

Excerpt from Applied Pharmaceuticals' annual report:

> The keys to our business are consistent and timely new product introductions and manufacturing process integrity. The new product introduction side of the equation is a function of research and development (R&D) yield (e.g., the number of marketable drug compounds created relative to the total number of potential compounds pursued). We seek to optimize our R&D yield and first-to-market capability by investing in state-of-the-art technology, hiring the highest possible percentage of the "best and the brightest" engineers that we pursue, and providing world-class training to those engineers. Manufacturing process integrity is all about establishing world-class quality specifications and then relentlessly engaging in prevention and appraisal activities to minimize defect rates. Our customers must have an awareness of and respect for our brand image of being "first to market and first in quality." If we deliver on this pledge to our customers, then our financial goal of increasing our return on stockholders' equity should take care of itself.

Excerpt from Destination Resorts International's annual report:

> Our business succeeds or fails based on the quality of the service that our front-line employees provide to customers. Therefore, it is imperative that we strive to maintain high employee morale and minimize employee turnover. In addition, it is critical that we train our employees to use technology to create one seamless worldwide experience for our repeat customers. Once an employee enters a customer preference (e.g., provide two extra pillows in the room, deliver fresh brewed coffee to the room at 8:00 A.M., etc.) into our database, our worldwide workforce strives to ensure that a customer will never need to repeat it at any of our destination resorts. If we properly train and retain a motivated workforce, we should see continuous improvement in our percentage of error-free repeat customer check-ins, the time taken to resolve customer complaints, and our independently assessed room cleanliness. This in turn should drive improvement in our customer retention, which is the key to meeting our revenue growth goals.

Required:

1. Based on the excerpts above, compare and contrast the strategies of Applied Pharmaceuticals and Destination Resorts International.

2. Select balanced scorecard measures for each company and link the scorecard measures using the framework from Exhibit 9–12. Use arrows to show the causal links between the performance measures and show whether the performance measure should increase or decrease over time. Feel free to create measures that may not be specifically mentioned in the chapter, but nonetheless make sense given the strategic goals of each company.
3. What hypotheses are built into each balanced scorecard? Why do the hypotheses differ between the two companies?

PROBLEM 9-21 Internal Business Process Performance Measures [LO6]

Exeter Corporation has recently begun a continuous improvement campaign. As a consequence, there have been many changes in operating procedures. Progress has been slow, particularly in trying to develop new performance measures for the factory.

Management has been gathering the following data over the past four months:

	Month			
	1	2	3	4
Quality control measures:				
Customer complaints as a percentage of units sold	1.4%	1.3%	1.1%	1.0%
Warranty claims as a percentage of units sold	2.3%	2.1%	2.0%	1.8%
Defects as a percentage of units produced	4.6%	4.2%	3.7%	3.4%
Material control measures:				
Scrap as a percentage of total cost.	3.2%	2.9%	3.0%	2.7%
Machine performance measures:				
Percentage of machine availability	80%	82%	81%	79%
Use as a percentage of availability	75%	73%	71%	70%
Average setup time (hours)	2.7	2.5	2.5	2.6
Delivery performance measures:				
Throughput time.	?	?	?	?
Manufacturing cycle efficiency.	?	?	?	?
Delivery cycle time	?	?	?	?
Percentage of on-time deliveries.	84%	87%	91%	95%

The president has attended conferences at which the importance of throughput time, manufacturing cycle efficiency, and delivery cycle time were stressed, but no one at the company is sure how they are computed. The data to compute these measures have been gathered and appear below:

	Month			
	1	2	3	4
Wait time per order before start of production, in days.	16.7	15.2	12.3	9.6
Inspection time per unit, in days	0.1	0.3	0.6	0.8
Process time per unit, in days	0.6	0.6	0.6	0.6
Queue time per unit, in days	5.6	5.7	5.6	5.7
Move time per unit, in days	1.4	1.3	1.3	1.4

Required:

1. For each month, compute the following operating performance measures:
   a. Throughput time.
   b. Manufacturing cycle efficiency (MCE).
   c. Delivery cycle time.
2. Using the performance measures given in the problem and those you computed in (1) above, do the following:
   a. Identify areas where the company seems to be improving.
   b. Identify areas where the company seems to be deteriorating or stagnating.
   c. Explain why you think some specific areas are improving while others are not.
3. Refer to the move time, process time, and so forth, given above for month 4.
   a. Assume that in month 5 the move time, process time, and so forth, are the same as for month 4, except that through the implementation of lean production, the company is able to

completely eliminate the queue time during production. Compute the new throughput time and MCE.

b. Assume that in month 6 the move time, process time, and so forth, are the same as for month 4, except that the company is able to completely eliminate both the queue time during production and the inspection time. Compute the new throughput time and MCE.

PROBLEM 9-22 Building a Balanced Scorecard [LO5]

Deer Creek ski resort was for many years a small, family-owned resort serving day skiers from nearby towns. Deer Creek was recently acquired by Mountain Associates, a major ski resort operator with destination resorts in several western states. The new owners have plans to upgrade the resort into a destination resort for vacationers staying for a week or more. As part of this plan, the new owners would like to make major improvements in the Lynx Lair Lodge, the resort's on-the-hill fast-food restaurant. The menu at the Lodge is very limited—hamburgers, hot dogs, chili, tuna fish sandwiches, french fries, and packaged snacks. The previous owners of the resort had felt no urgency to upgrade the food service at the Lodge since there is little competition. If skiers want lunch on the mountain, the only alternatives are the Lynx Lair Lodge or a brown bag lunch brought from home.

As part of the deal when acquiring Deer Creek, Mountain Associates agreed to retain all of the current employees of the resort. The manager of the Lodge, while hardworking and enthusiastic, has very little experience in the restaurant business. The manager is responsible for selecting the menu, finding and training employees, and overseeing daily operations. The kitchen staff prepares food and washes dishes. The dining room staff takes orders, serves as cashiers, and cleans the dining room area.

Shortly after taking over Deer Creek, management of Mountain Associates held a day-long meeting with all of the employees of the Lynx Lair Lodge to discuss the future of the ski resort and management's plans for the Lodge. At the end of this meeting, top management and Lodge employees created a balanced scorecard for the Lodge that would help guide operations for the coming ski season. Almost everyone who participated in the meeting seemed to be enthusiastic about the scorecard and management's plans for the Lodge.

The following performance measures were included on the balanced scorecard for the Lynx Lair Lodge:

- Customer satisfaction with service, as measured by customer surveys.
- Total Lynx Lair Lodge profit.
- Dining area cleanliness, as rated by a representative from Mountain Associates management.
- Average time to prepare an order.
- Customer satisfaction with menu choices, as measured by surveys.
- Average time to take an order.
- Percentage of kitchen staff completing institutional cooking course at the local community college.
- Sales.
- Percentage of dining room staff completing hospitality course at the local community college.
- Number of menu items.

Mountain Associates will pay for the costs of staff attending courses at the local community college.

Required:

1. Using the above performance measures, construct a balanced scorecard for the Lynx Lair Lodge. Use Exhibit 9–12 as a guide. Use arrows to show causal links and indicate with a + or − whether the performance measure should increase or decrease.
2. What hypotheses are built into the balanced scorecard for the Lynx Lair Lodge? Which of these hypotheses do you believe are most questionable? Why?
3. How will management know if one of the hypotheses underlying the balanced scorecard is false?

PROBLEM 9-23 Developing Standard Costs [LO1]

Le Forestier, S.A., is a small company that processes wild mushrooms found in the forests of central France. For many years, Le Forestier's products have had strong sales in France. However, companies from other countries in the European common market such as Italy and Spain have begun marketing similar products in France, and price competition has become increasingly intense. Jean Leveque, the company's controller, is planning to implement a standard cost system for Le Forestier and has gathered considerable information from the purchasing and production managers concerning production and material requirements for Le Forestier's products. Leveque believes that the use of standard costing will allow Le Forestier to improve cost control and thereby better compete with the new entrants into the French market.

Le Forestier's most popular product is dried chanterelle mushrooms, which are sold in small vacuum-packed jars. Each jar contains 15 grams of dried mushrooms. Fresh mushrooms are purchased for €60 per kilogram in bulk from individuals who gather them from local forests. (€ stands for euro, the currency used in France, and a kilogram is 1,000 grams.) Because of imperfections in the mushrooms and normal spoilage, one-quarter of the fresh mushrooms are discarded. Fifteen minutes is the direct labor time required for inspecting and sorting per kilogram of fresh mushrooms. After sorting and inspecting, the acceptable mushrooms are flash-dried, which requires 10 minutes of direct labor time per kilogram of acceptable, sorted, and inspected fresh mushrooms. The flash-drying removes most of the moisture content of the mushrooms and therefore drastically reduces their weight. Flash-drying reduces the weight of the acceptable mushrooms by 80%. As a consequence, a kilogram of *acceptable* fresh mushrooms yields only about 200 grams of dried mushrooms. After drying, the mushrooms are vacuum-packed in small jars and labels are applied.

Direct labor is paid at the rate of €12 per hour. The cost of the glass jars, lids, and labels is €10 per 100 jars. The labor time required to pack 100 jars is 10 minutes.

Required:

1. Develop the standard cost for the direct labor and materials cost components of a single jar of dried chanterelle mushrooms, including the costs of the mushrooms, inspecting and sorting, drying, and packing.
2. Jean Leveque wonders who should be held responsible—the purchasing manager or the production manager—for the materials variances for the chanterelle mushrooms.
   a. Who should be held responsible for the materials price variances for the chanterelle mushrooms? Explain.
   b. Who should be held responsible for the materials quantity variances for the chanterelle mushrooms? Explain.

PROBLEM 9-24 Materials and Labor Variances; Computations from Incomplete Data [LO1, LO2, LO3]

Topaz Company produces a single product. The company has set standards as follows for materials and labor:

	Direct Materials	Direct Labor
Standard quantity or hours per unit	? pounds	2.5 hours
Standard price or rate	? per pound	$9 per hour
Standard cost per unit	?	$22.50

During the past month, the company purchased 6,000 pounds of direct materials at a cost of $16,500. All of this material was used in the production of 1,400 units of product. Direct labor cost totaled $28,500 for the month. The following variances have been computed:

Materials quantity variance	$1,200 U
Total materials variance	$300 F
Labor efficiency variance	$4,500 F

Required:

1. For direct materials:
   a. Compute the standard price per pound for materials.
   b. Compute the standard quantity allowed for materials for the month's production.
   c. Compute the standard quantity of materials allowed per unit of product.
2. For direct labor:
   a. Compute the actual direct labor cost per hour for the month.
   b. Compute the labor rate variance.

(Hint: In completing the problem, it may be helpful to move from known to unknown data either by using the variance formulas or by using the columnar format shown in Exhibits 9–4 and 9–6.)

PROBLEM 9-25 Comprehensive Variance Analysis [LO2, LO3, LO4]
Helix Company produces several products in its factory, including a karate robe. The company uses a standard cost system to assist in the control of costs. According to the standards that have been set for the robes, the factory should work 780 direct labor-hours each month and produce 1,950 robes. The standard costs associated with this level of production are as follows:

	Total	Per Unit of Product
Direct materials	$35,490	$18.20
Direct labor	$7,020	3.60
Variable manufacturing overhead (based on direct labor-hours)	$2,340	1.20
		$23.00

During April, the factory worked only 760 direct labor-hours and produced 2,000 robes. The following actual costs were recorded during the month:

	Total	Per Unit of Product
Direct materials (6,000 yards)	$36,000	$18.00
Direct labor	$7,600	3.80
Variable manufacturing overhead	$3,800	1.90
		$23.70

At standard, each robe should require 2.8 yards of material. All of the materials purchased during the month were used in production.

Required:
Compute the following variances for April:
1. The materials price and quantity variances.
2. The labor rate and efficiency variances.
3. The variable manufacturing overhead spending and efficiency variances.

PROBLEM 9-26 Comprehensive Variance Analysis [LO1, LO2, LO3, LO4]
Vitalite, Inc., produces a number of products, including a body-wrap kit. Standard variable costs relating to a single kit are given below:

	Standard Quantity or Hours	Standard Price or Rate	Standard Cost
Direct materials	?	$6 per yard	$?
Direct labor	?	?	?
Variable manufacturing overhead	?	$2 per direct labor-hour	?
Total standard cost per kit			$42

During August, 500 kits were manufactured and sold. Selected information relating to the month's production is given below:

	Materials Used	Direct Labor	Variable Manufacturing Overhead
Total standard cost*	?	$8,000	$1,600
Actual costs incurred	$10,000	?	$1,620
Materials price variance	?		
Materials quantity variance	$600 U		
Labor rate variance		?	
Labor efficiency variance		?	
Variable overhead spending variance			?
Variable overhead efficiency variance			?

*For the month's production.

The following additional information is available for August's production of kits:

Actual direct labor-hours	900
Difference between standard and actual cost per kit produced during August	$0.14 U

Required:

1. What was the total standard cost of the materials used during August?
2. How many yards of material are required at standard per kit?
3. What was the materials price variance for August?
4. What is the standard direct labor rate per hour?
5. What was the labor rate variance for August? The labor efficiency variance?
6. What was the variable overhead spending variance for August? The variable overhead efficiency variance?
7. Complete the standard cost card for one kit shown at the beginning of the problem.

Cases

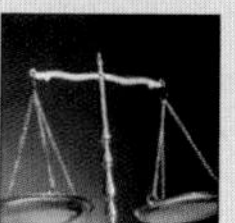

CASE 9-27 Ethics and the Manager; Rigging Standards [LO1]

Stacy Cummins, the newly hired controller at Merced Home Products, Inc., was disturbed by what she had discovered about the standard costs at the Home Security Division. In looking over the past several years of quarterly earnings reports at the Home Security Division, she noticed that the first-quarter earnings were always poor, the second-quarter earnings were slightly better, the third-quarter earnings were again slightly better, and the fourth quarter always ended with a spectacular performance in which the Home Security Division managed to meet or exceed its target profit for the year. She also was concerned to find letters from the company's external auditors to top management warning about an unusual use of standard costs at the Home Security Division.

When Ms. Cummins ran across these letters, she asked the assistant controller, Gary Farber, if he knew what was going on at the Home Security Division. Gary said that it was common knowledge in the company that the vice president in charge of the Home Security Division, Preston Lansing, had rigged the standards at his division in order to produce the same quarterly earnings pattern every year. According to company policy, variances are taken directly to the income statement as an adjustment to cost of goods sold.

Favorable variances have the effect of increasing net operating income, and unfavorable variances have the effect of decreasing net operating income. Lansing had rigged the standards so that there were always large favorable variances. Company policy was a little vague about when these variances have to be reported on the divisional income statements. While the intent was clearly to recognize variances on the income statement in the period in which they arise, nothing in the company's accounting manuals actually explicitly required this. So for many years Lansing had followed a practice of saving up the favorable variances and using them to create a nice smooth pattern of earnings growth in the first three quarters, followed by a big "Christmas present" of an extremely good fourth quarter. (Financial reporting regulations forbid carrying variances forward from one year to the next on the annual audited financial statements, so all of the variances must appear on the divisional income statement by the end of the year.)

Ms. Cummins was concerned about these revelations and attempted to bring up the subject with the president of Merced Home Products but was told that "we all know what Lansing's doing, but as long as he continues to turn in such good reports, don't bother him." When Ms. Cummins asked if the board of directors was aware of the situation, the president somewhat testily replied, "Of course they are aware."

Required:

1. How did Preston Lansing probably "rig" the standard costs—are the standards set too high or too low? Explain.
2. Should Preston Lansing be permitted to continue his practice of managing reported earnings?
3. What should Stacy Cummins do in this situation?

CASE 9-28 Balanced Scorecard [LO5]

Weierman Department Store is located in the downtown area of a medium-sized city in the American Midwest. While the store had been profitable for many years, it is facing increasing competition from large national chains that have set up stores in the city's suburbs. Recently the downtown area has been undergoing revitalization, and the owners of Weierman Department Store are somewhat optimistic that profitability can be restored.

In an attempt to accelerate the return to profitability, the management of Weierman Department Store is in the process of designing a balanced scorecard for the company. Management believes the company should focus on two key problems. First, customers are taking longer and longer to pay the bills they incur on the department store's charge card, and they have far more bad debts than are normal for the industry. If this problem were solved, the company would have more cash to make much needed renovations. Investigation has revealed that much of the problem with late payments and unpaid bills is apparently due to disputed bills that are the result of incorrect charges on the customer bills. These incorrect charges usually occur because salesclerks enter data incorrectly on the charge account slip. Second, the company has been incurring large losses on unsold seasonal apparel. Such items are ordinarily resold at a loss to discount stores that specialize in such distress items.

The meeting in which the balanced scorecard approach was discussed was disorganized and ineffectively led—possibly because no one other than one of the vice presidents had read anything about how to put a balanced scorecard together. Nevertheless, a number of potential performance measures were suggested by various managers. These potential performance measures are:

Performance measures suggested by various managers:

- Total sales revenue.
- Percentage of salesclerks trained to correctly enter data on charge account slips.
- Customer satisfaction with accuracy of charge account bills from monthly customer survey.
- Sales per employee.
- Travel expenses for buyers for trips to fashion shows.
- Average age of accounts receivables.
- Courtesy shown by junior staff members to senior staff members based on surveys of senior staff.
- Unsold inventory at the end of the season as a percentage of total cost of sales.
- Sales per square foot of floor space.
- Percentage of suppliers making just-in-time deliveries.
- Quality of food in the staff cafeteria based on staff surveys.
- Written-off accounts receivables (bad debts) as a percentage of sales.
- Percentage of charge account bills containing errors.
- Percentage of employees who have attended the city's cultural diversity workshop.
- Total profit.
- Profit per employee.

Required:

1. As someone with more knowledge of the balanced scorecard than almost anyone else in the company, you have been asked to build an integrated balanced scorecard. In your scorecard, use only performance measures suggested by the managers above. You do not have to use all of the performance measures suggested by the managers, but you should build a balanced scorecard that

reveals a strategy for dealing with the problems with accounts receivable and with unsold merchandise. Construct the balanced scorecard following the format used in Exhibit 9–12. Do not be particularly concerned with whether a specific performance measure falls within the learning and growth, internal business process, customer, or financial perspective. However, clearly show the causal links between the performance measures with arrows and whether the performance measures should show increases or decreases.

2. Assume that the company adopts your balanced scorecard. After operating for a year, there are improvements in some performance measures but not in others. What should management do next?
3. *a.* Suppose that customers express greater satisfaction with the accuracy of their charge account bills but the performance measures for the average age of accounts receivable and for bad debts do not improve. Explain why this might happen.
   b. Suppose that the performance measures for the average age of accounts receivable, bad debts, and unsold inventory improve, but total profits do not. Explain why this might happen. Assume in your answer that the explanation lies within the company.

RESEARCH AND APPLICATION 9-29 [LO5]

The questions in this exercise are based on the Nordstrom, Inc., 2004 annual report at http://phx.corporate-ir.net/phoenix.zhtml?c=93295&p=irol-reportsAnnual. You do not need to print the annual report in order to answer the questions.

Required:

1. What is Nordstrom's strategy for success in the marketplace? Does the company rely primarily on a customer intimacy, operational excellence, or product leadership customer value proposition? What evidence supports your conclusion?
2. Page 3 of the annual report summarizes six measures that Nordstrom collectively refers to as its scorecard. Do these measures constitute a balanced scorecard? Why or why not?
3. Identify four measures that Nordstrom could include in the financial perspective of a balanced scorecard. How do the measures that you have chosen differ from one another? Ideally, should each measure increase or decrease over time?
4. Identify four measures that Nordstrom could include in the customer perspective of a balanced scorecard. Feel free to create measures that are not explicitly mentioned in the annual report. What statements in the annual report motivated your choices? Ideally, should each of your measures increase or decrease over time?
5. Identify four measures that Nordstrom could include in the internal business process perspective of a balanced scorecard. Feel free to create measures that are not explicitly mentioned in the annual report. What statements in the annual report motivated your choices? Ideally, should each of your measures increase or decrease over time?
6. Identify four measures that Nordstrom could include in the learning and growth perspective of a balanced scorecard. Feel free to create measures that are not explicitly mentioned in the annual report. What statements in the annual report motivated your choices? Ideally, should each of your measures increase or decrease over time?
7. Create four hypothesis statements (in "if-then" form) that demonstrate four of the causal links between measures that you have chosen.

Chapter

10

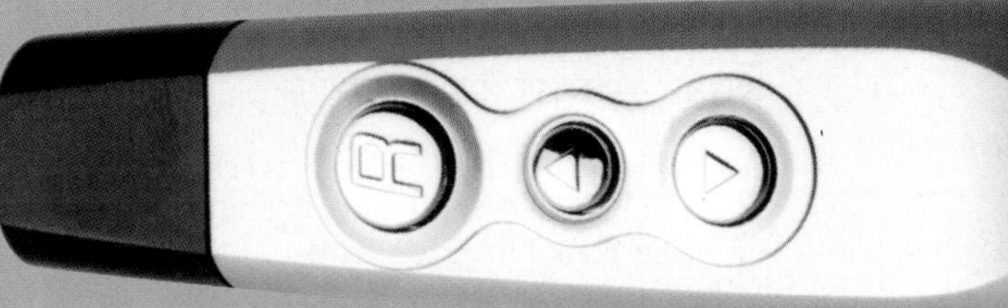

Learning Objectives

After studying Chapter 10, you should be able to:

LO1 Prepare a flexible budget and explain the advantages of the flexible budget approach over the static budget approach.

LO2 Prepare a performance report for both variable and fixed overhead costs using the flexible budget approach.

LO3 Use a flexible budget to prepare a variable overhead performance report containing only a spending variance.

LO4 Use a flexible budget to prepare a variable overhead performance report containing both a spending and an efficiency variance.

LO5 Compute the predetermined overhead rate and apply overhead to products in a standard cost system.

LO6 Compute and interpret the fixed overhead budget and volume variances.

LP 10

Flexible Budgets and Overhead Analysis

Controlling Costs—Rain or Shine

BUSINESS FOCUS

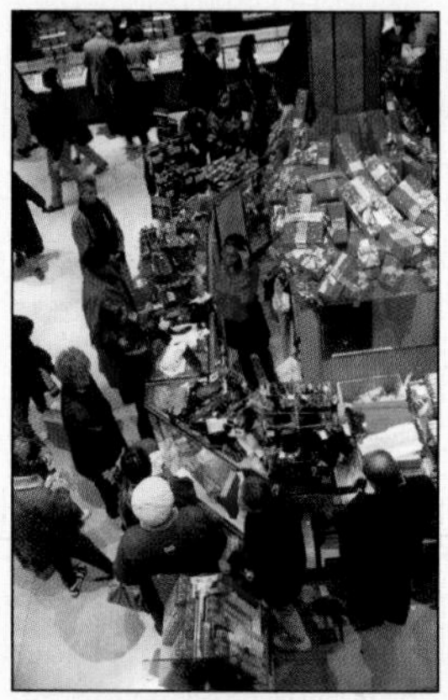

Totes»Isotoner Corporation is the world's largest marketer of umbrellas, gloves, rainwear, and other weather-related accessories. One of the company's costs is a "flex advertising" fee that it pays to department stores based on the stores' sales of totes»Isotoner products. The company prepares a management report that compares actual flex advertising costs *as a percentage of actual sales* to budgeted flex advertising costs *as a percentage of budgeted sales.* This is done because management expects a variable cost, such as flex advertising, to stay constant on a per sales dollar basis.

The company purposely does not compare its actual and budgeted *total dollar amounts* of flex advertising expense because it provides misleading feedback about managerial performance. For example, if actual sales exceed budgeted sales, a highly efficient manager could be naively penalized for incurring actual variable costs that exceed budgeted variable costs. Conversely, if actual sales are less than budgeted sales, an inefficient manager could be naively rewarded for incurring actual variable costs that are less than budgeted variable costs.

When it comes to fixed costs, totes»Isotoner monitors total dollar amounts rather than percentages. For example, the Information Technology (IT) Department incurs numerous costs that are not affected by sales variation within the relevant range. If percentages were used to manage these costs, an increase in sales would decrease the IT Department's total fixed costs as a percentage of sales, thereby sending misleading signals about managerial efficiency.

In addition to cost information, totes»Isotoner uses other non-financial performance measures to ensure its employees do not fixate on minimizing costs to the detriment of customers. ■

Source: Author's conversation with Donna Deye, senior vice president and CFO, totes»Isotoner Corporation.

Overhead is a major cost, if not *the* major cost, in many organizations. For example, it costs Microsoft very little to make copies of its software for sale to customers; almost all of Microsoft's costs are in research and development and marketing—elements of overhead. Or consider Disney World. The only direct cost of serving a particular guest is the cost of the food the guest consumes at the park; virtually all of the other costs of running the amusement park are overhead. Even Boeing, a manufacturer, has huge amounts of overhead in the form of engineering salaries, buildings, insurance, administrative salaries, and marketing costs. Not surprisingly, controlling overhead costs is a major preoccupation of managers.

IN BUSINESS

FOCUS ON OVERHEAD COSTS

Overhead costs now account for as much as 66% of the costs incurred by companies in service industries and up to 37% of the total costs of manufacturers. Consequently, overhead reduction is a recurring theme in many organizations. However, the extent of the reductions must be considered in light of competitive pressures to improve services and product quality. Managers must avoid cutting costs that add value to the organization.

Source: Nick Develin, "Unlocking Overhead Value," *Management Accounting*, December 1999, pp. 22–34.

Since overhead is usually made up of many separate costs, including everything from disposable coffee cups in the visitors' waiting area to the president's salary, it is more difficult to control than direct materials and direct labor. Overhead control is further complicated by the fact that overhead costs can be variable, fixed, or a mixture of variable and fixed. However, these complications can be largely overcome by using flexible budgets. In this chapter, we learn how to prepare flexible budgets and how they can be used to control costs. We also expand the study of overhead variances that we started in Chapter 9.

Let's start with a simple example. Imagine that you work as a baggage handler for an airline. Your boss has said that you should be able to unload 20 pieces of luggage from an airplane per minute. Flight 2707 from Boston carries *on average* 300 pieces of luggage. Today flight 2707 is scheduled to arrive from Boston and your boss has decided that you should be able to unload the luggage on the flight in 15 minutes (300 pieces of luggage ÷ 20 pieces per minute). However, it takes you 20 minutes instead of 15 minutes to unload the luggage and consequently your boss yells at you. But, the flight actually contained 460 pieces of luggage. How would you feel? You might do some quick math as follows. Since there were 460 pieces of luggage on this flight and you are expected to unload 20 pieces per minute, then you should have been expected to unload the luggage on this flight in 23 minutes (460 pieces of luggage ÷ 20 pieces per minute). You did it in just 20 minutes instead of 23 minutes. Therefore, you should be getting a pat on the back, not yelled at! Notice, your natural inclination was to "flex" the budget of 15 minutes, which was based on 300 pieces of luggage, to reflect what the budget should be for 460 pieces of luggage—23 minutes. Now, let's proceed by applying dollars and cents to this concept.

Flexible Budgets

Characteristics of a Flexible Budget

LEARNING OBJECTIVE 1
Prepare a flexible budget and explain the advantages of the flexible budget approach over the static budget approach.

The budgets that we studied in Chapter 8 were *static budgets.* A **static budget** is prepared at the beginning of the budgeting period and is valid for only the planned level of activity. A static budget is suitable for planning but is inappropriate for evaluating how well costs are controlled. If the actual level of activity differs from what was planned, it would be misleading to compare actual costs to the static budget. If activity is higher than expected, variable

Video 10–1

costs should be higher than expected; and if activity is lower than expected, variable costs should be lower than expected.

Flexible budgets take into account how changes in activity affect costs. A **flexible budget** makes it easy to estimate what costs should be for any level of activity within a specified range. When a flexible budget is used in performance evaluation, actual costs are compared to what the *costs should have been for the actual level of activity during the period* rather than to the budgeted costs from the original budget. This is a very important distinction—particularly for variable costs. If adjustments for the level of activity are not made, it is very difficult to interpret discrepancies between budgeted and actual costs.

IN BUSINESS

WHY DO COMPANIES NEED FLEXIBLE BUDGETS?

The difficulty of accurately predicting future financial performance can be readily understood by reading the annual report of any publicly traded company. For example Nucor Corporation, a steel manufacturer headquartered in Charlotte, North Carolina, cites numerous reasons why its actual results may differ from expectations, including the following: (1) the supply and cost of raw materials, electricity, and natural gas may change unexpectedly; (2) the market demand for steel products may change; (3) competitive pressures from imports and substitute materials may intensify; (4) uncertainties regarding the global economy may affect customer demand; (5) changes to U.S. and foreign trade policy may alter current importing and exporting practices; and (6) new government regulations could significantly increase environmental compliance costs. Each of these factors could cause static budget revenues and/or costs to differ from actual results.

Source: Nucor Corporation 2004 annual report, p. 3.

Deficiencies of the Static Budget

Video 10–1

To illustrate the difference between a static budget and a flexible budget, consider the case of Rick's Hairstyling, an upscale hairstyling salon located in Beverly Hills that is owned and managed by Rick Manzi. The salon has very loyal customers—many of whom are associated with the film industry. Recently Rick has been attempting to get better control of his overhead, and at the urging of his accounting and business adviser Victoria Kho, he has begun to prepare monthly budgets. Victoria Kho is an accountant in independent practice who specializes in small service-oriented businesses like Rick's Hairstyling.

At the end of February, Rick carefully prepared the March budget for overhead items that appears in Exhibit 10–1. Rick believes that the number of customers served in a month

EXHIBIT 10–1

Rick's Hairstyling
Static Budget
For the Month Ended March 31

Budgeted number of client-visits	5,000
Budgeted variable overhead costs:	
Hairstyling supplies (@$1.20 per client-visit)	$ 6,000
Client gratuities (@$4.00 per client-visit)	20,000
Electricity (@$0.20 per client-visit)	1,000
Total variable overhead cost	27,000
Budgeted fixed overhead costs:	
Support staff wages and salaries	8,000
Rent	12,000
Insurance	1,000
Utilities other than electricity	500
Total fixed overhead cost	21,500
Total budgeted overhead cost	$48,500

is the best way to measure the overall level of activity in his salon. He refers to these visits as client-visits. A customer who comes into the salon and has his or her hair styled is counted as one client-visit. After some discussion with Victoria Kho, Rick identified three major categories of variable overhead costs—hairstyling supplies, client gratuities, and electricity—and four major categories of fixed costs—support staff wages and salaries, rent, insurance, and utilities other than electricity. Client gratuities consist of flowers, candies, and glasses of champagne that Rick gives to his customers while they are in the salon. Rick considers electricity to be a variable cost because almost all of the electricity in the salon is consumed by running blow-dryers, curling irons, and other hairstyling equipment.

To develop the budget for variable overhead, Rick estimated that the average cost per client-visit should be $1.20 for hairstyling supplies, $4.00 for client gratuities, and $0.20 for electricity. Based on his estimate of 5,000 client-visits in March, Rick budgeted for $6,000 ($1.20 per client-visit × 5,000 client-visits) in hairstyling supplies, $20,000 ($4.00 per client-visit × 5,000 client-visits) in client gratuities, and $1,000 ($0.20 per client-visit × 5,000 client-visits) in electricity.

The budget for fixed overhead items was based on Rick's records of how much he had spent on these items in the past. The budget included $8,000 for support staff wages and salaries, $12,000 for rent, $1,000 for insurance, and $500 for utilities other than electricity.

At the end of March, Rick prepared a report comparing actual to budgeted costs. That report appears in Exhibit 10–2. The problem with that report, as Rick immediately realized, is that it compares costs at one level of activity (5,200 client-visits) to costs at a different level of activity (5,000 client-visits). Since Rick had 200 more client-visits than expected, some of his costs *should* be higher than budgeted. The static budget performance report confuses control over activity and control over costs. From Rick's standpoint, the increase in activity was good and should be counted as a favorable variance, but the increase in activity has an apparently negative impact on the costs in the report. Rick knew that something would have to be done to make the report more meaningful, but he was unsure of what to do. So he made an appointment to meet with Victoria Kho to discuss the next step.

MANAGERIAL ACCOUNTING IN ACTION
The Issue

Victoria: How is the budgeting going?

Rick: Pretty well. I didn't have any trouble putting together the overhead budget for March. I also prepared a report comparing the actual costs for March to the budgeted costs, but that report isn't giving me what I really want to know.

EXHIBIT 10–2

Rick's Hairstyling
Static Budget Performance Report
For the Month Ended March 31

	Actual	Budgeted	Variance
Client-visits	5,200	5,000	200 F
Variable overhead costs:			
Hairstyling supplies	$ 6,400	$ 6,000	$ 400 U*
Client gratuities	22,300	20,000	2,300 U*
Electricity	1,020	1,000	20 U*
Total variable overhead cost	29,720	27,000	2,720 U*
Fixed overhead costs:			
Support staff wages and salaries	8,100	8,000	100 U
Rent	12,000	12,000	0
Insurance	1,000	1,000	0
Utilities other than electricity	470	500	30 F
Total fixed overhead cost	21,570	21,500	70 U
Total overhead cost	$51,290	$48,500	$2,790 U*

*The cost variances for variable costs and for total overhead are useless for evaluating how well costs were controlled since they have been derived by comparing actual costs at one level of activity to budgeted costs at a different level of activity.

Victoria: Because your actual level of activity didn't match your budgeted activity?
Rick: Right. I know the level of activity shouldn't affect my fixed costs, but we had a lot more client-visits than I had expected and that had to affect my variable costs.
Victoria: So you want to know whether the actual costs are justified by the actual level of activity you had in March?
Rick: Precisely.
Victoria: If you leave your reports and data with me, I can work on it later today, and by tomorrow I'll have a report to show to you.

How a Flexible Budget Works

A flexible budget approach recognizes that a budget can be adjusted to show what costs *should be* for the actual level of activity. To illustrate how flexible budgets work, Victoria prepared the report in Exhibit 10–3. It shows how overhead costs should be expected to change, depending on the monthly level of activity. Within the activity range of 4,900 to 5,200 client-visits, the fixed costs are expected to remain the same. For the variable overhead costs, Victoria multiplied Rick's per-client costs ($1.20 for hairstyling supplies, $4.00 for client gratuities, and $0.20 for electricity) by the appropriate number of client-visits in each column. For example, the $1.20 cost of hairstyling supplies was multiplied by 4,900 client-visits to give the total cost of $5,880 for hairstyling supplies at that level of activity.

Topic Tackler

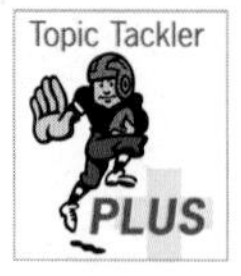

10–1

Using the Flexible Budgeting Concept in Performance Evaluation

LEARNING OBJECTIVE 2
Prepare a performance report for both variable and fixed overhead costs using the flexible budget approach.

To get a better idea of how well Rick controlled his variable overhead costs in March, Victoria applied the flexible budgeting concept to create a budget based on the *actual* number of client-visits for the month (Exhibit 10–4). This new budget is prepared by multiplying the actual level of activity by the cost formula for each of the variable cost categories. For example, using the $1.20 per client-visit for hairstyling supplies, the total cost for this item *should be* $6,240 for 5,200 client-visits ($1.20 per client-visit × 5,200 client-visits). Since

EXHIBIT 10–3
Illustration of the Flexible Budgeting Concept

Rick's Hairstyling
Flexible Budget
For the Month Ended March 31

Budgeted number of client-visits	5,000				
	Cost Formula (per client-visit)	Activity (in client-visits)			
Overhead Costs		4,900	5,000	5,100	5,200
Variable overhead costs:					
Hairstyling supplies	$1.20	$ 5,880	$ 6,000	$ 6,120	$ 6,240
Client gratuities	4.00	19,600	20,000	20,400	20,800
Electricity (variable)	0.20	980	1,000	1,020	1,040
Total variable overhead cost	$5.40	26,460	27,000	27,540	28,080
Fixed overhead costs:					
Support staff wages and salaries		8,000	8,000	8,000	8,000
Rent		12,000	12,000	12,000	12,000
Insurance		1,000	1,000	1,000	1,000
Utilities other than electricity		500	500	500	500
Total fixed overhead cost		21,500	21,500	21,500	21,500
Total overhead cost		$47,960	$48,500	$49,040	$49,580

EXHIBIT 10–4

Rick's Hairstyling
Flexible Budget Performance Report
For the Month Ended March 31

Budgeted number of client-visits	5,000			
Actual number of client-visits	5,200			
Overhead Costs	Cost Formula (per client-visit)	Actual Costs Incurred for 5,200 Client-Visits	Flexible Budget Based on 5,200 Client-Visits	Variance
Variable overhead costs:				
Hairstyling supplies	$1.20	$ 6,400	$ 6,240	$ 160 U
Client gratuities	4.00	22,300	20,800	1,500 U
Electricity (variable)	0.20	1,020	1,040	20 F
Total variable overhead cost	$5.40	29,720	28,080	1,640 U
Fixed overhead costs:				
Support staff wages and salaries		8,100	8,000	100 U
Rent		12,000	12,000	0
Insurance		1,000	1,000	0
Utilities other than electricity		470	500	30 F
Total fixed overhead cost		21,570	21,500	70 U
Total overhead cost		$51,290	$49,580	$1,710 U

the actual cost for hairstyling supplies was $6,400, the unfavorable variance is $160. This differs from the $400 unfavorable variance shown for hairstyling supplies in Exhibit 10–2. The difference arises because Exhibit 10–2 uses a static budget approach that compares actual costs at one level of activity to budgeted costs at a different level of activity. This is like comparing apples to oranges. Because actual activity was higher by 200 client-visits than budgeted activity, the total cost of hairstyling supplies *should* have been $240 ($1.20 per client-visit × 200 client-visits) higher than budgeted. As a result, $240 of the $400 "unfavorable" variance in the static budget performance report in Exhibit 10–2 is spurious.

The flexible budget performance report in Exhibit 10–4 provides a more valid assessment of performance because actual costs are compared to what costs should have been at the actual level of activity. In other words, apples are compared to apples. When this is done, we see that the hairstyling supplies variance is $160 unfavorable rather than $400 unfavorable as it was in the original static budget performance report. In some cases, as with electricity in Rick's report, an unfavorable static budget variance may be transformed into a favorable variance when an increase in activity is properly taken into account.

Video 10–1

The following discussion took place the next day at Rick's salon.

MANAGERIAL ACCOUNTING IN ACTION
The Wrap-Up

Victoria: Let me show you what I've got. [Victoria shows the report contained in Exhibit 10–4.] For the variable costs all I did was multiply the costs per client-visit by the number of client-visits you actually had in March. That allowed me to come up with a better benchmark for what the variable costs should have been.

Rick: That's what you labeled the "flexible budget based on 5,200 client-visits"?

Victoria: That's right. Your original budget was based on 5,000 client-visits, so it understated what the variable overhead costs should be when you actually serve 5,200 customers.

Rick: That's clear enough. These variances aren't quite as shocking as the variances on my first report.

Victoria: Yes, but you still have an unfavorable variance of $1,500 for client gratuities.

Rick: I know how that happened. In March there was a big Democratic Party fundraising dinner that I forgot about when I prepared the March budget.

Rick: To fit all of our regular clients in, we had to push them through here pretty fast. Everyone still got top-rate service, but I felt bad about not being able to spend as much time with each customer. I wanted to give my customers a little extra something to compensate them for the less personal service, so I ordered a lot of flowers which I gave away by the bunch.

Victoria: With the prices you charge, Rick, I am sure the gesture was appreciated.

Rick: One thing bothers me about the report. Why are some of my actual fixed costs different from what I budgeted? Doesn't fixed mean that they are not supposed to change?

Victoria: We call these costs *fixed* because they shouldn't be affected by *changes in the level of activity.* However, that doesn't mean that they can't change for other reasons. For example, your utilities bill, which includes natural gas for heating, varies with the weather.

Rick: I can see that. March was warmer than normal, so my utilities bill was lower than I had expected.

Victoria: The use of the term *fixed* also suggests to people that the cost can't be controlled, but that isn't true. It is often easier to control fixed costs than variable costs. For example, it would be fairly easy for you to change your insurance bill by adjusting the amount of insurance you carry. It would be much more difficult for you to reduce the electricity bill—a variable cost that is a necessary part of serving customers.

Rick: I think I understand, but it *is* confusing.

Victoria: Just remember that a cost is called variable if it is proportional to activity; it is called fixed if it does not depend on the level of activity. However, fixed costs can change for reasons unrelated to changes in the level of activity. And controllability has little to do with whether a cost is variable or fixed. Fixed costs are often more controllable than variable costs.

IN BUSINESS

FOCUS ON OPPORTUNITIES

The late management guru Peter F. Drucker cautioned managers that "almost without exception, the first page of the [monthly] report presents the areas in which results fall below expectations or in which expenditures exceed the budget. It focuses on problems. Problems cannot be ignored. But . . . enterprises have to focus on opportunities. That requires a small but fundamental procedural change: a new first page to the monthly report, one that precedes the page that shows the problems. The new page should focus on where results are better than expected. As much time should be spent on that new first page as traditionally was spent on the problem page."

Source: Peter F. Drucker, "Change Leaders," *Inc.* magazine, June 1999, pp. 65–72.

Using the flexible budget approach, Rick Manzi now has a better way of assessing whether overhead costs are under control. The analysis is not so simple, however, in companies that provide a variety of products and services. The number of units produced or customers served may not be an adequate measure of overall activity. For example, does it make sense to count a Sony CD player, worth less than $50, as equivalent to a large-screen Sony HD-TV? If the number of units produced is used as a measure of overall activity, then the CD player and the large-screen HD-TV would be counted as equivalent. Clearly, the number of units produced (or customers served) may not be appropriate as an overall measure of activity when the organization has a variety of products or services; a common denominator may be needed.

The Measure of Activity—A Critical Choice

What should be used as the measure of activity when a company produces a variety of products and services? At least three factors are important in selecting an activity base for an overhead flexible budget:

1. Changes in the activity base should cause, or at least be highly correlated with, changes in the variable overhead costs in the flexible budget. Ideally, the variable overhead costs

in the flexible budget should vary in direct proportion to changes in the activity base. For example, in a carpentry shop specializing in handmade wood furniture, the costs of miscellaneous supplies such as glue, wooden dowels, and sandpaper should vary with the number of direct labor-hours. Direct labor-hours would therefore be a good measure of activity to use in a flexible budget for the costs of such supplies.

2. The activity base should not be expressed in dollars or some other currency. For example, direct labor cost is usually a poor choice for an activity base in flexible budgets because changes in wage rates affect the activity base but do not usually result in a proportionate change in overhead. For example, we would not ordinarily expect to see a 5% increase in the consumption of glue in a carpentry shop if the workers receive a 5% increase in pay. Therefore, it is best to use physical rather than financial measures of activity in flexible budgets.
3. The activity base should be simple and easily understood, otherwise it will result in confusion and misunderstanding. It is difficult to control costs if people don't understand the reports or do not accept them as valid.

Variable Overhead Variances—A Closer Look

When the flexible budget is based on *hours* of activity (such as direct labor-hours) rather than on units of product or number of customers served, the flexible budget on the performance report can be based on either the actual hours used *or* the standard hours allowed for the actual output. Which should be used?

10–2

Video 10–1

Actual versus Standard Hours

To explain these two options, we will use an example involving MicroDrive Corporation, a manufacturer of precision computer disk-drive motors for military applications. Data concerning the company's variable manufacturing overhead costs are shown in Exhibit 10–5.

MicroDrive uses machine-hours as the activity base in its flexible budget because its managers believe most of the company's overhead costs are driven by machine-hours. At the beginning of the year, MicroDrive estimated that it would produce 25,000 motors. Since the company's standard allowance is 2 machine-hours per motor, the budgeted level of activity for the year was 50,000 machine-hours. During the year the company actually produced 20,000 motors that *should* have been produced in 40,000 machine-hours (40,000 machine-hours = 2 machine-hours allowed per motor × 20,000 motors); however, the company actually used 42,000 machine-hours to makes these motors.

EXHIBIT 10–5
MicroDrive Corporation Data

Budgeted production	25,000 motors
Actual production	20,000 motors
Standard machine-hours per motor	2 machine-hours per motor
Budgeted machine-hours (2 × 25,000)	50,000 machine-hours
Standard machine-hours allowed for the actual output (2 × 20,000)	40,000 machine-hours
Actual machine-hours	42,000 machine-hours
Variable overhead costs per machine-hour:	
Indirect labor	$0.80 per machine-hour
Lubricants	$0.30 per machine-hour
Power	$0.40 per machine-hour
Actual total variable overhead costs:	
Indirect labor	$36,000
Lubricants	11,000
Power	24,000
Total actual variable overhead cost	$71,000

In preparing an overhead performance report for the year, MicroDrive could use the 42,000 machine-hours actually worked during the year *or* the 40,000 machine-hours that should have been worked according to the standard. If the actual hours are used, only a spending variance will be computed. If the standard hours are used, both a spending *and* an efficiency variance will be computed. Both of these approaches are illustrated in the following sections.

Spending Variance Alone

LEARNING OBJECTIVE 3
Use a flexible budget to prepare a variable overhead performance report containing only a spending variance.

If MicroDrive Corporation bases its overhead performance report on the 42,000 machine-hours actually worked during the year, then the performance report will show only a spending variance for variable overhead. Exhibit 10–6 shows a performance report prepared in this way.

The formula for the spending variance was introduced in the preceding chapter. That formula is:

$$\text{Variable overhead spending variance} = (AH \times AR) - (AH \times SR)$$

where AH = Actual hours, AR = Actual rate, SR = Standard rate.

Or, in factored form:

$$\text{Variable overhead spending variance} = AH(AR - SR)$$

The report in Exhibit 10–6 is structured around the first, or unfactored, format.

EXHIBIT 10–6

MicroDrive Corporation
Variable Overhead Performance Report
For the Year Ended December 31

Budget allowances are based on 42,000 machine-hours actually worked.

Comparing the flexible budget to actual overhead cost yields only a spending variance.

Budgeted machine-hours	50,000
Actual machine-hours	42,000
Standard machine-hours allowed	40,000

Overhead Costs	Cost Formula (per machine-hour)	Actual Costs Incurred 42,000 Machine-Hours ($AH \times AR$)	Flexible Budget Based on 42,000 Machine-Hours ($AH \times SR$)	Spending Variance
Variable overhead costs:				
Indirect labor	$0.80	$36,000	$33,600*	$2,400 U
Lubricants	0.30	11,000	12,600	1,600 F
Power	0.40	24,000	16,800	7,200 U
Total variable overhead cost	$1.50	$71,000	$63,000	$8,000 U

*42,000 machine-hours × $0.80 per machine-hour = $33,600. Other budget allowances are computed in the same way.

Interpreting the Spending Variance The variable overhead spending variance is useful only to the extent that the cost driver for variable overhead really is the actual hours worked. Then the flexible budget based on the actual hours worked is a valid benchmark that tells us how much *should* have been spent in total on variable overhead items during the period. The actual overhead costs are larger than this benchmark, resulting in an unfavorable variance, if either (1) the variable overhead items cost more to purchase than the standards allow or (2) more variable overhead items were used than the standards allow. So the spending variance includes both price and quantity variances.

Both Spending and Efficiency Variances

LEARNING OBJECTIVE 4
Use a flexible budget to prepare a variable overhead performance report containing both a spending and an efficiency variance.

If management of MicroDrive Corporation wants to compute variable overhead spending and efficiency variances, then it should compute budget allowances for *both* the 40,000 machine-hour and the 42,000 machine-hour levels of activity. Exhibit 10–7 shows a performance report prepared in this way.

Note that the spending variance in Exhibit 10–7 is the same as the spending variance shown in Exhibit 10–6. The performance report in Exhibit 10–7 has simply been expanded to also include an efficiency variance. Together, the spending and efficiency variances make up the total variance.

Interpreting the Efficiency Variance Like the variable overhead spending variance, the variable overhead efficiency variance is useful only to the extent that the cost

EXHIBIT 10–7

MicroDrive Corporation
Variable Overhead Performance Report
For the Year Ended December 31

Budget allowances are based on 40,000 machine-hours—the time it *should have taken* to produce the year's actual output of 20,000 motors—as well as on the 42,000 *actual* machine-hours worked.

This approach yields both a spending and an efficiency variance.

Budgeted machine-hours	50,000
Actual machine-hours	42,000
Standard machine-hours allowed	40,000

Overhead Costs	Cost Formula (per machine-hour)	(1) Actual Costs Incurred 42,000 Machine-Hours (*AH* × *AR*)	(2) Flexible Budget Based on 42,000 Machine-Hours (*AH* × *SR*)	(3) Flexible Budget Based on 40,000 Machine-Hours (*SH* × *SR*)	Total Variance (1) − (3)	Breakdown of the Total Variance: Spending Variance (1) − (2)	Breakdown of the Total Variance: Efficiency Variance (2) − (3)
Variable overhead costs:							
Indirect labor	$0.80	$36,000	$33,600*	$32,000	$ 4,000 U	$2,400 U	$1,600 U
Lubricants	0.30	11,000	12,600	12,000	1,000 F	1,600 F	600 U
Power	0.40	24,000	16,800	16,000	8,000 U	7,200 U	800 U
Total variable overhead cost	$1.50	$71,000	$63,000	$60,000	$11,000 U	$8,000 U	$3,000 U

*42,000 machine-hours × $0.80 per machine-hour = $33,600. Other budget allowances are computed in the same way.

driver for variable overhead really is the actual hours worked. Then any increase in hours actually worked should result in additional variable overhead costs. Consequently, if too many hours are used to create the actual output, this is presumed to result in an increase in variable overhead. The variable overhead efficiency variance is an estimate of the effect on variable overhead costs of inefficiency in the use of the base (i.e., hours). In a sense, the term *variable overhead efficiency variance* is a misnomer. It seems to suggest that it measures the efficiency with which variable overhead resources are used. It does not. It is an estimate of the indirect effect on variable overhead costs of inefficiency in the use of the activity base.

Recall from the preceding chapter that the variable overhead efficiency variance is a function of the difference between the actual hours incurred and the hours that should have been used to produce the period's output:

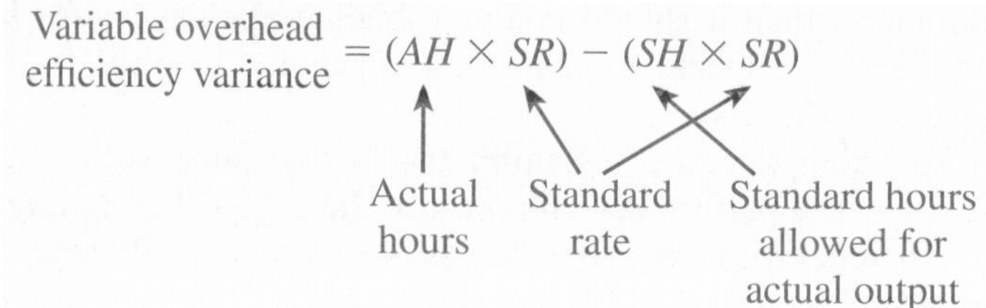

Or, in factored form:

$$\text{Variable overhead efficiency variance} = SR(AH - SH)$$

If more hours are worked than are allowed at standard, then the overhead efficiency variance will be unfavorable. However, as discussed above, the inefficiency is not in the use of overhead *but rather in the use of the base itself.*

This point can be illustrated by looking again at Exhibit 10–7. Two thousand more machine-hours were used during the period than should have been used to produce the period's output. Each of these hours presumably required the incurrence of $1.50 of variable overhead cost, resulting in an unfavorable variance of $3,000 (2,000 machine-hours × $1.50 per machine-hour = $3,000). Although this $3,000 variance is called an overhead efficiency variance, it could better be called a machine-hours efficiency variance, since it results from using too many machine-hours rather than from inefficient use of overhead resources.

Control of the Efficiency Variance Who is responsible for control of the overhead efficiency variance? Since the variance reflects efficiency in the utilization of the base underlying the flexible budget, whoever is responsible for control of this base is responsible for control of the variance. If the base is direct labor-hours, then the supervisor responsible for the use of labor time is responsible for any overhead efficiency variance.

Activity-Based Costing and the Flexible Budget

It is unlikely that all of the variable overhead in a complex organization is driven by a single factor such as the number of units produced or the number of labor-hours or machine-hours. The flexible budgeting approach can be easily adapted to accommodate a number of cost drivers. The cost formula for each variable cost element can depend on its own cost driver rather than on a single organization-wide measure of activity. For example, in a medical clinic the variable overhead cost of providing clinic staff with latex gloves might be driven by the number of patient-visits whereas the variable overhead cost of sterile wiping pads to prepare injection sites might be driven by the number of injections administered. In the flexible budget, the cost formula for latex gloves would be stated in terms of patient-visits whereas the cost formula for sterile wiping pads would be stated in terms of injections administered.

Overhead Rates and Fixed Overhead Analysis

LEARNING OBJECTIVE 5
Compute the predetermined overhead rate and apply overhead to products in a standard cost system.

As we shall see, fixed overhead variances are fundamentally different from variable overhead variances. To understand fixed overhead variances, we will need to review how predetermined overhead rates are established and used.

Flexible Budgets and Overhead Rates

Fixed costs come in large chunks that by definition do not vary with changes in the level of activity within the relevant range. This creates a problem in product costing, since the average fixed cost per unit will vary with the level of activity. Consider the data in the following table:

Video 10–1

Month	(1) Total Fixed Overhead Cost	(2) Number of Units Produced	Average Fixed Cost per Unit (1) ÷ (2)
January.	$6,000	1,000	$6.00
February	$6,000	1,500	$4.00
March	$6,000	800	$7.50

Notice that the large number of units produced in February results in a low unit cost ($4.00), whereas the smaller number of units produced in March results in a higher unit cost ($7.50). This occurs because the fixed cost is spread across more units in February than in March. One of the major reasons for using a predetermined overhead rate is to avoid such fluctuations in unit costs. A predetermined overhead rate can be set for an entire year, resulting in the same unit cost being recorded in the accounting system throughout the year.

Throughout the remainder of this chapter, we will be analyzing the fixed overhead costs of MicroDrive Corporation. To assist us in that task, the flexible budget of the company—including fixed costs—is displayed in Exhibit 10–8. Note that the total fixed overhead costs amount to $300,000 within the range of activity in the flexible budget.

EXHIBIT 10–8

MicroDrive Corporation
Flexible Budgets at Various Levels of Activity

Overhead Costs	Cost Formula (per machine-hour)	Activity (in machine-hours) 40,000	45,000	50,000	55,000
Variable overhead costs:					
Indirect labor	$0.80	$ 32,000	$ 36,000	$ 40,000	$ 44,000
Lubricants	0.30	12,000	13,500	15,000	16,500
Power.	0.40	16,000	18,000	20,000	22,000
Total variable overhead cost. .	$1.50	60,000	67,500	75,000	82,500
Fixed overhead costs:					
Depreciation.		100,000	100,000	100,000	100,000
Supervisory salaries		160,000	160,000	160,000	160,000
Insurance		40,000	40,000	40,000	40,000
Total fixed overhead cost. . . .		300,000	300,000	300,000	300,000
Total overhead cost.		$360,000	$367,500	$375,000	$382,500

Denominator Activity The formula that we used in Chapter 3 to compute the predetermined overhead rate was:

$$\text{Predetermined overhead rate} = \frac{\text{Estimated total manufacturing overhead cost}}{\text{Estimated total amount of the base (MH, DLH, etc.)}}$$

The estimated total amount of the base in the formula for the predetermined overhead rate is called the **denominator activity.** Recall from our discussion in Chapter 3 that once an estimated activity level (denominator activity) has been chosen, it remains unchanged throughout the year, even if the actual level of activity differs from what was estimated. The reason for not changing the denominator is to keep the amount of overhead applied to each unit of product the same regardless of when it is produced during the year.

IN BUSINESS

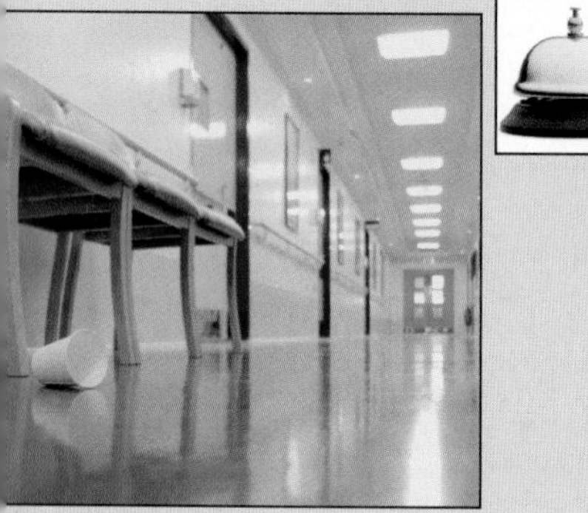

KNOW YOUR COSTS

Understanding the difference between fixed and variable costs can be critical. Kennard T. Wing, of OMG Center for Collaborative Learning, reports that a large health care system made the mistake of classifying all of its costs as variable. As a consequence, when volume dropped, managers felt that costs should be cut proportionately and more than 1,000 people were laid off—even though "the workload of most of them had no direct relation to patient volume. The result was that morale of the survivors plummeted and within a year the system was scrambling to replace not only those it had let go, but many others who had quit. The point is, the accounting systems we design and implement really do affect management decisions in significant ways. A system built on a bad model of the business will either not be used or, if used, will lead to bad decisions."

Source: Kennard T. Wing, "Using Enhanced Cost Models in Variance Analysis for Better Control and Decision Making," *Management Accounting Quarterly,* Winter 2000, pp. 27–35.

Computing the Overhead Rate When we discussed predetermined overhead rates in Chapter 3, we didn't explain how the estimated total manufacturing cost was determined. This figure can be derived using a flexible budget. The flexible budget can be used to determine the total amount of overhead cost that should be incurred at the denominator level of activity. The predetermined overhead rate can then be computed using the following variation on the basic formula for the predetermined overhead rate:

$$\text{Predetermined overhead rate} = \frac{\text{Overhead from the flexible budget at the denominator level of activity}}{\text{Denominator level of activity}}$$

To illustrate, refer to MicroDrive Corporation's flexible budget for manufacturing overhead in Exhibit 10–8. Suppose that the budgeted activity level for the year is 50,000 machine-hours and that this will be used as the denominator activity in the formula for the predetermined overhead rate. The numerator in the formula is the estimated total overhead cost of \$375,000 when the activity level is 50,000 machine-hours. This amount is taken from the flexible budget in Exhibit 10–8. Thus, the predetermined overhead rate for MicroDrive Corporation is computed as follows:

$$\text{Predetermined overhead rate} = \frac{\$375{,}000}{50{,}000 \text{ MHs}} = \$7.50 \text{ per machine-hour (MH)}$$

Or the company can break its predetermined overhead rate down into its variable and fixed components:

$$\text{Variable component: } \frac{\$75{,}000}{50{,}000 \text{ MHs}} = \$1.50 \text{ per MH}$$

$$\text{Fixed component: } \frac{\$300{,}000}{50{,}000 \text{ MHs}} = \$6.00 \text{ per MH}$$

For every standard machine-hour recorded, work in process will be charged with $7.50 of overhead, of which $1.50 will be variable overhead and $6.00 will be fixed overhead. Since a disk-drive motor should take two machine-hours to complete, its cost will include $3.00 of variable overhead and $12.00 of fixed overhead, as shown on the following standard cost card:

Standard Cost Card—Per Motor	
Direct materials (assumed)	$14.00
Direct labor (assumed)	6.00
Variable overhead (2 MHs at $1.50 per MH)	3.00
Fixed overhead (2 MHs at $6.00 per MH)	12.00
Total standard cost per motor	$35.00

In sum, the flexible budget provides the estimated overhead cost needed to compute the predetermined overhead rate. Thus, the flexible budget plays a key role in determining the amount of fixed and variable overhead cost that will be charged to units of product.

Overhead Application in a Standard Cost System

To understand fixed overhead variances, we first have to understand how overhead is applied to work in process in a standard cost system. Recall that in Chapter 3 we applied overhead to work in process on the basis of the actual level of activity. This procedure was correct, since at the time we were dealing with a normal cost system.[1] However, we are now dealing with a standard cost system. In such a system, overhead is applied to work in process on the basis of the *standard hours allowed for the actual output of the period* rather than on the basis of the actual number of hours worked. Exhibit 10–9 illustrates this point. In a standard cost system, every unit of product is charged with the same amount of overhead cost, regardless of how much time the unit actually requires for processing.

The Fixed Overhead Variances

LEARNING OBJECTIVE 6
Compute and interpret the fixed overhead budget and volume variances.

To illustrate the computation of fixed overhead variances, we will refer again to the data for MicroDrive Corporation.

Denominator activity in machine-hours	50,000
Budgeted fixed overhead costs	$300,000
Fixed portion of the predetermined overhead rate (computed earlier)	$6 per machine-hour

EXHIBIT 10–9
Applied Overhead Costs: Normal Cost System versus Standard Cost System

Normal Cost System		Standard Cost System	
Manufacturing Overhead		Manufacturing Overhead	
Actual overhead costs incurred.	Applied overhead costs: Actual hours × Predetermined overhead rate.	Actual overhead costs incurred.	Applied overhead costs: Standard hours allowed for actual output × Predetermined overhead rate.
Underapplied or overapplied overhead		Underapplied or overapplied overhead	

[1] Normal cost systems are discussed on page 85 in Chapter 3.

Let's assume that the following actual operating results were recorded for the year:

Actual machine-hours	42,000
Standard machine-hours allowed*	40,000
Actual fixed overhead costs:	
Depreciation	$100,000
Supervisory salaries	172,000
Insurance	36,000
Total actual fixed overhead cost	$308,000

*For the actual production of the year.

From these data, two variances are computed for fixed overhead—a *budget variance* and a *volume variance*. The variances are shown in Exhibit 10–10.

Notice from the exhibit that overhead has been applied to work in process on the basis of 40,000 standard hours allowed for the actual output of the year rather than on the basis of 42,000 actual hours worked. This keeps unit costs from being affected by variations in efficiency.

The Budget Variance—A Closer Look

The **budget variance** is the difference between the actual fixed overhead costs incurred during the period and the original budgeted fixed overhead costs for the period. It can be computed as shown in Exhibit 10–10 or by using the following formula:

$$\text{Budget variance} = \text{Actual fixed overhead cost} - \text{Budgeted fixed overhead cost}$$

Applying this formula to MicroDrive Corporation, the budget variance would be computed as follows:

$$\$308{,}000 - \$300{,}000 = \$8{,}000 \text{ U}$$

The variances computed for the fixed costs at Rick's Hairstyling in Exhibit 10–4 are all budget variances, since they represent the difference between the actual fixed overhead cost and the budgeted fixed overhead cost.

An expanded overhead performance report for MicroDrive Corporation appears in Exhibit 10–11. This report includes the budget variances for fixed overhead as well as the spending variances for variable overhead from Exhibit 10–6.

EXHIBIT 10–10
Computation of the Fixed Overhead Variances

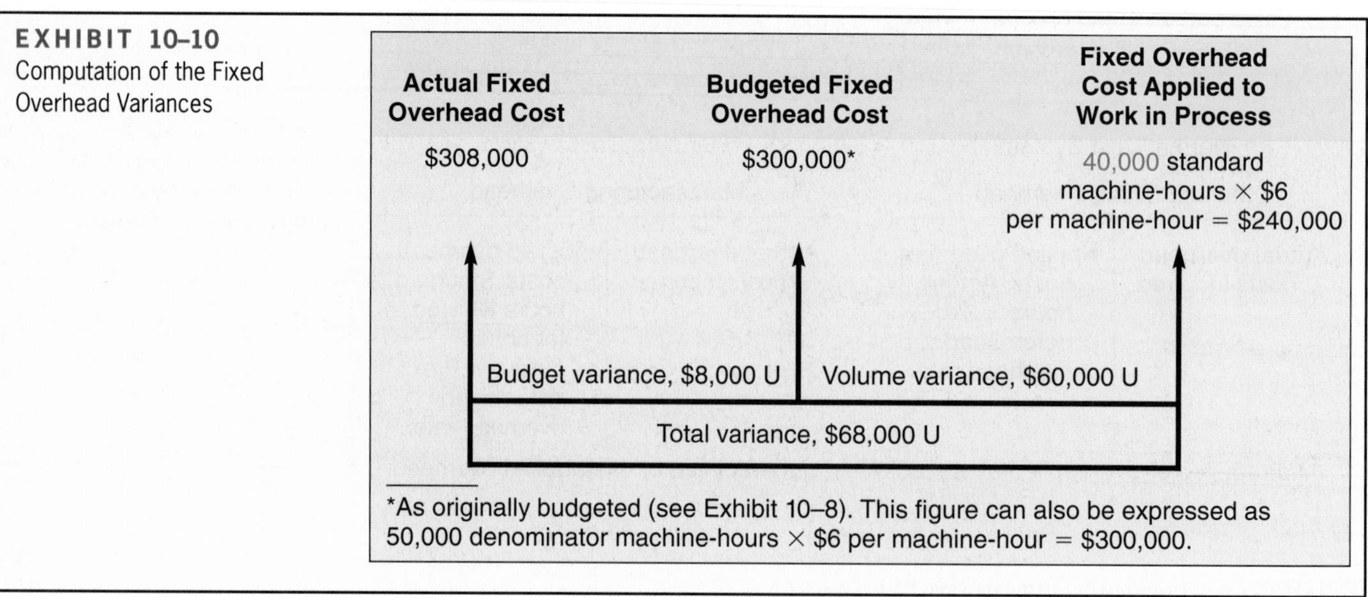

*As originally budgeted (see Exhibit 10–8). This figure can also be expressed as 50,000 denominator machine-hours × $6 per machine-hour = $300,000.

EXHIBIT 10–11
Fixed Overhead Costs on the Overhead Performance Report

MicroDrive Corporation
Overhead Performance Report
For the Year Ended December 31

Budgeted machine-hours	50,000
Actual machine-hours	42,000
Standard machine-hours allowed	40,000

	Cost Formula (per machine-hour)	Actual Costs 42,000 Machine-Hours	Flexible Budget Based on 42,000 Machine-Hours	Spending or Budget Variance
Overhead Costs				
Variable overhead costs:				
Indirect labor	$0.80	$ 36,000	$ 33,600	$ 2,400 U
Lubricants	0.30	11,000	12,600	1,600 F
Power	0.40	24,000	16,800	7,200 U
Total variable overhead cost	$1.50	71,000	63,000	8,000 U
Fixed overhead costs:				
Depreciation		100,000	100,000	0
Supervisory salaries		172,000	160,000	12,000 U
Insurance		36,000	40,000	4,000 F
Total fixed overhead cost		308,000	300,000	8,000 U
Total overhead cost		$379,000	$363,000	$16,000 U

The budget variances for fixed overhead can be very useful, since they represent the difference between how much *should* have been spent (according to the original budget) and how much was actually spent. For example, Exhibit 10–11 shows that supervisory salaries has a $12,000 unfavorable variance. This large variance should be explained. Was it due to an increase in salaries? Was it due to overtime? Was another supervisor hired? If so, why was another supervisor hired?

The Volume Variance—A Closer Look

The **volume variance** measures utilization of facilities. The variance arises whenever the standard hours allowed for the actual output of a period are different from the denominator activity level that was planned when the period began. It can be computed as shown in Exhibit 10–10 or by using the following formula:

$$\text{Volume variance} = \text{Fixed component of the predetermined overhead rate} \times \left(\text{Denominator hours} - \text{Standard hours allowed}\right)$$

Applying this formula to MicroDrive Corporation, the volume variance would be computed as follows:

$$\$6 \text{ per MH } (50{,}000 \text{ MHs} - 40{,}000 \text{ MHs}) = \$60{,}000 \text{ U}$$

Note that this computation agrees with the volume variance shown in Exhibit 10–10. As stated earlier, the volume variance is a measure of facility utilization. Or, to be more precise, it is a measure of how much actual output departed from the planned output that determined the denominator level of activity. An unfavorable variance, as above, means that the company's actual output was *less* than planned. A favorable variance would mean that the company's actual output was *greater* than planned.

It is important to note that the volume variance does not measure overspending or underspending. A company normally would incur the same dollar amount of fixed overhead cost regardless of whether the period's activity was above or below the planned (denominator) level. In short, the volume variance is an activity-related variance. It is explainable only by activity and is controllable only through activity.

To summarize:

1. If the denominator activity and the standard hours allowed for the actual output of the period are the same, the volume variance is zero.
2. If the denominator activity is greater than the standard hours allowed for the actual output of the period, then the volume variance is unfavorable. This indicates that facilities were utilized less than was planned.
3. If the denominator activity is less than the standard hours allowed for the actual output of the period, then the volume variance is favorable. This indicates that facilities were utilized more than was planned.

Graphic Analysis of Fixed Overhead Variances

Exhibit 10–12 shows a graphic analysis that offers insights into the fixed overhead budget and volume variances. As shown in the graph, fixed overhead cost is applied to work in process at the predetermined rate of $6 for each standard hour of activity. (The applied-cost line is the upward-sloping line on the graph.) Since a denominator level of 50,000 machine-hours was used in computing the $6 rate, the applied-cost line crosses the budget-cost line at exactly 50,000 machine-hours. If the denominator hours and the standard hours allowed for the actual output are the same, there is no volume variance. It is only when the standard hours differ from the denominator hours that a volume variance arises.

In MicroDrive's case, the standard hours allowed for the actual output (40,000 hours) are less than the denominator hours (50,000 hours). The result is an unfavorable volume

EXHIBIT 10–12
Graphic Analysis of Fixed Overhead Variances

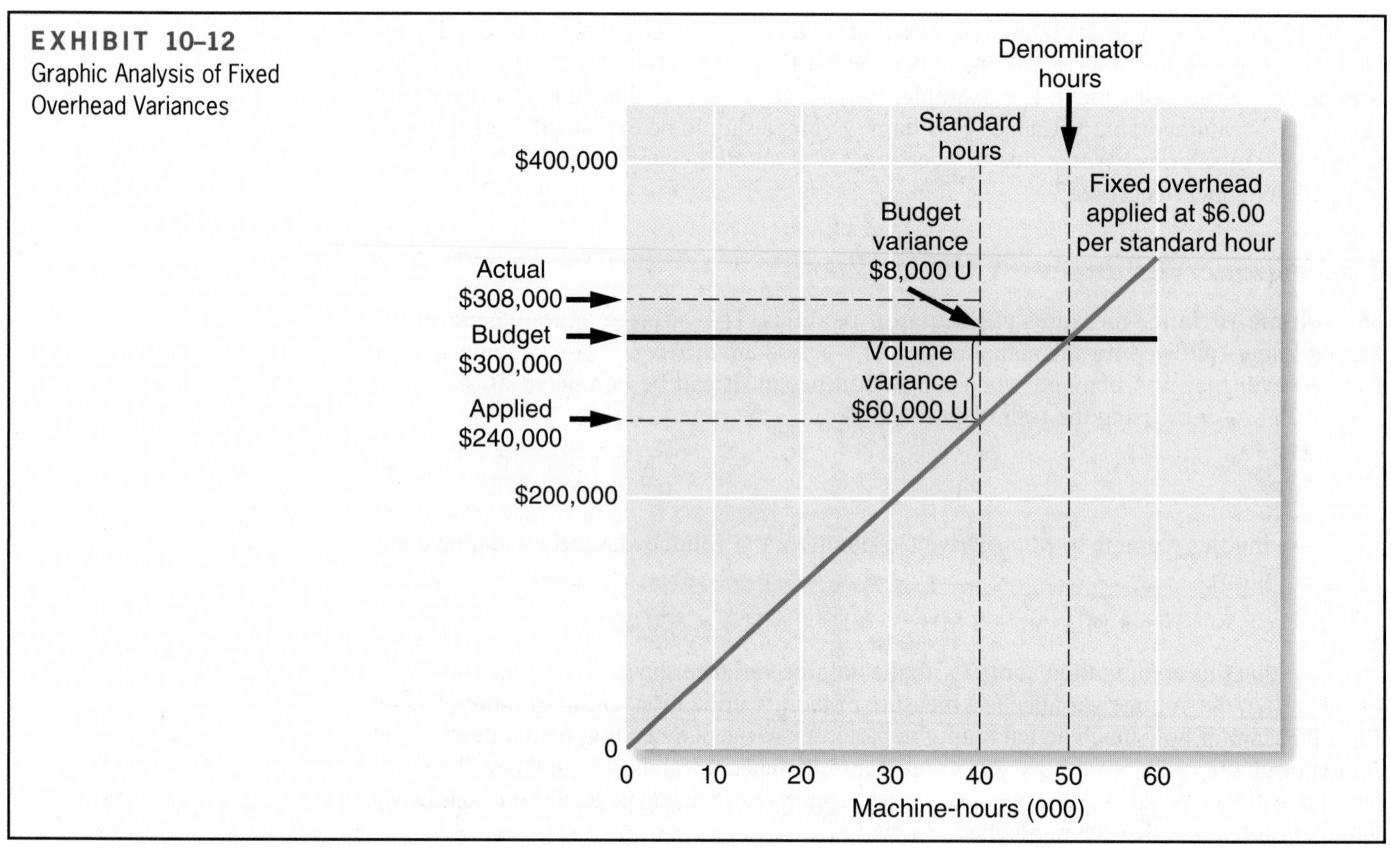

variance because less cost was applied to production than was originally budgeted. If the situation had been reversed and the standard hours allowed for the actual output had exceeded the denominator hours, then the volume variance on the graph would have been favorable.

Cautions in Fixed Overhead Analysis

A volume variance for fixed overhead arises because when applying the costs to work in process, we act *as if* the fixed costs are variable. The graph in Exhibit 10–12 illustrates this point. Notice from the graph that fixed overhead costs are applied to work in process at a rate of $6 per hour *as if* they are variable. Treating these costs as if they are variable is necessary for product costing purposes, but some real dangers lurk here. Managers can easily be misled into thinking that fixed costs are *in fact* variable.

Keep clearly in mind that fixed overhead costs come in large chunks. Expressing fixed costs on a unit or per hour basis, though necessary for product costing for external reports, is artificial. Increases or decreases in activity in fact have no effect on total fixed costs within the relevant range of activity. Even though fixed costs are expressed on a unit or per hour basis, they are *not* proportional to activity. In a sense, the volume variance is the error that occurs as a result of treating fixed costs as variable costs in the costing system.

Overhead Variances and Underapplied or Overapplied Overhead Cost

Four variances relating to overhead cost have been computed for MicroDrive Corporation in this chapter. These four variances are as follows:

Variable overhead spending variance (p. 404)	$ 8,000 U
Variable overhead efficiency variance (p. 405)	3,000 U
Fixed overhead budget variance (p. 410)	8,000 U
Fixed overhead volume variance (p. 410)	60,000 U
Total overhead variance	$79,000 U

Recall from Chapter 3 that underapplied or overapplied overhead is the difference between the amount of overhead applied to products and the actual overhead costs incurred during a period. Basically, the overhead variances we have computed in this chapter break the underapplied or overapplied overhead down into variances that can be used by managers for control purposes. *The sum of the overhead variances equals the underapplied or overapplied overhead cost for a period.*

Furthermore, in a standard cost system, unfavorable variances are equivalent to underapplied overhead and favorable variances are equivalent to overapplied overhead. Unfavorable variances occur because more was spent on overhead than the standards allow. Underapplied overhead occurs when more was spent on overhead than was applied to products during the period. But in a standard costing system, the standard amount of overhead allowed is exactly the same as the amount of overhead applied to products. Therefore, in a standard costing system, unfavorable variances and underapplied overhead are the same thing, as are favorable variances and overapplied overhead.

For MicroDrive Corporation, the total overhead variance is $79,000 unfavorable. Therefore, its overhead cost is underapplied by $79,000 for the year. To solidify this point in your mind, *carefully study the review problem at the end of the chapter!* This review problem provides a comprehensive summary of overhead analysis, including the computation of underapplied or overapplied overhead cost in a standard cost system.

IN BUSINESS

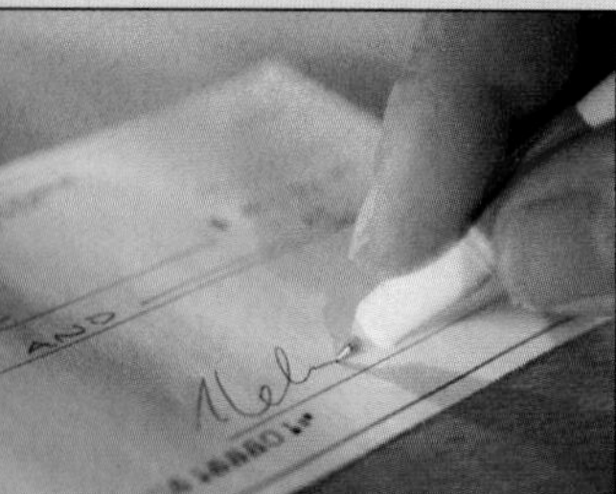

OVERHEAD ACCOUNTS: FERTILE GROUND FOR FRAUD

Particularly in small companies, the controller may be the only person who understands concepts such as overhead variances and overapplied and underapplied overhead. Furthermore, a small company controller may be able to both authorize cash disbursements and account for them. Since small, closely held companies often do not hire external auditors, these circumstances create an ideal environment for fraud.

Such was the case in a small manufacturing company with 100 employees and $30 million in annual sales. The controller embezzled nearly $1 million from the company over three years by writing checks to himself. The consultant who uncovered the fraud was tipped off by the unusually high overhead variances that resulted from the controller recording fictitious expenses in the overhead accounts to offset his fraudulent cash withdrawals. After the fraud was exposed, the company implemented various controls to reduce the risk of future problems. These controls included hiring an internal auditor and requiring periodic review of overhead variances to identify and explain significant discrepancies.

Source: John B. MacArthur, Bobby E. Waldrup, and Gary R. Fane, "Caution: Fraud Overhead," *Strategic Finance*, October 2004, pp. 28–32.

Summary

When analyzing overhead costs, it is essential to distinguish between variable overhead and fixed overhead. Total variable overhead costs vary in total in proportion to changes in activity whereas total fixed costs do not change within the relevant range. This distinction is important when constructing flexible budgets and when computing overhead variances.

A flexible budget shows what costs should be for various levels of activity. The flexible budget amount for a specific level of activity is determined differently depending on whether a cost is variable or fixed. If a cost is variable, the flexible budget amount is computed by multiplying the cost per unit of activity by the level of activity specified for the flexible budget. If a cost is fixed, the original total budgeted fixed cost is used as the flexible budget amount.

The two variances for variable overhead discussed in the chapter are the variable overhead spending and variable overhead efficiency variances. These variances were also covered in the previous chapter.

Two variances for fixed overhead are covered in the chapter. One—the budget variance—is quite simple; the other is considerably more complex. The budget variance is the difference between the actual total fixed overhead cost incurred and the total amount of fixed overhead cost that was originally budgeted. The volume variance is the difference between the amount of fixed overhead cost applied to inventory and the total amount of fixed overhead cost that was originally budgeted. The budget variance is a straightforward measure of the degree to which fixed overhead spending was under control. The volume variance is a consequence of treating a fixed cost as if it were variable and is more difficult to interpret meaningfully.

The sum of all four overhead variances equals the overhead overapplied or underapplied for the period. Unfavorable variances are equivalent to underapplied overhead and favorable variances are equivalent to overapplied overhead.

Review Problem: Overhead Analysis

(This problem provides a comprehensive review of Chapter 10, including the computation of underapplied or overapplied overhead and its breakdown into the four overhead variances.)

Data for the manufacturing overhead of Aspen Company are as follows:

Overhead Costs	Cost Formula (per machine-hour)	Machine-Hours 5,000	6,000	7,000
Variable overhead costs:				
Supplies	$0.20	$ 1,000	$ 1,200	$ 1,400
Indirect labor.	0.30	1,500	1,800	2,100
Total variable overhead cost	$0.50	2,500	3,000	3,500
Fixed overhead costs:				
Depreciation		4,000	4,000	4,000
Supervision.		5,000	5,000	5,000
Total fixed overhead cost.		9,000	9,000	9,000
Total overhead cost		$11,500	$12,000	$12,500

Five hours of machine time are required per unit of product. The company has set its denominator activity for the coming period at 6,000 machine-hours (or 1,200 units). The predetermined overhead rate is computed as follows:

$$\text{Total: } \frac{\$12{,}000}{6{,}000 \text{ MHs}} = \$2.00 \text{ per machine-hour}$$

$$\text{Variable component: } \frac{\$3{,}000}{6{,}000 \text{ MHs}} = \$0.50 \text{ per machine-hour}$$

$$\text{Fixed component: } \frac{\$9{,}000}{6{,}000 \text{ MHs}} = \$1.50 \text{ per machine-hour}$$

Assume the following *actual* results for the period:

Number of units produced	1,300 units
Actual machine-hours	6,800 machine-hours
Standard machine-hours allowed*	6,500 machine-hours
Actual variable overhead cost	$4,200
Actual fixed overhead cost	$9,400

*1,300 units × 5 machine-hours per unit.

Therefore, the company's Manufacturing Overhead account would appear as follows at the end of the period:

Manufacturing Overhead

	Debit	Credit	
Actual overhead costs	13,600*	13,000†	Applied overhead costs
Underapplied overhead	600		

*$4,200 variable + $9,400 fixed = $13,600.
†6,500 standard machine-hours × $2 per machine-hour = $13,000. In a standard cost system, overhead is applied on the basis of standard hours, not actual hours.

Required:
Analyze the $600 underapplied overhead in terms of:
1. The variable overhead spending variance.
2. The variable overhead efficiency variance.
3. The fixed overhead budget variance.
4. The fixed overhead volume variance.

Solution to Review Problem

Variable Overhead Variances

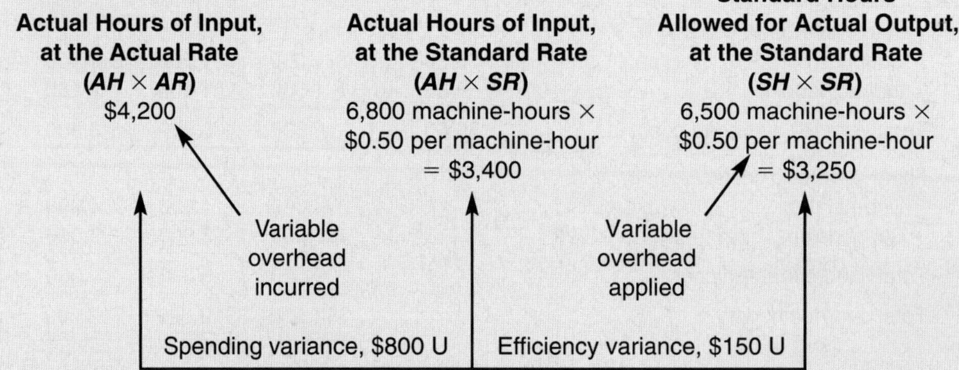

These same variances can be computed as follows:

Variable overhead spending variance:

$$\text{Spending variance} = (AH \times AR) - (AH \times SR)$$

$$= \text{Total actual variable overhead} - (AH \times SR)$$

$$\$4{,}200 - (6{,}800 \text{ machine-hours} \times \$0.50 \text{ per machine-hour}) = \$800 \text{ U}$$

Variable overhead efficiency variance:

$$\text{Efficiency variance} = SR(AH - SH)$$

$$\$0.50 \text{ per machine-hour } (6{,}800 \text{ machine-hours} - 6{,}500 \text{ machine-hours}) = \$150 \text{ U}$$

Fixed Overhead Variances

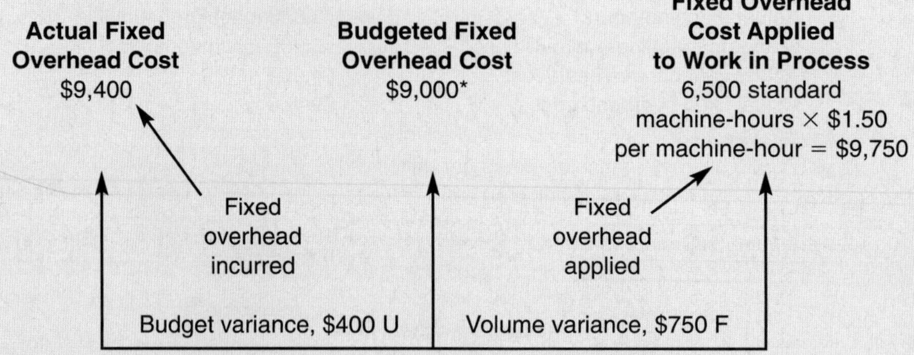

*Can be expressed as: 6,000 denominator machine-hours × $1.50 per machine-hour = $9,000.

These same variances can be computed as follows:

Fixed overhead budget variance:

$$\text{Budget variance} = \text{Actual fixed overhead cost} - \text{Budgeted fixed overhead cost}$$

$$\$9{,}400 - \$9{,}000 = \$400 \text{ U}$$

Fixed overhead volume variance:

$$\text{Volume variance} = \text{Fixed portion of the predetermined overhead rate} \times (\text{Denominator hours} - \text{Standard hours})$$

$$\$1.50 \text{ per machine-hour } (6{,}000 \text{ machine-hours} - 6{,}500 \text{ machine-hours}) = \$750 \text{ F}$$

Summary of Variances

The four overhead variances are summarized below:

Variable overhead:	
Spending variance	$800 U
Efficiency variance	150 U
Fixed overhead:	
Budget variance	400 U
Volume variance	750 F
Underapplied overhead	$600

Notice that the sum of the variances agrees with the underapplied balance in the company's Manufacturing Overhead account.

Glossary

Budget variance The difference between the actual fixed overhead costs incurred and the budgeted fixed overhead costs in the flexible budget. (p. 410)

Denominator activity The level of activity used to compute the predetermined overhead rate. (p. 408)

Flexible budget A budget that can be used to estimate what costs should be for any level of activity within a specified range. (p. 398)

Static budget A budget created at the beginning of the budgeting period that is valid only for the planned level of activity. (p. 397)

Volume variance The variance that arises whenever the standard hours allowed for the actual output of a period are different from the denominator activity level that was used to compute the predetermined overhead rate. It is computed by multiplying the fixed component of the predetermined overhead rate by the difference between the denominator hours and the standard hours allowed for the actual output. (p. 411)

Quiz 10

Multiple-choice questions are provided on the text Web site at www.mhhe.com/noreen1e.

Questions

10-1 What is a static budget?

10-2 What is a flexible budget and how does it differ from a static budget?

10-3 Name three criteria that should be considered in choosing an activity base on which to construct a flexible budget.

10-4 In a performance report for variable overhead, what variance(s) will be produced if the flexible budget is based on actual hours worked? On both actual hours worked and standard hours allowed?

10-5 What is meant by the term *standard hours allowed?*

10-6 How does the variable manufacturing overhead spending variance differ from the materials price variance?

10-7 Why is the term *overhead efficiency variance* potentially misleading?

10-8 What is meant by the term *denominator level of activity?*

10-9 Why do we apply overhead to work in process on the basis of standard hours allowed in Chapter 10 when we applied it on the basis of actual hours in Chapter 3? What is the difference in costing systems between the two chapters?

10-10 In a standard cost system, what two variances are computed for fixed manufacturing overhead?

10-11 What does the fixed overhead budget variance measure?

10-12 Under what circumstances would you expect the volume variance to be favorable? Unfavorable? Does the variance measure deviations in spending for fixed overhead items? Explain.

10-13 What is the danger in expressing fixed costs on a per unit basis?

10-14 Underapplied or overapplied overhead can be broken down into what four variances?

10-15 If factory overhead is overapplied for August, would you expect the total of the overhead variances to be favorable or unfavorable?

Exercises 

EXERCISE 10-1 Prepare a Flexible Budget [LO1]

The cost formulas for Swan Company's manufacturing overhead costs are given below. The costs cover a range of 8,000 to 10,000 machine-hours.

Overhead Costs	Cost Formula
Supplies	$0.20 per machine-hour
Indirect labor	$10,000 plus $0.25 per machine-hour
Utilities	$0.15 per machine-hour
Maintenance	$7,000 plus $0.10 per machine-hour
Depreciation	$8,000

Required:

Prepare a flexible budget in increments of 1,000 machine-hours. Include all costs in your flexible budget.

EXERCISE 10-2 Preparing a Flexible Budget Performance Report [LO2]

Canyonland Boat Charter Service rents live-aboard houseboats for cruising on the lake that traverses most of the Glen Canyon National Recreation area in Southern Utah. The company bases its overhead cost budgets on the following data:

Variable overhead costs:	
Cleaning	$72.50 per charter
Maintenance	$56.25 per charter
Park usage fees	$15.75 per charter
Fixed overhead costs:	
Salaries and wages	$7,860 per month
Depreciation	$13,400 per month
Utilities	$720 per month
Moorage	$3,670 per month

Each time a boat is chartered, whether it is for one day or a week, certain costs must be incurred. Those costs are listed above under the variable overhead costs. For example, each time a boat returns from a charter, it must be thoroughly cleaned, which costs $72.50 on average.

In August, the following actual costs were incurred for 140 charters:

Cleaning	$10,360
Maintenance	$7,630
Park usage fees	$2,210
Salaries and wages	$7,855
Depreciation	$14,450
Utilities	$735
Moorage	$3,950

Due to an unanticipated surge in demand for charters, the company purchased a new boat in August to add to its charter fleet.

Required:

1. Construct a Flexible Budget Performance Report for Canyonland Boat Charter Service for August, following the format in Exhibit 10–4.
2. What is apparently the major cause of the total overall overhead variance for the month? Explain.

EXERCISE 10-3 Variable Overhead Performance Report with Just a Spending Variance [LO3]

Jessel Corporation bases its variable overhead performance report on the actual direct labor-hours of the period. Data concerning the most recent year that ended on December 31 are as follows:

Budgeted direct labor-hours	42,000
Actual direct labor-hours	44,000
Standard direct labor-hours allowed	45,000
Cost formula (per direct labor-hour):	
Indirect labor	$0.90
Supplies	$0.15
Electricity	$0.05
Actual costs incurred:	
Indirect labor	$42,000
Supplies	$6,900
Electricity	$1,800

Required:

Prepare a variable overhead performance report using the format in Exhibit 10–6. Compute just the variable overhead spending variances; do not compute the variable overhead efficiency variances.

EXERCISE 10-4 Variable Overhead Performance Report with Both Spending and Efficiency Variances [LO4]

Refer to the data in Exercise 10-3 for Jessel Corporation. Management would like to compute both spending and efficiency variances for variable overhead in the company's variable overhead performance report.

Required:

Prepare a variable overhead performance report using the format in Exhibit 10–7. Compute both the variable overhead spending and efficiency variances.

EXERCISE 10-5 Applying Overhead in a Standard Costing System [LO5]

Mosbach Corporation has a standard cost system in which it applies overhead to products based on the standard direct labor-hours allowed for the actual output of the period. Data concerning the most recent year appear below:

Variable overhead cost per direct labor-hour	$3.50
Total fixed overhead cost per year	$600,000
Budgeted standard direct labor-hours (denominator level of activity)	80,000
Actual direct labor-hours	84,000
Standard direct labor-hours allowed for the actual output	82,000

Required:

1. Compute the predetermined overhead rate for the year.
2. Determine the amount of overhead that would be applied to the output of the period.

EXERCISE 10-6 Fixed Overhead Variances [LO6]

Lusive Corporation has a standard cost system in which it applies overhead to products based on the standard direct labor-hours allowed for the actual output of the period. Data concerning the most recent year appear below:

Total budgeted fixed overhead cost for the year	$400,000
Actual fixed overhead cost for the year	$394,000
Budgeted standard direct labor-hours (denominator level of activity)	50,000
Actual direct labor-hours	51,000
Standard direct labor-hours allowed for the actual output	48,000

Required:

1. Compute the fixed portion of the predetermined overhead rate for the year.
2. Compute the fixed overhead budget and volume variances.

EXERCISE 10-7 Preparing a Flexible Budget [LO1]

An incomplete flexible budget for overhead is given below for AutoPutz, Gmbh, a German company that owns and operates a large automatic carwash facility near Köln. The German currency is the euro, which is denoted by €.

Autoputz, Gmbh
Flexible Budget

Overhead Costs	Cost Formula (per car)	Activity (cars) 7,000	8,000	9,000
Variable overhead costs:				
Cleaning supplies	?	?	€ 6,000	?
Electricity	?	?	4,800	?
Maintenance	?	?	1,200	?
Total variable overhead cost	?	?	?	?
Fixed overhead costs:				
Operator wages		?	10,000	?
Depreciation		?	20,000	?
Rent		?	8,000	?
Total fixed overhead cost		?	?	?
Total overhead cost		?	?	?

Required:

Fill in the missing data in the flexible budget.

EXERCISE 10-8 Using a Flexible Budget [LO1]

Refer to the data in Exercise 10-7. AutoPutz, Gmbh's owner-manager would like to prepare a budget for August assuming an activity level of 8,200 cars.

Required:

Prepare a static budget for August. Use Exhibit 10–1 in the chapter as your guide.

EXERCISE 10-9 Flexible Budget Performance Report [LO2]

Refer to the data in Exercise 10-7. AutoPutz, Gmbh's actual level of activity during August was 8,300 cars, although the owner had constructed his static budget for the month assuming the level of activity would be 8,200 cars. The actual overhead costs incurred during August are given below:

	Actual Costs Incurred for 8,300 Cars
Variable overhead costs:	
Cleaning supplies	€6,350
Electricity	€4,865
Maintenance	€1,600
Fixed overhead costs:	
Operator wages	€10,050
Depreciation	€20,200
Rent	€8,000

Required:

Prepare a flexible budget performance report for both the variable and fixed overhead costs for August. Use Exhibit 10–4 in the chapter as your guide.

EXERCISE 10-10 Variable Overhead Performance Report [LO3]

The variable portion of Whaley Company's flexible budget for manufacturing overhead is as follows:

Overhead Costs	Cost Formula (per machine-hour)	Machine-Hours		
		10,000	18,000	24,000
Utilities	$1.20	$12,000	$21,600	$ 28,800
Supplies	0.30	3,000	5,400	7,200
Maintenance	2.40	24,000	43,200	57,600
Rework	0.60	6,000	10,800	14,400
Total variable overhead cost	$4.50	$45,000	$81,000	$108,000

During a recent period, the company recorded 16,000 machine-hours of activity. The variable overhead costs incurred were as follows:

Utilities	$20,000
Supplies	$4,700
Maintenance	$35,100
Rework	$12,300

The budgeted activity for the period had been 18,000 machine-hours.

Required:

1. Prepare a variable overhead performance report for the period. Indicate whether variances are favorable (F) or unfavorable (U). Show only a spending variance on your report.
2. Discuss the significance of the variances. Might some variances be the result of others? Explain.

EXERCISE 10-11 Predetermined Overhead Rate; Overhead Variances [LO4, LO5, LO6]

Weller Company's flexible budget for manufacturing overhead (in condensed form) follows:

Overhead Costs	Cost Formula (per machine-hour)	Machine-Hours		
		8,000	9,000	10,000
Variable cost	$1.05	$ 8,400	$ 9,450	$10,500
Fixed cost		24,800	24,800	24,800
Total overhead cost		$33,200	$34,250	$35,300

The following information is available for a recent period:

a. The denominator activity of 8,000 machine-hours was chosen to compute the predetermined overhead rate.

b. At the 8,000 standard machine-hours level of activity, the company should produce 3,200 units of product.

c. The company's actual operating results were as follows:

Number of units produced	3,500
Actual machine-hours	8,500
Actual variable overhead costs	$9,860
Actual fixed overhead costs	$25,100

Required:

1. Compute the predetermined overhead rate and break it down into variable and fixed cost elements.
2. What were the standard hours allowed for the year's actual output?
3. Compute the variable overhead spending and efficiency variances and the fixed overhead budget and volume variances.

EXERCISE 10-12 Using Fixed Overhead Variances [LO6]

The standard cost card for the single product manufactured by Prince Company is given below:

Standard Cost Card—Per Unit	
Direct materials, 3.5 feet at \$4 per foot	\$14.00
Direct labor, 0.8 direct labor-hours at \$18 per direct labor-hour	14.40
Variable overhead, 0.8 direct labor-hours at \$2.50 per direct labor-hour	2.00
Fixed overhead, 0.8 direct labor-hours at \$6 per direct labor-hour	4.80
Total standard cost per unit	\$35.20

Last year, the company produced 10,000 units of product and worked 8,200 actual direct labor-hours. Manufacturing overhead cost is applied to production on the basis of direct labor-hours. Selected data relating to the company's fixed manufacturing overhead cost for the year are shown below:

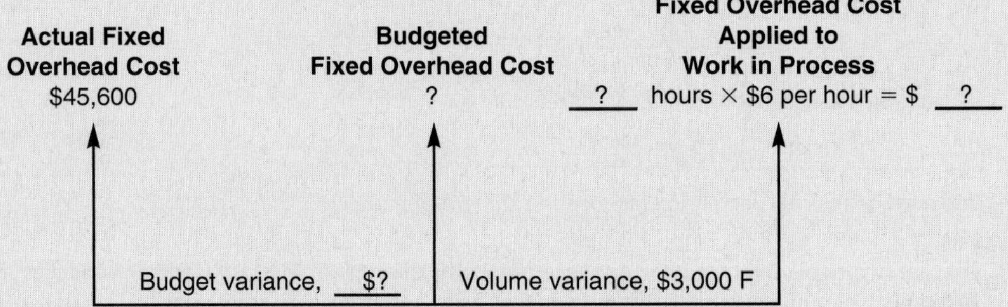

Required:

1. What were the standard hours allowed for the year's production?
2. What was the amount of budgeted fixed overhead cost for the year?
3. What was the budget variance for the year?
4. What denominator activity level did the company use in setting the predetermined overhead rate for the year?

EXERCISE 10-13 Variable Overhead Performance Report with Both Spending and Efficiency Variances [LO4]

The check-clearing office of San Juan Bank is responsible for processing all checks that come to the bank for payment. Managers at the bank believe that variable overhead costs are essentially proportional to the number of labor-hours worked in the office, so labor-hours are used as the activity base when preparing variable overhead budgets and performance reports. Data for October, the most recent month, appear below:

Budgeted labor-hours	865
Actual labor-hours	860
Standard labor-hours allowed for the actual number of checks processed	880

	Cost Formula (per labor-hour)	Actual Costs Incurred in October
Variable overhead costs:		
Office supplies	\$0.15	\$ 146
Staff coffee lounge	0.05	124
Indirect labor	3.25	2,790
Total variable overhead cost	\$3.45	\$3,060

Required:

Prepare a variable overhead performance report for October for the check-clearing office that includes both spending and efficiency variances. Use Exhibit 10–7 as a guide.

EXERCISE 10-14 Relations Among Fixed Overhead Variances [LO5, LO6]
Selected information relating to the fixed overhead costs of Westwood Company for the most recent year is given below:

Activity:	
Number of units produced	9,500
Standard machine-hours allowed per unit	2
Denominator activity (machine-hours)	20,000
Costs:	
Actual fixed overhead costs incurred	$79,000
Budget variance	$1,000 F

Overhead cost is applied to products on the basis of standard machine-hours.

Required:
1. What was the fixed portion of the predetermined overhead rate?
2. What were the standard machine-hours allowed for the period's production?
3. What was the volume variance?

EXERCISE 10-15 Predetermined Overhead Rates [LO5]
Operating at a normal level of 24,000 direct labor-hours, Trone Company produces 8,000 units of product. The direct labor wage rate is $12.60 per hour. Two pounds of raw materials go into each unit of product at a cost of $4.20 per pound. A flexible budget is used to plan and control overhead costs:

	Flexible Budget Data			
	Cost Formula (per direct	Direct Labor-Hours		
Overhead Costs	labor-hour)	20,000	22,000	24,000
Variable cost	$1.60	$ 32,000	$ 35,200	$ 38,400
Fixed cost		84,000	84,000	84,000
Total overhead cost		$116,000	$119,200	$122,400

Required:
1. Using 24,000 direct labor-hours as the denominator activity, compute the predetermined overhead rate and break it down into fixed and variable elements.
2. Complete the standard cost card below for one unit of product:

Direct materials, 2 pounds at $4.20 per pound	$8.40
Direct labor, ?.	?
Variable overhead, ?	?
Fixed overhead, ?.	?
Total standard cost per unit	$?

EXERCISE 10-16 Fixed Overhead Variances [LO6]

Selected operating information on three different companies for a recent period is given below:

	Company		
	X	Y	Z
Full-capacity direct labor-hours	20,000	9,000	10,000
Budgeted direct labor-hours*	19,000	8,500	8,000
Actual direct labor-hours	19,500	8,000	9,000
Standard direct labor-hours allowed for actual output	18,500	8,250	9,500

*Denominator activity for computing the predetermined overhead rate.

Required:
For each company, state whether the volume variance would be favorable or unfavorable; also, explain in each case *why* the volume variance would be favorable or unfavorable.

Problems 

PROBLEM 10-17 Preparing an Overhead Performance Report [LO2]

Shipley Company has had a comprehensive budgeting system in operation for several years. Feelings vary among the managers as to the value and benefit of the system. The line supervisors are very happy with the reports being prepared on their performance, but upper management often expresses dissatisfaction over the reports being prepared on various phases of the company's operations. A typical manufacturing overhead performance report for a recent period is shown below:

Shipley Company
Overhead Performance Report—Milling Department
For the Quarter Ended June 30

	Actual	Budget	Variance
Machine-hours	25,000	30,000	
Variable overhead:			
Indirect labor	$ 20,000	$ 22,500	$2,500 F
Supplies	5,400	6,000	600 F
Utilities	27,000	30,000	3,000 F
Rework	14,000	15,000	1,000 F
Total variable overhead cost	66,400	73,500	7,100 F
Fixed overhead:			
Maintenance	61,900	60,000	1,900 U
Inspection	90,000	90,000	0
Total fixed overhead cost	151,900	150,000	1,900 U
Total overhead cost	$218,300	$223,500	$5,200 F

After receiving a copy of this performance report, the supervisor of the Milling Department stated, "No one can complain about my department; our variances have been favorable for over a year now. We've saved the company thousands of dollars by our excellent cost control."

The budget data above are for the original planned level of activity for the quarter.

Required:

1. The production superintendent is uneasy about the performance reports being prepared and would like you to evaluate their usefulness to the company.
2. What changes, if any, should be made in the overhead performance report to give better insight into how well the supervisor is controlling costs?
3. Prepare a new overhead performance report for the quarter, incorporating any changes you suggested in (2) above. Include both the variable and the fixed costs in your report.

PROBLEM 10-18 Comprehensive Standard Cost Variances [LO4, LO6]

"It certainly is nice to see that small variance on the income statement after all the trouble we've had lately in controlling manufacturing costs," said Linda White, vice president of Molina Company. "The $12,250 overall manufacturing variance reported last period is well below the 3% limit we have set for variances. We need to congratulate everybody on a job well done."

The company produces and sells a single product. The standard cost card for the product follows:

Standard Cost Card—Per Unit

Direct materials, 4 yards at $3.50 per yard	$14
Direct labor, 1.5 direct labor-hours at $12 per direct labor-hour	18
Variable overhead, 1.5 direct labor-hours at $2 per direct labor-hour	3
Fixed overhead, 1.5 direct-labor hours at $6 per direct labor-hour	9
Standard cost per unit	$44

The following additional information is available for the year just completed:

a. The company manufactured 20,000 units of product during the year.
b. A total of 78,000 yards of material was purchased during the year at a cost of $3.75 per yard. All of this material was used to manufacture the 20,000 units. There were no beginning or ending inventories for the year.
c. The company worked 32,500 direct labor-hours during the year at a cost of $11.80 per hour.
d. Overhead cost is applied to products on the basis of standard direct labor-hours. Data relating to manufacturing overhead costs follow:

Denominator activity level (direct labor-hours)	25,000
Budgeted fixed overhead costs (from the flexible budget)	$150,000
Actual fixed overhead costs	$148,000
Actual variable overhead costs	$68,250

Required:

1. Compute the direct materials price and quantity variances for the year.
2. Compute the direct labor rate and efficiency variances for the year.
3. For manufacturing overhead, compute the following:
   a. The variable overhead spending and efficiency variances for the year.
   b. The fixed overhead budget and volume variances for the year.
4. Total the variances you have computed, and compare the net amount with the $12,250 mentioned by the vice president. Do you agree that everyone should be congratulated for a job well done? Explain.

PROBLEM 10-19 Applying Overhead; Overhead Variances [LO4, LO5, LO6]

Highland Shortbread, Ltd., of Aberdeen, Scotland, produces a single product and uses a standard cost system to help control costs. Manufacturing overhead is applied to production on the basis of standard machine-hours. According to the company's flexible budget, the following overhead costs should be incurred at an activity level of 18,000 machine-hours (the denominator activity level chosen for the year):

Variable manufacturing overhead cost	£ 31,500
Fixed manufacturing overhead cost	72,000
Total manufacturing overhead cost	£103,500

During the year, the following operating results were recorded:

Actual machine-hours worked	15,000
Standard machine-hours allowed	16,000
Actual variable manufacturing overhead cost incurred	£26,500
Actual fixed manufacturing overhead cost incurred	£70,000

At the end of the year, the company's Manufacturing Overhead account contained the following data:

Manufacturing Overhead

Actual costs	96,500	Applied costs	92,000
	4,500		

Management would like to determine the cause of the £4,500 underapplied overhead.

Required:

1. Compute the predetermined overhead rate for the year. Break it down into variable and fixed cost elements.
2. Show how the £92,000 "Applied costs" figure in the Manufacturing Overhead account was computed.
3. Analyze the £4,500 underapplied overhead figure in terms of the variable overhead spending and efficiency variances and the fixed overhead budget and volume variances.
4. Explain the meaning of each variance that you computed in (3) above.

PROBLEM 10-20 Applying the Flexible Budget Approach [LO2]

The KGV Blood Bank, a private charity partly supported by government grants, is located on the Caribbean island of St. Lucia. The blood bank has just finished its operations for September, which was a particularly busy month due to a powerful hurricane that hit neighboring islands, causing many injuries. The hurricane largely bypassed St. Lucia, but residents of St. Lucia willingly donated their blood to help people on other islands. As a consequence, the blood bank collected and processed over 25% more blood than had been originally planned for the month.

A report prepared by a government official comparing actual costs to budgeted costs for the blood bank appears below. (The currency on St. Lucia is the East Caribbean dollar.) Continued support from the government depends on the blood bank's ability to demonstrate control over its costs.

KGV Blood Bank
Cost Control Report
For the Month Ended September 30

	Actual	Budget	Variance
Liters of blood collected	780	600	180
Variable costs:			
Medical supplies	$ 9,252	$ 7,110	$2,142 U
Lab tests	10,782	8,610	2,172 U
Refreshments for donors	1,186	960	226 U
Administrative supplies	189	150	39 U
Total variable cost	21,409	16,830	4,579 U
Fixed costs:			
Staff salaries	13,200	13,200	0
Equipment depreciation	2,100	1,900	200 U
Rent	1,500	1,500	0
Utilities	324	300	24 U
Total fixed cost	17,124	16,900	224 U
Total cost	$38,533	$33,730	$4,803 U

The managing director of the blood bank was very unhappy with this report, claiming that his costs were higher than expected due to the emergency on the neighboring islands. He also pointed out that the additional costs had been fully covered by payments from grateful recipients on the other islands. The government official who prepared the report countered that all of the figures had been submitted by the blood bank to the government; he was just pointing out that actual costs were a lot higher than promised in the budget.

Required:

1. Prepare a new performance report for September using the flexible budget approach. (Note: Even though some of these costs might be classified as direct costs rather than as overhead, the flexible budget approach can still be used to prepare a flexible budget performance report.)
2. Do you think any of the variances in the report you prepared should be investigated? Why?

PROBLEM 10-21 Comprehensive Standard Cost Variances [LO4, LO5, LO6]

Dresser Company uses a standard cost system and sets predetermined overhead rates on the basis of direct labor-hours. The following data are taken from the company's budget for the current year:

Denominator activity (direct labor-hours)	9,000
Variable manufacturing overhead cost at 9,000 direct labor-hours	$34,200
Fixed manufacturing overhead cost	$63,000

The standard cost card for the company's only product is given below:

Direct materials, 4 pounds at $2.60 per pound	$10.40
Direct labor, 2 direct labor-hours at $9 per direct labor-hour	18.00
Overhead, 120% of direct labor cost	21.60
Standard cost per unit	$50.00

During the year, the company produced 4,800 units of product and incurred the following costs:

Materials purchased, 30,000 pounds at $2.50 per pound	$75,000
Materials used in production (in pounds)	20,000
Direct labor cost incurred, 10,000 direct labor-hours at $8.60 per direct labor-hour	$86,000
Variable manufacturing overhead cost incurred	$35,900
Fixed manufacturing overhead cost incurred	$64,800

Required:

1. Redo the standard cost card in a clearer, more usable format by detailing the variable and fixed overhead cost elements.
2. Prepare an analysis of the variances for materials and labor for the year.
3. Prepare an analysis of the variances for variable and fixed overhead for the year.
4. What effect, if any, does the choice of a denominator activity level have on standard unit costs? Is the volume variance a controllable variance from a spending point of view? Explain.

PROBLEM 10-22 Flexible Budgets and Overhead Analysis [LO1, LO4, LO5, LO6]

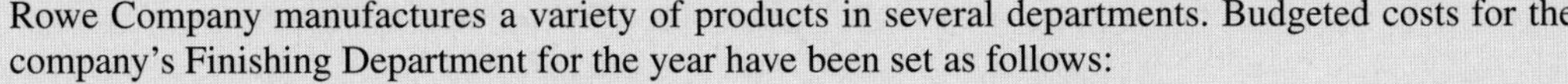

Rowe Company manufactures a variety of products in several departments. Budgeted costs for the company's Finishing Department for the year have been set as follows:

Variable costs:	
Direct materials	$ 600,000
Direct labor....................	450,000
Indirect labor..................	30,000
Utilities	50,000
Maintenance.....................	20,000
Total variable cost	1,150,000
Fixed costs:	
Supervisory salaries............	60,000
Insurance	5,000
Depreciation....................	190,000
Equipment rental	45,000
Total fixed cost................	300,000
Total budgeted cost	$1,450,000
Budgeted direct labor-hours	50,000

After careful study, the company has determined that operating activity in the Finishing Department is best measured by direct labor-hours. The cost formulas used to develop the budgeted costs above are valid over a relevant range of 40,000 to 60,000 direct labor-hours per year.

Required:

1. Prepare a manufacturing overhead flexible budget for the Finishing Department using increments of 10,000 hours. (The company does not include direct materials and direct labor costs in the flexible budget.)
2. Assume that the company computes predetermined overhead rates by department. Compute the rates, variable and fixed, that will be used to apply Finishing Department overhead costs to production.
3. Suppose that during the year the following actual activity and costs are recorded in the Finishing Department:

Actual direct labor-hours worked	46,000
Standard direct labor-hours allowed for the output of the year........	45,000
Actual variable manufacturing overhead cost incurred..............	$89,700
Actual fixed manufacturing overhead cost incurred	$296,000

a. A T-account for manufacturing overhead costs in the Finishing Department is given below. Determine the amount of applied overhead cost for the year, and compute the underapplied or overapplied overhead.

Manufacturing Overhead

Actual costs	385,700	

b. Analyze the underapplied or overapplied overhead in terms of the variable overhead spending and efficiency variances and the fixed overhead budget and volume variances.

PROBLEM 10-23 Comprehensive Problem: Flexible Budget; Overhead Performance Report [LO1, LO2, LO3, LO4]

Elgin Company has recently introduced budgeting as an integral part of its corporate planning process. An inexperienced member of the accounting staff was given the assignment of constructing a flexible budget for manufacturing overhead costs and prepared it in the format that follows:

Percentage of Capacity	80%	100%
Machine-hours	40,000	50,000
Utilities	$ 41,000	$ 49,000
Supplies	4,000	5,000
Indirect labor	8,000	10,000
Maintenance	37,000	41,000
Supervision	10,000	10,000
Total manufacturing overhead cost	$100,000	$115,000

The company assigns manufacturing overhead costs to production on the basis of standard machine-hours. The cost formulas used to prepare the budgeted figures above are relevant over a range of 80% to 100% of capacity in a month. The managers who will be working under these budgets have control over both fixed and variable manufacturing overhead costs.

Required:

1. Redo the company's flexible budget, presenting it in better format. Show the budgeted costs at 80%, 90%, and 100% levels of capacity. (Use the high-low method to separate fixed and variable costs.)
2. Express the flexible budget prepared in (1) above using a single cost formula for all overhead costs.
3. During May, the company operated at 86% of machine-hour capacity. Actual manufacturing overhead costs incurred during the month were as follows:

Utilities	$ 42,540
Supplies	6,450
Indirect labor	9,890
Maintenance	35,190
Supervision	10,000
Total actual manufacturing overhead cost	$104,070

   Fixed costs had no budget variances. Prepare an overhead performance report for May. Include both fixed and variable costs in your report (in separate sections). Structure your report so that it shows only a spending variance for overhead. The company originally budgeted to work 40,000 machine-hours during the month; standard hours allowed for the month's production totaled 41,000 machine-hours.
4. Explain possible causes of the spending variance for supplies.
5. Compute an efficiency variance for *total* variable overhead cost, and explain the nature of the variance.

PROBLEM 10-24 Applying Overhead; Overhead Variances [LO4, LO5, LO6]

Wymont Company produces a single product that requires a large amount of labor time. Overhead cost is applied on the basis of standard direct labor-hours. The company's condensed flexible budget for manufacturing overhead is given below:

Overhead Costs	Cost Formula (per DLH)	Direct Labor-Hours 24,000	30,000	36,000
Variable manufacturing overhead cost	$2	$ 48,000	$ 60,000	$ 72,000
Fixed manufacturing overhead cost		180,000	180,000	180,000
Total manufacturing overhead cost		$228,000	$240,000	$252,000

The company's product requires 4 feet of direct material that has a standard cost of $3 per foot. The product requires 1.5 hours of direct labor time. The standard labor rate is $12 per hour.

During the year, the company had planned to operate at a denominator activity level of 30,000 direct labor-hours and to produce 20,000 units of product. Actual activity and costs for the year were as follows:

Number of units produced	22,000
Actual direct labor-hours worked	35,000
Actual variable manufacturing overhead cost incurred	$63,000
Actual fixed manufacturing overhead cost incurred	$181,000

Required:

1. Compute the predetermined overhead rate for the year. Break the rate down into variable and fixed components.
2. Prepare a standard cost card for the company's product; show the details for all manufacturing costs on your standard cost card.
3. *a.* Compute the standard direct labor-hours allowed for the year's production.
   b. Complete the following Manufacturing Overhead T-account for the year:

Manufacturing Overhead	
?	?
?	?

4. Determine the reason for the underapplied or overapplied overhead from (3) above by computing the variable overhead spending and efficiency variances and the fixed overhead budget and volume variances.
5. Suppose the company had chosen 36,000 direct labor-hours as the denominator activity rather than 30,000 hours. State which, if any, of the variances computed in (4) above would have changed, and explain how the variance(s) would have changed. No computations are necessary.

PROBLEM 10-25 Flexible Budget and Overhead Performance Report [LO1, LO2, LO4]

Durrant Company has had great difficulty in controlling manufacturing overhead costs. At a recent convention, the president heard about a control device for overhead costs known as a flexible budget, and he has hired you to implement this budgeting program in Durrant Company. After some effort, you have developed the following cost formulas for the company's Machining Department. These costs are based on a normal operating range of 10,000 to 20,000 machine-hours per month:

Overhead Cost	Cost Formula
Utilities	$0.70 per machine-hour
Lubricants.	$1.00 per machine-hour plus $8,000 per month
Machine setup	$0.20 per machine-hour
Indirect labor.	$0.60 per machine-hour plus $120,000 per month
Depreciation	$32,000 per month

During March, the first month after your preparation of the above data, the Machining Department worked 18,000 machine-hours and produced 9,000 units of product. The actual manufacturing overhead costs for March were as follows:

Utilities	$ 12,000
Lubricants.	24,500
Machine setup	4,800
Indirect labor	132,500
Depreciation.	32,000
Total manufacturing overhead cost	$205,800

Fixed costs had no budget variances. The department had originally been budgeted to work 20,000 machine-hours during March.

Required:

1. Prepare a flexible budget for the Machining Department in increments of 5,000 hours. Include both variable and fixed costs in your budget.
2. Prepare an overhead performance report for the Machining Department for the month of March. Include both variable and fixed costs in the report (in separate sections). Show only a spending variance on the report.
3. What additional information would you need to compute an overhead efficiency variance for the department?

PROBLEM 10-26 Evaluting an Overhead Performance Report [LO2, LO4]

Ronald Davis, superintendent of Mason Company's Milling Department, is very happy with his performance report for the past month. The report follows:

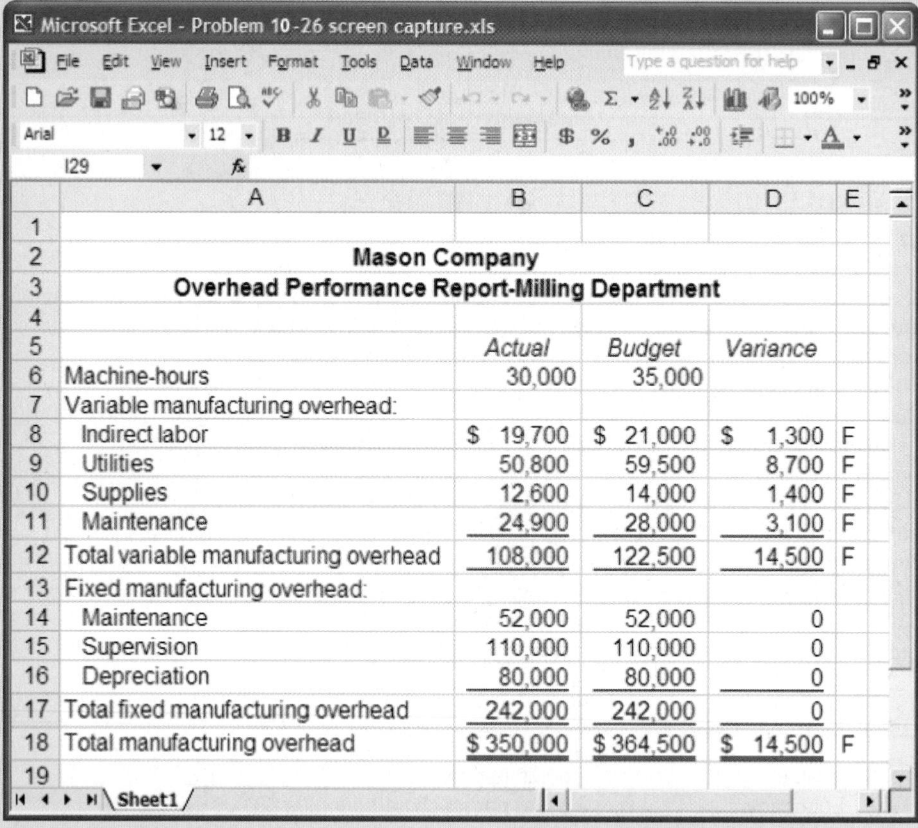

Mason Company
Overhead Performance Report-Milling Department

	Actual	Budget	Variance	
Machine-hours	30,000	35,000		
Variable manufacturing overhead:				
Indirect labor	$ 19,700	$ 21,000	$ 1,300	F
Utilities	50,800	59,500	8,700	F
Supplies	12,600	14,000	1,400	F
Maintenance	24,900	28,000	3,100	F
Total variable manufacturing overhead	108,000	122,500	14,500	F
Fixed manufacturing overhead:				
Maintenance	52,000	52,000	0	
Supervision	110,000	110,000	0	
Depreciation	80,000	80,000	0	
Total fixed manufacturing overhead	242,000	242,000	0	
Total manufacturing overhead	$ 350,000	$ 364,500	$ 14,500	F

Upon receiving a copy of this report, John Arnold, the production manager, commented, "I've been getting these reports for months now, and I still can't see how they help me assess efficiency and cost control in that department. I agree that the budget for the month was 35,000 machine-hours, but that represents 17,500 units of product, since it should take two hours to produce one unit. The department produced only 14,000 units during the month, and took 30,000 machine-hours to do it. Why do all the variances turn up favorable?"

Required:

1. In answer to Mr. Arnold's question, why are all the variances favorable? Evaluate the performance report.
2. Prepare a new overhead performance report that will help Mr. Arnold assess efficiency and cost control in the Milling Department. (Hint: Exhibit 10–7 may be helpful in structuring your report; however, include both variable and fixed costs in the report.)

PROBLEM 10-27 Selection of a Denominator; Overhead Analysis; Standard Cost Card [LO4, LO5, LO6]

The condensed flexible budget for manufacturing overhead of the Scott Company is as follows:

Overhead Costs	Cost Formula (per DLH)	Direct Labor-Hours 30,000	40,000	50,000
Variable manufacturing overhead cost	$2.50	$ 75,000	$100,000	$125,000
Fixed manufacturing overhead cost		320,000	320,000	320,000
Total manufacturing overhead cost		$395,000	$420,000	$445,000

The company produces a single product that requires 2.5 direct labor-hours to complete. The direct labor wage rate is $20 per hour. Three yards of raw material are required for each unit of product, at a cost of $5 per yard.

Demand for the company's product differs widely from year to year. Expected activity for this year is 50,000 direct labor-hours; normal activity is 40,000 direct labor-hours per year.

Required:

1. Assume that the company chooses 40,000 direct labor-hours as the denominator level of activity. Compute the predetermined overhead rate, breaking it down into fixed and variable cost components.
2. Assume that the company chooses 50,000 direct labor-hours as the denominator level of activity. Repeat the computations in (1) above.
3. Complete two standard cost cards as outlined below.

Denominator Activity: 40,000 DLHs	
Direct materials, 3 yards at $5 per yard	$15.00
Direct labor, ?.	?
Variable manufacturing overhead, ?	?
Fixed manufacturing overhead, ?	?
Total standard cost per unit.................	$?

Denominator Activity: 50,000 DLHs	
Direct materials, 3 yards at $5 per yard	$15.00
Direct labor, ?.	?
Variable manufacturing overhead, ?	?
Fixed manufacturing overhead, ?	?
Total standard cost per unit.................	$?

4. Assume that 48,000 actual hours are worked during the year, and that 18,500 units are produced. Actual manufacturing overhead costs for the year are as follows:

Variable manufacturing overhead cost	$124,800
Fixed manufacturing overhead cost	321,700
Total manufacturing overhead cost	$446,500

a. Compute the standard hours allowed for the year's actual output.

b. Compute the missing items from the Manufacturing Overhead account below. Assume that the company uses 40,000 direct labor-hours (normal activity) as the denominator activity figure in computing overhead rates, as you have used in (1) above.

Manufacturing Overhead

Debit		Credit
Actual costs	446,500	?
	?	?

c. Analyze your underapplied or overapplied overhead balance in terms of variable overhead spending and efficiency variances and fixed overhead budget and volume variances.

5. Looking at the variances that you have computed, what appears to be the major disadvantage of using normal activity rather than expected actual activity as a denominator in computing the predetermined overhead rate? What advantages can you see to offset this disadvantage?

PROBLEM 10-28 Variable Overhead Performance Report [LO4]

Ronson Products, Ltd., an Australian company, has the following cost formulas (expressed in Australian dollars) for variable overhead costs in one of its machine shops:

Variable Overhead Cost	Cost Formula (per machine-hour)
Supplies	$0.70
Power	1.20
Lubrication	0.50
Wearing tools	3.10
Total	$5.50

During July, the machine shop was scheduled to work 3,200 machine-hours and to produce 16,000 units of product. The standard machine time per unit of product is 0.2 hours. A severe storm during the month forced the company to close for several days, which reduced the level of output for the month. Actual results for July were as follows:

Actual machine-hours worked	2,700
Actual number of units produced	14,000

Actual costs for July were:

Variable Overhead Cost	Total Actual Cost	Per Machine-Hour
Supplies	$ 1,836	$0.68
Power	3,348	1.24
Lubrication	1,485	0.55
Wearing tools	8,154	3.02
Total	$14,823	$5.49

Required:

Prepare an overhead performance report for the machine shop for July. Use column headings in your report as shown below:

Overhead Item	Cost Formula (per MH)	Actual Costs Incurred, 2,700 MHs	Flexible Budget Based on ? MHs	Flexible Budget Based on ? MHs	Total Variance	Breakdown of the Total Variance: Spending Variance	Breakdown of the Total Variance: Efficiency Variance

Cases

CASE 10-29 Activity-Based Costing and the Flexible Budget Approach [LO2]

The Munchkin Theater is a nonprofit organization devoted to staging theater productions of plays for children in Toronto, Canada. The theater has a very small full-time professional administrative staff. Through a special arrangement with the actors' union, actors and directors rehearse without pay and are paid only for actual performances.

During 2006, The Munchkin Theater had five different productions—each of which was performed 12 times. The costs of 2006's operations were as follows:

The Munchkin Theater Cost Report For the Year Ended 31 December 2006	
Number of productions	5
Number of performances of each production	12
Total number of performances	60
Actual costs incurred:	
Actors and directors' wages	$144,000
Stagehands' wages	27,000
Ticket booth personnel and ushers' wages	10,800
Scenery, costumes, and props	43,000
Theater hall rent	45,000
Printed programs	10,500
Publicity	13,000
Administrative expenses	43,200
Total actual cost incurred	$336,500

Some of the costs vary with the number of productions, some with the number of performances, and some are relatively fixed and depend on neither the number of productions nor the number of performances. The costs of scenery, costumes, props, and publicity vary with the number of productions. It doesn't make any difference how many times Peter the Rabbit is performed, the cost of the scenery is the same. Likewise, the cost of publicizing a play with posters and radio commercials is the same whether there are 10, 20, or 30 performances of the play. On the other hand, the wages of the actors, directors, stagehands, ticket booth personnel, and ushers vary with the number of performances. The greater the number of performances, the higher the wage costs will be. Similarly, the costs of renting the hall and printing the programs will vary with the number of performances. Administrative expenses are more difficult to pin down, but the best estimate is that approximately 75% of these costs are fixed, 15% depend on the number of productions staged, and the remaining 10% depend on the number of performances.

At the end of 2006, the board of directors of the theater authorized changing the theater's program in 2007 to four productions, with 16 performances each. Actual costs for 2007 were higher than the costs for 2006. (Grants from donors and ticket sales were also correspondingly higher.) Data concerning 2007's operations appear below:

The Munchkin Theater Cost Report For the Year Ended 31 December 2007	
Number of productions	4
Number of performances of each production	16
Total number of performances	64
Actual costs incurred:	
Actors and directors' wages	$148,000
Stagehands' wages	28,600
Ticket booth personnel and ushers' wages	12,300
Scenery, costumes, and props	39,300
Theater hall rent	49,600
Printed programs	10,950
Publicity	12,000
Administrative expenses	41,650
Total actual cost incurred	$342,400

Even though many of the costs above may be considered direct costs rather than overhead, the flexible budget approach covered in the chapter can be used to evaluate how well these costs are controlled. The principles are the same whether a cost is a direct cost or is overhead.

Required:

1. Use the actual results from 2006 to estimate the cost formulas for the flexible budget for The Munchkin Theater. Keep in mind that the theater has two measures of activity—the number of productions and the number of performances.
2. Prepare a performance report for 2007 using the flexible budget approach and both measures of activity. Assume inflation was insignificant. (Note: To evaluate administrative expenses, first determine the flexible budget amounts for the three elements of administrative expenses. Then compare the total of the three elements to the actual administrative expense of $41,650.)
3. If you were on the board of directors of the theater, would you be pleased with how well costs were controlled during 2007? Why or why not?
4. The cost formulas provide figures for the average cost per production and average cost per performance. How accurate do you think these figures would be for predicting the cost of a new production or of an additional performance of a particular production?

CASE 10-30 Selling Expense Flexible Budget [LO2]

Mark Fletcher, president of SoftGro Inc., was looking forward to seeing the performance reports for November because he knew the company's sales for the month had exceeded budget by a considerable margin. SoftGro, a distributor of educational software packages, had been growing steadily for approximately two years. Fletcher's biggest challenge at this point was to ensure that the company did not lose control of expenses during this growth period. When Fletcher received the November reports, he was dismayed to see the large unfavorable variance in the company's monthly selling expense report that is presented below:

SoftGro Inc.
Monthly Selling Expense Report
November

		November		
	Annual Budget	Budget	Actual	Variance
Unit sales	2,000,000	280,000	310,000	30,000 F
Dollar sales	$80,000,000	$11,200,000	$12,400,000	$1,200,000 F
Orders processed	54,000	6,500	5,800	700 U
Salespersons per month	90	90	96	6 U
Expenses:				
Advertising	$19,800,000	$ 1,650,000	$ 1,660,000	$ 10,000 U
Staff salaries	1,500,000	125,000	125,000	0
Sales salaries	1,296,000	108,000	115,400	7,400 U
Commissions	3,200,000	448,000	496,000	48,000 U
Per diem expense	1,782,000	148,500	162,600	14,100 U
Office expense	4,080,000	340,000	358,400	18,400 U
Shipping expense	6,750,000	902,500	976,500	74,000 U
Total expense	$38,408,000	$ 3,722,000	$ 3,893,900	$ 171,900 U

Fletcher called in the company's new controller, Susan Porter, to discuss the implications of the variances reported for November and to plan a strategy for improving performance. Porter suggested that the reporting format that the company had been using might not be giving Fletcher a true picture of the company's operations and proposed that SoftGro implement flexible budgeting for reporting purposes. Porter offered to redo the monthly selling expense report for November using flexible budgeting so that Fletcher could compare the two reports and see the advantages of flexible budgeting.

After some analysis, Porter derived the following data about the company's selling expenses:

a. The total compensation paid to the sales force consists of both a monthly base salary and a commission. The commission varies with sales dollars.
b. Sales office expense is a mixed cost with the variable portion related to the number of orders processed. The fixed portion of office expense is $3,000,000 annually and is incurred uniformly throughout the year.

c. Subsequent to the adoption of the annual budget for the current year, SoftGro decided to open a new sales territory. As a consequence, approval was given to hire six additional salespersons effective November 1. Porter decided that these additional six people should be recognized in her revised report.
d. Per diem reimbursement to the sales force, while a fixed amount per day, is variable with the number of salespersons and the number of days spent traveling. SoftGro's original budget was based on an average sales force of 90 persons throughout the year with each salesperson traveling 15 days per month.
e. The company's shipping expense is a mixed cost with the variable portion, $3 per unit, dependent on the number of units sold. The fixed portion is incurred uniformly throughout the year.

Using the data above, Porter believed she would be able to redo the November report and present it to Fletcher for his review.

Required:

1. Describe the benefits of flexible budgeting, and explain why Susan Porter would propose that SoftGro use flexible budgeting in this situation.
2. Prepare a revised monthly selling expense report for November that would permit Mark Fletcher to more clearly evaluate SoftGro's control over selling expenses. The report should have a line for *each* selling expense item showing the appropriate budgeted amount, the actual selling expense, and the variance for November.

(CMA, adapted)

CASE 10-31 Ethics and the Manager [LO2]

Lance Prating is the controller of the Colorado Springs manufacturing facility of Advance Macro, Incorporated. Among the many reports that must be filed with corporate headquarters is the annual overhead performance report. The report covers the year which ends on December 31 and is due at corporate headquarters shortly after the beginning of the new year. Prating does not like putting work off to the last minute, so just before Christmas he put together a preliminary draft of the overhead performance report. Some adjustments would later be required for the few transactions that occur between Christmas and New Year's Day. A copy of the preliminary draft report, which Prating completed on December 21, follows:

Colorado Springs Manufacturing Facility
Overhead Performance Report
December 21 Preliminary Draft

Budgeted machine-hours	100,000
Actual machine-hours	90,000

Overhead Costs	Cost Formula (per machine-hour)	Actual Costs for 90,000 Machine-Hours	Flexible Budget Based on 90,000 Machine-Hours	Spending or Budget Variance
Variable overhead costs:				
Power	$0.03	$ 2,840	$ 2,700	$ 140 U
Supplies	0.86	79,060	77,400	1,660 U
Abrasives	0.34	32,580	30,600	1,980 U
Total variable overhead cost	$1.23	114,480	110,700	3,780 U
Fixed overhead costs:				
Depreciation		228,300	226,500	1,800 U
Supervisory salaries		187,300	189,000	1,700 F
Insurance		23,000	23,000	0
Industrial engineering		154,000	160,000	6,000 F
Factory building lease		46,000	46,000	0
Total fixed overhead cost		638,600	644,500	5,900 F
Total overhead cost		$753,080	$755,200	$2,120 F

Tab Kapp, the general manager at the Colorado Springs facility, asked to see a copy of the preliminary draft report at 4:45 P.M. on December 23. Prating carried a copy of the report to Kapp's office where the following discussion took place:

Kapp: Wow! Almost all of the variances on the report are unfavorable. The only thing that looks good at all are the favorable variances for supervisory salaries and for industrial engineering. How did we have an unfavorable variance for depreciation?

Prating: Do you remember that milling machine that broke down because the wrong lubricant was used by the machine operator?

Kapp: Only vaguely.

Prating: It turned out we couldn't fix it. We had to scrap the machine and buy a new one.

Kapp: This report doesn't look good. I was raked over the coals last year when we had just a few unfavorable variances.

Prating: I'm afraid the final report is going to look even worse.

Kapp: Oh?

Prating: The line item for industrial engineering on the report is for work we hired Sanchez Engineering to do for us on a contract basis. The original contract was for $160,000, but we asked them to do some additional work that was not in the contract. Under the terms of the contract, we have to reimburse Sanchez Engineering for the costs of the additional work. The $154,000 in actual costs that appear on the preliminary draft report reflects only their billings up through December 21. The last bill they had sent us was on November 28, and they completed the project just last week. Yesterday I got a call from Maria over at Sanchez and she said they would be sending us a final bill for the project before the end of the year. The total bill, including the reimbursements for the additional work, is going to be . . .

Kapp: I am not sure I want to hear this.

Prating: $176,000.

Kapp: Ouch!

Prating: The additional work we asked them to do added $16,000 to the cost of the project.

Kapp: No way can I turn in a performance report with an overall unfavorable variance. They'll kill me at corporate headquarters. Call up Maria at Sanchez and ask her not to send the bill until after the first of the year. We have to have that $6,000 favorable variance for industrial engineering on the performance report.

Required:

What should Lance Prating do? Explain.

Chapter 11

Segment Reporting and Decentralization

Centralizing Communications

Ingersoll-Rand, a global conglomerate that traces its roots to the early 1870s, has about 46,000 employees. The company has received numerous recognitions and awards, including being named the *Industryweek* Best Managed Company for several years in a row. Even so, the company decided that it needed to restructure its organization to effectively compete in the current economic environment.

Previously comprising 8 autonomous companies, Ingersoll-Rand now operates as 13 separate business units. To improve communications, its computer systems were integrated to provide information to managers and headquarters in real time. The company continues to operate in a decentralized fashion. Even though many of its functions have been centralized, such as purchasing, payroll, and accounts receivable and payable, decision making is still spread throughout the organization. For example, factory managers continue to be responsible for deciding what must be purchased. However, instead of directly issuing purchase orders to vendors, requisitions are communicated to headquarters, which then issues the purchase orders. As a result of this centralized approach to purchasing, the company has been able to negotiate better discounts with suppliers.

Analysts estimate the cost of the restructuring at $50 million. Don Janson, director of common administrative resources implementations at Ingersoll-Rand, predicts that the changes will pay for themselves within three years. ■

Sources: Ingersoll-Rand Company website; and Steve Konicki, "A Company Merges Its Many Units—Successfully," *Informationweek*, May 8, 2000, pp. 174–178.

BUSINESS FOCUS

Learning Objectives

After studying Chapter 11, you should be able to:

LO1 Prepare a segmented income statement using the contribution format and explain the difference between traceable fixed costs and common fixed costs.

LO2 Compute return on investment (ROI) and show how changes in sales, expenses, and assets affect ROI.

LO3 Compute residual income and understand its strengths and weaknesses.

LO4 (Appendix 11A) Determine the range, if any, within which a negotiated transfer price should fall.

LO5 (Appendix 11B) Charge operating departments for services provided by service departments.

LP 11

It is impossible for the top manager to make decisions about everything except in very small organizations. For example, the CEO of the Hyatt Hotel chain cannot be expected to decide whether a particular hotel guest at the Hyatt Hotel on Maui should be allowed to check out later than the normal checkout time. It makes sense for the CEO to authorize employees at Maui to make this decision. As in this example, managers in large organizations have to delegate some decisions to those who are at lower levels in the organization.

Decentralization in Organizations

In a **decentralized organization,** decision-making authority is spread throughout the organization rather than being confined to a few top executives. All large organizations are decentralized to some extent out of necessity. At one extreme, a strongly decentralized organization empowers even the lowest-level managers and employees to make decisions. At the other extreme, a strongly centralized organization provides lower-level managers with little freedom to make decisions. Most organizations fall somewhere between these two extremes.

Video 11–1

Advantages and Disadvantages of Decentralization

The major advantages of decentralization include:

1. By delegating day-to-day problem solving to lower-level managers, top management can concentrate on bigger issues such as overall strategy.
2. Empowering lower-level managers to make decisions puts the decision-making authority in the hands of those who tend to have the most detailed and up-to-date information about day-to-day operations.
3. By eliminating layers of decision making and approvals, organizations can respond more quickly to customers and to changes in the operating environment.
4. Granting decision-making authority helps train lower-level managers for higher-level positions.
5. Empowering lower-level managers to make decisions can increase their motivation and job satisfaction.

The major disadvantages of decentralization include:

1. Lower-level managers may make decisions without fully understanding the big picture.
2. If lower-level managers make their own decisions, coordination may be lacking.
3. Lower-level managers may have objectives that clash with the objectives of the entire organization.[1] For example, a manager may be more interested in increasing the size of his or her department, leading to more power and prestige, than in increasing the department's effectiveness.

---

[1] Similar problems exist with top-level managers as well. The shareholders of the company delegate their decision-making authority to the top managers. Unfortunately, top managers may abuse that trust by rewarding themselves and their friends too generously, spending too much company money on palatial offices, and so on. The issue of how to ensure that top managers act in the best interests of the company's owners continues to puzzle experts. To a large extent, the owners rely on performance evaluation using return on investment and residual income measures as discussed later in the chapter and on bonuses and stock options. The stock market is also an important disciplining mechanism. If top managers squander the company's resources, the price of the company's stock will almost surely fall—resulting in a loss of prestige, bonuses, and possibly a job. And, of course, particularly outrageous self-dealing may land a CEO in court, as recent events have demonstrated.

4. Spreading innovative ideas may be difficult in a decentralized organization. Someone in one part of the organization may have a terrific idea that would benefit other parts of the organization, but without strong central direction the idea may not be shared with, and adopted by, other parts of the organization. This problem can be reduced by effective use of intranet systems that make it easier for information to be shared across departments.

IN BUSINESS

DECENTRALIZATION: A DELICATE BALANCE

Decentralization has its advantages and disadvantages. Bed Bath & Beyond, a specialty retailer, benefits from allowing its local store managers to choose 70% of their store's merchandise based on local customer tastes. For example, the company's Manhattan stores stock wall paint, but its suburban stores do not because home improvement giants in the suburbs, such as Home Depot, meet this customer need.

On the other hand, Nestle, the Swiss consumer food products company, has been working to overcome glaring inefficiencies resulting from its decentralized management structure. For example, in Switzerland "each candy and ice cream factory was ordering its own sugar. Moreover, different factories were using different names for the identical grade of sugar, making it almost impossible for bosses at headquarters to track costs." Nestle hopes to significantly reduce costs and simplify recordkeeping by centralizing its raw materials purchases.

Sources: Nanette Byrnes, "What's Beyond for Bed Bath & Beyond?" *BusinessWeek*, January 19, 2004, pp. 44–50; and Carol Matlack, "Nestle Is Starting to Slim Down at Last," *BusinessWeek*, October 27, 2003, pp. 56–57.

Responsibility Accounting

Decentralized organizations need *responsibility accounting systems* that link lower-level managers' decision-making authority with accountability for the outcomes of those decisions. The term **responsibility center** is used for any part of an organization whose manager has control over and is accountable for cost, profit, or investments. The three primary types of responsibility centers are *cost centers, profit centers,* and *investment centers.*[2]

Cost, Profit, and Investment Centers

Cost Center The manager of a **cost center** has control over costs, but not over revenue or the use of investment funds. Service departments such as accounting, finance, general administration, legal, and personnel are usually classified as cost centers. In addition, manufacturing facilities are often considered to be cost centers. The managers of cost centers are expected to minimize costs while providing the level of products and services demanded by other parts of the organization. For example, the manager of a manufacturing facility would be evaluated at least in part by comparing actual costs to how much costs should have been for the actual level of output during the period. Standard cost variances and flexible budget variances, such as those discussed in Chapters 9 and 10, are often used to evaluate cost center performance.

Video 11–1

Profit Center The manager of a **profit center** has control over both costs and revenue, but not over the use of investment funds. For example, the manager in charge of a Six Flags amusement park would be responsible for both the revenues and costs, and hence the profits, of the amusement park, but may not have control over major investments in the park. Profit center managers are often evaluated by comparing actual profit to targeted or budgeted profit.

[2] Some companies classify business segments that are responsible mainly for generating revenue, such as an insurance sales office, as *revenue centers.* Other companies would consider this to be just another type of profit center, since costs of some kind (salaries, rent, utilities) are usually deducted from the revenues in the segment's income statement.

IN BUSINESS

RESPONSIBILITY ACCOUNTING: A CHINESE PERSPECTIVE

For years Han Dan Iron and Steel Company was under Chinese government control. During this period, the company's management accounting system focused on complying with government mandates rather than responding to the market. As a market-oriented economy began to emerge, the company realized that its management accounting system was obsolete. Managers were preoccupied with meeting production quotas imposed by the government rather than controlling costs and meeting profit targets or encouraging productivity improvements. To remedy this situation, the company implemented what it called a *responsibility cost control system* that (1) set cost and profit targets, (2) assigned target costs to responsibility center managers, (3) evaluated the performance of responsibility center managers based on their ability to meet the targets, and (4) provided incentives to improve productivity.

Source: Z. Jun Lin and Zengbiao Yu, "Responsibility Cost Control System in China: A Case of Management Accounting Application," *Management Accounting Research*, December 2002, pp. 447–467.

Investment Center The manager of an **investment center** has control over cost, revenue, and investments in operating assets. For example, the vice president of the Truck Division at General Motors would have a great deal of discretion over investments in the division. This vice president would be responsible for initiating investment proposals, such as funding research into more fuel-efficient engines for sport-utility vehicles. Once the proposal has been approved by General Motor's top-level managers and board of directors, the vice president of the Truck Division would then be responsible for making sure that the investment pays off. Investment center managers are usually evaluated using return on investment (ROI) or residual income measures, as discussed later in the chapter.

IN BUSINESS

EXTREME INCENTIVES

In 2003, Tyco International, Ltd., was rocked by a series of scandals including disclosure of $2 billion of accounting-related problems, investigations by the Securities and Exchange Commission, and a criminal trial of its ex-CEO, Dennis Kozlowski, on charges of more than $600 million in unauthorized compensation and fraudulent stock sales. Was any of this foreseeable? Well, in a word, yes.

BusinessWeek reported in 1999 that the CEO of Tyco International, Ltd., was putting unrelenting pressure on his managers to deliver growth. "Each year, [the CEO] sets targets for how much each manager must increase his or her unit's earnings in the coming year. The targets are coupled with a powerful incentive system. If they meet or exceed these targets, managers are promised a bonus that can be many times their salary. But if they fall even a bit short, the bonus plummets." This sounds good, but "to many accounting experts, the sort of all-or-nothing bonus structure set up at Tyco is a warning light. If top executives set profit targets too high or turn a blind eye to how managers achieve them, the incentive for managers to cut corners is enormous. Indeed, a blue-ribbon panel of accounting experts who were trying to improve corporate auditing standards several years ago . . . identified just such extreme incentives as a red flag. 'If you're right under the target, there's a tremendous economic interest to accelerate earnings,' says David F. Larcker, a professor of accounting at the Wharton School. 'If you're right over it, there is an incentive to push earnings into the next period.'"

Sources: *Reuters*, "Tyco Says to Restate Several Years of Results," June 16, 2003; Jeanne King, *Reuters*, "New York Trial of ex-Tyco CEO Koslowski Can Proceed," June 23, 2003; and, William C. Symonds, Diane Brady, Geoffrey Smith, and Lorraine Woellert, "Tyco: Aggressive or Out of Line?" *BusinessWeek*, November 1, 1999, pp. 160–165.

An Organizational View of Responsibility Centers

Superior Foods Corporation, a company that manufactures and distributes snack foods and beverages, provides an example of the various kinds of responsibility centers. Exhibit 11–1 shows a

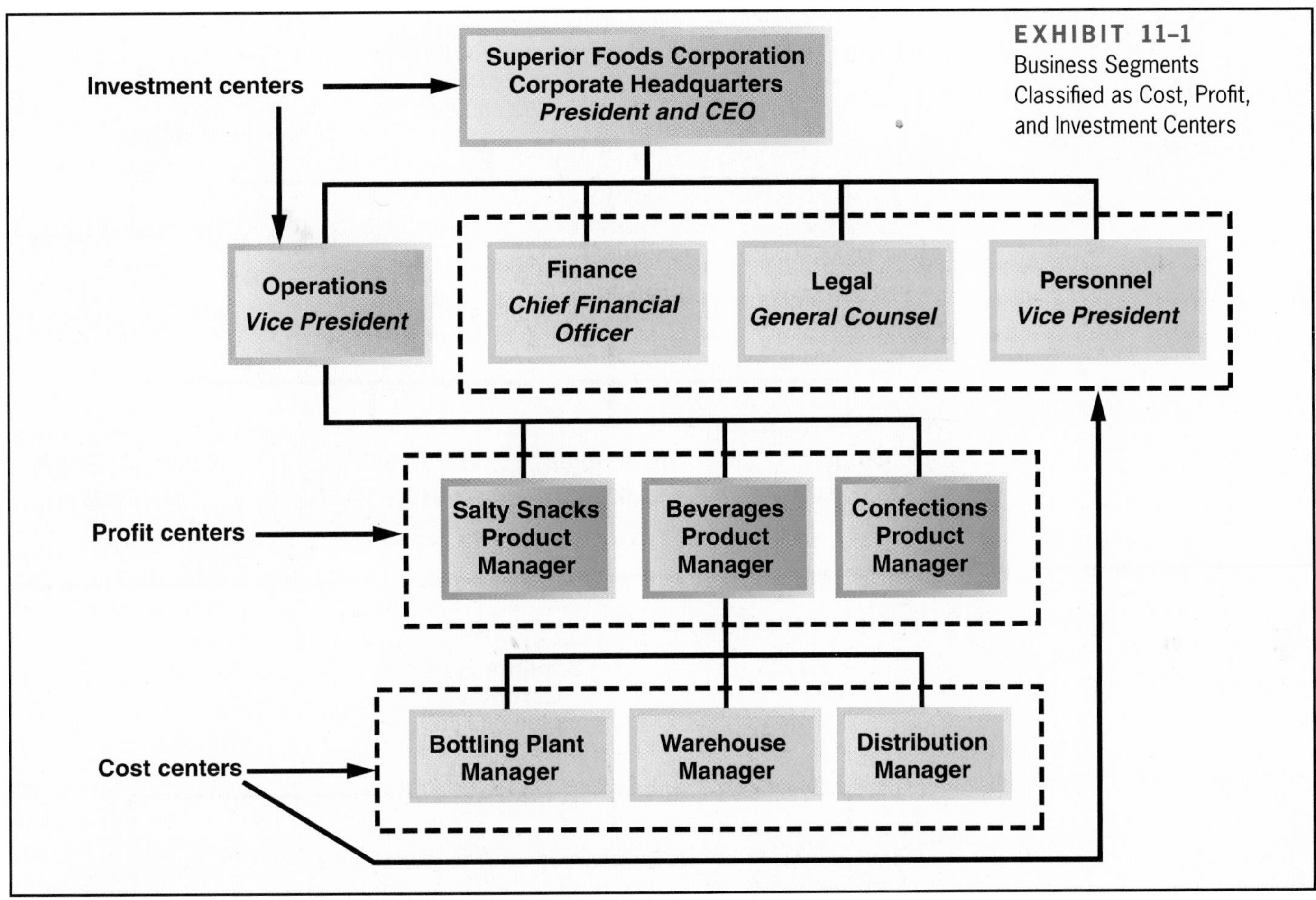

EXHIBIT 11–1
Business Segments Classified as Cost, Profit, and Investment Centers

partial organization chart for Superior Foods that displays its cost, profit, and investment centers. The departments and work centers that do not generate significant revenues by themselves are classified as cost centers. These are staff departments—such as finance, legal, and personnel—and operating units—such as the bottling plant, warehouse, and beverage distribution center. The profit centers generate revenues, and they include the salty snacks, beverages, and confections product families. The vice president of operations oversees the allocation of investment funds across the product families and is responsible for the profits of those product families. And finally, corporate headquarters is an investment center, since it is responsible for all revenues, costs, and investments.

Decentralization and Segment Reporting

LEARNING OBJECTIVE 1
Prepare a segmented income statement using the contribution format and explain the difference between traceable fixed costs and common fixed costs.

Effective decentralization requires *segmented reporting*. In addition to the companywide income statement, reports are needed for individual segments of the organization. A **segment** is a part or activity of an organization about which managers would like cost, revenue, or profit data. Cost, profit, and investment centers are segments as are sales territories, individual stores, service centers, manufacturing plants, marketing departments, individual customers, and product lines. A company's operations can be segmented in many ways. For example, Exhibit 11–2 (page 442) shows several ways in which Superior Foods could segment its business. The top half of the exhibit shows Superior segmenting its $500 million in revenue by geographical region, and the bottom half shows Superior segmenting its total

EXHIBIT 11–2
Superior Foods Corporation: Revenue Segmented by Geographic Region and Customer Channel

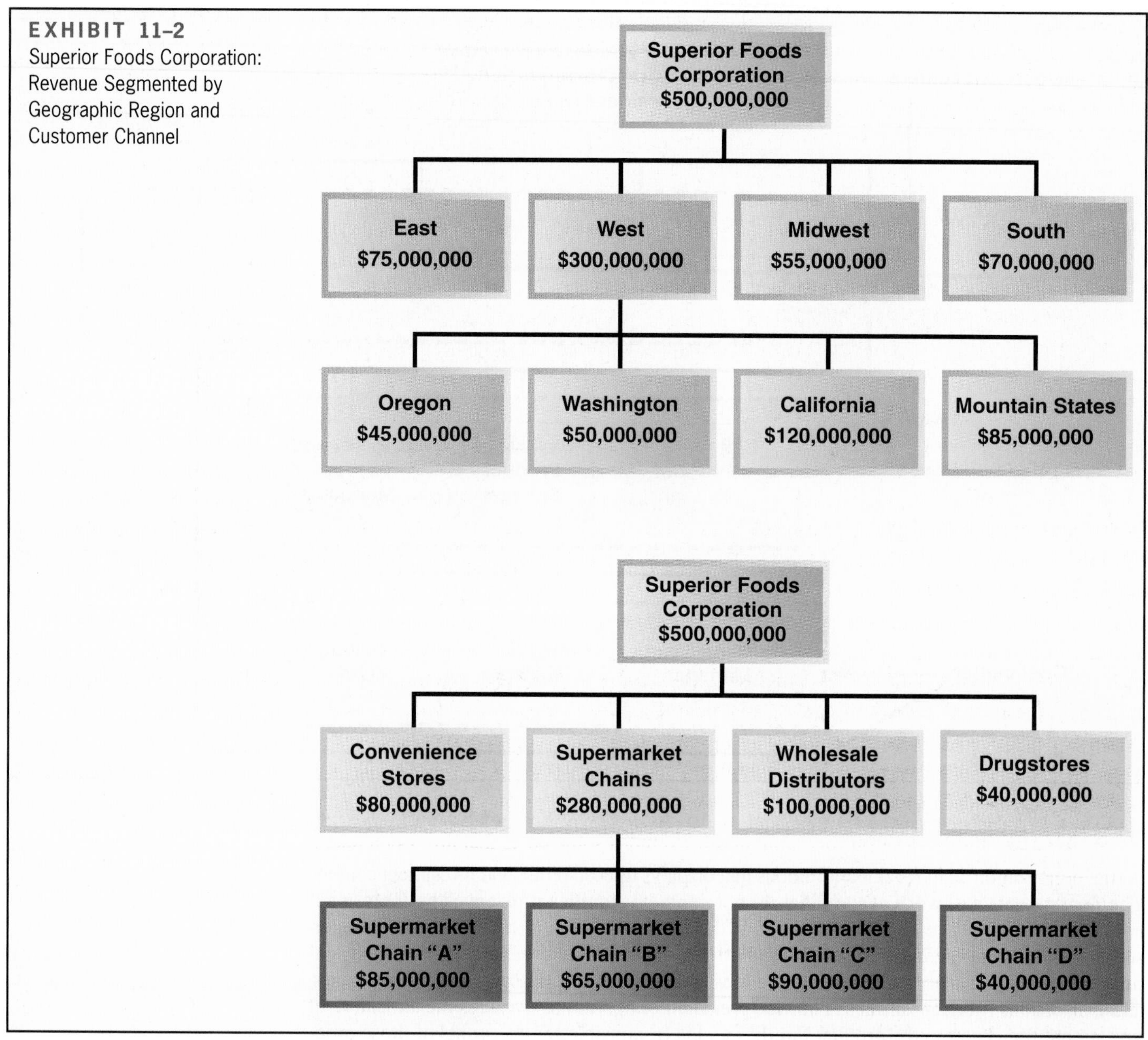

revenue by customer channel. With the appropriate database and software, managers could easily drill even further down into the organization. For example, the sales in California could be segmented by product family, then by product line. This drill-down capability helps managers to identify the sources of strong or weak overall financial performance. In this chapter, we learn how to construct income statements for business segments. These segmented income statements are useful in analyzing the profitability of segments and in measuring the performance of segment managers.

Building a Segmented Income Statement

Several important principles are involved in constructing a useful segmented income statement. These principles are illustrated in the following example.

MANAGERIAL ACCOUNTING IN ACTION
The Issue

SoftSolutions, Inc., is a rapidly growing computer software company founded by Lori Saffer, who had previously worked in a large software company, and Marjorie Matsuo, who had previously worked in the hotel industry as a general manager. They formed the company to develop and market user-friendly accounting and operations software designed specifically for hotels. They quit their jobs, pooled their savings, hired several programmers, and got down to work.

The first sale was by far the most difficult. No hotel wanted to be the first to use an untested product from an unknown company. After overcoming this obstacle with persistence, good luck, dedication to customer service, and a very low introductory price, the company's sales grew.

The company quickly developed similar business software for other specialized markets and then branched out into clip art and computer games. Within four years of its founding, the organization had grown to the point where Saffer and Matsuo were no longer able to personally direct all of the company's activities. Decentralization had become a necessity.

Accordingly, the company was split into two divisions—Business Products and Consumer Products. By mutual consent, Matsuo took the title president and Saffer took the title vice president of the Business Products Division. Chris Worden, a programmer who had spearheaded the drive into the clip art and computer games markets, was designated vice president of the Consumer Products Division.

Almost immediately, the issue arose of how best to evaluate the performance of the divisions. Matsuo called a meeting to consider this issue and asked Saffer, Worden, and the controller, Bill Carson, to attend. The following discussion took place at that meeting:

Marjorie: We need to find a better way to measure the performance of our divisions.

Chris: I agree. Consumer Products has been setting the pace in this company for the last two years, and we should be getting more recognition.

Lori: Chris, we are delighted with the success of the Consumer Products Division.

Chris: I know. But it is hard to figure out just how successful we are with the present accounting reports. All we have are sales and cost of goods sold figures for the division.

Bill: What's the matter with those figures? They are prepared using generally accepted accounting principles.

Chris: The sales figures are fine. However, cost of goods sold includes some costs that really aren't the costs of our division, and it excludes some costs that are. Let's take a simple example. Everything we sell in the Consumer Products Division has to pass through the automatic bar-coding machine, which applies a unique bar code to the product.

Lori: That's true for items from the Business Products Division as well as for items from the Consumer Products Division.

Chris: That's precisely the point. Whether an item comes from the Business Products Division or the Consumer Products Division, it must pass through the automatic bar-coding machine after the software has been packaged. How much of the cost of the automatic bar coder would be saved if we didn't have any consumer products?

Marjorie: Since we have only one automatic bar coder and we would need it anyway to code the business products, I guess none of the cost would be saved.

Chris: That's right. And since none of the cost could be saved even if the entire Consumer Products Division were eliminated, how can we logically say that some of the cost of the automatic bar coder is a cost of the Consumer Products Division?

Lori: Just a minute, Chris, are you saying that my Business Products Division should be charged with the entire cost of the automatic bar coder?

Chris: No, that's not what I am saying.

Marjorie: But Chris, I don't see how we can have sensible performance reports without making someone responsible for costs like the cost of the automatic bar coder. Bill, as our accounting expert, what do you think?

Bill: I have some ideas for handling issues like the automatic bar coder. The best approach would probably be for me to put together a draft performance report. We can discuss it at the next meeting when everyone has something concrete to look at.

Marjorie: Okay, let's see what you come up with.

Bill Carson, the controller of SoftSolutions, realized that segmented income statements would be required to more appropriately evaluate the performance of the two divisions. To construct the segmented reports, he would have to carefully segregate costs that are attributable to the segments from costs that are not. Since most of the disputes over costs would be about fixed costs such as the automatic bar-coding machine, he knew he would also have to separate fixed from variable costs. The conventional absorption costing income statement prepared for the entire company commingles variable and fixed manufacturing costs in the cost of goods sold.

Largely for these reasons, Bill Carson decided to use the contribution format income statement based on variable costing that was discussed in earlier chapters. Recall that when the contribution format is used: (1) the cost of goods sold consists only of the variable manufacturing costs; (2) variable and fixed costs are listed in separate sections; and (3) a contribution margin is computed. When such a statement is segmented as in this chapter, fixed costs are broken down further into what are called traceable and common costs as discussed later. This breakdown allows a *segment margin* to be computed for each segment of the company. The segment margin is a valuable tool for assessing the long-run profitability of a segment and is also a much better tool for evaluating performance than absorption costing reports.

Levels of Segmented Statements

A portion of the segmented report Bill Carson prepared is shown in Exhibit 11–3. The contribution format income statement for the entire company appears at the very top of the exhibit under the column labeled Total Company. Immediately to the right of this column are two columns—one for each of the two divisions. We can see that the Business Products Division's segment margin is $60,000 and the Consumer Products Division's is $40,000. These segment margins show the company's divisional managers how much each of their divisions is contributing to the company's profits.

However, segmented income statements can be prepared for activities at many levels in a company. To provide more information to the company's divisional managers, Bill Carson has further segmented the divisions according to their major product lines. In the case of the Consumer Products Division, the product lines are clip art and computer games. Going even further, Bill Carson has segmented each of the product lines according to how they are sold—in retail computer stores or over the Internet. In Exhibit 11–3, this further segmentation is illustrated for the computer games product line. Notice that as we go from one segmented statement to another, we look at smaller and smaller pieces of the company. While not shown in Exhibit 11–3, Bill Carson also prepared segmented income statements for the major product lines in the Business Products Division.

IN BUSINESS

COMPUTING SEGMENT MARGINS HELPS AN ENTREPRENEUR

In 2001, Victoria Pappas Collection, a small company specializing in women's sportswear, reported a net loss of $280,000 on sales of $1 million. When the company's founder, Vickie Giannukos, segmented her company's income statement into the six markets that she was serving, the results were revealing. The Dallas and Atlanta markets generated $825,000 of sales and incurred $90,000 of traceable fixed costs. The other four markets combined produced $175,000 of sales and also incurred $90,000 of traceable fixed costs. Given her average contribution margin ratio of 38%, the Dallas and Atlanta markets earned a segment margin of $223,500 [($825,000 × 38%) − $90,000] while the other four markets combined incurred a loss of $23,500 [($175,000 × 38%) − $90,000].

Vicky had made a common mistake—she chased every possible dollar of sales without knowing if her efforts were profitable. Based on her segmented income statements, she discontinued operations in three cities and hired a new sales representative in Los Angeles. She decided to focus on growing sales in Dallas and Atlanta while deferring expansion into new markets until it could be done profitably.

Source: Norm Brodsky, "The Thin Red Line," *Inc.* magazine, January 2004, pp. 49–52.

EXHIBIT 11–3
SoftSolutions, Inc.—Segmented Income Statements in the Contribution Format

Segments Defined as Divisions

		Divisions	
	Total Company	Business Products Division	Consumer Products Division
Sales	$500,000	$300,000	$200,000
Variable expenses:			
Variable cost of goods sold	180,000	120,000	60,000
Other variable expenses	50,000	30,000	20,000
Total variable expenses	230,000	150,000	80,000
Contribution margin	270,000	150,000	120,000
Traceable fixed expenses	170,000	90,000	80,000*
Divisional segment margin	100,000	$ 60,000	$ 40,000
Common fixed expenses not traceable to individual divisions	85,000		
Net operating income	$ 15,000		

Segments Defined as Product Lines of the Consumer Products Division

		Product Line	
	Consumer Products Division	Clip Art	Computer Games
Sales	$200,000	$ 75,000	$125,000
Variable expenses:			
Variable cost of goods sold	60,000	20,000	40,000
Other variable expenses	20,000	5,000	15,000
Total variable expenses	80,000	25,000	55,000
Contribution margin	120,000	50,000	70,000
Traceable fixed expenses	70,000	30,000	40,000
Product-line segment margin	50,000	$ 20,000	$ 30,000
Common fixed expenses not traceable to individual product lines	10,000		
Divisional segment margin	$ 40,000		

Segments Defined as Sales Channels for One Product Line, Computer Games, of the Consumer Products Division

		Sales Channels	
	Computer Games	On-Line Sales	Retail Stores
Sales	$125,000	$100,000	$ 25,000
Variable expenses:			
Variable cost of goods sold	40,000	32,000	8,000
Other variable expenses	15,000	5,000	10,000
Total variable expenses	55,000	37,000	18,000
Contribution margin	70,000	63,000	7,000
Traceable fixed expenses	25,000	15,000	10,000
Sales-channel segment margin	45,000	$ 48,000	$ (3,000)
Common fixed expenses not traceable to individual sales channels	15,000		
Product-line segment margin	$ 30,000		

*Notice that this $80,000 in traceable fixed expenses is divided into two parts when the Consumer Products Division is broken down into product lines—$70,000 traceable and $10,000 common. The reasons for this are discussed later in the section "Traceable Costs Can Become Common Costs."

Sales and Contribution Margin

To prepare a segmented income statement, variable expenses are deducted from sales to yield the contribution margin for the segment. The contribution margin tells us what happens to profits as volume changes—holding a segment's capacity and fixed costs constant. The contribution margin is especially useful in decisions involving temporary uses of capacity such as special orders. These types of decisions often involve only variable costs and revenues—the two components of contribution margin. Such decisions will be discussed in detail in Chapter 12.

Traceable and Common Fixed Costs

The most puzzling aspect of Exhibit 11–3 is probably the treatment of fixed costs. The report has two kinds of fixed costs—traceable and common. Only the *traceable fixed costs* are charged to particular segments. If a cost is not traceable to a segment, then it is not assigned to the segment.

A **traceable fixed cost** of a segment is a fixed cost that is incurred because of the existence of the segment—if the segment had never existed, the fixed cost would not have been incurred; and if the segment were eliminated, the fixed cost would disappear. Examples of traceable fixed costs include the following:

- The salary of the Fritos product manager at PepsiCo is a *traceable* fixed cost of the Fritos business segment of PepsiCo.
- The maintenance cost for the building in which Boeing 747s are assembled is a *traceable* fixed cost of the 747 business segment of Boeing.
- The liability insurance at Disney World is a *traceable* fixed cost of the Disney World business segment of the Disney Corporation.

A **common fixed cost** is a fixed cost that supports the operations of more than one segment, but is not traceable in whole or in part to any one segment. Even if a segment were entirely eliminated, there would be no change in a true common fixed cost. For example:

- The salary of the CEO of General Motors is a *common* fixed cost of the various divisions of General Motors.
- The cost of heating a Safeway or Kroger grocery store is a *common* fixed cost of the store's various departments—groceries, produce, bakery, meat, etc.
- The cost of the automatic bar-coding machine at SoftSolutions is a *common* fixed cost of the Consumer Products Division and of the Business Products Division.
- The cost of the receptionist's salary at an office shared by a number of doctors is a *common* fixed cost of the doctors. The cost is traceable to the office, but not to individual doctors.

Identifying Traceable Fixed Costs The distinction between traceable and common fixed costs is crucial in segment reporting, since traceable fixed costs are charged to segments and common fixed costs are not. In an actual situation, it is sometimes hard to determine whether a cost should be classified as traceable or common.

The general guideline is to treat as traceable costs *only those costs that would disappear over time if the segment itself disappeared.* For example, if the Consumer Products Division were sold or discontinued, it would no longer be necessary to pay the division manager's salary. Therefore the division manager's salary should be classified as a traceable fixed cost of the division. On the other hand, the president of the company undoubtedly would continue to be paid even if the Consumer Products Division were dropped. In fact, he or she might even be paid more if dropping the division was a good idea. Therefore, the president's salary is common to both divisions and should not be charged to either division.

When assigning costs to segments, the key point is to resist the temptation to allocate costs (such as depreciation of corporate facilities) that are clearly common and that will continue regardless of whether the segment exists or not. *Any allocation of common costs to segments reduces the value of the segment margin as a measure of long-run segment profitability and segment performance.*

Activity-Based Costing Some costs are easy to identify as traceable costs. For example, the cost of advertising Crest toothpaste on television is clearly traceable to Crest. A more difficult situation arises when a building, machine, or other resource is shared by two or more segments. For example, assume that a multiproduct company leases warehouse space that is used for storing the full range of its products. Would the lease cost of the warehouse be a traceable or a common cost of the products? Managers familiar with activity-based costing might argue that the lease cost is traceable and should be assigned to the products according to how much space the products use in the warehouse. In like manner, these managers would argue that order processing costs, sales support costs, and other selling and administrative expenses should also be charged to segments according to the segments' consumption of selling and administrative resources.

To illustrate, consider Holt Corporation, a company that manufactures concrete pipe for industrial uses. The company has three products—9-inch pipe, 12-inch pipe, and 18-inch pipe. Space is rented in a large warehouse on a yearly basis as needed. The rental cost of this space is $4 per square foot per year. The 9-inch pipe occupies 1,000 square feet of space, the 12-inch pipe occupies 4,000 square feet, and the 18-inch pipe occupies 5,000 square feet. The company also has an order processing department that incurred $150,000 in order processing costs last year. Management believes that order processing costs are driven by the number of orders placed by customers. Last year 2,500 orders were placed, of which 1,200 were for 9-inch pipe, 800 were for 12-inch pipe, and 500 were for 18-inch pipe. Given these data, the following costs would be assigned to each product using the activity-based costing approach:

Warehouse space cost:	
9-inch pipe: $4 per square foot × 1,000 square feet	$ 4,000
12-inch pipe: $4 per square foot × 4,000 square feet	16,000
18-inch pipe: $4 per square foot × 5,000 square feet	20,000
Total cost assigned	$ 40,000
Order processing costs:	
$150,000 ÷ 2,500 orders = $60 per order	
9-inch pipe: $60 per order × 1,200 orders	$ 72,000
12-inch pipe: $60 per order × 800 orders	48,000
18-inch pipe: $60 per order × 500 orders	30,000
Total cost assigned	$150,000

This method of assigning costs combines the strength of activity-based costing with the power of the contribution approach and greatly enhances the manager's ability to measure the profitability and performance of segments. However, managers must still ask themselves if the costs would in fact disappear over time if the segment itself disappeared. In the case of Holt Corporation, it is clear that the $20,000 in warehousing costs for the 18-inch pipe would be eliminated if 18-inch pipes were no longer being produced. The company would simply rent less warehouse space the following year. However, suppose the company owns the warehouse. Then it is not so clear that $20,000 of warehousing cost would really disappear if the 18-inch pipes were discontinued. The company might be able to sublease the space, or use it for other products, but then again the space might simply be empty while the warehousing costs continue to be incurred.

Traceable Costs Can Become Common Costs

Fixed costs that are traceable to one segment may be a common cost of another segment. For example, an airline might want a segmented income statement that shows the segment margin for a particular flight from Los Angeles to Paris further broken down into first-class, business-class, and economy-class segment margins. The airline must pay a substantial landing fee at Charles DeGaulle airport in Paris. This fixed landing fee is a traceable cost of the flight, but it is a common cost of the first-class, business-class, and economy-class segments. Even if the first-class cabin is empty, the entire landing fee must be paid. So the landing fee is not a traceable cost of the first-class cabin. But on the other hand, paying the fee is necessary in order to have any first-class, business-class, or economy-class passengers. So the landing fee is a common cost of these three classes.

The dual nature of some fixed costs can be seen in Exhibit 11–4. Notice from the diagram that when segments are defined as divisions, the Consumer Products Division has $80,000 in traceable fixed expenses. However, when we drill down to the product lines, only $70,000 of the $80,000 cost that was traceable to the Consumer Products Division is traceable to the product lines. The other $10,000 becomes a common cost of the two product lines of the Consumer Products Division.

Why would $10,000 of traceable fixed cost become a common cost when the division is divided into product lines? The $10,000 is the monthly salary of the manager of the Consumer Products Division. This salary is a traceable cost of the division as a whole, but it is a common cost of the division's product lines. The manager's salary is a necessary cost of having the two product lines, but even if one of the product lines were discontinued entirely, the manager's salary would probably not be cut. Therefore, none of the manager's salary can really be traced to the individual products.

The $70,000 traceable fixed cost of the product lines consists of the costs of product specific advertising. A total of $30,000 was spent on advertising clip art and $40,000 was spent on advertising computer games. These costs can clearly be traced to the individual product lines.

Segment Margin

Observe from Exhibit 11–3 that the **segment margin** is obtained by deducting the traceable fixed costs of a segment from the segment's contribution margin. It represents the margin available after a segment has covered all of its own costs. *The segment margin is the best gauge of the long-run profitability of a segment* because it includes only those costs that are caused by the segment. If a segment can't cover its own costs, then that segment probably should be dropped (unless it has important side effects on other segments). Notice from Exhibit 11–3, for example, that the Retail Stores sales channel has a negative segment margin. This means that the segment is not generating enough revenue to cover its own costs. Retention or elimination of product lines and other segments is covered in more depth in Chapter 12.

EXHIBIT 11–4
Reclassification of Traceable Fixed Expenses from Exhibit 11–3

	Total Company	Segment: Business Products Division	Segment: Consumer Products Division
Contribution margin	$270,000	$150,000	$120,000
Traceable fixed expenses	170,000	90,000	80,000

	Consumer Products Division	Segment: Clip Art	Segment: Computer Games
Contribution margin	$120,000	$50,000	$70,000
Traceable fixed expenses	70,000	30,000	40,000
Product-line segment margin	50,000	$20,000	$30,000
Common fixed expenses	10,000		
Divisional segment margin	$ 40,000		

From a decision-making point of view, the segment margin is most useful in major decisions that affect capacity such as dropping a segment. By contrast, as we noted earlier, the contribution margin is most useful in decisions involving short-run changes in volume, such as pricing special orders that involve temporary use of existing capacity.

IN BUSINESS

SEGMENT INFORMATION MAKES PROFITS RISE

Great Harvest bakeries use freshly milled Montana whole wheat to make soft-crust specialty breads. The company was founded by Pete and Laura Wakeman and is headquartered in Dillon, Montana. Great Harvest encourages each of its over 100 franchised bakeries to experiment with new approaches to business management, customer service, and marketing and uses several methods to spread the best innovations throughout the system. Staffers at the headquarters in Dillon "provide franchisees with a **top 10 list** of the 10 best-performing bakeries in 14 statistical and financial categories. . . . Got a problem controlling labor expenses at your store? Call up the bakery owners who've got that figured out and get their advice." In addition, bakery owners who join the Numbers Club agree to open their books to the other owners in the club. "Franchisees can spot other owners whose situations might be similar to theirs (same size bakery and market, say, or the same level of owner's labor)—and who appear to have found better solutions to problems. They can identify the perfectly useful peer—and call him or her up."

Source: Michael Hopkins, "Zen and the Art of the Self-Managing Company," *Inc.* magazine, November 2000, pp. 54–63.

MANAGERIAL ACCOUNTING IN ACTION
The Wrap-up

Shortly after Bill Carson, the SoftSolutions, Inc., controller, completed the segmented income statement, he sent copies to the other managers and called a meeting in which the report could be explained—Marjorie Matsuo, Lori Saffer, and Chris Worden were all in attendance.

Lori: I think these segmented income statements are fairly self-explanatory. However, there is one thing I wonder about.

Bill: What's that?

Lori: What is this common fixed expense of $85,000 listed under the total company? And who is going to be responsible for it if neither Chris nor I have responsibility?

Bill: The $85,000 of common fixed expenses represents expenses like administrative salaries and the costs of common production equipment such as the automatic bar-coding machine. Marjorie, do you want to respond to the question about responsibility for these expenses?

Marjorie: Sure. Since I'm the president of the company, I'm responsible for those costs. Some things can be delegated, others cannot be. It wouldn't make any sense for either you or Chris to make strategic decisions about the bar coder because it affects both of you. That's an important part of my job—making decisions about resources that affect all parts of the organization. This report makes it much clearer who is responsible for what. I like it.

Chris: So do I—my division's segment margin is higher than the net operating income for the entire company.

Marjorie: Don't get carried away, Chris. Let's not misinterpret what this report means. The segment margins *have* to be big to cover the common costs of the company. We can't let the big segment margins lull us into a sense of complacency. If we use these reports, we all have to agree that our objective is to increase all of our segment margins over time.

Lori: I'm willing to give it a try.

Chris: The reports make sense to me.

Marjorie: So be it. Then the first item of business would appear to be a review of the Retail Stores channel for selling computer games, where we appear to be losing money. Chris, could you brief us on this at our next meeting?

Chris: Yes. I have been suspecting for some time that our retail sales strategy could be improved.

Marjorie: We look forward to hearing your analysis.

IN BUSINESS

WHAT'S IN A SEGMENT?

Continental Airlines could figure out the profitability of a specific route on a monthly basis—for example, Houston to Los Angeles—but management did not know the profitability of a particular flight on that route. The company's new chief financial officer (CFO), Larry Kellner, placed top priority on developing a flight profitability system that would break out the profit (or loss) for each individual flight. Once completed, the flight profitability system revealed such money-losing flights as two December flights that left Houston for London within a four-hour period with only about 30 passengers each. "If those flights are blurred in with the whole month of December, they just don't jump off the page," says Kellner. With the data on the profitability of individual flights, Continental was able to design more appropriate schedules.

Source: Tim Reason, "Making Continental Airlines' Turnaround Permanent Meant Installing Some High-Flying IT Systems," *CFO,* October 2000, pp. 61–64.

Segmented Financial Information in External Reports

The Financial Accounting Standards Board (FASB) now requires that companies in the United States include segmented financial and other data in their annual reports and that the segmented reports prepared for external users *must use the same methods and definitions that the companies use in internal segmented reports that are prepared to aid in making operating decisions.* This is a very unusual requirement. Companies are not ordinarily required to report the same data to external users that are reported internally for decision-making purposes. This may seem like a reasonable requirement for the FASB to make, but it has some serious drawbacks. First, segmented data are often highly sensitive and companies are reluctant to release such data to the public for the simple reason that their competitors will then have access to the data. Second, segmented statements prepared in accordance with GAAP do not distinguish between fixed and variable costs and between traceable and common costs. Indeed, the segmented income statements illustrated earlier in this chapter do not conform to GAAP for that reason. To avoid the complications of reconciling non-GAAP segment earnings with GAAP consolidated earnings, it is likely that at least some managers will choose to construct their segmented financial statements in a manner that conforms with GAAP. This will result in more occurrences of the problems discussed in the following section.

Hindrances to Proper Cost Assignment

Costs must be properly assigned to segments. All of the costs attributable to a segment—and only those costs—should be assigned to the segment. Unfortunately, companies often make mistakes when assigning costs to segments. They omit some costs, inappropriately assign traceable fixed costs, and arbitrarily allocate common fixed costs.

Omission of Costs

The costs assigned to a segment should include all costs attributable to that segment from the company's entire value chain as discussed in Chapter 1. All of these functions, from research and development, through product design, manufacturing, marketing, distribution, and customer service, are required to bring a product or service to the customer and generate revenues.

However, as discussed in Chapters 2, 3, and 6, only manufacturing costs are included in product costs under absorption costing, which is widely regarded as required for external financial reporting. To avoid having to maintain two costing systems and to provide consistency between internal and external reports, many companies also use absorption costing for their internal reports such as segmented income statements. As a result, such companies omit from their profitability analysis part or all of the "upstream" costs in the value chain, which consist of research and development and product design, and the "downstream" costs, which consist of marketing, distribution, and customer service. Yet these nonmanufacturing costs are just as essential in determining product profitability as are the manufacturing costs. These upstream and downstream costs, which are usually included in selling and administrative expenses on the income statement, can represent half or more of the total costs of an organization. If either the upstream or downstream costs are omitted in profitability analysis, then the product is undercosted and management may unwittingly develop and maintain products that in the long run result in losses.

Inappropriate Methods for Assigning Traceable Costs among Segments

In addition to omitting costs, many companies do not correctly handle traceable fixed expenses on segmented income statements. First, they may not trace fixed expenses to segments even when it is feasible to do so. Second, they may use inappropriate allocation bases to allocate traceable fixed expenses to segments.

Failure to Trace Costs Directly

Costs that can be traced directly to a specific segment should be charged directly to that segment and should not be allocated to other segments. For example, the rent for a branch office of an insurance company should be charged directly to the branch office rather than included in a companywide overhead pool and then spread throughout the company.

Inappropriate Allocation Base

Some companies use arbitrary allocation bases to allocate costs to segments. For example, some companies allocate selling and administrative expenses on the basis of sales revenues. Thus, if a segment generates 20% of total company sales, it would be allocated 20% of the company's selling and administrative expenses as its "fair share." This same basic procedure is followed if cost of goods sold or some other measure is used as the allocation base.

Costs should be allocated to segments for internal decision-making purposes only when the allocation base actually drives the cost being allocated (or is very highly correlated with the real cost driver). For example, sales should be used to allocate selling and administrative expenses only if a 10% increase in sales will result in a 10% increase in selling and administrative expenses. To the extent that selling and administrative expenses are not driven by sales volume, these expenses will be improperly allocated—with a disproportionately high percentage of the selling and administrative expenses assigned to the segments with the largest sales.

Arbitrarily Dividing Common Costs among Segments

The third business practice that leads to distorted segment costs is the practice of assigning nontraceable costs to segments. For example, some companies allocate the common costs of the corporate headquarters building to products on segment reports. However, in a multiproduct company, no single product is likely to be responsible for any significant amount of this cost. Even if a product were eliminated entirely, there would usually be no significant effect on any of the costs of the corporate headquarters building. In short, there is no cause-and-effect relation between the cost of the corporate headquarters building and the existence of any one product. As a consequence, any allocation of the cost of the corporate headquarters building to the products must be arbitrary.

Common costs like the costs of the corporate headquarters building are necessary, of course, to have a functioning organization. The practice of arbitrarily allocating common costs to segments is often justified on the grounds that "someone" has to "cover the common costs." While it is undeniably true that the common costs must be covered, arbitrarily allocating common costs to segments does not ensure that this will happen. In fact, adding a share of common costs to the real costs of a segment may make an otherwise profitable segment appear to be unprofitable. If a manager eliminates the apparently unprofitable segment, the real traceable costs of the segment will be saved, but its revenues will be lost. And what happens to the common fixed costs that were allocated to the segment? They don't disappear; they are reallocated to the remaining segments of the company. That makes all of the remaining segments appear to be less profitable—possibly resulting in dropping other segments. The net effect will be to reduce the overall profits of the company and make it even more difficult to "cover the common costs."

Additionally, common fixed costs are not manageable by the manager to whom they are arbitrarily allocated; they are the responsibility of higher-level managers. Allocating common fixed costs to responsibility centers is counterproductive in a responsibility accounting system. When common fixed costs are allocated to managers, they are held responsible for those costs even though they cannot control them.

In sum, the way many companies handle segment reporting results in cost distortion. This distortion results from three practices—the failure to trace costs directly to a specific segment when it is feasible to do so, the use of inappropriate bases for allocating costs, and the allocation of common costs to segments. These practices are widespread. One study found that 60% of the companies surveyed made no attempt to assign selling and administrative costs to segments on a cause-and-effect basis.[3]

IN BUSINESS

THE BIG GOUGE?

The Big Dig in Boston is a $14 billion-plus project to bury major roads underground in downtown Boston. Two companies—Bechtel and Parsons Brinckerhoff (PB)—manage the 20-year project, which is $1.6 billion over budget. The two companies will likely collect in excess of $120 million in fixed fees for their work on the project—not including reimbursements for overhead costs. Bechtel and PB have many projects underway at any one time and many common fixed costs. These common fixed costs are not actually caused by the Big Dig project and yet portions of these costs have been claimed as reimbursable expenses. "Bechtel and PB say they don't collect a penny more for overhead than they are entitled to." A Bechtel spokesman says, "Our allocation of overhead [on the Big Dig] is rigorously audited . . . " This is undoubtedly true; in practice, fixed common costs are routinely (and arbitrarily) allocated to segments for cost reimbursement and other purposes. Managers at Bechtel, PB, and other companies argue that someone must pay for these costs. While this too is true, who actually pays for these costs will depend on how the common fixed costs are arbitrarily allocated among segments. Massachusetts has lodged a number of complaints concerning Bechtel's cost recovery claims. Such complaints are almost inevitable when common fixed costs are allocated to segments. It might be better to simply set an all-inclusive fixed fee up front with no cost recovery and hence no issues concerning what costs are really attributable to the project.

Source: Nathan Vardi, "Desert Storm," *Forbes*, June 23, 2003, pp. 63–66.

Evaluating Investment Center Performance—Return on Investment

LEARNING OBJECTIVE 2
Compute return on investment (ROI) and show how changes in sales, expenses, and assets affect ROI.

Thus far, the chapter has focused on how to properly assign costs to responsibility centers and how to construct segmented income statements. These are vital steps when evaluating cost and profit centers. However, evaluating an investment center's performance requires more than accurate cost and segment margin reporting. In addition, an investment center is responsible for earning an adequate return on investment. This section and the next section

[3] James R. Emore and Joseph A. Ness, "The Slow Pace of Meaningful Change in Cost Systems," *Journal of Cost Management* 4, no. 4, p. 39.

of the chapter present two methods for evaluating this aspect of an investment center's performance. The first method, covered in this section, is called *return on investment (ROI).* The second method, covered in the next section, is called *residual income.*

The Return on Investment (ROI) Formula

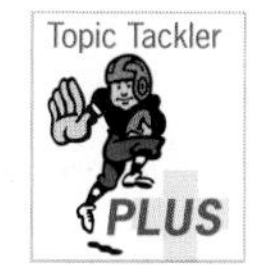

11–1

Return on investment (ROI) is defined as net operating income divided by average operating assets:

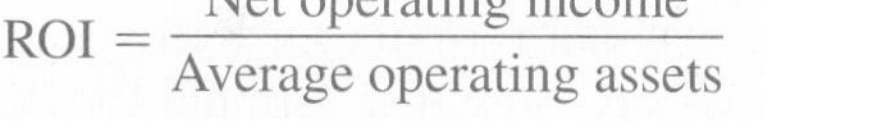

$$\text{ROI} = \frac{\text{Net operating income}}{\text{Average operating assets}}$$

The higher a business segment's return on investment (ROI), the greater the profit earned per dollar invested in the segment's operating assets.

Net Operating Income and Operating Assets Defined

Note that *net operating income,* rather than net income, is used in the ROI formula. **Net operating income** is income before interest and taxes and is sometimes referred to as EBIT (earnings before interest and taxes). Net operating income is used in the formula because the base (i.e., denominator) consists of *operating assets.* To be consistent, we use net operating income in the numerator.

Operating assets include cash, accounts receivable, inventory, plant and equipment, and all other assets held for operating purposes. Examples of assets that are not included in operating assets (i.e., examples of nonoperating assets) include land held for future use, an investment in another company, or a building rented to someone else. These assets are not held for operating purposes and therefore are excluded from operating assets. The operating assets base used in the formula is typically computed as the average of the operating assets between the beginning and the end of the year.

Most companies use the net book value (i.e., acquisition cost less accumulated depreciation) of depreciable assets to calculate average operating assets. This approach has drawbacks. An asset's net book value decreases over time as the accumulated depreciation increases. This decreases the denominator in the ROI calculation, thus increasing ROI. Consequently, ROI mechanically increases over time. Moreover, replacing old depreciated equipment with new equipment increases the book value of depreciable assets and decreases ROI. Hence, using net book value in the calculation of average operating assets results in a predictable pattern of increasing ROI over time as accumulated depreciation grows and discourages replacing old equipment with new, updated equipment. An alternative to using net book value is the gross cost of the asset, which ignores accumulated depreciation. Gross cost stays constant over time because depreciation is ignored; therefore, ROI does not grow automatically over time, and replacing a fully depreciated asset with a comparably priced new asset will not adversely affect ROI.

Nevertheless, most companies use the net book value approach to computing average operating assets because it is consistent with their financial reporting practices of recording the net book value of assets on the balance sheet and including depreciation as an operating expense on the income statement. In this text, we will use the net book value approach unless a specific exercise or problem directs otherwise.

Understanding ROI

The equation for ROI, net operating income divided by average operating assets, does not provide much help to managers interested in taking actions to improve their ROI. It only offers two levers for improving performance—net operating income and average operating assets. Fortunately, ROI can also be expressed as follows:

$$\text{ROI} = \text{Margin} \times \text{Turnover}$$

where

$$\text{Margin} = \frac{\text{Net operating income}}{\text{Sales}}$$

and

$$\text{Turnover} = \frac{\text{Sales}}{\text{Average operating assets}}$$

Note that the sales terms in the margin and turnover formulas cancel out when they are multiplied together, yielding the original formula for ROI stated in terms of net operating income and average operating assets. So either formula for ROI will give the same answer. However, the margin and turnover formulation provides some additional insights.

From a manager's perspective, **margin** and **turnover** are very important concepts. Margin is ordinarily improved by increasing sales or reducing operating expenses, including cost of goods sold and selling and administrative expenses. The lower the operating expenses per dollar of sales, the higher the margin earned. Some managers tend to focus too much on margin and ignore turnover. However, turnover incorporates a crucial area of a manager's responsibility—the investment in operating assets. Excessive funds tied up in operating assets (e.g., cash, accounts receivable, inventories, plant and equipment, and other assets) depress turnover and lower ROI. In fact, inefficient use of operating assets can be just as much of a drag on profitability as excessive operating expenses, which depress margin.

E.I. du Pont de Nemours and Company (better know as DuPont) pioneered the use of ROI and recognized the importance of looking at both margin and turnover in assessing a manager's performance. ROI is now widely used as the key measure of investment center performance. ROI reflects in a single figure many aspects of the manager's responsibilities. It can be compared to the returns of other investment centers in the organization, the returns of other companies in the industry, and to the past returns of the investment center itself.

DuPont also developed the diagram that appears in Exhibit 11–5. This exhibit helps managers understand how they can improve ROI. Any increase in ROI must involve at least one of the following:

1. Increased sales
2. Reduced operating expenses
3. Reduced operating assets

Many actions involve combinations of changes in sales, expenses, and operating assets. For example, a manager may make an investment in (i.e., increase) operating assets to reduce operating expenses or increase sales. Whether the net effect is favorable or not is judged in terms of its overall impact on ROI.

IN BUSINESS

J. CREW PULLS THE ROI LEVERS

J. Crew has adopted an interesting strategy for improving its ROI. The company has started selling "super-premium products—such as $1,500 cashmere coats and $1,500 beaded tunics—in limited editions, sometimes no more than 100 pieces nationwide." The intentional creation of scarcity causes many items to sell out within weeks as shoppers snatch them up before they are gone for good.

This strategy is helping boost J. Crew's ROI in two ways. First, the company earns higher margins on premium-priced products where customer demand dramatically exceeds supply. Second, the company is slashing its inventories because such small quantities of each item are purchased from suppliers. While J. Crew sacrifices some sales from customers who would have purchased sold out items, the overall effect on profits has been favorable. "Tighter inventories mean that J. Crew is no longer putting reams of clothes on sale, a move that kills profit margins and trains shoppers to wait for discounts. At one point . . . half of J. Crew's clothing sold at a discount. Today only a small percentage of it does."

Source: Julia Boorstin, "Mickey Drexler's Second Coming," *Fortune,* May 2, 2005, pp. 101–104.

EXHIBIT 11–5
Elements of Return on Investment (ROI)

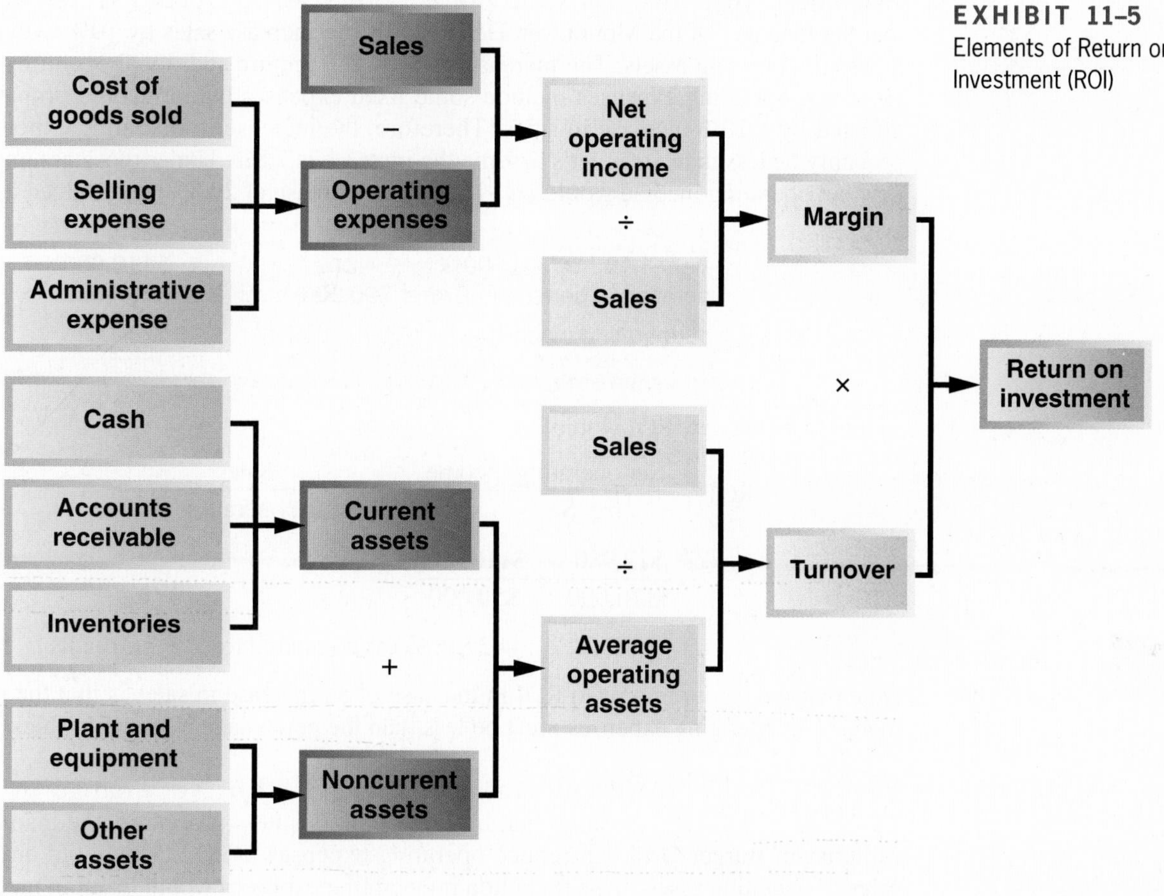

To illustrate how ROI is impacted by various actions, we will use the Monthaven outlet of the Burger Grill chain as an example. Burger Grill is a small chain of upscale casual restaurants that has been rapidly adding outlets via franchising. The Monthaven franchise is owned by a group of local surgeons who have little time to devote to management and little expertise in business matters. Therefore, they delegate operating decisions—including decisions concerning investments in operating assets such as inventories—to a professional manager they have hired. The manager is evaluated largely based on the ROI the franchise generates.

The following data represent the results of operations for the most recent month:

Sales	$100,000
Operating expenses	$90,000
Net operating income	$10,000
Average operating assets	$50,000

The return on investment (ROI) for the month is computed as follows:

$$\text{ROI} = \frac{\text{Net operating income}}{\text{Sales}} \times \frac{\text{Sales}}{\text{Average operating assets}}$$

$$= \frac{\$10,000}{\$100,000} \times \frac{\$100,000}{\$50,000}$$

$$= 10\% \times 2 = 20\%$$

Example 1: Increased Sales without Any Increase in Operating Assets Assume that the manager of the Monthaven Burger Grill can increase sales by 10% without any increase in operating assets. The increase in sales will require additional operating expenses. However, operating expenses include some fixed expenses, which would probably not be affected by a 10% increase in sales. Therefore, the increase in operating expenses would probably be less than 10%; let's assume the increase is 7.8%. Under those assumptions, the new net operating income would be $12,980, an increase of 29.8%, determined as follows:

Sales (1.10 × $100,000)	$110,000
Operating expenses (1.078 × $90,000)	97,020
Net operating income	$ 12,980

In this case, the new ROI would be:

$$\text{ROI} = \frac{\text{Net operating income}}{\text{Sales}} \times \frac{\text{Sales}}{\text{Average operating assets}}$$

$$= \frac{\$12{,}980}{\$110{,}000} \times \frac{\$110{,}000}{\$50{,}000}$$

$$= 11.8\% \times 2.2 = 25.96\% \text{ (as compared to 20\% originally)}$$

Note that the key to improved ROI in the case of an increase in sales is that the percentage increase in operating expenses must be less than the percentage increase in sales.

Example 2: Decreased Operating Expenses with No Change in Sales or Operating Assets Assume that by improving business processes, the manager of the Monthaven Burger Grill can reduce operating expenses by $1,000 without any effect on sales or operating assets. This reduction in operating expenses would result in increasing net operating income by $1,000, from $10,000 to $11,000. The new ROI would be:

$$\text{ROI} = \frac{\text{Net operating income}}{\text{Sales}} \times \frac{\text{Sales}}{\text{Average operating assets}}$$

$$= \frac{\$11{,}000}{\$100{,}000} \times \frac{\$100{,}000}{\$50{,}000}$$

$$= 11\% \times 2 = 22\% \text{ (as compared to 20\% originally)}$$

When margins or profits are being squeezed, the first line of attack is often to cut costs. Discretionary fixed costs are particularly vulnerable to cuts. However, managers must be careful not to cut too much or in the wrong place. Inappropriate cost cutting can lead to decreased sales, increased costs elsewhere, and a drop in morale.

Example 3: Decreased Operating Assets with No Change in Sales or Operating Expenses Assume that the manager of the Monthaven Burger Grill uses lean production techniques to reduce inventories by $10,000. This might actually have a positive effect on sales (through fresher ingredients) and on operating expenses (through reduced inventory spoilage), but for the sake of illustration, suppose the reduction in inventories has no effect on sales or operating expenses. The reduction in inventories will reduce average operating assets by $10,000, from $50,000 down to $40,000. The new ROI would be:

$$\text{ROI} = \frac{\text{Net operating income}}{\text{Sales}} \times \frac{\text{Sales}}{\text{Average operating assets}}$$

$$= \frac{\$10{,}000}{\$100{,}000} \times \frac{\$100{,}000}{\$40{,}000}$$

$$= 10\% \times 2.5 = 25\% \text{ (as compared to 20\% originally)}$$

In this example, Lean Production was used to reduce operating assets. Another common tactic for reducing operating assets is to speed up the collection of accounts receivable. For example, many companies encourage customers to pay electronically rather than by mail.

IN BUSINESS

JIT AND ROI IMPROVEMENT

A study of companies that adopted just-in-time (JIT) in comparison to a control group that did not adopt JIT, found that the JIT adopters improved their ROIs more. The JIT adopters' success resulted from improvements in both profit margins and asset turnover. The elimination of inventories in JIT reduces total assets, but more important, it leads to process improvements as production problems are exposed. When production problems and non-value-added activities are eliminated, costs go down.

Source: Michael R. Kinney and William F. Wempe, "Further Evidence on the Extent and Origins of JIT's Profitability Effects," *The Accounting Review,* January 2002, pp. 203–225.

Example 4: Invest in Operating Assets to Increase Sales Assume that the manager of the Monthaven Burger Grill invests $2,000 in a state-of-the-art soft-serve ice cream machine that can dispense a number of different flavors. This new machine will boost sales by $4,000, but will require additional operating expenses of $1,000. Thus, net operating income will increase by $3,000, to $13,000. The new ROI will be:

$$\text{ROI} = \frac{\text{Net operating income}}{\text{Sales}} \times \frac{\text{Sales}}{\text{Average operating assets}}$$

$$= \frac{\$13{,}000}{\$104{,}000} \times \frac{\$104{,}000}{\$52{,}000}$$

$$= 12.5\% \times 2 = 25\% \text{ (as compared to 20\% originally)}$$

In this particular example, the investment had no effect on turnover, which remained at 2, so there had to be an increase in margin in order to improve the ROI.

IN BUSINESS

MCDONALD CHIC

McDonald's France has been spending lavishly to remodel its restaurants to blend with local architecture and to make their interiors less uniform and sterile. For example, some outlets in the Alps have wood-and-stone interiors similar to those of alpine chalets. The idea is to defuse the negative feelings many of the French people have toward McDonald's as a symbol of American culture and, perhaps more importantly, to try to entice customers to linger over their meals and spend more. This investment in operating assets has apparently been successful—even though a Big Mac costs about the same in Paris as in New York, the average French customer spends about $9 per visit versus only about $4 in the U.S.

Source: Carol Matlack and Pallavi Gogoi, "What's This? The French Love McDonald's?" *BusinessWeek,* January 13, 2003, p. 50.

ROI and the Balanced Scorecard

The DuPont scheme, which is illustrated in Exhibit 11–5, provides managers with *some* guidance about how to increase ROI. Generally speaking, ROI can be increased by increasing sales, decreasing costs, and/or decreasing investments in operating assets. However, it may not be obvious to managers *how* they are supposed to increase sales, decrease costs, and decrease investments in a way that is consistent with the company's strategy. For example, a manager who is given inadequate guidance may cut back on investments that are critical to implementing the company's strategy.

For that reason, as discussed in Chapter 9, managers should be evaluated using a balanced scorecard approach. ROI, or residual income (discussed below), is typically included as one of the financial performance measures on a company's balanced scorecard. However, this measure is supplemented by other measures that indicate *how* the company intends to improve its financial performance. A well-constructed balanced scorecard should answer questions like: "What internal business processes should be improved?" and "Which customers should be targeted and how will they be attracted and retained at a profit?" In short, a well-constructed balanced scorecard provides managers with a road map that indicates how the company intends to increase its ROI. In the absence of such a road map of the company's strategy, managers may have difficulty understanding what they are supposed to do to increase ROI and they may work at cross-purposes rather than in harmony with the overall strategy of the company.

Criticisms of ROI

Although ROI is widely used in evaluating performance, it is subject to the following criticisms:

1. Just telling managers to increase ROI may not be enough. Managers may not know how to increase ROI; they may increase ROI in a way that is inconsistent with the company's strategy; or they may take actions that increase ROI in the short run but harm the company in the long run (such as cutting back on research and development). This is why ROI is best used as part of a balanced scorecard. A balanced scorecard can provide concrete guidance to managers, making it more likely that their actions are consistent with the company's strategy and reducing the likelihood that they will boost short-run performance at the expense of long-term performance.
2. A manager who takes over a business segment typically inherits many committed costs over which the manager has no control. These committed costs may be relevant in assessing the performance of the business segment as an investment but they make it difficult to fairly assess the performance of the manager.
3. As discussed in the next section, a manager who is evaluated based on ROI may reject investment opportunities that are profitable for the whole company but that would have a negative impact on the manager's performance evaluation.

IN BUSINESS

LET THE BUYER BEWARE

Those who sell products and services to businesses are well aware that many potential customers look very carefully at the impact the purchase would have on ROI before making a purchase. Unfortunately, some salespersons make extravagant ROI claims. For example, businesspeople complain that software salespersons routinely exaggerate the impact that new software will have on ROI. Some of the tricks used by salespersons include: inflating the salaries of workers who are made redundant by productivity gains; omitting costs such as training costs and implementation costs; inflating expected sales increases; and using former clients as examples of ROI gains when the clients were given the software for free or for nominal cost. The message? Be skeptical of salespersons' claims with respect to ROI gains from purchasing their products and services.

Source: Scott Leibs, "All Hail the ROI," *CFO,* April 2002, pp. 27–28.

Residual Income

LEARNING OBJECTIVE 3
Compute residual income and understand its strengths and weaknesses.

Residual income is another approach to measuring an investment center's performance. **Residual income** is the net operating income that an investment center earns above the minimum required return on its operating assets. In equation form, residual income is calculated as follows:

$$\text{Residual income} = \text{Net operating income} - \left(\text{Average operating assets} \times \text{Minimum required rate of return}\right)$$

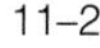
11–2

Economic Value Added (EVA®) is an adaptation of residual income that has been adopted by many companies.[4] Under EVA, companies often modify their accounting principles in various ways. For example, funds used for research and development are often treated as investments rather than as expenses.[5] These complications are best dealt with in a more advanced course; in this text we will not draw any distinction between residual income and EVA.

When residual income or EVA is used to measure performance, the objective is to maximize the total amount of residual income or EVA, not to maximize ROI. This is an important distinction. If the objective were to maximize ROI, then every company should divest all of its products except the single product with the highest ROI.

A wide variety of organizations have embraced some version of residual income or EVA, including Bausch & Lomb, Best Buy, Boise Cascade, Coca-Cola, Dun and Bradstreet, Eli Lilly, Federated Mogul, Georgia-Pacific, Guidant Corporation, Hershey Foods, Husky Injection Molding, J.C. Penney, Kansas City Power & Light, Olin, Quaker Oats, Silicon Valley Bank, Sprint, Toys R Us, Tupperware, and the United States Postal Service. In addition, financial institutions such as Credit Suisse First Boston now use EVA—and its allied concept, market value added—to evaluate potential investments in other companies.

For purposes of illustration, consider the following data for an investment center—the Ketchikan Division of Alaskan Marine Services Corporation.

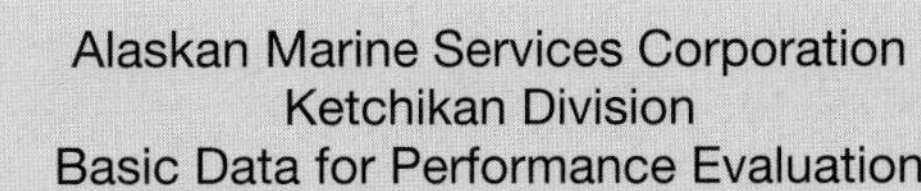

Alaskan Marine Services Corporation Ketchikan Division Basic Data for Performance Evaluation	
Average operating assets	$100,000
Net operating income	$20,000
Minimum required rate of return	15%

Alaskan Marine Services Corporation has long had a policy of using ROI to evaluate its investment center managers, but it is considering switching to residual income. The controller of the company, who is in favor of the change to residual income, has provided the table on the following page that shows how the performance of the division would be evaluated under each of the two methods:

[4] The basic idea underlying residual income and economic value added has been around for over 100 years. In recent years, economic value added has been popularized and trademarked by the consulting firm Stern, Stewart & Co.

[5] Over 100 different adjustments could be made for deferred taxes, LIFO reserves, provisions for future liabilities, mergers and acquisitions, gains or losses due to changes in accounting rules, operating leases, and other accounts, but most companies make only a few. For further details, see John O'Hanlon and Ken Peasnell, "Wall Street's Contribution to Management Accounting: the Stern Stewart EVA® Financial Management System," *Management Accounting Research* 9, 1998, pp. 421–444.

Alaskan Marine Services Corporation Ketchikan Division		
	Alternative Performance Measures	
	ROI	Residual Income
Average operating assets (a)	$100,000	$100,000
Net operating income (b)	$ 20,000	$ 20,000
ROI, (b) ÷ (a)	20%	
Minimum required return (15% × $100,000)		15,000
Residual income		$ 5,000

The reasoning underlying the residual income calculation is straightforward. The company is able to earn a rate of return of at least 15% on its investments. Since the company has invested $100,000 in the Ketchikan Division in the form of operating assets, the company should be able to earn at least $15,000 (15% × $100,000) on this investment. Because the Ketchikan Division's net operating income is $20,000, the residual income above and beyond the minimum required return is $5,000. If residual income is adopted as the performance measure to replace ROI, the manager of the Ketchikan Division would be evaluated based on the growth in residual income from year to year.

Motivation and Residual Income

One of the primary reasons why the controller of Alaskan Marine Services Corporation would like to switch from ROI to residual income relates to how managers view new investments under the two performance measurement schemes. The residual income approach encourages managers to make investments that are profitable for the entire company but that would be rejected by managers who are evaluated using the ROI formula.

To illustrate this problem with ROI, suppose that the manager of the Ketchikan Division is considering purchasing a computerized diagnostic machine to aid in servicing marine diesel engines. The machine would cost $25,000 and is expected to generate additional operating income of $4,500 a year. From the standpoint of the company, this would be a good investment because it promises a rate of return of 18% ($4,500 ÷ $25,000), which exceeds the company's minimum required rate of return of 15%.

If the manager of the Ketchikan Division is evaluated based on residual income, she would be in favor of the investment in the diagnostic machine as shown below:

Alaskan Marine Services Corporation Ketchikan Division Performance Evaluated Using Residual Income			
	Present	New Project	Overall
Average operating assets	$100,000	$25,000	$125,000
Net operating income	$ 20,000	$ 4,500	$ 24,500
Minimum required return	15,000	3,750*	18,750
Residual income	$ 5,000	$ 750	$ 5,750

*$25,000 × 15% = $3,750.

Since the project would increase the residual income of the Ketchikan Division by $750, the manager would choose to invest in the new diagnostic machine.

Now suppose that the manager of the Ketchikan Division is evaluated based on ROI. The effect of the diagnostic machine on the division's ROI is computed below:

Alaskan Marine Services Corporation Ketchikan Division Performance Evaluated Using ROI			
	Present	New Project	Overall
Average operating assets (a)	$100,000	$25,000	$125,000
Net operating income (b)	$20,000	$4,500	$24,500
ROI, (b) ÷ (a)	20%	18%	19.6%

The new project reduces the division's ROI from 20% to 19.6%. This happens because the 18% rate of return on the new diagnostic machine, while above the company's 15% minimum required rate of return, is below the division's current ROI of 20%. Therefore, the new diagnostic machine would decrease the division's ROI even though it would be a good investment from the standpoint of the company as a whole. If the manager of the division is evaluated based on ROI, she will be reluctant to even propose such an investment.

Generally, a manager who is evaluated based on ROI will reject any project whose rate of return is below the division's current ROI even if the rate of return on the project is above the company's minimum required rate of return. In contrast, managers who are evaluated using residual income will pursue any project whose rate of return is above the minimum required rate of return because it will increase their residual income. Because it is in the best interests of the company as a whole to accept any project whose rate of return is above the minimum required rate of return, managers who are evaluated based on residual income will tend to make better decisions concerning investment projects than managers who are evaluated based on ROI.

Divisional Comparison and Residual Income

The residual income approach has one major disadvantage. It can't be used to compare the performance of divisions of different sizes. Larger divisions often have more residual income than smaller divisions, not necessarily because they are better managed but simply because they are bigger.

As an example, consider the following residual income computations for the Wholesale Division and the Retail Division of Sisal Marketing Corporation:

	Wholesale Division	Retail Division
Average operating assets (a)	$1,000,000	$250,000
Net operating income	$ 120,000	$ 40,000
Minimum required return: 10% × (a)	100,000	25,000
Residual income	$ 20,000	$ 15,000

Observe that the Wholesale Division has slightly more residual income than the Retail Division, but that the Wholesale Division has $1,000,000 in operating assets as compared to only $250,000 in operating assets for the Retail Division. Thus, the Wholesale Division's greater residual income is probably due to its larger size rather than the quality of its management. In fact, it appears that the smaller division may be better managed, since it has been able to generate nearly as much residual income with only one-fourth as much in operating assets. When comparing investment centers, it is probably better to focus on the percentage change in residual income from year to year rather than on the absolute amount of the residual income.

IN BUSINESS

HEADS I WIN, TAILS YOU LOSE

A number of companies, including AT&T, Armstrong Holdings, and Baldwin Technology, have stopped using residual income measures of performance after trying them. Why? Reasons differ, but "bonus evaporation is often seen as the Achilles' heel of value-based metrics [like residual income and EVA]—and a major cause of plans being dropped." Managers tend to love residual income and EVA when their bonuses are big, but clamor for changes in performance measures when bonuses shrink.

Source: Bill Richard and Alix Nyberg, "Do EVA and Other Value Metrics Still Offer a Good Mirror of Company Performance?" *CFO*, March 2001, pp. 56–64.

Summary

For purposes of evaluating performance, business units are classified as cost centers, profit centers, and investment centers. Cost centers are commonly evaluated using standard cost and flexible budget variances as discussed in prior chapters. Profit centers and investment centers are evaluated using the techniques discussed in this chapter.

Segmented income statements provide information for evaluating the profitability and performance of divisions, product lines, sales territories, and other segments of a company. Under the contribution approach covered in this chapter, variable costs and fixed costs are clearly distinguished from each other and only those costs that are traceable to a segment are assigned to the segment. A cost is considered traceable to a segment only if the cost is caused by the segment and could be avoided by eliminating the segment. Fixed common costs are not allocated to segments. The segment margin consists of revenues, less variable expenses, less traceable fixed expenses of the segment.

Return on investment (ROI) and residual income and its cousin EVA are widely used to evaluate the performance of investment centers. ROI suffers from the underinvestment problem—managers are reluctant to invest in projects that would decrease their ROI but whose returns exceed the company's required rate of return. The residual income and EVA approaches solve this problem by giving managers full credit for any returns in excess of the company's required rate of return.

Review Problem 1: Segmented Statements

The business staff of the law firm Frampton, Davis & Smythe has constructed the following report which breaks down the firm's overall results for last month into two main business segments—family law and commercial law:

	Total	Family Law	Commercial Law
Revenues from clients	$1,000,000	$400,000	$600,000
Variable expenses	220,000	100,000	120,000
Contribution margin	780,000	300,000	480,000
Traceable fixed expenses	670,000	280,000	390,000
Segment margin	110,000	20,000	90,000
Common fixed expenses	60,000	24,000	36,000
Net operating income	$ 50,000	$ (4,000)	$ 54,000

However, this report is not quite correct. The common fixed expenses such as the managing partner's salary, general administrative expenses, and general firm advertising have been allocated to the two segments based on revenues from clients.

Required:

1. Redo the segment report, eliminating the allocation of common fixed expenses. Would the firm be better off financially if the family law segment were dropped? (Note: Many of the firm's commercial law clients also use the firm for their family law requirements such as drawing up wills.)
2. The firm's advertising agency has proposed an ad campaign targeted at boosting the revenues of the family law segment. The ad campaign would cost $20,000, and the advertising agency claims that it would increase family law revenues by $100,000. The managing partner of Frampton, Davis & Smythe believes this increase in business could be accommodated without any increase in fixed expenses. What effect would this ad campaign have on the family law segment margin and on the firm's overall net operating income?

Solution to Review Problem 1

1. The corrected segmented income statement appears below:

	Total	Family Law	Commercial Law
Revenues from clients	$1,000,000	$400,000	$600,000
Variable expenses	220,000	100,000	120,000
Contribution margin	780,000	300,000	480,000
Traceable fixed expenses	670,000	280,000	390,000
Segment margin	110,000	$ 20,000	$ 90,000
Common fixed expenses	60,000		
Net operating income	$ 50,000		

No, the firm would not be financially better off if the family law practice were dropped. The family law segment is covering all of its own costs and is contributing $20,000 per month to covering the common fixed expenses of the firm. While the segment margin for family law is much lower than for commercial law, it is still profitable. Moreover, family law may be a service that the firm must provide to its commercial clients in order to remain competitive.

2. The ad campaign would increase the family law segment margin by $55,000 as follows:

Increased revenues from clients	$100,000
Family law contribution margin ratio ($300,000 ÷ $400,000)	× 75%
Incremental contribution margin	$ 75,000
Less cost of the ad campaign	20,000
Increased segment margin	$ 55,000

Since there would be no increase in fixed expenses (including common fixed expenses), the increase in overall net operating income is also $55,000.

Review Problem 2: Return on Investment (ROI) and Residual Income

The Magnetic Imaging Division of Medical Diagnostics, Inc., has reported the following results for last year's operations:

Sales	$25 million
Net operating income	$3 million
Average operating assets	$10 million

Required:

1. Compute the Magnetic Imaging Division's margin, turnover, and ROI.
2. Top management of Medical Diagnostics, Inc., has set a minimum required rate of return on average operating assets of 25%. What is the Magnetic Imaging Division's residual income for the year?

Solution to Review Problem 2

1. The required calculations follow:

$$\text{Margin} = \frac{\text{Net operating income}}{\text{Sales}}$$

$$= \frac{\$3{,}000{,}000}{\$25{,}000{,}000}$$

$$= 12\%$$

$$\text{Turnover} = \frac{\text{Sales}}{\text{Average operating assets}}$$

$$= \frac{\$25{,}000{,}000}{\$10{,}000{,}000}$$

$$= 2.5\%$$

$$\text{ROI} = \text{Margin} \times \text{Turnover}$$

$$= 12\% \times 2.5$$

$$= 30\%$$

2. The Magnetic Imaging Division's residual income is computed as follows:

Average operating assets	$10,000,000
Net operating income	$ 3,000,000
Minimum required return (25% × $10,000,000)	2,500,000
Residual income	$ 500,000

Glossary

Common fixed cost A fixed cost that supports more than one business segment, but is not traceable in whole or in part to any one of the business segments. (p. 446)

Cost center A business segment whose manager has control over cost but has no control over revenue or investments in operating assets. (p. 439)

Decentralized organization An organization in which decision-making authority is not confined to a few top executives but rather is spread throughout the organization. (p. 438)

Economic Value Added (EVA) A concept similar to residual income in which a variety of adjustments may be made to GAAP financial statements for performance evaluation purposes. (p. 459)

Investment center A business segment whose manager has control over cost, revenue, and investments in operating assets. (p. 440)

Margin Net operating income divided by sales. (p. 454)

Net operating income Income before interest and income taxes have been deducted. (p. 453)

Operating assets Cash, accounts receivable, inventory, plant and equipment, and all other assets held for operating purposes. (p. 453)

Profit center A business segment whose manager has control over cost and revenue but has no control over investments in operating assets. (p. 439)

Residual income The net operating income that an investment center earns above the minimum required return on its operating assets. (p. 459)

Responsibility center Any business segment whose manager has control over costs, revenues, or investments in operating assets. (p. 439)

Return on investment (ROI) Net operating income divided by average operating assets. It also equals margin multiplied by turnover. (p. 453)

Segment Any part or activity of an organization about which managers seek cost, revenue, or profit data. (p. 441)

Segment margin A segment's contribution margin less its traceable fixed costs. It represents the margin available after a segment has covered all of its own traceable costs. (p. 448)

Traceable fixed cost A fixed cost that is incurred because of the existence of a particular business segment and that would be eliminated if the segment were eliminated. (p. 446)

Turnover Sales divided by average operating assets. (p. 454)

Appendix 11A: Transfer Pricing

Divisions in a company often supply goods and services to other divisions within the same company. For example, the truck division of Toyota supplies trucks to other Toyota divisions to use in their operations. When the divisions are evaluated based on their profit, return on investment, or residual income, a price must be established for such a transfer—otherwise, the division that produces the good or service will receive no credit. The price in such a situation is called a *transfer price.* A **transfer price** is the price charged when one segment of a company provides goods or services to another segment of the same company. For example, most companies in the oil industry, such as Shell, have petroleum refining and retail sales divisions that are evaluated on the basis of ROI or residual income. The petroleum refining division processes crude oil into gasoline, kerosene, lubricants, and other end products. The retail sales division takes gasoline and other products from the refining division and sells them through the company's chain of service stations. Each product has a price for transfers within the company. Suppose the transfer price for gasoline is $0.80 a gallon. Then the refining division gets credit for $0.80 a gallon of revenue on its segment report and the retailing division must deduct $0.80 a gallon as an expense on its segment report. Clearly, the refining division would like the transfer price to be as high as possible, whereas the retailing division would like the transfer price to be as low as possible. However, the transaction has no direct effect on the entire company's reported profit. It is like taking money out of one pocket and putting it into the other.

Managers are intensely interested in how transfer prices are set because they can have a dramatic effect on the reported profitability of their divisions. Three common approaches are used to set transfer prices:

1. Allow the managers involved in the transfer to negotiate their own transfer price.
2. Set transfer prices at cost using either variable cost or full (absorption) cost.
3. Set transfer prices at the market price.

We will consider each of these transfer pricing methods in turn, beginning with negotiated transfer prices. Throughout the discussion, keep in mind that *the fundamental objective in setting transfer prices is to motivate the managers to act in the best interests of the overall company.* In contrast, **suboptimization** occurs when managers do not act in the best interests of the overall company or even in the best interests of their own division.

Negotiated Transfer Prices

A **negotiated transfer price** results from discussions between the selling and buying divisions. Negotiated transfer prices have several important advantages. First, this approach preserves the autonomy of the divisions and is consistent with the spirit of decentralization. Second, the managers of the divisions are likely to have much better information about the potential costs and benefits of the transfer than others in the company.

> **LEARNING OBJECTIVE 4**
> Determine the range, if any, within which a negotiated transfer price should fall.

When negotiated transfer prices are used, the managers who are involved in a proposed transfer within the company meet to discuss the terms and conditions of the transfer. They may decide not to go through with the transfer, but if they do, they must agree to a transfer price. Generally speaking, we cannot predict the exact transfer price they will agree to. However, we can confidently predict two things: (1) the selling division will agree to the transfer only if its profits increase as a result of the transfer, and (2) the buying division will agree to the transfer only if its profits also increase as a result of the transfer. This may seem obvious, but it is an important point.

Clearly, if the transfer price is below the selling division's cost, the selling division will incur a loss on the transaction and it will refuse to agree to the transfer. Likewise, if the transfer price is set too high, it will be impossible for the buying division to make any profit on the transferred item. For any given proposed transfer, the transfer price has both a lower limit (determined by the selling division) and an upper limit (determined by the buying division). The actual transfer price agreed to by the two division managers can fall anywhere between those two limits. These limits determine the **range of acceptable**

transfer prices—the range of transfer prices within which the profits of both divisions participating in a transfer would increase.

An example will help us to understand negotiated transfer prices. Harris & Louder, Ltd., owns fast-food restaurants and snack food and beverage manufacturers in the United Kingdom. One of the restaurants, Pizza Maven, serves a variety of beverages along with pizzas. One of the beverages is ginger beer, which is served on tap. Harris & Louder has just purchased a new division, Imperial Beverages, that produces ginger beer. The managing director of Imperial Beverages has approached the managing director of Pizza Maven about purchasing Imperial Beverages ginger beer for sale at Pizza Maven restaurants rather than its usual brand of ginger beer. Managers at Pizza Maven agree that the quality of Imperial Beverages' ginger beer is comparable to the quality of their regular brand. It is just a question of price. The basic facts are as follows (the currency in this example is pounds, denoted here as £):

Imperial Beverages:		
Ginger beer production capacity per month.	10,000 barrels	
Variable cost per barrel of ginger beer		£8 per barrel
Fixed costs per month.	£70,000	
Selling price of Imperial Beverages ginger beer on the outside market		£20 per barrel
Pizza Maven:		
Purchase price of regular brand of ginger beer		£18 per barrel
Monthly consumption of ginger beer	2,000 barrels	

The Selling Division's Lowest Acceptable Transfer Price The selling division, Imperial Beverages, will be interested in a proposed transfer only if its profit increases. Clearly, the transfer price must not fall below the variable cost per barrel of £8. In addition, if Imperial Beverages has insufficient capacity to fill the Pizza Maven order while supplying its regular customers, then it would have to sacrifice some of its regular sales. Imperial Beverages would expect to be compensated for the contribution margin on these lost sales. In sum, if the transfer has no effect on fixed costs, then from the selling division's standpoint, the transfer price must cover both the variable costs of producing the transferred units and any opportunity costs from lost sales.

Seller's perspective:

$$\text{Transfer price} \geq \begin{matrix}\text{Variable cost}\\ \text{per unit}\end{matrix} + \frac{\text{Total contribution margin on lost sales}}{\text{Number of units transferred}}$$

The Buying Division's Highest Acceptable Transfer Price The buying division, Pizza Maven, will be interested in a transfer only if its profit increases. In cases like this where a buying division has an outside supplier, the buying division's decision is simple. Buy from the inside supplier if the price is less than the price offered by the outside supplier.

Purchaser's perspective:

$$\text{Transfer price} \leq \text{Cost of buying from outside supplier}$$

Or, if an outside supplier does not exist:

$$\text{Transfer price} \leq \text{Profit to be earned per unit sold (not including the transfer price)}$$

We will consider several different hypothetical situations and see what the range of acceptable transfer prices would be in each situation.

Selling Division with Idle Capacity Suppose that Imperial Beverages has sufficient idle capacity to satisfy the demand for ginger beer from Pizza Maven without sacrificing sales of ginger beer to its regular customers. To be specific, let's suppose that Imperial Beverages is selling only 7,000 barrels of ginger beer a month on the outside market. That leaves unused capacity of 3,000 barrels a month—more than enough to satisfy Pizza Maven's requirement of 2,000 barrels a month. What range of transfer prices, if any, would make both divisions better off with the transfer of 2,000 barrels a month?

1. The selling division, Imperial Beverages, will be interested in the transfer only if:

$$\text{Transfer price} \geq \begin{matrix}\text{Variable cost}\\ \text{per unit}\end{matrix} + \frac{\text{Total contribution margin on lost sales}}{\text{Number of units transferred}}$$

   Since Imperial Beverages has ample idle capacity, there are no lost outside sales. And since the variable cost per unit is £8, the lowest acceptable transfer price for the selling division is £8.

$$\text{Transfer price} \geq £8 + \frac{£0}{2{,}000} = £8$$

2. The buying division, Pizza Maven, can buy similar ginger beer from an outside vendor for £18. Therefore, Pizza Maven would be unwilling to pay more than £18 per barrel for Imperial Beverages' ginger beer.

$$\text{Transfer price} \leq \text{Cost of buying from outside supplier} = £18$$

3. Combining the requirements of both the selling division and the buying division, the acceptable range of transfer prices in this situation is:

$$£8 \leq \text{Transfer price} \leq £18$$

   Assuming that the managers understand their own businesses and that they are cooperative, they should be able to agree on a transfer price within this range.

Selling Division with No Idle Capacity Suppose that Imperial Beverages has *no* idle capacity; it is selling 10,000 barrels of ginger beer a month on the outside market at £20 per barrel. To fill the order from Pizza Maven, Imperial Beverages would have to divert 2,000 barrels from its regular customers. What range of transfer prices, if any, would make both divisions better off transferring the 2,000 barrels within the company?

1. The selling division, Imperial Beverages, will be interested in the transfer only if:

$$\text{Transfer price} \geq \begin{matrix}\text{Variable cost}\\ \text{per unit}\end{matrix} + \frac{\text{Total contribution margin on lost sales}}{\text{Number of units transferred}}$$

   Since Imperial Beverages has no idle capacity, there *are* lost outside sales. The contribution margin per barrel on these outside sales is £12 (£20 − £8).

$$\text{Transfer price} \geq £8 + \frac{(£20 - £8) \times 2{,}000}{2{,}000} = £8 + (£20 - £8) = £20$$

   Thus, as far as the selling division is concerned, the transfer price must at least cover the revenue on the lost sales, which is £20 per barrel. This makes sense since the cost of producing the 2,000 barrels is the same whether they are sold on the inside market or on the outside. The only difference is that the selling division loses the revenue of £20 per barrel if it transfers the barrels to Pizza Maven.
2. As before, the buying division, Pizza Maven, would be unwilling to pay more than the £18 per barrel it is already paying for similar ginger beer from its regular supplier.

$$\text{Transfer price} \leq \text{Cost of buying from outside supplier} = £18$$

3. Therefore, the selling division would insist on a transfer price of at least £20. But the buying division would refuse any transfer price above £18. It is impossible to satisfy

both division managers simultaneously; there can be no agreement on a transfer price and no transfer will take place. Is this good? The answer is yes. From the standpoint of the entire company, the transfer doesn't make sense. Why give up sales of £20 to save costs of £18?

Basically, the transfer price is a mechanism for dividing between the two divisions any profit the entire company earns as a result of the transfer. If the company as a whole loses money on the transfer, there will be no profit to divide up, and it will be impossible for the two divisions to come to an agreement. On the other hand, if the company as a whole makes money on the transfer, there will be a profit to share, and it will always be possible for the two divisions to find a mutually agreeable transfer price that increases the profits of both divisions. If the pie is bigger, it is always possible to divide it up in such a way that everyone has a bigger piece.

Selling Division Has Some Idle Capacity Suppose now that Imperial Beverages is selling 9,000 barrels of ginger beer a month on the outside market. Pizza Maven can only sell one kind of ginger beer on tap. It cannot buy 1,000 barrels from Imperial Beverages and 1,000 barrels from its regular supplier; it must buy all of its ginger beer from one source.

To fill the entire 2,000-barrel a month order from Pizza Maven, Imperial Beverages would have to divert 1,000 barrels from its regular customers who are paying £20 per barrel. The other 1,000 barrels can be made using idle capacity. What range of transfer prices, if any, would make both divisions better off transferring the 2,000 barrels within the company?

1. As before, the selling division, Imperial Beverages, will insist on a transfer price that at least covers its variable cost and opportunity cost:

$$\text{Transfer price} \geq \frac{\text{Variable cost}}{\text{per unit}} + \frac{\text{Total contribution margin on lost sales}}{\text{Number of units transferred}}$$

   Since Imperial Beverages does not have enough idle capacity to fill the entire order for 2,000 barrels, there *are* lost outside sales. The contribution margin per barrel on the 1,000 barrels of lost outside sales is £12 (£20 − £8).

$$\text{Transfer price} \geq £8 + \frac{(£20 - £8) \times 1{,}000}{2{,}000} = £8 + £6 = £14$$

   Thus, as far as the selling division is concerned, the transfer price must cover the variable cost of £8 plus the average opportunity cost of lost sales of £6.

2. As before, the buying division, Pizza Maven, would be unwilling to pay more than the £18 per barrel it pays its regular supplier.

$$\text{Transfer price} \leq \text{Cost of buying from outside suppliers} = £18$$

3. Combining the requirements for both the selling and buying divisions, the range of acceptable transfer prices is:

$$£14 \leq \text{Transfer price} \leq £18$$

   Again, assuming that the managers understand their own businesses and that they are cooperative, they should be able to agree on a transfer price within this range.

No Outside Supplier If Pizza Maven has no outside supplier for the ginger beer, the highest price the buying division would be willing to pay depends on how much the buying division expects to make on the transferred units—excluding the transfer price. If, for example, Pizza Maven expects to earn £30 per barrel of ginger beer after paying its own expenses, then it should be willing to pay up to £30 per barrel to Imperial Beverages. Remember, however, that this assumes Pizza Maven cannot buy ginger beer from other sources.

Evaluation of Negotiated Transfer Prices As discussed earlier, if a transfer within the company would result in higher overall profits for the company, there is always a range of transfer prices within which both the selling and buying division would also have higher profits if they agree to the transfer. Therefore, if the managers understand their own businesses and are cooperative, then they should always be able to agree on a transfer price if it is in the best interests of the company that they do so.

Unfortunately, not all managers understand their own businesses and not all managers are cooperative. As a result, negotiations often break down even when it would be in the managers' own best interests to come to an agreement. Sometimes that is the fault of the way managers are evaluated. If managers are pitted against each other rather than against their own past performance or reasonable benchmarks, a noncooperative atmosphere is almost guaranteed. Nevertheless, even with the best performance evaluation system, some people by nature are not cooperative.

Given the disputes that often accompany the negotiation process, most companies rely on some other means of setting transfer prices. Unfortunately, as we will see below, all of the alternatives to negotiated transfer prices have their own serious drawbacks.

Transfers at the Cost to the Selling Division

Many companies set transfer prices at either the variable cost or full (absorption) cost incurred by the selling division. Although the cost approach to setting transfer prices is relatively simple to apply, it has some major defects.

First, the use of cost—particularly full cost—as a transfer price can lead to bad decisions and thus suboptimization. Return to the example involving the ginger beer. The full cost of ginger beer can never be less than £15 per barrel (£8 per barrel variable cost + £7 per barrel fixed cost at capacity). What if the cost of buying the ginger beer from an outside supplier is less than £15—for example, £14 per barrel? If the transfer price were set at full cost, then Pizza Maven would never want to buy ginger beer from Imperial Beverages, since it could buy its ginger beer from an outside supplier at a lower price. However, from the standpoint of the company as a whole, ginger beer should be transferred from Imperial Beverages to Pizza Maven whenever Imperial Beverages has idle capacity. Why? Because when Imperial Beverages has idle capacity, it only costs the company £8 in variable cost to produce a barrel of ginger beer, but it costs £14 per barrel to buy from outside suppliers.

Second, if cost is used as the transfer price, the selling division will never show a profit on any internal transfer. The only division that shows a profit is the division that makes the final sale to an outside party.

Third, cost-based prices do not provide incentives to control costs. If the actual costs of one division are simply passed on to the next, there is little incentive for anyone to work to reduce costs. This problem can be overcome by using standard costs rather than actual costs for transfer prices.

Despite these shortcomings, cost-based transfer prices are commonly used in practice. Advocates argue that they are easily understood and convenient to use.

Transfers at Market Price

Some form of competitive **market price** (i.e., the price charged for an item on the open market) is often regarded as the best approach to the transfer pricing problem—particularly if transfer price negotiations routinely become bogged down.

The market price approach is designed for situations in which there is an *outside market* for the transferred product or service; the product or service is sold in its present form to outside customers. If the selling division has no idle capacity, the market price is the perfect choice for the transfer price. This is because, from the company's perspective, the real cost of the transfer is the opportunity cost of the lost revenue on the outside sale. Whether the item is transferred internally or sold on the outside market, the production costs are exactly the same. If the market price is used as the transfer price, the selling division manager will not lose anything by making the transfer, and the buying division manager will get the correct signal about how much it really costs the company for the transfer to take place.

While the market price works beautifully when the selling division has no idle capacity, difficulties occur when the selling division has idle capacity. Recalling once again the ginger beer example, the outside market price for the ginger beer produced by Imperial Beverages is £20 per barrel. However, Pizza Maven can purchase all of the ginger beer it wants from outside suppliers for £18 per barrel. Why would Pizza Maven ever buy from Imperial Beverages if Pizza Maven is forced to pay Imperial Beverages' market price? In some market price-based transfer pricing schemes, the transfer price would be lowered to £18, the outside vendor's market price, and Pizza Maven would be directed to buy from Imperial Beverages as long as Imperial Beverages is willing to sell. This scheme can work reasonably well, but a drawback is that managers at Pizza Maven will regard the cost of ginger beer as £18 rather than the £8, which is the real cost to the company when the selling division has idle capacity. Consequently, the managers of Pizza Maven will make pricing and other decisions based on an incorrect cost.

Unfortunately, none of the possible solutions to the transfer pricing problem are perfect—not even market-based transfer prices.

Divisional Autonomy and Suboptimization

The principles of decentralization suggest that companies should grant managers autonomy to set transfer prices and to decide whether to sell internally or externally. It may be very difficult for top managers to accept this principle when their subordinate managers are about to make a suboptimal decision. However, if top management intervenes, the purposes of decentralization are defeated. Furthermore, to impose the correct transfer price, top managers would have to know details about the buying and selling divisions' outside market, variable costs, and capacity utilization. The whole premise of decentralization is that local managers have access to better information for operational decisions than top managers at corporate headquarters.

Of course, if a division manager consistently makes suboptimal decisions, the performance of the division will suffer. The offending manager's compensation will be adversely affected and promotion will become less likely. Thus, a performance evaluation system based on divisional profits, ROI, or residual income provides some built-in checks and balances. Nevertheless, if top managers wish to create a culture of autonomy and independent profit responsibility, they must allow their subordinate managers to control their own destiny—even to the extent of granting their managers the right to make mistakes.

International Aspects of Transfer Pricing

The objectives of transfer pricing change when a multinational corporation is involved and the goods and services being transferred cross international borders. The objectives of international transfer pricing, as compared to domestic transfer pricing, are summarized in Exhibit 11A–1.[1]

As shown in the exhibit, the objectives of international transfer pricing focus on minimizing taxes, duties, and foreign exchange risks, along with enhancing a company's competitive

EXHIBIT 11A–1
Domestic and International Transfer Pricing Objectives

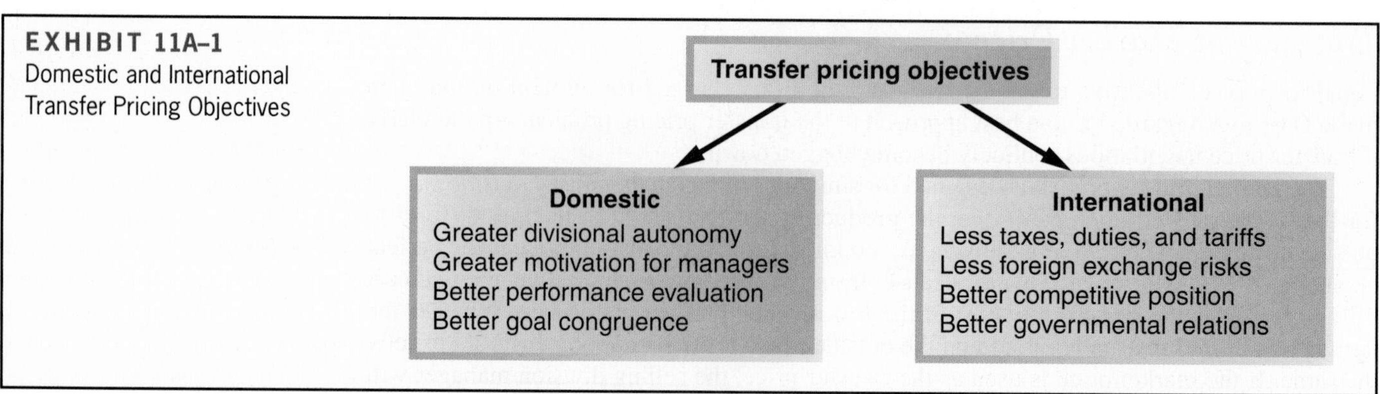

[1] The exhibit is adapted from Wagdy M. Abdallah, "Guidelines for CEOs in Transfer Pricing Policies," *Management Accounting* 70, no. 3, p. 61.

position and improving its relations with foreign governments. Although domestic objectives such as managerial motivation and divisional autonomy are always important, they often become secondary when international transfers are involved. Companies will focus instead on charging a transfer price that reduces its total tax bill or that strengthens a foreign subsidiary.

For example, charging a low transfer price for parts shipped to a foreign subsidiary may reduce customs duty payments as the parts cross international borders, or it may help the subsidiary to compete in foreign markets by keeping the subsidiary's costs low. On the other hand, charging a high transfer price may help a multinational corporation draw profits out of a country that has stringent controls on foreign remittances, or it may allow a multinational corporation to shift income from a country that has high income tax rates to a country that has low rates.

Review Problem 3: Transfer Pricing

Situation A

Collyer Products, Inc., has a Valve Division that manufactures and sells a standard valve:

Capacity in units	100,000
Selling price to outside customers	$30
Variable costs per unit	$16
Fixed costs per unit (based on capacity)	$9

The company has a Pump Division that could use this valve in one of its pumps. The Pump Division is currently purchasing 10,000 valves per year from an overseas supplier at a cost of $29 per valve.

Required:

1. Assume that the Valve Division has ample idle capacity to handle all of the Pump Division's needs. What is the acceptable range, if any, for the transfer price between the two divisions?
2. Assume that the Valve Division is selling all of the valves that it can produce to outside customers. What is the acceptable range, if any, for the transfer price between the two divisions?
3. Assume again that the Valve Division is selling all of the valves that it can produce to outside customers. Also assume that $3 in variable expenses can be avoided on transfers within the company, due to reduced selling costs. What is the acceptable range, if any, for the transfer price between the two divisions?

Solution to Situation A

1. Since the Valve Division has idle capacity, it does not have to give up any outside sales to take on the Pump Division's business. Applying the formula for the lowest acceptable transfer price from the viewpoint of the selling division, we get:

$$\text{Transfer price} \geq \begin{matrix}\text{Variable cost}\\ \text{per unit}\end{matrix} + \frac{\text{Total contribution margin on lost sales}}{\text{Number of units transferred}}$$

$$\text{Transfer price} \geq \$16 + \frac{\$0}{10{,}000} = \$16$$

The Pump Division would be unwilling to pay more than $29, the price it is currently paying an outside supplier for its valves. Therefore, the transfer price must fall within the range:

$$\$16 \leq \text{Transfer price} \leq \$29$$

2. Since the Valve Division is selling all of the valves that it can produce on the outside market, it would have to give up some of these outside sales to take on the Pump Division's business. Thus, the Valve Division has an opportunity cost, which is the total contribution margin on lost sales:

$$\text{Transfer price} \geq \begin{matrix}\text{Variable cost}\\ \text{per unit}\end{matrix} + \frac{\text{Total contribution margin on lost sales}}{\text{Number of units transferred}}$$

$$\text{Transfer price} \geq \$16 + \frac{(\$30 - \$16) \times 10{,}000}{10{,}000} = \$16 + \$14 = \$30$$

Since the Pump Division can purchase valves from an outside supplier at only $29 per unit, no transfers will be made between the two divisions.

3. Applying the formula for the lowest acceptable transfer price from the viewpoint of the selling division, we get:

$$\text{Transfer price} \geq \frac{\text{Variable cost}}{\text{per unit}} + \frac{\text{Total contribution margin on lost sales}}{\text{Number of units transferred}}$$

$$\text{Transfer price} \geq (\$16 - \$3) + \frac{(\$30 - \$16) \times 10{,}000}{10{,}000} = \$13 + \$14 = \$27$$

In this case, the transfer price must fall within the range:

$$\$27 \leq \text{Transfer price} \leq \$29$$

Situation B

Refer to the original data in situation A above. Assume that the Pump Division needs 20,000 special high-pressure valves per year. The Valve Division's variable costs to manufacture and ship the special valve would be $20 per unit. To produce these special valves, the Valve Division would have to reduce its production and sales of regular valves from 100,000 units per year to 70,000 units per year.

Required:

As far as the Valve Division is concerned, what is the lowest acceptable transfer price?

Solution to Situation B

To produce the 20,000 special valves, the Valve Division will have to give up sales of 30,000 regular valves to outside customers. Applying the formula for the lowest acceptable transfer price from the viewpoint of the selling division, we get:

$$\text{Transfer price} \geq \frac{\text{Variable cost}}{\text{per unit}} + \frac{\text{Total contribution margin on lost sales}}{\text{Number of units transferred}}$$

$$\text{Transfer price} \geq \$20 + \frac{(\$30 - \$16) \times 30{,}000}{20{,}000} = \$20 + \$21 = \$41$$

Glossary (Appendix 11A)

Market price The price charged for an item on the open market. (p. 469)

Negotiated transfer price A transfer price agreed on between buying and selling divisions. (p. 465)

Range of acceptable transfer prices The range of transfer prices within which the profits of both the selling division and the buying division would increase as a result of a transfer. (p. 465)

Suboptimization An overall level of profits that is less than a segment or a company is capable of earning. (p. 465)

Transfer price The price charged when one division or segment provides goods or services to another division or segment of an organization. (p. 465)

Appendix 11B: Service Department Charges

LEARNING OBJECTIVE 5
Charge operating departments for services provided by service departments.

Most large organizations have both *operating departments* and *service departments.* The central purposes of the organization are carried out in the **operating departments.** In contrast, **service departments** do not directly engage in operating activities. Instead, they provide services or assistance to the operating departments. Examples of operating departments include the Surgery Department at Mt. Sinai Hospital, the Geography Department at the University of Washington, the Marketing Department at Allstate Insurance Company, and production departments at manufacturers such as Mitsubishi, Hewlett-Packard, and Michelin.

Examples of service departments include Cafeteria, Internal Auditing, Human Resources, Cost Accounting, and Purchasing.

Service department costs are charged to operating departments for a variety of reasons including:

- To encourage operating departments to make wise use of service department resources. If the services were provided for free, operating managers would be inclined to waste these resources.
- To provide operating departments with more complete cost data for making decisions. Actions taken by operating departments have impacts on service department costs. For example, hiring another employee will increase costs in the human resources department. Such service department costs should be charged to the operating departments, otherwise the operating departments will not take them into account when making decisions.
- To help measure the profitability of operating departments. Charging service department costs to operating departments provides a more complete accounting of the costs incurred as a consequence of activities in the operating departments.
- To create an incentive for service departments to operate efficiently. Charging service department costs to operating departments provides a system of checks and balances in the sense that cost-conscious operating departments will take an active interest in keeping service department costs low.

In Appendix 11A, we discussed *transfer prices* that are charged within an organization when one part of an organization provides a product to another part of the organization. The service department charges considered in this appendix can be viewed as a transfer price that is charged for services provided by service departments to operating departments.

Charging Costs by Behavior

Whenever possible, variable and fixed service department costs should be charged to operating departments separately to provide more useful data for planning and control of departmental operations.

Variable Costs

Variable costs vary in total in proportion to changes in the level of service provided. For example, the cost of food in a cafeteria is a variable cost that varies in proportion to the number of persons using the cafeteria or the number of meals served.

As a general rule, a variable cost should be charged to consuming departments according to whatever activity causes the incurrence of the cost. For example, variable costs of a maintenance department that are caused by the number of machine-hours worked in the operating departments should be charged to the operating departments using machine-hours as the charge-out base. This will ensure that these costs are properly traced to departments, products, and customers.

Fixed Costs

The fixed costs of service departments represent the costs of making capacity available for use. These costs should be charged to consuming departments in *predetermined lump-sum amounts.* By predetermined lump-sum amounts we mean that the total amount charged to each consuming department is determined in advance and, once determined, does not change. The lump-sum amount charged to a department can be based either on the department's peak-period or long-run average servicing needs. The logic behind lump-sum charges of this type is as follows:

When a service department is first established, its capacity will be determined by the needs of the departments that it will serve. This capacity may reflect the peak-period needs of the other departments, or it may reflect their long-run average or "normal" servicing needs. Depending on how much servicing capacity is provided for, it will be necessary to make a commitment of resources, which will be reflected in the service department's fixed costs. These fixed costs should be borne by the consuming departments in proportion to the amount of capacity each consuming department requires. That is, if available capacity in the service department has been provided to meet the peak-period needs of consuming departments, then the fixed costs of the service department should be charged in predetermined lump-sum amounts to consuming departments on that basis. If available capacity has been provided only to meet "normal" or long-run average needs, then the fixed costs should be charged on that basis.

Once set, charges should not vary from period to period, since they represent the cost of having a certain level of service capacity available and on line for each consuming department. The fact that a consuming department does not need the peak level or even the "normal" level of service every period is immaterial; the capacity to deliver this level of service must be available. The consuming departments should bear the cost of that availability.

To illustrate this idea, assume that Novak Company has just organized a Maintenance Department to service all machines in the Cutting, Assembly, and Finishing Departments. In determining the capacity of the newly organized Maintenance Department, the various operating departments estimated that they would have the following peak-period needs for maintenance:

Department	Peak-Period Maintenance Needs in Terms of Number of Hours of Maintenance Work Required	Percent of Total Hours
Cutting	900	30%
Assembly	1,800	60
Finishing	300	10
	3,000	100%

Therefore, 30% of the Maintenance Department fixed costs should be charged to the Cutting Department, 60% to the Assembly Department, and 10% to the Finishing Department. These lump-sum charges *will not change* from period to period unless peak-period servicing needs change.

Should Actual or Budgeted Costs Be Charged?

Should the *actual* or *budgeted* costs of a service department be charged to operating departments? The answer is that budgeted costs should be charged because allocating actual costs would burden the operating departments with any inefficiencies in the service department. In other words, if actual costs are charged, any lack of cost control on the part of the service department is simply buried in the charges to other departments.

Any variance over budgeted costs is the responsibility of the service department and that variance should be retained in the service department. Operating department managers justifiably complain bitterly if they are forced to absorb service department inefficiencies.

In effect, management says, "You will be charged X dollars for every unit of service that you consume or capacity that you require. You can consume as much or as little as you desire; the total charge you bear will vary proportionately." The purpose of making such charges is to ensure that the managers of the operating departments are fully aware of all of the costs of their actions—including costs that are incurred in service departments. This helps operating department managers make appropriate trade-offs when deciding, for example, whether to purchase a service from an external provider or to obtain it from a service department inside the company.

Guidelines for Service Department Charges

The following guidelines summarize how service department costs should be charged out to other departments:

- Variable and fixed service department costs should be charged separately.
- Variable service department costs should be charged using a predetermined rate applied to the actual services consumed.
- Fixed costs represent the costs of having service capacity available. These costs should be charged in lump sums to each department in proportion to their peak-period needs or long-run average needs. The lump-sum amounts should be based on budgeted fixed costs, not actual fixed costs.

Implementing the Guidelines

Seaboard Airlines has two operating divisions: a Freight Division and a Passenger Division. The company has a Maintenance Department that provides servicing to both divisions. Variable servicing costs are budgeted at $10 per flight-hour. The department's fixed costs are budgeted at $750,000 for the year. The fixed costs of the Maintenance Department are budgeted based on the peak-period demand, which occurs during the Thanksgiving to New Year's holiday period. The airline wants to make sure that none of its aircraft are grounded during this key period due to unavailability of maintenance facilities. Approximately 40% of the maintenance during this period is performed on the Freight Division's equipment, and 60% is performed on the Passenger Division's equipment. These figures and the budgeted flight-hours for the coming year are as follows:

	Percent of Peak Period Capacity Required	Budgeted Flight-Hours
Freight Division.	40%	9,000
Passenger Division.	60	15,000
Total	100%	24,000

Year-end records show that actual variable and fixed costs in the aircraft Maintenance Department for the year were $260,000 and $780,000, respectively. One division logged more flight-hours during the year than planned, and the other division logged fewer flight-hours than planned, as shown below:

	Flight-Hours	
	Budgeted (see above)	Actual
Freight Division	9,000	8,000
Passenger Division	15,000	17,000
Total flight-hours	24,000	25,000

The amount of Maintenance Department cost charged to each division for the year would be as follows:

				Division	
			Actual activity	Freight	Passenger
Budgeted variable rate	Variable cost charges:				
	$10 per flight-hour	×	8,000 flight-hours . . .	$ 80,000	
	$10 per flight-hour	×	17,000 flight-hours . . .		$170,000
Peak-period capacity required	Fixed cost charges:				
	40%	×	$750,000	300,000	
	60%	×	$750,000		450,000
	Total charges			$380,000	$620,000
			Budgeted fixed cost		

Notice that variable servicing costs are charged to the operating divisions based on the budgeted rate ($10 per hour) and the *actual activity* for the year. In contrast, the charges for fixed costs are based entirely on budgeted data. Also note that the two operating divisions are *not* charged for the actual costs of the service department, which may be influenced by inefficiency in the service department and may be beyond the control of the managers of the operating divisions. Instead, the service department is held responsible for the actual costs not charged to other departments as shown below:

	Variable	Fixed
Total actual costs incurred	$260,000	$780,000
Total charges (above)	250,000*	750,000
Spending variance—responsibility of the Maintenance Department	$ 10,000	$ 30,000

*$10 per flight-hour × 25,000 actual flight-hours = $250,000.

Some Cautions in Allocating Service Department Costs

Pitfalls in Allocating Fixed Costs

Rather than charge fixed costs to using departments in predetermined lump-sum amounts, some companies allocate them using a *variable* allocation base that fluctuates from period to period. This practice can distort decisions and create serious inequities between departments. The inequities arise from the fact that the fixed costs allocated to one department are heavily influenced by what happens in *other* departments.

To illustrate, assume that Kolby Products has an auto service center that provides maintenance work on the fleet of autos used in the company's two sales territories. The auto service center costs are all fixed. Contrary to good practice, the company allocates these fixed costs to the sales territories on the basis of actual miles driven (a variable allocation base). Selected cost data for the last two years follow:

	Year 1	Year 2
Auto service center costs (all fixed) (a)	$120,000	$120,000
Western sales territory—miles driven.	1,500,000	1,500,000
Eastern sales territory—miles driven	1,500,000	900,000
Total miles driven (b)	3,000,000	2,400,000
Allocation rate per mile, (a) ÷ (b)	$0.04	$0.05

Notice that the Western sales territory maintained an activity level of 1,500,000 miles driven in both years. On the other hand, activity in the Eastern sales territory dropped from 1,500,000 miles in Year 1 to only 900,000 miles in Year 2. The auto service center costs that would be allocated to the two sales territories over the two-year span using actual miles driven as the allocation base are as follows:

Year 1:	
Western sales territory: 1,500,000 miles at $0.04 per mile	$ 60,000
Eastern sales territory: 1,500,000 miles $0.04 per mile	60,000
Total cost allocated	$120,000

Year 2:	
Western sales territory: 1,500,000 miles at $0.05 per mile	$ 75,000
Eastern sales territory: 900,000 miles $0.05 per mile	45,000
Total cost allocated	$120,000

In Year 1, the two sales territories share the service department costs equally. In Year 2, however, the bulk of the service department costs are allocated to the Western sales territory. This is not because of any increase in activity in the Western sales territory; rather, it is because of the *decrease* in activity in the Eastern sales territory. Even though the Western sales territory maintained the same level of activity in both years, it is penalized with a heavier cost allocation in Year 2 because of what happened in *another* part of the company.

This kind of inequity is almost inevitable when a variable allocation base is used to allocate fixed costs. The manager of the Western sales territory undoubtedly will be upset about the additional costs forced on his territory, but he will feel powerless to do anything about it. The result will be a loss of confidence in the system and considerable ill will.

Beware of Sales Dollars as an Allocation Base

Sales dollars is a popular base for allocating or charging service department costs. One reason is that a sales dollars base is simple, straightforward, and easy to work with. Another reason is that people tend to view sales dollars as a measure of ability to pay, and, hence, as a measure of how readily costs can be absorbed from other parts of the organization.

Unfortunately, sales dollars are often a very poor base for allocating or charging costs, for the reason that sales dollars vary from period to period, whereas the costs are often largely *fixed.* As discussed earlier, if a variable allocation base is used to allocate fixed costs, the costs allocated to one department will depend in large part on what happens in *other* departments. A letup in sales effort in one department will shift allocated costs from that department to other, more successful departments. In effect, the departments putting forth the best sales efforts are penalized in the form of higher allocations. The result is often bitterness and resentment on the part of the managers of the better departments.

Consider the following situation encountered by one of the authors:

A large men's clothing store has one service department and three sales departments—Suits, Shoes, and Accessories. The service department's costs total $60,000 per period and are allocated to the three sales departments according to sales dollars. A recent period showed the following allocation:

	Departments			
	Suits	Shoes	Accessories	Total
Sales by department	$260,000	$40,000	$100,000	$400,000
Percentage of total sales	65%	10%	25%	100%
Allocation of service department costs, based on percentage of total sales	$39,000	$6,000	$15,000	$60,000

In the following period, the manager of the Suits Department launched a very successful program to expand sales by $100,000 in his department. Sales in the other two departments remained unchanged. Total service department costs also remained unchanged, but the allocation of these costs changed substantially, as shown below:

	Departments			
	Suits	Shoes	Accessories	Total
Sales by department	$360,000	$40,000	$100,000	$500,000
Percentage of total sales	72%	8%	20%	100%
Allocation of service department costs, based on percentage of total sales	$43,200	$4,800	$12,000	$60,000
Increase (or decrease) from prior allocation	$4,200	$(1,200)	$(3,000)	$0

The manager of the Suits Department complained that as a result of his successful effort to expand sales in his department, he was being forced to carry a larger share of the service department costs. On the other hand, the managers of the departments that showed no improvement in sales were relieved of a portion of the costs that they had been carrying. Yet there had been no change in the amount of services provided for any department.

The manager of the Suits Department viewed the increased service department cost allocation to his department as a penalty for his outstanding performance, and he wondered whether his efforts had really been worthwhile in the eyes of top management.

Sales dollars should be used as a base for allocating or charging costs only in those cases where service department costs are driven by sales. In those situations where service department costs are fixed, they should be charged according to the three guidelines discussed earlier in the chapter.

Glossary (Appendix 11B)

Operating department A department in which the central purposes of the organization are carried out. (p. 472)

Service department A department that does not directly engage in operating activities; rather, it provides services or assistance to the operating departments. (p. 472)

Questions

11-1 What is meant by the term *decentralization?*
11-2 What benefits result from decentralization?
11-3 Distinguish between a cost center, a profit center, and an investment center.
11-4 What is a segment of an organization? Give several examples of segments.
11-5 What costs are assigned to a segment under the contribution approach?
11-6 Distinguish between a traceable cost and a common cost. Give several examples of each.
11-7 Explain how the segment margin differs from the contribution margin.
11-8 Why aren't common costs allocated to segments under the contribution approach?
11-9 How is it possible for a cost that is traceable to a segment to become a common cost if the segment is divided into further segments?
11-10 What is meant by the terms *margin* and *turnover* in ROI calculations?
11-11 What is meant by residual income?
11-12 In what way can the use of ROI as a performance measure for investment centers lead to bad decisions? How does the residual income approach overcome this problem?
11-13 (Appendix 11A) What is meant by the term *transfer price,* and why are transfer prices needed?
11-14 (Appendix 11A) From the standpoint of a selling division that has idle capacity, what is the lowest acceptable transfer price for an item?
11-15 (Appendix 11A) From the standpoint of a selling division that has *no* idle capacity, what is the lowest acceptable transfer price for an item?
11-16 (Appendix 11A) What are the advantages and disadvantages of cost-based transfer prices?
11-17 (Appendix 11A) If a market price for a product can be determined, why isn't it always the best transfer price?
11-18 (Appendix 11B) How should the variable costs of a service department be charged to operating departments?
11-19 (Appendix 11B) How should the fixed costs of a service department be charged to operating departments?

Quiz 11

Multiple-choice questions are provided on the text Web site at www.mhhe.com/noreen1e.

Exercises

EXERCISE 11-1 Basic Segmented Income Statement [LO1]
Caltec, Inc., produces and sells recordable CD and DVD packs. Revenue and cost information relating to the products follow:

	Product	
	CD	DVD
Selling price per pack	$8.00	$25.00
Variable expenses per pack	$3.20	$17.50
Traceable fixed expenses per year	$138,000	$45,000

Common fixed expenses in the company total $105,000 annually. Last year the company produced and sold 37,500 CD packs and 18,000 DVD packs.

Required:
Prepare a contribution format income statement for the year segmented by product lines.

EXERCISE 11-2 Compute the Return on Investment (ROI) [LO2]
Tundra Services Company, a division of a major oil company, provides various services to the operators of the North Slope oil field in Alaska. Data concerning the most recent year appear below:

Sales	$18,000,000
Net operating income	$5,400,000
Average operating assets	$36,000,000

Required:

1. Compute the margin for Tundra Services Company.
2. Compute the turnover for Tundra Services Company.
3. Compute the return on investment (ROI) for Tundra Services Company.

EXERCISE 11-3 Residual Income [LO3]

Midlands Design Ltd. of Manchester, England, is a company specializing in providing design services to residential developers. Last year the company had net operating income of £400,000 on sales of £2,000,000. The company's average operating assets for the year were £2,200,000 and its minimum required rate of return was 16%.

Required:

Compute the company's residual income for the year.

EXERCISE 11-4 (Appendix 11A) Transfer Pricing Situations [LO4]

In each of the cases below, assume that Division X has a product that can be sold either to outside customers or to Division Y of the same company for use in its production process. The managers of the divisions are evaluated based on their divisional profits.

	Case	
	A	B
Division X:		
Capacity in units	100,000	100,000
Number of units being sold to outside customers	100,000	80,000
Selling price per unit to outside customers	$50	$35
Variable costs per unit	$30	$20
Fixed costs per unit (based on capacity)	$8	$6
Division Y:		
Number of units needed for production	20,000	20,000
Purchase price per unit now being paid to an outside supplier	$47	$34

Required:

1. Refer to the data in case A above. Assume that $2 per unit in variable selling costs can be avoided on intracompany sales. If the managers are free to negotiate and make decisions on their own, will a transfer take place? If so, within what range will the transfer price fall? Explain.
2. Refer to the data in case B above. In this case there will be no reduction in variable selling costs on intracompany sales. If the managers are free to negotiate and make decisions on their own, will a transfer take place? If so, within what range will the transfer price fall? Explain.

EXERCISE 11-5 (Appendix 11B) Service Department Charges [LO5]

Gutherie Oil Company has a Transport Services Department that provides trucks to transport crude oil from docks to the company's Arbon Refinery and Beck Refinery. Budgeted costs for the transport services consist of $0.30 per gallon variable cost and $200,000 fixed cost. The level of fixed cost is determined by peak-period requirements. During the peak period, Arbon Refinery requires 60% of the capacity and the Beck Refinery requires 40%.

During the year, the Transport Services Department actually hauled the following amounts of crude oil for the two refineries: Arbon Refinery, 260,000 gallons; and Beck Refinery, 140,000 gallons. The Transport Services Department incurred $365,000 in cost during the year, of which $148,000 was variable cost and $217,000 was fixed cost.

Required:

1. Determine how much of the $148,000 in variable cost should be charged to each refinery.
2. Determine how much of the $217,000 in fixed cost should be charged to each refinery.
3. Will any of the $365,000 in the Transport Services Department cost not be charged to the refineries? Explain.

EXERCISE 11-6 Segmented Income Statement [LO1]

Bovine Company, a wholesale distributor of DVDs, has been experiencing losses for some time, as shown by its most recent monthly contribution format income statement below:

Sales	$1,500,000
Variable expenses	588,000
Contribution margin	912,000
Fixed expenses	945,000
Net operating loss	$ (33,000)

In an effort to isolate the problem, the president has asked for an income statement segmented by geographic market. Accordingly, the Accounting Department has developed the following data:

	Geographic Market		
	South	Central	North
Sales	$400,000	$600,000	$500,000
Variable expenses as a percentage of sales	52%	30%	40%
Traceable fixed expenses	$240,000	$330,000	$200,000

Required:

1. Prepare a contribution format income statement segmented by geographic market, as desired by the president.
2. The company's sales manager believes that sales in the Central geographic market could be increased by 15% if monthly advertising were increased by $25,000. Would you recommend the increased advertising? Show computations to support your answer.

EXERCISE 11-7 Computing and Interpreting Return on Investment (ROI) [LO2]

Selected operating data on the two divisions of York Company are given below:

	Division	
	Eastern	Western
Sales	$1,000,000	$1,750,000
Average operating assets	$500,000	$500,000
Net operating income	$90,000	$105,000
Property, plant, and equipment	$250,000	$200,000

Required:

1. Compute the rate of return for each division using the return on investment (ROI) formula stated in terms of margin and turnover.
2. Which divisional manager seems to be doing the better job? Why?

EXERCISE 11-8 Evaluating New Investments Using Return on Investment (ROI) and Residual Income [LO2, LO3]

Selected sales and operating data for three divisions of three different companies are given below:

	Division A	Division B	Division C
Sales	$6,000,000	$10,000,000	$8,000,000
Average operating assets	$1,500,000	$5,000,000	$2,000,000
Net operating income	$300,000	$900,000	$180,000
Minimum required rate of return	15%	18%	12%

Required:

1. Compute the return on investment (ROI) for each division, using the formula stated in terms of margin and turnover.
2. Compute the residual income for each division.
3. Assume that each division is presented with an investment opportunity that would yield a rate of return of 17%.
   a. If performance is being measured by ROI, which division or divisions will probably accept the opportunity? Reject? Why?
   b. If performance is being measured by residual income, which division or divisions will probably accept the opportunity? Reject? Why?

EXERCISE 11-9 (Appendix 11A) Transfer Pricing from Viewpoint of the Entire Company [LO4]
Division A manufactures picture tubes for TVs. The tubes can be sold either to Division B of the same company or to outside customers. Last year, the following activity was recorded in Division A:

Selling price per tube	$175
Variable cost per tube	$130
Number of tubes:	
Produced during the year	20,000
Sold to outside customers	16,000
Sold to Division B	4,000

Sales to Division B were at the same price as sales to outside customers. The tubes purchased by Division B were used in a TV set manufactured by that division. Division B incurred $300 in additional variable cost per TV and then sold the TVs for $600 each.

Required:

1. Prepare income statements for last year for Division A, Division B, and the company as a whole.
2. Assume that Division A's manufacturing capacity is 20,000 tubes per year. Next year, Division B wants to purchase 5,000 tubes from Division A, rather than only 4,000 tubes as in last year. (Tubes of this type are not available from outside sources.) From the standpoint of the company as a whole, should Division A sell the 1,000 additional tubes to Division B, or should it continue to sell them to outside customers? Explain.

EXERCISE 11-10 (Appendix 11B) Service Department Charges [LO5]
Reed Corporation operates a Medical Services Department for its employees. Charges to the company's operating departments for the variable costs of the Medical Services Department are based on the actual number of employees in each department. Charges for the fixed costs of the Medical Services Department are based on the long-run average number of employees in each operating department.

Variable Medical Services Department costs are budgeted at $60 per employee. Fixed Medical Services Department costs are budgeted at $600,000 per year. Actual Medical Services Department costs for the most recent year were $105,400 for variable costs and $605,000 for fixed costs. Data concerning employees in the three operating departments follow:

	Cutting	Milling	Assembly
Budgeted number of employees	600	300	900
Actual number of employees for the most recent year	500	400	800
Long-run average number of employees	600	400	1,000

Required:

1. Determine the Medical Services Department charges for the year to each of the operating departments—Cutting, Milling, and Assembly.
2. How much, if any, of the actual Medical Services Department costs for the year should not be allocated to the operating departments?

EXERCISE 11-11 Working with a Segmented Income Statement [LO1]
Marple Associates is a consulting firm that specializes in information systems for construction and landscaping companies. The firm has two offices—one in Houston and one in Dallas. The firm classifies the direct costs of consulting jobs as variable costs. A segmented contribution format income statement for the company's most recent year is given below:

	Total Company		Office			
			Houston		Dallas	
Sales	$750,000	100.0%	$150,000	100%	$600,000	100%
Variable expenses	405,000	54.0	45,000	30	360,000	60
Contribution margin	345,000	46.0	105,000	70	240,000	40
Traceable fixed expenses	168,000	22.4	78,000	52	90,000	15
Office segment margin	177,000	23.6	$ 27,000	18%	$150,000	25%
Common fixed expenses not traceable to offices	120,000	16.0				
Net operating income	$ 57,000	7.6%				

Required:
1. By how much would the company's net operating income increase if Dallas increased its sales by $75,000 per year? Assume no change in cost behavior patterns.
2. Refer to the original data. Assume that sales in Houston increase by $50,000 next year and that sales in Dallas remain unchanged. Assume no change in fixed costs.
   a. Prepare a new segmented income statement for the company using the above format. Show both amounts and percentages.
   b. Observe from the income statement you have prepared that the CM ratio for Houston has remained unchanged at 70% (the same as in the above data) but that the segment margin ratio has changed. How do you explain the change in the segment margin ratio?

EXERCISE 11-12 Working with a Segmented Income Statement [LO1]
Refer to the data in Exercise 11-11. Assume that Dallas's sales by major market are as follows:

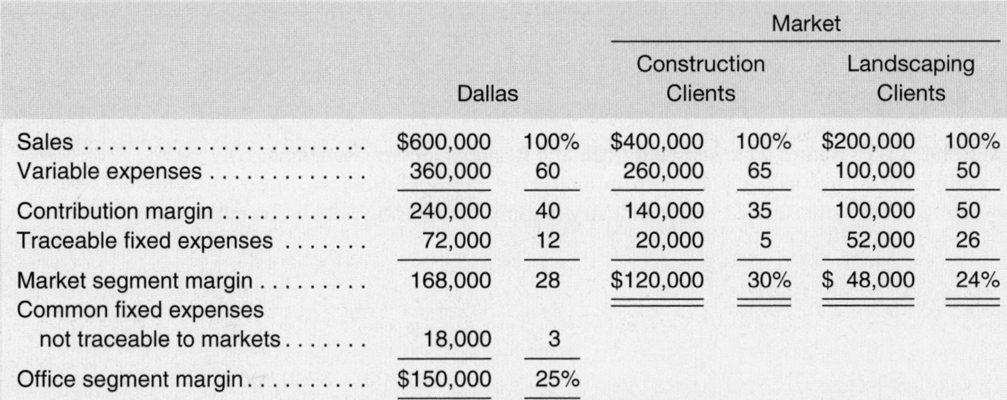

	Dallas		Market			
			Construction Clients		Landscaping Clients	
Sales	$600,000	100%	$400,000	100%	$200,000	100%
Variable expenses	360,000	60	260,000	65	100,000	50
Contribution margin	240,000	40	140,000	35	100,000	50
Traceable fixed expenses	72,000	12	20,000	5	52,000	26
Market segment margin	168,000	28	$120,000	30%	$ 48,000	24%
Common fixed expenses not traceable to markets	18,000	3				
Office segment margin	$150,000	25%				

The company would like to initiate an intensive advertising campaign in one of the two markets during the next month. The campaign would cost $8,000. Marketing studies indicate that such a campaign would increase sales in the construction market by $70,000 or increase sales in the landscaping market by $60,000.

Required:
1. In which of the markets would you recommend that the company focus its advertising campaign? Show computations to support your answer.
2. In Exercise 11-11, Dallas shows $90,000 in traceable fixed expenses. What happened to the $90,000 in this exercise?

EXERCISE 11-13 Contrasting Return on Investment (ROI) and Residual Income [LO2, LO3]

Rains Nickless Ltd. of Australia has two divisions that operate in Perth and Darwin. Selected data on the two divisions follow:

	Division	
	Perth	Darwin
Sales	$9,000,000	$20,000,000
Net operating income	$630,000	$1,800,000
Average operating assets	$3,000,000	$10,000,000

Required:

1. Compute the return on investment (ROI) for each division.
2. Assume that the company evaluates performance using residual income and that the minimum required rate of return for any division is 16%. Compute the residual income for each division.
3. Is the Darwin Division's greater residual income an indication that it is better managed? Explain.

EXERCISE 11-14 Effects of Changes in Sales, Expenses, and Assets on ROI [LO2]

BusServ.com Corporation provides business-to-business services on the Internet. Data concerning the most recent year appear below:

Sales	$8,000,000
Net operating income	$800,000
Average operating assets	$3,200,000

Required:

Consider each question below independently. Carry out all computations to two decimal places.

1. Compute the company's return on investment (ROI).
2. The entrepreneur who founded the company is convinced that sales will increase next year by 150% and that net operating income will increase by 400%, with no increase in average operating assets. What would be the company's ROI?
3. The Chief Financial Officer of the company believes a more realistic scenario would be a $2 million increase in sales, requiring an $800,000 increase in average operating assets, with a resulting $250,000 increase in net operating income. What would be the company's ROI in this scenario?

EXERCISE 11-15 Return on Investment (ROI) and Residual Income Relations [LO2, LO3]

A family friend has asked your help in analyzing the operations of three anonymous companies operating in the same service sector industry. Supply the missing data in the table below:

	Company		
	A	B	C
Sales	$400,000	$750,000	$600,000
Net operating income	$?	$45,000	$?
Average operating assets	$160,000	?	$150,000
Return on investment (ROI)	20%	18%	?
Minimum required rate of return:			
Percentage	15%	?	12%
Dollar amount	$?	$50,000	$?
Residual income	$?	$?	$6,000

EXERCISE 11-16 (Appendix 11A) Transfer Pricing Basics [LO4]

Nelcro Company's Electrical Division produces a high-quality transformer. Sales and cost data on the transformer follow:

Selling price per unit on the outside market	$40
Variable costs per unit	$21
Fixed costs per unit (based on capacity)	$9
Capacity in units	60,000

Nelcro Company has a Motor Division that would like to begin purchasing this transformer from the Electrical Division. The Motor Division is currently purchasing 10,000 transformers each year from another company at a cost of $38 per transformer. Nelcro Company evaluates its division managers on the basis of divisional profits.

Required:

1. Assume that the Electrical Division is now selling only 50,000 transformers each year to outside customers.
   a. From the standpoint of the Electrical Division, what is the lowest acceptable transfer price for transformers sold to the Motor Division?
   b. From the standpoint of the Motor Division, what is the highest acceptable transfer price for transformers acquired from the Electrical Division?
   c. If left free to negotiate without interference, would you expect the division managers to voluntarily agree to the transfer of 10,000 transformers from the Electrical Division to the Motor Division? Why or why not?
   d. From the standpoint of the entire company, should a transfer take place? Why or why not?
2. Assume that the Electrical Division is now selling all of the transformers it can produce to outside customers.
   a. From the standpoint of the Electrical Division, what is the lowest acceptable transfer price for transformers sold to the Motor Division?
   b. From the standpoint of the Motor Division, what is the highest acceptable transfer price for transformers acquired from the Electrical Division?
   c. If left free to negotiate without interference, would you expect the division managers to voluntarily agree to the transfer of 10,000 transformers from the Electrical Division to the Motor Division? Why or why not?
   d. From the standpoint of the entire company, should a transfer take place? Why or why not?

EXERCISE 11-17 (Appendix 11B) Sales Dollars as an Allocation Base for Fixed Costs [LO5]

Lacey's Department Store allocates its fixed administrative expenses to its four operating departments on the basis of sales dollars. During 2007, the fixed administrative expenses totaled $900,000. These expenses were allocated as follows:

	Men's	Women's	Shoes	Housewares	Total
Total sales—2007	$600,000	$1,500,000	$2,100,000	$1,800,000	$6,000,000
Percentage of total sales	10%	25%	35%	30%	100%
Allocation (based on the above percentages)	$90,000	$225,000	$315,000	$270,000	$900,000

During 2008, the following year, the Women's Department doubled its sales. The sales levels in the other three departments remained unchanged. The company's 2008 sales data were as follows:

	Department				
	Men's	Women's	Shoes	Housewares	Total
Total sales—2008	$600,000	$3,000,000	$2,100,000	$1,800,000	$7,500,000
Percent of total sales	8%	40%	28%	24%	100%

Fixed administrative expenses remained unchanged at $900,000 during 2008.

Required:

1. Using sales dollars as an allocation base, show the allocation of the fixed administrative expenses among the four departments for 2008.
2. Compare your allocation from (1) above to the allocation for 2007. As the manager of the Women's Department, how would you feel about the administrative expenses that have been charged to you for 2008?
3. Comment on the usefulness of sales dollars as an allocation base.

EXERCISE 11-18 Return on Investment (ROI) Relations [LO2]
Provide the missing data in the following table:

	Division		
	Fab	Consulting	IT
Sales	$800,000	$?	$?
Net operating income	$72,000	$?	$40,000
Average operating assets	$?	$130,000	$?
Margin	?	4%	8%
Turnover	?	5	?
Return on investment (ROI)	18%	?	20%

EXERCISE 11-19 Cost-Volume-Profit Analysis and Return on Investment (ROI) [LO2]
Images.com is a small Internet retailer of high-quality posters. The company has $800,000 in operating assets and fixed expenses of $160,000 per year. With this level of operating assets and fixed expenses, the company can support sales of up to $5 million per year. The company's contribution margin ratio is 10%, which means that an additional dollar of sales results in additional contribution margin, and net operating income, of 10 cents.

Required:

1. Complete the following table showing the relationship between sales and return on investment (ROI).

Sales	Net Operating Income	Average Operating Assets	ROI
$4,500,000	$290,000	$800,000	?
$4,600,000	?	$800,000	?
$4,700,000	?	$800,000	?
$4,800,000	?	$800,000	?
$4,900,000	?	$800,000	?
$5,000,000	?	$800,000	?

2. What happens to the company's return on investment (ROI) as sales increase? Explain.

EXERCISE 11-20 Effects of Changes in Profits and Assets on Return on Investment (ROI) [LO2]
The Abs Shoppe is a regional chain of health clubs. The managers of the clubs, who have authority to make investments as needed, are evaluated based largely on return on investment (ROI). The Abs Shoppe reported the following results for the past year:

Sales	$800,000
Net operating income	$16,000
Average operating assets	$100,000

Required:
The following questions are to be considered independently. Carry out all computations to two decimal places.

1. Compute the club's return on investment (ROI).

2. Assume that the manager of the club is able to increase sales by $80,000 and that as a result net operating income increases by $6,000. Further assume that this is possible without any increase in operating assets. What would be the club's return on investment (ROI)?
3. Assume that the manager of the club is able to reduce expenses by $3,200 without any change in sales or operating assets. What would be the club's return on investment (ROI)?
4. Assume that the manager of the club is able to reduce operating assets by $20,000 without any change in sales or net operating income. What would be the club's return on investment (ROI)?

Problems

PROBLEM 11-21 Restructuring a Segmented Income Statement [LO1]

Brabant NV of the Netherlands is a wholesale distributor of Dutch cheeses that it sells throughout the European Community. Unfortunately, the company's profits have been declining, which has caused considerable concern. To help understand the condition of the company, the managing director of the company has requested that the monthly income statement be segmented by sales territory. Accordingly, the company's accounting department has prepared the following statement for March, the most recent month. (The Dutch currency is the euro which is designated by €.)

	Sales Territory		
	Southern Europe	Middle Europe	Northern Europe
Sales	€300,000	€800,000	€700,000
Territorial expenses (traceable):			
Cost of goods sold	93,000	240,000	315,000
Salaries	54,000	56,000	112,000
Insurance	9,000	16,000	14,000
Advertising	105,000	240,000	245,000
Depreciation	21,000	32,000	28,000
Shipping	15,000	32,000	42,000
Total territorial expenses	297,000	616,000	756,000
Territorial income (loss) before corporate expenses	3,000	184,000	(56,000)
Corporate expenses:			
Advertising (general)	15,000	40,000	35,000
General administrative	20,000	20,000	20,000
Total corporate expenses	35,000	60,000	55,000
Net operating income (loss)	€(32,000)	€124,000	€(111,000)

Cost of goods sold and shipping expenses are both variable; other costs are all fixed. Brabant NV purchases cheeses at auction and from farmers' cooperatives, and it distributes them in the three territories listed above. Each of the three sales territories has its own manager and sales staff. The cheeses vary widely in profitability; some have a high margin and some have a low margin. (Certain cheeses, after having been aged for long periods, are the most expensive and carry the highest margins.)

Required:

1. List any disadvantages or weaknesses that you see to the statement format illustrated above.
2. Explain the basis that is apparently being used to allocate the corporate expenses to the territories. Do you agree with these allocations? Explain.
3. Prepare a new segmented contribution format income statement for May. Show a Total column as well as data for each territory. Include percentages on your statement for all columns. Carry percentages to one decimal place.
4. Analyze the statement that you prepared in (3) above. What points that might help to improve the company's performance would you bring to management's attention?

PROBLEM 11-22 Comparison of Performance Using Return on Investment (ROI) [LO2]

Comparative data on three companies in the same service industry are given below:

	Company		
	A	B	C
Sales	$4,000,000	$1,500,000	$?
Net operating income	$560,000	$210,000	$?
Average operating assets	$2,000,000	?	$3,000,000
Margin	?	?	3.5%
Turnover	?	?	2
Return on investment (ROI)	?	7%	?

Required:

1. What advantages are there to breaking down the ROI computation into two separate elements, margin and turnover?
2. Fill in the missing information above, and comment on the relative performance of the three companies in as much detail as the data permit. Make *specific recommendations* about how to improve the ROI.

(Adapted from National Association of Accountants, *Research Report No. 35,* p. 34)

PROBLEM 11-23 Return on Investment (ROI) and Residual Income [LO2, LO3]

"I know headquarters wants us to add that new product line," said Fred Halloway, manager of Kirsi Products' East Division. "But I want to see the numbers before I make a move. Our division's return on investment (ROI) has led the company for three years, and I don't want any letdown."

Kirsi Products is a decentralized wholesaler with four autonomous divisions. The divisions are evaluated on the basis of ROI, with year-end bonuses given to divisional managers who have the highest ROI. Operating results for the company's East Division for last year are given below:

Sales	$21,000,000
Variable expenses	13,400,000
Contribution margin	7,600,000
Fixed expenses	5,920,000
Net operating income	$ 1,680,000
Divisional operating assets	$ 5,250,000

The company had an overall ROI of 18% last year (considering all divisions). The company's East Division has an opportunity to add a new product line that would require an investment of $3,000,000. The cost and revenue characteristics of the new product line per year would be as follows:

Sales	$9,000,000
Variable expenses	65% of sales
Fixed expenses	$2,520,000

Required:

1. Compute the East Division's ROI for last year; also compute the ROI as it would appear if the new product line is added.
2. If you were in Fred Halloway's position, would you accept or reject the new product line? Explain.
3. Why do you suppose headquarters is anxious for the East Division to add the new product line?
4. Suppose that the company's minimum required rate of return on operating assets is 15% and that performance is evaluated using residual income.
   a. Compute the East Division's residual income for last year; also compute the residual income as it would appear if the new product line is added.
   b. Under these circumstances, if you were in Fred Halloway's position would you accept or reject the new product line? Explain.

PROBLEM 11-24 (Appendix 11A) Basic Transfer Pricing [LO4]

In cases 1-3 below, assume that Division A has a product that can be sold either to Division B of the same company or to outside customers. The managers of both divisions are evaluated based on their own division's return on investment (ROI). The managers are free to decide if they will participate in any internal transfers. All transfer prices are negotiated. Treat each case independently.

	Case			
	1	2	3	4
Division A:				
Capacity in units	50,000	300,000	100,000	200,000
Number of units now being sold to outside customers	50,000	300,000	75,000	200,000
Selling price per unit to outside customers	$100	$40	$60	$45
Variable costs per unit	$63	$19	$35	$30
Fixed costs per unit (based on capacity)	$25	$8	$17	$6
Division B:				
Number of units needed annually	10,000	70,000	20,000	60,000
Purchase price now being paid to an outside supplier	$92	$39	$60*	—

*Before any purchase discount.

Required:

1. Refer to case 1 above. A study has indicated that Division A can avoid $5 per unit in variable costs on any sales to Division B. Will the managers agree to a transfer and if so, within what range will the transfer price be? Explain.
2. Refer to case 2 above. Assume that Division A can avoid $4 per unit in variable costs on any sales to Division B.
   a. Would you expect any disagreement between the two divisional managers over what the transfer price should be? Explain.
   b. Assume that Division A offers to sell 70,000 units to Division B for $38 per unit and that Division B refuses this price. What will be the loss in potential profits for the company as a whole?
3. Refer to case 3 above. Assume that Division B is now receiving a 5% price discount from the outside supplier.
   a. Will the managers agree to a transfer? If so, within what range will the transfer price be?
   b. Assume that Division B offers to purchase 20,000 units from Division A at $52 per unit. If Division A accepts this price, would you expect its ROI to increase, decrease, or remain unchanged? Why?
4. Refer to case 4 above. Assume that Division B wants Division A to provide it with 60,000 units of a *different* product from the one that Division A is now producing. The new product would require $25 per unit in variable costs and would require that Division A cut back production of its present product by 30,000 units annually. What is the lowest acceptable transfer price from Division A's perspective?

PROBLEM 11-25 (Appendix 11B) Service Department Charges [LO5]

Northstar Company has two operating divisions—Machine Tools and Special Products. The company has a maintenance department that services the equipment in both divisions. The costs of operating the maintenance department are budgeted at $80,000 per month plus $0.50 per machine-hour. The fixed costs of the maintenance department are determined by peak-period requirements. The Machine Tools Division requires 65% of the peak-period capacity, and the Special Products Division requires 35%.

For October, the Machine Tools Division estimated that it would operate at 90,000 machine-hours of activity and the Special Products Division estimated that it would operate at 60,000 machine-hours of activity. However, due to labor unrest and an unexpected strike, the Machine Tools Division worked only 60,000 machine-hours during the month. The Special Products Division worked 60,000 machine-hours as planned.

Cost records in the maintenance department show that actual fixed costs for October totaled $85,000 and that actual variable costs totaled $78,000.

Required:

1. How much maintenance department cost should be charged to each division for October?
2. Assume that the company follows the practice of allocating *all* maintenance department costs incurred each month to the divisions in proportion to the actual machine-hours recorded in each division for the month. On this basis, how much cost would be allocated to each division for October?
3. What criticisms can you make of the allocation method used in part (2) above?
4. If managers of operating departments know that fixed service costs are going to be allocated on the basis of peak-period requirements, what will be their probable strategy as they report their estimate of peak-period requirements to the company's budget committee? As a member of top management, what would you do to neutralize any such strategies?

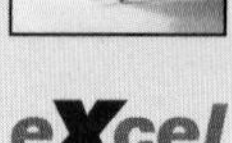

PROBLEM 11-26 Segment Reporting and Decision Making [LO1]

The most recent monthly contribution format income statement for Reston Company is given below:

Reston Company Income Statement For the Month Ended May 31		
Sales	$900,000	100.0%
Variable expenses	408,000	45.3
Contribution margin	492,000	54.7
Fixed expenses	465,000	51.7
Net operating income	$ 27,000	3.0%

Management is disappointed with the company's performance and is wondering what can be done to improve profits. By examining sales and cost records, you have determined the following:

a. The company is divided into two sales territories—Central and Eastern. The Central Territory recorded $400,000 in sales and $208,000 in variable expenses during May. The remaining sales and variable expenses were recorded in the Eastern Territory. Fixed expenses of $160,000 and $130,000 are traceable to the Central and Eastern Territories, respectively. The rest of the fixed expenses are common to the two territories.
b. The company is the exclusive distributor for two products—Awls and Pows. Sales of Awls and Pows totaled $100,000 and $300,000, respectively, in the Central Territory during May. Variable expenses are 25% of the selling price for Awls and 61% for Pows. Cost records show that $60,000 of the Central Territory's fixed expenses are traceable to Awls and $54,000 to Pows, with the remainder common to the two products.

Required:

1. Prepare contribution format segmented income statements, first showing the total company broken down between sales territories and then showing the Central Territory broken down by product line. Show both Amount and Percent columns for the company in total and for each segment. Round percentage computations to one decimal place.
2. Look at the statement you have prepared showing the total company segmented by sales territory. What points revealed by this statement should be brought to management's attention?
3. Look at the statement you have prepared showing the Central Territory segmented by product lines. What points revealed by this statement should be brought to management's attention?

PROBLEM 11-27 Return on Investment (ROI) and Residual Income [LO2, LO3]

Financial data for Bridger, Inc., for last year are as follows:

Bridger, Inc. Balance Sheet	Ending Balance	Beginning Balance
Assets		
Cash	$ 130,000	$ 125,000
Accounts receivable	480,000	340,000
Inventory	490,000	570,000
Plant and equipment, net	820,000	845,000
Investment in Brier Company	430,000	400,000
Land (undeveloped)	250,000	250,000
Total assets	$2,600,000	$2,530,000
Liabilities and Stockholders' Equity		
Accounts payable	$ 340,000	$ 380,000
Long-term debt	1,000,000	1,000,000
Stockholders' equity	1,260,000	1,150,000
Total liabilities and stockholders' equity	$2,600,000	$2,530,000

Bridger, Inc. Income Statement		
Sales		$4,180,000
Operating expenses		3,553,000
Net operating income		627,000
Interest and taxes:		
Interest expense	$120,000	
Tax expense	200,000	320,000
Net income		$ 307,000

The company paid dividends of $197,000 last year. The "Investment in Brier Company" on the balance sheet represents an investment in the stock of another company.

Required:

1. Compute the company's margin, turnover, and return on investment (ROI) for last year.
2. The board of directors of Bridger, Inc., has set a minimum required return of 20%. What was the company's residual income last year?

PROBLEM 11-28 (Appendix 11A) Transfer Pricing with an Outside Market [LO4]

Galati Products, Inc., has just purchased a small company that specializes in the manufacture of electronic tuners that are used as a component part of TV sets. Galati Products, Inc., is a decentralized company, and it will treat the newly acquired company as an autonomous division with full profit responsibility. The new division, called the Tuner Division, has the following revenue and costs associated with each tuner that it manufactures and sells:

Selling price		$20
Expenses:		
Variable	$11	
Fixed (based on a capacity of 100,000 tuners per year)	6	17
Net operating income		$3

Galati Products also has an Assembly Division that assembles TV sets. This division is currently purchasing 30,000 tuners per year from an overseas supplier at a cost of $20 per tuner, less a 10% purchase discount. The president of Galati Products is anxious to have the Assembly Division begin purchasing its tuners from the newly acquired Tuner Division in order to "keep the profits within the corporate family."

Required:

For (1) through (2) below, assume that the Tuner Division can sell all of its output to outside TV manufacturers at the normal $20 price.

1. Are the managers of the Tuner and Assembly Divisions likely to voluntarily agree to a transfer price for 30,000 tuners each year? Why or why not?
2. If the Tuner Division meets the price that the Assembly Division is currently paying to its overseas supplier and sells 30,000 tuners to the Assembly Division each year, what will be the effect on the profits of the Tuner Division, the Assembly Division, and the company as a whole?

For (3) through (6) below, assume that the Tuner Division is currently selling only 60,000 tuners each year to outside TV manufacturers at the stated $20 price.

3. Are the managers of the Tuner and Assembly Divisions likely to voluntarily agree to a transfer price for 30,000 tuners each year? Why or why not?
4. Suppose that the Assembly Division's overseas supplier drops its price (net of the purchase discount) to only $16 per tuner. Should the Tuner Division meet this price? Explain. If the Tuner Division does *not* meet this price, what will be the effect on the profits of the company as a whole?
5. Refer to (4) above. If the Tuner Division refuses to meet the $16 price, should the Assembly Division be required to purchase from the Tuner Division at a higher price for the good of the company as a whole? Explain.
6. Refer to (4) above. Assume that due to inflexible management policies, the Assembly Division is required to purchase 30,000 tuners each year from the Tuner Division at $20 per tuner. What will be the effect on the profits of the company as a whole?

PROBLEM 11-29 Basic Segmented Statement; Activity-Based Cost Assignment [LO1]

Vega Foods, Inc., has recently purchased a small mill that it intends to operate as one of its subsidiaries. The newly acquired mill has three products that it offers for sale—wheat cereal, pancake mix, and flour. Each product sells for $10 per package. Materials, labor, and other variable production costs are $3.00 per bag of wheat cereal, $4.20 per bag of pancake mix, and $1.80 per bag of flour. Sales commissions are 10% of sales for any product. All other costs are fixed.

The mill's income statement for the most recent month is given below:

		Product Line		
	Total Company	Wheat Cereal	Pancake Mix	Flour
Sales	$600,000	$200,000	$300,000	$100,000
Expenses:				
Materials, labor, and other	204,000	60,000	126,000	18,000
Sales commissions	60,000	20,000	30,000	10,000
Advertising	123,000	48,000	60,000	15,000
Salaries	66,000	34,000	21,000	11,000
Equipment depreciation	30,000	10,000	15,000	5,000
Warehouse rent	12,000	4,000	6,000	2,000
General administration	90,000	30,000	30,000	30,000
Total expenses	585,000	206,000	288,000	91,000
Net operating income (loss)	$ 15,000	$ (6,000)	$ 12,000	$ 9,000

The following additional information is available about the company:

a. The same equipment is used to mill and package all three products. In the above income statement, equipment depreciation has been allocated on the basis of sales dollars. An analysis of equipment usage indicates that it is used 40% of the time to make wheat cereal, 50% of the time to make pancake mix, and 10% of the time to make flour.
b. All three products are stored in the same warehouse. In the above income statement, the warehouse rent has been allocated on the basis of sales dollars. The warehouse contains 24,000 square feet of space, of which 8,000 square feet are used for wheat cereal, 14,000 square feet are used for pancake mix, and 2,000 square feet are used for flour. The warehouse space costs the company $0.50 per square foot to rent.
c. The general administration costs relate to the administration of the company as a whole. In the above income statement, these costs have been divided equally among the three product lines.
d. All other costs are traceable to the product lines.

Vega Foods' management is anxious to improve the mill's 2.5% margin on sales.

Required:

1. Prepare a new contribution format segmented income statement for the month. Adjust the allocation of equipment depreciation and warehouse rent as indicated by the additional information provided.
2. After seeing the income statement in the main body of the problem, management has decided to eliminate the wheat cereal, since it is not returning a profit, and to focus all available resources on promoting the pancake mix.
   a. Based on the statement you have prepared, do you agree with the decision to eliminate the wheat cereal? Explain.
   b. Based on the statement you have prepared, do you agree with the decision to focus all available resources on promoting the pancake mix? Assume that an ample market is available for all three products. (Hint. compute the contribution margin ratio for each product.)

PROBLEM 11-30 Return on Investment (ROI) Analysis [LO2]

The contribution format income statement for Westex, Inc., for its most recent period is given below:

Microsoft Excel - Problem 11-30 screen capture.xls

	A	B	C	D
1			*Total*	*Unit*
2	Sales		$1,000,000	$50.00
3	Variable expenses		600,000	30.00
4	Contribution margin		400,000	20.00
5	Fixed expenses		320,000	16.00
6	Net operating income		80,000	4.00
7	Income taxes @	40%	32,000	1.60
8	Net income		$ 48,000	$ 2.40
9				

The company had average operating assets of $500,000 during the period.

Required:

1. Compute the company's return on investment (ROI) for the period using the ROI formula stated in terms of margin and turnover.

For each of the following questions, indicate whether the margin and turnover will increase, decrease, or remain unchanged as a result of the events described, and then compute the new ROI figure. Consider each question separately, starting in each case from the original ROI computed in (1) above.

2. The company achieves a cost savings of $10,000 per period by using less costly materials.
3. Using Lean Production, the company is able to reduce the average level of inventory by $100,000. (The released funds are used to pay off bank loans.)
4. Sales are increased by $100,000; operating assets remain unchanged.
5. The company issues bonds and uses the proceeds to purchase $125,000 in machinery and equipment at the beginning of the period. Interest on the bonds is $15,000 per period. Sales remain unchanged. The new, more efficient equipment reduces production costs by $5,000 per period.
6. The company invests $180,000 of cash (received on accounts receivable) in a plot of land that is to be held for possible future use as a plant site.
7. Obsolete inventory carried on the books at a cost of $20,000 is scrapped and written off as a loss.

PROBLEM 11-31 (Appendix 11A) Market-Based Transfer Price [LO4]

Damico Company's Board Division manufactures an electronic control board that is widely used in high-end DVD players. The cost per control board is as follows:

Variable cost per board	$120
Fixed cost per board	30*
Total cost per board	$150

*Based on a capacity of 800,000 boards per year.

Part of the Board Division's output is sold to outside manufacturers of DVD players, and part is sold to Damico Company's Consumer Products Division, which produces a DVD player under the Damico name. The Board Division charges a selling price of $190 per control board for all sales, both internally and externally.

The costs, revenues, and net operating income associated with the Consumer Products Division's DVD player are given below:

Selling price per player		$580
Variable costs per player:		
Cost of the control board	$190	
Variable cost of other parts	230	
Total variable costs		420
Contribution margin		160
Fixed costs per player		85*
Net operating income per player		$ 75

*Based on a capacity of 200,000 DVD players per year.

The Consumer Products Division has an order from an overseas distributor for 5,000 DVD players. The distributor wants to pay only $400 per DVD player.

Required:

1. Assume that the Consumer Products Division has enough idle capacity to fill the 5,000-unit order. Is the division likely to accept the $400 price, or to reject it? Explain.
2. Assume that both the Board Division and the Consumer Products Division have idle capacity. Under these conditions, would rejecting the $400 price be advantageous for the company as a whole, or would it result in the loss of potential profits? Show computations to support your answer.
3. Assume that the Board Division is operating at capacity and could sell all of its control boards to outside manufacturers of DVD players. Assume, however, that the Consumer Products Division has enough idle capacity to fill the 5,000-unit order. Under these conditions, compute the profit impact to the Consumer Products Division of accepting the order at the $400 price.
4. What conclusions do you draw concerning the use of market price as a transfer price in intra-company transactions?

PROBLEM 11-32 (Appendix 11B) Service Department Charges [LO5]

Björnson A/S of Norway has only one service department—a cafeteria, in which meals are provided for employees in the company's Milling and Finishing departments. The costs of the cafeteria are all paid by the company as a fringe benefit to its employees. These costs are charged to the Milling and Finishing departments on the basis of meals served to employees in each department. Cost and other data relating to the Cafeteria and to the Milling and Finishing departments for the most recent year are provided below. (The Norwegian unit of currency is the krone, which is indicated below by K.)

Cafeteria:

	Budget	Actual
Variable costs for food	300,000K*	384,000K
Fixed costs	200,000K	215,000K

*Budgeted at 20K per meal served.

Milling and Finishing departments:

	Percent of Peak-Period Capacity Required	Number of Meals Served	
		Budget	Actual
Milling Department	70%	10,000	12,000
Finishing Department	30%	5,000	4,000
Total	100%	15,000	16,000

The level of fixed costs in the Cafeteria is determined by peak-period requirements.

Required:

Management would like data to assist in comparing actual performance to planned performance in the Cafeteria and in the other departments.

1. How much Cafeteria cost should be charged to the Milling Department and to the Finishing Department?
2. Should any portion of the actual Cafeteria costs not be charged to the other departments? If so, compute the amount that should not be charged, and explain why it should not be charged.

PROBLEM 11-33 Finely Segmented Income Statements [LO1]

Severo S.A. of Sao Paulo, Brazil, is organized into two divisions. The company's contribution format segmented income statement (in terms of the Brazilian currency Real) for last month is given below:

	Total Company	Divisions	
		Cloth	Leather
Sales	R3,500,000	R2,000,000	R1,500,000
Variable expenses	1,721,000	960,000	761,000
Contribution margin	1,779,000	1,040,000	739,000
Traceable fixed expenses:			
Advertising	612,000	300,000	312,000
Administration	427,000	210,000	217,000
Depreciation	229,000	115,000	114,000
Total traceable fixed expenses	1,268,000	625,000	643,000
Divisional segment margin	511,000	R 415,000	R 96,000
Common fixed expenses	390,000		
Net operating income	R 121,000		

Top management can't understand why the Leather Division has such a low segment margin when its sales are only 25% less than sales in the Cloth Division. As one step in isolating the problem, management has directed that the Leather Division be further segmented into product lines. The following information is available on the product lines in the Leather Division:

	Leather Division Product Lines		
	Garments	Shoes	Handbags
Sales	R500,000	R700,000	R300,000
Traceable fixed expenses:			
Advertising	R80,000	R112,000	R120,000
Administration	R30,000	R35,000	R42,000
Depreciation	R25,000	R56,000	R33,000
Variable expenses as a percentage of sales	65%	40%	52%

Analysis shows that R110,000 of the Leather Division's administration expenses are common to the product lines.

Required:

1. Prepare a contribution format segmented income statement for the Leather Division with segments defined as product lines.
2. Management is surprised by the handbag product line's poor showing and would like to have the product line segmented by market. The following information is available about the markets in which the handbag line is sold:

	Handbag Markets	
	Domestic	Foreign
Sales	R200,000	R100,000
Traceable fixed expenses:		
Advertising	R40,000	R80,000
Variable expenses as a percentage of sales	43%	70%

All of the handbag product line's administration expenses and depreciation are common to the markets in which the product is sold. Prepare a contribution format segmented income statement for the handbag product line with segments defined as markets.

3. Refer to the statement prepared in (1) above. The sales manager wants to run a special promotional campaign on one of the product lines over the next month. A marketing study indicates that such a campaign would increase sales of the garment product line by R200,000 or sales of the shoes product line by R145,000. The campaign would cost R30,000. Show computations to determine which product line should be chosen.

Cases

CASE 11-34 Service Organization; Segment Reporting [LO1]

The American Association of Acupuncturists is a professional association for acupuncturists that has 10,000 members. The association operates from a central headquarters but has local chapters throughout North America. The association's monthly journal, *American Acupuncture,* features recent developments in the field. The association also publishes special reports and books, and it sponsors courses that qualify members for the continuing professional education credit required by state certification boards. The association's statement of revenues and expenses for the current year is presented below:

American Association of Acupuncturists Statement of Revenues and Expenses For the Year Ended December 31	
Revenues	$970,000
Expenses:	
Salaries	440,000
Occupancy costs	120,000
Distributions to local chapters	210,000
Printing	82,000
Mailing	24,000
Continuing education instructors' fees	60,000
General and administrative	27,000
Total expenses	963,000
Excess of revenues over expenses	$ 7,000

The board of directors of the association has requested that you construct a segmented income statement that shows the financial contribution of each of the association's four major programs—membership service, journal, books and reports, and continuing education. The following data have been gathered to aid you:

a. Membership dues are $60 per year, of which $15 covers a one-year subscription to the association's journal. The other $45 pays for general membership services.
b. One-year subscriptions to *American Acupuncture* are sold to nonmembers and libraries at $20 per subscription. A total of 1,000 of these subscriptions were sold last year. In addition to subscriptions, the journal generated $50,000 in advertising revenues. The costs per journal subscription, for members as well as nonmembers, were $4 for printing and $1 for mailing.
c. A variety of technical reports and professional books were sold for a total of $70,000 during the year. Printing costs for these materials totaled $25,000, and mailing costs totaled $8,000.
d. The association offers a number of continuing education courses. The courses generated revenues of $230,000 last year.
e. Salary costs and space occupied by each program and the central staff follow:

	Salaries	Space Occupied (square feet)
Membership services	$170,000	3,000
Journal	60,000	1,000
Books and reports	40,000	1,000
Continuing education........	50,000	2,000
Central staff	120,000	3,000
Total....................	$440,000	10,000

f. The $120,000 in occupancy costs incurred last year includes $20,000 in rental cost for a portion of the warehouse used by the Membership Services program for storage purposes. The association has a flexible rental agreement that allows it to pay rent only on the warehouse space it uses.
g. Printing costs other than for journal subscriptions and for books and reports related to Continuing Education.
h. Distributions to local chapters are for general membership services.
i. General and administrative expenses include costs relating to overall administration of the association as a whole. The association's central staff does some mailing of materials for general administrative purposes.
j. The expenses that can be traced or assigned to the central staff, as well as any other expenses that are not traceable to the programs, will be treated as common costs. It is not necessary to distinguish between variable and fixed costs.

Required:

1. Prepare a contribution format segmented income statement for the American Association of Acupuncturists for last year. This statement should show the segment margin for each program as well as results for the association as a whole.
2. Give arguments for and against allocating all costs of the association to the four programs.

(CMA, adapted)

CASE 11-35 (Appendix 11A) Transfer Pricing; Divisional Performance [LO4]

Stanco, Inc., is a decentralized organization with five divisions. The company's Electronics Division produces a variety of electronics items, including an XL5 circuit board. The division (which is operating at capacity) sells the XL5 circuit board to regular customers for $12.50 each. The circuit boards have a variable production cost of $8.25 each.

The company's Clock Division has asked the Electronics Division to supply it with a large quantity of XL5 circuit boards for only $9 each. The Clock Division, which is operating at only 60% of capacity, will put the circuit boards into a timing device that it will produce and sell to a large oven manufacturer. The cost of the timing device being manufactured by the Clock Division follows:

XL5 circuit board (desired cost)	$ 9.00
Other purchased parts (from outside vendors)	30.00
Other variable costs	20.75
Fixed overhead and administrative costs	10.00
Total cost per timing device	$69.75

The manager of the Clock Division feels that she can't quote a price greater than $70 per timing device to the oven manufacturer if her division is to get the job. As shown above, in order to keep the price at $70 or less, she can't pay more than $9 per unit to the Electronics Division for the XL5 circuit boards. Although the $9 price for the XL5 circuit boards represents a substantial discount from the normal $12.50 price, she feels that the price concession is necessary for her division to get the oven manufacturer contract and thereby keep its core of highly trained people.

The company uses return on investment (ROI) to measure divisional performance.

Required:

1. Assume that you are the manager of the Electronics Division. Would you recommend that your division supply the XL5 circuit boards to the Clock Division for $9 each as requested? Why or why not? Show all computations.
2. Would it be profitable for the company as a whole for the Electronics Division to supply the Clock Division with the circuit boards for $9 each? Explain your answer.
3. In principle, should it be possible for the two managers to agree to a transfer price in this particular situation? If so, within what range would that transfer price lie?
4. Discuss the organizational and manager behavior problems, if any, inherent in this situation. What would you advise the company's president to do in this situation?

(CMA, adapted)

RESEARCH AND APPLICATION 11–36 [LO1, LO2, LO3]

The questions in this exercise are based on FedEx Corporation. To answer the questions you will need to download FedEx's Form 10-K for the fiscal year ended May 31, 2005 at www.sec.gov/edgar/searchedgar/companysearch.html. Once at this website, input CIK code 1048911 and hit enter. In the gray box on the right-hand side of your computer screen define the scope of your search by inputting 10-K and then pressing enter. Select the 10-K with a filing date of July 14, 2005. You do not need to print this document to answer the questions.

Required:

1. What is FedEx's strategy for success in the marketplace? Does the company rely primarily on a customer intimacy, operational excellence, or product leadership customer value proposition? What evidence supports your conclusion?
2. What are FedEx's four main business segments? Provide two examples of traceable fixed costs for each of FedEx's four business segments. Provide two examples of common costs that are not traceable to the four business segments.
3. Identify one example of a cost center, a profit center, and an investment center for FedEx.
4. Provide three examples of fixed costs that can be traceable or common depending on how FedEx defines its business segments.
5. Compute the margin, turnover, and return on investment (ROI) in 2005 for each of FedEx's four business segments. (Hint: page 99 reports total segment assets for each business segment).
6. Assume that FedEx established a minimum required rate of return of 15% for each of its business segments. Compute the residual income earned in 2005 in each of FedEx's four segments.
7. Assume that the senior managers of FedEx Express and FedEx Ground each have an investment opportunity that would require $20 million of additional operating assets and that would increase operating income by $4 million. If FedEx evaluates all of its senior managers using ROI, would the managers of both segments pursue the investment opportunity? If FedEx evaluates all of its senior managers using residual income, would the managers of both segments pursue the investment opportunity?

Chapter 12

Relevant Costs for Decision Making

Massaging the Numbers

BUSINESS FOCUS

Building and expanding convention centers appears to be an obsession with politicians. Indeed, billions of dollars are being spent to build or expand convention centers in 44 cities across the United States—adding more than 7 million square feet of convention space to the 64 million square feet that already exists. Given that trade show attendance across the country has been steadily declining, how do politicians justify these enormous investments? Politicians frequently rely on consultants who produce studies that purport to show the convention center will have a favorable economic impact on the area.

These economic impact studies are bogus in two respects. First, a large portion of the so-called favorable economic impact that is cited by consultants would be realized by a city even if it did not invest in a new or expanded convention center. For example, Portland, Oregon, voters overwhelmingly opposed spending $82 million to expand their city's convention center. Nonetheless, local politicians proceeded with the project. After completing the expansion, more than 70% of the people spending money at trade shows in Portland were from the Portland area. How much of the money spent by these locals would have been spent in Portland anyway if the convention center had not been expanded? We don't know, but in all likelihood much of this money would have been spent at the zoo, the art museum, the theater, local restaurants, and so on. This portion of the "favorable" economic impact cited by consultants and used by politicians to justify expanding convention centers should be ignored. Second, since the supply of convention centers throughout the United States substantially exceeds demand, convention centers must offer substantial economic incentives, such as waiving rental fees, to attract trade shows. The cost of these concessions, although often excluded from consultants' projections, further erodes the genuine economic viability of building or expanding a convention center. ■

Source: Victoria Murphy, "The Answer Is Always Yes," *Forbes*, February 28, 2005, pp. 82–84.

Learning Objectives

After studying Chapter 12, you should be able to:

LO1 Identify relevant and irrelevant costs and benefits in a decision.

LO2 Prepare an analysis showing whether a product line or other business segment should be dropped or retained.

LO3 Prepare a make or buy analysis.

LO4 Prepare an analysis showing whether a special order should be accepted.

LO5 Determine the most profitable use of a constrained resource and the value of obtaining more of the constrained resource.

LO6 Prepare an analysis showing whether joint products should be sold at the split-off point or processed further.

LP 12

Managers constantly must decide what products to sell, whether to make or buy component parts, what prices to charge, what channels of distribution to use, whether to accept special orders at special prices, and so forth. Making such decisions is often a difficult task that is complicated by numerous alternatives and massive amounts of data, only some of which may be relevant.

Every decision involves choosing from among at least two alternatives. In making a decision, the costs and benefits of one alternative must be compared to the costs and benefits of other alternatives. Costs that differ between alternatives are called **relevant costs.** Distinguishing between relevant and irrelevant costs and benefits is critical for two reasons. First, irrelevant data can be ignored—saving decision makers tremendous amounts of time and effort. Second, bad decisions can easily result from erroneously including irrelevant costs and benefits when analyzing alternatives. To be successful in decision making, managers must be able to tell the difference between relevant and irrelevant data and must be able to correctly use the relevant data in analyzing alternatives. The purpose of this chapter is to develop these skills by illustrating their use in a wide range of decision-making situations. These decision-making skills are as important in your personal life as they are to managers. After completing your study of this chapter, you should be able to think more clearly about decisions in many facets of your life.

Cost Concepts for Decision Making

LEARNING OBJECTIVE 1
Identify relevant and irrelevant costs and benefits in a decision.

Four cost terms discussed in Chapter 2 are particularly applicable to this chapter. These terms are *differential costs, incremental costs, opportunity costs,* and *sunk costs.* You may find it helpful to turn back to Chapter 2 and refresh your memory concerning these terms before reading on.

Identifying Relevant Costs and Benefits

Video 12–1

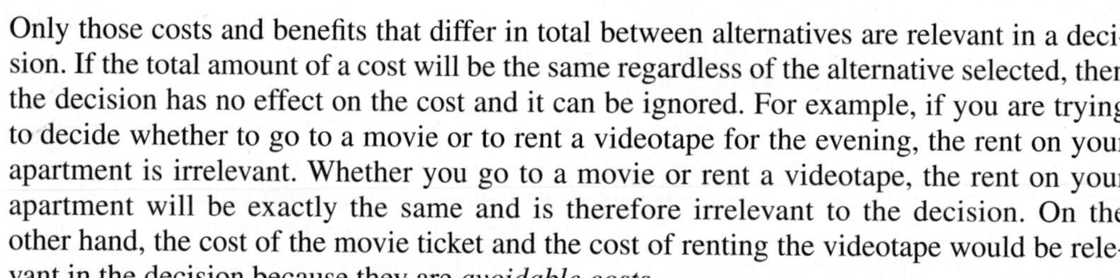

Only those costs and benefits that differ in total between alternatives are relevant in a decision. If the total amount of a cost will be the same regardless of the alternative selected, then the decision has no effect on the cost and it can be ignored. For example, if you are trying to decide whether to go to a movie or to rent a videotape for the evening, the rent on your apartment is irrelevant. Whether you go to a movie or rent a videotape, the rent on your apartment will be exactly the same and is therefore irrelevant to the decision. On the other hand, the cost of the movie ticket and the cost of renting the videotape would be relevant in the decision because they are *avoidable costs.*

An **avoidable cost** is a cost that can be eliminated in whole or in part by choosing one alternative over another. By choosing the alternative of going to the movie, the cost of renting the videotape can be avoided. By choosing the alternative of renting the videotape, the cost of the movie ticket can be avoided. Therefore, the cost of the movie ticket and the cost of renting the videotape are both avoidable costs. On the other hand, the rent on the apartment is not an avoidable cost of either alternative. You would continue to rent your apartment under either alternative. Avoidable costs are relevant costs. Unavoidable costs are irrelevant costs.

Two broad categories of costs are never relevant in decisions. These irrelevant costs are:

1. Sunk costs.
2. Future costs that do not differ between the alternatives.

As we learned in Chapter 2, a **sunk cost** is a cost that has already been incurred and cannot be avoided regardless of what a manager decides to do. For example, suppose a used car dealer purchased a five-year-old Toyota Camry for $12,000. The amount paid for the Camry is a sunk cost because it has already been incurred and the transaction cannot be undone. Sunk costs are always the same no matter what alternatives are being considered; therefore, they are irrelevant and should be ignored when making decisions. Future costs that do not differ between alternatives should also be ignored when making decisions. Continuing with the example discussed earlier, suppose you intend to order a pizza after you go to the movie theater or you rent a video. In that case, if you are going to buy the same pizza regardless of your choice of entertainment, its cost is irrelevant to the choice of whether you go to the movie theater or rent a video. Notice, the cost of the pizza is not a sunk cost because it has not yet been incurred. Nonetheless, the cost of the pizza is irrelevant to the entertainment decision because it is a future cost that does not differ between the alternatives.

The term **differential cost** was also introduced in Chapter 2. In managerial accounting, the terms *avoidable cost, differential cost, incremental cost,* and *relevant cost* are often used interchangeably. To identify the costs that are avoidable in a particular decision situation and are therefore relevant, these steps should be followed:

1. Eliminate costs and benefits that do not differ between alternatives. These irrelevant costs consist of (a) sunk costs and (b) future costs that do not differ between alternatives.
2. Use the remaining costs and benefits that do differ between alternatives in making the decision. The costs that remain are the differential, or avoidable, costs.

IN BUSINESS

THE RELEVANT COST OF EXECUTIVE PERKS

The Securities and Exchange Commission is concerned about CEOs who use company-owned airplanes for personal travel. For example, consider a CEO who uses his employers' Gulfstream V luxury airplane to transport his family on a 2,000 mile roundtrip vacation from New York City to Orlando, Florida. The standard practice among companies with personal travel reimbursement policies would be to charge their CEO $1,500 for this flight based on a per-mile reimbursement rate established by the Internal Revenue Service (the IRS rates are meant to approximate the per-mile cost of a first-class ticket on a commercial airline). However, critics argue that using IRS reimbursement rates grossly understates the flight costs that are borne by shareholders. Some of these critics claim that the $11,000 incremental cost of the flight, including fuel, landing fees, and crew hotel charges, should be reimbursed by the CEO. Still others argue that even basing reimbursements on incremental costs understates the true cost of a flight because it excludes fixed costs such as the cost of the airplane, crew salaries, and insurance. These costs are relevant because the excessive amount of personal travel by corporate executives essentially requires their employers to purchase, insure, and staff additional airplanes. This latter group of critics argues that the relevant cost of the trip from New York City to Orlando is $43,000—the market price that would have to be paid to charter a comparable size airplane for this flight. What do you think should be the relevant cost of this flight? Should shareholders expect their CEO to reimburse $0 (as is the practice at some companies), $1,500, $11,000, or $43,000? Or, should all companies disallow personal use of corporate assets?

Source: Mark Maremont, "Amid Crackdown, the Jet Perk Suddenly Looks a Lot Pricier," *The Wall Street Journal,* May 25, 2005, pp. A1 and A8.

Different Costs for Different Purposes

We need to recognize a fundamental concept of managerial accounting from the outset of our discussion—costs that are relevant in one decision situation are not necessarily relevant in another. This means that *managers need different costs for different purposes.* For one purpose, a particular group of costs may be relevant; for another purpose, an entirely different group of costs may be relevant. Thus, *each* decision situation must be carefully analyzed to isolate the relevant costs. Otherwise, irrelevant data may cloud the situation and lead to a bad decision.

The concept of "different costs for different purposes" is basic to managerial accounting; we shall frequently see its application in the pages that follow.

An Example of Identifying Relevant Costs and Benefits

Cynthia is currently a student in an MBA program in Boston and would like to visit a friend in New York City over the weekend. She is trying to decide whether to drive or take the train. Because she is on a tight budget, she wants to carefully consider the costs of the two alternatives. If one alternative is far less expensive than the other, that may be decisive in her choice. By car, the distance between her apartment in Boston and her friend's apartment in New York City is 230 miles. Cynthia has compiled the following list of items to consider:

Automobile Costs		
Item	Annual Cost of Fixed Items	Cost per Mile (based on 10,000 miles per year)
(a) Annual straight-line depreciation on car [($24,000 original cost − $10,000 estimated resale value in 5 years)/5 years]	$2,800	$0.280
(b) Cost of gasoline ($1.60 per gallon ÷ 32 miles per gallon)		0.050
(c) Annual cost of auto insurance and license	$1,380	0.138
(d) Maintenance and repairs		0.065
(e) Parking fees at school ($45 per month × 8 months)	$360	0.036
(f) Total average cost per mile		$0.569

Additional Data	
Item	
(g) Reduction in the resale value of car due solely to wear and tear	$0.026 per mile
(h) Cost of round-trip Amtrak ticket from Boston to New York City	$104
(i) Benefit of relaxing and being able to study during the train ride rather than having to drive	?
(j) Cost of putting the dog in a kennel while gone	$40
(k) Benefit of having a car available in New York City	?
(l) Hassle of parking the car in New York City	?
(m) Cost of parking the car in New York City	$25 per day

Which costs and benefits are relevant in this decision? Remember, only those costs and benefits that differ between alternatives are relevant. Everything else is irrelevant and can be ignored.

Start at the top of the list with item (a): the original cost of the car is a sunk cost. This cost has already been incurred and therefore can never differ between alternatives. Consequently, it is irrelevant and should be ignored. The same is true of the accounting depreciation of $2,800 per year, which simply spreads the sunk cost across five years.

Item (b), the cost of gasoline consumed by driving to New York City, is a relevant cost. If Cynthia takes the train, this cost would not be incurred. Hence, the cost differs between alternatives and is therefore relevant.

Item (c), the annual cost of auto insurance and license, is not relevant. Whether Cynthia takes the train or drives on this particular trip, her annual auto insurance premium and her auto license fee will remain the same.[1]

[1] If Cynthia has an accident while driving to New York City or back, this might affect her insurance premium when the policy is renewed. The increase in the insurance premium would be a relevant cost of this particular trip, but the normal amount of the insurance premium is not relevant in any case.

Item (d), the cost of maintenance and repairs, is relevant. While maintenance and repair costs have a large random component, over the long run they should be more or less proportional to the number of miles the car is driven. Thus, the average cost of $0.065 per mile is a reasonable estimate to use.

Item (e), the monthly fee that Cynthia pays to park at her school during the academic year is not relevant. Regardless of which alternative she selects—driving or taking the train—she will still need to pay for parking at school.

Item (f) is the total average cost of $0.569 per mile. As discussed above, some elements of this total are relevant, but some are not relevant. Since it contains some irrelevant costs, it would be incorrect to estimate the cost of driving to New York City and back by simply multiplying the $0.569 by 460 miles (230 miles each way × 2). This erroneous approach would yield a cost of driving of $261.74. Unfortunately, such mistakes are often made in both personal life and in business. Since the total cost is stated on a per-mile basis, people are easily misled. Often people think that if the cost is stated as $0.569 per mile, the cost of driving 100 miles is $56.90. But it is not. Many of the costs included in the $0.569 cost per mile are sunk and/or fixed and will not increase if the car is driven another 100 miles. The $0.569 is an average cost, not an incremental cost. Beware of such unitized costs (i.e., costs stated in terms of a dollar amount per unit, per mile, per direct labor-hour, per machine-hour, and so on)—they are often misleading.

Item (g), the decline in the resale value of the car that occurs as a consequence of driving more miles, is relevant in the decision. Because she uses the car, its resale value declines, which is a real cost of using the car that should be taken into account. Cynthia estimated this cost by accessing the *Kelly Blue Book* website at www.kbb.com. The reduction in resale value of an asset through use or over time is often called *real* or *economic depreciation.* This is different from accounting depreciation, which attempts to match the sunk cost of an asset with the periods that benefit from that cost.

Item (h), the $104 cost of a round-trip ticket on Amtrak, is relevant in this decision. If she drives, she would not have to buy the ticket.

Item (i) is relevant to the decision, even if it is difficult to put a dollar value on relaxing and being able to study while on the train. It is relevant because it is a benefit that is available under one alternative but not under the other.

Item (j), the cost of putting Cynthia's dog in the kennel while she is gone, is irrelevant in this decision. Whether she takes the train or drives to New York City, she will still need to put her dog in a kennel.

Like item (i), items (k) and (l) are relevant to the decision even if it is difficult to measure their dollar impacts.

Item (m), the cost of parking in New York City, is relevant to the decision.

Bringing together all of the relevant data, Cynthia would estimate the relevant costs of driving and taking the train as follows:

Relevant financial cost of driving to New York City:	
Gasoline (460 miles at $0.050 per mile)	$ 23.00
Maintenance and repairs (460 miles @ $0.065 per mile)	29.90
Reduction in the resale value of car due solely to wear and tear (460 miles @ $0.026 per mile)	11.96
Cost of parking the car in New York City (2 days @ $25 per day)	50.00
Total	$114.86
Relevant financial cost of taking the train to New York City:	
Cost of round-trip Amtrak ticket from Boston to New York City	$104.00

What should Cynthia do? From a purely financial standpoint, it would be cheaper by $10.86 ($114.86 − $104.00) to take the train than to drive. Cynthia has to decide if the convenience of having a car in New York City outweighs the additional cost and the disadvantages of being unable to relax and study on the train and the hassle of finding parking in the city.

In this example, we focused on identifying the relevant costs and benefits—everything else was ignored. In the next example, we include all of the costs and benefits—relevant or not. Nonetheless, we'll still get the correct answer because the irrelevant costs and benefits will cancel out when we compare the alternatives.

IN BUSINESS

CRUISING ON THE CHEAP

Cruise ship operators such as Princess Cruises sometimes offer deep discounts on popular cruises. For example, a 10-day Mediterranean cruise on the Norwegian Dream was offered at up to 75% off the list price. A seven-day cruise to Alaska could be booked for a $499–$700 discount. The cause? "An ambitious fleet expansion left the cruise industry grappling with a tidal wave of capacity. . . . Most cruise costs are fixed whether all the ship's berths are filled or not, so it is better to sell cheap than not at all. . . . In the current glut, discounting has made it possible for the cruise lines to keep berths nearly full."

Source: Martin Brannigan, *The Wall Street Journal,* July 17, 2000, pp. B1 and B4.

Reconciling the Total and Differential Approaches

Oak Harbor Woodworks is considering a new labor-saving machine that rents for $3,000 per year. The machine will be used on the company's butcher block production line. Data concerning the company's annual sales and costs of butcher blocks with and without the new machine are shown below:

	Current Situation	Situation with the New Machine
Units produced and sold	5,000	5,000
Selling price per unit	$40	$40
Direct materials cost per unit	$14	$14
Direct labor cost per unit	$8	$5
Variable overhead cost per unit	$2	$2
Fixed costs, other	$62,000	$62,000
Fixed costs, rental of new machine	—	$3,000

Given the data above, the net operating income for the product under the two alternatives can be computed as shown in Exhibit 12–1.

Note that the net operating income is $12,000 higher with the new machine, so that is the better alternative. Note also that the $12,000 advantage for the new machine can be obtained in two different ways. It is the difference between the $30,000 net operating income with the new machine and the $18,000 net operating income for the current situation. It is also the sum of the differential costs and benefits as shown in the last column of Exhibit 12–1. A positive number in the Differential Costs and Benefits column indicates that the difference between the alternatives favors the new machine; a negative number indicates that the difference favors the current situation. A zero in that column simply means that the total amount for the item is exactly the same for both alternatives. Thus, since the difference in the net operating incomes equals the sum of the differences for the individual items, any cost or benefit that is the same for both alternatives will have no impact on which alternative is preferred. This is the reason that costs and benefits that do not differ between alternatives are irrelevant and can be ignored. If we properly account for them, they will cancel out when we compare the alternatives.

EXHIBIT 12–1
Total and Differential Costs

	Current Situation	Situation with New Machine	Differential Costs and Benefits
Sales (5,000 units @ $40 per unit)	$200,000	$200,000	$ 0
Variable expenses:			
Direct materials (5,000 units @ $14 per unit)	70,000	70,000	0
Direct labor (5,000 units @ $8 and $5 per unit)	40,000	25,000	15,000
Variable overhead (5,000 units @ $2 per unit)	10,000	10,000	0
Total variable expenses	120,000	105,000	
Contribution margin	80,000	95,000	
Fixed expenses:			
Other	62,000	62,000	0
Rent of new machine	0	3,000	(3,000)
Total fixed expenses	62,000	65,000	
Net operating income	$ 18,000	$ 30,000	$12,000

We could have arrived at the same solution much more quickly by completely ignoring the irrelevant costs and benefits.

- The selling price per unit and the number of units sold do not differ between the alternatives. Therefore, the total sales revenues are exactly the same for the two alternatives as shown in Exhibit 12–1. Since the sales revenues are exactly the same, they have no effect on the difference in net operating income between the two alternatives. That is shown in the last column in Exhibit 12–1, which shows a $0 differential benefit.
- The direct materials cost per unit, the variable overhead cost per unit, and the number of units produced and sold do not differ between the alternatives. Consequently, the total direct materials cost and the total variable overhead cost will be the same for the two alternatives and can be ignored.
- The "other" fixed expenses do not differ between the alternatives, so they can be ignored as well.

Indeed, the only costs that do differ between the alternatives are direct labor costs and the fixed rental cost of the new machine. Hence, the two alternatives can be compared based only on these relevant costs:

Net Advantage of Renting the New Machine	
Decrease in direct labor costs (5,000 units at a cost savings of $3 per unit)	$15,000
Increase in fixed expenses	(3,000)
Net annual cost savings from renting the new machine	$12,000

If we focus on just the relevant costs and benefits, we get exactly the same answer as when we listed all of the costs and benefits—including those that do not differ between the alternatives and hence are irrelevant. We get the same answer because the only costs and benefits that matter in the final comparison of the net operating incomes are those that differ between the two alternatives and hence are not zero in the last column of Exhibit 12–1. Those two relevant costs are both listed in the above analysis showing the net advantage of renting the new machine.

Why Isolate Relevant Costs?

In the preceding example, we used two different approaches to analyze the alternatives. First, we considered all costs, both those that were relevant and those that were not; and second, we considered only the relevant costs. We obtained the same answer under both approaches. It would be natural to ask, "Why bother to isolate relevant costs when total costs will do the job just as well?" Isolating relevant costs is desirable for at least two reasons.

First, only rarely will enough information be available to prepare a detailed income statement for both alternatives. Assume, for example, that you are called on to make a decision relating to a portion of a single business process in a multidepartmental, multiproduct company. Under these circumstances, it would be virtually impossible to prepare an income statement of any type. You would have to rely on your ability to recognize which costs are relevant and which are not in order to assemble the data necessary to make a decision.

Second, mingling irrelevant costs with relevant costs may cause confusion and distract attention from the information that is really critical. Furthermore, the danger always exists that an irrelevant piece of data may be used improperly, resulting in an incorrect decision. The best approach is to ignore irrelevant data and base the decision entirely on relevant data.

Relevant cost analysis, combined with the contribution approach to the income statement, provides a powerful tool for making decisions. We will investigate various uses of this tool in the remaining sections of this chapter.

IN BUSINESS

ENVIRONMENTAL COSTS ADD UP

A decision analysis can be flawed by incorrectly including irrelevant costs such as sunk costs and future costs that do not differ between alternatives. It can also be flawed by omitting future costs that *do* differ between alternatives. This is a problem particularly with environmental costs because they have dramatically increased in recent years and are often overlooked by managers.

Consider the environmental complications posed by a decision of whether to install a solvent-based or powder-based system for spray-painting parts. In a solvent painting system, parts are sprayed as they move along a conveyor. The paint that misses the part is swept away by a wall of water, called a water curtain. The excess paint accumulates in a pit as sludge that must be removed each month. Environmental regulations classify this sludge as hazardous waste. As a result, a permit must be obtained to produce the waste and meticulous records must be maintained of how the waste is transported, stored, and disposed of. The annual costs of complying with these regulations can easily exceed $140,000 in total for a painting facility that initially costs only $400,000 to build. The costs of complying with environmental regulations include the following:

- The waste sludge must be hauled to a special disposal site. The typical disposal fee is about $300 per barrel, or $55,000 per year for a modest solvent-based painting system.
- Workers must be specially trained to handle the paint sludge.
- The company must carry special insurance.
- The company must pay substantial fees to the state for releasing pollutants (i.e., the solvent) into the air.
- The water in the water curtain must be specially treated to remove contaminants. This can cost tens of thousands of dollars per year.

In contrast, a powder-based painting system avoids almost all of these environmental costs. Excess powder used in the painting process can be recovered and reused without creating a hazardous waste. Additionally, the powder-based system does not release contaminants into the atmosphere. Therefore, even though the cost of building a powder-based system may be higher than the cost of building a solvent-based system, over the long run the costs of the powder-based system may be far lower due to the high environmental costs of a solvent-based system. Managers need to be aware of such environmental costs and take them fully into account when making decisions.

Source: Germain Böer, Margaret Curtin, and Louis Hoyt, "Environmental Cost Management," *Management Accounting*, September 1998, pp. 28–38.

Adding and Dropping Product Lines and Other Segments

LEARNING OBJECTIVE 2
Prepare an analysis showing whether a product line or other business segment should be dropped or retained.

Decisions relating to whether product lines or other segments of a company should be dropped and new ones added are among the most difficult that a manager has to make. In such decisions, many qualitative and quantitative factors must be considered. Ultimately, however, any final decision to drop a business segment or to add a new one is going to hinge primarily on the impact the decision will have on net operating income. To assess this impact, costs must be carefully analyzed.

An Illustration of Cost Analysis

Video 12–1

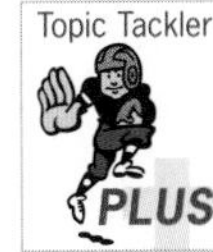

12–1

Exhibit 12–2 provides sales and cost information for the preceding month for the Discount Drug Company and its three major product lines—drugs, cosmetics, and housewares. A quick review of this exhibit suggests that dropping the housewares segment would increase the company's overall net operating income by $8,000. However, this would be a flawed conclusion because the data in Exhibit 12–2 do not distinguish between fixed expenses that can be avoided if a product line is dropped and common fixed expenses that cannot be avoided by dropping any particular product line.

In this scenario, the two alternatives under consideration are keeping the housewares product line and dropping the housewares product line. Therefore, only those costs that differ between these two alternatives (i.e., that can be avoided by dropping the housewares product line) are relevant. In deciding whether to drop housewares, it is crucial to identify which costs can be avoided, and hence are relevant to the decision, and which costs cannot be avoided, and hence are irrelevant. The decision should be analyzed as follows.

If the housewares line is dropped, then the company will lose $20,000 per month in contribution margin, but by dropping the line it may be possible to avoid some fixed costs such as salaries or advertising costs. If dropping the housewares line enables the company to avoid more in fixed costs than it loses in contribution margin, then its overall net operating income will improve by eliminating the product line. On the other hand, if the company is not able to avoid as much in fixed costs as it loses in contribution margin, then the housewares line should be kept. In short, the manager should ask, "What costs can I avoid if I drop this product line?"

As we have seen from our earlier discussion, not all costs are avoidable. For example, some of the costs associated with a product line may be sunk costs. Other costs may be allocated fixed costs that will not differ in total regardless of whether the product line is dropped or retained.

EXHIBIT 12–2
Discount Drug Company Product Lines

		Product Line		
	Total	Drugs	Cosmetics	Housewares
Sales	$250,000	$125,000	$75,000	$50,000
Variable expenses	105,000	50,000	25,000	30,000
Contribution margin	145,000	75,000	50,000	20,000
Fixed expenses:				
Salaries	50,000	29,500	12,500	8,000
Advertising	15,000	1,000	7,500	6,500
Utilities	2,000	500	500	1,000
Depreciation—fixtures	5,000	1,000	2,000	2,000
Rent	20,000	10,000	6,000	4,000
Insurance	3,000	2,000	500	500
General administrative	30,000	15,000	9,000	6,000
Total fixed expenses	125,000	59,000	38,000	28,000
Net operating income (loss)	$ 20,000	$ 16,000	$12,000	$ (8,000)

To show how to proceed in a product-line analysis, suppose that Discount Drug Company has analyzed the fixed costs being charged to the three product lines and has determined the following:

1. The salaries expense represents salaries paid to employees working directly on the product. All of the employees working in housewares would be discharged if the product line is dropped.
2. The advertising expense represents advertisements that are specific to each product line and are avoidable if the line is dropped.
3. The utilities expense represents utilities costs for the entire company. The amount charged to each product line is an allocation based on space occupied and is not avoidable if the product line is dropped.
4. The depreciation expense represents depreciation on fixtures used to display the various product lines. Although the fixtures are nearly new, they are custom-built and will have no resale value if the housewares line is dropped.
5. The rent expense represents rent on the entire building housing the company; it is allocated to the product lines on the basis of sales dollars. The monthly rent of $20,000 is fixed under a long-term lease agreement.
6. The insurance expense is for insurance carried on inventories within each of the three product lines. If housewares is dropped, the related inventories will be liquidated and the insurance premiums will decrease accordingly.
7. The general administrative expense represents the costs of accounting, purchasing, and general management, which are allocated to the product lines on the basis of sales dollars. These costs will not change if the housewares line is dropped.

With this information, management can determine that $15,000 of the fixed expenses associated with the housewares product line are avoidable and $13,000 are not:

Fixed Expenses	Total Cost Assigned to Housewares	Not Avoidable*	Avoidable
Salaries	$ 8,000		$ 8,000
Advertising	6,500		6,500
Utilities	1,000	$ 1,000	
Depreciation—fixtures	2,000	2,000	
Rent	4,000	4,000	
Insurance	500		500
General administrative	6,000	6,000	
Total	$28,000	$13,000	$15,000

*These fixed costs represent either sunk costs or future costs that will not change whether the housewares line is retained or discontinued.

As stated earlier, if the housewares product line were dropped, the company would lose the product's contribution margin of $20,000, but would save its associated avoidable fixed expenses. We now know that those avoidable fixed expenses total $15,000. Therefore, dropping the housewares product line would result in a $5,000 *reduction* in net operating income as shown below:

Contribution margin lost if the housewares line is discontinued (see Exhibit 12–2)	$(20,000)
Less fixed costs that can be avoided if the housewares line is discontinued (see above)	15,000
Decrease in overall company net operating income	$ (5,000)

In this case, the fixed costs that can be avoided by dropping the housewares product line ($15,000) are less than the contribution margin that will be lost ($20,000). Therefore, based on the data given, the housewares line should not be discontinued unless a more profitable use can be found for the floor and counter space that it is occupying.

A Comparative Format

This decision can also be approached by preparing comparative income statements showing the effects of either keeping or dropping the product line. Exhibit 12–3 contains such an analysis for the Discount Drug Company. As shown in the last column of the exhibit, if the housewares line is dropped, then overall company net operating income will decrease by $5,000 each period. This is the same answer, of course, as we obtained when we focused just on the lost contribution margin and avoidable fixed costs.

Beware of Allocated Fixed Costs

Go back to Exhibit 12–2. Does this exhibit suggest that the housewares product line should be kept—as we have just concluded? No, it does not. Exhibit 12–2 suggests that the housewares product line is losing money. Why keep a product line that is showing a loss? The explanation for this apparent inconsistency lies in part with the common fixed costs that are being allocated to the product lines. As we observed in Chapter 11, one of the great dangers in allocating common fixed costs is that such allocations can make a product line (or other segment of a business) look less profitable than it really is. In this instance, allocating the common fixed costs among all product lines makes the housewares product line appear to be unprofitable. However, as we have shown above, dropping the product line would result in a decrease in the company's overall net operating income. This point can be seen clearly if we redo Exhibit 12–2 by eliminating the allocation of the common fixed costs. Exhibit 12–4 (page 510) uses the segmented approach from Chapter 11 to estimate the profitability of the product lines.

Exhibit 12–4 gives us a much different perspective of the housewares line than does Exhibit 12–2. As shown in Exhibit 12–4, the housewares line is covering all of its own traceable fixed costs and generating a $3,000 segment margin toward covering the common fixed costs of the company. Unless another product line can be found that will generate a segment margin greater than $3,000, the company would be better off keeping the housewares line.

EXHIBIT 12–3
A Comparative Format for Product-Line Analysis

	Keep Housewares	Drop Housewares	Difference: Net Operating Income Increase (or Decrease)
Sales	$50,000	$ 0	$(50,000)
Variable expenses	30,000	0	30,000
Contribution margin	20,000	0	(20,000)
Fixed expenses:			
Salaries	8,000	0	8,000
Advertising	6,500	0	6,500
Utilities	1,000	1,000	0
Depreciation—fixtures	2,000	2,000	0
Rent	4,000	4,000	0
Insurance	500	0	500
General administrative	6,000	6,000	0
Total fixed expenses	28,000	13,000	15,000
Net operating income (loss)	$ (8,000)	$(13,000)	$ (5,000)

EXHIBIT 12–4
Discount Drug Company Product Lines—Recast in Contribution Format (from Exhibit 12–2)

		Product Line		
	Total	Drugs	Cosmetics	House-wares
Sales	$250,000	$125,000	$75,000	$50,000
Variable expenses	105,000	50,000	25,000	30,000
Contribution margin	145,000	75,000	50,000	20,000
Traceable fixed expenses:				
Salaries	50,000	29,500	12,500	8,000
Advertising	15,000	1,000	7,500	6,500
Depreciation—fixtures	5,000	1,000	2,000	2,000
Insurance	3,000	2,000	500	500
Total traceable fixed expenses	73,000	33,500	22,500	17,000
Product-line segment margin	72,000	$ 41,500	$27,500	$ 3,000*
Common fixed expenses:				
Utilities	2,000			
Rent	20,000			
General administrative	30,000			
Total common fixed expenses	52,000			
Net operating income	$ 20,000			

*If the housewares line is dropped, this $3,000 in segment margin will be lost to the company. In addition, we have seen that the $2,000 depreciation on the fixtures is a sunk cost that cannot be avoided. The sum of these two figures ($3,000 + $2,000 = $5,000) would be the decrease in the company's overall profits if the housewares line were discontinued. Of course, the company may later choose to drop the product if circumstances change—such as a pending decision to replace the fixtures.

By keeping the line, the company's overall net operating income will be higher than if the product line were dropped.

Additionally, managers may choose to retain an unprofitable product line if the line helps sell other products or if it serves as a "magnet" to attract customers. Bread, for example, may not be an especially profitable line in some food stores, but customers expect it to be available, and many of them would undoubtedly shift their buying elsewhere if a particular store decided to stop carrying it.

The Make or Buy Decision

LEARNING OBJECTIVE 3
Prepare a make or buy analysis.

Video 12–1

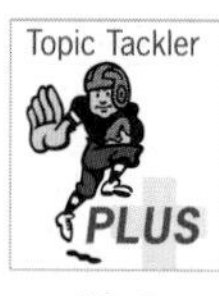

12–2

Providing a product or service to a customer involves many steps. For example, consider all of the steps that are necessary to develop and sell a product such as tax preparation software in retail stores. First the software must be developed, which involves highly skilled software engineers and a great deal of project management effort. Then the product must be put into a form that can be delivered to customers. This involves burning the application onto a blank CD or DVD, applying a label, and packaging the result in an attractive box. Then the product must be distributed to retail stores. Then the product must be sold. And finally, help lines and other forms of after-sale service may have to be provided. And we should not forget that the blank CD or DVD, the label, and the box must of course be made by someone before any of this can happen. All of these activities, from development, to production, to after-sales service are called a *value chain.*

Separate companies may carry out each of the activities in the value chain or a single company may carry out several. When a company is involved in more than one activity in the entire value chain, it is **vertically integrated.** Vertical integration is very common.

Some companies control all of the activities in the value chain from producing basic raw materials right up to the final distribution of finished goods and provision of after-sales service. Other companies are content to integrate on a smaller scale by purchasing many of the parts and materials that go into their finished products. A decision to carry out one of the activities in the value chain internally, rather than to buy externally from a supplier, is called a **make or buy decision.** Quite often these decisions involve whether to buy a particular part or to make it internally. Make or buy decisions also involve decisions concerning whether to outsource development tasks, after-sales service, or other activities.

IN BUSINESS

EMPLOYEE HEALTH BENEFITS—MAKE OR BUY?

With health care insurance premiums rising by over 10% per year, companies have been searching for ways to reduce the costs of providing health care to their employees. Some companies have adopted the unconventional approach of providing health care services in-house. Quad/Graphics, a printing company with 14,000 employees, hired its own doctors and nurses to provide primary health care on-site. By "making" its own health care for employees rather than "buying" it through the purchase of insurance, the company claims that its health care costs have risen just 6% annually and that their spending on health care is now 17% less than the industry average.

Source: Kimberly Weisul, "There's a Doctor in the House," *BusinessWeek*, December 16, 2002, p. 8

Strategic Aspects of the Make or Buy Decision

Vertical integration provides certain advantages. An integrated company is less dependent on its suppliers and may be able to ensure a smoother flow of parts and materials for production than a nonintegrated company. For example, a strike against a major parts supplier can interrupt the operations of a nonintegrated company for many months, whereas an integrated company that is producing its own parts would be able to continue operations. Also, some companies feel that they can control quality better by producing their own parts and materials, rather than by relying on the quality control standards of outside suppliers. In addition, an integrated company realizes profits from the parts and materials that it is "making" rather than "buying," as well as profits from its regular operations.

The advantages of vertical integration are counterbalanced by the advantages of using external suppliers. By pooling demand from a number of companies, a supplier may be able to enjoy economies of scale. These economies of scale can result in higher quality and lower costs than would be possible if the company were to attempt to make the parts or provide the service on its own. A company must be careful, however, to retain control over activities that are essential to maintaining its competitive position. For example, Hewlett-Packard controls the software for laser printers that it makes in cooperation with Canon Inc. of Japan. The present trend appears to be toward less vertical integration, with companies like Sun Microsystems and Hewlett-Packard concentrating on hardware and software design and relying on outside suppliers for almost everything else in the value chain. These factors suggest that the make or buy decision should be weighed very carefully.

An Example of Make or Buy

To provide an illustration of a make or buy decision, consider Mountain Goat Cycles. The company is now producing the heavy-duty gear shifters used in its most popular line of mountain bikes. The company's Accounting Department reports the following costs of producing 8,000 units of the shifter internally each year:

	Per Unit	8,000 Units
Direct materials	$ 6	$ 48,000
Direct labor	4	32,000
Variable overhead	1	8,000
Supervisor's salary	3	24,000
Depreciation of special equipment	2	16,000
Allocated general overhead	5	40,000
Total cost	$21	$168,000

An outside supplier has offered to sell 8,000 shifters a year to Mountain Goat Cycles at a price of only $19 each. Should the company stop producing the shifters internally and buy them from the outside supplier? As always, the focus should be on the relevant costs—those that differ between the alternatives. And the costs that differ between the alternatives consist of the costs that could be avoided by purchasing the shifters from the outside supplier. If the costs that can be avoided by purchasing the shifters from the outside supplier total less than $19, then the company should continue to manufacture its own shifters and reject the outside supplier's offer. On the other hand, if the costs that can be avoided by purchasing the shifters from the outside supplier total more than $19, the outside supplier's offer should be accepted.

Note that depreciation of special equipment is listed as one of the costs of producing the shifters internally. Since the equipment has already been purchased, this depreciation is a sunk cost and is therefore irrelevant. If the equipment could be sold, its salvage value would be relevant. Or if the machine could be used to make other products, this could be relevant as well. However, we will assume that the equipment has no salvage value and that it has no other use except making the heavy-duty gear shifters.

Also note that the company is allocating a portion of its general overhead costs to the shifters. Any portion of this general overhead cost that would actually be eliminated if the gear shifters were purchased rather than made would be relevant in the analysis. However, it is likely that the general overhead costs allocated to the gear shifters are in fact common to all items produced in the factory and would continue unchanged even if the shifters were purchased from the outside. Such allocated common costs are not relevant costs (since they do not differ between the make or buy alternatives) and should be eliminated from the analysis along with the sunk costs.

The variable costs of producing the shifters can be avoided by buying the shifters from the outside supplier so they are relevant costs. We will assume in this case that the variable costs include direct materials, direct labor, and variable overhead. The supervisor's salary is also relevant if it could be avoided by buying the shifters. Exhibit 12–5 contains the relevant

EXHIBIT 12–5
Mountain Goat Cycles Make or Buy Analysis

	Total Relevant Costs—8,000 units	
	Make	Buy
Direct materials (8,000 units @ $6 per unit)	$ 48,000	
Direct labor (8,000 units @ $4 per unit)	32,000	
Variable overhead (8,000 units @ $1 per unit)	8,000	
Supervisor's salary	24,000	
Depreciation of special equipment (not relevant)		
Allocated general overhead (not relevant)		
Outside purchase price		$152,000
Total cost	$112,000	$152,000
Difference in favor of continuing to make	$40,000	

cost analysis of the make or buy decision assuming that the supervisor's salary can indeed be avoided.

Since it costs $40,000 less to make the shifters internally than to buy them from the outside supplier, Mountain Goat Cycles should reject the outside supplier's offer. However, the company may wish to consider one additional factor before coming to a final decision—the opportunity cost of the space now being used to produce the shifters.

IN BUSINESS

OUTSOURCING R&D

A few years ago many experts felt that U.S. companies were unlikely to outsource their research and development (R&D) activities to lower labor cost Asian countries. However, these experts were wrong. Companies such as Procter & Gamble, Boeing, Dell, Eli Lilly, and Motorola are increasingly relying on Asian business partners to meet their R&D needs. In fact, research shows that U.S. technology companies outsource 70% of their personal digital assistant (PDA) designs, 65% of their notebook personal computer designs, and 30% of their digital camera designs.

Allen J. Delattre, head of Accenture's high-tech consulting practice, says "R&D is the single remaining controllable expense to work on. Companies either will have to cut costs or increase R&D productivity." In light of this stark reality, most Western companies are creating a global model of innovation that leverages the skills of Indian software developers, Taiwanese engineers, and Chinese factories. The lower labor rates available in these countries coupled with their strong technology orientation makes "buying" R&D capability from overseas more attractive to U.S. companies than relying solely on their domestic workforce to "make" R&D breakthroughs.

Source: Pete Engardio and Bruce Einhorn, "Outsourcing Innovation," *BusinessWeek*, March 21, 2005, pp. 82–94.

Opportunity Cost

If the space now being used to produce the shifters *would otherwise be idle,* then Mountain Goat Cycles should continue to produce its own shifters and the supplier's offer should be rejected, as stated above. Idle space that has no alternative use has an opportunity cost of zero.

But what if the space now being used to produce shifters could be used for some other purpose? In that case, the space would have an opportunity cost equal to the segment margin that could be derived from the best alternative use of the space.

To illustrate, assume that the space now being used to produce shifters could be used to produce a new cross-country bike that would generate a segment margin of $60,000 per year. Under these conditions, Mountain Goat Cycles should accept the supplier's offer and use the available space to produce the new product line:

	Make	Buy
Total annual cost (see Exhibit 12–5)	$112,000	$152,000
Opportunity cost—segment margin forgone on a potential new product line	60,000	
Total cost	$172,000	$152,000
Difference in favor of purchasing from the outside supplier.	$20,000	

Opportunity costs are not recorded in the organization's general ledger because they do not represent actual dollar outlays. Rather, they represent economic benefits that are *forgone* as a result of pursuing some course of action. The opportunity cost for Mountain Goat Cycles is sufficiently large in this case to change the decision.

IN BUSINESS

TOUGH CHOICES

Brad and Carole Karafil own and operate White Grizzly Adventures, a snowcat skiing and snowboarding company in Meadow Creek, British Columbia. While rare, it does sometimes happen that the company is unable to operate due to bad weather. Guests are housed and fed, but no one can ski. The contract signed by each guest stipulates that no refund is given in the case of an unavoidable cancellation that is beyond the control of the operators. So technically, Brad and Carole are not obligated to provide any refund if they must cancel operations due to bad weather. However, 70% of their guests are repeat customers and a guest who has paid roughly $300 a day to ski is likely to be unhappy if skiing is cancelled even though it is no fault of White Grizzly.

What costs, if any, are saved if skiing is cancelled and the snowcat does not operate? Not much. Guests are still housed and fed and the guides, who are independent contractors, are still paid. Some snowcat operating costs are avoided, but little else. Therefore, there would be little cost savings to pass on to guests.

Brad and Carole could issue a credit to be used for one day of skiing at another time. If a customer with such a credit occupied a seat on a snowcat that would otherwise be empty, the only significant cost to Brad and Carole would be the cost of feeding the customer. However, an empty seat basically doesn't exist—the demand for seats far exceeds the supply and the schedule is generally fully booked far in advance of the ski season. Consequently, the real cost of issuing a credit for one day of skiing is high. Brad and Carole would be giving up $300 from a paying customer for every guest they issue a credit voucher to. Issuing a credit voucher involves an opportunity cost of $300 in forgone sales revenues.

What would you do if you had to cancel skiing due to bad weather? Would you issue a refund or a credit voucher, losing money in the process, or would you risk losing customers? It's a tough choice.

Source: Brad and Carole Karafil, owners and operators of White Grizzly Adventures, www.whitegrizzly.com.

Special Orders

LEARNING OBJECTIVE 4
Prepare an analysis showing whether a special order should be accepted.

Managers must often evaluate whether a *special order* should be accepted, and if the order is accepted, the price that should be charged. A **special order** is a one-time order that is not considered part of the company's normal ongoing business. To illustrate, Mountain Goat Cycles has just received a request from the Seattle Police Department to produce 100 specially modified mountain bikes at a price of $279 each. The bikes would be used to patrol some of the more densely populated residential sections of the city. Mountain Goat Cycles can easily modify its City Cruiser model to fit the specifications of the Seattle Police. The normal selling price of the City Cruiser bike is $349, and its unit product cost is $282 as shown below:

Direct materials	$186
Direct labor	45
Manufacturing overhead	51
Unit product cost	$282

The variable portion of the above manufacturing overhead is $6 per unit. The order would have no effect on the company's total fixed manufacturing overhead costs.

The modifications requested by the Seattle Police Department consist of welded brackets to hold radios, nightsticks, and other gear. These modifications would require $17 in incremental variable costs. In addition, the company would have to pay a graphics design studio $1,200 to design and cut stencils that would be used for spray painting the Seattle Police Department's logo and other identifying marks on the bikes.

This order should have no effect on the company's other sales. The production manager says that she can handle the special order without disrupting any of the company's regular scheduled production.

What effect would accepting this order have on the company's net operating income?

Only the incremental costs and benefits are relevant. Since the existing fixed manufacturing overhead costs would not be affected by the order, they are not relevant. The incremental net operating income can be computed as follows:

	Per Unit	Total 100 Bikes
Incremental revenue	$279	$27,900
Less incremental costs:		
Variable costs:		
Direct materials	186	18,600
Direct labor	45	4,500
Variable manufacturing overhead	6	600
Special modifications	17	1,700
Total variable cost	$254	25,400
Fixed cost:		
Purchase of stencils		1,200
Total incremental cost		26,600
Incremental net operating income		$ 1,300

Therefore, even though the $279 price on the special order is below the normal $282 unit product cost and the order would require additional costs, the order would increase net operating income. In general, a special order is profitable if the incremental revenue from the special order exceeds the incremental costs of the order. However, it is important to make sure that there is indeed idle capacity and that the special order does not cut into normal unit sales or undercut prices on normal sales. For example, if the company was operating at capacity, opportunity costs would have to be taken into account as well as the incremental costs that have already been detailed above.

IN BUSINESS

FLY THE FRIENDLY AISLES

Shoppers at Safeway can now earn United Airlines frequent flier miles when they buy their groceries. Airlines charge marketing partners such as Safeway about 2¢ per mile. Since airlines typically require 25,000 frequent flier miles for a domestic round-trip ticket, United is earning about $500 per frequent-flier ticket issued to Safeway customers. This income to United is higher than many discounted fares. Moreover, United carefully manages its frequent flier program so that few frequent flier passengers displace regular fare-paying customers. The only incremental costs of adding a frequent flier passenger to a flight may be food, a little extra fuel, and some administrative costs. All of the other costs of the flight would be incurred anyway. Thus, the miles that United sells to Safeway are almost pure profit.

Source: Wendy Zellner, *BusinessWeek*, March 6, 2000, pp. 152–154.

Utilization of a Constrained Resource

LEARNING OBJECTIVE 5
Determine the most profitable use of a constrained resource and the value of obtaining more of the constrained resource.

Managers routinely face the problem of deciding how constrained resources are going to be used. A department store, for example, has a limited amount of floor space and therefore cannot stock every product that may be available. A manufacturer has a limited number of machine-hours and a limited number of direct labor-hours at its disposal. When a limited resource of some type restricts the company's ability to satisfy demand, the company has a **constraint.** Since the company cannot fully satisfy demand, managers must decide which products or services should be cut back. In other words, managers must decide which products or services make the best use of the constrained resource. Fixed costs are usually unaffected by such choices, so the course of action that will maximize the company's total contribution margin should ordinarily be selected.

Contribution Margin per Unit of the Constrained Resource

If some products must be cut back because of a constraint, the key to maximizing the total contribution margin may seem obvious—favor the products with the highest unit contribution margins. Unfortunately, that is not quite correct. Rather, the correct solution is to favor the products that provide the highest *contribution margin per unit of the constrained resource.* To illustrate, in addition to its other products, Mountain Goat Cycles makes saddlebags for bicycles called *panniers.* These panniers come in two models—a touring model and a mountain model. Cost and revenue data for the two models of panniers follow:

	Mountain Pannier	Touring Pannier
Selling price per unit	$25	$30
Variable cost per unit	10	18
Contribution margin per unit	$15	$12
Contribution margin (CM) ratio	60%	40%

The mountain pannier appears to be much more profitable than the touring pannier. It has a $15 per unit contribution margin as compared to only $12 per unit for the touring model, and it has a 60% CM ratio as compared to only 40% for the touring model.

But now let us add one more piece of information—the plant that makes the panniers is operating at capacity. This does not mean that every machine and every person in the plant is working at the maximum possible rate. Because machines have different capacities, some machines will be operating at less than 100% of capacity. However, if the plant as a whole cannot produce any more units, some machine or process must be operating at capacity. The machine or process that is limiting overall output is called the **bottleneck**—it is the constraint.

At Mountain Goat Cycles, the bottleneck (i.e., constraint) is a stitching machine. The mountain pannier requires two minutes of stitching time per unit, and the touring pannier requires one minute of stitching time per unit. By definition, since the stitching machine is a bottleneck, the stitching machine does not have enough capacity to satisfy the existing demand for mountain panniers and touring panniers Therefore, some orders for the products will have to be turned down. Naturally, managers will want to know which product is less profitable. To answer this question, they should focus on the contribution margin per unit of the constrained resource. This figure is computed by dividing a product's contribution margin per unit by the amount of the constrained resource required to make a unit of that product. These calculations are carried out below for the mountain and touring panniers:

	Mountain Pannier	Touring Pannier
Contribution margin per unit (a)	$15.00	$12.00
Stitching machine time required to produce one unit (b)	2 minutes	1 minute
Contribution margin per unit of the constrained resource, (a) ÷ (b)	$7.50 per minute	$12.00 per minute

It is now easy to decide which product is less profitable and should be deemphasized. Each minute on the stitching machine that is devoted to the touring pannier results in an increase of $12.00 in contribution margin and profits. The comparable figure for the mountain pannier is only $7.50 per minute. Therefore, the touring model should be emphasized. Even though the mountain model has the larger contribution margin per unit and the larger CM ratio, the touring model provides the larger contribution margin in relation to the constrained resource.

To verify that the touring model is indeed the more profitable product, suppose an hour of additional stitching time is available and that unfilled orders exist for both products. The additional hour on the stitching machine could be used to make either 30 mountain panniers (60 minutes ÷ 2 minutes per mountain pannier) or 60 touring panniers (60 minutes ÷ 1 minute per touring pannier), with the following profit implications:

	Mountain Pannier	Touring Pannier
Contribution margin per unit	$ 15	$ 12
Additional units that can be processed in one hour	× 30	× 60
Additional contribution margin	$450	$720

Since the additional contribution margin would be $720 for the touring panniers and only $450 for the mountain panniers, the touring panniers make the most profitable use of the company's constrained resource—the stitching machine.

This example clearly shows that looking at unit contribution margins alone is not enough; the contribution margin must be viewed in relation to the amount of the constrained resource each product requires.

IN BUSINESS

THEORY OF CONSTRAINTS SOFTWARE

Indalex Aluminum Solutions Group is the largest producer of soft alloy extrusions in North America. The company has installed a new generation of business intelligence software created by pVelocity, Inc., of Toronto, Canada. The software "provides decision makers across our entire manufacturing enterprise with time-based financial metrics using TOC concepts to identify bottlenecks." And, it "shifts the focus of a manufacturing company from traditional cost accounting measurements to measuring the generation of dollars per unit of time." For example, instead of emphasizing products with the largest gross margins or contribution margins, the software helps managers to identify and emphasize the products that maximize the contribution margin per unit of the constrained resource.

Source: Mike Alger, "Managing a Business as a Portfolio of Customers," *Strategic Finance,* June 2003, pp. 54–57.

Managing Constraints

Effectively managing an organization's constraints is a key to increased profits. Effective management of a bottleneck constraint involves selecting the most profitable product mix and finding ways to increase the capacity of the bottleneck operation. As discussed above, if the constraint is a bottleneck in the production process, the most profitable product mix consists of the products with the highest contribution margin per unit of the constrained resource. In addition, as discussed below, increasing the capacity of the bottleneck operation should lead to increased production and sales. Such efforts will often pay off in an almost immediate increase in profits.

It is often possible for a manager to increase the capacity of the bottleneck, which is called **relaxing (or elevating) the constraint.** For example, the stitching machine operator could be asked to work overtime. This would result in more available stitching time and hence the production of more finished goods that can be sold. The benefits from relaxing the constraint are often enormous and can be easily quantified. The manager should first ask, "What would I do with additional capacity at the bottleneck if it were available?" In our example, if unfilled orders exist for both the touring and mountain panniers, the additional capacity would be used to process more touring panniers, since they earn a contribution margin of $12 per minute, or $720 per hour. Given that the overtime pay for the operator is likely to be much less than $720 per hour, running the stitching machine on overtime would be an excellent way to increase the company's profits while at the same time satisfying more customers.

To reinforce this concept, suppose that there are only unfilled orders for the mountain pannier. How much would it be worth to the company to run the stitching machine overtime in this situation? Since the additional capacity would be used to make the mountain pannier, the value of that additional capacity would drop to $7.50 per minute or $450 per hour. Nevertheless, the value of relaxing the constraint would still be quite high.

These calculations indicate that managers should pay great attention to the bottleneck operation. If a bottleneck machine breaks down or is ineffectively utilized, the losses to the company can be quite large. In our example, for every minute the stitching machine is down due to breakdowns or setups, the company loses between $7.50 and $12.00.[2] The losses on an hourly basis are between $450 and $720! In contrast, there is no such loss of contribution margin if time is lost on a machine that is not a bottleneck—such machines have excess capacity anyway.

The implications are clear. Managers should focus much of their attention on managing the bottleneck. As we have discussed, managers should emphasize products that most profitably utilize the constrained resource. They should also make sure that products are processed smoothly through the bottleneck, with minimal lost time due to breakdowns and setups. And they should try to find ways to increase the capacity at the bottleneck.

The capacity of a bottleneck can be effectively increased in a number of ways, including:

- Working overtime on the bottleneck.
- Subcontracting some of the processing that would be done at the bottleneck.
- Investing in additional machines at the bottleneck.
- Shifting workers from processes that are not bottlenecks to the process that is the bottleneck.
- Focusing business process improvement efforts such as Six Sigma on the bottleneck.
- Reducing defective units. Each defective unit that is processed through the bottleneck and subsequently scrapped takes the place of a good unit that could have been sold.

The last three methods of increasing the capacity of the bottleneck are particularly attractive because they are essentially free and may even yield additional cost savings.

---

[2] Setups are required when production switches from one product to another. For example, consider a company that makes automobile side panels. The panels are painted before shipping them to an automobile manufacturer for final assembly. The customer might require 100 blue panels, 50 black panels, and 20 yellow panels. Each time the color is changed, the painting equipment must be purged of the old paint color, cleaned with solvents, and refilled with the new paint color. This takes time. In fact, some equipment may require such lengthy and frequent setups that it is unavailable for actual production more often than not.

The methods and ideas discussed in this section are all part of the Theory of Constraints, which was introduced in Chapter 1. A number of organizations have successfully used the Theory of Constraints to improve their performance, including Avery Dennison, Bethlehem Steel, Binney & Smith, Boeing, Champion International, Ford Motor Company, General Motors, ITT, Monster Cable, National Semiconductor, Pratt and Whitney Canada, Pretoria Academic Hospital, Procter and Gamble, Texas Instruments, United Airlines, United Electrical Controls, United States Air Force Logistics Command, and United States Navy Transportation Corps.

IN BUSINESS

ELEVATING A CONSTRAINT

The Odessa Texas Police Department was having trouble hiring new employees. Its eight-step hiring process was taking 117 days to complete and the best-qualified job applicants were accepting other employment offers before the Odessa Police Department could finish evaluating their candidacy. The constraint in the eight-step hiring process was the background investigation that required an average of 104 days. The other seven steps—filling out an application and completing a written exam, an oral interview, a polygraph exam, a medical exam, a psychological exam, and a drug screen—took a combined total of only 13 days. The Odessa Police Department elevated its constraint by hiring additional background checkers. This resulted in slashing its application processing time from 117 days to 16 days.

Source: Lloyd J. Taylor III, Brian J. Moersch, and Geralyn McClure Franklin, "Applying the Theory of Constraints to a Public Safety Hiring Process," *Public Personnel Management,* Fall 2003, pp. 367–382.

The Problem of Multiple Constraints

What does a company do if it has more than one potential constraint? For example, a company may have limited raw materials, limited direct labor-hours available, limited floor space, and limited advertising dollars to spend on product promotion. How would it determine the right combination of products to produce? The proper combination or "mix" of products can be found by use of a quantitative method known as *linear programming,* which is covered in quantitative methods and operations management courses.

Joint Product Costs and the Contribution Approach

LEARNING OBJECTIVE 6
Prepare an analysis showing whether joint products should be sold at the split-off point or processed further.

In some industries, a number of end products are produced from a single raw material input. For example, in the petroleum refining industry a large number of products are extracted from crude oil, including gasoline, jet fuel, home heating oil, lubricants, asphalt, and various organic chemicals. Another example is provided by the Santa Maria Wool Cooperative of New Mexico. The company buys raw wool from local sheepherders, separates the wool into three grades—coarse, fine, and superfine—and then dyes the wool using traditional methods that rely on pigments from local materials. Exhibit 12–6 on page 520 contains a diagram of the production process.

At Santa Maria Wool Cooperative, coarse wool, fine wool, and superfine wool are produced from one input—raw wool. Two or more products that are produced from a common input are known as **joint products.** The **split-off point** is the point in the manufacturing process at which the joint products can be recognized as separate products. This does not occur at Santa Maria Cooperative until the raw wool has gone through the separating process. The term **joint cost** is used to describe the costs incurred up to the split-off point. At Santa Maria Wool Cooperative, the joint costs are the $200,000 cost of the raw wool and the $40,000 cost of separating the wool. The undyed wool is called an *intermediate product*

EXHIBIT 12–6
Santa Maria Wool Cooperative

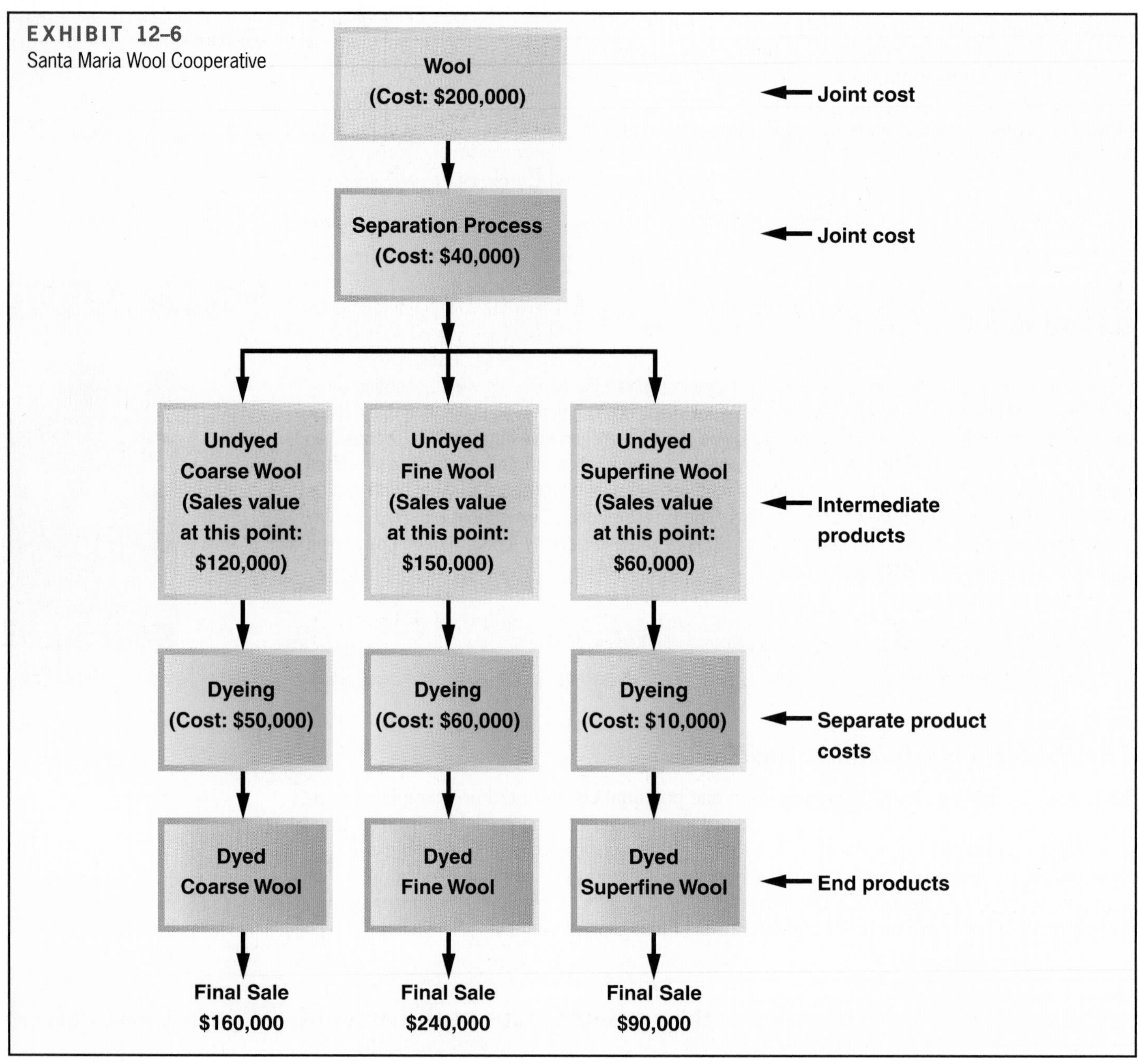

because it is not finished at this point. Nevertheless, a market does exist for undyed wool—although at a significantly lower price than finished, dyed wool.

The Pitfalls of Allocation

Joint costs are common costs that are incurred to simultaneously produce a variety of end products. These joint costs are traditionally allocated among the different products at the split-off point. A typical approach is to allocate the joint costs according to the relative sales value of the end products.

Although allocation of joint product costs is needed for some purposes, such as balance sheet inventory valuation, allocations of this kind are extremely misleading for decision making. The In Business box "Getting It All Wrong" on page 599 illustrates an incorrect decision that resulted from using such an allocated joint cost. You should stop now and read that box before proceeding further.

IN BUSINESS

GETTING IT ALL WRONG

A company located on the Gulf of Mexico produces soap products. Its six main soap product lines are produced from common inputs. Joint product costs up to the split-off point constitute the bulk of the production costs for all six product lines. These joint product costs are allocated to the six product lines on the basis of the relative sales value of each line at the split-off point.

A waste product results from the production of the six main product lines. The company loaded the waste onto barges and dumped it into the Gulf of Mexico, since the waste was thought to have no commercial value. The dumping was stopped, however, when the company's research division discovered that with some further processing the waste could be sold as a fertilizer ingredient. The further processing costs $175,000 per year. The waste was then sold to fertilizer manufacturers for $300,000.

The accountants responsible for allocating manufacturing costs included the sales value of the waste product along with the sales value of the six main product lines in their allocation of the joint product costs at the split-off point. This allocation resulted in the waste product being allocated $150,000 in joint product cost. This $150,000 allocation, when added to the further processing costs of $175,000 for the waste, made it appear that the waste product was unprofitable—as shown in the table below. When presented with this analysis, the company's management decided that further processing of the waste should be stopped. The company went back to dumping the waste in the Gulf.

Sales value of the waste product after further processing	$300,000
Less costs assignable to the waste product	325,000
Net loss	$ (25,000)

Sell or Process Further Decisions

Joint costs are irrelevant in decisions regarding what to do with a product from the split-off point forward. Once the split-off point is reached, the joint costs have already been incurred and nothing can be done to avoid them. Furthermore, even if the product were disposed of in a landfill without any further processing, all of the joint costs must be incurred to obtain the other products that come out of the joint process. None of the joint costs are avoidable by disposing of any one of the products that emerge from the split-off point. Therefore, none of the joint costs are economically attributable to any one of the intermediate or end products. The joint costs are a common cost of all of the intermediate and end products and should not be allocated to them for purposes of making decisions about the individual products. In the case of the soap company in the accompanying In Business box "Getting It All Wrong," the $150,000 in allocated joint costs should not have been permitted to influence what was done with the waste product from the split-off point forward. Even ignoring the negative environmental impact of dumping the waste in the Gulf of Mexico, a correct analysis would have shown that the company was making money by further processing the waste into a fertilizer ingredient. The analysis should have been done as follows:

	Dump in Gulf	Process Further
Sales value of fertilizer ingredient	0	$300,000
Additional processing costs	0	175,000
Contribution margin	0	$125,000
Advantage of processing further	$125,000	

Decisions of this type are known as **sell or process further decisions.** It is profitable to continue processing a joint product after the split-off point *so long as the incremental revenue from such processing exceeds the incremental processing cost incurred after the split-off point.* Joint costs that have already been incurred up to the split-off point are always irrelevant in decisions concerning what to do from the split-off point forward.

To provide a detailed example of the sell or process further decision, return to the data for Santa Maria Wool Cooperative in Exhibit 12–6. We can answer several important questions using this data. First, is the company making money if it runs the entire process from beginning to end? Assuming there are no costs other than those displayed in Exhibit 12–6, the company is indeed making money as follows:

Analysis of the profitability of the overall operation:		
Combined final sales value		
($160,000 + $240,000 + $90,000)		$490,000
Less costs of producing the end products:		
Cost of wool	$200,000	
Cost of separating wool	40,000	
Combined costs of dyeing		
($50,000 + $60,000 + $10,000)	120,000	360,000
Profit		$130,000

Note that the joint costs of buying the wool and separating the wool *are* relevant when considering the profitability of the entire operation. This is because these joint costs *could* be avoided if the entire operation were shut down. However, these joint costs are *not* relevant when considering the profitability of any one product. As long as the process is being run to make the other products, no additional joint costs are incurred to make the specific product in question.

Even though the company is making money overall, it may be losing money on one or more of the products. If the company buys wool and runs the separation process, it will get all three intermediate products. Nothing can be done about that. However, each of these products can be sold *as is* without further processing. It may be that the company would be better off selling one or more of the products prior to dyeing to avoid the dyeing costs. The appropriate way to make this choice is to compare the incremental revenues to the incremental costs from further processing as follows:

Analysis of sell or process further:	Coarse Wool	Fine Wool	Superfine Wool
Final sales value after further processing	$160,000	$240,000	$90,000
Less sales value at the split-off point	120,000	150,000	60,000
Incremental revenue from further processing	40,000	90,000	30,000
Less cost of further processing (dyeing)	50,000	60,000	10,000
Profit (loss) from further processing	$ (10,000)	$ 30,000	$20,000

As this analysis shows, the company would be better off selling the undyed coarse wool as is rather than processing it further. The other two products should be processed further and dyed before selling them.

Note that the joint costs of the wool ($200,000) and of the wool separation process ($40,000) play no role in the decision to sell or further process the intermediate products. These joint costs are relevant in a decision of whether to buy wool and to run the wool separation process, but they are not relevant in decisions about what to do with the intermediate products once they have been separated.

Activity-Based Costing and Relevant Costs

As discussed in Chapter 7, activity-based costing can be used to help identify potentially relevant costs for decision-making purposes. Activity-based costing improves the traceability of costs by focusing on the activities caused by a product or other segment. However, managers should exercise caution against reading more into this "traceability" than really exists. People have a tendency to assume that if a cost is traceable to a segment, then the cost is automatically an avoidable cost. That is not true. As emphasized in Chapter 7, the costs provided by a well-designed activity-based costing system are only *potentially* relevant. Before making a decision, managers must still decide which of the potentially relevant costs are actually avoidable. Only those costs that are avoidable are relevant and the others should be ignored.

To illustrate, refer again to the data relating to the housewares line in Exhibit 12–4. The $2,000 fixtures depreciation is a traceable cost of the housewares lines because it directly relates to activities in that department. We found, however, that the $2,000 is not avoidable if the housewares line is dropped. The key lesson here is that the method used to assign a cost to a product or other segment does not change the basic nature of the cost. A sunk cost such as depreciation of old equipment is still a sunk cost regardless of whether it is traced directly to a particular segment on an activity basis, allocated to all segments on the basis of labor-hours, or treated in some other way in the costing process. Regardless of the method used to assign costs to products or other segments, the principles discussed in this chapter must be applied to determine the costs that are avoidable in each situation.

Summary

Everything in this chapter consists of applications of one simple but powerful idea. Only those costs and benefits that differ between alternatives are relevant in a decision. All other costs and benefits are irrelevant and should be ignored. In particular, sunk costs are irrelevant as are future costs that do not differ between alternatives.

This simple idea was applied in a variety of situations including decisions that involve making or buying a component, adding or dropping a product line, accepting or rejecting a special order, processing a joint product further, and using a constrained resource. This list includes only a small sample of the possible applications of the relevant cost concept. Indeed, any decision involving costs hinges on the proper identification and analysis of the costs that are relevant. We will continue to focus on the concept of relevant costs in the following chapter where long-run investment decisions are considered.

Review Problem: Relevant Costs

Charter Sports Equipment manufactures round, rectangular, and octagonal trampolines. Sales and expense data for the past month follow:

		Trampoline		
	Total	Round	Rectangular	Octagonal
Sales	$1,000,000	$140,000	$500,000	$360,000
Variable expenses	410,000	60,000	200,000	150,000
Contribution margin	590,000	80,000	300,000	210,000
Fixed expenses:				
Advertising—traceable	216,000	41,000	110,000	65,000
Depreciation of special equipment	95,000	20,000	40,000	35,000
Line supervisors' salaries	19,000	6,000	7,000	6,000
General factory overhead*	200,000	28,000	100,000	72,000
Total fixed expenses	530,000	95,000	257,000	178,000
Net operating income (loss)	$ 60,000	$ (15,000)	$ 43,000	$ 32,000

*A common fixed cost that is allocated on the basis of sales dollars.

Management is concerned about the continued losses shown by the round trampolines and wants a recommendation as to whether or not the line should be discontinued. The special equipment used to produce the trampolines has no resale value. If the round trampoline model is dropped, the two line supervisors assigned to the model would be discharged.

Required:

1. Should production and sale of the round trampolines be discontinued? The company has no other use for the capacity now being used to produce the round trampolines. Show computations to support your answer.
2. Recast the above data in a format that would be more useful to management in assessing the profitability of the various product lines.

Solution to Review Problem

1. No, production and sale of the round trampolines should not be discontinued. Computations to support this answer follow:

Contribution margin lost if the round trampolines are discontinued		$(80,000)
Less fixed costs that can be avoided:		
Advertising—traceable	$41,000	
Line supervisors' salaries	6,000	47,000
Decrease in net operating income for the company as a whole		$(33,000)

The depreciation of the special equipment represents a sunk cost, and therefore it is not relevant to the decision. The general factory overhead is allocated and will presumably continue regardless of whether or not the round trampolines are discontinued; thus, it is not relevant.

2. If management wants a clearer picture of the profitability of the segments, the general factory overhead should not be allocated. It is a common cost and therefore should be deducted from the total product-line segment margin, as shown in Chapter 11. A more useful income statement format would be as follows:

		Trampoline		
	Total	Round	Rectangular	Octagonal
Sales	$1,000,000	$140,000	$500,000	$360,000
Variable expenses	410,000	60,000	200,000	150,000
Contribution margin	590,000	80,000	300,000	210,000
Traceable fixed expenses:				
Advertising—traceable	216,000	41,000	110,000	65,000
Depreciation of special equipment	95,000	20,000	40,000	35,000
Line supervisors' salaries	19,000	6,000	7,000	6,000
Total traceable fixed expenses..........	330,000	67,000	157,000	106,000
Product-line segment margin	260,000	$ 13,000	$143,000	$104,000
Common fixed expenses	200,000			
Net operating income (loss)	$ 60,000			

Glossary

Avoidable cost A cost that can be eliminated (in whole or in part) by choosing one alternative over another in a decision. This term is synonymous with *relevant cost* and *differential cost.* (p. 500)

Bottleneck A machine or some other part of a process that limits the total output of the entire system. (p. 516)

Constraint A limitation under which a company must operate, such as limited available machine time or raw materials, that restricts the company's ability to satisfy demand. (p. 516)

Differential cost Any cost that differs between alternatives in a decision-making situation. This term is synonymous with *avoidable cost* and *relevant cost.* (p. 501)

Joint costs Costs that are incurred up to the split-off point in a process that produces joint products. (p. 519)

Joint products Two or more products that are produced from a common input. (p. 519)

Make or buy decision A decision concerning whether an item should be produced internally or purchased from an outside supplier. (p. 511)

Relaxing (or elevating) the constraint An action that increases the amount of a constrained resource. Equivalently, an action that increases the capacity of the bottleneck. (p. 518)

Relevant cost A cost that differs between alternatives in a decision. This term is synonymous with *avoidable cost* and *differential cost.* (p. 500)

Sell or process further decision A decision as to whether a joint product should be sold at the split-off point or sold after further processing. (p. 522)

Special order A one-time order that is not considered part of the company's normal ongoing business. (p. 514)

Split-off point That point in the manufacturing process where some or all of the joint products can be recognized as individual products. (p. 519)

Sunk cost Any cost that has already been incurred and that cannot be changed by any decision made now or in the future. (p. 500)

Vertical integration The involvement by a company in more than one of the activities in the entire value chain from development through production, distribution, sales, and after-sales service. (p. 510)

Quiz 12

Multiple-choice questions are provided on the text website at www.mhhe.com/noreen1e.

Questions

12-1 What is a *relevant cost?*

12-2 Define the following terms: *incremental cost, opportunity cost,* and *sunk cost.*

12-3 Are variable costs always relevant costs? Explain.

12-4 "Sunk costs are easy to spot—they're simply the fixed costs associated with a decision." Do you agree? Explain.

12-5 "Variable costs and differential costs mean the same thing." Do you agree? Explain.

12-6 "All future costs are relevant in decision making." Do you agree? Why?

12-7 Prentice Company is considering dropping one of its product lines. What costs of the product line would be relevant to this decision? Irrelevant?

12-8 "If a product line is generating a loss, then it should be discontinued." Do you agree? Explain.

12-9 What is the danger in allocating common fixed costs among product lines or other segments of an organization?

12-10 How does opportunity cost enter into the make or buy decision?

12-11 Give at least four examples of possible constraints.

12-12 How will relating product contribution margins to the amount of the constrained resource they consume help a company maximize its profits?

12-13 Define the following terms: *joint products, joint costs,* and *split-off point.*

12-14 From a decision-making point of view, should joint costs be allocated among joint products?

12-15 What guideline should be used in determining whether a joint product should be sold at the split-off point or processed further?

12-16 Airlines sometimes offer reduced rates during certain times of the week to members of a businessperson's family if they accompany him or her on trips. How does the concept of relevant costs enter into the decision by the airline to offer reduced rates of this type?

Exercises

EXERCISE 12-1 Identifying Relevant Costs [LO1]

A number of costs are listed on the next page that may be relevant in decisions faced by the management of Poulsen & Sonner A/S, a Danish furniture manufacturer:

Item	Case 1 Relevant	Case 1 Not Relevant	Case 2 Relevant	Case 2 Not Relevant
a. Sales revenue				
b. Direct materials				
c. Direct labor				
d. Variable manufacturing overhead				
e. Book value—Model A3000 machine				
f. Disposal value—Model A3000 machine				
g. Depreciation—Model A3000 machine				
h. Market value—Model B3800 machine (cost)				
i. Fixed manufacturing overhead (general)				
j. Variable selling expense				
k. Fixed selling expense				
l. General administrative overhead				

Required:

Copy the information above onto your answer sheet and place an X in the appropriate column to indicate whether each item is relevant or not relevant in the following situations. Requirement 1 relates to Case 1 above, and requirement 2 relates to Case 2. Consider the two cases independently.

1. The company chronically runs at capacity and the old Model A3000 machine is the company's constraint. Management is considering the purchase of a new Model B3800 machine to use in addition to the company's present Model A3000 machine. The old Model A3000 machine will continue to be used to capacity as before, with the new Model B3800 being used to expand production. The increase in volume will be large enough to require increases in fixed selling expenses and in general administrative overhead, but not in the general fixed manufacturing overhead.
2. The old Model A3000 machine is not the company's constraint, but management is considering replacing it with a new Model B3800 machine because of the potential savings in direct materials cost with the new machine. The Model A3000 machine would be sold. This change will have no effect on production or sales, other than some savings in direct materials costs due to less waste.

EXERCISE 12-2 Dropping or Retaining a Segment [LO2]

Jackson County Senior Services is a nonprofit organization devoted to providing essential services to seniors who live in their own homes within the Jackson County area. Three services are provided for seniors—home nursing, meals on wheels, and housekeeping. In the home nursing program, nurses visit seniors on a regular basis to check on their general health and to perform tests ordered by their physicians. The meals on wheels program delivers a hot meal once a day to each senior enrolled in the program. The housekeeping service provides weekly housecleaning and maintenance services. Data on revenue and expenses for the past year follow:

	Total	Home Nursing	Meals on Wheels	House-keeping
Revenues	$900,000	$260,000	$400,000	$240,000
Variable expenses	490,000	120,000	210,000	160,000
Contribution margin	410,000	140,000	190,000	80,000
Fixed expenses:				
Depreciation	68,000	8,000	40,000	20,000
Liability insurance	42,000	20,000	7,000	15,000
Program administrators' salaries	115,000	40,000	38,000	37,000
General administrative overhead*	180,000	52,000	80,000	48,000
Total fixed expenses	405,000	120,000	165,000	120,000
Net operating income (loss)	$ 5,000	$ 20,000	$ 25,000	$ (40,000)

*Allocated on the basis of program revenues.

The head administrator of Jackson County Senior Services, Judith Miyama, is concerned about the organization's finances and considers the net operating income of $5,000 last year to be razor-thin. (Last year's results were very similar to the results for previous years and are representative of what would be expected in the future.) She feels that the organization should be building its financial reserves at a more rapid rate in order to prepare for the next inevitable recession. After seeing the above report, Ms. Miyama asked for more information about the financial advisability of perhaps discontinuing the housekeeping program.

The depreciation in housekeeping is for a small van that is used to carry the housekeepers and their equipment from job to job. If the program were discontinued, the van would be donated to a charitable organization. Depreciation charges assume zero salvage value. None of the general administrative overhead would be avoided if the housekeeping program were dropped, but the liability insurance and the salary of the program administrator would be avoided.

Required:

1. Should the housekeeping program be discontinued? Explain. Show computations to support your answer.
2. Recast the above data in a format that would be more useful to management in assessing the long-run financial viability of the various services.

EXERCISE 12-3 Make or Buy a Component [LO3]

Climate-Control, Inc., manufactures a variety of heating and air-conditioning units. The company is currently manufacturing all of its own component parts. An outside supplier has offered to sell a thermostat to Climate-Control for $20 per unit. To evaluate this offer, Climate-Control, Inc., has gathered the following information relating to its own cost of producing the thermostat internally:

	Per Unit	15,000 Units per Year
Direct materials	$ 6	$ 90,000
Direct labor	8	120,000
Variable manufacturing overhead	1	15,000
Fixed manufacturing overhead, traceable	5*	75,000
Fixed manufacturing overhead, common, but allocated	10	150,000
Total cost	$30	$450,000

*40% supervisory salaries; 60% depreciation of special equipment (no resale value).

Required:

1. Assuming that the company has no alternative use for the facilities now being used to produce the thermostat, should the outside supplier's offer be accepted? Show all computations.
2. Suppose that if the thermostats were purchased, Climate-Control, Inc., could use the freed capacity to launch a new product. The segment margin of the new product would be $65,000 per year. Should Climate-Control, Inc., accept the offer to buy the thermostats from the outside supplier for $20 each? Show computations.

EXERCISE 12-4 Evaluating a Special Order [LO4]

Miyamoto Jewelers is considering a special order for 10 handcrafted gold bracelets to be given as gifts to members of a wedding party. The normal selling price of a gold bracelet is $389.95 and its unit product cost is $264.00 as shown below:

Direct materials	$143.00
Direct labor	86.00
Manufacturing overhead	35.00
Unit product cost	$264.00

Most of the manufacturing overhead is fixed and unaffected by variations in how much jewelry is produced in any given period. However, $7 of the overhead is variable with respect to the number of bracelets produced. The customer who is interested in the special bracelet order would like special filigree applied to the bracelets. This filigree would require additional materials costing $6 per bracelet and would also require acquisition of a special tool costing $465 that would have no other use once the special order is completed. This order would have no effect on the company's regular sales and the order could be fulfilled using the company's existing capacity without affecting any other order.

Required:

What effect would accepting this order have on the company's net operating income if a special price of $349.95 is offered per bracelet for this order? Should the special order be accepted at this price?

EXERCISE 12-5 Utilization of a Constrained Resource [LO5]

Banner Company produces three products: A, B, and C. The selling price, variable costs, and contribution margin for one unit of each product follow:

	Product		
	A	B	C
Selling price	$60	$90	$80
Variable costs:			
Direct materials	27	14	40
Direct labor	12	32	16
Variable manufacturing overhead	3	8	4
Total variable cost	42	54	60
Contribution margin	$18	$36	$20
Contribution margin ratio	30%	40%	25%

Due to a strike in the plant of one of its competitors, demand for the company's products far exceeds its capacity to produce. Management is trying to determine which product(s) to concentrate on next week in filling its backlog of orders. The direct labor rate is $8 per hour, and only 3,000 hours of labor time are available each week.

Required:

1. Compute the amount of contribution margin that will be obtained per hour of labor time spent on each product.
2. Which orders would you recommend that the company work on next week—the orders for product A, product B, or product C? Show computations.
3. By paying overtime wages, more than 3,000 hours of direct labor time can be made available next week. Up to how much should the company be willing to pay per hour in overtime wages as long as there is unfilled demand for the three products? Explain.

EXERCISE 12-6 Sell or Process Further [LO6]

Solex Company manufactures three products from a common input in a joint processing operation. Joint processing costs up to the split-off point total $100,000 per year. The company allocates these costs to the joint products on the basis of their total sales value at the split-off point. These sales values are as follows: product X, $50,000; product Y, $90,000; and product Z, $60,000.

Each product may be sold at the split-off point or processed further. Additional processing requires no special facilities. The additional processing costs and the sales value after further processing for each product (on an annual basis) are shown below:

Product	Additional Processing Costs	Sales Value
X	$35,000	$80,000
Y	$40,000	$150,000
Z	$12,000	$75,000

Required:

Which product or products should be sold at the split-off point, and which product or products should be processed further? Show computations.

EXERCISE 12-7 Identification of Relevant Costs [LO1]

Steve has just returned from salmon fishing. He was lucky on this trip and brought home two salmon. Steve's wife, Wendy, disapproves of fishing, and to discourage Steve from further fishing trips, she has presented him with the following cost data. The cost per fishing trip is based on an average of 10 fishing trips per year.

Cost per fishing trip:	
Depreciation on fishing boat* (annual depreciation of $1,500 ÷ 10 trips)	$150
Boat moorage fees (annual rental of $1,200 ÷ 10 trips)	120
Expenditures on fishing gear, except for snagged lures (annual expenditures of $200 ÷ 10 trips)	20
Snagged fishing lures	7
Fishing license (yearly license of $40 ÷ 10 trips)	4
Fuel and upkeep on boat per trip	25
Junk food consumed during trip	8
Total cost per fishing trip	$334
Cost per salmon ($334 ÷ 2 salmon)	$167

*The original cost of the boat was $15,000. It has an estimated useful life of 10 years, after which it will have no resale value. The boat does not wear out through use, but it does become less desirable for resale as it becomes older.

Required:

1. Assuming that the salmon fishing trip Steve has just completed is typical, what costs are relevant to a decision as to whether he should go on another trip this year?
2. Suppose that on Steve's next fishing trip he gets lucky and catches three salmon in the amount of time it took him to catch two salmon on his last trip. How much would the third salmon have cost him to catch? Explain.
3. Discuss the costs that are relevant in a decision of whether Steve should give up fishing.

EXERCISE 12-8 Dropping or Retaining a Segment [LO2]

Boyle's Home Center, a retailing company, has two departments, Bath and Kitchen. The company's most recent monthly contribution format income statement follows:

		Department	
	Total	Bath	Kitchen
Sales	$5,000,000	$1,000,000	$4,000,000
Variable expenses	1,900,000	300,000	1,600,000
Contribution margin	3,100,000	700,000	2,400,000
Fixed expenses	2,700,000	900,000	1,800,000
Net operating income (loss)	$ 400,000	$ (200,000)	$ 600,000

A study indicates that $370,000 of the fixed expenses being charged to the Bath Department are sunk costs or allocated costs that will continue even if the Bath Department is dropped. In addition, the elimination of the Bath Department would result in a 10% decrease in the sales of the Kitchen Department.

Required:

If the Bath Department is dropped, what will be the effect on the net operating income of the company as a whole?

EXERCISE 12-9 Make or Buy a Component [LO3]

For many years, Diehl Company has produced a small electrical part that it uses in the production of its standard line of diesel tractors. The company's unit product cost for the part, based on a production level of 60,000 parts per year, is as follows:

	Per Part	Total
Direct materials	$ 4.00	
Direct labor	2.75	
Variable manufacturing overhead	0.50	
Fixed manufacturing overhead, traceable	3.00	$180,000
Fixed manufacturing overhead, common (allocated on the basis of labor-hours)	2.25	$135,000
Unit product cost	$12.50	

An outside supplier has offered to supply the electrical parts to the Diehl Company for only $10.00 per part. One-third of the traceable fixed manufacturing cost is supervisory salaries and other costs that can be eliminated if the parts are purchased. The other two-thirds of the traceable fixed manufacturing costs consist of depreciation of special equipment that has no resale value. Economic depreciation on this equipment is due to obsolescence rather than wear and tear. The decision to buy the parts from the outside supplier would have no effect on the common fixed costs of the company, and the space being used to produce the parts would otherwise be idle.

Required:

Prepare computations showing how much profits would increase or decrease as a result of purchasing the parts from the outside supplier rather than making them inside the company.

EXERCISE 12-10 Special Order [LO4]

Glade Company produces a single product. The costs of producing and selling a single unit of this product at the company's current activity level of 8,000 units per month are:

Direct materials	$2.50
Direct labor	$3.00
Variable manufacturing overhead	$0.50
Fixed manufacturing overhead	$4.25
Variable selling and administrative expenses	$1.50
Fixed selling and administrative expenses	$2.00

The normal selling price is $15 per unit. The company's capacity is 10,000 units per month. An order has been received from a potential customer overseas for 2,000 units at a price of $12.00 per unit. This order would not affect regular sales.

Required:

1. If the order is accepted, by how much will monthly profits increase or decrease? (The order would not change the company's total fixed costs.)
2. Assume the company has 500 units of this product left over from last year that are inferior to the current model. The units must be sold through regular channels at reduced prices. What unit cost is relevant for establishing a minimum selling price for these units? Explain.

EXERCISE 12-11 Utilization of a Constrained Resource [LO5]

Shelby Company produces three products: product X, product Y, and product Z. Data concerning the three products follow (per unit):

	Product X	Product Y	Product Z
Selling price	$80	$56	$70
Less variable expenses:			
Direct materials	24	15	9
Labor and overhead	24	27	40
Total variable expenses	48	42	49
Contribution margin	$32	$14	$21
Contribution margin ratio	40%	25%	30%

Demand for the company's products is very strong, with far more orders each month than the company can produce with the available raw materials. The same material is used in each product. The material costs $3 per pound, with a maximum of 5,000 pounds available each month.

Required:

Which orders would you advise the company to accept first, those for product X, for product Y, or for product Z? Which orders second? Third?

EXERCISE 12-12 Sell or Process Further [LO6]

Morrell Company produces several products from processing krypton, a rare mineral. Material and processing costs total $30,000 per ton, one-third of which are allocated to the product merifulon. The merifulon produced from a ton of krypton can either be sold at the split-off point, or processed further at a cost of $13,000 and then sold for $60,000. The sales value of merifulon at the split-off point is $40,000.

Required:

Should merifulon be processed further or sold at the split-off point?

EXERCISE 12-13 Identification of Relevant Costs [LO1]

Samantha Ringer purchased a used automobile for $10,000 at the beginning of last year and incurred the following operating costs:

Depreciation ($10,000 ÷ 5 years)	$2,000
Insurance	$960
Garage rent	$480
Automobile tax and license	$60
Variable operating cost	8¢ per mile

The variable operating costs consist of gasoline, oil, tires, maintenance, and repairs. Samantha estimates that at her current rate of usage the car will have zero resale value in five years, so the annual straight-line depreciation is $2,000. The car is kept in a garage for a monthly fee.

Required:

1. Samantha drove the car 10,000 miles last year. Compute the average cost per mile of owning and operating the car.
2. Samantha is unsure about whether she should use her own car or rent a car to go on an extended cross-country trip for two weeks during spring break. What costs above are relevant in this decision? Explain.
3. Samantha is thinking about buying an expensive sports car to replace the car she bought last year. She would drive the same number of miles regardless of which car she owns and would rent the same parking space. The sports car's variable operating costs would be roughly the same as the variable operating costs of her old car. However, her insurance and automobile tax and license costs would go up. What costs are relevant in estimating the incremental cost of owning the more expensive car? Explain.

EXERCISE 12-14 Dropping or Retaining a Segment [LO2]

Dexter Products, Inc., manufactures and sells a number of items, including an overnight case. The company has been experiencing losses on the overnight case for some time, as shown on the following contribution format income statement:

Dexter Products, Inc. Income Statement—Overnight Cases For the Quarter Ended June 30		
Sales		$450,000
Variable expenses:		
Variable manufacturing expenses	$130,000	
Sales commissions	48,000	
Shipping	12,000	
Total variable expenses		190,000
Contribution margin		260,000
Fixed expenses:		
Salary of product-line manager	21,000	
General factory overhead	104,000*	
Depreciation of equipment (no resale value)	36,000	
Advertising—traceable	110,000	
Insurance on inventories	9,000	
Purchasing department	50,000†	
Total fixed expenses		330,000
Net operating loss		$ (70,000)

*Allocated on the basis of machine-hours.
†Allocated on the basis of sales dollars.

Discontinuing the overnight cases would not affect sales of other product lines and would have no noticeable effect on the company's total general factory overhead or total purchasing department expenses.

Required:

Would you recommend that the company discontinue the manufacture and sale of overnight cases? Support your answer with appropriate computations.

EXERCISE 12-15 Make or Buy a Component [LO3]

Royal Company manufactures 20,000 units of part R-3 each year for use on its production line. At this level of activity, the cost per unit for part R-3 follows:

Direct materials	$ 4.80
Direct labor	7.00
Variable manufacturing overhead	3.20
Fixed manufacturing overhead	10.00
Total cost per part	$25.00

An outside supplier has offered to sell 20,000 units of part R-3 each year to Royal Company for $23.50 per part. If Royal Company accepts this offer, the facilities now being used to manufacture part R-3 could be rented to another company at an annual rental of $150,000. However, Royal Company has determined that $6 of the fixed manufacturing overhead being applied to part R-3 would continue even if part R-3 were purchased from the outside supplier.

Required:

Prepare computations showing how much profits will increase or decrease if the outside supplier's offer is accepted.

Problems

PROBLEM 12-16 Dropping or Retaining a Tour [LO2]

Blueline Tours, Inc., operates tours throughout the United States. A study has indicated that some of the tours are not profitable, and consideration is being given to dropping these tours to improve the company's overall operating performance.

One such tour is a two-day Historic Mansions bus tour conducted in the southern states. An income statement from a typical Historic Mansions tour is given below:

Ticket revenue (100 seat capacity × 40% occupancy × $75 ticket price per person)	$3,000	100%
Variable expenses ($22.50 per person)	900	30
Contribution margin	2,100	70%
Tour expenses:		
Tour promotion	$ 600	
Salary of bus driver	350	
Fee, tour guide	700	
Fuel for bus	125	
Depreciation of bus	450	
Liability insurance, bus	200	
Overnight parking fee, bus	50	
Room and meals, bus driver and tour guide	175	
Bus maintenance and preparation	300	
Total tour expenses	2,950	
Net operating loss	$ (850)	

The following additional information is available about the tour:

a. Bus drivers are paid fixed annual salaries; tour guides are paid for each tour conducted.
b. The "Bus maintenance and preparation" cost above is an allocation of the salaries of mechanics and other service personnel who are responsible for keeping the company's fleet of buses in good operating condition.
c. Depreciation of buses is due to obsolescence. Depreciation due to wear and tear is negligible.
d. Liability insurance premiums are based on the number of buses in the company's fleet.
e. Dropping the Historic Mansions bus tour would not allow Blueline Tours to reduce the number of buses in its fleet, the number of bus drivers on the payroll, or the size of the maintenance and preparation staff.

Required:

1. Prepare an analysis showing what the impact will be on the company's profits if this tour is discontinued.
2. The company's tour director has been criticized because only about 50% of the seats on Blueline's tours are being filled as compared to an industry average of 60%. The tour director has explained that Blueline's average seat occupancy could be improved considerably by eliminating about 10% of its tours, but that doing so would reduce profits. Explain how this could happen.

PROBLEM 12-17 Sell or Process Further [LO6]

(Prepared from a situation suggested by Professor John W. Hardy.) Abilene Meat Processing Corporation is a major processor of beef and other meat products. The company has a large amount of T-bone steak on hand, and it is trying to decide whether to sell the T-bone steaks as is or to process them further into filet mignon and New York cut steaks.

Management believes that a 1-pound T-bone steak would yield the following profit:

Wholesale selling price ($2.25 per pound)	$2.25
Less joint costs incurred up to the split-off point where T-bone steak can be identified as a separate product	1.70
Profit per pound	$0.55

As mentioned above, instead of being sold as is, the T-bone steaks could be further processed into filet mignon and New York cut steaks. Cutting one side of a T-bone steak provides the filet mignon, and cutting the other side provides the New York cut. One 16-ounce T-bone steak cut in this way will yield one 6-ounce filet mignon and one 8-ounce New York cut; the remaining ounces are waste. The cost of processing the T-bone steaks into these cuts is $0.20 per pound. The filet mignon can be sold for $3.60 per pound, and the New York cut can be sold wholesale for $2.90 per pound.

Required:

1. Determine the profit per pound from processing the T-bone steaks further into filet mignon and New York cut steaks.
2. Would you recommend that the T-bone steaks be sold as is or processed further? Why?

PROBLEM 12-18 Close or Retain a Store [LO2]

Thrifty Markets, Inc., operates three stores in a large metropolitan area. The company's segmented absorption costing income statement for the last quarter is given below:

Thrifty Markets, Inc.
Income Statement
For the Quarter Ended March 31

	Total	Uptown Store	Downtown Store	Westpark Store
Sales	$2,500,000	$900,000	$600,000	$1,000,000
Cost of goods sold	1,450,000	513,000	372,000	565,000
Gross margin	1,050,000	387,000	228,000	435,000
Selling and administrative expenses:				
Selling expenses:				
Direct advertising	118,500	40,000	36,000	42,500
General advertising*	20,000	7,200	4,800	8,000
Sales salaries	157,000	52,000	45,000	60,000
Delivery salaries	30,000	10,000	10,000	10,000
Store rent	215,000	70,000	65,000	80,000
Depreciation of store fixtures	46,950	18,300	8,800	19,850
Depreciation of delivery equipment	27,000	9,000	9,000	9,000
Total selling expenses	614,450	206,500	178,600	229,350
Administrative expenses:				
Store management salaries	63,000	20,000	18,000	25,000
General office salaries*	50,000	18,000	12,000	20,000
Utilities	89,800	31,000	27,200	31,600
Insurance on fixtures and inventory	25,500	8,000	9,000	8,500
Employment taxes	36,000	12,000	10,200	13,800
General office expenses—other*	25,000	9,000	6,000	10,000
Total administrative expenses	289,300	98,000	82,400	108,900
Total operating expenses	903,750	304,500	261,000	338,250
Net operating income (loss)	$ 146,250	$ 82,500	$ (33,000)	$ 96,750

*Allocated on the basis of sales dollars.

Management is very concerned about the Downtown Store's inability to show a profit, and consideration is being given to closing the store. The company has asked you to make a recommendation as to what course of action should be taken. The following additional information is available on the store:

a. The manager of the store has been with the company for many years; he would be retained and transferred to another position in the company if the store were closed. His salary is $6,000 per month, or $18,000 per quarter. If the store were not closed, a new employee would be hired to fill the other position at a salary of $5,000 per month.

b. The lease on the building housing the Downtown Store can be broken with no penalty.
c. The fixtures being used in the Downtown Store would be transferred to the other two stores if the Downtown Store were closed.
d. The company's employment taxes are 12% of salaries.
e. A single delivery crew serves all three stores. One delivery person could be discharged if the Downtown Store were closed; this person's salary amounts to $7,000 per quarter. The delivery equipment would be distributed to the other stores. The equipment does not wear out through use, but it does eventually become obsolete.
f. One-third of the Downtown Store's insurance relates to its fixtures.
g. The general office salaries and other expenses relate to the general management of Thrifty Markets, Inc. The employee in the general office who is responsible for the Downtown Store would be discharged if the store were closed. This employee's compensation amounts to $8,000 per quarter.

Required:

1. Prepare a schedule showing the change in revenues and expenses and the impact on the overall company net operating income that would result if the Downtown Store were closed.
2. Based on your computations in (1) above, what recommendation would you make to the management of Thrifty Markets, Inc.?
3. Assume that if the Downtown Store were closed, sales in the Uptown Store would increase by $200,000 per quarter due to loyal customers shifting their buying to the Uptown Store. The Uptown Store has ample capacity to handle the increased sales, and its gross margin is 43% of sales. What effect would these factors have on your recommendation concerning the Downtown Store? Show computations.

PROBLEM 12-19 Make or Buy Decision [LO3]

Bronson Company manufactures a variety of ballpoint pens. The company has just received an offer from an outside supplier to provide the ink cartridge for the company's Zippo pen line, at a price of $0.48 per dozen cartridges. The company is interested in this offer, since its own production of cartridges is at capacity.

Bronson Company estimates that if the supplier's offer were accepted, the direct labor and variable manufacturing overhead costs of the Zippo pen line would be reduced by 10% and the direct materials cost would be reduced by 20%.

Under present operations, Bronson Company manufactures all of its own pens from start to finish. The Zippo pens are sold through wholesalers at $4 per box. Each box contains one dozen pens. Fixed manufacturing overhead costs charged to the Zippo pen line total $50,000 each year. (The same equipment and facilities are used to produce several pen lines.) The present cost of producing one dozen Zippo pens (one box) is given below:

Direct materials	$1.50
Direct labor	1.00
Manufacturing overhead	0.80*
Total cost	$3.30

*Includes both variable and fixed manufacturing overhead, based on production of 100,000 boxes of pens each year.

Required:

1. Should Bronson Company accept the outside supplier's offer? Show computations.
2. What is the maximum price that Bronson Company should be willing to pay the outside supplier per dozen cartridges? Explain.
3. Due to the bankruptcy of a competitor, Bronson Company expects to sell 150,000 boxes of Zippo pens next year. As stated above, the company presently has enough capacity to produce the cartridges for only 100,000 boxes of Zippo pens annually. By incurring $30,000 in added fixed cost each year, the company could expand its production of cartridges to satisfy the anticipated

demand for Zippo pens. The variable cost per unit to produce the additional cartridges would be the same as at present. Under these circumstances, how many boxes of cartridges should be purchased from the outside supplier and how many should be made by Bronson? Show computations to support your answer.

4. What qualitative factors should Bronson Company consider in determining whether it should make or buy the ink cartridges?

(CMA, adapted)

PROBLEM 12-20 Accept or Reject a Special Order [LO4]

Pietarsaari Oy, a Finnish company, produces cross-country ski poles that it sells for €32 a pair. (The Finnish unit of currency, the euro, is denoted by €.) Operating at capacity, the company can produce 50,000 pairs of ski poles a year. Costs associated with this level of production and sales are given below:

	Per Pair	Total
Direct materials	€12	€ 600,000
Direct labor	3	150,000
Variable manufacturing overhead	1	50,000
Fixed manufacturing overhead	5	250,000
Variable selling expenses	2	100,000
Fixed selling expenses	4	200,000
Total cost	€27	€1,350,000

Required:

1. The Finnish army would like to make a one-time-only purchase of 10,000 pairs of ski poles for its mountain troops. The army would pay a fixed fee of €4 per pair, and in addition it would reimburse the Pietarsaari Oy company for its unit manufacturing costs (both fixed and variable). Due to a recession, the company would otherwise produce and sell only 40,000 pairs of ski poles this year. (Total fixed manufacturing overhead cost would be the same whether 40,000 pairs or 50,000 pairs of ski poles were produced.) The company would not incur its usual variable selling expenses with this special order.

   If the Pietarsaari Oy company accepts the army's offer, by how much would net operating income increase or decrease from what it would be if only 40,000 pairs of ski poles were produced and sold during the year?

2. Assume the same situation as described in (1) above, except that the company is already operating at capacity and could sell 50,000 pairs of ski poles through regular channels. Thus, accepting the army's offer would require giving up sales of 10,000 pairs at the normal price of €32 a pair. If the army's offer is accepted, by how much will net operating income increase or decrease from what it would be if the 10,000 pairs were sold through regular channels?

PROBLEM 12-21 Shutting Down or Continuing to Operate a Plant [LO2]

(Note: This type of decision is similar to dropping a product line.)

Hallas Company manufactures a fast-bonding glue in its Northwest plant. The company normally produces and sells 40,000 gallons of the glue each month. This glue, which is known as MJ-7, is used in the wood industry to manufacture plywood. The selling price of MJ-7 is $35 per gallon, variable costs are $21 per gallon, fixed manufacturing overhead costs in the plant total $230,000 per month, and the fixed selling costs total $310,000 per month.

Strikes in the mills that purchase the bulk of the MJ-7 glue have caused Hallas Company's sales to temporarily drop to only 11,000 gallons per month. Hallas Company's management estimates that the strikes will last for two months, after which sales of MJ-7 should return to normal. Due to the current low level of sales, Hallas Company's management is thinking about closing down the Northwest plant during the strike.

If Hallas Company does close down the Northwest plant, fixed manufacturing overhead costs can be reduced by $60,000 per month and fixed selling costs can be reduced by 10%. Start-up costs at the end of the shutdown period would total $14,000. Since Hallas Company uses Lean Production methods, no inventories are on hand.

Required:

1. Assuming that the strikes continue for two months, would you recommend that Hallas Company close the Northwest plant? Explain. Show computations to support your answer.
2. At what level of sales (in gallons) for the two-month period should Hallas Company be indifferent between closing the plant or keeping it open? Show computations. (Hint: This is a type of break-even analysis, except that the fixed cost portion of your break-even computation should include only those fixed costs that are relevant [i.e., avoidable] over the two-month period.)

PROBLEM 12-22 Relevant Cost Analysis in a Variety of Situations [LO2, LO3, LO4]

Barker Company has a single product called a Zet. The company normally produces and sells 80,000 Zets each year at a selling price of $40 per unit. The company's unit costs at this level of activity are given below:

Direct materials	$ 9.50
Direct labor	10.00
Variable manufacturing overhead	2.80
Fixed manufacturing overhead	5.00 ($400,000 total)
Variable selling expenses	1.70
Fixed selling expenses	4.50 ($360,000 total)
Total cost per unit	$33.50

A number of questions relating to the production and sale of Zets are given below. Each question is independent.

Required:

1. Assume that Barker Company has sufficient capacity to produce 100,000 Zets each year without any increase in fixed manufacturing overhead costs. The company could increase sales by 25% above the present 80,000 units each year if it were willing to increase the fixed selling expenses by $150,000. Would the increased fixed selling expenses be justified?
2. Assume again that Barker Company has sufficient capacity to produce 100,000 Zets each year. The company has an opportunity to sell 20,000 units in an overseas market. Import duties, foreign permits, and other special costs associated with the order would total $14,000. The only selling costs that would be associated with the order would be $1.50 per unit shipping cost. Compute the per unit break-even price on this order.
3. One of the materials used in the production of Zets is obtained from a foreign supplier. Civil unrest in the supplier's country has caused a cutoff in material shipments that is expected to last for three months. Barker Company has enough material on hand to operate at 25% of normal levels for the three-month period. As an alternative, the company could close the plant down entirely for the three months. Closing the plant would reduce fixed manufacturing overhead costs by 40% during the three-month period and the fixed selling expenses would continue at two-thirds of their normal level. What would be the impact on profits of closing the plant for the three-month period?
4. The company has 500 Zets on hand that were produced last month and have small blemishes. Due to the blemishes, it will be impossible to sell these units at the normal price. If the company wishes to sell them through regular distribution channels, what unit cost figure is relevant for setting a minimum selling price? Explain.
5. An outside manufacturer has offered to produce Zets and ship them directly to Barker's customers. If Barker Company accepts this offer, the facilities that it uses to produce Zets would be idle; however, fixed manufacturing overhead costs would continue at 30%. Since the outside manufacturer would pay for all shipping costs the variable selling expenses would be reduced by 60%. Compute the unit cost that is relevant for comparison to the price quoted by the outside manufacturer.

PROBLEM 12-23 Make or Buy Analysis [LO3]

"That old equipment for producing subassemblies is worn out," said Paul Taylor, president of Timkin Company. "We need to make a decision quickly." The company is trying to decide whether it should rent new equipment and continue to make its subassemblies internally or whether it should discontinue production of its subassemblies and purchase them from an outside supplier. The alternatives follow:

Alternative 1: Rent new equipment for producing the subassemblies for $60,000 per year.
Alternative 2: Purchase subassemblies from an outside supplier for $8 each.

Timkin Company's present costs per unit of producing the subassemblies internally (with the old equipment) are given below. These costs are based on a current activity level of 40,000 subassemblies per year:

Direct materials	$ 2.75
Direct labor	4.00
Variable overhead	0.60
Fixed overhead ($0.75 supervision, $0.90 depreciation, and $2 general company overhead)	3.65
Total cost per unit	$11.00

The new equipment would be more efficient and, according to the manufacturer, would reduce direct labor costs and variable overhead costs by 25%. Supervision cost ($30,000 per year) and direct materials cost per unit would not be affected by the new equipment. The new equipment's capacity would be 60,000 subassemblies per year.

The total general company overhead would be unaffected by this decision.

Required:

1. The president is unsure what the company should do and would like an analysis showing the unit costs and total costs for each of the two alternatives given above. Assume that 40,000 subassemblies are needed each year. Which course of action would you recommend to the president?
2. Would your recommendation in (1) above be the same if the company's needs were (*a*) 50,000 subassemblies per year, or (*b*) 60,000 subassemblies per year? Show computations in good form.
3. What other factors would you recommend that the company consider before making a decision?

PROBLEM 12-24 Utilization of a Constrained Resource [LO5]

The Brandilyn Toy Company manufactures a line of dolls and a doll dress sewing kit. Demand for the dolls is increasing, and management requests assistance from you in determining the best sales and production mix for the coming year. The company has provided the following data:

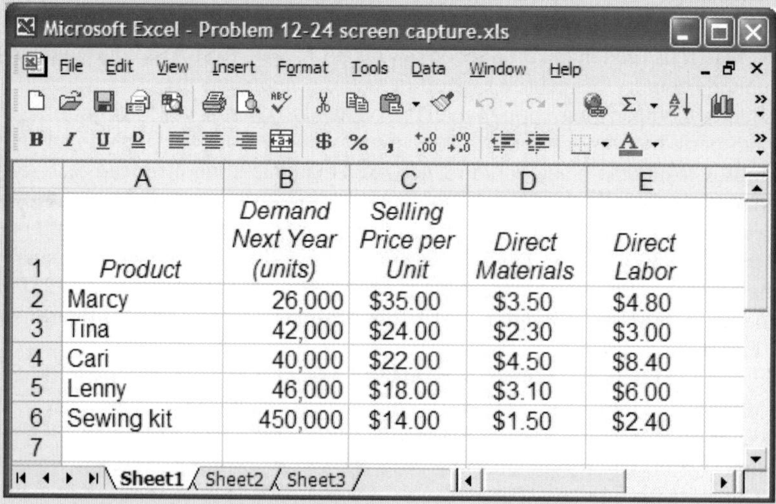
Microsoft Excel - Problem 12-24 screen capture.xls

	A	B	C	D	E
1	Product	Demand Next Year (units)	Selling Price per Unit	Direct Materials	Direct Labor
2	Marcy	26,000	$35.00	$3.50	$4.80
3	Tina	42,000	$24.00	$2.30	$3.00
4	Cari	40,000	$22.00	$4.50	$8.40
5	Lenny	46,000	$18.00	$3.10	$6.00
6	Sewing kit	450,000	$14.00	$1.50	$2.40
7					

The following additional information is available:

a. The company's plant has a capacity of 150,000 direct labor-hours per year on a single-shift basis. The company's present employees and equipment can produce all five products.

b. The direct labor rate of $12.00 per hour is expected to remain unchanged during the coming year.

c. Fixed costs total $356,000 per year. Variable overhead costs are $4.00 per direct labor-hour.

d. All of the company's nonmanufacturing costs are fixed.

e. The company's finished goods inventory is negligible and can be ignored.

Required:

1. Determine the contribution margin per direct labor-hour expended on each product.
2. Prepare a schedule showing the total direct labor-hours that will be required to produce the units estimated to be sold during the coming year.
3. Examine the data you have computed in (1) and (2) above. How would you allocate the 150,000 direct labor-hours of capacity to Brandilyn Toy Company's various products?
4. What is the highest price, in terms of a rate per hour, that Brandilyn Toy Company should be willing to pay for additional capacity (that is, for added direct labor time)?
5. Identify ways in which the company might be able to obtain additional output so that it would not have to leave some demand for its products unsatisfied.

(CMA, adapted)

PROBLEM 12-25 Sell or Process Further [LO6]

The Heather Honey Company purchases honeycombs from beekeepers for $2.00 a pound. The company produces two main products from the honeycombs—honey and beeswax. Honey is drained from the honeycombs, and then the honeycombs are melted down to form cubes of beeswax. The beeswax is sold for $1.50 a pound.

The honey can be sold in raw form for $3.00 a pound. However, some of the raw honey is used by the company to make honey drop candies. The candies are packed in a decorative container and are sold in gift and specialty shops. A container of honey drop candies sells for $4.40.

Each container of honey drop candies contains three quarters of a pound of honey. The other variable costs associated with making the candies are as follows:

Decorative container	$0.40
Other ingredients	0.25
Direct labor	0.20
Variable manufacturing overhead	0.10
Total variable manufacturing cost	$0.95

The monthly fixed manufacturing overhead costs associated with making the candies follow:

Master candy maker's salary	$3,880
Depreciation of candy making equipment	400
Total fixed manufacturing cost	$4,280

The master candy maker has no duties other than to oversee production of the honey drop candies. The candy making equipment is special-purpose equipment that was constructed specifically to make this particular candy. The equipment has no resale value and does not wear out through use.

A salesperson is paid $2,000 per month plus a commission of 5% of sales to market the honey drop candies.

The company had enjoyed robust sales of the candies for several years, but the recent entrance of a competing product into the marketplace has depressed sales of the candies. The management of the company is now wondering whether it would be more profitable to sell all of the honey rather than converting some of it into candies.

Required:

1. What is the incremental contribution margin per container from further processing the honey into candies?
2. What is the minimum number of containers of candy that must be sold each month to justify the continued processing of honey into candies? Explain. Show all computations.

(CMA, adapted)

Cases 

CASE 12-26 Integrative Case: Relevant Costs; Pricing [LO1, LO4]

Jenco Incorporated's only product is a combination fertilizer-weed killer called Fertikil. Fertikil is sold nationwide through normal marketing channels to retail nurseries and garden stores.

Taylor Nursery plans to sell a similar fertilizer weed killer compound through its regional nursery chain under its own private label. Taylor does not have manufacturing facilities of its own, so it has asked Jenco (and several other companies) to submit a bid for manufacturing and delivering a 25,000 pound order of the private brand compound to Taylor. While the chemical composition of the Taylor compound differs from that of Fertikil, the manufacturing processes are very similar.

The Taylor compound would be produced in 1,000 pound lots. Each lot would require 30 direct labor-hours and the following chemicals:

Chemicals	Quantity in Pounds
CW–3	400
JX–6	300
MZ–8	200
BE–7	100

The first three chemicals (CW–3, JX–6, and MZ–8) are all used in the production of Fertikil. BE–7 was used in another compound that Jenco discontinued several months ago. The supply of BE–7 that Jenco had on hand when the other compound was discontinued was not discarded. Jenco could sell its supply of BE–7 at the prevailing market price less $0.10 per pound selling and handling expenses.

Jenco also has on hand a chemical called CN–5, which was manufactured for use in another product that is no longer produced. CN–5, which cannot be used in Fertikil, can be substituted for CW–3 on a one-for-one basis without affecting the quality of the Taylor compound. The CN–5 in inventory has a salvage value of $500.

Inventory and cost data for the chemicals that can be used to produce the Taylor compound are as shown below:

Raw Material	Pounds in Inventory	Actual Price per Pound When Purchased	Current Market Price per Pound
CW–3	22,000	$0.80	$0.90
JX–6	5,000	0.55	0.60
MZ–8.	8,000	1.40	1.60
BE–7.	4,000	0.60	0.65
CN–5.	5,500	0.75	(Salvage)

The current direct labor rate is $14 per hour. The predetermined overhead rate is based on direct labor-hours (DLH). The predetermined overhead rate for the current year, based on a two-shift capacity of 400,000 total DLH with no overtime, is as follows:

Variable manufacturing overhead	$ 4.50 per DLH
Fixed manufacturing overhead.	7.50 per DLH
Combined rate	$12.00 per DLH

Jenco's production manager reports that the present equipment and facilities are adequate to manufacture the Taylor compound. Therefore, the order would have no effect on total fixed manufacturing overhead costs. However, Jenco is within 400 hours of its two-shift capacity this month. Any additional hours beyond 400 hours must be done in overtime. If need be, the Taylor compound could be produced on regular time by shifting a portion of Fertikil production to overtime. Jenco's rate for overtime hours is 1½ times the regular pay rate, or $21 per hour. There is no allowance for any overtime premium in the predetermined overhead rate.

Required:

1. Jenco, has decided to submit a bid for a 25,000 pound order of Taylor Nursery's new compound. The order must be delivered by the end of the current month. Taylor Nursery has indicated that this is a one-time order that will not be repeated. Calculate the lowest price that Jenco could bid for the order without reducing its net operating income.
2. Refer to the original data. Assume that Taylor Nursery plans to place regular orders for 25,000 pound lots of the new compound during the coming year. Jenco expects the demand for Fertikil to remain strong. Therefore, the recurring orders from Taylor Nursery would put Jenco over its two-shift capacity. However, production could be scheduled so that 60% of each Taylor Nursery order could be completed during regular hours. As another option, some Fertikil production could be shifted temporarily to overtime so that the Taylor Nursery orders could be produced on regular time. Current market prices are the best available estimates of future market prices.

   Jenco's standard markup policy for new products is 40% of the full manufacturing cost, including fixed manufacturing overhead. Calculate the price that Jenco would quote Taylor Nursery for each 25,000 pound lot of the new compound, assuming that it is to be treated as a new product and this pricing policy is followed.

(CMA, adapted)

CASE 12-27 Ethics and the Manager; Shut Down or Continue Operations [LO2]

Marvin Braun had just been appointed vice president of the Great Basin Region of the Financial Services Corporation (FSC). The company provides check processing services for small banks. The banks send checks presented for deposit or payment to FSC, which then records the data on each check in a computerized database. FSC sends the data electronically to the nearest Federal Reserve Bank check-clearing center where the appropriate transfers of funds are made between banks. The Great Basin Region consists of three check processing centers in Eastern Idaho—Pocatello, Idaho Falls, and Ashton. Prior to his promotion to vice president, Mr. Braun had been manager of a check processing center in Indiana.

Immediately upon assuming his new position, Mr. Braun requested a complete financial report for the just-ended fiscal year from the region's controller, Lance Whiting. Mr. Braun specified that the financial report should follow the standardized format required by corporate headquarters for all regional performance reports. That report appears below:

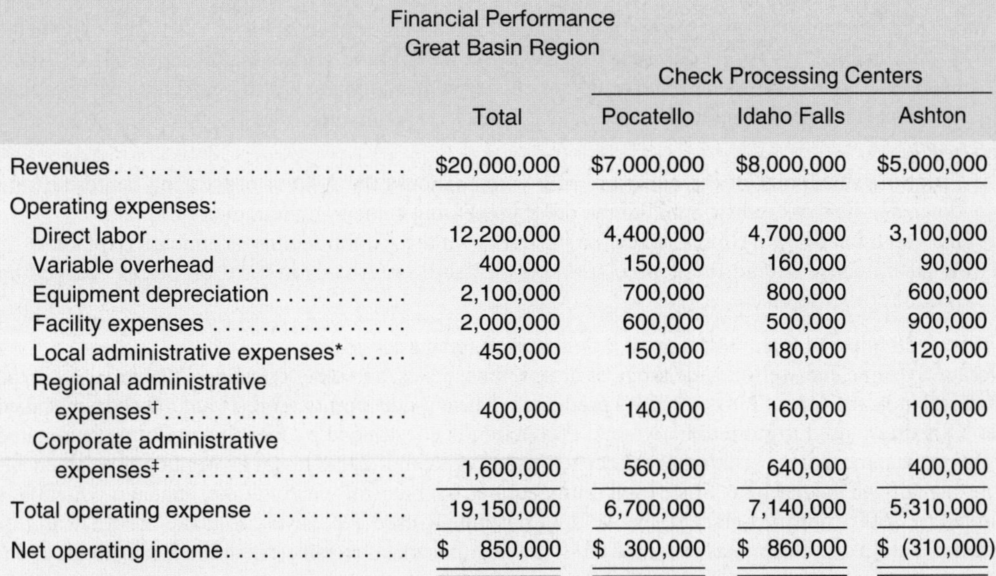

Financial Performance
Great Basin Region

	Total	Check Processing Centers		
		Pocatello	Idaho Falls	Ashton
Revenues	$20,000,000	$7,000,000	$8,000,000	$5,000,000
Operating expenses:				
Direct labor	12,200,000	4,400,000	4,700,000	3,100,000
Variable overhead	400,000	150,000	160,000	90,000
Equipment depreciation	2,100,000	700,000	800,000	600,000
Facility expenses	2,000,000	600,000	500,000	900,000
Local administrative expenses*	450,000	150,000	180,000	120,000
Regional administrative expenses†	400,000	140,000	160,000	100,000
Corporate administrative expenses‡	1,600,000	560,000	640,000	400,000
Total operating expense	19,150,000	6,700,000	7,140,000	5,310,000
Net operating income	$ 850,000	$ 300,000	$ 860,000	$ (310,000)

*Local administrative expenses are the administrative expenses incurred at the check processing centers.
†Regional administrative expenses are allocated to the check processing centers based on revenues.
‡Corporate administrative expenses represent a standard 8% charge against revenues.

Upon seeing this report, Mr. Braun summoned Lance Whiting for an explanation.

Braun: What's the story on Ashton? It didn't have a loss the previous year, did it?

Whiting: No, the Ashton facility has had a nice profit every year since it was opened six years ago, but Ashton lost a big contract this year.

Braun: Why?

Whiting: One of our national competitors entered the local market and bid very aggressively on the contract. We couldn't afford to meet the bid. Ashton's costs—particularly their facility expenses—are just too high. When Ashton lost the contract, we had to lay off a lot of employees, but we could not reduce the fixed costs of the Ashton facility.

Braun: Why is Ashton's facility expense so high? It's a smaller facility than either Pocatello or Idaho Falls and yet its facility expense is higher.

Whiting: The problem is that we are able to rent suitable facilities very cheaply at Pocatello and Idaho Falls. No such facilities were available at Ashton, so we had them built. Unfortunately, there were big cost overruns. The contractor we hired was inexperienced at this kind of work and in fact went bankrupt before the project was completed. After hiring another contractor to finish the work, we were way over budget. The large depreciation charges on the facility didn't matter at first because we didn't have much competition at the time and could charge premium prices.

Braun: Well, we can't do that anymore. The Ashton facility will obviously have to be shut down. Its business can be shifted to the other two check processing centers in the region.

Whiting: I would advise against that. The $900,000 in depreciation charges at the Ashton facility are misleading. That facility should last indefinitely with proper maintenance. And it has no resale value; there is no other commercial activity around Ashton.

Braun: What about the other costs at Ashton?

Whiting: If we shifted Ashton's business over to the other two processing centers in the region, we wouldn't save anything on direct labor or variable overhead costs. We might save $60,000 or so in local administrative expenses, but we would not save any regional administrative expense. And corporate headquarters would still charge us 8% of our revenues as corporate administrative expenses.

In addition, we would have to rent more space in Pocatello and Idaho Falls to handle the work transferred from Ashton; that would probably cost us at least $400,000 a year. And don't forget that it will cost us something to move the equipment from Ashton to Pocatello and Idaho Falls. And the move will disrupt service to customers.

Braun: I understand all of that, but a money-losing processing center on my performance report is completely unacceptable.

Whiting: And if you do shut down Ashton, you are going to throw some loyal employees out of work.

Braun: That's unfortunate, but we have to face hard business realities.

Whiting: And you would have to write off the investment in the facilities at Ashton.

Braun: I can explain a write-off to corporate headquarters; hiring an inexperienced contractor to build the Ashton facility was my predecessor's mistake. But they'll have my head at headquarters if I show operating losses every year at one of my processing centers. Ashton has to go. At the next corporate board meeting, I am going to recommend that the Ashton facility be closed.

Required:

1. From the standpoint of the company as a whole, should the Ashton processing center be shut down and its work redistributed to the other processing centers in the region? Explain.
2. Do you think Marvin Braun's decision to shut down the Ashton facility is ethical? Explain.
3. What influence should the depreciation on the facilities at Ashton have on prices charged by Ashton for its services?

CASE 12-28 Make or Buy; Utilization of a Constrained Resource [LO1, LO3, LO5]

Storage Systems, Inc., sells a wide range of drums, bins, boxes, and other containers that are used in the chemical industry. One of the company's products is a heavy-duty corrosion-resistant metal drum, called the XSX drum, used to store toxic wastes. Production is constrained by the capacity of an automated welding machine that is used to make precision welds. A total of 2,000 hours of welding time are available annually on the machine. Since each drum requires 0.8 hours of welding time, annual production is limited to 2,500 drums. At present, the welding machine is used exclusively to make the XSX drums. The accounting department has provided the following financial data concerning the XSX drums:

		XSX Drums
Selling price per drum		$154.00
Cost per drum:		
Direct materials	$44.50	
Direct labor ($18 per hour)	4.50	
Manufacturing overhead	3.15	
Selling and administrative expense	15.40	67.55
Margin per drum		$ 86.45

Management believes 3,000 XSX drums could be sold each year if the company had sufficient manufacturing capacity. As an alternative to adding another welding machine, management has looked into the possibility of buying additional drums from an outside supplier. Metal Products, Inc., a supplier of quality products, would be able to provide up to 1,800 XSX-type drums per year at a price of $120 per drum, which Storage Systems would resell to its customers at its normal selling price after appropriate relabeling.

Jasmine Morita, Storage Systems' production manager, has suggested that the company could make better use of the welding machine by manufacturing premium mountain bike frames, which would require only 0.2 hours of welding time per frame. Jasmine believes that Storage Systems could sell up to 3,500 mountain bike frames per year to mountain bike manufacturers at a price of $65 per frame. The accounting department has provided the following data concerning the proposed new product:

Mountain Bike Frames		
Selling price per frame		$65.00
Cost per frame:		
Direct materials	$17.50	
Direct labor ($18 per hour)	22.50	
Manufacturing overhead	15.75	
Selling and administrative expense	6.50	62.25
Margin per frame		$ 2.75

The mountain bike frames could be produced with existing equipment and personnel. Manufacturing overhead is allocated to products on the basis of direct labor-hours. Most of the manufacturing overhead consists of fixed common costs such as rent on the factory building, but some of it is variable. The variable manufacturing overhead has been estimated at $1.05 per XSX drum and $0.60 per mountain bike frame. The variable manufacturing overhead cost would not be incurred on drums acquired from the outside supplier.

Selling and administrative expenses are allocated to products on the basis of revenues. Almost all of the selling and administrative expenses are fixed common costs, but it has been estimated that variable selling and administrative expenses amount to $0.85 per XSX drum and would be $0.40 per mountain bike frame. The variable selling and administrative expenses of $0.85 per drum would be incurred when drums acquired from the outside supplier are sold to the company's customers.

All of the company's employees—direct and indirect—are paid for full 40-hour workweeks and the company has a policy of laying off workers only in major recessions.

Required:

1. Given the margins of the two products as indicated in the reports submitted by the accounting department, does it make any sense to even consider producing the mountain bike frames? Explain.
2. Compute the contribution margin per unit for:
   a. Purchased XSX drums.
   b. Manufactured XSX drums.
   c. Manufactured mountain bike frames.
3. Determine the number of XSX drums (if any) that should be purchased and the number of XSX drums and/or mountain bike frames (if any) that should be manufactured. What is the improvement in net income that would result from this plan over current operations?

As soon as your analysis was shown to the top management team at Storage Systems, several managers got into an argument concerning how direct labor costs should be treated when making this decision. One manager argued that direct labor is always treated as a variable cost in textbooks and in practice and has always been considered a variable cost at Storage Systems. After all, "direct" means you can directly trace the cost to products. If direct labor is not a variable cost, what is? Another manager argued just as strenuously that direct labor should be considered a fixed cost at Storage Systems. No one had been laid off in over a decade, and for all practical purposes, everyone at the plant is on a monthly salary. Everyone classified as direct labor works a regular 40-hour workweek and overtime has not been necessary since the company adopted Lean Production techniques. Whether the welding machine is used to make drums or frames, the total payroll would be exactly the same. There is enough slack, in the form of idle time, to accommodate any increase in total direct labor time that the mountain bike frames would require.

4. Redo requirements (2) and (3) above, making the opposite assumption about direct labor from the one you originally made. In other words, if you treated direct labor as a variable cost, redo the analysis treating it as a fixed cost. If you treated direct labor as a fixed cost, redo the analysis treating it as a variable cost.
5. What do you think is the correct way to treat direct labor in this situation—as a variable cost or as a fixed cost?

CASE 12-29 Sell or Process Further Decision [LO6]

Midwest Mills has a plant that can mill wheat grain into a cracked wheat cereal and then further mill the cracked wheat into flour. The company can sell all the cracked wheat cereal that it can produce at a selling price of $490 per ton. In the past, the company has sold only part of its cracked wheat as cereal and has retained the rest for further milling into flour. The flour has been selling for $700 per ton, but recently the price has become unstable and has dropped to $625 per ton. The costs and revenues associated with a ton of flour follow:

		Per Ton of Flour
Selling price		$625
Cost to manufacture:		
Raw materials:		
Enrichment materials	$ 80	
Cracked wheat	470	
Total raw materials	550	
Direct labor	20	
Manufacturing overhead	60	630
Manufacturing profit (loss)		$ (5)

Because of the weak price for flour, the sales manager believes that the company should discontinue milling flour and use its entire milling capacity to produce cracked wheat to sell as cereal.

The same milling equipment is used for both products. Milling one ton of cracked wheat into one ton of flour requires the same capacity as milling one ton of wheat grain into one ton of cracked wheat. Hence, the choice is between one ton of flour and two tons of cracked wheat. Current cost and revenue data on the cracked wheat cereal follow:

		Per Ton of Cracked Wheat
Selling price		$490
Cost to manufacture:		
Wheat grain	$390	
Direct labor	20	
Manufacturing overhead	60	470
Manufacturing profit		$ 20

The sales manager argues that since the present $625 per ton price for the flour results in a $5 per ton loss, the milling of flour should not be resumed until the price per ton rises above $630.

The company assigns manufacturing overhead cost to the two products on the basis of milling hours. The same amount of time is required to mill either a ton of cracked wheat or a ton of flour. Virtually all manufacturing overhead costs are fixed. Materials and labor costs are variable.

The company can sell all of the cracked wheat and flour it can produce at the current market prices.

Required:

1. Do you agree with the sales manager that the company should discontinue milling flour and use the entire milling capacity to mill cracked wheat if the price of flour remains at $625 per ton? Support your answer with computations and explanations.
2. What is the lowest price that the company should accept for a ton of flour? Again support your answer with computations and explanations.

CASE 12-30 Plant Closing Decision [LO1, LO2]

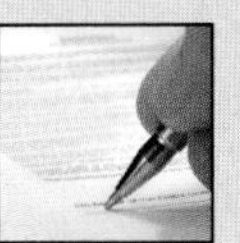

Mobile Seating Corporation manufactures seats for automobiles, vans, trucks, and boats. The company has a number of plants, including the Greenville Cover Plant, which makes seat covers.

Miriam Restin is the plant manager at the Greenville Cover Plant but also serves as the regional production manager for the company. Her budget as the regional manager is charged to the Greenville Cover Plant.

Restin has just heard that Mobile Seating has received a bid from an outside vendor to supply the equivalent of the entire annual output of the Greenville Cover Plant for $21 million. Restin was astonished at the low outside bid because the budget for the Greenville Cover Plant's operating costs for the coming year was set at $24.3 million. If this bid is accepted, the Greenville Cover Plant will be closed down.

The budget for the Greenville Cover Plant's operating costs for the coming year is presented below. Additional facts regarding the plant's operations are as follows:

a. Due to the Greenville Cover Plant's commitment to use high-quality fabrics in all of its products, the Purchasing Department was instructed to place blanket purchase orders with major suppliers to ensure the receipt of sufficient materials for the coming year. If these orders are canceled as a consequence of the plant closing, termination charges would amount to 25% of the cost of direct materials.
b. Approximately 350 employees will lose their jobs if the plant is closed. This includes all of the direct laborers and supervisors, management and staff, and the plumbers, electricians, and other skilled workers classified as indirect plant workers. Some of these workers would have difficulty finding new jobs. Nearly all the production workers would have difficulty matching the Greenville Cover Plant's base pay of $12.50 per hour, which is the highest in the area. A clause in Greenville Cover's contract with the union may help some employees; the company must provide employment assistance and job training to its former employees for 12 months after a plant closing. The estimated cost to administer this service would be $0.8 million.
c. Some employees would probably choose early retirement because Mobile Seating Corporation has an excellent pension plan. In fact, $0.7 million of the annual pension expense would continue whether the Greenville Cover Plant is open or not.
d. Restin and her regional staff would not be affected by the closing of the Greenville Cover Plant. They would still be responsible for running three other area plants.
e. If the Greenville Cover Plant were closed, the company would realize about $2 million salvage value for the equipment in the plant. If the plant remains open, there are no plans to make any significant investments in new equipment or buildings. The old equipment is adequate for the job and should last indefinitely.

Greenville Cover Plant
Annual Budget for Operating Costs

Materials		$ 8,000,000
Labor:		
Direct	$6,700,000	
Supervision	400,000	
Indirect plant	1,900,000	9,000,000
Overhead:		
Depreciation—equipment	1,300,000	
Depreciation—building	2,100,000	
Pension expense	1,600,000	
Plant manager and staff	600,000	
Corporate expenses*	1,700,000	7,300,000
Total budgeted costs		$24,300,000

*Fixed corporate expenses allocated to plants and other operating units based on total budgeted wage and salary costs.

Required:

1. Without regard to costs, identify the advantages to Mobile Seating Corporation of continuing to obtain covers from its own Greenville Cover Plant.
2. Mobile Seating Corporation plans to prepare a financial analysis that will be used in deciding whether or not to close the Greenville Cover Plant. Management has asked you to identify:
   a. The annual budgeted costs that are relevant to the decision regarding closing the plant (show the dollar amounts).
   b. The annual budgeted costs that are not relevant to the decision regarding closing the plant and explain why they are not relevant (again show the dollar amounts).
   c. Any nonrecurring costs that would arise due to the closing of the plant and explain how they would affect the decision (again show any dollar amounts).
3. Looking at the data you have prepared in (2) above, should the plant be closed? Show computations and explain your answer.
4. Identify any revenues or costs not specifically mentioned in the problem that Mobile Seating Corporation should consider before making a decision.

(CMA, adapted)

Chapter 13

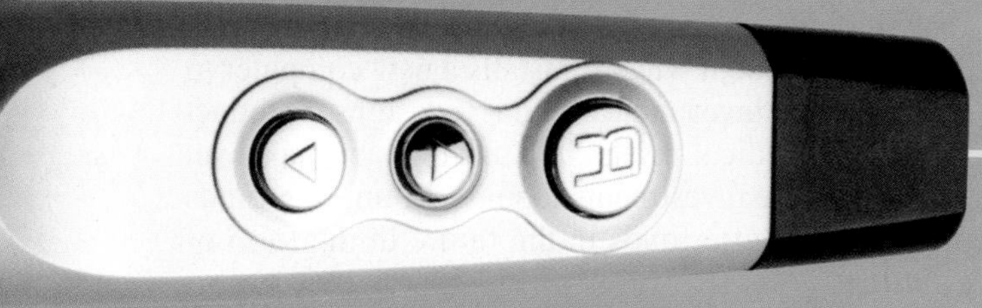

Capital Budgeting Decisions

LP 13

Capital Investments: A Key to Profitable Growth

BUSINESS FOCUS

Cintas Corporation, headquartered in Cincinnati, Ohio, has experienced 37 years of uninterrupted growth in sales and profits. The company provides highly specialized services to businesses of all types throughout North America, but the backbone of its success is providing corporate identity uniforms to more than five million North American workers. Cintas has 350 uniform rental facilities, 15 manufacturing plants, and seven distribution centers across North America. While these numbers are certain to grow in the future, the challenge for Cintas is choosing among competing capital expansion opportunities.

At Cintas, each capital investment proposal must be accompanied by a financial analysis that estimates the cash inflows and outflows associated with the project. The job of Paul Carmichael, the Controller of Cintas' Rental Division, is to challenge the validity of the assumptions underlying the financial estimates. Is the cost to build the new facility underestimated? Are future revenue growth rates overly optimistic? Is it necessary to build a new facility, or could an existing facility be refurbished or expanded? Asking these types of constructive questions helps Cintas channel its limited investment funds to the growth opportunities that will create the most long-term value for shareholders. ■

Source: Author's conversation with Paul Carmichael, Controller, Rental Division, Cintas Corporation.

Learning Objectives

After studying Chapter 13, you should be able to:

LO1 Evaluate the acceptability of an investment project using the net present value method.

LO2 Evaluate the acceptability of an investment project using the internal rate of return method.

LO3 Evaluate an investment project that has uncertain cash flows.

LO4 Rank investment projects in order of preference.

LO5 Determine the payback period for an investment.

LO6 Compute the simple rate of return for an investment.

LO7 (Appendix 13A) Understand present value concepts and the use of present value tables.

LO8 (Appendix 13C) Include income taxes in a capital budgeting analysis.

Managers are often involved in making decisions that involve an investment today in the hope of realizing future profits. For example, Tri-Con Global Restaurants, Inc. makes an investment when it opens a new Pizza Hut restaurant. L. L. Bean makes an investment when it installs a new computer to handle customer billing. DaimlerChrysler makes an investment when it redesigns a product such as the Jeep Eagle. Merck & Co. invests in medical research. Amazon.com makes an investment when it redesigns its website. All of these investments require committing funds today with the expectation of earning a return on those funds in the future in the form of additional cash inflows or reduced cash outflows.

The term **capital budgeting** is used to describe how managers plan significant investments in projects that have long-term implications such as the purchase of new equipment or the introduction of new products. Most companies have many more potential projects than can actually be funded. Hence, managers must carefully select those projects that promise the greatest future return. How well managers make these capital budgeting decisions is a critical factor in the long-run profitability of the company.

Capital Budgeting—Planning Investments

Video 13–1

Typical Capital Budgeting Decisions

Any decision that involves an outlay now in order to obtain a future return is a capital budgeting decision. Typical capital budgeting decisions include:

1. Cost reduction decisions. Should new equipment be purchased to reduce costs?
2. Expansion decisions. Should a new plant, warehouse, or other facility be acquired to increase capacity and sales?
3. Equipment selection decisions. Which of several available machines should be purchased?
4. Lease or buy decisions. Should new equipment be leased or purchased?
5. Equipment replacement decisions. Should old equipment be replaced now or later?

Capital budgeting decisions fall into two broad categories—*screening decisions* and *preference decisions.* **Screening decisions** relate to whether a proposed project is acceptable—whether it passes a preset hurdle. For example, a company may have a policy of accepting projects only if they promise a return of 20% on the investment. The required rate of return is the minimum rate of return a project must yield to be acceptable. **Preference decisions,** by contrast, relate to selecting from among several acceptable alternatives. To illustrate, a company may be considering several different machines to replace an existing machine on the assembly line. The choice of which machine to purchase is a preference decision. In this chapter, we first discuss screening decisions and then move on to preference decisions toward the end of the chapter.

The Time Value of Money

As stated earlier, capital investments usually earn returns that extend over fairly long periods of time. Therefore, it is important to recognize *the time value of money* when evaluating investment proposals. A dollar today is worth more than a dollar a year from now if for no other reason than that you could put a dollar in a bank today and have more than a dollar a year from now. Therefore, projects that promise earlier returns are preferable to those that promise later returns.

Capital budgeting techniques that recognize the time value of money involve *discounting cash flows.* We will spend most of this chapter showing how to use discounted cash flow methods in making capital budgeting decisions. If you are not already familiar with discounting and the use of present value tables, you should read Appendix 13A: The Concept of Present Value at the end of this chapter.

IN BUSINESS

CHOOSING A CAT

Sometimes a long-term decision does not have to involve present value calculations or any other sophisticated analytical technique. White Grizzly Adventures of Meadow Creek, British Columbia, needs two snowcats for its powder skiing operations—one for shuttling guests to the top of the mountain and one to be held in reserve in case of mechanical problems with the first. Bombardier of Canada sells new snowcats for $250,000 and used, reconditioned snowcats for $150,000. In either case, the snowcats are good for about 5,000 hours of operation before they need to be reconditioned. From White Grizzly's perspective, the choice is clear. Since both new and reconditioned snowcats last about 5,000 hours, but the reconditioned snowcats cost $100,000 less, the reconditioned snowcats are the obvious choice. They may not have all of the latest bells and whistles, but they get the job done at a price a small company can afford.

Bombardier snowcats do not have passenger cabs as standard equipment. To save money, White Grizzly builds its own custom-designed passenger cab for about $15,000, using recycled Ford Escort seats and industrial-strength aluminum for the frame and siding. If purchased at retail, a passenger cab would cost about twice as much and would not be as well-suited for snowcat skiing.

Source: Brad & Carole Karafil, owners and operators of White Grizzly Adventures, www.whitegrizzly.com.

Discounted Cash Flows—The Net Present Value Method

LEARNING OBJECTIVE 1
Evaluate the acceptability of an investment project using the net present value method.

Two approaches to making capital budgeting decisions use discounted cash flows. One is the *net present value method,* and the other is the *internal rate of return method.* The net present value method is discussed in this section; the internal rate of return method is discussed in the following section.

The Net Present Value Method Illustrated

Under the net present value method, the present value of a project's cash inflows is compared to the present value of the project's cash outflows. The difference between the present value of these cash flows, called the **net present value,** determines whether or not the project is an acceptable investment. To illustrate, consider the following data:

Example A: Harper Company is contemplating the purchase of a machine capable of performing certain operations that are now performed manually. The machine will cost $50,000, and it will last for five years. At the end of the five-year period, the machine will have a zero scrap value. Use of the machine will reduce labor costs by $18,000 per year. Harper Company requires a minimum pretax return of 20% on all investment projects.[1]

13–1

Video 13–1

Should the machine be purchased? Harper Company must determine whether a cash investment now of $50,000 can be justified if it will result in an $18,000 reduction in cost in each of the next five years. It may appear that the answer is obvious since the total cost savings is $90,000 ($18,000 per year × 5 years). However, the company can earn a 20% return by investing its money elsewhere. It is not enough that the cost reductions cover just the original cost of the machine; they must also yield a return of at least 20% or the company would be better off investing the money elsewhere.

[1] For simplicity, we ignore inflation and taxes. The impact of income taxes on capital budgeting decisions is discussed in Appendix 13C.

EXHIBIT 13–1
Net Present Value Analysis of a Proposed Project

Initial cost	$50,000
Life of the project	5 years
Annual cost savings	$18,000
Salvage value	$0
Required rate of return	20%

Item	Year(s)	Amount of Cash Flow	20% Factor	Present Value of Cash Flows
Annual cost savings	1–5	$ 18,000	2.991*	$53,838
Initial investment	Now	$(50,000)	1.000	(50,000)
Net present value				$ 3,838

*From Exhibit 13B–2 in Appendix 13B at the end of this chapter.

To determine whether the investment is desirable, the stream of annual $18,000 cost savings should be discounted to its present value and then compared to the cost of the new machine. Harper Company's minimum required return of 20% should be used as the *discount rate* in the discounting process. Exhibit 13–1 illustrates the computation of the net present value of this proposed project. The annual cost savings of $18,000 is multiplied by 2.991, the present value factor of a five-year annuity at the discount rate of 20%, to obtain $53,838.[2] This is the present value of the annual cost savings. The present value of the initial investment is computed by multiplying the investment amount of $50,000 by 1.000, the present value factor for any cash flow that occurs immediately.

According to the analysis, Harper Company should purchase the new machine. The present value of the cost savings is $53,838, whereas the present value of the required investment (cost of the machine) is only $50,000. Deducting the present value of the required investment from the present value of the cost savings yields the *net present value* of $3,838. Whenever the net present value is zero or greater, as in our example, an investment project is acceptable. Whenever the net present value is negative (the present value of the cash outflows exceeds the present value of the cash inflows), an investment project is not acceptable. In sum:

If the Net Present Value Is . . .	Then the Project Is . . .
Positive	Acceptable, since it promises a return greater than the required rate of return.
Zero	Acceptable, since it promises a return equal to the required rate of return.
Negative	Not acceptable, since it promises a return less than the required rate of return.

There is another way to interpret the net present value. Harper Company could spend up to $53,838 for the new machine and still obtain the minimum required 20% rate of return. The net present value of $3,838, therefore, shows the amount of "cushion" or "margin of error." One way to look at this is that the company could underestimate the cost of the new machine by up to $3,838, or overestimate the net present value of the future cash savings by up to $3,838, and the project would still be financially attractive.

[2] Unless otherwise stated, for the sake of simplicity we will assume in this chapter that all cash flows other than the initial investment occur at the ends of years.

Emphasis on Cash Flows

Accounting net income is based on accruals that ignore when cash flows occur. However, in capital budgeting, the timing of cash flows is critical. The present value of a cash flow depends on when it occurs. For that reason, cash flow rather than accounting net income is the focus in capital budgeting.[3] Examples of cash outflows and cash inflows that are often relevant to capital investment decisions are described below.

Typical Cash Outflows Most projects have at least three types of cash outflows. First, they often require an immediate cash outflow in the form of an initial investment in equipment, other assets, and installation costs. Any salvage value realized from the sale of old equipment can be recognized as a reduction in the initial investment or as a cash inflow. Second, some projects require a company to expand its working capital. **Working capital** is current assets (e.g., cash, accounts receivable, and inventory) less current liabilities. When a company takes on a new project, the balances in the current asset accounts often increase. For example, opening a new Nordstrom's department store requires additional cash in sales registers and more inventory. These additional working capital needs are treated as part of the initial investment in a project. Third, many projects require periodic outlays for repairs and maintenance and additional operating costs.

Typical Cash Inflows Most projects also have at least three types of cash inflows. First, a project will normally increase revenues or reduce costs. Either way, the amount involved should be treated as a cash inflow for capital budgeting purposes. Notice that from a cash flow standpoint, a reduction in costs is equivalent to an increase in revenues. Second, cash inflows are also frequently realized from selling equipment for its salvage value when a project ends, although the company may actually have to pay to dispose of some low-value or hazardous items. Third, any working capital that was tied up in the project can be released for use elsewhere at the end of the project and should be treated as a cash inflow at that time. Working capital is released, for example, when a company sells off its inventory or collects its accounts receivable.

IN BUSINESS

BEST BUY'S BIG GAMBLE

Best Buy is overhauling hundreds of its stores in an effort to tailor merchandise offerings and employee skills to meet the needs of each store's target customers. The cost to revamp one department of one store can easily exceed $600,000 for lighting and fixtures plus additional costs for employee training. While these initial cash outflows are readily quantifiable, the future cash inflows that they will generate are highly uncertain.

The first few dozen stores overhauled by Best Buy recorded sales growth that was three times greater than non-renovated stores. Best Buy reacted to these initial results by hastily renovating 154 more stores over the next three months. Shortly after completing these expensive renovations, the company had the misfortune of informing Wall Street that the newly revamped stores' growth rates were only slightly higher than non-renovated stores. This disappointing news apparently caused the market value of Best Buy's common stock to plummet by almost $3 billion in one day. Clearly, Wall Street analysts had serious concerns about the future cash flow generating ability of this capital investment project. Despite the "bump in the road," Best Buy remains committed to its course of action; however, the company has decided to slow down the pace of its implementation.

Source: Matthew Boyle, "Best Buy's Giant Gamble," *Fortune*, April, 3, 2006, pp. 69–75.

[3] Under certain conditions, capital budgeting decisions can be correctly made by discounting appropriately defined accounting net income. However, this approach requires advanced techniques that are beyond the scope of this book.

In summary, the following types of cash flows are common in business investment projects:

Cash outflows:
- Initial investment (including installation costs).
- Increased working capital needs.
- Repairs and maintenance.
- Incremental operating costs.

Cash inflows:
- Incremental revenues.
- Reduction in costs.
- Salvage value.
- Release of working capital.

Recovery of the Original Investment

The net present value method automatically provides for return of the original investment. Whenever the net present value of a project is positive, the project will recover the original cost of the investment plus sufficient excess cash inflows to compensate for tying up funds in the project. To demonstrate this point, consider the following situation:

Example B: Carver Hospital is considering the purchase of an attachment for its X-ray machine that will cost $3,170. The attachment will be usable for four years, after which time it will have no salvage value. It will increase net cash inflows by $1,000 per year in the X-ray department. The hospital's board of directors requires a rate of return of at least 10% on such investments in equipment.

A net present value analysis of the desirability of purchasing the X-ray attachment is presented in Exhibit 13–2. Notice that the attachment promises exactly a 10% return on the original investment, since the net present value is zero at a 10% discount rate.

Each annual $1,000 cash inflow arising from use of the attachment is made up of two parts. One part represents a recovery of a portion *of* the original $3,170 paid for the attachment, and the other part represents a return *on* this investment. The breakdown of each year's $1,000 cash inflow between recovery *of* investment and return *on* investment is shown in Exhibit 13–3.

The first year's $1,000 cash inflow consists of a return *on* investment of $317 (a 10% return *on* the $3,170 original investment), plus a $683 return *of* that investment. Since the amount of the unrecovered investment decreases each year, the dollar amount of the return on investment also decreases each year. By the end of the fourth year, all $3,170 of the original investment has been recovered.

EXHIBIT 13–2
Carver Hospital—Net Present Value Analysis of X-Ray Attachment

Initial cost	$3,170
Life of the project	4 years
Annual net cash inflow	$1,000
Salvage value	$0
Required rate of return	10%

Item	Year(s)	Amount of Cash Flow	10% Factor	Present Value of Cash Flows
Annual net cash inflow	1–4	$ 1,000	3.170*	$3,170
Initial investment	Now	$(3,170)	1.000	(3,170)
Net present value				$ 0

*From Exhibit 13B–2 in Appendix 13B.

EXHIBIT 13–3
Carver Hospital—Breakdown of Annual Cash Inflows

Year	(1) Investment Outstanding during the Year	(2) Cash Inflow	(3) Return on Investment (1) × 10%	(4) Recovery of Investment during the Year (2) − (3)	(5) Unrecovered Investment at the End of the Year (1) − (4)
1	$3,170	$1,000	$317	$ 683	$2,487
2	$2,487	$1,000	$249	751	$1,736
3	$1,736	$1,000	$173	827	$909
4	$909	$1,000	$91	909	$0
Total investment recovered				$3,170	

Simplifying Assumptions

Two simplifying assumptions are usually made in net present value analysis.

The first assumption is that all cash flows other than the initial investment occur at the end of periods. This is somewhat unrealistic in that cash flows typically occur *throughout* a period rather than just at its end. The purpose of this assumption is to simplify computations.

The second assumption is that all cash flows generated by an investment project are immediately reinvested at a rate of return equal to the discount rate. Unless these conditions are met, the net present value computed for the project will not be accurate. We used a discount rate of 10% for Carver Hospital in Exhibit 13–2. Unless the cash flows in each period are immediately reinvested at a 10% return, the net present value computed for the X-ray attachment will be misstated.

Choosing a Discount Rate

A positive net present value indicates that the project's return exceeds the discount rate. A negative net present value indicates that the project's return is less than the discount rate. Therefore, if the company's minimum required rate of return is used as the discount rate, a project with a positive net present value has a return that exceeds the minimum required rate of return and is acceptable. Contrarily, a project with a negative net present value has a return that is less than the minimum required rate of return and is unacceptable.

What is a company's minimum required rate of return? The company's *cost of capital* is usually regarded as the minimum required rate of return. The **cost of capital** is the average rate of return the company must pay to its long-term creditors and its shareholders for the use of their funds. If a project's rate of return is less than the cost of capital, the company does not earn enough to compensate its creditors and shareholders. Therefore, any project with a rate of return less than the cost of capital should be rejected.

The cost of capital serves as a *screening device.* When the cost of capital is used as the discount rate in net present value analysis, any project with a negative net present value does not cover the company's cost of capital and should be discarded as unacceptable.

An Extended Example of the Net Present Value Method

Example C provides an extended example of how the net present value method is used to analyze a proposed project. This example helps tie together and reinforce many of the ideas discussed thus far.

Example C: Under a special licensing arrangement, Swinyard Company has an opportunity to market a new product for a five-year period. The product would be purchased from the manufacturer, with Swinyard Company responsible for promotion and distribution costs. The licensing arrangement could be renewed at the end of the five-year period. After careful study, Swinyard Company estimated the following costs and revenues for the new product:

Cost of equipment needed	$60,000
Working capital needed	$100,000
Overhaul of the equipment in four years	$5,000
Salvage value of the equipment in five years	$10,000
Annual revenues and costs:	
Sales revenues	$200,000
Cost of goods sold	$125,000
Out-of-pocket operating costs (for salaries, advertising, and other direct costs)	$35,000

At the end of the five-year period, if Swinyard decides not to renew the licensing arrangement the working capital would be released for investment elsewhere. Swinyard Company uses a 14% discount rate. Would you recommend that the new product be introduced?

This example involves a variety of cash inflows and cash outflows. The solution is given in Exhibit 13–4.

Notice how the working capital is handled in this exhibit. It is counted as a cash outflow at the beginning of the project and as a cash inflow when it is released at the end of the project. Also notice how the sales revenues, cost of goods sold, and out-of-pocket costs are handled. **Out-of-pocket costs** are actual cash outlays for salaries, advertising, and other operating expenses.

Since the net present value of the proposal is positive, the new product is acceptable.

EXHIBIT 13–4
The Net Present Value Method—An Extended Example

Sales revenues	$200,000
Less cost of goods sold	125,000
Less out-of-pocket costs for salaries, advertising, etc.	35,000
Annual net cash inflows	$ 40,000

Item	Year(s)	Amount of Cash Flow	14% Factor	Present Value of Cash Flows
Purchase of equipment	Now	$(60,000)	1.000	$ (60,000)
Working capital needed	Now	$(100,000)	1.000	(100,000)
Overhaul of equipment	4	$(5,000)	0.592*	(2,960)
Annual net cash inflows from sales of the product line	1–5	$40,000	3.433†	137,320
Salvage value of the equipment	5	$10,000	0.519*	5,190
Working capital released	5	$100,000	0.519*	51,900
Net present value				$ 31,450

*From Exhibit 13B–1 in Appendix 13B.
†From Exhibit 13B–2 in Appendix 13B.

Discounted Cash Flows—The Internal Rate of Return Method

LEARNING OBJECTIVE 2
Evaluate the acceptability of an investment project using the internal rate of return method.

The **internal rate of return** is the rate of return promised by an investment project over its useful life. It is sometimes referred to simply as the *yield* on a project. The internal rate of return is computed by finding the discount rate that equates the present value of a project's cash outflows with the present value of its cash inflows. In other words, the internal rate of return is the discount rate that results in a net present value of zero.

The Internal Rate of Return Method Illustrated

To illustrate the internal rate of return method, consider the following data:

Video 13–1

Example D: Glendale School District is considering the purchase of a large tractor-pulled lawn mower. At present, the lawn is mowed using a small hand-pushed gas mower. The large, tractor-pulled mower will cost $16,950 and will have a useful life of 10 years. It will have a negligible scrap value, which can be ignored. The tractor-pulled mower would do the job faster than the old mower, resulting in labor savings of $3,000 per year.

To compute the internal rate of return promised by the new mower, we must find the discount rate that will cause the net present value of the project to be zero. How do we do this? The simplest and most direct approach *when the net cash inflow is the same every year* is to divide the investment in the project by the expected net annual cash inflow. This computation will yield a factor from which the internal rate of return can be determined. The formula is as follows:

$$\text{Factor of the internal rate of return} = \frac{\text{Investment required}}{\text{Net annual cash inflow}} \qquad (1)$$

The factor derived from formula (1) is then located in the present value tables to see what rate of return it represents. Using formula (1) and the data for the Glendale School District's proposed project, we get:

$$\frac{\text{Investment required}}{\text{Net annual cash inflow}} = \frac{\$16{,}950}{\$3{,}000} = 5.650$$

Thus, the discount factor that will equate a series of $3,000 cash inflows with a present investment of $16,950 is 5.650. Now we need to find this factor in Exhibit 13B–2 in Appendix 13B to see what rate of return it represents. We should use the 10-period line in Exhibit 13B–2 because the cash flows for the project continue for 10 years. If we scan along the 10-period line, we find that a factor of 5.650 represents a 12% rate of return. Therefore, the internal rate of return promised by the mower project is 12%. We can verify this by computing the project's net present value using a 12% discount rate. This computation is shown in Exhibit 13–5.

Notice from Exhibit 13–5 that using a 12% discount rate equates the present value of the annual cash inflows with the present value of the investment required for the project, leaving a zero net present value. The 12% rate therefore represents the internal rate of return promised by the project.

EXHIBIT 13–5
Evaluation of the Mower Purchase Using a 12% Discount Rate

Initial cost	$16,950
Life of the project	10 years
Annual cost savings	$3,000
Salvage value	$0

Item	Year(s)	Amount of Cash Flow	12% Factor	Present Value of Cash Flows
Annual cost savings	1–10	$3,000	5.650*	$16,950
Initial investment	Now	$(16,950)	1.000	(16,950)
Net present value				$ 0

*From Exhibit 13B–2 in Appendix 13B.

Salvage Value and Other Cash Flows

The technique just demonstrated works if a project's cash flows are identical every year. But what if they are not? For example, what if a project will have some salvage value at the end of its life in addition to the annual cash inflows? Under these circumstances, a trial-and-error process may be used to find the rate of return that will equate the cash inflows with the cash outflows. The trial-and-error process can be carried out by hand; however, computer software programs such as spreadsheets can perform the necessary computations in seconds. In short, erratic or uneven cash flows should not prevent an analyst from determining a project's internal rate of return.

Using the Internal Rate of Return

To evaluate a project, the internal rate of return is compared to the company's minimum required rate of return, which is usually the company's cost of capital. If the internal rate of return is equal to or greater than the required rate of return, then the project is considered to be acceptable. If the internal rate of return is less than the required rate of return, then the project is rejected.

In the case of the Glendale School District example, let us assume that the district has set a minimum required rate of return of 15% on all projects. Since the large mower's internal rate of return is only 12%, the project does not clear the 15% hurdle and should be rejected.

The Cost of Capital as a Screening Tool

As we have seen in preceding examples, the cost of capital often operates as a *screening* device, helping screen out undesirable investment projects. This screening is accomplished in different ways, depending on whether the company is using the internal rate of return method or the net present value method.

When the internal rate of return method is used, the cost of capital is used as the *hurdle rate* that a project must clear for acceptance. If the internal rate of return of a project is not great enough to clear the cost of capital hurdle, then the project is ordinarily rejected. We saw the application of this idea in the Glendale School District example, where the hurdle rate was set at 15%.

When the net present value method is used, the cost of capital is the *discount rate* used to compute the net present value of a proposed project. Any project yielding a negative net present value is rejected unless other factors are significant enough to warrant its acceptance.

The use of the cost of capital as a screening tool is summarized in Exhibit 13–6.

EXHIBIT 13–6
Capital Budgeting Screening Decisions

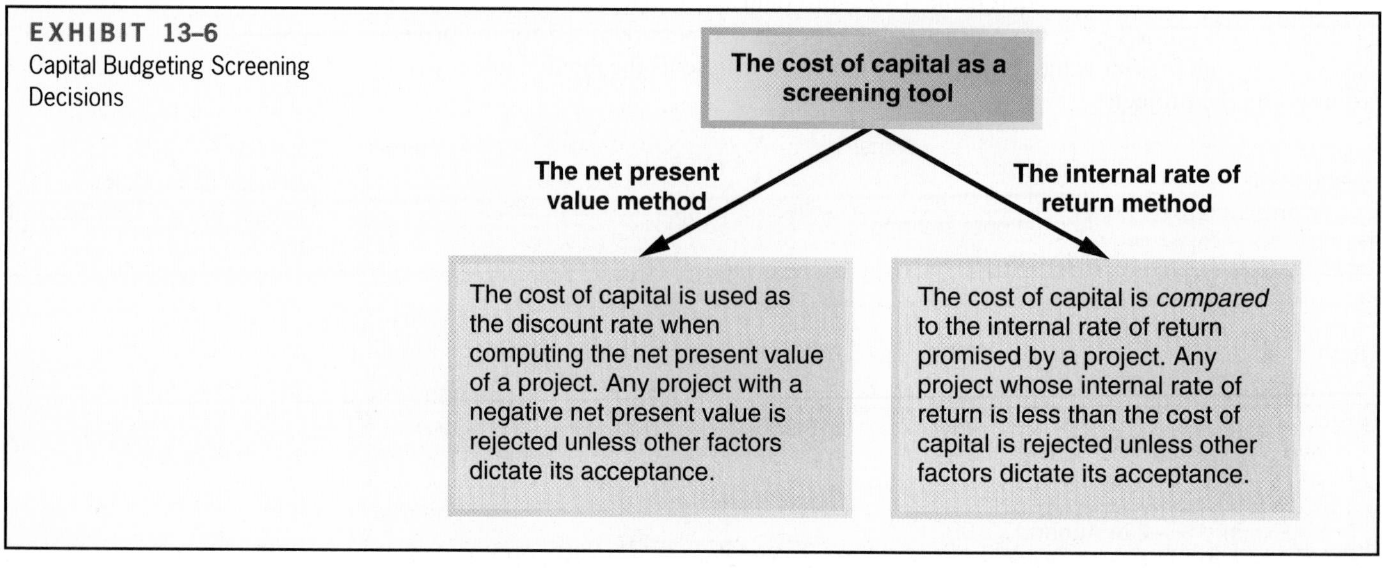

Comparison of the Net Present Value and Internal Rate of Return Methods

The net present value method has several important advantages over the internal rate of return method.

First, the net present value method is often simpler to use than the internal rate of return method. As mentioned earlier, the internal rate of return method may require hunting for the discount rate that results in a net present value of zero. This can be a very laborious trial-and-error process, although it can be automated using a computer.

Second, the internal rate of return method makes a questionable assumption. Both methods assume that cash flows generated by a project during its useful life are immediately reinvested elsewhere. However, the two methods make different assumptions concerning the rate of return that is earned on those cash flows. The net present value method assumes the rate of return is the discount rate, whereas the internal rate of return method assumes the rate of return is the internal rate of return on the project. Specifically, if the internal rate of return of the project is high, this assumption may not be realistic. It is generally more realistic to assume that cash inflows can be reinvested at a rate of return equal to the discount rate—particularly if the discount rate is the company's cost of capital or an opportunity rate of return. For example, if the discount rate is the company's cost of capital, this rate of return can be actually realized by paying off the company's creditors and buying back the company's stock with cash flows from the project. In short, when the net present value method and the internal rate of return method do not agree concerning the attractiveness of a project, it is best to go with the net present value method. Of the two methods, it makes the more realistic assumption about the rate of return that can be earned on cash flows from the project.

Expanding the Net Present Value Method

So far all of our examples have involved an evaluation of a single investment project. In the following section we expand the discussion of the net present value method to include evaluation of two alternative projects. In addition, we integrate relevant cost concepts into the discounted cash flow analysis. We use two approaches to compare competing investment projects—the *total-cost approach* and the *incremental-cost approach.* Each approach is illustrated in the next few pages.

The Total-Cost Approach

The total-cost approach is the most flexible method for comparing competing projects. To illustrate the mechanics of the approach, consider the following data:

Example E: Harper Ferry Company operates a high-speed passenger ferry service across the Mississippi River. One of its ferryboats is in poor condition. This ferry can be renovated at an immediate cost of $200,000. Further repairs and an overhaul of the motor will be needed five years from now at a cost of $80,000. In all, the ferry will be usable for 10 years if this work is done. At the end of 10 years, the ferry will have to be scrapped at a salvage value of $60,000. The scrap value of the ferry right now is $70,000. It will cost $300,000 each year to operate the ferry, and revenues will total $400,000 annually.

As an alternative, Harper Ferry Company can purchase a new ferryboat at a cost of $360,000. The new ferry will have a life of 10 years, but it will require some repairs costing $30,000 at the end of 5 years. At the end of 10 years, the ferry will have a scrap value of $60,000. It will cost $210,000 each year to operate the ferry, and revenues will total $400,000 annually.

Harper Ferry Company requires a return of at least 14% before taxes on all investment projects.

Should the company purchase the new ferry or renovate the old ferry? Exhibit 13–7 (page 558) shows the solution using the total-cost approach.

Two points should be noted from the exhibit. First, *all* cash inflows and *all* cash outflows are included in the solution under each alternative. No effort has been made to isolate those cash flows that are relevant to the decision and those that are not relevant. The inclusion of all cash flows associated with each alternative gives the approach its name—the *total-cost* approach.

EXHIBIT 13–7
The Total-Cost Approach to Project Selection

	New Ferry	Old Ferry
Annual revenues	$400,000	$400,000
Annual cash operating costs	210,000	300,000
Net annual cash inflows	$190,000	$100,000

Item	Year(s)	Amount of Cash Flows	14% Factor*	Present Value of Cash Flows
Buy the new ferry:				
Initial investment	Now	$(360,000)	1.000	$(360,000)
Salvage value of the old ferry	Now	$70,000	1.000	70,000
Repairs in five years	5	$(30,000)	0.519	(15,570)
Net annual cash inflows	1–10	$190,000	5.216	991,040
Salvage value of the new ferry	10	$60,000	0.270	16,200
Net present value				701,670
Keep the old ferry:				
Renovation	Now	$(200,000)	1.000	(200,000)
Repairs in five years	5	$(80,000)	0.519	(41,520)
Net annual cash inflows	1–10	$100,000	5.216	521,600
Salvage value of the old ferry	10	$60,000	0.270	16,200
Net present value				296,280
Net present value in favor of buying the new ferry				$ 405,390

*All present value factors are from Exhibits 13B–1 and 13B–2 in Appendix 13B.

Second, notice that a net present value is computed for each alternative. This is a distinct advantage of the total-cost approach because an unlimited number of alternatives can be compared side by side to determine the best option. For example, another alternative for Harper Ferry Company would be to get out of the ferry business entirely. If management desired, the net present value of this alternative could be computed to compare with the alternatives shown in Exhibit 13–7. Still other alternatives might be open to the company. In the case at hand, given only two alternatives, the data indicate that the most profitable choice is to purchase the new ferry.[4]

IN BUSINESS

DOES IT REALLY NEED TO BE NEW?

Tom Copeland, the director of Corporate Finance Practice at the consulting firm Monitor Group, observes: "If they could afford it, most people would like to drive a new car. Managers are no different . . . [I]n my experience, . . . [managers] routinely spend millions of dollars on new machines years earlier than they need to. In most cases, the overall cost (including the cost of breakdowns) is 30% to 40% lower if a company continues servicing an existing machine for five more years instead of buying a new one. In order to fight impulsive acquisitions of new machinery, companies should require unit managers to run the numbers on all alternative investment options open to them—including maintaining the existing assets or buying used ones."

Source: Tom Copeland, "Cutting Costs Without Drawing Blood," *Harvard Business Review*, September–October 2000, pp. 3–7.

[4] The alternative with the highest net present value is not always the best choice, although it is the best choice in this case. For further discussion, see the section Preference Decisions—The Ranking of Investment Projects.

EXHIBIT 13–8
The Incremental-Cost Approach to Project Selection

Item	Year(s)	Amount of Cash Flows	14% Factor*	Present Value of Cash Flows
Incremental investment to buy the new ferry	Now	$(160,000)	1.000	$(160,000)
Salvage value of the old ferry now	Now	$70,000	1.000	70,000
Difference in repairs in five years.	5	$50,000	0.519	25,950
Increase in net annual cash inflows	1–10	$90,000	5.216	469,440
Difference in salvage value in 10 years	10	$0	0.270	0
Net present value in favor of buying the new ferry. . .				$ 405,390

*All present value factors are from Exhibits 13B–1 and 13B–2 in Appendix 13B.

The Incremental-Cost Approach

When only two alternatives are being considered, the incremental-cost approach offers a simpler and more direct route to a decision. In the incremental-cost approach, only those costs and revenues that *differ* between the two alternatives are included in the analysis. To illustrate, refer again to the data in Example E relating to Harper Ferry Company. The solution using only differential costs is presented in Exhibit 13–8.[5]

Two things should be noted from the data in this exhibit. First, the net present value in favor of buying the new ferry of $405,390 shown in Exhibit 13–8 agrees with the net present value shown under the total-cost approach in Exhibit 13–7. The two approaches are just different roads to the same destination.

Second, the costs used in Exhibit 13–8 are just the differences between the costs shown for the two alternatives in the prior exhibit. For example, the $160,000 incremental investment required to purchase the new ferry in Exhibit 13–8 is the difference between the $360,000 cost of the new ferry and the $200,000 cost required to renovate the old ferry from Exhibit 13–7. The other figures in Exhibit 13–8 have been computed in the same way.

Least-Cost Decisions

Some decisions do not involve any revenues. For example, a company may be trying to decide whether to buy or lease an executive jet. The choice would be made on the basis of which alternative—buying or leasing—would be least costly. In situations such as these, where no revenues are involved, the most desirable alternative is the one with the *least total cost* from a present value perspective. Hence, these are known as least-cost decisions. To illustrate a least-cost decision, consider the following data:

Example F: Val-Tek Company is considering replacing an old threading machine with a new threading machine that would substantially reduce annual operating costs. Selected data relating to the old and new machines are presented below:

	Old Machine	New Machine
Purchase cost when new	$200,000	$250,000
Salvage value now	$30,000	—
Annual cash operating costs	$150,000	$90,000
Overhaul needed immediately	$40,000	—
Salvage value in six years	$0	$50,000
Remaining life	6 years	6 years

Val-Tek Company uses a 10% discount rate.

[5] Technically, the incremental-cost approach is misnamed, since it focuses on differential costs (that is, on both cost increases and decreases) rather than just on incremental costs. As used here, the term *incremental costs* should be interpreted broadly to include both cost increases and cost decreases.

EXHIBIT 13–9
The Total-Cost Approach (Least-Cost Decision)

Item	Year(s)	Amount of Cash Flows	10% Factor*	Present Value of Cash Flows
Buy the new machine:				
Initial investment	Now	$(250,000)	1.000	$(250,000)†
Salvage value of the old machine	Now	$30,000	1.000	30,000†
Annual cash operating costs	1–6	$(90,000)	4.355	(391,950)
Salvage value of the new machine	6	$50,000	0.564	28,200
Present value of net cash outflows				(583,750)
Keep the old machine:				
Overhaul needed now	Now	$(40,000)	1.000	$ (40,000)
Annual cash operating costs	1–6	$(150,000)	4.355	(653,250)
Present value of net cash outflows				(693,250)
Net present value in favor of buying the new machine				$ 109,500

*All factors are from Exhibits 13B–1 and 13B–2 in Appendix 13B.
†These two items could be netted into a single $220,000 incremental-cost figure ($250,000 − $30,000 = $220,000).

Exhibit 13–9 analyzes the alternatives using the total-cost approach. Because this is a least-cost decision, the present values are negative for both alternatives. However, the present value of the alternative of buying the new machine is $109,500 higher than the other alternative. Therefore, buying the new machine is the less costly alternative.

Exhibit 13–10 presents an analysis of the same alternatives using the incremental-cost approach. Once again, the total-cost and incremental-cost approaches arrive at the same answer.

IN BUSINESS

TRADING IN THAT OLD CAR?

Consumer Reports magazine provides the following data concerning the alternatives of keeping a four-year-old Ford Taurus for three years or buying a similar new car to replace it. The illustration assumes the car would be purchased and used in suburban Chicago.

	Keep the Old Taurus	Buy a New Taurus
Annual maintenance	$1,180	$650
Annual insurance	$370	$830
Annual license	$15	$100
Trade-in value in three years	$605	$7,763
Purchase price, including sales tax		$17,150

Consumer Reports is ordinarily extremely careful in its analysis, but in this instance it has omitted one financial item that differs substantially between the alternatives. What is it? To check your answer, go to the textbook website at www.mhhe.com/noreen1e. After accessing the site, click on the link to this chapter and then the link to the Internet Exercises.

Source: "When to Give Up on Your Clunker," *Consumer Reports*, August 2000, pp. 12–16.

EXHIBIT 13–10
The Incremental-Cost Approach (Least-Cost Decision)

Item	Year(s)	Amount of Cash Flows	10% Factor*	Present Value of Cash Flows
Incremental investment required to purchase the new machine	Now	$(210,000)	1.000	$(210,000)†
Salvage value of the old machine.	Now	$30,000	1.000	30,000†
Savings in annual cash operating costs	1–6	$60,000	4.355	261,300
Difference in salvage value in six years	6	$50,000	0.564	28,200
Net present value in favor of buying the new machine				$ 109,500

*All factors are from Exhibits 13B–1 and 13B–2 in Appendix 13B.
†These two items could be netted into a single $180,000 incremental-cost figure ($210,000 − $30,000 = $180,000).

Uncertain Cash Flows

Thus far, we have assumed that all future cash flows are known with certainty. However, future cash flows are often uncertain or difficult to estimate. A number of techniques are available for handling this complication. Some of these techniques are quite technical—involving computer simulations or advanced mathematical skills—and are beyond the scope of this book. However, we can provide some very useful information to managers without getting too technical.

LEARNING OBJECTIVE 3
Evaluate an investment project that has uncertain cash flows.

An Example

As an example of difficult-to-estimate future cash flows, consider the case of investments in automated equipment. The up-front costs of automated equipment and the tangible benefits, such as reductions in operating costs and waste, tend to be relatively easy to estimate. However, the intangible benefits, such as greater reliability, greater speed, and higher quality, are more difficult to quantify in terms of future cash flows. These intangible benefits certainly impact future cash flows—particularly in terms of increased sales and perhaps higher selling prices—but the cash flow effects are difficult to estimate. What can be done?

A fairly simple procedure can be followed when the intangible benefits are likely to be significant. Suppose, for example, that a company with a 12% discount rate is considering purchasing automated equipment that would have a 10-year useful life. Also suppose that a discounted cash flow analysis of just the tangible costs and benefits shows a negative net present value of $226,000. Clearly, if the intangible benefits are large enough, they could turn this negative net present value into a positive net present value. In this case, the amount of additional cash flow per year from the intangible benefits that would be needed to make the project financially attractive can be computed as follows:

Net present value excluding the intangible benefits (negative)	$(226,000)
Present value factor for an annuity at 12% for 10 periods (from Exhibit 13B–2 in Appendix 13B).	5.650

$$\frac{\text{Negative net present value to be offset, \$226,000}}{\text{Present value factor, 5.650}} = \$40,000$$

Thus, if the intangible benefits of the automated equipment are worth at least $40,000 a year to the company, then the automated equipment should be purchased. If, in the judgment of management, these intangible benefits are not worth $40,000 a year, then the automated equipment should not be purchased.

This technique can be used in other situations in which future cash flows are difficult to estimate. For example, this technique can be used when the salvage value is difficult to estimate. To illustrate, suppose that all of the cash flows from an investment in a supertanker have been estimated—other than its salvage value in 20 years. Using a discount rate of 12%, management has determined that the net present value of all of these cash flows is a negative $1.04 million. This negative net present value would be offset by the salvage value of the supertanker. How large would the salvage value have to be to make this investment attractive?

Net present value excluding salvage value (negative)	$(1,040,000)
Present value factor at 12% for 20 periods (from Exhibit 13B–1 in Appendix 13B)	0.104

$$\frac{\text{Negative net present value to be offset, \$1,040,000}}{\text{Present value factor, 0.104}} = \$10{,}000{,}000$$

Thus, if the salvage value of the tanker in 20 years is at least $10 million, its net present value would be positive and the investment would be made. However, if management believes the salvage value is unlikely to be as large as $10 million, the investment should not be made.

Real Options

The analysis in this chapter has assumed that an investment cannot be postponed and that, once started, nothing can be done to alter the course of the project. In reality, investments can often be postponed. Postponement is a particularly attractive option when the net present value of a project is modest using current estimates of future cash flows and the future cash flows involve a great deal of uncertainty that may be resolved over time. Similarly, once an investment is made, management can often exploit changes in the business environment and take actions that enhance future cash flows. For example, buying a supertanker provides management with a number of options, some of which may become more attractive as time unfolds. Instead of operating the supertanker itself, the company may decide to lease it to another operator if the rental rates become high enough. Or, if a supertanker shortage develops, management may decide to sell the supertanker and take a gain. In the case of an investment in automated equipment, management may initially buy only the basic model without costly add-ons, but keep the option open to add more capacity and capability later. The ability to delay the start of a project, to expand it if conditions are favorable, to cut losses if they are unfavorable, and to otherwise modify plans as business conditions change adds value to many investments. These advantages can be quantified using what is called *real options* analysis, but the techniques are beyond the scope of this book.

IN BUSINESS

THINKING AHEAD

With an eye on environmental concerns, the board of directors of Royal Dutch/Shell, the Anglo-Dutch energy company, has decided that all big projects must explicitly take into account the likely future costs of abating carbon emissions. Calculations must assume a cost of $5 per ton of carbon dioxide emission in 2005 through 2009, rising to $20 per ton from 2010 onward. A Shell manager explains: "We know that $5 and $20 are surely the wrong price, but everyone else who assumes a carbon price of zero in the future will be more wrong. This is not altruism. We see it as giving us a competitive edge."

Source: "Big Business Bows to Global Warming," *The Economist*, December 2, 2000, p. 81.

Preference Decisions—The Ranking of Investment Projects

LEARNING OBJECTIVE 4
Rank investment projects in order of preference.

Recall that when considering investment opportunities, managers must make two types of decisions—screening decisions and preference decisions. Screening decisions, which come first, pertain to whether or not a proposed investment is acceptable. Preference decisions come *after* screening decisions and attempt to answer the following question: "How do the remaining investment proposals, all of which have been screened and provide an acceptable rate of return, rank in terms of preference? That is, which one(s) would be *best* for the company to accept?"

Sometimes preference decisions are called rationing decisions, or ranking decisions. Limited investment funds must be rationed among many competing alternatives. Hence, the alternatives must be ranked. Either the internal rate of return method or the net present value method can be used in making preference decisions. However, as discussed earlier, if the two methods are in conflict, it is best to use the net present value method, which is more reliable.

Internal Rate of Return Method

When using the internal rate of return method to rank competing investment projects, the preference rule is: *The higher the internal rate of return, the more desirable the project.* An investment project with an internal rate of return of 18% is usually considered preferable to another project that promises a return of only 15%. Internal rate of return is widely used to rank projects.

Net Present Value Method

The net present value of one project cannot be directly compared to the net present value of another project unless the initial investments are equal. For example, assume that a company is considering two competing investments, as shown below:

	Investment	
	A	B
Investment required	$(10,000)	$(5,000)
Present value of cash inflows	11,000	6,000
Net present value	$ 1,000	$ 1,000

Although each project has a net present value of $1,000, the projects are not equally desirable if the funds available for investment are limited. The project requiring an investment of only $5,000 is much more desirable than the project requiring an investment of $10,000. This fact can be highlighted by dividing the net present value of the project by the investment required. The result, shown below in equation form, is called the **project profitability index.**

$$\text{Project profitability index} = \frac{\text{Net present value of the project}}{\text{Investment required}} \tag{2}$$

The project profitability indexes for the two investments above would be computed as follows:

	Investment	
	A	B
Net present value (a)	$1,000	$1,000
Investment required (b)	$10,000	$5,000
Project profitability index, (a) ÷ (b)	0.10	0.20

When using the project profitability index to rank competing investments projects, the preference rule is: *The higher the project profitability index, the more desirable the project.*[6] Applying this rule to the two investments above, investment B should be chosen over investment A.

The project profitability index is an application of the techniques for utilizing constrained resources discussed in Chapter 12. In this case, the constrained resource is the limited funds available for investment, and the project profitability index is similar to the contribution margin per unit of the constrained resource.

A few details should be clarified with respect to the computation of the project profitability index. The "Investment required" refers to any cash outflows that occur at the beginning of the project, reduced by any salvage value recovered from the sale of old equipment. The "Investment required" also includes any investment in working capital that the project may need.

Other Approaches to Capital Budgeting Decisions

The net present value and internal rate of return methods are widely used as decision-making tools. However, some managers also use the payback method and simple rate of return method to make capital budgeting decisions. Each of these methods will be discussed in turn.

The Payback Method

LEARNING OBJECTIVE 5
Determine the payback period for an investment.

The payback method focuses on the *payback period.* The **payback period** is the length of time that it takes for a project to recover its initial cost from the cash receipts that it generates. This period is sometimes referred to as "the time that it takes for an investment to pay for itself." The basic premise of the payback method is that the more quickly the cost of an investment can be recovered, the more desirable is the investment.

The payback period is expressed in years. *When the net annual cash inflow is the same every year,* the following formula can be used to compute the payback period:

Video 13–1

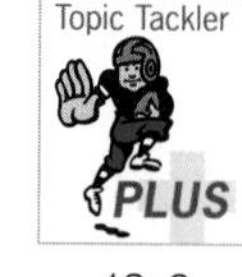

13–2

$$\text{Payback period} = \frac{\text{Investment required}}{\text{Net annual cash inflow}} \qquad (3)$$

To illustrate the payback method, consider the following data:

Example G: York Company needs a new milling machine. The company is considering two machines: machine A and machine B. Machine A costs $15,000, has a useful life of 10 years, and will reduce operating costs by $5,000 per year. Machine B costs only $12,000, will also reduce operating costs by $5,000 per year, but has a useful life of only five years.

Required:
Which machine should be purchased according to the payback method?

$$\text{Machine A payback period} = \frac{\$15{,}000}{\$5{,}000} = 3.0 \text{ years}$$

$$\text{Machine B payback period} = \frac{\$12{,}000}{\$5{,}000} = 2.4 \text{ years}$$

According to the payback calculations, York Company should purchase machine B because it has a shorter payback period than machine A.

[6] Because of the "lumpiness" of projects, the project profitability index ranking may not be perfect. Nevertheless, it is a good starting point. For further details, see the Profitability Analysis Appendix at the end of the book.

IN BUSINESS

ENTREPRENEURIAL INGENUITY AT ITS BEST

Jonathan Pratt owns two Ümani Cafés in Westchester County, New York. He used to pay $200 a month to dispose of the vegetable oil that is used to fry foods in his restaurants. Plus, he bought $700 of gas every month to operate his company's pick-up truck. Then Pratt got an idea. He purchased a diesel-powered Ford F250 on eBay for $11,000 and paid $1,500 to haul the truck from Arizona to New York. Next, he installed an $850 conversion kit on his new truck to enable it to run on vegetable oil. Since he no longer has to pay to dispose of vegetable oil or buy gasoline, Pratt figures that his investment will pay for itself in about 15 months ($13,350 ÷ $900 = 14.83 months). Furthermore, he now has the best smelling car in town—it smells like french fries when he drives down the road.

Source: Jean Chatzky, "Out of the Frying Pan, Into the Ford," *Money*, October, 2004, p. 28.

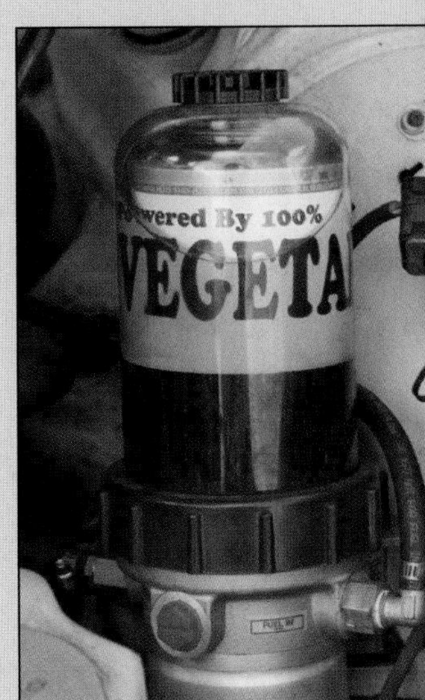

Evaluation of the Payback Method

The payback method is not a true measure of the profitability of an investment. Rather, it simply tells a manager how many years are required to recover the original investment. Unfortunately, a shorter payback period does not always mean that one investment is more desirable than another.

To illustrate, refer back to Example G above. Machine B has a shorter payback period than machine A, but it has a useful life of only 5 years rather than 10 years for machine A. Machine B would have to be purchased twice—once immediately and then again after the fifth year—to provide the same service as just one machine A. Under these circumstances, machine A would probably be a better investment than machine B, even though machine B has a shorter payback period. Unfortunately, the payback method ignores all cash flows that occur after the payback period.

A further criticism of the payback method is that it does not consider the time value of money. A cash inflow to be received several years in the future is weighed the same as a cash inflow received right now. To illustrate, assume that for an investment of $8,000 you can purchase either of the two following streams of cash inflows:

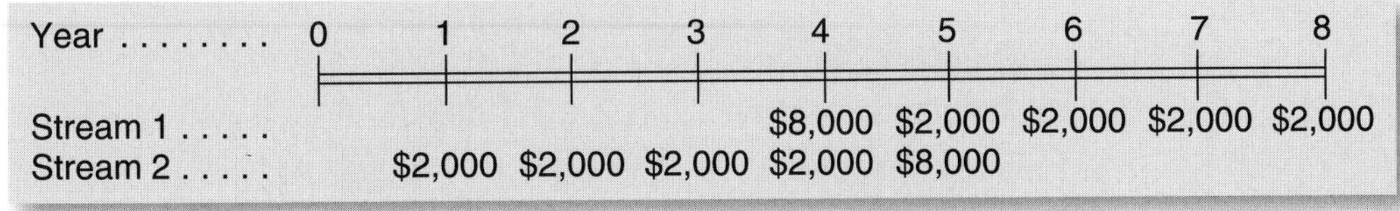

Year	0	1	2	3	4	5	6	7	8
Stream 1					$8,000	$2,000	$2,000	$2,000	$2,000
Stream 2		$2,000	$2,000	$2,000	$2,000	$8,000			

Which stream of cash inflows would you prefer to receive in return for your $8,000 investment? Each stream has a payback period of 4.0 years. Therefore, if payback alone is used to make the decision, the streams would be considered equally desirable. However, from a time value of money perspective, stream 2 is much more desirable than stream 1.

On the other hand, under certain conditions the payback method can be very useful. For one thing, it can help identify which investment proposals are in the "ballpark." That is, it can be used as a screening tool to help answer the question, "Should I consider this proposal further?" If a proposal doesn't provide a payback within some specified period, then there may be no need to consider it further. In addition, the payback period is often of great importance to new companies that are "cash poor." When a company is cash poor, a project with a short payback period but a low rate of return might be preferred over another project with a high rate of return but a long payback period. The reason is that the company may simply need a faster return of its cash investment. And finally, the payback method is sometimes used in industries where products become obsolete very rapidly—such as consumer electronics. Since products may last only a year or two, the payback period on investments must be very short.

IN BUSINESS

CONSERVATION IS NOT SELF-DENIAL

Amory Lovins, the director of the Rocky Mountain Institute in Snowmass, Colorado, is a passionate advocate of energy efficiency as a means of conserving natural resources and reducing pollution. Rather than cutting energy consumption by adopting more austere lifestyles, Lovins believes that energy consumption can be radically cut by using energy more efficiently. This approach has the virtues of combining energy conservation with cash savings and better living standards. He claims that America's annual electric bill of $220 billion could be cut in half by making investments with a payback period of one year or less. To illustrate his point, Lovins designed the institute's headquarters to require no furnace or air conditioning. During the cold winters, daytime solar heat enters the building through a built-in greenhouse, is soaked up by massive stone walls and foundations, and is then released at night. The institute is hardly a chilling, austere structure. Its passive heating system supports a small stand of tropical fruit trees, a mini fish farm, an indoor waterfall, and a hot tub. Lovins claims that the building's efficient design added only $6,000 to its construction costs and the payback period on this investment was only 10 months.

Source: David Stipp, "Can This Man Solve America's Energy Crisis?" *Fortune,* May 13, 2002, pp. 100–110.

An Extended Example of Payback

As shown by formula (3) given earlier, the payback period is computed by dividing the investment in a project by the net annual cash inflows that the project will generate. If new equipment is replacing old equipment, then any salvage value to be received when disposing of the old equipment should be deducted from the cost of the new equipment, and only the *incremental* investment should be used in the payback computation. In addition, any depreciation deducted in arriving at the project's net operating income must be added back to obtain the project's expected net annual cash inflow. To illustrate, consider the following data:

Example H: Goodtime Fun Centers, Inc., operates amusement parks. Some of the vending machines in one of its parks provide very little revenue, so the company is considering removing the machines and installing equipment to dispense soft ice cream. The equipment would cost $80,000 and have an eight-year useful life with no salvage value. Incremental annual revenues and costs associated with the sale of ice cream would be as follows:

Sales	$150,000
Variable expenses	90,000
Contribution margin	60,000
Fixed expenses:	
Salaries	27,000
Maintenance	3,000
Depreciation	10,000
Total fixed expenses	40,000
Net operating income	$ 20,000

The vending machines can be sold for a $5,000 scrap value. The company will not purchase equipment unless it has a payback period of three years or less. Does the ice cream dispenser pass this hurdle?

EXHIBIT 13–11
Computation of the Payback Period

Step 1: *Compute the net annual cash inflow.* Since the net annual cash inflow is not given, it must be computed before the payback period can be determined:

Net operating income (given above)	$20,000
Add: Noncash deduction for depreciation	10,000
Net annual cash inflow	$30,000

Step 2: *Compute the payback period.* Using the net annual cash inflow figure from above, the payback period can be determined as follows:

Cost of the new equipment	$80,000
Less salvage value of old equipment	5,000
Investment required	$75,000

$$\text{Payback period} = \frac{\text{Investment required}}{\text{Net annual cash inflow}}$$

$$= \frac{\$75,000}{\$30,000} = 2.5 \text{ years}$$

Exhibit 13–11 computes the payback period for the ice cream dispenser. Several things should be noted. First, depreciation is added back to net operating income to obtain the net annual cash inflow from the new equipment. Depreciation is not a cash outlay; thus, it must be added back to adjust net operating income to a cash basis. Second, the payback computation deducts the salvage value of the old machines from the cost of the new equipment so that only the incremental investment is used in computing the payback period.

Since the proposed equipment has a payback period of less than three years, the company's payback requirement has been met.

IN BUSINESS

COUNTING THE ENVIRONMENTAL COSTS

Companies often grossly underestimate how much they are spending on environmental costs. Many of these costs are buried in broad cost categories such as manufacturing overhead. Kestrel Management Services, LLC, a management consulting firm specializing in environmental matters, found that one chemical facility was spending five times as much on environmental expenses as its cost system reported. At another site, a small manufacturer with $840,000 in pretax profits thought that its annual safety and environmental compliance expenses were about $50,000 but, after digging into the accounts, found that the total was closer to $300,000. Alerted to this high cost, management of the company invested about $125,000 in environmental improvements, anticipating a three- to six-month payback period. By taking steps such as more efficient dust collection, the company improved its product quality, reduced scrap rates, decreased its consumption of city water for cooling, and reduced the expense of discharging wastewater into the city's sewer system. Further analysis revealed that spending $50,000 to improve energy efficiency would reduce annual energy costs by about $45,000. Few of these costs were visible in the company's traditional cost accounting system.

Source: Thomas P. Kunes, "A Green and *Lean* Workplace?" *Strategic Finance,* February 2001, pp. 71–73, 83.

Payback and Uneven Cash Flows

When the cash flows associated with an investment project change from year to year, the simple payback formula that we outlined earlier cannot be used. Consider the following data:

Year	Investment	Cash Inflow
1	$4,000	$1,000
2		$0
3		$2,000
4	$2,000	$1,000
5		$500
6		$3,000
7		$2,000

What is the payback period on this investment? The answer is 5.5 years, but to obtain this figure it is necessary to track the unrecovered investment year by year. The steps involved in this process are shown in Exhibit 13–12. By the middle of the sixth year, sufficient cash inflows will have been realized to recover the entire investment of $6,000 ($4,000 + $2,000).

EXHIBIT 13–12
Payback and Uneven Cash Flows

Year	Investment	Cash Inflow	Unrecovered Investment*
1	$4,000	$1,000	$3,000
2		$0	$3,000
3		$2,000	$1,000
4	$2,000	$1,000	$2,000
5		$500	$1,500
6		$3,000	$0
7		$2,000	$0

*Year X unrecovered investment = Year X-1 unrecovered investment + Year X investment − Year X cash inflow

The Simple Rate of Return Method

LEARNING OBJECTIVE 6
Compute the simple rate of return for an investment.

The **simple rate of return** method is another capital budgeting technique that does not involve discounting cash flows. The simple rate of return is also known as the accounting rate of return or the unadjusted rate of return.

Unlike the other capital budgeting methods that we have discussed, the simple rate of return method focuses on accounting net operating income rather than cash flows. To obtain the simple rate of return, the annual incremental net operating income generated by a project is divided by the initial investment in the project as shown below.

$$\text{Simple rate of return} = \frac{\text{Annual incremental net operating income}}{\text{Initial investment}} \qquad (4)$$

Two additional points should be made. First, depreciation charges that result from making the investment should be deducted when determining the annual incremental net operating income. Second, the initial investment should be reduced by any salvage value realized from the sale of old equipment.

Example I: Brigham Tea, Inc., is a processor of low-acid tea. The company is contemplating purchasing equipment for an additional processing line. The additional processing line would increase revenues by $90,000 per year. Incremental cash operating expenses would be $40,000 per year. The equipment would cost $180,000 and have a nine-year life with no salvage value.

To apply the formula for the simple rate of return, we must first determine the annual incremental net operating income from the project:

Annual incremental revenues		$90,000
Annual incremental cash operating expenses	$40,000	
Annual depreciation ($180,000 − $0)/9	20,000	
Annual incremental expenses		60,000
Annual incremental net operating income		$30,000

Given that the annual incremental net operating income from the project is $30,000 and the initial investment is $180,000, the simple rate of return is 16.7% as shown below:

$$\text{Simple rate of return} = \frac{\text{Annual incremental net operating income}}{\text{Initial investment}}$$

$$= \frac{\$30{,}000}{\$180{,}000}$$

$$= 16.7\%$$

Example J: Midwest Farms, Inc., hires people on a part-time basis to sort eggs. The cost of this hand-sorting process is $30,000 per year. The company is investigating an egg-sorting machine that would cost $90,000 and have a 15-year useful life. The machine would have negligible salvage value, and it would cost $10,000 per year to operate and maintain. The egg-sorting equipment currently being used could be sold now for a scrap value of $2,500.

This project is slightly different from the preceding project because it involves cost reductions with no additional revenues. Nevertheless, the annual incremental net operating income can be computed by treating the annual cost savings as if it were incremental revenues as follows:

Annual incremental cost savings		$30,000
Annual incremental cash operating expenses	$10,000	
Annual depreciation ($90,000 − $0)/15	6,000	
Annual incremental expenses		16,000
Annual incremental net operating income		$14,000

Thus, even though the new equipment would not generate any additional revenues, it would reduce costs by $14,000 a year. This would have the effect of increasing net operating income by $14,000 a year.

Finally, the salvage value of the old equipment offsets the initial cost of the new equipment as follows:

Cost of the new equipment	$90,000
Less salvage value of the old equipment	2,500
Initial investment	$87,500

Given the annual incremental net operating income of $14,000 and the initial investment of $87,500, the simple rate of return is 16.0% computed as follows:

$$\text{Simple rate of return} = \frac{\text{Annual incremental net operating income}}{\text{Initial investment}}$$
$$= \frac{\$14,000}{\$87,500}$$
$$= 16.0\%$$

IN BUSINESS

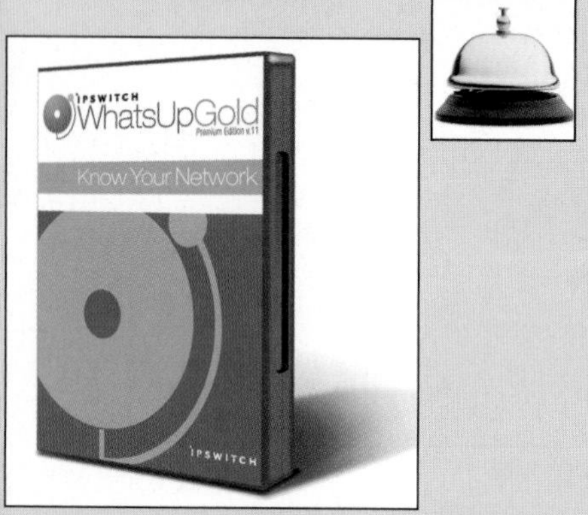

AN AMAZING RETURN

Ipswitch, Inc., a software developer and seller, has moved much of its business to the Web. Potential customers can download free trial copies of the company's software at www.ipswitch.com. After the trial period, a customer must return to the Web site to purchase and download a permanent copy of the software. The initial investment in setting up a Web site was modest—roughly $190,000. The cost of keeping the Web site up and running and updated with the latest product information is about $1.3 million a year—mainly in the form of salaries and benefits for eight employees. The company estimates that additional revenues brought in by the Web amount to about $13 million per year and that the company saves about $585,000 per year in direct mail advertising costs by using the Web for much of its advertising instead. Assuming that the cost of sales is almost zero for downloaded software, the accounting rate of return on the initial investment in the Web site is 6,466% ([$13,000,000 − $1,300,000 + $585,000] ÷ $190,000)!

Source: Karen N. Kroll, "Many Happy Returns," *Inc.* magazine, November 30, 2001, pp. 150–152.

Criticisms of the Simple Rate of Return

The simple rate of return method ignores the time value of money. It considers a dollar received 10 years from now to be as valuable as a dollar received today. Thus, the simple rate of return method can be misleading if the alternatives have different cash flow patterns. Additionally, many projects do not have constant incremental revenues and expenses over their useful lives. As a result, the simple rate of return will fluctuate from year to year, with the possibility that a project may appear to be desirable in some years and undesirable in others. In contrast, the net present value method provides a single number that summarizes all of the cash flows over the entire useful life of the project.

Postaudit of Investment Projects

After an investment project has been approved and implemented, a *postaudit* should be conducted. A **postaudit** involves checking whether or not expected results are actually realized. This is a key part of the capital budgeting process because it helps keep managers honest in their investment proposals. Any tendency to inflate the benefits or downplay the costs in a proposal should become evident after a few postaudits have been conducted. The postaudit also provides an opportunity to reinforce and possibly expand successful projects and to cut losses on floundering projects.

The same capital budgeting method should be used in the postaudit as was used in the original approval process. That is, if a project was approved on the basis of a net present value analysis, then the same procedure should be used in performing the postaudit. However, the data used in the postaudit analysis should be *actual observed data* rather than estimated data. This gives management an opportunity to make a side-by-side comparison to see how well the project has succeeded. It also helps assure that estimated data received on future proposals will be carefully prepared, since the persons submitting the data knows that their estimates will be compared to actual results in the postaudit process. Actual results that are far out of line with original estimates should be carefully reviewed.

IN BUSINESS

CAPITAL BUDGETING IN PRACTICE

A survey of Fortune 1000 companies—the largest companies in the United States—asked CFOs how often various capital budgeting methods are used in their companies. Some of the results of that survey are displayed below:

Capital Budgeting Tool	Frequency of Use				
	Always	Often	Sometimes	Rarely	Never
Net present value	50%	35%	11%	3%	1%
Internal rate of return	45%	32%	15%	6%	2%
Payback	19%	33%	22%	17%	9%
Accounting rate of return	5%	9%	19%	16%	50%

Many companies use more than one method—for example, they may use both the net present value and the internal rate of return methods to evaluate capital budgeting projects. Note that the two discounted cash flow methods—net present value and internal rate of return—are by far the most commonly used in practice.

A similar survey of companies in the United Kingdom yielded the following results:

Capital Budgeting Tool	Frequency of Use			
	Always	Mostly	Often	Rarely
Net present value	43%	20%	14%	7%
Internal rate of return	48%	20%	10%	5%
Payback	30%	16%	17%	14%
Accounting rate of return	26%	15%	18%	7%

Note that while the results were quite similar for the U.S. and U.K. companies, the U.K. companies were more likely to use the payback and accounting rate of return methods than the U.S. companies.

Sources: Patricia A. Ryan and Glenn P. Ryan, "Capital Budgeting Practices of the Fortune 1000: How Have Things Changed?" *Journal of Business and Management,* Fall 2002, pp. 355–364; and Glen C. Arnold and Panos D. Hatzopoulus, "The Theory-Practice Gap in Capital Budgeting: Evidence from the United Kingdom," *Journal of Business Finance & Accounting* 27(5) & 27(6), June/July 2000, pp. 603–626.

Summary

Investment decisions should take into account the time value of money because a dollar today is more valuable than a dollar received in the future. The net present value and internal rate of return methods both reflect this fact. In the net present value method, future cash flows are discounted to their present value. The difference between the present value of the cash inflows and the present value of the cash outflows is called a project's net present value. If the net present value of a project is negative, the project is rejected. The discount rate in the net present value method is usually based on a minimum required rate of return such as a company's cost of capital.

The internal rate of return is the rate of return that equates the present value of the cash inflows and the present value of the cash outflows, resulting in a zero net present value. If the internal rate of return is less than a company's minimum required rate of return, the project is rejected.

After rejecting projects whose net present values are negative or whose internal rates of return are less than the minimum required rate of return, more projects may remain than can be supported with available funds. The remaining projects can be ranked using either the project profitability index or internal rate of return. The project profitability index is computed by dividing the net present value of the project by the required initial investment.

Some companies prefer to use either the payback method or the simple rate of return to evaluate investment proposals. The payback period is the number of periods that are required to fully recover the initial investment in a project. The simple rate of return is determined by dividing a project's accounting net operating income by the initial investment in the project.

Review Problem 1: Basic Present Value Computations

Each of the following situations is independent. Work out your own solution to each situation, and then check it against the solution provided.

1. John plans to retire in 12 years. Upon retiring, he would like to take an extended vacation, which he expects will cost at least $40,000. What lump-sum amount must he invest now to have $40,000 at the end of 12 years if the rate of return is:
   a. Eight percent?
   b. Twelve percent?
2. The Morgans would like to send their daughter to a music camp at the end of each of the next five years. The camp costs $1,000 a year. What lump-sum amount would have to be invested now to have $1,000 at the end of each year if the rate of return is:
   a. Eight percent?
   b. Twelve percent?
3. You have just received an inheritance from a relative. You can either receive a $200,000 lump-sum amount at the end of 10 years or receive $14,000 at the end of each year for the next 10 years. If your discount rate is 12%, which alternative would you prefer?

Solution to Review Problem 1

1. *a.* The amount that must be invested now would be the present value of the $40,000, using a discount rate of 8%. From Exhibit 13B–1 in Appendix 13B, the factor for a discount rate of 8% for 12 periods is 0.397. Multiplying this discount factor by the $40,000 needed in 12 years will give the amount of the present investment required: $40,000 × 0.397 = $15,880.
   b. We will proceed as we did in (*a*) above, but this time we will use a discount rate of 12%. From Exhibit 13B–1 in Appendix 13B, the factor for a discount rate of 12% for 12 periods is 0.257. Multiplying this discount factor by the $40,000 needed in 12 years will give the amount of the present investment required: $40,000 × 0.257 = $10,280.
   Notice that as the discount rate (desired rate of return) increases, the present value decreases.
2. This part differs from (1) above in that we are now dealing with an annuity rather than with a single future sum. The amount that must be invested now is the present value of the $1,000 needed at the end of each year for five years. Since we are dealing with an annuity, or a series of annual cash flows, we must refer to Exhibit 13B–2 in Appendix 13B for the appropriate discount factor.
   a. From Exhibit 13B–2 in Appendix 13B, the discount factor for 8% for five periods is 3.993. Therefore, the amount that must be invested now to have $1,000 available at the end of each year for five years is $1,000 × 3.993 = $3,993.
   b. From Exhibit 13B–2 in Appendix 13B, the discount factor for 12% for five periods is 3.605. Therefore, the amount that must be invested now to have $1,000 available at the end of each year for five years is $1,000 × 3.605 = $3,605.
   Again, notice that as the discount rate increases, the present value decreases. When the rate of return increases, less must be invested today to yield a given amount in the future.
3. For this part we will need to refer to both Exhibits 13B–1 and 13B–2 in Appendix 13B. From Exhibit 13B–1, we will need to find the discount factor for 12% for 10 periods, then apply it to the $200,000 lump sum to be received in 10 years. From Exhibit 13B–2, we will need to find the discount factor for 12% for 10 periods, then apply it to the series of $14,000 payments to be received over the 10-year period. Whichever alternative has the higher present value is the one that should be selected.

$$\$200{,}000 \times 0.322 = \$64{,}400$$

$$\$14{,}000 \times 5.650 = \$79{,}100$$

Thus, you should prefer to receive the $14,000 per year for 10 years rather than the $200,000 lump sum. This means that you could invest the $14,000 received at the end of each year at 12% and have *more* than $200,000 at the end of 10 years.

Review Problem 2: Comparison of Capital Budgeting Methods

Lamar Company is considering a project that would have an eight-year life and require a $2,400,000 investment in equipment. At the end of eight years, the project would terminate and the equipment would have no salvage value. The project would provide net operating income each year as follows:

Sales		$3,000,000
Variable expenses		1,800,000
Contribution margin		1,200,000
Fixed expenses:		
Advertising, salaries, and other fixed out-of-pocket costs	$700,000	
Depreciation	300,000	
Total fixed expenses		1,000,000
Net operating income		$ 200,000

The company's discount rate is 12%.

Required:

1. Compute the net annual cash inflow from the project.
2. Compute the project's net present value. Is the project acceptable?
3. Find the project's internal rate of return to the nearest whole percent.
4. Compute the project's payback period.
5. Compute the project's simple rate of return.

Solution to Review Problem 2

1. The net annual cash inflow can be computed by deducting the cash expenses from sales:

Sales	$3,000,000
Variable expenses	1,800,000
Contribution margin	1,200,000
Advertising, salaries, and other fixed out-of-pocket costs	700,000
Net annual cash inflow	$ 500,000

Or the net annual cash inflow can be computed by adding depreciation back to net operating income:

Net operating income	$200,000
Add: Noncash deduction for depreciation	300,000
Net annual cash inflow	$500,000

2. The net present value is computed as follows:

Item	Year(s)	Amount of Cash Flows	12% Factor	Present Value of Cash Flows
Cost of new equipment	Now	$(2,400,000)	1.000	$(2,400,000)
Net annual cash inflow	1–8	$500,000	4.968	2,484,000
Net present value				$ 84,000

Yes, the project is acceptable because it has a positive net present value.

3. The formula for computing the factor of the internal rate of return is:

$$\text{Factor of the internal rate of return} = \frac{\text{Investment required}}{\text{Net annual cash inflow}}$$

$$= \frac{\$2{,}400{,}000}{\$500{,}000} = 4.800$$

Looking in Exhibit 13B–2 in Appendix 13B at the end of the chapter and scanning along the 8-period line, we find that a factor of 4.800 represents a rate of return of about 13%.

4. The formula for the payback period is:

$$\text{Payback period} = \frac{\text{Investment required}}{\text{Net annual cash flow}}$$

$$= \frac{\$2{,}400{,}000}{\$500{,}000}$$

$$= 4.8 \text{ years}$$

5. The formula for the simple rate of return is:

$$\text{Simple rate of return} = \frac{\text{Annual incremental net operating income}}{\text{Initial investment}}$$

$$= \frac{\$200{,}000}{\$2{,}400{,}000}$$

$$= 8.3\%$$

Glossary

Capital budgeting The process of planning significant investments in projects that have long-term implications such as the purchase of new equipment or the introduction of a new product. (p. 548)

Cost of capital The average rate of return a company must pay to its long-term creditors and shareholders for the use of their funds. (p. 553)

Internal rate of return The discount rate at which the net present value of an investment project is zero; the rate of return promised by a project over its useful life. (p. 555)

Net present value The difference between the present value of an investment project's cash inflows and the present value of its cash outflows. (p. 549)

Out-of-pocket costs Actual cash outlays for salaries, advertising, repairs, and similar costs. (p. 554)

Payback period The length of time that it takes for a project to fully recover its initial cost out of the cash receipts that it generates. (p. 564)

Postaudit The follow-up after a project has been approved and implemented to determine whether expected results were actually realized. (p. 570)

Preference decision A decision in which the alternatives must be ranked. (p. 548)

Project profitability index The ratio of the net present value of a project's cash flows to the investment required. (p. 563)
Screening decision A decision as to whether a proposed investment project is acceptable. (p. 548)
Simple rate of return The rate of return computed by dividing a project's annual incremental accounting net operating income by the initial investment required. (p. 568)
Working capital Current assets less current liabilities. (p. 551)

Appendix 13A: The Concept of Present Value

A dollar received today is more valuable than a dollar received a year from now for the simple reason that if you have a dollar today, you can put it in the bank and have more than a dollar a year from now. Since dollars today are worth more than dollars in the future, cash flows that are received at different times must be weighted differently.

LEARNING OBJECTIVE 7
Understand present value concepts and the use of present value tables.

The Mathematics of Interest

If a bank pays 5% interest, then a deposit of \$100 today will be worth \$105 one year from now. This can be expressed as follows:

$$F_1 = P(1 + r) \quad (1)$$

where F_1 = the balance at the end of one period, P = the amount invested now, and r = the rate of interest per period.

In the case where \$100 is deposited in a savings account that earns 5% interest, P = \$100 and $r = 0.05$. Under these conditions, F_1 = \$105.

The \$100 present outlay is called the **present value** of the \$105 amount to be received in one year. It is also known as the *discounted value* of the future \$105 receipt. The \$100 represents the value in present terms of \$105 to be received a year from now when the interest rate is 5%.

Compound Interest What if the \$105 is left in the bank for a second year? In that case, by the end of the second year the original \$100 deposit will have grown to \$110.25:

Original deposit	\$100.00
Interest for the first year:	
\$100 × 0.05	5.00
Balance at the end of the first year	105.00
Interest for the second year:	
\$105 × 0.05	5.25
Balance at the end of the second year	\$110.25

Notice that the interest for the second year is \$5.25, as compared to only \$5.00 for the first year. This difference arises because interest is being paid on interest during the second year. That is, the \$5.00 interest earned during the first year has been left in the account and has been added to the original \$100 deposit when computing interest for the second year. This is known as **compound interest.** In this case, the compounding is annual. Interest can be compounded on a semiannual, quarterly, monthly, or even more frequent basis. The more frequently compounding is done, the more rapidly the balance will grow.

We can determine the balance in an account after n periods of compounding using the following equation:

$$F_n = P(1 + r)^n \quad (2)$$

where n = the number of periods of compounding.

If $n = 2$ years and the interest rate is 5% per year, then the balance in two years will be computed as follows:

$$F_2 = \$100(1 + 0.05)^2$$
$$F_2 = \$110.25$$

Present Value and Future Value Exhibit 13A–1 shows the relationship between present value and future value. As shown in the exhibit, if $100 is deposited in a bank at 5% interest compounded annually, it will grow to $127.63 by the end of five years.

Computation of Present Value

An investment can be viewed in two ways—either in terms of its future value or in terms of its present value. We have seen from our computations above that if we know the present value of a sum (such as our $100 deposit), the future value in n years can be computed by using equation (2). But what if the situation is reversed and we know the *future* value of some amount but we do not know its present value?

For example, assume that you are to receive $200 two years from now. You know that the future value of this sum is $200 because this is the amount that you will be receiving in two years. But what is the sum's present value—what is it worth *right now?* The present value of any sum to be received in the future can be computed by turning equation (2) around and solving for P:

$$P = \frac{F_n}{(1 + r)^n} \quad (3)$$

EXHIBIT 13A–1
The Relationship between Present Value and Future Value

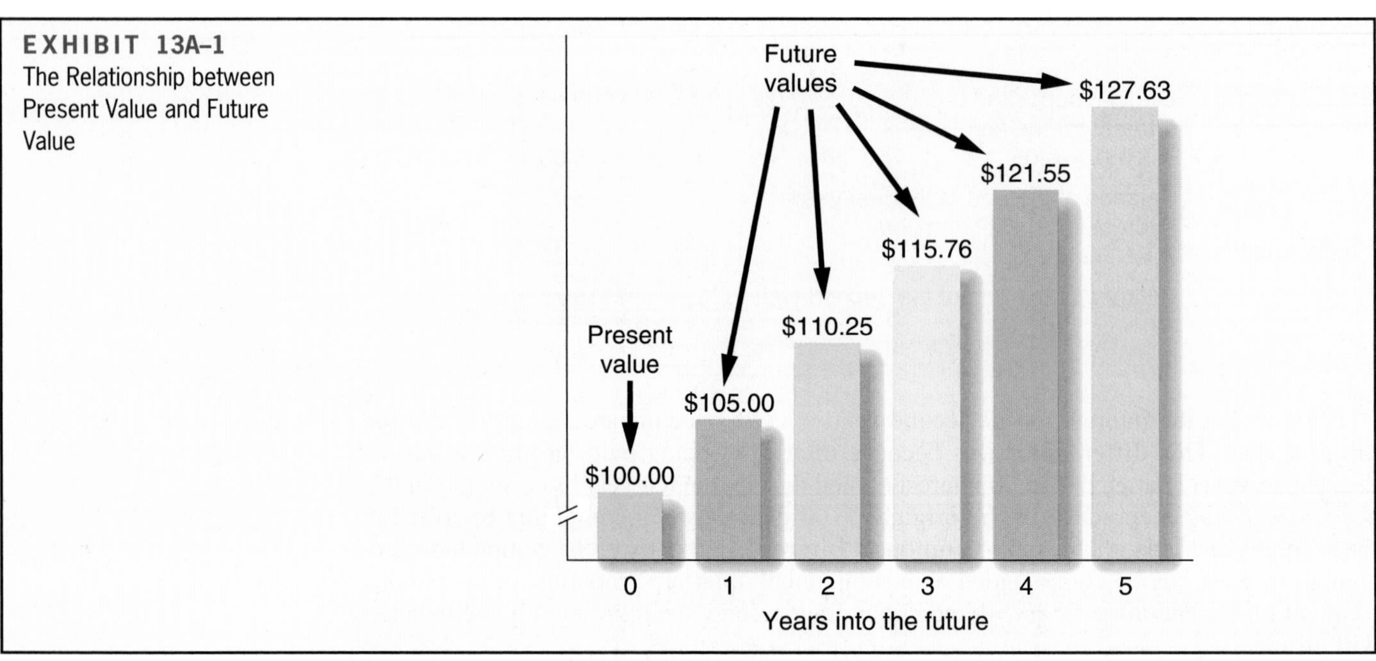

EXHIBIT 13B–2

Present Value of an Annuity of $1 in Arrears; $\frac{1}{r}\left[1 - \frac{1}{(1+r)^n}\right]$

Periods	4%	5%	6%	7%	8%	9%	10%	11%	12%	13%	14%	15%	16%	17%	18%	19%	20%	21%	22%	23%	24%	25%
1	0.962	0.952	0.943	0.935	0.926	0.917	0.909	0.901	0.893	0.885	0.877	0.870	0.862	0.855	0.847	0.840	0.833	0.826	0.820	0.813	0.806	0.800
2	1.886	1.859	1.833	1.808	1.783	1.759	1.736	1.713	1.690	1.668	1.647	1.626	1.605	1.585	1.566	1.547	1.528	1.509	1.492	1.474	1.457	1.440
3	2.775	2.723	2.673	2.624	2.577	2.531	2.487	2.444	2.402	2.361	2.322	2.283	2.246	2.210	2.174	2.140	2.106	2.074	2.042	2.011	1.981	1.952
4	3.630	3.546	3.465	3.387	3.312	3.240	3.170	3.102	3.037	2.974	2.914	2.855	2.798	2.743	2.690	2.639	2.589	2.540	2.494	2.448	2.404	2.362
5	4.452	4.329	4.212	4.100	3.993	3.890	3.791	3.696	3.605	3.517	3.433	3.352	3.274	3.199	3.127	3.058	2.991	2.926	2.864	2.803	2.745	2.689
6	5.242	5.076	4.917	4.767	4.623	4.486	4.355	4.231	4.111	3.998	3.889	3.784	3.685	3.589	3.498	3.410	3.326	3.245	3.167	3.092	3.020	2.951
7	6.002	5.786	5.582	5.389	5.206	5.033	4.868	4.712	4.564	4.423	4.288	4.160	4.039	3.922	3.812	3.706	3.605	3.508	3.416	3.327	3.242	3.161
8	6.733	6.463	6.210	5.971	5.747	5.535	5.335	5.146	4.968	4.799	4.639	4.487	4.344	4.207	4.078	3.954	3.837	3.726	3.619	3.518	3.421	3.329
9	7.435	7.108	6.802	6.515	6.247	5.995	5.759	5.537	5.328	5.132	4.946	4.772	4.607	4.451	4.303	4.163	4.031	3.905	3.786	3.673	3.566	3.463
10	8.111	7.722	7.360	7.024	6.710	6.418	6.145	5.889	5.650	5.426	5.216	5.019	4.833	4.659	4.494	4.339	4.192	4.054	3.923	3.799	3.682	3.571
11	8.760	8.306	7.887	7.499	7.139	6.805	6.495	6.207	5.938	5.687	5.453	5.234	5.029	4.836	4.656	4.486	4.327	4.177	4.035	3.902	3.776	3.656
12	9.385	8.863	8.384	7.943	7.536	7.161	6.814	6.492	6.194	5.918	5.660	5.421	5.197	4.988	4.793	4.611	4.439	4.278	4.127	3.985	3.851	3.725
13	9.986	9.394	8.853	8.358	7.904	7.487	7.103	6.750	6.424	6.122	5.842	5.583	5.342	5.118	4.910	4.715	4.533	4.362	4.203	4.053	3.912	3.780
14	10.563	9.899	9.295	8.745	8.244	7.786	7.367	6.982	6.628	6.302	6.002	5.724	5.468	5.229	5.008	4.802	4.611	4.432	4.265	4.108	3.962	3.824
15	11.118	10.380	9.712	9.108	8.559	8.061	7.606	7.191	6.811	6.462	6.142	5.847	5.575	5.324	5.092	4.876	4.675	4.489	4.315	4.153	4.001	3.859
16	11.652	10.838	10.106	9.447	8.851	8.313	7.824	7.379	6.974	6.604	6.265	5.954	5.668	5.405	5.162	4.938	4.730	4.536	4.357	4.189	4.033	3.887
17	12.166	11.274	10.477	9.763	9.122	8.544	8.022	7.549	7.120	6.729	6.373	6.047	5.749	5.475	5.222	4.990	4.775	4.576	4.391	4.219	4.059	3.910
18	12.659	11.690	10.828	10.059	9.372	8.756	8.201	7.702	7.250	6.840	6.467	6.128	5.818	5.534	5.273	5.033	4.812	4.608	4.419	4.243	4.080	3.928
19	13.134	12.085	11.158	10.336	9.604	8.950	8.365	7.839	7.366	6.938	6.550	6.198	5.877	5.584	5.316	5.070	4.843	4.635	4.442	4.263	4.097	3.942
20	13.590	12.462	11.470	10.594	9.818	9.129	8.514	7.963	7.469	7.025	6.623	6.259	5.929	5.628	5.353	5.101	4.870	4.657	4.460	4.279	4.110	3.954
21	14.029	12.821	11.764	10.836	10.017	9.292	8.649	8.075	7.562	7.102	6.687	6.312	5.973	5.665	5.384	5.127	4.891	4.675	4.476	4.292	4.121	3.963
22	14.451	13.163	12.042	11.061	10.201	9.442	8.772	8.176	7.645	7.170	6.743	6.359	6.011	5.696	5.410	5.149	4.909	4.690	4.488	4.302	4.130	3.970
23	14.857	13.489	12.303	11.272	10.371	9.580	8.883	8.266	7.718	7.230	6.792	6.399	6.044	5.723	5.432	5.167	4.925	4.703	4.499	4.311	4.137	3.976
24	15.247	13.799	12.550	11.469	10.529	9.707	8.985	8.348	7.784	7.283	6.835	6.434	6.073	5.746	5.451	5.182	4.937	4.713	4.507	4.318	4.143	3.981
25	15.622	14.094	12.783	11.654	10.675	9.823	9.077	8.422	7.843	7.330	6.873	6.464	6.097	5.766	5.467	5.195	4.948	4.721	4.514	4.323	4.147	3.985
26	15.983	14.375	13.003	11.826	10.810	9.929	9.161	8.488	7.896	7.372	6.906	6.491	6.118	5.783	5.480	5.206	4.956	4.728	4.520	4.328	4.151	3.988
27	16.330	14.643	13.211	11.987	10.935	10.027	9.237	8.548	7.943	7.409	6.935	6.514	6.136	5.798	5.492	5.215	4.964	4.734	4.524	4.332	4.154	3.990
28	16.663	14.898	13.406	12.137	11.051	10.116	9.307	8.602	7.984	7.441	6.961	6.534	6.152	5.810	5.502	5.223	4.970	4.739	4.528	4.335	4.157	3.992
29	16.984	15.141	13.591	12.278	11.158	10.198	9.370	8.650	8.022	7.470	6.983	6.551	6.166	5.820	5.510	5.229	4.975	4.743	4.531	4.337	4.159	3.994
30	17.292	15.372	13.765	12.409	11.258	10.274	9.427	8.694	8.055	7.496	7.003	6.566	6.177	5.829	5.517	5.235	4.979	4.746	4.534	4.339	4.160	3.995
40	19.793	17.159	15.046	13.332	11.925	10.757	9.779	8.951	8.244	7.634	7.105	6.642	6.233	5.871	5.548	5.258	4.997	4.760	4.544	4.347	4.166	3.999

Appendix 13B: Present Value Tables

EXHIBIT 13B–1

Present Value of \$1; $\frac{1}{(1+r)^n}$

Periods	4%	5%	6%	7%	8%	9%	10%	11%	12%	13%	14%	15%	16%	17%	18%	19%	20%	21%	22%	23%	24%	25%
1	0.962	0.952	0.943	0.935	0.926	0.917	0.909	0.901	0.893	0.885	0.877	0.870	0.862	0.855	0.847	0.840	0.833	0.826	0.820	0.813	0.806	0.800
2	0.925	0.907	0.890	0.873	0.857	0.842	0.826	0.812	0.797	0.783	0.769	0.756	0.743	0.731	0.718	0.706	0.694	0.683	0.672	0.661	0.650	0.640
3	0.889	0.864	0.840	0.816	0.794	0.772	0.751	0.731	0.712	0.693	0.675	0.658	0.641	0.624	0.609	0.593	0.579	0.564	0.551	0.537	0.524	0.512
4	0.855	0.823	0.792	0.763	0.735	0.708	0.683	0.659	0.636	0.613	0.592	0.572	0.552	0.534	0.516	0.499	0.482	0.467	0.451	0.437	0.423	0.410
5	0.822	0.784	0.747	0.713	0.681	0.650	0.621	0.593	0.567	0.543	0.519	0.497	0.476	0.456	0.437	0.419	0.402	0.386	0.370	0.355	0.341	0.328
6	0.790	0.746	0.705	0.666	0.630	0.596	0.564	0.535	0.507	0.480	0.456	0.432	0.410	0.390	0.370	0.352	0.335	0.319	0.303	0.289	0.275	0.262
7	0.760	0.711	0.665	0.623	0.583	0.547	0.513	0.482	0.452	0.425	0.400	0.376	0.354	0.333	0.314	0.296	0.279	0.263	0.249	0.235	0.222	0.210
8	0.731	0.677	0.627	0.582	0.540	0.502	0.467	0.434	0.404	0.376	0.351	0.327	0.305	0.285	0.266	0.249	0.233	0.218	0.204	0.191	0.179	0.168
9	0.703	0.645	0.592	0.544	0.500	0.460	0.424	0.391	0.361	0.333	0.308	0.284	0.263	0.243	0.225	0.209	0.194	0.180	0.167	0.155	0.144	0.134
10	0.676	0.614	0.558	0.508	0.463	0.422	0.386	0.352	0.322	0.295	0.270	0.247	0.227	0.208	0.191	0.176	0.162	0.149	0.137	0.126	0.116	0.107
11	0.650	0.585	0.527	0.475	0.429	0.388	0.350	0.317	0.287	0.261	0.237	0.215	0.195	0.178	0.162	0.148	0.135	0.123	0.112	0.103	0.094	0.086
12	0.625	0.557	0.497	0.444	0.397	0.356	0.319	0.286	0.257	0.231	0.208	0.187	0.168	0.152	0.137	0.124	0.112	0.102	0.092	0.083	0.076	0.069
13	0.601	0.530	0.469	0.415	0.368	0.326	0.290	0.258	0.229	0.204	0.182	0.163	0.145	0.130	0.116	0.104	0.093	0.084	0.075	0.068	0.061	0.055
14	0.577	0.505	0.442	0.388	0.340	0.299	0.263	0.232	0.205	0.181	0.160	0.141	0.125	0.111	0.099	0.088	0.078	0.069	0.062	0.055	0.049	0.044
15	0.555	0.481	0.417	0.362	0.315	0.275	0.239	0.209	0.183	0.160	0.140	0.123	0.108	0.095	0.084	0.074	0.065	0.057	0.051	0.045	0.040	0.035
16	0.534	0.458	0.394	0.339	0.292	0.252	0.218	0.188	0.163	0.141	0.123	0.107	0.093	0.081	0.071	0.062	0.054	0.047	0.042	0.036	0.032	0.028
17	0.513	0.436	0.371	0.317	0.270	0.231	0.198	0.170	0.146	0.125	0.108	0.093	0.080	0.069	0.060	0.052	0.045	0.039	0.034	0.030	0.026	0.023
18	0.494	0.416	0.350	0.296	0.250	0.212	0.180	0.153	0.130	0.111	0.095	0.081	0.069	0.059	0.051	0.044	0.038	0.032	0.028	0.024	0.021	0.018
19	0.475	0.396	0.331	0.277	0.232	0.194	0.164	0.138	0.116	0.098	0.083	0.070	0.060	0.051	0.043	0.037	0.031	0.027	0.023	0.020	0.017	0.014
20	0.456	0.377	0.312	0.258	0.215	0.178	0.149	0.124	0.104	0.087	0.073	0.061	0.051	0.043	0.037	0.031	0.026	0.022	0.019	0.016	0.014	0.012
21	0.439	0.359	0.294	0.242	0.199	0.164	0.135	0.112	0.093	0.077	0.064	0.053	0.044	0.037	0.031	0.026	0.022	0.018	0.015	0.013	0.011	0.009
22	0.422	0.342	0.278	0.226	0.184	0.150	0.123	0.101	0.083	0.068	0.056	0.046	0.038	0.032	0.026	0.022	0.018	0.015	0.013	0.011	0.009	0.007
23	0.406	0.326	0.262	0.211	0.170	0.138	0.112	0.091	0.074	0.060	0.049	0.040	0.033	0.027	0.022	0.018	0.015	0.012	0.010	0.009	0.007	0.006
24	0.390	0.310	0.247	0.197	0.158	0.126	0.102	0.082	0.066	0.053	0.043	0.035	0.028	0.023	0.019	0.015	0.013	0.010	0.008	0.007	0.006	0.005
25	0.375	0.295	0.233	0.184	0.146	0.116	0.092	0.074	0.059	0.047	0.038	0.030	0.024	0.020	0.016	0.013	0.010	0.009	0.007	0.006	0.005	0.004
26	0.361	0.281	0.220	0.172	0.135	0.106	0.084	0.066	0.053	0.042	0.033	0.026	0.021	0.017	0.014	0.011	0.009	0.007	0.006	0.005	0.004	0.003
27	0.347	0.268	0.207	0.161	0.125	0.098	0.076	0.060	0.047	0.037	0.029	0.023	0.018	0.014	0.011	0.009	0.007	0.006	0.005	0.004	0.003	0.002
28	0.333	0.255	0.196	0.150	0.116	0.090	0.069	0.054	0.042	0.033	0.026	0.020	0.016	0.012	0.010	0.008	0.006	0.005	0.004	0.003	0.002	0.002
29	0.321	0.243	0.185	0.141	0.107	0.082	0.063	0.048	0.037	0.029	0.022	0.017	0.014	0.011	0.008	0.006	0.005	0.004	0.003	0.002	0.002	0.002
30	0.308	0.231	0.174	0.131	0.099	0.075	0.057	0.044	0.033	0.026	0.020	0.015	0.012	0.009	0.007	0.005	0.004	0.003	0.003	0.002	0.002	0.001
40	0.208	0.142	0.097	0.067	0.046	0.032	0.022	0.015	0.011	0.008	0.005	0.004	0.003	0.002	0.001	0.001	0.001	0.000	0.000	0.000	0.000	0.000

The second point is that the computations used in Exhibit 13A–2 involved unnecessary work. The same present value of $54,075 could have been obtained more easily by referring to Exhibit 13B–2 in Appendix 13B. Exhibit 13B–2 contains the present value of $1 to be received each year over a *series* of years at various interest rates. Exhibit 13B–2 has been derived by simply adding together the factors from Exhibit 13B–1, as follows:

Year	Exhibit 13B–1 Factors at 12%
1	0.893
2	0.797
3	0.712
4	0.636
5	0.567
	3.605

The sum of the five factors above is 3.605. Notice from Exhibit 13B–2 that the factor for $1 to be received each year for five years at 12% is also 3.605. If we use this factor and multiply it by the $15,000 annual cash inflow, then we get the same $54,075 present value that we obtained earlier in Exhibit 13A–2.

$$\$15,000 \times 3.605 = \$54,075$$

Therefore, when computing the present value of a series of equal cash flows that begins at the end of period 1, Exhibit 13B–2 should be used.

To summarize, the present value tables in Appendix 13B should be used as follows:

Exhibit 13B–1: This table should be used to find the present value of a single cash flow (such as a single payment or receipt) occurring in the future.

Exhibit 13B–2: This table should be used to find the present value of a series of identical cash flows beginning at the end of the current period and continuing into the future.

The use of both of these tables is illustrated in various exhibits in the main body of the chapter. *When a present value factor appears in an exhibit, you should take the time to trace it back into either Exhibit 13B–1 or Exhibit 13B–2 to get acquainted with the tables and how they work.* (Review Problem 1 at the end of the chapter is designed for those who would like some practice in present value analysis before attempting the homework exercises and problems.)

Glossary (Appendix 13A)

Annuity A series of identical cash flows. (p. 577)

Compound interest The process of paying interest on interest in an investment. (p. 575)

Discount rate The rate of return that is used to find the present value of a future cash flow. (p. 577)

Discounting The process of finding the present value of a future cash flow. (p. 577)

Present value The value now of an amount that will be received in some future period. (p. 575)

In our example, F_n = \$200 (the amount to be received in the future), r = 0.05 (the annual rate of interest), and n = 2 (the number of years in the future that the amount will be received).

$$P = \frac{\$200}{(1 + 0.05)^2}$$

$$P = \frac{\$200}{1.1025}$$

$$P = \$181.40$$

As shown by the computation above, the present value of a \$200 amount to be received two years from now is \$181.40 if the interest rate is 5%. In effect, \$181.40 received *right now* is equivalent to \$200 received two years from now.

The process of finding the present value of a future cash flow, which we have just completed, is called **discounting.** We have *discounted* the \$200 to its present value of \$181.40. The 5% interest that we have used to find this present value is called the **discount rate.** Discounting future sums to their present value is a common practice in business, particularly in capital budgeting decisions.

If you have a power key (y^x) on your calculator, the above calculations are fairly easy. However, some of the present value formulas we will be using are more complex. Fortunately, tables are available in which many of the calculations have already been done. For example, Exhibit 13B–1 in Appendix 13B shows the discounted present value of \$1 to be received at various periods in the future at various interest rates. The table indicates that the present value of \$1 to be received two periods from now at 5% is 0.907. Since in our example we want to know the present value of \$200 rather than just \$1, we need to multiply the factor in the table by \$200:

$$\$200 \times 0.907 = \$181.40$$

This answer is the same as we obtained earlier using the formula in equation (3).

Present Value of a Series of Cash Flows

Although some investments involve a single sum to be received (or paid) at a single point in the future, other investments involve a *series* of cash flows. A series of identical cash flows is known as an **annuity.** To provide an example, assume that a company has just purchased some government bonds. The bonds will yield interest of \$15,000 each year and will be held for five years. What is the present value of the stream of interest receipts from the bonds? As shown in Exhibit 13A–2, if the discount rate is 12%, the present value of this stream is \$54,075. The discount factors used in this exhibit were taken from Exhibit 13B–1 in Appendix 13B.

Exhibit 13A–2 illustrates two important points. First, the present value of the \$15,000 interest declines the further it is into the future. The present value of \$15,000 received a year from now is \$13,395, as compared to only \$8,505 if received five years from now. This point simply underscores the time value of money.

EXHIBIT 13A–2
Present Value of a Series of Cash Receipts

Year	Factor at 12% (Exhibit 13B–1)	Interest Received	Present Value
1	0.893	\$15,000	\$13,395
2	0.797	\$15,000	11,955
3	0.712	\$15,000	10,680
4	0.636	\$15,000	9,540
5	0.567	\$15,000	8,505
			\$54,075

Appendix 13C: Income Taxes in Capital Budgeting Decisions

LEARNING OBJECTIVE 8
Include income taxes in a capital budgeting analysis.

We ignored income taxes in this chapter for two reasons. First, many organizations do not pay income taxes. Not-for-profit organizations, such as hospitals and charitable foundations, and governmental agencies are exempt from income taxes. Second, capital budgeting is complex and is best absorbed in small doses. Now that we have a solid foundation in the concepts of present value and discounting, we can explore the effects of income taxes on capital budgeting decisions.

The U.S. income tax code is enormously complex. We only scratch the surface here. To keep the subject within reasonable bounds, we have made many simplifying assumptions about the tax code. Among the most important of these assumptions are: (1) taxable income equals net income as computed for financial reports; and (2) the tax rate is a flat percentage of taxable income. The actual tax code is far more complex than this; indeed, experts acknowledge that no one person knows or can know it all. However, the simplifications that we make throughout this appendix allow us to cover the most important implications of income taxes for capital budgeting without getting bogged down in details.

The Concept of After-Tax Cost

Businesses, like individuals, must pay income taxes. In the case of businesses, the amount of income tax that must be paid is determined by the company's net taxable income. Tax deductible expenses (tax deductions) decrease the company's net taxable income and hence reduce the taxes the company must pay. For this reason, expenses are often stated on an *after-tax* basis. For example, if a company pays rent of $10 million a year but this expense results in a reduction in income taxes of $3 million, the after-tax cost of the rent is $7 million. An expenditure net of its tax effect is known as **after-tax cost.**

To illustrate, assume that a company with a tax rate of 30% is contemplating a training program that costs $60,000. What impact will this have on the company's taxes? To keep matters simple, let's suppose the training program has no immediate effect on sales. How much does the company actually pay for the training program after taking into account the impact of this expense on taxes? The answer is $42,000 as shown in Exhibit 13C–1 (page 582). While the training program costs $60,000 before taxes, it would reduce the company's taxes by $18,000, so its *after-tax* cost would be only $42,000.

The after-tax cost of any tax-deductible cash expense can be determined using the following formula:[1]

$$\frac{\text{After-tax cost}}{\text{(net cash outflow)}} = (1 - \text{Tax rate}) \times \text{Tax-deductible cash expense} \qquad (1)$$

We can verify the accuracy of this formula by applying it to the $60,000 training program expenditure:

$$(1 - 0.30) \times \$60{,}000 = \$42{,}000 \text{ after-tax cost of the training program}$$

This formula is very useful because it provides the actual amount of cash a company must pay after considering tax effects. It is this actual, after-tax, cash outflow that should be used in capital budgeting decisions.

Similar reasoning applies to revenues and other *taxable* cash inflows. Since these cash receipts are taxable, the company must pay out a portion of them in taxes. The **after-tax benefit,** or net cash inflow, realized from a particular cash receipt can be obtained by applying a simple variation of the cash expenditure formula used above:

$$\frac{\text{After-tax benefit}}{\text{(net cash inflow)}} = (1 - \text{Tax rate}) \times \text{Taxable cash receipt} \qquad (2)$$

[1] This formula assumes that a company is operating at a profit; if it is operating at a loss, the tax situation can be very complex. For simplicity, we assume in all examples, exercises, and problems that the company is operating at a profit.

EXHIBIT 13C–1
The Computation of After-Tax Cost

	Without Training Program		With Training Program
Sales	$850,000		$850,000
Less tax deductible expenses:			
Salaries, insurance, and other	700,000		700,000
New training program			60,000
Total expenses	700,000		760,000
Taxable income	$150,000		$ 90,000
Income taxes (30%)	$ 45,000		$ 27,000
Cost of new training program		$60,000	
Less: Reduction in income taxes ($45,000 − $27,000)		18,000	
After-tax cost of the new training program		$42,000	

We emphasize the term *taxable cash receipts* because not all cash inflows are taxable. For example, the release of working capital at the end of an investment project would not be a taxable cash inflow. It is not counted as income for either financial accounting or income tax reporting purposes since it is simply a recovery of the initial investment.

Depreciation Tax Shield

Depreciation is not a cash flow. For this reason, depreciation was ignored in Chapter 13 in all discounted cash flow computations. However, depreciation does affect the taxes that must be paid and therefore has an indirect effect on a company's cash flows.

To illustrate the effect of depreciation deductions on tax payments, consider a company with annual cash sales of $500,000 and cash operating expenses of $310,000. In addition, the company has a depreciable asset on which the depreciation deduction is $90,000 per year. The tax rate is 30%. As shown in Exhibit 13C–2, the depreciation deduction reduces the company's taxes by $27,000. In effect, the depreciation deduction of $90,000 *shields* $90,000 in revenues from taxation and thereby *reduces* the amount of taxes that the company must pay. Because depreciation deductions shield revenues from taxation, they are generally referred to as a **depreciation tax shield.**[2] The reduction in tax payments made possible by the depreciation tax shield is equal to the amount of the depreciation deduction, multiplied by the tax rate as follows:

$$\begin{array}{c}\text{Tax savings from the} \\ \text{depreciation tax shield}\end{array} = \text{Tax rate} \times \text{Depreciation deduction} \qquad (3)$$

We can verify this formula by applying it to the $90,000 depreciation deduction in our example:

$$0.30 \times \$90{,}000 = \$27{,}000 \text{ reduction in tax payments}$$

In this appendix, when we estimate after-tax cash flows for capital budgeting decisions, we will include the tax savings provided by the depreciation tax shield.

To keep matters simple, we will assume in all of our examples and problem materials that depreciation reported for tax purposes is straight-line depreciation, with no deduction for salvage value. In other words, we will assume that the entire original cost of the asset is written

[2] The term *depreciation tax shield* may convey the impression that there is something underhanded about depreciation deductions—that companies are getting some sort of a special tax break. However, to use the depreciation deduction, a company must have already acquired a depreciable asset—which typically requires a cash outflow. Essentially, the tax code requires companies to delay recognizing the cash outflow as an expense until depreciation charges are recorded.

EXHIBIT 13C–2
The Impact of Depreciation Deductions on Tax Payments

	Without Depreciation Deduction	With Depreciation Deduction
Sales	$500,000	$500,000
Cash operating expenses	310,000	310,000
Cash flow from operations	190,000	190,000
Depreciation expense	—	90,000
Taxable income	$190,000	$100,000
Income taxes (30%)	$ 57,000	$ 30,000

$27,000 lower taxes with the depreciation deduction

	Without Depreciation Deduction	With Depreciation Deduction
Cash flow comparison:		
Cash flow from operations (above)	$190,000	$190,000
Income taxes (above)	57,000	30,000
Net cash flow	$133,000	$160,000

$27,000 greater cash flow with the depreciation deduction

off evenly over its useful life. Since the net book value of the asset at the end of its useful life will be zero under this depreciation method, we will assume that any proceeds received on disposal of the asset at the end of its useful life will be taxed as ordinary income.

In actuality, the rules for depreciation are more complex than this and most companies take advantage of accelerated depreciation methods allowed under the tax code. These accelerated methods usually result in a reduction in current taxes and an offsetting increase in future taxes. This shifting of part of the tax burden from the current year to future years is advantageous from a present value point of view because a dollar today is worth more than a dollar in the future. A summary of the concepts we have introduced so far is given in Exhibit 13C–3.

Example of Income Taxes and Capital Budgeting

Armed with an understanding of after-tax cost, after-tax revenue, and the depreciation tax shield, we are now prepared to examine a comprehensive example of income taxes and capital budgeting.

EXHIBIT 13C–3
Tax Adjustments Required in a Capital Budgeting Analysis

Item	Treatment
Tax-deductible cash expense*	Multiply by (1 − Tax rate) to get after-tax cost.
Taxable cash receipt*	Multiply by (1 − Tax rate) to get after-tax cash inflow.
Depreciation deduction	Multiply by the tax rate to get the tax savings from the depreciation tax shield.

*Cash expenses can be deducted from the cash receipts and the difference multiplied by (1 − Tax rate). See the example at the top of Exhibit 13C–4.

Holland Company owns the mineral rights to land that has a deposit of ore. The company is uncertain if it should purchase equipment and open a mine on the property. After careful study, the company assembled the following data.

Cost of equipment needed	$300,000
Working capital needed	$75,000
Estimated annual cash receipts from sales of ore	$250,000
Estimated annual cash expenses for salaries, insurance, utilities, and other cash expenses of mining the ore	$170,000
Cost of road repairs needed in 6 years	$40,000
Salvage value of the equipment in 10 years	$100,000

The ore in the mine would be exhausted after 10 years of mining activity, at which time the mine would be closed. The equipment would then be sold for its salvage value. Holland Company uses the straight-line method, assuming no salvage value, to compute depreciation deductions for tax purposes. The company's after-tax cost of capital is 12% and its tax rate is 30%.

Should Holland Company purchase the equipment and open a mine on the property? The solution to the problem is given in Exhibit 13C–4. We suggest that you go through this solution item by item and note the following points:

Cost of new equipment. The initial investment of $300,000 in the new equipment is included in full with no reductions for taxes. This represents an *investment,* not an expense, so no tax adjustment is made. (Only revenues and expenses are adjusted for the effects of taxes.) However, this investment does affect taxes through the depreciation deductions that are considered below.

Working capital. Observe that the working capital needed for the project is included in full with no reductions for taxes. Like the cost of new equipment, working capital is an investment and not an expense so no tax adjustment is made. Also observe that no tax adjustment is made when the working capital is released at the end of the project's life. The release of working capital is not a taxable cash flow because it is a return of investment funds back to the company.

EXHIBIT 13C–4
Example of Income Taxes and Capital Budgeting

	Per Year
Cash receipts from sales of ore	$250,000
Less payments for salaries, insurance, utilities, and other cash expenses	170,000
Net cash receipts	$ 80,000

Items and Computations	Year(s)	(1) Amount	(2) Tax Effect*	After-Tax Cash Flows (1) × (2)	12% Factor	Present Value of Cash Flows
Cost of new equipment.	Now	$(300,000)	—	$(300,000)	1.000	$(300,000)
Working capital needed	Now	$(75,000)	—	$(75,000)	1.000	(75,000)
Net annual cash receipts (above)	1–10	$80,000	1 − 0.30	$56,000	5.650	316,400
Road repairs.	6	$(40,000)	1 − 0.30	$(28,000)	0.507	(14,196)
Annual depreciation deductions	1–10	$30,000	0.30	$9,000	5.650	50,850
Salvage value of equipment	10	$100,000	1 − 0.30	$70,000	0.322	22,540
Release of working capital	10	$75,000	—	$75,000	0.322	24,150
Net present value						$ 24,744

*Taxable cash receipts and tax-deductible cash expenses are multiplied by (1 − Tax rate) to determine the after-tax cash flow. Depreciation deductions are multiplied by the tax rate itself to determine the after-tax cash flow (i.e., tax savings from the depreciation tax shield).

Net annual cash receipts. The net annual cash receipts from sales of ore are adjusted for the effects of income taxes, as discussed earlier in the chapter. Note at the top of Exhibit 13C–4 that the annual cash expenses are deducted from the annual cash receipts to obtain the net cash receipts. This simplifies computations.

Road repairs. Since the road repairs occur just once (in the sixth year), they are treated separately from other expenses. Road repairs would be a tax-deductible cash expense, and therefore they are adjusted for the effects of income taxes, as discussed earlier in the chapter.

Depreciation deductions. The tax savings provided by depreciation deductions is essentially an annuity that is included in the present value computations in the same way as other cash flows.

Salvage value of equipment. Since the company does not consider salvage value when computing depreciation deductions, book value will be zero at the end of the life of an asset. Thus, any salvage value received is taxable as income to the company. The after-tax benefit is determined by multiplying the salvage value by (1 – Tax rate).

Since the net present value of the proposed mining project is positive, the equipment should be purchased and the mine opened. Study Exhibit 13C–4 thoroughly. *Exhibit 13C–4 is the key exhibit!*

Summary (Appendix 13C)

Unless a company is a tax-exempt organization, such as a not-for-profit school or a governmental unit, income taxes should be considered in making capital budgeting decisions. Tax-deductible cash expenditures and taxable cash receipts are placed on an after-tax basis by multiplying them by (1 – Tax rate). Only the after-tax amount should be used in determining the desirability of an investment proposal.

Although depreciation is not a cash outflow, it is a valid deduction for tax purposes and as such affects income tax payments. The depreciation tax shield—computed by multiplying the depreciation deduction by the tax rate itself—also results in savings in income taxes.

Glossary (Appendix 13C)

After-tax benefit The amount of net cash inflow realized from a taxable cash receipt after income tax effects have been considered. The amount is determined by multiplying the taxable cash receipt by (1 – Tax rate). (p. 581)

After-tax cost The amount of net cash outflow resulting from a tax-deductible cash expense after income tax effects have been considered. The amount is determined by multiplying the tax-deductible cash expense by (1 – Tax rate). (p. 581)

Depreciation tax shield A reduction in tax that results from depreciation deductions. The reduction in tax is computed by multiplying the depreciation deduction by the tax rate. (p. 582)

Quiz 13

Multiple-choice questions are provided on the text Web site at www.mhhe.com/noreen1e.

Questions

13-1 What is the difference between capital budgeting screening decisions and capital budgeting preference decisions?

13-2 What is meant by the term *time value of money?*

13-3 What is meant by the term *discounting?*

13-4 Why isn't accounting net income used in the net present value and internal rate of return methods of making capital budgeting decisions?

13-5 Why are discounted cash flow methods of making capital budgeting decisions superior to other methods?

13-6 What is net present value? Can it ever be negative? Explain.

13-7 Identify two simplifying assumptions associated with discounted cash flow methods of making capital budgeting decisions.

13-8 If a company has to pay interest of 14% on long-term debt, then its cost of capital is 14%. Do you agree? Explain.

13-9 What is meant by an investment project's internal rate of return? How is the internal rate of return computed?

13-10 Explain how the cost of capital serves as a screening tool when dealing with (*a*) the net present value method and (*b*) the internal rate of return method.

13-11 As the discount rate increases, the present value of a given future cash flow also increases. Do you agree? Explain.

13-12 Refer to Exhibit 13–4. Is the return on this investment proposal exactly 14%, more than 14%, or less than 14%? Explain.

13-13 How is the project profitability index computed, and what does it measure?

13-14 What is meant by the term *payback period?* How is the payback period determined? How can the payback method be useful?

13-15 What is the major criticism of the payback and simple rate of return methods of making capital budgeting decisions?

13-16 (Appendix 13C) What is meant by after-tax cost and how is the concept used in capital budgeting decisions?

13-17 (Appendix 13C) What is a depreciation tax shield and how does it affect capital budgeting decisions?

13-18 (Appendix 13C) Ludlow Company is considering the introduction of a new product line. Would an increase in the income tax rate tend to make the new investment more or less attractive? Explain.

13-19 (Appendix 13C) Assume that an old piece of equipment is sold at a loss. From a capital budgeting point of view, what two cash inflows will be associated with the sale?

13-20 (Appendix 13C) Assume that a new piece of equipment costs $40,000 and that the tax rate is 30%. Should the new piece of equipment be included in the capital budgeting analysis as a cash outflow of $40,000, or as a cash outflow of $28,000 [$40,000 × (1 − 0.30)]? Explain.

Exercises 

EXERCISE 13-1 Net Present Value Method [LO1]

The management of Opry Company, a wholesale distributor of suntan products, is considering the purchase of a $25,000 machine that would reduce operating costs in its warehouse by $4,000 per year. At the end of the machine's 10-year useful life, it will have no scrap value. The company's required rate of return is 12%.

Required:

(Ignore income taxes.)

1. Determine the net present value of the investment in the machine.
2. What is the difference between the total, undiscounted cash inflows and cash outflows over the entire life of the machine?

EXERCISE 13-2 Internal Rate of Return [LO2]

Pisa Pizza Parlor is investigating the purchase of a new $45,000 delivery truck that would contain specially designed warming racks. The new truck would have a six-year useful life. It would save $5,400 per year over the present method of delivering pizzas. In addition, it would result in the sale of 1,800 more pizzas each year. The company realizes a contribution margin of $2 per pizza.

Required:

(Ignore income taxes.)

1. What would be the total annual cash inflows associated with the new truck for capital budgeting purposes?
2. Find the internal rate of return promised by the new truck to the nearest whole percent.
3. In addition to the data above, assume that due to the unique warming racks, the truck will have a $13,000 salvage value at the end of six years. Under these conditions, compute the internal rate of return to the nearest whole percent. (Hint: You may find it helpful to use the net present value approach; find the discount rate that will cause the net present value to be closest to zero. Use the format shown in Exhibit 13–4.)

EXERCISE 13-3 Uncertain Future Cash Flows [LO3]
Union Bay Plastics is investigating the purchase of automated equipment that would save $100,000 each year in direct labor and inventory carrying costs. This equipment costs $750,000 and is expected to have a 10-year useful life with no salvage value. The company requires a minimum 15% rate of return on all equipment purchases. This equipment would provide intangible benefits such as greater flexibility and higher-quality output that are difficult to estimate and yet are quite significant.

Required:
(Ignore income taxes.)
What dollar value per year would the intangible benefits have to be worth in order to make the equipment an acceptable investment?

EXERCISE 13-4 Preference Ranking [LO4]
Information on four investment proposals is given below:

	Investment Proposal			
	A	B	C	D
Investment required	$(85,000)	$(200,000)	$(90,000)	$(170,000)
Present value of cash inflows	119,000	250,000	135,000	221,000
Net present value	$ 34,000	$ 50,000	$ 45,000	$ 51,000
Life of the project	5 years	7 years	6 years	6 years

Required:
1. Compute the project profitability index for each investment proposal.
2. Rank the proposals in terms of preference.

EXERCISE 13-5 Payback Method [LO5]
The management of Weimar Inc., a civil engineering design company, is considering an investment in a high-quality blueprint printer with the following cash flows:

Year	Investment	Cash Inflow
1	$38,000	$2,000
2	$6,000	$4,000
3		$8,000
4		$9,000
5		$12,000
6		$10,000
7		$8,000
8		$6,000
9		$5,000
10		$5,000

Required:
1. Determine the payback period of the investment.
2. Would the payback period be affected if the cash inflow in the last year were several times larger?

EXERCISE 13-6 Simple Rate of Return Method [LO6]
The management of Wallingford MicroBrew is considering the purchase of an automated bottling machine for $80,000. The machine would replace an old piece of equipment that costs $33,000 per year to operate. The new machine would cost $10,000 per year to operate. The old machine currently in use could be sold now for a scrap value of $5,000. The new machine would have a useful life of 10 years with no salvage value.

Required:
Compute the simple rate of return on the new automated bottling machine.

EXERCISE 13-7 (Appendix 13A) Basic Present Value Concepts [LO7]

Each of the following parts is independent. (Ignore income taxes.)

1. Largo Freightlines plans to build a new garage in three years to have more space for repairing its trucks. The garage will cost $400,000. What lump-sum amount should the company invest now to have the $400,000 available at the end of the three-year period? Assume that the company can invest money at:
   a. Eight percent.
   b. Twelve percent.
2. Martell Products, Inc., can purchase a new copier that will save $5,000 per year in copying costs. The copier will last for six years and have no salvage value. What is the maximum purchase price that Martell Products would be willing to pay for the copier if the company's required rate of return is:
   a. Ten percent?
   b. Sixteen percent?
3. Sally has just won the million-dollar Big Slam jackpot at a gambling casino. The casino will pay her $50,000 per year for 20 years as the payoff. If Sally can invest money at a 10% rate of return, what is the present value of her winnings? Did she really win a million dollars? Explain.

EXERCISE 13-8 (Appendix 13C) After-Tax Costs [LO8]

Solve each of the following parts independently:

a. Stoffer Company has hired a management consulting firm to review and make recommendations concerning Stoffer's organizational structure. The consulting firm's fee will be $100,000. What will be the after-tax cost of the consulting firm's fee if Stoffer's tax rate is 30%?
b. The Green Hills Riding Club has redirected its advertising toward a different sector of the market. As a result of this change in advertising, the club's annual revenues have increased by $40,000. If the club's tax rate is 30%, what is the after-tax benefit from the increased revenues?
c. The Golden Eagles Basketball Team has just installed an electronic scoreboard in its playing arena at a cost of $210,000. For tax purposes, the entire original cost of the electronic scoreboard will be depreciated over seven years, using the straight-line method. Determine the yearly tax savings from the depreciation tax shield. Assume that the income tax rate is 30%.

EXERCISE 13-9 Comparison of Projects Using Net Present Value [LO1]

Sharp Company has $15,000 to invest. The company is trying to decide between two alternative uses of the funds as follows:

	Invest in Project A	Invest in Project B
Investment required	$15,000	$15,000
Annual cash inflows	$4,000	$0
Single cash inflow at the end of 10 years		$60,000
Life of the project	10 years	10 years

Sharp Company uses a 16% discount rate.

Required:

(Ignore income taxes.) Which investment would you recommend that the company accept? Show all computations using net present value. Prepare separate computations for each investment.

EXERCISE 13-10 Basic Net Present Value Analysis [LO1]

On January 2, Fred Critchfield paid $18,000 for 900 shares of the common stock of Acme Company. Mr. Critchfield received an $0.80 per share dividend on the stock at the end of each year for four years. At the end of four years, he sold the stock for $22,500. Mr. Critchfield has a goal of earning a minimum return of 12% on all of his investments.

Required:

(Ignore income taxes.) Did Mr. Critchfield earn a 12% return on the stock? Use the net present value method and the general format shown in Exhibit 13–4. Round all computations to the nearest whole dollar.

EXERCISE 13-11 Internal Rate of Return and Net Present Value [LO1, LO2]

Scalia's Cleaning Service is investigating the purchase of an ultrasound machine for cleaning window blinds. The machine would cost $136,700, including invoice cost, freight, and training of employees to operate it. Scalia's has estimated that the new machine would increase the company's cash flows, net of expenses, by $25,000 per year. The machine would have a 14-year useful life with no expected salvage value.

Required:

(Ignore income taxes.)

1. Compute the machine's internal rate of return to the nearest whole percent.
2. Compute the machine's net present value. Use a discount rate of 16% and the format shown in Exhibit 13–5. Why do you have a zero net present value?
3. Suppose that the new machine would increase the company's annual cash flows, net of expenses, by only $20,000 per year. Under these conditions, compute the internal rate of return to the nearest whole percent.

EXERCISE 13-12 Uncertain Future Life [LO3]

Worldwide Travel Service has made an investment in certain equipment that cost the company $307,100. The equipment is expected to generate cash inflows of $50,000 each year.

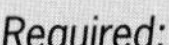

Required:

How many years will the equipment have to be used in order to provide the company with a 14% return on its investment?

EXERCISE 13-13 Basic Payback Period and Simple Rate of Return Computations [LO5, LO6]

Martin Company is considering the purchase of a new piece of equipment. Relevant information concerning the equipment follows:

Purchase cost	$180,000
Annual cost savings that will be provided by the equipment.	$37,500
Life of the equipment	12 years

Required:

(Ignore income taxes.)

1. Compute the payback period for the equipment. If the company rejects all proposals with a payback period of more than four years, would the equipment be purchased?
2. Compute the simple rate of return on the equipment. Use straight-line depreciation based on the equipment's useful life. Would the equipment be purchased if the company's required rate of return is 14%?

EXERCISE 13-14 (Appendix 13A) Basic Present Value Concepts [LO7]

Consider each of the following situations independently. (Ignore income taxes.)

1. Annual cash inflows from two competing investment opportunities are given below. Each investment opportunity will require the same initial investment. Compute the present value of the cash inflows for each investment using a 20% discount rate.

	Investment	
Year	X	Y
1.	$ 1,000	$ 4,000
2.	2,000	3,000
3	3,000	2,000
4	4,000	1,000
	$10,000	$10,000

2. At the end of three years, when you graduate from college, your father has promised to give you a used car that will cost $12,000. What lump sum must he invest now to have the $12,000 at the end of three years if he can invest money at:
   a. Six percent?
   b. Ten percent?
3. Mark has just won the grand prize on the "Hoot 'n' Holler" quiz show. He has a choice between (*a*) receiving $500,000 immediately and (*b*) receiving $60,000 per year for eight years plus a lump sum of $200,000 at the end of the eight-year period. If Mark can get a return of 10% on his investments, which option would you recommend that he accept? (Use present value analysis, and show all computations.)
4. You have just learned that you are a beneficiary in the will of your late Aunt Susan. The executrix of her estate has given you three options as to how you may receive your inheritance:
   a. You may receive $50,000 immediately.
   b. You may receive $75,000 at the end of six years.
   c. You may receive $12,000 at the end of each year for six years (a total of $72,000).
   If you can invest money at a 12% return, which option would you prefer?

EXERCISE 13-15 (Appendix 13C) After-Tax Cash Flows in Net Present Value Analysis [LO8]

Kramer Corporation is considering two investment projects, each of which would require $50,000. Cost and cash flow data concerning the two projects are given below:

	Project A	Project B
Investment in high-speed photocopier.	$50,000	
Investment in working capital.		$50,000
Net annual cash inflows.	$9,000	$9,000
Life of the project	8 years	8 years

The high-speed photocopier would have a salvage value of $5,000 in eight years. For tax purposes, the company computes depreciation deductions assuming zero salvage value and uses straight-line depreciation. The photocopier would be depreciated over eight years. At the end of eight years, the investment in working capital would be released for use elsewhere. The company requires an after-tax return of 10% on all investments. The tax rate is 30%.

Required:

Compute the net present value of each investment project. (Round to the nearest whole dollar.)

EXERCISE 13-16 Working With Net Present Value [LO1]

Mountain View Hospital has purchased new lab equipment for $134,650. The equipment is expected to last for three years and to provide cash inflows as follows:

Year 1	$45,000
Year 2	$60,000
Year 3	?

Required:

Assuming that the equipment will yield exactly a 16% rate of return, what is the expected cash inflow for Year 3?

EXERCISE 13-17 Basic Net Present Value and Internal Rate of Return Analysis [LO1, LO2]

(Ignore income taxes.) Consider each case below independently.

1. Minden Company's required rate of return is 15%. The company can purchase a new machine at a cost of $40,350. The new machine would generate cash inflows of $15,000 per year and have a four-year life with no salvage value. Compute the machine's net present value. (Use the format shown in Exhibit 13–1.) Is the machine an acceptable investment? Explain.
2. Leven Products, Inc., is investigating the purchase of a new grinding machine that has a projected life of 15 years. It is estimated that the machine will save $20,000 per year in cash operating costs. What is the machine's internal rate of return if it costs $111,500 new?

3. Sunset Press has just purchased a new trimming machine that cost $14,125. The machine is expected to save $2,500 per year in cash operating costs and to have a 10-year life. Compute the machine's internal rate of return. If the company's required rate of return is 16%, did it make a wise investment? Explain.

EXERCISE 13-18 Net Present Value Analysis of Two Alternatives [LO1]

Wriston Company has $300,000 to invest. The company is trying to decide between two alternative uses of the funds. The alternatives are as follows:

	A	B
Cost of equipment required	$300,000	$0
Working capital investment required	$0	$300,000
Annual cash inflows	$80,000	$60,000
Salvage value of equipment in seven years	$20,000	$0
Life of the project	7 years	7 years

The working capital needed for project B will be released for investment elsewhere at the end of seven years. Wriston Company uses a 20% discount rate.

Required:

(Ignore income taxes.) Which investment alternative (if either) would you recommend that the company accept? Show all computations using the net present value format. Prepare separate computations for each project.

EXERCISE 13-19 Payback Period and Simple Rate of Return [LO5, LO6]

The Heritage Amusement Park would like to construct a new ride called the Sonic Boom, which the park management feels would be very popular. The ride would cost $450,000 to construct, and it would have a 10% salvage value at the end of its 15-year useful life. The company estimates that the following annual costs and revenues would be associated with the ride:

Ticket revenues		$250,000
Less operating expenses:		
Maintenance	$40,000	
Salaries	90,000	
Depreciation	27,000	
Insurance	30,000	
Total operating expenses		187,000
Net operating income		$ 63,000

Required:

(Ignore income taxes.)

1. Assume that the Heritage Amusement Park will not construct a new ride unless the ride provides a payback period of six years or less. Does the Sonic Boom ride satisfy this requirement?
2. Compute the simple rate of return promised by the new ride. If Heritage Amusement Park requires a simple rate of return of at least 12%, does the Sonic Boom ride meet this criterion?

EXERCISE 13-20 (Appendix 13C) Net Present Value Analysis Including Income Taxes [LO8]

Press Publishing Company hires students from the local university to collate pages on various printing jobs. This collating is all done by hand, at a cost of $60,000 per year. A collating machine has just come onto the market that could be used in place of the student help. The machine would cost $140,000 and have a 10-year useful life. It would require an operator at an annual cost of $18,000 and have annual maintenance costs of $7,000. New roller pads would be needed on the machine in five years at a total cost of $20,000. The salvage value of the machine in 10 years would be $40,000.

For tax purposes, the company computes depreciation deductions assuming zero salvage value and uses straight-line depreciation. The collating machine would be depreciated over 10 years. Management requires a 14% after-tax return on all equipment purchases. The company's tax rate is 30%.

Required:

1. Determine the before-tax net annual cost savings that the new collating machine will provide.
2. Using the data from (1) above and other data from the exercise, compute the collating machine's net present value. (Round all dollar amounts to the nearest whole dollar.) Would you recommend that the machine be purchased?

Problems 

PROBLEM 13-21 Net Present Value Analysis; Uncertain Cash Flows [LO1, LO3]

Tiger Computers, Inc., of Singapore is considering the purchase of an automated etching machine for use in the production of its circuit boards. The machine would cost $900,000. (All currency amounts are in Singapore dollars.) An additional $650,000 would be required for installation costs and for software. Management believes that the automated machine would provide substantial annual reductions in costs, as shown below:

	Annual Reduction in Costs
Labor costs	$240,000
Material costs.	$96,000

The new machine would require considerable maintenance work to keep it in proper adjustment. The company's engineers estimate that maintenance costs would increase by $4,250 per month if the machine were purchased. In addition, the machine would require a $90,000 overhaul at the end of the sixth year.

The new etching machine would be usable for 10 years, after which it would be sold for its scrap value of $210,000. It would replace an old etching machine that can be sold now for its scrap value of $70,000. Tiger Computers, Inc., requires a return of at least 18% on investments of this type.

Required:

(Ignore income taxes.)

1. Compute the net annual cost savings promised by the new etching machine.
2. Using the data from (1) above and other data from the problem, compute the new machine's net present value. (Use the incremental-cost approach.) Would you recommend that the machine be purchased? Explain.
3. Assume that management can identify several intangible benefits associated with the new machine, including greater flexibility in shifting from one type of circuit board to another, improved quality of output, and faster delivery as a result of reduced throughput time. What dollar value per year would management have to attach to these intangible benefits in order to make the new etching machine an acceptable investment?

PROBLEM 13-22 Basic Net Present Value Analysis [LO1]

Renfree Mines, Inc., owns the mining rights to a large tract of land in a mountainous area. The tract contains a mineral deposit that the company believes might be commercially attractive to mine and sell. An engineering and cost analysis has been made, and it is expected that the following cash flows would be associated with opening and operating a mine in the area:

Cost of equipment required	$850,000
Net annual cash receipts	$230,000*
Working capital required	$100,000
Cost of road repairs in three years.	$60,000
Salvage value of equipment in five years	$200,000

*Receipts from sales of ore, less out-of-pocket costs for salaries, utilities, insurance, and so forth.

It is estimated that the mineral deposit would be exhausted after five years of mining. At that point, the working capital would be released for reinvestment elsewhere. The company's required rate of return is 14%.

Required:

(Ignore income taxes.) Determine the net present value of the proposed mining project. Should the project be accepted? Explain.

PROBLEM 13-23 Simple Rate of Return; Payback [LO5, LO6]

Lugano's Pizza Parlor is considering the purchase of a large oven and related equipment for mixing and baking "crazy bread." The oven and equipment would cost $120,000 delivered and installed. It would be usable for about 15 years, after which it would have a 10% scrap value. The following additional information is available:

a. Mr. Lugano estimates that purchase of the oven and equipment would allow the pizza parlor to bake and sell 72,000 loaves of crazy bread each year. The bread sells for $1.25 per loaf.
b. The cost of the ingredients in a loaf of bread is 40% of the selling price. Mr. Lugano estimates that other costs each year associated with the bread would be the following: salaries, $18,000; utilities, $9,000; and insurance, $3,000.
c. The pizza parlor uses straight-line depreciation on all assets, deducting salvage value from original cost.

Required:

(Ignore income taxes.)

1. Prepare a contribution format income statement showing the net operating income each year from production and sale of the crazy bread.
2. Compute the simple rate of return for the new oven and equipment. If a simple rate of return above 12% is acceptable to Mr. Lugano, will he purchase the oven and equipment?
3. Compute the payback period on the oven and equipment. If Mr. Lugano purchases any equipment with less than a six-year payback, will he purchase this equipment?

PROBLEM 13-24 (Appendix 13C) Basic Net Present Value Analysis Including Income Taxes [LO8]

Rapid Parcel Service has been offered an eight-year contract to deliver mail and small parcels between army installations. To accept the contract, the company would have to purchase several new delivery trucks at a total cost of $450,000. Other data relating to the contract follow:

Net annual cash receipts (before taxes) from the contract	$108,000
Cost of overhauling the motors in the trucks in five years	$45,000
Salvage value of the trucks at termination of the contract	$20,000

If the contract were accepted, several old, fully depreciated trucks would be sold at a total price of $30,000. These funds would be used to help purchase the new trucks. For tax purposes, the company computes depreciation deductions assuming zero salvage value and uses straight-line depreciation. The trucks would be depreciated over eight years. The company requires a 12% after-tax return on all equipment purchases. The tax rate is 30%.

Required:

Compute the net present value of this investment opportunity. Round all dollar amounts to the nearest whole dollar. Would you recommend that the contract be accepted?

PROBLEM 13-25 Basic Net Present Value Analysis [LO1]

Doughboy Bakery would like to buy a new machine for putting icing and other toppings on pastries. These are now put on by hand. The machine that the bakery is considering costs $90,000 new. It would last the bakery for eight years but would require a $7,500 overhaul at the end of the fifth year. After eight years, the machine could be sold for $6,000.

The bakery estimates that it will cost $14,000 per year to operate the new machine. The present manual method of putting toppings on the pastries costs $35,000 per year. In addition to reducing operating costs, the new machine will allow the bakery to increase its production of pastries by 5,000 packages per year. The bakery realizes a contribution margin of $0.60 per package. The bakery requires a 16% return on all investments in equipment.

Required:

(Ignore income taxes.)

1. What are the net annual cash inflows that will be provided by the new machine?
2. Compute the new machine's net present value. Use the incremental cost approach, and round all dollar amounts to the nearest whole dollar.

PROBLEM 13-26 Preference Ranking of Investment Projects [LO4]

Austin Company is investigating five different investment opportunities. Information on the four projects under study is given below:

	Project Number			
	1	2	3	4
Investment required.	$(480,000)	$(360,000)	$(270,000)	$(450,000)
Present value of cash inflows at a 10% discount rate.	567,270	433,400	336,140	522,970
Net present value	$ 87,270	$ 73,400	$ 66,140	$ 72,970
Life of the project	6 years	12 years	6 years	3 years
Internal rate of return	16%	14%	18%	19%

Since the company's required rate of return is 10%, a 10% discount rate has been used in the present value computations above. Limited funds are available for investment, so the company can't accept all of the available projects.

Required:

1. Compute the project profitability index for each investment project.
2. Rank the four projects according to preference, in terms of:
   a. Net present value
   b. Project profitability index
   c. Internal rate of return
3. Which ranking do you prefer? Why?

PROBLEM 13-27 Net Present Value Analysis [LO1]

Frank White will retire in six years. He wants to open some type of small business operation that can be managed in the free time he has available from his regular occupation, but that can be closed easily when he retires. He is considering several investment alternatives, one of which is to open a laundromat. After careful study, Mr. White has determined the following:

a. Washers, dryers, and other equipment needed to open the laundromat would cost $194,000. In addition, $6,000 in working capital would be required to purchase an inventory of soap, bleaches, and related items and to provide change for change machines. (The soap, bleaches, and related items would be sold to customers at cost.) After six years, the working capital would be released for investment elsewhere.
b. The laundromat would charge $1.50 per use for the washers and $0.75 per use for the dryers. Mr. White expects the laundromat to gross $1,800 each week from the washers and $1,125 each week from the dryers.
c. The only variable costs in the laundromat would be 7½ cents per use for water and electricity for the washers and 9 cents per use for gas and electricity for the dryers.
d. Fixed costs would be $3,000 per month for rent, $1,500 per month for cleaning, and $1,875 per month for maintenance, insurance, and other items.
e. The equipment would have a 10% disposal value in six years.

Mr. White will not open the laundromat unless it provides at least a 12% return.

Required:

(Ignore income taxes.)

1. Assuming that the laundromat would be open 52 weeks a year, compute the expected net annual cash receipts from its operation (gross cash receipts less cash disbursements). (Do not include the cost of the equipment, the working capital, or the salvage values in these computations.)

2. Would you advise Mr. White to open the laundromat? Show computations using the net present value method of investment analysis. Round all dollar amounts to the nearest whole dollar.

PROBLEM 13-28 Simple Rate of Return; Payback; Internal Rate of Return [LO2, LO5, LO6]
Chateau Beaune is a family-owned winery located in the Burgundy region of France, which is headed by Gerard Despinoy. The harvesting season in early fall is the busiest part of the year for the winery, and many part-time workers are hired to help pick and process grapes. Mr. Despinoy is investigating the purchase of a harvesting machine that would significantly reduce the amount of labor required in the picking process. The harvesting machine is built to straddle grapevines, which are laid out in low-lying rows. Two workers are carried on the machine just above ground level, one on each side of the vine. As the machine slowly crawls through the vineyard, the workers cut bunches of grapes from the vines, which then fall into a hopper. The machine separates the grapes from the stems and other woody debris. The debris are then pulverized and spread behind the machine as a rich ground mulch. Mr. Despinoy has gathered the following information relating to the decision of whether to purchase the machine:

a. The winery would save €190,000 per year in labor costs with the new harvesting machine. In addition, the company would no longer have to purchase and spread ground mulch—at an annual savings of €10,000. (The French currency is the euro, which is denoted by the symbol €.)
b. The harvesting machine would cost €480,000. It would have an estimated 12-year useful life and zero salvage value. The winery uses straight-line depreciation.
c. Annual out-of-pocket costs associated with the harvesting machine would be insurance, €1,000; fuel, €9,000; and a maintenance contract, €12,000. In addition, two operators would be hired and trained for the machine, and they would be paid a total of €70,000 per year, including all benefits.
d. Mr. Despinoy feels that the investment in the harvesting machine should earn at least a 16% rate of return.

Required:
(Ignore income taxes.)

1. Determine the annual net savings in cash operating costs that would be realized if the harvesting machine were purchased.
2. Compute the simple rate of return expected from the harvesting machine.
3. Compute the payback period on the harvesting machine. Mr. Despinoy will not purchase equipment unless it has a payback period of five years or less. Under this criterion, should the harvesting machine be purchased?
4. Compute (to the nearest whole percent) the internal rate of return promised by the harvesting machine. Based on this computation, does it appear that the simple rate of return is an accurate guide in investment decisions?

PROBLEM 13-29 Net Present Value; Uncertain Future Cash Flows; Postaudit [LO1, LO3]
"If we can get that new robot to combine with our other automated equipment, we'll have a complete flexible manufacturing system (FMS) in place in our Northridge plant," said Hal Swain, production manager for Diller Products.

"Let's just hope that reduced labor and inventory costs can justify its acquisition," replied Linda Wycoff, the controller. "Otherwise, we'll never get it. You know how the president feels about equipment paying for itself out of reduced costs."

Selected data relating to the robot are provided below:

Cost of the robot	$1,600,000
Software and installation	$700,000
Annual savings in labor costs	?
Annual savings in inventory carrying costs	$190,000
Monthly increase in power and maintenance costs	$2,500
Salvage value in 12 years	$90,000
Useful life	12 years

Engineering studies suggest that use of the robot will result in a savings of 20,000 direct labor-hours each year. The labor rate is $16 per hour. Also, the smoother work flow made possible by the FMS will allow the company to reduce the amount of inventory on hand by $300,000. The released funds will be available for use elsewhere in the company. This inventory reduction will take place in the first year of operation. The company's required rate of return is 20%.

Required:

(Ignore income taxes.)

1. Determine the net *annual* cost savings if the robot is purchased. (Do not include the $300,000 inventory reduction or the salvage value in this computation.)
2. Compute the net present value of the proposed investment in the robot. Based on these data, would you recommend that the robot be purchased? Explain.
3. Assume that the robot is purchased. At the end of the first year, Linda Wycoff has found that some items didn't work out as planned. Due to unforeseen problems, software and installation costs were $125,000 more than estimated, and direct labor has been reduced by only 17,500 hours per year, rather than by 20,000 hours. Assuming that all other cost data were accurate, does it appear that the company made a wise investment? Show computations, using the net present value format as in (2) above. (Hint: It might be helpful to place yourself back at the beginning of the first year, with the new data.)
4. Upon seeing your analysis in (3) above, the president stated, "That robot is the worst investment we've ever made. And here we'll be stuck with it for years."
   a. Explain to the president what benefits other than cost savings might accrue from using the new robot and FMS.
   b. Compute for the president the dollar amount of cash inflow that would be needed each year from the benefits in (*a*) above in order for the equipment to yield a 20% rate of return.

PROBLEM 13-30 Internal Rate of Return; Sensitivity Analysis [LO2]

Dr. Heidi Black is the managing partner of the Crestwood Dental Clinic. Dr. Black is trying to determine whether or not the clinic should move patient files and other items out of a spare room in the clinic and use the room for dental work. She has determined that it would require an investment of $142,950 for equipment and related costs of getting the room ready for use. Based on receipts being generated from other rooms in the clinic, Dr. Black estimates that the new room would generate a net cash inflow of $37,500 per year. The equipment purchased for the room would have a seven-year estimated useful life.

Required:

(Ignore income taxes.)

1. Compute the internal rate of return on the equipment for the new room to the nearest whole percent. Verify your answer by computing the net present value of the equipment using the internal rate of return you have computed as the discount rate.
2. Assume that Dr. Black will not purchase the new equipment unless it promises a return of at least 14%. Compute the amount of annual cash inflow that would provide this return on the $142,950 investment.
3. Although seven years is the average life for dental equipment, Dr. Black knows that due to changing technology this life can vary substantially. Compute the internal rate of return to the nearest whole percent if the life of the equipment were (*a*) five years and (*b*) nine years, rather than seven years. Is there any information provided by these computations that you would be particularly anxious to show Dr. Black?
4. Dr. Black is unsure about the estimated $37,500 annual cash inflow from the room. She thinks that the actual cash inflow could be as much as 20% greater or less than this figure.
   a. Assume that the actual cash inflow each year is 20% greater than estimated. Recompute the internal rate of return to the nearest whole percent.
   b. Assume that the actual cash inflow each year is 20% less than estimated. Recompute the internal rate of return to the nearest whole percent.
5. Refer to the original data. Assume that the equipment is purchased and that the room is opened for dental use. However, due to an increasing number of dentists in the area, the clinic is able to generate only $30,000 per year in net cash receipts from the new room. At the end of five years, the clinic closes the room and sells the equipment to a newly licensed dentist for a cash price of $61,375. Compute the internal rate of return to the nearest whole percent that the clinic earned on its investment over the five-year period. Round all dollar amounts to the nearest whole dollar. (Hint: A useful way to proceed is to find the discount rate that will cause the net present value of the investment to be equal to, or near, zero).

PROBLEM 13-31 Net Present Value Analysis of a Lease or Buy Decision [LO1]

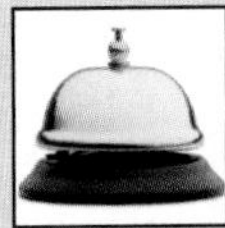

Blinko Products wants an airplane for use by its corporate staff. The airplane that the company wishes to acquire, a Zephyr II, can be either purchased or leased from the manufacturer. The company has made the following evaluation of the two alternatives:

Purchase alternative. If the Zephyr II is purchased, then the costs incurred by the company would be as follows:

Purchase cost of the plane	$850,000
Annual cost of servicing, licenses, and taxes	$9,000
Repairs:	
First three years, per year	$3,000
Fourth year	$5,000
Fifth year	$10,000

The plane would be sold after five years. Based on current resale values, the company would be able to sell it for about one-half of its original cost at the end of the five-year period.

Lease alternative. If the Zephyr II is leased, then the company would have to make an immediate deposit of $50,000 to cover any damage during use. The lease would run for five years, at the end of which time the deposit would be refunded. The lease would require an annual rental payment of $200,000 (the first payment is due at the end of Year 1). As part of this lease cost, the manufacturer would provide all servicing and repairs, license the plane, and pay all taxes. At the end of the five-year period, the plane would revert to the manufacturer, as owner.

Blinko Products' required rate of return is 18%.

Required:

(Ignore income taxes.)

1. Use the total-cost approach to determine the present value of the cash flows associated with each alternative.
2. Which alternative would you recommend that the company accept? Why?

PROBLEM 13-32 Simple Rate of Return; Payback [LO5, LO6]

Nagoya Amusements Corporation places electronic games and other amusement devices in supermarkets and similar outlets throughout Japan. Nagoya Amusements is investigating the purchase of a new electronic game called Mystic Invaders. The manufacturer will sell 20 games to Nagoya Amusements for a total price of ¥180,000. (The Japanese currency is yen, which is denoted by the symbol ¥.) Nagoya Amusements has determined the following additional information about the game:

a. The game would have a five-year useful life and a negligible salvage value. The company uses straight-line depreciation.
b. The game would replace other games that are unpopular and generating little revenue. These other games would be sold for a total of ¥30,000.
c. Nagoya Amusements estimates that Mystic Invaders would generate annual incremental revenues of ¥200,000 (total for all 20 games). Annual incremental out-of-pocket costs would be (in total): maintenance, ¥50,000; and insurance, ¥10,000. In addition, Nagoya Amusements would have to pay a commission of 40% of total revenues to the supermarkets and other outlets in which the games were placed.

Required:

(Ignore income taxes.)

1. Prepare a contribution format income statement showing the net operating income each year from Mystic Invaders.
2. Compute the simple rate of return on Mystic Invaders. Will the game be purchased if Nagoya Amusements accepts any project with a simple rate of return greater than 14%?
3. Compute the payback period on Mystic Invaders. If the company accepts any investment with a payback period of less than three years, will the game be purchased?

PROBLEM 13-33 Preference Ranking of Investment Projects [LO4]

Yancey Company has limited funds available for investment and must ration the funds among four competing projects. Selected information on the four projects follows:

Project	Investment Required	Net Present Value	Life of the Project (years)	Internal Rate of Return
A	$800,000	$221,615	7	18%
B	$675,000	$210,000	12	16%
C	$500,000	$175,175	7	20%
D	$700,000	$152,544	3	22%

The net present values above have been computed using a 10% discount rate. The company wants your assistance in determining which project to accept first, which to accept second, and so forth. The company's investment funds are limited.

Required:

1. Compute the project profitability index for each project.
2. In order of preference, rank the four projects in terms of:
   a. Net present value.
   b. Project profitability index.
   c. Internal rate of return.
3. Which ranking do you prefer? Why?

PROBLEM 13-34 Net Present Value Analysis of a New Product [LO1]

Atwood Company has an opportunity to produce and sell a revolutionary new smoke detector for homes. To determine whether this would be a profitable venture, the company has gathered the following data on probable costs and market potential:

a. New equipment would have to be acquired to produce the smoke detector. The equipment would cost $100,000 and be usable for 12 years. After 12 years, it would have a salvage value equal to 10% of the original cost.
b. Production and sales of the smoke detector would require a working capital investment of $40,000 to finance accounts receivable, inventories, and day-to-day cash needs. This working capital would be released for use elsewhere after 12 years.
c. An extensive marketing study projects sales in units over the next 12 years as follows:

Year	Sales in Units
1	4,000
2	7,000
3	10,000
4–12.	12,000

d. The smoke detectors would sell for $45 each; variable costs for production, administration, and sales would be $25 per unit.
e. To gain entry into the market, the company would have to advertise heavily in the early years of sales. The advertising program follows:

Year	Amount of Advertising
1–2	$70,000
3	$50,000
4–12	$40,000

f. Other fixed costs for salaries, insurance, maintenance, and straight-line depreciation on equipment would total $127,500 per year. (Depreciation is based on cost less salvage value.)
g. The company's required rate of return is 20%.

Required:
(Ignore income taxes.)
1. Compute the net cash inflow (cash receipts less yearly cash operating expenses) anticipated from sale of the smoke detectors for each year over the next 12 years.
2. Using the data computed in (1) above and other data provided in the problem, determine the net present value of the proposed investment. Would you recommend that Atwood Company accept the smoke detector as a new product?

PROBLEM: 13-35 (Appendix 13C) A Comparison of Investment Alternatives Including Income Taxes [LO8]

Ms. Keri Lee, an expert in retrofitting buildings to meet seismic safety standards, has just received a $200,000 after-tax bonus for the successful completion of a project on time and under budget. Business has been so good that she is planning to retire in 12 years, spending her time relaxing in the sun, skiing, and doing charitable work. Ms. Lee is considering two alternatives for investing her bonus.

Alternative 1. Municipal bonds can be purchased that mature in 12 years and that bear interest at 8%. This interest would be tax-free and paid semiannually. (In discounting a cash flow that occurs semiannually, the procedure is to halve the discount rate and double the number of periods. Use the same procedure for discounting the principal returned when the bonds reach maturity.)

Alternative 2. A small discount perfume shop is available for sale at a nearby factory outlet center. The business can be purchased from its current owner for $200,000. The following information relates to this alternative:

a. Of the purchase price, $80,000 would be for fixtures and other depreciable items. The remainder would be for the company's working capital (inventory, accounts receivable, and cash). The fixtures and other depreciable items would have a remaining useful life of at least 12 years but would be depreciated for tax reporting purposes over eight years using the following allowances published by the Internal Revenue Service:

Year	Percentage of Original Cost Depreciated
1	14.3%
2	24.5
3	17.5
4	12.5
5	8.9
6	8.9
7	8.9
8	4.5
	100.0%

Salvage value is not deducted when computing depreciation for tax purposes. At any rate, at the end of 12 years, these depreciable items would have a negligible salvage value; however, the working capital would be released for reinvestment elsewhere.

b. Store records indicate that sales have averaged $400,000 per year, and out-of-pocket costs have averaged $370,000 per year (*not* including income taxes). These out-of-pocket costs include rent on the building, cost of goods sold, utilities, and wages and salaries for the sales staff and the store manager. Ms. Lee plans to entrust the day-to-day operations of the store to the manager.
c. Ms. Lee's tax rate is 40%.

Required:
Advise Ms. Lee as to which alternative should be selected. Use the total-cost approach to discounted cash flow in your analysis and a discount rate of 8%. (Round all dollar amounts to the nearest whole dollar.)

PROBLEM: 13-36 Net Present Value; Total and Incremental Approaches [LO1]

Eastbay Hospital has an auxiliary generator that is used when power failures occur. The generator is worn out and must be either overhauled or replaced with a new generator. The hospital has assembled the following information:

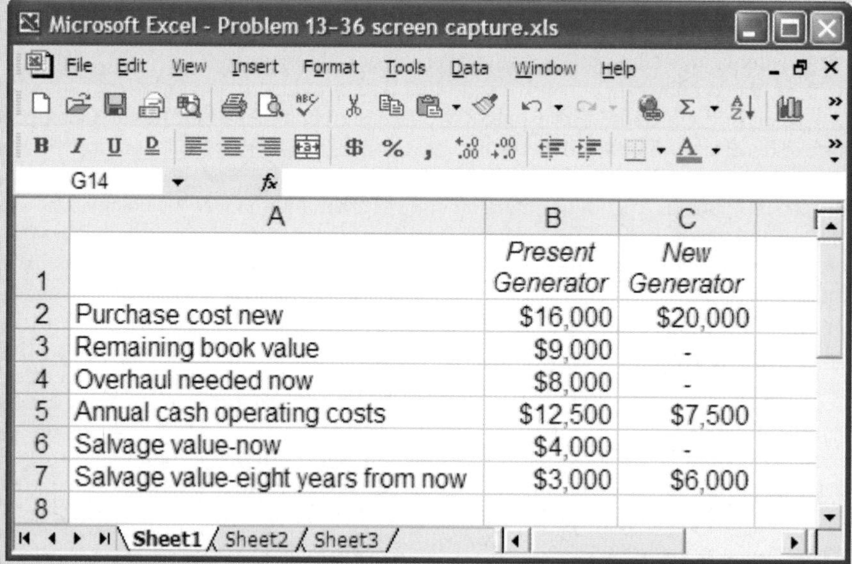

Microsoft Excel - Problem 13-36 screen capture.xls

	A	B	C
1		*Present Generator*	*New Generator*
2	Purchase cost new	$16,000	$20,000
3	Remaining book value	$9,000	-
4	Overhaul needed now	$8,000	-
5	Annual cash operating costs	$12,500	$7,500
6	Salvage value-now	$4,000	-
7	Salvage value-eight years from now	$3,000	$6,000
8			

If the company keeps and overhauls its present generator, then the generator will be usable for eight more years. If a new generator is purchased, it will be used for eight years, after which it will be replaced. The new generator would be diesel-powered, resulting in a substantial reduction in annual operating costs, as shown above.

The hospital computes depreciation on a straight-line basis. All equipment purchases are evaluated using a 16% discount rate.

Required:

(Ignore income taxes.)

1. Should Eastbay Hospital keep the old generator or purchase the new one? Use the total-cost approach to net present value in making your decision.
2. Redo (1) above, this time using the incremental-cost approach.

PROBLEM: 13-37 (Appendix 13C) Net Present Value Analysis Including Income Taxes [LO8]

The Crescent Drilling Company owns the drilling rights to several tracts of land on which natural gas has been found. The amount of gas on some of the tracts is somewhat marginal, and the company is unsure whether it would be profitable to extract and sell the gas that these tracts contain. One such tract is tract 410, on which the following information has been gathered:

Investment in equipment needed for extraction work	$600,000
Working capital investment needed	$85,000
Annual cash receipts from sale of gas, net of related cash operating expenses (before taxes)	$110,000
Cost of restoring land at completion of extraction work	$70,000

The natural gas in tract 410 would be exhausted after 10 years of extraction work. The equipment would have a useful life of 15 years, but it could be sold for only 15% of its original cost when extraction was completed. For tax purposes, the company would depreciate the equipment over 10 years using straight-line depreciation and assuming zero salvage value. The tax rate is 30%, and the company's after-tax discount rate is 10%. The working capital would be released for use elsewhere at the completion of the project.

Required:

1. Compute the net present value of tract 410. Round all dollar amounts to the nearest whole dollar.
2. Would you recommend that the investment project be undertaken?

Cases

CASE 13-38 Ethics and the Manager; Postaudit

After five years with a national CPA firm with mostly large manufacturing clients, Amy Kimbell joined Hi-Quality Productions Inc. (Hi-Q) as manager of Manufacturing Accounting. Amy has both CPA and CMA credentials.

Hi-Q is a publicly held company producing automotive components. One operation in the Alpha Division requires a highly automated process. Hi-Q's top management and board of directors had outsourced this particular high-tech operation to another company to avoid making a large investment in technology they viewed as constantly changing.

Each operating division of Hi-Q has a budget committee. Two years ago, the Alpha Division budget committee presented to the board its proposal to bring the high-tech operation in house. This would require a capital investment of approximately $4 million but would lead to more than enough cost savings to justify this expenditure. The board approved the proposal, and the investment was made. Later the same year, Amy Kimbell was promoted to assistant corporate controller. In this position, she sits on the budget committee of all divisions.

A little more than a year after the high-tech process was put into operation, the board requested a postaudit review of the actual cost savings. When the board requests such a review, the data are supplied by the management of the affected division and are reviewed by the division's budget committee. When the data were sent to the budget committee for review, Amy Kimbell noted that several of the projections in the original proposal were very aggressive. These included a very high salvage value for the equipment as well as a very long useful life over which cost savings were projected to occur. If more realistic projections had been used, Amy doubted that the board would have agreed to make the investment.

Also in the postaudit review, Amy noted that substantial amounts of incremental service department operating costs directly caused by the new investment were not being attributed to the high-tech operation. Instead, these costs were being allocated as general overhead to all departments. In addition, she noted that the estimated rate for spoiled and defective work contained in the proposal was being used in the review rather than the actual rate, which was considerably higher.

When Amy Kimbell brought these points to the attention of the division's budget committee, she was told that as a new member of the committee she would not be held responsible for decisions, such as the investment in the high-tech operation, that were made prior to her arrival. Accordingly, she should let the seasoned members of the committee handle this particular review. When Amy continued to express her concerns, she was firmly informed that it had been the unanimous decision of the committee to approve the original proposal because it was thought to be in the best long-run interest of the company. And given this consensus, it was felt that certain "adjustments and exceptions" to the postaudit review were justified to ensure the overall long-run well-being of the company.

Required:

1. What should Amy do? (Refer to the IMA's Statement of Ethical Professional Practice for guidance.)
2. Do you have any suggestions for revising the way in which postaudits are conducted at Hi-Q?

(Adapted from Roland L. Madison and Curtis C. Verschoor, "New Position Brings Ethical Dilemma," *Strategic Finance,* December 2000, pp. 22, 24. Used with permission from the IMA, Montvale, NJ, USA, www.imanet.org.)

CASE 13-39 Net Present Value Analysis of a Lease or Buy Decision [LO1]

Wyndham Stores operates a regional chain of upscale department stores. The company is going to open another store soon in a prosperous and growing suburban area. In discussing how the company can acquire the desired building and other facilities needed to open the new store, Harry Wilson, the company's marketing vice president, stated, "I know most of our competitors are starting to lease facilities, rather than buy, but I just can't see the economics of it. Our development people tell me that we can buy the building site, put a building on it, and get all the store fixtures we need for $14 million. They also say that property taxes, insurance, maintenance, and repairs would run $200,000 a year. When you figure that we plan to keep a site for 20 years, that's a total cost of $18 million. But then when you realize that the building and property will be worth at least $5 million in 20 years, that's a net cost to us of only $13 million. Leasing costs a lot more than that."

"I'm not so sure," replied Erin Reilley, the company's executive vice president. "Guardian Insurance Company is willing to purchase the building site, construct a building and install fixtures to our specifications, and then lease the facility to us for 20 years for an annual lease payment of only $1 million."

"That's just my point," said Harry. "At $1 million a year, it would cost us $20 million over the 20 years instead of just $13 million. And what would we have left at the end? Nothing! The building would belong to the insurance company! I'll bet they would even want the first lease payment in advance."

"That's right," replied Erin. "We would have to make the first payment immediately and then one payment at the beginning of each of the following 19 years. However, you're overlooking a few things. For one thing, we would have to tie up a lot of our funds for 20 years under the purchase alternative. We would have to put $6 million down immediately if we buy the property, and then we would have to pay the other $8 million off over four years at $2 million a year."

"But that cost is nothing compared to $20 million for leasing," said Harry. "Also, if we lease, I understand we would have to put up a $400,000 security deposit that we wouldn't get back until the end. And besides that, we would still have to pay all the repair and maintenance costs just like we owned the property. No wonder those insurance companies are so rich if they can swing deals like this."

"Well, I'll admit that I don't have all the figures sorted out yet," replied Erin. "But I do have the operating cost breakdown for the building, which includes $90,000 annually for property taxes, $60,000 for insurance, and $50,000 for repairs and maintenance. If we lease, Guardian will handle its own insurance costs and will pay the property taxes, but we'll have to pay for the repairs and maintenance. I need to put all this together and see if leasing makes any sense with our 12% before-tax required rate of return. The president wants a presentation and recommendation in the executive committee meeting tomorrow."

Required:

(Ignore income taxes.)

1. Using the net present value approach, determine whether Wyndham Stores should lease or buy the new store. Assume that you will be making your presentation before the company's executive committee.
2. How will you reply in the meeting if Harry Wilson brings up the issue of the building's future sales value?

CASE 13-40 Comparison of Alternatives Using Net Present Value Analysis [LO1]

Woolrich Company's market research division has projected a substantial increase in demand over the next several years for one of the company's products. To meet this demand, the company will need to produce units as follows:

Year	Production in Units
1	20,000
2	30,000
3	40,000
4–10.	45,000

At present, the company is using a single model 2600 machine to manufacture this product. To increase its productive capacity, the company is considering two alternatives:

Alternative 1. The company could purchase another model 2600 machine that would operate along with the one it now owns. The following information is available on this alternative:

a. The model 2600 machine now in use was purchased for $165,000 four years ago. Its present book value is $99,000, and its present market value is $90,000.
b. A new model 2600 machine costs $180,000 now. The old model 2600 machine will have to be replaced in six years at a cost of $200,000. The replacement machine will have a market value of about $100,000 when it is four years old.
c. The variable cost required to produce one unit of product using the model 2600 machine is given under the "general information" below.
d. Repairs and maintenance costs each year on a single model 2600 machine total $3,000.

Alternative 2. The company could purchase a model 5200 machine and use the old model 2600 machine as standby equipment. The model 5200 machine is a high-speed unit with double the capacity of the model 2600 machine. The following information is available on this alternative:

a. The cost of a new model 5200 machine is $250,000.
b. The variable cost required to produce one unit of product using the model 5200 machine is given under the "general information" below.

c. The model 5200 machine is more costly to maintain than the model 2600 machine. Repairs and maintenance on a model 5200 machine and on a model 2600 machine used as standby would total $4,600 per year.

The following general information is available on the two alternatives:

a. Both the model 2600 machine and the model 5200 machine have a 10-year life from the time they are first used in production. The scrap value of both machines is negligible and can be ignored. Straight-line depreciation is used by the company.
b. The two machine models are not equally efficient. Comparative variable costs per unit of product are as follows:

	Model 2600	Model 5200
Direct materials per unit	$0.36	$0.40
Direct labor per unit	0.50	0.22
Supplies and lubricants per unit	0.04	0.08
Total variable cost per unit.	$0.90	$0.70

c. No other factory costs would change as a result of the decision between the two machines.
d. Woolrich Company uses an 18% discount rate.

Required:

(Ignore income taxes.)

1. Which alternative should the company choose? Use the net present value approach. (Round to the nearest whole dollar.)
2. Suppose that the cost of direct materials increases by 50%. Would this make the model 5200 machine more or less desirable? Explain. No computations are needed.
3. Suppose that the cost of direct labor increases by 25%. Would this make the model 5200 machine more or less desirable? Explain. No computations are needed.

Appendix

A

Pricing Products and Services

Learning Objectives

After studying this appendix, you should be able to:

LO1 Compute the profit-maximizing price of a product or service using the price elasticity of demand and variable cost.

LO2 Compute the selling price of a product using the absorption costing approach.

LO3 Compute the target cost for a new product or service.

Introduction

Some products have an established market price. Consumers will not pay more than this price and there is no reason for a supplier to charge less—it can sell all that it produces at this price. Under these circumstances, the company simply charges the prevailing market price for the product. Markets for basic raw materials such as farm products and minerals follow this pattern.

In this appendix, we are concerned with the more common situation in which a business is faced with the problem of setting its own prices. Clearly, the pricing decision can be critical. If the price is set too high, customers won't buy the company's products. If the price is set too low, the company's costs won't be covered.

The usual approach in pricing is to *mark up* cost.[1] A product's **markup** is the difference between its selling price and its cost and is usually expressed as a percentage of cost.

$$\text{Selling price} = (1 + \text{Markup percentage}) \times \text{Cost}$$

For example, a company that uses a markup of 50% adds 50% to the costs of its products to determine selling prices. If a product costs $10, then the company would charge $15 for the product. This approach is called **cost-plus pricing** because a predetermined markup percentage is applied to a cost base to determine the selling price.

Two key issues must be addressed with the cost-plus approach to pricing. First, what cost should be used? Second, how should the markup be determined? Several alternative approaches are considered in this appendix, starting with the approach generally favored by economists.

The Economists' Approach to Pricing

LEARNING OBJECTIVE 1
Compute the profit-maximizing price of a product or service using the price elasticity of demand and variable cost.

If a company raises the price of a product, unit sales ordinarily fall. Because of this, pricing is a delicate balancing act in which the benefits of higher revenues per unit are traded off against the lower volume that results from charging a higher price. The sensitivity of unit sales to changes in price is called the *price elasticity of demand.*

Elasticity of Demand

A product's price elasticity should be a key element in setting its price. The **price elasticity of demand** measures the degree to which a change in price affects the unit sales of a product or service. Demand for a product is said to be *inelastic* if a change in price has little effect on the number of units sold. The demand for designer perfumes sold by trained personnel at cosmetic counters in department stores is relatively inelastic. Raising or lowering prices on these luxury goods has little effect on unit sales. On the other hand, demand for a product is *elastic* if a change in price has a substantial effect on the volume of units sold. An example of a product whose demand is elastic is gasoline. If a gas station raises its price for gasoline, unit sales will drop as customers seek lower prices elsewhere.

Price elasticity is very important in determining prices. Managers should set higher markups over cost when customers are relatively insensitive to price (i.e., demand is inelastic) and lower markups when customers are relatively sensitive to price (i.e., demand is

[1] There are some legal restrictions on prices. Antitrust laws prohibit "predatory" prices, which are generally interpreted by the courts to mean a price below average variable cost. "Price discrimination"—charging different prices to customers in the same market for the same product or service—is also prohibited by the law.

elastic). This principle is followed in department stores. Merchandise sold in the bargain basement has a much lower markup than merchandise sold elsewhere in the store because customers who shop in the bargain basement are much more sensitive to price (i.e., demand is elastic).

The price elasticity of demand for a product or service, ϵ_d, can be estimated using the following formula.[2,3]

$$\epsilon_d = \frac{\ln(1 + \%\text{ change in quantity sold})}{\ln(1 + \%\text{ change in price})}$$

For example, suppose that the managers of Nature's Garden believe that a 10% increase in the selling price of their apple-almond shampoo would result in a 15% decrease in the number of bottles of shampoo sold.[4] The price elasticity of demand for this product would be computed as follows:

$$\epsilon_d = \frac{\ln[1 + (-0.15)]}{\ln[1 + (0.10)]} = \frac{\ln(0.85)}{\ln(1.10)} = -1.71$$

For comparison purposes, the managers of Nature's Garden believe that another product, strawberry glycerin soap, would experience a 20% drop in unit sales if its price is increased by 10%. (Purchasers of this product are more sensitive to price than the purchasers of the apple-almond shampoo.) The price elasticity of demand for the strawberry glycerin soap is:

$$\epsilon_d = \frac{\ln[1 + (-0.20)]}{\ln[1 + (0.10)]} = \frac{\ln(0.80)}{\ln(1.10)} = -2.34$$

Both of these products, like other normal products, have a price elasticity that is less than -1.

Note that the price elasticity of demand for the strawberry glycerin soap is larger (in absolute value) than the price elasticity of demand for the apple-almond shampoo. This indicates that the demand for strawberry glycerin soap is more elastic than the demand for apple-almond shampoo.

In the next subsection, the price elasticity of demand will be used to compute the selling price that maximizes the profits of the company.

The Profit-Maximizing Price

Under certain conditions, the profit-maximizing price can be determined by marking up *variable cost* using the following formula:[5]

$$\text{Profit-maximizing markup on variable cost} = \frac{-1}{1 + \epsilon_d}$$

Using the above markup, the selling price would be set using the formula:

$$\text{Profit-maximizing price} = (1 + \text{Profit-maximizing markup on variable cost}) \times \text{Variable cost per unit}$$

---

[2] The term "ln( )" is the natural log function. You can compute the natural log of any number using the LN or ln$x$ key on your calculator. For example, $\ln(0.85) = -0.1625$.

[3] This formula assumes that the price elasticity of demand is constant. This occurs when the relation between the selling price, p, and the unit sales, q, can be expressed in the following form: $\ln(q) = a + \epsilon_d \ln(p)$. Even if this is not precisely true, the formula provides a useful way to estimate a product's price elasticity.

[4] The estimated change in unit sales should take into account competitors' responses to a price change.

[5] The formula assumes that (a) the price elasticity of demand is constant; (b) Total cost = Total fixed cost + Variable cost per unit × Quantity sold; and (c) the price of the product has no effect on the sales or costs of any other product. The formula can be derived using calculus.

IN BUSINESS

WHAT DID THAT SALMON DISH COST?

Restaurants mark up food costs by an average of 300% to cover their overhead and generate a profit, but the markup is not the same for all items on the menu. Some ingredients—especially prime cuts of beef and exotic seafood such as fresh scallops—are so costly that diners would not tolerate a 300% markup. So restaurants make it up on the cheap stuff—vegetables, pasta, and salmon. Why salmon? The farmed variety is only $2.50 per pound wholesale, much cheaper than prime restaurant-quality beef. At the Docks restaurant in New York City, a 10-ounce salmon dinner garnished with potatoes and coleslaw is $19.50. The actual cost of the ingredients is only $1.90.

To take another example, the ingredients of the best-selling Angus beef tenderloin at the Sunset Grill in Nashville, Tennessee, costs the restaurant $8.42. Applying the average 300% markup, the price of the meal would be $33.68. But few diners would order the meal at that price. So instead the restaurant charges just $25. In contrast, the restaurant charges $9 for its Grill vegetable plate—whose ingredients cost only $1.55.

Source: Eileen Daspin, "Entrée Economics," *The Wall Street Journal,* March 10, 2000, pp. W1 and W4.

The profit-maximizing prices for the two Nature's Garden products are computed below using these formulas:

Apple-Almond Shampoo

$$\text{Profit-maximizing markup on variable cost} = \left(\frac{-1}{1 + (-1.71)}\right) = 1.41$$

$$\text{Profit-maximizing price} = (1 + 1.41)\$2.00 = \$4.82$$

Strawberry Glycerin Soap

$$\text{Profit-maximizing markup on variable cost} = \left(\frac{-1}{1 + (-2.34)}\right) = 0.75$$

$$\text{Profit-maximizing price} = (1 + 0.75)\$0.40 = \$0.70$$

Note that the 75% markup for the strawberry glycerin soap is lower than the 141% markup for the apple-almond shampoo. The reason for this is that the purchasers of strawberry glycerin soap are more sensitive to price than the purchasers of apple-almond shampoo. Strawberry glycerin soap is a relatively common product with close substitutes available in nearly every grocery store.

Exhibit A–1 shows how the profit-maximizing markup is generally affected by how sensitive unit sales are to price. For example, if a 10% increase in price leads to a 20% decrease in unit sales, then the optimal markup on variable cost according to the exhibit is 75%—the figure computed above for the strawberry glycerin soap. Note that the optimal markup drops as unit sales become more sensitive to price.

Caution is advised when using these formulas to establish a selling price. The formulas rely on simplifying assumptions and the estimate of the percentage change in unit sales that would result from a given percentage change in price is likely to be inexact. Nevertheless, the formulas can provide valuable clues regarding whether prices should be increased or decreased. Suppose, for example, that the strawberry glycerin soap is currently being sold for $0.60 per bar. The formula indicates that the profit-maximizing price is $0.70 per bar. Rather than increasing the price by $0.10, it would be prudent to increase the price by a more modest amount to observe what happens to unit sales and to profits.

The formula for the profit-maximizing price conveys a very important lesson. If the total fixed costs are the same whether the company charges $0.60 or $0.70, they cannot be relevant in the decision of which price to charge for the soap. The optimal selling price should depend on two factors—the variable cost per unit and how sensitive unit sales are to changes in price. Fixed costs play no role in setting the optimal price. Fixed costs are relevant when

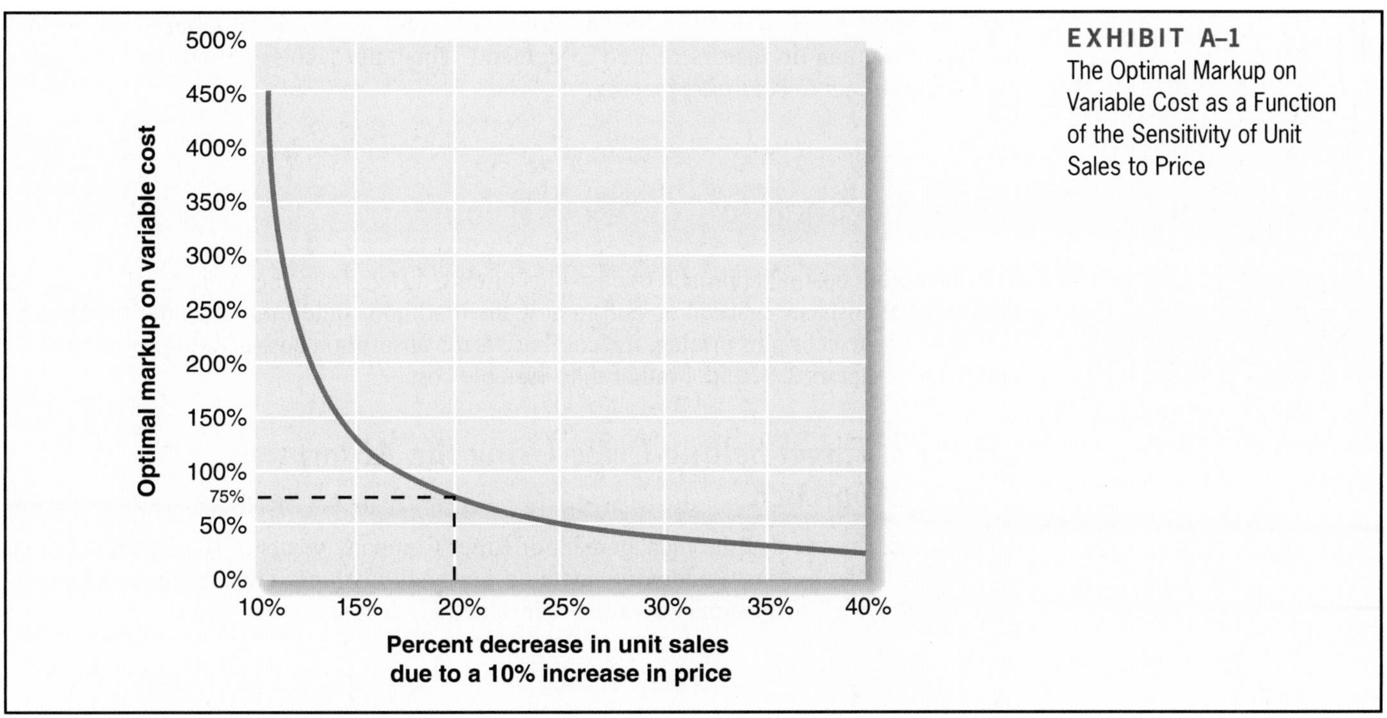

EXHIBIT A–1
The Optimal Markup on Variable Cost as a Function of the Sensitivity of Unit Sales to Price

deciding whether to offer a product but are not relevant when deciding how much to charge for the product.

We can directly verify that an increase in selling price for the strawberry glycerin soap from the current price of \$0.60 per bar is warranted, based just on the forecast that a 10% increase in selling price would lead to a 20% decrease in unit sales. Suppose, for example, that Nature's Garden is currently selling 200,000 bars of the soap per year at the price of \$0.60 a bar. If the change in price has no effect on the company's fixed costs or on other products, the effect on profits of increasing the price by 10% can be computed as follows:

	Present Price	Higher Price
Selling price	\$0.60	\$0.60 + (0.10 × \$0.60) = \$0.66
Unit sales	200,000	200,000 − (0.20 × 200,000) = 160,000
Sales	\$120,000	\$105,600
Variable cost (\$0.40 per unit)	80,000	64,000
Contribution margin	\$ 40,000	\$ 41,600

Despite the apparent optimality of prices based on marking up variable costs according to the price elasticity of demand, surveys consistently reveal that most managers approach the pricing problem from a completely different perspective.[6] They prefer to

[6] One study found that 83% of the 504 large manufacturing companies surveyed used some form of full cost (either absorption cost or absorption cost plus selling and administrative expenses) as the basis for pricing. The remaining 17% used only variable costs as a basis for pricing decisions. See V. Govindarajan and Robert N. Anthony, "How Firms Use Cost Data in Pricing Decisions," *Management Accounting,* July 1983, pp. 30–36. A more recent, but less extensive, survey by Eunsup Shim and Ephraim F. Sudit, "How Manufacturers Price Products," *Management Accounting,* February 1995, pp. 37–39, found similar results.

On the other hand, a survey of small-company executives summarized in *Inc.* magazine, November 1996, p. 84, revealed that only 41% set prices based on cost. The others charge what they think customers are willing to pay or what the market demands.

mark up some version of full, not variable, costs, and the markup is based on desired profits rather than on factors related to demand. This approach is called the *absorption costing approach to cost-plus pricing.*

The Absorption Costing Approach to Cost-Plus Pricing

LEARNING OBJECTIVE 2
Compute the selling price of a product using the absorption costing approach.

The absorption costing approach to cost-plus pricing differs from the economists' approach both in what costs are marked up and in how the markup is determined. Under the absorption approach to cost-plus pricing, the cost base is the absorption costing unit product cost as defined in Chapters 2, 3, and 4 rather than variable cost.

Setting a Target Selling Price Using the Absorption Costing Approach

To illustrate, assume that the management of Ritter Company wants to set the selling price on a product that has just undergone some design modifications. The Accounting Department has provided cost estimates for the redesigned product as shown below:

	Per Unit	Total
Direct materials	$6	
Direct labor.	$4	
Variable manufacturing overhead	$3	
Fixed manufacturing overhead		$70,000
Variable selling and administrative expenses	$2	
Fixed selling and administrative expenses		$60,000

The first step in the absorption costing approach to cost-plus pricing is to compute the unit product cost. For Ritter Company, this amounts to $20 per unit at a volume of 10,000 units, as computed below:

Direct materials	$ 6
Direct labor	4
Variable manufacturing overhead.	3
Fixed manufacturing overhead ($70,000 ÷ 10,000 units)	7
Unit product cost	$20

Ritter Company has a general policy of marking up unit product costs by 50%. A price quotation sheet for the company prepared using the absorption approach is presented in Exhibit A–2. Note that selling and administrative expenses are not included in the cost base. Instead, the markup is supposed to cover these expenses.

EXHIBIT A–2
Price Quotation Sheet—Absorption Basis (10,000 Units)

Direct materials	$ 6
Direct labor	4
Variable manufacturing overhead.	3
Fixed manufacturing overhead (based on 10,000 units)	7
Unit product cost	20
Markup to cover selling and administrative expenses and desired profit—50% of unit manufacturing cost	10
Target selling price	$30

Determining the Markup Percentage

Ritter Company's markup percentage of 50% could be a widely used rule of thumb in the industry or just a company tradition that seems to work. The markup percentage may also be the result of an explicit computation. As we have discussed, the markup over cost should be largely determined by market conditions. However, many companies base their markup on cost and desired profit. The reasoning goes like this. The markup must be large enough to cover selling and administrative expenses and provide an adequate return on investment (ROI). Given the forecasted unit sales, the markup can be computed as follows:

$$\text{Markup percentage on absorption cost} = \frac{(\text{Required ROI} \times \text{Investment}) + \text{Selling and administrative expenses}}{\text{Unit product cost} \times \text{Unit sales}}$$

To show how this formula is applied, assume Ritter Company invests \$100,000 in operating assets such as equipment to produce and market 10,000 units of the product each year. If Ritter Company requires a 20% ROI, then the markup for the product would be determined as follows:

$$\text{Markup percentage on absorption cost} = \frac{(20\% \times \$100{,}000) + (\$2 \text{ per unit} \times 10{,}000 \text{ units} + \$60{,}000)}{\$20 \text{ per unit} \times 10{,}000 \text{ units}}$$

$$= \frac{(\$20{,}000) + (\$80{,}000)}{\$200{,}000} = 50\%$$

As shown earlier, this markup of 50% leads to a target selling price of \$30 for Ritter Company. *If the company actually sells 10,000 units* of the product at this price, the company's ROI on this product will indeed be 20%. This is verified in Exhibit A–3. However, if it turns out that more than 10,000 units are sold at this price, the ROI will be greater than 20%. If less than 10,000 units are sold, the ROI will be less than 20%. *The required ROI will be attained only if the forecasted unit sales volume is attained.*

EXHIBIT A–3
Income Statement and ROI Analysis—Ritter Company Actual Unit Sales = 10,000 Units; Selling Price = \$30

Direct materials	\$ 6
Direct labor	4
Variable manufacturing overhead	3
Fixed manufacturing overhead (\$70,000 ÷ 10,000 units)	7
Unit product cost	\$20

Ritter Company
Absorption Costing Income Statement

Sales (\$30 per unit × 10,000 units)	\$300,000
Cost of goods sold (\$20 per unit × 10,000 units)	200,000
Gross margin	100,000
Selling and administrative expenses (\$2 per unit × 10,000 units + \$60,000)	80,000
Net operating income	\$ 20,000

ROI

$$\text{ROI} = \frac{\text{Net operating income}}{\text{Average operating assets}}$$

$$= \frac{\$20{,}000}{\$100{,}000}$$

$$= 20\%$$

IN BUSINESS

COST-BASED OR MARKET-BASED PRICES?

Jerry Bernstein, the director of Emerson Electric Co.'s price improvement team, says that setting prices used to be easy: "You developed a product, looked at the costs, and said, 'I need to make *X*,' and you marked it up accordingly—and people would buy it." Now the company charges based on what customers are willing to pay rather than its own costs. For example, a new compact sensor for factories that measures the flow of fluids would have been priced at $2,650 based on its cost. However, careful analysis revealed that customers would be willing to pay 20% more for the sensors than the company had planned to charge. The company settled on a price of $3,150.

Source: Timothy Aeppel, "Survival Strategies: After Cost Cutting, Companies Turn Toward Price Rises," *The Wall Street Journal*, September 18, 2002, pp. A1 and A12.

Problems with the Absorption Costing Approach

The absorption costing approach makes pricing decisions look deceptively simple. All a company needs to do is compute its unit product cost, decide how much profit it wants, and then set its price. It appears that a company can ignore demand and arrive at a price that will safely yield whatever profit it wants. However, as noted above, the absorption costing approach relies on a forecast of unit sales. Neither the markup nor the unit product cost can be computed without such a forecast.

The absorption costing approach essentially assumes that customers *need* the forecasted unit sales and will pay whatever price the company decides to charge. However, customers have a choice. If the price is too high, they can buy from a competitor or they may choose not to buy at all. Suppose, for example, that when Ritter Company sets its price at $30, it sells only 7,000 units rather than the 10,000 units forecasted. As shown in Exhibit A–4, the

EXHIBIT A–4
Income Statement and ROI Analysis—Ritter Company Actual Unit Sales = 7,000 Units; Selling Price = $30

Direct materials	$ 6
Direct labor	4
Variable manufacturing overhead	3
Fixed manufacturing overhead ($70,000 ÷ 7,000 units)	10
Unit product cost	$23

Ritter Company
Absorption Costing Income Statement

Sales ($30 per unit × 7,000 units)	$210,000
Cost of goods sold ($23 per unit × 7,000 units)	161,000
Gross margin	49,000
Selling and administrative expenses ($2 per unit × 7,000 units + $60,000)	74,000
Net operating income	$ (25,000)

ROI

$$\text{ROI} = \frac{\text{Net operating income}}{\text{Average operating assets}}$$

$$= \frac{-\$25{,}000}{\$100{,}000}$$

$$= -25\%$$

company would then have a loss of $25,000 on the product instead of a profit of $20,000.[7] Some managers believe that the absorption costing approach to pricing is safe. This is an illusion. The absorption costing approach is safe only if customers choose to buy at least as many units as managers forecasted they would buy.

Target Costing

LEARNING OBJECTIVE 3
Compute the target cost for a new product or service.

Our discussion thus far has presumed that a product has already been developed, has been costed, and is ready to be marketed as soon as a price is set. In many cases, the sequence of events is just the reverse. That is, the company already *knows* what price should be charged, and the problem is to *develop* a product that can be marketed profitably at the desired price. Even in this situation, where the normal sequence of events is reversed, cost is still a crucial factor. The company can use an approach called *target costing.* **Target costing** is the process of determining the maximum allowable cost for a new product and then developing a prototype that can be profitably made for that maximum target cost figure. A number of companies have used target costing, including Compaq, Culp, Cummins Engine, Daihatsu Motors, DaimlerChrysler, Ford, Isuzu Motors, ITT Automotive, Komatsu, Matsushita Electric, Mitsubishi Kasei, NEC, Nippodenso, Nissan, Olympus, Sharp, Texas Instruments, and Toyota.

The target cost for a product is computed by starting with the product's anticipated selling price and then deducting the desired profit, as follows:

$$\text{Target cost} = \text{Anticipated selling price} - \text{Desired profit}$$

The product development team is then given the responsibility of designing the product so that it can be made for no more than the target cost.

Reasons for Using Target Costing

The target costing approach was developed in recognition of two important characteristics of markets and costs. The first is that many companies have less control over price than they would like to think. The market (i.e., supply and demand) really determines price, and a company that attempts to ignore this does so at its peril. Therefore, the anticipated market price is taken as a given in target costing. The second observation is that most of a product's cost is determined in the design stage. Once a product has been designed and has gone into production, not much can be done to significantly reduce its cost. Most of the opportunities to reduce cost come from designing the product so that it is simple to make, uses inexpensive parts, and is robust and reliable. If the company has little control over market price and little control over cost once the product has gone into production, then it follows that the major opportunities for affecting profit come in the design stage where valuable features that customers are willing to pay for can be added and where most of the costs are really determined. So that is where the effort is concentrated—in designing and developing the product. The difference between target costing and other approaches to product development is profound. Instead of designing the product and then finding out how much it costs, the target cost is set first and then the product is designed so that the target cost is attained.

[7] It may be *impossible* to break even using an absorption costing approach when the company has more than one product—even when it would be possible to make substantial profits using the economists' approach to pricing. For details, see Eric Noreen and David Burgstahler, "Full Cost Pricing and the Illusion of Satisficing," *Journal of Management Accounting Research,* 9 (1997).

IN BUSINESS

MANAGING COSTS IN THE PRODUCT DESIGN STAGE

The Boeing Company is building the airframe of its 787 Dreamliner jet using carbon fiber-reinforced plastic. While this type of plastic has been used in golf club shafts and tennis rackets, it has never been used to construct the exterior of an airplane. Boeing is excited about this innovative raw material because it allows enormous cost savings. For example, Boeing's Dreamliner should be 20% more fuel efficient than the Boeing 767 or Airbus A330, its maintenance costs should be 30% less than aluminum planes, and the number of fasteners needed to assemble its fuselage should be 80% less than conventional airplanes. In addition, aluminum airplanes require costly corrosion inspections after 6 years of service, while the Dreamliner can fly 12 years before it would need a comparable inspection. To Boeing's delight, the Dreamliner's sales have "taken off" because "customers get tremendous bang for their bucks. For $120 million—about what they paid for the comparable Boeing 767-300 back in the 1980s—airlines get an all-new aircraft that flies faster than the competition and costs substantially less to operate."

Source: Stanley Holmes, "A Plastic Dream Machine," *BusinessWeek*, June 20, 2005, pp. 32–36.

An Example of Target Costing

To provide a simple example of target costing, assume the following situation: Handy Company wishes to invest $2,000,000 to design, develop, and produce a new hand mixer. The company's Marketing Department surveyed the features and prices of competing products and determined that a price of $30 would enable Handy to sell an estimated 40,000 hand mixers per year. Since the company desires a 15% ROI, the target cost to manufacture, sell, distribute, and service one mixer is $22.50 as computed below:

Projected sales (40,000 mixers × $30 per mixer)	$1,200,000
Less desired profit (15% × $2,000,000)	300,000
Target cost for 40,000 mixers	$ 900,000
Target cost per mixer ($900,000 ÷ 40,000 mixers)	$22.50

This $22.50 target cost would be broken down into target costs for the various functions: manufacturing, marketing, distribution, after-sales service, and so on. Each functional area would be responsible for keeping its actual costs within target.

Summary

Pricing involves a delicate balancing act. Higher prices result in more revenue per unit but drive down unit sales. Exactly where to set prices to maximize profit is a difficult problem, but, in general, the markup over cost should be highest for those products where customers are least sensitive to price. The demand for such products is said to be price inelastic.

Managers often rely on cost-plus formulas to set target prices. From the economists' point of view, the cost base for the markup should be variable cost. In contrast, in the absorption costing approach the cost base is the absorption costing unit product cost and the markup is computed to cover both nonmanufacturing costs and to provide an adequate return on investment. With the absorption approach, costs will not be covered and return on investment will not be adequate unless the unit sales forecast used in the cost-plus formula is accurate. If applying the cost-plus formula results in a price that is too high, the unit sales forecast will not be attained.

Some companies take a different approach to pricing. Instead of starting with costs and then determining prices, they start with prices and then determine allowable costs. Companies that use target costing estimate what a new product's market price is likely to be based on its anticipated features and prices of products already on the market. They subtract desired profit from the estimated market price to arrive at the product's target cost. The design and development team is then given the responsibility of ensuring that the actual cost of the new product does not exceed the target cost.

Glossary

Cost-plus pricing A pricing method in which a predetermined markup is applied to a cost base to determine the target selling price. (p. 606)

Markup The difference between the selling price of a product or service and its cost. The markup is usually expressed as a percentage of cost. (p. 606)

Price elasticity of demand A measure of the degree to which a change in price affects the unit sales of a product or service. (p. 606)

Target costing The process of determining the maximum allowable cost for a new product and then developing a prototype that can be profitably made for that maximum target cost figure. (p. 613)

Questions

A-1 What is cost-plus pricing?

A-2 What does the price elasticity of demand measure? What is inelastic demand? What is elastic demand?

A-3 According to the economists' approach to setting prices, the profit-maximizing price should depend on what two factors?

A-4 Which product should have a larger markup over variable cost, a product whose demand is elastic or a product whose demand is inelastic?

A-5 When the absorption costing approach to cost-plus pricing is used, what is the markup supposed to cover?

A-6 What assumption does the absorption costing approach make about how consumers react to prices?

A-7 Discuss the following statement: "Full cost can be viewed as a floor of protection. If a company always sets its prices above full cost, it will never have to worry about operating at a loss."

A-8 What is target costing? How do target costs enter into the pricing decision?

Exercises

EXERCISE A-1 The Economists' Approach to Pricing [LO1]

Kimio Nakimura owns an ice cream stand that she operates during the summer months in Jackson Hole, Wyoming. Her store caters primarily to tourists passing through town on their way to Yellowstone National Park.

Kimio is unsure of how she should price her ice cream cones and has experimented with two prices in successive weeks during the busy August season. The number of people who entered the store was roughly the same each week. During the first week, she priced the cones at $1.79 and 860 cones were sold. During the second week, she priced the cones at $1.39 and 1,340 cones were sold. The variable cost of a cone is $0.41 and consists solely of the costs of the ice cream and of the cone itself. The fixed expenses of the ice cream stand are $425 per week.

Required:

1. Did Kimio make more money selling the cones for $1.79 or for $1.39?
2. Estimate the price elasticity of demand for the ice cream cones.
3. Estimate the profit-maximizing price for ice cream cones.

EXERCISE A-2 Absorption Costing Approach to Setting a Selling Price [LO2]
Naylor Company is considering the introduction of a new product. Management has gathered the following information:

Number of units to be produced and sold each year	12,500
Unit product cost	$30
Projected annual selling and administrative expenses	$60,000
Estimated investment required by the company	$500,000
Desired return on investment (ROI)	18%

The company uses the absorption costing approach to cost-plus pricing.

Required:

1. Compute the markup required to achieve the desired ROI.
2. Compute the target selling price per unit.

EXERCISE A-3 Target Costing [LO3]
Eastern Auto Supply, Inc., produces and distributes auto supplies. The company is anxious to enter the rapidly growing market for long-life batteries that is based on lithium technology. Management believes that to be fully competitive, the price of the new battery that the company is developing cannot exceed $65. At this price, management is confident that the company can sell 50,000 batteries per year. The batteries would require an investment of $2,500,000, and the desired ROI is 20%.

Required:

Compute the target cost of one battery.

Problems 

PROBLEM A-4 Standard Costs; Absorption Costing Approach to Setting Prices [LO2]
Euclid Fashions, Inc., is introducing a sports jacket. A standard cost card has been prepared for the new jacket, as shown below:

	Standard Quantity or Hours	Standard Price or Rate	Standard Cost
Direct materials	2.0 yards	$4.60 per yard	$ 9.20
Direct labor	1.4 hours	$10.00 per hour	14.00
Manufacturing overhead (⅙ variable)	1.4 hours	$12.00 per hour	16.80
Total standard cost per jacket			$40.00

The following additional information relating to the new jacket is available:

a. The only variable selling and administrative cost will be $4 per jacket for shipping. Fixed selling and administrative costs will be (per year):

Salaries	$ 90,000
Advertising and other	384,000
Total	$474,000

b. Since the company manufactures many products, no more than 21,000 direct labor-hours per year can be devoted to production of the new jackets.
c. An investment of $900,000 will be necessary to carry inventories and accounts receivable and to purchase some new equipment. The company's required rate of return is 24%.
d. Manufacturing overhead costs are allocated to products on the basis of direct labor-hours.

Required:

1. Assume that the company uses the absorption approach to cost-plus pricing.
   a. Compute the markup that the company needs on the jackets to achieve a 24% ROI if it sells all of the jackets it can produce using 21,000 hours of labor time.
   b. Using the markup you have computed, prepare a price quote sheet for a single jacket.
   c. Assume that the company is able to sell all of the jackets that it can produce. Prepare an income statement for the first year of activity, and compute the company's ROI for the year on the jackets, using the ROI formula from Chapter 11.
2. After marketing the jackets for several years, the company is experiencing a falloff in demand due to an economic recession. A large retail outlet will make a bulk purchase of jackets if its label is sewn in and if an acceptable price can be worked out. What is the minimum acceptable price for this order?

PROBLEM A-5 The Economists' Approach to Pricing [LO1]

The postal service of St. Lucia, an island in the West Indies, obtains a significant portion of its revenues from sales of special souvenir sheets to stamp collectors. The souvenir sheets usually contain several high-value St. Lucia stamps depicting a common theme, such as the anniversary of Princess Diana's funeral. The souvenir sheets are designed and printed for the postal service by Imperial Printing, a stamp agency service company in the United Kingdom. The souvenir sheets cost the postal service $0.60 each. (The currency in St. Lucia is the East Caribbean dollar.) St. Lucia has been selling these souvenir sheets for $5.00 each and ordinarily sells 50,000 units. To test the market, the postal service recently priced a new souvenir sheet at $6.00 and sales dropped to 40,000 units.

Required:

1. Does the postal service of St. Lucia make more money selling souvenir sheets for $5.00 each or $6.00 each?
2. Estimate the price elasticity of demand for the souvenir sheets.
3. Estimate the profit-maximizing price for souvenir sheets.
4. If Imperial Printing increases the price it charges to the St. Lucia postal service for souvenir sheets to $0.70 each, how much should the St. Lucia postal service charge its customers for the souvenir sheets?

PROBLEM A-6 The Economists' Approach to Pricing; Absorption Costing Approach to Cost-Plus Pricing [LO1, LO2]

Softway, Inc., was started by two young software engineers to market AdBlocker, a software application they had written that blocks ads when surfing the Internet. Sales of the software have been good at 20,000 units a month, but the company has been losing money as shown below:

Sales (20,000 units × $18.95 per unit)	$379,000
Variable cost (20,000 units × $5.90 per unit)	118,000
Contribution margin	261,000
Fixed expenses	264,000
Net operating income (loss)	$ (3,000)

The company's only variable cost is the $5.90 fee it pays to another company to reproduce the software on CDs, print manuals, and package the result in an attractive box for sale to consumers. Monthly fixed selling and administrative expenses are $264,000.

The company's marketing manager has been arguing for some time that the software is priced too high. She estimates that every 10% decrease in price will yield a 20% increase in unit sales. The marketing manager would like your help in preparing a presentation to the company's owners concerning the pricing issue.

Required:

1. To help the marketing manager prepare for her presentation, she has asked you to fill in the blanks in the following table. The selling prices in the table were computed by successively decreasing the selling price by 10%. The estimated unit sales were computed by successively increasing the unit sales by 20%. For example, $17.06 is 10% less than $18.95 and 24,000 units are 20% more than 20,000 units.

Selling Price	Unit Sales	Sales	Variable Cost	Fixed Cost	Operating Income
$18.95	20,000	$379,000	$118,000	$264,000	$(3,000)
$17.06	24,000	$409,440	$141,600	$264,000	$ 3,840
$15.35	28,800	?	?	?	?
$13.82	34,560	?	?	?	?
$12.44	41,472	?	?	?	?
$11.20	49,766	?	?	?	?
$10.08	59,719	?	?	?	?
$9.07	71,663	?	?	?	?
$8.16	85,996	?	?	?	?
$7.34	103,195	?	?	?	?

2. Using the data from the table, construct a graph that shows the net operating income as a function of the selling price. Put the selling price on the *X*-axis and the net operating income on the *Y*-axis. Using the graph, estimate the approximate selling price at which net operating income is maximized.
3. Compute the price elasticity of demand for the AdBlocker software. Based on this calculation, what is the profit-maximizing price?
4. The owners have invested $120,000 in the company and feel that they should be earning at least 2% per month on these funds. If the absorption costing approach to pricing were used, what would be the target selling price based on the current sales of 20,000 units? What do you think would happen to the net operating income of the company if this price were charged?
5. If the owners of the company are dissatisfied with the net operating income and return on investment at the selling price you computed in (3) above, should they increase the selling price? Explain.

PROBLEM A-7 Missing Data; Markup Computations; Return on Investment; Pricing [LO2]
Rest Easy, Inc., has designed a new puncture-proof, self-inflating sleeping pad that is unlike anything on the market. Because of the unique properties of the new sleeping pad, the company anticipates that it will be able to sell all the pads that it can produce. On this basis, the following budgeted income statement for the first year of activity is available:

Sales (__?__ pads at __?__ per pad)	$?
Cost of goods sold (__?__ pads at __?__ per pad)	4,000,000
Gross margin	?
Selling and administrative expenses	2,160,000
Net operating income	$?

Additional information on the new sleeping pad is given below:

a. The company will hire enough workers to commit 100,000 direct labor-hours to the manufacture of the pads.
b. A partially completed standard cost card for the new sleeping pad follows:

	Standard Quantity or Hours	Standard Price or Rate	Standard Cost
Direct materials	5 yards	$6 per yard	$30
Direct labor	2 hours	$? per hour	?
Manufacturing overhead	? hours	$? per hour	?
Total standard cost per sleeping pad			$?

c. An investment of $3,500,000 will be necessary to carry inventories and accounts receivable and to purchase some new equipment. Management has decided that the design of the new pad is unique enough that the company should set a selling price that will yield a 24% return on investment (ROI).

d. Other information relating to production and costs follows:

Variable manufacturing overhead cost (per pad)	$7
Variable selling expense (per pad)	$5
Fixed manufacturing overhead cost (total)	$1,750,000
Fixed selling and administrative expense (total)	$?
Number of pads produced and sold (per year)	?

e. Manufacturing overhead costs are allocated to production on the basis of direct labor-hours.

Required:

1. Complete the standard cost card for a single pad.
2. Assume that the company uses the absorption approach to cost-plus pricing.
   a. Compute the markup that the company needs on the pads to achieve a 24% return on investment (ROI).
   b. Using the markup you have computed, prepare a price quotation sheet for a single pad.
   c. Assume, as stated, that the company can sell all the pads that it can produce. Complete the income statement for the first year of activity, and then compute the company's ROI for the year.
3. Assume that direct labor is a variable cost. How many units would the company have to sell at the price you computed in (2) above to achieve the 24% ROI? How many units would have to be produced and sold to just break even?

PROBLEM A-8 Target Costing [LO3]

Choice Culinary Supply, Inc., sells restaurant equipment and supplies throughout most of the United States. Management is considering adding a gelato machine to its line of ice cream making machines. Management will negotiate the price of the gelato machine with its Italian manufacturer.

Management of Choice Culinary Supply believes the gelato machines can be sold to its customers in the United States for $3,795 each. At that price, annual sales of the gelato machine should be 80 units. If the gelato machine is added to Choice Culinary Supply's product lines, the company will have to invest $50,000 in inventories and special warehouse fixtures. The variable cost of selling the gelato machines would be $350 per machine.

Required:

1. If Choice Culinary Supply requires a 20% return on investment (ROI), what is the maximum amount the company would be willing to pay the Italian manufacturer for the gelato machines?
2. Management would like to know how the purchase price of the machines would affect Choice Culinary Supply's ROI. Construct a graph that shows Choice Culinary Supply's ROI as a function of the purchase price of the gelato machine. Put the purchase price on the *X*-axis and the resulting ROI on the *Y*-axis. Plot the ROI for purchase prices between $2,400 and $3,400 per machine.
3. After many hours of negotiations, management has concluded that the Italian manufacturer is unwilling to sell the gelato machine at a low enough price for Choice Culinary Supply to earn its 20% required ROI. Apart from simply giving up on the idea of adding the gelato machine to Choice Culinary Supply's product lines, what could management do?

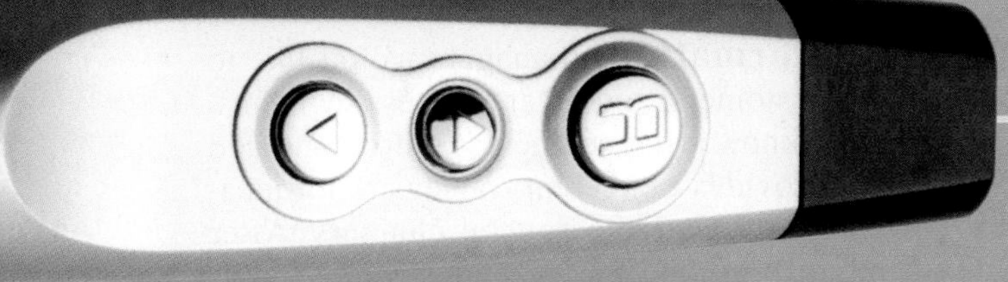

Appendix

B

Profitability Analysis

Learning Objectives

After studying this appendix, you should be able to:

LO1 Compute the profitability index and use it to select from among possible actions.

LO2 Compute and use the profitability index in volume trade-off decisions.

LO3 Compute and use the profitability index in other business decisions.

Introduction

Perhaps more than any other information, managers would like to know the profitability of their products, customers, and other business segments. They want this information so that they know what segments to drop and add and which to emphasize. This appendix provides a coherent framework for measuring profitability, bringing together relevant materials from several chapters. After studying this appendix you should have a firm grasp of the principles underlying profitability analysis. The first step is to distinguish between *absolute profitability* and *relative profitability.*

IN BUSINESS

TRIMMING THE PRODUCT LINE

A large pharmaceutical company eliminated 20% of its products, despite protests from the marketing department. This resulted in a 5% reduction in sales, but a 60% increase in net profits. Why? The products that were dropped were *absolutely* unprofitable. The company was better off simply dropping them.

Source: Tim Allen, "Are Your Products Profitable?" *Strategic Finance,* March 2002, pp. 33–37.

Absolute Profitability

Absolute profitability is concerned with the impact on the organization's overall profits of adding or dropping a particular segment such as a product or customer—without making any other changes. For example, if Coca-Cola were considering closing down its operations in the African country of Zimbabwe, managers would be interested in the absolute profitability of those operations. Measuring the absolute profitability of an existing segment is conceptually straightforward—compare the revenues that would be lost from dropping the segment to the costs that would be avoided. When considering a new potential segment, compare the additional revenues from adding the segment to the additional costs that would be incurred. In each case, include only the additional costs that would actually be avoided or incurred. All other costs are irrelevant and should be ignored.

In practice, figuring out what costs would change and what costs would not change if a segment were dropped (or added) can be very difficult. Activity-based costing can help in identifying such costs, but all costs should be carefully analyzed to determine whether they would really change. For example, an activity-based costing study of Coca-Cola's Zimbabwe operations might include charges for staff support provided to the Zimbabwe operations by Coca-Cola's corporate headquarters in Atlanta. However, if eliminating the Zimbabwe operations would have no impact on actual costs in Atlanta, then these costs are not relevant and should be excluded when measuring the absolute profitability of the Zimbabwe operations.

For examples of the measurement of absolute profitability see "Appendix 7A: ABC Action Analysis," the sections "Decentralization and Segment Reporting" in Chapter 11 and "Adding and Dropping Product Lines and Other Segments" in Chapter 12.

IN BUSINESS

KRAFT BULKS UP AND THEN SLIMS DOWN

In 2000, Kraft Foods Inc. acquired Nabisco for $19 billion. This acquisition coupled with nine others pushed Kraft's annual sales above $32 billion. Indeed, Kraft had assembled an impressive portfolio of brands including Oreo cookies, Oscar Mayer meats, Post cereals, Maxwell House Coffees, and DiGiorno pizzas, to name a few. However, Kraft's CEO, Roger K. Deromedi, has decided that it is time to slim the company down a bit. In 2004, Kraft sold its Life Savers and Altoids brands to Wm. Wrigley Jr. Co. for $1.5 billion in cash. Deromedi sold these laggard brands to enable Kraft to "concentrate on the blockbuster brands that can be tops in their categories worldwide." Presumably, Kraft considered Life Savers and Altoids to be relatively unprofitable compared to the other brands within the organization that were competing for scarce investment funds.

Source: Michael Arndt, "Why Kraft Is on a Crash Diet," *BusinessWeek*, November 29, 2004, p. 46.

Relative Profitability

LEARNING OBJECTIVE 1
Compute the profitability index and use it to select from among possible actions.

Even when every segment is *absolutely* profitable, managers often want to know which segments are most and least profitable. **Relative profitability** is concerned with ranking products, customers, and other business segments to determine which should be emphasized.

Why are managers interested in ranking segments or determining the relative profitability of segments? The answer to this deceptively simple question provides the key to measuring relative profitability. The only reason to rank segments is if something forces you to make trade-offs among them. If trade-offs are not necessary, the solution is simple—keep every segment that is absolutely profitable. What would force a manager to make trade-offs among profitable segments? There is only one answer—a *constraint.* In the absence of a constraint, all segments that are absolutely profitable should be pursued. On the other hand, if a constraint is present, then by definition the company cannot pursue every profitable opportunity. Choices have to be made. Thus, measuring relative profitability makes sense only when a constraint exists that forces trade-offs. This point cannot be overemphasized; constraints are fundamental to understanding and measuring relative profitability.

How should relative profitability be measured? Divide each segment's measure of absolute profitability, which is the incremental profit from that segment, by the amount of the constraint required by the segment. For example, refer to the data below for two of the many segments within a company:

	Segment A	Segment B
Incremental profit	$100,000	$200,000
Amount of constrained resource required.	100 hours	400 hours

Segment B may seem more attractive than Segment A because its incremental profit is twice as large, but it requires four times as much of the constrained resource. In fact, Segment B would not be the best use of the constrained resource because it generates only $500 of incremental profit per hour ($200,000 ÷ 400 hours), whereas Segment A generates $1,000 of incremental profit per hour ($100,000 ÷ 100 hours). Another way to look at this is to suppose that 400 hours of the constrained resource are available. Would you rather use the hours on four segments like Segment A, generating a total incremental profit of $400,000, or on one segment like Segment B, which generates $200,000 in incremental profit?

In general, the relative profitability of segments should be measured by the **profitability index** as defined below:

$$\text{Profitability index} = \frac{\text{Incremental profit from the segment}}{\text{Amount of the constrained resource required by the segment}}$$

The profitability index is computed below for the two segments in the example:

	Segment A	Segment B
Incremental profit (a)	$100,000	$200,000
Amount of constrained resource required (b)	100 hours	400 hours
Profitability index (a) ÷ (b)	$1,000 per hour	$500 per hour

We have already encountered several examples of the profitability index in previous chapters. For example, in Chapter 13 the project profitability index was defined as:

$$\text{Project profitability index} = \frac{\text{Net present value of the project}}{\text{Amount of investment required by the project}}$$

The project profitability index is used when a company has more long-term projects with positive net present values than it can fund. In this case, the incremental profit from the segment is the net present value of the project. And since the investment funds are the constraint, the amount of the constrained resource required by the segment is the amount of investment required by the project.

As an example of the use of the profitability index, consider the case of Quality Kitchen Design, a small company specializing in designing kitchens for upscale homes. Management is considering the 10 short-term projects listed in Panel A of Exhibit B–1. The incremental profit from each project is listed in the second column. For example, the incremental profit from Project A is $9,180. This incremental profit consists of the revenues from the project less any costs that would be incurred by the company as a consequence of accepting the project. The company's constraint is the lead designer's time. Project A would require 17 hours of the lead designer's time. If all of the projects were accepted, they would require a total of 100 hours. Unfortunately, only 46 hours are available. Consequently, management will have to turn down some projects. The profitability index will be used in deciding which projects to accept and which to turn down. The profitability index for a project is computed by dividing its incremental profit by the amount of the lead designer's time required for the project. In the case of Project A, the profitability index is $540 per hour.

The projects are ranked in order of the profitability index in Panel B of Exhibit B–1. The last column in that panel shows the cumulative amount of the constrained resource (i.e., lead designer's time) required to do the projects at that point in the list and higher. For example, the 7 hours listed to the right of Project J in the cumulative column represents the sum of the 4 hours required for Project F plus the 3 hours required for Project J.

To find the best combination of projects within the limits of the constrained resource, go down the list in Panel B to the point where all of the available constrained resource is used. In this case, since 46 hours of lead designer time are available, that would be the point above the solid line drawn in Panel B of Exhibit B–1. Projects F, J, B, I, D, and A lie above that line and would require a total of exactly 46 hours of lead designer time. The optimal plan consists of accepting these six projects and turning down the others. The total incremental profit from accepting these projects would be $32,930 as shown in Panel C of Exhibit B–1. No other feasible combination of projects would yield a higher total incremental profit.[1]

We should reinforce a very important point that may be forgotten in the midst of these details. The profitability index is based on *incremental* profit. When computing the incremental

[1] In this example, the top projects exactly consumed all of the available constrained resource. That won't always happen. For example, assume that only 45 hours of lead designer time are available. This small change complicates matters considerably. Because of the "lumpiness" of the projects, the optimal plan isn't necessarily to do projects F, J, B, I, and D—stopping at Project D on the list and a cumulative requirement of 29 hours. That would leave 16 hours of unused lead designer time. The best use of this time may be Project C, which has an incremental profit of $7,040. However, other possibilities exist too. Finding and evaluating all of the most likely possibilities can take a lot of time and ingenuity. When the constrained resource is not completely exhausted by the top projects on the list, some tinkering with the solution may be necessary. For this reason, the list generated by ranking based on the profitability index should be viewed as a starting point rather than as a definitive solution when the projects are "lumpy" and take big chunks of the constrained resource.

EXHIBIT B–1
Ranking Segments Based on the Profitability Index

Panel A: Computation of the Profitability Index

	Incremental Profit (A)	Amount of the Constrained Resource Required (B)	Profitability Index (A) ÷ (B)
Project A	$9,180	17 hours	$540 per hour
Project B	$7,200	9 hours	$800 per hour
Project C	$7,040	16 hours	$440 per hour
Project D	$5,680	8 hours	$710 per hour
Project E	$5,330	13 hours	$410 per hour
Project F	$4,280	4 hours	$1,070 per hour
Project G	$4,160	13 hours	$320 per hour
Project H	$3,720	12 hours	$310 per hour
Project I	$3,650	5 hours	$730 per hour
Project J	$2,940	3 hours	$980 per hour
		100 hours	

Panel B: Ranking Based on the Profitability Index

	Profitability Index	Amount of the Constrained Resource Required	Cumulative Amount of the Constrained Resource Used
Project F	$1,070 per hour	4 hours	4 hours
Project J	$980 per hour	3 hours	7 hours
Project B	$800 per hour	9 hours	16 hours
Project I	$730 per hour	5 hours	21 hours
Project D	$710 per hour	8 hours	29 hours
Project A	$540 per hour	17 hours	46 hours
Project C	$440 per hour	16 hours	62 hours
Project E	$410 per hour	13 hours	75 hours
Project G	$320 per hour	13 hours	88 hours
Project H	$310 per hour	12 hours	100 hours

Panel C: The Optimal Plan

	Incremental Profit
Project F	$ 4,280
Project J	2,940
Project B	7,200
Project I	3,650
Project D	5,680
Project A	9,180
	$32,930

profit for a segment such as a product, customer, or project, only the *incremental* costs of the segment should be included. Those are the costs that could be avoided—whether fixed or variable—if the segment is eliminated. All other costs are not relevant and should be ignored—including allocations of common costs.

Volume Trade-Off Decisions

Earlier we stated that you have already encountered several examples of the profitability index in this book. One was the project profitability index in Chapter 13. The other example of the profitability index is in the section "Utilization of a Constrained Resource" in Chapter 12. That section deals with situations in which a company does not have enough capacity to

LEARNING OBJECTIVE 2
Compute and use the profitability index in volume trade-off decisions.

satisfy demand for all of its products. Therefore, the company must produce less than the market demands of some products. This is called a volume trade-off decision because the decision, at the margin, consists of trading off units of one product for units of another. Fixed costs are typically unaffected by such decisions—capacity will be fully utilized, it is just a question of how it will be utilized. In volume trade-off decisions where fixed costs are irrelevant, the profitability index takes the special form:

$$\text{Profitability index for a volume trade-off decision} = \frac{\text{Unit contribution margin}}{\text{Amount of the constrained resource required by one unit}}$$

This profitability index is identical to the "contribution margin per unit of the constrained resource" that was used in Chapter 12 to decide which products should be emphasized. An example of a volume trade-off decision is presented in Exhibit B–2. In this example, the company makes three products that use the constrained resource—a machine that is available 2,200 minutes per week. As shown in Panel B of Exhibit B–2, producing all three products up to demand would require 2,700 minutes per week—500 more minutes than are available. Consequently, the company cannot fully satisfy demand for these three products and some product or products must be cut back.

The profitability index for this decision is computed in Panel C of Exhibit B–2. For example, the profitability index for product RX200 is $3 per minute. The comparable figure for product VB30 is $5 per minute and for product SQ500 is $4 per minute. Consequently, the correct ranking of the products is VB30 followed by SQ500, then followed by RX200.

The optimal production plan is laid out in Panel D of Exhibit B–2. The most profitable products, VB30 and SQ500, are produced up to demand and the remaining time on the constraint is used to make 200 units of RX200 (1,000 available minutes ÷ 5 minutes per unit).

The total contribution margin from following this plan is computed in Panel E of Exhibit B–2. The total contribution margin of $8,600 is higher than the contribution margin that could be realized from following any other feasible plan. Assuming that fixed costs are not affected by the decision of which products to emphasize, this plan will also yield a higher total profit than any other feasible plan.

Managerial Implications

LEARNING OBJECTIVE 3
Compute and use the profitability index in other business decisions.

In addition to the add-or-drop and volume trade-off decisions discussed above, the profitability index can be used in other ways. For example, which products would you rather have your salespersons emphasize—those with a low profitability index or those with a high profitability index? The answer is, of course, that salespersons should be encouraged to emphasize sales of the products with the highest profitability indexes. However, if salespersons are paid commissions based on sales, what products will they try to sell? The selling prices of products RX200, VB30, and SQ500 appear below:

	Products		
	RX200	VB30	SQ500
Unit selling price.	$40	$30	$35

If salespersons are paid a commission based on gross sales, they will prefer to sell product RX200, which has the highest selling price. But that is the *least* profitable product given the current constraint. It has a profitability index of only $3 per minute compared to $5 per minute for VB30 and $4 per minute for SQ500.

This suggests that salespersons should be paid commissions based on the profitability index and the amount of constraint time sold rather than on sales revenue. This would encourage them to sell the most profitable products, rather than the products with the highest selling prices. How would such a compensation system work? Prior to making a sales call, a salesperson would

EXHIBIT B–2
Using the Profitability Index in a Volume Trade-Off Decision

Panel A: Product Data

	Products		
	RX200	VB30	SQ500
Unit contribution margin	$15 per unit	$10 per unit	$16 per unit
Demand per week	300 units	400 units	100 units
Amount of the constrained resource required	5 minutes per unit	2 minutes per unit	4 minutes per unit

Panel B: Total Demand on the Constrained Resource

	Products			
	RX200	VB30	SQ500	Total
Demand per week (a)	300 units	400 units	100 units	
Amount of the constrained resource required (b)	5 minutes per unit	2 minutes per unit	4 minutes per unit	
Total amount of the constraint required per week to meet demand (a) × (b)	1,500 minutes	800 minutes	400 minutes	2,700 minutes

Panel C: Computation of the Profitability Index

	Products		
	RX200	VB30	SQ500
Unit contribution margin (a)	$15 per unit	$10 per unit	$16 per unit
Amount of the constrained resource required (b)	5 minutes per unit	2 minutes per unit	4 minutes per unit
Profitability index (contribution margin per unit of the constrained resource) (a) ÷ (b)	$3 per minute	$5 per minute	$4 per minute

Panel D: The Optimal Plan

Amount of constrained resource available	2,200 minutes
Less: Constrained resource required for production of 400 units of VB30	800 minutes
Remaining constrained resource available	1,400 minutes
Less: Constrained resource required for production of 100 units of SQ500	400 minutes
Remaining constrained resource available	1,000 minutes
Less: Constrained resource required for production of 200 units of RX200*	1,000 minutes
Remaining constrained resource available	0 minutes

*1,000 minutes available ÷ 5 minutes per unit of RX200 = 200 units of RX200.

Panel E: The Total Contribution Margin under the Optimal Plan

	Products			
	RX200	VB30	SQ500	Total
Unit contribution margin (a)	$15 per unit	$10 per unit	$16 per unit	
Optimal production plan (b)	200 units	400 units	100 units	
Contribution margin (a) × (b)	$3,000	$4,000	$1,600	$8,600

receive an up-to-date report indicating how much of the constrained resource is currently available and a listing of all products showing the amount of the constraint each requires and the profitability index. Such a report would appear as follows:

Marketing Data Report

	Products		
	RX200	VB30	SQ500
Unit selling price	$40	$30	$35
Unit variable cost	25	20	19
Unit contribution margin (a)	$15	$10	$16
Amount of the constrained resource required per unit (b)	5 minutes	2 minutes	4 minutes
Profitability index (a) ÷ (b)	$3 per minute	$5 per minute	$4 per minute

Total available time on the constrained resource: 100 minutes

The key here is to realize that the salesperson is really selling time on the constraint. A salesperson who is paid based on the profitability index will prefer to sell product VB30 since the salesperson would get credit for sales of $500 if all 100 minutes are used on product VB30 ($5 per minute × 100 minutes), whereas the credit would be only $300 for product RX200 or $400 for product SQ500.[2]

The profitability index also has implications for pricing new products. Suppose that the company has designed a new product, WR6000, whose variable cost is $30 per unit and that requires 6 minutes of the constrained resource per unit. Since the company is currently using all of its capacity, the new product would necessarily displace production of existing products. Consequently, the price of the new product should cover not only its variable cost, but it should also cover the opportunity cost of displacing existing products. What product would be displaced? Production of RX200 should be cut first because it is the least profitable existing product. And how much is a minute of the constrained resource worth if it would otherwise be used to make product RX200? A minute of the constrained resource is worth $3 per minute, the profitability index of product RX200. Therefore, the selling price of the new product should at least cover the costs laid out below:[3]

$$\begin{array}{c}\text{Selling price of}\\ \text{new product}\end{array} \geq \begin{array}{c}\text{Variable cost of}\\ \text{the new product}\end{array} + \left(\begin{array}{c}\text{Opportunity}\\ \text{cost per unit of}\\ \text{the constrained}\\ \text{resource}\end{array} \times \begin{array}{c}\text{Amount of the}\\ \text{constrained resource}\\ \text{required by a unit of}\\ \text{the new product}\end{array}\right)$$

In the case of the new product WR6000, the calculations would be:

$$\begin{array}{c}\text{Selling price of}\\ \text{WR6000}\end{array} \geq \$30 + (\$3 \text{ per minute} \times 6 \text{ minutes}) = \$30 + \$18 = \$48$$

WR6000 should sell for at least $48 or the company would be better off continuing to use the available capacity to produce RX200.[4]

---

[2] Equivalent incentives would be provided by commissions based on total contribution margin. If all 100 available minutes are used to make product VB30, 50 units could be produced (100 minutes ÷ 2 minutes per unit), for which the total contribution margin would be $500 ($10 per unit × 50 units). Likewise, the total contribution margin for product RX200 would be $300, and the total contribution margin would be $400 for product SQ500 if all available minutes were used to make just those products.

[3] In addition, the selling price of a new product should cover any avoidable fixed costs of the product. This is easier said than done, however, since achieving this goal involves estimating how many units will be sold—which in turn depends on the selling price.

[4] If production of WR6000 eventually completely displaces production of RX200, the opportunity cost would change. It would increase to $4 per minute, the profitability index of the next product in line to be cut back.

IN BUSINESS

DEALING WITH UNPROFITABLE CUSTOMERS

One retailer discovered that many of the biggest spending customers in their "loyalty" program were unprofitable because they bought only sale items and returned lots of items. The company stopped sending these customers notices of upcoming "private" sales.

Source: Larry Selden and Geoffrey Colvin, "Will this Customer Sink Your Stock?" *Fortune*, September 30, 2002, pp. 127–132.

Summary

A strong distinction should be made between absolute profitability and relative profitability. A segment is considered profitable in an absolute sense if dropping it would result in lower overall profits. Absolute profitability is measured by the segment's incremental profit, which is the difference between the revenues from the segment and the costs that could be avoided by dropping the segment.

A relative profitability measure is used to rank segments. Such rankings are necessary only if a constraint forces the organization to make trade-offs among segments. To appropriately measure relative profitability, three things must be known. First, the constraint must be identified. Second, the incremental profit associated with each segment must be computed. Third, the amount of the constrained resource required by each segment must be determined. Relative profitability is determined by the profitability index, which is the incremental profit from the segment divided by the amount of the constrained resource required by the segment. The profitability index can be used in a variety of situations, including selections of projects and volume trade-off decisions.

Glossary

Absolute profitability The impact on the organization's overall profits of adding or dropping a particular segment such as a product or customer—without making any other changes. (p. 622)

Profitability index The measure of relative profitability, which is computed by dividing the incremental profit from a segment by the amount of the constrained resource required by the segment. (p. 623)

Relative profitability A ranking of products, customers, or other business segments for purposes of making trade-offs among segments. This is necessary when a constraint exists. (p. 623)

Questions

B-1 What is meant by *absolute* profitability?

B-2 What is meant by *relative* profitability?

B-3 A successful owner of a small business stated: "We have the best technology, the best products, and the best people in the world. We have no constraints." Do you agree?

B-4 What information is needed to measure the *absolute* profitability of a segment?

B-5 What information is needed to measure the *relative* profitability of a product?

B-6 How should the relative profitability of products be determined in a volume trade-off decision?

B-7 What costs should be covered by the selling price of a new product?

Exercises

EXERCISE B-1 Ranking Projects Based on the Profitability Index [LO1]

Atlantic Amusements is in the process of reviewing proposals for new rides at its theme parks in cities scattered throughout the Atlantic coast. The company's only experienced safety engineer must carefully review plans and monitor construction on each and every project—this constraint makes it impossible to build all of the new rides this year. The net present values and the amount of safety engineer time required for the proposed rides are listed below:

Proposed Ride	Net Present Value	Safety Engineer Time Required (hours)
Ride 1	$ 741,400	220
Ride 2	382,500	150
Ride 3	850,500	350
Ride 4	450,500	170
Ride 5	620,400	220
Ride 6	1,004,400	310
Ride 7	953,800	380
Ride 8	332,500	190
Ride 9	385,500	150
Ride 10	680,400	270
Total	$6,401,900	2,410

Required:

1. The safety engineer is available to work on new rides for 1,220 hours during the year. Which of the proposed rides should the company build this year? (Note: The incremental profit of a long-term project such as constructing a new ride is its net present value.)
2. What would be the total net present value of the rides built under your plan?

EXERCISE B-2 Volume Trade-Off Decision [LO2]

Bateaux du Bois, Ltd., makes reproductions of classic wooden boats. The bottleneck in the production process is fitting wooden planks to build up the curved sections of the hull. This process requires the attention of the shop's most experienced craftsman. A total of 1,800 hours are available per year in this bottleneck operation. Data concerning the company's four products appear below:

	Trader	Trapper	Quebec	Runner
Unit contribution margin	$444	$464	$312	$462
Annual demand (units)	80	80	70	120
Hours required in the bottleneck operation per unit	6	8	4	7

No fixed costs could be avoided by modifying how many units are produced of any product or even by dropping any one of the products.

Required:

1. Is there sufficient capacity in the bottleneck operation to satisfy demand for all products?
2. What is the optimal production plan for the year?
3. What would be the total contribution margin for the optimal production plan you have proposed?

EXERCISE B–3 Pricing a New Product [LO3]

Java Stop owns and operates a chain of popular coffee stands that serve over 30 different coffee-based beverages. The constraint at the coffee stands is the amount of time required to fill an order, which can be considerable for the more complex beverages. Sales are often lost because customers leave after seeing a long waiting line to place an order. Careful analysis of the company's existing products has revealed that the opportunity cost of order-filling time is $3.40 per minute.

The company is considering introducing a new product, amaretto cappuccino, to be made with almond extract and double-fine sugar. The variable cost of the standard size amaretto cappuccino would be $0.46 and the time required to fill an order for the beverage would be 45 seconds.

Required:

What is the minimum acceptable selling price for the new amaretto cappuccino product?

Problems

PROBLEM B-4 Ranking Alternatives and Managing with a Constraint [LO1, LO3]

Terri's Baking Company has developed a reputation for producing superb, one-of-a-kind wedding cakes in addition to its normal fare of breads and pastries. While the wedding cake business is a major moneymaker, it creates some problems for the bakery's owner, Terri Chavez—particularly in June. The company's reputation for wedding cakes is largely based on the skills of Megan Easterling, who decorates all of the cakes. Unfortunately, last year the company accepted too many cake orders for some June weekends, with the result that Megan was worked to a frazzle and almost quit. To prevent a recurrence, Terri has promised Megan that she will have to work no more than 33 hours in any week to prepare the wedding cakes for the upcoming weekend. (Megan also has other duties at the bakery, so even with the 33-hour limitation, she would be working more than full time in June.)

A number of reservations for wedding cakes for the first weekend in June had already been received from customers by early May. When a customer makes a reservation, Ms. Chavez gets enough information concerning the size of the wedding party and the desires of the customer to determine the cake's price, the cost to make it, and the amount of time that Megan will need to spend decorating it. The reservations for the first weekend in June are listed below:

Customer	Incremental Profit	Megan's Time Required (hours)
Audet	$ 140	4
Boyer	124	4
Comfort	160	5
Donaghe	96	3
Due	190	5
Dupuy	288	8
Ebberts	93	3
Imm	136	4
Mulgrew	234	6
Paulding	204	6
Total	$1,665	48

For example, the Audet cake would require 4 hours of Megan's time and would generate a profit of $140 for the bakery. Following industry practice, pricing for the cakes is based on their size and standard formulas and does not reflect how much decorating would be required.

Required:

1. Ms. Chavez feels that she must cancel enough cake reservations to reduce Megan's workload to the promised level. She knows that customers whose reservations have been canceled will be disappointed, but she intends to refer all of those customers to an excellent bakery across town. If the sole objective is to maximize the company's total profit, which reservations should be canceled?
2. What would be the total profit if your recommendation in part (1) above is followed?
3. Assume that for competitive reasons it would not be practical for Terri's Baking Company to change the pricing of its wedding cakes. What recommendations would you make to Ms. Chavez concerning taking reservations in the future?
4. Assume that Terri's Baking Company could change the way it prices its wedding cakes. What recommendations would you make to Ms. Chavez concerning how she should set the prices of wedding cakes in the future?
5. What might Ms. Chavez be able to do to keep both Megan and her customers happy while increasing her profits? Be creative. (Hint: Review the section on managing constraints in Chapter 12.)

PROBLEM B-5 Interpreting Common Practice [LO1]

In practice, many organizations measure the relative profitability of their segments by dividing the segments' margins by their revenues. The segment margin for this purpose is the segment's revenue less its fully allocated costs—including allocations of fixed common costs. For example, a hospital might compute the relative profitability of its major segments as follows:

Memorial Hospital Profitability Report (in thousands of dollars)				
	Emergency Room	Surgery	Acute Care	Total
Revenue	$8,650	$14,870	$12,120	$35,640
Fully allocated cost	8,360	14,490	11,760	34,610
Margin	$ 290	$ 380	$ 360	$ 1,030
Profitability (Margin ÷ Revenue)	3.4%	2.6%	3.0%	2.9%

The hospital's net operating income for this period was $1,030,000.

Required:

1. Evaluate the use of the margin, as defined above, in the numerator of the profitability measure.
2. Evaluate the use of revenue in the denominator of the profitability measure.

PROBLEM B-6 Volume Trade-Off Decision; Managing the Constraint [LO2, LO3]
Enumclaw Brick, Inc., manufactures bricks using clay deposits on the company's property. Raw clays are blended and then extruded into molds to form unfired bricks. The unfired bricks are then stacked onto movable metal platforms and rolled into the kiln where they are fired until dry. The dried bricks are then packaged and shipped to retail outlets and contractors. The bottleneck in the production process is the kiln, which is available for 2,000 hours per year. Data concerning the company's four main products appear below. Products are sold by the pallet.

	Traditional Brick	Textured Facing	Cinder Block	Roman Brick
Gross revenue per pallet	$789	$1,264	$569	$836
Contribution margin per pallet	$370	$497	$328	$390
Annual demand (pallets)	120	80	180	70
Hours required in the kiln per pallet	5	7	4	6

No fixed costs could be avoided by modifying how much is produced of any product.

Required:

1. Is there sufficient capacity in the kiln to satisfy demand for all products?
2. What is the production plan for the year that would maximize the company's profit?
3. What would be the total contribution margin for the production plan you have proposed?
4. The kiln could be operated for more than 2,000 hours per year by running it after normal working hours. Up to how much per hour should the company be willing to pay in overtime wages, energy costs, and other incremental costs to operate the kiln additional hours?
5. The company is considering introducing a new product, glazed Venetian bricks, that would have a variable cost of $530 per pallet and would require 11 hours in the kiln. What is the minimum acceptable selling price for this new product?
6. Salespersons are currently paid a commission of 5% of gross revenues. Will this motivate the salespersons to make the right choices concerning which products to sell most aggressively?

PROBLEM B-7 Customer Profitability and Managerial Decisions [LO1, LO3]
FirstLine Pharmaceuticals, Inc., is a wholesale distributor of prescription drugs to independent retail and hospital-based pharmacies. Management believes that top-notch customer representatives are the key factor in determining whether the company will be successful in the future. Customer representatives serve as the company's liaison with customers—helping pharmacies monitor their stocks, delivering drugs when customer stocks run low, and providing up-to-date information on drugs from many different companies. Customer representatives must be ultra-reliable and are highly trained. Good customer representatives are hard to come by and are not easily replaced.

Customer representatives routinely record the amount of time they spend serving each pharmacy. This time includes travel time to and from the company's central warehouse as well as time spent replenishing stocks, dealing with complaints, answering questions about drugs, informing pharmacists of the latest developments and newest products, reviewing bills, explaining procedures, and so on. Some pharmacies require more hand-holding and attention than others and consequently they consume more of the representatives' time.

Recently, customer representative have increasingly complained that it is impossible to do their jobs without working well beyond normal working hours. This has led to an alarming increase in the number of customer representatives quitting for jobs in other organizations. As a consequence, management is considering dropping some customers to reduce the workload on customer representatives. Data concerning a representative sample of the company's customers appears below:

	Willows Pharmacy	Swedish Hospital Pharmacy	Georgetown Clinic Pharmacy	Kristen Pharmacy
Total revenues	$344,880	$1,995,200	$1,414,170	$154,800
Cost of drugs sold	$263,340	$1,446,520	$1,047,660	$120,960
Customer service costs	$12,240	$62,640	$39,900	$4,500
Customer representative time	180	1,160	570	90

Customer service costs include all of the costs—other than the costs of the drugs themselves—that could be avoided by dropping the customer. These costs include the hourly wages of the customer representatives, their sales commissions, the mileage-related costs of the customer representatives' company-provided vehicles, and so on.

Required:

1. Rank the four customers in terms of their profitability.
2. Customer representatives are currently paid $25 per hour plus a commission of 1% of sales revenues. If these four pharmacies are indeed representative of the company's customers, could the company afford to pay its customer representatives more in order to attract and retain customer representatives?

 Cases

CASE B-8 Redirecting Effort [LO2]

Prevala Corporation recently suffered from its fourth straight decline in quarterly earnings—despite modest increases in sales. Unfortunately, Prevala's industry is highly competitive, so the company is reluctant to increase its prices. However, management believes that profits would improve if the efforts of its sales force were redirected toward the more profitable products in its offerings.

Several years ago Prevala decided that its core competencies were strategy, design, and marketing and that production should be outsourced. Consequently, Prevala subcontracts all of its production.

Prevala's salespersons are paid salaries and commissions. All of the company's salespersons sell the company's full line of products. The commissions are 6% of the revenue generated by a salesperson and average about 70% of a salesperson's total compensation. There has been some discussion of increasing the size of the sales force, but management prefers for the present to redirect the efforts of salespersons towards the more profitable products. While management is reluctant to tinker with the sales compensation scheme, revenue targets for the various products will be set for the regional sales managers based on the products that management wants to push most aggressively. The regional sales managers will be paid a bonus if the sales targets are met.

The company computes product margins for all of its products using the following formula:

Selling price
Less: Sales commissions
Less: Cost of sales
Less: Operating expenses
= Product margin

The cost of sales in the product margin formula is the amount Prevala pays to its production subcontractors. The operating expenses represent fixed costs. Each product is charged a fair share of those costs, calculated this year as 37.2% of the product's selling price.

Management is convinced that the best way to improve overall profits is to redirect the efforts of the company's salespersons. There are no plans to add or drop any products.

Required:

How would you measure the relative profitability of the company's products in this situation? Assume that it is not feasible to change the way salespersons are compensated. Also assume that the only data you have available are the selling price, the sales commissions, the cost of sales, the operating expenses, and the product margin for each product.

Photo Credits

1	© Ryan McVay/Getty Images
4	© AP Photo/The Indianapolis Star, Robert Sheer
5	© Ryan McVay/Getty Images
16	© Ryan McVay/Getty Images
38	© AP Photo
40	© Plus Pix/age fotostock
54	Courtesy of Sandee Noreen
56	© Royalty-Free/CORBIS
78	Courtesy of University Tees, Inc.
83	© Renault communication/CURTET, Patrick
98	© Ryan McVay/Getty Images
120	Courtesy of Eric Noreen
123	© Rob Melnychuk/Getty Images
127	Courtesy of Sandee Noreen.
129	© Steve Allen/Getty Images
134	Courtesy of Sandee Noreen.
165	Courtesy of Joi de Vivre Hospitality
173	© AFP/Getty Images
181	© AP Photo/M. Spencer Green
183	© Jason Reed/Ryan McVay/Getty Images
208	© John Madere/CORBIS
211	© Tom Stewart/CORBIS
223	© Sacha Orlov/Getty Images
242	© Digital Vision/PunchStock
243	© Gabriel M. Covian/Getty Images
246	Courtesy of Sandee Noreen
252	© The McGraw-Hill Companies, Inc./Andrew Resek, photographer
297	© Walt Disney Productions/PHOTOFEST
302	© Rob Melnychuk/Getty Images
316	© Brand X Pictures/PunchStock
343	© Jean-Michel Turpin/GAMMA
344	© Cleve Bryant/PhotoEdit
368	© PhotoAlto
374	© Steve Mason/Getty Images
396	© AP Photo/Marty Lederhandler
398	© Mario Beauregard/CORBIS
408	© Getty Images
414	© Nick Koudis/Getty Images
437	© Michael Rosenfeld/Getty Images
439	© AP Photo/Kevork Djansezian
454	© AP Photo/Marcio Jose Sanchez
457	© Tony Freeman/PhotoEdit
499	© Gonzalo Azumendi/AGE Photostock
501	© Blend Images/SuperStock
514	Courtesy of Sandee Noreen
519	© AP Photo/Stew Milne
547	Courtesy of Cintas Headquarters
551	© AP Photo/Paul Sakuma
565	© AFP/Getty Images
570	Courtesy of Ipswitch, Inc.

Logos

77	The Dell logo is trademark of Dell, Inc.
119	© 2006 Toll Brothers, Inc.
163	© Blue Nile, 2006. Used with permission.
295	© 2006. JetBlue, Inc. Used with permission.

Index